EVIDENCE

PRINCIPLES AND PROBLEMS

Sixth Edition

by

Ronald Joseph Delisle

B.Sc., LL.B., LL.M.

Faculty of Law
Queen's University

and

Don Stuart

B.A., LL.B., Dip. Crim., D. Phil.

Faculty of Law
Queen's University

CARSWELL

A THOMSON COMPANY

The paper used in this publication meets the minimum requirements of the American National Standard for Information Sciences — Permanence of Paper for Printed Library Materials, ANSI Z39.48-1984.

National Library of Canada Cataloguing in Publication Data

Delisle, R. J.
    Evidence : principles and problems

6th ed.
Includes index.
ISBN 0-459-24029-3

1. Evidence (Law) — Canada — Cases.   I. Stuart, Don, 1943-
II. Title.

KE8440.D44 2001   347.71'06   C2001-902576-9

 CARSWELL

A THOMSON COMPANY

One Corporate Plaza   Customer Relations:
2075 Kennedy Road   Toronto 1-416-609-3800
Toronto, Ontario   Elsewhere in Canada/U.S. 1-800-387-5164
M1T 3V4   Fax 1-416-298-5094

For Gloria and Pam

PREFACE TO SIXTH EDITION

In the last couple of years there have been major Supreme Court rulings on almost every facet of the law of evidence. To make way for consideration of the latest issues older material now redundant had to be pruned. We worked together through every page and topic in an effort to update and elucidate for anyone wanting to understand the history and principles underlying this most important, practical and controversial subject. To facilitate review in this edition problems have been interspersed throughout chapters rather than put at the end of each chapter. Although the structure of the book remains largely intact we have made some changes of order.

The introductory first chapter is now largely devoted to a discussion of sources and applicability of the rules of evidence. We include material of formal admissions of fact which dispenses with the need for proof. The chapter also introduces the reader to the controversial issue of whether rules of evidence should be codified.

We have moved up to Chapter 2 consideration of burdens of proof with special attention given to the distinction between persuasive and evidentiary burdens, measures of proof, and the thorny issue of presumptions including the presumption of innocence now entrenched in the Canadian Charter of Rights and Freedoms. We have included the *Arcuri* ruling that there should be "limited weighing" of circumstantial evidence at preliminary inquiries.

Given their centrality the topics of relevance and discretion to exclude at common law and now under the Charter are separately considered in Chapter 3. Under the Charter our focus is on the uncertain discretion the Supreme Court now recognizes (see, for example, *Harrer* and *White*) to exclude evidence to ensure a fair trial. We concentrate less (see Chapter 11) on the Charter discretion in section 24(2) to exclude evidence obtained in violation of a Charter right. Since one of the central considerations under section 24(2) is the nature and seriousness of the Charter breach we are of the view that that topic is better considered in Criminal Procedure courses. See our *Learning Canadian Criminal Procedure* (6th ed., Carswell, 2000) pp. 396-492.

As in previous editions Chapter 4 on Character Evidence provides a test case for consideration of principles of relevance and discretion to exclude. We pay particular attention to the continuing debate as to whether similar fact evidence may be admitted to show propensity, contrasting in this edition the recent approach of the Ontario Court of Appeal in *L.B.* and *Batte* with that of the Supreme Court in *Arp*. We also highlight the controversial topic of rape shield laws, including the Supreme Court's recent ruling in *Darrach* and the unresolved issue of whether evidence of the complainant's prior sexual conduct *with the accused* should be treated differently. We also consider the significance of the recent recognition in *Mills* and *Darrach* of enforceable equality rights for complainants in sexual assault cases.

Chapters 5, 6 and 7 deal with the positive side of the laws of evidence: how matters are proved by the admission of evidence. Chapter 5 deals with cases where proof is not required under the controversial and still evolving doctrine of judicial notice. We have added consideration of recent Supreme Court pronouncements in the context of screening potential jurors for bias in *Williams* and *Find*. In Chapter 6 on Real Evidence we have added a consideration of practical topics such as how to file exhibits and how to authenticate. We have added a section on demonstrative evidence. The lengthy Chapter 7 on Witnesses is much as before except that we have moved up to here, under the topic of competence and compellability, a discussion of the special position of accused. This includes discussion of the common law privilege against self-incrimination and the emergence under the Charter of a pre-trial and trial right to silence and a wide principle against self-incrimination. We give further attention to the issue of competency hearings for children where the law is still controversial and in flux. Under the issue of cross-examination of prior inconsistent statements under sections 10 and 11 of the Canada Evidence Act we have added advocacy advice. We have also added this dimension to the section concerning cross-examination on declarations of adversity under sections 9(1) and (2), using as a hard example the prosecution of domestic assault where the principal witness has recanted.

The next three chapters cover the major exclusionary principles of Hearsay, Opinion and Privilege. Chapter 8 now includes the major decision of the Supreme Court in *Starr* that pigeonhole exceptions to the hearsay rule may now be subject to review under the *Khan/Smith* principled approach. We also consider the controversial ruling in *Starr* that corroborating extrinsic evidence cannot be considered on the issue of reliability of a hearsay statement. Chapter 9 now starts with a consideration of the opinion rule. On the issue of expert testimony we have shifted the focus to the Supreme Court's recent pronouncements in *Mohan* and *D.D.* Chapter 10 on privilege starts with a consideration of the leading decision in *Gruenke* and its distinction between class and case-by-case privilege. Under solicitor-client privilege we consider the Supreme Court's latest pronouncements in *Smith v. Jones* and *McClure*. The chapter concludes with the Charter balancing approach adopted on the issue of access to therapeutic records of complainants in sexual assault cases. We focus on the most recent legislation as interpreted in *Mills*.

We thank our longtime friend and colleague, Allan Manson, for many hours of stimulating discussion and insight into evidence issues. We are also grateful to our new colleague, Gary Trotter, for being so generous in his time and advice.

We thank Rebecca Duncan at Carswell for allowing us to produce this new edition ahead of schedule. Finally, we thank Dennis Brennan, our content editor, for his extraordinary commitment to excellence. He caught mistakes and inconsistencies that we missed. He has much improved our work at every point and worked tirelessly and efficiently to make all the production deadlines. We are deeply indebted.

R.J. Delisle
Don Stuart

Kingston
September 1, 2001

I am most privileged to have been asked by my friend and colleague to co-author the latest edition of his well known book. I am very much a junior partner to one long preeminent in the field of the laws of evidence. As with other co-authored books with Ron I have found the work incredibly worthwhile, informative and stimulating.

Don Stuart

Kingston
September 1, 2001

PREFACE TO FIFTH EDITION

As the courts find more and more discretion in the applications of the rules of evidence, counsel needs more and more to be familiar with the principles underlying the rules so that intelligent arguments may be put with regard to their implementation. This book accordingly emphasizes a principled approach to the rules.

I thank my close friends and colleagues, Don Stuart and Alan Manson, for their continued support and helpful advice. I thank Hugh Lawford, a colleague and founder of QL Systems Limited, for providing a wonderful research tool. I thank Alan Gold for his database Gold on QL for keeping me current. I thank Litza Anderson for helping me with my research. Finally I thank Bev Stone and Suzanne Conway, Product Development Managers at Carswell and most particularly Debbie Bowen, the best editor I have ever had.

I have tried to state the law accurately as of November 1998.

R. J. Delisle

Kingston
May, 1999

PREFACE TO FOURTH EDITION

The trend towards greater admissibility of evidence and the more frequent use of discretion continues. To be effective as counsel one needs to be aware not just of the rules of evidence but of their underlying purpose so that intelligent arguments can be fashioned as to whether or not a particular rule should be applied. The book continues to emphasize this principled approach.

Our appellate courts are quite active in the area. Well over a hundred new cases were seen to be worth discussion. Some pruning of other cases was necessary to keep the book at a manageable length. The reader will hopefully recognize that severe editing of some of the cases was necessary as the appellate courts, particularly our highest court, continue to write extremely long decisions, frequently with many opinions. I hope the editing while severe was wise. I have tried to describe the law accurately as of January, 1996.

I continue to thank my colleagues Don Stuart and Alan Manson for their support and for being there to consider my questions and to offer advice. I thank Hugh Lawford, a colleague, an evidence teacher and the founder of QL Systems Limited. That research tool has been invaluable to me in trying to keep current in this area. I would like to thank fellow evidence teachers and friends, Professor Lee Stuesser at Manitoba and Professor Rollie Thompson at Dalhousie, for their helpful comments. I thank the Law School at the University of New South Wales for providing me accommodation as I put the finishing touches to the book. The Head of School, Susan Armstrong, and Professors Jill Hunter and Mark Aronson made me feel very much at home and therefore made the task that much easier. I thank Julia Gulej, Acquisitions Editor, and John Morris, Production Co-ordinator at Carswell. They made the final tasks pleasurable.

R. J. Delisle

Kingston
April, 1996

ix

PREFACE TO THIRD EDITION

Our courts continue their trend toward greater admissibility and increased recognition of the centrality of discretion's place in the law of evidence. With those developments come the burdens of articulating the guidelines for the exercise of discretion and the cautions that need to be addressed to the trier of fact regarding the weight to be given to evidence that formerly would have been rejected. All of this makes it more important than ever that the lawyer be fully aware of the reasons and policy choices that underlie the rules that have been fashioned over the years.

The Third Edition continues to emphasize the problem approach with text providing a principled analytical framework within which the reader can consider the approaches taken by the courts. The book recognizes, however, that in a number of instances the reader would be shortchanged if given only a paraphrase of a court's thinking. Often the court itself does a better job than this writer in articulating why evidence deserves receipt or rejection. This Edition therefore includes even more case material than the Second Edition. I hope the proper mix has been achieved. I hope as well that I have reasonably accurately described the law as of January, 1993.

I would like to publicly thank my colleagues Don Stuart and Alan Manson. They are always open to my questions and they force me to better articulate my positions. I would like to thank my colleague Hugh Lawford. A fellow evidence teacher who shares insights on the subject, he also is the founder of QL Systems Limited. That research tool has made the task of keeping current in the law of evidence so much easier and efficient. Thanks are also due to David Keeshan, Managing Editor, and Kimberly Aiken, Production Editor, at Carswell; they made the final tasks pleasurable. Finally, I thank my secretary Sandra Tallen for her patience and industry in getting the job done.

R. J. Delisle

Kingston
April, 1993

PREFACE TO SECOND EDITION

I still believe that it is best to teach the law of evidence by the problem method. It is simply more efficient to set out the general principles and underlying philosophy in textual form, rather than forcing the student to spend valuable time discovering the same for herself by reading the original materials. The student and the teacher are then freed to discuss solutions to problems as they might arise in practise; the student learns to use the law of evidence, rather than simply being equipped with the ability to describe the law. For the Second Edition, a good deal of new text has been added throughout the book but particularly in the beginning when dealing with the most basic concepts. A thorough understanding of the make-up and meaning of relevancy, materiality, prejudice, fairness and the importance of judicial discretion are absolutely necessary before the student goes on to consider topics of competence, hearsay, opinion and the like.

I have been persuaded, however, by fellow evidence teachers (notably Stuart, McKinnon and Cromwell) that the students should be afforded the ready opportunity of reading at least some of the primary materials for themselves. A notable change in the Second Edition, therefore, is the inclusion of 30 to 40 cases. Many of these cases are recent decisions by the Supreme Court of Canada and, may I respectfully acknowledge, they do provide excellent expositions of the subject.

A number of new problems have been added and some of the old ones, which didn't seem to work, have been deleted. Special thanks are due to Marc Rosenberg, who contributed several intriguing questions to the Problems segment of the Hearsay chapter. Over the past five years of teaching with this book, I have supplemented my instruction with video-tapes illustrating the problems in action. I have found this technique to be well received by the students and copies are readily available, for the asking, should others like to try it.

I was given a deadline by the publisher, of February 1, and I do hope that I have reasonably accurately described the law of evidence in Canada as of that date. I have deleted most references to the Uniform Evidence Bill. At the time of the First Edition I believed, and hoped, that the Bill would achieve passage and Canada would have a comprehensive statement of the law to the advantage of all. Such was not to be the case and the references served only to confuse the student.

I would like to thank my students whose questions have forced me to a better understanding of the subject and my colleagues, Don Stuart and Allan Manson, who give freely of their time and encouragement and make Queen's a fine place to be. Thanks are also due to the staff at Carswell, particularly Production Editor Peter Enman. I am indebted particularly to Rosella Cornaviera for her industry, creativity and patience in providing valuable research assistance in the preparation of this Second Edition.

R. J. Delisle

Kingston
May, 1989

PREFACE TO FIRST EDITION

After teaching the basic course in evidence for a number of years I concluded that the traditional method of using case analysis can be wasteful of time and energy. While that method is obviously useful for the purpose of developing analytical skills it is not efficient, particularly when it comes to teaching procedural subjects. The principles which students are expected to glean by case analysis can be communicated much more easily by text. With the time gained the students can then afford to consider more deeply the policies which underlie the principles, the historical background that gave them birth, their inherent logic or lack of logic, ethical issues in their use, and attempts at reform. This book then is basically a textbook, although there are some lengthy extracts from leading cases to directly evidence the judicial approach. For each area, problems have been devised and it is these which are intended to form the basis of classroom discussion. Students are expected to introduce themselves to the basics by reading assigned text and to come to class prepared to discuss the problems and debate alternative approaches to their resolution; it is anticipated that there will be frequent recourse to role playing. Some of the problems were generated by actual cases and in those instances the cases are cited; students are advised, however, to consider the problem against the background of principles learned from the text before examining and comparing the judicial resolution with their own. It is hoped that this format will promote a better appreciation of the philosophy which underlies the law and an improved ability to make practical use of the rules.

There is presently before the Senate a bill which would in large measure restate, and in some instances reform, the law of evidence. It was born out of an attempt by the provinces and the federal government to achieve uniformity in the law of evidence, to state the rules clearly, and to effect improvements. At the end of each topic the relevant statutory provisions of the Bill are canvassed so the reader might compare.

The book attempts to state and review the law of evidence in Canada as of the spring of 1984. Aside from describing the law as found, some effort has been devoted to critical analysis and comparison with the law in other jurisdictions.

I would like to thank my friend and colleague, Don Stuart, for his advice, his criticisms, always constructive, and for his encouragement to see the book through to publication.

I would like to thank Moira Calderwood, my summer research assistant in 1983, for her industry in ensuring the accuracy of citations and her talent in the preliminary editing. I thank Candy Randall and Theresa Brown for coping so pleasantly with such a large typing task.

I thank the staff at Carswell's for smoothing the way, and particularly Kathy Hurd for her editing skills and dedication in the production of this book.

I thank Queen's University for granting me a sabbatical in 1982-83, and the Social Science and Humanities Research Council of Canada for their support in the form of a Leave Fellowship.

Finally, I would thank the masters of the law of evidence, Wigmore, McCormick, Morgan, Cross and the great Thayer for providing the insights so necessary to anyone who seeks to seriously study this fascinating subject.

Ronald Delisle

Kingston
April, 1984

TABLE OF CONTENTS

WD
– handout
contrast

not on exam

not on exam

Khan, Smith, KGB = important

not on exam

TABLE OF CASES

C

Q

R

XYZ

1

Introduction

1. ADVERSARY SYSTEM

The method of inquiry in our courts is quite distinct from the scientific method; our method of ascertaining the facts is known as adversarial, while the scientific might be labelled inquisitorial. The principal distinguishing characteristic between the two methods resides in the relative passivity of the decision-maker, the judge, in the adversary method. Her function is to make the ultimate finding of facts, but she does not herself investigate; rather, she judges the merits of two positions that are put before her. The tradition in the English-speaking world is to regard the "over-speaking judge [as] no well-tuned cymbal."[1] Should a trial judge intervene too frequently during the trial, she runs the risk of being reversed on appeal and of a new trial being ordered. A frank description of our method of inquiry is seen in the decision of the Ontario Court of Appeal, *Phillips v. Ford Motor Co.*[2] Evans, J.A. wrote:

> Our mode of trial procedure is based upon the adversary system in which the contestants seek to establish through relevant supporting evidence, before an impartial trier of facts, those events or happenings which form the bases of their allegations. This procedure assumes that the litigants, assisted by their counsel, will fully and diligently present all the material facts which have evidentiary value in support of their respective positions and that these disputed facts will receive from a trial Judge a dispassionate and impartial consideration in order to arrive at the truth of the matters in controversy. A trial is not intended to be a scientific exploration with the presiding Judge assuming the role of a research director; it is a forum established for the purpose of providing justice for the litigants. Undoubtedly a Court must be concerned with truth, in the sense that it accepts as true certain sworn evidence and rejects other testimony as unworthy of belief, but it cannot embark upon a quest for the "scientific" or "technological" truth when such an adventure does violence to the primary function of the Court, which has always been to do justice, according to law.

In *Phillips* the plaintiff sued for damages arising out of an automobile accident. The issue was whether the accident was caused by a defective brake mechanism or driver error. What had the trial judge done that deserved such criticism? He had appointed an expert pursuant to the rules of court, which then stated:

---

1. Lord Chancellor Bacon, as quoted by Lord Denning in *Jones v. Nat. Coal Bd.*, [1957] 2 Q.B. 55, 64 (C.A.).
2. (1971), 18 D.L.R. (3d) 641, 661 (C.A.). Contrast the remarks of Frankfurter, J. in *Johnson v. U.S.*, 333 U.S. 46, 53-54 (1948):
   > While a court room is not a laboratory for the scientific pursuit of truth, a trial judge is surely not confined to an account, obviously fragmentary, of the circumstances of a happening. . . . A trial is not a game of blind man's bluff; and the trial judge — particularly in a case where he himself is the trier of the facts upon which he is to pronounce the law — need not blindfold himself by failing to call an available vital witness simply because the parties, for reasons of trial tactics, choose to withhold his testimony. . . . Federal judges are not referees at prize-fights but functionaries of justice.

The court may obtain the assistance of merchants, engineers, accountants, actuaries or scientific persons, in such way as it thinks fit, the better to enable it to determine any matter of fact in question in any cause or proceeding.

The parties had called their experts but so did the judge. The judge's expert did more than simply interpret the evidence of the other experts; he provided input of his own. The judge also involved himself very much in the conduct of the proceedings. The parties were Nathan Phillips, elderly and retired mayor of Toronto, and the Ford Motor Company. Might it be that the adversaries were seen by the trial judge to be not evenly balanced in resources?

The "work product" of Ford's solicitors, engineering reports commissioned by them, was protected from disclosure by an evidence rule which we'll later examine privileging solicitor-client communications.[3] This privilege is normally justified as necessary to the proper workings of an adversary system.

Suppose you were counsel for the Ford Motor Company and an engineering report you had ordered showed your client was negligent. Would you disclose this to the other side? Would you file any adverse report received from an expert in your waste basket and get another, more favourable report to present to the Court? Would you be content to defeat what you regard to be a just claim?

Justice Evans appeared to strike the balance in the *Phillips* case in favour of justice over truth. Consider *R. v. Levogiannis*.[4] There an attack was made on the constitutional validity of a Criminal Code provision, section 486(2.1), which permits young complainants to testify behind a screen. The accused challenged the provision on the grounds that it violated his right to a fair trial guaranteed by sections 7 and 11(*d*) of the Canadian Charter of Rights and Freedoms. In deciding that the provision was constitutional Justice L'Heureux-Dubé wrote for the Court. In the course of her judgment she wrote:

The examination of whether an accused's rights are infringed encompasses multifaceted considerations, such as the rights of witnesses, in this case children, the rights of accused and courts' duties to ascertain the truth. The goal of the court process is truth seeking and, to that end, the evidence of all those involved in judicial proceedings must be given in a way that is most favourable to eliciting the truth. . . . [O]ne cannot ignore the fact that, in many instances, the court process is failing children, especially those who have been victims of abuse, who are then subjected to further trauma as participants in the judicial process.[5]

In *R. v. Darrach*,[6] Gonthier, J., for a unanimous court, dealt with rape shield legislation designed to protect the complainants in sexual assault cases. The accused complained that the legislation was unconstitutional as it deprived him of his fair trial rights. Justice Gonthier wrote:

The current version of s. 276 is carefully crafted to comport with the principles of fundamental justice. It protects the integrity of the judicial process while at the same

---

3.   See generally Wilson, "Privilege in Experts' Working Papers" (1997), 76 Can. Bar Rev. 346.
4.   [1993] 4 S.C.R. 475.
5.   *Ibid.*, at p. 483.
6.   [2000] 2 S.C.R. 443, 450, para. 3, 461-462, para. 24

time respecting the rights of the people involved. The complainant's privacy and dignity are protected by a procedure that also vindicates the accused's right to make full answer and defence. The procedure does not violate the accused's s. 7 *Charter* right to a fair trial nor his s. 11(*c*) right not to testify against himself or his s. 11(*d*) right to a fair hearing.

. . .

. . . while the right to make full answer and defence and the principle against self-incrimination are certainly core principles of fundamental justice, they can be respected without the accused being entitled to "the most favourable procedures that could possibly be imagined". Nor is the accused entitled to have procedures crafted that take only his interests into account. Still less is he entitled to procedures that would distort the truth-seeking function of a trial by permitting irrelevant and prejudicial material at trial. [Citations omitted.]

It is perhaps noteworthy that there are two bronzes in front of the Supreme Court of Canada building. One is entitled Truth and the other Justice. Throughout the materials in this volume we will witness the ever present tension in the decision-making process as justice and truth vie for attention.

The adversary method has been justified over the years by many lawyers as capable of promoting the finest approximation to the truth. Jerome Frank noted:

Many lawyers maintain that the best way for the court to discover the facts in a suit is to have each side strive as hard as it can, in a keenly partisan spirit, to bring to the court's attention the evidence favourable to that side. Macauley said that we obtain the fairest decision "when two men argue, as unfairly as possible, on opposite sides" for then "it is certain that no important consideration will altogether escape notice."[7]

The diligence of the parties in ferreting out evidence favourable to their side and the vigour with which they attack their opponent's case are seen by many as finer guarantees of approximating the historical truth than giving the problem for resolution to some government official whose motivation can rarely be of the magnitude of the parties.[8] Also, it is believed that the bias of the decision-maker can be minimized if he plays a much less active role than is demanded in the inquisitorial method.[9] The judge who himself conducts the examination of witnesses "descends into the arena and is liable to have his vision clouded by the dust of the conflict. Unconsciously he deprives himself of the advantage of calm and dispassionate observation."[10]

The Supreme Court of Canada ordered a new trial when the trial judge's interruptions were so frequent and of such a nature that justice was not seen to be done. Speaking for the court, Lamer, J., *Brouillard v. R.*,[11] said:

---

7.   *Courts on Trial* (1949), at p. 80.
8.   See Brooks, *The Judge and The Adversary System*, *The Canadian Judiciary* (A. Linden, ed., 1976).
9.   See Lind, Thibault and Walker, "Cross-Cultural Comparison of the Effect of Adversary and Inquisitorial Processes on Bias in Legal Decision-Making" (1976), 62 Va. L. Rev. 271.
10. Lord Greene, M.R. in *Yuill v. Yuill*, [1945] 1 All E.R. 183, 189 (C.A.).
11. (1985), 16 D.L.R. (4th) 447, 450, 451, 453 (S.C.C.); the court reproduces instances from the transcript illustrating the nature of the remarks addressed to the accused and to his witness.

The role of a trial judge is sometimes very demanding, owing to the nature of the case and the conduct of the litigants (parties). Like anyone, a judge may occasionally lose patience. He may then step down from his judge's bench and assume the role of counsel. When this happens, and, *a fortiori*, when this happens to the detriment of an accused, it is important that a new trial be ordered, even when the verdict of guilty is not unreasonable having regard to the evidence, and the judge has not erred with respect to the law applicable to the case and has not incorrectly assessed the facts.

The reason for this is well known. It is one of the most fundamental principles of our case-law, the best-known formulation of which is to be found in Lord Hewart C.J.'s judgment in *R. v. Sussex Justices, Ex p. McCarthy*, [1924] 1 K.B. 256 at p. 259: "[it] is of fundamental importance that justice should not only be done, but should manifestly and undoubtedly be seen to be done". . . .

. . . it is clear that judges are no longer required to be as passive as they once were; to be what I call sphinx judges. We now not only accept that a judge may intervene in the adversarial debate, but also believe that it is sometimes essential for him to do so for justice in fact to be done. Thus a judge may and sometimes must ask witnesses questions, interrupt them in their testimony and if necessary call them to order. . . .

Finally, prudence and the resulting judicial restraint must be all the greater where the accused is a witness. He must be allowed to proceed, within limits, of course, but always bearing in mind that at the end of the day he is the only one who may be leaving the court in handcuffs.

In conclusion, although the judge may and must intervene for justice to be done, he must none the less do so in such way that justice *is seen to be done*. It is all a question of manner.

Compare Justice L'Heureux-Dubé in *R. v. L. (D.O.)*,[12] dealing with the accused's complaint that the trial judge had exhibited bias:

The final issue raised by the respondent is whether the trial judge may have acted in such a manner as to raise a reasonable apprehension of bias, as per *R. v. Brouillard*, [1985] 1 S.C.R. 39. In *Brouillard, supra*, Lamer J., for the court held that the judiciary should not be seen as "entering the ring" or acting on behalf of one of the parties. . . .

It is my view that, in the case at hand as well as in other cases involving fragile witnesses such as children, the trial judge has a responsibility to ensure that the child understands the questions being asked and that the evidence given by the child is clear and unambiguous. To accomplish this end, the trial judge may be required to clarify and rephrase questions asked by counsel and to ask subsequent questions to the child to clarify the child's responses. In order to ensure the appropriate conduct of the trial, the judge should provide a suitable atmosphere to ease the tension so that the child is relaxed and calm. The trial judge, in this case, did not prevent the mounting of a proper defence, nor did he demonstrate favouritism toward the witness in such a way as to preclude a fair trial. I find that the trial judge in this instance did nothing more than "intervene for justice to be done".[13]

Whether the adversary method will more closely approximate truth is certainly open to question. The lawyer is trained to seek success for her client, to win the game. Her goal is to present the best picture of her client's position and not the most complete picture at her disposal. Also, the adversary system

---

12.   (1994), 25 C.R. (4th) 285 (S.C.C.).
13.   *Ibid.*, at pp. 322-23.

presupposes for success some equality between the parties; when this is lacking, the "truth" becomes too often simply the view of the more powerful. Most judges will confess to the frequent temptation to reach out and "even the match" although the system cautions against such practice. Perhaps most importantly, while it is true that in deciding between the validity of two competing theories the decision-maker may be considerably aided by advocates on each side presenting their respective positions in the strongest arguments possible, it is certainly questionable whether such a technique is valuable in ensuring that all of the available evidence has been presented by the parties for examination. As Professor Peter Brett has noted:

> . . . observe the practice of scientists and historians in carrying out their investigations . . . a lengthy search will fail to reveal one competent practitioner in either discipline who will willingly and in advance confine himself, in deciding any question involving factual data, to a choice between two sets of existing data proffered to him by rival claimants. In short, the inquisitorial method is the one used by every genuine seeker of the truth in every walk of life (not merely scientific and historical investigations) with only one exception . . . the trial system in the common-law world.[14]

And Jerome Frank expressed his concern:

> But frequently the partisanship of the opposing lawyers blocks the uncovering of vital evidence or leads to a presentation of vital testimony in a way that distorts it. We have allowed the fighting spirit to become dangerously excessive. . . . In short, the lawyer aims at victory, at winning in the fight, not at aiding the court to discover the facts. He does not want the trial court to reach a sound educated guess, if it is likely to be contrary to his client's interests. Our present trial method is thus the equivalent of throwing pepper in the eyes of a surgeon when he is performing an operation.[15]

A major impediment to our search for truth is that the facts to be discovered by our courts are almost always past facts. Our method of discovering them is normally through the oral testimony of witnesses who have personal knowledge about what happened. This personal "knowledge" might perhaps better be described as personal beliefs about what they now remember of facts which they believe they observed. The trier of fact then has regard to what the witness says, and based on her observations of what the witness said and how he said it, she comes to her own belief as to whether that is an honest belief. She can do no more. She cannot, as the scientist might, duplicate in her laboratory the actual facts and test the hypothesis proposed. Facts as found by the court are really then only guesses about the actual facts. As an illustration:

> When Jack Spratt, as a witness, testifies to a fact, he is merely stating his belief or opinion about that past fact. When he says, "I saw McCarthy hit Schmidt," he means, "I believe that is what happened." When a trial judge or jury, after hearing that testimony, finds as a fact that McCarthy hit Schmidt, the finding means no more than the judge's or jury's belief that the belief of the witness Spratt is an honest belief, and that his belief accurately reflects what actually happened. A trial court's findings of fact is, then, at best, its belief or opinion about someone else's belief or opinion.[16]

---

14. See Brett, "Legal Decision Making and Bias: A Critique of an 'Experiment' " (1973), 45 U. Col. L. Rev. 1 at 23.
15. *Courts on Trial, supra*, note 7 at pp. 81 and 85.
16. *Ibid.*, at p. 22.

Justice Haines in *R. v. Lalonde* described it this way:

> A trial is not a faithful reconstruction of the events as if recorded on some giant television screen. It is an historical recall of that part of the events to which witnesses may be found and presented in an intensely adversary system *where the object is quantum of proof.* Truth may be only incidental.[17]

In *Lalonde*, a murder case, accused's counsel had sought an order from the trial judge commanding Crown counsel to provide a list of witnesses interviewed by the police who the Crown did not intend to call at trial. The judge refused because:

1. The accused's right to a fair trial, his right to discovery to aid in the search for truth, had to be balanced by the need to maintain effective channels of investigation by the police. Potential witnesses were seen as vulnerable to tampering and intimidation.
2. Witnesses may be reluctant to give statements if they know they'll be given to opposing counsel who'll use them to pick apart their testimony in court.
3. A trial judge should be concerned with the interests of justice, which are not necessarily the same as the interests of the accused.

However, in *R. v. Stinchcombe*[18] the Supreme Court of Canada mandated the Crown's obligation to make disclosure to the defence. The judgment of the Court was delivered by Sopinka, J.:

> Production and discovery were foreign to the adversary process of adjudication in its earlier history when the element of surprise was one of the accepted weapons in the arsenal of the adversaries. This applied to both criminal and civil proceedings. Significantly, in civil proceedings this aspect of the adversary process has long since disappeared, and full discovery of documents and oral examination of parties and even witnesses are familiar features of the practice. This change resulted from acceptance of the principle that justice was better served when the element of surprise was eliminated from the trial and the parties were prepared to address issues on the basis of complete information of the case to be met. Surprisingly, in criminal cases in which the liberty of the subject is usually at stake, this aspect of the adversary system has lingered on. While the prosecution bar has generally co-operated in making disclosure on a voluntary basis, there has been considerable resistance to the enactment of comprehensive rules which would make the practice mandatory. This may be attributed to the fact that proposals for reform in this regard do not provide for reciprocal disclosure by the defence. . . .
>
> It is difficult to justify the position which clings to the notion that the Crown has no legal duty to disclose all relevant information. The arguments against the existence of such a duty are groundless while those in favour, are, in my view, overwhelming. The suggestion that the duty should be reciprocal may deserve consideration by this Court in the future but is not a valid reason for absolving the Crown of its duty. . . .
>
> I would add that the fruits of the investigation which are in the possession of counsel for the Crown are not the property of the Crown for use in securing a conviction but the property of the public to be used to ensure that justice is done. In contrast, the defence has no obligation to assist the prosecution and is entitled to

---

17.   (1971), 15 C.R.N.S. 1, 4 (Ont. H.C.) [emphasis added].
18.   [1991] 3 S.C.R. 326.

assume a purely adversarial role toward the prosecution. The absence of a duty to disclose can, therefore, be justified as being consistent with this role.[19]

In *R. v. Peruta*,[20] the Crown unsuccessfully maintained that he was entitled to discovery of prior statements of the defence witnesses just as he was obliged to provide prior statements of his witnesses. In denying the thought Justice Proulx explained:

> The discovery of evidence is a constitutional guarantee for the accused which tries fundamentally to balance the forces involved in the trial.[21] . . .
> It would be presumptuous to assert that this balance has now been reached and that the two parties, as they do in a civil trial, can mutually claim the total disclosure of the evidence.[22]

Ought there to be reciprocity in disclosure in criminal cases?[23]

Besides searching for a different truth than the scientist, our methods are also circumscribed by other considerations, which require our fact-finding to be done in a way which is acceptable to the parties and to society. Our courts provide a forum for the purpose of resolving disputes between parties which they themselves have been unable to resolve in any other way. Our modern form of trial began simply as a substitute for private duels and feuds which had later been dignified by the process of trial by battle. Resolution of conflict now must be done in a way which ensures social tranquility generally, and which is also acceptable to the individual parties. The parties should be able to leave the court feeling that they have had their say, that their case has been presented in the best possible light, and that they have been judged by an impartial trier.[24] In judging the efficacy of the legal system's method of fact-finding we must remember:

> A contested law suit is society's last line of defense in the indispensable effort to secure the peaceful settlement of social conflicts. . . . It is a last-ditch process in which something more is at stake than the truth only of the specific matter in contest. There is at stake also that confidence of the public generally in the impartiality and fairness of public settlement of disputes which is essential if the ditch is to be held and the settlements accepted peaceably.
>
> . . . While it is of course important that the court be right . . . a decision must be made now, one way or the other. . . . To require certainty . . . would be impracticable and undesirable. The law thus compromises.[25]

---

19. *Ibid.*, at pp. 332-33.
20. (1993), 78 C.C.C. (3d) 350 (Que. C.A.), leave to appeal refused, 81 C.C.C. (3d) vi (S.C.C.).
21. "For in criminal cases, the State has in the police, an agency for the discovery of evidence, superior to anything which even the wealthiest defendant could employ": "Devlin Report on Evidence of Identification" (1976), H.C. 338, para. 1.17. [Proulx, J.A.'s footnote.]
22. *Supra*, note 20, at p. 370.
23. Compare Tanovich and Crocker, "Dancing with Stinchcombe's Ghost: A Modest Proposal for Reciprocal Defence Disclosure" (1994), 26 C.R. (4th) 333; and Davison, "Putting Ghosts to Rest: A Reply to the Modest Proposal for Defence Disclosure" (1995), 43 C.R. (4th) 105.
24. See authorities described by Brooks, *supra*, note 8, at pp. 98 *et seq.*
25. Hart and McNaughton, *Evidence and Inference in the Law* (D. Lerner, ed.); "Evidence and Inference" (Hayden Colloquium, 1958), pp. 52-53.

As we examine the material in the pages that follow we should ask ourselves whether the compromises we have made are the best that we can do.

2. SOURCES

The law of evidence is primarily judge-made. Numerous procedural reforms were accomplished by statute in England in the 19th century and these were largely copied in Canada. In Canada procedure in criminal matters is entrusted to the federal Parliament[26] and procedure in civil matters to the provincial legislatures.[27] Legislation enacted pursuant to these powers, the Canada Evidence Act and the various provincial Evidence Acts, covers only a small portion of the law of evidence, and the bulk of it is still governed by the common law.

A further source of evidence law, and especially so in criminal law, is the entrenched Charter of Rights and Freedoms. We will in this course address in particular the rule against compellability of accused in section 11(c), the principle against self-incrimination in section 7, the right to a fair trial under sections 7 and 11(d), the presumption of innocence in section 11(d), the ability to exclude evidence in section 24 and equality rights for complainants in sexual assault cases under section 15.

3. CODIFICATION

There was an attempt at codification by the Law Reform Commission of Canada in 1975[28] but this was not well received by the profession.[29] In 1977 the Federal/Provincial Task Force on Uniform Rules of Evidence was established[30] and its product, the proposed Canada Evidence Act, 1986, was much more comprehensive than existing legislation. No one has yet enacted this legislation.

In 1975 in the United States the Federal Rules of Evidence were legislated. This was a comprehensive scheme providing for the rules of evidence in federal courts. Since that time the majority of the states has enacted similar schemes patterned on the federal model. In 1995 the Australian Capital Territory enacted a similar comprehensive scheme. Within months Australia's largest state, New South Wales, copied them for use in its courts. Canada, which in the 19th century had adopted the English Draft Code to cover substantive criminal law and criminal procedure, does not appear ready for a similar venture into the area of evidence.

Arguments for a Comprehensive Statement

1.   The main advantage of a comprehensive statement would be accessibility

---

26.   S. 91(27), Constitution Act, 1867.
27.   S. 92(14), Constitution Act, 1867.
28.   *Report on Evidence* (1975), Information Canada, Ottawa.
29.   See generally Brooks, "The Law Reform Commission of Canada's Evidence Code" (1978), 16 Osgoode Hall L.J. 241; Brooks, "The Common Law and the Evidence Code: Are They Compatible?" (1978), 27 U.N.B.L.J. 27; and Anderson, "A Criticism of the Evidence Code" (1976), 11 U.B.C.L. Rev. 163.
30.   See generally *Report of the Federal/Provincial Task Force on Uniform Rules of Evidence* (1982).

— bringing together into one document all the evidentiary rules. In Canada today the law of evidence is partly judge-made and partly made by legislation. A comprehensive legislated statement would bring it all together. Obviously this would be preferable to having some evidence rules regarding the use of evidence in judicial decisions while others appear in statutory form.

2. When an objection is made at trial the judge needs to make an immediate ruling. Wouldn't it be wonderful if we were all on the same page, aiming at the same target? At the very least the comprehensive statement would be, if not the definitive word, a good beginning to the argument. The Federal Rules of Evidence in the United States are available in a 4-inch by 5-inch pamphlet of about 50 pages. Based on our experience in the courtroom, the present rules are handled, to be kind, unevenly, and a comprehensive, ready-to-hand statement would necessarily improve the present situation. Both the evidentiary arguments and the results would be better based.

3. A comprehensive statement of the rules, written in terms of the underlying principles, would also create a better understanding of how the rules are meant to operate. This is particularly so if the rules were to be accompanied by explanatory notes. Such a rendition would minimize what some have referred to as "rampant conceptualism": the tendency of many lawyers to discuss the rules of evidence in terms of the meanings of the labels attached to them rather than in terms of their underlying rationale.

4. A comprehensive statement of the rules, written in terms of the underlying principles, would recognize a discretion in the judge in the application of the law of evidence, room for choice, room for judgment. The evidence rules are there to promote efficiency, fairness and the best approximation of the truth. Discretion in dealing with each particular case is necessary as it is inherent in the nature of the exercise. Recognizing that within each rule there must exist a fair amount of discretion, by articulating the rule in principled terms you thereby begin the process of describing the guidelines for a sound exercise of discretion. The simplicity of the process makes the law clearer and the discretion of the judge is better brought under control. Counsel then can make arguments based on principle rather than on technical interpretations of a mechanical rule and the judge will similarly be obliged to make decisions based on principle. Indeed, once it is recognized that discretion already exists, and must necessarily exist, we make the law much more certain than it ever was before and the trial more fair.

5. Teaching the beginning student through an examination of a comprehensive statement would better prepare them for the world of practice.

6. Through a comprehensive statement the law becomes more accessible, not only because it is gathered together in one place, but also because it would tend to resolve many of the present ambiguities which give differing results depending on the individual judge. The law becomes more uniform. A comprehensive statement might also encourage uniformity among the various legislatures, easing the burden on the practitioner who goes back and forth between civil and criminal law encountering different pieces of legislation. If uniformity was achieved among the provincial and federal governments, we would all be farther ahead as we generate judicial decisions and academic commentary regarding the rules, such writing coming from a common larger base.

7. Enacting a comprehensive statement of the rules would provide a forum within which reform of the law of evidence would be facilitated. It is true that much of the judge-made law can be reformed by judicial action but such reforms are by their nature piecemeal and also often resisted by the conservatism of the legal profession.

8. A comprehensive statement would also make the law of evidence more accessible to the citizenry. Bentham was moved in his calls for reform in the 19th century to better equip the ordinary man to understand. The present law of evidence is, for many, often unclear and difficult to ascertain. For those who see the rules as eight volumes of Wigmore with innumerable exceptions, the task is overly complex and daunting. Success often goes to the advocate best equipped with a memory for precedent and the ability to articulate the mechanical rule with precision. For many looking on, the adversary system is seen as too much of a game with the outcome dependent on the skill of the adversaries. If, on the other hand, we recognize precedent as valuable only as a vehicle for the expression of principle and focus on understanding the principle, there will be a more genuine communication between counsel and the judge and a better appreciation by the onlooker as to why a particular piece of evidence was accepted or rejected. Resistance to a comprehensive statement might be partly attributed to the lawyers' self-interest in their wish to keep the law as complicated as possible and thus keep it to themselves.

Arguments Against a Comprehensive Statement

1. The present law of evidence is accessible and known to those who are willing to make the effort. The law of evidence is like any other body of law and can be discovered and learned. It is folly to think that the rules can be made so simple that a lay person would understand without the assistance of a lawyer. A suitable text can inform the profession and the judiciary as well as any legislated statement of the rules.

2. Enacting a comprehensive statute will produce years of extensive litigation with arguments as to whether the legislature intended to effect change in the area or intended to enact the status quo. While there may be some ambiguity in the existing rules, even a restatement will produce argument as to the meaning of the words chosen. Judicial interpretations will vary for a lengthy period of time and uniformity will be an elusive object.

3. A comprehensive statute, which is codification by another name, will freeze the law of evidence and the courts will no longer be vehicles for change. Judges will no longer be able to create a rule or an exception to do justice in an individual case but will be limited to interpreting the legislation. The limits on proper judicial statutory interpretation will strait-jacket the judiciary. Changes will only be available by legislative action and delay will be the natural consequence. In addition, it is the judiciary and the litigation bar who are the experts in the law of evidence; it is they who actually know how the system works, and we ought not to forfeit their expertise.

4. Discretion in the trial judge equates, for many, to greater admissibility of evidence. The trial judge will no longer be as concerned with rejecting evidence as insufficiently reliable and will be moved to leave it to the trier of fact to assess worth given the totality of the evidence. Opponents who

voice these concerns are normally found in those members of the bar who do not generally have the burden of proof. As their function is often seen to be preventing evidence being admitted, anything that increases admissibility is to be resisted.

5. A comprehensive legislative scheme runs the risk of being subject to political influence and this will particularly prejudice the accused in criminal cases. Prosecutors in the past, who have had difficulties in certain prosecutions, have been known to lobby, successfully, for changes in admissibility of evidence or changes with respect to the burdens of proof. Criminal lawyers believe that there is greater protection for an accused from a non-elected judge than from a legislator who feels he must give a fair hearing and respond to concerns of the community toward crime. Given the growing victims' rights movement, defence counsel are increasingly concerned about legislative action. They recognize that accused persons do not have a lobby in the legislature. If changes are to be made to the law of evidence by the legislature, as opposed to the judiciary, the criminal defence bar may feel, with some justification, that the accused's interests will not be well served.

As we explore the laws of evidence you may wish to consider whether you accept this view that legislation is not necessary.

For more discussion on the value or not of a comprehensive statement see Delisle, "A Comprehensive Statement of Evidence Rules?" and Paciocco, "The Case Against Legislated Text in Matters of Proof", both pieces to be found in *Towards a Clear and Just Criminal Law: A Criminal Reports Forum* (Carswell, 1999), at pp. 1-84.

4. APPLICABILITY OF LAWS OF EVIDENCE

when do rules of ev. vary

The rules of evidence we will be examining are rules which cover court proceedings, civil and criminal. There are, of course, a number of administrative tribunals functioning in Canada and each, by its enacting legislation, may describe its own rules of procedure. Aside from the legislation governing the particular tribunal, there may also be more general legislation applicable. For example, the Statutory Powers Procedure Act[31] of Ontario provides:

15.(1) Subject to subsections (2) and (3), a tribunal may admit as evidence at a hearing, whether or not given or proven under oath or affirmation or admissible as evidence in a court,

(a) any oral testimony; and

(b) any document or other thing,

relevant to the subject matter of the proceeding and may act on such evidence, but the tribunal may exclude anything unduly repetitious.

(2) Nothing is admissible in evidence at a hearing,

(a) that would be inadmissible in a court by reason of any privilege under the law of evidence; or

(b) that is inadmissible by the statute under which the proceeding arises or any other statute.

---

31. R.S.O. 1990, c. S.22.

(3) Nothing in subsection (1) overrides the provisions of any Act expressly limiting the extent to or purposes for which any oral testimony, documents or things may be admitted or used in evidence in any proceeding.[32]

The case of *R. v. Barber*[33] is instructive. Section 37(7)(*c*) of the then Ontario Labour Relations Act[34] read:

An arbitrator or an arbitration board, as the case may be, has power . . . to accept such oral or written evidence as the arbitrator or the arbitration board, as the case may be, in its discretion considers proper, whether admissible in a court of law or not.

The arbitrator, Barber, decided that the clause of the collective agreement under review was ambiguous and received extrinsic evidence consisting of oral evidence as to past practice and a master policy unilaterally secured by the company. The award was quashed on *certiorari* on the basis that the clause was not ambiguous. The Court of Appeal, in dismissing the appeal, wrote about section 37(7)(*c*):

By that clause the Legislature recognized that arbitrations will frequently be presented before arbitration boards by lay persons. Accordingly, it relaxed the strict rules as to the admissibility of evidence and in particular allowed hearsay evidence to be adduced without objection. However, that provision does not relieve a board from acting only on evidence having cogency in law. For instance, a board may admit evidence which is inadmissible on the ground of irrelevancy, but the section does not permit it to then act illegally by drawing inferences from wholly irrelevant evidence.[35]

In *Re City of Toronto and C.U.P.E., Local 79*,[36] the arbitrator had refused to admit into evidence the report of a Commission of Inquiry. On appeal the union sought to uphold his decision to exclude on the basis that a number of established rules of evidence rendered the report inadmissible; eight or nine rules, including the hearsay rule and the best evidence rule, were mentioned. The court referred to the broad discretion conferred by the above section and wrote:

The argument made to this Court that the Board would have been prevented from doing so by exclusionary rules applicable in the Courts is singularly without merit. It is plain that the Board was not bound by the rules of evidence and the argument addressed to us by the Union and the arbitration board decisions cited by

---

32. See, however, the remarks of Reid, J. in *Re Northwestern Gen. Hosp. Bd. of Governors and Brown* (1985), 52 O.R. (2d) 591, 600 (Div. Ct.):

The Board has a wide discretion with respect to evidence pursuant to the *Statutory Powers Procedure Act* . . . it was not entitled, in my opinion, to make a ruling based on some policy it has adopted and without regard to the merits of the issue. Thus, I think that the Board was not only wrong in its given reasons but wrong in its apparent resolution by way of a rigid policy.

33. [1968] 2 O.R. 245 (C.A.).
34. See now S.O. 1995, c. 1, Sched. A, s. 12.
35. *Supra*, note 33, at p. 252. See also *Re Girvin and Consumers' Gas Co.* (1973), 1 O.R. (2d) 421 (Div. Ct.) and *Re Windsor Bd. of Educ.* (1982), 3 L.A.C. (3d) 426 (Gorsky); and see generally Gorsky, *Evidence and Procedure in Canadian Labour Arbitration* (1981), at p. 141.
36. (1982), 133 D.L.R. (3d) 94, 106 (Ont. C.A.); leave to appeal to S.C.C. refused 36 O.R. (2d) 386.

it fly in the face of the statute. A decision by any board to refuse to admit evidence because it was not admissible in the Courts or because the board was bound by decisions of other arbitration boards would constitute an obvious error of law. In addition, the discretion of a board obviously would be improperly exercised if it acted in the belief that these legal rules or prior arbitration decisions were binding upon it. It is beyond question that any board so acting would fetter its discretion.

Presumably, however, an arbitrator could refuse hearsay if he decided, in his discretion, that it was "proper" so to do. The arbitrator could reason that:

> For this Board rejection [of hearsay] is justified by consideration of the effects were hearsay freely used. Free use, at least on central issues, would unfairly disadvantage the opposing party. At the same time, it would reduce the arbitrator's ability to judge the weight of evidence as they determine the facts. Together both would endanger respect for the arbitration process itself. These factors — and not the simple dictates of the Judge-made hearsay rule — justify rejection.[37]

While the legislators may decide that formal rules of evidence may inhibit the inquiry, some of the rules are regarded as so essential to a fair inquiry that administrative tribunals may be moved to follow the example set by the courts.[38] Rules of evidence applicable in a court proceeding may also be varied by specific legislation. For example, the Child and Family Services Act[39] provides:

> 50.—(1) Despite anything in the *Evidence Act*, in any proceeding under this Part,
>
> (a) the court may consider the past conduct of a person toward any child if that person is caring for or has access to or may care for or have access to a child who is the subject of the proceeding; and
>
> (b) any oral or written statement or report that the court considers relevant to the proceeding, including a transcript, exhibit or finding or the reasons for a decision in an earlier civil or criminal proceeding, is admissible into evidence.

Judicial interpretation of this section and its predecessor, s. 28(4) of the Child Welfare Act,[40] has varied. In *Re C.A.S. Metro Toronto and N.H.B.*[41] the court received various documents from another case involving the same mother and different children: court orders, judgments, clinic reports and transcripts from previous hearings. The court believed the section gave a very wide discretion to admit hearsay. In *Re Jennifer C.*[42] the court, however, refused to admit certain hospital records:

---

37. *Re Ont. Jockey Club* (1977), 15 L.A.C. (2d) 273, 276 (Schiff). But compare *Chrysler Can. Ltd. v. U.A.W., Loc. 1285* (1983), 11 L.A.C. (3d) 415 (Palmer), and contrast Lord Denning's acceptance of hearsay by administrative tribunals in *Miller v. Min. of Housing & Loc. Govt.*, [1968] 1 W.L.R. 992 (C.A.).

38. See *O.P.S.E.U. v. Min. of Correctional Services* (1984), 2 O.A.C. 351, 358 (Div. Ct.). See generally Adell, "Arbitral Discretion in the Admission of Evidence" in *Labour Arbitration Yearbook 1999-2000*, at pp. 1-38 and see Evans, Janisch and Mullan, *Administrative Law* (4th ed., Emond Montgomery), at pp. 634-5, 637-40.

39. R.S.O. 1990, c. C.11, s. 50(1).

40. R.S.O. 1980, c. 66.

41. (1980), 5 A.C.W.S. 66 (Ont. Prov. Ct.), per Walmsley, Prov. J.

42. (1984), 39 R.F.L. (2d) 244 (Ont. Prov. Ct.), per Weisman, Prov. J. Compare *Re C.A.S., Metro. Toronto and R. (K.)*, [1983] W.D.F.L. 1320, per Thomson, Prov. J. See generally,

. . . I can see no reason to permit the society to use s. 28(4) [now s. 46(1)] to prove the very conduct complained of by recorded hearsay, thereby depriving the mother of her right to cross-examine on this pivotal issue.

In *Central Burner Service Inc. v. Texaco Canada Inc.*[43] the defendant to a civil action brought in Provincial Court appealed on the basis that the judge had relied on hearsay evidence with respect to a critical issue. The appeal was dismissed. The court decided:

Counsel conceded that most, if not all, of the relevant evidence was hearsay. Hearsay evidence is not admissible to prove the truth of its contents in regular court proceedings, particularly where it goes to the root of an issue. However, s. 80(1) of the Courts of Justice Act, S.O. 1984, c. 11, provides as follows:

80(1) Subject to subsections (2) and (3), the Provincial Court (Civil Division) may admit as evidence at a hearing, whether or not given or proven under oath or affirmation or admissible as evidence in any other court,

(a)   any oral testimony; and

(b)   any document or other thing,

relevant to the subject-matter of the proceeding and may act on such evidence, but the court may exclude anything unduly repetitious.

Prior to the enactment of s. 80, hearsay evidence was not generally allowed in the Small Claims Court. The question is to what extent has s. 80 changed the law. Counsel for the defendants contends that if hearsay evidence is admitted with respect to critical issues at trial the opposing party will not have the opportunity to test that evidence by cross-examination. While that may be so, the weight to be given to any kind of evidence is for the trial judge to decide. Normally, hearsay evidence should be given less weight than direct evidence.

In my opinion, s. 80 allows hearsay evidence of all oral testimony and all documents or other things, provided they are relevant and not unduly repetitious. There is nothing in s. 80 that draws a distinction between critical issues and more peripheral issues. The object of s. 80 is to avoid technical procedures and the additional cost of calling extra witnesses in cases involving small claims.

The trial judge was entitled to rely on hearsay evidence. In the present case the transcript shows that she clearly understood that much of the evidence was hearsay and she stated that she would give it the appropriate weight. Therefore, there was evidence upon which she could come to her conclusion and that she properly weighed it.

In addition, the courts will often take a different attitude toward the rules and procedures if the subject-matter warrants. For example, in *Gordon v. Gordon*,[44] the Ontario Court of Appeal wrote:

Bala and Anweiler, "Allegations of Sexual Abuse in a Parental Custody Dispute" (1987), 2 C.F.L.Q. 343. See also *Roman Catholic C.A.S. (Essex) v. H. (L.)*, [1987] O.J. No. 1845 (Ont. Fam. Ct.), dealing with s. 47(7) [now s. 51(7)] of the Child and Family Services Act which provides that in an interim proceeding, "the court may admit and act on evidence that the court considers credible and trustworthy in the circumstances." And see *R. v. Hajdu* (1984), 14 C.C.C. (3d) 563 (Ont. H.C.) commenting upon s. 457.3(1)(*e*) [now s. 518(*e*)] of the Criminal Code, a section providing that a justice conducting a bail hearing "may receive and base his decision on evidence considered credible or trustworthy by him in the circumstance of each case."

43.   (1989), 36 O.A.C. 239, 240 (C.A.).

44.   (1980), 23 R.F.L. (2d) 266, 271.

A custody case, where the best interest of the child is the only issue, is not the same as ordinary litigation and requires, in our view, that the person conducting the hearing take a more active role than he ordinarily would take in the conduct of a trial. Generally, he should do what he reasonably can to see to it that his decision will be based upon the most relevant and helpful information available.

In *Official Solicitor v. K.*,[45] Lord Evershed stated:

It is not in doubt that a judicial enquiry concerning the proper steps to be taken for the care and maintenance of a ward of Court is subject — and necessarily subject because of the nature and purpose of the enquiry — to a procedure in many respects quite special.[46]

And Lord Devlin agreed:

But a principle of judicial enquiry, whether fundamental or not, is only a means to an end. If it can be shown in any particular class of case that the observance of a principle of this sort does not serve the ends of justice, it must be dismissed, otherwise it would become the master instead of the servant of justice. Obviously the ordinary principles of judicial enquiry are requirements for all ordinary cases and it can only be in an extraordinary class of case that any one of them can be discarded.[47]

In *R. v. Zeolkowski*[48] the court was concerned with the rules to be applied when a judge conducted a hearing pursuant to the Criminal Code to determine whether a person should possess firearms. It appeared that a police sergeant was going to testify that a prohibition order should go on the basis that the person's wife had told the sergeant that he had threatened her. The wife would not be called. The Provincial Court judge ruled that hearsay evidence was inadmissible, in that evidence at a hearing under section 98(6) of the Code was limited to that which would be admissible at a criminal trial. Appeals in Manitoba confirmed the ruling. The Supreme Court reversed:

The provincial court judge must simply be satisfied that the peace officer had reasonable grounds to believe as he or she did: in other words, that there is an objective basis for the reasonable grounds on which the peace officer acted. . . . Accordingly, I am prepared to hold that hearsay evidence is admissible at a firearm prohibition hearing under s. 98(6).

Finally, the rules of evidence may vary within a court proceeding depending on the stage of the proceedings. For example, in *R. v. Gardiner*[49] the Crown argued that the burden of proof at sentencing should be less than the traditional criminal onus of beyond a reasonable doubt which applies at trial to the determination of guilt. The Supreme Court of Canada decided that the burdens

---

45. [1965] A.C. 201 (H.L.).
46. *Ibid.*, at p. 218.
47. *Ibid.*, at p. 238. See also *Lucier v. R.* (1982), 65 C.C.C. (2d) 150 (S.C.C.), indicating that a rule of evidence can operate differently depending on whether it is in the interest of the Crown or the accused. And see *R. v. Rowbotham* (1988), 63 C.R. (3d) 113, 164 (Ont. C.A.), that application of a technical rule which denies justice to an accused should be ignored.
48. (1989), 50 C.C.C. (3d) 566, 572 (S.C.C.).
49. (1982), 68 C.C.C. (2d) 477, 513 (S.C.C.). See also the excellent discussion by Grenier, J. in *R. v. Alarie* (1980), 28 C.R. (3d) 73 (C.S.P. Qué.). And see *R. v. Albright*, [1987] 2 S.C.R. 383.

of proof should be the same but also decided that the rules could vary. Justice Dickson wrote:

> One of the hardest tasks confronting a trial judge is sentencing. The stakes are high for society and for the individual. Sentencing is the critical stage of the criminal justice system, and it is manifest that the judge should not be denied an opportunity to obtain relevant information by the imposition of all the restrictive evidential rules common to a trial. Yet the obtaining and weighing of such evidence should be fair. A substantial liberty interest of the offender is involved and the information obtained should be accurate and reliable.
>
> It is a commonplace that the strict rules which govern at trial do not apply at a sentencing hearing and it would be undesirable to have the formalities and technicalities characteristic of the normal adversary proceeding prevail. The hearsay rule does not govern the sentencing hearing. Hearsay evidence may be accepted where found to be credible and trustworthy. The judge traditionally has had wide latitude as to the sources and types of evidence upon which to base his sentence. He must have the fullest possible information concerning the background of the accused if he is to fit the sentence to the offender rather than to the crime. . . .
>
> To my mind, the facts which justify the sanction are no less important than the facts which justify the conviction; both should be subject to the same burden of proof. Crime and punishment are inextricably linked.

Are you satisfied that the burden of proof must be the same but the rules governing admissibility can vary? Why should the hearsay rule govern the determination of the crime but not the punishment?[50]

Although the strict rules of evidence do not apply at sentencing hearings, the basic principles of justice must be adhered to. At a sentencing hearing on a charge of sexual assault, the trial judge admitted evidence given by the 17-year-old mentally handicapped victim of other sexual acts with the accused, her stepfather. The victim's testimony was uncorroborated and unsworn and the testimony of her mother concerning circumstances surrounding the other occasions of sexual activity was largely hearsay. The Newfoundland Court of Appeal reduced the accused's sentence, stating:

> In the case before us, the accused was charged with and pleaded guilty to a single charge of sexual assault. Crown counsel put before the court evidence, from one witness, for the most part, hearsay, and from another, unsworn and uncorroborated, relating to prior uncharged and unproven offences, all over the strenuous objection of counsel for the accused, which could only be perceived as inviting the court to increase the punishment to be imposed. The trial judge was in error in accepting into the record the evidence complained of and we are not satisfied that his judgment was not influenced by it. . . .
>
> A basic principle of justice requires an accused be tried and convicted of a crime before being subjected to punishment for it. If the Crown has any grounds to believe charges could be laid for other acts by the appellant, it can lay those charges. In such eventuality any convictions resulting would be a factor in his sentencing but unproven allegations may not be. With respect, it is evident that the learned trial judge took unproven allegations into account in the sentence and it is for this reason the sentence has been varied.[51]

---

50.   Adopting *Gardiner*-like provisions in recent amendments, see ss. 723 and 724 of the Criminal Code.

51.   *R. v. J.C.L.* (1987), 36 C.C.C. (3d) 32, 42 (Nfld. C.A.).

5. FORMAL ADMISSIONS OF FACT

In civil cases pleadings are designed to narrow issues and determine facts not in dispute. Failure to admit facts can result in an award of costs. Admissions of fact, law or mixed law and facts can occur in a number of ways such as in pleadings, a failure to respond, an agreed statement in a signed letter, or orally at trial.

In criminal trials sections 655 and 795 of the Criminal Code allow the accused or his counsel to admit any fact alleged against him thereby dispensing with the need for proof.

CASTELLANI v. R.
[1970] S.C.R. 310, 9 C.R.N.S. 111, [1970] 4 C.C.C. 287

CARTWRIGHT C.J.C.:— This is an appeal from the unanimous judgment of the Court of Appeal for British Columbia, pronounced on July 19, 1968, dismissing the appellant's appeal from his conviction before Dryer J. and a jury on October 6, 1967, of the capital murder of his wife.

. . . .

The grounds of appeal relied upon by the appellant in the Court of Appeal are accurately summarized as follows in the reasons of Norris J.A. and of Bull J.A.:

1. The learned trial Judge erred in refusing to allow the appellant or his counsel to admit at the trial certain facts under Section 562 (now s. 655) of the *Criminal Code*.

. . . .

As to the first of these grounds, it appears that on September 25, 1967, the first day of the trial, after the evidence of one Crown witness had been heard, counsel for the appellant tendered a formal written admission of facts "for the purpose of freeing the Crown of the responsibility for proving same" and asked that this be received pursuant to s. 562 of the *Criminal Code* which reads as follows:

562. Where an accused is on trial for an indictable offence he or his counsel may admit any fact alleged against him for the purpose of dispensing with proof thereof.

The document tendered consisted of eight paragraphs; following the style of cause it read as follows:

Pursuant to the provisions of section 562 of the *Criminal Code* of Canada, Counsel for Rene Emile Castellani hereby admit the following facts:

1. That at the Vancouver General Hospital, in the City of Vancouver in the County of Vancouver, in the Province of British Columbia, on July 12th, 1965, an autopsy was performed by Dr. Frank H. Anderson on the body of Esther Castellani, deceased.

2. That on July 14th, 1965, at Forest Lawn Memorial Park in the Municipality of Burnaby, in the Province of British Columbia, the body of Esther Castellani, deceased, was buried in a casket placed in a closed cement crypt.

3. That on August 3rd, 1965, the body of Esther Castellani, deceased, was exhumed from the cement crypt of Forest Lawn Memorial Park in the Municipality of Burnaby, and delivered to the morgue in the City of Vancouver where a post-mortem examination was conducted by Dr. Thomas Redo Harmon.

4. That control specimens of embalming fluid from the same source as were used by the undertakers who embalmed the body of Esther Castellani, deceased and

who buried her, namely Simmons & McBride Ltd. of the City of Vancouver, were delivered to Eldon Rideout at the City of Vancouver on August 3rd, 1965.

5. That on July 28th, 1965, at the Broadway and Cambie Branch of the Canadian Imperial Bank of Commerce in the City of Vancouver, Rene Emile Castellani signed a certain application for a loan from from the Kinross Mortgage Corporation, in the presence of Mr. R.S. Keyes.

6. That no action or proceeding for dissolution of the marriage between Rene Emile Castellani and Esther Castellani, which marriage was solemnized on July 16th, 1946, was ever commenced in any Court having jurisdiction to hear such an action.

7. That scientific tests known as X-ray diffraction procedures were done by Mrs. Thompson at the Ontario Attorney-General's Crime Detection Laboratory, in an effort to determine from the hair samples removed from the body of Esther Castellani what salt or compound the arsenic had originated from, but the results were inconclusive because there was not a sufficient quantity of hair.

8. That Rene Emile Castellani and Adelaide Miller mutually engaged in an extra-marital sexual relationship from approximately the Fall of A.D., 1964 to the Spring of A.D., 1966.

It was dated September 25, 1967, and signed by both the counsel who appeared for the appellant at the trial.

Counsel for the Crown objected and the question was adjourned to the following day for argument. During the adjournment counsel for both parties agreed that the first seven paragraphs should be admitted but Crown counsel objected to the inclusion of para. 8 while counsel for the appellant insisted that under s. 562 he had the right to make that admission and intended to do so.

Following argument in the absence of the jury the learned trial Judge, after expressing regret that counsel for the Crown had not seen fit to accept the admissions as tendered, ruled that while the Crown's case was being put in the defence did not have the right to make an admission unless the Crown were willing to accept it. Later the admission consisting of the seven paragraphs was signed and filed with the consent of both parties but counsel for the appellant maintained that they had the right to insist on also making the admission contained in para. 8.

The Court of Appeal were of the view that the learned trial Judge should have permitted the admission set out in para. 8 to be made, interpreting the words of s. 562 as giving the accused an unqualified right to make an admission of any fact alleged against him. They held therefore that the learned trial Judge had erred in law but went on to hold that the error had caused no prejudice to the appellant and that no substantial wrong or miscarriage of justice had occurred. If I were in agreement with the Court of Appeal that the learned trial Judge had erred in law in the manner stated I would also have agreed with their conclusion that this occasioned no substantial wrong or miscarriage of justice; but, with respect, I do not agree that the learned trial Judge was in error in the ruling which he made.

In a criminal case, there being no pleadings, there are no precisely worded allegations of fact which are susceptible of categorical admission. An accused cannot admit a fact alleged against him until the allegation has been made. When recourse is proposed to be had to s. 562 it is for the Crown, not for the defence, to state the fact or facts which it alleges against the accused and of which it seeks admission. The accused, of course, is under no obligation to admit the fact so alleged but his choice is to admit it or to decline to do so. He cannot frame the wording of the allegation to suit his own purposes and then insist on admitting it. To permit such a course could only lead to confusion. The idea of the admission of an allegation involves action by two persons, one who makes the allegation and another who admits it.

. . . .

In my opinion the purpose of enacting s. 562 and its predecessors was to alter the common law rule by eliminating the necessity, on the trial of an indictable offence, of proof by the Crown of any fact which it desires to prove and which the accused is prepared to admit at his trial.

R. v. PROCTOR
(1991), 11 C.R. (4th) 200, 69 C.C.C. (3d) 436 (Man. C.A.)

[The accused was charged with first degree murder. The victim, a 21-year-old woman, had been raped and strangled. The trial began with the Crown's argument that he should be permitted to tell the jury in his opening address about similar attacks made by the accused on two teenagers a few weeks after the killing. Crown counsel argued that the evidence was probative of the killer's identity but defence counsel argued that identity was not in issue. Defence counsel said the only issue was the accused's sanity at the time of the killing. The evidence was led as relevant to state of mind. The conviction was set aside.]

TWADDLE J.A.:—

Counsel had previously agreed to the proof of some facts by admission. Although these facts consisted mainly of minutiae, they were probably enough when added together to enable the jury to infer that the accused was the killer. In any event, defence counsel made it crystal clear that the accused did not dispute his role as the killer: the only issue was his sanity at the time of the killing.

. . . .

The usual practice where the admissibility of similar fact evidence is in dispute is for Crown counsel to refrain from mentioning it in his opening address. Then, as the case develops, and the nature of the defence is known, the relevance of the disputed evidence can better be determined by the trial judge. This practice avoids the necessity of relying upon the mere statement of the accused's counsel as to what his client's defence will be and enables the judge to determine the admissibility of the similar fact evidence on the basis of its relevance to an issue which is really in dispute.

. . . .

The *Criminal Code* contains provision enabling an accused person to admit facts for the purpose of dispensing with proof of them. Whilst it is true that such admissions must first be accepted by the Crown (*Castellani v. R.*, [1970] S.C.R. 310, I do not think the Crown is entitled to refuse acceptance where its purpose in doing so is to keep an issue alive artificially. In my opinion, evidence which shows the accused to have committed another crime of moral turpitude should not ordinarily be admitted where its only relevance is to an issue which the accused does not dispute. The accused must, of course, make all necessary admissions. But, if the accused is willing to make them, the Crown should not be allowed to gain entry for prejudicial evidence by refusing to accept the admissions.

If the admissions made by the accused in the case at bar had been read into the record before the application with respect to the teenagers' evidence had been made, it would have been apparent that the accused's identity as the killer was not in dispute. The absence of an express admission to that effect was clearly due to the refusal of the Crown to accept it. The learned trial judge, correctly in my view, recognized this fact and found that identity was not an issue on which the teenagers' evidence should be admitted.

. . . .

In view of the disposition I propose, further comments on how much of the teenagers' evidence should have been admitted in rebuttal of the insanity defence should not be made. The extent to which such evidence should be admitted, at the proper time, is a matter for the trial judge to decide. He will no doubt be aware of the evidence which the teenagers will be expected to give and of the fact that such evidence, detailing as it does their harrowing encounter with the accused, is enough to make a petrified mummy cry. In that circumstance, he will no doubt give much thought to the words of McLachlin J. in *R. v. B. (C.R.)*, [1990] 1 S.C.R. 717, where she said (at p. 735):

> In a case such as the present, where the similar fact evidence sought to be adduced is prosecution evidence of a morally repugnant act committed by the accused, the potential prejudice is great and the probative value must be high indeed to permit its reception.

. . . .

The role of prosecuting counsel in Canada is to promote the cause of justice. It is not his function to persuade a jury to convict other than by reason. His function is to ensure that all the proper evidence, and all the proper inferences that may be drawn from it, are placed before the jury, together with a reasoned argument as to the conclusion to which such evidence and inferences lead. . . .

In *R. v. B. (L.)*,[52] Justice Charron, discussing the proper assessment of probative value and prejudice with the admission of similar fact evidence, relying on *Proctor*, noted:

> The extent to which the matter sought to be proved is an issue in the trial is important to the assessment of the probative value. If the issue in question is but a minor one the evidence will have less probative value and may not be worth receiving given its prejudicial effect. If the matter is not in issue at all, the evidence should not be admitted because it is irrelevant. See *R. v. Proctor* (1992), 11 C.R. (4th) 200 (Man. C.A.). In some circumstances, it may be necessary to postpone the ruling on the question of admissibility to a later stage in the trial when all relevant issues are known.

Identifying the issue in the trial to which the proposed evidence relates is particularly important given the prejudice which may arise from the admission of evidence of discreditable conduct. It is important to keep in mind what is meant by prejudice in this context. The danger which must be guarded against is that the trier of fact, in relying on the evidence of discreditable conduct, may conclude that the accused committed the offence with which he is charged based, not on the strength of the evidence which has a connection to the issues in the case, but rather, on the strength of the evidence that he is "a bad person" who would have a tendency to commit this offence.

It is because of the prejudice which is inherent to this type of evidence that courts have often focused on the requirement that the evidence of discreditable conduct relate to an issue in the trial before it can be admitted. Indeed this particular factor, which must be considered in assessing the probative value of the proposed evidence, is often stated as a separate facet of the similar fact evidence rule. In many cases, the Supreme Court of Canada has adopted a more classic two-part formulation of the rule stating that the proposed evidence will be

---

52.   (1997), 9 C.R. (5th) 38, 57, para. 40 (Ont. C.A.).

test for admission

admissible if "(1) relevant to some other issue beyond disposition or character, and (2) the probative value outweighs the prejudicial effect."

Another type of formal admission of fact is a plea of guilt. The evidentiary requirements for a guilty plea and admissions of fact was considered by Lamer, J. in *Matheson v. R.*[53] as follows:

> A person may be convicted for an offence only after having been accused of that offence and after a trial at which proof of that person's guilt has been adduced before a judge (or judge and jury) having jurisdiction to hear the case. An accused may waive (subject to that waiver being accepted by the judge) his right to a trial by a plea of guilty. Short of that there must be compliance with the rule that guilt must be established during the trial before the trier of fact. As regards evidence by witnesses, strict compliance means their being sworn or affirmed and heard at the trial before the trier of fact. An accused may, if the Crown consents and the Court accepts, waive *strict* compliance with that rule in many ways and in various degrees; indeed, he may relieve the Crown from proving certain facts by admitting them; he may dispense with the swearing in of witnesses and the taking of their evidence by admitting what their evidence would be as regards certain facts if those witnesses were called; he may, if the evidence has already been adduced at a previous proceeding, accept that the evidence be read or even be deemed to be read into the trial proceedings; he may even accept, when, as in this case, the trial judge is the same person before whom the witnesses testified in the previous proceedings, that their evidence be deemed read into the record of his trial without even awaiting the filing of the transcript of their oral evidence. But, whatever be the method chosen for satisfying at least substantial compliance, there are two prerequisites to be met, short either one of which there is no compliance at all (save the exception found in the *Code* at s. 485(3)(b): that the consent by the accused and the Crown departing from strict compliance be conveyed to the Court in the course of the trial, and then that the evidence in some way, be it by the filing of transcripts or even by some reference to previous judicial proceedings, enter the record sometime during that trial. In the present case neither was met. As a result the evidence adduced prior to the re-election cannot form any part of the trial.

See also *R. v. Adgey*[54] regarding the role of the trial judge on a plea of guilty.

---

53.   (1981), 22 C.R. (3d) 289, 291-292, para. 5 (S.C.C.).
54.   [1975] 2 S.C.R. 426.

2

Burdens of Proof and Presumptions

1. BURDENS OF PROOF

(a) Terminology

To the confusion of both the student and the profession, the term "burden of proof" is used in the cases to signify different things. Sometimes the term is used to refer to the requirement of satisfying the trier of fact that a certain material proposition has been made out. If the party who has this burden of proof is unable to persuade the trier that his alleged version of the facts actually occurred, that party will lose the case. Sometimes the term is used to signify the obligation of ensuring that there is evidence in the case concerning an issue. Failing to satisfy this burden will prevent the issue from being considered by the trier.

Cases seeking to distinguish the two uses sometimes refer to the former as the "persuasive burden," the "legal burden," the "ultimate," "major," or "primary" burden and to the latter as the "evidential burden," the "tactical burden," the "minor" or "secondary" burden or "the duty of going forward."

Chief Justice Dickson described the chaos and brought order to bear in *R. v. Schwartz*:[1]

> Judges and academics have used a variety of terms to try to capture the distinction between the two types of burdens. The burden of establishing a case has been referred to as the "major burden," the "primary burden," the "legal burden" and the "persuasive burden." The burden of putting an issue in play has been called the "minor burden," the "secondary burden," the "evidential burden," the "burden of going forward," and the "burden of adducing evidence." While any combination of phrases has its advantages and drawbacks, I prefer to use the terms "persuasive burden" to refer to the requirement of proving a case or disproving defences, and "evidential burden" to mean the requirement of putting an issue into play by reference to evidence before the court. The party who has the persuasive burden is required to persuade the trier of fact, to convince the trier of fact that a certain set of facts existed. Failure to persuade means that the party loses. The party with an evidential burden is not required to convince the trier of fact of anything, only to point out evidence which suggests that certain facts existed. The phrase "onus of proof" should be restricted to the persuasive burden, since an issue can be put into play without being proven. The phrases "burden of going forward" and "burden of adducing evidence" should not be used, as they imply that the party is required to produce his or her own evidence on an issue. As we have seen, in a criminal case the accused can rely on evidence produced by the Crown to argue for a reasonable doubt.
>
> It is important not to identify the evidential burden solely with the accused. The Crown has the evidential burden of leading evidence which, if believed, would prove each element of the offence charged. If the Crown does not even meet this evidential requirement, the case never goes to the trier of fact; the accused has a right to a directed verdict of acquittal.

---

1.   [1988] 2 S.C.R. 443, 466.

In *R. v. Osolin*,[2] Justice Cory described the role of the trial judge in determining whether the accused had satisfied his evidential burden. He was there discussing the defence of honest but mistaken belief in consent in a sexual assault case:

> . . . a defence should not be put to the jury if a reasonable jury properly instructed would have been unable to acquit on the basis of the evidence tendered in support of that defence. On the other hand, if a reasonable jury properly instructed could acquit on the basis of the evidence tendered with regard to that defence, then it must be put to the jury. It is for the trial judge to decide whether the evidence is sufficient to warrant putting a defence to a jury as this is a question of law alone. . . . There is thus a two step procedure which must be followed. First, the trial judge must review all the evidence and decide if it is sufficient to warrant putting the defence to the jury. Second, if the evidence meets that threshold, the trial judge must put the defence to the jury, which in turn will weigh it and decide whether it raises a reasonable doubt. . . .

> . . . .

> It is trite law that a trial judge must instruct the jury only upon those defences for which there is a real factual basis. A defence for which there is no evidentiary foundation should not be put to the jury. This rule extends well beyond the defence of mistaken belief in consent and is of long standing. . . .

> . . . .

> . . . A juror should not be required to listen to instructions on defences which simply cannot be applicable to the case that they have heard. . . .

> . . . .

> It can be seen that this Court has consistently held that the defence of mistake of fact in a sexual assault trial will be put to the jury so long as it meets the same threshold requirement as that demanded of all defences. The term "air of reality" simply means that the trial judge must determine if the evidence put forward is such that, if believed, a reasonable jury properly charged could have acquitted. If the evidence meets that test then the defence must be put to the jury. This is no more than an example of the basic division of tasks between judge and jury. It is the judge who must determine if evidence sought to be adduced is relevant and admissible. In the same way, it is the judge who determines if there is sufficient evidence adduced to give rise to the defence. If there has been sufficient evidence put forward, then the jury must be given the opportunity to consider that defence along with all the other evidence and other defences left with them in coming to their verdict.

A leading case which illustrates the damage that can result from confusing the two burdens is *Woolmington v. Director of Public Prosecutions*.[3] The accused was convicted of murdering his bride. The accused admitted the shooting but testified that it was an accident. The trial judge charged the jury:

> If you come to the conclusion that she died in consequence of injuries from the gun which he was carrying, you are put by the law of this country into this position: The killing of a human being is homicide, however he may be killed, and all homicide is presumed to be malicious and murder, unless the contrary appears from

---

2.   [1993] 4 S.C.R. 595, 676, 677, 680, 681, 682.
3.   [1935] A.C. 462 (H.L.). See also *R. v. Stoddart* (1909), 2 Cr. App. R. 217, 233 and 242 (C.C.A.).

circumstances of alleviation, excuse, or justification. "In every charge of murder, the fact of killing being first proved, all the circumstances of accident, necessity, or infirmity are to be satisfactorily proved by the prisoner, unless they arise out of the evidence produced against him; for the law will presume the fact to have been founded in malice, unless the contrary appeareth." That has been the law of this country for all time since we had law. Once it is shown to a jury that somebody has died through an act of another, that is presumed to be murder, unless the person who has been guilty of the act which causes the death can satisfy a jury that what happened was something less, something which might be alleviated, something which might be reduced to a charge of manslaughter, or was something which was accidental, or was something which could be justified.[4]

The Court of Appeal dismissed the accused's appeal as it recognized "ample authority for that statement of law."[5] The House of Lords traced the authority to Sir Michael Foster's text in 1762, written at a time when "the law of evidence was in a very fluid condition."[6] The Lords also noted that there had been many changes in procedure in the intervening two centuries, including the prisoner's right to give evidence, to counsel, to an appeal. Viscount Sankey explained the true meaning of earlier authorities:

> All that is meant is that if it is proved that the conscious act of the prisoner killed a man and nothing else appears in the case, there is evidence upon which the jury may, not must, find him guilty of murder. It is difficult to conceive so bare and meagre a case, but that does not mean that the onus is not still on the prosecution.
>
> . . . Just as there is evidence on behalf of the prosecution so there may be evidence on behalf of the prisoner which may cause a doubt as to his guilt. In either case, he is entitled to the benefit of the doubt. But while the prosecution must prove the guilt of the prisoner, there is no such burden laid on the prisoner to prove his innocence and it is sufficient for him to raise a doubt as to his guilt; he is not bound to satisfy the jury of his innocence.
>
> . . . where intent is an ingredient of a crime there is no onus on the defendant to prove that the act alleged was accidental. Throughout the web of the English Criminal Law one golden thread is always to be seen, that it is the duty of the prosecution to prove the prisoner's guilt subject to what I have already said as to the defence of insanity and subject also to any statutory exception. If at the end of and on the whole of the case, there is a reasonable doubt, created by the evidence given by either the prosecution or the prisoner, as to whether the prisoner killed the deceased with a malicious intention, the prosecution has not made out the case and the prisoner is entitled to an acquittal. No matter what the charge or where the trial, the principle that the prosecution must prove the guilt of the prisoner is part of the common law of England and no attempt to whittle it down can be entertained. When dealing with a murder case the Crown must prove (a) death as the result of a voluntary act of the accused and (b) malice of the accused. It may prove malice either expressly or by implication. For malice may be implied where death occurs as the result of a voluntary act of the accused which is (i) intentional and (ii) unprovoked. When evidence of death and malice has been given (this is a question for the jury) the accused is entitled to show, by evidence or by examination of the circumstances adduced by the Crown that the act on his part which caused death was either unintentional or provoked. If the jury are either satisfied with his explanation or, upon

golden thread

4.   *Ibid.*, at pp. 472-73.
5.   *Ibid.*, at p. 473.
6.   *Ibid.*, at p. 478.

a review of all the evidence, are left in reasonable doubt whether, even if his explanation be not accepted, the act was unintentional or provoked, the prisoner is entitled to be acquitted.[7]

(b) Allocation of Burdens

How do we decide the allocation of responsibility between the parties? Thayer believed we should have regard to the principles of pleading and in attending to these:

> We shall sometimes find ourselves involved in an analysis of the substantive law of the particular case and perhaps in an inquiry into things obsolete, anomolous and forgotten. . . .
>
> Clearly one has no right to look to the law of evidence for a solution of such questions as these, and I am not proposing to answer them.[8]

Later commentators on the law of evidence have attempted to distill from the cases some general principles, but the furthest they have been able to take us is to note that problems of allocation involve "considerations of policy, fairness and probability."[9]

(i) Civil Cases

FONTAINE v. INSURANCE CORPORATION OF BRITISH COLUMBIA
[1998] 1 S.C.R. 424

[The plaintiff claimed damages with respect to the death of her husband. His body and that of his hunting companion, which was still buckled in the driver's seat, were in the companion's badly damaged truck which had been washed along a flood-swollen creek flowing alongside a mountain highway. No one saw the accident and no one knew precisely when it occurred. A great deal of rain had fallen in the vicinity of the accident the weekend of their hunting trip. The trial judge found that negligence had not been proven against the driver and dismissed the plaintiff's case. An appeal to the Court of Appeal was dismissed.]

MAJOR J. (for the court):—This appeal provides another opportunity to consider the so-called maxim of *res ipsa loquitur*. What is it? When does it arise? And what effect does its application have?

. . . .

7.   *Ibid.*, at pp. 480-82.
8.   Thayer, *A Preliminary Treatise on Evidence at the Common Law* (1898), p. 355.
9.   Cleary, "Presuming and Pleading: An Essay on Juristic Immaturity" (1959), 12 Stan. L. Rev. 5 at 11. To the same effect, and using the same words, see James, "Burdens of Proof" (1961), 47 Va. L. Rev. 51 at 58-61; Morgan, *Some Problems of Proof Under the Anglo-American System of Litigation* (1956), p. 76; and 9 Wigmore, *Evidence* (Chad. Rev.), s. 2486, p. 291. Considerations of policy, fairness and probability can of course change: see, *e.g.*, *R. v. Jackson* (1984), 14 C.R.R. 248 (B.C. Co. Ct.), regarding the presumption that a husband is in possession and control of the premises and their contents.

A. *When does res ipsa loquitur apply?*

Res ipsa loquitur, or "the thing speaks for itself", has been referred to in negligence cases for more than a century. In *Scott v. London and St. Katherine Docks Co.* (1865), 159 E.R. 665 . . . at p. 667 . . ., Erle C.J. defined what has since become known as *res ipsa loquitur* in the following terms:

> There must be reasonable evidence of negligence.
> But where the thing is shewn to be under the management of the defendant or his servants, and the accident is such as in the ordinary course of things does not happen if those who have the management use proper care, it affords reasonable evidence, in the absence of explanation by the defendants, that the accident arose from want of care.

. . . .

For *res ipsa loquitur* to arise, the circumstances of the occurrence must permit an inference of negligence attributable to the defendant. The strength or weakness of that inference will depend on the factual circumstances of the case. As described in *Canadian Tort Law* (5th ed. 1993), by Allen M. Linden, at p. 233, "[t]here are situations where the facts merely whisper negligence, but there are other circumstances where they shout it aloud."

As the application of *res ipsa loquitur* is highly dependent upon the circumstances proved in evidence, it is not possible to identify in advance the types of situations in which *res ipsa loquitur* will arise. The application of *res ipsa loquitur* in previous decisions may provide some guidance as to when an inference of negligence may be drawn, but it does not serve to establish definitive categories of when *res ipsa loquitur* will apply. It has been held on numerous occasions that evidence of a vehicle leaving the roadway gives rise to an inference of negligence. Whether that will be so in any given case, however, can only be determined after considering the relevant circumstances of the particular case.

. . . .

B. *Effect of the application of res ipsa loquitur*

As in any negligence case, the plaintiff bears the burden of proving on a balance of probabilities that negligence on the part of the defendant caused the plaintiff's injuries. The invocation of *res ipsa loquitur* does not shift the burden of proof to the defendant. Rather, the effect of the application of *res ipsa loquitur* is as described in *The Law of Evidence in Canada* (1992), by John Sopinka, Sidney N. Lederman and Alan W. Bryant, at p. 81:

> *Res ipsa loquitur*, correctly understood, means that circumstantial evidence constitutes reasonable evidence of negligence. Accordingly, the plaintiff is able to overcome a motion for a non-suit and the trial judge is required to instruct the jury on the issue of negligence. The jury may, but need not, find negligence: a permissible fact inference. If, at the conclusion of the case, it would be equally reasonable to infer negligence or no negligence, the plaintiff will lose since he or she bears the legal burden on this issue. Under this construction, the maxim is superfluous. It can be treated simply as a case of circumstantial evidence.

Should the trier of fact choose to draw an inference of negligence from the circumstances, that will be a factor in the plaintiff's favour. Whether that will be sufficient for the plaintiff to succeed will depend on the strength of the inference drawn and any explanation offered by the defendant to negate that inference. If the defendant produces a reasonable explanation that is as consistent with no negligence as the *res ipsa loquitur* inference is with negligence, this will effectively neutralize the inference of negligence and the plaintiff's case must fail. Thus, the strength of the explanation that the defendant must provide will vary in accordance with the strength of the inference sought to be drawn by the plaintiff.

. . . .

Whatever value *res ipsa loquitur* may have once provided is gone. Various attempts to apply the so-called doctrine have been more confusing than helpful. Its use has been restricted to cases where the facts permitted an inference of negligence and there was no other reasonable explanation for the accident. Given its limited use it is somewhat meaningless to refer to that use as a doctrine of law.

It would appear that the law would be better served if the maxim was treated as expired and no longer used as a separate component in negligence actions. After all, it was nothing more than an attempt to deal with circumstantial evidence. That evidence is more sensibly dealt with by the trier of fact, who should weigh the circumstantial evidence with the direct evidence, if any, to determine whether the plaintiff has established on a balance of probabilities a *prima facie* case of negligence against the defendant. Once the plaintiff has done so, the defendant must present evidence negating that of the plaintiff or necessarily the plaintiff will succeed.

C. *Application to this case*

. . . .

There are a number of reasons why the circumstantial evidence in this case does not discharge the plaintiff's onus. Many of the circumstances of the accident, including the date, time and precise location, are not known. Although this case has proceeded on the basis that the accident likely occurred during the weekend of November 9, 1990, that is only an assumption. There are minimal if any evidentiary foundations from which any inference of negligence could be drawn.

As well, there was evidence before the trial judge that a severe wind and rainstorm was raging at the presumed time of the accident. While it is true that such weather conditions impose a higher standard of care on drivers to take increased precautions, human experience confirms that severe weather conditions are more likely to produce situations where accidents occur and vehicles leave the roadway regardless of the degree of care taken. In these circumstances, it should not be concluded that the accident would ordinarily not have occurred in the absence of negligence.

. . . The trial judge's finding was not unreasonable and should not be interfered with on appeal.

. . . .

The appellant submitted that an inference of negligence should be drawn whenever a vehicle leaves the roadway in a single-vehicle accident. This bald proposition ignores the fact that whether an inference of negligence can be drawn is highly dependent upon the circumstances of each case. . . . The position advanced by the appellant would virtually subject the defendant to strict liability in cases such as the present one.

(ii) *Criminal Cases*

In the criminal law the presumption of innocence normally allocates the persuasive burden of proof to the Crown.

Since 1960, section 2(*f*) of the Canadian Bill of Rights has guaranteed that a person charged with an offence will be "presumed innocent until proved guilty according to law in a fair and public hearing by an independent and impartial tribunal". An identical guarantee is contained in section 11(*d*) of the Charter of Rights and Freedoms. The latter clearly operates irrespective of statutory wording *ie golden thread*

to both federal and provincial legislation. It has long been clear that the *Woolmington* rule applies also to provincial offences.

What values underlie this presumption? The presumption of innocence characterizes most civilized systems of criminal law and is the cornerstone of ours. In the leading interpretation of section 11(*d*), Chief Justice Dickson, for the Supreme Court of Canada in *Oakes*,[10] sees the presumption of innocence as embodying cardinal values lying at the very heart of criminal law which are protected expressly by section 11(*d*) but are also integral to the general protection of life, liberty and security of the person in section 7.

> The presumption of innocence protects the fundamental liberty and human dignity of any and every person accused by the state of criminal conduct. An individual charged with a criminal offence faces grave social and personal consequences, including potential loss of physical liberty, subjection to social stigma and ostracism from the community, as well as other social, psychological and economic harms. In light of the gravity of these consequences, the presumption of innocence is crucial. It ensures that, until the state proves an accused's guilt beyond all reasonable doubt, he or she is innocent. This is essential in a society committed to fairness and social justice. The presumption of innocence confirms our faith in humankind; it reflects our belief that individuals are decent and law-abiding members of the community until proven otherwise.

Our complex and expensive system of police and prosecutors gives the state a powerful advantage against an accused. If we did not presume innocence, an elementary sense of fairness would require us to radically revise our system and give the accused an equivalent fact-finding capability. Before tampering with the presumption of innocence, the whole pattern of present evidential rules would have to be changed. The rules are interrelated. A trial is not just a relentless search for truth. We risk setting some guilty free for fear of convicting the innocent. Our universally high conviction rates indicate minimal risk.

Some view the presumption of innocence as legalistic nonsense. Common sense indicates a *de facto* presumption of guilt since the police usually get the right person. The presumption is unnatural. Our police must have reasonable grounds for their belief in guilt, yet the presumption of innocence requires fact-finders to ignore this and deduce nothing from the workings of the system which brought the accused to court. Brett offers a blunt and persuasive reply:

> Common sense has apparently overlooked that if the police do in fact bring only the guilty to the bar of justice, it may well be because they know that they will have to adduce proof beyond reasonable doubt. Whether they would continue to be so careful if the accused men had to prove their innocence is open to doubt. Moreover, common sense, in assuming that those found guilty are in fact guilty, overlooks the realities of plea bargaining, the cost of defending oneself, the imperfections of the trial process, and so on.[11]

Insanity Defence — Persuasive or Evidential?

It is true that the judges in *M'Naghten's Case*[12] advised that every man shall be presumed sane until the contrary is proved, and the legislature has followed

---

10. (1986), 50 C.R. (3d) 1, 15 (S.C.C.).
11. Brett, "Strict Responsibility: Possible Solutions" (1974), 37 Mod. L. Rev. 417.
12. (1843), 8 E.R. 718 (H.L.).

that lead.[13] Is there anything gained from the imposition of a persuasive burden on the accused that couldn't be equally gained by the lesser evidential burden? According to *Woolmington,* the accused in a murder case is entitled to an acquittal when the trier of fact has a reasonable doubt regarding his intent. Is it not inconsistent or illogical to foreclose an acquittal when the trier has a reasonable doubt regarding the accused's capacity to form the necessary intent and to demand that the trier be satisfied that the accused was incapable? Harlan, J., in *Davis v. U.S.*,[14] rejected the idea that the presumption of sanity must be negatived by a preponderance of evidence in favour of a rule that the presumption simply called for evidence to be introduced to place the matter in issue:

> Upon whom then must rest the burden of proving that the accused, whose life it is sought to take under the forms of law, belongs to a class capable of committing crime? On principle, it must rest upon those who affirm that he has committed the crime for which he is indicted. That burden is not fully discharged, nor is there any legal right to take the life of the accused, until guilt is made to appear from all the evidence in the case. The plea of not guilty is unlike a special plea in a civil action, which, admitting the case averred, seeks to establish a substantive ground of defense by a preponderance of evidence. It is not in confession and avoidance, for it is a plea that controverts the existence of every fact essential to constitute the crime charged. Upon that plea the accused may stand, shielded by the presumption of his innocence, until it appears that he is guilty; and his guilt cannot in the very nature of things be regarded as proved, if the jury entertain a reasonable doubt from all the evidence whether he was legally capable of committing crime.

In *R. v. Chaulk*[15] it was argued that the presumption of sanity contained in section 16(4) of the Criminal Code, placing the onus of proving the defence of insanity on the accused, was an unconstitutional violation of the presumption of innocence in section 11(*d*). Chief Justice Lamer, writing for himself and four other judges, held that there had been a violation of section 11(*d*) but it could be justified under section 1. The objective of the presumption was to "avoid placing an impossible burden of proof on the Crown." Citing recent judgments of the court indicating that Parliament was not required to adopt the absolutely least intrusive means, Chief Justice Lamer saw the issue as "whether a less intrusive means would achieve the same objective or would achieve the same objective as effectively." The Chief Justice concluded that the alternative of an evidentiary burden requiring that the accused merely raise a reasonable doubt would not be as effective, accepting arguments by Attorneys General that it would be very easy for accused persons to "fake" such a defence.

---

13.   Criminal Code, R.S.C. 1985, c. C-46, s. 16.

14.   160 U.S. 469, 485-88 (1895). In *Leland v. Oregon*, 343 U.S. 790 (1952), the Supreme Court upheld *state* legislation which imposed a persuasive burden on the accused on the issue of insanity as not violative of due process and noted that the *Davis* case had announced a rule respecting federal cases as opposed to constitutional doctrine. And see Bridge, "Presumptions and Burdens" (1949), 12 Mod. L. Rev. 273, 286-88. Compare the reasoning that allows the Crown to institute *criminal* proceedings and to raise and prove that the accused was incapable of committing the crime: *R. v. Simpson* (1977), 35 C.C.C. (2d) 337 (Ont. C.A.), "explained" in *R. v. Saxell* (1980), 59 C.C.C. (2d) 176, 188-89 (Ont. C.A.).

15.   (1990), 2 C.R. (4th) 1 (S.C.C.).

The sole dissent on this point in *Chaulk* was Madam Justice Wilson, who held that this was not a case for relaxing the minimum impairment test. This might be done where a legislature, mediating between competing groups of citizens or allocating scarce resources, had to compromise on the basis of conflicting evidence. But in *Chaulk* the state was acting as "singular antagonists" of a very basic legal right of an accused and the strict standard of review in *Oakes* should be applied. The government's objective could be quite readily met by a mere burden on the accused to adduce evidence that made insanity "a live issue fit and proper to be left to the jury." Madam Justice Wilson noted the experience in the United States where an evidential burden was the order of the day, and believed the case for the imposition of a persuasive burden had not been made out.

Facts Peculiarly Within Knowledge of Accused

There is a dangerously attractive "doctrine" which is frequently invoked[16] to cast a burden of persuasion on the defendant in a criminal case. Its root is commonly accepted as residing in the judgment of Lord Ellenborough in *R. v. Turner*.[17] The accused in that case was convicted of having game in his possession. The accused argued that the game laws provided a number of exceptions and qualifications and that to support a conviction there must be evidence led to negative each of the same. The conviction was affirmed and Lord Ellenborough wrote:

> There are, I think, about ten different heads of qualification enumerated in the statute to which the proof may be applied. . . . The (accused's) argument really comes to this, that there would be a moral impossibility of ever convicting upon such an information. . . . Does not, then, common sense shew, that the burden of proof ought to be cast on the person, who, by establishing any one of the qualifications, will be well defended? . . . The proof of (the qualification) is easy on the one side, but almost impossible on the other.[18]

Bayley, J. agreed:

> I have always understood it to be a general rule, that if a negative averment be made by one party, which is peculiarly within the knowledge of the other, the party within whose knowledge it lies, and who asserts the affirmative is to prove it, and not he who avers the negative.[19]

In the context of that case there is much to be said for the doctrine. If in present day Ontario a defendant is prosecuted for fishing or hunting without a licence and it is seen that there are 500 persons authorized to issue licences throughout the province, it is relatively simple for the defendant to prove his licence and virtually impossible for the prosecution to negative. But, as MacFarlane, J. said:

---

16. See, *e.g.*, Goddard, L.J. in *Hill v. Baxter*, [1958] 1 Q.B. 277, 282; and Grove, J. in *Abrath v. N.E. Ry. Co.* (1883), 11 Q.B. 79, 82 (C.A.). See also Laidlaw, J.A. in *R. v. Roher* (1947), 89 C.C.C. 365 (Ont. C.A.).
17. (1816), 105 E.R. 1026.
18. *Ibid.*, p. 1028.
19. *Ibid.*

It is obvious that an unrestricted application of the principle would relieve the Crown from the burden of proof that rests on it always of making out a *prima facie* case against the accused and would make the presumption of innocence a mockery.[20]

How dangerous "the unrestricted application of the principle" can be is illustrated in the still oft-cited case of *R. v. McIver*.[21] The defendant was convicted of careless driving contrary to the provincial Highway Traffic Act, which provided:

> Every person is guilty of the offence of driving carelessly who drives a vehicle on a highway without due care and attention or without reasonable consideration for other persons using the highway and is liable to a fine of not less than $100 and not more than $500 or to imprisonment for a term of not more than three months, and in addition his licence or permit may be suspended for a period of not more than two years.[22]

The facts as found by the magistrate were that the defendant's vehicle had collided with a vehicle parked off the pavement on the shoulder of the road, the weather was clear, the road surface was snow covered but in good condition, straight and level, the area was well-lit and the defendant had an odour of alcohol on his breath. There was no direct evidence regarding the manner in which the accused had been driving prior to the accident. The question of law stated for the Supreme Court was whether there was evidence upon which the magistrate could base his finding of guilt. Chief Justice McRuer concluded that the magistrate was entitled to draw the inference and on further appeal Chief Justice Porter agreed that "there was evidence from which an inference *could* be drawn to the effect that the accused was driving carelessly."[23] Mackay, J.A., speaking for the remaining four justices, went much further. He regarded the legislation as creating an offence of strict liability and prohibiting

> . . . a defined type of conduct; it is silent as to intent or *mens rea*. In such case, the Crown need only prove that the accused committed the prohibited act and the accused will be convicted unless he can show that the forbidden act was done without negligence or fault on his part.
>
> If there were an explanation of this accident having occurred without fault on the part of the accused, it was wholly within his knowledge and the principle applied by the Court of Criminal Appeal in *John v. Humphreys*, [1955] 1 All E.R. 793, applies. In that case the accused was charged with not having a driver's licence. At p. 794 Lord Goddard, C.J., said:
>
> > . . . when an act of Parliament provides that a person shall not do a certain thing unless he has a licence, the onus is always on the defendant to prove that he has a licence *because it is a fact peculiarly within his own knowledge.* . . .
>
> . . . .
>
> On a charge laid under s. 60 of the *Highway Traffic Act,* it is open to the accused as a defence, to show an absence of negligence on his part. For example, that his conduct was caused by the negligence of some other person, or by showing that the cause was a mechanical failure, or other circumstance, that he could not reasonably have foreseen.

---

20. In *R. v. Billett* (1952), 105 C.C.C. 169 (B.C.S.C.).
21. [1965] 2 O.R. 475 (C.A.); affirmed [1966] S.C.R. 254.
22. R.S.O. 1960, c. 172, s. 60.
23. *McIver, supra,* note 21, at O.R. pp. 478-79.

In the present case it was open to the accused to show, if he could, that the collision of his car with the car parked on the shoulder of the road, occurred without fault or negligence on his part. He having failed to do so was properly convicted.[24]

The case of *John v. Humphreys* here relied on, a prosecution for driving without a licence, in turn relied on another licensing case, *R. v. Oliver*,[25] which in turn had relied on other licensing cases including our "fount of authority," *R. v. Turner*. The shift of the burden in such cases may be a matter of common sense but, as Lord Bowen said,[26] these cases are to be "explained on special grounds." Applying the doctrine to careless driving the majority in the Court of Appeal are led to state that the prosecution need only prove "the prohibited act" and the accused *must* be convicted unless he can establish an absence of negligence. This, despite the fact that binding precedent[27] established that the legislation prohibited negligent driving; the legislation did not make having an accident a "prohibited act."[28] Just how insidious the "doctrine" can be is shown in a later decision of the same court: *R. v. Peda*.[29] Binding precedent[30] had established that for the offence of dangerous driving contrary to the Criminal Code, advertent negligence in the accused, a state of awareness must be shown. Nevertheless, relying on the earlier judgment in *McIver*, Mackay, J.A. wrote:

> Whether the driving of his motor-car by the appellant was dangerous is a question of fact. On the evidence it is not open to question but that it was. The cause or reason for the dangerous driving is within the knowledge of the accused. It seldom can be within the knowledge of the Crown, so that once the Crown proves beyond a reasonable doubt that the driving was dangerous, an onus of explanation lies on the accused to give an explanation that will in law relieve him from liability under the section.[31]

Clearly, if we extend the "doctrine" without limit, we are compelled to reject the golden thread of *Woolmington;* nothing could be more "peculiarly within the knowledge of the accused" than whether he meant to cause death and on proof of a shooting he must be convicted unless he establishes lack of intent.[32]

The notion that an accused must prove matters peculiarly within his knowledge was part of the justification provided by Bastarache J. for a 5:4 majority

---

24. *Ibid.*, at pp. 480-81.
25. [1943] 2 All E.R. 800 (C.C.A.).
26. *Abrath v. N.E. Ry. Co., supra*, note 16. Regarding the danger of the peculiar knowledge doctrine, see *R. v. Edwards* (1974), 59 Cr. App. R. 213. For a description of the current English scene in this area, see *R. v. Hunt*, [1987] A.C. 352 (H.L.).
27. *O'Grady v. Sparling* (1960), 128 C.C.C. 1 (S.C.C.).
28. To be fair, the Ontario Court of Appeal later concluded in a unanimous judgment, MacKay, J. concurring, that
    > in each instance, the Crown must prove beyond a reasonable doubt that the accused either drove his vehicle on a highway without due care and attention, or that he operated it without reasonable consideration for other persons using the highway. One of these two ingredients must be proven to support a conviction under this section.
    Per Gale, C.J.O. in *R. v. Wilson*, [1971] 1 O.R. 349 (C.A.).
29. [1969] 1 O.R. 90 (C.A.); affirmed [1969] S.C.R. 905.
30. *Binus v. R.*, [1967] S.C.R. 594.
31. *Supra*, note 29, at p. 93.
32. See *R. v. Spurge*, [1961] 2 Q.B. 205, 212 (C.C.A.).

in *Stone*[33] for requiring the accused to prove a defence of sane automatism on a balance of probabilities. The majority also asserted a so-called presumption of voluntariness. For criticism see Delisle, "*Stone*: Judicial Activism Gone Awry to Presume Guilt" (1999), 24 C.R. (5th) 91; Editorial in (1999), 4 Can. Crim. L. Rev. 119; and Healy, "Automatism Confined" (2000), 45 McGill L.J. 87.

(c) Measure of Burden of Persuasion

(i) *Generally*

It is commonly said that the burden of persuasion in civil cases requires for satisfaction "a preponderance of evidence," or "proof on the balance of probability." Lord Denning expressed it:

> That degree is well settled. It must carry a reasonable degree of probability, but not so high as is required in a criminal case. If the evidence is such that the tribunal can say: "We think it more probable than not," the burden is discharged, but, if the probabilities are equal, it is not.[34]

It is common then to contrast the civil standard with the criminal standard which requires the trier to be "satisfied beyond a reasonable doubt." This higher standard, according to Phipson,

> . . . dates from the end of the eighteenth century, [and] was due to the reaction then setting in, against the rigours of the penal code, and was originally applied *in favorem vitae* to capital cases only.[35]

Despite the distinction, it is not unusual to see the courts in civil cases adopting the latter standard, or a third standard requiring "clear and convincing proof," where the issue to be proved involves the imputation of conduct which is criminal or quasi-criminal in nature.[36] This approach was rejected by the Supreme Court of Canada[37] though it was recognized that within each standard there were variations in the degree of satisfaction. Cartwright, J. wrote:

> . . . in every civil action before the tribunal can safely find the affirmative of an issue of fact required to be proved it must be reasonably satisfied, and that whether or not it will be so satisfied must depend upon the totality of the circumstances on which its judgment is formed including the gravity of the consequences of the finding.[38]

He adopted an earlier passage from Dixon, J. in the Australian High Court:

---

33. (1999), 24 C.R. (5th) 1 (S.C.C.).
34. *Miller v. Min. of Pensions*, [1947] 2 All E.R. 372, 374 (K.B.). See also Duff, J. in *Clark v. R.* (1921), 61 S.C.R. 608, 616: ". . . such a preponderance of evidence as to shew that the conclusion he seeks to establish is substantially the most probable of the possible views of the facts."
35. Phipson, *Evidence*, 9th ed. (1952), p. 8. Wigmore seems to agree: 9 Wigmore, *Evidence* (Chad. Rev.), s. 2497, p. 405. Compare, however, Thayer, *supra*, note 8, at p. 558 suggesting the rule is an ancient one traceable to the *Corpus Juris* of the fourth century.
36. See, *e.g.*, *Harasyn v. Harasyn* (1970), 13 D.L.R. (3d) 635 (Sask. Q.B.); *LeBlanc v. MacDonald* (1969), 1 D.L.R. (3d) 132 (N.S.S.C.); and *Welstead v. Brown*, [1952] 1 S.C.R. 3.
37. See *Smith v. Smith*, [1952] 2 S.C.R. 312; *Boykowych v. Boykowych*, [1955] S.C.R. 151; and *Hanes v. Wawanesa Mutual Ins. Co.* (1963), 36 D.L.R. (2d) 718 (S.C.C.).
38. In *Smith v. Smith, ibid.*, at pp. 331-32.

The seriousness of an allegation made, the inherent unlikelihood of an occurrence of a given description, or the gravity of the consequences flowing from a particular finding are considerations which must affect the answer to the question whether the issue has been proved to the reasonable satisfaction of the tribunal.[39]

The Supreme Court has also approved[40] Lord Denning's famous dictum in _Bater v. Bater:_

The difference of opinion which has been evoked about the standard of proof in these cases may well turn out to be more a matter of words than anything else. It is true that by our law there is a higher standard of proof in criminal cases than in civil cases, but this is subject to the qualification that there is no absolute standard in either case. In criminal cases the charge must be proved beyond reasonable doubt, but there may be degrees of proof within that standard. Many great judges have said that, in proportion as the crime is enormous, so ought the proof to be clear. So also in civil cases. The case may be proved by a preponderance of probability, but there may be degrees of probability within that standard. The degree depends on the subject-matter. A civil court, when considering a charge of fraud, will naturally require a higher degree of probability than that which it would require if considering whether negligence were established. It does not adopt so high a degree as a criminal court, even when it is considering a charge of a criminal nature, but still it does require a degree of probability which is commensurate with the occasion.[41]

Most recently, Laskin, C.J.C. observed that the trial judge

in dealing with the burden of proof could properly consider the cogency of the evidence offered to support proof on a balance of probabilities and this is what he did when he referred to proof commensurate with the gravity of the allegations or of the accusation of theft by the temporary driver. There is necessarily a matter of judgment involved in weighing evidence that goes to the burden of proof, and a trial judge is justified in scrutinizing evidence with greater care if there are serious allegations to be established by the proof that is offered.[42]

In _Beckon v. Ontario (Deputy Chief Coroner)_,[43] the Ontario Court of Appeal agreed that a coroner's jury verdict of suicide had to be quashed because the coroner had charged the jury:

[W]hat you must decide is, what on the balance of probability you think the means of death is. Considering all the facts, what do you think likely happened.

. . . .

. . . To my knowledge all civil cases, boards, tribunals operate on the balance of

39.   In _Briginshaw v. Briginshaw_ (1938), 60 C.L.R. 336, 362. See also Rand, J. in _Boykowych_ observing a criticism of this passage, [1955] S.C.R. 154-55.
40.   In _Hanes v. Wawanesa, supra,_ note 37, at p. 733, per Ritchie, J. and more recently in _Continental Ins. Co. v. Dalton Cartage Co.,_ [1982] 1 S.C.R. 164.
41.   [1950] 2 All E.R. 458, 459. And see _LeBlanc v. Allstate_ (1982), 40 N.B.R. (2d) 460 (Q.B.).
42.   In _Continental Ins. Co., supra,_ note 40, at p. 170, followed in _Kelly v. Phoenix Assur. Co._ (1985), 13 C.C.L.I. 235 (N.B.C.A.). See also _Gannon & Assoc. Ltd. v. Advocate Gen. Ins. Co. of Can._ (1984), 12 C.C.L.I. 61 (Man. Q.B.). In assessing the consequences of a decision, however, judges can have different views: contrast _Re S._ (1979), 10 R.F.L. (2d) 341, 350 (Ont. Prov. Ct.) and _Re Rachel H._ (1984), 27 A.C.W.S. (2d) 158. See generally, Pattenden, "The Risk of Non-Persuasion in Civil Trials: The Case Against a Floating Standard of Proof" (1988), 7 Civ. Just. Q. 220.
43.   (1992), 9 O.R. (3d) 256.

probability tests. And only criminal charges are decided using beyond reasonable doubt.[44]

Relying on _Continental Insurance Co._, the court decided the coroner had erred:

> [W]ith respect to proof of a serious allegation such as one of suicide, . . . the required standard of proof is not proof beyond a reasonable doubt but, rather, proof to a high degree of probability.

> . . . .

> Suicide is not to be presumed. In fact, there is a presumption against it. The finding must be against suicide unless the jury is satisfied, on a balance of probability, that the means of death was suicide. The degree of probability is a high one and, before being satisfied that it has been met, the jury should take into account that suicide is not a natural act and that the allegation of suicide is a serious one with grave consequences. The evidence establishing the probability of suicide should be clear and cogent.[45]

In criminal cases too there must be a difference in the standard of proof required in a murder prosecution from that required in a charge of impaired driving, despite the same formula of words being employed. Degrees of satisfaction must vary along a continuum dependent on all the circumstances and consequences of a particular case. Professor Fridman correctly analyzed the problem:

> The truth is submitted to be that standards of proof (whether civil or criminal) are impossible of precise and definitive distinction by mere words, however technical the language used. All that can be said is that judges and jurors alike must be "satisfied" of the truth of allegations or denials of fact. What amounts to "satisfaction" will vary with the issues involved. The more trivial the question, the more easily and swiftly will "satisfaction" materialize. The more momentous and serious its consequences, the greater the caution and deliberation demanded, that is, the greater amount of cogent evidence before there can be any "satisfaction" about where the truth lies.[46]

R. v. LIFCHUS
[1997] 3 S.C.R. 320, 9 C.R. (5th) 1, 118 C.C.C. (3d) 1

[The accused was charged with fraud. The trial judge told the jury in her charge on the burden of proof that she used the words " 'proof beyond a reasonable doubt' . . . in their ordinary, natural everyday sense", and that the words "doubt" and "reasonable" are "ordinary, everyday words that . . . you understand." The accused was convicted of fraud. On appeal, he contended that the trial judge had erred in instructing the jury on the meaning of the expression "proof beyond a reasonable doubt." The Court of Appeal allowed the appeal and ordered a new trial. The Supreme Court dismissed the Crown's appeal.]

CORY J. (LAMER C.J.C., and SOPINKA, MCLACHLIN, IACOBUCCI and MAJOR JJ. concurring):—

---

44.   _Ibid._, at pp. 266-67.
45.   _Ibid._, at pp. 270, 271-72.
46.   Fridman, "Standards of Proof" (1955), 33 Can. Bar Rev. 665, 670.

. . . .

The phrase "beyond a reasonable doubt", is composed of words which are commonly used in everyday speech. Yet, these words have a specific meaning in the legal context. This special meaning of the words "reasonable doubt" may not correspond precisely to the meaning ordinarily attributed to them. In criminal proceedings, where the liberty of the subject is at stake, it is of fundamental importance that jurors fully understand the nature of the burden of proof that the law requires them to apply. An explanation of the meaning of proof beyond a reasonable doubt is an essential element of the instructions that must be given to a jury. That a definition is necessary can be readily deduced from the frequency with which juries ask for guidance with regard to its meaning. It is therefore essential that the trial judge provide the jury with an explanation of the expression.

. . . .

Perhaps a brief summary of what the definition should and should not contain may be helpful. It should be explained that:

the standard of proof beyond a reasonable doubt is inextricably intertwined with that principle fundamental to all criminal trials, the presumption of innocence;

the burden of proof rests on the prosecution throughout the trial and never shifts to the accused;

a reasonable doubt is not a doubt based upon sympathy or prejudice;

rather, it is based upon reason and common sense;

it is logically connected to the evidence or absence of evidence;

it does not involve proof to an absolute certainty; it is not proof beyond any doubt nor is it an imaginary or frivolous doubt; and

more is required than proof that the accused is probably guilty, a jury which concludes only that the accused is probably guilty must acquit.

On the other hand, certain references to the required standard of proof should be avoided. For example:

describing the term "reasonable doubt" as an ordinary expression which has no special meaning in the criminal law context;

inviting jurors to apply to the task before them the same standard of proof that they apply to important, or even the most important, decisions in their own lives;

equating proof "beyond a reasonable doubt" to proof "to a moral certainty";

qualifying the word "doubt" with adjectives other than "reasonable", such as "serious", substantial" or "haunting", which may mislead the jury; and

instructing jurors that they may convict if they are "sure" that the accused is guilty, before providing them with a proper definition as to the meaning of the words "beyond a reasonable doubt".

A charge which is consistent with the principles set out in these reasons will suffice regardless of the particular words used by the trial judge. Nevertheless, it may be useful to set out a "model charge" which could provide the necessary instructions as to the meaning of the phrase beyond a reasonable doubt.

Suggested Charge

Instructions pertaining to the requisite standard of proof in a criminal trial of proof beyond a reasonable doubt might be given along these lines:

The accused enters these proceedings presumed to be innocent. That presumption of innocence remains throughout the case until such time as the Crown has on the evidence put before you satisfied you beyond a reasonable doubt that the accused is guilty.

What does the expression "beyond a reasonable doubt" mean? The term "beyond a reasonable doubt" has been used for a very long time and is a part of our history and traditions of justice. It is so engrained in our criminal law that some think it needs no explanation, yet something must be said regarding its meaning.

A reasonable doubt is not an imaginary or frivolous doubt. It must not be based upon sympathy or prejudice. Rather, it is based on reason and common sense. It is logically derived from the evidence or absence of evidence.

Even if you believe the accused is probably guilty or likely guilty, that is not sufficient. In those circumstances you must give the benefit of the doubt to the accused and acquit because the Crown has failed to satisfy you of the guilt of the accused beyond a reasonable doubt.

On the other hand you must remember that it is virtually impossible to prove anything to an absolute certainty and the Crown is not required to do so. Such a standard of proof is impossibly high.

In short if, based upon the evidence before the court, you are sure that the accused committed the offence you should convict since this demonstrates that you are satisfied of his guilt beyond a reasonable doubt.

This is not a magic incantation that needs to be repeated word for word. It is nothing more than a suggested form that would not be faulted if it were used. . . . . Further, it is possible that an error in the instructions as to the standard of proof may not constitute a reversible error. It was observed in *R. v. W. (D.)*, [1991] 1 S.C.R. 742, at p. 758, that the verdict ought not be disturbed "if the charge, when read as a whole, makes it clear that the jury could not have been under any misapprehension as to the correct burden and standard of proof to apply." On the other hand, if the charge as a whole gives rise to the reasonable likelihood that the jury misapprehended the standard of proof, then as a general rule the verdict will have to be set aside and a new trial directed.

R. v. STARR
[2000] 2 S.C.R. 144, 36 C.R. (5th) 1, 147 C.C.C. (3d) 449

[The accused had been convicted of two counts of first degree murder. The majority of the court decided that the reasonable doubt instruction given in the case fell prey to many of the same difficulties outlined in Lifchus, and likely misled the jury as to the content of the criminal standard of proof. In allowing the accused's appeal they gave further advice.]

IACOBUCCI, J. (MAJOR, BINNIE, ARBOUR and LEBEL, JJ. concurring): —

. . . .

In the present case, the trial judge did refer to the Crown's onus and to the presumption of innocence, and he stated that the appellant should receive the benefit of any reasonable doubt. The error in the charge is that the jury was not told *how a reasonable doubt is to be defined.* As was emphasized repeatedly in *Lifchus* and again in *Bisson, a jury must* be instructed that the standard of proof in a criminal trial is higher than the probability standard used in making everyday decisions and in civil trials. Indeed, it is this very requirement to go beyond probability that meshes the standard of proof in criminal cases with the presumption of innocence and the Crown's onus. However, as Cory J. explained in these earlier decisions, it is generally inappropriate to define the meaning of the term "reasonable doubt" through examples from daily life, through the use of synonyms, or through analogy to moral choices. The criminal standard of proof has a special significance unique to the legal process. It is an exacting standard of proof rarely encountered in everyday life, and there is no universally intelligible illustration of the concept, such as the scales of justice with respect to the balance of probabilities standard. Unlike absolute certainty or the balance of probabilities, reasonable doubt is not an easily quantifiable standard. It cannot be measured or described by analogy. It must be explained. However, precisely because it is not quantifiable, it is difficult to explain.

In my view, an effective way to define the reasonable doubt standard for a jury is to explain that it falls much closer to absolute certainty than to proof on a balance of probabilities. As stated in *Lifchus*, a trial judge is required to explain that something less than absolute certainty is required, and that something more than probable guilt is required, in order for the jury to convict. Both of these alternative standards are fairly and easily comprehensible. It will be of great assistance for a jury if the trial judge situates the reasonable doubt standard appropriately between these two standards. The additional instructions to the jury set out in *Lifchus* as to the meaning and appropriate manner of determining the existence of a reasonable doubt serve to define the space between absolute certainty and proof beyond a reasonable doubt. In this regard, I am in agreement with Twaddle J.A. in the court below, when he said, at p. 177:

> If standards of proof were marked on a measure, proof "beyond reasonable doubt" would lie much closer to "absolute certainty" than to "a balance of probabilities". Just as a judge has a duty to instruct the jury that absolute certainty is not required, he or she has a duty, in my view, to instruct the jury that the criminal standard is more than a probability. The words he or she uses to convey this idea are of no significance, but the idea itself must be conveyed. . . .

See further Patrick Healy, "Direction and Guidance on Reasonable Doubt in the Charge to the Jury" (2001), 6 Can. Crim. L.R. 161.

(ii) *Choosing Between Competing Versions*

In being satisfied to the requisite standard the trier of fact does not "choose" between competing versions of the incident. The plaintiff or the prosecutor makes allegations, seeks to disturb the status quo and bears the burden of satisfying the trier. In *R. v. Nadeau*,[47] the accused was convicted of murder. The accused testified and his version of the incident differed from that of the prosecution's witness. The trial judge told the jury that they had to choose between the two versions. A new trial was ordered and Lamer, J. wrote:

> With respect, this direction is in error. The accused benefits from any reasonable doubt at the outset, not merely if "the two versions are equally consistent with the evidence, are equally valid". Moreover, the jury does not have to choose between two versions. It is not because they would not believe the accused that they would then have to agree with Landry's version. The jurors cannot accept his version, or any part of it, unless they are satisfied beyond all reasonable doubt, having regard to all the evidence, that the events took place in this manner; otherwise, the accused is entitled, unless a fact has been established beyond a reasonable doubt, to the finding of fact the most favourable to him, provided of course that it is based on evidence in the record and not mere speculation.[48]

---

47. (1984), 42 C.R. (3d) 305 (S.C.C.).
48. *Ibid.*, at p. 310. And see *R. v. Finlay* (1985), 11 O.A.C. 279, 287: ". . . even if they entirely reject the defence evidence, they must nonetheless be satisfied on the evidence given by the prosecution that the guilt of the accused has been proved beyond a reasonable doubt." See also *R. v. P.M.* (1983), 31 C.R. (3d) 311 (Ont. C.A.).

R. v. W. (D.)
[1991] 1 S.C.R. 742, 3 C.R. (4th) 302, 63 C.C.C. (3d) 347

[The accused was convicted of sexual assault after a trial that pitted the credibility of the accused against that of the complainant. It was objected that the trial judge erred in his recharge in that he characterized the core issue to be determined by the jury as whether they believed the complainant or whether they believed the appellant.]

CORY, J.:—

A trial Judge might well instruct the jury on the question of credibility along these lines:

> First, if you believe the evidence of the accused, obviously you must acquit.
>
> Second, if you do not believe the testimony of the accused but you are left in reasonable doubt by it, you must acquit.
>
> Third, even if you are not left in doubt by the evidence of the accused, you must ask yourself whether, on the basis of the evidence which you do accept, you are convinced beyond a reasonable doubt by that evidence of the guilt of the accused.

formula

If that formula were followed, the oft-repeated error which appears in the recharge in this case would be avoided. The requirement that the Crown prove the guilt of the accused beyond a reasonable doubt is fundamental in our system of criminal law. Every effort should be made to avoid mistakes in charging the jury on this basic principle.[49]

W. (D.) is one of the most frequently cited authorities. For different views as to its wisdom see Gans, (2000), 43 Crim. L.Q. 345 and Plaxton, (2000), 43 Crim. L.Q. 443.

R. v. S. (W.D.)
[1994] 3 S.C.R. 521, 34 C.R. (4th) 1, 93 C.C.C. (3d) 1

[The accused was charged with sexual assault. The only evidence presented at the trial pertaining to the assault was that of the complainants and the accused. In the main charge the trial judge properly instructed the jury on all matters including directions as to the onus resting upon the Crown to prove the case against the accused beyond a reasonable doubt. At the conclusion of the charge, the jury retired to deliberate. Four hours later, they submitted a question to the trial judge stating that "[t]he jury is hung up" and requesting "an explanation of the guideline on the jury's duty regarding evidence and reasonable doubt". In the trial judge's response, he made certain statements that might suggest the jury had to choose between two competing versions, that of the complainants on the one hand and that of the accused on the other. The accused was convicted of one offence and acquitted of the other. The Court of Appeal dismissed the accused's appeal from his conviction.]

---

49.   *Ibid.*, at p. 310. In *R. v. Molnar* (1990), 76 C.R. (3d) 125 (C.A.) the accused was charged with arson. Expert evidence was called and there was conflict between them as to whether the fire was of incendiary origin or of accidental origin. The trial judge told the jury that they should resolve the conflict by accepting the opinion that they believed was entitled to the greater weight. This was held to be error.

Cory J. (Lamer C.J. and La Forest, Sopinka, and Major JJ. concurring):—

. . . .

The response of the trial judge to that question gives rise to difficulties presented in this case. He stated:

> The accused is entitled to a reasonable doubt on the issue of credibility; who is to be believed, either complainant in each of the counts or the accused. If you cannot reject his evidence, it must raise a reasonable doubt. If you believe his evidence, it raises a reasonable doubt. If you reject his evidence, in comparison to the evidence of either of the complainants and that complainant's evidence is accepted by you as being true, then you convict.
>
> It's as simple to say it as that. I know it is difficult to work out. You have two stories here. You have to decide whether one is strong enough — one of the complainants' evidence is strong enough to convince you of the guilt, and you can reject the accused's evidence. If it isn't that strong and you can't reject the accused's evidence, you must have a reasonable doubt. If it is that strong, and you can reject the accused's evidence, you should be able to say, I am convinced beyond a reasonable doubt.
>
> Now, I don't know what — if you want me to deal with evidence any further, any point of evidence or just what your duties are with respect to the evidence. I will tell you what they are. You weigh all of the evidence, and you look at the whole case, and you say, looking at everything, Am I convinced beyond a reasonable doubt that her evidence is correct and his evidence can't be accepted, and you do that with each count.

At the conclusion of these remarks, the jury then retired and continued its deliberations for another 4½ hours. They then returned and delivered the verdict acquitting the accused of the charge of assaulting V.D. but convicting him of the assault upon S.D.

. . . .

Was the Charge Erroneous?

In this case all the evidence presented at trial was that of the complainant and the appellant. There was nothing else before the jury. It therefore was essential that the jury, which had advised the judge that it was "hung up" on the issue of reasonable doubt, be properly directed with regard to the issue.

This was vital since this case turned completely on the question of credibility and the correct consideration by the jury of the onus of proof resting upon the Crown of proving the charge beyond a reasonable doubt.

. . . .

Obviously, it is not necessary to recite this formula [the formula spelled out in *R. v. W. (D.)*] word for word as some magic incantation. However, it is important that the essence of these instructions be given. It is erroneous to direct a jury that they must accept the Crown's evidence or that of the defence. To put forward such an either/or approach excludes the very real and legitimate possibility that the jury may not be able to select one version in preference to the other and yet on the whole of the evidence be left with a reasonable doubt. The effect of putting such a position to the jury is to shift a burden to the accused of demonstrating his or her innocence, since a jury might believe that the accused could not be acquitted unless the defence evidence was believed.

It seems to me that the recharge in this case suffers from the same flaw as the recharge in *R. v. W. (D.), supra.* . . .

Running through the recharge in this case is the notion of choosing between the credibility of the complainant and that of the accused.

no choosing

[Appeal allowed; new trial ordered.]

. . . .

McLACHLIN J. (dissenting) (L'HEUREUX-DUBÉ J. concurring):—

. . . .

I note in passing that the second branch [in *R.v. W. (D.)*] as stated by Cory J. has given rise to some academic debate: J. Gibson, "The Liars' Defence" (1993), 20 C.R. (4th) 96; A.D. Gold, "The 'Average, Nervous, Inadequate, Inarticulate, in Short, Typical' Accused's Defence" (1993), 22 C.R. (4th) 253; J.L. Gibson, "Misquote Changes Meaning" (1994), 24 C.R. (4th) 395; and A.D. Gold, "Typo Does Not Change Anything" (1994), 24 C.R. (4th) 397. It has been suggested that if one rejects the evidence of the accused, it is logically inconsistent to have a reasonable doubt with respect to it. Such a doubt, it is argued, would not be reasonable. Certainly if the jury rejected (as opposed to merely being undecided about) *all* of the evidence of the accused, it is difficult to see how that very evidence, having been rejected, could raise a reasonable doubt. However, a jury could reject part of the evidence of the accused and still reasonably entertain a doubt as to his guilt based on other parts of the accused's evidence, which the jury did not reject, but either accepted or was undecided about. It is in the latter sense that I read the second condition of Cory J. I note also that immediately preceding his three-part statement of the rule, Cory J. states the rule in two branches, rolling the second and third branch of the three-part statement into one . . . :

> Specifically, the trial judge is required to instruct the jury that they *must* acquit the accused in two situations. First, if they believe the accused. Second, if they do not believe the accused's evidence but still have a reasonable doubt as to his guilt after considering the accused's evidence in the context of the evidence as a whole.

I raise this point only for one purpose: when scholars of the criminal law themselves argue about how the second branch of the *W. (D.)* test should be phrased, it would be wrong to reverse a conviction merely because a particular formula was not repeated verbatim. We must remember that jurors are laypeople, not lawyers, and do not hear and interpret each and every word of the judge's charge with all the legal baggage that a career in the law may engender. An overly legalistic focus on the strict text of the judge's charge does not take this courtroom reality into account, nor accommodate the fact that the judge may have to formulate his or her remarks in various ways in order to make the jury understand that it must acquit regardless of what evidence it may accept or reject if it is left with a reasonable doubt when considering that evidence as a whole. What is required, to quote Sopinka J. in *R. v. Morin*, [1988] 2 S.C.R. 345, at p. 362, is that the "charge alerts [the jury] to the fact that, if the defence evidence leaves them in a state of doubt after considering it in the context of the whole of the evidence, then they are to acquit".

. . . .

Having considered the impugned passages of the trial judge's recharge and found them not to violate the requirements of law, I turn to the question of whether viewed globally the trial judge over-emphasized the credibility contest between the complainant and the accused. I cannot conclude that he did.

(iii) *Application of Persuasive Burden*

R. v. MORIN
[1988] 2 S.C.R. 345, 66 C.R. (3d) 1, 44 C.C.C. (3d) 193

[The accused was acquitted on a charge of first degree murder. His position at trial was that he was not the killer, but in the alternative, if he was the killer he was not guilty by reason of insanity. On appeal it was found that the trial judge had misdirected the jury. The trial judge invited the jury to apply the criminal standard of proof beyond a reasonable doubt to individual pieces of evidence. The Court of Appeal allowed the Crown's appeal and directed a new trial. The accused appealed. The Supreme Court confirmed the order of a new trial.]

SOPINKA J. (DICKSON C.J.C. and MCINTYRE and LA FOREST JJ. concurring):—

. . . .

The appellant submits that the charge, when read as a whole, did not invite the jury to subject individual pieces of evidence to the criminal standard, but rather the effect of the charge was that during the ''fact-finding'' stage items of evidence were to be examined in relation to other evidence. The residuum resulting from this process constitutes the ''whole of the evidence'', from which the jury determines whether guilt has been proved beyond a reasonable doubt.

This argument raises two questions:

(i) Is the appellant's interpretation of the charge correct?

(ii) Assuming that it is, is it misdirection to instruct the jury to apply the criminal standard at two stages as submitted?

. . . .

The following are the relevant excerpts from the charge to the jury set out in the order in which they occurred:

1. *Concerning Evidence*

You are not obliged to accept any part of the evidence of a witness just because there is no denial of it. If you have a reasonable doubt about any of the evidence, you will give the benefit of that doubt to the accused with respect to such evidence. *Having decided what evidence you consider worthy of belief, you will consider it as a whole, of course, in arriving at your verdict.* [emphasis added]

2. *Concerning Burden of Proof*

The accused is entitled to the benefit of reasonable doubt on the whole of the case and on each and every issue in the case.

Proof beyond a reasonable doubt does not apply to the individual items of evidence or the separate pieces of evidence in the case, but to the total body of evidence upon which the Crown relies to prove guilt. Before you can convict you must be satisfied beyond a reasonable doubt of his guilt.

3. *Concerning Hairs and Fibres*

It seems to me that this evidence does not go beyond proving that Christine could have been in the Honda motor vehicle and that the accused could have been at the scene of the killing, and of course that is not proof beyond a reasonable doubt.

4. *Concerning Appellant's Statements to Hobbs*

I was going to go on to say that, if you find that the evidence of the accused at trial here represents the correct interpretation of those tapes and transcripts, or parts of the tapes and transcripts, or if you have a reasonable doubt that that might be so, you will give him the benefit of the doubt as to those parts of the tapes or transcripts and adopt his interpretation.

5. *Concerning Appellant's Statement to Inmate May*

Now, as to that evidence, in relation to that part of the tape that I have just read, if you find the evidence of the accused at trial represents the correct interpretation of that exchange, or if you have a reasonable doubt that that may be so, you will give the benefit of the doubt to the accused and adopt his interpretation.

In my opinion, based on my reading of the charge as a whole, a jury would likely have concluded that in examining the evidence they were to give the accused the benefit of the doubt in respect of *any* evidence. This process of examination and elimination would occur during the so-called "fact-finding" stage, to use the appellant's phrase. The evidence as a whole to which the jury was to apply itself in order to determine guilt or innocence was the residuum after the "fact-finding" stage. There is no other way of reading the first excerpt from the charge.

. . . .

The argument in favour of a two-stage application of the criminal standard has superficial appeal in theory but in my respectful opinion is wrong in principle and unworkable in practice. In principle it is wrong because the function of a standard of proof is not the weighing of individual items of evidence but the determination of ultimate issues. Furthermore, it would require the individual member of the jury to rely on the same facts in order to establish guilt. The law is clear that the members of the jury can arrive at a verdict by different routes and need not rely on the same facts. Indeed, the jurors need not agree on any single fact except the ultimate conclusion: see Wigmore on Evidence, Chadbourn revision, vol. 9 (1981), para. 2497, at pp. 412-14; *R. v. Lynch* (1978), 40 C.C.C. (2d) 7 at 19 (Ont. C.A.); *R. v. Bouvier*, supra, Ont. C.A. at pp. 264-65; *R. v. Moreau* (1986), 51 C.R. (3d) 209, 26 C.C.C. (3d) 359 at 389 (Ont. C.A.); *R. v. Agbim*, [1979] Crim. L. Rev. 171 (C.A.); *R. v. Thatcher*, supra, Sask. C.A. at p. 510, S.C.C. at p. 697.

The matter is summed up in Cross at p. 146:

It has been held by the Court of Appeal that it is unnecessary for a judge to direct the jury that it must be unanimous with regard to even one item of evidence bearing upon a particular count before convicting on it. It seems to be enough that all members of the jury find the accused guilty upon the basis of some of the facts bearing upon that count.

In practice it is not practical, because the jury would have to agree on not only the same facts but what individual facts prove. Individual facts do not necessarily establish guilt, but are a link in the chain of ultimate proof. It is not possible, therefore, to require the jury to find facts proved beyond a reasonable doubt without identifying *what it is* that they prove beyond a reasonable doubt. Since the same fact may give rise to different inferences tending to establish guilt or innocence, the jury might discard such facts on the basis that there is doubt as to what they prove.

The concern which proponents of the two-stage process express is that facts which are doubtful will be used to establish guilt. The answer to this concern is that a chain is only as strong as its weakest link. If facts which are essential to a finding of guilt are still doubtful notwithstanding the support of other facts, this will produce a doubt in the mind of the jury that guilt has been proved beyond a reasonable doubt.

I conclude from the foregoing that the facts are for the jury to determine, subject to an instruction by the trial judge as to the law. While the charge may and often does include many helpful tips on the weighing of evidence, such as observing demeanour, taking into the account the interest of the witness and so forth, the law lays down only one basic requirement: during the process of deliberation the jury or other trier of fact must consider the evidence as a whole and determine whether guilt is established by the prosecution beyond a reasonable doubt. This of necessity requires that each element of the offence or issue be proved beyond a reasonable doubt. Beyond this injunction it is for the trier of fact to determine how to proceed. To intrude in this area is, as pointed out by North P., an intrusion into the province of the jury.

The reason we have juries is so that lay persons and not lawyers decide the facts. To inject into the process artificial legal rules with respect to the natural human activity of deliberation and decision would tend to detract from the value of the jury system. Accordingly, it is wrong for a trial judge to lay down additional rules for the weighing of the evidence. Indeed, it is unwise to attempt to elaborate on the basic requirement referred to above. I would make two exceptions. The jury should be told that the facts are not to be examined separately and in isolation with reference to the criminal standard. This instruction is a necessary corollary to the basic rule referred to above. Without it there is some danger that a jury might conclude that the requirement that each issue or element of the offence be proved beyond a reasonable doubt demands that individual items of evidence be so proved.

The second exception is that it is appropriate, where issues of credibility arise between the evidence for the prosecution and the defence, that the jury be charged as suggested by Morden J.A. in *Challice*, supra. There is a danger in such a situation that a jury might conclude that it is simply a matter as to which side they believe. The suggested charge alerts them to the fact that, if the defence evidence leaves them in a state of doubt after considering it in the context of the whole of the evidence, then they are to acquit.

Consequently, even if the appellant is correct in his interpretation of the charge to the jury, there was misdirection — although not as serious as the misdirection which I have found occurred.

R. v. WHITE
[1998] 2 S.C.R. 72, 16 C.R. (5th) 199, 125 C.C.C. (3d) 385

[The accused were charged with first degree murder. There was evidence that they had fled the jurisdiction after the killing and attempted to dispose of the murder weapon. An issue for the Court was whether the trial judge should have instructed the jury to apply the reasonable doubt standard to the evidence of the accused's post-offence conduct.]

MAJOR J. (L'HEUREUX-DUBÉ, GONTHIER, CORY, McLACHLIN, BASTARACHE and BINNIE JJ. concurring):—

. . . .

In cases where the post-offence conduct of an accused is put before the jury, the trial judge should provide an instruction regarding the proper use of that evidence. The purpose of such a charge is to counter the jury's natural tendency to leap from evidence of flight or concealment to a conclusion of guilt, and to ensure that alternative explanations for the accused's conduct are given full consideration. In particular, the trial judge should remind the jury that people sometimes flee or lie for entirely innocent reasons, and that even if the accused was motivated by a feeling of guilt, that feeling might be attributable to some culpable act other than the offence for which the accused is being tried. The jury should be instructed to keep these principles in mind when deciding how much weight, if any, to give such evidence in the final evaluation of guilt or innocence.

The jury charge in this case complied with those requirements, and the appellants do not claim that there was anything misleading about that charge so far as it went. It is contended, however, that the charge was insufficient because the trial judge did not specifically direct the jury to apply the criminal standard of proof to the evidence of the appellants' post-offence conduct. It is the appellants' submission that the jury should have been told that unless they were satisfied beyond a reasonable doubt that the appellants' post-offence conduct constituted flight or concealment, and moreover that those acts were motivated by the appellants' sense of culpability for Chiu's murder and not by some other explanation, the jury could draw no inference of guilt from the conduct, and must set it aside and proceed to consider the balance of evidence in the case.

It is settled that the criminal standard of proof applies only to the jury's final determination of guilt or innocence and is not to be applied to individual items or categories of evidence. It is improper for the jury to divide their deliberations into separate stages; their verdict must be based on the record as a whole, not merely on items of evidence which have previously been established beyond a reasonable doubt: see *Morin*. The kind of charge argued for by the appellants is facially inconsistent with these principles, and no persuasive reason has been advanced which would justify creating an exception for evidence of post-offence conduct. The trial judge in this case was not required to give such a charge and indeed he would have been in error had he done so. . . . . The inherent difficulty involved in distinguishing between different types of circumstantial evidence only reinforces the holding in *Morin* that jury deliberations are somewhat holistic in nature and should not be broken down in relation to individual pieces or categories of evidence.

. . . .

The appellants concede that as a general rule the criminal standard of proof does not apply to individual pieces of evidence. They contend, however, that because post-offence conduct can give rise to an inference that is tantamount to a finding of guilt itself, such conduct is unlike other kinds of circumstantial evidence and should benefit from an exception to the rule in *Morin*. Specifically, the appellants assert that an act of flight or concealment is not probative of guilt unless the jury is satisfied that the act was motivated by the accused's awareness of having committed the offence in question; but they point out that once the jury has drawn such an inference of "guilty consciousness", it follows as a matter of logic that the accused must in fact be guilty, unless he or she was somehow mistaken or delusional about having committed the crime. Because of this danger, the appellants contend that the jury should be required to apply the same standard of proof to its evaluation of post-offence conduct as it would apply to the ultimate issue of guilt, i.e., proof beyond a reasonable doubt.

That argument is not persuasive. There is no principled basis for the claim that evidence of after-the-fact conduct is substantively different from other kinds of circumstantial evidence, or that it should be accorded special status during jury deliberations. Other types of highly incriminating evidence which present essentially the same kinds of risks do not receive such treatment. In particular, a pretrial oral admission of guilt, which, as the Court of Appeal observed, "goes more directly to the ultimate issue than circumstantial evidence of consciousness of guilt", is not subject to a separate reasonable doubt analysis. As Weiler J.A. observed in *Peavoy*, "[t]here is nothing magical or unique about evidence of after-the-fact conduct." It is simply some evidence which is to be considered and weighed by the jury, together with the rest of the evidence, in deciding whether the accused is guilty or innocent. The fact that such evidence may by its nature be compelling and inculpatory does not have the effect of modifying the evidentiary threshold required by criminal law — namely, that all the evidence, when considered together, must give rise to proof beyond a reasonable doubt.

It is true that a jury may regard an act of flight or concealment as an admission of guilt by conduct, and there is a danger that such evidence could lead a jury to leap erroneously to a conclusion of guilt. As explained below, however, the proper remedy for that danger is not the imposition of a separate burden of proof, but rather an instruction to the jury to be cautious about drawing an incriminatory inference from such evidence and a reminder that all the evidence in the case must be considered.

As a practical matter, if the trial judge invoked the criminal standard of proof as a threshold test for using evidence of post-offence conduct, there would be a risk of confusing the jury and inviting them to short-circuit their deliberations. If the jury determined beyond a reasonable doubt that the accused fled or lied because he or she was aware of having committed the crime charged, they would be less likely to give full consideration to the rest of the evidence. If, on the other hand, the jury failed to determine the motivation of the accused to such a high standard of proof, they would be forced to exclude the evidence of post-offence conduct, which might otherwise be useful in the context of the case as a whole. In either case, the verdict is likely to be reached on the basis of less than all the evidence.

———————

White is also important for discouraging the use of the language of evidence as to "consciousness of guilt". It would be better to refer to "post-offence conduct." See further Stewart (1999), 43 Crim. L.Q. 17.

(d) "Rule" in Hodge's Case

This "rule", which, though derived from an English case, apparently existed only in Canada, may perhaps best be appreciated if we here reproduce the entire case, including the troublesome headnote:

Liverpool Sum. Assizes, 1838
HODGE'S CASE

(Where a charge depends upon circumstantial evidence, it ought not only to be consistent with the prisoner's guilt, but inconsistent with any other rational conclusion.)

The prisoner was charged with murder.

The case was one of circumstantial evidence altogether, and contained no one fact, which taken alone amounted to a presumption of guilt. The murdered party (a woman), who was also robbed, was returning from market with money in her pocket; but how much, or of what particular description of coin, could not be ascertained distinctly.

The prisoner was well acquainted with her, and had been seen near the spot (a lane), in or near which the murder was committed, very shortly before. There were also four other persons together in the same lane about the same period of time. The prisoner, also, was seen some hours after, and on the same day, but at a distance of some miles from the spot in question, burying something, which on the following day was taken up, and turned out to be money, and which corresponded generally as to amount with that which the murdered woman was supposed to have had in her possession when she set out on her return home from market, and of which she had been robbed.

Alderson, B., told the jury, that the case was made up of circumstances entirely; and that, before they could find the prisoner guilty, they must be satisfied, "not only that those circumstances were consistent with his having committed the act, but they must also be satisfied that the facts were such as to be inconsistent with any other rational conclusion than that the prisoner was the guilty person."

He then pointed out to them the proneness of the human mind to look for — and often slightly to distort the facts in order to establish such a proposition — forgetting that a single circumstance which is inconsistent with such a conclusion, is of more importance than all the rest, inasmuch as it destroys the hypothesis of guilt.

The learned Baron then summed up the facts of the case, and the jury returned a verdict of Not guilty.[50]

The important question for us is whether Baron Alderson coined a form of words for explaining to the jury how they might be satisfied beyond a reasonable doubt when the evidence was circumstantial, or whether he intended to erect a new and higher standard of persuasion for such cases.

In 1973 the issue came before the House of Lords in *McGreevy v. Director of Public Prosecutions*[51] on an appeal from Northern Ireland from a conviction for murder. The principal basis for the appeal was that the trial judge in a criminal case dependent on circumstantial evidence should not only direct the jury that they must be satisfied beyond a reasonable doubt but also must charge them in accordance with the so-called rule in *Hodge's Case*. In a unanimous opinion Lord Morris wrote:

> The painstaking research of counsel for the appellant showed that in some countries in the Commonwealth both learned judges and also legal writers have made reference to the "rule" in *Hodge's* case. I do not propose to refer to all the citations which counsel made. The singular fact remains that here in the home of the common law *Hodge's* case has not been given very special prominence: references to it are scant and do not suggest that it enshrines guidance of such compulsive power as to amount to a rule of law which if not faithfully followed will stamp a summing-up as defective. I think that this is consistent with the view that *Hodge's* case was reported not because it laid down a new rule of law but because it was thought to furnish a helpful example of one way in which a jury could be directed in a case where the evidence was circumstantial.[52]

In *R. v. Cooper*[53] the issue again came before the Supreme Court of Canada. The accused was charged that he did confer a benefit on a government employee with respect to dealings between the accused and the government. It was accepted that the evidence from which it was sought to prove that the conferring of the benefit was with respect to accused's dealings with the government, was almost entirely circumstantial. The trial judge charged the jury in accordance with the rule in *Hodge's Case*. The prosecution objected that the question of whether the benefits were with respect to the accused's dealings with the government involved a question of what the accused intended and, citing the *Mitchell* case in support, the instruction was not warranted. The trial judge recalled the jury and advised them to disregard his previous charge with respect to circumstantial evidence. On appeal to the Ontario Court of Appeal it was held that the question was a factual one and that the rule did apply. On the further appeal the court held that the question was one of the accused's intent, that according to *Mitchell* the rule did not apply, and that the trial judge was correct in advising the jury to disregard his previous charge. The accused argued, however, that in recharging the jury in this way the trial judge had diluted his charge as to reasonable doubt as the recharge

---

50.   168 E.R. 1136.
51.   [1973] 1 All E.R. 503 (H.L.).
52.   *Ibid.*, at p. 508.
53.   (1977), 74 D.L.R. (3d) 731 (S.C.C.), applied in *R. v. Elmosri* (1985), 23 C.C.C. (3d) 503 (Ont. C.A.). See also *R. v. Divizio* (1986), 32 C.C.C. (3d) 239 (Ont. Dist. Ct.).

would convey to the jury that his instruction previously given in the language of *Hodge's* case was neither a formula to assist in applying the accepted standard of proof nor a graphic illustration of the principle of reasonable doubt.[54]

The majority denied that such would be the case and Ritchie, J. wrote:

> ... when the charge, as corrected, is read as a whole and in light of this final admonition, I am of opinion that no reasonable juror could have been confused as to the obligation to be satisfied beyond a reasonable doubt before entering a conviction. Nothing was said to suggest any other standard of proof and in my opinion the instructions as to reasonable doubt are in no way diluted by charging the jury in accordance with the law established in this Court that the *Hodge's* formula does not apply in determining the "intention" of the accused. The language employed by Mr. Justice Spence in the passage from his reasons in *R. v. Mitchell, supra,* has been reaffirmed in this Court in *R. v. John, supra; R. v. Bagshaw,* (1971), 4 C.C.C. (2d) 303 at p. 307, [1972] S.C.R. at p. 6, and *R. v. Paul* (1975), 27 C.C.C. (2d) 1 at p. 4, 33 C.R.N.S. 328, and must, I think, be taken to have been accepted as confining the application of the *Hodge's Case* formula in the manner there stated. This is not to say that, even where the issue is one of identification, the exact words used by Baron Alderson must necessarily be incorporated in a Judge's charge. It is enough if it is made plain to the members of the jury that before basing a verdict of guilty on circumstantial evidence they must be satisfied beyond a reasonable doubt that the guilt of the accused is the only reasonable inference to be drawn from the proven facts. In this regard it will be seen that I agree with the Chief Justice in his rejection of the *Hodge* formula as an inexorable rule of law in Canada.[55]

Laskin, C.J.C., in a dissenting opinion, would go much further:

> There are a few observations I would make on *Hodge's Case* specifically. Intent is no less a question of fact than is identity or the *actus reus* of an offence. I would not condone a situation where a trial Judge may properly charge a jury under *Hodge's Case* in respect of identity, and all other issues except intent, and then in the same case tell them to approach the Crown's burden of proof on a different basis on the question of intent. There must be consistency in a charge where burden of proof is concerned; and to have two different formulae in one case is as unjust to the Crown as it is to an accused.
>
> The judgment of the House of Lords in *McGreevy v. Director of Public Prosecutions,* [1973] 1 All E.R. 503, rejects the notion that there ever was any rule arising from *Hodge's Case* which Judges in England were required to follow where all or most of the evidence in a jury trial was circumstantial. In *R. v. Comba* (1938), 70 C.C.C. p. 237 at p. 238, [1938] S.C.R. 396 at p. 397, this Court referred to the formula in *Hodge's Case* as "the long settled rule of the common law, which is the rule of law in Canada". Notwithstanding this pronouncement, this Court attenuated the rule in its judgment in *R. v. Mitchell, supra,* and manifested its discomfort with *Hodge's Case* in *R. v. John* (1970), 2 C.C.C. (2d) 157, [1971] S.C.R. 781. The time has come to reject the formula in *Hodge's Case* as an inexorable rule of law in Canada. Without being dogmatic against any use of the formula of the charge in *Hodge's Case* I would leave the matter to the good sense of the trial Judge (as was said in *McGreevy*), with the reminder that a charge in terms of the traditional formula of required proof beyond a reasonable doubt is the safest as well as the simplest way to bring a lay jury to the appreciation of the burden of proof resting on the Crown in a criminal case.[56]

---

54. *Ibid.,* at p. 745.
55. *Ibid.,* at p. 746.
56. *Ibid.,* at p. 735.

In *R. v. Charemski*,[57] Bastarache, J., Cory and Iacobucci, JJ. concurring, for the majority, wrote:

> In my view, the trial judge should have directed the jury according to the requirement that a finding of guilt could only be made where there was no other rational explanation for the circumstantial evidence but that the defendant committed the crime (*John v. The Queen*, [1971] S.C.R. 781, at pp. 791-92; *R. v. Cooper*, [1978] 1 S.C.R. 860, at p. 881; *Mezzo v. The Queen*, [1986] 1 S.C.R. 802, at p. 843).

Has the Rule in *Hodge's Case* been resurrected? The Manitoba Court of Appeal in *R. v. Khan*[58] read *Charemski* as having done so but the Ontario Court of Appeal took the opposite position in *R. v. Tombran*[59] and *R. v. Robert*.[60] — *Sharpe J. — no rescussitation*

(e) Measure of Evidential Burden

The evidential burden signifies the duty of going forward in the production of evidence, either at the outset of the trial or during its course. The party who entertains the burden and fails in its discharge not only risks loss at the hands of the trier but also risks loss at the hands of the judge; the party who fails to produce evidence may not get past the judge and into the hands of the jury. While our system is predicated on the right to a jury's verdict, the system has always provided a role for the judge to confine the jury within the parameters of rationality.

The trial judge must determine whether the jury, acting reasonably, *could* find a verdict for the proponent. A nice question arises. When the trial judge weighs the evidence should he assess it against the standard of persuasion fixed on the case? Should he, for example, in a criminal case let the prosecution case go to the jury only if he is satisfied that a jury *could* reasonably conclude guilt beyond a reasonable doubt? In the classic case of *R. v. Comba*[61] the Supreme Court of Canada was quite specific and express that the standard of proof should be incorporated. Duff, C.J.C. wrote for the court:

> It is admitted by the Crown, as the fact is, that the verdict rests solely upon a basis of circumstantial evidence. In such cases, by the long settled rule of the common law, which is the rule of law in Canada as in all countries of the British Empire, the jury, before finding a prisoner guilty upon such evidence, must be satisfied not only that the circumstances are consistent with a conclusion that the criminal act was committed by the accused, but also that the facts are such as to be inconsistent with any other rational conclusion than that the accused is the guilty person.
>
> We have no doubt that the facts adduced have not the degree of probative force that is required in order to satisfy the test formulated by this rule; which is one that Courts of justice in Canada are governed by and are bound to apply.
>
> We agree with the majority of the Court of Appeal, whose reasons for their judgment we find convincing and conclusive, that the learned trial Judge ought, on the application made by counsel for the prisoner at the close of the evidence for the

---

57.   [1998] 1 S.C.R. 679.
58.   (1998), 17 C.R. (5th) 221 (Man. C.A.).
59.   (2000), 31 C.R. (5th) 349 (Ont. C.A.).
60.   (2000), 31 C.R. (5th) 340 (Ont. C.A.).
61.   [1938] 3 D.L.R. 719 (S.C.C.).

Crown, to have told the jury that in view of the dubious nature of the evidence, it would be unsafe to find the prisoner guilty and to have directed them to return a verdict of acquittal accordingly.[62]

R. v. NELLES
(1982), 16 C.C.C. (3d) 97 (Ont. Prov. Ct.)

VANEK PROV. CT. J.:—

. . . .

In accordance with the foregoing principles of law, I have directed myself that in arriving at a decision whether or not to commit the accused for trial, it is not my function as a "justice" at a preliminary inquiry to weigh the evidence for the purpose of determining whether it is credible or trustworthy; that these matters fall within the sphere of the jury; and that I must consider, apart from credibility and accepting the evidence on the basis that it is true, whether it is "sufficient", under s. 475 of the *Criminal Code* and in accordance with the test of sufficiency laid down by Ritchie J. in *Sheppard*, to warrant committing the accused for trial.

. . . .

From my assessment of the evidence before me in this case I come to the following conclusions:

1. The evidence is entirely circumstantial.
2. There is no evidence of any motive.
3. In the case of Janice Estrella, there is no evidence to go before a jury that the accused was the person who murdered this child.
4. While the accused had access to each of Pacsai, Miller and Cook and therefore an opportunity to administer the dosage of digoxin that caused death, in none of these cases did she have exclusive access and opportunity; in each case other persons also had access to each of these infants at relevant times and the opportunity to administer the digoxin to them that caused death.
5. There is no evidence of any acts or conduct on the part of the accused in relation to any of the four babies that is out of the usual course of her duties as a registered nurse at the hospital, or which isolates and identifies her as the person who caused death by the administration of overdoses of digoxin to any of them.
6. The accused is an excellent nurse and enjoys an excellent reputation among her peers.
7. Each item or piece of evidence in support of the Crown's case, if consistent with guilt, is equally consistent with a rational conclusion, grounded in the evidence, that the accused is not the guilty person.
8. In addition, there is powerful evidence in disproof of the allegation that the accused is the person who caused the death of the four babies. This evidence is composed of proof that the accused could not be the person who caused the death of Janice Estrella or who administered an overdose of digoxin to baby Lombardo that likely caused his death, together with the strong likelihood that one person caused the death of all five children: Lombardo, Estrella, Pacsai, Miller and Cook.
9. There is evidence that points in a different direction.

Upon the whole of the evidence, it is my conclusion that there is no evidence to go before a jury on the count of murder in connection with Janice Estrella; that on each of the remaining counts, the evidence against the accused is at least equally consistent with the rational conclusion, grounded in the evidence, that the accused is innocent of the

---

62. *Ibid.*, at pp. 720-21.

offence charged as it is that the accused is the guilty person. The evidence viewed in its entirety is either of too dubious a nature or amounts to no evidence at all to go before a jury; in either case, a reasonable jury, properly instructed, could not find beyond a reasonable doubt that the guilt of the accused is the only reasonable inference to be drawn from the proven facts.

In my opinion, therefore, upon the whole of the evidence, no sufficient case is made out to put the accused on trial on any of the four charges included in the three informations before me.

Accordingly, with respect to each count, the accused must be discharged.

———————

The logic of incorporating the applicable standard seems inescapable. If a trial judge in a criminal case does not incorporate the criminal standard he runs the risk of an irrational verdict. If such incorporation were forbidden he would be obliged to leave the case to the jury when he believes a jury could reasonably conclude that the evidence preponderates in favour of the prosecution even though he believes that no jury could reasonably be satisfied beyond a reasonable doubt. If incorporation is forbidden the anomaly is produced that the trial judge must admonish the jury that they can convict only if they are satisfied beyond a reasonable doubt but leave the case with them though he is convinced that no reasonable jury could be so satisfied.

In *R. v. Syms*[63] the trial judge had directed an acquittal but on appeal a new trial was ordered. The trial judge had stated:

> Accordingly, I am ruling that *having regard to the standard of proof, that a jury would have to apply,* it is my view, that a jury properly instructed, acting as men of ordinary reason and fairness could not make a finding of exclusive opportunity and thereby reach a verdict of guilty based on the inferences to be drawn from the proven facts in the Crown's case. [Emphasis added.][64]

The Ontario Court of Appeal criticized the trial judge for demanding *exclusive* opportunity and later remarked:

> . . . as the appellant was not put to his election whether he was going to call evidence, it would have been inappropriate for the trial Judge to have applied his mind, at that stage of the proceedings, to the question of reasonable doubt.[65]

U.S.A. v. SHEPPARD
(1976), [1977] 2 S.C.R. 1067, 34 C.R.N.S. 207, 30 C.C.C. (2d) 424

[The case involved an application for extradition. The case has relevance here since the test for the extradition judge is, by statute,[66] the same test that

———————

63.   (1979), 47 C.C.C. (2d) 114 (Ont. C.A.).
64.   *Ibid.*, at p. 116.
65.   *Ibid.*, at p. 117. See also *R. v. Paul* (1975), 27 C.C.C. (2d) 1, 5 (S.C.C.) per Ritchie, J.:
      . . . the rule in *Hodge's Case* which was reaffirmed in *R. v. Comba*, was concerned with the weight to be attached to the evidence, whereas here the question is whether there was any evidence to weigh.
      And *R. v. Downie* (1972), 10 C.C.C. (2d) 335 (Man. C.A.):
      . . . we agree that the applicability of the rule in *Hodge's Case* arises not at the end of the Crown's case but only after the accused has made his election whether or not to call evidence.
66.   *Extradition Act,* R.S.C. 1985, c. E-23, s. 18(1)(*b*).

would justify a committal for trial after a preliminary hearing which, in turn, was judicially decided to be the same test which is applied on a motion for a directed verdict. The affidavit evidence filed on the hearing was that of an admitted drug dealer and alleged accomplice of Sheppard who by his affidavit admitted that he was purchasing immunity for himself by offering his accusation of Sheppard. The extradition judge, Hugessen, J., rejected this evidence as unworthy of belief and refused the extradition. The Supreme Court of Canada disagreed. Ritchie, J. for the majority stated:]

Credibility in my view must always be a question for the jury and if the function of an extradition Judge is equivalent to that of a Judge in determining whether or not a case should be left to the jury, it follows that credibility is not within his sphere.

MONTELEONE v. R.
[1987] 2 S.C.R. 154, 59 C.R. (3d) 97, 35 C.C.C (3d) 193

[The accused was the proprietor of a men's clothing store which occupied the ground floor of a three-storey building. He was charged with setting a fire which destroyed the building. The fire inspector testified that in his view the fire was set. He admitted that the actual cause of the fire could not be determined, but concluded that the fire was of incendiary origin because the investigation revealed no accidental cause. The accused gave a statement to the inspector that placed him at the scene shortly before the fire; he admitted that he smelled smoke but presumed it was from a defective vacuum cleaner that had overheated. A number of persons had access to the accused's shop. There was no evidence that the accused was in extreme financial difficulty, nor was it shown that he would profit in any substantial degree from the fire. At the close of the Crown's case, before the accused elected whether to call evidence, the trial judge acceded to a defence motion and directed a verdict of acquittal. The Crown appealed to the Court of Appeal, the appeal was allowed, and the accused appealed further.]

The judgment of the court was delivered by:

McIntyre J.:—

. . . .

To reach a conclusion in this case, some consideration of the evidence is involved. The Crown, in seeking to establish its case, tendered evidence which for our purposes may be grouped under four headings:

(1) the nature of the fire;
(2) the motive of the appellant;
(3) the opportunity on the part of the appellant; and
(4) contradictions within the appellant's own statement.

[The Court then examined the evidence that had been led on these matters.]

I do not suggest that the inculpatory evidence is conclusive or even persuasive. That is not the function of an appellate court. The resolution of that question is for the jury upon proper instructions on the law after having heard the evidence. I have made only slight reference to the inculpatory evidence, but I would note that at trial it was strongly challenged on many points. From cross-examination of principal creditors it appeared that the financial obligations of the appellant were not unusual, considering all circumstances and the nature of the business. No creditor expressed any fear as to its security prior to the fire, and the appellant was not being pressed by his creditors. This evidence might very well influence a jury to discount the inculpatory evidence and find in favour of the appellant. This they would do, however, in the exercise of the function imposed upon them by law as the true finders of fact. It is not open to a judge in a jury trial to consider the weight of the evidence. This is the function of the jury and it should be left to them. I am of the view that there was evidence before the trial judge which met the test propounded by Ritchie J. in *U.S. v. Shephard*, supra. I am in substantial agreement with the reasons for judgment of Lacourcière J.A. for the Ontario Court of Appeal and I would dismiss the appeal and confirm the order for a new trial.

Appeal dismissed.

In a companion case, *R. v. Yebes*,[67] handed down the same day as *Monteleone*, the court reviewed the role of an appellate court when a jury's verdict is disputed as "unreasonable or cannot be supported by the evidence" pursuant to section 686(1)(*a*)(i) of the Criminal Code:

> The court must determine on the whole of the evidence whether the verdict is one that a properly-instructed jury, acting judicially, could reasonably have rendered. While the Court of Appeal must not merely substitute its view for that of the jury, in order to apply the test the court must *re-examine* and to some extent *reweigh* and consider the effect of the evidence. [Emphasis added.][68]

Why is it that an appellate court can look back and re-weigh the evidence, and so determine whether the verdict was reasonable, but a trial judge cannot look forward and weigh the evidence to determine whether a verdict based thereon could be reasonable? Are appellate judges more able?

R. v. QUERCIA
(1990), 1 C.R. (4th) 385, 60 C.C.C. (3d) 380 (Ont. C.A.)

[The accused was charged with aggravated sexual assault. He denied any involvement in the offence and testified that he was at home with his mother when the assault occurred. His mother testified and corroborated the accused's evidence. The case against the accused rested entirely on the victim's identification of him. The accused was convicted after a trial before a judge and jury. He appealed on the ground that the verdict was unreasonable.

Held, the appeal should be allowed, the conviction quashed and an acquittal entered.]

DOHERTY J.A. (GALLIGAN and OSBORNE JJ.A. concurring):—

. . . .

The appellant raises three grounds of appeal:

(1) Did the learned trial judge err in not directing a verdict of not guilty at the close of the Crown's case?

---

67. (1987), 59 C.R. (3d) 108, 120 (S.C.C.). Regarding the appellate court assessing the reasonableness of a verdict, see also *R. v. Gale* (1984), 42 C.R. (3d) 94 (B.C.C.A.).
68. R.S.C. 1985, c. C-46.

(2) Did the learned trial judge err in failing to instruct the jury as to the reason behind the danger inherent in relying on eyewitness identification?

(3) Was the verdict unreasonable?

We did not call on the Crown on the first two grounds of appeal advanced. The first ground of appeal is determined against the appellant by the judgment of the Supreme Court of Canada in *R. v. Mezzo*. . . . With respect to the alleged non-direction, I cannot agree that the charge to the jury was deficient. The trial judge's instructions pertaining to the manner in which eyewitness identification should be approached and his review of the relevant evidence was marked by both clarity and thoroughness. The instructions to the jury were, at the least, fair to the appellant and were, in some respects, very favourable to him.

The third ground of appeal raises a much more difficult problem. This is a case in which the conviction of the appellant depends entirely on the identification of him by the victim. Where the Crown's case rests on eyewitness identification, one is always very concerned about the reliability of a finding of guilt.

. . . Where the verdict is said to be unreasonable or not supported by the evidence, the appellate court must independently examine and assess the evidence adduced at trial and reach its own conclusion as to the reasonableness of the verdict. In doing so, it must decide whether the totality of the evidence is such that the verdict is one that a "properly instructed jury acting judicially, could reasonably have rendered": *R. v. Yebes*. . . . In deciding whether a jury has exceeded the bounds of reasonableness, the court must give due deference to the advantageous position of the jury, who actually saw and heard the witnesses.

. . . .

Bearing in mind both my duty to weigh and assess the evidence independent of the jury's verdict and the limited scope of my review, I turn to the evidence in the case at bar. I begin by acknowledging that the victim was in every respect an honest witness. Honesty cannot, however, be equated with reliability where identification evidence is concerned.

. . . .

Considering the totality of the evidence describing the attack, and acknowledging the chilling horror of the circumstances in which the victim found herself, I regard this as a case where the victim, in part because of her heroic determination to observe the appellant, had a good opportunity to observe and accurately record in her mind the appearance of her attacker. This was no fleeting encounter. Having made that assessment, I hasten to add that a person in the victim's position could hardly be expected to observe and mentally record all of the salient features of her attacker, nor could she be expected to be completely accurate in her recollection of those observations.

. . . .

I acknowledge the victim's honesty and integrity and I applaud her courage, but I am driven to conclude that her evidence identifying the appellant as her assailant was significantly flawed and could not, standing alone, justify a conviction. There is virtually no other evidence confirming her identification. The weight of the remaining evidence points away from the appellant's involvement in the attack. In my judgment, the verdict is unreasonable and cannot be supported by the evidence. I would allow the appeal, quash the conviction, and enter an acquittal.

circumstantial evidence

R. v. CHAREMSKI

[1998] 1 S.C.R. 679, 15 C.R. (5th) 1, 123 C.C.C. (3d) 225

[The accused was charged with the murder of his estranged wife. The forensic evidence failed to establish definitively that the deceased had died from natural causes, or as a result of an accident, suicide, or homicide. The trial judge granted a motion for a directed verdict of acquittal after concluding that there was no evidence that the deceased had been murdered. He concluded that this gap in the evidence would preclude any reasonable jury from returning a verdict of guilty. The Court of Appeal set the directed verdict aside and ordered a new trial.]

Held: Appeal dismissed.

BASTARACHE J. (CORY and IACOBUCCI JJ. concurring):—

. . . .

Where the evidence is purely circumstantial, this Court made it quite clear, [in *Monteleone*], that the issue of whether the standard set in *Hodge's Case* has been met is a matter for the jury, and not the judge. In other words, whether or not there is a rational explanation for that evidence other than the guilt of the accused, is a question for the jury. To my mind, this view is dispositive of this case and the Court need go no further than to rely on this authority.

As noted above, in a murder prosecution, the Crown must adduce sufficient evidence on the issues of identity, causation, the death of the victim and the requisite mental state. The core issue in this appeal is whether the evidence led by the Crown at trial met the requirements of the *Shephard* test by adducing sufficient evidence of causation.

As the trial judge noted, the forensic evidence did not establish that the deceased was murdered and was inconclusive on this point. Two medical experts examined the body and were unable to determine definitively whether the deceased died from natural causes, or as a result of an accident, suicide or homicide. The trial judge concluded that "from an examination of the body, as a matter of law, there is no evidence that she met with foul play or that, in the words of the definition of homicide, that somebody caused her death". The evidence in the deceased's apartment also did not establish any foul play. The trial judge concluded that "with respect to the apartment, there is no evidence of a homicide other than the fact that the body is there". Finally, the Crown presented no direct evidence (e.g., fingerprints or eyewitness testimony) placing the accused in his wife's apartment on the night she died, and no evidence that he actually knew of the manner of her death before being informed by the police. On the basis of these observations, the trial judge concluded that there was no evidence on the issue of causation, a gap which would preclude any reasonable jury from returning a verdict of guilty.

It is necessary and useful to review the other evidence adduced by the Crown, and the possible inferences that could be drawn therefrom, before addressing the significance of the purportedly missing element of the Crown's case, as perceived by the trial judge. First, the Crown adduced evidence relating to animus and to motive. The appellant and the deceased had a difficult marriage marked by periods of separation. During one such period, the deceased began a relationship with another man, which the appellant found "shameful" and which had made him feel "like an idiot". The appellant told police that the deceased had taken lovers in the past and was always "making problems" for him. On one occasion, the deceased told her doctor that she was afraid of staying with her husband and wanted to move away from him, and the doctor told the deceased about a women's shelter. The deceased also once told a friend that the appellant was verbally abusive and that she was afraid of him. The Crown also led evidence suggesting the appellant may have had a financial motive to kill his wife. The appellant, who receives social assistance, held a life insurance policy on the deceased in the amount of $50,000. The Crown adduced evidence to establish that this represents a great deal of money in Poland, where the appellant (who is Polish) has been living on and off for the past five years. On the basis of these facts, the Crown, in my opinion, adduced sufficient evidence from which a jury, properly instructed, could have inferred the requisite mental state for the homicide. That is, the jury could have inferred from the evidence of animus and financial motive that the accused intended to kill his wife.

The issue of identity was not disputed. The appellant admitted that he was present at the deceased's apartment building on the night she died, and that he had telephoned her. This admission also allowed the Crown to present evidence of opportunity. The appellant clearly made a great effort to see his wife on Christmas Eve, travelling by plane and bus from Vancouver to London, Ontario. During the second telephone call to his wife, the appellant asked whether she was alone; the deceased then asked her friends to leave so that she could speak to the appellant. It is not clear whether she knew at that point that the appellant was in town, or whether she thought she would be speaking with him on the telephone from Vancouver. Finally, the appellant failed to account for the time between his arrival at the deceased's apartment building (11:00 p.m.) and the time he was picked up by a taxi and left for Toronto (12:30 a.m.). The deceased died at some point between 11:00 p.m. and 1:00 a.m. The deceased's key to her apartment could not be found. Clearly, a jury could infer from the evidence that the appellant had the opportunity to kill his wife.

The Crown also presented evidence that the appellant had premature knowledge of the manner of his wife's death. Three days after the deceased died, the police interviewed the appellant by telephone. The appellant stated in that conversation that the deceased had complained about being short of money, being sick, and forgetting things. He told police that she was in poor health and abused drugs. The appellant then volunteered that the deceased had complained to him about falling asleep in the bathtub sometimes for an hour or two, and that the deceased had told him she almost drowned on a couple of occasions. At that point in the conversation, the police had not yet discussed how the deceased had died, and the appellant had not yet heard from another source. The jury could have inferred that the appellant knew of the manner of his wife's death because he was present when she died, and further, because he caused her death.

Returning to the issue of causation, the Crown presented evidence related to the condition of the deceased's body. Although the forensic evidence was inconclusive in the sense that there was no proof of homicide (for example, neck trauma resulting from strangulation), it is also true that the forensic tests turned up no evidence consistent with death by natural causes, accident, drug overdose or suicide. Moreover, the location of the body in scalding water with the head near the faucets provided evidence from which a jury could have inferred that the deceased was in fact the victim of foul play.

In my opinion, the Crown thus presented sufficient evidence from which a reasonable jury, properly instructed, could return a verdict of guilty, notwithstanding the fact that the cause of death was unexplained. Both the position and condition of the body as found, and the indications of the appellant's premature knowledge of the manner of death, constitute circumstantial evidence pertaining to the cause of death. This conclusion is based largely on this Court's decision in *Monteleone*, where the appellant appealed the reversal of the trial's judge directed verdict on charges of arson. . . . . Just as was the case in *Monteleone*, "evidence of other matters — motive, opportunity, financial difficulty and possibility of gain — [could] be considered as evidence going to prove the crime", and it was not necessary for the Crown to adduce direct evidence of the corpus delicti. Indeed, I would suggest that there is in fact more evidence in this case than was available in *Monteleone*. There, there was no evidence whatsoever as to the cause of the fire; here, we have the deceased in the bathtub with her head at the faucet end. There are hot water burns on the skin, but not on the lungs. This constitutes at least some — albeit not compelling evidence — of foul play.

In my view, the trial judge should have directed the jury according to the requirement that a finding of guilt could only be made where there was no other rational explanation for the circumstantial evidence but that the defendant committed the crime (*John v. The Queen*, [1971] S.C.R. 781, at pp. 791-92; *R. v. Cooper*, [1978] 1 S.C.R. 860, at p. 881; *Mezzo v. The Queen*, [1986] 1 S.C.R. 802, at p.843). Making that finding is essentially a factual matter arising from an evaluation of the evidence. That assessment is properly left to the jury. Judges should not be hasty to encroach on that time-honoured function, particularly where well-established principles articulated in this Court provide clear guidance on the circumstances in which a question may be withheld from the jury.

McLACHLIN J. (MAJOR J. concurring), dissenting:— I have read the reasons of Justice Bastarache. I respectfully disagree.

This is said to be a murder case, although no one can be sure there has been a murder. The accused's wife, from whom he was separated, was found dead in her bathtub in the early hours of Christmas Day, 1992. Two pathologists examined the body; neither was able to conclude whether she died from natural causes, as the result of an accident, by suicide or by homicide. Her lungs were heavy, which was consistent with drowning. There were no signs of strangulation. There was no evidence of foul play in her apartment. Everything was neat and in order. Her bed was turned down for the night and her pyjamas laid out. No fingerprints of the accused were found in the apartment. The accused denied having been there, although he readily admitted to having wanted to see his wife that evening and to having telephoned her from the lobby asking to come up. The husband and wife had a joint life insurance policy worth $50,000, but there was no evidence the accused needed or wanted money. They were separated and had had difficulties in the past, but there is no evidence explaining why the accused might at this point, when they had established separate lives thousands of miles apart, have decided to kill his wife.

The Crown's case was woefully weak. The most glaring deficiency was the inability of the pathologists to determine whether a murder had been committed. The other evidence was, at best, equivocal. Not surprisingly, at the close of the Crown's case the accused made a motion for a directed verdict of acquittal. The trial judge granted the motion. Flinn J. reviewed the law in detail, then applied the test of whether any reasonable jury properly instructed could find the accused guilty of murder on the evidence. He concluded that no reasonable jury could and that therefore there was "no evidence". Accordingly, he directed a verdict of acquittal.

In my view the trial judge reached the correct conclusion. The Court of Appeal should not have disturbed his decision. Neither should this Court. The accused should not be subjected to another trial on evidence as flimsy as this.

The Test on a Motion for a Directed Verdict

The test on a motion for a directed verdict has been clear for over a century. It is a fundamental part of our criminal law. It is accepted throughout the common law world, including England and the United States. The test is whether a properly instructed jury could reasonably convict on the evidence. This Court has repeatedly affirmed this test, notably in *United States of America v. Shephard*, [1977] 2 S.C.R. 1067, *Mezzo v. The Queen*, [1986] 1 S.C.R. 802, and *R. v. Monteleone*, [1987] 2 S.C.R. 154.

A properly instructed jury acting reasonably is a jury that will convict only if it finds that the evidence establishes guilt beyond a reasonable doubt. To determine whether this could occur, the judge on the motion for a directed verdict must ask whether some or all of the admissible evidence is legally sufficient to permit the jury to find guilt beyond a reasonable doubt. In doing so, the trial judge is determining the sufficiency of the evidence. The question is whether the evidence is capable of supporting a verdict of guilt beyond a reasonable doubt. If it is not, the judge must direct an acquittal, since it would be impossible for a reasonable jury to convict legally on the evidence. The case against the accused has not been made out and there is no charge to answer. To permit the trial to continue would be to impinge on the accused's right to silence and right to be presumed innocent until proved guilty, and to risk a verdict that would necessarily be unreasonable.

While some judges have referred to a distinction between "no evidence" and "some evidence", this distinction is nonsensical. The question on a motion for a directed acquittal always relates to the ability of the evidence to support a verdict of guilt, that is, whether there is sufficient evidence to permit a properly instructed jury to reasonably convict: R. J. Delisle, "Evidence — Tests for Sufficiency of Evidence: *Mezzo v. The Queen*" (1987),

66 Can. Bar Rev. 389, at p. 393; and see also David M. Tanovich, "*Monteleone's* Legacy: Confusing Sufficiency with Weight" (1994), 27 C.R. (4th) 174, at pp. 175-76. . . . . As Professor Delisle puts it in *Evidence: Principles and Problems* (3rd ed. 1993), at p. 178, "[l]ogically . . . it would seem to be wrong to let a case go to the jury if the trial judge believed that no reasonable jury could be satisfied beyond a reasonable doubt" (as cited in Tanovich, *supra*, at p. 176).

. . . .

On any motion for a directed verdict, whether the evidence is direct or circumstantial, the judge, in assessing the sufficiency of the evidence must, by definition, weigh it. There is no way the judge can avoid this task of limited weighing, since the judge cannot answer the question of whether a properly instructed jury could reasonably convict without determining whether it is rationally possible to find that the fact in issue has been proved. In the case of circumstantial evidence, the issue is the reasonableness of the inference the Crown seeks to have drawn. As stated by Professor Delisle, in "Tests for Sufficiency of Evidence", *supra*, at p. 392, "[i]t is in evaluating the rationality of the necessary derivative inference, in testing its legitimacy, that the judge, either at preliminary, at trial or on appeal, performs the necessary weighing function". But weighing the evidence for this purpose is a very limited exercise. The judge does not ask him or herself whether he or she is personally satisfied by the evidence. Rather, the judge asks whether a jury, acting reasonably, could be satisfied by the evidence. Nor is the judge permitted to assess the credibility of the witnesses: see *Mezzo, supra*. It is for the jury to determine the credibility of the witnesses, to decide what evidence it accepts and what evidence it rejects, and ultimately, to determine if the evidence establishes guilt beyond a reasonable doubt. The difference between the judge's function on a motion for a directed verdict and the jury's function at the end of the trial is simply this: the judge assesses whether, hypothetically, a guilty verdict is possible; the jury determines whether guilt has actually been proved beyond a reasonable doubt.

. . . .

Until recently, no one questioned the rule that on a motion for a directed verdict the trial judge must determine whether there is sufficient evidence to permit a properly instructed jury, acting reasonably, to convict, with the implied correlative that the trial judge must weigh the evidence in the limited sense of determining whether it is capable of supporting essential inferences the Crown seeks to have the jury draw. However, in this case the Crown argues that the test has been altered in cases of circumstantial evidence by two decisions of this Court: *Mezzo, supra*, and *Monteleone, supra*. I do not agree. While some of the language of these cases is confusing, a closer reading suggests that the justices had no intention of discarding the time-hallowed and universally accepted test for directed acquittals.

. . . .

The ambiguities in *Mezzo* and *Monteleone* leave me far from certain that the judges who wrote in those cases intended to abandon the long-standing rule that trial judges on a motion for a directed verdict must determine whether the evidence is sufficient to permit a properly instructed jury acting reasonably to reach a verdict of guilt. On the contrary, the Court in both cases expressly reaffirm this principle. In my view, the comments in the decisions suggesting a possible contrary effect should not be read as negating this fundamental principle.

In my opinion, the test for a directed verdict in Canada remains the traditional one: whether a properly instructed jury acting reasonably could find guilt beyond a reasonable doubt. Where it is necessary to engage in a limited evaluation of inferences in order to answer this question, as in cases based on circumstantial evidence, trial judges may do so; indeed, they cannot do otherwise in order to discharge their obligation of determining whether the Crown has established a case that calls on the accused to answer or risk being convicted.

This conclusion is confirmed by the following considerations: it is the only conclusion that satisfies the logic of the trial process; it is the only conclusion that adequately safeguards the accused's rights; it is the rule that prevails in other common law jurisdictions; and it is the view that best harmonizes with the tests established for proceedings analogous to the motion for a directed verdict, such as preliminary inquiries and appeals on the reasonableness of a conviction.

Application of the Rule to This Case

. . . .

Bastarache J. correctly asserts that the Crown must adduce sufficient evidence on the issues of identity, causation, the death of the victim and the requisite mental state to pass the hurdle of a motion for a directed acquittal. To this I would add two further comments.

First, "sufficient evidence" must mean sufficient evidence to sustain a verdict of guilt beyond a reasonable doubt; merely to refer to "sufficient evidence" is incomplete since "sufficient" always relates to the goal or threshold of proof beyond a reasonable doubt. This must constantly be borne in mind when evaluating whether the evidence is capable of supporting the inferences necessary to establish the essential elements of the case. My second comment concerns the relationship between the elements of identity, causation, the death of victim and requisite mental state. "Identity" means "identity of the murderer". It is impossible to discuss identity unless one has evidence capable of supporting the finding, beyond a reasonable doubt, that a murder was committed. Similarly, the element of mental state presupposes a culpable homicide. Therefore, I do not agree that the fact that the accused was in the deceased's apartment block the night of the death establishes identity. Until there is a homicide, it is meaningless to speak of identity. The same goes for mental state. This means that the finding that there has been a homicide or culpable cause of death, is critical. Without that finding, we cannot even meaningfully discuss two of the other essential elements of murder. We have only a death and that alone cannot support a conviction for murder.

. . . .

The Crown argues that the corpus delicti can be proved by evidence of motive and opportunity. It relies on *Monteleone, supra,* in which this Court held that the corpus delicti of arson could be established by evidence of motive, opportunity, financial difficulty and possibility of gain. This argument fails for three reasons. First, the argument ignores the longstanding principle that on charges of murder, there is "the necessity of the most compelling proof of the corpus delicti": see *McWilliams, supra.* Second, the facts in *Monteleone* were more compelling than here. In *Monteleone* there was evidence of financial difficulty and clear evidence of opportunity. The evidence suggested that a valuable antique desk had been removed prior to the fire and that there was very little inventory. The accused admitted that he was in the building shortly before the fire. Here, by contrast, there is no evidence placing the accused in the deceased's apartment. There is no evidence of financial difficulty or need. The presence of a long-standing life insurance policy on one's spouse without more is hardly evidence of motive; such policies are common among even happily married couples. The fact that $50,000 is a lot of money in Poland is also not evidence of motive — presumably it is "a lot of money" in many places. Third, it seems that in *Monteleone* there was no other rational explanation for the fire; the fire marshall testified to this effect. The pathologists in the case at bar, on the contrary, testified to the reasonable possibility of other non-criminal causes of death.

In determining whether it was legally possible for a properly instructed jury acting reasonably to convict on the evidence, the central question — the question on which all other questions hinged — was whether the evidence was capable of permitting an inference, beyond a reasonable doubt, that the deceased had been killed. The medical evidence adduced by the two Crown pathologists provided two other reasonable explanations for the death — natural causes and suicide. Thus, the evidence was incapable of supporting an inference, beyond a reasonable doubt, that the death was wrongful. To paraphrase *McCormick on Evidence, supra,* at p. 435, an inference that the deceased was murdered was far beyond the "limits of reasonable inference from the facts proven". That being the case, there was no way that a reasonable jury, properly instructed, could have returned a verdict of guilty.

. . . .

No reasonable jury properly instructed could have convicted the accused of the murder of his wife on this evidence. There was no case for the accused to meet. The trial judge correctly allowed the motion for a directed verdict and entered the acquittal.

Is the majority in *Charemski* complaining that the trial judge erred in weighing the evidence or is it really complaining that the trial judge erred when he, after weighing the evidence, concluded that there was not sufficient evidence? In other words, is it okay to weigh but please get it right!? On October 8, 1998, the charges were withdrawn in *Charemski* because, *inter alia*, the Crown stated that there was no reasonable prospect of conviction: see (1998) ADGN/98-1585 (QUICKLAW database Gold).

R. v. ARCURI
[2001] S.C.J. No. 52

[The accused was charged with first degree murder. At the preliminary inquiry, the Crown's case was entirely circumstantial and the accused called two witnesses whose testimony was arguably exculpatory. The preliminary inquiry judge rejected the accused's contention that he must weigh the evidence and, after viewing the evidence as a whole, determined that the accused should be committed to trial for second degree murder. The accused's certiorari application was dismissed and that decision was affirmed by the Court of Appeal. The issue before the Supreme Court was whether the preliminary inquiry judge, in determining whether the evidence was sufficient to commit the accused to trial, erred in refusing to weigh the Crown's evidence against the allegedly exculpatory direct evidence adduced by the accused.]

McLACHLIN, C.J. (L'HEUREUX-DUBÉ, GONTHIER, IACOBUCCI, MAJOR, BASTARACHE, BINNIE, ARBOUR and LeBEL, JJ. concurring): —

. . . .

The question to be asked by a preliminary inquiry judge under s. 548(1) of the Criminal Code is the same as that asked by a trial judge considering a defence motion for a directed verdict, namely, "whether or not there is any evidence upon which a reasonable jury properly instructed could return a verdict of guilty": *Shephard, supra,* at p. 1080; see also *R. v. Monteleone,* [1987] 2 S.C.R. 154, at p. 160. Under this test, a preliminary inquiry judge must commit the accused to trial "in any case in which there is admissible evidence which could, if it were believed, result in a conviction": *Shephard, supra,* at p. 1080.

The test is the same whether the evidence is direct or circumstantial: see *R. v. Mezzo,* [1986] 1 S.C.R. 802, at p. 842—43; *Monteleone, supra,* at p. 161. The nature of the judge's task, however, varies according to the type of evidence that the Crown has advanced. Where the Crown's case is based entirely on direct evidence, the judge's task is straightforward. By definition, the only conclusion that needs to be reached in such a case is whether the evidence is true. . . .

The judge's task is somewhat more complicated where the Crown has not presented direct evidence as to every element of the offence. The question then becomes whether the remaining elements of the offence — that is, those elements as to which the Crown has not advanced direct evidence — may reasonably be inferred from the circumstantial evidence. Answering this question inevitably requires the judge to engage in a limited weighing of the evidence because, with circumstantial evidence, there is, by definition, an inferential gap between the evidence and the matter to be established — that is, an inferential gap beyond the question of whether the evidence should be believed. . . . The judge must therefore weigh the evidence, in the sense of assessing whether it is reasonably capable of supporting the inferences that the Crown asks the jury to draw. This weighing, however, is limited. The judge does not ask whether she herself would conclude that the accused is guilty. Nor does the judge draw factual inferences or assess credibility. The judge asks only whether the evidence, *if believed,* could reasonably support an inference of guilt.

. . . .

Notwithstanding certain confusing language in *Mezzo* and *Monteleone* nothing in this Court's jurisprudence calls into question the continuing validity of the common law rule. . . . In *Mezzo*, the issue was whether the Crown had proffered sufficient evidence as to identity. McIntyre J., writing for the majority, stated that a trial judge can direct an acquittal only if there is "no evidence" as to an essential element of the offence. . . . He also stated that the judge has no authority to "weigh and consider the quality of the evidence and to remove it from the jury's consideration". . . . Those statements, taken alone, might be understood to suggest that a preliminary inquiry judge must commit the accused to trial even if the Crown's evidence would not reasonably support an inference of guilt. However, as the dissent in *Charemski* . . . discusses, the remainder of McIntyre J.'s reasons make clear that by "no evidence" McIntyre J. meant "no evidence capable of supporting a conviction," and by "weighing" McIntyre J. was referring to the ultimate determination of guilt (a matter for the jury), as distinguished from the determination of whether the evidence can reasonably support an inference of guilt (a matter for the preliminary inquiry judge). His concern was to reject the argument that the judge must determine whether guilt is the only reasonable inference. His reasons cannot be read to call into question the traditional rule, namely, that the judge must determine whether the evidence can reasonably support an inference of guilt.

In *Monteleone*, the accused was charged with setting fire to his own clothing store. The evidence was entirely circumstantial. The question was whether the trial judge had erred in directing an acquittal on the grounds that the "cumulative effect [of the evidence] gives rise to suspicion only, and cannot justify the drawing of an inference of guilt". . . . In ordering a new trial, McIntyre J. wrote that "[i]t is not the function of the trial judge to weigh the evidence, [or] . . . to draw inferences of fact from the evidence before him". . . . Again, however, the remainder of the reasons make clear that by "weighing" McIntyre J. was referring to the final drawing of inferences from the facts (which task, again, is within the exclusive province of the jury), not to the task of assessing whether guilt could reasonably be inferred. Indeed, the reasons explicitly reaffirm the common law rule that the judge must determine whether "there is before the court any admissible evidence, . . . Whether direct or circumstantial, which, if believed by a properly charged jury acting reasonably, would justify a conviction". . . .

Contrary to the appellant's contention, *Charemski* . . . did not evidence disagreement in this Court as to the proper approach. The appellant in *Charemski* . . . had been charged with the murder of his wife. The trial judge directed a verdict of acquittal, principally because the forensic evidence did not affirmatively suggest that the deceased had been murdered. The question in this Court was whether the Court of Appeal erred in setting aside the trial judge's directed verdict of acquittal. There was no disagreement between the majority and the dissent as to the test that the preliminary inquiry justice must apply. On the contrary, both the majority and the dissent clearly reaffirmed *Shephard* . . . and its progeny. . . . Any disagreement concerned not the test for sufficiency but the question of whether sufficient evidence was led in that case. The majority conceded that forensic evidence had not affirmatively indicated that the deceased had been murdered, but reasoned that a properly instructed jury could reasonably infer guilt from the other evidence that the Crown had led. The dissent argued that, as it had not been established that the deceased had been murdered, it was meaningless to discuss identity and causation, two of the other essential elements of the offence. The dissent also argued that the accused's presence in the deceased's apartment could not reasonably be inferred from the accused's conceded presence in the lobby. The dissenting justices concluded that the circumstantial evidence could not reasonably support an inference of guilt.

. . . .

The question that arises in the case at bar is whether the preliminary inquiry judge's task differs where the defence tenders exculpatory evidence, as is its prerogative under s. 541. In my view, the task is essentially the same, in situations where the defence calls exculpatory evidence, whether it be direct or circumstantial. Where the Crown adduces direct evidence on all the elements of the offence, the case must proceed to trial, regardless of the existence of defence evidence, as by definition the only conclusion that needs to be reached is whether the evidence is true. However, where the Crown's evidence consists of, or includes, circumstantial evidence, the judge must engage in a limited weighing of the whole of the evidence (i.e. including any defence evidence) to determine whether a reasonable jury properly instructed could return a verdict of guilty.

In performing the task of limited weighing, the preliminary inquiry judge does not draw inferences from facts. Nor does she assess credibility. Rather, the judge's task is to determine whether, *if the Crown's evidence is believed*, it would be reasonable for a properly instructed jury to infer guilt. Thus, this task of "limited weighing" never requires consideration of the inherent reliability of the evidence itself. It should be regarded, instead, as an assessment of the reasonableness of the inferences to be drawn from the circumstantial evidence.

. . . .

With those principles in mind, I turn, then, to the question of whether Lampkin Prov. J. properly interpreted and applied the law in this case. . . .

. . . .

Notwithstanding . . . two reservations, I am not persuaded that Lampkin Prov. J. reached the wrong result. Before committing the appellant to trial, the preliminary inquiry justice thoroughly surveyed the circumstantial evidence that had been presented by the Crown. . . . Only after considering "the evidence as a whole" did Lampkin Prov. J. commit the appellant to trial.

. . . .

For the foregoing reasons, I conclude that the appeal should be dismissed.

For a comment see Delisle, "Limited Weighing of Circumstantial Evidence" (2001), 44 C.R. (5th) 227.

Timing and Procedure

For some time there existed in Canada a belief that a trial judge in a criminal case on a motion for a directed verdict of acquittal was entitled to reserve his ruling on the motion and to call on the accused to elect whether he was going to call any evidence.[69] This has now been corrected. In *R. v. Angelantoni*,[70] Brooke, J.A. wrote:

> The trial judge said at the beginning of the motion that he was going to reserve his judgment upon that motion and to put the appellant to his election as to whether or not he would call evidence when the argument concluded and he did so.
> In our opinion he erred in proceeding in this way. When a motion such as this is made in a criminal case it must be decided before the trial proceeds further.

In a civil case, however, the practice is different. As described by Watson, Borins and Williams:

> After the plaintiff's lawyer has called all of his witnesses he will close the case for the plaintiff. At this point in the trial the defendant's lawyer may wish to contend that the plaintiff has failed to adduce sufficient evidence to establish his case. In other words, he may apply for a *non-suit* and ask the judge to dismiss the plaintiff's action. The trial judge will not rule upon this motion unless the defendant's lawyer elects not to call any evidence. If the defendant's lawyer indicates that he intends to call witnesses the trial judge will reserve his decision on the motion until all of the evidence in the case has been completed. On the other hand, if the defendant's lawyer elects to call no evidence the trial judge may rule upon the motion for non-suit at once. However, because this is a jury trial the judge will only rule on the motion after the jury has had the opportunity to consider the evidence and reach their decision.[71]

In *McKenzie v. Bergin*[72] the plaintiff sought to recover damages for injuries sustained as the result of a dog's bite. The trial judge, of his own volition, directed a non-suit on the ground that defendant's ownership of the dog had not been established. On appeal the court found the judge had erred because there was sufficient evidence of ownership to submit to the jury. The Court of Appeal ordered a new trial to allow the defendant the opportunity to present evidence but expressed its regret that unnecessary expenses were thereby being incurred. The court reasoned:

> . . . if counsel for the defendant moves for a non-suit, it would be wise and convenient if the trial Judge would reserve his decision on the motion for non-suit and ask the defendant if he desires to put in evidence. If the defendant desires to put in evidence, the case should proceed and the jury's finding obtained. If the learned trial Judge then decided that the non-suit should be granted he could dismiss the action, and, if appeal were taken, this Court would have all the facts before it, including the assessment of damages, and if it should be of opinion that the non-suit should not have been granted the action could be finally disposed of.[73]

---

69. This may have been sparked by some confusing language in *R. v. Morabito* (1949), 7 C.R. 88 (S.C.C.).

70. (1975), 31 C.R.N.S. 342, 345 (Ont. C.A.). Followed in *R. v. Boissonneault* (1986), 29 C.C.C. (3d) 345 (Ont. C.A.).

71. *Canadian Civil Procedure*, 2d ed. (Toronto: Butterworths, 1977), pp. 1-9.

72. [1937] O.W.N. 200 (C.A.).

73. *Ibid.*, at p. 201. To similar effect see *Jurasits v. Nemes* (1957), 8 D.L.R. (2d) 659, 667 (Ont. C.A.) and *Bank of Montreal v. Horan* (1986), 54 O.R. (2d) 757 (H.C.). In England, see *Laurie v. Raglan Bldg. Co.*, [1941] 3 All E.R. 332 (C.A.) and *Parry v. Aluminum Co.* (1940), 162 L.T. 236 (C.A.). In the latter case, Lord Goddard described the practice as appropriate in negligence cases but thought in other cases, *e.g.*, slander and defamation cases, the defendant was entitled to an immediate ruling. In *Parry v. Aluminum*, Lord

The possibility of the motion for a non-suit being rendered redundant by the existing practice at civil law is bothersome. Although we do not speak of the defendant in a civil case having any right to silence, there seems to be some worth in his ability to have a judicial ruling as to whether the plaintiff has adduced sufficient evidence to warrant calling on the defence for a response. The plaintiff has made certain allegations in his statement of claim and seeks to disturb the status quo. The defendant should have the right to refuse to answer spurious claims.

The courts have evidently created their present practice out of concern that there may be unnecessary effort and expenses flowing from new trials when the trial judge rules incorrectly on a motion. If we posit the thought that trial judges are more often right than wrong, a change in the existing practice would be even more efficient. If there is no case to meet, the defendant is not put to the expense and effort of presenting a defence and the trial tribunal's time is not wasted. The procedure ought to be the same in civil and criminal cases and the protagonist's claim vetted by a judicial officer before the defendant need determine whether he cares to answer.

In *Canadian Labour Arbitration*[74] the learned authors analogize the procedure during a labour arbitration to the motion for non-suit in civil proceedings. They note:

> The usual procedure following such a motion is for the arbitrator to ask the defendant to elect whether or not to put in any evidence. If he does elect to call evidence, the hearing will proceed in the normal way and the motion for non-suit will become *redundant*. [Emphasis added.]

Again, if it is clear to the arbitrator that the party has failed to produce a case that warrants an answer, has failed to produce sufficient evidence to allow a rational verdict in his favour, the more efficient thing to do would be to rule immediately on the motion being made.

ONTARIO v. O.P.S.E.U.
(1990), 37 O.A.C. 218

[The employee was dismissed after he pleaded guilty to defrauding the employer and others. The employee was a loans officer and occupied a position of trust. He was suspended without pay when charges were laid and dismissed 17 months later. The Board granted a non-suit motion by the employee on the basis that there was no evidence to explain the dismissal. The Divisional Court decided the decision was fundamentally flawed and the errors destroyed the Board's jurisdiction.]

REID J.:—

. . . .

The non-suit motion rested on the ground that the employer had failed to make out a

---

Goddard approved the practice of the trial judge reserving on the ruling until all the evidence was in and then ruling whether, on the whole of the case, there was a case to go to the jury.

74.   Brown & Beatty (Aurora, Ont.: Canada Law Book, 1985), p. 135.

prima facie case of adequate grounds for dismissal. In light of the uncontested evidence setting out in detail how the frauds were accomplished it is difficult to understand why the non-suit was granted. In my respectful opinion, the reasoning which led to this conclusion was fatally flawed. It stemmed from the Board's misunderstanding of the nature of a non-suit.

. . . .

The standard of proof on a non-suit is that of a prima facie case, not a case on the balance of probabilities. If a prima facie case has been shown a non-suit must not be granted. It is erroneous to determine a non-suit motion on the basis of the higher onus of the balance of probabilities. A prima facie case is no more than a case for the defendant to answer.

> The term non-suit describes the modern practice of the defendant making an application for judgment at the close of the plaintiff's case on the ground that the plaintiff has failed to make out a case for the defendant to answer. Williston and Rolls, *The Conduct of an Action*, p. 45. (Butterworths)
>
> A motion for non-suit in modern practice is made by the defendant, contending that the trier of fact should not proceed to evaluate the evidence in the normal way, but should dismiss the action. The defendant must satisfy the trial judge that the evidence is such that no jury, acting judicially, could find in favour of the plaintiff. The decision of the judge in both jury and non-jury actions is a decision on a question of law. Sopinka, *The Trial of an Action*, p. 124 (Butterworths).

. . . .

Over the years there has been some variation in the practice on non-suits turning on the question whether the mover must concurrently elect to call no evidence. That has now been resolved. A motion will not be entertained without an election to call no evidence: see *Bank of Montreal v. Horan et al.* (1986), 54 O.R. (2d) 757.

There is no reason to think that a motion for a non-suit before an administrative tribunal should not conform with the law that governs the courts. The Board applied the wrong standard of proof, but beyond that, it was apparently unaware of its duty to lean in favour of a respondent to a non-suit motion and of its discretion to permit evidence omitted through inadvertence to be adduced.

Court practice is summed up neatly in the rule proposed by the Williston Committee referred to in the following passage from *The Principles of Non-Suit in Ontario*, by Allan M. Rock, Q.C., (in *Studies in Criminal Procedure*, Eric Gertner ed. (1979) Butterworths):

> In Ontario, as in England, the courts have shaped the practice and formed the tests in motions for non-suit: no statute or rules govern the procedure.
>
> In Ontario, however, the Williston Committee, in its *Working Draft of Proposed Ontario Rules of Civil Procedure* included, in the section entitled Trial Procedure, draft rule 54.14, which provides as follows:
>
> *54.14 Application for Non-Suit*
>
> When the evidence in chief on behalf of the plaintiff is concluded, the defendant, where he elects to call no evidence, may move for dismissal of the action on the ground that, having regard to the evidence and the law, the plaintiff has not made out a prima facie case.
>
> The simplicity of the draft rule is attractive: while codifying the three essential elements of the practice (the conclusion of the plaintiff's evidence prior to the motion, the election by the defendant not to call evidence and the test whether a prima facie case has been made out), the draft rule wisely refrains from seeking to regulate every aspect of the procedure.

Directed verdict

R. v. ROWBOTHAM
[1994] 2 S.C.R. 463, 30 C.R. (4th) 141, 90 C.C.C. (3d) 449

LAMER C.J. for the Court:—

. . . .

In the case at bar, the trial judge directed the jury to acquit the accused:

> Since the accused have been placed in your hands, it is not for me to acquit them. It is for you to do so. I told you at the beginning of the case you would have to take your law from me. It was not expected that you would take it in quite the straight forward and simple way in which I am going to direct you, but it is still in principle true, and I tell you as a matter of law that these accused are entitled to your verdict of not guilty for the reason I have just mentioned. I must therefore ask you to retire to your jury room to elect a foreperson to present your verdict and to return to the courtroom with a verdict finding each of the accused not guilty of the charges.

The jury left the courtroom at 3:05 p.m. and returned at 3:26 p.m. The registrar asked the members of the jury whether they had agreed upon their verdict and the following exchange took place:

> THE FOREPERSON: We have, your honour, but there are a number of questions that some of the jurors have and we would like permission to have some of them answered, if the court so wishes.

> THE COURT: If the jury have questions before rendering their verdict, we do the best we can to answer them. If they are necessary prior to your having reached a verdict to have these answered, then we should deal with them now. If they are questions that are not pertinent to the verdict, then we should have the verdict first and we can have a discussion if you wish afterwards, but if they're pertinent to the verdict then we'd better deal with them now.

> THE FOREPERSON: Could I have a moment?

> THE COURT: Certainly.

> —Discussion among the jury *sotto voce*.

> A JUROR: I don't think all of us think that it's not guilty. Sorry. Some of us still believe a guilty verdict should go through.

. . . .

A directed verdict is not a creature of statute but rather of the common law. Although the appropriate *test* for a directed verdict has been the source of great controversy, the actual *procedure* a judge should follow once he or she has decided to direct the jury to bring in an acquittal has been relatively uncontroversial:

> Where there is a jury present, the proper practice is for the judge, upon finding that there is no evidence to go before a jury, to direct the jury to acquit and discharge the accused. A judge who instead withdraws the case from the jury errs in so doing.

(Law Reform Commission of Canada, Working Paper 63, *Double Jeopardy, Pleas and Verdicts* (1991), at pp. 38-39.)

. . . .

The common theme in the case law is that a trial judge commits an error if he or she withdraws the case from the jury and enters an acquittal him- or herself rather than directing the jury to bring in a verdict of not guilty.

. . . .

I conclude that the common law procedure with respect to directed verdicts should be modified — in instances where in the past the trial judge would have directed the jury to return a particular verdict, the trial judge should now say "as a matter of law, I am withdrawing the case from you and I am entering the verdict I would otherwise direct you to give as a matter of law".

PROBLEMS

Problem 1

The accused is charged with possession of narcotics for the purpose of trafficking. He was seized on the street by undercover policemen who testified that during the altercation the accused threw something away. A young boy testified that he saw the accused throw a package and he retrieved the same and gave it to the police. On analysis the package was seen to contain heroin. At the close of the Crown's case, a motion for a directed verdict of acquittal was made. The trial judge reasoned:

> That is the whole issue. Did it come from the accused? Has the Crown satisfied me that this came from the accused? . . . I do not think there is any fabrication, but I am puzzled over the evidence of the boy. As you know I have to be satisfied beyond a reasonable doubt. I was analyzing the boy's evidence as he was giving it. . . . I have to decide on the evidence, beyond a reasonable doubt, that the parcel that he picked up was the parcel which had been in possession of the accused. I think the Crown has failed in that respect and on the motion, I find the accused not guilty, and discharge him from custody.

Are there grounds for appeal? Compare *R. v. Morabito,* [1948] 3 D.L.R. 513, 517 (Ont. C.A.); reversed [1949] 1 D.L.R. 609 (S.C.C.). Suppose the evidence was simply that when the accused was apprehended and searched no drugs were found but nearby on the ground a package of heroin was found with accused's address stamped thereon. Could accused then successfully move for a directed verdict of acquittal?

Problem 2

The accused is charged with auto theft. The information recites that "on the 25th day of December 1987 the accused stole a 1986 Chevrolet the property of one John Brown." John Brown has testified that an automobile found in the accused's possession on December 26, 1987 was stolen from the driveway at his residence on the evening of December 25. The investigating officer is in the stand:

Officer:	So I turned the corner and saw the accused with the Impala. I knew it had been stolen just hours before and I asked the accused where she had gotten it. She said she'd rather wait for her lawyer before saying anything.
Defence Counsel:	I take it, Officer, that she indicated that she wanted to wait for her lawyer after you had advised her of her right to counsel?
Officer:	No. I hadn't yet decided to charge her or arrest her. I was just making inquiries.

Defence Counsel:	I have no further questions, your Honour.
Crown Counsel:	That completes the case for the Crown.
Defence Counsel:	I am asking the court to direct a verdict of acquittal. I am reserving my right to call evidence should my motion be denied, but I am saying that at this point no jury, acting reasonably, could convict my client on the basis of this evidence. Further, we note that the information speaks of a 1986 Chevrolet automobile. I understand that the evidence is that my client was found in possession of an Impala. There is nothing before you to equate the two. An impala, I understand, is a deer-like creature that roams the forests of Africa.
Crown Counsel:	Your Honour, we rely on the doctrine of recent possession. When a person is found in possession of something which was stolen only hours before it is a matter of common sense to infer that the person is the thief. A jury at this stage would be quite reasonable in making that inference and defence motion should be denied. As to whether the evidence discloses theft of a 1986 Chevrolet, I understand, and I ask you to judicially notice, that an Impala is also the name of a Chevrolet automobile. If you're not prepared to do that, I ask leave to reopen my case to allow me to present evidence on the point.

Problem 3

The accused is charged with possession of marijuana. The crime carries the possibility of a heavy sentence and the jurisprudence is clear that the prosecution needs to establish knowledge of the nature of the substance possessed. The Crown at trial establishes that the accused was found in physical possession of some green plant-like material which later analyzed as marijuana. That is the totality of the Crown evidence. As we go to the courtroom the accused is addressing the court:

Counsel for Accused:	Your Honour, there's nothing here. I move to dismiss.
His Honour:	(testily) Perhaps you could let me know exactly what it is you're seeking by your motion.
Counsel:	I am making an application for a directed verdict of acquittal. At this point we submit that, taking the Crown's case at its highest, accepting as true all the testimony of the Crown witnesses, one cannot imagine a trier of fact rationally concluding guilt. We say that the Crown has not led sufficient evidence that would warrant calling on the accused for a defence.
Crown Counsel:	Your Honour, we submit that the facts speak for themselves. A natural inference, and I put it no higher than that, is that the accused, found in possession of marijuana, knew what it was and a jury, acting reasonably, could conclude guilt.
Defence Counsel:	They might conclude that he might probably have known but they wouldn't be reasonable if they found that they were satisfied beyond a reasonable doubt.
Crown:	At this stage, I needn't go that far.
His Honour:	I'm satisfied that Crown counsel is right and I refuse your application. When you made the motion I was about to ask whether you had another motion in mind.

Counsel for Accused: I'm getting the drift, your Honour. The defence is calling no evidence and moves for a dismissal on the basis that the Crown cannot have persuaded you of my client's guilt beyond a reasonable doubt.

Crown: We say that now all the evidence is in, and the accused electing not to testify, your Honour should be satisfied beyond a reasonable doubt that the accused was in possession of marijuana and knew that it was marijuana.

His Honour: Well, now that I am sure that all the evidence is in, I must put on the hat I wear as trier of fact. I am not now just the trier of law asking whether a trier of fact *could* reasonably conclude guilt, but rather I must ask whether *I* am so satisfied. In the result, I cannot say that I am and the case is dismissed. I note in passing that I think it very inappropriate to consider the accused's silence at this stage. He has been given a right to remain silent and his exercise of that right should not work to his prejudice.

Compare *R. v. Cahill* (1962), 40 C.R. 166 (P.E.I.S.C.) and *Mezzo v. R.* (1986), 52 C.R. (3d) 113 (S.C.C.). Consider also *R. v. Pelley* (1983), 34 C.R. (3d) 385 (Ont. Co. Ct.) and *R. v. Lafontaine* (1984), 43 C.R. (3d) 283 (Alta. Q.B.).

2. PRESUMPTIONS

(a) Introduction

Every writer of sufficient intelligence to appreciate the difficulties of the subject-matter has approached the topic of presumptions with a sense of hopelessness and has left it with a feeling of despair.[75]

Stanley presumed from certain basic facts that the man he was addressing was Dr. Livingstone. So, too, all presumptions in the law of evidence describe a process or a legal consequence whereby we infer the existence of a presumed fact when certain other basic facts have been established by evidence; the inference from the evidentiary fact is usually taken as a result of our own sense of logic or our own sense of experience but at times it may be statutorily or judicially directed to accommodate some extrinsic policy consideration.

The literature on the subject of presumptions is extensive and much of it is devoted to attempts to minimize the confusion by demonstrating the misuse or overuse of the term "presumption."[76]

---

75. Morgan, "Presumptions" (1937), 12 Wash. L. Rev. 255.
76. Among the classic expositions on the subject are Cleary, "Presuming and Pleading: An Essay on Juristic Immaturity" (1959), 12 Stan. L. Rev. 5; Stone, "Burden of Proof and the Judicial Process" (1944), 60 L.Q.R. 262, Morgan, "Some Observations Concerning Presumptions" (1931), 44 Harv. L. Rev. 906; McBaine, "Burden of Proof: Presumptions" (1955), 2 U.C.L.A. Law Rev. 13; Bohlen, "The Effect of Rebuttable Presumptions of Law Upon the Burden of Proof" (1920), 68 U. Pa. L. Rev. 307; Denning, "Presumptions and Burdens" (1945), 61 L.Q.R. 379. And see Helman, "Presumptions" (1944), 22 Can. Bar Rev. 117.

Professor Thayer, on whose thesis all other writers have built,[77] described presumptions as follows:

> Presumptions are aids to reasoning and argumentation, which assume the truth of certain matters for the purpose of some given inquiry. They may be grounded on general experience, or probability of any kind; or merely on policy and convenience. On whatever basis they rest, they operate in advance of argument or evidence, or irrespective of it, by taking something for granted; by assuming its existence. When the term is legitimately applied it designates a rule or a proposition which still leaves open to further inquiry the matter thus assumed. The exact scope and operation of these *prima facie* assumptions are to cast upon the party against whom they operate, the duty of going forward, in argument or evidence, on the particular point to which they relate. . . . Presumption, assumption, taking for granted, are simply so many names for an act or process which aids and shortens inquiry and argument. . . . Such is the nature of all rules to determine the legal effect of facts as contrasted with their logical effect. To prescribe and fix a certain legal equivalence of facts, is a very different thing from merely allowing that meaning to be given to them. A rule of presumption does not merely say that such and such a thing is a permissible and usual inference from other facts, but it goes on to say that this significance shall always, in the absence of other circumstances, be imputed to them, — sometimes passing first through the stage of saying that it *ought to be* imputed.[78]

Later writers interpreted the Thayerian view of presumptions as the "bursting bubble theory" by which was meant that the effect of any presumption was spent when the opponent led any evidence.[79] But Thayer never suggested that all presumptions should have this minimal effect, and he recognized that, depending on the need or purpose which gave rise to a recognition of the particular presumption, the onus on the opponent would vary. Later in his *Treatise* he wrote:

> How much evidence shall be required from the adversary to meet the presumption, or, as it is variously expressed, to overcome it or destroy it, is determined by no fixed rule. It may be merely enough to make it reasonable to require the other side to answer; it may be enough to make out a full *prima facie* case, and it may be a great weight of evidence, excluding all reasonable doubt. A mere presumption involves no rule as to the weight of evidence necessary to meet it. When a presumption is called a strong one, like the presumption of legitimacy, it means that it is accompanied by another rule relating to the weight of evidence to be brought in by him against whom it operates.[80]

From this framework we can profitably limit the use of the term presumption and so minimize the confusion.

(b) False Presumptions

Professor Thayer notes that the term "presumption" is legitimately used only when the matter presumed is left open to further inquiry. It is sometimes said

---

77. Interestingly, Wigmore refers to him simply as "the master in the law of evidence": 9 Wigmore, *Evidence* (Chad. Rev.), s. 2511, p. 533.
78. Thayer, *supra*, note 8, at pp. 314-17.
79. Cleary points out that this was due to "tearing his statement from its context, and popularized by Wigmore," *supra*, note 76, at p. 18. And see Helman, *supra*, note 76, at p. 122.
80. Thayer, *supra*, note 8, at pp. 575-76.

that given certain facts other facts shall be "conclusively presumed." For example, at common law it was said that a child under seven years of age was conclusively presumed to be incapable of the commission of a crime; he was *doli incapax*. The Criminal Code provides that "a place that is found to be equipped with a slot machine shall be conclusively presumed to be a common gaming house."[81] In truth these are not presumptions apportioning burdens of proof, but rather rules of substantive law; a "conclusive presumption" is a contradiction in terms. On proof of the basic fact the so-called "presumed fact" in such a case is actually immaterial; if the prosecution proves that the place was equipped with a slot machine the substantive law provides for conviction and whether the place is a common gaming house or not is immaterial.[82] It would be best then, in our quest to minimize confusion, to discard the use of the term "conclusive presumption." The above section could simply be reworded to provide that "a place that is found to be equipped with a slot machine is a common gaming house."

At the other end of the scale, we note that Thayer would deny the use of the term presumption to describe simply the permissible inference which flows from the logical effect of certain facts. For him a presumption *demands* an effect unless the opponent does something. When a material fact *may* be inferred from basic facts proved, as opposed to *must,* it would be best to label such simply as a justifiable inference. The cases sometimes refer to this process as a presumption of fact as opposed to a presumption of law, or a permissive presumption as opposed to a compelling presumption, but this is misleading and can be dangerous. Let us take two examples: the presumption that persons intend the natural consequences of their acts, and the "doctrine" of recent possession.

When a criminal offence requires the mental element of intention, the prosecution will need to establish the same, barring a confession, by proof of the accused's actions, asking the jury to infer from such actions that the requisite state of mind existed. The best statement of the process is by Lord Goddard in *R. v. Steane*:[83]

> No doubt, if the prosecution prove an act, the natural consequence of which would be a certain result and no evidence or explanation is given, then a jury may, on a proper direction, find that the prisoner is guilty of doing the act with the intent alleged, but if on the totality of the evidence there is room for more than one view as to the intent of the prisoner, the jury should be directed that it is for the prosecution to prove the intent to the jury's satisfaction, and if, on a review of the whole evidence, they either think that the intent did not exist or they are left in doubt as to the intent, the prisoner is entitled to be acquitted.

To explain this to the jury, judges have occasionally advised them that persons are presumed to intend the natural consequences of their acts. Lord Denning explained, however:

> When people say that a man must be taken to intend the natural consequences of his acts, they fall into error: there is no "must" about it; it is only "may." The presumption of intention is not a proposition of law but a proposition of ordinary good sense. It means this: that, as a man is usually able to foresee what are the natural

---

81. Section 198(2). For other examples of conclusive presumptions, see ss. 163(8), 356(2), 421(2), 436(2) and 588.
82. See 9 Wigmore, *Evidence* (Chad. Rev.), s. 2492.
83. [1947] 1 K.B. 997, 1004 (C.C.A.).

consequences of his acts, so it is, as a rule, reasonable to infer that he did foresee them and intend them. But, while that is an inference which may be drawn, it is not one which must be drawn. If on all the facts of the case it is not the correct inference, then it should not be drawn.[84]

In *R. v. Ortt*,[85] a murder prosecution, the trial judge instructed the jury in terms of the presumption and Jessup, J.A., delivering the opinion of the Ontario Court of Appeal, wrote:

> It has been held by this Court that it is error in law to tell a jury it is a presumption of law that a person intends the natural consequences of his acts. . . . Moreover the word "presumption" alone creates a difficulty in that it may suggest an onus on the accused. I agree with the comment of the authors of *Martin's Annual Criminal Code* (1968), p. 195:
>
> > The difficulty would not arise if the use of the word "presumption" were avoided. A presumption requires that a certain conclusion must be drawn, unless the accused takes steps to make that conclusion unwarranted. An inference, however, is no more than a matter of common sense and merely indicates that a certain conclusion may be drawn if warranted by the evidence. . . .
>
> In my opinion, therefore, the word "presumption" is to be avoided in this context and juries simply told that generally it is a reasonable inference that a man intends the natural consequences of his acts so that when, for instance, a man points a gun at another and fires it the jury may reasonably infer that he meant either to cause his death or to cause him bodily harm that he knew was likely to cause death reckless of whether death ensued or not.[86]

In *Stapleton v. R.*,[87] Dixon, C.J. of the Australian High Court was also critical of such a direction:

> The introduction of the maxim or statement that a man is presumed to intend the reasonable consequences of his act is seldom helpful and always dangerous. For it either does no more than state a self evident proposition of fact or it produces an illegitimate transfer of the burden of proof of a real issue of intent to the person denying the allegation.

The so-called legal doctrine of recent possession is, also on analysis, a matter of common sense and not of law.[88] An analysis of the early cases involving charges of theft or possession of stolen goods shows the courts applying common sense to an evaluation of a piece of circumstantial evidence, namely, possession in the accused of the recently stolen goods. The early case of *Clement*[89] has no need for the language of presumption or doctrine. The entire report of the case reads:

---

84. *Hosegood v. Hosegood* (1950), 66 T.L.R. 735, 738 (C.A.).
85. [1969] 1 O.R. 461 (C.A.).
86. *Ibid.*, at p. 463. And see *R. v. Berger* (1975), 27 C.C.C. (2d) 357, 383 (B.C.C.A.) per McIntyre, J.A.
87. (1952), 86 C.L.R. 358, 365 (H.C.).
88. See *R. v. Smythe* (1980), 72 Cr. App. R. 8, 11 (C.A.): "Nearly every reported case of recent possession is merely a decision of fact as an example of what is no more than a rule of evidence."
89. (1830), 168 E.R. 980.

Prisoner was indicted for horse-stealing. The evidence was, that he had the horse in his possession in Kirkcudbright, three days after it had been stolen, in the county of Cumberland.

Parke, J., held this to be sufficient evidence of a stealing by the prisoner in Cumberland.

In *R. v. Deer*[90] the accused was convicted by a jury of receiving property known to have been stolen. On his challenge of the verdict, observe the simple, common-sense evaluation of sufficiency by Pollock, C.B.:

In this case the prisoner was lodging in the house of the prosecutor, and disappeared under circumstances which are not disclosed. The prosecutor's wife afterwards left her home; and the prisoner is subsequently found with her and in possession of a large quantity of the prosecutor's property, some part being actually upon his person. We are of opinion that there is some evidence to support the conviction.

Conviction affirmed.[91]

Suppose that defendant Deer, on being apprehended by the prosecutor, told him that the prosecutor's wife had followed him and given him these things with the prosecutor's blessing. Would you then infer knowledge that the goods were stolen? Would you then be satisfied beyond a reasonable doubt that defendant did know? If the explanation given at the time was an explanation that "might reasonably be true" would you then have a reasonable doubt and acquit? Does it matter when the defendant gives the explanation? At the time of his apprehension or in the box?

Suppose you're acting for the Crown. You question the officer in the witness box. He says, "I found defendant in possession of stolen goods." Your brief indicates that defendant gave an explanation to the officer at the time. Will you ask the officer to relate the explanation?

Just as relevance is dictated by common sense and experience, so too is sufficiency.[92] These matters vary with the fact situation under review. Certain fact situations regularly recur and appellate opinions are produced expressing their concurrence that particular facts are relevant and that a certain measure of circumstantial evidence is sufficient to pass the judge and support a reasonable verdict. From an early time our courts have recognized that possession of goods recently stolen is relevant to the issue of whether the possessor is the thief, or knowing receiver, and sufficiently probative to permit the finding. The reasoning which underlies this finding of relevance and sufficiency is perhaps best expressed in *Wills on Circumstantial Evidence*.[93]

Since the desire of dishonest gain is the impelling motive to theft and robbery, it naturally follows that the possession of the fruits of crime recently after it has been committed, affords a strong and reasonable ground for the presumption that the party in whose possession they are found, was the real offender, unless he can account

---

90.   (1862), 169 E.R. 1380.
91.   *Ibid.*, at p. 1381.
92.   *Que. (A.G.) v. Hamel* (1987), 60 C.R. (3d) 174 (Que. C.A.); leave to appeal to S.C.C. refused 89 N.R. 80n (up to preliminary magistrate to draw inferences), applying *Dubois v. R.*, [1986] 1 S.C.R. 366.
93.   6th ed. (1912), pp. 82-83.

for such possession in some way consistent with his innocence. The force of this presumption has been recognized from the earliest times; and it is founded on the obvious consideration, that if such possession had been lawfully acquired, the party would be able, at least shortly after its acquisition, to give an account of the manner in which it was obtained; and his unwillingness or inability to afford such explanation is justly regarded as amounting to strong self-condemnatory evidence.

As the factual situation of theft and possession[94] regularly occurred and the practice of drawing the inference became standard, the courts, perhaps unfortunately, began speaking of the "presumption" which arises from the possession of recently stolen goods;[95] from there it was a short step to talk of the "doctrine" of recent possession. This is unfortunate as the clothing of legal language often serves to distract from the simplicity and common sense of the proposition and may place too heavy a burden on the accused. Viewed against this background the classic and oft-quoted statement on recent possession by Reading, C.J.C. in *R. v. Schama*,[96] is seen not as a technical treatise but rather as a simple statement on reasonable doubt:

> Where the prisoner is charged with receiving recently stolen goods, when the prosecution has proved the possession by the prisoner, and that the goods had been recently stolen, the jury should be told that they may, not that they must, in the absence of any reasonable explanation, find the prisoner guilty. But if an explanation is given which may be true, it is for the jury to say on the whole of the evidence whether the accused is guilty or not; that is to say, if the jury think the explanation may reasonably be true, though they are not convinced that it is true, the prisoner is entitled to an acquittal, because the Crown has not discharged the onus of proof imposed upon it of satisfying the jury beyond reasonable doubt of the prisoner's guilt.[97]

The process which permits, but does not demand, a finding does not deserve the label presumption.[98] Laskin, J., in *R. v. Graham*,[99] wrote:

> The use of the term "presumption", which has been associated with the doctrine (of recent possession), is too broad, and the word which properly ought to be substituted is "inference". . . . The inference of guilty knowledge which may be made upon proof of unexplained recent possession ought not to be magnified as some iniquity which necessarily stands out above all other evidence in the case. The misuse, in my opinion, of the term "presumption" in this connection may lead to injustice because of its strong connotation.[100]

---

94. In *R. v. Langmead* (1864), 169 E.R. 1459, it was urged that evidence of recent possession was only evidence of stealing and not of receiving or possession but Pollock, C.B. denied any such distinction: the evidence was sufficient and the jury would determine on the facts.

95. Kellock, J. in *R. v. Suchard* (1956), 114 C.C.C. 257, 263 (S.C.C.) commented: "The presumption is merely an inference of fact which has become crystallized into a rule of law."

96. (1914), 11 Cr. App. R. 45.

97. *Ibid.*, at p. 49.

98. See 9 Wigmore, *Evidence* (Chad. Rev.), s. 2513(4) for numerous citations indicating a proper trend toward repudiating presumptive language.

99. (1972), 7 C.C.C. (2d) 93 (S.C.C.).

100. *Ibid.*, at pp. 108, 110. See also *R. v. Raviraj* (1987), 85 Cr. App. R. 93, 103 (C.A.):
    The doctrine is only a particular aspect of the general proposition that where suspicious circumstances appear to demand an explanation and no explanation, or

PROBLEMS

Problem 1

The accused is charged with possession of stolen property. The property was stolen two years before the accused was found in possession. The accused has testified that he didn't know the property was stolen and was simply holding it as bailee for another. The accused's counsel has asked you as trial judge to direct the jury that if the accused's explanation was one that could reasonably be true, a verdict of not guilty should be rendered. Will you accede to his request? Compare *R. v. Palmer*, [1970] 3 C.C.C. 402 (B.C. C.A.).

Problem 2

There were three break-ins in the neighbourhood during the summer in each of which the owners of the burgled houses had recently died and the burglaries took place during the time of the pre-advertised funeral service. The accused's brother was arrested in the act of committing a theft. During questioning by the investigating officers he admitted that he committed the three break and enters in question. He then led the officers to a house that he shared with the accused. Here the officers found seventy-six items stolen during the break and enters described above. The accused was found in his bedroom. The door was closed and the police officer demanded that the accused come out. The accused stated that he would do so after he got dressed. Five minutes later the accused emerged from his bedroom. A police officer who had been stationed outside testified that the accused had opened the curtains, unlocked the window and attempted to lift the window, but upon seeing the officer had stopped these activities. Fourteen of the stolen items were found in the accused's bedroom. The items were grouped according to the separate break-ins. The accused was arrested and charged with three counts of break, enter and theft. When questioned by the police about his involvement in the burglaries the accused replied "All you got me for is possession. I'm not saying anything". He made no further comment and did not testify at his trial. You are sitting as a judge alone. Would you convict? Compare *R. v. Kowlyk*, [1988] 2 S.C.R. 59.

(c) True Presumptions

If satisfied that the language of conclusive and permissive presumptions should be discarded, we can then examine the true presumptions: devices which leave open to inquiry the matters presumed but which demand a finding if the opponent does nothing.

A true presumption compels the trier of fact to find a fact, the presumed fact, to be proved against a party when another fact, the basic fact, is proved. The trier is compelled to find the presumed fact unless the party against whom the presumption operates does something. That "something" depends on the

---

an entirely incredible explanation, is given, the lack of explanation may warrant an inference of guilty knowledge in the defendant. This again is only part of a wider proposition that guilt may be inferred from unreasonable behaviour of a defendant when confronted with facts which seem to accuse.

language of the particular presumptive device. It may be to ensure that there is evidence in the case contrary to the presumed fact or it may actually require the party to disprove the presumed fact. The former "something" imposes an evidential burden on the party and the latter a persuasive burden.

There are many true presumptions scattered throughout the cases and statutes created out of considerations of probabilities or substantive law policy. We will examine a few, as Professor Thayer cautioned that "any detailed consideration of the mass of legal presumptions [would be] an unprofitable and monstrous task."[101]

A good example of a presumptive device placing an evidential burden may be seen in the criminal case of *R. v. Proudlock*.[102] The accused was charged with break and enter with intent to commit an indictable offence contrary to section 306(1)(*a*) of the Criminal Code. The Code provided:

> 306.(2) For the purposes of proceedings under this section, evidence that an accused
>
> > (*a*) broke and entered a place is, in the absence of any evidence to the contrary, proof that he broke and entered with intent to commit an indictable offence therein.[103]

The crime charged required proof of an act and proof of an intention. An evidentiary assist was given to the prosecution with respect to the latter element. In *R. v. Proudlock*, the trial judge summarized the accused's evidence:

> When he testified, Proudlock said that he did not have an explanation and did not know what his motives had been. He acknowledged that it was "possible" he had told the janitor he was looking for soup, but said that would not have been a true statement of his purpose. He resolutely denied any intention to steal. . . . I did not find Proudlock's evidence, when he was asked why he broke and entered the restaurant to be convincing in the least degree. To put the matter simply, I did not believe him. . .
>
> In my opinion, Proudlock broke and entered the restaurant purposefully, and I do not believe that purpose has escaped his memory. . . . I do not believe Proudlock.[104]

Nevertheless, the trial judge acquitted the accused. He reasoned that evidence to the contrary was present, the presumption of intent was rebutted, and as the prosecution led no evidence of intent a material ingredient of the crime had not been established. The Supreme Court of Canada held that "evidence disbelieved by the trier of fact is not 'evidence to the contrary' "[105] and Pigeon, J. for the majority reasoned:

> The accused does not have to "establish" a defence or an excuse, all he has to do is to raise a reasonable doubt. If there is nothing in the evidence adduced by the Crown from which a reasonable doubt can arise, then the accused will necessarily have the burden of adducing evidence if he is to escape conviction. . . . The accused

---

101. Thayer, *supra*, note 8, at p. 313. Regarding the unfortunate and confusing phrase "*prima facie* evidence," see *R. v. Pye* (1984), 38 C.R. (3d) 375 (N.S.C.A.).

102. (1979), 43 C.C.C. (2d) 321 (S.C.C.).

103. This phrasing is repeated in a number of sections of the Criminal Code: see ss. 198(1), 212(3), 215(4), 338(3), 339(4), 349(2), 364(2), 396(2), 414, 421(1) and 446(4).

104. *Supra*, note 102, at p. 329.

105. *Ibid.*, at p. 323.

may remain silent, but, when there is a *prima facie* case against him and he is, as in the instant case, the only person who can give "evidence to the contrary" his choice really is to face *certain conviction* or to offer in testimony whatever explanation or excuse may be available to him. [Emphasis added.][106]

Since there had been no "evidence to the contrary" the accused had failed to discharge his evidential burden and the Supreme Court entered a conviction.

An example of a presumptive device placing an evidential burden on the opponent in a civil case is the presumption of testamentary capacity. Lord Dunedin, in *Robins v. National Trust*,[107] explained:

Those who propound a will must show that the will of which probate is sought is the will of the testator, and that the testator was a person of testamentary capacity. In ordinary cases if there is no suggestion to the contrary any man who is shown to have executed a will in ordinary form will be presumed to have testamentary capacity, but the moment the capacity is called in question then at once the onus lies on those propounding the will to affirm positively the testamentary capacity.

As an example of a presumptive device shifting a persuasive burden on a material ingredient to the accused in a criminal case, consider the case of *R. v. Appleby*.[108] The accused was charged with having the care and control of a motor vehicle while his ability to drive was impaired by alcohol. There was no question of the accused's impairment, and the only question was whether he had care and control. The Crown relied on a statutory presumption which provided:

224A(1) In any proceedings under section 222 or 224,

   (*a*)   where it is proved that the accused occupied the seat ordinarily occupied by the driver of a motor vehicle, he shall be deemed to have had the care or control of the vehicle unless he establishes that he did not enter or mount the vehicle for the purpose of setting it in motion.[109]

The trial judge convicted though he did make the finding of fact:

That the Defendant sought to rebut the presumption under Section 224A(1)(a) by testifying that he entered the driver's seat of the taxi to use the radio to summon a wrecker, rather than for the purpose of driving the vehicle and, although this evidence was unsupported by any other witness, it did raise a reasonable doubt in my mind.[110]

The conviction was entered then on the basis that the judge was not satisfied by a preponderance of evidence "that he did not enter or mount the motor vehicle for the purpose of setting it in motion." The British Columbia Court of Appeal found the trial judge had erred and that the presumptive effect was to cast only an evidential burden on the accused. The Supreme Court of Canada reversed and restored the conviction, holding that there had been an express enactment

---

106. *Ibid.*, at pp. 325 and 327. And see *R. v. Vanegas* (1987), 60 C.R. (3d) 169 (B.C.C.A.).
107. [1927] A.C. 515, 519 (P.C.). And see *Smith v. Nevins*, [1925] S.C.R. 619, 638. See also generally, Wright, "Testamentary Capacity" (1938), 16 Can. Bar Rev. 405. Other presumptions of validity of marriage, presumption of validity of a foreign divorce decree and the presumption in favour of the domicile of origin: *Powell v. Cockburn* (1976), 68 D.L.R. (3d) 700, 706 (S.C.C.).
108. (1971), 3 C.C.C. (2d) 354 (S.C.C.).
109. *Ibid.*, at p. 356.
110. *Ibid.*

exceptionally[111] placing a persuasive burden on the accused. Ritchie, J., for the majority, reasoned:

> With all respect, it appears to me that if the Court of Appeal of British Columbia were correct in holding that it is enough, to rebut the presumption created by the words "shall be deemed" as they occur in s. 224A(1)(a), for the accused to raise a reasonable doubt as to whether or not he entered the motor vehicle for the purpose of setting it in motion, then it would, in my view follow, that if the Crown has established the basis of the presumption beyond a reasonable doubt, it must also give similar proof of the facts which the statute deems to exist and expressly requires the accused to negate. This is exactly the burden which the Crown would have to discharge if the section had not been enacted, and in my view such a construction makes the statutory presumption ineffective and the section meaningless.[112]

Could the section have meaning by imposing an evidential burden?[113] That is, commanding a result if no contrary evidence was given?

An example of a presumptive device having the effect of shifting a persuasive burden to the opponent in a civil case is the presumption of legitimacy.[114] In

---

111. As to whether it is presently "exceptional" to place a persuasive burden on the accused in Canada, consider the fact that over 60 sections in the Criminal Code have language akin to that canvassed in *Appleby:*

    "Until the contrary is proved, be presumed," s. 16(4); "without lawful excuse, the proof of which lies upon him," ss. 57(3), 82, 104(3), 145(1)(b), 177, 215(2), 276(5), 349(1), 351(1), 352, 376(1)(b), (c); "without lawful authority, the proof of which lies upon him," ss. 125(c), 294(a), 417(1), (2), 419; "without lawful authority or excuse, the proof of which lies upon him," ss. 369, 405; "without lawful justification or excuse, the proof of which lies upon him," ss. 450, 451, 452, 458, 459; "unless the accused establishes," ss. 50(1)(a), 394(1); "unless he has consent . . . the proof of which lies upon him," s. 110(1)(b), (c); "no accused shall be convicted . . . where he proves," ss. 409(2), 429(2); "the burden of proving . . . is upon the accused," ss. 338(4), 339(5), 383(2), 794(2); "the onus of proving . . . is on the accused," s. 197(3); "no person shall be convicted . . . if he establishes," ss. 163(3), 420(2); "shall be deemed to have committed . . . unless he proves," s. 210(4); "shall be deemed to have committed . . . unless he establishes," ss. 255(1)(a), 290(4); "no person shall be deemed . . . where he proves," s. 311; "it shall be presumed . . . unless the court is satisfied," s. 362(4); "no person shall be convicted . . . where, to the satisfaction of the court or judge, he accounts . . . and shows," s. 402(2); "the burden of proof of which lies upon the accused," s. 440. Of course, many sections in other Acts in the Revised Statutes of Canada contain these operative words. The best known are s. 8 of the Narcotic Control Act, R.S.C. 1985, c. N-1, and s. 38 of the Food and Drugs Act, R.S.C. 1985, c. F-27. Although all of these sections have not, of course, been interpreted in the courts, they would all appear to place the burden of persuasion on the accused since the cases, in interpreting the words of the various sections, have not distinguished between the purpose of the section or whether the section required the accused to assert a positive or negative averment.

112. (1971), 3 C.C.C. (2d) 354, 360 (S.C.C.).

113. The court also denied that the legislation was in conflict with the Bill of Rights guarantee of a "presumption of innocence."

114. Another presumption having such an effect in civil cases is the presumption of death of a person not heard of for seven years: *Middlemiss v. Middlemiss*, [1955] 4 D.L.R. 801 (B.C.C.A.); *Re Bell*, [1946] O.R. 854 (C.A.). And see Treitel, "The Presumption of Death" (1954), 17 Mod. L. Rev. 530. The adversary must also persuade on the balance of

Welstead v. Brown[115] the plaintiff was successful at trial in his claim for damages for criminal conversation. The wife had given birth to a child and blood tests indicated it was *impossible* for the husband to be the father. The Supreme Court of Canada decided that on such evidence the presumption of legitimacy could be rebutted. But Cartwright, J. wrote:

> Had the doctors testified that the result of the tests indicated that it was in the highest degree improbable, but not impossible that the appellant be the father of the child it would, in my opinion, have been the duty of the trial Judge to direct the jury that as a matter of law such evidence could not avail against the presumption.[116]

And Kellock, J. wrote:

> In my view, a child born in lawful wedlock is still presumed to be a legitimate child, and *the presumption is to be overborne only by evidence excluding reasonable doubt.* [Emphasis added.][117]

(d) Presumption of Innocence and Charter

In *R. v. Appleby*[118] the accused argued that the reverse onus provision requiring him to establish the lack of an essential ingredient of the offence contravened the Canadian Bill of Rights, which provides that no law of Canada shall be construed or applied so as to

> 2(f) deprive a person charged with a criminal offence of the right to be presumed innocent until proved guilty according to law. . . .

The Supreme Court of Canada reasoned that this provision had not been contravened since the accused had been "proved guilty according to law" since the law was stated as stated in *Woolmington v. Director of Public Prosecutions.*[119] Viscount Sankey had there written:

> . . . it is the duty of the prosecution to prove the prisoner's guilt subject to what I have already said as to the defence of insanity *and subject also to any statutory exception.* [Emphasis added.][120]

Of course, on this thesis Parliament could enact any reverse onus provision and never contravene the Bill of Rights!

R. v. OAKES
[1986] 1 S.C.R. 103, 50 C.R. (3d) 1, 24 C.C.C. (3d) 321

[The Supreme Court was called on to deal with the constitutionality of section 8 of the Narcotic Control Act, which provided that a person found in possession

---

probabilities to rebut the presumption of advancement to show that no gift was intended: see *Dagle v. Dagle* (1990), 81 Nfld. & P.E.I.R. 245 (P.E.I.C.A.).

115. [1952] 1 D.L.R. 465 (S.C.C.). See also *Hiuser v. Hiuser,* [1962] O.W.N. 220 (C.A.) and *S. v. McC.,* [1972] A.C. 24 (H.L.).

116. *Ibid.,* at pp. 475-76.

117. *Ibid.,* at p. 483.

118. (1971), 3 C.C.C. (2d) 354 (S.C.C.); Canadian Bill of Rights, R.S.C. 1985, App. III.

119. [1935] A.C. 462 (H.L.).

120. *Ibid.,* at p. 481.

of a narcotic was presumed to be in possession for the purpose of trafficking unless he established the contrary.]

DICKSON C.J.C. (CHOUINARD, LAMER, WILSON and LE DAIN JJ. concurring):—

. . . .

[O]ne cannot but question the appropriateness of reading into the phrase "according to law" in s. 11(*d*) of the Charter the statutory exceptions acknowledged in *Woolmington*, supra, and in *Appleby*, supra. The *Woolmington* case was decided in the context of a legal system with no constitutionally-entrenched human rights document. In Canada, we have tempered Parliamentary supremacy by entrenching important rights and freedoms in the Constitution. Viscount Sankey L.C.'s statutory exception proviso is clearly not applicable in this context and would subvert the very purpose of the entrenchment of the presumption of innocence in the Charter. I do not, therefore, feel constrained in this case by the interpretation of s. 2(*f*) of the Canadian Bill of Rights presented in the majority judgment in *Appleby*. Section 8 of the Narcotic Control Act is not rendered constitutionally valid simply by virtue of the fact that it is a statutory provision.

. . . .

In general one must, I think, conclude that a provision which requires an accused to disprove on a balance of probabilities the existence of a presumed fact which is an important element of the offence in question violates the presumption of innocence in s. 11(*d*). If an accused bears the burden of disproving on a balance of probabilities an essential element of an offence, it would be possible for a conviction to occur despite the existence of a reasonable doubt. This would arise if the accused adduced sufficient evidence to raise a reasonable doubt as to his or her innocence but did not convince the jury on a balance of probabilities that the presumed fact was untrue.

The fact that the standard is only the civil one does not render a reverse onus clause constitutional. As Sir Rupert Cross commented in the Rede lecture "The Golden Thread of the English Criminal Law: The Burden of Proof", delivered in 1976 at the University of Toronto, at p. 11:

It is sometimes said that exceptions to the Woolmington rule are acceptable because, whenever the burden of proof on any issue in a criminal case is borne by the accused, he only has to satisfy the jury on the balance of probabilities, whereas on issues on which the Crown bears the burden of proof the jury must be satisfied beyond a reasonable doubt.

And at p. 13:

The fact that the standard is lower when the accused bears the burden of proof than it is when the burden of proof is borne by the prosecution is no answer to my objection to the existence of exceptions to the Woolmington rule as it does not alter the fact that a jury or bench of magistrates may have to convict the accused although they are far from sure of his guilt.

As we have seen, the potential for a rational connection between the basic fact and the presumed fact to justify a reverse onus provision has been elaborated in some of the cases discussed above and is now known as the "rational connection test". In the context of s. 11(*d*), however, the following question arises: if we apply the rational connection test to the consideration of whether s. 11(*d*) has been violated, are we adequately protecting the constitutional principle of the presumption of innocence? As Professors MacKay and Cromwell point out in their article "*Oakes*: A Bold Initiative Impeded by Old Ghosts" (1983), 32 C.R. (3d) 221, at p. 233:

The rational connection test approves a provision that *forces* the trier to infer a fact that may be simply rationally connected to the proved fact. Why does it follow that such a provision does not offend the constitutional right to be proved guilty beyond a reasonable doubt?

A basic fact may rationally tend to prove a presumed fact, but not prove its existence beyond a reasonable doubt. An accused person could thereby be convicted despite the presence of a reasonable doubt. This would violate the presumption of innocence.

I should add that this questioning of the constitutionality of the "rational connection test" as a guide to interpreting s. 11(d) does not minimize its importance. The appropriate stage for invoking the rational connection test, however, is under s. 1 of the Charter. This consideration did not arise under the Canadian Bill of Rights because of the absence of an equivalent to s. 1. At the Court of Appeal level in the present case, Martin J.A. sought to combine the analysis of s. 11(d) and s. 1 to overcome the limitations of the Canadian Bill of Rights jurisprudence. To my mind, it is highly desirable to keep s. 1 and s. 11(d) analytically distinct.

To return to s. 8 of the Narcotic Control Act, I am in no doubt whatsoever that it violates s. 11(d) of the Charter by requiring the accused to prove on a balance of probabilities that he was not in possession of the narcotic for the purpose of trafficking. Mr. Oakes is compelled by s. 8 to prove that he is *not* guilty of the offence of trafficking. He is thus denied his right to be presumed innocent and subjected to the potential penalty of life imprisonment unless he can rebut the presumption. This is radically and fundamentally inconsistent with the societal values of human dignity and liberty which we espouse, and is directly contrary to the presumption of innocence enshrined in s. 11(d). Let us turn now to s. 1 of the Charter.

V. Is S. 8 of the Narcotic Control Act a Reasonable and Demonstrably Justified Limit Pursuant to S. 1 of the Charter?

The Crown submits that, even if s. 8 of the Narcotic Control Act violates s. 11(d) of the Charter, it can still be upheld as a reasonable limit under s. 1, which, as has been mentioned, provides:

> 1. The *Canadian Charter of Rights and Freedoms* guarantees the rights and freedoms set out in it subject only to such reasonable limits prescribed by law as can be demonstrably justified in a free and democratic society.

The question whether the limit is "prescribed by law" is not contentious in the present case, since s. 8 of the Narcotic Control Act is a duly-enacted legislative provision. It is, however, necessary to determine if the limit on Mr. Oakes' right, as guaranteed by s. 11(d) of the Charter, is "reasonable" and "demonstrably justified in a free and democratic society" for the purpose of s. 1 of the Charter, and thereby saved from inconsistency with the Constitution.

It is important to observe at the outset that s. 1 has two functions: first, it constitutionally guarantees the rights and freedoms set out in the provisions which follow; and second, it states explicitly the exclusive justificatory criteria (outside of s. 33 of the Constitution Act, 1982) against which limitations on those rights and freedoms must be measured. Accordingly, any s. 1 inquiry must be premised on an understanding that the impugned limit violates constitutional rights and freedoms — rights and freedoms which are part of the supreme law of Canada. As Wilson J. stated in *Singh v. Min. of Employment & Immigration*, supra, at p. 218:

> . . . it is important to remember that the courts are conducting this inquiry in light of a commitment to uphold the rights and freedoms set out in the other sections of the *Charter*.

A second contextual element of interpretation of s. 1 is provided by the words "free and democratic society". Inclusion of these words as the final standard of justification for limits on rights and freedoms refers the court to the very purpose for which the Charter was originally entrenched in the Constitution: Canadian society is to be free and democratic. The court must be guided by the values and principles essential to a free and democratic society, which I believe embody, to name but a few, respect for the inherent dignity of the human person, commitment to social justice and equality, accommodation of a wide variety of beliefs, respect for cultural and group identity, and faith in social and political institutions which enhance the participation of individuals and groups in society. The underlying values and principles of a free and democratic society are the genesis of the rights and freedoms guaranteed by the Charter and the ultimate standard against which a limit on a right or freedom must be shown, despite its effect, to be reasonable and demonstrably justified.

The rights and freedoms guaranteed by the Charter are not, however, absolute. It may become necessary to limit rights and freedoms in circumstances where their exercise would be inimical to the realization of collective goals of fundamental importance. For this reason, s. 1 provides criteria of justification for limits on the rights and freedoms guaranteed by the Charter.

These criteria impose a stringent standard of justification, especially when understood in terms of the two contextual considerations discussed above, namely, the violation of a constitutionally-guaranteed right or freedom and the fundamental principles of a free and democratic society.

The onus of proving that a limit on a right or freedom guaranteed by the Charter is reasonable and demonstrably justified in a free and democratic society rests upon the party seeking to uphold the limitation. It is clear from the text of s. 1 that limits on the rights and freedoms enumerated in the Charter are exceptions to their general guarantee. The presumption is that the rights and freedoms are guaranteed unless the party invoking s. 1 can bring itself within the exceptional criteria which justify their being limited. This is further substantiated by the use of the word "demonstrably", which clearly indicates that the onus of justification is on the party seeking to limit: *Hunter v. Southam Inc.*, supra.

The standard of proof under s. 1 is the civil standard, namely, proof by a preponderance of probability. The alternative criminal standard, proof beyond a reasonable doubt, would, in my view, be unduly onerous on the party seeking to limit. Concepts such as "reasonableness", "justifiability" and "free and democratic society" are simply not amenable to such a standard. Nevertheless, the preponderance of probability test must be applied rigorously. Indeed, the phrase "demonstrably justified" in s. 1 of the Charter supports this conclusion. Within the broad category of the civil standard, there exist different degrees of probability depending on the nature of the case: see Sopinka and Lederman, The Law of Evidence in Civil Cases (Toronto, 1974), at p. 385. As Denning L.J. explained in *Bater v. Bater*, [1950] 2 All E.R. 458 at 459 (C.A.):

> The case may be proved by a preponderance of probability, but there may be degrees of probability within that standard. The degree depends on the subject-matter. A civil court, when considering a charge of fraud, will naturally require a higher degree of probability than that which it would require if considering whether negligence were established. It does not adopt so high a standard as a criminal court, even when considering a charge of a criminal nature, but still it does require a degree of probability which is commensurate with the occasion.

This passage was cited with approval in *Hanes v. Wawanesa Mut. Ins. Co.*, [1963] S.C.R. 154 at 161, [1963] 1 C.C.C. 321 [Ont.]. A similar approach was put forward by Cartwright J. in *Smith v. Smith*, [1952] 2 S.C.R. 312 at 331-32, [B.C.]:

> I wish, however, to emphasize that in every civil action before the tribunal can safely find the affirmative of an issue of fact required to be proved it must be satisfied, and that whether or not it will be so satisfied must depend on the totality of the circumstances on which its judgment is formed including the gravity of the consequences . . .

Having regard to the fact that s. 1 is being invoked for the purpose of justifying a violation of the constitutional rights and freedoms the Charter was designed to protect, a very high degree of probability will be, in the words of Denning L.J., "commensurate with the occasion". Where evidence is required in order to prove the constituent elements of a s. 1 inquiry, and this will generally be the case, it should be cogent and persuasive and make clear to the court the consequences of imposing or not imposing the limit: see *L.S.U.C. v. Skapinker*, supra, at p. 384; *Singh v. Min. of Employment & Immigration*, supra, at p. 217. A court will also need to know what alternative measures for implementing the objective were available to the legislators when they made their decisions. I should add, however, that there may be cases where certain elements of the s. 1 analysis are obvious or self-evident.

To establish that a limit is reasonable and demonstrably justified in a free and democratic society, two central criteria must be satisfied. First, the objective, which the measures responsible for a limit on a Charter right or freedom are designed to serve, must be "of sufficient importance to warrant overriding a constitutionally protected right or freedom": *R. v. Big M Drug Mart Ltd.*, supra, at p. 352. The standard must be high in order to ensure that objectives which are trivial or discordant with the principles integral to a free and democratic society do not gain s. 1 protection. It is necessary, at a minimum, that an objective relate to concerns which are pressing and substantial in a free and democratic society before it can be characterized as sufficiently important.

Second, once a sufficiently significant objective is recognized, then the party invoking s. 1 must show that the means chosen are reasonable and demonstrably justified. This involves "a form of proportionality test": *R. v. Big M Drug Mart Ltd.*, supra, at p. 352. Although the nature of the proportionality test will vary depending on the circumstances, in each case courts will be required to balance the interests of society with those of individuals and groups. There are, in my view, three important components of a proportionality test. First, the measures adopted must be carefully designed to achieve the objective in question. They must not be arbitrary, unfair or based on irrational considerations. In short, they must be rationally connected to the objective. Second, the means, even if rationally connected to the objective in this first sense, should impair "as little as possible" the right or freedom in question: *R. v. Big M Drug Mart Ltd.*, supra, at p. 352. Third, there must be a proportionality between the *effects* of the measures which are responsible for limiting the Charter right or freedom and the objective which has been identified as of "sufficient importance".

With respect to the third component, it is clear that the general effect of any measure impugned under s. 1 will be the infringement of a right or freedom guaranteed by the Charter; this is the reason why resort to s. 1 is necessary. The inquiry into effects must, however, go further. A wide range of rights and freedoms are guaranteed by the Charter, and an almost infinite number of factual situations may arise in respect of these. Some limits on rights and freedoms protected by the Charter will be more serious than others in terms of the nature of the right or freedom violated, the extent of the violation, and the degree to which the measures which impose the limit trench upon the integral principles of a free and democratic society. Even if an objective is of sufficient importance, and the first two elements of the proportionality test are satisfied, it is still possible that, because of the severity of the deleterious effects of a measure on individuals or groups, the measure will not be justified by the purposes it is intended to serve. The more severe the deleterious effects of a measure, the more important the objective must be if the measure is to be reasonable and demonstrably justified in a free and democratic society.

Having outlined the general principles of a s. 1 inquiry, we must apply them to s. 8 of the Narcotic Control Act. Is the reverse onus provision in s. 8 a reasonable limit on the right to be presumed innocent until proven guilty beyond a reasonable doubt as can be demonstrably justified in a free and democratic society?

The starting point for formulating a response to this question is, as stated above, the nature of Parliament's interest or objective which accounts for the passage of s. 8 of the Narcotic Control Act. According to the Crown, s. 8 of the Narcotic Control Act is aimed at curbing drug trafficking by facilitating the conviction of drug traffickers. In my opinion, Parliament's concern that drug trafficking be decreased can be characterized as substantial and pressing. The problem of drug trafficking has been increasing since the 1950s, at which time there was already considerable concern: see Report of the Special Committee on Traffic in Narcotic Drugs, Appendix to Debates of the Senate of Canada, session of 1955, pp. 690-700; see also Final Report, Commission of Inquiry into the Non-Medical Use of Drugs (Ottawa, 1973). Throughout this period, numerous measures were adopted by free and democratic societies, at both the international and national levels.

At the international level, on 23rd June 1953, the Protocol for Limiting and Regulating the Cultivation of the Poppy Plant, the Production of, International and Wholesale Trade in, and Use of Opium, to which Canada is a signatory, was adopted by the United Nations Opium Conference held in New York. The Single Convention on Narcotic Drugs (1961), was acceded to in New York on 30th March 1961. This treaty was signed by Canada on 30th March 1961. It entered into force on 13th December 1964. As stated in the preamble, "addiction to narcotic drugs constitutes a serious evil for the individual and is fraught with social and economic danger to mankind".

At the national level, statutory provisions have been enacted by numerous countries which, inter alia, attempt to deter drug trafficking by imposing criminal sanctions: see, for example, Misuse of Drugs Act, 1975 (New Zealand), no. 116; Misuse of Drugs Act, 1971 (Eng.), c. 38.

The objective of protecting our society from the grave ills associated with drug trafficking is, in my view, one of sufficient importance to warrant overriding a constitutionally-protected right or freedom in certain cases. Moreover, the degree of seriousness of drug trafficking makes its acknowledgement as a sufficiently important objective for the purposes of s. 1 to a large extent self-evident. The first criterion of a s. 1 inquiry, therefore, has been satisfied by the Crown.

The next stage of inquiry is a consideration of the means chosen by Parliament to achieve its objective. The means must be reasonable and demonstrably justified in a free and democratic society. As outlined above, this proportionality test should begin with a consideration of the rationality of the provision: Is the reverse onus clause in s. 8 rationally related to the objective of curbing drug trafficking? At a minimum, this requires that s. 8 be internally rational; there must be a rational connection between the basic fact of possession and the presumed fact of possession for the purpose of trafficking. Otherwise the reverse onus clause could give rise to unjustified and erroneous convictions for drug trafficking of persons guilty only of possession of narcotics.

In my view, s. 8 does not survive this rational connection test. As Martin J.A. of the Ontario Court of Appeal concluded, possession of a small or negligible quantity of narcotics does not support the inference of trafficking. In other words, it would be irrational to infer that a person had an intent to traffic on the basis of his or her possession of a very small quantity of narcotics. The presumption required under s. 8 of the Narcotic Control Act is overinclusive and could lead to results in certain cases which would defy both rationality and fairness. In light of the seriousness of the offence in question, which carries with it the possibility of imprisonment for life, I am further convinced that the first component of the proportionality test has not been satisfied by the Crown.

As I have concluded that s. 8 does not satisfy this first component of proportionality, it is unnecessary to consider the other two components.

VI. Conclusion

The Ontario Court of Appeal was correct in holding that s. 8 of the Narcotic Control Act violates the Canadian Charter of Rights and Freedoms and is therefore of no force or effect. Section 8 imposes a limit on the right guaranteed by s. 11(d) of the Charter which is not reasonable and is not demonstrably justified in a free and democratic society for the purpose of s. 1. Accordingly, the constitutional question is answered as follows:

Question: Is s. 8 of the Narcotic Control Act inconsistent with s. 11(d) of the Canadian Charter of Rights and Freedoms and thus of no force and effect?

Answer: Yes.

I would therefore dismiss the appeal.

Appeal dismissed.

In *R. v. Whyte*,[121] the Court amplified on its reasons in *Oakes* and Dickson C.J. provided:

> The distinction between elements of the offence and other aspects of the charge is irrelevant to the s. 11(*d*) inquiry. The real concern is not whether the accused must disprove an element or prove an excuse, but that an accused may be convicted while a reasonable doubt exists. When that possibility exists, there is a breach of the presumption of innocence. The exact characterization of a factor as an essential element, a collateral factor, an excuse, or a defence should not affect the analysis of the presumption of innocence. It is the final effect of a provision on the verdict that is decisive. If an accused is required to prove some fact on the balance of probabilities to avoid conviction, the provision violates the presumption of innocence because it permits a conviction in spite of a reasonable doubt in the mind of the trier of fact as to the guilt of the accused.

Section 16(4) of the Criminal Code, amended in 1991, formerly read:

16(4) Every one shall, until the contrary is proved, be presumed to be and to have been sane.

R. v. CHAULK
[1990] 3 S.C.R. 1303, 2 C.R. (4th) 1, 62 C.C.C. (3d) 193

LAMER C.J. (DICKSON, C.J.C., and LA FOREST and CORY JJ., concurring):—

. . . .

In my view, the principles enunciated in *Whyte* are applicable to this case and establish that the presumption of sanity embodied in s. 16(4) violates the presumption of innocence. If an accused is found to have been insane at the time of the offence, he will not be found guilty; thus the "fact" of insanity precludes a verdict of guilty. Whether the claim of insanity is characterized as a denial of *mens rea*, an excusing defence or, more generally, as an exemption based on criminal incapacity, the fact remains that sanity is essential for guilt. Section 16(4) allows a factor which is essential for guilt to be presumed rather than proven by the Crown beyond a reasonable doubt. Moreover, it requires an accused to disprove sanity (or prove insanity) on a balance of probabilities; it therefore violates the presumption of innocence because it permits a conviction in spite of a reasonable doubt in the mind of the trier of fact as to the guilt of the accused.

. . . .

Is s. 16(4) a Reasonable Limit Under s. 1 of the Charter?

. . . .

2. *As Little as Possible*

. . . In my view, the question to be addressed at this stage of the s. 1 inquiry is whether Parliament could reasonably have chosen an alternative means which would have achieved the identified objective as effectively.

---

121. (1988), 64 C.R. (3d) 123 (S.C.C.).

Recent judgments of this Court (*R. v. Edwards Books and Art Ltd.*, [1986] 2 S.C.R. 713; *Irwin Toy Ltd. v. Quebec (Attorney General)*, [1989] 1 S.C.R. 927; and *Reference re ss. 193 and 195.1(1)(c) of the Criminal Code (Man.)*, [1990] 1 S.C.R. 1123) indicate that Parliament is not required to search out and to adopt the absolutely least intrusive means of attaining its objective. Furthermore, when assessing the alternative means which were available to Parliament, it is important to consider whether a less intrusive means would achieve the "same" objective or would achieve the same objective as effectively.

. . . .

It is true that s. 16 will be seldom raised, given the substantial constraint on liberty which follows a successful insanity plea. Nonetheless, I have concluded that the objective of the current provision is "pressing and substantial", given the next to impossible burden which would be placed on the Crown if s. 16(4) did not exist. If insanity were easier for an accused to establish, the defence would be successfully invoked more often (even if, statistically, it is still infrequently raised). Thus, putting a lesser burden on the accused would not have achieved the objective which is achieved by s. 16(4).

. . . .

WILSON J.:—

. . . .

The issue under this part of the *Oakes* test is whether some other legislative provision could achieve the desired objective while impairing the *Charter* right "as little as possible". Lamer C.J. is of the view that Parliament is not required to seek and adopt "the absolutely least intrusive means of attaining its objective" (p. 1341). He indicates that he is unwilling to embark on a course of "second-guessing" the wisdom of Parliament's choice of legislative means and cites some recent decisions of this Court as authority for this deferential attitude. In my view, this is not a case for deference. In one of the cases on which the Chief Justice relies, *Irwin Toy Ltd. v. Quebec (Attorney General)*, [1989] 1 S.C.R. 927, this Court indicated that there might be exceptions to the stringent review called for under this part of the *Oakes* test. Whether or not such an exception was warranted would depend upon the role Parliament was fulfilling in enacting the impugned legislation.

As I understand this aspect of *Irwin Toy*, an exception may be made where the legislature mediating between the competing claims of groups of citizens or allocating scarce resources among them is forced to strike a compromise on the basis of conflicting evidence. In such cases there will be a substantial policy component to the choice of means selected by the legislature and that choice should be respected even if it cannot be said to represent the "least intrusive means". In my view, *Irwin Toy* does not stand for the proposition that in balancing the objective of government against the guaranteed right of the citizen under s. 1 different levels of scrutiny may be applied depending upon the nature of the right. The prerequisite for the exception to the minimal impairment test in *Oakes*, as I understand *Irwin Toy*, is that the guaranteed right of different groups of citizens cannot be fully respected; to respect to the full the right of one group will necessarily involve an infringement upon the right of the other. In such a circumstance *Irwin Toy* holds that it is appropriate for the government to fashion a compromise on the basis of policy considerations.

. . . .

For these reasons, I am not persuaded that s. 16(4) impairs the accused's right to be presumed innocent as little as is reasonably possible. Rather, I am of the view that the government's objective could be quite readily met by imposing a purely evidentiary burden on the accused. The infringement on s. 11(d) of the *Charter* resulting from s. 16(4) is accordingly not saved by s. 1.

Justices Gonthier, McLachlin and L'Heureux-Dubé found the provision did not violate the presumption of innocence as section 16 "should be read as relating to the fundamental pre-condition for the assignment of criminal responsibility rather than to the elements of an offence or to particular defences." Justice Sopinka dissented, but he agreed that section 16(4) of the Criminal Code was valid for the reasons expressed by the Chief Justice.

In 1991, the Code was amended to provide:

16(3) The burden of proof that an accused was suffering from a mental disorder so as to be exempt from criminal responsibility is on the party that raises the issue.

In *Re Boyle*,[122] the issue before the Ontario Court of Appeal concerned presumptions created by language of the Criminal Code "in the absence of any evidence to the contrary proof," a frequently-used legislative device. The Court held that, although such presumptions can be displaced merely by evidence which raises a reasonable doubt rather than proof on a balance of probabilities, there was a common feature in the mandatory nature of the conclusion required to be drawn. The trier of fact must find the presumed fact; there was no may about it. The obligation on the accused required mandatory presumptions to also receive protection under the Charter presumption of innocence. In *Boyle*, the Court held that the presumption that arises under section 354(2) on possession of a motor vehicle with an obliterated identification number, that the motor vehicle or part thereof was at some time obtained by the commission of an indictable offence, was entirely reasonable and constitutionally valid. However, the second presumption under section 354(2), that the person found in possession knows that the vehicle or part thereof was obtained by the commission of an indictable offence, was not constitutionally valid, since it was arbitrary and hence unreasonable.

R. v. DOWNEY
[1992] 2 S.C.R. 10, 13 C.R. (4th) 129, 72 C.C.C. (3d) 1

[The accused was charged with two counts of living on the avails of prostitution. The accused answered the agency's telephones, made up the receipts and did the banking. He knew the calls were for sexual services. Throughout the period he had no other employment. During the course of the trial an application was made for a declaration that section 195(2) of the Criminal Code was of no force or effect because of section 11(d) of the Charter. Section 195(2) [now section 212(3)] provides that "[e]vidence that a person lives with or is habitually in the company of a prostitute . . . is, in the absence of evidence to the contrary, proof that the person lives on the avails of prostitution. . . ." The application was dismissed. The accused was convicted and his appeals to the Court of Appeal and the Supreme Court of Canada were dismissed.]

CORY J. (L'HEUREUX-DUBÉ, SOPINKA and GONTHIER, JJ. concurring):—

---

122. (1983), 35 C.R. (3d) 34 (Ont. C.A.).

. . . .

The presumption contained in s. 195 infringes s. 11(*d*) of the *Charter* since it can result in the conviction of an accused despite the existence of a reasonable doubt. For example consider the situation of a spouse or companion of a prostitute, who is working, self-supporting and not dependent or relying upon the income garnered by the spouse or companion from prostitution. There is nothing parasitical about such a relationship. Neither being a prostitute nor being a spouse of a prostitute constitutes a crime. Yet as a result of the presumption, the spouse could be found guilty despite the existence of a reasonable doubt. The fact that someone lives with a prostitute does not lead inexorably to the conclusion that the person is living on avails. The presumption therefore infringes s. 11(*d*).

Downey is welcome in its extension of Charter protection to mandatory presumptions. However, its reasoning may be suspect. The *Oakes* case dealt with a persuasive burden being imposed on the accused. Is the test there formulated for determining a violation of section 11(*d*) appropriate to a similar determination of the validity of an evidential burden? Can a trier have a reasonable doubt as to whether the accused is living on the avails if there has been no evidence led on the matter? On the other hand, if there was evidence led that the accused was working, self-supporting and not dependent on the prostitute's earnings, the presumptive device would disappear and a result would not be mandated. Perhaps a different test would be more suitable:

> Any presumptive device which compels the trier of fact to find an essential element, or the absence of any material justification or excuse, to be proved beyond a reasonable doubt, though no direct positive evidence was led concerning the existence of either, must violate the presumption of innocence in section 11(*d*).

The majority, having found the provision violative of section 11(*d*) found it saved by section 1. La Forest, McLachlin and Iacobucci, JJ. agreed that the provision violated section 11(*d*); La Forest, J., "for the reasons given by Cory, J." and the other two because "living with a prostitute does not lead inexorably to the conclusion that the person is living on avails." The dissenters decided, however, that the provision could not be saved by section 1.

R. v. LABA
[1994] 3 S.C.R. 965, 34 C.R. (4th) 360, 94 C.C.C. (3d) 385

[The accused were charged under section 394(1)(*b*) of the Criminal Code, which provided:

(1) Every one is guilty of an indictable offence and liable to imprisonment for a term not exceeding five years who

. . . .

(*b*) sells or purchases any rock, mineral or other substance that contains precious metals or unsmelted, untreated, unmanufactured or partly smelted, partly treated or partly manufactured precious metals, unless he establishes that he is the owner or agent of the owner or is acting under lawful authority.

They brought a pre-trial motion challenging the constitutional validity of the section. The motions judge declared that section 394(1)(*b*) violated the presumption of innocence in section 11(*d*) of the Charter, was not saved by section 1 of the Charter, and so was of no force or effect. He granted the accused's application for a stay of proceedings. On appeal the Crown conceded that there was an infringement of section 11(d) but sought to reverse the ruling on the ground that the provision should have been saved under section 1. The Court of Appeal concluded that the Crown had not met the onus of proving that the reverse onus clause was a reasonable limit within the meaning of section 1. In its order it stated that the appeal was allowed to the extent that, with the exception of the words "he establishes that", which were struck out, the validity of the remainder of section 394(1)(b) was upheld.]

SOPINKA J. (CORY, McLACHLIN, IACOBUCCI and MAJOR JJ. concurring):—

. . . .

Both in this Court and in the Court of Appeal the Crown conceded that the reverse onus in s. 394(1)(b) violates s. 11(d) of the *Charter* because it is open for a person to be convicted under that provision even if there is a reasonable doubt as to whether he or she was entitled to buy or sell the precious metal. There is no doubt in my mind that this concession was properly made and that the parties were correct in proceeding on the basis that the only point in issue is whether s. 394(1)(b) of the *Criminal Code* constitutes a reasonable limit on the s. 11(d) *Charter* right pursuant to s.1 of the *Charter*.

. . . .

. . . Does s. 394(1)(b) pass the Oakes test?

. . . Taking into account the modification suggested by the Chief Justice in his reasons in *Dagenais v. Canadian Broadcasting Corp.*, [1994] 3 S.C.R. 835, released concurrently herewith, the test can be stated as follows:

1) In order to be sufficiently important to warrant overriding a constitutionally protected right or freedom the impugned provision must relate to concerns which are pressing and substantial in a free and democratic society;

2) The means chosen to achieve the legislative objective must pass a three-part proportionality test which requires that they (a) be rationally connected to the objective, (b) impair the right or freedom in question as little as possible and (c) have deleterious effects which are proportional to both their salutary effects and the importance of the objective which has been identified as being of "sufficient importance".

(i) *Pressing and Substantial Objective*

I agree with the Attorney General of Canada that the objective of s. 394(1)(b) is the deterrence of theft of precious metal ore. In furtherance of this general objective, the specific objective of the reverse onus clause is to facilitate the prosecution of offenders given the special problem of proof to which I have referred above. I also agree that s. 394(1)(b) creates a "true criminal offence" and that like other true criminal offences involving activity bereft of social utility, it is an expression of society's repugnance to the conduct proscribed. In these circumstances, the Court can conclude, in the absence of extrinsic evidence as to the importance of the objective, that the subsection meets the first branch of the *Oakes* test.

. . . .

(ii) *Rational Connection*

Parliament has chosen to achieve the objective of deterring theft of ore by proscribing trade in stolen ore and placing the onus upon the accused to show that the ore is not stolen. Both these measures strike me as rational responses to the problem posed by theft of precious metal ore. The criminalization of trade in stolen goods is a common and eminently sensible method of deterring theft. Where there is good reason to believe that it would be difficult for the Crown to prove that goods have been stolen it is rational to place some kind of burden of proving that they have not been stolen upon the accused. . . .

Before moving on to consider the next step in the *Oakes* test I would like to address the respondents' argument that s. 394(1)(*b*) fails the rational connection test because it creates an unreasonable presumption that any ore which has been purchased or sold was stolen. This argument is premised upon the notion that in order for a legislatively created presumption to pass this portion of the *Oakes* test it must be internally rational in the sense that there is a logical connection between the presumed fact and the fact substituted by the presumption. This argument was made by the appellant in *R. v. Downey*, [1992] 2 S.C.R. 10. It was contended that a presumption which is not internally rational unduly enmeshes the innocent in the criminal process. This argument was not accepted by the majority. Consequently, I regard it as settled that there is no general requirement that a presumption be internally rational in order to pass the rational connection phase of the proportionality test. The only relevant consideration at this stage of the analysis is whether the presumption is a logical method of accomplishing the legislative objective. Later in these reasons, I will consider the relevance of this factor in connection with the final phase of the proportionality test.

(iii) *Minimal Impairment*

. . . .

The legislature is entitled to some deference in choosing the means of attaining a given objective. As Lamer C.J. stated in *R. v. Chaulk*, [1990] 3 S.C.R. 1303 at p. 1341, "Parliament is not required to search out and to adopt the absolutely least intrusive means of attaining its objective". . . . However, it is also important to remember that this is not a case in which the legislature has attempted to strike a balance between the interests of competing individuals or groups. Rather it is a case in which the government (as opposed to other individuals or groups) can be characterized as the singular antagonist of an individual attempting to assert a legal right which is fundamental to our system of criminal justice. As the majority wrote in *Irwin Toy Ltd. v. Quebec (Attorney General)*, [1989] 1 S.C.R. 927 . . . , in such circumstances the courts are in as good a position as the legislature to assess whether the least drastic means of achieving the governmental purpose have been chosen, especially given the inherently legal nature of the rights in question and the courts' accumulated experience in dealing with such matters.

In drafting s. 394(1)(*b*) Parliament could have chosen merely to place an evidentiary burden rather than a full legal burden of proving ownership, agency or lawful authority upon the accused. Under such a provision the accused would simply be required to adduce or point to evidence which, if accepted, would be capable of raising a reasonable doubt as to whether he was the owner or agent of the owner or was acting under lawful authority. If he or she succeeded in raising such a doubt the burden would shift to the Crown to prove the contrary beyond a reasonable doubt. If the Crown failed to dispel a reasonable doubt, the accused would be acquitted. Knowledge of the availability of this option must be imputed to Parliament since evidentiary burdens of this kind are and were commonly used to relieve the Crown of the burden of proving that an accused did not legitimately acquire possession of property.

The appellant has not demonstrated to my satisfaction that Parliament has chosen the alternative which impairs s. 11(*d*) as little as is reasonably possible. . . . In my opinion, Parliament's purpose will be effectively served by the imposition of an evidential burden. A seller will have to testify or produce documents tending to show that he or she was either the owner or agent of the owner, or is duly authorized. A purchaser may be required to adduce *viva voce* evidence or produce a document tending to show that the person from whom he or she purchased the material was the owner, agent of the owner or duly authorized. In either case, the matter will have been narrowed to identify the basis of the seller's claim in the one case and the identity of the seller in the other. This will in most cases enable the Crown to produce testimony or documents disproving the claim that the seller or alleged seller is the owner or agent or is duly authorized.

. . . .

Remedy

. . . .

In view of the conclusion that I have reached on the s. 1 issue, the available alternative remedies are: (i) striking down the offending words, a remedy adopted by the Court of Appeal and supported in this Court by the respondents; and (ii) striking down the offending words coupled with reading in appropriate words to substitute an evidentiary burden.

. . . .

In *R. v. Holmes*, [1988] 1 S.C.R. 914, this Court acknowledged that the words "without lawful excuse, the proof of which lies upon him" were capable of creating a legal burden but interpreted them to require the accused to raise a reasonable doubt. This is an interpretation which could be adopted in this case but I would hesitate to do so in view of the many provisions in the *Criminal Code* and other statutes employing the same wording, some of which may validly create a legal burden. I do, however, conclude from the foregoing and the fact that there are many provisions in the *Criminal Code* and other federal statutes that place an evidentiary burden on the accused, that it is safe to assume that Parliament would have enacted the subsection in question in this appeal but restricted to an evidentiary burden, if the option of a legal burden had not been available.

. . . .

In the result I would allow the appeal in part by affirming the lifting of the stay but varying the Court of Appeal's order to state that, pursuant to s. 52 of the *Constitution Act, 1982*, s. 394(1)(*b*) should be read as follows:

> 394. (1) Every one is guilty of an indictable offence and liable to imprisonment for a term not exceeding five years who
>
> . . . .
>
> (*b*) sells or purchases any rock, mineral or other substance that contains precious metals or unsmelted, untreated, unmanufactured or partly smelted, partly treated or partly manufactured precious metals, in the absence of evidence which raises a reasonable doubt that he is the owner or agent of the owner or is acting under lawful authority.

[Lamer C.J. and La Forest, Gonthier, L'Heureux-Dubé, JJ. agreed with Sopinka, J. on the substantive issues.]

———————

The evidentiary device in *Laba* was seen to impose a persuasive burden on the accused to prove that he was the owner of the minerals when he sold them. The Court of Appeal had found the evidentiary device violative of section 11(*d*) and not salvageable under section 1 because it failed the first part of the *Oakes* test in that the objective was not sufficiently pressing to permit the violation of the presumption of innocence. The Ontario Court decided that removing the offending words, "he establishes that", would make the provision constitutional. Then the normal rules of a criminal case would apply. The Crown would have to prove that the accused was not the owner of the minerals and any evidence in the case, led by the Crown or by the defence, that created a reasonable doubt in that regard would enure to the benefit of the accused. If there was no evidence as to ownership the accused would have to be acquitted. The Supreme Court also decided that the section was violative of section 11(*d*) and could not be saved under section 1. The Supreme Court decided that the section was not salvageable because the section did not impair the constitutionally protected right as little as reasonably possible. The Supreme Court decided, however, that simply striking out the offending words was not sufficient. The court decided to write into the provision that guilt would be mandated "in the absence of evidence which raised a reasonable doubt" that he is the owner. If there was no evidence as to ownership the accused would have to be convicted. That result would be mandated by the words written in.

R. v. CURTIS
(1998), 14 C.R. (5th) 328, 123 C.C.C. (3d) 178 (Ont. C.A.)

[The accused were charged under section 215(2) of the Criminal Code with failing to provide the necessaries of life. That section provides that everyone commits an offence who, being under a legal duty within the meaning of section 215(1) of the Code, fails without lawful excuse, "the proof of which lies upon him", to perform that duty in certain specified circumstances. The accused applied for a declaration that section 215(2) was unconstitutional in that it requires a person to prove the defence of lawful excuse on the balance of probabilities. The trial judge found that section 215(2) violated the presumption of innocence guaranteed by section 11(*d*) of the Canadian Charter of Rights and Freedoms and that the section could not be saved under section 1 of the Charter. He declared the entire section unconstitutional and stayed the proceedings. The Crown's appeal was allowed.

On appeal, the Crown conceded that the reverse onus clause rendered section 215(2) in violation of section 11(*d*) of the Charter but sought to justify it under section 1. The Court decided there was a rational connection but found that the provision did not impair the accused's right "as little as possible." Observe the Court's solution.]

GOUDGE J.A. (DOHERTY and CARTHY JJ.A. concurring):—

. . . .

In my view, the fundamental question for the minimal impairment analysis is whether, if s. 215(2) simply permitted an accused to escape responsibility by raising a reasonable doubt as to a lawful excuse for not doing his duty, the Crown could show that the section would less effectively achieve Parliament's objective than it does now with the reverse onus language.

If the impugned language were removed, the section would merely require that, to take advantage of the defence of lawful excuse, the accused point to evidence which could leave a reasonable doubt as to his having a lawful excuse for not performing his duty. If such evidence existed, the Crown would have to prove beyond a reasonable doubt the absence of lawful excuse for there to be a conviction. In my view, the section changed in this way would not compromise at all the right of the accused to the presumption of innocence. Would the Crown, however, be able to demonstrate that the changed section would less effectively achieve its objective?

The Crown put forward no factual basis to suggest that without the reverse onus clause it would be easy for an accused to point to evidence sufficient to raise a reasonable doubt as to a lawful excuse for non-performance, when no such excuse actually existed. Nor did it demonstrate that if the accused attempted to raise a reasonable doubt as to lawful excuse the Crown would be handicapped in proving the absence of such an excuse.

. . . .

I would therefore conclude that the Crown has not shown that if s. 215(2) were shorn of the reverse onus clause, accused persons would more easily be excused for not doing their duty than under the section as presently worded. The Crown has thus not shown that s. 215(2), if it were changed in this way, would less effectively meet Parliament's objective. The reverse onus clause cannot, therefore, clear the minimal impairment hurdle.

. . . .

What remains, then, is the question of remedy. The trial judge, having concluded as I have, simply declared the entirety of s. 215 unconstitutional and of no effect pursuant to s. 52 of the *Constitution Act, 1982* and, as well, granted the accused a stay of proceedings.

In my opinion, he erred in doing so. In this case, the offending portion of s. 215(2) is clearly defined. It is the reverse onus clause, ''the proof of which lies upon him''. This language constitutes the extent to which the section is inconsistent with the provisions of the *Constitution*. The declaratory remedy available under s. 52 thus extends only to the impugned provision, not to the entire section. . . . I therefore agree with the remedy proposed by the Crown, namely that the reverse onus clause, ''the proof of which lies upon him'', be declared of no force or effect. Given that with this excision, s. 215(2) does not violate the presumption of innocence, there is no basis for a stay of proceedings of a charge under the section shorn of this language. I would therefore allow the appeal, declare the words ''the proof of which lies upon him'' in s. 215(2) to be of no force or effect, and otherwise set aside the order declaring s. 215 to be unconstitutional and of no effect. I would further set aside the order staying the proceedings and direct that this matter be remitted for trial.

Do you see the difference in the solution in *Curtis* from that arrived at in *Laba*? Which is preferable?

PROBLEMS

Problem 1

The accused is charged with possession of counterfeit money contrary to section 450 of the Criminal Code:

450(*b*) Every one who, without lawful justification or excuse, the proof of which lies on him, has in his custody or possession counterfeit money is guilty of an indictable offence. . . .

The accused was found to have four counterfeit $10 bills in his wallet. He advises you he didn't know they were counterfeit. What onus? He advises you he collects counterfeit money as a hobby. What onus? See *R. v. Santeramo* (1976), 32 C.C.C. (2d) 35 (Ont. C.A.) and *R. v. Freng* (1993), 86 C.C.C. (3d) 91 (B.C.C.A.).

Problem 2

The accused was convicted of driving while prohibited contrary to the Motor Vehicle Act. The Crown relied upon a certificate of the superintendent. The Act provides that such a certificate proves the prohibition and is proof that the defendant had knowledge of the prohibition unless the accused proves the contrary. Construct an argument for appeal. Compare *R. v. Alston* (1985), 36 M.V.R. 67 (B.C.C.A.) and *R. v. Burge* (1986), 55 C.R. (3d) 131 (B.C.C.A.).

Problem 3

The accused is charged with kidnapping contrary to section 279 of the Criminal Code. Section 279(3) provides:

> In proceedings under this section, the fact that the person in relation to whom the offence is alleged to have been committed did not resist is not a defence unless the accused proves that the failure to resist was not caused by threats, duress, force or exhibition of force.

Constitutional? Compare *R. v. Gough* (1985), 43 C.R. (3d) 297 (Ont. C.A.), and *R. v. Grift* (1986), 43 Alta. L.R. (2d) 365 (Q.B.).

Problem 4

The accused is charged with leaving the scene of an accident with intent to escape liability contrary to section 252(1) of the Criminal Code. Section 252(2) provides that evidence that an accused failed to stop and give his name and address is, in the absence of evidence to the contrary, proof of an intent to escape liability. What is the burden on the accused? Is it constitutional? Compare *R. v. S.D.T.* (1985), 33 M.V.R. 148 (N.S.C.A.).

Problem 5

The accused is charged with obtaining goods by false pretences. Section 362(4) of the Criminal Code provides that goods shall be presumed to have been obtained by a false pretence if obtained by a cheque that was dishonoured unless the court is satisfied that when the accused issued the cheque he reasonably believed it would be honoured. Burden on the accused? Rational connection? Constitutional? Compare *Bunka v. R.*, [1984] 4 W.W.R. 252 (Sask. Q.B.), and *R. v. Driscoll* (1987), 49 Alta. L.R. (2d) 383; affirmed [1987] 6 W.W.R. 748 (C.A.).

3

Relevance and Discretion to Exclude

1. RELEVANCE

(a) Tests

Professor Thayer described the function and limitations of the law of evidence created by the English common law:

> There is a principle — not so much a rule of evidence as a presupposition involved in the very conception of a rational system of evidence, as contrasted with the old formal and mechanical system — which forbids receiving anything irrelevant, not logically probative. How are we to know what these forbidden things are? Not by any rule of law. The law furnishes no test of relevancy. For this, it tacitly refers to logic and general experience, — assuming that the principles of reasoning are known to its judges and ministers, just as a vast multitude of other things are assumed as already sufficiently known to them.[1]

Thayer later explained that by "logic" he was not referring to the deductive logic of the syllogism, but the inductive logic of knowledge or science. He noted that his book used:

> . . . the word relevancy merely as importing a logical relation, that is to say, a relation determined by the reasoning faculty. . . . The law has no orders for the reasoning faculty, any more than the perceiving faculty, — for the eyes and ears.[2]

In *R. v. Watson,*[3] Doherty, J.A. explained:

> Relevance . . . requires a determination of whether as a matter of human experience and logic the existence of "Fact A" makes the existence or non-existence of "Fact B" more probable than it would be without the existence of "Fact A." If it does then "Fact A" is relevant to "Fact B". As long as "Fact B" is itself a material fact in issue or is relevant to a material fact in issue in the litigation then "Fact A" is relevant and prima facie admissible.

The concept of relevancy is ordered by our present insistence on a rational method of fact-finding and its substance, we say, is dictated by our common sense and experience. The law furnishes no test for relevancy and therefore, in the final analysis, the decision rests with the individual judge to value the probabilities in the particular case.[4] This decision, this judicial finding of relevance,

---

1. Thayer, *Preliminary Treatise on Evidence at the Common Law* (1898), pp. 264-69 [footnotes omitted].
2. "Law and Logic" (1900), 14 Harv. L. Rev. 139 in reply to a criticism by Fox at p. 39 of the same volume. Interestingly, Thayer's earlier version of the material in his "Treatise in Presumptions and the Law of Evidence" (1889-1890), 3 Harv. L. Rev. 141 at 144, refers only to logic as the test rather than to logic and general experience.
3. (1996), 50 C.R. (4th) 245, 257 (Ont. C.A.).
4. In his classic article "Relevancy, Probability and the Law" (1941), 29 Cal. L. Rev. 689, 696, Professor James explained that relevancy is a tendency to prove and commented:
   This tendency to prove can be demonstrated only in terms of some general proposition, based most often on the practical experience of the judge and jurors as men,

is a question of law reviewable on appeal.[5] While we cannot legally define relevance, and we, of necessity, must therefore leave it to the trial judge's sound exercise of discretion, subject to review, we need to recognize that "common sense and experience," and hence relevance, will vary depending on the judge's culture, gender, background, social origin and age. The judge's intuition that fact X frequently accompanies fact Y, making X's presence relevant to Y's, may not accord with another's and counsel may need to be provided with the opportunity to encourage the judge that the hunch is incorrect, and deserves to be rethought in light of the other's experience.[6]

We know that evidence is relevant if it has any tendency to make the proposition for which it is tendered more probable than that proposition would be without the evidence. For evidence to have any value there must be a premise, a generalization that one makes, allowing the inference to be made. Borrowing from Professors Binder and Bergman,[7] evidence that roses were in bloom, when tendered to prove that it was then springtime, has meaning only if we adopt the premise or generalization that roses usually bloom in the spring. The tendency of evidence to prove a proposition, and hence its relevance, depends on the validity of the premise which links the evidence to the proposition. The probative worth of the relevant evidence depends on the accuracy of the premise which supports the inference. Sometimes the premise will be indisputable, sometimes always true, sometimes often true and sometimes only rarely true. But a premise there must be. The next time someone says to you that the evidence is *clearly* relevant ask the proponent of the evidence to articulate for you what premise she is relying on. If she has no premise the evidence is irrelevant. If she has a premise you can debate with her the validity of the premise. What experience does she base it on? Is there contrary experience? Is the premise based on myth? Is the premise always true, sometimes or only rarely? These latter parameters do not affect relevance since relevance has a very low threshold but may affect the probative worth which may cause rejection of the evidence if the probative value is outweighed by competing considerations. Approaching discussions of relevance in this way may yield a more intelligent discussion than the oftentimes typical exchange of conclusory opinions.

(b) Materiality

Not only must the evidence tendered be rationally probative of the fact sought to be thereby established; the fact sought to be established must concern a matter

---

sometimes upon generalizations of science introduced into the trial to act as connecting links.

Professor McCormick wrote: "The answer must filter through the judge's experience, his judgment, and his knowledge of human conduct and motivation."

5. See, *e.g., R. v. Driver* (1984), 39 C.R. (3d) 297 (Ont. Dist. Ct.); *Parke, Davis & Co. v. Empire Laboratories Ltd.,* [1964] S.C.R. 351; and *R. v. Borg,* [1969] S.C.R. 551. See also *R. v. Hewitt* (1986), 55 C.R. (3d) 41 (Man. C.A.), regarding admission of irrelevant evidence being a violation of the principles of fundamental justice contrary to s. 7 of the Charter.
6. See Weyrauch, "Law as Mask — Legal Ritual and Relevance" (1978), 66 Cal. L. Rev. 699; and Weinstein, "Some Difficulties in Devising Rules for Determining Truth in Judicial Trials" (1966), 66 Cal. L. Rev. 223.
7. *Fact Investigation* (West Publishing, 1984), p. 82.

in issue between the parties, *i.e.*, it must be material. Another way of saying this is that the evidence must be relevant to a legal issue in the case. With this concept as well the law of evidence does not dictate the parameters, but rather the same is set down by the substantive law and the pleadings.

In civil cases the statements of claim and defence narrow the issues between the parties. In criminal cases the prosecution sets out in the information or indictment what is intended to be established. In our system of fact-finding the parties select a particular slice of life to be litigated and test their rights in that context against their understanding of the substantive law; they do not litigate all of history.[8]

The accused is charged with possession of undersized lobsters. Defence counsel tenders in evidence a witness who will testify that the accused didn't know that there were undersized lobsters in his catch. What do you, as prosecutor, say? "The evidence is immaterial".[9] Notice that by objecting that the evidence is immaterial the prosecutor is not arguing that the evidence would fail to rationally persuade a trier of fact regarding the accused's state of mind but rather that the accused's state of mind doesn't matter. It's immaterial. Our courts decided, as a matter of substantive law, that there is no *mens rea* requirement for the offence of possession of undersized lobster; the offence was decided to be one of strict liability. The evidence tendered was relevant to the matter sought to be established but what was sought to be established was beside the point; it was immaterial.

R. v. LAVALLEE

[1990] 1 S.C.R. 852, 76 C.R. (3d) 329, 55 C.C.C. (3d) 97

[The accused, a battered woman in a volatile common law relationship, killed her partner late one night by shooting him in the back of the head as he left her room. A psychiatrist described the accused's terror and her inability to escape the relationship. The psychiatrist opined that the shooting was the final desperate act of a woman who sincerely believed that she would be killed that night. The accused was acquitted at trial. The court had to decide whether the psychiatric evidence was properly received. Was the evidence relevant to a material issue?]

WILSON J.:—

. . . .

Expert evidence on the psychological effect of battering on wives and common law partners must, it seems to me, be both relevant and necessary in the context of the present case. How can the mental state of the appellant be appreciated without it? The average member of the public (or of the jury) can be forgiven for asking: Why would a woman put up with this kind of treatment? Why should she continue to live with such a man? How could she love a partner who beat her to the point of requiring hospitalization? We would expect the woman to pack her bags and go. Where is her self-respect? Why does she not cut loose and make a new life for herself? Such is the reaction of the average person confronted with the so-called "battered wife syndrome". We need help to understand it and help is available from trained professionals.

---

8. See 1 Wigmore, *Evidence* (3d ed.), s. 2, at p. 6. And see his homely example illustrating materiality at p. 5.
9. See *R. v. Pierce Fisheries Ltd.*, [1970] C.C.C. 193 (S.C.C.).

. . . .

The feature common to both s. 34(2)(*a*) and s. 34(2)(*b*) [the self-defence sections of the Criminal Code] is the imposition of an objective standard of reasonableness on the apprehension of death and the need to repel the assault with deadly force. . . .

If it strains credulity to imagine what the "ordinary man" would do in the position of a battered spouse, it is probably because men do not typically find themselves in that situation. Some women do, however. The definition of what is reasonable must be adapted to circumstances which are, by and large, foreign to the world inhabited by the hypothetical "reasonable man".

. . . .

It will be observed that subsection 34(2)(*a*) does not actually stipulate that the accused apprehend *imminent* danger when he or she acts. Case law has, however, read that requirement into the defence. . . . The sense in which "imminent" is used conjures up the image of "an uplifted knife" or a pointed gun. The rationale for the imminence rule seems obvious. The law of self-defence is designed to ensure that the use of defensive force is really necessary. It justifies the act because the defender reasonably believed that he or she had no alternative but to take the attacker's life. If there is a significant time interval between the original unlawful assault and the accused's response, one tends to suspect that the accused was motivated by revenge rather than self-defence. In the paradigmatic case of a one-time bar room brawl between two men of equal size and strength, this inference makes sense. How can one feel endangered to the point of firing a gun at an unarmed man who utters a death threat, then turns his back and walks out of the room? One cannot be certain of the gravity of the threat or his capacity to carry it out. Besides, one can always take the opportunity to flee or to call the police. If he comes back and raises his fist, one can respond in kind if need be. These are the tacit assumptions that underlie the imminence rule.

All of these assumptions were brought to bear on the respondent in *R. v. Whynot* (1983), 37 C.R. (3d) 198 (C.A.).

. . . .

Where evidence exists that an accused is in a battering relationship, expert testimony can assist the jury in determining whether the accused had a "reasonable" apprehension of death when she acted by explaining the heightened sensitivity of a battered woman to her partner's acts. Without such testimony I am skeptical that the average fact-finder would be capable of appreciating why her subjective fear may have been reasonable in the context of the relationship. After all, the hypothetical "reasonable man" observing only the final incident may have been unlikely to recognize the [batterer's] threat as potentially lethal. Using the case at bar as an example, the "reasonable man" might have thought, as the majority of the Court of Appeal seemed to, that it was unlikely that Rust would make good on his threat to kill the appellant that night because they had guests staying overnight.

For recent discussion of *Lavallee* and the proper instruction to the jury, see *R. v. Malott*.[10]

(c) Multiple Relevance

The same piece of evidence may be relevant to different matters. An awareness of the underlying policies for our rules will assist us in dealing with

---

10.   [1998] 1 S.C.R. 123.

the problems that arise when the evidence has multiple relevance. We will then appreciate that though evidence may be inadmissible when tendered for one purpose as violative of a certain policy it may nevertheless be admissible when tendered for another purpose. For example, evidence of character may be relevant to both credibility and disposition; rules of evidence could exclude such evidence if tendered to prove that the person acted in conformity with that character on the occasion under review, but admit the same if tendered to impact on the credibility of a witness. If we keep in mind the policy underlying the rule we should then be better able to judge whether the evidence ought to be received, with a limiting instruction to the trier of its limited utility, or rejected.

Suppose the accused is charged with fraud. The accused has a criminal record which includes convictions for obtaining money by false pretences, perjury and sexual assault. Are those convictions relevant to the material issue? To answer one must first ask what is the material issue? Did he commit fraud? Do the previous convictions make the proposition that he committed the fraud under review more probable than that proposition would be without the evidence of the previous convictions? Now suppose the accused takes the witness stand and testifies that he didn't know that his representations were false. Are the previous convictions relevant to the credibility of the accused *qua* witness? If the convictions are relevant to credibility they should be received. Suppose I now tell you that there is a rule of evidence, *i.e.* a rule that excludes relevant evidence, that evidence of the bad character of an accused cannot be led for the purpose of persuading the trier of fact that the accused on the occasion under review acted in conformity with that character and committed the dastardly deed.

What should the trial judge do? May counsel in cross-examination ask questions about the accused's prior record on the basis that the same is relevant to credibility? Should the trial judge admit for the one purpose and exclude for the other? What does the judge say to the jury? Will the jury understand?

(d) Relevancy and Circumstantial Evidence

When evidence about a material proposition is led, the proponent seeks to persuade the trier to draw the inference from the fact led to the proposition. If there is a rational connection between them, if the fact will, according to reason and experience, support the inference, the fact will be adjudged relevant and received. The facts tendered in evidence are normally classified as either testimonial or circumstantial, but in each case inferences are necessary and problems of relevancy therefore occur. With testimonial evidence, sometimes called direct evidence, the trier is asked to infer, from the fact that the witness made a statement, the truth of the matter stated. If the witness is seen to be sincere and possessed of an ability to observe and accurately recall, and if it is clear that he had the opportunity to see the matter in issue, there will be reason to draw the inference and his testimony will be credited. Though a true problem of relevance exists, it is more common, however, to examine and discuss the probative worth of such evidence under the heads of Testimonial Qualifications and Credibility.[11] Commonly we reserve the concept of relevancy for discussions

---

11.   See 2 Wigmore, *Evidence* (Chad. Rev.), pp. 5 and 475.

involving circumstantial evidence. In cases of circumstantial evidence certain facts connected with the material fact are proved and the trier is asked to infer from those facts that the material fact exists. If reason and experience support the connection the evidence led is relevant. John Robinette described it:

> All that circumstantial evidence is, is that you are seeking to prove circumstances, subordinate circumstances, subordinate facts, from which a trial tribunal may draw the inference that a principal issue of fact vital to your case has been established. Therefore, as a matter of logic, if an inference may be drawn from a subordinate fact that the principal fact occurred then evidence is admissible to prove the subordinate fact and that is what is loosely called circumstantial evidence.[12]

If a witness is willing to testify that she saw the accused shoot the deceased, this is direct evidence of that fact. The trial judge will first ensure the witness's competence to speak, then the evidence may be evaluated according to the trier of fact's assessment of the witness's credibility. If a witness is willing to testify that she heard the deceased scream and moments later saw the accused standing over the body holding a smoking gun this is circumstantial evidence of the accused shooting the deceased. The trial judge will assess the relevance of the evidence led; if received the trier of fact will then assess its sufficiency.

Notice that in the case of direct evidence there is but one source of error. The person who describes a stabbing she witnessed might be mistaken or lying. The witness who says she only saw certain circumstances, the wounds and the blood-stained knife, may also be mistaken or lying about those circumstances, but also even if she's accurate in her description the inference that the prosecutor wants the trier to draw may not be the correct one. That is why we say that circumstantial evidence has two sources of error. This leads some to conclude that circumstantial evidence is weaker than direct, but is it?

In a murder prosecution the Crown introduces into evidence letters written by the accused confessing a great love for the victim's wife. Relevant? Premise? Receivable? A Crown witness testifies that she saw the accused stab the victim. Relevant? Premise? Receivable? Which piece of evidence is stronger, more persuasive?

Suppose that during cross-examination of the eye-witness defence counsel is able to bring out that:

1. The opportunity to observe was momentary.
2. The room was dark.
3. The witness's eyesight was poor.
4. The witness had never seen the accused before.

Suppose the Crown leads additional circumstantial evidence that a knife capable of inflicting the stab wound was found in the accused's possession, that there were bloodstains on the accused's clothes matching the victim's blood-type, etc., etc. Which evidence is stronger?

It is a mistake to think of circumstantial evidence as inherently less probative than direct. Justice Hall explained how powerful circumstantial evidence can be:

---

12.   *Circumstantial Evidence*, [1955] L.S.U.C. Spec. Lect. 307. For the same author speaking in parables on the subject, see *Charge to the Jury in a Criminal Case*, [1959] L.S.U.C. Spec. Lect. 147 and 153.

The case against Truscott was predominantly but not exclusively one of circumstantial evidence. I recognize fully that guilt can be brought home to an accused by circumstantial evidence; that there are cases where the circumstances can be said to point inexorably to guilt more reliably than direct evidence; that direct evidence is subject to the everyday hazards of imperfect recognition or of imperfect memory or both. The circumstantial evidence case is built piece by piece until the final evidentiary structure completely entraps the prisoner in a situation from which he cannot escape. There may be missing from that structure a piece here and there and certain imperfections may be discernible, but the entrapping mesh taken as a whole must be continuous and consistent. The law does not require that the guilt of an accused be established to a demonstration but is satisfied when the evidence presented to the jury points conclusively to the accused as the perpetrator of the crime and excludes any reasonable hypothesis of innocence. The rules of evidence apply with equal force to proof by circumstantial evidence as to proof by direct evidence. The evidence in both instances must be equally credible, admissible and relevant.[13]

(e) Relevancy and Sufficiency

Relevancy of evidence must be distinguished from sufficiency of evidence and we need to recognize that to be receivable as relevant the piece of evidence being tendered need not by itself be compelling. Also, evidence objected to as irrelevant may need to be received on counsel's undertaking to link up the same with other expected evidence and so later demonstrate relevance. The trier may need to be advised to disregard such evidence conditionally received if the connection fails to materialize.[14] McCormick explained:

> This is the distinction between relevancy and sufficiency. The test of relevancy, which is to be applied by the trial judge in determining whether a particular item or group of items of evidence is to be admitted is a different and less stringent one than the standard used at a later stage in deciding whether all the evidence of the party on an issue is sufficient to permit the issue to go to the jury. A brick is not a wall.
>
> What is the standard of relevance or probative quality which evidence must meet if it is to be admitted? We have said that it must "tend to establish" the inference for which it is offered. How strong must this tendency be? Some courts have announced tests, variously phrased, which seem to require that the evidence offered must render the inference for which it is offered more probable than the other possible inferences or hypotheses, that is, the chances must appear to preponderate that the inference claimed is the true one.
>
> . . . .
>
> . . . It is believed that a more modest standard better reflects the actual practice of the courts, and that the most acceptable test of relevancy is the question, does the evidence offered render the desired inference *more probable than it would be without the evidence?*[15]

---

13. In *R. v. Truscott*, [1967] 2 C.C.C. 285, 360-61 (S.C.C.), relied on in *R. v. Kaysaywaysemat* (1992), 10 C.R. (4th) 317 (Sask. C.A.); leave to appeal to S.C.C. refused (1992), 97 Sask. R. 320 (note).

14. See *R. v. Dass* (1979), 47 C.C.C. (2d) 194, 203 (Man. C.A.); or a new trial may be necessary, *R. v. Spence* (1979), 47 C.C.C. (2d) 167 (Ont. C.A.).

15. McCormick, *Evidence* (2d ed.), pp. 436-38.

The present Federal Rules of Evidence in the United States reflect the current orthodoxy regarding the meaning of relevance:

"Relevant evidence" means evidence having any tendency to make the existence of any fact that is of consequence to the determination of the action more probable or less probable than it would be without the evidence.[16]

Compare, however, the remarks in the Supreme Court of Canada in *Wray v. R.*[17] The accused wished to lead evidence that, following the acquittal on his first trial, he was free to go where he pleased until he voluntarily surrendered himself two years later for the court-ordered second trial. Counsel for the accused argued that just as flight might be taken as indicative of a consciousness of guilt so too the accused's remaining was indicative of innocence and thus relevant. The evidence was rejected and the Ontario Court of Appeal dismissed his appeal. Arnup, J.A. explained:

... there may be a large number of reasons why an accused, although under suspicion, refrained from flight and (as in this case) voluntarily surrendered for his trial. It would not be a long step from the proposition advanced here to the stage where it would be submitted that an inference of innocence could be inferred from the fact that the accused was at large on only nominal bail and could easily have fled the jurisdiction without other than minor pecuniary loss.[18]

Ritchie, J. in the Supreme Court of Canada agreed:

...the appellant's voluntary appearance at his trial *does not necessarily give rise to any inference* except that he was doing what the law required ... the evidence of lack of flight and voluntary surrender ... has no probative value.[19]

While there may be other reasons why Wray didn't flee, does that make it irrelevant? While his remaining isn't determinative regarding his innocence, might it not be an appropriate "brick" that a jury should know about and be able to consider along with all the other evidence?

Later, in *Cloutier v. R.*,[20] Pratte, J., giving the majority opinion, wrote:

For one fact to be relevant to another, there must be a connection or nexus between the two which makes it possible to infer the existence of one from the existence of the other. One fact is not relevant to another if it does not have *real probative value* with respect to the latter (Cross, *Evidence*, 4th ed. (1974), p. 16).[21]

---

16.   Federal Rules of Evidence, 1974, R. 401.
17.   (1973), 10 C.C.C. (2d) 215 (S.C.C.).
18.   (1971), 4 C.C.C. (2d) 378, 383 (Ont. C.A.).
19.   *Supra*, note 17, at p. 220. Compare the passage quoted in the opinion from Wills, *Circumstantial Evidence*, 7th ed. (1937), p. 277. Professor McCormick, *supra*, note 15, at p. 438, would, on the other hand, say that
         [a trial judge] must ask himself, could a reasonable juror believe that the attempt makes it more probable that accused was conscious of guilt of the crime being tried, than it would be in the absence of the attempt; and if the answer is yes, the evidence is relevant.
20.   (1979), 48 C.C.C. (2d) 1 (S.C.C.).
21.   *Ibid.*, at p. 28.

The reference to Cross and the adjective "real" appear to be a regrettable purchase of the concept of "legal relevance" requiring a "plus value" over and above a minimum of probative value. Cross wrote:

> . . . all evidence which is *sufficiently relevant* to an issue before the court is admissible and all that is irrelevant, or *insufficiently relevant*, should be excluded. [Emphasis added.][22]

And Wigmore wrote:

> . . . the question of the uselessness, or the contrary, of the spending of time on evidence offered is . . . constantly required to be raised and settled at the outset.
>
> . . . .
>
> . . . [The court will] require a generally *higher degree of probative value for all evidence to be submitted to a jury* than would be asked in ordinary reasoning. The judge, in his efforts to prevent the jury from being satisfied by matters of slight value, capable of being exaggerated by prejudice and hasty reasoning, has constantly seen fit to exclude matter which does not rise to a clearly sufficient degree of value. In other words, legal relevancy denotes, first of all, *something more than a minimum of probative value*. Each single piece of evidence must have a plus value. [Emphasis added.][23]

It might be better to reason that <u>if the evidence is relevant, material and admissible, it may still be excluded if the trial judge, in his discretion,[24] believes there are competing considerations which outweigh the probative worth of the evidence.</u> The court could find the probative force tenuous and outweighed by the danger of undue prejudice, confusion of issues, undue consumption of time and unfair surprise to the witness or to the opposite party.[25] Frequently in the cases, we read of evidence being rejected as irrelevant though closer analysis will reveal a rational connection; the label "irrelevant" is then being used to mask a discretionary exercise based on one or more of the above factors, and by "irrelevant" the opinion writer truly means "insufficiently relevant."[26] Confining the use of the term relevant to describe rational connection would produce greater clarity of thought in this confused area.[27]

---

22. Cross, *Evidence* (5th ed.), p. 17. Cross at p. 18 adopts Stephen's definition of relevance; see the criticism by Thayer in his *Preliminary Treatise on Evidence at the Common Law* (1898), p. 266, note 1: "It is here that Mr. Justice Stephen's treatment of the law of evidence is perplexing, and has the aspect of a *tour de force*."

23. 1 Wigmore, *Evidence* (3d ed.), s. 28.

24. See, *e.g.*, *R. v. McNamara (No. 1)* (1981), 56 C.C.C. (2d) 193, 298 (Ont. C.A.); *R. v. Wray*, [1970] 4 C.C.C. 1 (S.C.C.); *Noor Mohammed v. R.*, [1949] 1 All E.R. 365 (P.C.); and *Selvey v. D.P.P.* (1968), 52 Cr. App. R. 443 (H.L.). See also *Draper v. Jacklyn* (1969), 9 D.L.R. (3d) 264 (S.C.C.). See generally McElroy, "Some Observations Concerning the Discretions Reposed in Trial Judges" (1942), Model Code of Evidence 356, and Trautman, "Logical or Legal Relevancy" (1952), 5 Vand. L. Rev. 385, and 1 Wigmore, *Evidence* (3d ed.), s. 29a. Compare Livesey, "Judicial Discretion to Exclude Prejudicial Evidence," [1968] Camb. L.J. 291.

25. See McCormick, *Evidence* (2d ed.), p. 441.

26. See Hoffman, "Similar Facts After Boardman" (1975), 91 L.Q. R. 193 at 205.

27. See generally the illuminating article by James, "Relevancy, Probability and the Law" (1940-41), 29 Cal. L. Rev. 689.

2. DISCRETION AND LAW OF EVIDENCE

(a) Common Law

In the proposed Code of Evidence,[28] the most important sections, indeed the Code's heart and soul, were:

> 4.(1) All relevant evidence is admissible except as provided in this Code or any other Act.
>
> (2) "Relevant evidence" means evidence that has any tendency in reason to prove a fact in issue in a proceeding.
>
> 5. Evidence may be excluded if its probative value is substantially outweighed by the danger of undue prejudice, confusing the issues, misleading the jury, or undue consumption of time.

broader than irrelevant

This was essentially a copy of a provision in the Federal Rules of Evidence in the United States. Federal Rule 403 reads:

> Although relevant, evidence may be excluded if its probative value is substantially outweighed by the danger of unfair prejudice, confusion of the issues, or misleading the jury, or by considerations of undue delay, waste of time or needless presentation of cumulative evidence.

The Code was not accepted by the profession. Antonio Lamer was the Vice-Chairman of the Law Reform Commission at the time and G.V. La Forest was the Commissioner in charge of the Evidence Project. Ask yourself, when reading the next two cases, whether they were able to accomplish judicially what they were unable to accomplish legislatively.

In *Morris v. R.*[29] the Supreme Court of Canada adopted the Thayerian view of relevance, explained the *Cloutier* decision, and denied that there was any minimum probative value before a piece of information could be labelled relevant.

MORRIS v. R.
[1983] 2 S.C.R. 190, 36 C.R. (3d) 1, 7 C.C.C. (3d) 97

McIntyre J. (Ritchie, Beetz and Estey JJ. concurring):—I have had the opportunity of reading the reasons for judgment prepared in this case [an appeal from (1982), 68 C.C.C. (2d) 115] by my brother Lamer. I agree with his observation on the subject of the relevancy of evidence. I also agree with his exposition of the reason for and the development of the exclusionary rule which applies to evidence in criminal cases dealing only with the question of disposition and character of the accused. I am unable, however, to agree with his characterization of the newspaper clipping in this case as evidence indicating only a disposition on the part of the appellant.

In my view, an inference could be drawn from the unexplained presence of the newspaper clipping among the possessions of the appellant that he had an interest in and had informed himself on the question of sources of supply of heroin, necessarily a subject of vital interest to one concerned with the importing of the narcotic.

---

28. Law Reform Commission of Canada, 1975.

29. (1983), 7 C.C.C. (3d) 97, 104, 106 (S.C.C.), per Lamer, J. Though this was a dissenting opinion the majority opinion of McIntyre, J. expressly agreed with his observations on relevance. But see *R. v. Pugliese* (1992), 71 C.C.C. (3d) 295 (Ont. C.A.) writing that the evidence was receivable because it "satisfied the requirements of admissibility and probative value set out in *Cloutier v. The Queen*."

. . . .

I agree that the probative value of such evidence may be low, especially since the newspaper article here concerns the heroin trade in Pakistan rather than in Hong Kong, which was apparently the source of the heroin involved in this case. However, admissibility of evidence must not be confused with weight. If the article had concerned the heroin trade in Hong Kong, it would of course have had greater probative value. If the article had been a manual containing a step-by-step guide to importing heroin into Vancouver from Hong Kong, the probative value would have been still greater. The differences between these examples, however, and the facts at bar are differences in degree, not kind. In other words, the differences go to weight and not to admissibility.

The weight to be given to evidence is a question for the trier of fact, subject of course to the discretion of the trial judge to exclude evidence where the probative value is minimal and the prejudicial effect great: see *R. v. Wray*, [1971] S.C.R. 272. In the present case the trial judge did not consider that the evidence should be thus excluded. In my opinion it would not be proper in the circumstances of this case for this court to substitute its view on this matter of discretion for that of the trial judge. In my opinion the trial judge made no error in law in admitting evidence of the newspaper clipping, and I would therefore dismiss the appeal.

LAMER J. (dissenting) (DICKSON and WILSON JJ. concurring):— The appellant, one Gary Robert Morris, was convicted in Vancouver, by a County Court Judge sitting without a jury, of having conspired with others to import and traffic heroin. He appealed from his conviction to the British Columbia Court of Appeal. His appeal was heard by a panel of three judges and was dismissed [(1982), 68 C.C.C. (2d) 115]. One of the judges, Anderson J.A., dissented and would have allowed the appeal and ordered a new trial on the following ground of law, namely:

> That the learned trial judge erred in admitting into evidence and in taking into consideration a newspaper clipping entitled, 'The Heroin Trade Moves to Pakistan', being Exhibit 26 at the Appellant's trial.

. . . .

THE LAW

While I agree with Anderson J.A. that the clipping should not have been admitted in evidence, it is not because I believe the clipping irrelevant, but because it was, in my view, not admissible. His reference to the clipping as having "no probative value in proving the offence charged" is understandable given the language this court resorted to when dealing with analogous evidence in the case of *Cloutier*. Cloutier was charged with importing a narcotic into Canada, namely, 20 pounds of cannabis (marihuana). The evidence was that the merchandise was concealed in the false bottom of a dresser arriving from South America, which the appellant asked his mother to store in her home, and it was there that the police made the seizure.

One of the grounds of appeal in this court was that the trial judge refused to admit in evidence certificates of analysis to establish that the items seized at the accused's home, a cigarette butt, a pipe and a green substance, indicated that the accused was a user of marihuana.

Pratte J., writing for a majority of this court, stated the following, at p. 731:

> For one fact to be relevant to another, there must be a connection or nexus between the two which makes it possible to infer the existence of one from the existence of the other. One fact is not relevant to another if it does not have real probative value with respect to the latter (Cross, *On Evidence*, 4th ed. [1974], at p. 16).

Thus, apart from certain exceptions which are not applicable here, evidence is not admissible if its only purpose is to prove that the accused is the type of man who is more likely to commit a crime of the kind with which he is charged; such evidence is viewed as having no real probative value with regard to the specific crime attributed to the accused: there is no sufficient logical connection between the one and the other.

It has been said that some might read in these comments (see Report of the Federal/ Provincial Task Force on Uniform Rules of Evidence (1982), at p. 62 et seq.) a pronouncement by this court indicating a departure from Thayer's premise in A Preliminary Treatise on Evidence at the Common Law, of relevancy, logic and experience, and an adoption of Wigmore's concept of "legal relevancy" of which "the effect is to require a generally *higher degree of probative value for all evidence to be submitted to a jury*" and that "legal relevancy denotes, first of all, *something more than a minimum of probative value*. Each single piece of evidence must have a plus value.": Wigmore on Evidence, 3rd ed., vol. 1 (1940), para. 28, pp. 409-10. I do not think that it was intended by the majority in this court in *Cloutier*, supra, that such a departure be made. All agreed that the evidence could not be admitted to prove the accused's propensity, including the dissenting judges. In fact, the whole case, in my view, turned upon whether the evidence was relevant and admissible as tending to establish motive.

. . . .

Thayer's statement of the law, which is still the law in Canada, was as follows (p. 530):

(1) that nothing is to be received which is not logically probative of some matter requiring to be proved; and (2) that everything which is thus probative should come in, unless a clear ground of policy or law excludes it.

To this general statement should be added the discretionary power judges exercise to exclude logically relevant evidence (p. 266):

. . . as being of too slight a significance, or as having too conjectural and remote a connection; others, as being dangerous, in their effect on the jury, and likely to be misused or overestimated by that body; others, as being impolitic, or unsafe on public grounds; others, on the bare ground of precedent. It is this sort of thing, as I said before, — the rejection on one or another practical ground, of what is really probative, — which is the characteristic thing in the law of evidence; stamping it as the child of the jury system.

It was through the exercise of this discretionary power that judges developed rules of exclusion. As said by Thayer at p. 265, when speaking of the rule of general admissibility of what is logically probative:

. . . in an historical sense it has not been the fundamental thing, to which the different exclusions were exceptions. What has taken place, in fact, is the shutting out by the judges of one and another thing from time to time; and so, gradually, the recognition of this exclusion under a rule. These rules of exclusion have had their exceptions; and so the law has come into the shape of a set of primary rules of exclusion; and then a set of exceptions to these rules.

Thus came about, as a primary rule of exclusion, the following: disposition, i.e., the fact that the accused is the sort of person who would be likely to have committed the offence, though relevant, is not admissible. As a result, evidence adduced *solely* for the purpose of proving disposition is itself inadmissible, or, to put it otherwise, evidence the sole relevancy of which to the crime committed is through proof of disposition is inadmissible.

. . . .

Now to consider the "clipping". The presence of the clipping in the room tends to prove that the accused either clipped it or received it and kept it for future reference. Had the article referred to movement of drugs in Hong Kong, to a laxity in that colony on the part of the customs officials, and so forth, it would have found its relevancy as proving the accused's participation in the conspiracies through his possession of a document that might have been instrumental to the commission of the crimes. But such is not the case. Its sole relevancy is through proof of the accused's disposition, the reasoning being as follows, that, because persons who are traffickers are more likely to keep such information than not, people who keep such information are more likely to be traffickers than people who do not, and that a person who trafficks is more likely to have committed the alleged offence than a person who does not. The ultimate purpose of placing the accused in the first category (people who keep such information for future reference) is to put him in a category of people the character of which indicates a propensity to commit the offences of which he was charged. This is clearly inadmissible evidence.

. . . .

I have read the evidence and agree with Anderson J.A. that this is not the proper case for the application of s. 613(1)(*b*)(iii). I cannot say, however, that, once the clipping and the answers of the accused when cross-examined as to the reasons for its presence in his room are excluded, there is left no evidence upon which a trier of fact might reasonably convict. As a result, I would allow the appeal, quash the conviction and order a new trial.

Appeal dismissed.

Sometimes you will hear a lawyer argue that a piece of evidence should be excluded because the evidence is prejudicial. This is not a ground of exclusion. Of course the evidence is prejudicial to the opponent's case. That's why proponent is offering it! If the evidence wasn't prejudicial it wouldn't be relevant to a material issue. There is however a power to exclude if the evidence, though relevant, would unfairly prejudice the opponent. If the unfairness of the evidence outweighs its probative value it deserves to be excluded. The unfairness may occur in different ways. The trier of fact may:

1. exaggerate the probative value that the evidence deserves,
2. disregard the real issue in the case or become confused as to what the real issues are, or
3. use the evidence for an improper purpose.

The law of evidence principally consists of the study of canons of exclusion, rules regarding admissibility, which deny receipt into evidence of information which is rationally probative of a matter in issue between the parties.[30] Since these canons of exclusion interfere with the rational decision-making process, excluding information which is relevant to a material issue, they need constant justification and the advocate who would exclude is seen to bear the onus.[31]

The rules of evidence will guide us in most cases. By and large they are sound compromises worked out over the years by knowledgeable judges and thoughtful legislators. We need to recognize, however, that in the application of the rules of evidence there is usually room for a sound exercise of discretion, *i.e.,* judgment. A good understanding of the principles that underlie the particular rule is necessary to permit the trial judge to exercise her judgment and wisely apply the rule. A good understanding may also alert the trial judge to the fact that in her particular case the rule is otherwise satisfied by the circumstances and need not in that case be mechanically or slavishly applied.

---

30. See generally Montrose, "Basic Concepts of the Law of Evidence" (1954), 70 L.Q.R. 527 at 535.
31. See generally Cmnd. 2964 (1966).

Recognizing a discretion in the trial judge recognizes room for choice, room for judgment. It's inherent in the nature of the exercise. We should not fear it nor should we insist on certainty in all our rules of evidence. The so-called "rules" of evidence were designed largely by trial judges seeking justice in their individual cases and were not meant to be a calculus rigidly applied. The best that we can do is to catalogue factors which are important to the sound exercise of discretion. Nor should discretion be feared as some form of palm-tree justice which is unreviewable. Protection against a trial judge's abuse of discretion should always be available by appeal.[32] Appellate court judges at the same time should recognize, however,

> . . . the vantage point of the trial judge, the superiority of his position. It's not that he knows more. It's that he sees more, and sometimes smells more.[33]

What do we mean by "discretion"? Consider these contrasting views:

> The discretion of a Judge is the Law of Tyrants; it is always unknown; it is different in different men; it is casual and depends on constitution, temper and passion. In the best it is often times caprice, in the worst it is every vice, folly and passion to which human nature is liable.[34]

> Discretion when applied to a court of justice means sound discretion guided by law. It must be governed by rule not by humour; it must not be arbitrary, vague and fanciful, but legal and regular.[35]

No one would speak in favour of the former type of discretion; no one however can deny the necessity of the latter. Discretion is endemic to the law of evidence and essential to any model of adjudication. There is a need to recognize that fact and to get on with the task of articulating the guidelines necessary to exercise the judicial function.

It is somewhat odd to see resistance to discretion in the application of the rules of evidence when we remind ourselves that in bench trials we regularly equip the trial judge with the ultimate discretion of finding guilt or innocence. When a judge seeks to reach a conclusion of fact from the evidence of witnesses, he discriminates as to weight and cogency. Jerome Frank referred to this exercise as "fact discretion."[36] A witness describes a past event. On analysis, the witness is stating his present recall of what he believes he then saw. The trier of fact observes the demeanour of the witness, sees him tested on cross-examination, and expresses his opinion regarding the correctness of the witness's belief. We have "subjectivity piled on subjectivity"; guesses upon guesses.[37] In this exercise, which is the best we can do, we trust in the judge to exercise her discretion in a sound manner and to discriminate wisely.

---

32.   See *R. v. Collins* (1987), 56 C.R. (3d) 193, where the Supreme Court of Canada recognized that s. 24(2) of the Charter called for an exercise of discretion in deciding whether or not to exclude improperly obtained evidence but also noted that the decision "is a question of law from which an appeal will generally lie" (at p. 204). See also *R. v. Cook* (1959), 2 Q.B. 340, 348 and *Selvey v. D.P.P.* (1968), [1970] A.C. 304 (H.L.) regarding reviewability of discretionary rulings.

33.   Rosenberg, "Judicial Discretion" (1965), 38 The Ohio Bar 819.

34.   Lord Camden in *Doe d. Hindson v. Kersey* (1765).

35.   Lord Mansfield in *R. v. Wilkes* (1770), 4 Burr 2527, 2539 (H.L.).

36.   *Courts on Trial*, 1949, p. 57.

37.   *Ibid.*, Ch. III, Facts are Guesses.

(b) Charter

CORBETT v. R.

[1988] 1 S.C.R. 670, 64 C.R. (3d) 1, 41 C.C.C. (3d) 385

[The accused was convicted of murder. He appealed, arguing that he was deprived of his right to a fair hearing by reason of the introduction of evidence of his earlier conviction of another murder. The accused had sought a ruling that, if he was called as a witness, section 12 of the Canada Evidence Act would not apply to him because of section 11(*d*) of the Charter and he could not be cross-examined as to his prior criminal record. The evidence of his previous conviction was elicited after a negative ruling by the trial judge. While Justice La Forest dissented on the facts in the case his opinion was accepted by the majority as to the law.]

DICKSON C.J.C. (LAMER J. concurring):—

. . . .

I agree with La Forest J. that there is a discretion to exclude evidence of prior convictions of an accused. However, as I take a different view as to the manner in which the trial judge's discretion should have been exercised, it will be necessary for me to deal with the constitutional validity of s. 12 of the Canada Evidence Act.

. . . .

Before calling any evidence, Corbett's counsel sought a ruling that, if the accused were called, s. 12 of the Canada Evidence Act would not apply to him because of s. 11(*d*) of the Charter, and therefore that Corbett could not be cross-examined as to his prior criminal record. The trial judge ruled against Corbett on this issue, following the decision of the British Columbia Supreme Court in *R. v. Jarosz* (1982), 3 C.R.R. 333. The accused was then called, and in order "to soften the blow" his own counsel put to him his criminal record, which Corbett admitted. The record is as follows:

— 23 April 1954   armed robbery, receiving stolen property, breaking, entering and theft (four counts)

— 12 May 1954   escaping custody

— 6 Dec. 1954   theft of auto, breaking and entering

— 8 Nov. 1971   non-capital murder

In his evidence, Corbett denied shooting Pinsonneault and swore that he left his hotel room only once during the night, to get some liquor and cigarettes from his car, the hotel clerk having testified that he had let Corbett back into the hotel at 3:10 a.m.

In charging the jury, the trial judge stated as follows with regard to the relevance of Corbett's criminal record:

There was evidence tendered by the accused that he was previously convicted of a number of Criminal Code offences, including the offence of non-capital murder, which conviction was registered on November 8th 1971. Evidence of previous convictions is admissible only in respect to the credibility of the witness. It can only be used to assess the credibility of the accused, and for no other purpose. Because the accused was previously convicted of murder, it must not be used by you, the jury, as evidence to prove that the accused person committed the murder of which he stands charged. You, the jury, must not take the person's previous convictions into account in your deliberations when determining whether the Crown has proven beyond a reasonable doubt that the accused committed the murder with which he is charged.

This warning could hardly have been more explicit.

. . . .

It is my view that on the facts of the present case a serious imbalance would have arisen had the jury not been apprised of Corbett's criminal record. Counsel for Corbett vigorously attacked the credibility of the Crown witnesses and much was made of the prior criminal records of Marcoux and Bergeron. What impression would the jury have had if Corbett had given his evidence under a regime whereby the Crown was precluded from bringing to the jury's attention the fact that Corbett had a serious criminal record? It would be impossible to explain to the jury that one set of rules applies to ordinary witnesses, while another applies to the accused, for the very fact of such an explanation would undermine the purpose of the exclusionary rule. Had Corbett's criminal record not been revealed, the jury would have been left with the quite incorrect impression that, while all the Crown witnesses were hardened criminals, the accused had an unblemished past. It cannot be the case that nothing short of this entirely misleading situation is required to satisfy the accused's right to a fair trial.

There is perhaps a risk that, if told of the fact that the accused has a criminal record, the jury will make more than it should of that fact. But concealing the prior criminal record of an accused who testifies deprives the jury of information relevant to credibility, and creates a serious risk that the jury will be presented with a misleading picture.

In my view, the best way to balance and alleviate these risks is to give the jury all the information, but at the same time give a clear direction as to the limited use they are to make of such information. Rules which put blinders over the eyes of the trier of fact should be avoided except as a last resort. It is preferable to trust the good sense of the jury and to give the jury all relevant information, so long as it is accompanied by a clear instruction in law from the trial judge regarding the extent of its probative value. . . .

In my view, it would be quite wrong to make too much of the risk that the jury *might* use the evidence for an improper purpose. This line of thinking could seriously undermine the entire jury system. The very strength of the jury is that the ultimate issue of guilt or innocence is determined by a group of ordinary citizens who are not legal specialists and who bring to the legal process a healthy measure of common sense. The jury is, of course, bound to follow the law as it is explained by the trial judge. Jury directions are often long and difficult, but the experience of trial judges is that juries do perform their duty according to the law. We should regard with grave suspicion arguments which assert that depriving the jury of all relevant information is preferable to giving them everything, with a careful explanation as to any limitations on the use to which they may put that information. So long as the jury is given a clear instruction as to how it may and how it may not use evidence of prior convictions put to an accused on cross-examination, it can be argued that the risk of improper use is outweighed by the much more serious risk of error should the jury be forced to decide the issue in the dark. . . .

I agree with La Forest J. that the trial judge has a discretion to exclude prejudicial evidence of previous convictions in an appropriate case.

However, I respectfully disagree with my colleague La Forest J. that this discretion should have been exercised in favour of the appellant in the circumstances of the present case. In his reasons, La Forest J. provides a useful catalogue of factors to which reference may be had in determining how this discretion is to be exercised. In my view, however, my colleague gives too little weight to the fact that in this case the accused appellant made a deliberate attack on the credibility of Crown witnesses, largely based upon their prior records.

LA FOREST J. (dissenting):—

. . . .

GENERAL PRINCIPLES

As is true with respect to the resolution of most, if not all, issues relating to the law of evidence, resort must be had first and foremost to its animating or first principles, for it is only with reference to these that the more specific rules of evidence can be understood and evaluated. Failure to so reference discussion often results in the unhappy divorce of legal reasoning from common sense, with the consequence that rules of evidence are apt to be viewed as both self-sustaining and self-justifying. The present case further illustrates that statutory rules of evidence must also be interpreted in light of these guiding principles.

The organizing principles of the law of evidence may be simply stated. All relevant evidence is admissible, subject to a discretion to exclude matters that may unduly prejudice, mislead or confuse the trier of fact, take up too much time, or should otherwise be excluded on clear grounds of law or policy. Questions of relevancy and exclusion are, of course, matters for the trial judge, but over the years many specific exclusionary rules have been developed for the guidance of the trial judge, so much so that the law of evidence may superficially appear to consist simply of a series of exceptions to the rules of admissibility, with exceptions to the exceptions, and their sub-exceptions. . . .

I agree with Professor Friedland that the law's sedulously fostered position, that the character of an accused may not be considered unless he first raises the issue or unless the Crown meets the criteria of similar fact evidence, ought not to easily yield to what a Law Reform Commission of Canada paper has described as "the fallacy [in s. 12] that it is rational to treat the accused like an ordinary non-party witness" (Evidence Study Paper 3, Credibility (1972), at p. 8). Furthermore, I think it self-evident that the law cannot profess to learn from common sense and experience and yet selectively ignore such lessons. I also think it significant that I have not unearthed any academic or empirical evidence tending to undermine these observations. Indeed, quite the contrary is true: see Wissler and Saks, "On the Inefficacy of Limiting Instructions: When Jurors Use Prior Conviction Evidence to Decide on Guilt" (1985), 9 L. & Human Behavior 37; also Ratushny and Friedland.

. . . .

Having satisfied myself that the risk of prejudice is by no means speculative or illusory, I now turn to the question whether s. 12 admits of a discretion in the trial judge to prevent such prejudice materializing.

[Having found that there was a discretion, he continued.]

It is impossible to provide an exhaustive catalogue of the factors that are relevant in assessing the probative value or potential prejudice of such evidence, but among the most important are the nature of the previous conviction and its remoteness or nearness to the present charge.

. . . .

. . . [T]he more similar the offence to which the previous conviction relates to the conduct for which the accused is on trial, the greater the prejudice harboured by its admission.

. . . .

I think that a court should be very chary of admitting evidence of a previous conviction for a similar crime, especially when the rationale for the stringent test for admitting "similar fact" evidence is kept in mind. . . .

. . . .

As I indicated in my earlier comments respecting the admission into evidence of previous convictions for offences similar to that for which the accused is on trial, I think it self-evident that the prejudicial potential harboured by the admission at a trial for murder of a previous conviction for non-capital murder is manifestly profound. Furthermore, the probative value of this item of evidence in relation to credibility (which is the only use to which it legitimately could be put) is, at best, trifling, certainly in this case. The foregoing alone appears to satisfy a narrow reading of the test in *Wray*.

However, as I mentioned earlier, discretion cannot be judicially exercised in a vacuum; it is only with reference to the circumstances of the case that its exercise becomes meaningful. The circumstances of the present case, however, rather than "indicat[ing] strong reasons for disclosure" (*Gordon*, supra, at p. 940), militate strenuously for exclusion. It is true that the appellant had assailed the credibility of Crown witnesses, and indeed that credibility was the vital issue at trial. However, the circumstances of the case itself, indicating a violation by the appellant of his parole conditions, and the substance of the appellant's defence, indicating clearly the appellant's involvement in cocaine transactions, would have served to bring home to the jury the unsavoury criminal character of the appellant and, on the theory that such evidence affects credibility, this objective would have been fulfilled. This, along with the evidence of the appellant's previous convictions for theft and breaking and entering, amply served the purpose of impeaching his credibility. Indeed, the convictions for theft and breaking and entering, though quite remote in time, would appear far more probative of a disposition for dishonesty than a conviction for murder. The latter, in the circumstances of the case, added very little, if anything, to the jury's perception of the appellant's character for veracity; on the other hand, in the words of Hutcheon J.A. in the court below [p. 230], "it might well be that the fact that he had been convicted some years before of a similar offence might have been the last ounce which turned the scales against him". The jury's actions at trial in this case in no way diminish this possibility.

CONCLUSION

I conclude, therefore, that s. 12 of the Canada Evidence Act, when read in conjunction with the salutary common law discretion to exclude prejudicial evidence, does not violate an accused's right to a fair trial or deprive him of his liberty except in accordance with the principles of fundamental justice. Here, the trial judge erred in law in failing to recognize the existence of the exclusionary discretion described above, and consequently in admitting into evidence the previous conviction for murder. Given my belief that the introduction of this evidence was, in the circumstances of the case, unjustifiably prejudicial to the fairness of the appellant's trial, I am unable to conclude that no substantial wrong or miscarriage of justice was occasioned thereby. I would therefore allow the appeal, quash the conviction and order a new trial pursuant to s. 613(2)(*b*) of the Criminal Code. I would answer the first constitutional question in the negative, and consequently find it unnecessary to answer the second constitutional question.

Appeal dismissed.[38]

———————————

See Knazan, "Putting Evidence Out of Your Mind" (1999), 42 Crim. L.Q. 501. For how the discretion under section 12 of the Canada Evidence Act has been exercised, see Chapt. 7, 3(c) Character of the Witness, *infra*.

In *R. v. Potvin*[39] the Supreme Court had to deal with the admissibility at trial of former testimony. The accused and two others, D. and T., were charged with murder. The Crown proceeded against the accused first, and called D. as a witness. Although D. had testified at the preliminary inquiry, he refused to testify at the trial. The transcript of D.'s testimony at the preliminary was received into evidence at trial pursuant to section 643 [now section 715] of the Criminal Code,

———————————

38.   See generally Delisle, "Case Note to *Corbett v. R.*" (1988), 67 Can. Bar. Rev. 706.
39.   (1989), 68 C.R. (3d) 193 (S.C.C.).

*TJ = discretion to exclude if prejudicial effect outweighs its probative value.

DISCRETION AND THE LAW OF EVIDENCE   115

and the accused was convicted. An appeal from his conviction was dismissed, and the accused appealed further. The Supreme Court allowed the appeal and ordered a new trial. The court decided that the statutory provision did not violate section 7 or section 11(d) of the Charter. All five judges concluded, however, that a trial judge has a discretion to exclude former testimony, even though the statutory conditions have been met, and determined that the trial judge in this case had failed to exercise that discretion. Madam Justice Wilson, Justices Lamer and Sopinka concurring, wrote:

> . . . In my view there are two main types of mischief at which the discretion might be aimed. First, the discretion could be aimed at situations in which there has been unfairness in the manner in which the evidence was obtained. . . . An example of unfairness in obtaining the testimony might be a case in which, although the witness was temporarily absent from Canada, the Crown could have obtained the witness's attendance at trial with a minimal degree of effort. Another example might be a case in which the Crown was aware at the time when the evidence was initially taken that the witness would not be available to testify at the trial but did not inform the accused of this fact so that he could make best use of the opportunity to cross-examine the witness at the earlier proceeding. . . .
> A different concern at which the discretion might have been aimed is the effect of the admission of the previously-taken evidence on the fairness of the trial itself. This concern flows from the principle of the law of evidence that evidence may be excluded if it is highly prejudicial to the accused and of only modest probative value.
>
> . . . .
>
> In my view, . . . s. 643(1) of the Code should be construed as conferring a discretion on the trial judge broader than the traditional evidentiary principle that evidence should be excluded if its prejudicial effect exceeds its probative value.[40]

Madam Justice Wilson stressed that even evidence of high probative value could be excluded if admission would render the trial unfair. She noted that the credibility of the witness in this case was critical, the jury had no opportunity to observe the witness's demeanour, and the trial judge had failed to consider this possible lack of fairness.

Similar discretionary treatment was accorded the reception of videotaped interviews under section 715.1 in the Criminal Code. In *R. v. L. (D.O.)*[41] the Supreme Court dealt with the admissibility of videotaped statements of young complainants in sexual assault cases pursuant to section 715.1 of the Criminal Code. The question was whether the statutory provision was consistent with principles of fundamental justice. The court of appeal had held that section 715.1 contravened sections 7 and 11(d) of the Charter and could not be sustained under section 1. The Supreme Court decided that the statutory provision did not violate the Charter as there was discretion in the trial judge in the application of the section. Lamer, C.J., La Forest, Sopinka, Cory, McLachlin and Iacobucci, JJ., concurring, wrote:

> [T]he incorporation of judicial discretion into s. 715.1, which permits a trial judge to edit or refuse to admit videotaped evidence where its prejudicial effect outweighs its

---

40. *Ibid.*, at pp. 236-37.
41. [1993] 4 S.C.R. 419.

probative value, ensures that s. 715.1 is consistent with fundamental principles of justice and the right to a fair trial protected by ss. 7 and 11(*d*) of the *Charter*.[42]

L'Heureux-Dubé, J. (Gonthier, J., concurring), wrote:

[T]he wording of s. 715.1 itself supports the interpretation that such a provision accommodates traditional rules of evidence and judicial discretion. Thus, in addition to the power to expunge or edit statements where necessary, the trial judge has discretion to refuse to admit the videotape in evidence if its prejudicial effect outweighs its probative value. Properly used, this discretion to exclude admissible evidence ensures the validity of s. 715.1 and is conversant with fundamental principles of justice necessary to safeguard the right to a fair trial enshrined in the *Charter*.[43]

Notice that in both *Potvin* and in *L. (D.O.)* the statutory provisions say nothing about discretion in the trial judge. The judges in the Supreme Court of Canada, to ensure a fair trial, read the requirement in.

R. v. HARRER
[1995] 3 S.C.R. 562, 42 C.R. (4th) 269, 101 C.C.C. (3d) 193

[The accused's boyfriend escaped from custody in Vancouver while awaiting extradition to the United States. The United States immigration officers began an investigation which led them to the accused. The accused was herself suspected of being illegally in the United States. The accused was arrested and she was given the "Miranda" warning against self-incrimination. She was later taken to a State Police post. The immigration officers left her with U.S. Marshals and advised that the Marshals wanted to question her. At some point the interview shifted to the accused's alleged criminal participation in her boyfriend's escape, but she was not given another warning as would be required under the Canadian Charter of Rights. American law does not require a second warning. The accused was returned to Canada, the Marshals forwarded her statements to police in Vancouver, and she was charged with assisting in an escape from custody, contrary to section 147(*a*) of the Criminal Code. At trial, the Crown attempted to adduce the statement to the United States Marshals but the judge ruled that the interrogation violated section 10(*b*) of the Charter, which guarantees the right of a person arrested or detained to retain and instruct counsel without delay. The evidence was rejected on the basis that its admission would bring the administration of justice into disrepute. Accordingly, the accused was acquitted. On appeal, a new trial was ordered on the ground that the Charter has no application to interrogations conducted in the United States. The accused appealed. The appeal was dismissed. The Supreme Court decided that the rights flowing from section 10(*b*) to persons arrested or detained had no application in this case. The Charter applied when the Canadian police began proceedings against the accused. If the admission of crucial evidence, such as the out-of-court self-incriminatory statement, would violate the principles of fundamental justice, the trial would not be fair. Although dicta, the following excerpt emphasizes the trial judge's role in conducting a fair trial.]

La Forest J. (Lamer C.J.C., L'Heureux-Dubé, Sopinka, Gonthier, Cory, and Iacobucci JJ. concurring):—

---

42.   *Ibid.*, at p. 429.
43.   *Ibid.*, at p. 461.

. . . .

I would be inclined to think that evidence obtained following a *Miranda* warning should ordinarily be admitted in evidence at a trial unless in the light of other circumstances the court has reason to think the admission of the evidence would make the trial unfair.

There were no such circumstances here — quite the opposite. As I mentioned, not only was the *Miranda* warning given at the outset of the questioning by the Immigration agents; it was also later recalled to the appellant when the police began their questioning. As well, before the relevant statements were made, the interrogating Marshal impressed upon the appellant the seriousness of her situation and his knowledge that she was involved in the escape. On a reading of the judge's findings, it is abundantly clear that the appellant (whom the trial judge, despite her age, described as a "cagey witness" and as "a street wise and sophisticated young woman" intimately associated with a fugitive sought on charges of high level cocaine trafficking) knew full well that she was being questioned in relation to the very matter in respect of which it is argued a second warning should have been given. Under these circumstances, I am at a loss to understand how these statements would, if admitted, result in the trial being unfair.

I should add that, had the circumstances been such that the admission of the evidence would lead to an unfair trial, I would have had no difficulty rejecting the evidence by virtue of the *Charter*. I would not take this step under s. 24(2), which is addressed to the rejection of evidence that has been wrongfully obtained. Nor would I rely on s. 24(1), under which a judge of competent jurisdiction has the power to grant such remedy to a person who has suffered a *Charter* breach as the court considers just and appropriate. Rather, I would reject the evidence on the basis of the trial judge's duty, now constitutionalized by the enshrinement of a fair trial in the *Charter*, to exercise properly his or her judicial discretion to exclude evidence that would result in an unfair trial.

I shall, however, attempt to put more flesh on this approach because the argument was strongly advanced that since there was no breach of the *Charter* in obtaining the evidence, a prerequisite to the power to exclude evidence under s. 24(2) of the *Charter*, there was no *Charter* based jurisdiction to exclude evidence. The difficulty with this contention is that it fails to appreciate the full nature of a fair trial. As I mentioned, while s. 24(2) is directed to the exclusion of evidence obtained in a manner that infringed a *Charter* right, it does not operate until there is a *Charter* breach. What we are concerned with here is not the remedy for a breach but with the manner in which a trial must be conducted if it is to be fair.

The law of evidence has developed many specific rules to prevent the admission of evidence that would cause a trial to be unfair, but the general principle that an accused is entitled to a fair trial cannot be entirely reduced to specific rules. In *R. v. Corbett*, [1988] 1 S.C.R. 670, a majority of this court made it clear that a judge has a discretion to exclude evidence that would, if admitted, undermine a fair trial; see also *R. v. Potvin*, [1989] 1 S.C.R. 525. . . . In *Thomson Newspapers*, supra, I attempted to explain that this approach is a necessary adjunct to a fair trial as guaranteed by s. 11(*d*) of the Charter in the following passage:

> There can really be no breach of the *Charter* until unfair evidence is admitted. Until that happens, there is no violation of the principles of fundamental justice and no denial of a fair trial. Since the proper admission or rejection of derivative evidence does not admit of a general rule, a flexible mechanism must be found to deal with the issue contextually. That can only be done by the trial judge.

I went on to further explain, as I had in *Corbett*, supra, that the common law principle had now been constitutionalized by the *Charter's* guarantee of a fair trial under s. 11(*d*) of the *Charter*. I continued:

> The fact that this discretion to exclude evidence is grounded in the right to a fair trial has obvious constitutional implications. The right of an accused to a fair hearing is

constitutionalized by s. 11(*d*), a right that would in any event be protected under s. 7 as an aspect of the principles of fundamental justice.

The effect of s. 11(*d*), then, is to transform this high duty of the judge at common law to a constitutional imperative. As I noted in *Thomson Newspapers*, judges must, as guardians of the Constitution, exercise this discretion where necessary to give effect to the *Charter's* guarantee of a fair trial. In a word, there is no need to resort to s. 24(2), or s. 24(1) for that matter. In such circumstances, the evidence is excluded to conform to the constitutional mandate guaranteeing a fair trial, i.e., to prevent a trial from being unfair at the outset.

McLACHLIN, J. (MAJOR, J. concurring):—

. . . .

[T]he argument [is] that the conduct of the American police prior to the taking of the statement requires its exclusion from evidence to preserve a fair trial in Canada. The argument is simply put. Every person charged in Canada has a right to a fair trial. The Canadian courts are bound to provide this fair trial, and to this end may exclude evidence which would render a trial unfair. Admission of Harrer's second statement would render her trial unfair. Therefore the trial judge correctly excluded it.

The first premise of this argument does not permit of dissent. Every person tried in Canada is entitled to a fair trial. The right to a fair trial is the foundation upon which our criminal justice system rests. It can neither be denied nor compromised. The common law has for centuries proclaimed it, and the Canadian Charter confirms it. Section 11(d) provides that "Any person charged with an offence has the right . . . to be presumed innocent until proven guilty according to law in a fair and public hearing by an independent and impartial tribunal". The right to a fair trial is also a "principle of fundamental justice" which s. 7 of the Charter requires to be observed where the liberty of the subject is at stake.

The second premise of the argument, that judges have the power to exclude evidence where its admission would render the trial unfair, while less obvious, is readily resolved. At common law, a trial judge has a discretion to exclude evidence "if the strict rules of admissibility would operate unfairly against the accused": *Kuruma v. The Queen*. Similarly, in Canada, the discretion allows exclusion of evidence that "would undermine the right to a fair trial": *R. v. Corbett*, considering s. 12 of the Canada Evidence Act. . . .

In addition to the common law exclusionary power, the Charter guarantees the right to a fair trial (s. 11(d)) and provides new remedies for breaches of the legal rights accorded to an accused person. Evidence obtained in breach of the Charter may only be excluded under s. 24(2): *R. v. Therens*, [1985] 1 S.C.R. 613. Evidence not obtained in breach of the Charter but the admission of which may undermine the right to a fair trial may be excluded under s. 24(1), which provides for "such remedy as the court considers appropriate and just in the circumstances" for Charter breaches. Section 24(1) applies to prospective breaches, although its wording refers to "infringe" and "deny" in the past tense: *Operation Dismantle Inc. v. The Queen*, [1985] 1 S.C.R. 441. It follows that s. 24(1) permits a court to exclude evidence which has not been obtained in violation of the Charter, but which would render the trial unfair contrary to s. 11(d) of the Charter.

. . . .

Whether a particular piece of evidence would render a trial unfair is often a matter of some difficulty. . . .

At base, a fair trial is a trial that appears fair, both from the perspective of the accused and the perspective of the community. A fair trial must not be confused with the most advantageous trial possible from the accused's point of view: *R. v. Lyons*, [1987] 2 S.C.R. 309, at p. 362, per La Forest J. Nor must it be conflated with the perfect trial; in the real world, perfection is seldom attained. A fair trial is one which satisfies the public interest in getting at the truth, while preserving basic procedural fairness to the accused.

Evidence may render a trial unfair for a variety of reasons. The way in which it was taken may render it unreliable. Its potential for misleading the trier of fact may outweigh such minimal value it might possess. Again, the police may have acted in such an abusive fashion that the court concludes the admission of the evidence would irremediably taint the fairness of the trial itself. In the case at bar, police abuse or unfairness is the only ground raised, and hence the only one with which we need concern ourselves.

. . . .

The question is whether the failure of the foreign police to comply with the procedures required under the Charter in Canada so taints the evidence that its admission would result in an unfair trial. In my view, it does not. This is because the police conduct of which Harrer complains was, viewed in all the circumstances of this case, including the expectations of Harrer in the place where the evidence was taken, neither unfair or abusive. Since the police conduct was not unfair, it follows necessarily that its admission cannot render the trial unfair.

R. v. WHITE

[1999] 2 S.C.R. 417, 24 C.R. (5th) 201, 135 C.C.C. (3d) 257

[The accused was charged under the Criminal Code with leaving the scene of an accident. Provincial legislation required persons involved in a traffic accident to complete an accident report. The Court needed to decide whether the accused's statements made under compulsion in the traffic report were admissible in criminal proceedings.]

IACOBUCCI, J. (LAMER, C.J. and GONTHIER, McLACHLIN, BASTARACHE and BINNIE, JJ. concurring):—

. . . .

Although I agree with the majority position in *Harrer* that it may not be necessary to use s. 24(1) in order to exclude evidence whose admission would render the trial unfair, I agree also with McLachlin J.'s finding in that case that s. 24(1) may appropriately be employed as a discrete source of a court's power to exclude such evidence. In the present case, involving an accused who is entitled under s. 7 to use immunity in relation to certain compelled statements in subsequent criminal proceedings, exclusion of the evidence is required. Although the trial judge could have excluded the evidence pursuant to his common law duty to exclude evidence whose admission would render the trial unfair, he chose instead to exclude the evidence pursuant to s. 24(1) of the Charter. I agree that he was entitled to do so.

[Justice L'Heureux-Dubé dissented on the basis that there was evidence to conclude that the third statement, which was made after the police officer had informed the accused of her section 10(*b*) Charter rights and her right to silence, was admissible, since it was voluntary and freely made.]

In addition to the discretion witnessed above we should recognize of course that there is given in the Charter an express discretion to exclude evidence obtained in violation of an accused's rights. Section 24 provides:

24. (1) Anyone whose rights or freedoms, as guaranteed by this Charter, have been infringed or denied may apply to a court of competent jurisdiction to obtain such remedy as the court considers appropriate and just in the circumstances.

(2) Where, in proceedings under subsection (1), a court concludes that evidence was obtained in a manner that infringed or denied any rights or freedoms guaranteed

by this Charter, the evidence shall be excluded if it is established that, having regard to all the circumstances, the admission of it in the proceedings would bring the administration of justice into disrepute.

We will touch on this briefly in the final chapter of this book. A major consideration in the exclusion of evidence under this section is the seriousness of the violation and we therefore determined that a thorough treatment of this would be better done in a Criminal Procedure course.

A sound exercise of discretion is absolutely essential to the proper application of the rules of evidence and recognition of that fact will likely produce greater actual certainty at the sacrifice only of apparent certainty. In answer to those who fear discretion, listen to Professor Rosenberg:

> Discretion need not be, as Lord Camden said, a synonym for lawlessness or tyranny, if those who created it wield it and review its use are sensitive to the risks and responsibilities it raises, and if they play fair with the system; for the difference between government of law and government of man is not that the lawyers decide cases in one and fools in the other. Men, that is the judges, always decide. The difference is in whether judges are aware of their power, sensitive to their responsibilities and true to the tradition of the common law.[44]

We, properly, trust our judges to make all manner of preliminary and final decisions affecting the outcome of a case. It would be incongruous then to deny them the right to exercise discretion in judging how, and what evidence will be heard by the trier of fact. We should always then be conscious of the policy on which the rule is based, so that we may gauge whether that policy is actually being advanced in the particular application of the rule and whether the policy that gave birth to the rule continues as a viable support.

PROBLEMS

Problem 1

The accused was charged with arson. The incinerated premises had been the home of John Doe. At trial the prosecution tenders into evidence a photograph showing the remains of John's house. In the foreground John Doe's sad face is clearly seen. Is the photograph relevant? Prejudicial? Receivable? If you were acting as counsel for the accused how would you prevent the introduction of the photograph? See *Draper v. Jacklyn*, [1970] S.C.R. 192 and compare *R. v. Wade* (1994), 18 O.R. (3d) 33 (C.A.).

Problem 2

In a prosecution for fraud it was alleged that the accused had misrepresented the effectiveness of a device purportedly useful for forecasting weather. At the trial the accused testified that she had made 100 tests of the device. The prosecutor leads scientific evidence that the tests employed by the accused were not such that a reasonable person could rely on them. Was accused's testimony

---

44.   Rosenberg, *supra*, note 33, at p. 826.

irrelevant? Could you argue that the evidence was nevertheless admissible? How?

Problem 3

In a prosecution for assault causing bodily harm the accused argued self-defence. The incident occurred at Joe's Bar. The accused wants to lead evidence that the alleged victim had a reputation as a bully. That the alleged victim regularly beat on newcomers to the bar. Relevant? Receivable? Does it matter whether the accused was aware of the alleged victim's reputation prior to the incident? Why? If you say the evidence is relevant, what is the premise that rationally connects the evidence offered with the proposition sought to be established? Is that premise indisputable? Usually true? Sometimes true? Rarely true?

Problem 4

The accused was charged with speeding. He allegedly travelled 30 K.P.H. in a school zone that prescribed a limit of 20 K.P.H. The prosecutor wants to call a witness who will testify that he saw the accused, a block away from the school zone, travelling at 40 K.P.H. in a 30 K.P.H. zone. Relevant? Why? Premise? Always or sometimes true? Suppose the observation was made three blocks away? A mile away? Accused wants to tender evidence that the police officer who gave him the speeding ticket that had been told by his superior that week that if he didn't issue his quota of speeding tickets he'd be suspended. Relevant? Prejudicial? Receivable?

Problem 5

The accused is charged with the theft of a rare stamp. The Crown wants to lead evidence that the accused is a stamp collector. Relevant? Premise? Receivable? Sufficient?

Problem 6

The accused is charged with aggravated assault. The charge resulted from a stabbing which occurred during a fight. The accused admitted punching the victim but testified that he fled the scene when he saw S stab the victim. Is accused's flight relevant? Premise? Receivable? What instruction should the judge give to the jury? Suppose the accused didn't flee the scene but rather assisted the medics in treating the victim and gave an exculpatory statement to the police. Is this information relevant? For discussion of "after-the-fact conduct" see *R. v. Arcangioli* (1994), 27 C.R. (4th) 1 (S.C.C.); *R. v. Peavoy* (1997), 9 C.R. (5th) 83 (Ont. C.A.); *R. v. B. (S.C.)* (1997), 10 C.R. (5th) 302 (Ont. C.A.) and *R. v. White*, [1998] 2 S.C.R. 72. See also Kapoor, "Of Unconscious Guilt" (1997), 2 Can. Crim. L.R. 31.

Problem 7

Smith sues Jones for damages arising out of a motor vehicle accident. Jones earlier pleaded guilty to a charge of dangerous driving arising out of the same incident and Smith seeks to tender this fact in evidence. Relevant? Receivable?

See *English v. Richmond*, [1956] S.C.R. 383. If Jones had pleaded not guilty would that fact be relevant? Receivable when tendered by Jones? If he was acquitted would that fact be receivable? If convicted? See *Hollington v. F. Hewthorn & Co.*, [1943] 2 All E.R. 35 (C.A.). Compare *Kennedy v. Tomlinson* (1959), 20 D.L.R. (2d) 273 (Ont. C.A.). See now *Demeter v. Br. Pac. Life Ins. Co.* (1985), 48 O.R. (2d) 266 (C.A.) and *Re Del Core and Ont. College of Pharmacists* (1985), 51 O.R. (2d) 1 (C.A.); leave to appeal to S.C.C. refused (1987), 57 O.R. (2d) 296n (S.C.C.).

Problem 8

The accused is charged with possession of a weapon for a purpose dangerous to the public peace. In his bedroom the police found a loaded .25 calibre pistol. From a kitchen cupboard they seized notes handwritten in Italian. The notes have been translated and an expert has testified that they are a constitution of a secret Italian criminal organization related to the Mafia and that anyone in possession of them almost certainly had to belong to the organization. Are the notes relevant? Receivable? Compare *R. v. Caccamo* (1975), 29 C.R.N.S. 78 (S.C.C.).

Problem 9

Plaintiff sues defendant bus company for personal injuries sustained as the result of negligent operation of a bus claimed to belong to the defendant. On the facts presented the defendant concedes that the evidence warranted the submission to the jury of the question of the operator's negligence in the management of the bus. The accident occurred on Main Street at 1:00 a.m. and the only description of the bus came from the plaintiff who was able to describe the bus simply as "a great big, long, wide affair." Records at City Hall indicate that the defendant bus company was the only bus company licensed to operate on that street. The defendant's timetable shows its buses scheduled to leave North Square for South Square via Main Street at 12:15 a.m., 12:45 a.m., 1:15 a.m., and 1:45 a.m. Are these records relevant? Receivable? Sufficient? Compare *Smith v. Rapid Transit Inc.*, 58 N.E. 2d 754 (Mass. Sup. Ct., 1945). See also *People v. Collins*, 438 P. 2d 33 (Cal. Sup. Ct., 1968).

Problem 10

In a suit for damages alleging negligence in the defendant's failure to maintain his property in a safe condition plaintiff tenders evidence of repairs made by the defendant to his premises subsequent to the incident. Are such repairs relevant to the issue of negligence? Is there relevance by way of indicating the defendant's belief that his premises were defective and that an injury was reasonably foreseeable? If the evidence is relevant should it be received? For competing points of view see the judgments in *Algoma Central Railway v. Herb Fraser & Associates Ltd.* (1988), 66 O.R. (2d) 330 (Ont. Div. Ct.).

Problem 11

In a civil suit for negligence plaintiff seeks to tender evidence that the defendant is insured. Relevant? Plaintiff argues that it is rational to infer that a person who is insured is less apt to careful, as he is fully protected against loss, and to then infer that he was careless on the particular occasion under review. Defendant argues that being insured marks him as one of those careful and wise individuals who take all appropriate precautions against risk. If the evidence is relevant ought it to be received? See *Bowhey v. Theakston*, [1951] S.C.R. 679 and *Dickison v. Montgomery*, [1960] O.R. 544 (C.A.). Compare *Didluck v. Evans* (1968), 63 W.W.R. 555 (Sask. C.A.) and *Currie v. Nova Scotia Trust Co.* (1969), 7 D.L.R. (3d) 588 (N.S.T.D.).

Problem 12

The plaintiff sued to recover the proceeds of life insurance policies covering his deceased wife. The insurance company resisted the claim on the basis that public policy precluded any person benefiting from his own criminal act. Is the accused's conviction of murdering his wife relevant? Receivable? Compare *Hollington v. Hewthorn*, [1943] 2 All E.R. 35 (C.A.) and *Demeter v. British Pacific Life Ins. Co.* (1983), 43 O.R. (2d) 33, affirmed (1984), 48 O.R. (2d) 266 (C.A.).

Problem 13

After his arrest for the murder of David, the accused, while at the police station, asked to make a phone call to his father. The officer who took the accused to the telephone heard the accused say during the call "... I killed David ...". The officer stated that he did not hear what was said before and after those three words. Relevant? Receivable? Compare the different points of view in *R. v. Ferris*, (1994), 27 C.R. (4th) 141 (Alta. C.A.).

4

Character Evidence

1. HABIT

Evidence of how a person acted on another occasion is evidence of a circumstance from which we ask the trier of fact to infer that the person acted in a similar fashion on the occasion being litigated. If the evidence is that the person always, invariably, acted in a certain way, the circumstantial evidence is very probative and deserves to be received. We label this as evidence of Habit but see it for what it is — a piece of circumstantial evidence, more specific than evidence of the person's general character but differing only in degree and not in kind. If the circumstantial evidence indicates invariable habit the evidence is very powerful. If the evidence is that the person normally acted in that way the circumstantial evidence is less powerful. If the evidence is that he acted in that way occasionally the court may have concerns that the time necessary to hear the evidence may not be justified given the low probative value. If the evidence is of the person's general character or personality trait, the court recognizes that, even though the person' s character or trait has relevance, the probative value may be outweighed by competing considerations and should be excluded. The court recognizes that even so-called "good people" sometimes do bad things and "bad people" do good things. Plumbing the depths of their character may not be worth the time and trouble. Determining receivability is thus seen to be a matter for the trial judge's discretion where she weighs probative value against the dangers of consumption of time, confusion of the issues and prejudice to the proper outcome of the trial.

McCormick distinguished between habit and character:

> Character and habit are close akin. Character is a generalized description of one's disposition, or of one's disposition in respect to a general trait, such as honesty, temperance, or peacefulness. "Habit" in modern usage, both lay and psychological, is more specific. It describes one's regular response to a repeated specific situation. If we speak of character for care, we think of the person's tendency to act prudently in all the varying situations of life, in business, family life, in handling automobiles and in walking across the street. A habit, on the other hand, is the person's regular practice of meeting a particular kind of situation with a specific type of conduct, such as the habit of going down a particular stairway two stairs at a time, or of giving the hand signal for a left turn, or of alighting from railway cars while they are moving. The doing of the habitual acts may become semi-automatic.
>
> Character may be thought of as the sum of one's habits though doubtless it is more than this. But unquestionably the uniformity of one's response to habit is far greater than the consistency with which one's conduct conforms to character or disposition.[1]

---

1. McCormick, *Evidence* (3d ed.), p. 462.

BELKNAP v. MEAKES
(1989), 64 D.L.R. (4th) 452 (B.C.C.A.)

[The Court allowed an appeal from a finding of negligence.]

SEATON, J.A. (HUTCHEON and WALLACE, JJ.A. concurring):—

. . . .

The defence had a difficult time putting its case. Dr. Meakes was prevented from saying what he did before the operation. He could not specifically remember it. That is understandable. Nearly three years elapsed between the operation and the trial, and two and one-half years elapsed between the operation and the time the allegation of negligent blood pressure management was raised. Dr. Meakes said that his "pre-operative assessment is a very standard part of my practice" and that he could say what had happened "because this is a habit from which I do not waiver". The trial judge said that he did not think the evidence was admissible unless the witness could "remember what he said to Mr. Belknap" and that if the evidence of Dr. Meakes's practice from which he did not waiver was admitted it carried so little weight that it would be "not much help to me at all".

If a person can say of something he regularly does in his professional life that he invariably does it in a certain way, that surely is evidence and possibly convincing evidence that he did it in that way on the day in question.

Wigmore on Evidence, vol. IA (Tillers rev. 1983), states that there is no reason why habit should not be used as evidence either of negligent action or of careful action (para. 97), and that habit should be admissible as a substitute for present recollection. *Phipson on Evidence*, 13th ed. (1982), paras. 9-22, reaches a similar conclusion.

Similar reasoning admits evidence of a general course of business, a question dealt with by the New Brunswick Court of Appeal in *Medical Arts Ltd. v. Minister of Municipal Affairs* (1977), 17 N.B.R. (2d) 147 at p. 152:

> The evidence adduced on behalf of the Minister of the usual course of business in the district office together with the certificate of the post office employee date stamped September 3, 1974 were admissible to prove the sending to the respondent of the documents referred to in s. 25(4) of the Act. *Phipson on Evidence*, 7th ed. states at p. 102:
>
>> To prove that an act has been done, it is admissible to prove any general course of business or office, whether public or private, according to which it would ordinarily have been done; there being a probability that the general course will be followed in the particular case.

The reasoning of Dixon, J. in *Martin v. Osborne*[2] is instructive with respect to the distinction between character and habit. The defendant was prosecuted for driving a commercial passenger vehicle without a licence. As part of the evidence to establish that the passengers were carried for reward on the day complained of, the prosecution tendered evidence that the defendant carried passengers between the same termini on the two preceding days, that different passengers were carried on each journey and possessed no common characteristic, that the vehicle stood at convenient rendezvous for passengers and that the journey was in each instance by the same route. The defendant objected that this evidence was irrelevant. Dixon, J. wrote:

2.　(1936), 55 C.L.R. 367 (H.C.).

The moral tendencies of persons, their proneness to acts or omissions of a particular description, their reputations and their associations are in general not matters which it is lawful to take into account, and evidence disclosing them, if not otherwise relevant, is rigidly excluded. But the class of acts and occurrences that may be considered includes circumstances whose relation to the fact in issue consists in the probability, or increased probability, judged rationally upon common experience, that they would not be found unless the fact to be proved also existed. . . .

The acts of a party are admissible against him whenever they form a component in a combination of circumstances which is unlikely to occur without the fact in issue also occurring. The repetition of acts or occurrences is often the very thing which makes it probable that they are accompanied by some further fact. The frequency with which a set of circumstances recurs or the regularity with which a course of conduct is pursued may exclude, as unreasonable, any other explanation or hypothesis than the truth of the fact to be proved. For example, the probability that the neglected condition of a barber's implements was the cause of his customer contracting barber's itch becomes much higher when it appears that about the same time two more of his habitual customers also contracted the disease (*Hales v. Kerr*). If four close relatives of a woman, dwelling in her house and eating meals prepared by her, die of arsenical poisoning one after another within a few months, the inference that she wilfully administered the poison has more support than if one death only occurred in such circumstances (*R. v. Geering*). The discovery of a number of dead bodies of infants buried in the ground at different premises lately occupied by a baby farmer greatly increases the probability of her having murdered an infant entrusted to her charge which has disappeared (*R. v. Makin; R. v. Knorr*). An inference from circumstances that on a specific occasion an act of adultery or of incest took place between a man and a woman may be uncertain until it appears that a previous sexual relationship existed between them, but the addition of that fact may remove doubt (*R. v. Ball; McConville v. Bayley; R. v. Goldsworthy*). For a medical man or midwife frequently to procure abortion makes it unlikely that his or her proved association with a specific case of abortion was not criminal (*R. v. Bond; R. v. Graham*). The repetition by an accounting party of the same error or kind of error in calculating at excessive amounts the totals of his disbursements makes it probable that the overstatement was fraudulent (*R. v. Richardson*; cf. *R. v. Proud; R. v. Garsed; R. v. Hiddilston; Hardgrave v. The King; R. v. Finlayson*). In the same way repeated utterings of coins or notes in fact counterfeit or forged, and repeated obtainings of money by representations in fact untrue increase the probability that on a specific occasion a coin was uttered or a pretence made with guilty knowledge and intent (*R. v. Whiley; R. v. Forster; R. v. Weeks; R. v. Francis*).

In the present case the evidence to which the defendant objected, when combined with that describing the actual journey laid as the offence, shows that for three consecutive days the Hupmobile car behaved exactly as service cars do, and that for the greater part of that time it was under the control of the defendant. . . .

In my opinion such evidence was admissible, because it tended to show that the defendant was operating the car regularly for the carriage of passengers between the two cities, and thus to make it improbable that the passengers were not carried for reward.[3]

R. v. WATSON — *leading case*

(1996), 50 C.R. (4th) 245, 108 C.C.C. (3d) 310 (Ont. C.A.)

[The accused was charged with murder. The Crown took the position that the accused, with Headley and Cain, went to the deceased's premises, armed,

---

3.   *Ibid.*, at pp. 375-76; numerous citations for each of the examples are here omitted.

with the intention of killing the deceased. The deceased went to the rear of the premises while the accused remained near the front office. The Crown took the position that the accused remained on guard in the front area and was guilty as an aider and abetter. The accused took the position that the shooting was the result of a dispute which arose in the context of a private drug transaction between the deceased and Headley. According to the accused, the deceased was hit five times by Headley, and the deceased shot Cain, who was standing some distance away, unarmed. The accused claimed to have panicked, then fled the scene with Headley and Cain.

The accused wanted to introduce the evidence of Mair, a good friend of the deceased, to demonstrate that the deceased had a habit of carrying a gun. In a statement to the police, Mair had said that the deceased always carried a gun; in fact, the gun was like a credit card for the deceased, since he never left home without it. The trial judge found that this evidence was irrelevant. He concluded that there was no viable issue of self-defence, that there was no evidence that the deceased had a gun on the day in question, and that there was no evidence that he fired a gun, if he did have a gun in his possession on that date.

The accused was convicted of manslaughter and successfully appealed.]

DOHERTY J.A. (MORDEN A.C.J.O. and ARBOUR J.A. concurring): —

. . . .

Where a person's conduct in given circumstances is in issue, evidence that the person repeatedly acted in a certain way when those circumstances arose in the past has been received as circumstantial evidence that the person acted in conformity with past practice on the occasion in question: *Cross and Tapper on Evidence*, 8th ed. (1995) at pp. 25-26; *Wigmore on Evidence*: Tillers Rev. (1983) Vol. 1A, pp. 1607-1610; R. Delisle, *Evidence Principles and Problems*, 4th ed. (1996) at p. 38; *McCormick on Evidence*, 4th ed. (1992), Vol. I, pp. 825-830. For example, in *McCormick* at p. 826 it is said:

> Surely any sensible person in investigating whether a given individual did a particular act would be greatly helped in his inquiry by evidence as to whether that individual was in the habit of doing it.

The position taken in these authorities is, in my opinion, consistent with human experience and logic. The fact that a person is in the habit of doing a certain thing in a given situation suggests that on a specific occasion in which those circumstances arose the person acted in accordance with established practice. It makes the conclusion that the person acted in a particular way more likely than it would be without the evidence of habit. Evidence of habit is therefore properly viewed as circumstantial evidence that a person acted in a certain way on the occasion in issue.

Evidence of habit is closely akin to, but not identical to, evidence of disposition. Evidence of habit involves an inference of conduct on a given occasion based on an established pattern of past conduct. It is an inference of conduct from conduct. Evidence of disposition involves an inference of the existence of a state of mind (disposition) from a person's conduct on one or more previous occasions and a further inference of conduct on the specific occasion based on the existence of that state of mind. Evidence of habit proceeds on the basis that repeated conduct in a given situation is a reliable predictor of conduct in that situation. Evidence of disposition is premised on the belief that a person's disposition is a reliable predictor of conduct in a given situation.

The distinction between evidence of habit and evidence of disposition is demonstrated by a comparison of this case and the facts in *Scopelliti*. Here the defence wanted to show that the deceased habitually carried a gun in the past and to invite the jury to infer from that prior conduct that he had a gun when he was shot. In *Scopelliti*, the defence wanted to show that the deceased had on occasions in the past been the aggressor in physical confrontations with others and to invite the jury to infer, first that the deceased was a physically aggressive person (his disposition), and second that the deceased's actions at the relevant time were in keeping with his physically aggressive nature. Like evidence of habit, evidence of disposition can constitute circumstantial evidence of conduct on a specific occasion. The inferences necessary to render disposition evidence relevant to prove conduct on a specific occasion may be more difficult to draw than those required where evidence of habit is tendered.

The recognition that evidence of habit is relevant to prove conduct on a specific occasion begs the more fundamental question — what is a habit? *McCormick* at p. 826 describes habit as:

> the person's regular practice of responding to a particular kind of situation with a specific type of conduct.

Habit therefore involves a repeated and specific response to a particular situation.

Mair's graphic assertion that the deceased carried a gun "like a credit card. He never left home without it" strongly suggests repeated and specific conduct. Mair's statement does not suggest that the deceased's possession of a weapon was limited to any particular situation. To the contrary, Mair indicated that the deceased always carried a gun. The general nature of the habit described by Mair does not affect the relevance of the evidence, but would, along with other aspects of the evidence (e.g., the duration and regularity of the habit), go to the weight to be given to the evidence by the jury.

Having concluded that evidence that the deceased always carried a gun was relevant to the question of whether he had a gun when he was shot, I turn to the second level of the relevance inquiry. Mair's evidence may put the deceased in possession of a gun at the material time, but standing alone it cannot support the inference that he fired the gun at that time. In fact, Mair's evidence did not suggest that the deceased had ever used his gun. The further inference from possession to use of the weapon is essential to make Mair's evidence relevant to any issue in the trial. The availability of that inference requires a consideration of the rest of the evidence.

There were at most three people at the back of the warehouse. The deceased and Cain were shot and the evidence does not suggest that Cain shot himself. He must have been shot by either Headley or the deceased. Headley definitely shot the deceased and at least two of the bullets which hit the deceased came from a different gun than the one used to shoot Cain. There were, therefore, two possibilities. Either Cain was shot by the deceased or Headley fired two different guns hitting the deceased with one and Cain with the other. In my opinion, a jury, having concluded that the deceased was armed, could have inferred that Cain was shot not by his friend Headley, but by the deceased who was the target of Headley's assault.

I am further satisfied, had the jury inferred that the deceased was armed and fired a weapon, that those inferences could logically have influenced the jury's conclusion as to the origins of the shooting. If the deceased was unarmed, the circumstances strongly suggest a preconceived plan to shoot the deceased. If the deceased was armed and used his weapon, then the possibility that the shooting was a result of a spontaneous confrontation between Headley and the deceased, both of whom were armed, becomes a viable one. If the shooting was the product of an armed confrontation between the two men it could reasonably be inferred that the confrontation arose during the discussion involving Headley and the deceased. If the confrontation arose in this manner, it offered strong support for the appellant's contention that he was not party to any plan to kill or do harm to the deceased. Therefore, evidence supporting the inferences that the deceased was armed and used a weapon during the confrontation made the defence position as to the appellant's non-involvement in any plan to kill or do harm to the deceased more viable than it would have been if those inferences were not available. Mair's proposed evidence, which provided the basis for those inferences, was, therefore, relevant to a material fact in issue. In so concluding, I do not pass on the cogency of the inferences relied on by the defence or attempt to measure the effect of the proposed evidence on the jury's assessment of the appellant's liability. I limit myself to the inquiry demanded by our concept of relevancy.

2. CHARACTER

(a) Introduction

Before examining the evidence rules concerning character we need to recognize that character evidence may be relevant in different ways. A person's conduct or reputation previous to the event being litigated may be relevant to a material issue in the case without the necessity of the trier of fact inferring that the person acted in conformity with his or her previous conduct or reputation on the occasion under review. For example, in a case of assault, a claim of self-defence might be founded on the accused's belief, based on his understanding of the victim's previous conduct or reputation, that the victim had a disposition towards violent behaviour; such a belief, if honestly held, could cause the accused to view the victim's conduct with apprehension and so cause the accused to strike out at the victim. In a prosecution for sexual assault, the accused may defend on the basis of a mistaken belief in consent and may seek to demonstrate the reasonableness of such belief as founded in his understanding of the victim's disposition toward indiscriminate sexual intercourse which in turn was founded on his appreciation of the victim's previous conduct or reputation. The chain of reasoning which we ask the trier of fact to follow in these cases does not involve the necessity of inferring that the person acted in conformity with his or her character. The evidence of character is led, and the trier is asked simply to infer from it that the accused's belief was genuine.

Occasionally the character of a person is not just relevant to a fact in issue but rather is itself a material point in the case; an operative fact which dictates rights and liabilities. For example, in an action for defamation in which justification is pleaded, the plaintiff's reputation or character is the determining matter. An action for wrongful dismissal might include as a material issue the lack of fitness or competency of the employee.

When the character of a person is relevant to a fact in issue other than by inferring from the character to the conduct of the person, or when the substantive law makes the character material as the very core of the inquiry, evidence of it must be admitted. This part of the chapter is concerned, however, with the canons of exclusion which the law of evidence has created for the reception of character as circumstantial evidence of how a person acted during the material incident; character evidence of this sort is seen to be relevant on the premise that character reflects disposition and a person's disposition to act, think or feel in a particular way is evidence from which it might be inferred that he or she behaved in conformity with that character on the particular occasion.

The common law assumes that character evidence is predictive of behaviour; that a person's behaviour is governed by personality traits. The common law assumes, for example, that if there is evidence that the accused has behaved aggressively in the past, that evidence has probative worth in determining if he committed the assault with which he is now charged. Some disagree:

> Empirical research, however, has not only failed to validate trait theory but has generally rejected it. As Walter Mischel notes: "The initial assumptions of trait-state

theory were logical, inherently plausible, and also consistent with common sense and intuitive impressions about personality. Their real limitation turned out to be empirical — they simply have not been supported adequately." Instead, the research shows that behaviour is largely shaped by specific situational determinants that do not lend themselves easily to predictions about individual behaviour. . . . From this psychological perspective, evidence that a witness has been convicted of a felony involving dishonesty or has cheated on his taxes may or may not tell us anything about whether he was truthful on the stand. Likewise, evidence that the accused was engaged in an altercation after a New Year's Eve party may tell us nothing about his behaviour during a peace demonstration. These findings threaten the common law's basic assumptions about the probative value of character evidence.[4]

While empirical findings may threaten, the common law nevertheless continues with its assumptions.

R. v. CLARKE
(1998), 18 C.R. (5th) 219, 129 C.C.C. (3d) 1 (Ont. C.A.)

[The issue concerned the admissibility of evidence of a witness's reputation for veracity. It was resolved that questions could be put to an impeaching witness concerning a witness's reputation, or character, for truth-telling. In the course of approving such evidence the court offered the following advice.]

ROSENBERG J.A. (MCMURTRY C.J.O. and LABROSSE J.A. concurring): —

The theory upon which the admissibility of this evidence is based, the "trait or generality theory" has been criticized. It has been argued that there is no such thing as stable personality traits from which one could reasonably predict how a person would act in a given situation. To the contrary, it is argued that a theory of "situationism" provides a more reasonable basis for predicting behaviour. According to this theory, behaviour is determined almost exclusively by environmental factors, by the situation in which the actors find themselves. However, even this theory has been found to be flawed and trait theory has come back into its own. Susan M. Davies describes the understanding of social scientists, S.M. Davies, "Evidence of Character to Prove Conduct: A Reassessment of Relevancy" (1991), 27 Crim. L.B. 504 at 516-17:

Using improved methodology, trait theorists are now able to demonstrate the existence in individuals of consistent behavioral tendencies over a sample of situations, and to predict average behaviour accurately. In fact, the usefulness of trait information in predicting behaviour is no longer controverted by members of the psychology community. The most outspoken critic of trait theory has conceded that traits exist and that trait theorists 'can predict many things about people at levels of confidence that are reasonable for various goals and purposes.' Even more significant for the forensic consideration of character is the fact that most psychologists now recognize that, as a general matter, a lay person, given information about a subject's past behaviour, can predict the subject's future behaviour with a significant degree of accuracy.

(b) Character of Parties in Civil Cases

A person's character or disposition is commonly taken into account when we seek to forecast how the person will respond to a future situation or to judge

---

4.   Mendez, "California's New Law on Character Evidence: The Impact of Recent Psychological Studies" (1984), 31 U.C.L.A. Law Rev. 1003, 1052.

how he did respond to a past situation. From our common sense and experience we view his character as rationally probative and hence his character may be regarded as relevant in judicial proceedings.

Generally speaking, the character of the plaintiff or defendant in a civil case is not receivable for the purpose of proving that the litigant acted in conformity therewith on the occasion under review. In the old case of *A.G. v. Radloff,*[5] Baron Martin "reasoned":

> In criminal cases evidence of the good character of the accused is most properly and with good reason admissible in evidence, because there is a fair and just presumption that a person of good character would not commit a crime; but in civil cases such evidence is with equal good reason not admitted, because no presumption would fairly arise, in the very great proportion of such cases, from the good character of the defendant, that he did not commit the breach of contract or of civil duty alleged against him.

The reasoning is clearly strained. If character is relevant in one instance it must be relevant in the other. Perhaps the distinction is to be justified on the basis that in a criminal case, with the disparity in resources between the litigants and the consequences for the accused, the accused is entitled to lead any evidence that could possibly affect the result. In civil cases the character evidence is excluded, not because it is irrelevant, but because it may confuse the issues and may unfairly surprise the opposing litigants.

(c) Character of Accused in Criminal Cases

(i) *When Character Evidence May be Led*

Shortly stated, the accused is entitled to lead evidence of his own good character but, generally speaking, the prosecution is not entitled to lead evidence of the accused's bad character. As with most general rules there are exceptions: the prosecution is entitled to lead evidence of bad character if the accused leads evidence of good character thereby choosing to put his character in issue and will also be entitled to introduce evidence of the accused's previous bad conduct if this meets certain tests for what is known as "similar fact evidence."

In criminal prosecutions from an early period, the prosecutor has had the right to the last word with the jury unless the accused calls no evidence. In *R. v. Stannard*[6] the accused called no evidence directly bearing upon the facts of the case, but did call witnesses to his good character and the court was asked to rule whether the prosecutor had the right to address the jury last. Patterson, J. ruled:

> I cannot in principle make any distinction between evidence of facts, and evidence of character: the latter is equally laid before the jury as the former, as being relevant to the question of guilty or not guilty: the object of laying it before the jury is to induce them to believe, from the improbability that a person of good character should have conducted himself as alleged, that there is some mistake or misrepresentation in the evidence on the part of the prosecution, and it is strictly evidence in the case.[7]

[handwritten margin note: - if ACC calls only character evidence, may still address the jury last]

---

5.   (1854), 156 E.R. 366, 371.
6.   (1837), 173 E.R. 295 (N.P.); and see *R. v. McMillan* (1975), 23 C.C.C. (2d) 160, 167 (Ont. C.A.); affirmed [1977] 2 S.C.R. 824.
7.   *Ibid.,* at p. 296.

It was at one time thought that character evidence was only useful in borderline cases. Martin, J.A., in _R. v. Tarrant_,[8] wrote:

> Evidence of good character is evidence which has a bearing on the improbability of the accused committing the offence and also is relevant to his credibility. The effect of the charge by the learned trial Judge was to deprive character evidence of any use unless the jury was in doubt or the scales were evenly balanced. It need scarcely be pointed out that if the jury were in doubt or if the scales were equally balanced it would be their duty to acquit whether or not there was evidence of good character. The evidence of good character may, along with all the other evidence, create or result in the jury having a reasonable doubt.

Just as good character is relevant, so too evidence of the accused's bad character is relevant to whether he committed the complained of act. We might rationally infer that on the occasion under review the accused may have acted in conformity with his character, his disposition. While it is relevant, the law has created a canon of exclusion lest the trier of fact give it more probative force than it warrants or be diverted from judging the action to judging the man. In the leading case of _R. v. Rowton_[9] Willes, J. wrote of character evidence:

> It is strictly relevant to the issue; but such evidence is not admissible upon the part of the prosecution ... because if the prosecution were allowed to go into such evidence we should have the whole life of the prisoner ripped up, and as has been witnessed in the proceedings of jurisdictions where such evidence is admissible upon a charge preferred, you might begin by showing that when a boy at school he had robbed an orchard and so read the rest of his conduct and the whole of his life; and the result would be that a man on his trial would be overwhelmed by prejudice instead of being convicted on affirmative evidence, which the law of this country requires. The prosecution is prevented from giving such evidence for reasons rather of policy and humanity than because proof that the prisoner was a bad character is not relevant to the issue, — it is relevant to the issue, but it is expedient for the sake of letting in all the evidence which might possibly throw light upon the subject; you might arrive at justice in one case and you might do injustice in ninety-nine.

And Baron Parke in _Attorney General v. Hitchcock_:[10]

> We cannot enter into a collateral question as to the man's having committed a crime on some former occasion, one reason being, that it would lead to complicated issues and long inquiries; and another, that a party cannot be expected to be prepared to defend the whole of the actions of his life.

Should the accused lead evidence of his own good character, however, the prosecution is entitled to lead evidence of bad character in rebuttal lest the trier

---

8.   (1982), 63 C.C.C. (2d) 385, 388 (Ont. C.A.). And see _R. v. Yadollahi_ (1987), 36 C.C.C. (3d) 478 (Ont. C.A.) ordering a new trial because the trial judge in a sexual assault case omitted to give the jury any instruction as to the use that could be made of character evidence adduced on behalf of the accused showing a good reputation for honesty and integrity. Contrast _R. v. Smith_ (1985), 8 O.A.C. 241 (C.A.) where the court held that the trial judge's failure to review good character evidence in a sexual assault case was not error because "the relevance of a good reputation for honesty has less relevance in relation to sexual offences than a charge of possession of stolen goods."

9.   (1865), 10 Cox. C.C. 25, 38. See the description of French trials where character evidence was freely used.

10. (1847), 1 Ex. 91.

of fact be deceived. It was said by Martin, J.A., however, in *R. v. McNamara*[11] that

> . . . the evidence of bad character cannot be used to show that the person was likely from his character to have committed the offence

but rather has the limited use of refuting the defendant's claim that he has a good one. Following such a limiting instruction could prove difficult!

(ii) *How Character May be Proved*

Having examined *when* the character of the accused may be evidenced, we turn now to the separate question of *how* that character may be shown. Three methods suggest themselves as rational: first, by reports of the accused's reputation in the community for the pertinent character trait; second, by the opinion of one who knows the accused's character; and, finally, by description of specific acts of conduct or misconduct from which his general disposition or character might be inferred.[12] The last method was viewed by the courts as of little probative value and carried the danger of multiplicity of issues and unfair surprise. Willes, J. explained:

> You exclude particular facts on the part of the prisoner because a person who is a robber may do an act or acts of generosity, and the proof of such acts are, therefore, irrelevant to the question whether he was likely to have committed the particular act of robbery or not; and, on the one hand, I agree that particular acts must be excluded on the part of the prosecution partly for the reason that excludes them in the first instance, and partly for the reason that no notice has been given to the prisoner that you are going into an inquiry as to particular facts.[13]

Prior to the landmark decision of *Rowton* the normal technique of informing the trier of the accused's character was by the opinions of those who knew him, bolstered at times by their reports of his reputation. Curiously, this practice was there suddenly reversed.[14] Rowton was charged with having committed an indecent assault upon a 14-year-old boy. The accused called several witnesses who gave him an excellent character as a moral and well-conducted man. The prosecution called in reply a witness who knew the accused and when asked:

> What is the defendant's general character for decency and morality of conduct?

he replied:

> I know nothing of the neighbourhood's opinion, because I was only a boy at school when I knew him; but my own opinion, and the opinion of my brothers who were also pupils of his, is, that his character is that of a man capable of the grossest indecency and the most flagrant immorality.

This evidence was received over the objections of the accused, the accused was convicted, and the question was reserved for the opinion of 12 judges. The

---

11.   (1981), 56 C.C.C. (2d) 193, 352 (Ont. C.A.), relying on 1 Wigmore, *Evidence* (3d ed.), s. 58.
12.   Character inferred from demeanour in court: *R. v. Owens* (1986), 55 C.R. (3d) 386, 393 (Ont. C.A.).
13.   *R. v. Rowton* (1865), 10 Cox. C.C. 25, 39.
14.   See 7 Wigmore, *Evidence* (3d ed.), s. 1981, at p. 210 for a description of how *Rowton* surprised the legal profession.

majority[15] held this to be error and the conviction was quashed. Since that time evidence of character was usually limited to evidence of reputation, and character witnesses are commanded that they are not to speak from their own experience of the accused but rather to report on the rumours in the community. As Wurtele, J. later summarized:

> In criminal prosecutions evidence respecting the general character of the defendant is admissible for the purpose of raising a presumption of innocence or of guilt, but the party who tenders such evidence must restrict himself to evidence of mere general reputation, and the question to be put to a witness to character is: What is the defendant's reputation for honesty, morality or humanity? as the case may be. The Crown has no right, however, in making out its case to put in evidence of bad character, but, on the other hand, the defendant is at liberty to give evidence of his general good character; and then the counsel for the Crown can cross-examine the witnesses as to particular or isolated facts and as to the ground of their belief, and may also call witnesses to prove the general bad reputation of the defendant, and thus to contradict his witnesses.[16]

The character witness must have knowledge of the person's reputation in the community. Our jurisprudence reflects the fact, however, that the nature of the community changes with the times.

R. v. LEVASSEUR
(1987), 56 C.R. (3d) 335, 35 C.C.C. (3d) 136 (Alta. C.A.)

[The accused was charged with break, enter and theft. The defence sought to introduce evidence of the accused's good character through testimony of her employer, who had discussed the accused's general reputation with 15 of their business acquaintances. The trial judge ruled the evidence was inadmissible because the evidence was not of her reputation in the community in which she lived.]

HARRADENCE J.A.:—

. . . .

Scrutiny by a modern appellate court can only result in the conclusion that the neighbourhood requirement is no longer justifiable. While it may have been appropriate in the days of the redoubtable Duke of Wellington, who regretted the advent of the British railroad system because it would allow the lower classes to move about, it is not appropriate to a society which has supersonic transport available to it.

The laws of evidence must not continue to reflect this parochial attitude; as Lord Ellenborough pointed out, "The rules of evidence must expand according to the exigencies of society" (*Pritt v. Fairclough* (1812), 170 E.R. 1391 at 1392). . . .

Credibility is crucial to the issue of whether the appellant committed the offence of breaking and entering. The appellant claims that she was told to remove the vehicles from the warehouse bay and therefore had colour of right. Had the jurors heard evidence of her good character, their conclusion might have differed.

---

15. Willes, J. and Erle, C.J. dissented.
16. *R. v. Barsalou* (1901), 4 C.C.C. 347, 348 (Que. K.B.). And see *Michelson v. U.S.*, 335 U.S. 469 (1948). See also *R. v. Grosse* (1983), 9 C.C.C. (3d) 465 (N.S.C.A.); leave to appeal to S.C.C. refused 61 N.S.R. (2d) 447n.

[A new trial was ordered.]

How probative is character in sexual assault cases?

R. v. PROFIT
(1992), 16 C.R. (4th) 332, 85 C.C.C. (3d) 232 (Ont. C.A.)

[The accused, a school principal, was convicted of sexual offences involving students. The accused appealed.]

GOODMAN J.A. (BLAIR J.A. concurring):—

. . . .

Twenty-two character witnesses testified on behalf of the appellant. Fifteen were colleagues or school board employees who had worked either for or with the appellant. Three were associated with the appellant through volunteer or church organizations. Two were independent businessmen from the appellant's community and two were personal friends. Some of them had, as children, attended camps where the appellant was a director and in later years had acted as counsellors in the camp under the appellant's supervision. All of these witnesses had seemingly impeccable backgrounds and were well qualified to give evidence with respect to the reputation of the appellant in the community with respect to honesty, integrity and morality.

A fair résumé of their evidence with respect to their personal knowledge was that they had never seen the appellant conduct himself in a sexually inappropriate manner, nor had they ever heard the appellant make a statement that they would consider sexually inappropriate. None of them had ever received a complaint about the appellant's conduct.

. . . .

The trial judge, however, made no reference whatsoever to the use of character evidence as a basis of an inference that the appellant was unlikely to have committed the crime charged.

. . . .

[W]here the character witnesses have given evidence as to the moral behaviour of an accused with respect to children in cases alleging sexual offences against children and have given evidence with respect to the general reputation of an accused for not only honesty and integrity but also morality, in the broader sense, such evidence has the same degree of relevance and weight to establish the improbability that the accused committed the offence, as evidence of general reputation with respect to honesty has in the case of an alleged offence involving a theft or a fraudulent transaction. In each case it is only one part of the evidence to be considered by the finder of fact along with all other evidence in determining the culpability of an accused and its weight will no doubt vary with the circumstances of each case. . . . . [T]he character evidence in the case at bar dealt specifically with the appellant's behaviour with his students and his general reputation with respect to morality.

. . . .

Accordingly, I would allow the appeal and quash the convictions.

GRIFFITHS J.A. (dissenting):—

. . . .

[W]hile such evidence may be relevant in cases involving crimes of commercial dishonesty, it has little probative value in cases involving sexual misconduct against children by persons in positions of trust or control.

Recently there have been a number of cases involving persons who enjoyed impeccable reputations in the community for honesty, integrity and morality, such as teachers, scout leaders, priests and others who, in breach of their positions of trust, have committed acts of sexual assault. In these cases, the sexual assaults were generally shrouded in secrecy, and the flaw in the character of the offender frequently did not come to light until he had been charged and convicted.

R. v. PROFIT

[1993] 3 S.C.R. 637, 24 C.R. (4th) 279, 85 C.C.C. (3d) 232

SOPINKA J.:—We agree with the conclusion of Griffiths J.A. in his dissenting reasons. When the reasons of the trial judge are considered as a whole, we are satisfied that he dealt with the character evidence tendered in this case adequately. The reasons of the trial judge must be viewed in light of the fact that as a matter of common sense, but not as a principle of law, a trial judge may take into account that in sexual assault cases involving children, sexual misconduct occurs in private and in most cases will not be reflected in the reputation in the community of the accused for morality. As a matter of weight, the trial judge is entitled to find that the propensity value of character evidence as to morality is diminished in such cases.

Accordingly, the appeal is allowed and the convictions restored.

With whom do you agree on this issue? Compare *R. v. Lizzi.*[17]

R. v. MOHAN

[1994] 2 S.C.R. 9, 29 C.R. (4th) 243, 89 C.C.C. (3d) 402

[The accused, a practising paediatrician, was charged with sexually assaulting four of his female patients, who were aged thirteen to sixteen at the relevant time. The alleged sexual assaults were perpetrated during the course of medical examinations. Counsel for the accused sought to call a psychiatrist who would testify that the perpetrator of the offences alleged to have been committed would be one of a limited and unusual group of individuals, and that the accused did not fall within that narrow class because he did not possess the characteristics belonging to that group. The trial judge ruled that the evidence would not be admitted. The jury found the accused guilty as charged. The Court of Appeal allowed the accused's appeal, quashed the convictions and ordered a new trial. The Court of Appeal found that the rejected evidence was admissible to show that the accused was not a member of either of the unusual groups of aberrant personalities which could have committed the offenses alleged. The Crown appealed. The Court discussed the admissibility generally of expert opinion evidence and the need for the trial judge to find (a) relevance; (b) necessity in assisting the trier of fact; (c) the absence of any exclusionary rule and (d) a properly qualified expert. We'll discuss later in Chapter 5 the admissibility generally of expert opinion evidence. Here we'll deal only with the admissibility of expert opinion as to character or disposition.]

---

17. (1996), 2 C.R. (5th) 95 (Ont. Gen. Div.).

SOPINKA J. (LAMER C.J. and LA FOREST, L'HEUREUX-DUBÉ, GONTHIER, CORY, MCLACHLIN, IACOBUCCI and MAJOR JJ. concurring):—

. . . .

Expert Evidence as to Disposition

The accused is permitted to adduce evidence as to disposition both in his or her own evidence or by calling witnesses. The general rule is that evidence as to character is limited to evidence of the accused's reputation in the community with respect to the relevant trait or traits. The accused in his or her own testimony, however, may rely on specific acts of good conduct. . . . Evidence of an expert witness that the accused, by reason of his or her mental make-up or condition of the mind, would be incapable of committing or disposed to commit the crime does not fit either of these categories. A further exception, however, has developed that is limited in scope. I propose to examine the extent of this exception.

. . . .

With respect to the development of the exception in Canada, *R. v. Lupien, supra*, is a good starting point. It involved a respondent who was convicted of attempting to commit an act of gross indecency, and whose defence was that he lacked the requisite intent to commit the act because he thought his companion was a woman. He sought to prove his "lack of intent" by tendering psychiatric evidence which showed that he reacted violently against any type of homosexual activity and, therefore, could not have knowingly engaged in an act of gross indecency. Ritchie J. concluded . . . that the evidence was admissible for the following reasons:

> I am far from saying that as a general rule psychiatric evidence of a man's disinclination to commit the kind of crime with which he is charged should be admitted, but the present case is concerned with gross indecency between two men and I think that crimes involving homosexuality stand in a class by themselves in the sense that the participants frequently have characteristics which make them more readily identifiable as a class than ordinary criminals. . . . In any event, it appears to me that the question of whether or not a man is homosexually inclined or otherwise sexually perverted is one upon which an experienced psychiatrist is qualified to express an opinion and that if such opinion is relevant it should be admitted at a trial such as this even if it involves the psychiatrist in expressing his conclusion that the accused does not have the capacity to commit the crime with which he is charged.

It is this passage that created the abnormal group exception which is often sought to be applied to various contexts other than the homosexual context.

The Ontario Court of Appeal . . . further looked into this exception of proving the disposition of the accused through psychiatric evidence in . . . *R. v. McMillan* . . . and *R. v. Robertson*.

. . . .

I question whether use of the terms "abnormal" and "normal" is the best way to describe the concept that underlies their use. The term "abnormal" is derived from the English cases in which it usually connotes the mental state of insanity or diminished responsibility. . . . The basic rationale of these cases is that "normal" human behaviour is a matter which a judge or jury can assess without the assistance of expert evidence. Canadian cases have extended the exception to include what has been described as sexually deviant behaviour.

. . . .

In my opinion, the term "distinctive" more aptly defines the behavioural characteristics which are a pre-condition to the admission of this kind of evidence.

. . . .

Before an expert's opinion is admitted as evidence, the trial judge must be satisfied, as a matter of law, that either the perpetrator of the crime or the accused has distinctive behavioural characteristics such that a comparison of one with the other will be of material assistance in determining innocence or guilt. Although this decision is made on the basis of common sense and experience, as Professor Mewett suggests, it is not made in a vacuum. The trial judge should consider the opinion of the expert and whether the expert is merely expressing a personal opinion or whether the behavioural profile which the expert is putting forward is in common use as a reliable indicator of membership in a distinctive group. Put another way: Has the scientific community developed a standard profile for the offender who commits this type of crime? An affirmative finding on this basis will satisfy the criteria of relevance and necessity. Not only will the expert evidence tend to prove a fact in issue but it will also provide the trier of fact with assistance that is needed. Such evidence will have passed the threshold test of reliability which will generally ensure that the trier of fact does not give it more weight than it deserves. The evidence will qualify as an exception to the exclusionary rule relating to character evidence provided, of course, that the trial judge is satisfied that the proposed opinion is within the field of expertise of the expert witness.

Application to This Case

I take the findings of the trial judge to be that a person who committed sexual assaults on young women could not be said to belong to a group possessing behavioural characteristics that are sufficiently distinctive to be of assistance in identifying the perpetrator of the offences charged. Moreover, the fact that the alleged perpetrator was a physician did not advance the matter because there is no acceptable body of evidence that doctors who commit sexual assaults fall into a distinctive class with identifiable characteristics. Notwithstanding the opinion of Dr. Hill, the trial judge was also not satisfied that the characteristics associated with the fourth complaint identified the perpetrator as a member of a distinctive group. He was not prepared to accept that the characteristics of that complaint were such that only a psychopath could have committed the act. There was nothing to indicate any general acceptance of this theory. Moreover, there was no material in the record to support a finding that the profile of a pedophile or psychopath has been standardized to the extent that it could be said that it matched the supposed profile of the offender depicted in the charges. The expert's group profiles were not seen as sufficiently reliable to be considered helpful. In the absence of these *indicia* of reliability, it cannot be said that the evidence would be necessary in the sense of usefully clarifying a matter otherwise unaccessible, or that any value it may have had would not be outweighed by its potential for misleading or diverting the jury. Given these findings and applying the principles referred to above, I must conclude that the trial judge was right in deciding as a matter of law that the evidence was inadmissible.

R. v. B. (S.C.)
(1997), 10 C.R. (5th) 302, 119 C.C.C. (3d) 530 (Ont. C.A.)

[The accused was charged with sexual assault with a weapon, sexual assault causing bodily harm, and uttering a threat to cause death to the complainant. The only issue at trial was identity. There was compelling evidence that the accused was the perpetrator. The accused testified and denied committing the offences. The accused led expert evidence from a psychiatrist, Dr. Motayne, that the accused was not the type of person capable of committing the attack described by the complainant. The accused was acquitted. The Crown's appeal was allowed.]

DOHERTY and ROSENBERG JJ.A. (MCKINLAY J.A. concurring): —

. . . .

Dr. Greg Motayne, a psychiatrist, was called by the defence. He was described as an expert in sexual behaviour including child and adolescent sexual behaviour. He had been provided with some of the Crown disclosure describing the nature of the attack upon the complainant. He had also examined the respondent and administered certain tests to him. As we understand it, the defence hoped to show through this expert evidence that the perpetrator of these offences had an abnormal disposition and that the respondent as a normal adolescent did not fit the psychiatric profile of the perpetrator.

The admissibility of this expert evidence depends on the application of the principles set down in *R. v. Mohan* (1994), 89 C.C.C. (3d) 402 (S.C.C.). Those principles may be summarized as follows:

- Psychiatric evidence to the effect that the accused, because of his or her mental makeup, is unlikely to have committed the crime alleged is generally inadmissible;

- The defence may, however, lead expert evidence of an accused's disposition where the crime alleged is one that was committed by a person who is part of a group possessing distinct and identifiable behavioural characteristics. In those cases, the defence may lead evidence to show that the accused's mental makeup or behavioural characteristics excluded him or her from that group.

. . . .

At trial, after setting out a hypothetical which tracked the facts of the case, defence counsel asked Dr. Motayne whether the assailant described in the hypothetical "fit a profile that you are familiar with in the course of your work, a unique and relatively limited segment of the population?" Dr. Motayne did not respond directly to counsel's question. Instead, he indicated that there were "features" of the hypothetical which fit the description of a sexual sadist or the description of a person suffering from an anti-social personality disorder. These two conditions were specific categories of mental illness which were well recognized in the psychiatric community. Dr. Motayne then described the tests he had performed on the respondent and advanced his opinion that the respondent did not fit within either of the two categories described above. He said that he could not "completely" rule out the possibility that the respondent had committed these acts, but nothing indicated that the respondent endorsed the beliefs of a sexual sadist or suffered from an anti-social personality disorder.

In cross-examination, the following exchange occurred:

Q. You would agree with me, doctor, that there is another category, a wider category called a rapist. Is that not right?

A. That is not defined in the SM4. I think when one speaks of a rapist one includes both categories, both the anti-social personality disorder and the sexual sadist.

Q. Well, is it correct to say that there is no such thing as a typical rapist?

A. That's a difficult question for me to answer. I can only answer it in terms of what is defined under the SM4 and for me, if somebody would commit extremely violent acts and happen to do a sexual act I would suggest that that person is a psychopath or an anti-social personality disorder. If the act is driven by a sexual drive or the need to satisfy a sexual urge by degrading somebody I would call that individual a sexual sadist.

. . . .

In-chief, Dr. Motayne did no more than indicate that some features of the hypothetical presented to him were consistent with the acts of a sexual sadist or a person suffering from an anti-social personality disorder. Dr. Motayne did not suggest that others who did not fall within either of those categories could be excluded as possible perpetrators. Dr. Motayne's evidence in-chief did not address the question of whether the scientific community has developed "a standard profile for the offender who commits this type of crime" (*R. v. Mohan*). Dr. Motayne's evidence in-chief went no further than to identify two recognized types of mental disorder and to opine that certain features of the hypothetical were consistent with a person who suffered from one or the other of those disorders.

    ... In cross-examination, Dr. Motayne testified to the effect that he believed that anyone who would commit the kinds of acts described in the hypothetical must fall within one of the two categories he had described. However, Dr. Motayne did not suggest that this view was generally accepted within the psychiatric community. His evidence on cross-examination, set out above, comes down to an assertion of a personal belief and does not meet the standard set down in *Mohan*. The evidence should have been excluded.

Compare *R. v. B. (S.C.)* with *R. v. J.J.*,[18] where the expert would testify that the accused had none of the personality traits of a pedophile.

An exception to the general rule forbidding the evidencing of character by specific acts of the accused was created by the legislature in England[19] and now finds itself exampled in section 666 of the Criminal Code, which provides:

Where, at a trial, the accused adduces evidence of his good character, the prosecutor may, in answer thereto, before a verdict is returned, adduce evidence of the previous conviction of the accused for any offences, including any previous conviction by reason of which a greater punishment may be imposed.

The legislation was enacted

... to defeat the scandalous attempt often made by persons, who had been repeatedly convicted of felony, bringing witnesses, or cross-examining the witnesses for the prosecution, to prove that the prisoner had previously borne a good character for honesty.[20]

Note that the legislation allows for proof of specific acts only when the act resulted in a conviction.

(iii) *When Does Accused Put his Character into Evidence?*

When does the accused put his character into issue and thereby open the door for the prosecution to rebut? In *R. v. Shrimpton*[21] the accused maintained that he had not given evidence of good character as he had not called witnesses to that fact but rather elicited the same in cross-examination of a prosecution witness. It was held:

---

18. [1998] A.Q. No. 2493 (C.A.).
19. See An Act to Prevent the Fact of a Previous Conviction being given on Evidence to the Jury, 1836 (6 & 7 Will. 4, c. 111), and An Act for the Better Prevention of Offences, 1851 (14 & 15 Vict., c. 19), s. 9. See also *R. v. Nealy* (1987), 17 O.A.C. 164 (C.A.).
20. *R. v. Shrimpton* (1851), 5 Cox. C.C. 387. Consider the legislative history of s. 666 as prior to the 1955 revision. It apparently was limited to prosecutions for offences which called for a greater penalty on a second conviction.
21. (1851), 5 Cox. C.C. 387.

If, either by calling witnesses on his part, or by cross-examination of the witnesses for the Crown, the prisoner relies upon his good character, it is lawful for the prosecutor to give the previous conviction in evidence.

At that time, of course, the accused was incapable of giving evidence. When he now takes the stand and denies the charge, does he open the door to character evidence being led by the prosecution? Let us compare two cases.

In *R. v. Demyen (No. 2)* [22] the accused, Dennis Demyen, was charged with the murder of an infant, the daughter of his wife. The child had died from a severe blow to the stomach which the accused denied inflicting. At trial the Crown was permitted to introduce, pursuant to section 666 of the Criminal Code, evidence of a previous conviction for assault on a child of the same age and sex as the deceased. The "good character evidence" which permitted this rebuttal was found by the trial judge in the following cross-examination of a Crown witness:

> Q. Now you have known Dennis for quite a few years, about five years or so. What would you say about his attitude towards children generally? Did he like children?
>
> A. Yes.
>
> Q. Would you say he was a gentle and decent person in his relationship with children?
>
> A. Yes.
>
> Q. And with people generally?
>
> A. Yes.
>
> Q. Was he an easy person to get along with?
>
> A. Oh yes.

The Saskatchewan Court of Appeal ordered a new trial on the basis that the above did not amount to evidence of character since the witness had not described the accused's reputation but had given his own opinion of the accused's disposition. The court held that this evidence ought not to have been received at trial, and so evidence of the previous conviction was also inadmissible.

In *R. v. McFadden* [23] the accused was charged with first degree murder. The Crown's theory was that the accused had killed the deceased in the course of an indecent assault. In cross-examination of the accused it was suggested that he had gone to the deceased's place to satisfy his sexual urge and that he had stabbed her when she resisted. The accused replied: "I have the most beautiful wife in the world. I worship the ground that girl walks on." The British Columbia Court of Appeal held that the accused had thereby placed his character for sexual morality in issue because he meant to convey that he would not get sexually involved with any other woman. Craig, J.A. said:

> The purpose of evidence of good character is to show the accused is a person who is not likely to have committed the act with which he is charged and, also, to enhance his credibility. An accused may adduce evidence of good character (1) by calling witnesses; (2) by cross-examining Crown witnesses on the subject; (3) by giving testimony. Normally, he may lead evidence of good character by adducing evidence only of his general reputation, not by adducing evidence of specific acts

---

22. (1976), 31 C.C.C. (2d) 383 (Sask. C.A.).
23. (1981), 65 C.C.C. (2d) 9 (B.C.C.A.).

which might tend to establish his character. The Crown may call evidence of bad character in rebuttal, but such evidence, also, must relate only to general reputation: *R. v. Rowton* (1865), 169 E.R. 1497. An accused may put his character in issue in the course of giving his testimony, not by giving evidence of his general reputation, but by making assertions which tend to show that he is a person of good character, particularly with regard to the aspect of his character which is in issue. Obviously, the Crown may rebut this testimony by calling evidence of bad character, but may the Crown call evidence only of general reputation or may the Crown call evidence other than the evidence of general reputation? In some circumstances, the Crown may call evidence of specific incidents in rebutting evidence of good character. For example, under the provisions of s. 593 of the *Criminal Code*, the Crown could prove previous convictions as evidence of bad character. The Crown may, also, adduce similar fact evidence to rebut evidence of good character: *Guay v. The Queen* (1979), 42 C.C.C. (2d) 536, [1979] 1 S.C.R. 18.[24]

R. v. McNamara[25] was a prosecution of a number of companies and individuals for conspiracy to defraud by agreeing on who should bid the successful bid on dredging contracts. A principal Crown witness, Rindress, was the president of two companies, J.P. Porter and Richelieu, which were part of a corporate structure of which the accused Jean Simard was a director. Rindress testified that he assumed he had a mandate from Simard to bid-rig. In Simard's examination-in-chief he was asked as to the mandate he had given Rindress:

Q.   Mr. Rindress in giving his evidence has told us that what he considered his mandate was in connection with the operation of the Porter Company and the Richelieu Company, what did you consider was the mandate of Mr. Rindress in connection with operating the company?

A.   The mandate that Mr. Rindress had is to run the company like a company should be run, legally.

Q.   I am sorry?

A.   Like any company should be run, legally.

The trial judge ruled that the accused had put his character into issue, and the Crown was permitted to cross-examine Simard with respect to an otherwise unrelated building transaction which inpugned Simard's character for honesty. The Ontario Court of Appeal held:

Manifestly, an accused does not put his character in issue by denying his guilt and repudiating the allegations made against him, nor by giving an explanation of matters which are essential to his defence. An accused is not entitled, however, under the guise of repudiating the allegations against him to assert expressly or impliedly that he would not have done the things alleged against him because he is a person of good character; if he does, he puts his character in issue.

The difficult question is whether the appellant crossed over the line of permissible repudiation of the charge and asserted that he was an honest man. . . .

The appellant Jean Simard in response to his counsel's question as to the scope of Rindress' mandate did not confine himself to saying that the mandate was to run the company legally. The appellant said that Rindress' mandate was to run the company like a company should be run, legally. He followed that answer by repeating that Rindress' mandate was to run the company "like any company should be run, legally". The appellant's evidence is consistent only with his intention to assert that

---

24.   *Ibid.*, at p. 13.
25.   (1981), 56 C.C.C. (2d) 193, 343 (Ont. C.A.).

he would not knowingly permit a Simard company to be operated other than legally. If there were any doubt whether the appellant, by these answers, intended to project the image of a law-abiding citizen, these answers, when taken together with his subsequent evidence, make it clear that the appellant intended to project the image of a man of integrity and of an ethical businessman.[26]

The holding in *McNamara* is confined to receipt of evidence in rebuttal in the form of questioning the accused and not in the form of extrinsic evidence and to cases where the accused himself has testified to his own character. In *R. v. Close*[27] Crown witnesses, in cross-examination, had deposed to the accused's good character and the trial judge allowed the Crown to advance evidence of the accused's previous convictions pursuant to section 593 [now section 666] of the Criminal Code. The Ontario Court of Appeal ordered a new trial distinguishing the *McNamara* decision as a case where the accused *in his own evidence* had projected a good character.[28]

In *R. v. Shortreed*[29] the accused was charged with a number of sexual assaults. He testified in chief that he never sexually assaulted anyone. The accused later explained that what he meant by that was that he had not attacked any of the victims in this case. The court held that the accused had not placed his character in issue and the Crown should not therefore have been permitted to cross-examine the accused as to facts underlying a prior conviction for wounding:

> Having regard to the qualification of his general statement when he was asked in-chief to explain its meaning, it is apparent that the appellant was not attempting to rely on his non-violent nature, but merely intended to deny having assaulted any of the five complainants. He was not adducing evidence of good character within the meaning of s. 666 of the *Criminal Code*. . . .

> . . . .

> An accused person does not place his character in issue by denying his guilt and repudiating the allegations made against him. Neither do the introductory routine questions as to education, marital status, religious affiliation have the effect of rendering the accused's character relevant.[30]

R. v. A. (W.A.)
(1996), 3 C.R. (5th) 388, 112 C.C.C. (3d) 83 (Man. C.A.)

[The accused was charged with sexually assaulting his stepdaughter. At trial, the stepdaughter's long cross-examination attacked her character and truthfulness. The accused's wife, who was the stepdaughter's natural mother, gave evidence for the accused as to her daughter's bad behaviour, and the

---

26. *Ibid.*, at pp. 346-47.
27. (1982), 137 D.L.R. (3d) 655 (Ont. C.A.).
28. See also *R. v. Farrant* (1983), 147 D.L.R. (3d) 511, 526 (S.C.C.), following the *McNamara* position without citing the same. Compare *R. v. Baird* (1990), 105 A.R. 265 (C.A.): the Crown, in a murder prosecution, rebutting accused's evidence of good character, given in chief, by evidence, elicited in cross-examination, that the accused had forged rent receipts and participated in numerous altercations in various bars.
29. (1990), 54 C.C.C. (3d) 292 (Ont. C.A.).
30. *Ibid.*, at p. 307.

accused's lack of opportunity to commit the crime. During the Crown's cross-examination as to why she considered her daughter a liar, the wife said, "I know my husband." The trial judge then let the Crown cross-examine the wife as to the family's dynamics. Under further cross-examination, the wife admitted that the accused had once assaulted her, that he had committed himself to a mental health centre, and that he had had an angry meeting with the stepdaughter's teacher. The trial judge cautioned the members of the jury that the cross-examination evidence was useful only to give them a balanced insight into the accused's temperament and that it was not relevant as to the accused's propensity to commit the offence charged. The accused was convicted, and he appealed.]

SCOTT C.J.M. (HUBAND and MONNIN JJ.A. concurring): —

. . . .

In my opinion, the accused did not put his "character" in issue through answers given by Mrs. A. during cross-examination by Crown counsel. The line of questioning pursued by Crown counsel that led Mrs. A. to make the response "I know my husband" was directly attributable to Crown counsel's persistence in cross-examination in querying why she was supportive of the accused and not her daughter, the complainant.

In any event there is clear authority that, while the accused may put his own character in issue by introducing such evidence himself, when dealing with defence witnesses it is only through their examination-in-chief that an accused's character may be put in issue. . . . In my opinion, limiting the ways of putting character in issue through defence witnesses to evidence-in-chief makes eminent good sense as illustrated by the very facts of this case where the approbation by Mrs. A. of her husband's "character" was not volunteered, but was elicited as a direct response to a line of questioning only pursued during cross-examination. If it were otherwise, the Crown could put the accused's character in issue through clever cross-examination of defence witnesses and thus frustrate the rule against it.

The evidence brought out during the cross-examination of Mrs. A. is simply incapable of constituting character evidence introduced by or on behalf of the accused. Indeed, the point is so obvious that I have not been able to find any authorities directly on point. See, for example, *R. v. Valeanu* (1995), 97 C.C.C. (3d) 338 (Ont. C.A.), where the Crown conceded on appeal that questioning such as occurred here was clearly improper cross-examination.

Since it is not now strictly necessary to review the scope of character evidence once the accused has put it in issue, I simply note that authorities of many years' standing make it clear that it ordinarily refers to evidence of reputation and not to evidence of disposition. This is normally attested to by evidence as to the accused's general reputation within the community. Thus the evidence brought out during cross-examination is not character evidence in the traditional sense since it deals with specific incidents involving the accused and members of his household during the period relevant to the indictment.

(d) Similar Facts

The classic and oft-repeated statement of the rule regarding the reception in evidence of similar facts was that of Lord Herschell, L.C.in *Makin v. Attorney-General for New South Wales*:[31]

> It is undoubtedly not competent for the prosecution to adduce evidence tending to shew that the accused has been guilty of criminal acts other than those covered by

---

31.   [1894] A.C. 57, 65.

the indictment, for the purpose of leading to the conclusion that the accused is a person likely from his criminal conduct or character to have committed the offence for which he is being tried. On the other hand, the mere fact that the evidence adduced tends to shew the commission of other crimes does not render it inadmissible if it be relevant to an issue before the jury, and it may be so relevant if it bears upon the question whether the acts alleged to constitute the crime charged in the indictment were designed or accidental, or to rebut a defence which would otherwise be open to the accused. The statement of these general principles is easy, but it is obvious that it may often be very difficult to draw the line and to decide whether a particular piece of evidence is on the one side or the other.

This statement, however, has been the cause of considerable confusion and difficulty both for the law student and the courts as it seeks to distinguish between different kinds of relevance. If the evidence is relevant only as showing the accused to be by his nature or disposition a person likely to commit the crime alleged, the evidence is inadmissible. If, on the other hand, the evidence is relevant in some other way to an issue before the jury, it is admissible. This approach led to the judicial creation over the years of categories of relevance[32] which would admit similar facts if the evidence "rebutted the defence of accident," "rebutted a defence of legitimate association for honest purpose," "demonstrated system," "went to identity," and so on. While this pigeon-hole method of analysis can be used to explain most of the similar fact cases, some cases continued to be troubling[33] and after repeated attempts at resolution the House of Lords opted for a quite different approach.

In *R. v. Boardman*[34] the accused was charged and convicted of buggery and incitement to commit buggery. The victims, pupils at the accused's school, testified concerning the particular acts committed on each, and the trial judge ruled that the evidence of each could be taken as corroborative of the other as the acts were similar. The Court of Appeal dismissed the accused's appeal but certified a point of law of general public importance:

> Whether, on a charge involving an allegation of homosexual conduct there is evidence that the accused person is a man whose homosexual proclivities take a particular form, that evidence is thereby admissible although it tends to show that the accused has been guilty of criminal acts other than those charged.[35]

---

32.   See the numerous categories detailed in Cross, *Evidence* (5th ed.), pp. 378-93. See the pigeon-hole approach in *Leblanc v. R.,* [1977] 1 S.C.R. 339.

33.   Cases such as *R. v. Straffen*, [1952] 2 Q.B. 911 (C.C.A.); *Thompson v. R.*, [1918] A.C. 221; and *R. v. Ball*, [1911] A.C. 47 (C.C.A.); the opinions profess to follow *Makin*, but on analysis the only relevance of the similar facts lies in showing the accused to be one "likely from his criminal conduct or character to have committed the offence for which he is being tried." See analysis by Hoffman, "Similar Facts after Boardman" (1975), 91 L.Q. R. 193.

34.   [1975] A.C. 421 (H.L.). For commentaries see also: Williams, "The Problem of Similar Fact Evidence" (1979), 5 Dalhousie L. Rev. 281; Turcott, "Similar Fact Evidence: The Boardman Legacy" (1978), 21 Crim. L.Q. 43; Tapper, "Similar Facts; Peculiarity and Credibility" (1975), 38 Mod. L. Rev. 206; Eggleston, *Evidence, Proof and Probability* (1978); Sklar, "Similar Fact Evidence — Catchwords and Cartwheels" (1977), 23 McGill L.J. 60; Cross, "Fourth Time Lucky — Similar Fact Evidence in the House of Lords", [1975] Crim. L.R. 62; Killeen, "Recent Developments in the Law of Evidence" (1975), 18 Crim. L.Q. 103 at 120; Cross, *Evidence*, 5th ed. (1979), pp. 374-76; Piragoff, *Similar Fact Evidence* (1981), p. 161.

35.   *Boardman, ibid.,* at p. 437.

The Lords were unanimous in declining to create, or recognize, a "category of relevance" giving "automatic admissibility to evidence where proclivities take a particular form."[36] Rather the approach was to be based on principle and the trial judge in each case was to assess the probative worth of the evidence compared to the possibilities of prejudice and confusion of issues. The Law Lords followed the lead of Lord Simon in *Director of Public Prosecutions v. Kilbourne* when he interpreted the classic passage from Lord Herschell's opinion in *Makin*:

> That what was declared to be inadmissible in the first sentence of this passage is nevertheless relevant (i.e., logically probative) can be seen from numerous studies of offences in which recidivists are matched against first offenders. . . . All relevant evidence is prima facie admissible. The reason why the type of evidence referred to by Lord Herschell L.C. in the first sentence of the passage is inadmissible is, not because it is irrelevant, but because its logically probative significance is considered to be grossly outweighed by its prejudice to the accused, so that a fair trial is endangered if it is admitted; the law therefore exceptionally excludes this relevant evidence: whereas in the circumstances referred to in the second sentence the logically probative significance of the evidence is markedly greater.[37]

Lord Wilberforce in *Boardman* wrote:

> The basic principle must be that the admission of similar fact evidence (of the kind now in question) is exceptional and requires a strong degree of probative force. This probative force is derived, if at all, from the circumstance that the facts testified to by the several witnesses bear to each other such a striking similarity that they must, when judged by experience and common sense, either all be true, or have arisen from a cause common to the witnesses or from pure coincidence. The jury may, therefore, properly be asked to judge whether the right conclusion is that all are true, so that each story is supported by the other(s).[38]

Lord Cross agreed:

> the reason for this general rule is not that the law regards such evidence as inherently irrelevant but that it is believed that if it were generally admitted jurors would in many cases think that it was more relevant than it was, so that, as it is put, its prejudicial effect would outweigh its probative value. Circumstances, however, may arise in which such evidence is so very relevant that to exclude it would be an affront to common sense. Take, for example, *Reg. v. Straffen* [1952] 2 Q.B. 911. There a young girl was found strangled. It was a most unusual murder for there had been no attempt to assault her sexually or to conceal the body though this might easily have been done. The accused, who had just escaped from Broadmoor and was in the neighbourhood at the time of the crime, had previously committed two murders of young girls, each of which had the same peculiar features. It would, indeed, have been a most extraordinary coincidence if this third murder had been committed by someone else and though an ultra-cautious jury might still have acquitted him it would have been absurd for the law to have prevented the evidence of the other murders being put before them although it was simply evidence to show that Straffen was a man likely to commit a murder of that particular kind. . . . The question must always be whether the similar fact evidence taken together with the other evidence would

---

36.   *Ibid.*, at p. 441 per Lord Morris of Borth-y-Gest.
37.   [1973] A.C. 729, 757. But see the opinion of Lord Hailsham in *Boardman, supra,* note 34, at p. 451, that adds, as "another" reason or theory for excluding similar fact evidence, that it is irrelevant!
38.   *Supra*, note 34, at p. 444.

do no more than raise or strengthen a suspicion that the accused committed the offence with which he is charged or would point so strongly to his guilt that only an ultra-cautious jury, if they accepted it as true, would acquit in face of it. In the end — although the admissibility of such evidence is a question of law, not of discretion — the question as I see it must be one of degree.[39]

Lord Morris of Borth-y-Gest similarly opined:

> where what is important is the application of principle, the use of labels or definitive descriptions cannot be either comprehensive or restrictive. . . . Evidence of other occurrences which merely tend to deepen suspicion does not go to prove guilt: so evidence of "similar facts" should be excluded unless such evidence has a really material bearing on the issues to be decided. . . . There may be cases where a judge, having both limbs of Lord Herschell's famous proposition in mind, considers that the interests of justice (of which the interests of fairness form so fundamental a component) make it proper that he should permit a jury when considering the evidence on a charge concerning one fact or set of facts also to consider the evidence concerning another fact or set of facts if between the two there is such a close or striking similarity or such an underlying unity that probative force could fairly be yielded.[40]

Viewed in this way, the so-called similar fact evidence rule may be stated in terms of its underlying rationale. Previous misconduct of the accused which is similar to the activity presently charged is relevant thereto but in our concern for a fair trial we erect a canon of exclusion lest the accused be prejudiced by its reception. Prejudice in this context does not mean that the evidence might increase the chances of conviction but rather that the evidence may be improperly used by the trier of fact. The trier who learns of the accused's previous misconduct may then view the accused as a bad man, one who deserves punishment regardless of his guilt of the instant offence and may be less critical of the evidence presently marshalled against him. The only true relevance of the previous activity follows a chain of reasoning through the accused's disposition and the law recognizes that frequently such chain is tenuous in its nature as people can change and dispositions vary. The law then erects a canon of exclusion for similar fact evidence which is tenuous in nature when viewed against the possibility of prejudice. If, however, the similar fact evidence is *not* tenuous in nature, if it has sufficient relevance, if it has genuine probative worth when taken together with the other evidence and is not then outweighed by considerations of prejudice, the reason for the canon of exclusion disappears. The first principle of rational fact-finding, that all relevant evidence should be received, then controls.

The classic statement of Lord Herschell continues to be troublesome. While Lords Cross and Wilberforce did not even mention *Makin* in their opinions, Lord Hailsham, in *Boardman*, sought to continue its force and "*explained*" the rule:

> It is perhaps helpful to remind oneself that what is *not* to be admitted is a chain of reasoning and not necessarily a state of facts. If the inadmissible chain of reasoning is the *only* purpose for which the evidence is adduced as a matter of law, the evidence itself is not admissible. If there is some other relevant, probative purpose than for

---

39. *Ibid.*, at p. 456.
40. *Ibid.*, at pp. 439-41.

the forbidden type of reasoning, the evidence is admitted, but should be made subject to a warning from the judge that the jury must eschew the forbidden reasoning.[41]

As Hoffman[42] points out, while this may be an accurate paraphrase of the *Makin* rule, it is impossible to reconcile it with many of the other classic cases on similar fact evidence.

(i) *Need for Connection Between Previous Acts and Accused*

Before similar facts can be considered as evidence in the case there must be seen to be a connection between the previous acts and the accused. If the previous acts cannot be tied to the accused they have no relevance at all. Canadian courts have recognized this fact but have not clearly articulated an appropriate test.

Should the prosecution have to establish beyond a reasonable doubt that the accused committed the earlier acts? On a balance of probabilities? To whose satisfaction? The judge as a preliminary condition of admissibility? The jury who decides everything at the end of the case?[43]

The following two cases provide some guidance.

SWEITZER v. R.
[1982] 1 S.C.R. 949, 29 C.R. (3d) 97, 68 C.C.C. (2d) 193

[The accused had originally been committed to trial on 15 counts of (what is now) sexual assault. The various counts were severed prior to trial. At the trial of the first count, the circumstances surrounding the 14 other offences were admitted into evidence. In 11 of these offences, including count 1, the victims were unable to identify their assailant. The only evidence of identification was to be found in the fact that the conduct of the assailant in the episodes where he was unidentifiable was similar to his conduct where he was identified and in one episode caught at the scene. The Court of Appeal dismissed the accused's appeal against conviction. Before ordering a new trial, McIntyre, J., for the full court, reviewed the law on similar fact evidence.]

The question of the admissibility of similar fact evidence has been the subject of much legal writing to be found in the decided cases and textbooks and in the academic articles and commentaries. The general principle stated by Lord Herschell L.C. in *Makin and Makin v. A.-G. for New South Wales*, [1894] A.C. 57 at p. 65, has been largely accepted as the basis for the admission of this evidence. . . .

Over the years in seeking to apply this principle judges have tended to create a list of categories or types of cases in which similar fact evidence could be admitted, generally by reference to the purpose for which the evidence was adduced. Evidence of similar facts has been adduced to prove intent, to prove a system, to prove a plan, to show malice, to

41.   [1975] A.C. 421, 453 (H.L.).
42.   See "Similar Facts After Boardman" (1975), 91 L.Q. Rev. 193 at 198.
43.   See generally, Tanovich, "Probative Value and the Issue of Proof in Similar Fact Evidence Cases" (1994), 23 C.R. (4th) 157, and more recently, Tanovich, "Revisiting the *Sweitzer* Issue of Proof" (1997), 9 C.R. (5th) 74.

rebut the defence of accident or mistake, to prove identity, to rebut the defence of innocent association and for other similar and related purposes. This list is not complete.

This approach has been useful because similar fact evidence by its nature is frequently adduced for its relevance to a single issue in the case under trial. It has however involved, in my opinion, a tendency to overlook the true basis upon which evidence of similar facts is admissible. The general principle described by Lord Herschell may and should be applied in all cases where similar fact evidence is tendered and its admissibility will depend upon the probative effect of the evidence balanced against the prejudice caused to the accused by its admission whatever the purpose of its admission. This approach finds support in *Boardman v. Director of Public Prosecutions*, [1974] 3 All E.R. 887, and is implicit in the words of Lord Herschell in the *Makin* case.

. . . .

The general principle enunciated in the *Makin* case by Lord Herschell, should be borne in mind in approaching this problem. The categories, while sometimes useful, remain only as illustrations of the application of that general rule.

Before evidence may be admitted as evidence of similar facts, there must be a link between the allegedly similar facts and the accused. In other words there must be some evidence upon which the trier of fact can make a proper finding that the similar facts to be relied upon were in fact the acts of the accused for it is clear that if they were not his own but those of another they have no relevance to the matters at issue under the indictment.

. . . .

Dealing with the 11 episodes I say at once that in my view evidence relating to them was inadmissible and ought not to have been admitted. I put that proposition simply upon the footing that they afford no evidence of identification of the appellant, because, despite the existence of varying degrees of similarity between the acts revealed in the evidence and the facts of the case under trial, there is no evidence which connects the appellant with any of those episodes.

Appeal allowed; new trial ordered.

R. v. MILLAR
(1989), 71 C.R. (3d) 78, 49 C.C.C. (3d) 193 (Ont. C.A.)

[The accused was charged with manslaughter. The victim was his nine-week-old son. The cause of death was subdural haemorrhage as a result of the child having been shaken by the accused. It was the theory of the Crown that the accused had shaken the baby excessively using more force than was necessary to assist the infant, or that he shook the infant in anger. The defence maintained that the accused shook the infant because he had stopped breathing. The Crown adduced evidence of a number of other injuries including fractures to the child's ribs. These injuries had occurred some weeks before. On appeal, objection was taken to the admissibility of the evidence of other injuries to the child. This ground of appeal failed. The appeal was allowed on other grounds and a new trial ordered.]

MORDEN J.A. (GRIFFITH and CARTHY JJ. concurring):—

. . . .

2. *The admission of the evidence of other injuries*

The appellant's basic submission with respect to this evidence is that it was inadmissible because it had little probative value and strong prejudicial effect. The appellant concedes that evidence of other injuries to the victim is potentially relevant. . . . Evidence of this kind is potentially relevant to the state of mind with which the accused person kills the victim and, where relevant, to the fact that he killed him. The appellant, however, submits that notwithstanding its potential relevance this evidence should have been excluded because it was incapable of supporting two inferences:

(1) that the injuries were not the result of mere accident, but were the consequence of aggression towards the victim; and

(2) that the injuries were inflicted by the appellant.

With respect to (1), although there was evidence to the contrary — that is, that the other injuries could have been the result of accidents — it is clear that there was evidence sufficient for consideration by the jury that the injuries were not the result of accidents but were intentionally inflicted.

With respect to (2), there is, however, more difficulty. Because there was no objection to the admissibility of this evidence at the trial we do not have the benefit of the trial judge's consideration of this issue. It is clear that there must, at least, be some evidence capable of reasonably supporting a finding that the appellant was implicated in the other injuries.

. . . .

The only evidential basis for considering that the appellant was implicated in the earlier injuries is that the deceased was in the appellant's custody for the whole of his short life. This was not, however, exclusive custody. No doubt he spent more time alone with his mother than with the appellant alone. There is really no evidence of the deceased's being in the care of anyone else apart from the appellant's sister for one night at the Millar residence and Mrs. Chouinard, the grandmother, from time to time at the campsite. Both of these persons gave evidence and I do not think it could be said from a reading of the record as a whole that there was a reasonable possibility that either of these persons caused the injuries. Mrs. Millar testified that after Michael had been with his grandmother there never was any indication that he could have been hurt and, further, that she never saw any mishap when other people were holding the child that could have caused the injuries.

When the Crown had completed its case I do not think that there was any basis on which the jury could more reasonably conclude, assuming that the injuries were intentionally caused, that it was the appellant rather than Mrs. Millar who had caused the injuries. When, however, all of the evidence at the trial had been given I think that the picture changed.

Mrs. Millar gave evidence that she had been charged with manslaughter with respect to the death of the child. Although it is not stated clearly in the record it may be inferred that she was discharged following the preliminary inquiry. Mrs. Millar was never asked point blank whether she had caused the injuries. However, at more than one point in her evidence she testified that she had had no idea of the injuries that Michael was subsequently discovered to have suffered. She speculated in her evidence that the rib injuries could have occurred during birth, and also that the injuries could have occurred on the two occasions when Sean carried the baby or when the baby had apparently fallen out of bed. She also referred to the occasion when the baby fell out of the appellant's arms.

Although, certainly, there is no positive suggestion in Mrs. Millar's evidence that the appellant caused the injuries, if the jury accepted her evidence that she was ignorant of the injuries before August 1st and rejected the appellant's evidence that he had not caused the injuries, then there was an evidentiary basis which could reasonably support a finding that the appellant had caused the other injuries.

The Crown, at the end of the case, was entitled to rely upon all of the evidence in the record. Accordingly, I think that this ground of appeal should fail.

. . . .

It should be emphasized that the evidence of the other injuries was before the jury solely on the issue of the accused's state of mind at the time he shook the baby; it could not be used to support a general inference that the appellant was the sort of person likely to have committed the crime in question: *Makin v. A.-G. N.S.W.*, [1894] A.C. 57 at p. 65 (P.C.).

At the new trial the wife would be a competent witness only for the defence. As defence counsel would you call her?

(ii) *How are Similar Facts Relevant?*

R. v. B. (C.R.)
[1990] 1 S.C.R. 717, 76 C.R. (3d) 1, 55 C.C.C. (3d) 1

[The accused was charged with sexual offences against a young child, his natural daughter. The daughter testified that the acts of sexual misconduct by the accused began in 1981 when she was 11 years old and continued for almost two years. In support of the child's testimony, the Crown sought to introduce evidence that the accused had had sexual relations in 1975 with a 15-year-old girl, the daughter of his common law wife, with whom he had enjoyed a father-daughter relationship. The trial judge admitted the evidence and convicted the accused. The majority of the Court of Appeal held that the similar fact evidence was properly admitted and upheld the conviction. The accused appealed further.]

MCLACHLIN J. (DICKSON C.J.C. and WILSON, L'HEUREUX-DUBÉ and GONTHIER JJ. concurring):—

. . . .

The common law has traditionally taken a strict view of similar fact evidence, regarding it with suspicion. In recent years, the courts have moved to loosen the formalistic strictures which had come to encumber the rule. The old category approach determining what types of similar fact evidence is admissible has given way to a more general test which balances the probative value of the evidence against its prejudice.

Despite the apparent simplicity of the modern rule for the admission of similar fact evidence, the rule remains one of considerable difficulty in application. The problems stem in part from a tendency to view the modern formulation of the rule in isolation from the historical context from whence it springs. While the contemporary formulation may permit a more flexible, less restricted analysis, the dangers which it addresses and the principles upon which it rests remain unchanged.

. . . .

Problems with the category approach to similar fact evidence became increasingly apparent in the less formalistic 20th century. On the one hand, the effect of the categories and the frequently referred to requirement of "striking similarity" was that similar fact evidence, which from the point of view of common sense had great relevance, might be excluded — a result which provoked one judge to declaim (*R. v. Hall* (1987), 5 N.Z.L.R. 93 at 108-10 (C.A)):

Viewed in the light of science . . . or common sense, there is without doubt a nexus . . . The common law must often result in what the public may regard as a failure of justice. That is really not our concern.

Other judges reacted to the tendency of the rule to exclude probative evidence by drawing distinctions that were fundamentally unworkable or imaginary in order to admit evidence which common sense told them should be admitted. On the other hand, the rule sometimes permitted reception of evidence of doubtful worth. Provided it fell within one of the accepted categories, evidence of prior misconduct or inclination might be admitted even though its relevance was suspect.

From the point of view of theory too, the category approach associated with *Makin* was subject to criticism. The categories focussed attention on the *purpose* for which the similar fact evidence was adduced, rather than the real question — its *relevance*: see J.A. Andrews and M. Hirst, Criminal Evidence (1987), para. 15.34. As Sklar stated ("Similar Fact Evidence — Catchwords and Cartwheels" (1977), 23 McGill L.J. 60 at 62), "Whether the evidence was really *relevant* to the issue by whatever the rationale and whether, if it was, it was *relevant enough* to justify its reception despite its nearly uncontrollable tendency to damn the accused in the minds of the jury, was lost in the shuffle" (emphasis added in original). If the evidence fell within a recognizable category, it was admitted even if its relevance may have been suspect. Moreover, the emphasis on the need for the evidence to relate to an issue other than disposition was arguably artificial. As Professor Andrews and Mr. Hirst have commented at pp. 342-43:

15.37 Although the courts made a great show of relying on the categories of relevance and of avoiding the forbidden chain of reasoning [guilt from propensity], their whole approach was really based upon a fundamental misconception. In reality, similar fact evidence can hardly ever show design or rebut a defence except by encouraging the court or jury to utilise the forbidden chain of reasoning. Whether the judges realised this or not, the undeniable fact is that in many of the leading cases evidence was admitted where it could only have been relevant because it showed disposition or propensity.

Provided some element, however small, other than disposition could be found to which the evidence related, it went in, although the effect might be almost entirely related to disposition.

Difficulties such as these led the House of Lords to readdress the question of similar fact evidence in *D.P.P. v. Boardman*, [1975] A.C. 421. On its face, *Boardman* constitutes no great departure from *Makin*, with three of the five Law Lords (Lords Morris, Hailsham and Salmon) expressly affirming the validity of *Makin*. However, all five judges rejected the category approach that had become associated with *Makin*, emphasizing that similar fact evidence is not automatically admissible merely because it fits into a prescribed category. The admissibility of similar fact evidence was to be based on general principle, not categories and catch phrases. That general principle was relevance.

While the five separate and sometimes conflicting opinions delivered in *Boardman* may not provide a comprehensive picture of the various ways in which cogency may be found, the ratio decidendi of the case is clear: the admissibility of similar fact evidence depends on its bearing a very high degree of probative value — sufficient to outweigh the inherent prejudice likely to flow from its reception.

. . . .

The Canadian jurisprudence since *Boardman* is generally consistent with the approach advocated in that case. It has followed *Boardman* in rejecting the category approach to the admission of similar fact evidence. At the same time, cases in Canada have on the whole maintained an emphasis on the general rule that evidence of mere propensity is inadmissible, and have continued to emphasize the necessity that such evidence possess high probative value in relation to its potential prejudice.

. . . .

While our courts have affirmed the general exclusionary rule for evidence of disposition and propensity, they have for the most part cast it in terms of *Boardman* rather than *Makin*. It is no longer necessary to hang the evidence tendered on the peg of some issue other than disposition. While the language of some of the assertions of the exclusionary rule admittedly might be taken to suggest that mere disposition evidence can *never* be admissible, the preponderant view prevailing in Canada is the view taken by the majority in *Boardman* — evidence of propensity, while generally inadmissible, may exceptionally be admitted where the probative value of the evidence in relation to an issue in question is so high that it displaces the heavy prejudice which will inevitably inure to the accused where evidence of prior immoral or illegal acts is presented to the jury.

. . . .

Catchwords have gone the same way as categories. Just as English courts have expressed doubts about the necessity of showing "striking similarity" . . . , so in *Robertson* Wilson J. rejected the validity of this phrase as a legal test.

A third feature of this court's treatment of the similar fact rule since *Boardman* is the tendency to accord a high degree of respect to the decision of the trial judge, who is charged with the delicate process of balancing the probative value of the evidence against its prejudicial effect. . . . This deference to the trial judge may in part be seen as a function of the broader, more discretionary nature of the modern rule at the stage where the probative value of the evidence must be weighed against its prejudicial effect.

. . . .

. . . In a case such as the present, where the similar fact evidence sought to be adduced is prosecution evidence of a morally repugnant act committed by the accused, the potential prejudice is great and the probative value of the evidence must be high indeed to permit its reception. The judge must consider such factors as the degree of distinctiveness or uniqueness between the similar fact evidence and the offences alleged against the accused, as well as the connection, if any, of the evidence to issues other than propensity, to the end of determining whether, in the context of the case before him, the probative value of the evidence outweighs its potential prejudice and justifies its reception.

Against this background, I turn to the facts in this case and the ruling of the trial judge.

. . . .

The main similarity is that in each case the accused, shortly after establishing a father-daughter relationship with the victim, is alleged to have engaged her in a sexual relationship. Additionally, the trial judge detailed similarities relating to the place and manner in which the relations occurred in the two situations. The age of the girls was different; one was sexually mature, the other only a child when the acts began. One girl was a blood relation, the other was not. . . .

That said, it cannot be concluded that the evidence necessarily fails the test indicated by the authorities to which I earlier referred. The fact that in each case the accused established a father-daughter relationship with the girl before the sexual violations began might be argued to go to showing, if not a system or design, a pattern of similar behaviour suggesting that the complainant's story is true. The question then is whether the probative value of the evidence outweighs its prejudicial effect. While I may have found this case to have been a borderline case of admissibility if I had been the trial judge, I am not prepared to interfere with the conclusion of the trial judge, who was charged with the task of weighing the probative value of the evidence against its prejudicial effect in the context of the case as a whole.

I would dismiss the appeal and affirm the conviction.

SOPINKA J. (LAMER J. concurring), dissenting:

. . . .

There is no special rule with relation to similar fact evidence in sexual offences. . . . There is no support in the cases in our court for the theory that the rule has special application in sexual offences. Accordingly, evidence that the accused has a propensity to molest children or his or her own children is never admissible solely for that purpose.

. . . .

To have probative value the evidence must be susceptible of an inference relevant to the issues in the case other than the inference that the accused committed the offence because he or she has a disposition to the type of conduct charged: *Morris v. R.*, supra, . . . As in the case of relevance, evidence can be logically probative but not legally probative. When the term "probative value" is employed in the cases, reference is made to legally probative value.

The principal reason for the exclusionary rule relating to propensity is that there is a natural human tendency to judge a person's action on the basis of character. Particularly with juries there would be a strong inclination to conclude that a thief has stolen, a violent man has assaulted and a pedophile has engaged in pedophilic acts. Yet the policy of the law is wholly against this process of reasoning. This policy is reflected not only in similar acts cases, but as well in the rule excluding evidence of the character of the accused unless placed in issue by him. The stronger the evidence of propensity, the more likely it is that the forbidden inference will be drawn and, therefore, the greater the prejudice.

I am unable therefore to subscribe to the theory that in exceptional cases propensity alone can be the basis for admissibility. To say that propensity may have probative value in a sufficiently high degree to be admissible is a contradiction in terms. It is tantamount to saying that when the danger of the application of the forbidden line of reasoning is the strongest, the evidence can go in. The view has been expressed that this change in the principles outlined above was made in *Boardman*, supra (see Hoffmann, "Similar Facts after *Boardman*" (1975), 91 L.Q. Rev. 193 at 202).

The suggestion that *Boardman* effected a radical change in the law is not borne out by an analysis of the respective speeches in the House of Lords. . . .

. . . .

In considering the admissibility of the evidence in this case, I observe that no attempt appears to have been made to negative the possibility of collaboration. No questions were directed to Crown witnesses to determine whether this possibility existed. The Crown, who must persuade the trial judge that the evidence has probative value, has the burden of proof. . . . In my view, the Crown must negative conspiracy or collaboration in accordance with the criminal standard. This is a requirement that applies whenever a preliminary finding of fact is a precondition to the admissibility of evidence tendered by the Crown. . . .

There is then the further question of coincidence. Are the common characteristics in the evidence of the two girls so unusual that it would be against common sense to conclude that they are not both telling the truth? In this connection, the observation of Lord Cross in *Boardman*, quoted above, is helpful. We have only two instances and should proceed with caution. They are separated by a considerable passage of time and as well there are material differences which are detailed in the reasons of Harradence J.A. in the Court of Appeal. McLachlin J. stresses that in each case the appellant established a father relationship. As her statement of the facts indicates, the appellant was the father of one child and he enjoyed a father-daughter relationship with the other. These are not unusual facts and indeed are neutral. In any case, where it is alleged that a father has had an incestuous relationship with two of his children, this fact will be common to both. If one or both girls are not telling the truth, is it unlikely that they would both have said that the appellant established a father relationship with them? Obviously not, because that happened irrespective of whether the balance of their evidence is true.

. . . .

. . . I am unable to say what would have occurred if the similar fact evidence had been rejected by the trial judge. Accordingly, I would direct a new trial. The appeal is therefore allowed and a new trial directed.

R. v. LEPAGE

[1995] 1 S.C.R. 654, 36 C.R. (4th) 145, 95 C.C.C. (3d) 385

[The accused was charged with possession of LSD for the purpose of trafficking. In a search of the house the accused was renting the police had found a clear plastic bag under the sofa containing blotting paper impregnated with 682 hits of LSD. The only identifiable fingerprints on the bag were those of the accused. T, one of the subtenants, on behalf of the Crown, stated that the LSD found under the sofa belonged to the accused and indicated that the basis of this knowledge was that the accused was the only major dealer in the house. The accused was convicted. The Court of Appeal set aside the conviction and directed a new trial. The Crown successfully appealed.]

SOPINKA J. (GONTHIER and IACOBUCCI JJ. concurring):—

. . . .

In support of the trial judge's conclusion, it appears that she relied at least in part on the testimony of Thelland. The following portion of Thelland's testimony is relevant for the purpose of inferring whether the respondent was in possession of the LSD:

Q. What do you know about that LSD?
A. I know it belonged to John Paul Lepage.
Q. How do you know that?
A. He's the only one that was the major dealer in the house.
Q. When you say major dealer, what do you mean by that?
A. Well, quantity.
Q. Of what?
A. Of any narcotic that was coming in.
Q. What can you tell me about this specific bundle of drugs?
A. It belongs to John Lepage.
Q. How do you know that?
A. Because I lived at the house. I knew that he was dealing.
Q. How did you know that?
A. Well, I've seen. Most of his friends are my friends, too, and I've seen all kinds of it around. So I knew basically who he was hanging around with and stuff like that, too.
Q. Were these narcotics yours?
A. No they were not.

The respondent asserts that the evidence of Thelland ought not to have been admissible as it was evidence of bad character adduced for the purpose of showing that the respondent was the type of person who would possess LSD.

It is true that the testimony of Thelland can be construed as character evidence relevant to show the disposition of the respondent or his propensity to traffic in narcotics. Clearly, this would be an inadmissible purpose for adducing the evidence. However, evidence which demonstrates bad character may nonetheless be admissible if it is also relevant to an issue at trial, apart from propensity or disposition. In *R. v. B. (F.F.)*, [1993] 1 S.C.R. 697, Iacobucci J. explained the appropriate principles. . . .

In the present case, the testimony of Thelland is not merely relevant to the character of the respondent, but is also relevant to possession which is a key issue in the case. In the circumstances of this case, there were three people living in the house and it was clear that the drugs belonged to one of the three. Surely, it is relevant to the issue of possession to have one of the three testify that the drugs were not his and furthermore, indicate that the respondent is in the business and therefore it is more likely that he was the owner of the drugs.

The evidence is not being adduced solely for the purpose of showing that the respondent is likely to have committed the crime because he is the type of person who

*remember: general exclusion of character
    evidence, it relates solely to propensity
- exception: LePage - ok if also relates to
    a main issue in case

CHARACTER   157

would be likely to possess drugs. As I stated above, this would be inadmissible character evidence based on the criminal disposition or propensity of an individual. Rather, the evidence of Thelland merely illustrates that someone who is in the business of dealing narcotics has more opportunity and is more likely to be in possession of narcotics.

MAJOR J. (CORY J., concurring):—

. . . .

[T]he essential nature of Thelland's testimony [related] solely to the character and disposition of the accused, rather than to the specific facts of the offence with which he was charged. Thelland did not testify that he had seen Lepage handle the bag of LSD or have the bag in his possession. He did not testify that he saw Lepage place the bag under the couch. Nor did he testify that Lepage had admitted possessing the LSD. The only purpose of this evidence in my view was to show the disposition of the accused, or his propensity to traffic in narcotics and associate with dealers. This is an impermissible purpose.

. . . In Justice Sopinka's view, the evidence of Thelland was relevant not solely to character, but also to possession, in that someone in the business of dealing narcotics had more opportunity and was more likely to be in possession of narcotics. With respect, this is evidence of propensity to deal in drugs, and nothing more. This is what is precluded by the general exclusion of character evidence. The accused is only forced to stand trial for the transactions forming the subject matter of the charge for which he is being tried. The Crown must therefore demonstrate more than a "likelihood" or "opportunity" arising from the past history of the accused. It must demonstrate, beyond a reasonable doubt, that this accused person was in possession of the drugs which form the subject matter of the charge. The testimony of Thelland, in my view, could not assist the Crown in this respect. The prejudicial effect of such testimony would clearly outweigh its minimal probative value with respect to the charge of possession for the purposes of trafficking.

R. v. B. (L.)
(1997), 9 C.R. (5th) 38, 116 C.C.C. (3d) 481 (Ont. C.A.)

[B was charged with sexually assaulting his stepdaughter. She testified that the accused had sexually assaulted her on a number of occasions when she was 8 to 12 years of age. The Crown was allowed to introduce evidence from three other women who alleged sexual abuse at the hands of the accused when they were young girls. The main ground of appeal against conviction concerned the admissibility of similar fact evidence.]

CHARRON J.A. (McMURTRY C.J.O. and DOHERTY J.A. concurring): —

. . . .

The expression "similar fact evidence" is neither very accurate nor descriptive of the type of evidence that is governed by this particular set of evidentiary rules; it is also misleading in some ways. Therefore, when I refer to this type of evidence I will call it evidence of discreditable conduct. However, since the terminology is so deeply ingrained, I will refer to the principles governing the admissibility of this kind of evidence as the "similar fact evidence rule".

Unfortunately, it is not only the label ascribed to this kind of evidence which is unhelpful. It can be quite a perplexing task to discern from the case law the evidentiary rule which effectively governs its admissibility. Indeed, cases on this issue are sometimes difficult, and at times impossible, to reconcile. In my view, it is important to consider the similar fact evidence rule in the context of more general principles of admissibility in order to better understand its application. Some of these principles will be reviewed below.

A. *The Similar Fact Evidence Rule*

(Rule)

The Supreme Court of Canada has considered the similar fact evidence rule, its historical context and its application in numerous cases in the last decade. It is clear that the law has moved from the inception of the rule and from the "old category approach" that followed, to a more modern formulation. The House of Lords in *Boardman v. Director of Public Prosecutions* (1974), [1975] A.C. 421 (U.K. H.L.) revisited the question of similar fact evidence and rejected the category approach that had developed since Makin in favour of a more flexible test: the probative force of the evidence must outweigh its potential prejudice in all the circumstances of the case before it will be admitted. As noted in *R. v. B. (C.R.)*, [1990] 1 S.C.R. 717, 730, "The Canadian jurisprudence since *Boardman* is generally consistent with the approach advocated in that case." In a nutshell, the similar fact evidence rule can be stated as follows: evidence of discreditable conduct of the accused, sought to be introduced by the prosecution, will be inadmissible except when its probative value outweighs its prejudicial effect.

. . . .

The trial judge who is charged with the delicate process of balancing the probative value of the proposed evidence against its prejudicial effect should inquire into the following matters.

TJ must inquire about:

1. Is the conduct, which forms the subject-matter of the proposed evidence, that of the accused?
2. If so, is the proposed evidence relevant and material?
3. If relevant and material, is the proposed evidence discreditable to the accused?
4. If discreditable, does its probative value outweigh its prejudicial effect?

Although the rule can be stated with relative ease, the cases reveal that it can be difficult to apply to specific situations. One difficulty undoubtedly arises from the fact that people have different subjective interpretations of the probative value of evidence. Trial judges must usually draw from their own knowledge and experience when assessing the various factors affecting the probative value of the proposed evidence. It is therefore inevitable that there will often be differences of opinion on any given set of facts. It was perhaps in an effort to achieve greater consistency that the courts had adopted the category approach. However, the category approach is subject to different criticism. If highly prejudicial evidence is admitted whenever it fits into a particular category regardless of its probative value, the purpose of the rule is largely defeated. Conversely, the trier of fact may be deprived of the benefit of highly probative evidence whose prejudicial effect is minimal simply because the evidence does not fall within an accepted category.

The modern formulation of the similar fact evidence rule, which requires a more "purposive and principled case-by-case approach", is consistent with many other recent developments in the law of evidence. Despite its inherent imperfections, and until the wisdom of experience persuades us otherwise, it is believed that this modern approach can better achieve fairness than the rigid application of set rules. I will now review some of the matters which should be considered in answering the above-noted questions.

1. *Is the alleged discreditable conduct that of the accused?*

The Supreme Court has defined the threshold which must be met before evidence of the discreditable conduct other than which forms the subject-matter of the charge may be admitted in *R. v. Sweitzer*, [1982] 1 S.C.R. 949 (S.C.C.):

Before evidence may be admitted as evidence of similar facts, there must be a link between the allegedly similar facts and the accused. In other words there must be some evidence upon which the trier of fact can make a proper finding that the similar facts to be relied upon were in fact the acts of the accused for it is clear that if they were not his own but those of another they have no relevance to the matters at issue under the indictment.

As can be readily observed, this "threshold test" is simply the first step in the inquiry into the relevance of the proposed evidence. The inquiry into relevance and materiality in fact constitutes the threshold test for admissibility of all evidence.

2. Is the proposed evidence relevant and material?

A cardinal principle of our law of evidence is that any information that has any tendency to prove a fact in issue may be admitted in evidence. Therefore, before any evidence can be admitted, it must be relevant and material. It is relevant "where it has some tendency as a matter of logic and human experience to make the proposition for which it is advanced more likely than that proposition would appear to be in the absence of that evidence." It is material if it is directed at a matter in issue in the case.

This threshold test for admissibility is not any different where the Crown seeks to introduce evidence of the accused's conduct other than that which forms the subject-matter of the charge. Despite the label, "similar fact evidence", usually attached to this type of evidence, the initial inquiry is *not* about the degree of similarity between the other conduct and the conduct for which the accused stands trial. Rather, it is about *relevance and materiality*. Generally, this basic threshold of relevance and materiality can be tested by asking what inference is sought to be made from the proposed evidence and whether it has some tendency to advance the inquiry before the court.

Evidence of the conduct of an accused other than that which forms the subject-matter of the charge is a form of character evidence and, as with other forms of character evidence, its relevance usually depends on the proposition that persons tend to act consistently with their character. Even though we know from human experience that this proposition is not always true, the law has proceeded on the basis that, in deciding how a person has acted on a particular occasion, the trier of fact may be assisted by evidence of how he or she has acted before and since. Hence the inference which is sought to be drawn from this kind of evidence is that the accused has acted in a like manner on the occasion which forms the subject-matter of the charge as he or she has acted on other occasions.

Therefore, as a matter of logic and human experience, it will generally be considered relevant in deciding whether a person has sexually assaulted his child or his pupil on a particular occasion to know that he has done so on other occasions. Since the inference which is sought to be drawn from the proposed evidence is that the accused acted in the manner alleged in the charge, the proposed evidence relates to an issue at trial and hence is also material. Therefore, this kind of evidence will usually meet the threshold test for admissibility.

3. Is the proposed evidence discreditable to the accused?

Of course, as we know, passing the threshold test is not always enough for proposed evidence to gain admission at trial. Depending on the nature of the evidence or its potential effect, policy considerations may require further screening before it can be admitted. Where the Crown seeks to introduce evidence of the conduct of an accused other than which forms the subject-matter of the charge, it is the adverse reflection that this evidence may have on the accused's character that signals the need for further investigation. One should ask, is the prior conduct discreditable? If it is not, the rationale underlying the similar fact evidence rule will not apply. Unless the proposed evidence, which does not discredit the accused, triggers the application of some other exclusionary rule of evidence, it is admissible. However, where the other conduct is sufficiently discreditable that it may prejudice the trier of fact against the accused, the similar fact evidence rule does apply and its probative value must outweigh its prejudicial effect before it will be admitted.

Professors Paciocco and Stuesser set out an example that distinguishes well between discreditable conduct and other conduct which does not discredit the accused:

So, evidence that the accused was in the habit of carrying a concealed, illegal weapon should be inadmissible unless it conforms to the similar fact evidence rule. By contrast, the similar fact evidence rule does not apply to evidence that the accused was in the habit of smoking a particular brand of cigarette that was found at the scene of a crime.

Because evidence of discreditable conduct other than that which forms the subject-matter of the charge presents a serious risk of prejudice to the accused, it must not only be relevant and material to gain admission at trial, but must be subject to further screening to ensure that it is worth receiving.

It is important to define what is meant by prejudice in this context. In its widest sense, any evidence that tends to prove guilt can be said to be prejudicial to the accused since it is detrimental to his or her position. Obviously that is not the kind of prejudice that calls for special evidentiary rules. Professor Delisle defines the meaning of prejudice in this context succinctly as follows:

> Prejudice in this context, of course, does not mean that the evidence might increase the chances of conviction but rather that the evidence might be improperly used by the trier of fact. It is one thing for evidence to operate unfortunately for an accused but it is quite another matter for the evidence to operate unfairly. The trier who learns of the accused's previous misconduct may view the accused as a bad man, one who deserves punishment regardless of his guilt of the instant offence and may be less critical of the evidence presently marshalled against him.

4. Does the probative value of the proposed evidence outweigh its prejudicial effect?

In assessing the probative value of the proposed evidence, consideration should be given to such matters as:

(i) the strength of the evidence;

(ii) the extent to which the proposed evidence supports the inference(s) sought to be made from it (this factor will often correspond to the degree of similarity between the prior misconduct and the conduct forming the subject-matter of the charge); and

(iii) the extent to which the matters it tends to prove are at issue in the proceedings.

In assessing the prejudicial effect of the proposed evidence, consideration should be given to such matters as:

(i) how discreditable it is;

(ii) the extent to which it may support an inference of guilt based solely on bad character;

(iii) the extent to which it may confuse issues; and

(iv) the accused's ability to respond to it.

These lists are not meant to be exhaustive. The matters that should be considered depend largely on the particular circumstances of the case. I propose to make a few general comments on some of these matters.

The strength of the proposed evidence

The extent to which the discreditable conduct can be proven has a direct bearing on its probative value. In cases where the accused denies his or her involvement in the prior acts, the issue of proof may be important to the inquiry into its probative value. As seen earlier, this factor will be determinative of the issue in cases where the proposed evidence is so weak as to be incapable of supporting any rational inference. In such cases, the threshold test set out in *Sweitzer* will not have been met and the inquiry will have ended. Once the threshold is met, the strength of the proposed evidence relates to its probative value. The more compelling the proof, the greater its probative value will be.

The accused may have admitted the prior conduct, hence increasing its probative value. In some cases, the discreditable conduct will have been the subject-matter of a conviction and, provided the evidence remains available, it will be capable of proof beyond a reasonable doubt. In other cases, the proposed evidence may be weak or questionable thereby decreasing its probative value. In all cases, the strength of the evidence of discreditable conduct is one factor to be taken into account in the overall assessment of its probative value as it compares to its prejudicial effect.

The problem of the possibility of collaboration among the witnesses who testify to similar acts committed by an accused is one circumstance which may affect the probative value of the proposed evidence. As will be discussed further below, the probative value of evidence of discreditable conduct essentially lies in the improbability of witnesses giving accounts of events of such similarity unless the events occurred. Therefore collusion between witnesses may deprive the evidence of much, if not all, of its force. A question arises as to whether circumstances giving rise to the possibility of collusion should weigh so heavily as to preclude the admissibility of the proposed evidence in all such cases. In my view, the possibility of collusion is but one factor to be considered by the trial judge in assessing the probative value of the evidence and it is not in any way determinative of the question of admissibility. However, there appears to be some uncertainty on this issue.

The issue was recently canvassed by the Supreme Court of Canada in *R. v. Burke,* [1996] 1 S.C.R. 474. . . . In considering this issue, Sopinka J., writing for the court, stated as follows:

> There is a considerable body of authority to the effect that when an issue of the possibility of collusion or collaboration is raised, evidence of similar acts should not be admitted absent a finding by the trial judge that there is no real possibility of collusion or collaboration. See *Cross on Evidence* (7th ed. 1990), at pp. 364-65, and *Hoch v. The Queen* (1988), 165 C.L.R. 292 (H.C. Austr.).
>
> . . . .
>
> As a result of its more recent decisions in *Director of Public Prosecutions v. P.*, [1991] 2 A.C. 447, and *R. v. H.*, [1995] 2 A.C. 596, the House of Lords is now of the view that, generally, the possibility of collusion is not a factor to be applied by the trial judge in determining the admissibility of this type of evidence. This Court has not decided the question although it was my view in my dissent in *R. v. B. (C.R.)*, [1990] 1 S.C.R. 717, that before similar fact evidence is admitted, the risk of collusion must be negatived by a finding by the trial judge. The majority did not express an opinion on the point.
>
> . . . .

The Supreme Court adopted the following approach:

> On the assumption that the evidence is admissible, I am prepared to adopt the more conventional approach which would leave it to the trier of fact to determine what weight, if any, is to be given to evidence that is alleged to have been concocted by means of collusion or collaboration. Under this approach, the trier of fact is obliged to consider the reliability of the evidence having regard to *all* the circumstances, including the opportunities for collusion or collaboration to concoct the evidence and the possibility that these opportunities were used for such a purpose. [Emphasis in original.]

In light of the above, it is my view that, in determining the question of admissibility, the trial judge does not have to reach a conclusion as to the existence of collusion or any other factor affecting the veracity of the witnesses who will testify to the discreditable conduct. The issue will be one for the trier of fact to determine. While the trial judge does not have to make any preliminary finding of facts on the veracity of the proposed evidence, it is my view that the strength of the proposed evidence is nonetheless a factor to be considered in the assessment of its probative value for the purpose of determining admissibility.

. . . .

It is clear from the above excerpt, [in *Lepage*] and from many other cases as well, that propensity reasoning in and of itself is not prohibited. Indeed, it is usually inevitable, given the nature of the evidence and the reason for its admission. Therefore, the trier of fact is entitled to infer from the evidence of prior misconduct (Lepage having dealt in narcotics) that he is *more likely to be* in possession of the narcotics in question and therefore guilty of the offence with which he is charged.

It is propensity reasoning that is based solely on the general bad character of the accused, as revealed through this evidence of discreditable conduct, which is prohibited. Consider, for example, if Lepage had been charged with trafficking in a narcotic as a result of a sale of a piece of cocaine to a police agent, and the sole issue at trial was identification. Evidence that Lepage was a major dealer in drugs without more would have probative value, but only to show that he is the type of person who could well have been selling narcotics as alleged. In this example, there is nothing about the evidence of prior discreditable conduct that connects it to the sole issue in the case, identification. The risk of prejudice, in the sense described above, would be substantial. There would be a real risk that the trier of fact who learns that the accused is a major drug dealer "may view him as a bad man, one who deserves punishment regardless of his guilt of the instant offence and may be less critical of the evidence presently marshalled against him." (See Delisle (1992), 16 Prov. Judges J. 13 at 15.) No matter what probative value can be attached to the fact that he is a major dealer in drugs, the evidence would not be admissible since it is not connected to an issue in the case other than the accused's general disposition to commit the type of offence with which he is charged. If, on the other hand, the sale of the cocaine to the police agent had been carried out in unusual circumstances which bore some distinctive features and the evidence of prior drug dealings bore many of the same features, a connection may well be made to the issue of identification, and the evidence could be admitted if its probative value exceeded its prejudicial effect.

. . . .

Therefore, in assessing this aspect of the probative value of the evidence, it is important to circumscribe the meaning of "disposition" or "propensity", much in the same way as the notion of prejudice described above. The forbidden line of reasoning is that which leads to the conclusion that the accused committed the offence with which he is charged based, not on the strength of the evidence which has a connection to the issues in the case, but rather, on the strength of the evidence that he is "a bad person" who would have a tendency to commit this offence.

Admittedly, the distinction may not always be an easy one to make. But, given the potentially high prejudice inherent in evidence of this kind, this requirement is meant to ensure that only evidence with a real connection to the case will be admitted as opposed to evidence that merely adds to the risk of a wrongful conviction. And, as a final safeguard, whenever this kind of evidence is admitted, the jury must be directed to consider it in relation to the relevant issues in the case and to guard against jumping to unwarranted conclusions based on bad character alone.

———————

For discussion and justification of a similar approach, see Delisle, "The Direct Approach To Similar Fact Evidence" (1996), 50 C.R. (4th) 286.

R. v. ARP

[1998] 3 S.C.R. 339, 20 C.R. (5th) 1, 129 C.C.C. (3d) 321

[Two women, U and B, were murdered some two-and-a-half years apart in the same city and in similar circumstances. The accused was charged with first degree murder of both women. Defence counsel unsuccessfully applied to sever the two murder counts in the indictment. The Crown opposed the application and asserted that even in the case of severance, it would seek to adduce the evidence of each offence in the other trial as similar fact evidence. The Crown conceded that unless the evidence concerning the one murder was admissible to establish that the accused committed the other murder, there should be a severance of the two counts. However, the Crown argued that there were many similarities between the two events indicative of pattern and design.

The trial judge charged the jury that, if they concluded both counts were likely committed by the same person, they could use the evidence on each count to assist in deciding the accused's guilt on both counts. He stated that the evidence on the B killing was admissible in proving the guilt of the accused for the U killing and vice versa. When examining the evidence on both counts, they were instructed not to conclude that the appellant was a person whose character or disposition was such that he likely committed the offences. The trial judge stated that they could infer from the evidence, although they were not required to do so, that the incident mentioned in the B count and the incident mentioned in the U count had characteristics in common that were so strikingly similar that it was likely that they were committed by one person.

The trial judge reviewed the evidence related to the murder of U. The trial judge noted that the Crown submitted the crimes were similar in that the victims were young single females who were vulnerable and who were without funds or transportation in the early morning hours; there was evidence that each was picked up by the accused in a grey pickup truck; the U case clearly involved sexual intercourse, while in the B murder a sexual purpose could be inferred; the victims were left in isolated but accessible areas outside Prince George; the victims' clothes were found discarded nearby; there was evidence that in both cases a sharp-edged instrument such as a knife was used.

The accused was convicted and his appeal dismissed.]

CORY, J. (LAMER, C.J. and L'HEUREUX-DUBʹE, GONTHIER, MCLACHLIN, IACOBUCCI, MAJOR, BASTARACHE and BINNIE, JJ. concurring): —

. . . .

Admissibility of Similar Fact Evidence

Probative Value

This appeal concerns the proper charge to a jury on the use of similar fact evidence. This issue necessarily requires a careful review of the role of the trial judge in considering the admission of similar fact evidence. This is necessary in order to place the function of the jury in weighing similar fact evidence in its proper context.

. . . .

Evidence of propensity or disposition (e.g., evidence of prior bad acts) is relevant to the ultimate issue of guilt, in so far as the fact that a person has acted in a particular way in the past tends to support the inference that he or she has acted that way again. Though this evidence may often have little probative value, it is difficult to say it is not relevant. In this regard, I disagree in part with Lord Hailsham's judgment in *Director of Public Prosecutions v. Boardman*, [1975] A.C. 421. He wrote, at p. 451, that "[w]hen there is nothing to connect the accused with a particular crime except bad character or similar crimes committed in the past, the probative value of the evidence is nil and the evidence is rejected on that ground". I think this statement may go too far. . . .

Thus evidence of propensity or disposition may be relevant to the crime charged, but it is usually inadmissible because its slight probative value is ultimately outweighed by its highly prejudicial effect. As Sopinka J. noted in *R. v. D. (L.E.)*, [1989] 2 S.C.R. 111, at pp. 127-28, there are three potential dangers associated with evidence of prior bad acts: (1) the jury may find that the accused is a "bad person" who is likely to be guilty of the offence charged; (2) they may punish the accused for past misconduct by finding the accused guilty of the offence charged; or (3) they may simply become confused by having their attention deflected from the main purpose of their deliberations, and substitute their verdict on another matter for their verdict on the charge being tried. Because of these very serious dangers to the accused, evidence of propensity or disposition is excluded as an exception to the general rule that all relevant evidence is admissible.

However, as Lord Hailsham stated in *Boardman, supra*, at p. 453, "what is *not* to be admitted is a chain of reasoning and not necessarily a state of facts" (emphasis added). That is, disposition evidence which is adduced *solely* to invite the jury to find the accused guilty because of his or her past immoral conduct is inadmissible. However, evidence of similar past misconduct may exceptionally be admitted where the prohibited line of reasoning may be avoided.

[Justice Cory then reviewed the majority opinion of McLachlin, J. in *R. v. B. (C.R.)* and concluded.]

It can be seen that in considering whether similar fact evidence should be admitted the basic and fundamental question that must be determined is whether the probative value of the evidence outweighs its prejudicial effect. As well it must be remembered that a high degree of deference must be given to the decision of a trial judge on this issue. . . .

It follows that where identity is at issue in a criminal case and the accused is shown to have committed acts which bear a striking similarity to the alleged crime, the jury is not asked to infer from the accused's habits or disposition that *he is the type of person* who would commit the crime. Instead, the jury is asked to infer from the degree of distinctiveness or uniqueness that exists between the commission of the crime and the similar act that *the accused is the very person* who committed the crime. This inference is made possible only if the high degree of similarity between the acts renders the likelihood of coincidence objectively improbable. See *Hoch v. The Queen* (1988), 165 C.L.R. 292 (Aust. H.C.). That is, there is always a possibility that by coincidence the perpetrator of the crime and the accused share certain predilections or that the accused may become implicated in crimes for which he is not responsible. However, where the evidence shows a distinct pattern to the acts in question, the possibility that the accused would repeatedly be implicated in strikingly similar offences purely as a matter of coincidence is greatly reduced.

. . . .

[A] principled approach to the admission of similar fact evidence will in all cases rest on the finding that the accused's involvement in the alleged similar acts or counts is unlikely to be the product of coincidence. This conclusion ensures that the evidence has sufficient probative force to be admitted, and will involve different considerations in different contexts. Where, as here, similar fact evidence is adduced on the issue of identity, there must be a high degree of similarity between the acts for the evidence to be admitted. For example, a unique trademark or signature will automatically render the alleged acts "strikingly similar" and therefore highly probative and admissible. In the same way, a number of significant similarities, taken together, may be such that by their cumulative effect, they warrant admission of the evidence. Where identity is at issue ordinarily, the trial judge should review the manner in which the similar acts were committed — that is to say, whether the similar acts involve a unique trademark or reveal a number of significant similarities. This review will enable him or her to decide whether the alleged similar acts were all committed by the same person. This preliminary determination establishes the objective improbability that the accused's involvement in the alleged acts is the product of coincidence and thereby gives the evidence the requisite probative force. Thus, where the similar fact evidence is adduced to prove identity, once this preliminary determination is made, the evidence related to the similar act (or count, in a multi-count indictment) may be admitted to prove the commission of another act (or count).

. . . .

revised Test re: identity

In summary, in considering the admissibility of similar fact evidence, the basic rule is that the trial judge must first determine whether the probative value of the evidence outweighs its prejudicial effect. In most cases where similar fact evidence is adduced to prove identity it might be helpful for the trial judge to consider the following suggestions in deciding whether to admit the evidence:

(1) Generally where similar fact evidence is adduced to prove identity a high degree of similarity between the acts is required in order to ensure that the similar fact evidence has the requisite probative value of outweighing its prejudicial effect to be admissible. The similarity between the acts may consist of a unique trademark or signature on a series of significant similarities.

(2) In assessing the similarity of the acts, the trial judge should only consider the manner in which the acts were committed and not the evidence as to the accused's involvement in each act.

(3) There may well be exceptions but as a general rule if there is such a degree of similarity between the acts that it is likely that they were committed by the same person then the similar fact evidence will ordinarily have sufficient probative force to outweigh its prejudicial effect and may be admitted.

(4) The jury will then be able to consider all the evidence related to the alleged similar acts in determining the accused's guilt for any one act.

Once again these are put forward not as rigid rules but simply as suggestions that may assist trial judges in their approach to similar fact evidence.

Link to the Accused — *Sweitzer: just need same evidence, not conclude (proof)*

Where the similar fact evidence adduced to prove identity suggests that the same person committed the similar acts, then logically this finding makes the evidence linking the accused to each similar act relevant to the issue of identity for the offence being tried. Similarly, in a multi-count indictment, the link between the accused and any one count will be relevant to the issue of identity on the other counts which disclose a striking similarity in the manner in which those offences were committed.

A link between the accused and the alleged similar acts is, however, also a precondition to admissibility. This requirement was set forth in *R. v. Sweitzer*, [1982] 1 S.C.R. 949, at p. 954. . . .

. . . .

Should the trial judge be required to conclude *not only* that the evidence suggests that the acts are the work of one person with sufficient force to outweigh the prejudicial effect of the evidence, but that they also are likely the acts of the accused? This is the approach advocated by Professor R. Mahoney in "Similar Fact Evidence and the Standard of Proof", [1993] Crim. L. Rev. 185, at pp. 196-97, and is implicitly favoured by those courts which have endorsed the "anchor" or "sequential" approach to similar fact evidence. See, e.g., *R. v. Ross*, [1980] 5 W.W.R. 261 (B.C. C.A.); *R. v. J.T.S.*, [1997] A.J. No. 125 (C.A.).

The suggestion that the evidence linking the accused to the similar acts must also link the acts to the accused goes too far. Once the trial judge has concluded that the similar acts were likely the work of one person and that there is some evidence linking the accused to the alleged similar acts, it is not necessary to conclude that the similar acts were likely committed by the accused. The answer to this question may well determine guilt or innocence. This is the very question which the trier of fact must determine on the basis of all the evidence related to the similar acts, including of course the accused's involvement in each act. The standard set out in *Sweitzer* should be maintained. This only requires that the trial judge be satisfied that there is some evidence which links the accused to the similar acts.

. . . .

The general principles enunciated in these cases indicate that the jury should determine, on a balance of the probabilities, whether the similarities between the acts establishes that the two counts were committed by the same person. If that threshold is met, the jury can then consider all the evidence relating to the similar acts in determining whether, beyond a reasonable doubt, the accused is guilty.

However, the general rule that preliminary findings of fact may be determined on a balance of probabilities is departed from in those certainly rare occasions when admission of the evidence may itself have a conclusive effect with respect to guilt. For example, where the Crown adduces a statement of the accused made to a person in authority, the trial judge must be satisfied beyond a reasonable doubt of the voluntariness of the statement. That evidence may of itself, if accepted as true, provide conclusive proof of guilt. Since doubt about the statement's voluntariness also casts doubt on its reliability, proof beyond a reasonable doubt is warranted. See *Ward v. The Queen*, [1979] 2 S.C.R. 30. If this were not the rule, the jury would be permitted to rely on evidence which it could accept as extremely cogent even though the inherent reliability of that evidence was in doubt.

Similar fact evidence, on the other hand, as circumstantial evidence, must be characterized differently, since, by its nature, it does not carry the potential to be conclusive of guilt. It is just one item of evidence to be considered as part of the Crown's overall case. Its probative value lies in its ability to support, through the improbability of coincidence, other inculpatory evidence. As with all circumstantial evidence, the jury will decide what weight to attribute to it. The mere fact that in a particular case, similar fact evidence might be assigned a high degree of weight by the trier is entirely different from the concept that, by its very nature, the evidence has the potential to be decisive of guilt.

R. v. BATTE
(2000), 34 C.R. (5th) 197, 145 C.C.C. (3d) 449 (Ont. C.A.)

[The accused was charged with sexually assaulting two sisters, D.D. and D.S.D, in the late 1970s when the complainants were young teenagers. The trial turned on the credibility of the complainants. The trial judge admitted evidence of the accused's sexual abuse of the complainants at places and times not encompassed within the indictment.]

DOHERTY, J.A. (MCMURTRY, C.J.O. and ROSENBERG, J.A. concurring): —

. . . .

Counsel's argument regarding the trial judge's failure to caution the jury against resort to propensity reasoning assumes that propensity reasoning could have no proper role in the jury's analysis of the evidence. I do not accept that assumption. While a jury must never convict based on a finding that an accused engaged in misconduct other than that alleged, and must never convict based on an assessment that the accused is a bad person, there will be cases in which a more focused form of propensity reasoning is entirely appropriate. I think this was such a case.

Propensity reasoning involves two inferences. First, one infers from conduct on occasions other than the occasion in issue that a person has a certain disposition (state of mind). Second, one infers from the existence of that disposition that a person acted in a certain way on the occasion in issue: *R. v. Watson* (1996), 108 C.C.C. (3d) 310 (Ont. C.A.) at p. 325. Assuming the evidence can reasonably support both inferences, there is nothing irrational or illogical in using propensity reasoning to infer that an accused committed the act alleged. Viewed in this way, the evidence of the accused's discreditable conduct is a form of circumstantial evidence and meets the legal relevance criterion: *R. v. Arp*, *supra*, at pp. 338-9 S.C.R.

Despite its relevance, evidence that depends on propensity reasoning for its admissibility is usually excluded because its potential prejudicial effect outweighs its probative value: *R. v. Arp*, *supra*, at p. 339 S.C.R. Often the evidence has little probative value because either or both of the necessary inferences needed to give the evidence probative force are tenuous. For example, the inference that an accused has a certain disposition based on evidence of a single discreditable act could be so tenuous as to have virtually no probative value. Similarly, where discreditable evidence is probative of a disposition, the inference that an accused acted in accordance with that disposition on the occasion in question will often be a very weak one. For example, evidence that an accused repeatedly abused "A" would not, standing alone, support the inference that he was disposed to abuse "B" on the occasion alleged in the indictment.

Even where the discreditable conduct is such as to reasonably permit the inferences necessary to give propensity reasoning probative value, that evidence can still be misused by the jury. Often, evidence which can support propensity reasoning will have a much greater potential to improperly prejudice the jury against the accused. As Sopinka J. observed in *R. v. D. (L.E.)*, [1989] 2 S.C.R. 111 at pp. 127-28, 50 C.C.C. (3d) 142, a jury may assume from the evidence of discreditable conduct that the accused is a bad person and convict on that basis, or they may convict in order to punish the accused for the discreditable conduct, or they may become embroiled in a determination of whether the accused committed the alleged discreditable acts and lose sight of the real question — did he commit the acts alleged in the indictment? The risk that the jury will be led astray by evidence of discreditable conduct usually overcomes the probative force of that evidence where the probative force rests entirely on propensity reasoning.

Propensity reasoning also imperils the overall fairness of the criminal trial process. It is a fundamental tenet of our criminal justice system that persons are charged and tried based on specific allegations of misconduct. If an accused is to be convicted, it must be because the Crown has proved that allegation beyond a reasonable doubt and not because of the way the accused has lived the rest of his or her life. An accused must be tried for what he or she did and not for who he or she is. The criminal law's reluctance to permit inferences based on propensity reasoning reflects its commitment to this fundamental tenet: *McCormick on Evidence*, 5th ed., p. 658; R. Lempert and S. Saltzburg, *A Modern Approach to Evidence*, 2nd ed. (West Publishing Co., 1982), at p. 219.

The wisdom of excluding evidence which relies entirely for its cogency on propensity reasoning is beyond doubt. In most situations, the evidence will provide little or no assistance in determining how an accused acted on the occasion in issue. It may, however, leave the jury with the clear sense that this accused is a bad person who merits punishment or at least does not merit the benefit of any reasonable doubt.

The criminal law's resistance to propensity reasoning is not, however, absolute. There will be situations in which the probative force of propensity reasoning is so strong that it overcomes the potential prejudice and cannot be ignored if the truth of the allegation is to be determined. The probative force of propensity reasoning reaches that level where the evidence, if accepted, suggests a strong disposition to do the very act alleged in the indictment. For example, if an accused is charged with assaulting his wife, evidence that the accused beat his wife on a regular basis throughout their long marriage would be admissible. Evidence of the prior beatings does much more than suggest that the accused is a bad person or that the accused has a general disposition to act violently and commit assaults. The evidence suggests a strong disposition to do the very act in issue — assault his wife. In such cases, the jury is permitted to reason, assuming it accepts the evidence of the prior assaults, that the accused was disposed to act violently towards his wife and that he had that disposition on the occasion in issue. The existence of the disposition is a piece of circumstantial evidence that may be considered in deciding whether the accused committed the alleged assault.

The admissibility of prior assaults as evidence that the accused assaulted the same person on the occasion in issue is well established in the authorities: e.g., *R. v. F. (D.S.)* (1999), 132 C.C.C. (3d) 97 (Ont. C.A.); *McCormick on Evidence, supra*, pp. 665-66. While the authorities refer to the evidence as relevant to demonstrate motive or animus, these labels merely describe the disposition that is established by the discreditable conduct evidence. They do not detract from the fact that the evidence derives its probative force through propensity reasoning: R. Lempert, S. Saltzburg, *A Modern Approach to Evidence, supra*, pp. 226-27, 229-30.

. . . .

My colleague [Charron, J.A. in *R. v. B. (L.)*] has captured the crucial issue to be addressed when determining whether discreditable conduct evidence should be admitted on the basis of propensity reasoning. Evidence which tends to show no more than a general disposition must be distinguished from evidence which demonstrates a disposition to do the very thing alleged in the indictment. If the evidence of the discreditable conduct is such that it shows a strong disposition to do the very act alleged in the very circumstances alleged, then the evidence has a "real connection" to the very issue to be decided — did the accused commit the act: see R. Delisle, "Similar Facts: Here We Go Again" (1999), 20 C.R. (5th) 38 at p. 41. The probative potential of propensity reasoning will be highest where the discreditable conduct is temporally connected to the allegations in the indictment and involves repeated acts of the same kind with the same complainant as those alleged in the indictment.

Some commentators have suggested that *R. v. Arp, supra*, is inconsistent with the approach taken by Charron, J.A. in *R. v. B. (L.), supra*, to propensity reasoning: see V. Maric, "Similar Fact Evidence: Preferring *B. (L.)* to *Arp*" (1999), 23 C.R. (5th) 57; R. Delisle, "Similar Facts: Here We Go Again", *supra*, at pp. 41-42. I do not agree. Both judgments drew on the same authorities from the Supreme Court of Canada, particularly *R. v. B. (C.R.), supra*. Factually, however, they were very different cases. Arp was charged with two murders, one of which was committed some two years before the other. The issue at trial was identity. The Crown contended that the evidence of the accused's involvement in each homicide was admissible to establish his guilt on the other homicide. It was in this factual context that Cory J. described propensity reasoning as an improper basis upon which to receive or use the evidence of one homicide in considering Arp's guilt on the other.

The facts in *Arp* could not reasonably permit the drawing of either of the inferences necessary for legitimate propensity reasoning. It is difficult to see how a single act of violence demonstrates a disposition to act violently, much less a disposition to act violently in different circumstances some two and one-half years earlier or later. The danger of misusing propensity reasoning by inferring that Arp was a "bad person" who therefore committed both crimes was, however, great. Consequently, Cory J. held that if the evidence of one homicide was to be admitted on the other, the Crown had to demonstrate a legitimate process of reasoning which would avoid reasoning through propensity. This led Cory J.

to a consideration of whether the circumstances were such as to permit, apart entirely from any inference to be drawn from propensity, the inference that it was likely that the two acts were committed by the same person. His summary of the elements of an appropriate charge where discreditable conduct is admitted (at p. 356 S.C.R.) is also directed to cases, like *R. v. Arp, supra,* in which propensity reasoning is inappropriate.

R. v. Arp, supra, does not hold that propensity reasoning is never permissible. Cory J., at p. 361 S.C.R., p. 339 C.C.C., recognized that evidence of propensity is "usually inadmissible". He strongly reaffirmed the dangers associated with that form of reasoning and reiterated the exclusionary rule where inferences based on propensity reasoning are simply too weak to overcome the prejudice associated with drawing inferences based on propensity.

. . . .

In *R. v. B. (L.), supra,* as in this case, the issue was whether sexual assaults occurred. The evidence of the accused's sexual misconduct towards the other young girls in his charge was sufficiently connected to that issue to make the inferences to be drawn from propensity reasoning sufficiently cogent to warrant the admissibility of the evidence and the use of that reasoning. This was so even though the evidence, coming from three other witnesses, carried the potential prejudice inherent where evidence of discreditable conduct is given by witnesses other than the complainant. In the present case, the cogency of the propensity reasoning was arguably stronger since the misconduct involved the same complainants. The risk of prejudice was reduced since the evidence came from the same complainants and there was no risk that their credibility would be enhanced by the evidence of third parties.

Neither the Crown nor the defence asked the trial judge to instruct the jury for or against the use of propensity reasoning. The trial judge approached the evidence, as counsel had, as going to the credibility of the complainants. The trial judge could have told the jury that they should not infer from the evidence of the appellant's discreditable conduct that he was the type of person who would engage in the criminal activity alleged against him: *R. v. M. (B.)* (1998), 42 O.R. (3d) 1 (C.A.) at p. 10. Had he elected to warn against the misuse of propensity reasoning, however, the trial judge would also have had to instruct the jury on its proper use. He would have had to instruct the jury that if they accepted the complainants' evidence, they could infer that the appellant had consistently, over a prolonged period, extracted sexual services from the complainants while they were under his control as his entitlement in return for the benefits he bestowed upon them. The trial judge would further have had to instruct the jury that if they were satisfied that the appellant had consistently extracted those services, they could infer that the appellant had done the same thing during the time frame set out in the indictment and could consider that evidence in determining whether the Crown had proved the allegations in the indictment beyond a reasonable doubt.

I have no doubt that, on balance, an instruction which explained both the proper and improper uses of propensity reasoning would have operated against the appellant's interests. I see no error in the alleged non-direction.

For comments see Delisle, "*Batte*: Similar Fact Evidence Is a Matter of Propensity" (2000), 34 C.R. (5th) 240, and Peck and Harris, "Propensity Evidence Reclaims Its Name: The Potential Impact of *R. v. Batte*" (2000), 34 C.R. (5th) 243.

PROBLEMS

Problem 1

Plaintiff in a suit for damages for criminal conversation sought to show that on the evening in question his wife and the defendant stayed overnight in a hotel, and when they registered as Mr. and Mrs. Miller they had baggage with them. The significance of the baggage would be in its confirmation of an intended overnight sojourn. To prove the presence of the baggage the plaintiff called as a witness the hotel room clerk. The clerk is prepared to testify that the room was not paid for in advance and that it was the uniform practice of the hotel to require payment in advance for lodging when the registrant was without luggage. Relevant? How uniform must the practice be? See *Baldridge v. Matthews*, 106 A. 2d 809 (Pa. S.C., 1954) and *Joy v. Phillips, Mills & Co.*, [1916] 1 K.B. 849 (C.A.).

Problem 2

A is charged with the murder of B, a woman with whom he was then living. The cause of B's death was arsenical poisoning. The prosecution seeks to tender evidence that A's wife died of arsenical poisoning two years earlier. Relevant? Receivable? Compare *Noor Mohammed v. R.*, [1949] A.C. 182 (P.C.).

Problem 3

Plaintiff, a young newsboy, sues defendant for personal injuries suffered as the result of the negligence of the defendant's servants while he was boarding a street-car owned by defendant; the defendant maintains that the accident was caused by the boy's own negligence in that he attempted to board the street-car while it was moving. The defendant offers in evidence that the boy within a month of the accident had been seen on two occasions boarding moving street-cars. Relevant? Receivable? Compare *Manenti v. Melbourne and Metropolitan Tramways Board*, [1954] V.L.R. 115. If you feel the evidence is irrelevant would you change your mind if the boy had been seen boarding moving street-cars on more than two occasions? How many more? If such evidence is rejected could the defendant offer evidence that the boy had been twice warned of the danger of boarding moving street-cars? Relevant? Material? Fair? Receivable? Limiting instructions?

Problem 4

The accused is charged with sexual assault. The victim is the daughter of the accused, aged 16. The prosecution seeks to tender in evidence a previous conviction of the accused for sexual assault. Relevant? Receivable? Would your opinion change if the victim of the previous rape is the sister of the present victim? Compare *R. v. Chenier* (1981), 63 C.C.C. (2d) 36 (Que. C.A.) and *R. v. C. (J.R.)* (1996), 1 C.R. (5th) 334 (Sask. C.A.).

Problem 5

The accused is charged with arson. The building destroyed housed the accused's business and was heavily insured. The prosecution tenders in evidence the fact that twice in the past three years heavily insured business premises owned by the accused were destroyed by fire. He is prepared to show that the accused was found at the scene of each fire, that in his possession on each occasion were keys to the premises, and in all three instances the premises appeared to have been secure at the time of the fire. Relevant? Receivable? Compare *R. v. Carpenter* (1981), 61 C.C.C. (2d) 481 (Ont. C.A.).

Problem 6

The accused is charged with murder. The victim was one of his children, aged three, and there is no doubt from the evidence that the child died as the result of external violence. Two prosecution witnesses have testified in graphic detail the manner in which the accused allegedly beat the child into unconsciousness. The defence is an outright denial. The prosecution wishes to tender in evidence descriptions of other occasions on which the accused beat the child. Relevant? Receivable? Of other occasions when the accused beat the other children. Of occasions when he abused the family dog. Relevant? Receivable? Compare *R. v. Drysdale*, [1969] 2 C.C.C. 141 (Man. C.A., 1968), *R. v. Roud* (1981), 58 C.C.C. (2d) 226 (Ont. C.A.), *R. v. Speid* (1985), 46 C.R. (3d) 22 (Ont. C.A.), and *R. v. Gottschall* (1983), 10 C.C.C. (3d) 447 (N.S. C.A.).

(iii) *Civil Cases*

There are far fewer reported civil cases involving the problem of similar facts than criminal cases. In those reported, the approach is commonly said to be the same.

The oft-cited decision of *Hales v. Kerr* [44] is instructive. The plaintiff was a customer of the defendant and had been shaved on October 9, 1907. The plaintiff contracted a disease known as barber's itch. The plaintiff called two witnesses who testified that they had been shaved in the defendant's shop in September and had contracted the same disorder. Channel, J. analogized to the rule in criminal cases and recognized that thereby evidence of previous misconduct was inadmissible when such evidence was simply tendered to show that he is "a likely person to have committed the offence charged." Channell, J. wrote:

> In civil proceedings the rules are not dissimilar. It is not legitimate to charge a man with an act of negligence on a day in October and to ask a jury to infer that he was negligent on that day because he was negligent on every day in September. The defendant may have mended his ways before the day named in October; moreover, he does not come to trial prepared to meet all the allegations of previous negligence.[45]

The same underlying concern is being voiced; though the evidence may be relevant it is not fair to the defendant who may be taken by surprise and who may also be prejudiced in the eyes of the jury. Nevertheless, the court ruled the evidence was receivable as it went to establish a dangerous practice carried on in the defendant's establishment, from which a legitimate inference could be taken that such practice having caused injury on those occasions it caused injury in the plaintiff's case also. By this "technique" the court sought to avoid a chain of reasoning which would involve imputations against the defendant's character for care; a chain of reasoning that would suggest the defendant was a "likely person" to have been negligent on the occasion under review.

---

44.   [1908] 2 K.B. 601 (Div. Ct.).
45.   *Ibid.*, at pp. 604-05.

Has the court accomplished its aim? Could we more straightforwardly confront the problem? The problems of surprise and prejudice are real and it may be wise to generally exclude evidence of similar facts. But when the similar facts have a high degree of probative worth can we not then simply recognize that fact and ask whether it is sufficiently relevant that the dangers are overcome? Consider the approach of Lord Reid in *McWilliams v. Sir William Arrol & Co.*[46] In that case, a steel erector had fallen 70 feet from a tower in the building of which the victim was assisting. His widow sued his employer for damages for failing to provide a safety belt. Safety belts had been available on the job site until two or three days before the accident but had then been removed to another site. The employers resisted the claim, arguing that while they had breached their statutory duty in failing to provide safety belts such breach was not the cause of the accident as the deceased would not have worn a safety belt if it had been provided. Several witnesses testified that they had never seen McWilliams wear a safety belt, but one witness said he had seen him wear a belt on two occasions when working in an exposed position. Lord Reid reasoned:

> . . . it appears to me to be a natural, and indeed almost inevitable inference that he would not have worn a belt on this occasion even if it had been available. And that inference is strengthened by the general practice of other men not to wear belts.
>
> It was argued that the law does not permit such an inference to be drawn because what a man did on previous occasions is no evidence of what he would have done on a later similar occasion. This argument was based on the rule that you cannot infer that a man committed a particular crime or delict from the fact that he has previously committed other crimes or delicts. But even that is not an unqualified rule, and there are reasons for that rule which would not apply to a case like the present. *It would not be right to draw such an inference too readily because people do sometimes change their minds unexpectedly. But the facts of this case appear to me to be overwhelming.* [Emphasis added.][47]

Consider also the more recent civil case of *Mood Music Publishing Co. v. De Wolfe Ltd.*[48] following the lead of *Boardman*. The plaintiffs in a copyright action alleged infringement, and the defence was that the similarity was coincidental and not the result of copying. The plaintiffs tendered in evidence other works produced by defendants which were markedly similar to works of well known composers which were still in copyright. The plaintiffs maintained that this showed the defendants in other cases had been reproducing musical works which were subject to copyright and so may have done the same in regard to their work. Lord Denning ruled the evidence receivable:

> The criminal courts have been very careful not to admit such evidence unless its probative value is so strong that it should be received in the interests of justice: and its admission will not operate unfairly to the accused. In civil cases the courts have followed a similar line but have not been so chary of admitting it. In civil cases the courts will admit evidence of similar facts if it is logically probative, that is, if it is logically relevant in determining the matter which is in issue: provided that it is not oppressive or unfair to the other side: and also that the other side has fair notice of it and is able to deal with it. . . . *the evidence of these three matters is of sufficient*

---

46.   [1962] 1 All E.R. 623 (H.L.).
47.   *Ibid.*, at pp. 630-31.
48.   [1976] 2 W.L.R. 451 (C.A.).

probative weight to be relevant to this issue and should be admitted. [Emphasis added.][49]

In the British Columbia Court of Appeal, in *MacDonald v. Canada Kelp Co.*,[50] the plaintiffs sought rescission and damages for fraudulent misrepresentation with respect to the sale of certain shares. The defendant denied the representations alleged and the plaintiffs sought to show that similar representation had been made by the defendant to others at about the same general period of time. The defendants conceded that such evidence would be receivable if it was led, per one of the categories of relevance, to show intent, state of mind, *mens rea*, identity, or to negative accident, but maintained that where the only issue was whether the statements were in fact made, evidence of similar statements made to other people was not receivable. The court rejected this reasoning and held simply:

> *When there is a real and substantial nexus or connection* between the act or allegation made, whether it be a crime or a fraud (but not, of course, limited to those), and facts relating to previous or subsequent transactions are sought to be given in evidence, then those facts have relevancy and are admissible not only to rebut a defence, such as lack of intent, accident, *mens rea* or the like, but to prove the fact of the act or allegations made. [Emphasis added.][51]

TESKEY v. CANADIAN NEWSPAPERS CO.
(1989), 68 O.R. (2d) 737, 59 D.L.R. (4th) 709 (C.A.)

[In a civil suit for damages the plaintiff needed to show malice in the defendant. On appeal it was objected that the trial judge had received evidence of wrongful allegations of misconduct made by the defendant in the past.]

. . . .

The problem created by the admission of similar fact evidence is well known and was recently reviewed by McIntyre J. in *Sweitzer v. The Queen* (1982), 137 D.L.R. (3d) 702 at pp. 705-7, 68 C.C.C. (2d) 193, [1982] 1 S.C.R. 949. Such evidence is not admissible to show, from past conduct, a person's disposition to commit certain types of acts, in this case, the making of charges against persons holding public offices or appointments. Nevertheless, such evidence is admissible if it is relevant to issues before a jury. McIntyre J. listed examples where evidence had been admitted for this purpose at p. 706:

> Over the years in seeking to apply this principle judges have tended to create a list of categories or types of cases in which similar fact evidence could be admitted, generally by reference to the purpose for which the evidence was adduced. Evidence of similar facts has been adduced to prove intent, to prove a system, to prove a plan, *to show malice*, to rebut the defence of accident or mistake, to prove identity, to rebut the defence of innocent association and for other similar and related purposes. This list is not complete.

---

49.   *Ibid.*, at p. 456. Followed in *Re Bianchi and Aquanno* (1983), 42 O.R. (2d) 76 (Div. Ct.) and in *Berger v. Raymond Sun*, [1984] 1 W.L.R. 625.
50.   (1973), 39 D.L.R. (3d) 617 (B.C.C.A.).
51.   *Ibid.*, at p. 626 per Bull, J.A. Compare the older view, "distinguished" in *MacDonald* in *Larson v. Boyd* (1919), 58 S.C.R. 275, and the dissenting opinion of Robertson, J.A. in *MacDonald*, which saw *Larson v. Boyd* as controlling to reject.

(Emphasis added.) Such evidence is only admissible if its probative value is not outweighed by the prejudice caused by its admission.

I think that Fitzpatrick J. properly admitted this evidence. His ruling stated that the evidence might "well have considerable probative value with respect to the issue of malice". After balancing its relevance on this issue with the possibility of prejudice, he admitted the evidence with the observation that, if prejudice resulted, he might be able "to repair that damage in my charge". Mrs. Block objected to his charge because he made no mention of prejudice but, in view of the over-all evidence of malice, to which I will refer later, there was no requirement, in my opinion, for him to do so.

The court says that evidence of similar facts "is not admissible to show, from past conduct, a person's disposition to commit certain types of facts." But, the court says, "such evidence is admissible if it is relevant to issues before a jury." No information is admissible unless it is relevant to issues before a jury; that's the first rule of evidence. The second comment of the court adds nothing then of particular significance to the admissibility of similar fact evidence. Ask yourselves how the past conduct in *Teskey* was relevant to the issue of malice before the jury save and except through exhibiting the defendant's disposition. Recall that in *Sweitzer*, in the paragraph that follows the quotation chosen by the court in *Teskey*, the Supreme Court of Canada referred to the fact that the creation of a list of categories has served to obscure the true basis for the admission of similar fact evidence which is simply that "admissibility will depend upon the probative effect of the evidence balanced against the prejudice caused by its admission."

(e) Character of Victim

Chief Justice Cardozo sought to justify a difference in treatment of character evidence depending on whether it was of the accused or the victim:

> In a very real sense a defendant starts his life afresh when he stands before a jury, a prisoner at the bar. There has been a homicide in a public place. The killer admits the killing, but urges self-defence and sudden impulse. Inflexibly the law has set its face against the endeavour to fasten guilt upon him by proof of character or experience predisposing to an act of crime. At times, when the issue has been self-defence, testimony has been admitted as to the murderous propensity of the deceased, the victim of the homicide, but never of such a propensity on the part of the killer. The principle back of the exclusion is one, not of logic, but of policy. There may be cogency in the argument that a quarrelsome defendant is more likely to start a quarrel than one of a milder type, a man of dangerous mode of life more likely than a shy recluse. The law is not blind to this, but equally it is not blind to the peril of the innocent if character is accepted as probative of crime. "The natural and inevitable tendency of the tribunal — whether judge or jury — is to give excessive weight to the vicious record of crime thus exhibited, and either to allow it to bear too strongly on the present charge, or to take the proof of it as justifying a condemnation irrespective of guilt of the present charge."[52]

---

52. *People v. Zackowitz*, 172 N.E. 466 (1930). The quotation in this excerpt is from 1 Wigmore, *Evidence*, s. 194.

(i) *Self-defence*

Are you satisfied with this justification?

The accused is charged with murder and she offers self-defence as an excuse. The accused maintains that she viewed the deceased's actions as threatening since she believed him to be a violent man. The accused offers in evidence the deceased's character, his reputation, his violent acts, to support her defence.

Is this evidence relevant? To what? Can you articulate the "rational connection"? Is it receivable?[53]

Notice the evidence is not being offered for a circumstantial use. The trier is not being asked to infer from the victim's character that the victim acted in conformity with it on the occasion under review. The material fact in issue is the accused's state of mind, and the evidence offered is relevant to her/his belief that the character apprehended was there to be perceived. The evidence is being tendered to show the reasonableness of the accused's belief. If it is relevant to a material issue, the evidence is receivable unless there is a clear policy to argue against admissibility.

Can you articulate any policy reasons for exclusion of such evidence?[54]

Suppose, however, that in the manslaughter case the deceased's character or disposition towards violence was not known to the accused at the time of the incident.

On a plea of self-defence is the deceased's character for violence relevant?

In this case we ask the trier to infer that the persons acted in conformity with their character. Since here we are offering the character evidence as circumstantial evidence from which we ask the trier of fact to infer that the victim acted in conformity with their character, a problem of relevance arises. The law provides no answer to such a problem. Rather, we must rely on our common sense and experience to guide us.

In *R. v. Scopelliti*[55] the accused was charged with two counts of murder. The principal defence was self-defence. The accused testified to his apprehension caused by the deceased's actions. The trial judge allowed the defence to intoduce evidence of three prior acts of violence or threats of violence, *not known to the accused*, committed by the deceased and directed at other persons. On appeal from the acquittal the Ontario Court of Appeal, presented with no authorities on the issue, reasoned from basic principles:

---

53. See *R. v. Whynot (Stafford)* (1983), 37 C.R. (3d) 198 (N.S.C.A.).
54. See *R. v. Drouin* (1909), 15 C.C.C. 205, 207 (Que. Q.B.) and *R. v. Scott* (1910), 15 C.C.C. 442 (Ont. H.C.).
55. (1981), 63 C.C.C. (2d) 481 (Ont. C.A.). *Scopelliti* was followed in *R. v. Ryan* (1989), 49 C.C.C. (3d) 490 (Nfld. C.A.): evidence of violent acts by the deceased was receivable in evidence in a murder prosecution to support the reasonableness of the accused's state of mind and also to indicate who was the agressor on the occasion under review. See also *R. v. Yaeck* (1991), 10 C.R. (4th) 1 (Ont. C.A.), considering both *Scopelliti* and *Seaboyer*, *infra*.

. . . the admission of such evidence accords in principle with the view expressed by this Court that the disposition of a person to do a certain act is relevant to indicate the probability of his having done or not having done the act. The law prohibits the prosecution from introducing evidence for the purpose of showing that the *accused* is a person who by reason of his criminal character (disposition) is likely to have committed the crime charged, on policy grounds, not because of lack of relevance. There is, however, no rule of policy which excludes evidence of the disposition of a third person for violence where that disposition has probative value on some issue before the jury.[56]

Interestingly, the court, following Wigmore,[57] saw "no substantial reason against evidencing the character by particular instances of violent or quarrelsome conduct." While not necessary to its decision, the court went on to hold that in a case such as this the Crown would be entitled to rebut the defence evidence by character evidence showing the deceased to be of a peaceable disposition.[58] The court left open the question of whether the Crown was also then entitled to lead evidence of the accused's disposition towards violence.

Recognizing that evidence of the victim's character for violence is relevant to whether he was the aggressor on the occasion under review, is there any policy presented that might argue for exclusion?

In *Scopelliti* the court recognized the need for a weighing by the trial judge of the probative worth of the evidence against the possibility of an irrational decision by the jury:

> Since evidence of prior acts of violence by the deceased is likely to arouse feelings of hostility against the deceased, there must inevitably be some element of discretion in the determination whether the proferred evidence has sufficient probative value for the purpose for which it is tendered to justify its admission.[59]

The Crown in *Scopelliti* argued that there was insufficient probative value as none of the prior acts were life-threatening, and the acts simply tended to show a general disposition toward violence which would make it likely that the deceased were the aggressors. This attempt to provide a limitation on such evidence akin to the limitation on the introduction of similar facts against an accused was rejected by the court.[60]

---

56.   *Scopelliti, ibid.*, at p. 493.

57.   1 Wigmore, *Evidence* (3d ed.), s. 198.

58.   See and compare *Comm. of Pennsylvania v. Castellana*, 121 A. 50 (Pa., 1923) and *R. v. Johnson* (1965), 49 C.R. 176 (N.S.C.A.), and *R. v. Dejong* (1998), 16 C.R. (5th) 372 (B.C.C.A.).

59.   *Supra*, note 55, at p. 496. For a recent approval of the existence of this discretion see *R. v. Yaeck* (1991), 10 C.R. (4th) 1, 23 (Ont. C.A.).

60.   Compare *R. v. Davis*, [1980] 1 N.Z.L.R. 257 (C.A.). The accused had been convicted of manslaughter arising out of a street fight in which he knifed the deceased. The accused appealed arguing that he ought to have been entitled to bring out in cross-examination of a detective the criminal record of the deceased. The appeal was dismissed. The record disclosed convictions for, *inter alia*, four separate charges of common assault, threatening to do grievous bodily harm, rape and assault on a female.

(ii) Sexual Assault

When dealing with evidence of the alleged victims's character in sexual assault cases there are hazards. Professor Estrich describes the difficulties of teaching in this area.[61] She writes:

> I know many students, and even a few professors, who believe that the women are always right and the men are always wrong; that if she didn't consent fully and voluntarily, it is rape, no matter what she said or did, or what he did or did not realize. Everything about his past should be admitted, and nothing about hers. And that's what they want to hear in class.
>
> This kind of orthodoxy is not only bad educationally but, in the case of rape, it also misses the point. Society is not so orthodox in its views. There is a debate going on in courthouses and prosecutors' offices, and around coffee machines and dinner tables, about whether Mike Tyson was guilty or not, and whether William Kennedy Smith ever should have been prosecuted; about when women should be believed, and what counts as consent. There's a debate going on in America as to what is reasonable when it comes to sex. Turn on the radio and you will hear it. To silence that debate in the classroom is to remove the classroom from reality, and to make ourselves irrelevant. It may be hard for some students, but ultimately the only way to change things — and that's usually the goal of those who find the discussions most difficult — is to confront the issues squarely, not to pretend that they don't exist. Besides, the purpose of education, in my classes anyway, is to prepare our students to participate in the controversies that animate the law, not to provide them with a shelter from reality.
>
> . . . .
>
> Judges and juries these days are less inclined to accept male conduct that only a few years ago was tolerated as understandably macho. I don't find as many students in my classes these days who believe that a man has the right to ignore the fact that a woman is saying no. And I don't think the reason for this change is that feminists have defined what is "politically correct" in the classroom; I think instead that most of my students, male and female, actually believe that a man should listen to a woman's words, and take her at her word.
>
> This shift in our thinking about the elements of culpability leaves credibility as the only defense game in town. After all, rapes rarely take place in front of witnesses. If no doesn't mean yes, if bruises aren't necessary, and if no unusual force is required, then in many cases there's not going to be much physical evidence to rely on. She gives her version and he gives his. If you are the defense attorney, your job is to convince the jury not to believe what she says — which means that the only way to defend may be to destroy the credibility of the victim.
>
> The key question in many acquaintance rape cases today thus becomes not what counts as rape but rather what we need to know about the victim, and the defendant, in order to decide who is telling the truth.
>
> . . . .
>
> It is one thing to exclude evidence of a woman's sexual past or of psychiatric treatment when she has been beaten and burned; it is easy to argue there that admitting such evidence does almost nothing except to deter legitimate prosecutions and to victimize the victim. But it is surely a harder case when there have been no

---

61.   Susan Estrich, "Teaching Rape Law" (1992), Yale L.J. 509. See also Tomkovicx, "Teaching Rape: Reasons, Risks and Rewards" (1992), Yale L.J. 481.

weapons and no bruises, and when the man's liberty depends on convincing a jury not to believe a woman who appears at least superficially credible.

Many of the traditional rules of rape liability were premised on the notion that women lie; Wigmore went so far as to view rape complainants as fundamentally deranged. I don't buy that for a moment nor, I expect, do most of my students. Yet even if only one of a hundred men, or one of a thousand, is falsely accused, the question is still how we can protect that man's right to disprove his guilt. Assume for a moment, I tell my students, that it was you, or your brother, or your boyfriend or your son, who was accused of rape by a casual date with a history of psychiatric problems, or by a woman he met in a bar who had a history of one-night stands. Would you exclude that evidence? What else can the man do to avoid a felony conviction and a ruined life? Where do you draw the line? But if you don't exclude the evidence, will some women as a result become unrapable, at least as a matter of law? That is, will women who have histories of mental instability or of "promiscuity" ever be able to convince juries who know those histories that they really were raped?

Similar issues arise with respect to the man's credibility. The first question many people asked when Anita Hill charged that Clarence Thomas had harassed her was whether there were other women who had been similarly mistreated. The first significant ruling in the Smith case, indeed the decisive ruling, was the judge's pretrial decision to exclude the testimony of three other women who claimed that they had been sexually abused by the defendant. If the testimony of only one woman cannot be believed — unless she is a Sunday school teacher, camera in hand, as Desiree Washington was, and the defendant is a black man who has made a host of inconsistent statements, as Mike Tyson did — is it fair to exclude the testimony of the other women? And if the testimony is not excluded, do we risk convicting a defendant for being a bad man, indeed being a rapist, rather than committing the particular act charged?

One answer is to say that we need symmetry: exclude all the evidence about both of them. That's the approach the judge followed in the William Kennedy Smith case. On the surface, it is neat and appealing. The only problem is that it's a false symmetry that is being enforced. After all, evidence that a man has abused other women is much more probative of rape than evidence that a woman has had consensual sex with other men is probative of consent. Most women have had sexual experiences, and unless those experiences fall into some kind of unusual pattern, the mere fact that a woman has had lovers tells us almost nothing about whether she consented on the particular occasion that she is charging as rape. But won't we all look at a defendant differently if three other women have also come forward to say they were abused? The danger with such evidence is not that it proves so little, but that it may prove too much. Symmetry won't get you out of this hole, at least not in my classroom.

Thus, even if most students can agree these days that no means no, and that force can be established if you push a woman down, there's very little agreement about what we need to know about her or him before deciding whether she in fact said yes or no, and whether he actually pushed her down or just lay down with her. The consensus on what counts as rape is more apparent than real. These days, society's continued ambivalence towards acquaintance rape is increasingly being expressed in evidentiary rules and standards of credibility rather than in the definitions of force and consent. The questions have shifted; answering them is no easier.[62]

---

62.   Estrich, *ibid.*, at pp. 515-20.

Common Law

The position at common law regarding evidence of the character of the alleged victim in sexual assault cases was summarized by the English Court of Appeal in *R. v. Krausz*:[63]

> It is settled law that she who complains of rape or attempted rape can be cross-examined about (1) her general reputation and moral character, (2) sexual intercourse between herself and the defendant on other occasions, and (3) sexual intercourse between herself and other men; and that evidence can be called to contradict her on (1) and (2) but that no evidence can be called to contradict her denials of (3).

The common law regarded evidence of (1) and (2) as relevant to the material issue of consent[64] but evidence of (3) as irrelevant to the issue of consent but relevant to credit. As (3) was only relevant to credit the matter was collateral and the witness could not be contradicted. Osler, J.A. in the Ontario Court of Appeal remarked:

> ... she may be asked, but, inasmuch as the question is one going strictly to her credit, she is not generally compellable to answer whether she has had connection with persons other than the prisoner. This seems to rest to some extent in the discretion of the trial Judge. Whether, however, she answers it or not that is an end of the matter, otherwise as many collateral, and therefore irrelevant issues might be raised as there were specific charges of immorality suggested, and the prosecutrix could not be expected to come prepared to meet them, though she might well be prepaared to repel an attack upon her general character for chastity.[65]

While most of the older authorities state that evidence of particular acts of intercourse with persons other than the accused is irrelevant to the issue of consent, can it be argued that on our understanding of the meaning of the term "relevant," i.e., "does the evidence offered render the desired inference more probable than it would be without the evidence?", the evidence may, in exceptional cases, be relevant? Though relevant the evidence could nevertheless still be excluded because of considerations of fairness to the victim-witness and because of prejudice to the outcome of the trial through improper use of the evidence. Cardozo, J. deplored the existence of the inflexible rule based on "irrelevancy" and argued for a discretion in the trial judge, who could assess probative worth against the dangers in his particular case.[66]

---

63. (1973), 57 Cr. App. R. 466, 472. See *R. v. Finnessey* (1906), 11 O.L.R. 338, 341 (C.A.) for a similar outline of the common law. And see *R. v. Basken* (1974), 21 C.C.C. (2d) 321, 337 (Sask. C.A.) approving this description. See also *Gross v. Brodrecht* (1897), 24 O.A.R. 687 (C.A.).

64. For examples of cases where evidence of the complainant's reputation and general habits for promiscuity was received, see *R. v. Krausz* (1973), 57 Cr. App. R. 466; *R. v. Barker* (1829), 172 E.R. 558 (N.P.); and *R. v. Bashir*, [1969] 3 All E.R. 692 (Q.B.).

65. In *R. v. Finnessey, supra*, note 63, at p. 341. The historical development of the common law position is concisely presented in Julie Taylor, "Rape and Women's Credibility: Problems of Recantations and False Accusations Echoed in the Case of Cathleen Crowell Webb and Gary Dotson" (1987), 10 Harvard Women's L.J. 59 at 74-81.

66. Cardozo, *The Nature of the Judicial Process* (1921), p. 156. Wigmore argued for admissibility of the particular acts: 1 Wigmore, *Evidence* (3d ed.), s. 200. See also Scutt, "Admissibility of Sexual History Evidence and Allegations in Rape Cases" (1979), 53 Aust. L.J. 817 and Bohmer Blumberg, "Twice Traumatized: The Rape Victim and the Court" (1975), 58 Judicature 391.

Arguments have been advanced, however, that prior sexual history with others is not relevant to the issue of consent. In a speech given on sexual harassment, Professor Catherine MacKinnon stated:

> The question of prior sexual history is one area in which the issue of sexual credibility is directly posed. Evidence of the defendant's sexual harassment of other women in the same institutional relation or setting is increasingly being considered admissible, and it should be. The other side of the question is whether evidence of a victim's prior sexual history should be discoverable or admissible, and it seems to me it should not be. Perpetrators often seek out victims with common qualities or circumstances or situations — we are fungible to them so long as we are similarly accessible — but victims do not seek out victimization at all, and their nonvictimized sexual behavior is no more relevant to an allegation of sexual force than is the perpetrator's consensual sex life, such as it may be.
>
> So far the leading case, consistent with the direction of rape law, has found that the victim's sexual history with other individuals is not relevant, although consensual history with the individual perpetrator may be.[67]

Professor Christine Boyle has argued:[68]

> The tendency in this area has been, unfortunately, simply to assert or deny the relevance of the sexual activity of the complainant. One can appreciate the reluctance of those concerned about the abuse of such evidence in the past to concede its relevance in any context, but the problems have arisen with respect to the introduction of the evidence to suggest consent or to undermine the credibility of the complainant. Its use for these purposes is unjustifiable since the tests of relevance, common sense and human experience, suggest that people exercise choice over each sexual partner. Moreover, there is no evidence to suggest that sexual activity has any link with credibility.

An intermediate approach to this issue focuses on the assumptions underlying findings of relevance of the victim's prior sexual history. The position advanced is that though evidence of prior sexual acts may be relevant in certain limited circumstances, the identification of those circumstances must be based on a reevaluation of the assumptions upon which findings of relevance have traditionally been based.

Professor Adler explains the premise upon which the intermediate approach is based:

> According to one authority on evidence, "relevant" means that "any two facts to which it is applied are so related to each other that according to the common course of events one either taken by itself or in connection with other facts proves or renders probable the past, present or future existence or non-existence of another." Thus, if one "fact" is the complainant's sexual experience, and the other, her consent to intercourse on the occasion of the alleged rape, there must be a link of some sort between the two for evidence of the former to be relevant and hence admissible in court. In practice, such a link almost invariably involves some alleged or actual aspect of the complainant's past sexual behaviour which is argued to bear some similarity to the incident involved in the trial. The similarity may be in the mere fact of her having had sexual intercourse in the past, or additional factors inherent in the situation may be drawn upon to imply greater relevance.

---

67. MacKinnon, *Feminism Unmodified: Discourses on Life and Law* (1987), at p. 113.
68. *Sexual Assault* (1984), at p. 137.

The main question currently open to judicial interpretation concerns the nature, logic and strength of such links. Few would wish to argue that a woman's past experience of consensual intercourse with her husband makes her more likely to have consented to another defendant. But where the line is to be drawn is far from clear, and without explicit guidelines, decisions in individual cases remain diverse and uneven.[69]

Professor Adler notes that one difficulty with leaving determinations of relevance of previous sexual history to the discretion of the trial judge is the subjectivity inherent in the exercise of discretion.

Compare the remarks of Susan Brownmiller in *Against Our Will:*[70]

Not only is the victim's response during the act measured and weighed, her past sexual history is scrutinized under the theory that it relates to her "tendency to consent," or that it reflects on her credibility, her veracity, her predisposition to tell the truth or to lie. Or so the law says. As it works out in practice, juries presented with evidence concerning a woman's past sexual history make use of such information to form a moral judgment on her character, and here all the old myths of rape are brought into play, for the feeling persists that a virtuous woman either cannot get raped or does not get into situations that leave her open to assault. Thus the questions in the jury room become "Was she or wasn't she asking for it?"; "If she had been a decent woman, wouldn't she have fought to death to defend her 'treasure'?"; and "Is this bimbo worth the ruination of a man's career and reputation?"

The crime of rape must be totally separated from all traditional concepts of chastity, for the very meaning of chastity presupposes that it is a woman's duty (but not a man's) to refrain from sex outside the matrimonial union. That sexual activity renders a woman "unchaste" is a totally male view of the female as *his* pure vessel. The phrase "prior chastity" as well as the concept must be stricken from the legal lexicon, along with "prosecutrix," as inflammatory and prejudicial to a complainant's case.

A history of sexual activity with many partners may be indicative of a female's healthy interest in sex, or it may be indicative of a chronic history of victimization and exploitation in which she could not assert her own inclinations; it may be indicative of a spirit of adventure, a spirit of rebellion, a spirit of curiosity, a spirit of joy or a spirit of defeat. Whatever the reasons, and there are many, prior consensual intercourse between a rape complainant and other partners of her choosing should not be scrutinized as an indicator of purity or impurity of mind or body, not in this day and age at any rate, and it has no place in jury room deliberation as to whether or not, in the specific instance in question, an act of forcible sex took place. Prior consensual intercourse between the complainant and *the defendant* does have some relevance and such information probably should not be barred.

An overhaul of present laws and a fresh approach to sexual assault legislation must go hand in hand with a fresh approach to enforcing the law. The question of who interprets and who enforces the statutes is as important as the contents of the law itself. At present, female victims of sexual crimes of violence who seek legal justice must rely on a series of male authority figures whose masculine orientation, values and fears place them securely in the offender's camp.

---

69.   Adler, "The Relevance of Sexual History Evidence in Rape: Problems of Subjective Interpretation", [1985] Crim. L. Rev. 769, 772.

70.   (New York: Simon & Schuster, 1975), pp. 385-86.

Charter of Rights

R. v. SEABOYER
[1991] 2 S.C.R. 577, 7 C.R. (4th) 117, 66 C.C.C. (3d) 321

[The accused were each charged with sexual assault. At their preliminary hearings they sought to cross-examine the respective complainants with respect to their previous sexual conduct. In each case the judge ruled that such cross-examination was foreclosed by the Criminal Code. Each accused applied to the Supreme Court for an order quashing their committals for trial on the ground that the judge, in enforcing the then existing sections 276 and 277 of the Criminal Code, had exceeded his jurisdiction and deprived the accused of his right to make full answer and defence. The orders were granted on the ground that sections 276 and 277 violated the Charter of Rights and Freedoms. The cases were remitted to the preliminary inquiry judges for a ruling on the evidentiary issues unhampered by the statutory provisions. An appeal to the Court of Appeal was allowed on the ground that the preliminary inquiry judges lacked the jurisdiction to determine the constitutional validity of the impugned sections and accordingly had not erred in applying the sections. The Court of Appeal went on however to consider the constitutional validity of the sections. The majority of the court held that section 276 was capable of contravening an accused's rights under the Charter in some circumstances. The majority held that the section would generally be operative and the appropriate course was for the trial judge to decline to apply it in those limited and rare instances where it could lead to a Charter breach. The accused appealed. On the appeal, constitutional questions were stated putting in issue the constitutional validity of sections 276 and 277.]

McLACHLIN, J. (LAMER, C.J.C., LA FOREST, SOPINKA, CORY, STEVENSON and IACOBUCCI, JJ. concurring):—

. . . .

These cases raise the issue of the constitutionality of ss. 276 and 277 of the *Criminal Code,* . . . commonly known as the "rape-shield" provisions. The provisions restrict the right of the defence on a trial for a sexual offence to cross-examine and lead evidence of a complainant's sexual conduct on other occasions. The question is whether these restrictions offend the guarantees accorded to an accused person by the *Canadian Charter of Rights and Freedoms.*

My conclusion is that one of the sections in issue, s. 276, offends the *Charter.* While its purpose—the abolition of outmoded, sexist-based use of sexual conduct evidence—is laudable, its effect goes beyond what is required or justified by that purpose. At the same time, striking down s. 276 does not imply reversion to the old common law rules, which permitted evidence of the complainant's sexual conduct even though it might have no probative value to the issues on the case and, on the contrary, might mislead the jury. Instead, relying on the basic principles that actuate our law of evidence, the courts must seek a middle way that offers the maximum protection to the complainant compatible with the maintenance of the accused's fundamental right to a fair trial.

. . . .

I deal first with *Seaboyer.* The accused was charged with sexual assault of a woman with whom he had been drinking in a bar. On the preliminary inquiry the judge refused to allow the accused to cross-examine the complainant on her sexual conduct on other occasions. The appellant contends that he should have been permitted to cross-examine as to other acts of sexual intercourse which may have caused bruises and other aspects of the complainant's condition which the Crown had put in evidence. While the theory of the defence has not been detailed at this early stage, such evidence might arguably be relevant to consent, since it might provide other explanations for the physical evidence tendered by the Crown in support of the use of force against the complainant.

The *Gayme* case arose in different circumstances. The complainant was 15, the appellant 18. They were friends. The Crown alleges that the appellant sexually assaulted her at his school. The defence, relying on the defences of consent and honest belief in consent, contends that there was no assault and that the complainant was the sexual aggressor. In pursuance of this defence, the appellant at the preliminary inquiry sought to cross-examine and present evidence of prior and subsequent sexual conduct of the complainant. . . .

. . . .

It should be noted that the admissibility of the evidence sought to be tendered in the two cases is not at issue. In neither case did the preliminary inquiry judge consider whether the evidence would have been relevant or admissible in the absence of ss. 276 or 277 of the *Criminal Code*.

Relevant Legislation

Criminal Code, s. 276:

276. (1) In proceedings in respect of an offence under section 271, 272 or 273, no evidence shall be adduced by or on behalf of the accused concerning the sexual activity of the complainant with any person other than the accused unless

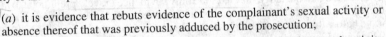

(*a*) it is evidence that rebuts evidence of the complainant's sexual activity or absence thereof that was previously adduced by the prosecution;

(*b*) it is evidence of specific instances of the complainant's sexual activity tending to establish the identity of the person who had sexual contact with the complainant on the occasion set out in the charge; or

(*c*) it is evidence of sexual activity that took place on the same occasion as the sexual activity that forms the subject-matter of the charge, where that evidence relates to the consent that the accused alleges he believed was given by the complainant.

(2) No evidence is admissible under paragraph (1)(*c*) unless

(*a*) reasonable notice in writing has been given to the prosecutor by or on behalf of the accused of his intention to adduce the evidence together with particulars of the evidence sought to be adduced; and

(*b*) a copy of the notice has been filed with the clerk of the court.

(3) No evidence is admissible under subsection (1) unless the judge, provincial court judge or justice, after holding a hearing in which the jury and the members of the public are excluded and in which the complainant is not a compellable witness, is satisfied that the requirements of this section are met.

Criminal Code, s. 277:

277. In proceedings in respect of an offence under section 271, 272 or 273, evidence of sexual reputation, whether general or specific, is not admissible for the purpose of challenging or supporting the credibility of the complainant.

. . . .

Everyone, under s. 7 of the *Charter*, has the right to life, liberty and security of person and the right not to be deprived thereof except in accordance with the principles of fundamental justice.

. . . .

The real issue under s. 7 is whether the potential for deprivation of liberty flowing from ss. 276 and 277 takes place in a manner that conforms to the principles of fundamental justice.

. . . .

All the parties agree that the right to a fair trial—one which permits the trier of fact to get at the truth and properly and fairly dispose of the case—is a principle of fundamental justice. Nor is there any dispute that encouraging reporting of sexual offences and protection of the complainant's privacy are legitimate goals provided they do not interfere with the primary objective of a fair trial. Where the parties part company is on the issue of whether ss. 276 and 277 of the *Criminal Code* in fact infringe the right to a fair trial. The supporters of the legislation urge that it furthers the right to a fair trial by eliminating evidence of little or no worth and considerable prejudice. The appellants, on the other hand, say that the legislation goes too far and in fact eliminates relevant evidence which should be admitted notwithstanding the possibility of prejudice.

. . . .

This Court has affirmed the trial judges' power to exclude Crown evidence the prejudicial effect of which outweighs its probative value in a criminal case, but a narrower formula than that articulated by McCormick has emerged. In *Wray*, *supra*, at p. 293, the Court stated that the judge may exclude only "evidence gravely prejudicial to the accused, the admissibility of which is tenuous, and whose probative force in relation to the main issue before the court is trifling". More recently, in *Sweitzer v. The Queen*, [1982] 1 S.C.R. 949, at p. 953, an appeal involving a particularly difficult brand of circumstantial evidence offered by the Crown, the Court said that "admissibility will depend upon the probative effect of the evidence balanced against the prejudice caused to the accused by its admission". In *Morris*, *supra*, at p. 193, the Court without mentioning *Sweitzer* cited the narrower *Wray* formula. But in *R. v. Potvin*, [1989] 1 S.C.R. 525, La Forest J. (Dickson C.J. concurring) affirmed in general terms "the rule that the trial judge may exclude admissible evidence if its prejudicial effect substantially outweighs its probative value" (p. 531).

I am of the view that the more appropriate description of the general power of a judge to exclude relevant evidence on the ground of prejudice is that articulated in *Sweitzer* and generally accepted throughout the common law world. . . .

The Canadian cases cited above all pertain to evidence tendered by the Crown against the accused. The question arises whether the same power to exclude exists with respect to defence evidence. Canadian courts, like courts in most common law jurisdictions, have been extremely cautious in restricting the power of the accused to call evidence in his or her defence, a reluctance founded in the fundamental tenet of our judicial system that an innocent person must not be convicted. It follows from this that the prejudice must substantially outweigh the value of the evidence before a judge can exclude evidence relevant to a defence allowed by law.

. . . .

Section 277 excludes evidence of sexual reputation for the purpose of challenging or supporting the credibility of the plaintiff. The idea that a complainant's credibility might be affected by whether she has had other sexual experience is today universally discredited. There is no logical or practical link between a woman's sexual reputation and whether she is a truthful witness. It follows that the evidence excluded by s. 277 can serve no legitimate purpose in the trial. Section 277, by limiting the exclusion to a purpose which is clearly illegitimate, does not touch evidence which may be tendered for valid purposes, and hence does not infringe the right to a fair trial.

I turn then to s. 276. Section 276, unlike s. 277, does not condition exclusion on use of the evidence for an illegitimate purpose. Rather, it constitutes a blanket exclusion, subject to three exceptions—rebuttal evidence, evidence going to identity, and evidence relating to consent to sexual activity on the same occasion as the trial incident. The question is whether this may exclude evidence which is relevant to the defence and the probative value of which is not substantially outweighed by the potential prejudice to the trial process. To put the matter another way, can it be said *a priori*, as the Attorney General for Ontario contends, that any and all evidence excluded by s. 276 will necessarily be of such trifling weight in relation to the prejudicial effect of the evidence that it may fairly be excluded?

In my view, the answer to this question must be negative. The Canadian and American jurisprudence affords numerous examples of evidence of sexual conduct which would be excluded by s. 276 but which clearly should be received in the interests of a fair trial, notwithstanding the possibility that it may divert a jury by tempting it to improperly infer consent or lack of credibility in the complainant.

Consider the defence of honest belief. It rests on the concept that the accused may honestly but mistakenly (and not necessarily reasonably) have believed that the complainant was consenting to the sexual act. If the accused can raise a reasonable doubt as to his intention on the basis that he honestly held such a belief, he is not guilty under our law and is entitled to an acquittal. The basis of the accused's honest belief in the complainant's consent may be sexual acts performed by the complainant at some other time or place. Yet section 276 would preclude the accused leading such evidence.

Another category of evidence eliminated by s. 276 relates to the right of the defence to attack the credibility of the complainant on the ground that the complainant was biased or had motive to fabricate the evidence. In *State v. Jalo*, 557 P.2d 1359 (Or. Ct. App. 1976), a father accused of sexual acts with his young daughter sought to present evidence that the source of the accusation was his earlier discovery of the fact that the girl and her brother were engaged in intimate relations. The defence contended that when the father stopped the relationship, the daughter, out of animus toward him, accused him of the act. The father sought to lead this evidence in support of his defence that the charges were a concoction motivated by animus. Notwithstanding its clear relevance, this evidence would be excluded by s. 276. The respondent submits that the damage caused by its exclusion would not be great, because all that would be forbidden would be evidence of the sexual activities of the children, and the father could still testify that his daughter was angry with him. But surely the father's chance of convincing the jury of the validity of his defence would be greatly diminished if he were reduced to saying, in effect, "My daughter was angry with me, but I can't say why or produce any corroborating evidence." As noted above, to deny a defendant the building blocks of his defence is often to deny him the defence itself.

Other examples abound. Evidence of sexual activity excluded by s. 276 may be relevant to explain the physical conditions on which the Crown relies to establish intercourse or the use of force, such as semen, pregnancy, injury or disease—evidence which may go to consent: . . . In the case of young complainants where there may be a tendency to believe their story on the ground that the detail of their account must have come from the alleged encounter, it may be relevant to show other activity which provides an explanation for the knowledge: . . .

Even evidence as to pattern of conduct may on occasion be relevant. Since this use of evidence of prior sexual conduct draws upon the inference that prior conduct infers similar subsequent conduct, it closely resembles the prohibited use of the evidence and must be carefully scrutinized: . . . Yet such evidence might be admissible in non-sexual cases under the similar fact rule. Is it fair then to deny it to an accused, merely because the trial relates to a sexual offence? . . .

. . . .

These examples leave little doubt that s. 276 has the potential to exclude evidence of critical relevance to the defence. Can it honestly be said, as the Attorney General for Ontario contends, that the value of such evidence will always be trifling when compared with its potential to mislead the jury? I think not. The examples show that the evidence may well be of great importance to getting at the truth and determining whether the accused is guilty or innocent under the law—the ultimate aim of the trial process. They demonstrate that s. 276, enacted for the purpose of helping judges and juries arrive at the proper and just verdict in the particular case, overshoots the mark, with the result that it may have the opposite effect of impeding them in discovering the truth.

. . . .

2. *Is s. 276 Saved by s. 1 of the Charter?* — NO

Is s. 276 of the *Criminal Code* justified in a free and democratic society, notwithstanding the fact that it may lead to infringements of the *Charter*?

The first step under s. 1 is to consider whether the legislation addresses a pressing and substantial objective: . . .

The second requirement under s. 1 is that the infringement of rights be proportionate to the pressing objective. . . . In creating exceptions to the exclusion of evidence of the sexual activity of the complainant on other occasions, Parliament correctly recognized that justice requires a measured approach, one which admits evidence which is truly relevant to the defence notwithstanding potential prejudicial effect. Yet Parliament at the same time excluded other evidence of sexual conduct which might be equally relevant to a legitimate defence and which appears to pose no greater danger of prejudice than the exceptions it recognizes. To the extent the section excludes relevant defence evidence whose value is not clearly outweighed by the danger it presents, the section is overbroad.

I turn finally to the third aspect of the proportionality requirement — the balance between the importance of the objective and the injurious effect of the legislation. The objective of the legislation, as discussed above, is to eradicate the erroneous inferences from evidence of other sexual encounters that the complainant is more likely to have consented to the sexual act in issue or less likely to be telling the truth. The subsidiary aims are to promote fairer trials and increased reporting of sexual offences and to minimize the invasion of the complainant's privacy. In this way the personal security of women and their right to equal benefit and protection of the law are enhanced. The effect of the legislation, on the other hand, is to exclude relevant defence evidence, the value of which outweighs its potential prejudice. As indicated in the discussion of s. 7, all parties agree that a provision which rules out probative defence evidence which is not clearly outweighed by the prejudice it may cause to the trial strikes the wrong balance between the rights of complainants and the rights of the accused. The line must be drawn short of the point where it results in an unfair trial and the possible conviction of an innocent person. Section 276 fails this test.

I conclude that s. 276 is not saved by s. 1 of the Charter.

. . . .

4. *What Follows From Striking Down s. 276?*

The first question is whether the striking down of s. 276 revives the old common law rules of evidence permitting liberal and often inappropriate reception of evidence of the complainant's sexual conduct. . . .

The answer to this question is no. The rules in question are common law rules. Like other common law rules of evidence, they must be adapted to conform to current reality. As all counsel on these appeals accepted, the reality in 1991 is that evidence of sexual conduct and reputation in itself cannot be regarded as logically probative of either the complainant's credibility or consent. Although they still may inform the thinking of many, the twin myths which s. 276 sought to eradicate are just that—myths—and have no place in a rational and just system of law. It follows that the old rules which permitted evidence of sexual conduct and condoned invalid inferences from it solely for these purposes have no place in our law.

The inquiry as to what the law is in the absence of s. 276 of the *Code* is thus remitted to consideration of the fundamental principles governing the trial process and the reception of evidence. Harking back to <u>Thayer's</u> maxim, relevant evidence should be admitted, and irrelevant evidence excluded, subject to the qualification that the value of the evidence must outweigh its potential prejudice to the conduct of a fair trial. Moreover, the focus must be not on the evidence itself, but on the use to which it is put. As Professor Galvin puts it, our aim is "to abolish the outmoded, sexist-based use of sexual conduct evidence while permitting other uses of such evidence to remain": *supra*, at p. 809.

This definition of the problem suggests an approach which abolishes illegitimate uses and inferences, while preserving legitimate uses. There is wide agreement that the approach of a general exclusion supplemented by categories of exceptions is bound to fail because of the impossibility of predicting in advance what evidence may be relevant in a particular case: see Galvin, *supra*, Doherty, *supra*, and Elliott, *supra*. On the other hand, judges are not free to act on whim. As Professor Vivian Berger puts it in her article "Man's Trial, Woman's Tribulation: Rape Cases in the Courtroom" (1977), 77 *Colum. L. Rev.* 1, at p. 69:

> The problem is to chart a course between inflexible legislative rules and wholly untrammelled judicial discretion: The former threatens the rights of defendants; the latter may ignore the needs of complainants.

. . . .

Galvin's proposal, with some modification, reflects an appropriate response to the problem of avoiding illegitimate inferences from evidence of the complainant's sexual conduct, while preserving the general right to a fair trial. It is, moreover, a response which is open to trial judges in the absence of legislation. It reflects, in essence, an application of the fundamental common law notions which govern the reception of evidence on trials. The general prohibition on improper use of evidence of sexual conduct reflects the fact that it is always open to a judge to warn against using a particular piece of evidence for an inference on an issue for which that evidence has no probative force. Similarly, the mandate to the judge to determine when the evidence may be properly receivable is a reflection of the basic function of the trial hudge of determining the relevance of evidence and whether it should be received, bearing in mind the balance between its probative value and its potential prejudice.

As for the procedures which should govern the determination of whether the sexual conduct evidence should be admitted, Galvin proposes a written motion followed by an in camera hearing. The devices of a preliminary affidavit and an in camera hearing are designed to minimize the invasion of the complainant's privacy. If the affidavit does not show the evidence to be relevant, it will not be heard at all. Where this threshold is met, the evidence will be heard in camera so that, in the event the judge finds its value is outweighed by its potential prejudice, it will not enter the public domain. Such procedures do not require legislation. It has always been open to the Courts to devise such procedures as may be necessary to ensure a fair trial. The requirements of a voir dire before a confession can be admitted, for example, is judge-made law.

While accepting the premise and the general thrust of Galvin's proposal, I suggest certain modifications. There seems little purpose in having separate rules for the use of sexual conduct evidence for illegitimate inferences of consent and credibility in the Canadian context. Again, I question whether evidence of other sexual conduct with the accused should automatically be admissible in all cases; sometimes the value of such evidence might be little or none. The word "complainant" is more compatible with the presumption of innocence of the accused than the word "victim". Professor Galvin's reference to the defence of "reasonable belief in consent must be adapted to meet Canadian law, which does not require reasonableness. And the need to warn the jury clearly against improper uses of the evidence should be emphasized, in my view.

In the absence of legislation, it is open to this Court to suggest guidelines for the reception and use of sexual conduct evidence. Such guidelines should be seen for what they are—an attempt to describe the consequences of the application of the general rules of evidence governing relevance and the reception of evidence—and not as judicial legislation cast in stone.

In my view the trial judge under this new regime shoulders a dual responsibility. First, the judge must assess with a high degree of sensitivity whether the evidence proffered by the defence meets the test of demonstrating a degree of relevance which outweighs the damages and disadvantages presented by the admission of such evidence. The examples presented earlier suggest that while cases where such evidence will carry sufficient probative value will exist, they will be exceptional. The trial judge must ensure that evidence is tendered for a legitimate purpose, and that it logically supports a defence. The fishing expeditions which unfortunately did occur in the past should not be permitted. The trial judge's discretion must be exercised to ensure that neither the *in camera* procedure nor the trial become forums for demeaning and abusive conduct by defence counsel.

The trial judge's second responsibility will be to take special care to ensure that, in the exceptional case where circumstances demand that such evidence be permitted, the jury is fully and properly instructed as to its appropriate use. The jurors must be cautioned that they should not draw impermissible inferences from evidence of previous sexual activity. While such evidence may be tendered for a purpose logically probative of the defence to be presented, it may be important to remind jurors that they not allow the allegations of past sexual activity to lead them to the view that the complainant is less worthy of belief, or was more likely to have consented for that reason. It is hoped that a sensitive and responsive exercise of discretion by the judiciary will reduce and even eliminate the concerns which provoked legislation such as s. 276, while at the same time preserving the right of an accused to a fair trial.

I would summarize the applicable principles as follows:

1.   On a trial for a sexual offence, evidence that the complainant has engaged in consensual sexual conduct on other occasions (including past sexual conduct with the accused) is not admissible solely to support the inference that the complainant is by reason of such conduct:

     (*a*)   more likely to have consented to the sexual conduct at issue in the trial;

     (*b*)   less worthy of belief as a witness.

2.   Evidence of consensual sexual conduct on the part of the complainant may be admissible for purposes other than an inference relating to the consent or credibility of the complainant where it possesses probative value on an issue in the trial and where that probative value is not substantially outweighed by the danger of unfair prejudice flowing from the evidence.

    By way of illustration only, and not by way of limitation, the following are examples of admissible evidence:

    (A)   Evidence of specific instances of sexual conduct tending to prove that a person other than the accused caused the physical consequences of the rape alleged by the prosecution;

    (B)   Evidence of sexual conduct tending to prove bias or motive to fabricate on the part of the complainant;

    (C)   Evidence of prior sexual conduct, known to the accused at the time of the act charged, tending to prove that the accused believed that the complainant was consenting to the act charged (without laying down absolute rules, normally one would expect some proximity in time between the conduct that is alleged to have given rise to an honest belief and the conduct charged);

(D) Evidence of prior sexual conduct which meets the requirements for the reception of similar act evidence, bearing in mind that such evidence cannot be used illegitimately merely to show that the complainant consented or is an unreliable witness;

(E) Evidence tending to rebut proof introduced by the prosecution regarding the complainant's sexual conduct.

3.   Before evidence of consensual sexual conduct on the part of a victim is received, it must be established on a *voir dire* (which may be held *in camera*) by affidavit or the testimony of the accused or third parties, that the proposed use of the evidence of other sexual conduct is legitimate.

4.   Where evidence that the complainant has engaged in sexual conduct on other occasions is admitted on a jury trial, the judge should warn the jury against inferring from the evidence of the conduct itself, either that the complainant might have consented to the act alleged, or that the complainant is less worthy of credit.

[L'Heureux-Dubé, J., Gonthier, J. concurring, decided that section 276 did not violate sections 7 or 11(*d*) and, if it did, it would be saved by section 1.]

L'HEUREUX-DUBÉ, J. (GONTHIER, J. concurring), dissenting in part:—

. . . .

Sexual assault is not like any other crime. In the vast majority of cases the target is a woman and the perpetrator is a man. . . . Unlike other crimes of a violent nature, it is for the most part unreported. Yet, by all accounts, women are victimized at an alarming rate and there is some evidence that an already frighteningly high rate of sexual assault is on the increase. The prosecution and conviction rates for sexual assault are among the lowest for all violent crimes. Perhaps more than any other crime, the fear and constant reality of sexual assault affects how women conduct their lives and how they define their relationship with the larger society. Sexual assault is not like any other crime.

. . . .

There are a number of reasons why women may not report their victimization: fear of reprisal, fear of a continuation of their trauma at the hands of the police and the criminal justice system, fear of a perceived loss of status and lack of desire to report due to the typical effects of sexual assault such as depression, self-blame or loss of self-esteem. Although all of the reasons for failing to report are significant and important, more relevant to the present inquiry are the numbers of victims who choose not to bring their victimization to the attention of the authorities due to their perception that the institutions with which they would have to become involved will view their victimization in a stereotypical and biased fashion. . . .

. . . .

The woman who comes to the attention of the authorities has her victimization measured against the current rape mythologies, i.e., who she should be in order to be recognized as having been, in the eyes of the law, raped; who her attacker must be in order to be recognized, in the eyes of the law, as a potential rapist; and how injured she must be in order to be believed. If her victimization does not fit the myths, it is unlikely that an arrest will be made or a conviction obtained. As prosecutors and police often suggest, in an attempt to excuse their application of stereotype, there is no point in directing cases toward the justice system if juries and judges will acquit on the basis of their stereotypical perceptions of the "supposed victim" and her "supposed" victimization. . . .

. . . .

More specifically, police rely in large measure upon popular conceptions of sexual assault in order to classify incoming cases as "founded" or "unfounded". It would appear as though most forces have developed a convenient shorthand regarding their decisions to proceed in any given case. This shorthand is composed of popular myth regarding rapists (distinguishing them from men as a whole), and stereotype about women's character and sexuality. Holmstrom and Burgess, *supra*, at pp. 174-99, conveniently set out and explain the most common of these myths and stereotypes:

1. *Struggle and Force: Woman As Defender of Her Honor.* There is a myth that a woman cannot be raped against her will, that if she really wants to prevent a rape she can.
   The prosecution attempts to show that she did struggle, or had no opportunity to do so, while the defence attempts to show that she did not.

Women know that there is no response on their part that will assure their safety. The experience and knowledge of women is borne out by the *Canadian Urban Victimization Survey: Female Victims of Crime* (1985). At page 7 of the report the authors note:

Sixty percent of those who tried reasoning with their attackers, and 60% of those who resisted actively by fighting or using weapon [*sic*] were injured. Every sexual assault incident is unique and so many factors are unknown (physical size of victims and offenders, verbal or physical threats, etc.) that no single course of action can be recommended unqualifiedly.

2. *Knowing the Defendant: The Rapist As a Stranger.* There is a myth that rapists are strangers who leap out of bushes to attack their victims. . . . the view that interaction between friends or between relatives does not result in rape is prevalent.

The defence uses the existence of a relationship between the parties to blame the victim. . . .

3. *Sexual Reputation: The Madonna-Whore Complex.* . . . women . . . are categorized into one-dimensional types. They are maternal or they are sexy. They are good or they are bad. They are madonnas or they are whores.

The legal rules use these distinctions.

4. *General Character: Anything Not 100 Percent Proper and Respectable.* . . . Being on welfare or drinking or drug use could be used to discredit anyone, but where women are involved, these issues are used to imply that the woman consented to sex with the defendant or that she contracted to have sex for money.

5. *Emotionality of Females.* Females are assumed to be 'more emotional' than males. The expectation is that if a woman is raped, she will get hysterical during the event and she will be visibly upset afterward. If she is able to 'retain her cool,' then people assume that "nothing happened". . . .

6. *Reporting Rape.* Two conflicting expectations exist concerning the reporting of rape. One is that if a woman is raped she will be too upset and ashamed to report it, and hence most of the time this crime goes unreported. The other is that if a woman is raped she will be so upset that she will report it. Both expectations exist simultaneously.

7. *Woman as Fickle and Full of Spite.* Another stereotype is that the feminine character is especially filled with malice. Woman is seen as fickle and as seeking revenge on past lovers.

8. *The Female Under Surveillance: Is the Victim Trying to Escape Punishment? . . .* It is assumed that the female's sexual behavior, depending on her age, is under the surveillance of her parents or her husband, and also more generally of the community. Thus, the defense argues, if a woman says she was raped it must be because she consented to sex that she was not supposed to have. She got caught, and now she wants to get back in the good graces of whomever's surveillance she is under.

9. *Disputing That Sex Occurred.* That females fantasize rape is another common stereotype. Females are assumed to make up stories that sex occurred when in fact nothing happened. . . . Similarly, women are thought to fabricate the sexual activity not as part of a fantasy life, but out of spite.

10. *Stereotype of the Rapist.* One stereotype of the rapist is that of a stranger who leaps out of the bushes to attack his victim and later abruptly leaves her. . . . stereotypes of the rapist can be used to blame the victim. She tells what he did. And because it often does not match what jurors think rapists do, his behavior is held against her.

. . . .

This list of stereotypical conceptions about women and sexual assault is by no means exhaustive. Like most stereotypes, they operate as a way, however flawed, of understanding the world and, like most such constructs, operate at a level of consciousness that makes it difficult to root them out and confront them directly. This mythology finds its way into the decisions of the police regarding their "founded"/"unfounded" categorization, operates in the mind of the Crown when deciding whether or not to prosecute, influences a judge's or juror's perception of guilt or innocence of the accused and the "goodness" or "badness" of the victim, and finally, has carved out a niche in both the evidentiary and substantive law governing the trial of the matter.

. . . .

Absolutely pivotal to an understanding of the nature and purpose of the provisions and constitutional questions at issue in this case is the realization of how widespread the stereotypes and myths about rape are, notwithstanding their inaccuracy.

The appellants argue that we, as a society, have become more enlightened, that prosecutors, police, judges and jurors can be trusted to perform their tasks without recourse to discriminatory views about women manifested through rape myth. Unfortunately, social science evidence suggests otherwise. Rape myths still present formidable obstacles for complainants in their dealings with the very system charged with discovering the truth. Their experience in this regard is illustrated by the following remarks of surprisingly recent vintage:

> Women who say no do not always mean no. It is not just a question of saying no, it is a question of how she says it, how she shows and makes it clear. If she doesn't want it she has only to keep her legs shut and she would not get it without force and there would be marks of force being used.

(Judge David Wild, Cambridge Crown Court, 1982, quoted in Elizabeth Sheehy, "Canadian Judges and the Law of Rape: Should the Charter Insulate Bias?" (1989), 21 *Ottawa L. Rev.* 741, at p. 741.)

> Unless you have no worldly experience at all, you'll agree that women occasionally resist at first but later give in to either persuasion or their own instincts.

(Judge Frank Allen, Manitoba Provincial Court, 1984, quoted in Sheehy, *supra*, at p. 741.)

> . . . it is easy for a man intent upon his own desires to mistake the intentions of a woman or girl who may herself be in two minds about what to do. Even if he makes

no mistake it is not unknown for a woman afterwards either to take fright or for some other reason to regret what has happened and seek to justify herself retrospectively by accusing the man of rape.

(Howard, *Criminal Law* (3rd ed. 1977), at p. 149.)

Modern psychiatrists have amply studied the behavior of errant young girls and women coming before the courts in all sorts of cases. Their psychic complexes are multifarious, distorted partly by inherent defects, partly by diseased derangements or abnormal instincts, partly by bad social environment, partly by temporary physiological or emotional conditions. One form taken by these complexes is that of contriving false charges of sexual offenses by men.

(Wigmore, *Evidence in Trials at Common Law*, vol. 3A (1970), at p. 736.)

Regrettably, these remarks demonstrate that many in society hold inappropriate stereotypical beliefs and apply them when the opportunity presents itself.

. . . .

Traditional definitions of what is relevant include "whatever accords with common sense" (McWilliams, *Canadian Criminal Evidence* (3rd ed. 1990), at p. 3-5); " 'relevant' means that any two facts to which it is applied are so related to each other that according to the common course of events one either taken by itself or in connection with other facts proves or renders probable the past, present or future existence or non-existence of the other" (Stephens, *A Digest of the Law of Evidence* (12th ed. 1946), art. 1), and finally Thayer's "logically probative" test with relevance as an affair of logic and not of law, a test adopted by this Court in *Morris, infra.*

Whatever the test, be it one of experience, common sense or logic, it is a decision particularly vulnerable to the application of private beliefs. Regardless of the definition used, the content of any relevancy decision will be filled by the particular judge's experience, common sense and/or logic. For the most part there will be general agreement as to that which is relevant and the determination will not be problematic. However, there are certain areas of inquiry where experience, common sense and logic are informed by stereotype and myth. As I have made clear, this area of the law has been particularly prone to the utilization of stereotype in determinations of relevance and again, as was demonstrated earlier, this appears to be the unfortunate concomitant of a society which, to a large measure, holds these beliefs. It would also appear that recognition of the large role that stereotype may play in such determinations has had surprisingly little impact in this area of the law. . . .

. . . .

Once the mythical bases of relevancy determinations in this area of the law are revealed (discussed at greater length later in these reasons), the irrelevance of most evidence of prior sexual history is clear. Nevertheless, Parliament has provided broad avenues for its admissibility in the setting out of the exceptions to the general rule in s. 246.6 (now s. 276). Moreover, all evidence of the complainant's previous sexual history with the accused is *prima facie* admissible under those provisions. Evidence that is excluded by these provisions is simply, in a myth- and stereotype-free decision-making context, irrelevant.

For comments on *Seaboyer* see Christine Boyle and Marilyn MacCrimmon, "*R. v. Seaboyer*. A Lost Cause?" (1992), 7 C.R. (4th) 225 and a reply by Anthony Allman in (1992), 10 C.R. (4th) 153. See, too, Paciocco, "Techniques for Eviscerating the Concept of Relevance" (1995), 33 C.R. (4th) 365.

Most would agree that receiving evidence of the complainant's previous sexual history on a trial of sexual assault will so prejudice the trial that the same should rarely be admitted. Has the court drawn the proper line?

While striking down the complainant's statutory protection, the court recognized the possibility that the then existing common law rules could permit the inappropriate reception of evidence of the complainant's sexual conduct and the majority therefore changed the common law. The majority said it was suggesting "guidelines for the reception of sexual conduct evidence" and these were not to be seen as "judicial legislation cast in stone". Rather they were "an attempt to describe the consequences of the application of the general rules of evidence governing relevance and the reception of evidence". While the majority wrote that it was not legislating but only offering "guidelines", if the "guidelines" are the Supreme Court of Canada's thoughts on the common law of today, their expression differs little from the exercise of legislating. There will surely be no different result waiting for the trial judge who decides not to follow the guidelines.

The new regime announced in *Seaboyer* offers greater protection to the complainant than did the legislative provision that was struck down. The old section 276 forbade the introduction of evidence "concerning the sexual activity of the complainant with any person other than the accused". The common law had always recognized that previous sexual conduct with the accused was relevant to the issue of whether the complainant consented on the occasion under review. The majority's opinion "question[ed] whether evidence of other sexual conduct with the accused should automatically be admissible in all cases; sometimes the value of such evidence might be little or none". While sometimes the value of such evidence will be little or none the majority decided to exclude it in all cases: "evidence that the complainant has engaged in consensual sexual conduct on other occasions (including past sexual conduct with the accused) is not admissible solely to support the inference that [she] is more likely to have consented".

Suppose A and B have been living together for a year. The evidence is clear and undisputed that the parties regularly engaged in consensual sexual intercourse. On the evening brought into question before the court sexual intercourse occurred. A says it was consensual and B says it was not. The court in *Seaboyer* says that evidence of the previous consensual activity is not admissible. Such evidence cannot come in if the sole purpose is to show consent. No one, of course, would suggest that such previous conduct would be determinative of the issue, but is it relevant and at least worth considering along with the other evidence?

The commonly accepted meaning of relevance, we noted earlier, bespeaks a very low threshold: does the evidence offered render the desired inference more probable than it would be without the evidence? Consider the absolute nature of the prohibition which operates regardless of whether the probative value of the evidence outweighs the potential prejudice to the proper outcome of the trial. There is no discretion in the trial judge to receive the evidence if, in her opinion, the probative value outweighs the prejudice.

The majority in *Seaboyer* cited frequently and quoted heavily from Professor Galvin's article, "Shielding Rape Victims in the State and Federal Courts: A

Proposal for the Second Decade". Galvin's proposed rape shield law, however, was confined to the exclusion of evidence of sexual conduct with persons other than the accused. The majority in *Seaboyer* wrote "Galvin's proposal, with some modification, reflects an appropriate response to the problem . . . ." One "modification" eliminates the distinction regarding sexual conduct with the accused. This is a major modification. Professor Galvin wrote:

> Even the most ardent reformers acknowledged the high probative value of past sexual conduct in at least two instances. The first is when the defendant claims consent and establishes prior consensual relations between himself and the complainant. . . . Although the evidence is offered to prove consent, its probative value rests on the nature of the complainant's specific mindset toward the accused rather than on her general unchaste character. . . . All 25 statutes adopting the Michigan approach (to rape shield laws) allow the accused to introduce evidence of prior sexual conduct between himself and the complainant. The high probative value and minimal prejudicial effect of this evidence have been discussed.

Another article quoted by the majority in *Seaboyer* is Professor Vivian Berger's "Man's Trial, Woman's Tribulation". Professor Berger justified the reception of evidence of sexual conduct with the accused in this way:

> The inference from past to present behaviour does not, as in cases of third party acts, rest on highly dubious beliefs about "women who do and women who don't" but rather relies on common sense and practical psychology. Admission of the proof supplies the accused with a circumstance making it probable that he did not obtain by violence what he might have secured by persuasion.

Another major modification to Galvin's proposal is with respect to so-called similar fact evidence. Galvin proposed that "evidence of a pattern of sexual conduct so distinctive and so closely resembling the accused's version of the alleged encounter with the victim as to tend to prove that the victim consented to the act charged" could be received. The majority in *Seaboyer* wrote that "similar fact evidence cannot be used illegitimately merely to show that the complainant consented" and where evidence of sexual conduct on other occasions is admitted, the trial judge should warn the jury against this prohibited use. Why? This major modification of Galvin's proposal is not explained unless we are to take it as a given that previous sexual conduct of the complainant can never be indicative of a propensity, a disposition, a willingness, to have sexual intercourse, from which a trier could infer that she acted in conformity with that character.

Suppose the evidence is that the accused and complainant met in Sam's Bar one Saturday night and left to go to her apartment. It's agreed that sexual intercourse occurred but the parties disagree on the issue of consent. The accused's evidence is that he was sitting at the bar when complainant approached him, offered him a drink and propositioned him. Should the accused be able to call Sam to testify that every Saturday night for the previous four weeks the complainant came into his bar, offered a stranger a drink, propositioned him and left in his company?

On the issue of receiving similar fact evidence tendered by the accused, Professor Berger wrote:

> What if the accused were offering to show that the victim habitually goes to bars on Saturday nights, picks up strangers and takes them home to bed with her, and that over the past 12 months she has done so on more than 20 occasions. Now

could one assert with assurance that this particular sexual record does not substantially reinforce the defendant's version of the night's events? And if it does, should he not be permitted as a matter of constitutional right to place this evidence before the jury?

New Legislation — Bill C-49

Seaboyer produced an immediate outcry on the basis that it would mean that women and children would be even less likely to pursue charges of sexual assault given that there would be unrestricted cross-examination of their prior sexual history. Such comments were quite unfair to the majority of the Supreme Court of Canada. For the majority, Madam Justice McLachlin had been quite alive to the dangers of leaving this crucial issue to unfettered judicial discretion and had crafted what she considered to be careful guidelines as to the admissibility of such evidence. She had also extended the protection to prior sexual conduct with the accused. One of the sources of the vehement reaction was that the majority took but a line to hold that, although victims might have equality rights, these had to give way to the accused's right to make full answer and defence.

The response from the Minister of Justice, the Honourable Kim Campbell, was swift. She announced that Parliament would better respond to protect women and children. She called a meeting of national and regional women's groups and thereafter worked very closely with them in drafting and revising a Bill. The coalition of some 60 women's groups reached unanimity at each point and agreed to oppose any attempt to water down the Bill.

Bill C-49 was tabled on December 12, 1991. It was referred to committee after second reading on April 16, 1992. It quickly passed through the House of Commons and Senate and received Royal Assent on June 23, 1992. Bill C-49 was proclaimed to be in force on August 15, 1992.

See Sheila McIntyre, "Redefining Reformism: The Consultations that Shaped Bill C-49" in J. Roberts and R. Mohr (eds.), *Confronting Sexual Assault. A Decade of Legal and Social Change* (1994), chapter 12.

The new section 276, regarding the admissibility of evidence of the complainant's sexual activity, provides:

> **276.**(1) In proceedings in respect of an offence under section 151, 152, 153, 155 or 159, subsection 160(2) or (3) or section 170, 171, 172, 173, 271, 272 or 273, evidence that the complainant has engaged in sexual activity, whether with the accused or with any other person, is not admissible to support an inference that, by reason of the sexual nature of that activity, the complainant
>
> > (a)   is more likely to have consented to the sexual activity that forms the subject-matter of the charge; or
> >
> > (b)   is less worthy of belief.
>
> (2) In proceedings in respect of an offence referred to in subsection (1), no evidence shall be adduced by or on behalf of the accused that the complainant has engaged in sexual activity other than the sexual activity that forms the subject-matter of the charge, whether with the accused or with any other person, unless the judge, provincial court judge or justice determines, in accordance with the procedures set out in sections 276.1 and 276.2, that the evidence
>
> > (a)   is of specific instances of sexual activity;

but can't be relevant to consent, p16 that would violate one of the twin myths

(b)   is relevant to an issue at trial; and

(c)   has significant probative value that is not substantially outweighed by the danger of prejudice to the proper administration of justice.

(3) In determining whether evidence is admissible under subsection (2), the judge, provincial court judge or justice shall take into account

(a)   the interests of justice, including the right of the accused to make a full answer and defence;

(b)   society's interest in encouraging the reporting of sexual assault offences;

(c)   whether there is a reasonable prospect that the evidence will assist in arriving at a just determination in the case;

(d)   the need to remove from the fact-finding process any discriminatory belief or bias;

(e)   the risk that the evidence may unduly arouse sentiments of prejudice, sympathy or hostility in the jury;

(f)   the potential prejudice to the complainant's personal dignity and right of privacy;

(g)   the right of the complainant and of every individual to personal security and to the full protection and benefit of the law; and

(h)   any other factor that the judge, provincial court judge or justice considers relevant.

The new section 276.1 imposes a requirement of written notice for a hearing to determine admissibility under section 276(2). Section 276.2 provides for the exclusion of the public at the hearing and the non-compellability of the complainant at the hearing. The new section 276.4 requires the trial judge to instruct the jury as to the proper use of the evidence received.

Does the new legislation give more or less discretion to judges than did *Seaboyer*? What are the differences?

→ evidence admitted — credibility in issue, not really about consent

R. v. CROSBY
[1995] 2 S.C.R. 912, 39 C.R. (4th) 315, 98 C.C.C. (3d) 225

[The accused was charged with sexual assault. The complainant testified that she had been attacked by the accused and another man and forced to engage in non-consensual sexual acts with both. The accused testified that the complainant had consented throughout. In a voir dire before the commencement of the trial, the defence sought permission from the trial judge to lead evidence or cross-examine the complainant on certain statements which referred in some way to sexual activity other than that which formed the subject matter of the charge. This application triggered section 276 scrutiny.

In her original statement to police, the complainant admitted to having engaged in consensual sexual intercourse with the accused three days before the alleged assault. She also admitted that when she visited the accused on the day of the alleged assault she did so with the intention of having sexual intercourse with him again. At the preliminary hearing, the complainant testified that she did not visit the accused with the intention of having sex with him. The material inconsistency was inextricably linked in the police questioning to a reference to the earlier, consensual sexual contact between the complainant and the accused. Relying upon section 276 of the Code, the trial judge prohibited defence counsel from cross-examining the complainant on her original statement made to police. The accused was convicted of sexual assault. He appealed on the basis that the trial judge erred in excluding the evidence of the statements. The majority in the Court of Appeal upheld his conviction.

Held: Appeal allowed; new trial ordered.]

L'HEUREUX-DUBÉ J. (LAMER C.J., LA FOREST, and GONTHIER JJ. concurring):—

. . . .

In her original statement to police, the complainant admitted to having engaged in consensual sexual intercourse with Crosby on November 1, 1991, three days before the alleged assault. She also admitted that when she visited Crosby on November 4, she did so with the intention of having sexual intercourse with him again:

Q: Have you had sex with Scott before?
A: The Friday night before I did.
Q: Is that the reason you went there on Monday?
A: Yup.
Q: Why did you change your mind?
A: Because I didn't feel right with John there and I didn't want to have to have sex with him.

By contrast, at the preliminary hearing, the complainant testified that she did not visit Crosby on November 4, 1991 with the intention of having sex with him:

Q: O.K. Were you hoping to have sex with Scott again that night?
A: No.

There was an apparent inconsistency between these two statements.

Ordinarily, nothing would prevent defence counsel from cross-examining the complainant on an inconsistency which related to her intentions in going to the accused's house on the day of the alleged assault. Material inconsistencies are relevant to the complainant's credibility. Unfortunately for the accused in this case, however, the material inconsistency was inextricably linked in the police questioning to a reference to the earlier, consensual sexual contact between the complainant and the accused. Defence counsel (and apparently the trial judge) thought that it was necessary to place into evidence the actual excerpts from the interview between the complainant and the police.

This created a dilemma. If the actual questions and answers were placed before the jury, then the jury would also have been alerted to the prior sexual activity between the complainant and Crosby on November 1. Relying upon s. 276 of the Code, the trial judge therefore prohibited defence counsel from cross-examining the complainant on this entire portion of her original statement made to police. When the complainant was cross-examined at trial, the following exchange occurred between defence counsel and the complainant:

Q: Now when you went to Mr. Crosby's home on November 7th, did you want to have sex with Mr. Crosby?
A: November 7th?
Q: Or sorry, November 4th, the day this happened with you and Rines . . .
A: No.
Q: You didn't?
A: No.

As a result of the s. 276 ruling, counsel for the appellant was precluded from pursuing this inconsistency between the complainant's trial testimony and her original statement to the police.

With respect, the trial judge erred in excluding this statement, and therefore in preventing defence counsel from cross-examining the complainant on this material inconsistency in her statements.

Where the defence of honest but mistaken belief is not realistically advanced by the accused at trial, then evidence of prior, unrelated sexual activity between the complainant and the accused will seldom be relevant to an issue at trial. . . . However, although the defence of honest but mistaken belief in consent was not realistically at issue in the present case, the circumstances were nonetheless somewhat exceptional. In particular, it appears from the transcripts that the only reason the unrelated sexual activity of November 1 was at all implicated was because it was directly referred to *by police* while posing a question which did, indeed, bear on the sexual activity which formed the subject matter of the charge. The effect of the trial judge's invocation of s. 276 in this case was therefore to exclude otherwise admissible evidence (the complainant's prior statement as to her original intention in going to Crosby's house) by piggybacking it atop otherwise *prima facie* inadmissible evidence (the evidence of the unrelated sexual activity). In my view, it would be unfair for an accused person to be denied access to evidence which is otherwise admissible and relevant to his defence if the prejudice related to admitting that evidence is uniquely attributable to the authorities' conduct. I do not believe that s. 276 was ever designed or intended to be employed to prevent cross-examination in a situation such as this.

. . . Section 276 cannot be interpreted so as to deprive a person of a fair defence. This is not its purpose. This does not mean, of course, that the accused is entitled to the most beneficial procedures possible. . . . Rather, it is evident from the majority's remarks in *Seaboyer* and from the criteria enumerated in s. 276(3) that judges must undertake a balancing exercise under s. 276 that is sensitive to many differing, and potentially conflicting, interests.

In the present case, however, consideration of those factors favoured admission of the complainant's earlier statement. The versions told by the complainant and the accused were diametrically opposed in every material respect, and credibility was consequently the central issue at trial. An inconsistency on a material and pertinent issue is highly relevant in such circumstances. The interests of justice, including the right of the accused to make full answer and defence, therefore militated in favour of admitting the evidence (s. 276(3)(*a*)). So, too, did the fact that there was a reasonable prospect that the evidence would have assisted the jury in arriving at a just determination in the case (section 276(3)(*c*)).

[Sopinka, J., Iacobucci and Major, JJ. concurring, agreed with the reasons for judgment of Justice L'Heureux-Dubé, with respect to the admissibility of the complainant's statement to the police.]

In *Crosby* all the justices agreed that evidence of the statement to the police should have been admitted as it was necessary to ensure a fair trial for the accused. This was despite the fact that the first statement referred to previous sexual activity with the accused. This discretionary exercise, or reading down or into section 276, may signal that it is only a matter of time before a majority of the Supreme Court squarely recognizes that to make section 276 constitutional, the next step is to recognize that a similar discretion or reading down is necessary when the issue is not credibility but whether or not there was consent. Is it not possible to imagine that in some instances evidence of previous consensual sexual conduct with the accused would not only be relevant to the issue of consent but also have sufficient probative force that it would outweigh the possibility of prejudice to the correct disposal of the case? Then, despite section 276, the evidence would need to be admitted if the accused is to have a fair trial and a discretion will have to be recognized.

Section 276(1) seems to contain an express blanket prohibition on what is commonly referred to as the "twin myths" reasoning. It prohibits the use of prior sexual history of the complainant on the issue of consent or to show that the complainant was less worthy of belief. This seemed to make it unconstitutional because *Seaboyer* had called for discretion (see Delisle, "Potential Charter Challenges to the New Rape Shield Law" (1992), 13 C.R. (4th) 390).

However, Professor David Paciocco, "The New Rape Shield Provisions in Section 276 Should Survive Charter Challenge" (1993), 21 C.R. (4th) 223, suggested that the legislation could be read down. Section 276(1) only prohibited general stereotypical inferences. Evidence of prior sexual history with the accused could be admitted under section 276(2) where the defence could establish that a specific inference can be drawn from such evidence to an issue relevant in the trial. In Charter challenges in lower courts the Paciocco position carried the day and was increasingly relied on as the proper interpretation.

When the Supreme Court finally considered the constitutionality of the "new" statutory scheme in *Darrach* a unanimous court had little difficulty in declaring the "new" rape shield provisions constitutional.

R. v. DARRACH
[2000] 2 S.C.R. 443, 36 C.R. (5th) 223, 148 C.C.C. (3d) 97

[The accused was charged with sexual assault and, at his trial, attempted to introduce evidence of the complainant's sexual history. He unsuccessfully challenged the constitutionality of section 276.1 (2)(*a*) of the Criminal Code (which requires that the affidavit contain "detailed particulars" about the evidence), sections 276(1) and 276(2)(*c*) (which govern the admissibility of sexual conduct evidence generally), and section 276.2(2) (which provides that the complainant is not a compellable witness at the hearing determining the admissibility of evidence of prior sexual activity). After a voir dire, the trial judge refused to allow the accused to adduce the evidence of the complainant's sexual history. The accused was convicted and the Court of Appeal dismissed the accused's appeal, concluding that the impugned provisions did not violate the accused's right to make full answer and defence, his right not to be compelled to testify against himself or his right to a fair trial as protected by sections 7, 11(*c*) and 11(*d*) of the Canadian Charter of Rights and Freedoms. Here we consider the accused's argument that section 276(1) was unconstitutional.]

GONTHIER, J. (MCLACHLIN, C.J.C., L'HEUREUX-DUBÉ, IACOBUCCI, MAJOR, BASTARACHE, BINNIE, ARBOUR and LEBEL, JJ. concurring): —

. . . .

The current s. 276 categorically prohibits evidence of a complainant's sexual history only when it is used to support one of two general inferences. These are that a person is more likely to have consented to the alleged assault and that she is less credible as a witness by virtue of her prior sexual experience. Evidence of sexual activity may be admissible, however, to substantiate other inferences. . . .

. . . .

The current version of s. 276 is in essence a codification by Parliament of the Court's guidelines in *Seaboyer*.

must examine all the principles of fund. justice that s.7 is designed to protect.

. . . .

[T]he Court's jurisprudence . . . has consistently held that the principles of fundamental justice enshrined in s. 7 protect more than the rights of the accused. . . . One of the implications of this analysis is that while the right to make full answer and defence and the principle against self-incrimination are certainly core principles of fundamental justice, they can be respected without the accused being entitled to "the most favourable procedures that could possibly be imagined" (*R. v. Lyons*, [1987] 2 S.C.R. 309, at p. 362; cited in *Mills*, *supra*, at para. 72). Nor is the accused entitled to have procedures crafted that take only his interests into account. Still less is he entitled to procedures that would distort the truth-seeking function of a trial by permitting irrelevant and prejudicial material at trial.

new propositions

strong approval of twin-myth hypothesis

In *Seaboyer*, the Court found that the principles of fundamental justice include the three purposes of s. 276 identified above: protecting the integrity of the trial by excluding evidence that is misleading, protecting the rights of the accused, as well as encouraging the reporting of sexual violence and protecting "the security and privacy of the witnesses" (p. 606). This was affirmed in *Mills*, *supra*, at para. 72. The Court crafted its guidelines in *Seaboyer* in accordance with these principles, and it is in relation to these principles that the effects of s. 276 on the accused must be evaluated.

3 purposes of s. 276

The Court in *Mills* upheld the constitutionality of the provisions in the Criminal Code that control the use of personal and therapeutic records in trials of sexual offences. The use of these records in evidence is analogous in many ways to the use of evidence of prior sexual activity, and the protections in the Criminal Code surrounding the use of records at trial are motivated by similar policy considerations. L'Heureux-Dubé J. has warned that therapeutic records should not become a tool for circumventing s. 276: "[w]e must not allow the defence to do indirectly what it cannot do directly" (*R. v. O'Connor*, [1995] 4 S.C.R. 411, at para. 122, and *R. v. Osolin*, [1993] 4 S.C.R. 595, at p. 624). Academic commentators have observed that the use of therapeutic records increased with the enactment of s. 276 nonetheless (see K. D. Kelly, "'You must be crazy if you think you were raped': Reflections on the Use of Complainants' Personal and Therapy Records in Sexual Assault Trials" (1997), 9 C.J.W.L. 178, at p. 181).

. . . .

full answer defence / 1-privacy / 2-privacy / 3-equality

(T)he test for admissibility in s. 276(2) requires not only that the evidence be relevant but also that it be more probative than prejudicial. *Mills* dealt with a conflict among the same three Charter principles that are in issue in the case at bar: full answer and defence, privacy and equality (at para. 61). The Court defined these rights relationally: "the scope of the right to make full answer and defence must be determined in light of privacy and equality rights of complainants and witnesses" (paras. 62-66 and 94). The exclusionary rule was upheld. The privacy and equality concerns involved in protecting the records justified interpreting the right to make full answer and defence in a way that did not include a right to all relevant evidence.

. . . .

In the case at bar, I affirm the reasons in *Seaboyer* and find that none of the accused's rights are infringed by s. 276 as he alleges. *Seaboyer* provides a basic justification for the legislative scheme in s. 276, including the determination of relevance as well as the prejudicial and probative value of the evidence. *Mills* and *White* show how the impact of s. 276 on the principles of fundamental justice relied on by the accused should be assessed in light of the other principles of fundamental justice that s. 276 was designed to protect. The reasons in *Mills* are apposite because they demonstrate how the same principles of equality, privacy and fairness can be reconciled. I shall show below how the procedure created by s. 276 to protect the trial process from distortion and to protect complainants is consistent with the principles of fundamental justice. It is fair to the accused and properly reconciles the divergent interests at play, as the Court suggested in *Seaboyer*.

kind of like Pacioco, but Gontier uses "specific" instead of general

. . . .

Section 276(1) — The Exclusionary Rule

The accused objects to the exclusionary rule itself in s. 276(1) on the grounds that it is a "blanket exclusion" that prevents him from adducing evidence necessary to make full answer and defence, as guaranteed by ss. 7 and 11(d) of the Charter. He is mistaken in his characterization of the rule. Far from being a "blanket exclusion", s. 276(1) only prohibits the use of evidence of past sexual activity when it is offered to support two specific, illegitimate inferences. These are known as the "twin myths", namely that a complainant is more likely to have consented or that she is less worthy of belief "by reason of the sexual nature of the activity" she once engaged in.

This section gives effect to McLachlin J.'s finding in *Seaboyer* that the "twin myths" are simply not relevant at trial. They are not probative of consent or credibility and can severely distort the trial process. Section 276(1) also clarifies *Seaboyer* in several respects. Section 276 applies to all sexual activity, whether with the accused or with someone else. It also applies to non-consensual as well as consensual sexual activity, as this Court found implicitly in *R. v. Crosby*, [1995] 2 S.C.R. 912, at para. 17. Although the *Seaboyer* guidelines referred to "consensual sexual conduct" (pp. 634-35), Parliament enacted the new version of s. 276 without the word "consensual". Evidence of non-consensual sexual acts can equally defeat the purposes of s. 276 by distorting the trial process when it is used to evoke stereotypes such as that women who have been assaulted must have deserved it and that they are unreliable witnesses, as well as by deterring people from reporting assault by humiliating them in court. The admissibility of evidence of non-consensual sexual activity is determined by the procedures in s. 276. Section 276 also settles any ambiguity about whether the "twin myths" are limited to inferences about "unchaste" women in particular; they are not (as discussed by C. Boyle and M. MacCrimmon, "The Constitutionality of Bill C-49: Analyzing Sexual Assault As If Equality Really Mattered" (1999), 41 Crim. L.Q. 198, at pp. 231-32).

The Criminal Code excludes all discriminatory generalizations about a complainant's disposition to consent or about her credibility based on the *sexual nature* of her past sexual activity on the grounds that these are improper lines of reasoning. This was the import of the Court's findings in *Seaboyer* about how sexist beliefs about women distort the trial process. The text of the exclusionary rule in s. 276(1) diverges very little from the guidelines in *Seaboyer*. The mere fact that the wording differs between the Court's guidelines and Parliament's enactment is itself immaterial. In *Mills, supra*, the Court affirmed that "[t]o insist on slavish conformity" by Parliament to judicial pronouncements "would belie the mutual respect that underpins the relationship" between the two institutions (para. 55). In this case, the legislation follows the Court's suggestions very closely.

The phrase "by reason of the sexual nature of that activity" in s. 276 is a clarification by Parliament that it is inferences from the *sexual nature* of the activity, as opposed to inferences from other potentially relevant features of the activity, that are prohibited. If evidence of sexual activity is proffered for its non-sexual features, such as to show a pattern of conduct or a prior inconsistent statement, it may be permitted. The phrase "by reason of the sexual nature of that activity" has the same effect as the qualification "solely to support the inference" in *Seaboyer* in that it limits the exclusion of evidence to that used to invoke the "twin myths" (p. 635).

. . . .

An accused has never had a right to adduce irrelevant evidence. Nor does he have the right to adduce misleading evidence to support illegitimate inferences: "the accused is not permitted to distort the truth-seeking function of the trial process" (*Mills, supra*, at para. 74). Because s. 276(1) is an evidentiary rule that only excludes material that is not relevant, it cannot infringe the accused's right to make full answer and defence. Section 276(2) is more complicated, and I turn to it now.

Section 276(2)(c) — "Significant Probative Value"

If evidence is not barred by s. 276(1) because it is tendered to support a permitted inference, the judge must still weigh its probative value against its prejudicial effect to determine its admissibility. This essentially mirrors the common law guidelines in *Seaboyer* which contained this balancing test (at p. 635). The accused takes issue with the fact that s. 276(2)(c) specifically requires that the evidence have "significant probative value". The word "significant" was added by Parliament but it does not render the provision unconstitutional by raising the threshold for the admissibility of evidence to the point that it is unfair to the accused.

. . . .

The context of the word "significant" in the provision in which it occurs substantiates this interpretation. Section 276(2)(c) allows a judge to admit evidence of *"significant* probative value that is not *substantially* outweighed by the danger of prejudice to the proper administration of justice" (emphasis added). The adverb "substantially" serves to protect the accused by raising the standard for the judge to exclude evidence once the accused has shown it to have significant probative value. In a sense, both sides of the equation are heightened in this test, which serves to direct judges to the serious ramifications of the use of evidence of prior sexual activity for all parties in these cases.

In light of the purposes of s. 276, the use of the word "significant" is consistent with both the majority and the minority reasons in *Seaboyer*. Section 276 is designed to prevent the use of evidence of prior sexual activity for improper purposes. The requirement of "significant probative value" serves to exclude evidence of trifling relevance that, even though not used to support the two forbidden inferences, would still endanger the "proper administration of justice". The Court has recognized that there are inherent "damages and disadvantages presented by the admission of such evidence" (*Seaboyer, supra*, at p. 634). As Morden A.C.J.O. puts it, evidence of sexual activity must be significantly probative if it is to overcome its prejudicial effect. The Criminal Code codifies this reality.

By excluding misleading evidence while allowing the accused to adduce evidence that meets the criteria of s. 276(2), s. 276 enhances the fairness of trials of sexual offences. Section 11(d) guarantees a fair trial. Fairness under s. 11(d) is determined in the context of the trial process as a whole (*R. v. Stoddart* (1987), 37 C.C.C. (3d) 351 (Ont. C.A.), at pp. 365-66). As L'Heureux-Dubé J. wrote in *Crosby, supra*, at para. 11, "[s]ection 276 cannot be interpreted so as to deprive a person of a fair defence." At the same time, the accused's right to make full answer and defence, as was held in *Mills, supra*, at para. 75, is not "automatically breached where he or she is deprived of relevant information". Nor is it necessarily breached when the accused is not permitted to adduce relevant information that is not "significantly" probative, under a rule of evidence that protects the trial from the distorting effects of evidence of prior sexual activity.

. . . .

Thus the threshold criteria that evidence be of "significant" probative value does not prevent an accused from making full answer and defence to the charges against him. Consequently his Charter rights under ss. 7 and 11(d) are not infringed by s. 276(2)(c).

The Procedural Sections to Determine Relevance: The Affidavit and Voir Dire

The constitutionality of the procedure that must be followed to introduce evidence of prior sexual activity has also been challenged. It requires that whoever seeks to introduce it "by or on behalf of the accused" must present an affidavit and establish on a voir dire that the evidence is admissible in accordance with the criteria in the Criminal Code.

[The Court determined that the procedural provisions were not violative of the accused's constitutional rights. In the course of its analysis the court later commented on relevance and probative value of evidence of previous sexual activity.]

consent is still murder ↗

Although the Supreme Court has determined the issue of constitutionality, it seems very likely that *Darrach* has not resolved the question of the proper application of sections 276(1) and (2), especially in the context of prior sexual history with the accused where the issue is consent. We have seen that the Court in (Darrach) at one point says that such evidence is not relevant then in the next breath it says it may be admitted. Towards the end of the judgment this is put in yet another way:

> Evidence of prior sexual activity will rarely be relevant to support a denial that sexual activity took place or to establish consent (C.R., para. 58).

That judges have different views on the issue of the relevance and probative value of evidence of prior sexual history with the accused on the issue of consent is reflected in the views of the Ontario Court of Appeal in the court below in *Darrach*, which were not addressed in the Supreme Court. According to Morden, A.C.J.O. for the court, (1998), 13 C.R. (5th) 283, 122 C.C.C. (3d) 225 (Ont. C.A.), (Osborne and Doherty, JJ.A. concurring):

> It will likely be that evidence of previous sexual activity with the accused will satisfy the requirements of admissibility in s. 276(2) more often than that relating to sexual activity with others. This does not mean that this evidence should always be admissible (C.R. at 299).

✳

Trial judges appear to regularly admit evidence of a prior or ongoing relationship where there is a viable issue of consent. Otherwise the trial would be devoid of context and potentially unfair to accused. That is not to say that such evidence is determinative.

flouting SCC

For a comprehensive review of case law on section 276 see Chapman, "Section 276 of the Criminal Code and the Admissibility of Sexual Activity Evidence" (1999), 25 Queen's Law Journal 121.

R. v. A.
[2001] H.L.J. No. 25, May 17, 2001

[On a charge of rape the trial judge had ruled that the accused could not cross-examine the complainant as to her previous sexual relationship with the accused. The Court of Appeal reversed the accused's conviction. The Court of Appeal certified the following question:

> May a sexual relationship between a defendant and complainant be relevant to the issue of consent so as to render its exclusion under section 41 of the Youth Justice and Criminal Evidence Act 1999 a contravention of the defendant's right to a fair trial?

The House of Lords dismissed the Crown's appeal.]

LORD SLYNN OF HADLEY: —

The need to protect women from harassment in the witness box is fundamental. It must not be lost sight of but I suspect that the man or woman in the street would find it strange that evidence that two young people who had lived together or regularly as part of a happy relationship had had sexual acts together, must be wholly excluded on the issue of consent unless it is immediately contemporaneous. The question whether such evidence should be believed and whether it is sufficient to establish consent or even belief in consent are different matters. The man and woman in the street might also find it strange that evidence may be given and cross examination allowed as to belief in consent but not to consent itself when the same evidence was being relied on. That distinction has been recognised in the cases but without in any way resiling from a strong insistence on the need to protect women from humiliating cross examination and prejudicial but valueless evidence. It seems to me clear that these restrictions in section 41 prima facie are capable of preventing an accused person from putting forward relevant evidence which may be evidence critical to his defence, whether it is as to consent or to belief that the woman consented. If thus construed section 41 does prevent the accused from having a fair trial then it must be declared to be incompatible with the Convention.

LORD STEYN: —

As a matter of common sense, a prior sexual relationship between the complainant and the accused may, depending on the circumstances, be relevant to the issue of consent. It is a species of prospectant evidence which may throw light on the complainant's state of mind. It cannot, of course, prove that she consented on the occasion in question. Relevance and sufficiency of proof are different things. The fact that the accused a week before an alleged murder threatened to kill the deceased does not prove an intent to kill on the day in question. But it is logically relevant to that issue. After all, to be relevant the evidence need merely have some tendency in logic and common sense to advance the proposition in issue. It is true that each decision to engage in sexual activity is always made afresh. On the other hand, the mind does not usually blot out all memories. What one has been engaged on in the past may influence what choice one makes on a future occasion. Accordingly, a prior relationship between a complainant and an accused may sometimes be relevant to what decision was made on a particular occasion.

. . . .

Following *R v Seaboyer* section 276 of the Criminal Code was amended. Subsequently the Supreme Court held that section 276 as amended was valid. As amended it was not viewed as a blanket exclusion: *R v Darrach* (2000) 191 DLR (4th) 539. Unfortunately, the Secretary of State's understanding of the Canadian position was flawed. *R v Seaboyer* is largely concerned with the irrelevance of sexual experience between the complainant and third parties. In her leading judgment McLachlin J placed general reliance upon an article of Galvin, who emphasises the probative value of prior sexual conduct between a complainant and an accused to the issue of consent: "Shielding Rape Victims in the State and Federal Courts: A Proposal for the Second Decade" (1986) 70 Minn L Rev 763. Moreover, McLachlin J made a telling comment on prior sexual history with the accused. It is to the following effect, at 83 DLR (4th) 193, 280D:

> I question whether evidence of other sexual conduct with the accused should automatically be admissible in all cases; sometimes the value of such evidence might be little or none.

R v Seaboyer does not justify the breadth of the exclusionary provisions of section 41 in respect of previous sexual experience between a complainant and a defendant.

LORD HOPE OF CRAIGHEAD: —

It is plain a balance must be struck between the right of the defendant to a fair trial and the right of the complainant not to be subjected to unnecessary humiliation and distress when giving evidence. The right of the defendant to a fair trial has now been reinforced by the incorporation into our law of article 6 of the European Convention for the Protection of Human Rights and Fundamental Freedoms by the Human Rights Act 1998. But the principles which are enshrined in that article have for long been part of our common law. The common law recognises that a defendant has the right to cross-examine the prosecutor's witnesses and to give and lead evidence. The guiding principle as to the extent of that right is that prima facie all evidence which is relevant to the question whether the defendant is guilty or innocent is admissible. As the fact that the act of sexual intercourse was without the consent of the complainant is one of the essential elements in the charge which the prosecutor must establish, the defendant must be given an opportunity to cross-examine the prosecutor's witnesses and to give and lead evidence on that issue. That is an essential element of his right to a fair trial.

. . . .

While section 41(3) imposes very considerable restrictions, it needs to be seen in its context. I would hold that the required level of unfairness to show that in every case where previous sexual behaviour between the complainant and the accused is alleged the solution adopted is not proportionate has not been demonstrated. I emphasise the words "every case", because I believe that it would only be if there was a material risk of incompatibility with the article 6 Convention right in all such cases that it would be appropriate to lay down a rule of general application as to how, applying section 3 of the Human Rights Act 1998, section 41(3) ought to be read in a way that is compatible with the Convention right or, if that were not possible, to make a declaration of general incompatibility. I do not accept that there is such a risk.

LORD CLYDE: —

The Canadian experience shows how important it is to secure a proper balance between the necessity to provide sufficient protection for the victim of a sexual offence at the trial of the person accused of the offence and the corresponding necessity to secure that the accused has the opportunity to present any relevant defence which he has to the charge. It is right that the victim be protected. But it is also right that an accused should be allowed a fair trial.

. . . .

But there is one vital distinction which must be recognised among the generalities which are sometimes adopted in this context, and that is the distinction between a history of intercourse with the defendant and a history of intercourse with other men. To an extent that distinction has been recognised in the past. While questions could be asked in cross-examination of the complainant about someone other than the defendant evidence could not be called to contradict her answer since that would open the way to an inquiry into a multitude of collateral issues (*R v Holmes* (1871) LR 1 CCR 334). On the other hand evidence could be led to counter an answer where the question had been asked in relation to intercourse with the defendant (*R v Riley* (1887) 18 QBD 481). But the distinction should be recognised as going further. It may readily be accepted that some evidence at least relating to sexual behaviour with the defendant outside the particular event which is the subject of the trial may be relevant as casting light on the question of the complainant's consent. But I do not consider that evidence of her behaviour with other men should now be accepted as relevant for that purpose.

LORD HUTTON: —

My Lords, in a criminal trial there are two principal objectives of the law. One is that a defendant should not be convicted of the crime with which he is charged when he has not committed it. The other is that a defendant who is guilty of the crime with which he is charged should be convicted. But where the crime charged is that of rape, the law must have a third objective which is also of great importance: it is to ensure that the woman who complains that she has been raped is treated with dignity in court and is given protection against cross-examination and evidence which invades her privacy unnecessarily and which subjects her to humiliating questioning and accusations which are irrelevant to the charge against the defendant. The need to protect a witness against unfair questioning applies, of course, to all trials but it is of special importance in a trial for rape. Linked to the third objective is the further consideration that allegations relating to the sexual history of the complainant may distort the course of the trial and divert the jury from the issue which they have to determine.

It is the need to achieve both the objective of protecting an innocent defendant and the objective of protecting a woman complainant which gives rise to the difficult and important issue before the House on this appeal. The issue is difficult because in some cases where an innocent defendant wishes to give evidence that prior to the sexual intercourse which gives rise to the charge against him he had had consensual sexual intercourse with the complainant on previous occasions, it may be necessary to permit him to give such evidence and the complainant to be cross-examined on the matter in order to enable the jury to come to a just verdict. On the other hand there will be other cases where the adducing of evidence of the complainant's past sexual conduct and cross-examination about it will be unnecessary to ensure that justice is done and may prevent the conviction of a guilty defendant.

PROBLEMS

Problem 1

Three correctional officers were dismissed from their employment for using excessive force on an inmate. Their union grieved these dismissals to the Grievance Settlement Board. Regulations made pursuant to the Ministry of Correctional Services Act specify when force may be used but also provides:

> ... the amount of force used shall be reasonable and not excessive, having regard to the nature of the threat posed by the inmate and *all other circumstances of the case*. [Emphasis added.]

The Grievance Settlement Board dismissed the grievances. In the course of its reasons it noted its inability to decide how the incident had started and the irrelevance of the inmate's previous acts of violence. The union is now arguing on its application for judicial review.

Counsel for
Applicant: In deciding whether the Ministry was justified in dismissing these employees the Board was obliged by the Regulations to measure the amount of force against "all the circumstances". One of the most critical of these circumstances is "How did it all start?" It was impossible to decide the major question without first deciding how the incident was initiated. This amounted to an error of law and the matter must be remitted back to the Board for a new hearing. The Board deliberately closed its eyes to the evidence of previous acts of violence committed by the inmate. The Board referred to this evidence as irrelevant. Clearly, if one is attempting to figure out how a violent altercation occurred, one does not close its eyes to the propensity for violence of one of the participants. The evidence shows the inmate to be a violent person and it is reasonable to assume that he may have acted on this occasion

in conformity with his disposition. His disposition may not be conclusive but it is certainly relevant.

Counsel for
Responsent:

The inmates of a correctional institution are often individuals who have committed violent acts. And yet even these are entitled to be treated in a civilized way. The regulations which govern these three employees prohibit excessive force. The focus for the Grievance Settlement Board was just that. Did the officers use more force than was reasonable, in "all the circumstances"? The Board found itself able to answer that question. The issue of who began the incident was properly seen by them to be immaterial. Correctional officers have the responsibility for dealing with whatever situations arise and dealing with them within certain constraints. The Board made a finding of fact, not open to review, that the employees did not act reasonably and the Ministry was justified to dismiss. Furthermore, leading evidence of past acts of violence would be extremely prejudicial to the interests of the state and to the victim of this assault and deserves exclusion on that ground as well.

Judge:

Thank you, counsel. Now would you please articulate for me the rational connection that you see in this evidence that renders it relevant.

Compare *O.P.S.E.U. v. Min. of Correctional Services* (1984), 2 O.A.C. 351 (Div. Ct.).

Problem 2

The accused is charged with assault. The Crown called the victim, who testified the accused had punched him two or three times about the head. The victim, in his evidence, alluded to two other youths known to the victim who were standing close by and who probably saw it all. The accused gave evidence that he pushed the victim once and that was only after the victim had punched him. The accused, in cross-examination, allows that the two youths standing near the incident are classmates at his high school.

Defence Counsel: Your Honour, the Crown has the obligation of satisfying you beyond a reasonable doubt. The Crown has the obligation of calling all witnesses it believes are credible. The Crown has the obligation of calling all the witnesses who may advance our search for the truth. In considering whether you are satisfied I ask that you be concerned about the credibility of this alleged victim since the Crown did not call the bystanders to confirm his account.

Crown Counsel: Your Honour, my friend's position is preposterous. Failing to call witnesses has no probative worth whatsoever. It's irrelevant. Further, the Crown has the obligation of keeping the length of these trials to a minimum. Efficiency does count for something. If the assault had occurred in front of the bleachers at Exhibition Stadium, would he have me call all the spectators who could possibly shed light on the matter? Besides, we've heard that these bystanders are friends of the accused. If there are to be any inferences drawn, they should be drawn against the accused.

Compare *R. v. Zehr* (1980), 54 C.C.C. (2d) 65 (Ont. C.A.), *Vieczorek v. Piersma* (1987), 58 O.R. (2d) 583 (C.A.), and *R. v. Rooke* (1988), 22 B.C.L.R. (2d) 145 (C.A.).

Problem 3

The accused is charged with robbery. The accused testifies that at the critical moment he was at home with his grandmother. The identification evidence against the accused is weak. The grandmother testified in support of the alibi defence, but in cross-examination she broke down and admitted that she made up her story because the accused had asked her to do so. This witness has just been excused and the Crown Attorney is making submissions relating to her testimony.

Crown Attorney: Your Honour, I have some submissions as to the use of the grandmother's testimony. We have heard the accused's *only* alibi witness state, under oath, that her evidence supporting the accused's alibi is a fabrication and that she lied at the request of the accused. I ask this court to draw an inference of consciousness of guilt from this false alibi and to view this inference as indicating a state of mind of the accused which only the robber would have possessed and which would further support the identification evidence so far adduced.

Judge: You want me to draw this inference as a result of the grandmother's lies?

Crown Attorney: . . . and more importantly from the evidence given that the accused asked her to fabricate those lies.

Judge: (to defence counsel) Do you have any submissions?

Defence Counsel: Yes, your Honour. The law on this point has been clearly stated by the Supreme Court of Canada in *Mahoney*. An inference of consciousness of guilt can be drawn from *proof* of fabrication of a false alibi. But this inference is not to be drawn where the trier of fact simply rejects the alibi evidence. Now, this distinction is subtle but can be amplified if seen in this way: The trier of fact may accept or reject the grandmother's testimony. If they accept her testimony that the accused asked her to support his alibi by lies then the acceptance has the effect of removing the alibi from consideration as a barrier to the acceptance of the case for the prosecution. Nothing more. In other words, the alibi is negated BUT no inference of consciousness can be drawn because there is no extrinsic evidence to support this inference. The rejection of the alibi evidence cannot be treated as an additional piece of circumstantial evidence to prove guilt without any extrinsic evidence. So, if the trier of fact finds that the grandmother did in fact lie for her grandson, this would simply produce a disbelief in the alibi and is not sufficient to constitute grounds for drawing an inference of consciousness of guilt.

Judge: Huh?

See *R. v. Zehr* (1980), 54 C.C.C. (2d) 65 and *R. v. Mahoney* (1979), 50 C.C.C. (2d) 380 (Ont. C.A.); affirmed (1982), 136 D.L.R. (3d) 608 (S.C.C.). See also Peter J. Connelly, "Alibi: Proof of Falsehood and Consciousness of Guilt" (1982-83), 25 Crim. L.Q. 165.

Problem 4

A robbery occurred at a corner convenience store. When the robber fled, his cap flew off. The police have shown various photographs to the store owner and she has selected the photo of John Black. Constable Jones, the investigating officer, is testifying.

Constable Jones: I attended on John Black at his residence that evening. I asked him for a sample of his hair. He asked me why. I told him that we had a suspicion concerning his possible involvement in a robbery and that the robber had left behind his cap. I told him we'd found hairs in the cap and we wanted to make a comparison.

Crown Counsel: Did the accused co-operate?

Defence Counsel: Objection, your Honour.

Crown Counsel: Then what happened?

Constable Jones: I asked him if he would come down to the station and participate in a line-up and he said "No way".

Defence Counsel: Your Honour, please . . .

Constable Jones: So, I asked him if he wanted to tell me where he was at 8:00 p.m. that evening. He said he'd rather wait until he had spoken with his lawyer.

Defence Counsel: Your Honour, I must protest.

Crown Counsel: Your Honour, I understood the defence wants to later lead an alibi defence when presenting his case, and I am simply anticipating that.

What are the objections being made? Would you object in this way? Does His Honour need to know more or should he guess? How should he rule? Compare *R. v. Smith*, [1985] Crim. L. Rev. 590, *R. v. Eden*, [1970] 2 O.R. 161 (C.A.), *R. v. Itwaru*, [1970] 4 C.C.C. 206 (N.S. C.A.), *Marcoux v. R.* (1975), 60 D.L.R. (3d) 119 (S.C.C.).

Problem 5

The accused is charged with criminal negligence in the operation of a motor vehicle causing death. The incident occurred when the accused was driving the wrong way on a one-way street and while he was impaired. The Crown wants to introduce into evidence that two years before this incident the accused was convicted under the Highway Traffic Act for driving the wrong way on a one-way street and one year ago was convicted of impaired driving. Relevant? Receivable? Compare *R. v. Hamilton* (1984), 3 O.A.C. 232.

Problem 6

The accused is charged with conspiracy to traffic in narcotics. The Crown proposes to call on someone who will testify that he met the accused at Kingston Penitentiary and that the accused enticed him with tales of unlimited wealth should he join the accused's drug organization on their release from prison. The accused asks that any reference to his previous incarceration be eliminated. Rule. Compare *R. v. Rowbotham* (1984), 42 C.R. (3d) 175 (Ont. H.C.); affirmed (1988), 63 C.R. (3d) 113 (Ont. C.A.). Suppose the charge is murder and the killing occurred in the penitentiary. See *R. v. Nygaard* (1987), 36 C.C.C. (3d) 199 (Alta. C.A.); leave to appeal to S.C.C. granted (1988), 38 C.C.C. (3d) vi, and *R. v. Nielsen* (1984), 16 C.C.C. (3d) 39 (Man. C.A.); leave to appeal to S.C.C. refused (1985), 31 Man. R. (2d) 240.

Problem 7

The accused is charged with having performed an illegal abortion. The accused in his testimony admits having used instruments as deposed to by the chief witness for the Crown, but he denies his intent to produce a miscarriage averring that miscarriage had in fact already begun before his intervention, and that his purpose was merely to obviate septic poisoning. The Crown seeks to tender evidence of the use by the accused of similar instruments in two other cases for the purpose of procuring miscarriage. Defence objects. Rule on the objection. Relevant? Fair? Receivable? Compare *Brunet v. R.* (1918), 42 D.L.R. 405 (S.C.C.). If the accused's defence was not lack of criminal intent but simply complete denial of the act, would your answer differ? Compare *Brunet v. R.,* [1928] 3 D.L.R. 822 (S.C.C.) and see also the differing opinions in *R. v. Campbell*, [1947] 1 D.L.R. 904 (B.C. C.A.). Should there be different "standards of relevancy" depending on whether the evidence is led to establish act or intent? See *R. v. Scarrott*, [1978] 1 Q.B. 1016 (C.A.).

Problem 8

Plaintiff is suing for damages for injuries received when struck by defendant's plane during a low pass made by defendant. Plaintiff proposes to call witnesses who will describe defendant's reputation for carelessness. Plaintiff also proposes to call evidence that on two previous occasions the defendant violated the Aeronautics Act by flying too low, and that on one of these occasions a person was injured and the defendant settled the matter out of court. Is the evidence receivable? See *Leblanc v. R.*, [1977] 1 S.C.R. 339. See also *Rock v. Canadian Northern Railway Co.*, [1922] 1 W.W.R. 496 (Sask. C.A.), *R. v. Royal Bank*, [1920] 1 W.W.R. 198 (Man. C.A.), and *Brown v. Eastern & Midlands Railway Co.* (1889), 22 Q.B.D. 391.

5

Judicial Notice

1. INTRODUCTION

> . . . [T]o require that a judge should affect a cloistered aloofness from facts that every other man in Court is fully aware of, and should insist on having proof on oath of what, as a man of the world, he knows already better than any witness can tell him, is a rule that may easily become pedantic and futile. . . . Judicial notice . . . involves that, at the stage when evidence of material facts can be properly received, certain facts may be deemed to be established, although not proved by sworn testimony, or by the production, out of the proper custody, of documents, which speak for themselves. Judicial notice refers to facts, which a judge can be called upon to receive and to act upon, either from his general knowledge of them, or from inquiries to be made by himself for his own information from sources to which it is proper for him to refer. . . .[1]

> The judicial process cannot construct every case from scratch, like Descartes creating a world based on the postulate Cogito, ergo sum.[2]

We do not prove by evidence, indeed we cannot prove by evidence, all the facts that are necessary to a judicial decision. Certain matters are so well known in the community or so easily determinable as to be indisputable.

Consider a civil suit for damages for injuries sustained in an automobile accident. The defendant describes his speed and handling of the car. He maintains that the accident was unavoidable as he was unable to bring his vehicle to a stop. The plaintiff maintains that the defendant was negligent in that he was driving too fast for the conditions of the road at the time of the accident. The evidence indicates that it was raining at the time of the accident. To resolve the issue of liability, do we need evidence to be led to establish that rain makes road surfaces wet, that the coefficient of friction between tires and asphalt is thereby reduced, that such a fact is known to most drivers, and that careful drivers lower their speed in such conditions? Such matters are so well known in the community as to be indisputable. This material need not be proved according to the normal rules of evidence. This knowledge is assumed to be already possessed by the judge and the party who has the burden on the issue may simply call on the judge to judicially notice those facts which are necessary to the determination of the question. The judge, at times, may not herself have the knowledge and may need to be informed, but when the judge is informed about such matters it is not through material filtered through the various rules of evidence. Dictionaries, atlases and the like are ready at hand and may freely be consulted by her. In some cases she may even need to be informed by testimony on the matter; but in such cases the testimony is to inform the judge and the fact is decided by her, is judicially noticed by her, and is not left open for a contrary decision by the

---

1. *Commonwealth Shipping Representative v. P. & O. Branch Service*, [1923] A.C. 191, 211-12 (H.L.) per Lord Sumner.
2. Advisory Committee's Note to Rule 201 of the U.S. Federal Rules of Evidence.

jury. In *McQuaker v. Goddard*[3] the plaintiff had been bitten by a camel at the defendant's zoo. In his suit for damages the plaintiff maintained that a camel is a wild animal and that, therefore, as a matter of substantive law, its owner was absolutely liable for any damage and there was no need for the plaintiff to show that the owner was aware of the animal's propensity to attack humans. The Court of Appeal upheld the trial judge's ruling that camels are domestic animals. Scott, L.J. wrote:

> It was quite clearly established by the defendant's witnesses, in my view, that camels do not exist anywhere in the world to-day . . . as wild animals. . . . In every country in the world where camels exist, they are domestic animals used for carrying either people or loads, or for draught purposes.

> . . . .

> [I]t is also well to remember that it is the function of the judge, and not of the jury, to decide whether an animal belongs to the class of domestic animals or to the class of wild animals.[4]

And Clauson, L.J. explained:

> I should like to add a word as to the part taken in the matter by the evidence given as to the facts of nature in regard to camels. That evidence is not, it must be understood, in the ordinary sense bearing upon an issue of fact. In my view, the exact position is this. The judge takes judicial notice of the ordinary course of nature, and, in this particular case, of the ordinary course of nature in regard to the position of camels, among other animals. The reason why the evidence was given was so that it might assist the judge in forming his view as to what the ordinary course of nature in this regard in fact is, a matter of which he is supposed to have complete knowledge.[5]

In *R. v. Zundel*[6] the Ontario Court of Appeal explained:

> It is well established that the court may take judicial notice of an historical fact. The court may, on its own initiative, consult historical works or documents, or the court may be referred to them: see *Read v. Lincoln (Bishop)*, [1892] A.C. 644 (P.C.); *R. v. Bartleman*, 55 B.C.L.R. 78, [1984] 3 C.N.L.R. 114, 13 C.C.C. (3d) 488 at 491-92, 12 D.L.R. (4th) 73 (C.A.). The court may even hear sworn testimony before judicial notice is taken: see *McQuaker v. Goddard*, [1940] 1 K.B. 687, [1940] 1 All E.R. 471 (C.A.).

> As Professor Cross points out, the distinction between the process of taking judicial notice and the reception of evidence begins to fade when the judge makes inquiries before deciding to take judicial notice of a matter. He points out that if learned treatises are consulted it is not easy to say whether evidence is being received under an exception to the hearsay rule or whether the judge is equipping himself to take judicial notice. The resemblance of taking judicial notice to the reception of evidence is even more marked when sworn testimony is heard before judicial notice is taken. He concludes, however, that, even where the processes of taking judicial notice and receiving evidence approximate most closely, they are essentially different: see Cross

---

3.   [1940] 1 All E.R. 471 (C.A.).
4.   *Ibid.*, at pp. 474-75.
5.   *Ibid.*, at p. 478.
6.   (1987), 56 C.R. (3d) 1, 56.

on Evidence, pp. 67-68. The essential difference is that, when the judge is equipping himself to take judicial notice, the hearsay rule does not apply.[7]

2. BOUNDARIES OF JUDICIAL NOTICE

Illustrations from reported cases give us a notion of what is traditionally described as judicial notice. For example, we see court rulings that evidence is not necessary to establish that Victoria is in British Columbia,[8] that Toronto is in Canada,[9] that L.S.D. can be a mind destroying drug,[10] that Colonel By Drive in Ottawa is National Commission property,[11] that big horn sheep are mountain sheep,[12] that a pizza costs less than $200,[13] that "O.D.'d" means overdosed on a drug,[14] or that the incidence of a particular crime has reached such a high level that deterrence is mandated.[15] All these things can be judicially noticed. The judge does not need to be informed about these matters by evidence.

Judicially noticing geographic locations and the meaning of words presents few real problems. When the facts are indisputable, no one has a basis to object. But suppose a judge notices or assumes something about which there are different opinions. Is this also judicial notice? Is it permissible?

There are different schools of thought concerning the boundaries of judicial notice. Professor Thayer regarded judicial notice not as belonging peculiarly to the law of evidence, but rather

to the general topic of legal or judicial reasoning. It is, indeed, woven into the very texture of the judicial function. In conducting a process of judicial reasoning, as of

---

7. The court recognized that it was fitting and proper to judicially notice historical facts. The court in *Zundel* recognized that the fact of the Holocaust was generally known and accepted and that the trial judge would be entitled, therefore, to judicially notice it. The court decided, however, that judicial notice was a discretionary matter and that the trial judge was right to refuse the Crown's application for judicial notice and to insist that the Crown prove it. The court exhibited concern that judicially noticing that the Holocaust occurred would be "gravely prejudicial" to the accused's defence. Ask yourself whether it is proper to refuse to judicially notice that which is generally known and accepted. Should the accused be provided an opportunity to try to prove, in a courtroom, the opposite of what everyone knows, and accepts as true? See Delisle, annotation to *R. v. Zundel* (1987), 56 C.R. (3d) 77 at 94 criticizing the court's interpretation of Professor Thayer. Professor Thayer had written: "Courts may judicially notice much which they cannot be required to notice." The court relied on this sentence for saying that a judge had a discretion whether or not to judicially notice. But Thayer was saying that besides noticing things that they were required to notice, things which were indisputable, judges could also judicially notice other things. He never said that a judge could refuse to notice things that were indisputable! The court repeated this "error" when sitting on appeal from the second *Zundel* trial: *R. v. Zundel* (1990), 53 C.C.C. (3d) 161 (Ont. C.A.).
8. *R. v. Kuhn* (1970), 1 C.C.C. (2d) 132 (B.C. Co. Ct.).
9. *R. v. Cerniuk* (1948), 91 C.C.C. 56 (B.C.C.A.).
10. *R. v. Shaw* (1977), 36 C.R.N.S. 358 (Ont. C.A.).
11. *R. v. Potts* (1982), 134 D.L.R. (3d) 227 (Ont. C.A.).
12. *R. v. Quinn* (1975), 27 C.C.C. (2d) 543 (Alta. S.C.). See also *Sigeareak v. R.*, [1966] S.C.R. 645.
13. *Re Livingstone and R.* (1975), 29 C.C.C. (2d) 557 (B.C.S.C.).
14. *R. v. MacAulay* (1975), 25 C.C.C. (2d) 1 (N.B.C.A.).
15. See, *e.g.*, *R. v. McNicol*, [1969] 3 C.C.C. 56 (Man. C.A.) and *R. v. Adelman*, [1968] 3 C.C.C. 311 (B.C.C.A.).

other reasoning, not a step can be taken without assuming something which has not been proved; and the capacity to do this, with competent judgment and efficiency, is imputed to judges and juries as part of their necessary mental outfit. . . . What are the things of which judicial tribunals may take notice, and should take notice, without proof? It is possible to indicate with exactness only a part of these matters. Some things are thus dealt with by virtue of express statutory law; some in a manner that is referable merely to precedent — to the actual decision, which have selected some things and omitted others in a way that is not always explicable upon any general principle; others upon a general maxim of reason and good sense, the application of which must rest mainly with the discretion of the tribunal, and, in any general discussion, must rather be illustrated than defined.[16]

Cross on Evidence similarly concludes:

The tacit applications of the doctrine of judicial notice are more numerous and more important that the express ones. A great deal is taken for granted when any question of relevance is considered or assumed. For example, evidence is constantly given that persons accused of burglary were found in possession of jemmies or skeleton keys, that the accused became confused when charged; these are relevant only provided there is a common practice to use such things in the commission of crime, or provided that guilty people tend more to become confused when charged, but no one ever thinks of calling evidence on such a subject.[17]

Professor Morgan, on the other hand, in his classic article on the subject, so viewed the purpose of judicial notice that he limited its application to those facts which were indisputable:

Just as the court cannot function unless the judge knows the law and unless the judge and jury have the fund of information common to all intelligent men in the community as well as the capacity to use the ordinary processes of reasoning, so it cannot adjust legal relations among members of society and thus fulfil the sole purpose of its creation if it permits the parties to take issue on, and thus secure results contrary to, what is so notoriously true as not to be the subject of reasonable dispute, or what is capable of immediate and accurate demonstration by resort to sources of indisputable accuracy easily accessible to men in the situation of members of the court. This, it is submitted, is the rock of reason and policy upon which judicial notice of facts is built. . . . To warrant judicial notice the probability must be so great as to make the truth of the proposition notoriously indisputable among reasonable men.[18]

It has been noted that the Morgan thesis thrived in an era dominated by a mood of judicial restraint.[19] How the particular judge views his role will probably dictate how much he or she will rely on materials not introduced by the parties. It depends on "whether he will play an affirmative or quiescent role in the performance of his duties."[20]

---

16. Thayer, *A Preliminary Treatise on Evidence at the Common Law* (1898), pp. 279 and 299.

17. *Cross and Tapper on Evidence*, 8th ed., p. 79.

18. Morgan, "Judicial Notice" (1944), 57 Harv. L. Rev. 269, 273-74.

19. Roberts, "Preliminary Notes Toward a Study of Judicial Notice" (1966-67), 52 Cornell Law Q. 210, 230.

20. Weinstein's Evidence, 200-04. The authors note that this phrase was termed "the most important decision the judge makes for himself" by Judge Breitel, "Ethical Problems in the Performance of the Judicial Function" (Chicago University Conference of Judicial Ethics) 65.

While we see that in many instances the judicially noticed facts are indisputable, and the court then *must* notice them, Professor Thayer believed that there were other instances when a court, in its discretion, might judicially notice facts which could not be demonstrated as being indisputable. While Professor Morgan saw the purpose of judicial notice as ensuring that courts did not make decisions contrary to nature, and therefore would confine it to instances where the facts were notoriously indisputable, Professor Thayer saw another purpose for the doctrine: efficiency. Professor Thayer wrote:

> Taking judicial notice does not import that the matter is indisputable. It is not necessarily anything more than a *prima facie* recognition, leaving the matter still open to controversy. . . . Courts may judicially notice much which they cannot be required to notice. That is well worth emphasizing, for it points to a great possible usefulness in this doctrine, in helping to shorten and simplify trials; it is an instrument of great capacity in the hands of a competent judge; and is not nearly as much used, in the region of practice and evidence, as it should be.[21]

Professor Davis, also disagreeing with Morgan's thesis, wrote:

> The plain fact is, however, that judges and administrative officers necessarily use extra-record facts which are neither indisputable nor found in sources of indisputable accuracy. A human being is probably unable to consider a problem — whether of fact, law, policy, judgment or discretion — without using his past experience, much of which may be factual and much highly disputable. Judges and administrators are at their best when they are well informed; their understanding and information must be used to the full if their decisions are to be wise and sound. Fact finding, law making, and policy formulation should be guided by experience and understanding, not limited to wooden judgments predicated upon the literal words of witnesses.[22]

In his textbook, Davis later emphasized that judicial notice was *not* based simply on ensuring that courts were protected from making findings which did not accord with reality, but that

> the basic principle is that extra-record facts should be assumed whenever it is convenient to assume them, except that convenience should always yield to the

---

21. *Supra*, note 16 at pp. 308-09.
22. Davis, "Judicial Notice" (1955), 55 Col. L. Rev. 945, 948-49. In Davis, *A System of Judicial Notice Based on Fairness and Convenience, Perspectives of Law* (1964), 69, 74, Davis explained that the boundaries of judicial notice coincide with those of judicial reasoning: When the judge reads a pleading or listens to a witness testify, he cannot know the meaning of the words used except through extra-record information, and apart from the meaning of words, he cannot understand the significance of the ideas expressed unless he uses his general background of knowledge — knowledge that cannot conceivably be captured and penned up within the pages of a formal record. As judges go about their workaday tasks, they assume facts all along the line without either thinking or speaking in terms of judicial notice. They assume facts without mentioning that they do so, and when they mention that they do so, they are more likely to say that they "assume" the facts than that they "take judicial notice" of them. Nothing hinges — and nothing should hinge — on the form of words that happen to be used. Compare Carter, "Do Courts Decide According to the Evidence?" (1988), 22 U.B.C.L. Rev. 51, 363: When assessing any evidence given in court, the trier of fact must obviously draw upon a vast mass of previously acquired factual information, knowledge and experience. The use of the terminology of judicial notice to describe this may be confusing. This is not a question of judicial notice, but of the tribunal relying on its own experience as to the ordinary course of human affairs.

requirement of procedural fairness that parties should have an opportunity to meet in the appropriate fashion all facts that influence the disposition of the case.[23]

Professor Roberts commented:

> The Davis theory of judicial notice is just as much a product of the times as was the Morgan theory. Courts seen as super-legislatures must be allowed to roam far and wide and must at all costs not be inhibited by any requirement that the facts with which they deal must be either found in the record or attributable to common knowledge or sources of indisputable accuracy. The law, in short, must be seen as a creative process and the rules of judicial notice recast to expedite this creativity.[24]

Whichever view one takes of the doctrine, one needs to recognize the necessity for procedural fairness to the parties and that the parties need to be advised of the court's intention of taking judicial notice so that they might present information and argument regarding its propriety. Failing to do this would be a denial of natural justice.[25]

R. v. S. (R.D.)
[1997] 3 S.C.R. 484, 10 C.R. (5th) 1, 118 C.C.C. (3d) 353

[The accused, a black 15-year-old, was charged with a series of offences arising out of an incident wherein a white police officer had arrested the accused for interfering with the arrest of another youth. The police officer and the accused were the only witnesses at trial. Their accounts of the relevant events differed widely. The trial judge weighed the evidence and determined that the accused should be acquitted. While delivering her oral reasons, the trial judge, who was also black, remarked:

> The Crown says, well, why would the officer say that events occurred the way in which he has relayed them to the Court this morning? I am not saying that the Constable has misled the court, although police officers have been known to do that in the past. I am not saying that the officer overreacted, but certainly police officers do overreact, particularly when they are dealing with non-white groups. That to me indicates a state of mind right there that is questionable. I believe that probably the situation in this particular case is the case of a young police officer who overreacted. I do accept the evidence of [R.D.S.] that he was told to shut up or he would be under arrest. It seems to be in keeping with the prevalent attitude of the day. At any rate, based upon my comments and based upon all the evidence before the court I have no other choice but to acquit.

The Crown challenged these comments as raising a reasonable apprehension of bias. The Crown's appeal was allowed and a new trial ordered. This judgment was upheld by a majority of the Nova Scotia Court of Appeal. The accused appealed further.]

Held: Appeal allowed; acquittals restored.

23. Davis, *Administrative Law*, 3d ed. (1972), p. 314.
24. Roberts, *supra*, note 19, at p. 233.
25. See *R. v. Haines* (1980), 52 C.C.C. (2d) 558, 563 (B.C. Co. Ct.); affirmed (1981), 63 C.C.C. (2d) 348 (B.C.C.A.), and *Pfizer Co. v. Deputy M.N.R.* (1975), 68 D.L.R. (3d) 9, 15 (S.C.C.).

CORY J. (IACOBUCCI J. concurring):—

. . . .

In some circumstances it may be acceptable for a judge to acknowledge that racism in society might be, for example, the motive for the overreaction of a police officer. This may be necessary in order to refute a submission that invites the judge as trier of fact to presume truthfulness or untruthfulness of a category of witnesses, or to adopt some other form of stereotypical thinking. Yet it would not be acceptable for a judge to go further and suggest that all police officers should therefore not be believed or should be viewed with suspicion where they are dealing with accused persons who are members of a different race. Similarly, it is dangerous for a judge to suggest that a particular person overreacted because of racism unless there is evidence adduced to sustain this finding. It would be equally inappropriate to suggest that female complainants, in sexual assault cases, ought to be believed more readily than male accused persons solely because of the history of sexual violence by men against women.

If there is no evidence linking the generalization to the particular witness, these situations might leave the judge open to allegations of bias on the basis that the credibility of the individual witness was prejudged according to stereotypical generalizations. This does not mean that the particular generalization — that police officers have historically discriminated against visible minorities or that women have historically been abused by men — is not true, or is without foundation. The difficulty is that reasonable and informed people may perceive that the judge has used this information as a basis for assessing credibility instead of making a genuine evaluation of the evidence of the particular witness' credibility. As a general rule, judges should avoid placing themselves in this position.

. . . .

The Crown contended that the real problem arising from Judge Sparks' remarks was the inability of the Crown and Constable Stienburg to respond to the remarks. In other words, the Crown attempted to put forward an argument that the trial was rendered unfair for failure to comply with "natural justice". This cannot be accepted. Neither Constable Stienburg nor the Crown was on trial. Rather, it is essential to consider whether the remarks of Judge Sparks gave rise to a reasonable apprehension of bias. This is the only basis on which this trial could be considered unfair.

. . . .

However, there was no evidence before Judge Sparks that would suggest that anti-black bias influenced this particular police officer's reactions. Thus, although it may be incontrovertible that there is a history of racial tension between police officers and visible minorities, there was no evidence to link that generalization to the actions of Constable Stienburg. The reference to the fact that police officers may overreact in dealing with non-white groups may therefore be perfectly supportable, but it is nonetheless unfortunate in the circumstances of this case because of its potential to associate Judge Sparks' findings with the generalization, rather than the specific evidence. This effect is reinforced by the statement "[t]hat to me indicates a state of mind right there that is questionable" which immediately follows her observation.

There is a further troubling comment. After accepting R.D.S.'s evidence that he was told to shut up, Judge Sparks added that "[i]t seems to be in keeping with the prevalent attitude of the day". Again, this comment may create a perception that the findings of credibility have been made on the basis of generalizations, rather than the conduct of the particular police officer. Indeed these comments standing alone come very close to indicating that Judge Sparks predetermined the issue of credibility of Constable Stienburg on the basis of her general perception of racist police attitudes, rather than on the basis of his demeanour and the substance of his testimony.

The remarks are worrisome and come very close to the line. Yet, however troubling these comments are when read individually, it is vital to note that the comments were not made in isolation. It is necessary to read all of the comments in the context of the whole proceeding, with an awareness of all the circumstances that a reasonable observer would be deemed to know.

The reasonable and informed observer at the trial would be aware that the Crown had made the submission to Judge Sparks that "there's absolutely no reason to attack the credibility of the officer". She had already made a finding that she preferred the evidence of R.D.S. to that of Constable Stienburg. She gave reasons for these findings that could appropriately be made based on the evidence adduced. A reasonable and informed person hearing her subsequent remarks would conclude that she was exploring the possible reasons why Constable Stienburg had a different perception of events than R.D.S. Specifically, she was rebutting the unfounded suggestion of the Crown that a police officer by virtue of his occupation should be more readily believed than the accused. Although her remarks were inappropriate they did not give rise to a reasonable apprehension of bias.

. . . .

A high standard must be met before a finding of reasonable apprehension of bias can be made. Troubling as Judge Sparks' remarks may be, the Crown has not satisfied its onus to provide the cogent evidence needed to impugn the impartiality of Judge Sparks. Although her comments, viewed in isolation, were unfortunate and unnecessary, a reasonable, informed person, aware of all the circumstances, would not conclude that they gave rise to a reasonable apprehension of bias. Her remarks, viewed in their context, do not give rise to a perception that she prejudged the issue of credibility on the basis of generalizations, and they do not taint her earlier findings of credibility.

. . . .

I must add that since writing these reasons I have had the opportunity of reading those of Major J. It is readily apparent that we are in agreement as to the nature of bias and the test to be applied in order to determine whether the words or actions of a trial judge raise a reasonable apprehension of bias. The differences in our reasons lies in the application of the principles and test we both rely upon to the words of the trial judge in this case. The principles and the test we have both put forward and relied upon are different from and incompatible with those set out by Justices L'Heureux-Dubé and McLachlin.

MAJOR J. (LAMER C.J.C. and SOPINKA J. concurring):— The trial judge stated that "police officers have been known to [mislead the court] in the past" and that "police officers do overreact, particularly when they are dealing with non-white groups" and went on to say "[t]hat to me indicates a state of mind right there that is questionable." She in effect was saying, "sometimes police lie and overreact in dealing with non-whites, therefore I have a suspicion that this police officer may have lied and overreacted in dealing with this non-white accused." This was stereotyping all police officers as liars and racists, and applied this stereotype to the police officer in the present case. The trial judge might be perceived as assigning less weight to the police officer's evidence because he is testifying in the prosecution of an accused who is of a different race. Whether racism exists in our society is not the issue. The issue is whether there was evidence before the court upon which to base a finding that this particular police officer's actions were motivated by racism. There was no evidence of this presented at the trial.

. . . .

Trial judges have to base their findings on the evidence before them. It was open to the appellant to introduce evidence that this police officer was racist and that racism motivated his actions or that he lied. This was not done. For the trial judge to infer that based on her general view of the police or society is an error of law. For this reason there should be a new trial.

. . . .

The life experience of this trial judge, as with all trial judges, is an important ingredient in the ability to understand human behaviour, to weigh the evidence, and to determine credibility. It helps in making a myriad of decisions arising during the course of most trials. It is of no value, however, in reaching conclusions for which there is no evidence. The fact that on some other occasions police officers have lied or overreacted is irrelevant. Life experience is not a substitute for evidence. There was no evidence before the trial judge to support the conclusions she reached.

. . . .

Canadian courts have, in recent years, criticized the stereotyping of people into what is said to be predictable behaviour patterns. If a judge in a sexual assault case instructed the jury or him or herself that because the complainant was a prostitute he or she probably consented, or that prostitutes are likely to lie about such things as sexual assault, that decision would be reversed. Such presumptions have no place in a system of justice that treats all witnesses equally. Our jurisprudence prohibits tying credibility to something as irrelevant as gender, occupation or perceived group predisposition. . . . It can hardly be seen as progress to stereotype police officer witnesses as likely to lie when dealing with non-whites. This would return us to a time in the history of the Canadian justice system that many thought had past. This reasoning, with respect to police officers, is no more legitimate than the stereotyping of women, children or minorities.

. . . .

I agree with the approach taken by Cory J. with respect to the nature of bias and the test to be used to determine if the words or actions of a judge give rise to apprehension of bias. However, I come to a different conclusion in the application of the test to the words of the trial judge in this case. It follows that I disagree with the approach to reasonable apprehension of bias put forward by Justices L'Heureux-Dubé and McLachlin.

L'HEUREUX-DUBÉ J. (McLACHLIN J. concurring):—

. . . .

Lhallow all experiences of judge to play a role

In our view, the test for reasonable apprehension of bias established in the jurisprudence is reflective of the reality that while judges can never be neutral, in the sense of purely objective, they can and must strive for impartiality. It therefore recognizes as inevitable and appropriate that the differing experiences of judges assist them in their decision-making process and will be reflected in their judgments, so long as those experiences are relevant to the cases, are not based on inappropriate stereotypes, and do not prevent a fair and just determination of the cases based on the facts in evidence. We find that on the basis of these principles, there is no reasonable apprehension of bias in the case at bar. Like Cory J. we would, therefore, overturn the findings by the Nova Scotia Supreme Court (Trial Division) and the majority of the Nova Scotia Court of Appeal that a reasonable apprehension of bias arises in this case, and restore the acquittal of R.D.S. This said, we disagree with Cory J.'s position that the comments of Judge Sparks were unfortunate, unnecessary, or close to the line. Rather, we find them to reflect an entirely appropriate recognition of the facts in evidence in this case and of the context within which this case arose — a context known to Judge Sparks and to any well-informed member of the community.

. . . .

Cardozo recognized that objectivity was an impossibility because judges, like all other humans, operate from their own perspectives. As the Canadian Judicial Council noted in Commentaries on Judicial Conduct (1991), at p. 12, "[t]here is no human being who is not the product of every social experience, every process of education, and every human contact". What is possible and desirable, they note, is impartiality:

The wisdom required of a judge is to recognize, consciously allow for, and perhaps to question, all the baggage of past attitudes and sympathies that fellow citizens are free to carry, untested, to the grave.

True impartiality does not require that the judge have no sympathies or opinions; it requires that the judge nevertheless be free to entertain and act upon different points of view with an open mind.

. . . .

As discussed above, judges in a bilingual, multiracial and multicultural society will undoubtedly approach the task of judging from their varied perspectives. They will certainly have been shaped by, and have gained insight from, their different experiences, and cannot be expected to divorce themselves from these experiences on the occasion of their appointment to the bench. In fact, such a transformation would deny society the benefit of the valuable knowledge gained by the judiciary while they were members of the Bar. As well, it would preclude the achievement of a diversity of backgrounds in the judiciary. The reasonable person does not expect that judges will function as neutral ciphers; however, the reasonable person does demand that judges achieve impartiality in their judging.

. . . .

An understanding of the context or background essential to judging may be gained from testimony from expert witnesses in order to put the case in context: *R. v. Lavallee, R. v. Parks*, and *Moge v. Moge*, from academic studies properly placed before the Court; and from the judge's personal understanding and experience of the society in which the judge lives and works. This process of enlargement is not only consistent with impartiality; it may also be seen as its essential precondition. A reasonable person far from being troubled by this process, would see it as an important aid to judicial impartiality.

where can we get evidence from

. . . .

It is important to note that having already found R.D.S. to be credible, and having accepted a sufficient portion of his evidence to leave her with a reasonable doubt as to his guilt, Judge Sparks necessarily disbelieved at least a portion of the conflicting evidence of Constable Stienburg. At that point, Judge Sparks made reference to the submissions of the Crown that "there's absolutely no reason to attack the credibility of the officer", and then addressed herself to why there might, in fact, be a reason to attack the credibility of the officer in this case. It is in this context that Judge Sparks made the statements which have prompted this appeal. [The trial judge's] remarks do not support the conclusion that Judge Sparks found Constable Stienburg to have lied. In fact, Judge Sparks did quite the opposite. She noted firstly, that she was not saying Constable Stienburg had misled the court, although that could be an explanation for his evidence. She then went on to remark that she was not saying that Constable Stienburg had overreacted, though she was alive to that possibility given that it had happened with police officers in the past, and in particular, it had happened when police officers were dealing with non-white groups. Finally, Judge Sparks concluded that, though she was not willing to say that Constable Stienburg did overreact, it was her belief that he probably overreacted. And, in support of that finding, she noted that she accepted the evidence of R.D.S. that "he was told to shut up or he would be under arrest".

At no time did Judge Sparks rule that the probable overreaction by Constable Stienburg was motivated by racism. Rather, she tied her finding of probable overreaction to the evidence that Constable Stienburg had threatened to arrest the appellant R.D.S. for speaking to his cousin. At the same time, there was evidence capable of supporting a finding of racially motivated overreaction. At an earlier point in the proceedings, she had accepted the evidence that the other youth arrested that day, was handcuffed and thus secured when R.D.S. approached. This constitutes evidence which could lead one to question why it was necessary for both boys to be placed in choke holds by Constable Stienburg, purportedly to secure them. In the face of such evidence, we respectfully disagree with the views of our colleagues Cory and Major JJ. that there was no evidence on which Judge Sparks could have found "racially motivated" overreaction by the police officer.

. . . .

While it seems clear that Judge Sparks did not in fact relate the officer's probable overreaction to the race of the appellant R.D.S., it should be noted that if Judge Sparks had chosen to attribute the behaviour of Constable Stienburg to the racial dynamics of the situation, she would not necessarily have erred. As a member of the community, it was open to her to take into account the well-known presence of racism in that community and to evaluate the evidence as to what occurred against that background. That Judge Sparks recognized that police officers sometimes overreact when dealing with non-white groups simply demonstrates that in making her determination in this case, she was alive to the well-known racial dynamics that may exist in interactions between police officers and visible minorities.

. . . .

Judge Sparks' oral reasons show that she approached the case with an open mind, used her experience and knowledge of the community to achieve an understanding of the reality of the case, and applied the fundamental principle of proof beyond a reasonable doubt. Her comments were based entirely on the case before her, were made after a consideration of the conflicting testimony of the two witnesses and in response to the Crown's submissions, and were entirely supported by the evidence. In alerting herself to the racial dynamic in the case, she was simply engaging in the process of contextualized judging which, in our view, was entirely proper and conducive to a fair and just resolution of the case before her.

GONTHIER J. (LA FOREST J. concurring):—I agree with Cory J. and L'Heureux-Dubé and McLachlin JJ. as to the disposition of the appeal and with their exposition of the law on bias and impartiality and the relevance of context. However, I am in agreement with and adopt the joint reasons of L'Heureux-Dubé and McLachlin JJ. in their treatment of social context and the manner in which it may appropriately enter the decision-making process as well as their assessment of the trial judge's reasons and comments in the present case.

———————————

For competing views on *S. (R.D.)*, see Archibald, "The Lessons of the Sphinx: Avoiding Apprehensions of Judicial Bias in a Multi-racial, Multi-cultural Society" (1998), 10 C.R. (5th) 54 and Delisle, "An Annotation to *S. (R.D.)*" (1998), 10 C.R. (5th) 7.

3. LEGISLATIVE FACTS

Professor Davis drew a distinction between judicially noticing adjudicative facts and legislative facts. He wrote:

> When a court or an agency finds facts concerning the immediate parties — who did what, where, when, how, and with what motive or intent — the court or agency is performing an adjudicative function, and the facts so determined are conveniently called adjudicative facts. When a court or an agency develops law or policy, it is acting legislatively; the courts have created the common law through judicial

legislation, and the facts which inform the tribunal's legislative judgment are called legislative facts.[26]

These legislative facts, by their nature, are generally known or discovered by the judge from sources outside the formal proof offered by the parties. Unlike adjudicative facts they can seldom be indisputable and knowledge of them is more properly labelled belief:

> The bulk of social science probably cannot be called "clearly indisputable". Even though anyone would prefer to found lawmaking upon clearly indisputable facts, the practical choice is often between proceeding in ignorance and following the uncertain, tentative, and far from indisputable searchings of social science such as they are, for the simple reason that clearly indisputable facts are unavailable.[27]

These legislative facts are necessary, however, to an informed policy choice between competing rules or interpretations and also decisions on constitutional validity.[28] Judge Weinstein explains why consultation with the parties concerning notice of legislative fact is appropriate:

> In taking judicial notice of legislative facts, courts frequently take cognizance of matter which is neither indisputable nor easily verifiable. . . . Is such power compatible with our adversary system, which presupposes that disputed facts must be brought into the open, subject to cross-examination? . . . Legislative facts . . . relate to substantive law, and if the judge is to exercise the function of shaping the law he must have discretion to consider those factors essential to the process. Limitations in the form of indisputability or rigid and formal requirements of notice are inappropriate. . . . Once the court decides to advise itself in order to make new law, it ought not to add to the risk of a poor decision by denying itself whatever help on the facts it can with propriety obtain. Informal consultation with the parties enables the court to enlist their aid in obtaining further information, guarantees that differing points of view will be consulted, and is especially appropriate in those cases where the facts the judge is noticing may have adjudicative as well as legislative implications.[29]

Problems of fairness to the parties are generated in the silent use of legislative facts, as the parties must frequently guess at the judge's appreciation of the legislative facts and may not be given the opportunity of displaying contrary data to support a competing view. A notorious example from the cases is seen in *Hersees of Woodstock Ltd. v. Goldstein*.[30] In that case, the plaintiff sought an injunction to restrain the secondary picketing of his premises. The Ontario Court of Appeal reasoned:

---

26. Davis, "Judicial Notice", *supra*, note 22. The distinction was coined in an earlier article: Davis, "An Approach to Problems of Evidence in the Administrative Process" (1942), 55 Harv. L. Rev. 364.

27. Davis, *A System of Judicial Notice Based on Fairness and Convenience*, *supra*, note 22, at pp. 69 and 87, quoted in Weinstein's Evidence, at pp. 200-16.

28. When a court is involved in determining an appropriate remedy or penalty it frequently goes outside the record for assistance and notices the legislative facts that condition deterrence and rehabilitation. See Davis, "Judicial Notice", *supra*, note 22 at p. 960. And for examples of Canadian courts using such legislative facts, see *R. v. McNicol*, [1969] 3 C.C.C. 56 (Man. C.A.); *R. v. Adelman*, [1968] 3 C.C.C. 311 (B.C.C.A.).

29. Weinstein's Evidence, pp. 200-17.

30. (1963), 2 O.R. 81 (C.A.); leave to appeal to S.C.C. refused.

But even assuming that the picketing carried on by the respondents was lawful in the sense that it was merely peaceful picketing for the purpose only of communicating information, I think it should be restrained. Appellant has a right lawfully to engage in its business of retailing merchandise to the public. In the City of Woodstock where that business is being carried on, the picketing for the reasons already stated, has caused or is likely to cause damage to the appellant. *Therefore*, the right, if there be such a right of the respondents to engage in secondary picketing of appellant's premises must give way to appellant's right to trade; the former, assuming it to be a legal right, is exercised for the benefit of a particular class only while the latter is a right far more fundamental and of far greater importance, in my view, as one which in its exercise affects and is for the benefit of the community at large. If the law is to serve its purpose then in civil matters just as in matters within the realm of the criminal law, the interests of the community at large must be held to transcend those of the individual or a particular group of individuals. [Emphasis added.] [31]

Is the "therefore" self-evident? [32] Are property interests clearly more important than the community's interest in free speech? Is the property interest protected here clearly of benefit to the community at large? Is the picketing right here restrained only of benefit to this "particular class"? Must individual rights always bow to the community? Perhaps the court silently addressed all these questions before giving its answer. The record does not tell us. If the legislative facts believed in by the court were made known to the parties and the parties were given the opportunity to present competing legislative facts, the parties would probably be more satisfied with the decision and the court would be better informed. [33]

DAISHOWA INC. v. FRIENDS OF THE LUBICON
(1998), 39 O.R. (3d) 620 (Ont. Gen. Div.)

[The plaintiff sought an injunction to restrain the activities of the defendants. When discussions between the plaintiff and the Lubicon Cree failed to produce any agreement that the company not log the property until land rights were settled, the Friends of the Lubicon began a boycott campaign in Ontario, which was aimed both at customers of the plaintiff's paper products and at the consumers of the customers' goods and services, such as Pizza Pizza. The latter was carried out by picketing at the stores and businesses of the plaintiff's customers. The campaign was remarkably successful and the plaintiff brought an action seeking a permanent injunction against the Friends' consumer boycott activities. The application was dismissed.]

MacPherson J.:—

---

31. *Ibid.*, at p. 86.
32. See the case comment by Arthurs (1963), 41 Can. Bar Rev. 573, 580. Compare the opinions in *Harrison v. Carswell*, [1976] 2 S.C.R. 200.
33. See the solution of Frank, J., in *Repouille v. U.S.*, 165 F. 2d 152 (2d Cir., 1947). And see Laskin, J. in *A.G. Man. v. Manitoba Egg & Poultry Assn.* (1971), 19 D.L.R. (3d) 169, 181 (S.C.C.) deploring the absence of legislative facts in assessing the constitutional validity of legislation. See also the inclusion of such data in *Reference re Anti-Inflation Act, 1975 (Canada)*, [1976] 2 S.C.R. 373.

. . . .

The first and most important case cited by Daishowa on the picketing issue is *Hersees of Woodstock Ltd. v. Goldstein*. Daishowa relies heavily on this case because, as it puts it at para. 76 of its factum, "the Ontario Court of Appeal clearly established that the common law of Ontario prohibits secondary picketing as does the common law of other Canadian jurisdictions".

. . . .

In the passage from Aylesworth J.A.'s judgment set out earlier, he refers explicitly to a "right to trade". Moreover, he states that this right "is for the benefit of the community at large" and contrasts it with the union's speech through their picketing which he describes as being "exercised for the benefit of a particular class only". Without quarrelling with the ratio of *Hersees* and its continuing applicability in cases dealing with secondary picketing in a labour relations context, it strikes me that this component of Aylesworth J.A.'s reasoning is anachronistic today. The fact that freedom of expression is protected in the Canadian Charter of Rights and Freedoms, coupled with the absence of any economic rights, except for mobility to pursue the gaining of a livelihood, in the same document, is a clear indication that free speech is near the top of the values that Canadians hold dear. As expressed by MacIntyre J. in *Dolphin Delivery, supra*, at p. 583 S.C.R.:

> Freedom of expression . . . is one of the fundamental concepts that has formed the basis for the historical development of the political, social and educational institutions of western society. Representative democracy, as we know it today, which is in great part the product of free expression and discussion of varying ideas, depends upon its maintenance and protection.

Additionally, even if one accepts Aylesworth J.A.'s description of unions as representing "a particular class only", namely their own membership interested in their own economic well-being, this description does not apply to the Friends. They are interested in an issue, the plight of the Lubicon Cree, that presents an amalgam of historical, political, social, economic and even moral factors. The plight of the Lubicon is precisely the type of issue that should generate widespread public discussion. Moreover, there is not one penny of economic self-interest in the Friends' campaign.

With the advent of the Charter of Rights and the new task of determining the constitutional validity of legislation the courts are, of necessity, called on to judicially notice legislative facts. For example, in *R. v. Oakes* [34] the government had the task of justifying a violation of a constitutional right under section 1: to establish that the violation of the accused's right to be presumed innocent was justified as a reasonable limit in a free and democratic society. In that case, the court noted:

> Where evidence is required in order to prove the constituent elements of a s. 1 inquiry, *and this will generally be the case*, it should be cogent and persuasive and make clear to the court the consequences of imposing or not imposing the limit. [Emphasis added.] [35]

Nevertheless, the court, in deciding that the legislative objective was of sufficient importance to warrant overriding a constitutionally protected right relied on all manner of material to inform itself regarding the legislative facts. The court noted:

---

34.   (1986), 50 C.R. (3d) 1 (S.C.C.).
35.   *Ibid.*, at pp. 29-30.

In my opinion, Parliament's concern that drug trafficking be decreased can be characterized as substantial and pressing. The problem of drug trafficking has been increasing since the 1950s, at which time there was already considerable concern: see Report of the Special Committee on Traffic in Narcotic Drugs, Appendix to Debates of the Senate of Canada, session of 1955, pp. 690-700; see also Final Report, Commission of Inquiry into the Non-Medical Use of Drugs (Ottawa, 1973). Throughout this period, numerous measures were adopted by free and democratic societies, at both the international and national levels.

At the international level, on 23rd June 1953, the Protocol for Limiting and Regulating the Cultivation of the Poppy Plant, the Production of, International and Wholesale Trade in, and Use of Opium, to which Canada is a signatory, was adopted by the United Nations Opium Conference held in New York. The Single Convention on Narcotic Drugs (1961), was acceded to in New York on 30th March 1961. This treaty was signed by Canada on 30th March 1961. It entered into force on 13th December 1964. As stated in the preamble, "addiction to narcotic drugs constitutes a serious evil for the individual and is fraught with social and economic danger to mankind".

At the national level, statutory provisions have been enacted by numerous countries which, inter alia, attempt to deter drug trafficking by imposing criminal sanctions: see, for example, Misuse of Drugs Act, 1975 (New Zealand), no. 116; Misuse of Drugs Act, 1971 (Eng.), c. 38.

The objective of protecting our society from the grave ills associated with drug trafficking is, in my view, one of sufficient importance to warrant overriding a constitutionally-protected right or freedom in certain cases. Moreover, the degree of seriousness of drug trafficking makes its acknowledgement as a sufficiently important objective for the purposes of s. 1 to a large extent self-evident. The first criterion of a s. 1 inquiry, therefore, has been satisfied by the Crown.[36]

R. v. LAVALLEE
[1990] 1 S.C.R. 852, 76 C.R. (3d) 329, 55 C.C.C. (3d) 97

[The accused, a battered woman in a volatile common law relationship, killed her partner, Rust, late one night by shooting him in the back of the head as he left her room. The shooting occurred after an argument where the accused had been physically abused. She was fearful for her life after being taunted with the threat that either she kill him or he would get her. She had frequently been a victim of his physical abuse and had concocted excuses to explain her injuries to medical staff on those occasions. A psychiatrist with extensive professional experience in the treatment of battered wives prepared a psychiatric assessment of the appellant which was used in support of her defence of self-defence. The jury acquitted the accused but its verdict was overturned by a majority of the Manitoba Court of Appeal. The Supreme Court allowed the accused's appeal deciding that the expert's opinion was admissible as relevant to her claim of self-defence.

---

36.   Ibid., at pp. 31-32. See also R. v. Edwards Books & Art Ltd., [1986] 2 S.C.R. 713; R. v. Thomsen (1988), 63 C.R. (3d) 1 (S.C.C.) and R. v. Hufsky (1988), 63 C.R. (3d) 14 (S.C.C.). And see generally, Maybank, "Proof of Facts Under S. 1 of the Charter" (1990), 77 C.R. (3d) 260 and Morgan, "Proof of Facts in Charter Litigation" in Sharpe, ed., Charter Litigation (1987). See also McEachern, "Viva Voce Evidence in Charter Cases" (1989), 23 U.B.C. Law Rev. 591.

Notice the court's reasoning. Notice how it judicially notices legislative facts; how it decides; how it reforms the law to fit society's attitude. Notice the literature relied on which was not proved in evidence.]

WILSON J. (DICKSON C.J.C and LAMER, L'HEUREUX-DUBÉ, GONTHIER and CORY JJ. concurring):—

. . . .

The gravity, indeed, the tragedy of domestic violence can hardly be overstated. Greater media attention to this phenomenon in recent years has revealed both its prevalence and its horrific impact on women from all walks of life. Far from protecting women from it, the law historically sanctioned the abuse of women within marriage as an aspect of the husband's ownership of his wife and his "right" to chastise her. One need only recall the centuries old law that a man is entitled to beat his wife with a stick "no thicker than his thumb".

Laws do not spring out of a social vacuum. The notion that a man has a right to "discipline" his wife is deeply rooted in the history of our society. The woman's duty was to serve her husband and to stay in the marriage at all costs "till death do us part" and to accept as her due any "punishment" that was meted out for failing to please her husband. One consequence of this attitude was that "wife battering" was rarely spoken of, rarely reported, rarely prosecuted, and even more rarely punished. Long after society abandoned its formal approval of spousal abuse, tolerance of it continued and continues in some circles to this day.

Fortunately, there has been a growing awareness in recent years that no man has a right to abuse any woman under any circumstances. Legislative initiatives designed to educate police, judicial officers and the public, as well as more aggressive investigation and charging policies all signal a concerted effort by the criminal justice system to take spousal abuse seriously. However, a woman who comes before a judge or jury with the claim that she has been battered and suggests that this may be a relevant factor in evaluating her subsequent actions still faces the prospect of being condemned by popular mythology about domestic violence. Either she was not as badly beaten as she claims or she would have left the man long ago. Or, if she was battered that severely, she must have stayed out of some masochistic enjoyment of it.

. . . .

. . . Was the appellant "under reasonable apprehension of death or grievous bodily harm" from Rust as he was walking out of the room? The second is the assessment in s. 34(2)(b) of the magnitude of the force used by the accused. Was the accused's belief that she could not "otherwise preserve herself from death or grievous bodily harm" except by shooting the deceased based "on reasonable grounds"?

. . . .

If it strains credulity to imagine what the "ordinary man" would do in the position of a battered spouse, it is probably because men do not typically find themselves in that situation. Some women do, however. The definition of what is reasonable must be adapted to circumstances which are, by and large, foreign to the world inhabited by the hypothetical "reasonable man".

. . . .

The cycle described by Dr. Shane conforms to the Walker Cycle Theory of Violence named for clinical psychologist Dr. Lenore Walker, the pioneer researcher in the field of the battered wife syndrome. Dr. Shane acknowledged his debt to Dr. Walker in the course of establishing his credentials as an expert at trial. Dr. Walker first describes the cycle in the book The Battered Woman, (1979). In her 1984 book, The Battered Woman Syndrome,

Dr. Walker reports the results of a study involving 400 battered women. Her research was designed to test empirically the theories expounded in her earlier book. At pp. 95-96 of The Battered Woman Syndrome she summarizes the Cycle Theory as follows:

[There follows a lengthy extract from the book.]

Dr. Walker defines a battered woman as a woman who has gone through the battering cycle at least twice. As she explains in her introduction to The Battered Woman, at p. xv, "Any woman may find herself in an abusive relationship with a man once. If it occurs a second time, and she remains in the situation, she is defined as a battered woman."

. . . .

Another aspect of the cyclical nature of the abuse is that it begets a degree of predictability to the violence that is absent in an isolated violent enounter between two strangers. This also means that it may in fact be possible for a battered spouse to accurately predict the onset of violence before the first blow is struck, even if an outsider to the relationship cannot. Indeed, it has been suggested that a battered woman's knowledge of her partner's violence is so heightened that she is able to anticipate the nature and extent (though not the onset) of the violence by his conduct beforehand. In her article "Potential Uses for Expert Testimony: Ideas Toward the Representation of Battered Women Who Kill" (1986), 9 Women's Rights Law Reporter 227, psychologist Julie Blackman describes this characteristic, at p. 229:

[Another lengthy quote.]

. . . The requirement imposed in Whynot that a battered woman wait until the physical assault is "underway" before her apprehensions can be validated in law would, in the words of an American court, be tantamount to sentencing her to "murder by instalment": State v. Gallegos, 719 P.2d 1268 (N.M. 1986), at p. 1271. I share the view expressed by Willoughby in "Rendering Each Woman Her Due: Can a Battered Woman Claim Self-Defense When She Kills Her Sleeping Batterer" (1989), 38 Kan. L. Rev. 169, at p. 184, that "society gains nothing, except perhaps the additional risk that the battered woman will herself be killed, because she must wait until her abusive husband instigates another battering episode before she can justifiably act".

. . . .

. . . Was the appellant "under reasonable apprehension of death or grievous bodily harm" from Rust as he was walking out of the room?

. . . .

If it strains credulity to imagine what the "ordinary man" would do in the position of a battered spouse, it is probably because men do not typically find themselves in that situation. Some women do, however. The definition of what is reasonable must be adapted to circumstances which are, by and large, foreign to the world inhabited by the hypothetical "reasonable man".

. . . .

The cycle described by Dr. Shane conforms to the Walker Cycle Theory of Violence named for clinical psychologist, Dr. Lenore Walker, the pioneer researcher in the field of the battered wife syndrome. Dr. Shane acknowledged his debt to Dr. Walker in the course of establishing his credentials as an expert at trial. Dr. Walker first describes the cycle in the book The Battered Woman (1979). In her 1984 book, The Battered Woman Syndrome, Dr. Walker reports the results of a study involving 400 battered women. Her research was designed to test empirically the theories expounded in her earlier book. At pp. 95-96 of The Battered Woman Syndrome she summarizes the Cycle Theory as follows: [a lengthy quote from the book].

Dr. Walker defines a battered woman as a woman who has gone through the battering cycle at least twice. As she explains in her introduction to The Battered Woman at p. xv, "Any woman may find herself in an abusive relationship with a man once. If it occurs a second time, and she remains in the situation, she is defined as a battered woman".

. . . .

Another aspect of the cyclical nature of the abuse is that it begets a degree of predictability to the violence that is absent in an isolated violent encounter between two strangers. This also means that it may in fact be possible for a battered spouse to accurately predict the onset of violence before the first blow is struck, even if an outsider to the relationship cannot. Indeed, it has been suggested that a battered woman's knowledge of her partner's violence is so heightened that she is able to anticipate the nature and extent (though not the onset) of the violence by his conduct beforehand. In her article "Potential Uses for Expert Testimony: Ideas Toward the Representation of Battered Women Who Kill" (1986), 9 Women's Rights Law Reporter 227, psychologist Julie Blackman describes this characteristic at p. 229: [a lengthy quote].

. . . .

The requirement imposed in *Whynot* that a battered woman wait until the physical assault is "underway" before her apprehensions can be validated in law would, in the words of an American court, be tantamount to sentencing her to "murder by installment": *New Mexico v. Gallegos*, 719 P. 2d 1268, at 1271, 104 N.M. 247 (C.A., 1986). I share the view expressed by M. J. Willoughby in "Rendering Each Woman Her Due: Can a Battered Woman Claim Self-Defense When She Kills Her Sleeping Batterer" (1989), 38 Kan. L. Rev. 169, at p. 184, that "society gains nothing, except perhaps the additional risk that the battered woman will herself be killed, because she must wait until her abusive husband instigates another battering episode before she can justifiably act".

R. v. MALOTT
[1998] 1 S.C.R. 123, 12 C.R. (5th) 207, 121 C.C.C. (3d) 456

[The accused was charged with murder. The accused and the deceased had lived as common law spouses for almost 20 years. The deceased abused the accused physically, sexually, psychologically and emotionally. The jury found her guilty of second degree murder in the death of the deceased and of the attempted murder of his girlfriend. A majority of the Court of Appeal affirmed the convictions. The accused appealed, complaining about the adequacy of the trial judge's charge to the jury on the murder charge with regard to the issue of battered woman syndrome as a defence. The appeal was dismissed. Concurring in the result, Justice L'Heureux-Dubé, McLachlin J. concurring, noted that concerns had been expressed that the treatment of expert evidence on battered woman syndrome, admissible in order to combat the myths and stereotypes which society has about battered women, had led to a new stereotype of the battered woman.]

L'HEUREUX-DUBÉ, J. (MCLACHLIN, J. concurring):— I have read the reasons of my colleague Justice Major, and I concur with the result that he reaches. However, given that this Court has not had the opportunity to discuss the value of evidence of "battered woman syndrome" since *R. v. Lavallee*, [1990] 1 S.C.R. 852, and given the evolving discourse on "battered woman syndrome" in the legal community, I will make a few comments on the importance of this kind of evidence to the just adjudication of charges involving battered women.

. . . .

. . . Concerns have been expressed that the treatment of expert evidence on battered women syndrome, which is itself admissible in order to combat the myths and stereotypes which society has about battered women, has led to a new stereotype of the "battered woman": see, e.g., Martha Shaffer, "The battered woman syndrome revisited: Some complicating thoughts five years after *R. v. Lavallee*" (1997), 47 *U.T.L.J.* 1, at p. 9; Sheila Noonan, "Strategies of Survival: Moving Beyond the Battered Woman Syndrome", in Ellen Adelberg and Claudia Currie, eds., *In Conflict with the Law: Women and the Canadian Justice System* (1993), 247, at p. 254; Isabel Grant, "The 'syndromization' of women's experience", in Donna Martinson et al., "A Forum on *Lavallee v. R.*: Women and Self-Defence" (1991), 25 *U.B.C. L. Rev.* 23, 51, at pp. 53-54; and Martha R. Mahoney, "Legal Images of Battered Women: Redefining the Issue of Separation" (1991), 90 *Mich. L. Rev.* 1, at p. 42.

It is possible that those women who are unable to fit themselves within the stereotype of a victimized, passive, helpless, dependent, battered woman will not have their claims to self-defence fairly decided. For instance, women who have demonstrated too much strength or initiative, women of colour, women who are professionals, or women who might have fought back against their abusers on previous occasions, should not be penalized for failing to accord with the stereotypical image of the archetypal battered woman. See, e.g., Julie Stubbs and Julia Tolmie, "Race, Gender, and the Battered Woman Syndrome: An Australia Case Study" (1995), 8 *C.J.W.L.* 122. Needless to say, women with these characteristics are still entitled to have their claims of self-defence fairly adjudicated, and they are also still entitled to have their experiences as battered women inform the analysis. Professor Grant, *supra*, at p. 52, warns against allowing the law to develop such that a woman accused of killing her abuser must either have been "reasonable 'like a man' or reasonable 'like a battered woman'". I agree that this must be avoided. The "reasonable woman" must not be forgotten in the analysis, and deserves to be as much a part of the objective standard of the reasonable person as does the "reasonable man".

How should the courts combat the "syndromization", as Professor Grant refers to it, of battered women who act in self-defence? The legal inquiry into the moral culpability of a woman who is, for instance, claiming self-defence must focus on the *reasonableness* of her actions in the context of her personal experiences, and her experiences as a woman, not on her status as a battered woman and her entitlement to claim that she is suffering from "battered woman syndrome". This point has been made convincingly by many academics reviewing the relevant cases: see, e.g., Wendy Chan, "A Feminist Critique of Self-Defense and Provocation in Battered Women's Cases in England and Wales" (1994), 6 *Women & Crim. Just.* 39, at pp. 56-57; Elizabeth M. Schneider, "Describing and Changing: Women's Self-Defense Work and the Problem of Expert Testimony on Battering" (1992), 14 *Women's Rts. L. Rep.* 213, at pp. 216-17; and Marilyn MacCrimmon, "The social construction of reality and the rules of evidence", in Donna Martinson et al., *supra*, 36, at pp. 48-49. By emphasizing a woman's "learned helplessness", her dependence, her victimization, and her low self-esteem, in order to establish that she suffers from "battered woman syndrome", the legal debate shifts from the objective rationality of her actions to preserve her own life to those personal inadequacies which apparently explain her failure to flee from her abuser. Such an emphasis comports too well with society's stereotypes about women. Therefore, it should be scrupulously avoided because it only serves to undermine the important advancements achieved by the decision in Lavallee.

. . . .

My focus on women as the victims of battering and as the subjects of "battered woman syndrome" is not intended to exclude from consideration those men who find themselves in abusive relationships. However, the reality of our society is that typically, it is women who are the victims of domestic violence, at the hands of their male intimate partners. To assume that men who are victims of spousal abuse are affected by the abuse in the same way, without benefit of the research and expert opinion evidence which has informed the courts of the existence and details of "battered woman syndrome", would be imprudent.

Alan Gold, in response to *Malott*, ADGN/98-075 (QUICKLAW database Gold) advises that the reader might care to review the research and expert opinion that informed courts of the existence and details of battered woman syndrome in the recent article by Faigman and Wright, "The Battered Woman Syndrome in the Age of Science" (1997), 39 Ariz. L. Rev. 67. That article begins with a scathing denunciation of Lenore Walker's book, *The Battered Woman* (New York: Harper Collins, 1980), which figured so prominently in Justice Wilson's judgment in *R. v. Lavallee:*

> The battered woman syndrome illustrates all that is wrong with the law's use of science. The working hypothesis of the battered woman syndrome was first introduced in Lenore Walker's 1979 book, *The Battered Woman*. When it made its debut, this hypothesis had little more to support it beyond the clinical impressions of a single researcher. Five years later, Walker published a second book that promised a more thorough investigation of the hypothesis. However, this book contains little more than a patchwork of pseudo-scientific methods employed to confirm a hypothesis that its author and participating researchers never seriously doubted. Indeed, the 1984 book would provide an excellent case study for psychology graduate students on how not to conduct empirical research. Yet, largely based upon the same political ideology driving the researchers, judges have welcomed the battered woman syndrome into their courts. Because the law is driven by precedent, it quickly petrified around the original conception of the defense. Increasingly, observers are realizing that the evidence purportedly supporting the battered woman syndrome is without empirical foundation, and, perhaps more troubling, that the syndrome itself is inimical to the political ideology originally supporting it. In short, in the law's hasty effort to use science to further good policy, it is now obvious that the battered woman syndrome is not good science nor does it generate good policy.

In *Lavallee*, the Court announced a major change in the law. It was informed partly by the expert opinion given at the trial, but also by books and articles which the Court read for itself. The Court judicially noticed legislative facts outlined in Lenore Walker's books, and formed the law to fit the Court's view of society's present attitude. But the literature, before and after *Lavallee*, is replete with research disagreeing with Walker's description of battered woman syndrome, which description was adopted in *Lavallee*. Some are mentioned in Justice L'Heureux-Dubé's opinion in *Malott*. For citations to literature disagreeing with the court's description of battered woman syndrome, see Fischer, Vidmar & Ellis, "The Culture of Battering and the Role of Mediation in Domestic Violence Cases" (1993), 46 S.M.U. L. Rev. 2117.

It is a welcome advance that the Court in *Malott*, or at least two members of the Court, are now prepared to admit that the Court's earlier description of the battered woman was in error and too restrictive. Justice L'Heureux-Dubé in *Malott* speaks of courts having been informed by expert opinion evidence. In truth the Supreme Court frequently informs itself through its own research, judicially noticing facts found in the literature, and not by expert witnesses. Using expert witnesses has the advantage that their opinions can be challenged by cross-examination and by competing experts and a truer picture will then emerge. Also it would be fairer to the parties. To use *Lavallee* as but one example, the Court would have been better off, before issuing its opinion, had it advised counsel that it was about to rely on this book by Lenore Walker so that the parties might have had the opportunity to inform the court of other sources. When the courts decide to use science to inform the law they will be better informed if the parties are engaged. The joint endeavour will improve the court's ability to recognize junk science when it comes across it.

MOGE v. MOGE
[1992] 3 S.C.R. 813

[The parties were married in the mid-50's in Poland and moved to Canada in 1960. They separated in 1973 and divorced in 1980. The wife had a grade seven education and no special skills or training. During the marriage, she cared for the house and their three children and, except for a brief period, also worked six hours per day in the evenings cleaning offices. After the separation, she was awarded custody of the children and received $150 per month spousal and child support and continued to work cleaning offices. The husband remarried in 1984 and continued to pay support to his former wife. She was laid off in 1987 and, as a result of an application to vary, her spousal and child support was increased to $400. She was later able to secure part-time and intermittent cleaning work. In 1989, the husband was granted an order terminating support. The trial judge found that the former wife had had time to become financially independent and that her husband had supported her as long as he could be required to do. The Court of Appeal set aside the judgment and ordered spousal support in the amount of $150 per month for an indefinite period. The appeal to the Supreme Court of Canada was then to determine whether the wife was entitled to ongoing support for an indefinite period of time or whether spousal support should be terminated. The Court decided to reverse a series of cases that had been based on a self-suffiency model of spousal support. Justice L'Heureux-Dubé noted the heavy costs that would be involved if expert evidence was necessary and decided the answer lay in judicial notice. She was influenced by a number of writings.]

L'HEUREUX-DUBÉ, J. (LA FOREST, GONTHIER, CORY and IACOBUCCI, JJ. concurring):—

. . . .

In Canada, the feminization of poverty is an entrenched social phenomenon. Between 1971 and 1986 the percentage of poor women found among all women in this country more than doubled. During the same period the percentage of poor among all men climbed by 24 percent. The results were such that by 1986, 16 percent of all women in this country were considered poor: M. Gunderson, L. Muszynski and J. Keck, *Women and Labour Market Poverty* (1990), at p. 8.

Given the multiplicity of economic barriers women face in society, decline into poverty cannot be attributed entirely to the financial burdens arising from the dissolution of marriage: J.D. Payne, "The Dichotomy between Family Law and Family Crises on Marriage Breakdown" (1989), 20 *R.G.D.* 109, at pp. 116-17. However, there is no doubt that divorce and its economic effects are playing a role. Several years ago, L.J. Weitzman released her landmark study on divorce, The Divorce Revolution: The Unexpected Social and Economic Consequences for Women and Children in America (1985), and concluded at p. 323:

On a societal level, divorce increases female and child poverty and creates an ever-widening gap between the economic well-being of divorced men, on the one hand, and their children and former wives on the other.

. . . .

One proposal put forth by Professor Rogerson would be for Parliament to consider enacting a set of legislative guidelines. . . .

One possible disadvantage of such a solution lies in the risk that it may impose a strait-jacket which precludes the accommodation of the many economic variables susceptible to be encountered in spousal support litigation.

Another alternative might lie in the doctrine of judicial notice. The doctrine itself grew from a need to promote efficiency in the litigation process and may very well be applicable to spousal support. One classic statement of the content and purpose of the doctrine is outlined in *Varcoe v. Lee*, 181 P. 223 (Cal. 1919), at p. 226:

> The three requirements . . . — that the matter be one of common and general knowledge, that it be well established and authoritatively settled, be practically indisputable, and that this common, general, and certain knowledge exist in the particular jurisdiction — all are requirements dictated by the reason and purpose of the rule, which is to obviate the formal necessity for proof when the matter does not require proof.

As E.M. Morgan noted in "Judicial Notice" (1944), 57 Harv. L. Rev. 269, at p. 272:

> . . . the judge . . . must be assumed to have a fund of general information, consisting of both generalized capacity to relate it to what he has perceived during the proceeding, as well as the ability to draw reasonable deductions from the combination by using the ordinary processes of thought. That fund of general information must be at least as great as that of all reasonably well-informed persons in the community. He cannot be assumed to be ignorant of what is so generally accepted as to be incapable of dispute among reasonable men.

. . . .

Based upon the studies which I have cited earlier in these reasons, the general economic impact of divorce on women is a phenomenon the existence of which cannot reasonably be questioned and should be amenable to judicial notice. More extensive social science data are also appearing. Such studies are beginning to provide reasonable assessments of some of the disadvantages incurred and advantages conferred post-divorce. . . . While quantification will remain difficult and fact related in each particular case, judicial notice should be taken of such studies, subject to other expert evidence which may bear on them, as background information at the very least. . . .

In all events, whether judicial notice of the circumstances generally encountered by spouses at the dissolution of a marriage is to be a formal part of the trial process or whether such circumstances merely provide the necessary background information, it is important that judges be aware of the social reality in which support decisions are experienced when engaging in the examination of the objectives of the Act.

CRONK v. CANADIAN GENERAL INSURANCE CO.
(1995), 25 O.R. (3d) 505 (Ont. C.A.)

[The plaintiff was employed as a clerk-stenographer. In 1993, as a result of internal reorganization by the defendant, the plaintiff's employment was terminated. She brought an action for damages for wrongful dismissal and moved for summary judgment, seeking damages based on a notice period of 20 months.

The plaintiff was awarded damages of 20 months' salary and the defendant appealed.]

LACOURCIÈRE, J.A.:—

. . . .

In granting judgment in her favour, MacPherson J. noted that "the factors to be considered in determining reasonable notice have remained more or less constant for over 30 years", having been enunciated by McRuer C.J.H.C. in *Bardal v. Globe & Mail Ltd.*, [1960] O.W.N. 253 (H.C.J.) at p. 255:

> There could be no catalogue laid down as to what was reasonable notice in particular classes of cases. The reasonableness of the notice must be decided with reference to each particular case, having regard to the character of the employment, the length of service of the servant, the age of the servant and the availability of similar employment, having regard to the experience, training and qualifications of the servant.

. . . .

Addressing the role played by the character of employment in determining the requisite notice period, MacPherson J. observed that the length of notice requested by the respondent had traditionally been reserved for persons with positions more senior to hers. Having said that, he could find no principled reason why this should be so. He rejected the proposition that senior employees are more stigmatized by the loss of employment than are their underlings. Likewise, he could find no support for the notion, frequently articulated in the case-law, that senior, specialized employees have greater difficulty in securing new employment. Apart from the fact that the appellant had not provided any evidence to that effect, and the fact that the respondent was still out of work eight months after her dismissal, MacPherson J. found another basis on which to dismiss the proposition (at p. 25):

> Third, the reality is — as we are all told by our parents at a young age — that education and training *are* directly related to employment. The senior manager and the professional person are better, not worse, positioned to obtain employment, both initially and later in a post-dismissal context. Higher education and specialized training correlate directly with *increased* access to employment.

In support of this assertion, the learned motions court judge cited two studies published by the Council of Ontario Universities, as well as a May 21, 1994 article in the *Economist* magazine. He discovered these materials through his own research. For those reasons, he refused to accept the defendant's argument based on a managerial-clerical distinction.

. . . .

In my opinion, the learned motion court judge's reasons do not justify departing from the widely accepted principle. He erred in doing so on the basis of his own sociological research without providing counsel an opportunity to challenge or respond to the results of the two studies relied upon. I agree with the appellant that the factual conclusions which he drew from these studies are beyond the scope of proper judicial notice.

. . . .

The conclusion of the motions court judge based on the studies prepared by the Council of Ontario Universities are obviously not so generally known or accepted as to challenge the validity of an established principle which has found judicial acceptance for over three decades. It is not, as the respondent contended, an undisputed "social reality" as was the background information concerning the circumstances encountered by spouses at the dissolution of a marriage, in *Moge v. Moge*, [1992] 3 S.C.R. 813 at p. 874.

Before taking new matters into account based on statistics which have not been considered in the judgment under appeal, the adversarial process requires that the court ensure that the parties are given an opportunity to deal with the new information by making further submissions, oral or written, and allowing, if requested, fresh material in response.

The result arrived at has the potential of disrupting the practices of the commercial and industrial world, wherein employers have to predict with reasonable certainty the cost of downsizing or increasing their operations, particularly in difficult economic times. As well, legal practitioners specializing in employment law and the legal profession generally have to give advice to employers and employees in respect of termination of employment with reasonable certainty. Adherence to the doctrine of *stare decisis* plays an important role in that respect: *Cassell & Co. v. Broome*, [1972] 1 All E.R. 801 at p. 809, [1972] A.C. 1027 (H.L.).

. . . .

In my opinion, the character of the employment of the respondent does not entitle her to a lengthy period of notice.

. . . .

For these reasons, I would vary the judgment of MacPherson J. so that the plaintiff respondent will recover damages based on a salary calculation covering 12 months from September 9, 1993.

WEILER J.A. (dissenting in part):—

. . . .

The justification for placing less weight on the factor of character of employment in the case of a clerical employee is based on several factual propositions or assumptions put forward by the appellant. Lacourcière J.A. does not find it necessary to deal with the validity of these propositions because they were not challenged in argument before MacPherson J. MacPherson J. did, however, question the validity of these factual propositions. In my opinion he was not prevented from doing so although he erred in not giving the parties an opportunity to lead evidence and to make submissions respecting his rejection of these factual propositions.

. . . .

A trial is a search for the truth. When a trial judge reviews jurisprudence and finds it rests on a factual assumption, that may no longer be true or which may not apply in all cases, the judge is not obliged to continue to accept this assumption as a fact. Naturally, the judge wishes to avoid the expense and delay of requiring counsel to re-attend for further argument concerning the material he has discovered and upon which he seeks to rely. However, where a judicial approach rests on a factual proposition with which the judge disagrees, and counsel are unaware that the judge is considering a break with the past, I can see no alternative but for the judge to allow counsel an opportunity to call evidence and to make submissions. The reason for this is two-fold. The general studies or material that the judge sees as rebutting the factual proposition may, as a result of expert evidence, be susceptible to other interpretation. In addition, the parties have a right to expect that if a judge disagrees with a factual assumption, which has found its way into the jurisprudence and which has gone unchallenged, the judge will give the parties an opportunity to make submissions concerning the studies he sees as rebutting this assumption. MacPherson J. erred in not doing so. The parties should have been recalled.

. . . .

I would allow the appeal, set aside the judgment of MacPherson J. respecting reasonable notice, and in its place, substitute an order pursuant to rule 20.04(3) directing the trial of an issue as to the amount that Ms. Cronk is entitled to be paid in lieu of notice.

MORDEN, A.C.J.O.:— I have had the benefit of reading the reasons of Lacourcière J.A. and Weiler J.A. I agree with Lacourcière J.A.'s proposed disposition of this appeal and agree, generally, with his reasons. I shall state my particular reasons briefly.

. . . .

The parties were content to have MacPherson J. and this court dispose of Ms. Cronk's motion for summary judgment on the basis of the materials which they had filed with the court. They were satisfied that the court could come to a just conclusion on what was a reasonable notice period on these materials. Although this would involve the court's consideration of the parties' competing contentions on the application of the reasonable notice standard to differing views of the facts, a trial was not required for this purpose. There was no genuine issue requiring a trial: see *Ron Miller Realty v. Honeywell, Wotherspoon* (1991), 4 O.R. (3d) 492 (Gen. Div.). I think that the parties are to be commended for adopting this approach. In the light of this and, also, the consideration that character of employment is not commensurate with availability of other employment, and, even if it were, my doubt that this would necessarily result in the upward adjustment of notice periods for clerical employees (rather than the downward adjustment of those for senior employees), I do not think, with respect, that a trial should be directed.

Do you see why it was undisputed social reality in *Moge v. Moge* and therefore amenable to judicial notice, but not in *Cronk*?

R. v. PETER PAUL
(1998) 18 C.R. (5th) 360, 124 C.C.C. (3d) 1 (N.B.C.A.)

[The accused was acquitted of unlawfully removing timber from Crown lands without authorization. The judge of first instance, Judge Arsenault, concluded that harvesting trees was a treaty right and that the right could be exercised for commercial purposes. The Summary Conviction Appeal Court, Mr. Justice Turnbull, dismissed the Crown's appeal holding that the British Crown never obtained title to Indian lands and there was an aboriginal treaty right to harvest trees.]

HOYT, RICE, RYAN, TURNBULL AND DRAPEAU JJ.A.:—

. . . .

The scant historical evidence and lack of any other pertinent material underlines the limited focus of the proceedings before Judge Arsenault. Some documents upon which Judge Arsenault relied, as will be seen, have no application. The material upon which Mr. Justice Turnbull relied was not placed before him by the parties, but resulted from his independent historical research.

We compare the 25 pages of evidence and 12 exhibits before us, some of which do not have any relevance, with the evidence submitted in *Delgamuukw v. British Columbia*, [1997] 3 S.C.R. 1010, where Lamer, C.J., at p. 1028, described the trial:

> At the British Columbia Supreme Court, McEachern C.J. heard 374 days of evidence and argument. Some of that evidence was not in a form which is familiar to common law courts, including oral histories and legends. Another significant part was the evidence of experts in genealogy, linguistics, archaeology, anthropology, and geography.

Delgamuukw, a civil action for a declaration of title, involved, among other issues, what was required to establish aboriginal rights, the content of aboriginal title to land in British

Columbia and whether that Province could extinguish aboriginal rights after it joined Confederation in 1871.

What we have here, in stark contrast to *Delgamuukw*, are seven treaties, proclamations or promises, four of which, exhibits D-1, D-1A, D-2 and D-6 have little or no practical application. We are left with the three Promises (exhibits D-3, D-4 and D-5) relating to a treaty that is not in evidence. This shortcoming was noted by Judge Arsenault at p. 290:

> [N]either party to these proceedings attempted to submit historical data or viva voce evidence from historians or senior or elderly members of the MicMac or Maliseet tribes in respect of the territorial range of their pursuits.

He could have made the same observation about the absence of evidence of the historical context within which the various treaties were negotiated and of the lack of evidence regarding the intention of the parties to these treaties.

. . . .

On appeal, Mr. Justice Turnbull agreed with Judge Arsenault's result, but not with his rationale with respect to treaty acquired rights. . . . Turnbull, J. [concluded] that the English Monarch never obtained title to Indian lands. . . . [A]s acknowledged by the parties, he based his decision almost entirely on his post-hearing historical research. As a result, this matter has evolved from an alleged regulatory violation at trial to, as Mr. Allaby acknowledged during the hearing of the appeal, a land claim to the entire Province by the status Indians of New Brunswick.

Although the appellant and the intervenors have raised several points, they all relate to the four questions that must be resolved to determine the appeal, namely, one, could Mr. Justice Turnbull take judicial notice of disputable historical data, two, should he have used the results of his exclusive research after the hearing without notice to the parties, three, if so, does the evidence disclose a treaty or other right that exempts Mr. Peter Paul from the provisions of the *Crown Lands and Forests Act* and, four, if he has such an exemption, has pre-Confederation legislation extinguished that right?

To answer the first question, as will be seen, there is no authority for taking judicial notice of disputed facts, whether they be historical or otherwise.

Both the short and the long answer to the second question is that Mr. Justice Turnbull should not have decided the case on his independent historical research. The short answer is that the appeal provisions noted earlier restricted him to the trial transcript. The longer answer, which follows, is that there is neither authority for making such extensive use of historical material under the guise of judicial notice nor for using such material without giving notice to the parties.

. . . .

An authoritative statement of judicial notice is that of Lord Sumner in *Commonwealth Shipping Representative v. P. & O. Branch Service*, [1923] A.C. 191, where he said at p. 212:

> [C]ertain facts may be deemed to be established, although not proved by sworn testimony, or by the production, out of the proper custody, of documents, which speak for themselves. Judicial notice refers to facts, which a Judge can be called upon to receive and to act upon, either from his general knowledge of them, or from inquiries to be made by himself for his own information from sources to which it is proper for him to refer. In the present case the opportunity for introducing new evidence had passed.

More recently, in *Moge v. Moge*, [1992] 3 S.C.R. 813, L'Heureux-Dubé, J. had occasion to discuss the doctrine of judicial notice. She said at p. 873:

> One classic statement of the content and purpose of the doctrine is outlined in *Varcoe v. Lee*, 181 P. 223 (Cal. 1919), at p. 226:

The three requirements . . . – that the matter be one of common and general knowledge, that it be well established and authoritatively settled, be practically indisputable, and that this common, general, and certain knowledge exist in the particular jurisdiction – all are requirements dictated by the reason and purpose of the rule, which is to obviate the formal necessity for proof when the matter does not require proof.

As E.M. Morgan noted in "Judicial Notice" (1944), 57 *Harv. L. Rev.* 269, at p. 272:

> . . . the judge . . . must be assumed to have a fund of general information, consisting of both generalized knowledge and knowledge of specific facts, and the capacity to relate it to what he has perceived during the proceeding, as well as the ability to draw reasonable deductions from the combination by using the ordinary processes of thought. That fund of general information must be at least as great as that of all reasonably well-informed persons in the community. He cannot be assumed to be ignorant of what is so generally accepted as to be incapable of dispute among reasonable men.

Although Lamer, J., as he then was, in *Sioui*, endorsed the use of judicial notice of historical facts in cases involving aboriginal rights, there are, as noted, limits to the doctrine. Stratton, C.J.N.B., in *R. v. Augustine et al.; R. v. Barlow* (1986), 74 N.B.R. (2d) 156, (application for leave to appeal to Supreme Court of Canada refused, [1987] 1 S.C.R. v.), said at p. 171:

> The general rule or principle of judicial notice was stated by O Hearn, County Court Judge in *R. v. Bennett* (1971), 4 C.C.C. (2d) 55 at p. 66 as follows:
>
> > Courts will take judicial notice of what is considered by reasonable men of that time and place to be indisputable either by resort to common knowledge or to sources of indisputable accuracy easily accessible to men in the situation of members of that court.

In a recent case, also involving an Indian's alleged right to hunt, Mr. Justice Lambert of the British Columbia Court of Appeal examined evidence that was not presented at trial but was careful to note that he took "judicial notice of [only] indisputable, relevant, historical facts by reference to a readily obtainable and authoritative source, in accordance with the ordinary principles of judicial notice": see *R. v. Bartleman* (1984), 12 D.L.R. (4th) 73, at p. 77. Mr. Justice Lambert also added this:

> To the extent that these writings deal with facts, I have relied on them only to draw my attention to facts that I was then able to verify independently by examining the letters and the written component of the treaties, and no further. For the purposes of my own independent verification, I have reached only those conclusions that I regard as being beyond rational dispute.

See also *R. v. Pallett*, [1970] 2 O.R. 222. Furthermore, the text by J. Sopinka, S.N. Lederman and A.W. Bryant, *The Law of Evidence in Canada* (1992), at p. 976, states:

> Judicial notice is the acceptance by a Court or Judicial tribunal, in a civil or criminal proceeding, without the requirement of proof, of the truth of a particular fact or state of affairs. Facts which are (a) *so notorious as not to be the subject of dispute among reasonable persons*, or (b) *capable of immediate and accurate demonstration by resorting to readily accessible sources of indisputable accuracy* may be noticed by the court without proof of them by either party.

Turnbull, J. recognizes, at para. 19 of his decision, that the issues before him that involve aboriginal title are disputed facts. He said:

> I may have spent altogether too much time on this aspect of when and how England obtained Indian title to Nova Scotia. To me it is a mystery and *a matter of debate*.

At para. 21, he concedes the difficulty of doing historical research. In any event, the question of aboriginal title, upon which he based his decision, should have been raised with the parties. This is particularly true when the inferences that the Judge drew from his research determined the case.

Thus, as noted above, a case that was acknowledged by Justice Turnbull at para. 21 to have been argued "on the basis of a treaty right to trade" was transformed by him into one premised upon aboriginal title. This transition occurred without giving notice to the parties and without affording counsel the opportunity to address the issue with written or oral argument or to dispute the documents or the inferences drawn from them or to present evidence of any kind.

In *King et al. v. Canada (Attorney General) et al.* (1997), 187 N.B.R. (2d) 185, Hoyt, C.J. said at p. 196:

> Judges must resist the temptation to raise new issues, particularly those that are determinative, without giving the parties an opportunity to respond.

Similarly, in *R. v. Fraillon* (1990), 62 C.C.C. (3d) 474, Vallerand, J.A. said at p. 476:

> It is first wrong that the trial Judge ruled as he did without giving the parties an opportunity to argue the issue. Generally, it is open to the judge to point out to the parties that, in his mission to do justice, he is troubled by a point in the facts or in the law which neither one raised. This is especially the case where it is a right recognized by the Charter. But again, he must point it out to the parties and give them all the time necessary to completely argue the question before he rules on it. Here the parties to their great astonishment learned during the rendering of judgment that it was based, and based solely, on a question that the judge had only raised and resolved *proprio motu*. This manner of proceeding is inadmissible and is sufficient in and of itself to result in the granting of the appeal.

Even more authoritatively, and in a case involving aboriginal title, Dickson, J., as he then was, in *Kruger et al. v. The Queen*, [1978] 1 S.C.R. 104, said at p. 108-09:

> [A] sound rule to follow is that questions of title should only be decided when title is directly in issue. Interested parties should be afforded an opportunity to adduce evidence in detail bearing upon the resolution of the particular dispute. Claims to aboriginal title are woven with history, legend, politics and moral obligations. *If the claim of any Band in respect of any particular land is to be decided as a justiciable issue and not a political issue, it should be so considered on the facts pertinent to that Band and to that land, and not on any global basis.*

In this case, the arguments of counsel and the tendered evidence were not directed to the issue of aboriginal title globally or to any Micmac aboriginal title in the land at or near the Arseneau Road. This was not, therefore, a case upon which a court could properly assess any claim of aboriginal title to Crown lands in New Brunswick.

Thus, Turnbull, J. erred in not only relying on his exclusive post-argument historical research, research that formed the basis for his decision that Mr. Peter Paul could rely on aboriginal title as a defence, but also by using such research, particularly without giving the parties the right to respond. For that reason alone, the appeal should be allowed because, as noted, Turnbull, J. would otherwise have allowed the Crown's appeal from Judge Arsenault's decision.

. . . .

For the above reasons, we allow the appeal, direct that a conviction be entered and remit the matter to the Provincial Court for sentence.

For a criticism of the judgment in *Bartleman* see M.H. Ogilvie, "Evidence —

Judicial Notice — Historical Documents — Indian Treaty Rights" (1986), 64 Can. Bar Rev. 183.

A relatively recent development in criminal procedure in Canada has been the ability to challenge prospective jurors to determine if they have a bias which might interefere with the decision-making process. A nice question arises. To permit questions need there be evidence led concerning bias in the community and should there be evidence as to whether this bias can be put aside?

In *R. v. Parks* (1993), 24 C.R. (4th) 81 (Ont. C.A.), the Court decided that the trial judge should have permitted questions of prospective jurors regarding their ability to put aside racial prejudice when coming to a conclusion. The decision has had its share of critics. Robert Martin wrote:

> Doherty cited several documents prepared by the Ontario Human Rights Commission, as well as reports from the Canadian Human Rights Commission, Multiculturalism Canada, and a group called Equal Opportunity Consultants. He offered no comment on the methodologies employed by any of these organizations. Doherty cited at length a letter written by Stephen, tears-for-hire, Lewis to Robert K. Rae, Q.C. in June of 1992. If Mr. Lewis thinks Ontario is a wretchedly racist place, that, apparently, is good enough for Doherty. Doherty was not able to find a single Canadian study which based itself in empirical data. All he could do was cite three articles which hypothesized about the effects of racial prejudice on juries. None of the research which led to these conclusions was presented by the appellant. The judges dug it all out themselves, which meant, of course, it couldn't be subjected to critical analysis by the Crown. Why do our courts bother holding hearings any more? They could just issue regular pronouncements and save us bother and money. Lawyers Weekly, November 26, 1993.

Compare Justice Doherty in a later decision. In *R. v. Alli* (1996), 110 C.C.C. (3d) 283 (Ont. C.A.), the accused was convicted of sexual assault. He was found to have sexually assaulted another male prisoner while both were confined in the drunk tank of a local lock-up. The accused was Guyanese and the complainant was Vietnamese. The accused complained that the trial judge had improperly denied his right to challenge prospective jurors for cause. The accused had sought to challenge for cause on two grounds: the potential prejudice against homosexuals and the potential prejudice against the accused who is a member of a visible minority. The accused had called no evidence in support of either proposed ground. Justice Doherty wrote:

> In *Parks*, this court went outside the trial record and beyond the material submitted by the parties to find sociological and empirical support for its conclusions. That form of appellate activism, while appropriate in some cases, should be used sparingly: *Willick v. Willick*, [1994] 3 S.C.R. 670, per L'Heureux-Dubé J. at 699-705. Appellate analysis of untested social science data should not be regarded as the accepted means by which the scope of challenges for cause based on generic prejudice will be settled.
>
>   . . . Any proposed extension of *Parks* should be approached with caution. Where, as in this case, there was no evidence offered at trial to support the proposed extension, the court should decline to interfere with the trial judge's exercise of his or her discretion. Any extension of *Parks* should await a case in which an adequate evidentiary foundation has been laid at trial to permit an informed determination of whether the ratio of *Parks* should be extended to other forms of generic prejudice.

In *R. v. Williams*, (1994) 30 C.R. (4th) 277 (B.C.S.C.), the Court refused the challenge for cause process noting that a cost-benefit analysis did not warrant the same. Observe the Supreme Court's attitude on appeal.

R. v. WILLIAMS
[1998] 1 S.C.R. 1128, 15 C.R. (5th) 227, 124 C.C.C. (3d) 481

[The accused, an aboriginal, was charged with robbery. The trial court refused his request to challenge jurors for cause. The Court of Appeal dismissed an appeal from conviction. The courts accepted that there was widespread prejudice against aboriginal people in the community but questioned whether the evidence of widespread bias against aboriginal people in the community raised a realistic potential of partiality.]

McLACHLIN, J.:—

. . . .

The Crown argues that evidence of widespread racial bias against persons of the accused's race does not translate into a "realistic potential" for partiality. There is a presumption that jurors will act impartially, whatever their pre-existing views. Evidence of widespread bias does not rebut that presumption. More is required. The Crown does not detail what evidence might suffice. However, it emphasizes that the evidence must point to not only bias, but also partiality, or bias that may affect the outcome. What is required, in the Crown's submission, is concrete evidence showing prejudice that would not be capable of being set aside at trial. The Crown interprets *Parks, supra,* where challenges for cause for racial bias in the community were permitted, as being an exceptional case where the nature and extent of the racial bias was sufficiently extreme to establish a reasonable possibility of partiality.

. . . .

In my respectful view, the positions of the Crown, Esson C.J. and the Court of Appeal reflect a number of errors that lead to the evidentiary threshold for challenges for cause being set too high. . . .

. . . .

Section 638(2) requires two inquiries and entails two different decisions with two different tests. The first stage is the inquiry before the judge to determine whether challenges for cause should be permitted. The test at this stage is whether there is a realistic potential or *possibility* for partiality. The question is whether there is reason to suppose that the jury pool *may* contain people who are prejudiced and whose prejudice *might not* be capable of being set aside on directions from the judge. The operative verbs at the first stage are "may" and "might". Since this is a preliminary inquiry which may affect the accused's *Charter* rights, . . . a reasonably generous approach is appropriate.

If the judge permits challenges for cause, a second inquiry occurs on the challenge itself. The defence may question potential jurors as to whether they harbour prejudices against people of the accused's race, and if so, whether they are able to set those prejudices aside and act as impartial jurors. The question at this stage is whether the candidate in question *will* be able to act impartially. To demand, at the preliminary stage of determining whether a challenge for cause should be permitted, proof that the jurors in the jury pool will not be able to set aside any prejudices they may harbour and act impartially, is to ask the question more appropriate for the second stage.

. . . .

Impossibility of Proving That Racism in Society Will Lead to Juror Partiality

To require the accused to present evidence that jurors will in fact be unable to set aside their prejudices as a condition of challenge for cause is to set the accused an impossible task. It is extremely difficult to isolate the jury decision and attribute a particular portion of it to a given racial prejudice observed at the community level. Jury research based on the study of actual trials cannot control all the variables correlated to race. Studies of mock juries run into external validity problems because they cannot recreate an authentic trial experience: see Jeffrey E. Pfeiffer, "Reviewing the Empirical Evidence on Jury Racism: Findings of Discrimination or Discriminatory Findings?" (1990), 69 *Neb. L. Rev.* 230. As recognized by Doherty J.A. in *Parks, supra*, at p. 366, "[t]he existence and extent of [matters such as] racial bias are not issues which can be established in the manner normally associated with the proof of adjudicative facts".

"Concrete" evidence as to whether potential jurors can or cannot set aside their racial prejudices can be obtained only by questioning a juror. If the Canadian system permitted jurors to be questioned after trials as to how and why they made the decisions they did, there might be a prospect of obtaining empirical information on whether racially prejudiced jurors can set aside their prejudices. But s. 649 of the *Code* forbids this. So, imperfect as it is, the only way we have to test whether racially prejudiced jurors will be able to set aside their prejudices and judge impartially between the Crown and the accused, is by questioning prospective jurors on challenges for cause. In many cases, we can infer from the nature of widespread racial prejudice, that some jurors at least may be influenced by those prejudices in their deliberations. Whether or not this risk will materialize must be left to the triers of impartiality on the challenge for cause. To make it a condition of the right to challenge to cause is to require the defence to prove the impossible and to accept that some jurors may be partial.

. . . .

In the case at bar, the accused called witnesses and tendered studies to establish widespread prejudice in the community against aboriginal people. It may not be necessary to duplicate this investment in time and resources at the stage of establishing racial prejudice in the community in all subsequent cases. The law of evidence recognizes two ways in which facts can be established in the trial process. The first is by evidence. The second is by judicial notice. Tanovich, Paciocco and Skurka observe that because of the limitations on the traditional forms of proof in this context, "doctrines of judicial notice [will] play a significant role in determining whether a particular request for challenge for cause satisfies the threshold test": see *Jury Selection in Criminal Trials* (1997), at p. 138. Judicial notice is the acceptance of a fact without proof. It applies to two kinds of facts: (1) facts which are so notorious as not be the subject of dispute among reasonable persons; and (2) facts that are capable of immediate and accurate demonstration by resorting to readily accessible sources of indisputable accuracy: see Sopinka, Lederman and Bryant, *The Law of Evidence in Canada* (1992), at p. 976. The existence of racial prejudice in the community may be a notorious fact within the first branch of the rule. As Sopinka, Lederman and Bryant note, at p. 977, "[t]he character of a certain place or of the community of persons living in a certain locality has been judicially noticed". Widespread racial prejudice, as a characteristic of the community, may therefore sometimes be the subject of judicial notice. Moreover, once a finding of fact of widespread racial prejudice in the community is made on evidence, as here, judges in subsequent cases may be able to take judicial notice of the fact. "The fact that a certain fact or matter has been noted by a judge of the same court in a previous matter has precedential value and it is, therefore, useful for counsel and the court to examine the case law when attempting to determine whether any particular fact can be noted": see Sopinka, Lederman and Bryant, *supra*, at p. 977. It is also possible that events and documents of indisputable accuracy may permit judicial notice to be taken of widespread racism in the community under the second branch of the rule. For these reasons, it is unlikely that long inquiries into the existence of widespread racial prejudice in the community will become a regular feature of the criminal trial process. While these comments are not necessarily limited to challenges for cause, the question whether they are applicable to other phases of the criminal trial is not to be decided in the present case.

. . . .

Conclusion

Although they acknowledged the existence of widespread bias against aboriginals, both Esson C.J. and the British Columbia Court of Appeal held that the evidence did not demonstrate a reasonable possibility that prospective jurors would be partial. In my view, there was ample evidence that this widespread prejudice included elements that could have affected the impartiality of jurors. Racism against aboriginals includes stereotypes that relate to credibility, worthiness and criminal propensity. . . . There is evidence that this widespread racism has translated into systemic discrimination in the criminal justice system: see Royal Commission on Aboriginal Peoples, *Bridging the Cultural Divide: A Report on Aboriginal People and Criminal Justice in Canada*, at p. 33; Royal Commission on the Donald Marshall, Jr., Prosecution: *Findings and Recommendations*, vol. 1 (1989), at p. 162; *Report on the Cariboo-Chilcotin Justice Inquiry* (1993), at p. 11. . . .

. . . .

In these circumstances, the trial judge should have allowed the accused to challenge prospective jurors for cause. Notwithstanding the accused's defence that another aboriginal person committed the robbery, juror prejudice could have affected the trial in many other ways. Consequently, there was a realistic potential that some of the jurors might not have been indifferent between the Crown and the accused. The potential for prejudice was increased by the failure of the trial judge to instruct the jury to set aside any racial prejudices that they might have against aboriginals. It cannot be said that the accused had the fair trial by an impartial jury to which he was entitled. I would allow the appeal and direct a new trial.

R. v. FIND
42 C.R. (5th) 1, 154 C.C.C. (3d) 97 (S.C.C.)

[The accused was charged with 21 counts of sexual offences involving complainants ranging between 6 and 12 years of age at the time of the alleged offences. Prior to jury selection, he applied to challenge potential jurors for cause, arguing that the nature of the charges against him gave rise to a realistic possibility that some jurors might be unable to try the case against him impartially and solely on the evidence before them. The trial judge rejected the application. The accused was convicted on 17 of the 21 counts. The majority of the Court of Appeal dismissed the accused's appeal, upholding the trial judge's ruling not to permit the accused to challenge prospective jurors for cause.]

McLachlin, C.J.:—

. . . .

As a practical matter, establishing a realistic potential for juror partiality generally requires satisfying the court on two matters: (1) that a widespread bias exists in the community; and (2) that some jurors may be incapable of setting aside this bias, despite trial safeguards, to render an impartial decision. These two components of the challenge for cause test reflect, respectively, the *attitudinal* and *behavioural* components of partiality.

. . . .

Ultimately, the decision to allow or deny an application to challenge for cause falls to the discretion of the trial judge. However, judicial discretion should not be confused with judicial whim. Where a realistic potential for partiality exists, the right to challenge must flow. . . . If in doubt, the judge should err on the side of permitting challenges. Since the right of the accused to a fair trial is at stake, "[i]t is better to risk allowing what are in fact unnecessary challenges, than to risk prohibiting challenges which are necessary": see *Williams*. . . .

Proof: How a Realistic Potential for Partiality May Be Established

A party may displace the presumption of juror impartiality by calling evidence, by asking the judge to take judicial notice of facts, or both. In addition, the judge may draw inferences from events that occur in the proceedings and may make common sense inferences about how certain biases, if proved, may affect the decision-making process.

The first branch of the inquiry — establishing relevant widespread bias — requires evidence, judicial notice or trial events demonstrating a pervasive bias in the community. The second stage of the inquiry — establishing a behavioural link between widespread attitudes and juror conduct — may be a matter of proof, judicial notice, or simply reasonable inference as to how bias might influence the decision-making process. . . .

In this case, the appellant relies heavily on proof by judicial notice. Judicial notice dispenses with the need for proof of facts that are clearly uncontroversial or beyond reasonable dispute. Facts judicially noticed are not proved by evidence under oath. Nor are they tested by cross-examination. Therefore, the threshold for judicial notice is strict: a court may properly take judicial notice of facts that are either: (1) so notorious or generally accepted as not to be the subject of debate among reasonable persons; or (2) capable of immediate and accurate demonstration by resort to readily accessible sources of indisputable accuracy. . . .

The scientific and statistical nature of much of the information relied upon by the appellant further complicates this case. Expert evidence is by definition neither notorious nor capable of immediate and accurate demonstration. This is why it must be proved through an expert whose qualifications are accepted by the court and who is available for cross-examination. As Doherty J.A. stated in *R. v. Alli* (1996), 110 C.C.C. (3d) 283 (Ont. C.A.), at p. 285: "[a]ppellate analysis of untested social science data should not be regarded as the accepted means by which the scope of challenges for cause based on generic prejudice will be settled".

Were the Grounds for Challenge for Cause Present in this Case?

. . . .

. . . The appellant called no evidence, expert or otherwise, on the incidence or likely effect of prejudice stemming from the nature of the offences with which he is charged. Instead, he asks the Court to take judicial notice of a widespread bias arising from allegations of the sexual assault of children. The Crown, by contrast, argues that the facts on which it agrees do not translate into bias, much less widespread bias.

The appellant relies on the following: (a) the incidence of victimization and its effect on members of the jury pool; (b) the strong views held by many about sexual assault and the treatment of this crime by the criminal justice system; (c) myths and stereotypes arising from widespread and deeply entrenched attitudes about sexual assault; (d) the incidence of intense emotional reactions to sexual assault, such as a strong aversion to the crime or undue empathy for its victims; (e) the experience of Ontario trial courts, where hundreds of potential jurors in such cases have been successfully challenged as partial; and (f) social science research indicating a "generic prejudice" against the accused in sexual assault cases. He argues that these factors permit the Court to take judicial notice of widespread bias arising from charges of sexual assault of children.

. . .

Moldaver J.A. [in the Ontario Court of Appeal in a companion case] concluded that the prevalence of sexual assault in Canadian society and its traumatic and potentially lifelong effects, provided a realistic basis to believe that victims of this crime may harbor intense and deep-seated biases. In arriving at this conclusion, he expressly relied on an unpublished article by Professor David Paciocco, "Challenges for Cause in Jury Selection after *Regina v. Parks*: Practicalities and Limitations", Canadian Bar Association, Ontario, February 11, 1995, which he quoted at para. 176 for the proposition that "[o]ne cannot help but believe that these deep scars would, for some, prevent them from adjudicating sexual offence violations impartially".

This is, however, merely the statement of an assumption, offered without a supporting foundation of evidence or research. Courts must approach sweeping and untested "common sense" assumptions about the behaviour of abuse victims with caution: see *R. v. Seaboyer* [and] *R. v. Lavallee*. Certainly these assumptions are not established beyond reasonable dispute, or documented with indisputable accuracy, so as to permit the Court to take judicial notice of them. I conclude that while widespread victimization may be a factor to be considered, standing alone it fails to establish widespread bias that might lead jurors to discharge their task in a prejudicial and unfair manner.

Strongly Held Views Relating to Sexual Offences

The appellant submits that the politicized and gender-based nature of sexual offences gives rise to firmly held beliefs, opinions and attitudes that establish widespread bias in cases of sexual assault.

This argument found favour with Moldaver J.A. in *K. (A.)*. Moldaver J.A. judicially noticed the tendency of sexual assault to be committed along gender lines. He also took judicial notice of the systemic discrimination women and children have faced in the criminal justice system, and the fact that recent reforms have gone too far for some and not far enough for others. From this foundation of facts, he inferred that the gender-based and politicized nature of sexual offences leads to a realistic possibility that some members of the jury pool, as a result of their political beliefs, will harbour deep-seated and virulent biases that might prove resistant to judicial cleansing. Quoting from the work of Professor Paciocco, Moldaver J.A. emphasized that strong political convictions and impartiality are not necessarily incongruous, but that for some "feminists" "commitment gives way to zealotry and dogma". The conviction that the justice system and its rules are incapable of protecting women and children, it is argued, may lead some potential jurors to disregard trial directions and rules safeguarding the presumption of innocence. Little regard for judicial direction can be expected from "those who see the prosecution of sexual offenders as a battlefront in a gender-based war" (para. 177).

. . . .

The appellant's submission reduces to this: while strong views on the law do not ordinarily indicate bias, an exception arises in the case of sexual assaults on children. The difficulty, however, is that there is nothing in the material that supports this contention, nor is it self-evident. There is no indication that jurors are more willing to cross the line from opinion to prejudice in relation to sexual assault than for any other serious crime. It is therefore far from clear that strongly held views about sexual assault translate into bias, in the required sense of a tendency to act in an unfair and prejudicial manner.

Moreover, assuming that the strong views people may hold about sexual assault raise the possibility of bias, how widespread such views are in Canadian society remains a matter of conjecture. The material before the Court offers no measure of the prevalence in Canadian society of the specific attitudes identified by the appellant as corrosive of juror impartiality. Some people may indeed believe that the justice system is faltering in the face of an epidemic of abuse and that perpetrators of this crime too often escape conviction; yet, it is far from clear that these beliefs are prevalent in our society, let alone that they translate into bias on a widespread scale.

Myths and Stereotypes About Sexual Offences

The appellant suggests that the strong views that surround the crime of sexual assault may contribute to widespread myths and stereotypes that undermine juror impartiality. In any given jury pool, he argues, some people may reason from the prevalence of abuse to the conclusion that the accused is likely guilty; some may assume children never lie about abuse; and some may reason that the accused is more likely to be guilty because he is a man.

Again, however, the proof falls short. Although these stereotypical beliefs clearly amount to bias that might incline some people against the accused or toward conviction, it is neither notorious nor indisputable that they enjoy widespread acceptance in Canadian society. Myths and stereotypes do indeed pervade public perceptions of sexual assault. Some favour the accused, others the Crown. In the absence of evidence, however, it is difficult to conclude that these stereotypes translate into widespread bias.

Emotional Nature of Sexual Assault Trials

The appellant asks the Court to take judicial notice of the emotional nature of sexual assault trials and to conclude that fear, empathy for the victim, and abhorrence of the crime establish widespread bias in the community. His concern is that jurors, faced with allegations of sexual assaults of children, may act on emotion rather than reason. This is particularly the case, he suggests, for past victims of abuse, for whom the moral repugnancy of the crime may be amplified. He emphasizes that the presumption of innocence in criminal trials demands the acquittal of the "probably" guilty. An intense aversion to sexual crimes, he argues, may incline some jurors to err on the side of conviction in such circumstances. Undue empathy for the victim, he adds, may also prompt a juror to "validate" the complaint with a guilty verdict, rather than determine guilt or innocence according to the law.

Crimes commonly arouse deep and strong emotions. They represent a fundamental breach of the perpetrator's compact with society. Crimes make victims, and jurors cannot help but sympathize with them. Yet these indisputable facts do not necessarily establish bias, in the sense of an attitude that could unfairly prejudice jurors against the accused or toward conviction. Many crimes routinely tried by jurors are abhorrent. Brutal murders, ruthless frauds and violent attacks are standard fare for jurors. Abhorred as they are, these crimes seldom provoke suggestions of bias incompatible with a fair verdict.

One cannot automatically equate strong emotions with an unfair and prejudicial bias against the accused. Jurors are not expected to be indifferent toward crimes. Nor are they expected to remain neutral toward those shown to have committed such offences. If this were the case, prospective jurors would be routinely and successfully challenged for cause as a preliminary stage in the trial of all serious criminal offences. Instead, we accept that jurors often abhor the crime alleged to have been committed — indeed there would be cause for alarm if representatives of a community did *not* deplore heinous criminal acts. It would be equally alarming if jurors did not feel empathy or compassion for persons shown to be victims of such acts. These facts alone do not establish bias. There is simply no indication that these attitudes, commendable in themselves, unfairly prejudice jurors against the accused or toward conviction. They are common to the trial of many serious offences and have never grounded a right to challenge for cause.

. . . .

The History of Challenges for Cause in Ontario

The appellant refers this Court to the experience of Ontario trial courts where judges have allowed defence counsel to challenge prospective jurors for cause in cases involving allegations of sexual assault: see Vidmar, *supra*, at p. 5; D.M. Tanovich, D.M. Paciocco, S. Skurka, *Jury Selection in Criminal Trials: Skills, Science, and the Law* (1997), at pp. 239-42. These sources, cataloguing 34 cases, indicate that hundreds of potential jurors have been successfully challenged for cause as not indifferent between the Crown and the accused. It is estimated that 36 percent of the prospective jurors challenged were disqualified.

The appellant argues that the fact that hundreds of prospective jurors have been found to be partial is in itself sufficient evidence of widespread bias arising from sexual assault trials. This is proof, he asserts, that the social realities surrounding sexual assault trials give rise to prejudicial beliefs, attitudes and emotions on a widespread scale in Canadian communities.

. . . .

The first argument against the survey is that its methodology is unsound. The Crown raises a number of concerns: the survey is entirely anecdotal, not comprehensive or random; not all of the questions asked of prospective jurors are indicated; there is no way in which to assess the directions, if any, provided by the trial judge, especially in relation to the distinction between strong opinions or emotions and partiality; and no comparative statistics are provided contrasting these results with the experience in other criminal law contexts. The intervener CLA concedes that the survey falls short of scientific validity, but contends that it nevertheless documents a phenomenon of considerable significance. Hundreds of prospective jurors disqualified on the grounds of bias by impartial triers of fact must, it is argued, displace the presumption of juror impartiality. Nonetheless, the lack of methodological rigour and the absence of expert evidence undermine the suggestion that the Ontario experience establishes widespread bias.

The second argument against the survey is that the questions asked were so general, and the information elicited so scarce, that no meaningful inference can be drawn from the responses given by challenged jurors or from the number of potential jurors disqualified. Charron J.A., for the majority in *K. (A.)*, observed that prospective jurors in that case received no meaningful instruction on the nature of jury duty or the meaning and importance of impartiality. Further, they often indicated confusion at the questions posed to them or asked that the questions be repeated. In the end, numerous prospective jurors were disqualified for offering little more than that they would find it difficult to hear a case of this nature, or that they held strong emotions about the sexual abuse of children.

. . . .

Where potential jurors are challenged for racial bias, the risk of social disapprobation and stigma supports the veracity of admissions of potential partiality. No similar *indicia* of reliability attach to the frank and open admission of concern about one's ability to approach and decide a case of alleged child sexual abuse judiciously. While a prospective juror's admission of racial prejudice may suggest partiality, the same cannot be said of an admission of abhorrence or other emotional attitude toward the sexual abuse of children. We do not know whether the potential jurors who professed concerns about serving on juries for sexual assault charges were doing so because they were biased, or for other reasons. We do not know whether they were told that strong emotions and beliefs would not in themselves impair their duty of impartiality, or whether they were informed of the protections built into the trial process.

. . . .

It follows that the survey of past challenge for cause cases involving charges of sexual assault does not without more establish widespread bias arising from these charges.

Social Science Evidence of "Generic Prejudice"

The appellant argues that social science research, particularly that of Vidmar, supports the contention that social realities, such as the prevalence of sexual abuse and its politically charged nature, translate into a widespread bias in Canadian society.

In *Williams, supra*, the Court referred to Vidmar's research in concluding that the partiality targeted by s. 638(1)(b) was not limited to biases arising from a direct interest in the proceeding or pre-trial exposure to the case, but could arise from *any* of a variety of sources, including the "nature of the crime itself" (para. 10). However, recognition that the nature of an offence may give rise to "generic prejudice" does not obviate the need for proof. Labels do not govern the availability of challenges for cause. Regardless of how a case is classified, the ultimate issue is whether a realistic possibility exists that some potential jurors may try the case on the basis of prejudicial attitudes and beliefs, rather than the evidence offered at trial. The appellant relies on the work of Vidmar for the proposition that such a possibility does in fact arise from allegations of sexual assault.

Vidmar is known for the theory of a "generic prejudice" against accused persons in sexual assault trials and for the conclusion that the attitudes and beliefs of jurors are frequently reflected in the verdicts of juries on such trials. However, the conclusions of Vidmar do not assist in finding widespread bias. His theory that a "generic prejudice" exists against those charged with sexual assault, although in the nature of expert evidence, has not been proved. Nor can the Court take judicial notice of this contested proposition. With regard to the behaviour of potential jurors, the Court has no foundation in this case to draw an inference of partial juror conduct, as discussed in more detail below, under the behavioural stage of the partiality test.

. . . .

Conclusions on the Existence of a Relevant, Widespread Bias

Do the factors cited by the appellant, taken together, establish widespread bias arising from charges relating to sexual abuse of children? In my view, they do not. The material presented by the appellant, considered in its totality, falls short of grounding judicial notice of widespread bias in Canadian society against the accused in such trials. At best, it establishes that the crime of sexual assault, like many serious crimes, frequently elicits strong attitudes and emotions.

However, the two branches of the test for partiality are not water-tight compartments. Given the challenge of proving facts as elusive as the nature and scope of prejudicial attitudes, and the need to err on the side of caution, I prefer not to resolve this case entirely at the first, attitudinal stage. Out of an abundance of caution, I will proceed to consider the potential impact, if any, of the alleged biases on juror behaviour.

Is it Reasonable to Infer that Some Jurors May Be Incapable of Setting Aside Their Biases Despite Trial Safeguards?

. . . .

The applicant need not always adduce direct evidence establishing this link between the bias in issue and detrimental effects on the trial process. Even in the absence of such evidence, a trial judge may reasonably infer that some strains of bias by their very nature may prove difficult for jurors to identify and eliminate from their reasoning.

This inference, however, is not automatic. Its strength varies with the nature of the bias in issue, and its amenability to judicial cleansing. In *Williams*, the Court inferred a behavioural link between the pervasive racial prejudice established on the evidence and the possibility that some jurors, consciously or not, would decide the case based on prejudice and stereotype. Such a result, however, is not inevitable for every form of bias, prejudice or preconception. In some circumstances, the appropriate inference is that the "predispositions can be safely regarded as curable by judicial direction": *Williams, supra,* at para. 24.

. . . .

In the absence of evidence that such beliefs and attitudes may affect jury behaviour in an unfair manner, it is difficult to conclude that they will not be cleansed by the trial process. Only speculation supports the proposition that jurors will act on general opinions and beliefs to the detriment of an individual accused, in disregard of their oath or affirmation, the presumption of innocence, and the directions of the trial judge.

The appellant also contends that myths and stereotypes attached to the crime of sexual assault may unfairly inform the deliberation of some jurors. However, strong, sometimes biased, assumptions about sexual behaviour are not new to sexual assault trials. Traditional myths and stereotypes have long tainted the assessment of the conduct and veracity of complainants in sexual assault cases – the belief that women of "unchaste" character are more likely to have consented or are less worthy of belief; that passivity or even resistance may in fact constitute consent; and that some women invite sexual assault by reason of their dress or behaviour, to name only a few. Based on overwhelming evidence from relevant social science literature, this Court has been willing to accept the prevailing existence of such myths and stereotypes: see, for example, *Seaboyer, supra; R. v. Osolin*, [1993] 4 S.C.R. 595, at pp. 669-71; *R. v. Ewanchuk*, [1999] 1 S.C.R. 330, at paras. 94-97.

Child complainants may similarly be subject to stereotypical assumptions, such as the belief that stories of abuse are probably fabricated if not reported immediately, or that the testimony of children is inherently unreliable: *R. v. W. (R.)*, [1992] 2 S.C.R. 122; *R. v. D. (D.)*, [2000] 2 S.C.R. 275, 2000 SCC 43; N. Bala, "Double Victims: Child Sexual Abuse and the Canadian Criminal Justice System" in W. S. Tarnopolsky, J. Whitman and M. Ouellette, eds., *Discrimination in the Law and the Administration of Justice* (1993).

These myths and stereotypes about child and adult complainants are particularly invidious because they comprise part of the fabric of social "common sense" in which we are daily immersed. Their pervasiveness, and the subtlety of their operation, create the risk that victims of abuse will be blamed or unjustly discredited in the minds of both judges and jurors.

Yet the prevalence of such attitudes has never been held to justify challenges for cause as of right by Crown prosecutors. Instead, we have traditionally trusted the trial process to ensure that such attitudes will not prevent jurors from acting impartially. We have relied on the rules of evidence, statutory protections, and guidance from the judge and counsel to clarify potential misconceptions and promote a reasoned verdict based solely on the merits of the case.

Absent evidence to the contrary, there is no reason to believe that stereotypical attitudes about accused persons are more elusive of these cleansing measures than stereotypical attitudes about complainants. It follows that the myths and stereotypes alleged by the appellant, even if widespread, provide little support for any inference of a behavioural link between these beliefs and the potential for juror partiality.

. . . .

It follows that even if widespread bias were established, we cannot safely infer, on the record before the Court, that it would lead to unfair, prejudicial and partial juror behaviour. . . .

Conclusion

The case for widespread bias arising from the nature of charges of sexual assault on children is tenuous. Moreover, even if the appellant had demonstrated widespread bias, its link to actual juror behaviour is speculative, leaving the presumption that it would be cleansed by the trial process firmly in place. Many criminal trials engage strongly held views and stir up powerful emotions — indeed, even revulsion and abhorrence. Such is the nature of the trial process. Absent proof, we cannot simply assume that strong beliefs and emotions translate into a realistic potential for partiality, grounding a right to challenge for cause. I agree with the majority of the Court of Appeal that the appellant has not established that the trial judge erred in refusing to permit him to challenge prospective jurors for cause.

I would dismiss the appeal and affirm the conviction.

R. v. POPERT
(1981), 19 C.R. (3d) 393, 58 C.C.C. (2d) 505 (Ont. C.A.)

[The accused were charged that they made use of the mails for the purpose of transmitting indecent, immoral or scurrilous matter contrary to section 164 of the Criminal Code. The case was tried in the Provincial Court before His Honour Judge Harris, who acquitted the appellants. Judge Harris placed the acquittal of the appellants on four grounds. One of those grounds was that there was insufficient evidence to establish a community standard. This was held to be error.]

ZUBER J.:—

. . . .

[T]he real issue in this case is whether the article "Men Loving Boys Loving Men" published in The Body Politic is immoral or indecent. . . .

The determination of what is immoral or indecent is to be determined by a judge not by reference to his own standards of indecency or immorality but by reference to a community standard. The learned trial judge, however, was of the opinion that there rested on the Crown an obligation to produce evidence and prove a community standard. In his reasons for judgment he said:

> . . . in this case the trial Judge must determine on the evidence what is the community standard of acceptance of material that is or may be indecent, immoral or scurrilous.
> . . . I am of the opinion that all in all the evidence adduced from the majority of both Crown and Defence witnesses establishes nothing which really assists the Court in ascertaining the limits of community tolerance. . . . In the result, therefore, I, having found that there is insufficient evidence to establish a community standard . . . it follows that each of the accused is not guilty of this charge.

In my view, the learned trial judge was in error. The reference to a community standard imports an objective test into the ascertainment of indecency and immorality and while evidence with respect to community standards is admissible and sometimes helpful, it is not a fact which the Crown is obliged to prove as a part of its case.

Is the court in *Popert* sanctioning judicial notice of legislative facts or of adjudicative facts?

4. DIFFERENT SCHOOLS OF THOUGHT

In an article written by L'Heureux-Dubé which had justified her decision in *Moge v. Moge,* Justice L'Heureux-Dubé discussed the propriety of bringing social reality into the courtroom by way of judicial notice and concluded:

> By recognizing that exclusive reliance on the adversarial framework, and all of its accompanying legal baggage, may not be the best means by which to address family law concerns, we open the door for more innovative and co-operative solutions that should ultimately improve both the interpretation and application of family law in Canada.[37]

But not all agree! *Willick v. Willick*[38] was concerned with an application to vary the amount of child support which had been set in a separation agreement later incorporated into a divorce judgment. The Court was unanimous that the conditions necessary for a variation had been satisfied. There was a difference of opinion regarding the propriety of judicial notice. Justice Sopinka, La Forest,

---

37.   L'Heureux-Dubé, "Re-examining the Doctrine of Judicial Notice in the Family Law Context" (1994), 26 Ottawa L. Rev. 551.
38.   [1994] 3 S.C.R. 670.

Cory and Iacobucci JJ. concurring, decided that he was able to arrive at the same result as Justice L'Heureux-Dubé on the basis of the rules of statutory construction as to the proper statutory interpretation of s. 17(4) of the Divorce Act, without resort to extensive extrinsic materials. He wrote:

> A contextual approach to the interpretation of the statutory provisions is appropriate but does not require an examination of the broad policy grounds to which my colleague refers. Following that course would require us to resolve the thorny question of the use of extraneous materials such as studies, opinions and reports and whether it is appropriate to take judicial notice of them and what notice to counsel, if any, is required. We would also have to consider the extent to which our approach is different in a case such as this from a constitutional case in which wider latitude is allowed.

Justice L'Heureux-Dubé, Gonthier and McLachlin JJ. concurring, wrote:

> Social science research and socio-economic data are longstanding judicial tools in both Canada and the United States. The judiciary's long-recognized function as a policy finder sometimes compels it to consider social authority even when the parties do not, themselves, present relevant evidence on relevant questions of public policy. In the course of Charter interpretations, this Court has often taken judicial notice of reliable social research and socio-economic data in order to assist its contextual s. 1 analysis of a rights violation. Social authority can be an indispensable element to this approach and this Court has accepted its value in non-constitutional contexts which nonetheless raise broad questions of public policy. See *R. v. Lavallee*.

Justice L'Heureux-Dubé then went on to consider a variety of studies.

Judge Williams was critical of Justice L'Heureux-Dubé's willingness to use judicial notice without informing the parties and seeking their involvement.[39] Recently Justice L'Heureux-Dubé has responded and maintained her position:

> In his view, judicial notice of social framework evidence should not be undertaken without providing the parties with the opportunity to make submissions at trial on this evidence or other evidence which refutes it. I, on the other hand, believe that, while desirable in certain cases, strict procedural requirements applied uniformly to all cases may too readily ignore the very reasons for which judicial notice is both needed and appropriate in the family law context. I have already underlined the significance of cost and the unfairly onerous burden a lengthy trial may place on the spouse with more limited resources. I have also demonstrated the need for tempering the adversarial process in family law matters.[40]

But consider the concerns of Professor Davis, herself a former judge:

> The absence of traditions and procedures for regulating judicial notice of legislative facts provides the sitting judge with a dangerous freedom. As a former judge who has experienced the freedom granted by this permissive view, I have had cause to doubt its wisdom.[41]

Davis calls for some legislative response to encourage litigants and judges to address the issues directly and to ensure, as far as possible, a fair procedure and informed deliberation. There needs to be a procedure for the judge to solicit

---

39. Williams, "Grasping a Thorny Baton" (1996), 14 C.F.L.Q. 179.
40. L'Heureux-Dubé, "Making Equality Work in Family Law" (1997), 14 Can. J. Fam. Law 103, 119.
41. Commenting on the absence of any restrictions in the Federal Rules, see Davis, "There is a Book Out . . ." (1987), 100 Harv. L. Rev. 1539, 1541.

briefs, depositions of experts or to conduct hearings as to whether the judge should take notice of a disputable fact. No one presently denies the necessity of judges sometimes making law. To change the common law, to interpret a statute, to make a constitutional decision. Everyone recognizes as well that the decision should be informed by the facts. It is not too much to ask however that the judges, when they recognize that they are relying on extra-record disputable facts, advise the litigants so that they have an opportunity to agree or disagree.

Perhaps something along the lines of what was proposed in "Study Paper No. 6, Judicial Notice", published by the Law Reform Commission of Canada in 1973 could be used. The Evidence Project recommended legislation dealing with the subject:

> 2 (3) A judge may take judicial notice of scientific, economic and social facts in determining the law or in determining the constitutional validity of a statute.
>
> . . . .
>
> 4 (2) With respect to any fact referred to in subsection 2(3)
>
> (a) if the judge has been requested to take, or proposes to take, or has taken judicial notice, he shall, if requested, afford each party reasonable opportunity to make representations as to the fact or matter of law involved and as to the propriety of taking judicial notice; and
>
> (b) if the judge resorts to any source of information, including the advice of persons learned in the subject matter, that is not received in open court, that information and its source shall be made a part of the record in the proceedings and the judge shall, if requested, afford each party an opportunity to make representations as to the validity of that information.

5. JUDICIAL NOTICE OF PERSONAL KNOWLEDGE

The practice of county court judges of supplementing evidence by having recourse to their own knowledge and experience has been criticized, praised as most beneficial, objected to and encouraged in different decisions.[42]

A final problem with judicial notice of adjudicative facts concerns the distinction between the trier of fact's use of general information known commonly in the community and particular knowledge concerning the facts of the case. For example, in *R. v. Holmes*,[43] the accused was prosecuted for unlawful possession of an instrument suitable to the manufacture of spirits. The magistrate in convicting stated that he knew that a worm, a copper coil, produced as an exhibit, was suitable to the manufacture of spirits. On appeal the conviction was quashed as the fact noticed was regarded as a matter of special and not common knowledge. While the jury in its infancy was expected to act on its own particular knowledge, the growth of the adversary system caused the courts to seek to limit the trier's information to that presented by the parties. It was not desirable, nor indeed possible, to foreclose the trier's use of background information but should the matter noticed be in the forefront of the controversy, should the fact

---

42.   Per Lord Greene in *Reynolds v. Llanelly*, [1948] 1 All E.R. 140.

43.   (1922), 70 D.L.R. 851 (Alta. T.D.). See also *R. v. Savidant* (1945), 19 M.P.R. 448 (P.E.I. S.C.); *Yuill v. Yuill*, [1945] 1 All E.R. 183 (C.A.); and *R. v. Dickson* (1973), 5 N.S.R. (2d) 240 (C.A.).

be determinative, the law protected the adversary by insisting that the matter be so commonly known, and hence indisputable, that its notice could not prejudice the opponent. The principle seems plain, but drawing the line between the particular and the general is not always easy.[44]

Consider the case of *R. v. W. (S.)*.[45] The trial judge, in assessing the credibility of the complainant, on a trial of a charge of sexual assault, commented on the difficulty that was evident in the way she responded to questions. He convicted the accused however and put the complainant's difficulty down to a "compelling cultural disinclination to relive past events of an unpleasant nature." The judge evidently had some experience and knowledge not shared by all. The appellate court, mindful that we are engaged in an adversary system, decided that the judge should not rely on his or her own personal knowledge but rather confine the decision-making to evidence led at the trial:

> There was no evidence of such a "cultural disinclination," and the trial Judge was not entitled to take judicial notice of it.[46]

Should the Court of Appeal have also been critical that there was no evidence before the trial judge that reluctance or hesitancy in answering questions should cause a trier of fact to be concerned as to a witness's credibility? When trial judges make assessments of credibility based on demeanour are they judicially noticing indisputable facts?[47]

Compare *R. v. H. (R.A.)*.[48] The accused had been convicted of sexual assault. In his reasons for judgment, the trial judge had said, concerning the accused's testimony:

> Questions on direct examination were put to him in such a manner that he was able to mostly limit his responses to yes or no. The accused gave evidence in a manner designed to limit his exposure, and even then he did not strike the court as a particularly truthful witness.[49]

In the course of ordering a new trial, the Court of Appeal commented on the trial judge's reasons for not believing the accused:

> He is a young, First Nations person. So far as one can tell from reading the transcript, his answers were responsive to the questions he was asked. Many of those questions, including those asked by his own counsel, were leading questions. I think in those circumstances it would be dangerous for a judge to draw adverse inferences concerning the witness's credibility on the basis that his answers were short, or simply yes or no answers. I think that particularly to be the case where both the accused

---

44. See cases discussed in Phipson, *Evidence* (12th ed.), p. 48 and those collected in 9 Wigmore, *Evidence* (Chad. Rev.), s. 2569, note 4. See also Radin, "The Conscience of the Court" (1932), 48 L.Q.R. 506 and Manchester, "Judicial Notice and Personal Knowledge" (1979), 42 Mod. L. Rev. 22.

45. (1991), 6 C.R. (4th) 373 (Ont. C.A.).

46. *Ibid.*, at p. 374. At a judicial conference in Sudbury in May, 1997, the trial judge in *R. v. W. (S.)* advised that he had come by this information at a lecture to Family Court Judges at an earlier conference. A psychologist had presented a paper on the topic.

47. See Blumenthal, "A Wipe of the Hands, a Lick of the Lips: The Validity of Demeanour Evidence in Assessing Witness Credibility" (1993), 72 Nebraska Law Rev. 1157.

48. (1995), 61 B.C.A.C. 126 (C.A).

49. *Ibid.*, at p. 130.

and complainant are young, First Nations people, and where credibility is the central issue.[50]

In *R. v. J. (F.E.)* [51] the court decided that expert evidence could be received to explain that it was not uncommon for children who have been sexually abused and who have complained to later recant. A recantation then should not impact too negatively on the child's testimony given in the courtroom.

Do Ontario judges need expert assistance for that proposition anymore or may it now be judicially noticed?[52] Is that proposition the law now in Ontario? How about a judge in Alberta? Can a judge judicially notice and act on the scientific literature that she has read concerning the worth of evidence of children?[53] How about information gained at judges' educational conferences?

In *R. v. François* [54] the accused was charged with rape. The only evidence put before the jury was that of the complainant, who testified that she was raped on a number of occasions by the accused over a period of 12 months in 1980, when she was 13 years old. Her testimony in examination-in-chief was that she did not report the assaults until 1990 because she was afraid of what the accused might do to her. She was confronted in cross-examination with an affidavit she had sworn in wardship proceedings in 1986 stating that she had never been sexually abused, and with a second affidavit which she had sworn in 1989 in child support proceedings stating that she was a virgin prior to 1985. She admitted that these statements were untrue, but said that she believed them to be true because she had blocked the incidents involving the accused out of her memory, and that the memory returned to her in a flashback in 1990. On appeal from conviction Justice Robins wrote:

> The complainant's evidence of memory block and flashback was for the jury to evaluate along with her other evidence. This evidence cannot, as is suggested, be rejected as inherently implausible. The mental blocking of traumatic experience, such as sexual abuse suffered as a child, from memory, and the later incremental

50. *Ibid.*
51. (1990), 74 C.R. (3d) 269 (Ont. C.A.).
52. Regarding the process of proof before the courts evolving into judicial notice, see *U.S. v. Ridling*, 350 F.Supp. 90, 94 (E.D. Mich., 1972). In *U.S. v. Lopez*, 328 F.Supp. 1077 (E.D.N.Y., 1971), Weinstein, J., the court was concerned with the admissibility of heroin seized at an airport. The accused went through a machine called "Friskem," a security device that purportedly was able to detect metal weapons. U.S. Marshals were summoned when the accused's presence activated the machine. The accused challenged the admissibility of proof that the machine did what it was purported to have done. Justice Weinstein noted: "Since no opinion was brought to the Court's attention taking judicial notice of magnetometer capabilities, the Court also relied upon expert testimony adduced at the hearing. Such reliance is often the first step in a process that passes through judicial notice to acceptance on a theory of stare decisis. . . . This has been the experience in connection with such scientific techniques as use of fingerprints, ballistic comparison and radar."
53. *E.g.*, Haka-Ikse, "The Child as a Witness in Sexual Abuse Cases: A Developmental Perspective", as quoted in the next chapter of this book. Or, does the doctor have to repeat the words she has written and be subject to cross-examination?
54. (1993), 14 O.R. (3d) 191 (C.A.).

recollection of the abuse through flashbacks are widely recognized psychological processes. The courts have in various contexts made reference to this phenomenon: see, for example, *M. (K.) v. M. (H.)*, [1992] 3 S.C.R. 6; *R. v. L. (W.K.)*, [1991] 1 S.C.R. 1091, 64 C.C.C. (3d) 321; *R. v. C. (R.A.)* (1990), 57 C.C.C. (3d) 522, 78 C.R. (3d) 390 (B.C. C.A.). This jury saw and heard the complainant and in assessing her evidence was entitled to conclude without expert evidence that the shock and confusion engendered in this young girl by being sexually abused by a person in the position of trust of this appellant, together with the fear generated by his demand for secrecy and his accompanying threat, could lead her to block the events from her conscious memory.[55]

Is it unnecessary in future trials to lead expert evidence of the phenomenon of memory block?[56]

In *R. c. Désaulniers*,[57] the accused was convicted of sexual assault. The trial judge had relied on the Badgley Report) "The Report of the Committee on Sexual Offences Against Children and Youths in Canada", to refute expert evidence called by the defence. Tourigny J.A. wrote for the court:

> The present state of Canadian criminal law is to the effect that these works must be put in evidence either through expert witnesses or by being put during the cross-examination of the opposing party's expert witnesses so that they can discuss them, if they are so able to do . . . . Reference by a judge, of his own initiative and without there being any suggestion on the part of the parties, to a scientific work or report which sets out the opinions of experts, constitutes an error of law; obviously, this rule does not apply to consultation of legal works. I cannot, however, prevent myself from pointing out that one finds, in the jurisprudence of the 1990s, at least five decisions of the Supreme Court of Canada which specifically refer to the Badgley Report. However, it must be said that, in these cases one does not know how these documents were brought to the attention of the judge.[58]

Children's Aid Society of London & Middlesex v. W. (K.)[59] involved an application for Crown wardship without access. Vogelsang J. wrote:

> There was little, if any, evidence before me of the atrophy of the bonding between the respondents and the children. Mr. Lepine [counsel for the children] attempted to fill in that evidentiary hiatus by shaping his argument around a text written by Dr. Paul D. Steinhauer: *The Least Detrimental Alternative — A Systematic Guide to Case Planning and Decision Making for Children in Care* (Toronto: University of Toronto Press, 1991). Such a course is not proper where literature is not established in evidence at the trial.[60]

In *R. v. Morris*,[61] the accused was charged with sexual abuse of two young girls, then aged eight and six. The accused testified at trial and denied the allegations. The judge made a positive and clear finding on credibility in favour of the complainants and convicted. In allowing the appeal the Court wrote:

---

55. *Ibid.*, at pp. 195-96.
56. Compare Loftus & Ketcham, *The Myth of Repressed Memory* (N.Y.: St. Martins Press, 1994).
57. (1994), 93 C.C.C. (3d) 371 (Que. C.A.).
58. *Ibid.*, at pp. 376-77.
59. [1995] O.J. No. 4104 (Ont. Gen. Div.).
60. Para. 51.
61. (1995), 169 A.R. 167 (C.A.).

In his reasons for judgment, the trial judge referred to a number of articles and studies which were not in evidence at the trial and were not raised in argument. The material included the Badgley report, an article by Brenda Gutkin of the Child Protection Centre, Winnipeg, presented to a judicial seminar in 1990, an article by Hornik and Clark entitled *Child Custody, Legal and Developmental Issues*, and some unidentified United States' authority. The thrust of all of the material referred to by the trial judge was with respect to the reliability of evidence given by young complainants with respect to alleged sexual abuse. That material was referred to periodically throughout the reasons for judgment and was intermingled with considerations of the evidence given by the complainants and an assessment of their credibility. We are not satisfied that the trial judge was not influenced by the material he referred to in his reasons for judgment. It would be dangerous, we believe, to uphold convictions in these circumstances.[62]

In *R. v. P. (S.D.)*,[63] the accused was convicted of sexual assault. In the course of his reasons the trial judge noted that:

There is a good deal of literature, which is now virtually accepted by the courts and quoted with respect to child witnesses and the literature seems to be consistent that one of the weaknesses with child witnesses is as to recollection of precise dates.[64]

In dismissing the appeal Abella J.A. wrote:

While it might have been preferable had he been more specific about what he was referring to, his allusion to the literature does not mean that he erred in his examination of the complainant's evidence. The Supreme Court of Canada has recently and repeatedly expressed itself on the issue of child witnesses. (See *R. v. Khan*, [1990] 2 S.C.R. 531 and *R. v. W. (R.)*, [1992] 2 S.C.R. 122. See also Ontario Law Reform Commission, *Report on Child Witnesses* (Toronto: July 1991).) There was nothing inappropriate, therefore, in the trial judge indicating a familiarity with this jurisprudence; rather, the comment demonstrated an awareness of the factors the trial judge was obliged to consider in weighing this particular child's evidence.[65]

Justice Brooke said he did not entirely agree with the reasons delivered by Abella J.A. and delivered a judgment concurring in the result. In the course of it he wrote:

I agree with the appellant's submission with respect to the reference to literature in the reasons for judgment. It is not open to judges to rely upon such literature unless it has been accepted after being properly introduced and tested in evidence. However in my respectful view having regard to manner in which the trial judge dealt with this matter I am not satisfied that the appellant was prejudiced by what occurred.[66]

Justice Laskin wrote:

I have read the reasons of my colleagues. I agree with the reasons of Brooke J.A. I also agree with the reasons of Abella J.A. except for her discussion of the trial judge's use of literature and her application and discussion of *Burns* and *Francois*. I, too, would dismiss the appeal.[67]

---

62. *Ibid.*, at p. 168.
63. (1995), 98 C.C.C. (3d) 83 (Ont. C.A.).
64. *Ibid.*, at p. 90.
65. *Ibid.*
66. *Ibid.*, at p. 94.
67. *Ibid.*, at p. 95.

6. DETERMINING RELEVANCE

We regard our present system of fact-finding as a rational system. It's rational at least insofar as we do not engage in the earlier techniques of trial by ordeal or trial by battle. Each of those trials were attempts to call on the Almighty to directly provide us a witness as to who was in the right. Regarding our present system as rational, we insist that there be a rational connection between the evidence sought to be led and the conclusion that the proponent of the evidence hopes to be drawn therefrom — a rational connection between the evidence tendered and the proposition sought to be established thereby. We exclude from the trier of fact information which affects the senses only. We seek to include only those items which have a legitimate influence on reason. But how are we to know what is relevant? Professor Thayer wrote that this is a matter of common sense and experience. We need to recognize that "common sense and experience," judicially noticed, and hence relevance, may vary depending on the judge's culture, gender, background, education, social origin and age. The judge's intuition that fact X frequently accompanies fact Y, making X's presence relevant to Y's, may not accord with another's and counsel may need to be provided with the opportunity to encourage the judge that the judge's hunch is incorrect, and deserves to be rethought in light of the other's experience.[68] When we ask our judges to determine questions of relevance by using "common sense" the operative word is "common." We don't want the judge to determine matters in accordance just with his sense but rather in accordance with the sense that is commonly held, i.e., the sense of the community.

As with any matter judicially noticed, natural justice requires that the judge provide an opportunity for the party against whom the matter will operate to dissuade the judge from his point of view. A major difficulty of course is that while a judge's knowledge of the world may be deficient, unless he is prepared to recognize this possibility, it will not occur to him that his view is not shared by all and it will not occur to him that it's necessary to provide the opportunity to dissuade.

To ensure better rulings on relevancy and judicial notice more in accord with the community's understanding of life, recall the advice of Professor Tillers:

> We should attach more importance to answering the question of what types of factfinders and judicial processes are most likely to reflect faithfully the vision of man and nature to which our society is committed, since it is of great importance that the community believe, and with good reason, that any judgment rendered in a lawsuit is truly the judgment of the community rather than the judgment of any particular individual or class of individuals. . . . [W]e should take some care to see to it that our judges are schooled not only in the law but also in the sentiments and values that undergird our society. Otherwise, there is a serious danger that judges will bring bureaucratic visions to bear on the evidentiary process and will forget that they must speak faithfully for the community and reflect its visions and values.[69]

---

68.   See Weyrauch, "Law as Mask — Legal Ritual and Relevance" (1978), 66 Cal. L. Rev. 699 and Weinstein, "Some Difficulties in Devising Rules for Determining Truth in Judicial Trials" (1966), 66 Col. L. Rev. 223.

69.   1A Wigmore, *Evidence* (Tillers Rev. 1983), s. 37.7, pp. 1094-95. See also generally, Tillers' description of Modern Theories of Relevancy, *id.*, ss. 35-57.

The soundness of Tillers' solution, education, is highlighted by the fact that today arguments in the courtroom as to relevance often tend to be statements of conclusory opinions rather than attempts to logically persuade.

If a judge is judicially noticing when she makes a determination as to relevance, what is she doing when she exercises her discretion to exclude relevant evidence because in her view the probative value is outweighed by competing considerations of time, confusion and prejudice? Professors Lempert and Saltzburg pose an interesting problem:

> When a trial judge is required to balance the probative value of evidence against its prejudicial effect in order to determine whether or not to admit evidence, the judge must of necessity consider matters on which no proof has been offered. Does such consideration amount to judicial notice? Should the judge inform the parties of any sources she has consulted in making her ruling? Of rules of thumb she has relied upon? Should she inform the parties of the extra-record facts she intends to rely upon in reaching a decision on the merits of the case? Of the facts she relies upon in evaluating the credibility of witnesses in a bench trial?[70]

In *R. v. B. (L.)*,[71] Justice Charron wrote for the Court regarding the admissibility of similar fact evidence. She decided it was a matter of balancing the probative value of the evidence against its prejudicial impact and was not to be approached on the basis of categories. In the course of her opinion she noted:

> Because of the inherently prejudicial nature of evidence of discreditable conduct, it is subject to a general exclusionary rule unless the "scales tip in favour of probative value." The trial judge is charged with the delicate process of balancing the probative value of the proposed evidence against its prejudicial effect. . . . Although the rule can be stated with relative ease, the cases reveal that it can be difficult to apply to specific situations. One difficulty undoubtedly arises from the fact that people have different subjective interpretations of the probative value of evidence. Trial judges must usually draw from their own knowledge and experience when assessing the various factors affecting the probative value of the proposed evidence. It is therefore inevitable that there will often be differences of opinion on any given set of facts. It was perhaps in an effort to achieve greater consistency that the courts had adopted the category approach. However, the category approach is subject to different criticism. If highly prejudicial evidence is admitted whenever it fits into a particular category regardless of its probative value, the purpose of the rule is largely defeated. Conversely, the trier of fact may be deprived of the benefit of highly probative evidence whose prejudicial effect is minimal simply because the evidence does not fall within an accepted category.[72]

7. JUDICIAL NOTICE OF LAW

Professor Morgan well described the process of judicially noticing law and distinguished it from judicially noticing fact:

> In any lawsuit the litigants may be in disagreement as to the tenor of an applicable rule of domestic law, or as to the applicability of an unquestioned rule, or as to the facts, or as to two or more of these. A dispute as to the tenor or applicability of a rule of domestic law must be resolved by the judge; a dispute as to the facts is

---

70. Lempert and Saltzburg, *A Modern Approach to Evidence* (1977), p. 923, Problem X-27.
71. (1997), 9 C.R. (5th) 38 (Ont. C.A.).
72. *Ibid.*, at p. 46.

ordinarily decided by the jury in a court of common law, by the judge in a court of equity. The process of resolving the former is quite different from that of deciding the latter.

The judge is charged with the duty of knowing the domestic law. If he does not have the requisite knowledge, he must acquire it. Knowledge of the domestic law, or the capacity to acquire it, is part of his equipment for the office. The same is true as to his knowledge of the applicability of a rule of law to a given state of facts. The assumption that he has such knowledge is imperative. If he lacks it, or any element of it, what he has must serve for what he ought to have. The defects, if any, of a trial judge may be cured or corrected by the judges of the appellate courts; those of the judges of the court of last resort must be assumed not to exist.

In determining the content or applicability of a rule of domestic law, the judge is unrestricted in his investigation and conclusion. He may reject the propositions of either party or of both parties. He may consult the sources of pertinent data to which they refer, or he may refuse to do so. He may make an independent search for persuasive data or rest content with what he has or what the parties present. He may reach a conclusion in accord with the overwhelming weight of available data or against it. If he is a trial judge, his conclusion is subject to review. If he is a judge of a court of last resort and the majority of its members agree with him, his conclusion is final though contrary to the contentions of the parties and to theretofore accepted postulates, principles, and rules. In all this he is entitled to the assistance of the parties and their counsel, for he is acting for the sole purpose of reaching a proper solution of their controversy. But the parties do no more than to assist; they control no part of the process.

In describing the exercise of the judge's functions as to domestic law, it is commonly said that the judge takes judicial notice of the law, and, subject to the operation of the doctrine of invited error, is bound to do so. No fault can be found with this phraseology. It describes the qualification of a judge, distinguishing what he must be assumed to know from what he may actually know. It connotes the process by which he may make the assumption a fact. Both the assumption and the process are necessary concomitants of our system of administering justice. The judicial office in our system cannot be rationally administered on any other premise.[73]

When a judge in Canada is faced with a Charter argument and is called on to determine whether a limitation on a right is reasonable and demonstrably justified in a democratic society, is it a question of burden of proof or is it a question of judicial notice? Does it matter? How?

The common law position requiring the court to judicially notice domestic common and statute law has been supplemented by a variety of statutory enactments and some examples follow:

Canada Evidence Act[74]

17.   Judicial notice shall be taken of all Acts of the Imperial Parliament, of all ordinances made by the Governor in Council, or the lieutenant governor in council of any province or colony that, or some portion of which, now forms or hereafter may form part of Canada, and of all the Acts of the legislature of any such province or colony, whether enacted before or after the passing of the *British North America Act, 1867.*

18.   Judicial notice shall be taken of all Acts of the Parliament of Canada, public or private, without being specially pleaded.

---

73. Morgan, "Judicial Notice" (1944), 57 Harv. L. Rev. 269 at 270-72.
74. R.S.C. 1985, c. C-5, ss. 17,18.

Criminal Code[75]

781.(1) No order, conviction or other proceeding shall be quashed or set aside, and no defendant shall be discharged, by reason only that evidence has not been given

    (*a*)   of a proclamation or order of the Governor in Council or the lieutenant governor in council;

    (*b*)   of rules, regulations or by-laws, made by the Governor in Council under an Act of the Parliament of Canada or by the lieutenant governor in council under an Act of the legislature of the province; or

    (*c*)   of the publication of a proclamation, order, rule, regulation or by-law in the *Canada Gazette* or in the official gazette for the province.

(2) Proclamations, orders, rules, regulations and by-laws mentioned in subsection (1) and the publication thereof shall be judicially noticed.

The Interpretation Act (Ontario)[76]

7.(1) Every Act shall be judicially noticed by judges, justices of the peace and others without being specially pleaded.

(2) Every proclamation shall be judicially noticed by judges, justices of the peace and others without being specially pleaded.

Delegated legislation will frequently not have the notoriety or accessibility needed for judicial notice and will need to be proved as a fact.[77] Statutory provisions in each of the provinces and in the federal sphere ease the manner of their proof. For example in Ontario the Municipal Act[78] provides:

129.(4) A copy of a by-law purporting to be certified by the clerk, under the seal of the corporation, as a true copy, shall be received in evidence in all courts without proof of the seal or signature.

And in the Canada Evidence Act:[79]

33.(1) No proof shall be required of the handwriting or official position of any person certifying, in pursuance of this Act, to the truth of any copy of or extract from any proclamation, order, regulation, appointment, book or other document.

R. v. SMITH
[1988] O.J. No. 2551

HARRIS PROV. CT. J. (orally):—The short issue here is whether a municipal by-law, or a certified copy thereof, must be an Exhibit at a trial or may the party propounding it merely refer to it, or to a certified copy thereof, and ask the Court to take judicial notice thereof.

The argument in favour of judicial notice is as follows:

---

75.   R.S.C. 1985, c. C-46, s. 781.

76.   R.S.O. 1980, c. 219, s. 7.

77.   See *R. v. Snelling*, [1952] O.W.N. 214 (H.C.). Compare *R. v. Clark* (1974), 3 O.R. (2d) 716 (C.A.). See also *R. v. Jahn*, [1982] 3 W.W.R. 684 (Alta. C.A.) and *R. v. Lum*, [1982] 3 W.W.R. 694 (B.C. Co. Ct.).

78.   R.S.O. 1980, c. 302. See also, regarding the currency of the certificate, *R. v. Bleta*, [1966] 2 O.R. 108 (C.A.). And see *R. v. Clark* (1974), 1 O.R. (2d) 210 (H.C.).

79.   R.S.C. 1985, c. C-5, s. 33(1).

Section 7, subsection (1) of the Interpretation Act, R.S.O. 1980, c. 219, provides that every Act shall be judicially noticed by judges, justices of the peace and others without being specially pleaded.

Section 30, subsection (1) of the Interpretation Act provides that in every Act the word "Act" includes "enactment. . . . So, a municipal by-law is an "enactment"; an "enactment" is included within the meaning of the term "Act"; judicial notice shall be taken of an Act, and therefore of an enactment, and therefore of a municipal by-law.

The argument in favour of entering as an Exhibit is as follows:

Rogers on Municipal Law, paragraph 82 says it must be so entered and refers to Snelling; [1952] O.W.N. 2142, unless a statute otherwise directs: Priest (1955), 16 W.W.R. 556, at 558. The judicial notice proponents say that there is such statutory direction.

Mr. Justice Barlow in Snelling says, briefly, only that he has carefully perused the case law and is satisfied judicial notice cannot be taken. Unfortunately, he does not cite any of the case law to which he refers, nor does it appear that the Interpretation Act was argued to him.

I have concluded that the case law notwithstanding, the section 7 statutory argument is compelling, even though accepting it means a departure from long established practice. In my opinion that practice rests on flimsy foundations unsupported by ascertainable authority, whereas the statutory authority is clear and unambiguous.

However, because of the absence of any authoritative and easily available printed by-laws, similar to the R.S.O. or the R.R.O., it would be well if counsel for the prosecuting municipality would file with the Court at the trial, not the whole by-law but a certified copy of the relevant section or sections of the by-law, as amended, together with the enacting clause, penalty clause or clauses, and date or dates of passage — whether this be marked as an Exhibit or not, or merely become part of the record, should be left to the ruling of the trial judge or justice.

But contra, *Grand Central Ottawa Ltd. v. Ottawa (City)*.[80]

The court must judicially notice domestic law because the court is expected to have knowledge of the same by the nature of the office. The court is not expected to know foreign law and the same must therefore be proved by evidence, by the testimony of experts. In *Lazard Brothers & Co. v. Midland Bank Ltd.*[81] the issue was whether by Soviet law a certain bank, on a certain day, was an existing juristic person. Lord Wright wrote:

What the Russian Soviet Law is in that respect is a question of fact, of which the English Court cannot take judicial cognizance, even though the foreign law has already been proved before it in another case. The Court must act upon the evidence before it in the actual case. . . . The evidence it is clear must be that of qualified experts in the foreign law. If the law is contained in a code or written form, the question is not as to the language of the written law, but what the law is as shown by its exposition, interpretation and adjudication. . . . if there be a conflict of evidence of the experts, "you (the judge) must decide as well as you can on the conflicting testimony, but you must take the evidence from the witnesses." Hence the Court is not entitled to construe a foreign code itself: it has not "organs to know and to deal with the text of that law." . . . The text of the foreign law if put in evidence by the

---

80.   (1998), 39 O.R. (3d) 47 (Ont. Prov. Div.).
81.   [1933] A.C. 289 (H.L.).

experts may be considered, if at all, only as part of the evidence and as a help to decide between conflicting expert testimony.[82]

In an earlier decision in the Supreme Court of Canada, Duff, J. wrote with regard to the expert witnesses:

> . . . if the evidence of such witnesses is conflicting or obscure the Court may go a step further and examine and construe the passages cited for itself in order to arrive at a satisfactory conclusion.[83]

But in *Drew Brown Ltd. v. The Orient Trader,*[84] Laskin, J., relying on *Allen v. Hay*, wrote:

> [The expert's] evidence was that the weight of authority accorded with the view he expressed, and I do not think it is open to me to re-examine all the authorities to see if they, on balance . . . support his evidence. At the most, I may look to his sources to see if his reliance on them is borne out.

An example of the strictness with which Canadian courts demand proof of foreign law may be seen in *Walkerville Brewing Co. v. Mayrand.*[85] The trial judge had dismissed plaintiff's action and in doing so had found that there existed in Ontario the business of exporting liquor from Canada to the United States "in contravention of the constitution and laws of that country." The Ontario Court of Appeal set the judgment aside, saying:

> One country does not take judicial notice of the laws of another, but, like any other fact, they must be proved. In this case there is no evidence of any law making the importation of liquor into the United States unlawful. There may be no moral doubt of the existence of such a law, and every one may know — or thinks he knows — of its existence, but Courts require legal evidence of material facts.[86]

PROBLEMS

Problem 1

In determining relevance and in assessing probative force against prejudice the trial judge relies on his own life experience and intuition. Is this judicial notice? Do the parties have the right to know how he is coming to his conclusion before he finally arrives at it? Do the parties have the right to lead evidence and make submissions to persuade him to take a contrary point of view?

Problem 2

The accused is charged with possession of marijuana for the purpose of trafficking. The accused maintains that the marijuana found hidden in the truck in which he was a passenger was placed there without his knowledge. The

---

82. *Ibid.*, at pp. 297-98.
83. *Allen v. Hay* (1922), 69 D.L.R. 193, 195 (S.C.C.). See also *Bondholders Securities Corp. v. Manville (No. 2)*, [1935] 1 W.W.R. 452 (Sask. C.A.).
84. (1972), 34 D.L.R. (3d) 339, 366 (S.C.C.).
85. [1929] 2 D.L.R. 945 (Ont. C.A.).
86. *Ibid.*, at p. 946. Compare *Saxby v. Fulton*, [1909] 2 K.B. 208, 221 (C.A.) where the English Court of Appeal was prepared to assume that playing roulette was lawful in Monte Carlo.

accused testifies that there was an opportunity for this to happen when they stopped at a restaurant and he was inside eating pizza. A pizza box containing part of a pizza was found in the truck.

During defence counsel's summation the following conversation ensues:

Defence Counsel: The half-eaten pizza in the pizza box supports my client's testimony . . .

Judge: What? Hold on . . . he said he ate the pizza *in* the restaurant didn't he?

Defence Counsel: Yes, but . . .

Judge: Well, then, the pizza box in the truck certainly doesn't support that story. If anything, the evidence of the pizza box points out an inconsistency that has not been explained.

Defence Counsel: With respect, your Honour, there is no inconsistency. It is not uncommon for a person to ask for a doggie bag — it is no different when it comes to pizza. Although this fact had not been proven, I would ask you to take judicial notice that a pizza box could serve as a doggie bag.

Judge: Judicial notice, huh? I'd like to hear what you have to say about this, Mr. Crown Attorney.

Crown Attorney: Your Honour, the law is that you may take judicial notice of facts only when they are indisputable. If this fact is not indisputable, and it is my submission that it is not, then you cannot judicially notice it and it must be proven. Since it has not been proven, then, as your Honour has pointed out, it does show an inconsistency and I would ask your Honour to consider this inconsistency when assessing the accused's credibility.

Defence Counsel: Your Honour, the law on judicial notice is not as clear-cut as my friend suggests. There is authority for the proposition that judicial notice may be taken of facts which are not indisputable. Professor Thayer suggests that taking judicial notice of a fact is to simply presume it until there is a reason to dispel the presumption. We ask you to judicially notice that, although it is not indisputable, it is not uncommon for a restaurant to supply a pizza box to a patron who has not finished his meal and would like to take it with him. If my friend has any evidence to rebut this presumption, she should have tendered it. Since the presumption has not been rebutted, the inconsistency your Honour referred to disappears and the pizza box supports my client's story.

Argument? Compare *R. v. Boissonneault* (1986), 29 C.C.C. (3d) 345 (Ont. C.A.).

Problem 3

Husband petitions for divorce on the ground of his wife's adultery. The evidence is established that during the period between 186 and 360 days before the birth of a child to her he had been continuously absent abroad, and that there had been no opportunity for intercourse between them. No other evidence was led. Can the trier of fact be satisfied beyond a reasonable doubt that the child was conceived in adultery? Compare *Preston-Jones v. Preston-Jones*, [1951] A.C. 391 (H.L.) per Lord Simonds and per Lord Denning in the Court of Appeal, 65 T.L.R. 624.

Problem 4

Plaintiff sues defendant for damages for injuries received in a running-down case. The accident occurred at the corner of Yonge and Queen Streets in the city of Toronto. As part of its proof of negligence, the plaintiff maintained that the defendant was driving in excess of the speed limit. By municipal ordinance the speed limit for a "business district" is 30 k.p.h. and evidence was led that defendant was travelling at 40 k.p.h. No evidence was led regarding the character of the intersection. Can judgment be given for plaintiff? Compare *Varcoe v. Lee*, 181 P. 223 (Cal. S.C., 1919) and *R. v. Snelling*, [1952] O.W.N. 214 (H.C.).

Problem 5

The accused is charged with possession of obscene material, which is by statute defined to include "any publication a dominant characteristic of which is the undue exploitation of sex." The term "undue" has been judicially interpreted to require that the work offend contemporary community standards. Counsel for the accused asks leave to file with the court catalogues and books containing reproductions of the works of certain masters and eminent contemporary artists that have been exhibited in galleries, churches and museums, and asks the court to judicially notice the community standards exampled thereby. Rule on the request. Compare *R. v. Cameron*, [1966] 2 O.R. 777 (C.A.), and *Popert v. R.* (1981), 19 C.R. (3d) 393 (Ont. C.A.).

Problem 6

The accused is charged with speeding in that he did travel at 70 k.p.h. in a 50 k.p.h. zone in the city of Kingston, Ontario. The street on which the accused was clocked was duly posted in accordance with the Highway Traffic Act, R.S.O. 1980, c. 198. At the close of the prosecution's case, the accused has elected to call no evidence and moved for dismissal on the grounds that it had not been proved that the maximum rate of speed was 50 k.p.h. Rule on the motion. Compare *R. v. Clark* (1974), 3 O.R. (2d) 716 (C.A.). See also *R. v. Ross*, [1966] 2 O.R. 273 (C.A.).

Problem 7

Plaintiff seaman sues for damages for injuries received through the negligence of a fellow officer while the ship was on the high seas. Suit is brought in Quebec and at trial the court finds the *lex loci delicti* to be the law of British Columbia. In Quebec the law of common-employment or fellow-servant rule was not recognized; in British Columbia it is recognized as a defence. The defendant did not plead nor lead evidence of the law of British Columbia. May the Quebec court judicially notice the law of British Columbia? If the plaintiff is successful in Quebec courts may defendant on appeal to Supreme Court of Canada seek that court's reliance on judicial notice? Compare *Can. Nat. S.S. Co. v. Watson*, [1939] 1 D.L.R. 273 (S.C.C.) and *Logan v. Lee* (1907), 39 S.C.R. 311.

6

Real Evidence

Authentication

1. AUTHENTICATION

Wigmore distinguished the three modes by which a trier may acquire knowledge: testimonial evidence, circumstantial evidence, and real evidence:

> If, for example, it is desired to ascertain whether the accused has lost his right hand and wears an iron hook in place of it, one source of belief on the subject would be the testimony of a witness who had seen the arm; in believing this testimonial evidence, there is an inference from the human assertion to the fact asserted. A second source of belief would be the mark left on some substance grasped or carried by the accused; in believing this circumstantial evidence, there is an inference from the circumstance to the thing producing it. A third source of belief remains, namely, the *inspection by the tribunal* of the accused's arm. This source differs from the other two in omitting any step of conscious inference or reasoning, and in proceeding by direct self-perception, or autopsy. . . . From the point of view of the litigant party furnishing the source of belief, it may be termed *autoptic proference*.[1]

His term "autoptic proference" has not gained much acceptance and the third source of belief is commonly referred to in England and Canada as real evidence.[2] The types or kinds of real evidence are infinitely variable and may affect any of the senses. Here we are content to explore some general principles applicable to all.

To be receivable, real evidence must of course be relevant and it will only be relevant to the matters in issue if the item proffered is identified as genuine, i.e., if the item tendered as an exhibit is authenticated to be what it is represented to be by its proponent. In a prosecution for assault causing bodily harm, a blood-stained shirt is not relevant evidence unless it is identified as having been worn by the victim on the evening of the altercation. There are functions here for both the judge and the jury. The judge must be satisfied that there is sufficient evidence introduced to permit a rational finding by the jury that the item is as claimed; the jury then weighs the evidence and determines whether the item is authentic.

This process, and the division of labours, may be illustrated by *R. v. Parsons*.[3] The accused were charged with conspiracy to use forged documents as if they were genuine. The prosecution's case was entirely dependent upon evidence obtained by the interception of private telephone communications. The interception was purportedly in accord with an authorization given by a judge pursuant to the provisions of the Criminal Code. For such evidence to be received, the trial judge must be satisfied that the authorization was valid, that the

---

1. 4 Wigmore, *Evidence* (Chad. Rev.), s. 1150, p. 322.
2. See generally Nokes, "Real Evidence" (1949), 65 L.Q.R. 57. McCormick, *Evidence* (2d ed., 1972), at p. 524 notes that "it will be seen variously referred to as real, autoptic, demonstrative, tangible, and objective."
3. (1977), 37 C.C.C. (2d) 497 (Ont. C.A.); affirmed (*sub nom. Charette v. R.*) (1980), 51 C.C.C. (2d) 350 (S.C.C.).

investigation authorized was carried out in the manner provided therein, that the authorization allowed the intercept of the parties to the particular conversation and that notice of an intention to introduce such evidence was given to the opponent; these conditions are set by statute and the trial judge must be satisfied with their compliance on a *voir dire*. The trial judge in this case was persuaded as well that he must also be satisfied that the voice was that of the party. On appeal, Dubin, J.A. for the court wrote:

> The determination of whether the statutory conditions precedent have been fulfilled rests exclusively with the trial Judge and are properly determined in a *voir dire*.
>
> Once the statutory conditions have been met, what the Crown must show is that the intercepted private communications are those of the person against whom it is tendered and accurately reproduce his words. The Crown's proof as to the integrity of the tape, its accuracy, its continuity, and voice identification, and that there has been no tampering nor alterations in any way all relate to the proof that the evidence tendered is an accurate reproduction of what it is alleged the person against whom it is tendered said. The weight to be given to that evidence is for the jury, and the admissibility of such evidence is not subject to any statutory conditions precedent, and should be dealt with in the same manner as any other issues of fact, which arise in every jury trial.

In *Cross on Evidence,* 4th ed., p. 61, the following appears:

> The question whether the maker of a dying declaration was under a settled hopeless expectation of death, a condition precedent to its admissibility at a trial for homicide, should on principle be decided by the judge. By way of contrast, the question whether a tape-recording was the original, being one which must ultimately be determined by the jury, *the judge need do no more than decide whether there is sufficient evidence to leave the issue to it.* [Emphasis added].

Counsel for the respondent Charette forcefully urged that the issue of voice identification went to the lawfulness of the interception, a view apparently shared by the trial Judge. He submitted that the lawfulness of an intercepted private communication, and hence the admissibility of evidence of an intercepted private communication, depended, *inter alia,* on whether those persons identified in the authorization are those same persons who are identified as having been intercepted, and hence (voice identification) is not simply a question of fact for the trier of fact, but is part of the larger question, *i.e.,* the lawfulness of the interception. It followed, in his submission, that it was a matter initially for the trial Judge who had to be satisfied on this issue beyond a reasonable doubt before the evidence could be left with the jury. With respect, however, I do not agree.[4]

The court was properly critical of the extent of the *voir dire* conducted as it tended to usurp the function of the jury. The Evidence Code proposed by the Law Reform Commission of Canada suggested:

> When the relevancy of evidence depends upon its authenticity or identity, the requirement of authentication or identification is satisfied by evidence sufficient to support a finding that the matter in question is what its proponent claims.[5]

---

4.   *Ibid.,* at p. 502 (37 C.C.C.). Agreeing with this distinction see McCormick, *Evidence* (2d ed., 1972), p. 555.
5.   1975, s. 46.

In the absence of agreement of counsel, real evidence, whether this be the gun, the drugs, a photograph or a letter, must be tendered through witnesses and be authenticated. There is no set procedure or questions that must be asked. The usual steps for counsel seeking to tender a piece of real evidence are:

1.   call a witness with personal knowledge of the object,
2.   ask the witness to describe the object before showing it to the witness,
3.   allow the witness to examine and identify it as genuine, and
4.   ask that the object be entered as an exhibit, with an appropriate stamp applied by the clerk.

how to get real evidence in

Sometimes the witness will not be able to identify the object as that previously seen. In such cases the accepted practice is to have it marked as an "exhibit for identification". Hopefully there will be a later witness to call who can properly authenticate it so that it can then be marked as an exhibit as a piece of evidence in the case. If entered as an exhibit in jury trials the jury is usually allowed to take the exhibits into the jury room during their deliberations. See further Lee Stuesser, *An Advocacy Primer* (1990) pp. 98-103.

PROBLEMS

Problem 1

The plaintiff is suing a manufacturer for damages. Plaintiff claims that a tool manufactured by defendant was defective in its design and as a result plaintiff was hurt. Plaintiff seeks to tender into evidence the tool so that the jury might examine the same and observe first hand the design. How should plaintiff go about authenticating the tool?

Problem 2

In a narcotics case, the prosecutor seeks to introduce a package of a green plant-like material which the RCMP found in the accused's pocket. Advise the prosecutor concerning the steps he needs to follow to introduce the package.

Problem 3

Plaintiff claims he suffered psychological damage as a result of drinking a bottle of ginger beer and discovering a snail at the bottom. The bottle has etched in the glass the name of the defendant's company "Stevenson Bottling Works." Is that sufficient to prove that the bottle came from the defendant's company?

2. DEMONSTRATIVE EVIDENCE

One needs to recognize a distinction between real evidence and demonstrative evidence. Demonstrative evidence, charts, models and the like are tools to assist the trier in understanding the evidence. Real evidence, the gun, the narcotics, the bloodstained shirt, tendered as an object within the courtroom is not a helpful aid but rather is evidence itself. Real evidence needs to be authenticated. With demonstrative evidence their worth depends on whether they are accurate representations of what happened. The judge needs to be satisfied that the demonstration will genuinely assist the trier of fact and not distort the fact finding process. There is concern that the demonstration might overpower the trier. In the end we can do little more than trust the discretion of the trial judge.

R. v. HOWARD AND TRUDEL
(1983), 3 C.C.C. (3d) 399 (Ont. C.A.)

[The accused were charged with first degree murder. Over a period of some four days at the trial, expert evidence was called with respect to four footprints. Nineteen feet five inches south of the body a complete shoe impression was located. Twelve feet west and four feet north there was a partial heel print. Two inches from the victim's head two partial heel impressions were found with one superimposed upon the other. Both inked and plastic impressions of the heels of the accused T's shoes were obtained. In addition a rubber silicone mould of the heel was obtained and photographed. Expert witnesses called by the Crown testified that T's right shoe had made the impression. The expert called by the defence disagreed with the evidence of the Crown's experts that Trudel's heel had made the impression.]

HOWLAND, C.J.O. (BROOKE and LACOURCIERE, JJ.A concurring):—

. . . .

The trial judge refused to permit Dr. Watt, [the defence expert], when he was giving evidence, to make an impression of Trudel's heel in plasticine so that he could demonstrate that the shoe could not make the right angle mark that appeared in the photograph (of the footprint impression). The trial judge refused to permit the demonstration. He stated:

> Court room demonstrations are normally not acceptable, they are subject to distortion, the exact conditions under which comparisons are made cannot be duplicated, it involves confusion and delay, and in this particular one the material with which he would work is highly susceptible to transformation in the handling of it in the jury room, and it really amounts to the creation of evidence in court which in my view unless it is a very simple matter is not permissible and this is certainly a discretionary matter and in my discretion I refuse to permit the witness to make the cast which you requested him to make.

Bearing in mind the importance of the footprint evidence and the fact that the Crown had had the opportunity to make ink and plastic impressions and a rubber silicone mould to assist its witnesses in presenting its evidence, the defence expert should have been given equal latitude in presenting the defence. It is true that what he wanted to do was somewhat different. It was not merely a case of producing a plasticine mould in advance of the heel of Trudel's shoe, but of demonstrating to the jury when he was giving evidence that the heel of Trudel's shoe could not make the right angle mark that appeared in the photograph. Counsel for the Crown stated that the Crown never disputed that Trudel's right shoe could not make a right angle turn; in his view the real dispute was whether the photograph of the footprint showed the corner of the heel, and the demonstration would not have been of assistance on this point. In *McCormick's Handbook of the Law of Evidence*, 2nd ed. 1972, it is stated at p. 536:

> Whether demonstrations in the form of experiments in court are to be permitted is also largely subject to the discretion of the trial judge. Unlike experiments performed out of court, the results of which are generally communicated testimonially, in-court experimentation may involve considerable confusion and

delay, and the trial judge is viewed as in the best position to judge whether the game is worth the candle. Simple demonstrations by a witness are usually permitted, and may be strikingly effective in adding vividness to the spoken word.

While such courtroom demonstrations are only permitted in rare cases, in my opinion this was such a case. It was a demonstration which Dr. Watt had always performed in such cases and it seems appropriate that he should have been permitted to undertake it. However, I am not prepared to say that the trial judge proceeded on any wrong principle. In the last analysis the decision whether to permit the demonstration was within his discretion and his refusal to permit it was not reversible error.

R. v. MACDONALD ET AL.
(2000), 35 C.R. (5th) 130, 146 C.C.C. (3d) 525 (Ont. C.A.)

[The accused M was a fugitive from justice. He and his co-accused V were the targets of a police "takedown" which did not go smoothly. As a result, M was charged with two counts of aggravated assault and one count of dangerous driving, and V was charged with possession of a restricted weapon, possession of a weapon for a purpose dangerous to the public peace and assault with a weapon. Twenty months after the attempted takedown, the police made a video in which they attempted to reconstruct and re-enact the takedown. The finished product reflected the recollections of four police officers. Defence counsel objected to the admissibility of the video at trial on the ground that it was more prejudicial than probative. The trial judge ruled that the video was admissible. The Crown played the video twice during the examination-in-chief of one of the police officers.]

Per Curiam:—

. . . .

We will first describe how the video was made and its contents, then discuss the applicable principles governing its admissibility and, finally, apply the principles to this case.

The evidence on the *voir dire* explained how the video re-enactment was produced and what it showed. The police acquired a car similar to the car MacDonald was driving and another car to be positioned behind the "suspect car". During the takedown, the car behind had been a large sport-utility vehicle, a Ford Explorer; its replacement in the video was much smaller, a 1987 Toyota. The location chosen for the video, apparently a deserted sand quarry, differed from the location of the actual incident, a controlled intersection with a traffic light in the town of Markham. The video lasted 20 seconds. Officer Brown testified that it showed the cars moving "much slower" than they did during the actual incident and, therefore, the length of the video was also longer than the time of the incident.

The video re-enacts the police's version of what occurred during the attempted takedown. Four police officers — Brown, Wright, Rodgers and Giangrande — played themselves, recreating what each claimed to have done during the incident. The video shows the four officers getting out of the emergency response unit van, which is partly blocking the suspect car. Three officers take up positions several feet in front of the car with their guns aimed at the occupants. All three are shouting loudly: "Police, don't move." Four seconds elapse between the police first shouting and the suspect car backing up. The camera shows the police from behind facing the suspect car. The camera is then set inside the car to show the driver's perspective looking out at the officers through the windshield. The police are clearly visible to the driver of the suspect car.

After the suspect car backs up a considerable distance, the camera shows the car from the outside, advancing on the officers. Brown, the officer nearest the passenger side, shoots twice into the windshield on that side of the car. Rodgers, the officer at the driver's window, fires four shots in rapid succession at the windshield on the driver's side. Red lines were added to the video to show the trajectory of the bullets but the trial judge ruled they be deleted before the video was shown to the jury. As the car moves forward on the video it hits Brown, who rolls onto the hood in a fetal position. The video ends with the car driving away, Brown still on the hood.

The video re-enactment took two hours to make. The finished product reflected the recollections of the four officers. Although each officer tried to recreate his own actions, the four discussed the incident among themselves before making the video.

We turn now to the applicable legal principles. A serious concern with videotaped re-enactments, particularly those created without the participation of the accused, is their potential to unfairly influence the jury's decision-making. Because a video re-enactment has an immediate visual impact, jurors may be induced to give it more weight than it deserves and, correspondingly, to discount less compelling or less vivid evidence which is nonetheless more probative of the facts in dispute. Several commentators and courts have warned against this danger. Dean Wigmore adverted to it in his classic treatise on evidence, *Wigmore, Evidence in Trials at Common Law* (1970), at s. 798a:

> In so far as such a [motion] picture has any value beyond a still picture, this value depends on the correctness of the *artificial reconstruction* of a complex series of movements and erections, usually involving several actors, each of them the paid agent of the party and acting under his direction. Hence its reliability, as identical with the original scene, is decreased and may be minimized to the point of worthlessness.

> Where this possibility is serious, what should be done? Theoretically, of course, the motion picture can never be assumed to represent the actual occurrence: what is seen in it is merely what certain witnesses say was the thing that happened. And, moreover, the party's hired agents may so construct it as to go considerably further in his favor than the witnesses' testimony has gone. And yet, any motion picture is apt to cause forgetfulness of this and to impress the jury with the convincing impartiality of Nature herself . . .

So too did Professor McCormick in his evidence text, *McCormick on Evidence*, 4th ed. (1992), vol. 2, at pp. 3-4:

> It has already been noted that evidence from which the trier of fact may derive his own perceptions, rather than evidence consisting of the reported perceptions of others, possesses unusual force. Consequently, demonstrative evidence is frequently objected to as prejudicial, a term which is today generally defined as suggesting "decision on an improper basis, commonly, though not necessarily, an emotional one." A great deal of demonstrative evidence has the capacity to generate emotional responses such as pity, revulsion, or contempt, and where this capacity outweighs the value of the evidence on the issues in litigation, exclusion is appropriate. Again, even if no essentially emotional response is likely to result, demonstrative evidence may convey an impression of objective reality to the trier. Thus, the courts are frequently sensitive to the objection that the evidence is "misleading", and zealous to insure that there is no misleading differential between objective things offered at trial and the same or different objective things as they existed at the time of the events or occurrences in litigation.

This danger increases when the videotape depicts not just the undisputed positions of persons and things, but one side's version of disputed facts. McCormick makes this point in discussing the admissibility of photographs, at p. 17:

> A somewhat . . . troublesome problem is presented by posed or artificially reconstructed scenes, in which people, automobiles, and other objects are placed so as to conform to the descriptions of the original crime or collision given by the witnesses. When the posed photographs go no further than to portray the positions

of persons and objects as reflected in the undisputed testimony, their admission has long been generally approved. Frequently, however, a posed photograph will portray only the version of the facts supported by the testimony of the proponent's witness. The dangers inherent in this situation, i.e., the tendency of the photographs unduly to emphasize certain testimony and the possibility that the jury may confuse one party's reconstruction with objective fact, have led many courts to exclude photographs of this type . . . the current trend would appear to be to permit even photos of disputed reconstructions in some instances [e.g., if pressing necessity].

In a comprehensive article on the subject, "Manufacturing Evidence for Trial: The Prejudicial Implications of Videotaped Crime Scenery Re-enactments" (1994), 142 *U. Pa. L. R.* 2125, David B. Hennes examined the high sensory impact of video images and their tendency to stay at the front of the viewer's mind. He summarized why admitting videotaped re-enactments may be unfair at pp. 2179-80:

> The danger of unfair prejudice presented by the videotaped re-enactment is a function of both the manner of the presentation and the content of the presentation. That danger is only accentuated by its stark lack of probative value. The availability heuristic suggests that the re-enactment will be readily recalled and heavily relied upon during the decision-making process. Individuals learn more readily through sight, and a key component of the learning process comes through the use of the television, an everyday source of entertainment and information. A television videotape, much more than other forms of demonstrative visual evidence, leaves a lasting impression on jurors' mental processes, since its vividness dictates that it will be readily available for cognitive recall. The videotaped re-enactment, because of its mental impressionability, is exactly the type of vivid information to which the availability heuristic grants cognitive priority during decision-making.

Mr. Hennes approved of the majority opinion of the Texas Court of Appeals in *Lopez v. State*, 651 S.W. 2d 413 (1983) at p. 416, banning video re-enactments. Burdock J. wrote:

> . . . We find that any staged, re-enacted criminal acts or defensive issues involving human beings are impossible to duplicate in every minute detail and are therefore inherently dangerous, offer little in substance and the impact of re-enactments is too highly prejudicial to insure the State or the defendant a fair trial.

In addition to the concerns about video re-enactments discussed by courts and commentators, we cannot ignore the reality that usually only the Crown has the resources to produce a video and thus, in many cases, the re-enactment will be an "extra witness for the state".

Despite these concerns, however, we think it would be unwise to lay down rigid rules governing the admissibility of video re-enactments. In an era of rapidly changing technology we would take a step backward were we to prohibit the use of video re-enactments in the courtroom. Further, an outright prohibition would hinder the efforts of today's advocates to devise new and creative ways to promote their clients' causes.

In our view, the preferable approach recognizes the dangers of video re-enactments but adopts a case-by-case analysis. As with the admissibility of other kinds of evidence, the overriding principle should be whether the prejudicial effect of the video re-enactment outweighs its probative value. If it does, the video re-enactment should not be admitted. In balancing the prejudicial and probative value of a video re-enactment, trial judges should at least consider the video's relevance, its accuracy, its fairness, and whether what it portrays can be verified under oath: see *R. v. Creemer*, [1968] 1 C.C.C. 14 at p. 22 (N.S. C.A.). Other considerations may be material depending on the case. And as with rulings on the admissibility of other kinds of evidence, the trial judge's decision to admit or exclude a video re-enactment is entitled to deference on appeal.

The appellants contend that another consideration should be necessity, whether the video is needed in the light of the other evidence in the case. According to the appellants, if a taped re-enactment merely repeats what witnesses have already testified to, it adds nothing new and accordingly should not be admitted. This argument, however, applies equally to other kinds of demonstrative evidence — charts, graphs, diagrams and photographs — that courts routinely admit to help the trier of fact understand the testimony of witnesses. The question of necessity is, therefore, better dealt with as yet another aspect of evaluating the prejudicial effect and probative value of a video re-enactment in a given case.

With these principles in mind, we consider the use of the video by the Crown in this case. We accept that the video was relevant because it sought to portray the incident that gave rise to the charges against the appellants. We also accept that Officer Rodgers testified under oath about the video and explained it to the jury. In our view, however, the trial judge erred in admitting the video for two main reasons: first, he failed to appreciate that its many inaccuracies undermined its probative value; and, second, he was not sensitive enough to the prejudice caused by re-enacting one side's version of events.

A video's probative value rests on the accuracy of its re-enactment of undisputed facts. This video failed to meet this requirement. It did not accurately represent the undisputed facts and even ventured into the realm of disputed facts. Variation from the actual facts may be permissible but only if the variation can be fully explained to and properly understood by the trier of fact. No explanation was given to the jury in this case.

Accuracy imports many different factors. LeSage J. observed in *R. v. Maloney (No. 2)* (1976), 29 C.C.C. (2d) 431 (Ont. Co. Ct.) at p. 436 that accuracy means "consistent with facts, agreeing with reality . . . reality therefore includes not only material objects but also the immaterial such as light, sound, and the dimensions of space and *time*". Discrepancies in various factors may affect the accuracy of a videotaped re-enactment, including time of day, time of year, weather conditions, lighting or visibility, speed of action, distance, location, physical characteristics of the individuals portrayed, physical characteristics of the "props", and complexity of the events depicted. Many of these factors are inaccurately represented in this video re-enactment. The following table shows how the undisputed evidence at trial about the attempted takedown differed from the video re-enactment of it:

Facts	Actual Takedown	Video Re-enactment
Time of year	June 20	February
Time of day	4:00 p.m.	Morning
Location	Markham intersection at stop light	Deserted sand quarry
Speed	Actual	Slower
Distance (of suspect's car from Officer Rodgers)	3 – 4 feet	Inches
Type of car behind the suspect car	Ford Explorer	Toyota

These inaccuracies distorted the reality of the takedown. The jurors were given a powerful and misleading image of what occurred, which could only have undermined their ability to fairly determine the crucial fact in the case, whether MacDonald could see that those who surrounded his car were police officers. Moreover, the video re-enactment was superfluous. The jury heard ample evidence from the Crown and the defence about what happened during the takedown. They were also given maps and diagrams of the scene. Overall, in our view, the video re-enactment had little or no probative value.

In contrast, the video was highly prejudicial. The trial judge dismissed the claim of prejudice by stating that the video re-enactment "is not more prejudicial than oral testimony". This is surely wrong. All of the authorities say the opposite. The video permitted the prosecution to put before the jury its own version of what occurred, distilled into a neatly packaged, compressed, and easily assimilated sight and sound bite. The violent, visual, highly impressionistic imagery gave the Crown an unfair advantage in this trial. Courts must be sensitive to how a video re-enactment that depicts only the Crown's version of disputed facts may distort the jury's decision-making and thus prejudice an accused's right to a fair trial.

In this case, the Crown's video re-enactment contradicted in material ways not just MacDonald's testimony but even the evidence of the Crown's ballistics expert. For example, the video depicts the police van cutting off MacDonald's car; MacDonald testified that he did not see the van. In the video the police are yelling loudly; MacDonald testified that he did not hear the police announce their presence. In the video the police are plainly visible in front of the car; MacDonald said that he did not see the police at first and then mistook them. On the video MacDonald's car backs up; MacDonald testified that the unmarked police car bumped him from behind. The video showed two shots fired into the front windshield on the passenger's side and four shots into the windshield on the driver's side; MacDonald's evidence, supported by the Crown's ballistics expert, was that shots were fired through the window on the driver's door.

These examples demonstrate how one-sided the video re-enactment was. This one-sided depiction of what occurred, presented in vivid and forceful imagery, was highly prejudicial. The distortion of even undisputed facts only added to the prejudice.

. . . .

[Appeals against conviction were allowed, the convictions were set aside and a new trial was ordered.]

For a discussion of the recent developments in using computer animation to demonstrate a litigant's position see D'Angelo, "The Snoop Doggy Dogg Trial: A Look at How Computer Animation Will Impact Litigation in the Next Century" (1998), 32 Univ. of San. Fran. Law Rev. 561.

3. DOCUMENTS

Documents are the most common form of real evidence. Their authenticity may be established by calling the suggested writer, by calling one who saw him write the document or who has an awareness of his handwriting, by direct comparison of the handwriting in dispute with handwriting known to be that of the suggested writer,[6] by the testimony of experts, or by admission of authenticity by the party against whom the document is tendered.[7] In addition, there are some documents which so regularly have significance in legal proceedings that the common law has developed rules allowing the documents to authenticate themselves because of the circumstances in which they are generated or kept in custody.

Two examples of such rules allowing authentication by circumstantial evidence are those affecting ancient documents and reply letters. If a document is over 30 years old, there are no circumstances indicating fraud, and it is produced from a place where its custody is natural, the circumstances call for it to be presumed authentic; the courts were also moved by the fact that circumstantial evidence would often be necessary as the maker or witnesses

---

6.   See, *e.g.*, s. 8, Canada Evidence Act, R.S.C. 1985, c. C-5. See also *R. v. Ewing*, [1983] 2 All E.R. 645 (C.A.) and *R. v. Abdi* (1997), 11 C.R. (5th) 197 (Ont. C.A.).

7.   As to this last form of authentication see the various Rules of Court, *e.g.*, see Forms 51A, 51B to Ont. Rules of Civil Procedure, O. Reg. 560/84. See also *Gen. Host Corp. v. Chemalloy Minerals Ltd.*, [1972] 3 O.R. 142, 164 (H.C.).

might no longer be available.[8] If a letter is received purportedly signed by Smith, the law will presume the letter authentic if it was received in response to an earlier letter; the reply indicates knowledge in the signer which, relying on the habitual accuracy of the mails, could only have come from the earlier letter addressed to Smith.[9] In addition to the rules developed at common law, the various Evidence Acts in Canada and the Criminal Code are filled with provisions to aid the authentication of documents. For example, the Canada Evidence Act[10] provides:

> **19.** Every copy of any Act of Parliament, public or private, published by the Queen's Printer, is evidence of that Act and of its contents, and every copy purporting to be printed by the Queen's Printer shall be deemed to be so printed, unless the contrary is shown.

> **20.** Imperial proclamations, orders in council, treaties, orders, warrants, licences, certificates, rules, regulations, or other Imperial official records, Acts or documents may be proved

> (a)   in the same manner as they may from time to time be provable in any court in England;

> (b)   by the production of a copy of the *Canada Gazette*, or a volume of the Acts of Parliament purporting to contain a copy of the same or a notice thereof; or

> (c)   by the production of a copy thereof purporting to be published by the Queen's Printer.

> **21.** Evidence of any proclamation, order, regulation or appointment, made or issued by the Governor General or by the Governor in Council, or by or under the authority of any minister or head of any department of the Government of Canada and evidence of a treaty to which Canada is a party, may be given in all or any of the following ways:

> (a)   by the production of a copy of the *Canada Gazette*, or a volume of the Acts of Parliament purporting to contain a copy of the treaty, proclamation, order, regulation or appointment, or a notice thereof;

> (b)   by the production of a copy of the proclamation, order, regulation or appointment, purporting to be published by the Queen's Printer;

> (c)   by the production of a copy of the treaty purporting to be published by the Queen's Printer;

> (d)   by the production, in the case of any proclamation, order, regulation or appointment made or issued by the Governor General or by the Governor in Council, of a copy or extract purporting to be certified to be true by the clerk or assistant or acting clerk of the Queen's Privy Council for Canada; and

> (e)   by the production, in the case of any order, regulation or appointment made or issued by or under the authority of any minister or head of a department of the Government of Canada, of a copy or extract purporting to be certified to be true by the minister, by his deputy or acting deputy, or by the secretary or acting secretary of the department over which he presides.

---

8.   See *Montgomery v. Graham* (1871), 31 U.C.Q.B. 57 (C.A.). Note that the document though authenticated as genuine may still be held inadmissible as violative of the hearsay rule. A hearsay exception for ancient writings deserves further consideration.

9.   See *Stevenson v. Dandy*, [1920] 2 W.W.R. 643, 661 (Alta. C.A.).

10.   R.S.C. 1985, c. C-5. And when statutory provisions cannot be satisfied, do not forget the common law: see *R. v. Tatomir* (1989), 51 C.C.C. (3d) 321 (Alta. C.A.).

22. (1) Evidence of any proclamation, order, regulation or appointment made or issued by a lieutenant governor or lieutenant governor in council of any province, or by or under the authority of any member of the executive council, being the head of any department of the government of the province, may be given in all or any of the following ways:

(a)   by the production of a copy of the official gazette for the province purporting to contain a copy of the proclamation, order, regulation or appointment, or a notice thereof;

(b)   by the production of a copy of the proclamation, order, regulation or appointment purporting to be published by the government or Queen's Printer for the province; and

(c)   by the production of a copy or extract of the proclamation, order, regulation or appointment purporting to be certified to be true by the clerk or assistant or acting clerk of the executive council, by the head of any department of the government of a province, or by his deputy or acting deputy, as the case may be.

(2) Evidence of any proclamation, order, regulation or appointment made by the Lieutenant Governor or Lieutenant Governor in Council of the Northwest Territories, as constituted prior to September 1, 1905, or by the Commissioner in Council of the Yukon Territory, the Commissioner in Council of the Northwest Territories or the legislature for Nunavut, may be given by the production of a copy of the *Canada Gazette* purporting to contain a copy of the proclamation, order, regulation or appointment, or a notice thereof.

23. (1) Evidence of any proceeding or record whatever of, in or before any court in Great Britain, the Supreme Court, Federal Court or Tax Court of Canada, any court in any province, any court in any British colony or possession or any court of record of the United States, of any state of the United States or of any other foreign country, or before any justice of the peace or coroner in any province, may be given in any action or proceeding by an exemplification or certified copy of the proceeding or record, purporting to be under the seal of the court or under the hand or seal of the justice or coroner or court stenographer, as the case may be, without any proof of the authenticity of the seal or of the signature of the justice, coroner or court stenographer or other proof whatever.

(2) Where any court, justice, coroner or court stenographer referred to in subsection (1) has no seal, or so certifies, the evidence may be given by a copy purporting to be certified under the signature of a judge or presiding provincial court judge or of the justice or coroner or court stenographer, without any proof of the authenticity of the signature or other proof whatever.

It must be borne in mind that these provisions merely authenticate the writing, merely establish that in fact the statement was made. If the statement is to be introduced to establish the truth of the matter stated, its receivability will be conditioned by the hearsay rule which will be examined later.

4. BEST EVIDENCE RULE

In contrast to the above rules which *facilitate* the proof of a document there is a rule which *requires* that, when the terms of a document are material, proof of the terms of the document must be by production of the original. The documentary originals rule, sometimes called the best evidence rule, existed even before witnesses were called to testify before a jury,[11] but as the new system of

---

11.   Thayer, *A Preliminary Treatise on Evidence at the Common Law* (1898), p. 503.

inquiry took hold, the rule was retained, as it was seen to be beneficial; production of the original avoided possible errors in copying or in oral evidence regarding the contents. Some text-writers in the 19th century spoke of a wider best evidence rule applicable to *all* forms of evidence which *required* the best evidence that could be given and also *allowed* the best evidence that could be given. Thayer described this as "an old principle which had served a useful purpose for the century while rules of evidence had been forming and . . . was no longer fit to serve any purpose as a working rule of exclusion."[12] Restricting the rule's use to documents, perhaps jettisoning its use completely in favour of the name "documentary originals rule," would bring needed clarity. As opposed to a general rule of exclusion for the other forms of real evidence, we would have then simply the application of common sense that the failure to produce the best evidence available to the proponent might yield a distrust for the evidence that was produced. Lord Denning summed up the present impact of the old rule:

> . . . the old rule that a party must produce the best evidence that the nature of the case will allow, and that any less good evidence is to be excluded. That old rule has gone by the board long ago. The only remaining instance of it that I know is that if an original document is available in one's hands, one must produce it. One cannot give secondary evidence by producing a copy. Nowadays we do not confine ourselves to the best evidence. We admit all relevant evidence. The goodness or badness of it goes only to weight, and not to admissibility.[13]

Notice that the documentary originals rule requires production of the original unless the proponent is unable to do so. Secondary evidence may be introduced if the proponent can satisfy the court that the original is lost or destroyed or is in the possession of another and cannot be obtained.[14] In addition, various statutory provisions have been enacted to provide for the introduction of copies when to require the original would produce great inconvenience. For example, section 29 of the Canada Evidence Act[15] provides for the receipt of copies of entries in bankers' books, section 30(3) for copies of records made in the usual and ordinary course of business, and section 31(2)(*c*) for copies of records belonging to or deposited with any government or corporation there defined.

---

12. *Ibid.*, at p. 495.
13. *Garton v. Hunter*, [1969] 1 All E.R. 451, 453 (C.A.). Followed in *Kajala v. Noble* (1982), 75 Cr. App. R. 149, 152 (C.A.) per Arkner, L.J.: "In our judgment the old rule is limited and confined to written documents in the strict sense of the term, and has no relevance to tapes or films." See also *R. v. Donald* (1958), 121 C.C.C. 304, 306 (N.B.C.A.) and *R. v. Galarce* (1983), 35 C.R. (3d) 268 (Sask. Q.B.).
14. See, *e.g.*, *R. v. Wayte* (1983), 76 Cr. App. R. 110. In *R. v. Betterest Vinyl Manufacturing Ltd.* (1989), 52 C.C.C. (3d) 441, 447-48 (B.C.C.A.), following the lead of *Wayte* and many cases to similar effect, Taggart, J.A., for the court, wrote: "As I read the text writers and the authorities we are no longer bound to apply strictly the best evidence rule as it relates to copies of documents and especially to photocopies of them. . . .'An over-technical and strained application of the best evidence rule serves only to hamper the inquiry without at all advancing the cause of truth.' "
15. R.S.C. 1985, c. C-5.

R. v. SWARTZ ET AL.

(1977), 37 C.C.C. (2d) 409 (Ont. C.A.), affirmed (*sub nom. Papalia v. R.*)
[1979] 2 S.C.R. 256, 45 C.C.C. (2d) 1, (*sub nom. R. v. Swartz*) 7 C.R. (3d)
185, 11 C.R. (3d) 150

[The accused were charged with conspiracy to possess money obtained by extortion.]

JESSUP, J.A. (ARNUP and ZUBER, JJ.A. concurring):—

. . . .

The only evidence incriminating Violi and Cotroni, and essential evidence against Swartz and Papalia, consisted of the tape recordings of three conversations which took place in premises at Montreal. The recordings proffered in evidence were re-recordings. The explanation for this was that, after re-recording, the original recordings had been erased and the tapes of them reused. The reason was that at that time it was not the practice of the Montreal police to use tape recordings as evidence in Court. The further reason was that electronic surveillance of the premises in Montreal had extended over a protracted period and the storage of the many resultant tapes presented a problem. As a result, a record only of significant conversations was kept by re-recording such significant parts on fresh tapes which were preserved.

It was argued that the re-recordings proffered were inadmissible as not being the best evidence of the conversations they reproduced. However, counsel made the significant admission that no question was raised as to the authenticity of the re-recordings.

Of the "best evidence" rule Halsbury states in 17 Hals., 4th ed., pp. 8-9, para. 8:

> That evidence should be the best that the nature of the case will allow is, besides being a matter of obvious prudence, a principle with a considerable pedigree. However, any strict interpretation of this principle has long been obsolete, and the rule is now only of importance in regard to the primary evidence of private documents. The logic of requiring the production of an original document where it is available rather than relying on possibly unsatisfactory copies, or the recollections of witnesses, is clear, although modern techniques make objections to the first alternative less strong.

The rule itself, in its relatively modern form, did not absolutely exclude evidence. It is stated by Lord Esher, M.R., in *Lucas v. Williams & Sons*, [1892] 2 Q.B. 113 at p. 116:

> "Primary" and "secondary" evidence mean this: primary evidence is evidence which the law requires to be given first; secondary evidence is evidence which may be given in the absence of the better evidence which the law requires to be given first, when a proper explanation is given of the absence of that better evidence.

Lord Denning would remove the question of secondary evidence entirely from the area of admissibility to that of weight. In *Garton v. Hunter*, [1969] 2 Q.B. 37 at p. 44 he said:

> It is plain that Scott L.J. had in mind the old rule that a party must produce the best evidence that the nature of the case will allow, and that any less good evidence is to be excluded. That old rule has gone by the board long ago. The only remaining instance of it that I know is that if an original document is available in your hands, you must produce it. You cannot give secondary evidence by producing a copy. Nowadays we do not confine ourselves to the best evidence. We admit all relevant evidence. The goodness or badness of it goes only to weight, and not to admissibility.

However, the counsel of prudence mentioned by Halsbury accords with the principle stated by *McCormick's Handbook of the Law of Evidence*, 2nd ed. (1972), p. 571:

Rule

> If the original document has been destroyed by the person who offers evidence of its contents, the evidence is not admissible unless, by showing that the destruction was accidental or was done in good faith, without intention to prevent its use as evidence, he rebuts to the satisfaction of the trial judge, any inference of fraud.

The same principle should apply to tape recordings.

. . . .

held

. . . In my opinion, the learned trial Judge properly received in evidence in the present case the re-recordings proffered.

In *A.G. Ont. v. Bear Island Foundation*[16] each of the parties was claiming possession of certain lands. The defendants sought to prove that they were entitled by producing oral history. The court received the evidence:

> Indian oral history is admissible in aboriginal land-claim cases where their history was never recorded in writing. However, this does not detract from the basic principle that the court should always be given the best evidence. The court has an obligation, first, to weigh the evidence and consider what evidence is the best evidence and, second, if such best evidence is not introduced, to consider making an adverse finding against the person who has failed to produce it.

5. VIEWS

If it is physically impossible to bring the real evidence into the courtroom, the courtroom may have to go to the evidence and take a view. Statutory authority for taking a view in criminal cases is found in the Criminal Code:

> 652. (1) The judge may, where it appears to be in the interests of justice, at any time after the jury has been sworn and before it gives its verdict, direct the jury to have a view of any place, thing or person, and shall give directions respecting the manner in which, and the persons by whom, the place, thing or person shall be shown to the jury, and may for that purpose adjourn the trial.
>
> (2) Where a view is ordered under subsection (1), the judge shall give any directions that he considers necessary for the purpose of preventing undue communication by any person with members of the jury, but failure to comply with any directions given under this subsection does not affect the validity of the proceedings.
>
> (3) Where a view is ordered under subsection (1) the accused and the judge shall attend.

and in civil cases is located in the various rules of court. For example, the Ontario Rules[17] provide:

> 52.05 The judge or judge and jury by whom an action is being tried or the court before whom an appeal is being heard may, in the presence of the parties or their counsel, inspect any property concerning which any question arises in the action, or the place where the cause of action arose.

---

16. (1985), 49 O.R. (2d) 353, 368 (H.C.).
17. Rules of Civil Procedure, R.R.O 1990, Reg. 194.

The decision as to whether a view will be taken is properly within the discretion of the judge, who will assess the importance of the evidence against the disruption of the trial necessitated by the adjournment.[18]

On the question of whether a view is evidence or is only a device for better understanding the evidence the courts have divided. In *Chambers v. Murphy* [19] the trial judge had taken a view of the motor vehicle accident scene. He rejected the defendant's evidence as to how the accident had taken place:

> When the defendant Peter Murphy told me that he stopped, that his vision was obstructed, and that he started into Tashmoo Avenue so that he could see, he told me what was not so.[20]

A new trial was ordered as the Ontario Court of Appeal believed it was

> . . . well settled and beyond all controversy that the purpose of a view by a Judge or jury of any place is "in order to understand better the evidence". . . .
>
> I have no doubt that the learned Judge proceeded quite innocently in taking the course he did, and indeed counsel assented to that course and were present at the time of the making of the tests. Nevertheless the facts ascertained from those tests were evidence that might properly have been received from a witness at the trial, but was not so given. The learned Judge in reality supplied that evidence himself and erroneously acted upon it.[21]

The decision of the English Court of Appeal[22] relied on for this holding was, however, later regarded by that court, per Lord Denning, as

> unduly restrict[ive of] the function of a view. Everyday practice in these courts shows that, where the matter for decision is one of ordinary common sense, the judge of fact is entitled to form his own judgment on the real evidence of a view, just as much as on the oral evidence of witnesses.[23]

It is preferable to regard the view as evidence and allow all reasonable inferences to be drawn therefrom as

> it is unreasonable to assume that jurors, however they may be instructed, will apply the metaphysical distinction suggested and ignore the evidence of their own senses when it conflicts with the testimony of the witnesses.[24]

Nevertheless, two appellate courts in Canada have recently reiterated the old-fashioned view![25]

---

18. See generally 4 Wigmore, *Evidence* (Chad. Rev.), s. 1164.
19. [1953] 2 D.L.R. 705 (Ont. C.A.).
20. *Ibid.*, at p. 706.
21. *Ibid.* See criticism of this case by Milner (1953), 31 Can. Bar Rev. 305.
22. *London Gen. Omnibus Co. v. Lavell*, [1901] 1 Ch. 135 (C.A.).
23. *Buckingham v. Daily News Ltd.*, [1956] 2 All E.R. 904, 914 (C.A.). This opinion was accepted by the Manitoba Court of Appeal in *Meyers v. Govt. of Man.* (1960), 26 D.L.R. (2d) 550 in preference to *Chambers v. Murphy*, [1953] 2 D.L.R. 705 (Ont. C.A.). See also *Re Allen and Caledonia*, [1965] 1 O.R. 391 (C.A.).
24. McCormick, *Evidence* (1972), p. 539. Regarding the use of real evidence by the jury see *R. v. Pleich* (1980), 55 C.C.C. (2d) 13 (Ont. C.A.) and *R. v. McCrea*, [1970] 3 C.C.C. 77 (Sask. C.A.).
25. See *Triple A Invt. Ltd. v. Adams Bros. Ltd.* (1985), 56 Nfld. & P.E.I.R. 272 (Nfld. C.A.), and *Swadron v. North York* (1985), 8 O.A.C. 204 (Div. Ct.).

6. PHOTOGRAPHS

Professor Wigmore preferred to regard photographs and recordings as a form of non-verbal testimony.[26] He wrote:

> . . . a document purporting to be a map or diagram is, for evidential purposes, simply *nothing, except so far as it has a human being's credit to support it*. It is mere waste paper — testimonial nonentity. . . . We must somehow put a testimonial human being behind it (as it were) before it can be treated as having any testimonial standing in court. It is *somebody's testimony,* or it is nothing. . . . But whenever such a document is offered as proving *a thing to be as therein represented,* then it is offered testimonially and it *must be associated with a testifier.* . . . Upon like principles a photograph may be admissible as the testimony of a qualified witness who instead of verbalizing his knowledge of what the picture portrays, adopts it as a substitute for description with words.[27]

He relied on the early English decision of *R. v. Tolson,*[28] where Willes, J. described the process:

> The photograph was admissible because it is only a visible representation of the image or impression made upon the minds of the witnesses by the sight of the person or the object it represents; and, therefore is, in reality, only another species of the evidence which persons give of identity, when they speak merely from memory.

For Wigmore two consequences followed:

> On the one hand, the mere picture or map itself cannot be received except as a non-verbal expression of the *testimony of some witness* competent to speak to the facts represented. On the other hand, it is *immaterial whose hand prepared the thing,* provided it is presented to the tribunal by a competent witness as a representation of his knowledge.[29]

R. v. SCHAFFNER
(1988), 44 C.C.C. (3d) 507 (N.S.C.A.)

MATTHEWS J.A. (PACE and CHIPMAN JJ.A. concurring):— After a lengthy trial, on February 2, 1988, His Honour Judge John R. Nichols found the appellant guilty of stealing moneys between February 27, 1987 and April 10, 1987, the property of the Nova Scotia Liquor Commission, of a value not exceeding $1,000.00, contrary to s. 294(*b*)(ii) of the *Criminal Code*.

. . . .

Between May, 1986 and April 10, 1987, the appellant was employed as a clerk at the Middleton store of the Liquor Commission. Due to inordinately high shortages there, the Commission conducted an internal investigation and then the matter was turned over to the Middleton town police. They requested that the Commission use its video surveillance

---

26. See 4 Wigmore, *Evidence* (Chad. Rev.), s. 1156. Compare Gardner, "The Camera Goes to Court" (1946), 24 N.C.L.R. 233. For a bibliography on photographs, motion pictures as evidence, see appendix to the decision *R. v. Maloney (No. 2)* (1976), 29 C.C.C. (2d) 431, 437 (Ont. Co. Ct.).
27. 3 Wigmore, *Evidence* (Chad. Rev.), s. 790. Regarding x-ray photographs see *id.,* at s. 795.
28. (1864), 176 E.R. 488 (Surrey Assizes).
29. 4 Wigmore, *Evidence* (Chad. Rev.), s. 1156, p. 218.

equipment. During the *voir dire* in respect to the admissibility of the videotapes John Nield, in charge of security for the commission, testified that he directed the installation of that equipment in the attic of the store immediately above one of the cash registers. Prior to joining the Commission Nield was a member of the R.C.M.P. and had used such equipment while with the force.

The evidence disclosed that attached to the video cassette recorder were a time/date generator and a tape stacker. The generator imprinted directly on the videotape the date in day, month and year, and the time in hour, minute and second. The stacker held three tapes, each of which provided four and a half hours of recording and automatically ejected a recorded tape and inserted another tape in the machine. There was no operator present during the filming, the procedure was automatic. Once installed Nield determined that it was functioning properly. Frank Cress, the manager of the store, was instructed in the use of the equipment and to keep accurate notations of the videotapes. The equipment was operated during business hours between February 23 and April 10, 1987. When a day's recording had been completed, the tapes were collected by Cress and forwarded to Kenneth Cole, the regional supervisor for the commission. They were then viewed by Nield, Cole and Detective Brown. During the *voir dire* Nield showed and commented upon four tapes depicting irregularities on the part of the appellant in conjunction with the detailed cash-register tape for each particular day under study. Nield was able to match a particular transaction recorded on videotape with its corresponding notation on the cash register tape. He was able to properly identify the appellant and pointed out four separate irregularities in the handling of cash by the appellant amounting to a total of $23.

It was over the objection of appellant's counsel that the trial judge ruled that the tapes were admissible in evidence. The appellant now says that the trial judge erred in law in doing so. Briefly put, the appellant's submission is that a photograph is not admissible by itself. It must be verified on oath by a witness as to its accuracy and fairness. He urges that the same principles should apply in determining the admissibility of films or videotapes. He quoted from the interesting and informative article by Elliott Goldstein, "Photographic and Videotape Evidence in the Criminal Courts of England and Canada", [1987] Crim. L.R. 384, p. 386:

A photograph may be authenticated by

    (a) the photographer;
    (b) a person present when the photograph was taken;
    (c) a person qualified to state that the representation is accurate; or,
    (d) an expert witness.

Witnesses in categories one and two, who see the event as it is being photographed, are eye-witnesses. An eye-witness testifies to two things: (a) what he saw, from memory, and (b) whether what he sees in a courtroom in the photograph, is the same as what his memory tells him he saw at the scene. Witnesses in categories three and four are not eye-witnesses, but can still authenticate a photograph either because of their familiarity with its subject matter or their knowledge of the operation of the equipment that produced it.

The issue of the admissibility of evidence at trial is a question of law and thus properly before us.

A photograph is admissible in evidence if it accurately represents the facts, is not tendered with the intention to mislead and is verified on oath by a person capable to do so. . . . I agree with Judge O Hearn that "This can be proved by anybody who is able to attest to those qualities . . .": *R. v. Lorde and Johnson* (1978), 33 N.S.R. (2d) 376 at p. 378 (N.S. Co. Ct.).

Here Nield described the equipment used, where it was located, the reasons why it was so located, that it was operating properly, and how the detailed cash register tape matched the video. As earlier mentioned he testified that he had used similar equipment as a member of the R.C.M.P.

The trial judge in determining the admissibility of the videotapes considered the appropriate factors, and was satisfied as to the quality of the tapes. We are unanimously of the opinion that those tapes were properly "authenticated" and that the trial judge did not err in law in admitting them into evidence.

R. v. NIKOLOVSKI
[1996] 3 S.C.R. 1197, 3 C.R. (5th) 362, 111 C.C.C. (3d) 403

[The accused was convicted of robbing a convenience store. The sole witness, the store clerk, could not identify the accused with any certainty and, when shown a videotape of the robbery during his testimony, did not identify the person in the videotape as the accused. The Crown called no other identification evidence. The trial judge relied on her own comparison between the accused and the robber in the videotape to conclude that the accused was the robber.]

CORY J. (LAMER C.J. and LA FOREST, L'HEUREUX-DUBÉ, GONTHIER, McLACHLIN and IACOBUCCI JJ. concurring):—Can a videotape alone provide the necessary evidence to enable the trier of fact to identify the accused as the perpetrator of the crime? That is the question that must be resolved on this appeal.

. . . .

The courts have long recognized the frailties of identification evidence given by independent, honest and well-meaning eyewitnesses. This recognized frailty served to emphasize the essential need to cross-examine eyewitnesses. So many factors come into play with the human identification witness. As a minimum it must be determined whether the witness was physically in a position to see the accused and, if so, whether that witness had sound vision, good hearing, intelligence and the ability to communicate what was seen and heard. Did the witness have the ability to understand and recount what had been perceived? Did the witness have a sound memory? What was the effect of fear or excitement on the ability of the witness to perceive clearly and to later recount the events accurately? Did the witness have a bias or at least a biased perception of the event or the parties involved? This foreshortened list of the frailties of eyewitness identification may serve as a basis for considering the comparative strengths of videotape evidence.

It cannot be forgotten that a robbery can be a terrifyingly traumatic event for the victim and witnesses. Not every witness can have the fictional James Bond's cool and unflinching ability to act and observe in the face of flying bullets and flashing knives. Even Bond might have difficulty accurately describing his would be assassin. He certainly might earnestly desire his attacker's conviction and be biased in that direction.

The video camera on the other hand is never subject to stress. Through tumultuous events it continues to record accurately and dispassionately all that comes before it. Although silent, it remains a constant, unbiased witness with instant and total recall of all that it observed. The trier of fact may review the evidence of this silent witness as often as desired. The tape may be stopped and studied at a critical juncture.

So long as the videotape is of good quality and gives a clear picture of events and the perpetrator, it may provide the best evidence of the identity of the perpetrator. It is relevant and admissible evidence that can by itself be cogent and convincing evidence on the issue of identity. Indeed, it may be the only evidence available. For example, in the course of a robbery, every eyewitness may be killed yet the video camera will steadfastly continue to impassively record the robbery and the actions of the robbers. Should a trier of fact be denied the use of the videotape because there is no intermediary in the form of a human witness to make some identification of the accused? Such a conclusion would be contrary to common sense and a totally unacceptable result. It would deny the trier of fact the use of clear, accurate and convincing evidence readily available by modern technology. The powerful and probative record provided by the videotape should not be excluded when it can provide such valuable assistance in the search for truth. In the course of their deliberations, triers of fact will make their assessment of the weight that should be accorded the evidence of the videotape just as they assess the weight of the evidence given by viva voce testimony.

It is precisely because videotape evidence can present such very clear and convincing evidence of identification that triers of fact can use it as the sole basis for the identification of the accused before them as the perpetrator of the crime. It is clear that a trier of fact may, despite all the potential frailties, find an accused guilty beyond a reasonable doubt on the basis of the testimony of a single eyewitness. It follows that the same result may be reached with even greater certainty upon the basis of good quality video evidence. Surely, if a jury had only the videotape and the accused before them, they would be at liberty to find that the accused they see in the box was the person shown in the videotape at the scene of the crime committing the offence. If an appellate court, upon a review of the tape, is satisfied that it is of sufficient clarity and quality that it would be reasonable for the trier of fact to identify the accused as the person in the tape beyond any reasonable doubt then that decision should not be disturbed. Similarly, a judge sitting alone can identify the accused as the person depicted in the videotape.

. . . .

I viewed the tape and it is indeed of excellent quality and great clarity. The accused is depicted for a significant period of time. At one point, it is almost as though there was a close-up of the accused taken specifically for identification purposes. There is certainly more than adequate evidence on the tape itself from which the trial judge could determine whether or not the person before her was the one who committed the robbery. The fact that the store clerk could not identify the accused is not of great significance. When the tape is viewed, it is easy to appreciate that the clerk might not have been able to properly focus upon the identity of the robber. The violent and savagely menacing jab made by the robber with a large knife directed towards the clerk suggests that self-preservation, not identification, may very reasonably have been the clerk's prime concern at the time of the robbery. Yet, the tape remained cool, collected, unbiased and accurate. It provides as clear a picture of the robbery today as it did when the traumatic events took place. The evidence of the tape is of such clarity and strength that it was certainly open to the trial judge to conclude that the accused before her was the person depicted on the tape. The trial judge was aware of the difficulties and frailties of identification evidence and acknowledged them in her reasons. Nonetheless, she was entitled on the evidence before her to conclude beyond a reasonable doubt that the accused was guilty. There was no need for corroboration of this tape.

SOPINKA J. and MAJOR J. dissenting:—

. . . .

It is significant that the judge's observations are entirely untested by cross-examination. Cross-examination in identification is of special importance. Here, not only was there no opportunity to cross-examine, but the substance of the judge's observations was unknown until the case for both the Crown and defence was closed. Not only are the judge's subjective observations not tested by cross-examination but they cannot be tested on appeal. In order to evaluate the reasonableness of the evidence upon which a trier of fact relies, the Court of Appeal must be able to examine all the evidence. All we can do is see one side of a coin that has two sides. All the assurances about the clarity of the video are of no avail if we cannot see the person with whom the comparison is being made.

In summary, this conviction was based on evidence that amounted to no more than the untested opinion of the trial judge which was contradicted by other evidence that the trial judge did not reject. This included evidence that the victim, a few days after the robbery, identified a person other than the accused as the more likely perpetrator of the crime. The trial judge simply relied on her own observations, the accuracy of which we are not in a position to assess. Having regard for the inherent frailties in identification evidence, I conclude that the conviction rests on a shaky foundation and is unsafe and unsatisfactory. I am satisfied that the verdict is unreasonable and cannot be supported by the evidence.

PROBLEMS

Problem 1

The accused is charged with assault causing bodily harm arising out of an altercation during a hockey game. The prosecution seeks to introduce a video tape taken of the game. Portions of the tape depict the action in slow motion and there are also stop-action shots of the accused striking the victim with his hockey stick. Defense counsel objects that the tape should not be received as it does not accord with reality. Rule on the objection. Compare *R. v. Maloney (No. 2)* (1976), 29 C.C.C. (2d) 431 (Ont. Co. Ct.).

Problem 2

The accused is charged with the murder of Joseph Brown. The theory of the prosecution is that the deceased died as the result of a fire deliberately set by the accused. The defence is alibi. The prosecution has tendered photographs of the charred remains of a body. These photographs are identified as accurate portrayals of the remains of Joseph Brown, by the two doctors who conducted the post-mortem examination. Defence counsel objects to the receipt of the photographs as there is no evidence of who took the photographs or developed them. Rule on the objection. Compare *R. v. Bannister,* [1936] 2 D.L.R. 795 (N.B.C.A.). Are there any other reasons for exclusion? Compare *R. v. Wildman* (1981), 60 C.C.C. (2d) 289, 293 (Ont. C.A.); reversed [1984] 2 S.C.R. 311, and *Draper v. Jacklyn,* [1970] S.C.R. 92. See also the transcript in the *Truscott* case reported in Friedland, *Cases and Materials on Criminal Law and Procedure,* 4th ed. (1974), pp. 740-45 and 4 Wigmore, *Evidence* (Chad. Rev.), p. 1157. And see McFarlane, "Photographic Evidence: Its Probative Value at Trial and the Judicial Discretion to Exclude it from Evidence" (1973-74), 16 Crim. L.Q. 149.

Problem 3

The accused was charged with possession of marijuana for the purposes of trafficking. The pertinent facts were not contradicted and are simple. The respondent was checked by two constables on a Burnaby street and found to be in possession of a cigarette and several baggies each containing a substance which was alleged to be the narcotic being the subject of the charge. On search, another baggie containing a like substance was found in the respondent's shorts and, later, when his home was searched, further substance asserted to be marijuana was found. The constable in charge took personal possession of all the substances, and on returning to the police station marked and initialed them and placed them in narcotic exhibit envelopes, sealed the envelopes, marked them with the respondent's name, the number given to the case, the date and his own initials. The officer placed all envelopes in his locked personal locker, to which he had the only key. They remained there for almost two days until he took them from the locker and deposited them in a steel security box provided for the purpose. Envelopes can be put in the box but nothing can be removed except after the box is unlocked by the laboratory personnel who had the combination or key. Several days later the envelopes were returned to the officer having been opened and then resealed with a red wax resin seal. To each envelope was attached a certificate of a duly designated analyst who certified that he had received by depository box from the said officer "a sealed and unopened" package bearing the markings placed by the constable as indicated above. The certificates all certified that the contents of the envelopes from which samples were taken were cannabis (marijuana).

The learned Provincial Court judge, upon motion for dismissal by respondent's counsel, acquitted him, giving the following reasons:

> I have no evidence as to where the exhibit was from one o'clock on March the 3rd other than it was in the deposit locker until it was received in the Crime Lab. on March the 7th. I have also no evidence as to who had access to the drug locker, or how, or when the drug was taken from the lockers to the Crime Lab., and by whom.

Are there grounds for appeal? Compare *R. v. DeGraaf* (1981), 60 C.C.C. (2d) 315 (B.C.C.A.).

7

Witnesses

1. COMPETENCE AND COMPELLABILITY

(a) Introduction

The testimonial qualifications of any witness are to be gauged according to that witness's ability, first, to observe, second, to accurately recall her observation, and, third, to communicate her recollection to the trier of fact. The witness's ability to communicate has two aspects: the *intellectual* ability to understand questions and to give intelligent answers, and the *moral responsibility* to speak the truth.[1] Each of these qualifications provides fertile ground for the cross-examiner to explore, for the benefit of the trier of fact, the credibility of the testimony offered. The early common law also erected rules which completely forbade testimony from those witnesses who could be seen from the outset as incapable of exercising the necessary powers of observation, recollection and communication. These witnesses were regarded as incompetent, and their incompetency was determined not by the jury but by the trial judge. As the common law matured the blanket rules were refined.

(b) Organic Incapacity and Oath

At common law, to be a competent witness a person was obliged to take an oath. In the earlier modes of trial, the oath was a direct appeal to the Almighty to witness the justness of the party's claim, and since it was then believed that a false appeal would be immediately visited with punishment, the claim would be upheld if the party survived the oath. As the mode of trial changed and witnesses informed the trier, the oath was given to the witness to guard against false evidence; the witness was advised that he was undertaking a solemn obligation, and it was hoped that bringing to his mind the threat of retribution from some Superior Being would cause the witness to be truthful:

> The object of the law in requiring an oath is to get at the truth by obtaining a hold on the conscience of the witness.[2]

Since this is the purpose of the oath it must be determined what form, if any, would act as an assurance of trustworthiness. Although in Canada a fear of divine retribution may no longer be necessary,[3] there must be some belief in the witness of something sacred called to witness his evidence. The form of the oath must then vary according to the witness. This was recognized in 1744 in *Omychund v. Barker:*[4]

---

1. See 2 Wigmore, *Evidence* (Chad. Rev.), s. 506, approved in *R. v. Kendall* (1962), 132 C.C.C. 216, 220 (S.C.C.).
2. Best, *Evidence* (1849), s. 161 as quoted in 6 Wigmore, *Evidence* (Chad. Rev.), s. 1816.
3. See below, respecting child witnesses.
4. (1744), 26 E.R. 15, 30, 31 (C.A.) per Willes, L.C.J. See *R. v. Lai Ping* (1904), 11 B.C.R. 102 (C.A.), paper oath administered wherein witness writes his name on paper which is

But oaths are as old as the creation. . . .

The nature of an oath is not at all altered by Christianity, but only made more solemn from the sanction of rewards and punishments being more openly declared.

. . . .

The form of oaths varies in countries according to different laws and constitutions, but the substance is the same in all.

. . . .

There can be no evidence admitted without oath, it would be absurd for him to swear according to the Christian oath, which he does not believe; and therefore, out of necessity, he must be allowed to swear according to his own notion of an oath.

. . . .

I found my opinion upon the certificate, which says, the *Gentoos* believe in a God as the Creator of the universe, and that He is a rewarder of those who do well, and an avenger of those who do ill.

As emphasis that there is no "correct" form of oath, see the Ontario Evidence Act which provides:

16. Where an oath may be lawfully taken, it may be administered to a person while such person holds in his or her hand a copy of the Old or New Testament without requiring him or her to kiss the same, or, when the person objects to being sworn in this manner or declares that the oath so administered is not binding upon the person's conscience, then *in such manner and form and with such ceremonies as he or she declares to be binding.* [Emphasis added.][5]

The traditional form of oath which developed in England, and which will be normally administered in Canada unless the witness requests otherwise, varies slightly between criminal and civil cases. In criminal cases the witness is addressed:

You swear that the evidence to be given by you to the Court (and jury sworn between our Sovereign Lady the Queen and the prisoner at the Bar) shall be the truth, the whole truth, and nothing but the truth. So help you God.[6]

And in civil cases:

You swear that the evidence to be given by you to the Court (and jury sworn) touching the matters in question, shall be the truth, the whole truth, and nothing but the truth. So help you God.

R. v. KALEVAR
(1991), 4 C.R. (4th) 114 (Ont. Gen. Div.)

[The accused was charged with theft under $1,000. He represented himself at his trial. When he came forward to testify he objected to the Bible that was offered to him for taking the oath. The court instructed that he be affirmed. The accused sought to give notice that he wished to raise a constitutional question.

---

then burned, and *R. v. Lee Tuck* (1912), 4 Alta. L.R. 388 (S.C.). See also *R. v. Ah Wooey* (1902), 8 C.C.C. 25 (B.C.S.C.), chicken oath administered. And see generally Silving, *Essays on Criminal Procedure* (1964), for a thorough description of many forms of oaths.
5.   R.S.O. 1990, c. E-23.
6.   See *R. v. Budin* (1981), 58 C.C.C. (2d) 352, 354 (Ont. C.A.). See also 6 Wigmore, *Evidence* (Chad. Rev.), s. 1818 and Crankshaw's *Criminal Code of Canada*, 7th ed. (1959), p. 622.

The court admonished him that he was to give his evidence under oath or affirmation. In the result the accused gave no evidence. A conviction was entered and the accused appealed.]

March 20, 1991. HALEY J.: —

. . . .

. . . [T]he appellant gave no evidence and the matter was put over for submissions. On the subsequent hearing the Crown suggested to the Judge that the wording of the *Canada Evidence Act*, . . . dealing with oaths was such that an oath need not be taken on the Bible, and that some other religious oath could bind the appellant as a solemn oath so that he could give evidence in the proceedings. The Judge held that the appellant had refused to be affirmed, and there was no other course now open to him to permit him to give evidence except to give unsworn evidence as a ''dock statement'' from the body of the Court. The appellant refused and a conviction was entered.

On this appeal, the Crown took the position that the Judge had erred in not giving the appellant the right to a religious oath other than on the Bible and, accordingly, the appellant had not had the opportunity to make full answer and defence. In those circumstances the Crown agreed that the appeal should be allowed, the conviction set aside and an acquittal entered. This was done as I was in agreement that a solemn oath was not limited to one taken on the Bible.

Section 13 of the *Canada Evidence Act* reads as follows:

> Every court and judge, and every person having, by law or consent of parties, authority to hear and receive evidence, has power to administer an oath to every witness who is legally called to give evidence before that court, judge or person.

The *Shorter Oxford Dictionary* . . . defines oath as ''a solemn appeal to God (or something sacred) in witness that a statement is true, or a promise binding.''

The use of oaths other than those taken on the Bible are not unknown in this country. *R. v. Ah Wooey* (1902), 8 C.C.C. 25 (S.C.) was a case in the Supreme Court of British Columbia in which the following decision was taken [p. 25 C.C.C.]:

> For taking the evidence of a Canton Chinaman not a believer in Christianity, the oath known as the 'chicken oath' should be administered instead of the less solemn 'paper oath', if the trial is for a capital offence.

In those circumstances an oath in writing to the King of Heaven was signed by the witness. ''The oath was then read out loud by the witness, after which he wrapped it in Joss-paper as used in religious ceremonies, then laid the cock on the block and chopped its head off, and then set fire to the oath from the candles and held it until it was consumed'' [pp. 26-27].

Clearly, Canada's emerging multi-cultural society requires an acknowledgement in the courts that the Judaic-Christian form of oath is not necessarily the only form of religious oath to be administered, and that persons of other religious persuasions should not automatically be given affirmation as the only alternative.

The appellant wishes to go further and have me decide his appeal on the ground that his right to freedom of conscience and religion under the *Canadian Charter of Rights and Freedoms* has been breached by the offering to him of an oath on the Bible. He argues strenuously that this freedom has been offended by the presence of the Bible in the courtroom to the exclusion of all other holy books, and that steps should be taken to remove any suggestion of paramountcy of the Bible in the court process.

It is perhaps disappointing from the appellant's point of view that this ground is not necessary to the success of his appeal. Throughout the transcripts it is plain that his main concern was the making of the constitutional argument. However, in the circumstances anything I might decide on the *Charter* issue would be only obiter dicta as unnecessary for the appeal, and the argument must wait until a new case with the proper factual basis can be found to place the argument before the Court for decision.

One would have thought this issue had been long settled. It is disappointing that the accused had to go on appeal to have his rights recognized. The Canada Evidence Act provides no form of oath. Any form of oath that will bind the witness's conscience is permissible. Section 16 of the Ontario Evidence Act provides that an oath *may* be taken by holding a copy of the Old or New Testament or "in such manner and form and with such ceremonies as he [the person taking the oath] declares to be binding." In civil or criminal proceedings any form of oath is allowed.

Rather than automatically proffering a Bible to every witness who comes forward, it might be better to ask each witness whether he or she wishes to be sworn and, if so, in what manner. A witness is normally frightened attending court and the court taking this initiative would avoid yet another burden on the witness of objecting to the oath. Or, counsel might best inquire of the witness what he prefers and make the announcement for him as he goes to the witness stand. Or, one might see the wisdom of the "oath ceremony" devised by His Honour Judge Peter Nasmith.[7] His Honour described the way in which witnesses in his court, over the age of 12, had been treated. His clerk addressed the witness as follows:

> Do you know that it is a criminal offence to intentionally give false evidence in a judicial proceeding?
>
> Do you solemnly promise to tell the truth in this proceeding?

His Honour noted that the answers were invariably "Yes" and the witness was then considered to be under oath.

Though the common law developed some flexibility in the form of the oath, still there were people excluded as witnesses though they were competent in all other respects: those who were children and had not yet formed any religious beliefs, those who had religious beliefs which forbade taking an oath, for example Quakers, and those who were atheists. These groups were accommodated by legislation enacted during the 19th century. See now section 14 of the Canada Evidence Act,[8] which provides:

> **14.**(1) A person may, instead of taking an oath, make the following solemn affirmation:
>
> I solemnly affirm that the evidence to be given by me shall be the truth, the whole truth and nothing but the truth,
>
> (2) Where a person makes a solemn affirmation in accordance with subsection (1), his evidence shall be taken and have the same effect as if taken under oath.

The Ontario Evidence Act provides:

> **17.**(1) Where a person objects to being sworn from conscientious scruples, or on the ground of his or her religious belief, or on the ground that the taking of an oath would have no binding effect on the person's conscience, he or she may, in lieu of

---

7.   See "High Time for One Secular Oath" (1990), L. Soc. Gaz. 230.

8.   R.S.C. 1985, c. C-5; am. S.C. 1994, c. 44, s. 87.

taking an oath, make an affirmation or declaration that is of the same force and effect as if the person had taken an oath in the usual form.[9]

(i) *Immaturity*

In *R. v. Brasier,*[10] a case of assault with intent to commit rape committed on a child under seven years of age had been proved against the prisoner by the testimony of the child's mother and another woman to whom the child had complained. The child was not sworn or produced at trial and the question was submitted for the opinion of the 12 judges:

> The Judges assembled at Serjeants'-Inn Hall 29 April 1779, were unanimously of opinion, That no testimony whatever can be legally received except upon oath; and that an infant, though under the age of seven years, may be sworn in a criminal prosecution, provided such infant appears, on strict examination by the Court, to possess a sufficient knowledge of the nature and consequences of an oath . . . for there is no precise or fixed rule as to the time within which infants are excluded from giving evidence; but their admissibility depends upon the sense and reason they entertain of the danger and impiety of falsehood, which is to be collected from their answers to questions propounded to them by the Court; but if they are found incompetent to take an oath, their testimony cannot be received. The Judges determined, therefore, that the evidence of the information which the infant had given to her mother and the other witness, ought not to have been received. —The prisoner received a pardon.[11]

Rule (margin note)

held (margin note)

Although there is no "precise or fixed rule" regarding age limits, it seems gradually to have come to be understood that a child under 14 years of age would be presumed incompetent and one over 14 years of age would be presumed competent.[12] The child of tender years needs to be tested prior to being sworn regarding both his appreciation of the nature and consequences of an oath and his capacity to observe, recollect and communicate.[13]

In *Horsburgh v. R.,*[14] Evans, J.A. noted:

> There is no definition of the words "tender years" and the competency of a child witness to give sworn or unsworn evidence depends not upon the precise age of the child but rather upon the actual degree of intelligence possessed by the witness and his appreciation of his duty to be truthful. The determination of the degree of intelligence and understanding of the child and his obligation to tell the truth, in my opinion, depends not only upon the inquiry conducted by the trial Judge as to the capacity and intelligence of the child, his appreciation of the difference between truth and falsehood and his duty to tell the former but also upon the conclusions which the presiding Judge draws from observing the appearance, demeanour, manner of

9.   R.S.O. 1990, c. E-23.
10. (1779), 168 E.R. 202 (C.C.R.). *R. v. Travers* (1726), 93 E.R. 793 (K.B.) reviews authorities suggesting that no witness less than nine years of age had been accepted. But see also *Strachan v. McGinn*, [1936] 1 W.W.R. 412 (B.C.S.C.) allowing that a child under six might be sworn.
11. *Ibid.*, at pp. 202-03.
12. See *R. v. Nicholson* (1950), 98 C.C.C. 291 (B.C.S.C.); *R. v. Armstrong* (1959), 125 C.C.C. 56 (B.C.C.A.).
13. 2 Wigmore, *Evidence* (Chad. Rev.), ss. 505-06. Consider the case of *R. v. Kendall, supra,* note 1.
14. [1966] 1 O.R. 739, 746 (C.A.).

speaking and deportment of the witness. The inquiry may be quite exhaustive in some cases and rather limited in others but the various factors which led the presiding Judge to form his opinion cannot always be found, nor should they be expected to be found, in the record of the proceedings. There are certain intangibles, which cannot be isolated, but which contribute to the formation of an opinion.

. . . .

A child of 14 is presumed subject to conviction and punishment under the *Criminal Code* and in my opinion, a similar presumption must apply to the competency of such child to give sworn evidence.

Professor Wigmore argued for abandonment of this rule of incapacity as well:

Recognizing on the one hand the childish disposition to weave romances and to treat imagination for verity, and on the other the rooted ingenuousness of children and their tendency to speak straightforwardly what is in their minds, it must be concluded that the sensible way is to put the child upon the stand and let it tell its story for what it may seem to be worth. To this result legislation must come.[15]

Legislation was enacted in England in 1885 to provide for the receipt of a child's evidence in prosecutions for unlawfully having carnal knowledge of a girl under the age of 13. The Act provided:

Where, upon the hearing of a charge under this section, the girl in respect of whom the offence is charged to have been committed, or any other child of tender years who is tendered as a witness, does not, in the opinion of the court or justices, understand the nature of an oath, the evidence of such girl or other child of tender years may be received, though not given upon oath, if, in the opinion of the court or justices, as the case may be, such girl or other child of tender years is possessed of sufficient intelligence to justify the reception of the evidence, and understands the duty of speaking the truth: Provided that no person shall be liable to be convicted of the offence unless the testimony admitted by virtue of this section and given on behalf of the prosecution shall be corroborated by some other material evidence in support thereof implicating the accused.[16]

In 1890 this legislation was copied in Canada[17] and in 1893 the legislation was amended to provide for the reception of such evidence "in any legal proceeding where a child of tender years is tendered as a witness,"[18] and this legislation was continued as section 16 of the Canada Evidence Act,[19] which provided:

16.(1) In any legal proceeding where a child of tender years is offered as a witness, and such child does not, in the opinion of the judge, justice or other presiding officer, understand the nature of an oath, the evidence of such child may be received, though not given upon oath, if, in the opinion of the judge, justice or other presiding officer, as the case may be, the child is possessed

---

15. 2 Wigmore, *Evidence* (Chad. Rev.), s. 509.
16. Criminal Law Amendment Act, 1885 ("An Act to make further provision for the protection of Women and Girls"), 48 and 49 Vict., c. 69, s. 4.
17. Criminal Law Amendment Act, 1890, S.C. 53 Vict., c. 37, s. 13.
18. Canada Evidence Act, 1892, S.C. 56 Vict., c. 31, s. 25.
19. R.S.C. 1970, c. E-10 [see now R.S.C. 1985, c. C-5]. Almost identical language is used by the provinces: see, *e.g.*, s. 18 of the Ontario Evidence Act, R.S.O. 1980, c. 145. For a good historical account of the passage of this legislation see McEwan, "Note, Child Witness and the Nature of an Oath" (1981), 13 Ottawa L. Rev. 426.

of sufficient intelligence to justify the reception of the evidence, and understands the duty of speaking the truth.

(2) No case shall be decided upon such evidence alone, and it must be corroborated by some other material evidence.

Similar legislation was enacted in each of the provinces. It is worth noting that the legislation was designed to permit the reception of evidence from a witness who could not take an oath because she did not understand its nature. The section erected certain conditions that had to be met prior to the receipt of such unsworn evidence: the court had to be satisfied that the child was "possessed of sufficient intelligence to justify the reception of the evidence, and understands the duty of speaking the truth." The conditions demanded an examination of the child's capacity for observation, recollection and communication, the latter embracing both intelligence in understanding questions and framing answers and an awareness of a moral obligation to speak the truth. The section described the conditions necessary for receiving unsworn evidence. The section never intended and does not prescribe the conditions for the receipt of sworn evidence. There was no need to prescribe those conditions as they were settled by the common law.[20]

At common law the witness to be sworn was required to understand the nature and consequences of an oath. In the great case of *Omychund v. Barker*[21] the issue was the receipt in evidence of a deposition sworn to by a person of the Gentoo religion. It was objected that to be admissible in an English court the witness must "take the oath upon the holy Evangelists",[22] but it was ruled contrary, with Lord Chief Justice Willes stating:

> Though I have shewn that an Infidel in general cannot be excluded from being a witness, and though I am of opinion that infidels who believe a God, and future rewards and punishments in the other world, may be witnesses; yet I am as clearly of opinion, that if they do not believe a God, or future rewards and punishments, they ought not to be admitted as witnesses.[23]

After a period of uncertainty over whether the punishment apprehended must be in a future life, it was resolved in England:

> Therefore there is no necessity that the person taking the oath should believe that he will be liable to be punished in a future state. If there be any belief in a religion according to which it is supposed that a Supreme Being would punish a man in this world for doing wrong, that is enough; but if he does not believe in a God, or if believing in a God he does not think that God will either reward or punish him in this world or the next, in either case according to the law of England as here declared a man cannot be a witness in any case, or under any circumstances.[24]

---

20. See *R. v. Antrobus* (1946), 87 C.C.C. 118 (B.C.C.A.).
21. (1744), 26 E.R. 15 (C.A.).
22. The objector relied on Lord Coke but on this Willes, L.C.J. remembered: "Lord Coke is a very great lawyer, but our Saviour and St. *Peter* are in this respect much better authorities than a person possessed with such narrow notions . . . Our Saviour and St. *Peter* have said, *God is no respecter of persons.*" *Ibid.*, at p. 30.
23. *Ibid.*, at p. 31.
24. *A.G. v. Bradlaugh* (1885), 14 Q.B.D. 667, 697 per Brett, M.R. Curiously, the authority for his statement is another report of Willes, C.J. in *Omychund v. Barker.* Wigmore suggests

The requirement that the child display an awareness of both the nature and consequences of an oath, an awareness of retribution for falsehood from a Supreme Being, continued unchallenged as the law in Canada[25] until *R. v. Bannerman*.[26] In that case the child witness appeared to realize that it was "bad" to tell a lie, that at "catechism" they had told him to tell the truth, but he had no awareness of the consequences of a falsehood. The defence argued that the child could not be sworn unless he could answer that a lie would cause him to go to hell. The transcript on this point concludes:

Q.   (defence counsel, Walsh): Now what would happen to you if you didn't tell the truth, do you know?

A.   No.

Walsh: That is all I have to ask.

Crown: May the witness be sworn, your Honour?

Court: I see the Magistrate had him sworn. I didn't realize that. I think I would rule he should be sworn. I think he knows what it means.

The Court of Appeal dismissed the accused's appeal saying:

The question was phrased by counsel and had to be answered as it was put. The most learned moral theologian compelled to answer that particular question must have given the same answer as young Spence. By his answer this child was not admitting ignorance in an area where he ought to have been better informed.

It would be wrong to teach this child to give any other answer to the question. To encourage him to say that he *knew* as a fact that the result of not telling the truth was that he *would* go to hell or that he *would inevitably* be punished by God either in the present or future life would be to ask him to contradict his Christian belief in the forgiveness of sins and the mercy of God.

. . . .

In my opinion, all that is required when one speaks of an understanding of the "consequences" of an oath is that the child appreciates it is assuming a moral obligation.

. . . .

. . . the Canadian courts, in *Rex v. Antrobus* and in cases following that decision, have fallen into error: (1) In adopting the word "consequences" from *Rex v. Brasier*, and giving insufficient recognition to the absence of that word in sec. 16 of the *Canada Evidence Act*; and (2) Having adopted the word, interpreting it to mean "the spiritual retribution which follows the telling of a lie" rather than "the solemn assumption before God of a moral obligation to speak the truth."[27]

The court noted that the section under review did not use the word *consequences*, and only referred to understanding the *nature* of an oath. Since the purpose of the legislation was to define the conditions for receiving unsworn evidence, and

as if here kid did this logical reasoning in his head!!

---

the two reports of the same judgment gave rise to the earlier period of uncertainty: 6 Wigmore, *Evidence* (Chad. Rev.), s. 1817, p. 385.

25.   See *R. v. Antrobus*, *supra*, note 20, and followed after the *Bannerman* decision in *R. v. Hampton* (1966), 55 W.W.R. 432 (B.C.C.A.); *R. v. Dyer* (1971), 5 C.C.C. (2d) 376 (B.C.C.A.); and *R. v. McKay*, [1975] 4 W.W.R. 235 (B.C.C.A.).

26.   (1966), 55 W.W.R. 257 (Man. C.A.); affirmed without reasons (1966), 57 W.W.R. 736 (S.C.C.).

27.   *Ibid.*, at pp. 278, 282, 284 and 285.

not the requirements for taking an oath, quaere how much should be read into that omission. The court further noted that its interpretation was necessary, since otherwise a child witness who only understood the nature of an oath would be prohibited from giving sworn or unsworn evidence. Again, having regard to the purpose of the legislation, the intention is clear that a child witness who could not take an oath, who could not appreciate the nature or the consequences of an oath, would be permitted to give unsworn evidence. That part of the judgment which stresses that awareness of consequences forms no part of the requirement for sworn testimony produces a problem. The only requirement then remaining is that the child understands that there is a moral obligation to speak the truth. Indeed, in *Reference re R. v. Truscott*,[28] the majority in the Supreme Court of Canada wrote:

> We are of opinion that the learned trial judge properly exercised the discretion entrusted to him and that there were reasonable grounds for his concluding that both Jocelyne Goddette and Arnold George *understood the moral obligation of telling the truth.* [Emphasis added.]

Test

This was later referred to in *Horsburgh v. R.*[29] as

> the test so set out must be considered to be that upon which the competency of a child of tender years to be sworn must now be determined.

unsworn v sworn

If all that is required to give sworn evidence is that the child understand he has a moral obligation to speak the truth, how does that requirement differ from the requirement for giving unsworn evidence, which is that the child "understands the duty of speaking the truth"?[30]

Perhaps the answer lies in the second branch of *Bannerman*: that "consequences" deserves a new interpretation for this modern age[31] and is limited to a recognition by the witness that an oath is a "solemn assumption before God of a moral obligation to speak the truth."

In *R. v. Budin*[32] the Ontario Court of Appeal sought to distinguish:

> ... "*nature of an oath*" [is] required to be understood as opposed to a mere understanding of the "*duty of speaking the truth.*"

The court agreed that the child witness need not understand the spiritual consequences of an oath but maintained:

---

28. [1967] S.C.R. 309, 368.
29. (1967), 63 D.L.R. (2d) 699, 728 (S.C.C.) per Spence, J.
30. See the attempt in *R. v. Dinsmore*, [1974] 5 W.W.R. 121 (Alta. S.C., McDonald, J.) to "explain" *Bannerman* and *Sankey v. R.*, [1927] S.C.R. 436 that "consequences" may mean "temporal consequences" which in turn may mean "moral obligation." With respect, his rejection, at p. 125, of *R. v. Antrobus*, *supra*, note 19, as dated by new English legislation, is questionable.
31. In *Horsburgh v. R.*, [1966] 1 O.R. 739, 755 (C.A.) Laskin, J.A., as he then was, remarked: "... at a distance of some 200 years from *Omychund v. Barker* ... the contention that competency of a witness depends on demonstration that he or she is fearful of divine retribution (as an exclusive test) rather than earthly justice as the consequences of false testimony, is highly talismanic. The common law deserves better than that at the hands of the judiciary in the 20th century."
32. (1981), 58 C.C.C. (2d) 352, 355 (Ont. C.A.).

God &
truth speaking

. . . the trial Judge's questioning should establish whether or not the child believes in God or another Almighty and whether he appreciates that, in giving the oath, he is telling such Almighty that what he will say will be the truth. A moral obligation to tell the truth is implicit in such belief and appreciation.[33]

The *Budin* case also emphasized that the counsel who tenders the child witness should instruct the child in the nature of an oath, and the child should be examined by the court, and not cross-examined on the matter by opposing counsel.

-oven truth speaking

In *R. v. Fletcher* [34] the Ontario Court of Appeal, however, reversed its position and decided that no inquiry need be made as to whether the child believes or disbelieves in God or a Supreme Being when seeking to determine whether the child understands the nature of an oath. An awareness in the child of the moral obligation of speaking the truth is sufficient. Again the problem is raised, how does that differ from the duty to speak the truth? The court adopted the reasoning in an English case as apposite in establishing guidelines to be followed by the trial judge:

> The important consideration, we think, when a judge has to decide whether a child should properly be sworn, is whether the child has a sufficient appreciation of the solemnity of the occasion, and the added responsibility to tell the truth, which is involved in taking an oath, over and above the duty to tell the truth which is an ordinary duty of normal social conduct.[35]

R. v. KHAN
[1990] 2 S.C.R. 531, 79 C.R. (3d) 1, 59 C.C.C. (3d) 92

[At the trial of the accused on a charge of sexual assault, the Crown sought to have the victim of the assault testify. The Court of Appeal found that the trial judge was right in deciding that the child should not be sworn but applied the wrong test in determining that the child could not give unsworn evidence.]

McLACHLIN, J. (LAMER, C.J.C., WILSON, SOPINKA and GONTHIER, JJ., concurring):—

. . . .

T. was called as a witness at the trial. She was four years and eight months old. Questioning revealed that she did not understand what the Bible was and did not understand the nature of telling the truth "in court". The Crown did not contend that she was competent to give evidence under oath. It submitted, however, that her unsworn evidence should be received under s. 16 of the *Canada Evidence Act*. . . . The trial judge refused to receive T.'s unsworn evidence on the ground that while she possessed sufficient intelligence to justify the reception of the evidence, he was not satisfied that she understood the duty of speaking the truth.

. . . .

I agree with the Court of Appeal that the trial judge made the two errors to which it referred. He erred first in applying the *Bannerman* test to s. 16 of the *Evidence Act* and emphasizing that T. did not understand what it meant to lie "to the court". While the distinction between the ability to testify under oath and the ability to give unsworn evidence

---

33.   *Ibid.*, at p. 356. Followed in *Roberts v. R.* (1982), 27 C.R. (3d) 244 (Ont. H.C.).
34.   (1983), 1 C.C.C. (3d) 370 (Ont. C.A.).
35.   *Ibid.*, at p. 380, quoting Bridge, L.J. in *R. v. Hayes*, [1977] 2 All E.R. 288 (C.A.).

under s. 16 has been narrowed by rejection in cases such as *Bannerman* of the need for a religious understanding of the oath, it has not been eliminated. Before a person can give evidence under oath, it must be established that the oath in some way gets a hold on his conscience, that there is an appreciation of the significance of testifying in court under oath. It was wrong to apply this test, which T. clearly did not meet, to s. 16, where the only two requirements for reception of the evidence are sufficient intelligence and an understanding of the duty to tell the truth.

s. 16

The trial judge also erred in placing critical weight on the child's young age. The Act makes no distinction between children of different ages. The trial judge in effect found that T. met the two requirements for permitting a child to testify under s. 16, but, emphasizing her immaturity, rejected her evidence. He found that T. had sufficient intelligence, and conceded that she "seemed to be aware at least of the consequences of telling a lie". This is clear from T.'s evidence, as revealed by the following portions of the transcript:

Q.   Yes, and do you know what it is to tell the truth? You're sort of shrugging your shoulders there and smiling. Do you know what it is to tell a lie?

A.   U-hmm.

Q.   What's a lie?

A.   If you say you cleaned up the room and you didn't, and your mother and your father went to see it and it's messy, that's a lie.

Q.   I see. What happens when you tell a lie?

A.   The parent spank their bum.

. . . . .

Q.   I see. You're doing just fine. Tell me, what else happens to you if you tell a lie?

A.   I get spanked and I get sent in my room and I get cleaned up and I cry and I come back out and I not cry, and that's okay.

Q.   And then everything is fine, is it?

A.   (Nod)

Age shouldn't be a determinative issue

Having found that the two requirements for reception of the evidence under s. 16 had been fulfilled, the trial judge erred in letting himself be swayed by the young age of the child. Were that a determinative consideration, there would be danger that offences against very young children could never be prosecuted.[36]

It is important to recognize that even when sworn, the child's evidence has traditionally been regarded with some circumspection. In *Horsburgh v. R.*,[37] Spence, J. said:

The view expressed by the learned trial Judge is not only that the evidence of children, once sworn, must be received, but it must be treated as that of a competent adult witness. In my opinion, this is a serious misdirection, as the witnesses, despite the fact that it was determined, in my opinion properly, that they were capable of being sworn, were nevertheless child witnesses and their testimony bore all the frailties of testimony of children, such frailties as Judson, J., in this Court referred to

---

36.   See Bessner, "*Khan*: Important Strides Made by the Court Respecting Children's Evidence" (1990), 79 C.R. (3d) 15.

37.   [1968] 2 C.C.C. 288, 320 (S.C.C.).

in *R. v. Kendall* .... The evidence of such children was, as Judson, J., pointed out, subject to the difficulties related to (1) capacity of observation, (2) capacity to recollect, (3) capacity to understand questions put and frame intelligent answers, and (4) the moral responsibility of the witness. It is this fourth difficulty which is very marked in the present case.

We should note, however, that the difficulties enumerated as particularly referable to the evidence of children are, on reflection, the difficulties inherent in the testimony of all witnesses, including adults!

Dr. Haka-Ikse explained:

Children are not necessarily incompetent morally or cognitively to testify as implied by the present legal system. The assumptions about the testimonial limitations of children do not as an example take into consideration the significant differences between pre-school and adolescent children just under 14 years of age. Conversely, the law considers as competent witness any individual after his or her 14th birthday, which is a totally arbitrary division. Also, the law fails to consider the very wide range of verbal, cognitive and perceptual abilities between children of the same age. The assumption that every individual of older age has the necessary moral judgement, impartiality, objectivity and rationality to give competent testimony is at best questionable. Long pediatric experience in interviewing and coming to know sufficiently close large numbers of pre-latency and latency age children and their parents, indicate that children are able to talk about events that are important to them with simplicity, candor and without excursions to fantasy. The normal pre-schooler or young school age child may have fears about ghosts or the boogey man (and so do some adults by the way) but he or she does not mistake the parent, the babysitter or the teacher as the ghost or the monster. Many children have imaginary companions but they only play with or talk to them in the privacy of their room. The memory of children is often surprising. I have seen 4 and 5 year olds returning to the clinic for a visit after several months and remember where they had sat or where the toys were kept. Conversely the memory of some parents I interview is subjective, bound to interpretation rather than facts, indicating poor recall or understanding of events and often being colored by the parents' emotional status and wishful thinking. The competence of a person to present facts either in giving medical history or in testifying in court, depends on the particular individual's qualities and is not a function of age. I recall many situations when parents interviewed in the presence of their child turn to the child for assistance in answering some questions they ignore or cannot recall the answers. In other instances I recall children interrupting parents to correct or clarify what the parents are reporting. In terms of moral judgement although it is true that the younger the individual is the more he or she relies on authority figures to define or set moral standards rather than to absolute moral imperatives, and their actions are not perceived as "bad" as long as nobody knows about them. The same is true for a good number of adults. Discrimination against children by the law on such grounds is developmentally unfounded and unconstitutional.[38]

---

38.   Haka-Ikse, "The Child as Witness in Sexual Abuse Cases: A Developmental Perspective," unreported paper delivered September 10, 1985, University of Toronto. See also Goodman, "The Child Witness" (1984), 40 J. of Social Issues 157; Wehrspann and Steinhauer, "Assessing the Credibility of Young Children's Allegations of Sexual Abuse" (1987), 32 Can. J. of Psychiatry 610, 615.

R. v. W. (R.)

[1992] 2 S.C.R. 122, 13 C.R. (4th) 257, 74 C.C.C. (3d) 134

[The accused was charged with indecent assault, gross indecency and sexual assault against three young girls. The evidence of the oldest child, S.W., was internally consistent. The evidence of the two younger children, however, revealed a number of inconsistencies and was contradicted in some respects. The accused was convicted on all counts and appealed. The convictions were set aside on the basis that there was no confirmatory evidence and the evidence of the younger children was fraught with inaccuracy. The Crown appealed.]

McLACHLIN, J. (LA FOREST, L'HEUREUX-DUBÉ, GONTHIER, CORY, and IACOBUCCI, JJ. concurring):—

. . . .

The following is the text of the Court of Appeal's endorsement:

> This case has caused us very great concern. The case has been carefully argued. We recognize the advantage of the trial judge, but also the responsibility of this court. . . . Giving the matter our best consideration, we are all of the opinion that on this evidence these convictions cannot safely stand. There was really no confirmatory evidence, the evidence of the two younger children was fraught with inaccuracy and in the case of the older children [it was] perfectly clear that neither was aware or concerned that anything untoward occurred which is really the best test of the quality of the acts. The appeal is allowed, the conviction is set aside and an acquittal is entered.

. . . .

. . . I pause to consider the general question of how courts should approach the evidence of young children. The law affecting the evidence of children has undergone two major changes in recent years. The first is removal of the notion, found at common law and codified in legislation, that the evidence of children was inherently unreliable and therefore to be treated with special caution. Thus, for example, the requirement that a child's evidence be corroborated has been removed. . . . The repeal of provisions creating a legal requirement that children's evidence be corroborated does not prevent the judge or jury from treating a child's evidence with caution where such caution is merited in the circumstances of the case. But it does revoke the assumption formerly applied to all evidence of children, often unjustly, that children's evidence is always less reliable than the evidence of adults. So if a court proceeds to discount a child's evidence automatically, without regard to the circumstances of the particular case, it will have fallen into an error.

The second change in the attitude of the law toward the evidence of children in recent years is a new appreciation that it may be wrong to apply adult tests for credibility to the evidence of children. One finds emerging a new sensitivity to the peculiar perspectives of children. Since children may experience the world differently from adults, it is hardly surprising that details important to adults, like time and place, may be missing from their recollection. Wilson J. recognized this in *R. v. B. (G.)*, [1990] 2 S.C.R. 30, at pp. 54-55, when, in referring to submissions regarding the court of appeal judge's treatment of the evidence of the complainant, she said that:

> . . . it seems to me that he was simply suggesting that the judiciary should take a common sense approach when dealing with the testimony of young children and not impose the same exacting standard on them as it does on adults. However, this is not to say that the courts should not carefully assess the credibility of child witnesses and I do not read his reasons as suggesting that the standard of proof must be lowered when dealing with children as the appellants submit. Rather, he was expressing

concern that a flaw, such as a contradiction, in a child's testimony should not be given the same effect as a similar flaw in the testimony of an adult. I think his concern is well founded and his comments entirely appropriate. While children may not be able to recount precise details and communicate the when and where of an event with exactitude, this does not mean that they have misconceived what happened to them and who did it. In recent years we have adopted a much more benign attitude to children's evidence, lessening the strict standards of oath taking and corroboration, and I believe that this is a desirable development. The credibility of every witness who testifies before the courts must, of course, be carefully assessed but the standard of the 'reasonable adult' is not necessarily appropriate in assessing the credibility of young children.

As Wilson J. emphasized in *B. (G.)*, these changes in the way the courts look at the evidence of children do not mean that the evidence of children should not be subject to the same standard of proof as the evidence of adult witnesses in criminal cases. Protecting the liberty of the accused and guarding against the injustice of the conviction of an innocent person require a solid foundation for a verdict of guilt, whether the complainant be an adult or a child. What the changes do mean is that we approach the evidence of children not from the perspective of rigid stereotypes, but on what Wilson J. called a "common sense" basis, taking into account the strengths and weaknesses which characterize the evidence offered in the particular case.

It is neither desirable nor possible to state hard and fast rules as to when a witness's evidence should be assessed by reference to "adult" or "child" standards — to do so would be to create anew stereotypes potentially as rigid and unjust as those which the recent developments in the law's approach to children's evidence have been designed to dispel. Every person giving testimony in court, of whatever age, is an individual, whose credibility and evidence must be assessed by reference to criteria appropriate to her mental development, understanding and ability to communicate. But I would add this. In general, where an adult is testifying as to events which occurred when she was a child, her credibility should be assessed according to criteria applicable to her as an adult witness. Yet with regard to her evidence pertaining to events which occurred in childhood, the presence of inconsistencies, particularly as to peripheral matters such as time and location, should be considered in the context of the age of the witness at the time of the events to which she is testifying.

Against this background, I turn to a more particular consideration of the Court of Appeal's treatment of the evidence in this case. First, the Court referred to the fact that "there was really no confirmatory evidence". This suggests that the Court may have been applying the old rule that the evidence of a child could not found a conviction unless it was confirmed or corroborated by independent evidence. It may be that in considering the whole of the evidence in accordance with the *Yebes* test, a court of appeal will take into account, along with other factors, the presence or absence of confirmatory evidence. So the reference to lack of confirmatory evidence is not in itself an error of law. But standing as it does as a bald proposition unrelated to a detailed examination of the evidence, it does support the submission that the Court of Appeal was treating the evidence of the children as being inherently less reliable than adult evidence might be.

. . . .

The Court of Appeal next referred to the fact that the evidence of the younger children was fraught with inaccuracy. This is true, particularly with respect to B.W.'s evidence. Some of the inconsistencies are minor, for example an error on the distance from a van to a ball game many years ago. Others are more significant, relating to the sleeping arrangements of the three children, the location of bedrooms in the house and possibly the respondent's nighttime attire. While it was the proper task of the Court of Appeal to consider such inconsistencies, one finds no mention of the fact that the trial judge was alive to them and resolved them to his satisfaction in his reasons for judgment, nor of the fact that many of the inconsistencies may be explained by reference to the fact that a young child might not be paying particular attention to sleeping arrangements or clothing or that the children had lived in a variety of different arrangements, which might well have given rise to confusion on such details.

Finally, the Court of Appeal relied on the fact that neither of the older children was "aware or concerned that anything untoward occurred which is really the best test of the quality of the acts." This reference reveals reliance on the stereotypical but suspect view that the victims of sexual aggression are likely to report the acts, a stereotype which found expression in the now discounted doctrine of recent complaint. In fact, the literature suggests the converse may be true; victims of abuse often in fact do not disclose it, and if they do, it may not be until a substantial length of time has passed. . . .

In summary, the Court of Appeal was right to be concerned about the quality of the evidence and correct in entering upon a re-examination and reweighing, to some extent, of the evidence. It went too far, however, in finding lacunae in the evidence which did not exist and in applying too critical an approach to the evidence, an approach which appears to have placed insufficient weight on the trial judge's findings of credibility, influenced as the Court of Appeal appears to have been by the old stereotypes relating to the inherent unreliability of children's evidence and the "normal" behaviour of victims of sexual abuse.

Placing myself, as I must, in the position of the Court of Appeal . . . I conclude that we are here concerned with verdicts which "a properly instructed jury [or judge], acting judicially, could reasonably have rendered", to repeat the words of *Yebes*. I would allow the appeal and restore the convictions.

For commentary on *W. (R.)*, see Bala, "More Sensitivity to Child Witnesses" (1992), 13 C.R. (4th) 270 and Rauf, "Questioning the New Orthodoxy of the Proper Approach to Child Witnesses" (1993), 17 C.R. (4th) 305. Consider the Martensville cases involving several false charges of child abuse: see *R. v. S. (T.)* (1995), 40 C.R. (4th) 1 (Sask. C.A.). See also David Paciocco, "The Evidence of Children: Testing the Rule Against What We Know" (1996), 21 Queen's L.J. 345 and Nick Bala, "Developmentally Appropriate Questions for Child Witnesses" (1999), 25 Queen's L.J. 252 and "A Legal and Psychological Critique of the Present Approach to the Assessment of the Competence of Child Witnesses" (2001), Osgoode Hall L.J. (in press).

New Legislation

In 1987 and 1994 the Canada Evidence Act was amended, and section 16 now reads:

16.(1) Where a proposed witness is a person under fourteen years of age or a person whose mental capacity is challenged, the court shall, before permitting the person to give evidence, conduct an inquiry to determine

(*a*) whether the person understands the nature of an oath or a solemn affirmation; and

(*b*) whether the person is able to communicate the evidence.

(2) A person referred to in subsection (1) who understands the nature of an oath or a solemn affirmation and is able to communicate the evidence shall testify under oath or solemn affirmation.

(3) A person referred to in subsection (1) who does not understand the nature of an oath or a solemn affirmation but is able to communicate the evidence may,

notwithstanding any provision of any Act requiring an oath or a solemn affirmation, testify on promising to tell the truth.

(4) A person referred to in subsection (1) who neither understands the nature of an oath or a solemn affirmation nor is able to communicate the evidence shall not testify.

(5) A party who challenges the mental capacity of a proposed witness of fourteen years of age or more has the burden of satisfying the court that there is an issue as to the capacity of the proposed witness to testify under an oath or a solemn affirmation.[39]

see p. 309

put on 309

p. 309

The Ontario Evidence Act was recently amended to provide:

18.4(1) A witness under the age of 18 may testify behind a screen or similar device that allows the witness not to see an adverse party, if the court is of the opinion that this is likely to help the witness give complete and accurate testimony or that it is in the best interests of the witness, and if the condition set out in subsection (4) is satisfied.

(2) The court may order that closed-circuit television be used instead of a screen or similar device if the court is of the opinion that,

   (a)   a screen or similar device is insufficient to allow the witness to give complete and accurate testimony; or

   (b)   the best interests of the witness require the use of closed-circuit television.

(3) If the court makes an order under subsection (2), the witness shall testify outside the courtroom and his or her testimony shall be shown in the courtroom by means of closed-circuit television.

(4) When a screen or similar device or closed-circuit television is used, the judge and jury and the parties to the proceeding and their lawyers shall be able to see and hear the witness testify.

18.5(1) During the testimony of a witness under the age of 18, a support person chosen by the witness may accompany him or her.

(2) If the court determines that the support person chosen by the witness is not appropriate for any reason, the witness is entitled to choose another support person.

(3) The following are examples of reasons on the basis of which the court may determine that the support person chosen by a witness is not appropriate:

   1.   The court is of the opinion that the support person may attempt to influence the testimony of the witness.

   2.   The support person behaves in a disruptive manner.

   3.   The support person is also a witness in the proceeding.

18.6(1) The court may prohibit personal cross-examination of a witness under the age of 18 by an adverse party if the court is of the opinion that such a cross-examination,

   (a)   would be likely to affect adversely the ability of the witness to give evidence; or

   (b)   would not be in the best interests of the witness.

---

39.   R.S.C. 1985, c. C-5, s. 16; 1994, c. 44, s. 9. Adopted in British Columbia and about to be adopted in Ontario.

(2) If the court prohibits personal cross-examination by the adverse party, the cross-examination may be conducted in some other appropriate way (for example, by means of questions written by the adverse party and read to the witness by court).[40]

R. v. FERGUSON
(1996), 112 C.C.C. (3d) 342 (B.C.C.A.)

[The accused was convicted of sexual assault. The victim was five at the time of the trial. On appeal the accused argued that the trial judge had erred in failing to conduct the voir dire on competence in the presence of the jury.]

FINCH J.A. (CARROTHERS and NEWBURY JJ.A. concurring):—

. . . .

The leading English decision is *R. v. Reynolds*, [1950] 1 All E.R. 335, where the jury retired while the judge heard the evidence of the child's teacher as to her competence to testify. The English Court of Appeal held that this was wrong and that the conviction had to be quashed. The court explained

> although the duty of deciding whether the child may be sworn or not lies on the judge and is not a matter for the jury, it is most important that the jury should hear the answers which the child gives and see her demeanour when she is questioned by the court, for that enables them to come to a conclusion as to what weight they should attach to her evidence.

. . . .

I think there may be much to recommend conducting the inquiry in the jury's presence. This inquiry is somewhat analogous to the voir dire held into whether an expert witness is qualified to give opinion evidence on a certain subject matter. Juries hear that evidence even though it is for the judge to decide whether the witness is qualified to testify as an expert, because experts' evidence on their qualifications is relevant to their credibility and hence to the weight juries may attach to the experts' opinions if they are permitted to give them. In the case of a child witness, the evidence given by a prospective child witness on a s. 16 inquiry may very well assist the jury in weighing the child's evidence on the substance of the complaint if she is subsequently found competent to testify. For child witnesses, the questions of competence — to be determined by the judge — and of credibility — to be determined by the jury — are tightly entwined. Evidence relevant to one issue will be relevant to the other.

The only reason for not conducting the inquiry under s. 16 in the jury's presence would be the possibility of prejudice to an accused if the child were found by the trial judge to be not competent to testify. It is not clear to me that such prejudice would necessarily arise. In such circumstances, the jury would know the evidence on which the child was held to be not competent. That evidence need not, however, include any inquiry into the substance of the child's complaint. The possibility of prejudice to an accused is a matter to be discussed by the judge with counsel before the s.16 inquiry occurs.

While it may be advantageous, therefore, in some cases, to conduct the s. 16 inquiry in the presence of the jury, it was not a reversible error in this case to conduct that inquiry in the absence of the jury. Clearly the inquiry must be conducted in open court, but I see nothing in the legislation to require that the inquiry be held in the presence of the jury.

---

40. *Ibid.*

R. v. MARQUARD
[1993] 4 S.C.R. 223, 25 C.R. (4th) 1, 85 C.C.C. (3d) 193

[The accused was charged with the aggravated assault of her 3½-year-old granddaughter. The Crown alleged that the accused had put the child's face against a hot stove door in order to discipline her. The child's unsworn testimony, given on a promise to tell the truth, was that her "Nanna" had put her on the stove. The accused testified that she discovered the child early in the morning, screaming, after she had burned herself with a butane lighter. The jury found the accused guilty and the Court of Appeal upheld the conviction The accused appealed. This portion of the judgment deals with the inquiry mandated by the Canada Evidence Act and the charge to the jury.]

MCLACHLIN J. (LAMER C.J. and SOPINKA, CORY, IACOBUCCI and MAJOR JJ. concurring):—

. . . .

The Inquiry under s. 16(1)(b) of the Canada Evidence Act

The appellant, Mrs. Marquard, submits that the trial judge erred in failing to conduct an adequate inquiry into whether the complainant could rationally communicate evidence about the injury. The trial judge questioned Debbie-Ann on her schooling and on her appreciation of the duty to tell the truth. Several times the child reiterated that "You have to tell the truth". Asked whether it was important or unimportant to tell the truth, she responded that it was important. At the end of the questioning, the judge asked defence counsel whether she had omitted any questions. He replied, "I can't say that there's anything I think Your Honour has omitted." In further questioning by Crown counsel, Debbie-Ann demonstrated that she knew the difference between the truth and a lie. The judge indicated that while she did not believe the child capable of understanding an oath, her unsworn evidence should be accepted. Some further questioning on remembering took place, and Debbie-Ann told the judge that yesterday "I went down to the donut shop, and I got a drink and bubble gum." After promising to tell the truth, the child's evidence was taken.

. . . .

The appellant's argument turns on the meaning of the phrase "conduct an inquiry to determine . . . whether the person is able to communicate the evidence." She contends that it is not enough to explore the child's ability to understand the truth and communicate. The judge must, in her submission, be satisfied that the child is competent to testify about the events at issue in the trial. To this end, the trial judge must test the child's ability to perceive and interpret the events in question at the time they took place as well as the child's ability to recollect accurately and communicate them at trial. All the latter, she submits, are embraced by the phrase "able to communicate the evidence" in s. 16 of the Act.

The Crown, on the other hand, takes the position that Parliament, in choosing the infinitive "to communicate", evinced the intention to exclude all other aspects of testimonial competence. The ability of the witness to perceive and interpret the events at the time they occurred and the ability of the witness to recollect them at the time of trial are not part of the test. The only requirement is that the child be able to "communicate" the evidence.

It seems to me that the proper interpretation of s. 16 lies between these two extremes. In the case of a child testifying under s. 16 of the *Canada Evidence Act* testimonial competence is not presumed. The child is placed in the same position as an adult whose competence has been challenged. At common law, such a challenge required the judge to inquire into the competence of the witness to testify.

Testimonial competence comprehends: (1) the capacity to observe (including interpretation); (2) the capacity to recollect; and (3) the capacity to communicate: *McCormick on Evidence* (4th ed. 1991), vol. 1, at pp. 242-48; *Wigmore on Evidence* (Chadbourn Rev. 1979), Vol. 2, at pp. 636-38. The judge must satisfy him- or herself that the witness possesses these capacities. Is the witness capable of observing what was happening? Is he or she capable of remembering what he or she observes? Can he or she communicate what he or she remembers? The goal is not to ensure that the evidence is credible, but only to assure that it meets the minimum threshold of being receivable. The enquiry is into *capacity* to perceive, recollect and communicate, not whether the witness *actually* perceived, recollects and can communicate about the events in question. Generally speaking, the best gauge of capacity is the witness's performance at the time of trial. The procedure at common law has generally been to allow a witness who demonstrates capacity to testify at trial to testify. Defects in ability to perceive or recollect the particular events at issue are left to be explored in the course of giving the evidence, notably by cross-examination.

I see no indication in the wording of s. 16 that Parliament intended to revise this time-honoured process. The phrase "communicate the evidence" indicates more than mere verbal ability. The reference to "the evidence" indicates the ability to testify about the matters before the court. It is necessary to explore in a general way whether the witness is capable of perceiving events, remembering events and communicating events to the court. If satisfied that this is the case, the judge may then receive the child's evidence, upon the child's promising to tell the truth under s. 16(3). It is not necessary to determine in advance that the child perceived and recollects the very events at issue in the trial as a condition of ruling that the child's evidence be received. That is not required of adult witnesses, and should not be required for children.

My colleague, Justice L'Heureux-Dubé, contends that the standard I have outlined is one which is inconsistent with "the trend to do away with presumptions of unreliability and to expand the admissibility of children's evidence and may, in fact, subvert the purpose of legislative reform in this area." I disagree. The test I have expounded is not based on presumptions about the incompetency of children to be witnesses nor is it intended as a test which would make it difficult for children to testify. Rather, the test outlines the basic abilities that individuals need to possess if they are to testify. The threshold is not a high one. What is required is the basic ability to perceive, remember and communicate. This established, deficiencies of perception, recollection of the events at issue may be dealt with as matters going to the weight of the evidence.

The examination conducted in this case was sufficient to permit the trial judge to conclude that Debbie-Ann was capable of perceiving events, remembering events and recounting events to the court. This in turn permitted the trial judge to receive her evidence, upon Debbie-Ann's promise to tell the truth. What Debbie-Ann actually perceived and recollected of the events in question was a matter for the jury to determine after listening to her evidence in chief and in cross-examination.

. . . .

I conclude that the trial judge did not err in the inquiry she conducted under s. 16(1)(b) of the *Canada Evidence Act* or in receiving the evidence of the child.

. . . .

. . . Charge to the Jury on the Child's Evidence

The appellant submits that the trial judge failed to warn the jury adequately about frailties in the child's evidence. In particular, she alleges that the warning given by the trial judge failed to assist the jury in properly assessing the child's evidence, and that the charge on the confirmatory evidence was unhelpful, confusing and prejudicial to the appellant. The Crown submits that the trial judge's charge was more than adequate and in some respects unduly favourable to the defence.

With children as with adults, there can be no fixed and precise formula to be followed in warning a jury about potential problems with a witness' evidence.

. . . .

I am satisfied that the evidence of the child required a warning from the trial judge as to the risks of accepting it. The child was very young. She was unable to give much detail about the incident. And she had told a different story at an earlier time.

I am also satisfied that the trial judge fairly pointed out these problems to the jury. One of the last things she said to them before they began their deliberations was this:

> You will understand that as a matter of common sense that to convict on the unconfirmed and unsworn evidence of a child witness is fraught with dangers and in that you must use your common sense and all the evidence before you. She has not been sworn. She has promised to tell the truth. I found that she was intelligent enough to answer the questions on a promise to tell the truth.

Earlier the trial judge had pointed out particular deficiencies in the child's evidence. She spoke about the fact that the child had earlier told a different story. She said:

> You heard evidence, too, of the prior contradictory statement by the child, Debbie-Ann LeBlanc that in hospital she gave to Dr. Mian, an explanation which, to encapsulate, was effectively ''I was trying to light a cigarette and I burned myself,'' and then in Court, she said, ''nanna put me in the stove.'' The fact that a witness has on a prior occasion made a statement or statements that are contradictory to her evidence at this trial goes to the credibility or the truthfulness of a witness. The testimony of a witness may be discredited in whole or in part by showing that she previously made a statement which is inconsistent with her present testimony. . . . You are the sole judges as to whether there has been a contradiction of an earlier statement by the witness and the effect, if any, of such contradiction on the witness' credibility.

The trial judge directed the jury to the difficulty defence counsel had in getting responsive answers on cross-examination:

> There was some particular difficulty counsel for the defence had in examining the child, Debbie-Ann LeBlanc. You will recollect that when he attempted to examine her in cross-examination, virtually all of his questions were answered, ''I don't know'', or ''maybe'', or ''I don't remember'', and eventually, I think, there was nothing else he could do but give up on that cross-examination.

The trial judge also pointed out to the jury that there was ''very little embellishment'' by the child of the statement ''nanna put me in the stove.''

The trial judge explained the fact that while technical corroboration of a child's evidence was not required, the jury might consider whether other evidence in fact corroborated her testimony and explained the requirements of corroborative evidence. She concluded with this caution:

> Before leaving the evidence of the child, I should say that just because you find that her evidence has been corroborated by some other material evidence, that does not mean that you must accept the evidence of the child in whole or in part or that you must convict the accused.

Finally, the trial judge repeatedly warned the jury that the child had not been sworn, but was testifying under a promise to tell the truth. She stated: ''It is for you to decide . . . what weight is to be given to the child's promise to tell the truth.'' In my view, these cautions adequately warned the jury of the risks associated with accepting the child's evidence.

[L'Heureux-Dubé, Gonthier and La Forest, JJ. dissented with an opinion that "communicate" meant only verbal ability.]

The Supreme Court considered whether the trial judge had adequately warned the jury regarding the frailties in the child's evidence. Applying the lesson of *Vetrovec*, the court noted that it is wrong to apply negative stereotypes to the evidence of children generally but that rather each child should be approached as an individual. The court noted that there were some features about the child's evidence in *Marquard* that deserved to be emphasized to the jury: the child was very young, unable to give much detail, and had told a different story on another occasion. The court found that these were duly noted by the trial judge. Another "frailty" mentioned by the Court was the fact that the child had not been sworn but had given her evidence on a promise to tell the truth. The decision underlines what had been forecast when the new section 16 first came in: a hierarchy of values of testimony depending on how the witness was assessed following the inquiry. Under the former section 16 a witness could give her evidence sworn or unsworn. If given unsworn, corroboration was required. There is no corroboration requirement any more but evidently, according to the court, unsworn evidence, given on a promise, is not as valuable as sworn and the trial judge is required to so charge the jury. We need to remember that the inquiry takes place in front of the jury. Will the trier also give less weight if the child affirms rather than testify on oath?

poten. prob.

R. v. FARLEY
(1995), 40 C.R. (4th) 190, 99 C.C.C. (3d) 76

DOHERTY J.A. (ROBINS, and WEILER JJ.A. concurring):— The appellant was convicted of sexual assault and sentenced to three years in the penitentiary. . . .

The complainant was 26 years of age at the time of the trial. He is severely intellectually handicapped and has, according to one of his caregivers, the comprehension of a three-year-old child. Before the complainant testified, the trial judge conducted the inquiry required under s. 16 of the *Canada Evidence Act*, R.S.C. 1985, c. C-5. She determined that the complainant could not testify under oath or affirmation, but could testify upon promising to tell the truth.

. . . .

The appellant contends that the complainant should not have been found competent to give evidence. Apart from that contention, I see no error in the trial proceedings.

. . . .

Section 16(3) has two components. Before the prospective witness can testify pursuant to that section, he or she must:

• be able to communicate the evidence
   AND
• promise to tell the truth.

The phrase "able to communicate the evidence" refers to the cognitive and communicative capacity of the proposed witness. . . .

In *R. v. Caron* (1994), 94 C.C.C. (3d) 466 at 471 (Ont. C.A.), Arbour J.A. considered the above passage from *Marquard* and said:

In order to be found capable of communicating his or her evidence, a witness must demonstrate some ability not only to distinguish between fact and fiction, as this child did with respect to colour for instance, but also a capacity and a willingness, limited as it may be in the case of a young child, to relate to the court the essence of what happened to her.

In my opinion, the capacity to perceive entails not only an ability to perceive events as they occur, but also an ability to differentiate between that which is actually perceived and that which the person may have imagined, been told by others, or otherwise have come to believe. Similarly, the capacity to remember refers to the person's capacity to maintain a recollection of his or her actual perceptions of a prior event, and the ability to distinguish those retained perceptions from information provided to the person from other sources, such as statements made to the person by others. The capacity to communicate refers to the ability to understand questions and to respond to them in an intelligible fashion.

The cognitive and communicative components of the competence test found in s. 16(3) refer to capacity and not to the proposed witness's actual perception, recollection, and narration of the relevant events. A person may have the capacity to perceive, recall, and recount and yet be unable to perform one or more of those functions in a given situation. For example, a witness who genuinely has no recollection of the relevant events is not thereby rendered incompetent unless that inability to recall is a reflection of the absence of the capacity to recall. It must also be stressed that the cognitive and communicative components of s. 16(3) set a relatively low threshold for testimonial competence. Once the capacity to perceive, remember, and recount is established, any deficiencies in a particular witness's perception, recollection, or narration go to the weight of that witness's evidence and not the witness's competence to testify: *R. v. Marquard, supra*, at p. 220.

. . . .

If a proposed witness is able to communicate the evidence in the sense described above, s. 16(3) provides that the witness may testify only upon promising to tell the truth. Unless a promise to tell the truth is a meaningless formalism, it must impose a further prerequisite to testimonial competence beyond the above-described capacity to communicate the evidence.

. . . .

There is clearly a close relationship between an understanding of the duty to speak the truth and the making of a meaningful promise to tell the truth. The latter assumes the existence of the former.

. . . .

A proposed witness who can communicate the evidence should be allowed to testify under s. 16(3) only if he or she "understand[s] the duty to speak the truth in terms of . . . everyday social conduct." In the context of a witness called to describe a prior event, an understanding of the duty to speak the truth entails an appreciation by the witness that he or she must answer all questions in accordance with the witness's recollection of what actually happened.

. . . .

In holding that an understanding of the duty to tell the truth remains a precondition to giving unsworn or unaffirmed evidence, I do not mean to suggest that a proposed witness must make an actual commitment to tell the truth before being allowed to testify under s. 16(3). A witness who understands the duty to speak the truth, but is nonetheless prepared to ignore that obligation, is not thereby rendered an incompetent witness. A willingness to lie goes to credibility and not to competence.

The Ontario Evidence Act was recently amended to provide:

18.(1) A person of any age is presumed to be competent to give evidence.

(2) When a person's competence is challenged, the judge, justice or other presiding officer shall examine the person.

(3) However, if the judge, justice or other presiding officer is of the opinion that the person's ability to give evidence might be adversely affected if he or she examined the person, the person may be examined by counsel instead.

18.1(1) When the competence of a proposed witness who is a person under the age of 14 is challenged, the court may admit the person's evidence if the person is able to communicate the evidence, understands the nature of an oath or solemn affirmation and testifies under oath or solemn affirmation.

(2) The court may admit the person's evidence, if the person is able to communicate the evidence, even though the person does not understand the nature of an oath or solemn affirmation, if the person understands what it means to tell the truth and promises to tell the truth.

(3) If the court is of the opinion that the person's evidence is sufficiently reliable, the court has discretion to admit it, if the person is able to communicate the evidence, even if the person understands neither the nature of an oath or solemn affirmation nor what it means to tell the truth.

18.2(1) Evidence given by a person under the age of 14 need not be corroborated.

(2) It is not necessary to instruct the trier of fact that it is unsafe to rely on the uncorroborated evidence of a person under the age of 14.[41]

R. v. LEVOGIANNIS
[1993] 4 S.C.R. 475, 25 C.R. (4th) 325, 85 C.C.C. (3d) 327

[The accused was charged with touching a child for a sexual purpose. The Crown requested that the 12-year-old complainant be allowed to testify behind a screen pursuant to section 486(2.1) of the Code. The trial judge granted the Crown's motion following the testimony of a clinical psychologist who indicated that the complainant was experiencing a great deal of fear about testifying. The accused challenged the constitutional validity of section 486(2.1) on the grounds that it violated his right to a fair trial guaranteed by sections 7 and 11(*d*) of the Charter. Both the trial judge and the Court of Appeal held that section 486(2.1) of the Code did not infringe sections 7 and 11(*d*). The Court of Appeal added that even if section 486(2.1) infringed these sections, the infringement would be justified under section 1 of the Charter.]

L'HEUREUX-DUBÉ J.:—

. . . .

The examination of whether an accused's rights are infringed encompasses multifaceted considerations, such as the rights of witnesses, in this case children, the rights of accused and courts' duties to ascertain the truth. The goal of the court process is truth seeking and, to that end, the evidence of all those involved in judicial proceedings must be given in a way that is most favourable to eliciting the truth. In ascertaining the

---

41.   R.S.O. 1990, c. E.23 (as am. S.O. 1995, c. 6, s. 6).

constitutionality of s. 486(2.1) of the *Criminal Code*, one cannot ignore the fact that, in many instances, the court process is failing children, especially those who have been victims of abuse, who are then subjected to further trauma as participants in the judicial process.

. . . .

The plight of children who testify and the role courts must play in ascertaining the truth must not be overlooked in the context of the constitutional analysis in the case at hand. As this Court has said, children may require different treatment than adults in the courtroom setting.

. . . .

An order under s. 486(2.1) simply blocks the complainant's view of the accused and not vice versa. The wording of s. 486(2.1) merely provides that the screen "would allow the complainant not to see the accused". The screen does not obstruct the view of the complainant by the accused, his counsel, the Crown or the judge. All are present in court. The evidence is given and the trial is conducted in the usual manner, including cross-examination. As a result, the issue before this Court, is, simply put, whether a witness's obstructed view of an accused, infringes the rights of such accused under s. 7 or 11(*d*) of the *Charter*.

. . . .

In my view, the main objective pursued by the legislative enactment presently challenged is to better "get at the truth", by recognizing that a young child abuse victim's evidence may, in certain circumstances, be facilitated if the child is able to focus his or her attention on giving testimony, rather than experiencing difficulties in facing the accused. Section 486(2.1) of the *Criminal Code* recognizes that a child may react negatively to a face-to-face confrontation and, as a result, special procedures may be required to alleviate these concerns.

. . . .

The appellant submits that his right to "be presumed innocent until proven guilty according to law in a fair and public hearing by an independent and impartial tribunal" is violated, as the screen undermines the presumption of innocence, operates unfairly against the accused and hampers cross-examination. . . .

According to the appellant, the use of a screen lends an air of credence to the witness' testimony and, since the courtroom has been altered for the protection of the young complainant, the accused may appear guilty. In the case at bar, the appellant was tried before a judge sitting alone and, as a result, the issue of appearance to the jury is not relevant. Had a jury been present, however, I suggest that, properly informed, they would not have been swayed by the use of the screen. As Dickson C.J. said in *R. v. Corbett*, [1988] 1 S.C.R. 670, at p. 692:

In my view, it would be quite wrong to make too much of the risk that the jury might use the evidence for an improper purpose.

In a similar vein, I suggest that one should assume that a jury will follow judicial instruction and will not be biased by the use of such a device. In fact, in contrast to the perspective raised by the appellant, it has been remarked that Crown prosecutors are reluctant to request the use of screens because they are concerned that the young complainant may not come across as credible or the child's testimony may have less of an impact. . . . The use of a screen could very well be held against a child complainant, who might be judged to be an unreliable witness, because she or he is unable to look the accused in the eye, rather than against the accused. If screens were used more regularly as part of the courtroom procedure, as recommended by the Family Court Clinic in London, these perceptions may well be totally eliminated. Finally, while it is true, as the appellant contends, that s. 486(2.1) of the *Criminal Code*, similar in this regard to most sections of the *Code*, does not contain prescribed jury instructions, such instructions are routinely given by judges and such a caution is no more a constitutional prerequisite with respect to this section than with respect to any other section of the *Criminal Code*. Such caution may not be necessary or, if it is, it will be a function of the circumstances of the case.

(ii) *Mental Illness*

In *R. v. Hill*[42] the accused, an attendant at a lunatic asylum, was convicted for the manslaughter of one of the patients. It was objected that the chief prosecution witness was incompetent due to his lunacy. Evidence was given that the witness did suffer the delusion that spirits spoke to him, but he was also described as having a good memory and ability to give an account of events observed. The precedents at the time were in conflict over whether there should be a blanket rule of inadmissibility and the court answered:

Lord Campbell, C.J.:

> It has been argued that any particular delusion, commonly called monomania, makes a man inadmissible. This would be extremely inconvenient in many cases in the proof either of guilt or innocence: it might also cause serious difficulties in the management of lunatic asylums. I am, therefore, of opinion that the Judge must, in all such cases, determine the competency, and the jury the credibility. Before he is sworn, the insane person may be cross-examined, and witnesses called to prove circumstances which might shew him to be inadmissible; but, in the absence of such proof, he is *prima facie* admissible, and the jury must attach what weight they think fit to his testimony.

In the course of argument Lord Campbell spoke of the judge determining

> whether the insane person has the sense of religion in his mind, and whether he understands the nature and sanction of an oath,[43]

and concluded that the trial judge was right in swearing the witness as the uncontradicted evidence showed that the witness was able to give a rational account of matters observed. Although the witness had described his awareness of the consequences of a false oath, eternal damnation, and so demonstrated moral responsibility, the bulk of the evidence led on his testimonial qualifications concerned the quite separate aspects of his ability to accurately observe, recollect and rationally communicate.

Although, generally, the competency of a witness should be challenged before the witness is sworn, if the incompetency only becomes manifest later, the trial judge may stop the examination and order the evidence stricken.[44] The mental capacity of the witness will initially be presumed, but when challenged the offering party will be put to proof on a *voir dire* and the trial judge must then

---

42. (1851), 169 E.R. 495 (Crown Cases Reserved). Followed in *R. v. Dunning*, [1965] Crim. L.R. 372 (C.C.A.).
43. *Ibid.*, at p. 498.
44. See *R. v. Steinberg*, [1931] O.R. 222, 257 (C.A.) per Grant, J.A., quoted with approval in *R. v. Hawke* (1975), 22 C.C.C. (2d) 19, 43 (Ont. C.A.). And see *R. v. Deol* (1981), 58 C.C.C. (2d) 524 (Alta. C.A.) rejecting such an objection raised for the first time on a nonsuit application as not timely. See also *R. v. Clark* (1983), 35 C.R. (3d) 357 (Ont. C.A.).

make an express finding.[45] The *voir dire* should be in the presence of the jury "since the dispute would be for their use and their instruction."[46] The trial judge is advised

> that the derangement or defect, in order to disqualify, must be such as *substantially negatives trustworthiness* upon the specific subject of the testimony.[47]

Commentators have long argued for an abandonment of the present rule leaving it to the jury to consider what weight, if any, it will attach to the testimony of such a witness. In 1853 the Common Law Practice Commissioners recommended:

> Plain sense and reason would obviously suggest that any living witness who could throw light upon a fact in issue should be heard to state what he knows, subject always to such observations as may arise as to his means of knowledge or his disposition to tell the truth.[48]

R. v. PARROTT
[2001] 1 S.C.R. 178, 39 C.R. (5th) 255, 150 C.C.C. (3d) 449

[The accused was charged with offences in relation to a woman who suffered from Down's Syndrome. The complainant was considered to be mildly to moderately retarded and had been in institutional care for almost 20 years. The complainant made statements to the police when she was found, and to the doctor who first examined her. The police also conducted a videotaped interview the following day. We will see later, in the chapter dealing with Hearsay, that out-of-court statements may be received for their truth if there are grounds of necessity and the statements were made in circumstances that indicated they were reliable. This case deals with the requirement of necessity.]

BINNIE, J. (MAJOR, BASTARACHE and ARBOUR, JJ. concurring): — This appeal tests the limits of the principled hearsay exception that allows the Crown in exceptional circumstances to lead the out-of-court evidence of a complainant at a criminal trial without having him or her present in court and available for cross-examination by the defence.

In this case, the complainant in a kidnapping and sexual assault case was a mature woman who had suffered since birth from Down's Syndrome. She was considered mildly to moderately retarded and had been in institutional care for almost 20 years. Expert evidence was called to establish that her mental development was equivalent to that of a

---

45. See 2 Wigmore, *Evidence* (3d ed.), s. 497, approved as accurately reflecting the duty of the trial judge in *R. v. Hawke, ibid.*, at p. 27.

46. *Toohey v. Metro. Police Commr.*, [1965] 1 All E.R. 506, 512 (H.L.).

47. 2 Wigmore, *Evidence* (3d ed.), s. 492, adopted in *R. v. Hawke, supra*, note 44, at p. 27.

48. As quoted in 2 Wigmore, *Evidence* (Chad. Rev.), s. 501, note 2. See *R. v. Spencer; R. v. Smails*, [1986] 2 All E.R. 928 (H.L.) re duty to warn of danger of convicting on the uncorroborated evidence of a mental patient. See *R. v. Thurlow* (1994), 34 C.R. (4th) 53 (Ont. Gen. Div.), where Weekes, J. dealt with the difficult problem of the competency of a witness with multiple personalities. While giving evidence at the preliminary hearing she took the oath identifying herself as M.B. During cross-examination she explained that the person who was testifying was not M.B. but was, in fact, a persona she identified as "Me". Subsequently she purportedly transformed into a different persona, a male, who identified himself as "Alex". "Alex" gave evidence but, during this time, neither M. nor "Me" was present in the court. The witness appeared to the court to be in a dissociative state.

three- or four-year-old child and that her memory of events was poor. Her response to even the simplest questions was said to be not very coherent. The complainant herself was never called into the presence of the trial judge so that these attributes could be verified even though she was available and there was no suggestion that she would suffer any trauma or other adverse effect by appearing in court. Instead the court received evidence of out-of-court statements that she had earlier made to the police and to a doctor.

. . . .

Analysis

While in this country an accused does not have an absolute right to confront his or her accuser in the course of a criminal trial, the right to full answer and defence generally produces this result. In this case, unusually, the Crown precipitated an inquiry under s. 16 of the Canada Evidence Act not for the purpose of establishing the testimonial competence of "a proposed witness", namely the complainant, but to lay an evidentiary basis to keep her out of the witness box. Having satisfied the trial judge entirely through expert evidence that the complainant neither understood the nature of an oath nor could communicate her evidence, the Crown used the *voir dire* as a springboard to establish the admissibility of hearsay evidence of her out-of-court statements under the principles established in *Khan*.

This procedure raises two distinct though related issues, firstly the admissibility of the expert evidence at the *voir dire*, and secondly the admissibility of the complainant's out-of-court statements at the trial. In my view, these issues ought to have been resolved in favour of the respondent, as held by the majority judgment of the Newfoundland Court of Appeal, for the following reasons:

1. The expert evidence was improperly admitted at the *voir dire*. Trial judges are eminently qualified to assess the testimonial competence of a witness. The trial judge, after all, was to be at the receiving end of the complainant's communication, and could have determined whether or not she was able to communicate her evidence to him. If she had been called and it became evident that the trial judge required expert assistance to draw appropriate inferences from what he had heard her say (or not say), or if either the defence or the Crown had wished to pursue the issue of requiring an oath or solemn affirmation, expert evidence might then have become admissible to assist the judge. At the time the expert testimony was called, it had not been shown that expert evidence as such was necessary, and the testimony of Drs. Gillespie, Morley and Parsons was therefore inadmissible: *R. v. Mohan*, [1994] 2 S.C.R. 9.

2. Consequently, the trial judge erred in ruling at the conclusion of the *voir dire* that the complainant's out-of-court statements would be admissible at trial. Having dispensed with hearing from the complainant, and the expert medical testimony having been improperly admitted, the trial judge had no admissible evidence on which to exercise a discretion to admit the complainant's out-of-court statements.

. . . .

At the threshold stands the question of why expert evidence was admitted in the first place to establish the competency of a witness, a task which is specifically assigned by s. 16 of the Canada Evidence Act to the trial judge. In *R. v. Abbey*, [1982] 2 S.C.R. 24, the Court adopted as correct the statement that "[i]f on the proven facts a judge or jury can form their own conclusions without help, then the opinion of the expert is unnecessary".

The key and undisputed facts of this case are that the complainant was available to testify and there was no suggestion by anybody that she might be harmed thereby. She was not called simply because the Crown made the tactical decision to proceed without calling her. The medical experts were not called to assist the judge to interpret what he had seen or heard from the complainant in the witness box, but in substitution for any such opportunity of direct observation.

this should be file work of the TJ

The special role of the expert witness is not to testify to the facts, but to provide an opinion based on the facts, to assist the trier of fact to draw the appropriate inferences from the facts as found "which the judge and jury, due to the technical nature of the facts, are unable to formulate" (*Abbey, supra.*)

. . . .

Whether a complainant "is able to communicate the evidence" in this broad sense is a matter on which a trial judge can (and invariably does) form his or her own opinion. It is not a matter "outside the experience and knowledge of a judge or jury" (*Mohan, supra*, at p. 23). It is the very meat and potatoes of a trial court's existence.

LeBel, J. (L'Heureux-Dubé and Gonthier, JJ. concurring) dissenting: —

. . . The question at issue in this appeal is whether, on the *voir dire* to determine necessity, the Crown was *obliged* to put the complainant forward as a witness in order for the trial judge to evaluate her testimonial capacity. While I agree with my colleague, Binnie J., that it is generally a prudent practice to have the Crown do so, I would not elevate it to an absolute legal requirement in every case. In my view, the evidence before the trial judge in the present case amply supports his findings of necessity and reliability. . . .

. . . .

(c) Emotional Incapacity — Interest

When witnesses first began informing the jury in the 15th century, there was no bar against witnesses who were interested in the outcome. Indeed, witnesses who were disinterested were regarded as meddling and unless summoned by the court or the jury they might risk a maintenance prosecution.[49] Originally witnesses were interested in the outcome and as a result distinctly partisan. To this there was one major exception: the parties themselves. The party could plead or argue but could not be sworn since to do so would be to mix two kinds of proof; during the fifteenth century, and indeed continuing into the sixteenth, the party could elect trial by wager of law rather than by jury, and in that mode of proceeding he was entitled to the use of his own oath. Later, as trial by witnesses before a jury became the predominant mode of proceeding in civil cases, the disqualification of parties was extended, by analogy, to include other persons interested in the outcome and by 1650 the disqualification was firmly established. One particular group of readily identifiable interested persons were the spouses of the parties. Curiously, while the disqualification was extended to cover the spouse, the common law did not go further and extend it to children or other relatives; perhaps the extension to spouses was grounded on the then current notion of identity or merger of the two spouses into a single person. In criminal trials the accused had been entitled, like a party in a civil case, to plead and argue orally, by himself, and later, through his counsel. The accused then presented his own "evidence" and was questioned though he was not sworn.

---

49.   See Thayer, *Preliminary Treatise on Evidence at the Common Law* (1898), pp. 125-29. At p. 128 quoting Paston, J. in 1442: "If one who has no reason to meddle in the matter and is not learned in the law shows the jury, or the party himself, or his counsel, the truth of the matter and opens evidence of it as well and as fully as one who was learned in the law could, yet this is a maintenance in his person."

By analogy to the civil cases his statements were not to be regarded as testimony since he was disqualified as a witness from his own interest in the outcome.[50]

As in civil cases the spouse was incompetent in criminal trials:

> ... except in case of necessity, and that necessity is not a general necessity, as where no other witness can be had, but a particular necessity, as where, for instance, the wife would otherwise be exposed without remedy to personal injury.[51]

Inspired by Bentham, the reformers in the mid to late 19th century gradually discarded these disqualifications for interest, preferring that the proposed witness' interest be displayed to, and taken into account by, the trier of fact, who could then evaluate to what particular extent the interest may have impaired credibility. As Bentham noted:

> Any interest, interest of any sort and quantity, sufficient to prove mendacity? As rational would be it to say, any horse, or dog, or flea, put to a wagon, is sufficient to move it ...
>
> ... In the eyes of the English lawyer, one thing, and one thing only, has a value: that thing is money. On the will of man, if you believe the English lawyer, one thing, and one thing only, has influence: that thing is money. Such is his system of psychological dynamics. If you will believe the man of law, there is no such thing as the fear of God; no such thing as regard for reputation; no such thing as fear of legal punishment; no such thing as ambition; no such thing as the love of power; no such thing as filial, no such thing as parental, affection; no such thing as party attachment; no such thing as party enmity; no such thing as public spirit, patriotism, or general benevolence; no such thing as compassion; no such thing as gratitude; no such thing as revenge.[52]

The reforming legislation enacted in England was copied in Canada. The incremental nature of the change in England by individual statutes over a period of years is seen reflected in the provincial legislation, which in its present form consequently appears duplicative. For example the Ontario Evidence Act[53] provides:

> **6.** No person offered as a witness in an action shall be excluded from giving evidence by reason of any alleged incapacity from crime or interest.
>
> **7.** Every person offered as a witness shall be admitted to give evidence notwithstanding that he has an interest in the matter in question or in the event

---

50. The detailed history of the development here briefly described may be seen in 2 Wigmore, *Evidence* (Chad. Rev.), ss. 575, 601. See also *Coleman's Trial* (1678), 7 Howell's State Trials 1, 65: the prosecution witness maintained the prisoner's treasonous act was done about the 21st of August and the prisoner said to the court:
    Prisoner: I went out of town on the 10th of August, it was the latter end I came home.
    L.C.J.:   Have you any witness to prove that?
    Prisoner: I cannot say I have a witness.
    L.C.J.:   Then you say nothing. . . . You say you went out of town the 10th and came home the last of August; you say it is impossible that he should say right, but yet you do not prove it.

51. *Bentley v. Cooke* (1784), 99 E.R. 729, per Lord Mansfield.

52. Bentham, *Rationale of Judicial Evidence* (1827), cited in 2 Wigmore, *Evidence* (Chad. Rev.), s. 576.

53. R.S.O. 1990, c. E-23.

of the action and notwithstanding that he has been previously convicted of a crime or offence.

8.(1) The parties to an action and the persons on whose behalf it is brought, instituted, opposed or defended are, except as hereinafter otherwise provided, competent and compellable, to give evidence on behalf of themselves or of any of the parties, and the husbands and wives of such parties and persons are, except as hereinafter otherwise provided, competent and compellable to give evidence on behalf of any of the parties.

. . . .

10.(1) The parties to a proceeding instituted in consequence of adultery and the husbands and wives of such parties are competent to give evidence in such proceedings, . . .

The Canada Evidence Act[54] provides: *(this is the present law)*

3.   A person is not incompetent to give evidence by reason of interest or crime.

4.(1) Every person charged with an offence, and, except as otherwise provided in this section, the wife or husband, as the case may be, of the person so charged, is a competent witness for the defence, whether the person so charged is charged solely or jointly with any other person.

(2) The wife or husband of a person charged with an offence against subsection 50(1) of the Young Offenders Act or with an offence against any of sections 151, 152, 153, 155 or 159, subsection 160(2) or (3), or sections 170 to 173, 179, 212, 215, 218, 271 to 273, 280 to 283, 291 to 294 or 329 of the Criminal Code, or an attempt to commit any such offence, is a competent and compellable witness for the prosecution without the consent of the person charged.

. . . .

(4) The wife or husband of a person charged with an offence against any of sections 220, 221, 235, 236, 237, 239, 240, 266, 267, 268 or 269 of the Criminal Code where the complainant or victim is under the age of fourteen years is a competent and compellable witness for the prosecution without the consent of the person charged.

(5) Nothing in this section affects a case where the wife or husband of a person charged with an offence may at common law be called as a witness without the consent of that person.

(d) Spousal Compellability[55]

The general rule at common law just examined, spousal incompetence, disqualified witnesses from testifying for their spouse. Some hundred years earlier than that rule's establishment, the cases indicate a privilege in a witness to refuse to testify *against* their spouse. The policies underlying the two rules appear to be different: the former based on a concern for falsehood in one interested in the outcome, while the latter apparently based on some notion that to force disclosure would be repugnant and disruptive of marital harmony.[56] When

---

54. R.S.C. 1985, c. C-5 [s. 4 am. 1987, c. 24, s. 17].
55. Where the spouse is an accused other special rules apply, as discussed below.
56. See the criticism of the various "policies" given for the second rule in 8 Wigmore, *Evidence* (McNaughton Rev.), s. 2228.

exceptions were made to the former rule what effect did they have on the latter? What is the meaning of "competent" in the statutory provisions noted above?

In *Gosselin v. R.*[57] the Supreme Court of Canada interpreted "competent" in the predecessor to section 4 of the Canada Evidence Act as meaning competent and compellable and ruled therefore that the accused's wife could be compelled to give evidence against her husband in a prosecution for murder. The legislation at that time did not contain the words "for the defence" following "competent."[58] But in *R. v. Amway Corp.,* [1989] 1 S.C.R. 21, Justice Sopinka for the Court held:

> It is apparent from the words of s. [4(1)] that it addresses only one of the two components of the rights and obligations of a witness: that is, competence. It does not purport to deal with compellability. At common law an accused was neither competent nor compellable as a witness. By virtue of s. 4(1) of the Canada Evidence Act, first introduced in 1893 and amended by S.C. 1906, c. 10, s. 1, the common law was altered to make an accused a competent witness for the defence. These amendments left intact the common law with respect to the non-compellability of an accused person at the instance of the Crown.

The legislation continued in existence[59] the common law exception to the general rule which is vaguely described as involving those cases wherein the spouse's "person, liberty or health" were affected. In the early case of *Lord Audley's Trial,*[60] in 1631, the accused was charged with the rape of his own wife in assisting one of his servants to have intercourse with her against her will. The accused objected to his wife's evidence as incompetent, but it was held that she was competent "for she was the party wronged; otherwise she might be abused."[61] This exception was then founded on necessity but as Professor Wigmore criticized:

> The notion of necessity, indeed, might commendably have been a broader one; the necessity of doing justice to other persons in general, when the spouse's testimony was indispensable, would have been at least as great. But the common lawyers here kept their eyes upon the ground, and did not allow their survey to exceed the range of immediate and unavoidable vision. Anyone could see that an absolute privilege in a husband to close the mouth of the wife in testimony against him would be a vested license to injure her in secret with complete immunity. This much the common lawyers saw, and were willing to concede. Just how far the concession went, in concrete cases, was never precisely settled. It was given varying definitions at different times. It certainly extended to causes involving corporal violence to the wife, and it certainly did not extend to all wrongs done to the wife.[62]

---

57. (1903), 33 S.C.R. 255, followed in *Re Samwald and Mills* (1977), 78 D.L.R. (3d) 219 (B.C.S.C.). Compare *Ayotte v. Wachowicz* (1961), 36 W.W.R. 656 (Sask. C.A.).

58. Added later in 1906: An Act to Further Amend The Canada Evidence Act, 1893, S.C. 1906, 6 Edw. VII, c. 10.

59. Canada Evidence Act, R.S.C. 1970, c. E-10, s. 4(4).

60. (1631), 3 Howell's State Trials 401.

61. *Ibid.,* at pp. 402 and 414.

62. 8 Wigmore, *Evidence* (McNaughton Rev.), s. 2239. Compare *R. v. Bowles* (1967), 60 W.W.R. 276 (Alta. Mag. Ct.) and *R. v. Comiskey* (1973), 12 C.C.C. (2d) 410 (Ont. Prov. Ct.) for different views re the nature of the crime necessary to qualify. See also the trial judge's view (OHearn, Co. Ct. J.) in *R. v. Marchand* (1980), 55 C.C.C. (2d) 77, 85 (N.S.C.A.) that the subsection extended to "crimes of forgery and uttering forged documents as coming

If a spouse was at common law competent in such cases so that she might effect redress for her own injury, was she also compellable? Lord Edmund Davies, in a dissenting report, argued:

> The epoch-making decision in *Lord Audley's* case is sought to be explained away as arising simply ex necessitate, a spouse assaulted in secret having no redress were she denied a hearing in the courts. But the criminal law serves a dual purpose: to render aid to citizens who themselves seek its protection, and itself to take active steps to protect those other citizens who, though grievously in need of protection, for one reason or another do not themselves set the law in motion. And it does not follow that their failure should mean that, proceedings having nevertheless been instituted, the injured spouse should be less compellable as a Crown witness than one unrelated by marriage to the alleged assailant. I readily confess to a complete absence of any feeling of "repugnance" that, in the circumstances of the instant case, Mrs. Hoskyn was compelled to testify against the man who had three days earlier become her husband.[63]

This position has found favour in Canada.[64]

The breadth of the common law exception was extended in the case of *R. v. McPherson*.[65] The accused had been convicted of assaulting his six-year-old son, the principal Crown witness being the accused's wife. In extending the exception the court reasoned:

> In this day and age the principal reasons for spousal non-competency in child abuse cases, namely, the unity of husband and wife and a desire to avoid discord and dissension between them and to protect the legal relationship of marriage as one of full confidence and affection, must, in my opinion, take a subservient position to that of the welfare and protection of the child. This cannot be accomplished unless the criminal law can be enforced. The need of children to be protected calls out for an extension of the common law exceptions to spousal disqualification to allow one spouse to testify against the other in cases of child abuse.[66]

In 1982, section 4 of the Canada Evidence Act was amended[67] to provide for the compellability of spouses where the victim was a young child.

What is the meaning of "wife or husband of a person charged"? It is for the trial judge to determine if the witness is a spouse,[68] that is, whether the witness

---

within the ambit of 'person and liberty' of the wife." See also *R. v. Giroux* (1985), 38 Sask. R. 172 (Q.B.) and *R. v. Wood* (1982), 8 C.C.C. (3d) 217 (Ont. Prov. Ct.).

63. *Hoskyn v. Metro. Police Commissioner*, [1978] 2 All E.R. 136, 154 (H.L.).

64. *R. v. Czipps* (1979), 48 C.C.C. (2d) 166 (Ont. C.A.) which reasons on the point were agreed with in *R. v. Marchand*, supra, note 62, at p. 93. To similar effect see *R. v. Lonsdale* (1973), 15 C.C.C. (2d) 201 (Alta. C.A.).

65. (1980), 52 C.C.C. (2d) 547 (N.S.C.A.). In a strong dissenting opinion, Jones, J.A. recognized the need for an exception but believed it to be a case for Parliament to create. See also *R. v. McNamara* (1979), 48 C.C.C. (2d) 201 (Ont. Co. Ct.) and *R. v. Fellichle* (1979), 12 C.R. (3d) 207 (B.C.S.C.).

66. *Ibid.*, at p. 557. See also *R. v. Czipps, supra*, note 64, and *R. v. Sillars* (1978), 45 C.C.C. (2d) 283 (B.C.C.A.) that the charge itself need not allege interference with the spouse's person, liberty or health, but rather that it is sufficient if the evidence of the surrounding circumstances discloses a threat to her person, liberty or health.

67. S.C. 1980-81-82-83, c. 125, s. 29(2).

68. See *R. v. Mann*, [1971] 5 W.W.R. 84 (B.C.S.C.).

has entered into a legal marriage relationship[69] with the accused. Should the witness's status change if the marriage is dissolved before the trial? For some years it was believed the status remained insofar as the witness's right to speak to matters which arose during coverture,[70] but recently the Nova Scotia Supreme Court has expressed the view that there is no reason not to simply follow the plain grammatical meaning of the legislation and terminate incompetency after dissolution.[71]

Finally, one is driven to ask whether this privilege, fashioned in the 16th century, has any place in present day society. Professor Wigmore was clear in his views:

> This privilege has no longer adequate reason for retention. In an age which has so far rationalized, depolarized and dechivalrized the marital relation and the spirit of femininity as to be willing to enact complete legal and political equality and independence of man and woman, this marital privilege is the merest anachronism in legal theory and an indefensible obstruction to truth in practice. It is unfortunate that the United States Supreme Court, when handed the opportunity in 1958, failed to eliminate this relic from the impediments to justice in the federal courts.[72]

In 1980 the United States Supreme Court reversed itself, abandoned the privilege and wrote:

> The ancient foundations for so sweeping a privilege have long since disappeared. Nowhere in the common-law world — indeed in any modern society — is a woman regarded as chattel or demeaned by denial of a separate legal identity and the dignity associated with recognition as a whole human being. Chip by chip, over the years those archaic notions have been cast aside . . .
>
> The contemporary justification for affording an accused such a privilege is also unpersuasive. When one spouse is willing to testify against the other in a criminal proceeding — whatever the motivation — their relationship is almost certainly in disrepair; there is probably little in the way of marital harmony for the privilege to preserve. In these circumstances, a rule of evidence that permits an accused to prevent adverse spousal testimony seems far more likely to frustrate justice than to foster family peace.[73]

R. v. McGINTY
(1986), 52 C.R. (3d) 161, 27 C.C.C. (3d) 36 (Y.T.C.A.)

[The accused was charged with assault causing bodily harm. Three weeks before the trial she married the alleged victim. At the trial the victim said that he would rather not testify. The judge ruled that he was both a competent and a

---

69. See, *e.g., R. v. Coté* (1972), 22 D.L.R. (3d) 353 (Sask. C.A.). See also *R. v. Junaid Khan* (1987), 84 Cr. App. R. 44 (C.A.).

70. See *R. v. Algar,* [1954] 1 Q.B. 279 (C.C.A.) per Lord Goddard, and *R. v. Cooper (No. 1)* (1974), 51 D.L.R. (3d) 216 (Ont. H.C.). Marriage after the material incident but prior to trial makes the spouse incompetent: see *R. v. Lonsdale* (1973), 15 C.C.C. (2d) 201 (Alta. C.A.). But see *R. v. Bailey* (1983), 32 C.R. (3d) 337 (Ont. C.A.): divorced person permitted to testify about events occurring during marriage.

71. *R. v. Marchand* (1980), 55 C.C.C. (2d) 77 (N.S.C.A.).

72. 8 Wigmore, *Evidence* (McNaughton Rev.), s. 2228, p. 221.

73. *Trammel v. U.S.,* 445 U.S. 40, 52 (1980); overturning *Hawkins v. U.S.,* 358 U.S. 74 (1958).

compellable witness for the prosecution. The victim testified, the accused was convicted and appealed.]

McLachlin J.A.: —

. . . .

It emerges clearly from a review of the authorities that policy plays a large part in resolving the question of the compellability of a wife or husband to testify against his or her spouse in a case arising from an act of violence against the witness spouse. On the one hand, it is desirable that persons who commit crimes of violence against their spouses be effectively prosecuted. On the other, it is contended, compelling a husband or wife to testify against his spouse will disturb marital harmony and is repugnant to fair-minded persons. The issue is succinctly stated in the Criminal Law Revision Committee's Eleventh Report, Evidence (General), Cmnd. 4991 (1972), at p. 93:

> How far the wife of the accused should be competent and compellable for the prosecution, for the accused and for a co-accused is in these days essentially a question of balancing the desirability that all available evidence which might conduce to the right verdict should be before the court against (i) the objection on social grounds to disturbing marital harmony more than is absolutely necessary and (ii) what many regard as the harshness of compelling a wife to give evidence against her husband.

The interest of society in securing proper prosecution of persons who commit crimes of violence against their spouses is vital. Such crimes are common. Their consequences are frequently grave. Because they tend to be committed in the privacy of the home, very often it is impossible to prosecute them unless the victim-spouse testifies. And very often when the trial date arrives the spouse declines to testify, whether out of fear of further brutality or blandishments or a combination of the two. As Dean Weir noted in his comment on *Lapworth* at p. 221:

> Cases are frequently reported in the press in which a wife who has laid a charge against her husband for an offence involving injuries to her person, has later had a change of heart and has refused to give evidence when the time came. In such cases, if the prosecution is dependent on the spouse's evidence, the magistrate, probably with reluctance because he realizes that the wife's change of attitude may have been brought about by the 'kicks or kisses' or curses of her husband, has frequently considered himself as having no power to compel the recalcitrant wife to give evidence and has dismissed the case.

Unfortunately, these words are as true now as they were in 1931. If the victim spouse is given the option of whether to testify or not, the result is frequently that the guilty spouse is acquitted. It thus becomes possible for a spouse who has brutalized his or her mate to continue to commit crimes of violence with impunity. On the other hand, if the offending spouse knows that the victim has no choice but to testify, he or she is more likely to be deterred from committing crimes of violence or from inflicting further threats or violence to prevent him or her from testifying.

What then of the competing interests? The first is the disruption to matrimonial harmony which may be caused by compelling the spouse to testify; the second the "natural repugnance" to fair-minded persons of compelling him or her to testify. These interests were discussed by Craig J.A. in *R. v. Sillars, supra*, in the context of competence. In my view his comments are equally applicable to the issue of compellability. After referring to Wigmore on Evidence (McNaughton Revision, 1961), vol. 8, para. 2228, Craig J.A. stated at p. 286:

> The most common view for not permitting such evidence [Wigmore] suggests, is the 'danger of causing dissention and of disturbing the peace of families.' Wigmore opines that there is no merit whatsoever in this particular view. At p. 216 he says:

But if we are to ignore the futility of appealing to a reason which is never allowed in practice to be logically applied and are to treat it as a serious argument, the answer is, first, that the peace of families does not essentially depend on this immunity from compulsory testimony, and next, that so far as it might be affected, that result is not to be allowed to stand in the way of doing justice to others.

A second reason which is sometimes advanced for not permitting a spouse to testify against the other spouse is 'that there is a *natural repugnance* to every fair-minded person to compelling a wife or husband to be the means of the other's condemnation . . .' p. 217. With regard to these views, Wigmore says at pp. 217-8:

> . . . that the state and the complainant have a right to the truth; and that this high and solemn duty of doing justice and of establishing the truth is not to be obstructed by considerations of sentiment . . .

I adopt these comments with the following additional remarks. In my opinion, a rule which leaves to the husband or wife the choice of whether he or she will testify against his aggressor-spouse is more likely to be productive of family discord than to prevent it. It leaves the victim-spouse open to further threats and violence aimed at preventing him or her from testifying, and leaves him or her open to recriminations if he or she chooses to testify. It seems to me better to leave the spouse no choice and to extend to married persons the general policy of the law that victims are compellable witnesses against their aggressor.

With respect to the contention that fair-minded persons find it naturally abhorrent to require one spouse to testify against another, it must also be remembered that fair-minded persons generally find it abhorrent that persons who commit crimes go unprosecuted. A crime committed against a spouse is as much a crime as a crime against a stranger, and should bear the same consequences. Crimes of violence are particularly abhorrent, raising as they do the state's duty to protect the safety of its citizens, married and unmarried. Presumably it was for such reasons that the common law centuries ago concluded that a spouse ought to be permitted to testify against her spouse where the latter had inflicted violence upon her. The same reasons dictate that such spouses should be compellable.

For these reasons I conclude that as a matter of policy husbands and wives should be competent and compellable witnesses against each other in cases of crimes of violence perpetrated by the one upon the other.

Conclusion

On the basis of the authorities and policy, I conclude that the trial judge was correct in ruling that under s. 4(4) [now s. 4(5)] of the Canada Evidence Act spouses are competent and compellable witnesses against their spouses in cases involving violence against them. The husband in this case was properly required to testify. I would dismiss the appeal.

Appeal dismissed.

[Taggart, J.A. concurred with McLachlin, J.A.; Lambert, J.A. concurred in the result for somewhat different reasons.]

R. v. MOORE
(1986), 30 C.C.C. (3d) 328 (N.W.T.T.C.)

BOURASSA Terr. Ct. J.:— Judy Moore's current problems with the law may be traced to a policy of the Government of Canada made applicable to the Northwest Territories as set out in a government news release dated the 21st of December, 1983:

> All complaints of domestic violence involving spousal assault should be investigated immediately and thoroughly with a criteria of charges being laid for court prosecution, irrespective of whether the assaulted spouse wishes to proceed with the charges.

An early object of the investigation should be the protection and assistance of victims. It is the purpose of this directive to require the prosecution of spousal assault cases where there is sufficient evidence.

. . . .

[T]he defendant's choice not to testify was clear and unambiguous, polite and determined. The State's case against the accused Jack Storr was thereby totally frustrated and the State's valid interest in the protection of society and the prevention of violence was foreclosed in this case — the search for juridical truth terminated.

. . . .

The policy of "prosecution regardless", has, for a significant number of people not had the beneficial effect originally anticipated. In fact, its effect has been noticeably detrimental to certain people and institutions and in a number of ways. The problems created in trying to replace an imperfect system (police discretion) by another imperfect system may even be more severe than the problems that were to be originally eliminated. This has in fact been recognized in this jurisdiction, appropriately enough, in the report by the "Task Force on Spousal Assault", February 5, 1985, Government of the Northwest Territories, which observes at p. 44:

Two years ago the R.C.M.P. were directed to lay charges in spousal assault cases without requiring a complaint from the victim. This was an important policy change because it signaled the determination of the Parliament of Canada to have spousal assaults be treated as a crime. The policy change has led to problems, however, and is being used in the North in a discretionary way, though not consistently. The problems are:— when victims know the R.C.M.P. will lay charges they are sometimes reluctant to call the R.C.M.P. even to act as Peace Officers to break-up the incident.

— Victims now fear greater retribution when the R.C.M.P. are called than they did formerly. R.C.M.P. may lay charges which can not be successfully prosecuted because the victim is reluctant, sometimes afraid, to testify and will refuse to give evidence or decline to tell the truth where a batterer knows he can, by threats or promises to the victim, prevent her from giving evidence, his disrespect for the law and the court grows.

Recommendations

The Task Force therefore recommends:— because it appears to be more important to the victim that the R.C.M.P. investigate and restore the peace than whether batterers can be prosecuted, that the policy be reviewed.

Too often this court has presided over spousal assault cases where the witness takes the stand and through swollen lips and with eyes bruised shut suddenly becomes reticent and unable to recall when and how her injuries occurred.

Perversely, in some incidents spouses have conspired together to concoct a story to defeat the State's case and indeed the whole process of law — conspirators against the court and the rule of law. . . .

In a sense, the defendant is a victim, and a deterrent sentence would only serve to increase the degree of victimization. Rather than offering protection, peace and order, the courts become an institution to avoid, to subvert and denigrate.

However, from another perspective a deterrence sentence is called for: The criminal law of Canada applies to all persons equally which application does not depend upon the individual's consent. The State has a valid and continuing interest in maintaining peace between its citizens and intervening when the laws of the land are ignored or broken. This defendant's refusal to testify and contempt was deliberate, calculated, premeditated and without apology. No one person should be allowed, nor can they be allowed, to stand above the law of the land. This attitude, were the court dealing with sentencing on another matter, would be a most aggravating factor.

The defendant apparently does not want the protection of the law with respect to any difficulties she may experience in her personal relationship with her spouse. That relationship is such that it is more important to her than the possible or potential injury she may sustain within it. It would be perverse if the defendant should end up in jail as a result of these proceedings while it is equally unjust the alleged offender . . . should escape the consequences of his actions and it is not just, or right, that people should come to court and refuse to testify. There is no easy answer or resolution to this Gordian knot.

One may refer to the position taken by the Law Reform Commission in effect that people are not going to use the laws if they don't agree with them, in the result the laws will not function. It would appear, at least in this defendant's situation, that the existence of the criminal court, the police and the law by itself and with the well reasoned intentions behind a policy which ultimately brought this woman to court will not prevent spousal assaults, and will not resolve the problem of spousal assault. In my view there is nothing this court can do with respect to this matter before it, this criminal court cannot resolve all of society's problems, one of which being a witness who does not want to testify against her spouse.

There will be a fine of one dollar.

R. v. SALITURO
[1991] 3 S.C.R. 654, 9 C.R. (4th) 324, 68 C.C.C. (3d) 289

[The accused was charged with the forgery of his wife's signature on a cheque payable jointly to her and to him. The wife testified against her husband. There was evidence that at the time of the trial the accused and his wife were separated without any reasonable possibility of reconciliation. The trial judge accepted the wife's evidence and convicted. Without the wife's testimony the accused would not have been convicted. The accused's appeal was dismissed and he appealed further.]

IACOBUCCI, J. (LAMER, C.J.C. AND GONTHIER, CORY, and McLACHLIN, JJ. concurring):—

. . . .

A. *What Are the Limits on the Power of Judges to Change the Common Law?*

(1) *Introduction*

At one time, it was accepted that it was the role of judges to discover the common law, not to change it. In Book One of his *Commentaries on the Laws of England* (4th ed. 1770), Sir William Blackstone propounded a view of the common law as fixed and unchanging. . . .

. . . .

However, Blackstone's static model of the common law has gradually been supplanted by a more dynamic view. . . .

. . . .

In keeping with these developments, this Court has signalled its willingness to adapt and develop common law rules to reflect changing circumstances in society at large. In four recent cases, *Ares v. Venner*, [1970] S.C.R. 608, *Watkins v. Olafson, supra, R. v. Khan*, [1990] 2 S.C.R. 531, and *R. v. Seaboyer*, [1991] 2 S.C.R. 577, this Court has laid down guidelines for the exercise of the power to develop the common law. The common theme of these cases is that, while complex changes to the law with uncertain ramifications should be left to the legislature, the courts can and should make incremental changes to the common law to bring legal rules into step with a changing society. . . .

. . . .

These cases reflect the flexible approach that this Court has taken to the development of the common law. Judges can and should adapt the common law to reflect the changing social, moral and economic fabric of the country. Judges should not be quick to perpetuate rules whose social foundation has long since disappeared. Nonetheless, there are significant constraints on the power of the judiciary to change the law. . . . The judiciary should confine itself to those incremental changes which are necessary to keep the common law in step with the dynamic and evolving fabric of our society.

B. *The Policy of the Rule that a Spouse Is an Incompetent Witness for the Prosecution*

From an examination of the history of the rule making a spouse an incompetent witness for the prosecution, it is apparent that any policy justification which may at one time have existed in support of the rule has now disappeared in the context of divorced or irreconcilably separated spouses. The rule reflects a view of the role of women which is no longer compatible with the importance now given to sexual equality. In particular, the rule making an irreconcilably separated spouse an incompetent witness is inconsistent with the values enshrined in the *Canadian Charter of Rights and Freedoms*, and preserving the rule would be contrary to this Court's duty to see that the common law develops in accordance with the values of the *Charter*.

. . . .

The most important justification is that the rule protects marital harmony. . . . A second reason sometimes mentioned is what Wigmore called the "*natural repugnance* to every fair-minded person to compelling a wife or husband to be the means of the other's condemnation". . . .

The two justifications which have not survived are that a spouse is an incompetent witness because husband and wife are in law a single person, . . . and that husband and wife are disqualified from being witnesses for or against each other because their interests are identical.

. . . .

In the study paper "Competence and Compellability" by the Evidence Project of the Law Reform Commission of Canada, the rule was characterized as more a product of history than the reflection of any clear policy decision:

> . . . the rule, rather than the reflection of a clear-cut fundamental policy decision, appears to be simply a product of history. This is confirmed when we note that a fundamental policy decision surely would be based on concern not only for the married couple but for the family unit as a whole, and yet no one has suggested legislation making fathers and sons or mothers and daughters incompetent witnesses for the prosecution against their parents or children.

. . . .

There is in my opinion a more fundamental difficulty with the reasons for the rule. The grounds which have been used in support of the rule are inconsistent with respect for the freedom of all individuals, which has become a central tenet of the legal and moral fabric of this country particularly since the adoption of the *Charter*. In *R. v. Big M Drug Mart Ltd.*, [1985] 1 S.C.R. 295, Dickson J. (as he then was) defined freedom in this way (at p. 336): "Freedom must surely be founded in respect for the inherent dignity and the inviolable rights of the human person.'' The common law rule making a spouse an incompetent witness involves a conflict between the freedom of the individual to choose whether or not to testify and the interests of society in preserving the marriage bond. It is unnecessary for me to consider the difficult question of how this conflict ought to be resolved, because in this appeal we are concerned only with spouses who are irreconcilably separated. Where spouses are irreconcilably separated, there is no marriage bond to protect and we are faced only with a rule which limits the capacity of the individual to testify.

To give paramountcy to the marriage bond over the value of individual choice in cases of irreconcilable separation may have been appropriate in Lord Coke's time, when a woman's legal personality was incorporated in that of her husband on marriage, but it is inappropriate in the age of the *Charter*. . . .

. . . .

Where the principles underlying a common law rule are out of step with the values enshrined in the *Charter*, the courts should scrutinize the rule closely. If it is possible to change the common law rule so as to make it consistent with *Charter* values, without upsetting the proper balance between judicial and legislative action that I have referred to above, then the rule ought to be changed. The common law rule making an irreconcilably separated spouse an incompetent witness for the prosecution against the other spouse is inconsistent with the values in the *Charter*. Subject to consideration of the limits on the judicial role, the rule ought therefore to be changed. Society can have no interest in preserving marital harmony where spouses are irreconcilably separated because there is no marital harmony to be preserved.

The facts of this case do not raise the issue of whether a spouse who is a competent witness for the prosecution will also be compellable. That question is for another day. However, were it necessary to decide this question, the possibility that a competent spouse would be found also to be compellable is a real one, in light of the reasons in *R. v. McGinty* (1986), 27 C.C.C. (3d) 36 (Y.T.C.A.), *R. v. Marchand*, *supra*, *R. v. Czipps*, *supra*, and *R. v. Lonsdale* (1973), 15 C.C.C. (2d) 201 (Alta. S.C., App. Div.), although I would note that in the U.S., a spouse is a competent but not a compellable witness for the prosecution: *Trammel v. United States*, 445 U.S. 40 (1980).

. . . .

Concerns were raised before us that making an irreconcilably separated spouse a competent witness would increase the risk of violence to women. Violence against women is a very grave problem in our society, and any possibility of an increase in the risk of violence must be taken most seriously. But I find it difficult to accept that the proper response to the threat of violence is to limit the capacity of women in the hope that preventing women from testifying will decrease the risk of violence against them. If our expectations for a society founded on respect for the dignity of the human person are to have meaning, we must encourage and protect everyone in the exercise of their rights and responsibilities as equal members of our society. Furthermore, if a competent spouse is also compellable, I would note that McLachlin J.A. (as she then was) suggested in *McGinty*, *supra*, at p. 60, that making a spouse compellable may in fact reduce the risk of violence by giving the spouse no choice but to testify. The same argument was made by the Evidence Project of the Law Reform Commission of Canada in their study paper ''Competence and Compellability'', *supra*, at pp. 6-7.

. . . .

Absent parliamentary intervention, I would conclude that changing the common law rule to make spouses who are irreconcilably separated competent witnesses for the prosecution would be appropriate. . . .

. . . .

I would conclude that in appropriate cases, judges can and should change the common law. This is such a case. The common law should be the servant of society. While there are changes to the common law that are best left to the legislature, the change made by the Court of Appeal in the present case to the rule that a spouse is an incompetent witness for the prosecution is not an example of such a change.

Has the Court changed the common law or has it changed the statutory law? Both?

In *R. v. Jeffrey*[74] the accused was convicted of two counts of breaking and entering the unoccupied home of his estranged wife's parents and stealing. The trial judge held that she was a competent witness for the Crown on the principle that irreconcilably separated spouses were competent witnesses against each other in a criminal trial. On appeal the sole issue was the standard of proof of irreconcilable separation required to render a spouse a competent witness. The accused argued that the Crown's burden of proof was that beyond a reasonable doubt as against the standard of balance of probabilities adopted by the convicting judge. It was held that the proof of irreconcilable separation was to be decided under the civil standard of balance of probabilities

In *R. v. Thompson*[75] the accused was convicted of possession of a stolen motorcycle The Crown called as a witness Ms. Daisy MacDonald, who was identified as the "common-law spouse" of the accused. The evidence before the court with respect to the relationship was that MacDonald had lived with the accused "on and off for five years"; MacDonald and the accused were parents of a two-year-old child; MacDonald was pregnant with the appellant's child; there was no legal reason why the two could not marry; MacDonald had had no other relationships with men during the time she had been living with the appellant; plans between MacDonald and the accused to be married were "called off on a couple of previous occasions"; and MacDonald and the accused planned to get married in August 1993. The learned trial judge held that MacDonald was a common-law spouse of the appellant but held that section 4 of the Canada Evidence Act did not apply to "common-law spouses" and accordingly, MacDonald was directed to testify. On appeal the accused unsuccessfully argued that that such a distinction is a prohibited discrimination violating section 15(1) of the Charter. The Court noted:

> It is apparent that any attempt to define such a group becomes an arbitrary line-drawing exercise, defying classification as "discrete and insular". And no matter where the line is drawn, membership in the group is highly fluid, with people constantly flowing in or out, as criteria are met or lost.[76]

In *R. v. Marchand*,[77] the accused was charged with forging his ex-wife's signature on two mortgages. The trial judge decided the ex-wife could testify on the basis of the common law exception with respect to matters affecting the person, liberty or health of the spouse. On appeal the Court noted that the trial judge was correct on the issue of competence but for the wrong reason. Since

---

74.   (1993), 25 C.R. (4th) 104 (Alta. C.A.).
75.   (1994), 90 C.C.C. (3d) 519 (Alta. C.A.).
76.   *Ibid.*, at p. 525.
77.   (1980), 55 C.C.C. (2d) 77 (N.S.C.A.).

the parties were no longer married she was not a spouse within the meaning of section 4 of the Canada Evidence Act!

R. v. HAWKINS
[1996] 3 S.C.R. 1043, 2 C.R. (5th) 245, 111 C.C.C. (3d) 129

[The accused, H. and M., were charged with conspiracy to obstruct justice. The investigation with respect to H. and M. was commenced after H.'s then girlfriend G. provided information to the police. G. testified as a Crown witness at the preliminary inquiry and originally implicated the accused. However, at the end of her testimony at the preliminary inquiry, G. indicated that she had obtained advice from independent counsel. Her counsel informed the presiding judge that she wished to be recalled as a witness, and substantially recant her initial testimony. She was permitted to do so. Shortly after the preliminary inquiry was concluded, G. married H. At trial, the Crown nevertheless sought to call G. as a Crown witness. On the motion, the Crown adduced evidence tending to show that H.'s motivation for marrying G. was to render her an incompetent witness for the Crown. The trial judge held that G. was not a competent witness for the Crown. The trial judge also refused to admit G.'s evidence under s. 715 of the Criminal Code, or as an exception to the hearsay rule.]

LAMER C.J.C. and IACOBUCCI J. (GONTHIER and CORY JJ. concurring):—

. . . .

In our view, the circumstances of this case do not warrant modifying the common law rule of spousal incompetence. Both the trial judge and the Court of Appeal were correct in holding that Graham was not a competent witness for the Crown at the trial, as she had entered into a valid and genuine marriage with the co-appellant Hawkins.

. . . .

Numerous justifications for the rule have been advanced over the history of the common law, but only two appear to have survived to the modern era. As originally noted by Lord Coke, in his *Institutes of the Laws of England* (1832), the first justification for the rule is that it promotes conjugal confidences and protects marital harmony. The second justification is that the rule prevents the indignity of conscripting an accused's spouse to participate in the accused's own prosecution. However, as this Court recognized in *Salituro*, serious criticisms have been levelled against these two surviving justifications of the traditional rule. It has been called arbitrary for excluding other familial relationships, and antiquated, because it is based on outmoded notions of marriage. Perhaps most importantly, rendering a person incapable of testifying solely on the basis of marital status does strip an individual of key aspects of his or her autonomy.

. . . .

Some have suggested an alternative approach whereby a spouse could be declared competent against his or her spouse, but not compellable. The United Kingdom recently endorsed such a rule with the passage of s. 80 of the *Police and Criminal Evidence Act 1984* (U.K.), 1984, c. 60. The United States Supreme Court adopted a similar modification of the common law rule. The court held that under the Federal Rules of Evidence, a spouse is a competent but not compellable witness for the prosecution, with the witness spouse having the privilege to refuse to testify adversely: *Trammel v. United States*, 445 U.S. 40 (1980). While such alternative approaches to the rule of spousal incompetency may serve to promote the autonomy and dignity of an individual spouse, it is our opinion that any significant change to the rule should not be made by the courts, but should rather be left to Parliament.

The common law rule of spousal incompetence has remained largely unchanged for some 350 years. The respondent has submitted that there is ample scope for judicial development of the rule. While it is true that this Court has signalled its willingness to adapt and develop common law rules to reflect changing circumstances in society at large it is clear that the courts will only make incremental changes to the common law. So, for example, the change implemented in *Salituro*, did not strike at the original justifications of marital harmony and repugnance which animated the substance of the common law rule.

. . . .

In this instance, the Crown has conceded that the marriage of Hawkins and Graham is genuine. At the time of this Court's hearing, the couple were approaching their seventh wedding anniversary. There was no evidence that either of the two partners had failed to fulfil their reciprocal obligations of care and support. Under the circumstances, making Graham compellable by the Crown would threaten the couple's genuine marital harmony and undermine the purpose of the spousal incompetency rule. . . . Absent evidence that the marriage was a sham, we fail to see how the court can begin to inquire into the reasons for the marriage. There is no justification for such an inquiry unless there should be concrete evidence that the marriage was legally invalid. . . . We emphasize that the matter may be different if the evidence clearly established that the only purpose of the marriage was to avoid criminal responsibility by rendering a key witness uncompellable and that the partners had no intention of fulfilling their mutual obligations of care and support. In such circumstances, the marriage would be a "sham", and the court may be willing to take this into account. However, this is not the case in the Hawkins-Graham marriage.

[La Forest, L'Heureux-Dubé, Major, Sopinka and McLachlin JJ. agreed with the above position on competence and compellability.]

Justice Carthy in the Court of Appeal in *Salituro*, dissenting, noted that the change to the common law permitting the spouse to testify effected a change to the statutory law as well since Parliament had already decided where to draw the line between the interests of truth and justice and the interest of protection of marriage, and this line was altered by the Court. By its decision in *Salituro*, the Canada Evidence Act was effectively amended. It is one thing for the judges to modify the common law that they created to mirror their appreciation of Charter values, but changing legislation for similar reasons, although the statute is not seen to violate a section of the Charter, is quite another.

In *R. v. Hawkins* the Court decided that changing the common law and creating an exception to the rule as to spousal incompetency where the parties entered into the marriage after the events in issue, thus insulating the spouse from being called as a witness, would be more than an incremental change. Had the Court been persuaded by the Crown to effect this change, the Canada Evidence Act would again be altered. This restraint from entering the arena of legislative change is admirable, but the Court specifically noted that the marriage in *Hawkins* was a genuine marriage. The Court noted that the situation might be different

if the evidence clearly established that the only purpose of the marriage was to avoid criminal responsibility by rendering a key witness uncompellable and that the partners had no intention of fulfilling their mutual obligations of care and support.

The court may not be finished amending the legislation!

(e) Compellability of Accused

(i) *History of Privilege Against Self-incrimination*[78]

Prior to the 13th century, criminal procedure was basically accusatorial. Both on the continent and in England, a private person accused another, provided details of the complaint, conducted the prosecution and led the proof. The resultant trial might be by compurgation, battle, or ordeal. By the 13th century, trials by battle and compurgation had fallen into disfavour as they were increasingly seen as irrational and untrustworthy. In 1215, the church forbade its clergy from participating in trials by ordeal and new methods of proceeding became necessary. England retained the accusatorial method and gave its grand jury of presentment the additional task of finding a verdict. In England the perceived lack of partiality in the trier gradually gave birth to a separate, petit jury for the latter task. The ecclesiastical courts and the continental civilian courts on the other hand embraced the inquisitorial method as a replacement.

The inquisitorial method allowed the judge to fill all the roles; he was accuser, prosecutor and trier. The judge, and not a jury of presentment, decided whether there were sufficient grounds to call the individual to answer. The method also provided for a new oath to be taken by the accused at the beginning of the inquiry whereby he promised to answer all questions put to him though he be given no information regarding the charges against him nor the evidence, if any, which supported them. This type of oath became known as the oath *ex officio* as it was administered by the judge by virtue of his office.

The oath *ex officio* was introduced into the ecclesiastical courts in England in 1236, and was adopted by the judicial arm of the King's Council, the Court of Star Chamber, in 1487. In the common law courts at this time the accused was interrogated but he was not sworn. On taking the oath *ex officio* the accused was compelled to choose between offending his God and risking punishment for perjury or accusing himself of crime; failing to take the oath was regarded by the court as a confession of guilt. Placing an individual in such a dilemma was regarded by many as more cruel than physical torture. With no requirement of a charge in advance, much less a demonstrated basis for the same, the individual became his own accuser and his own means of destruction.

During the 16th and 17th centuries the *ex officio* oath was used in England by the Court of Star Chamber and the Court of the High Commission in Causes Ecclesiastical for the purposes of stamping out non-conforming political and religious views. Opposition to this method of inquiry, wide ranging and without benefit of accusation, steadily grew and reached its culmination in 1638 in the trial in the Court of Star Chamber of a young Puritan named John Lilburne. The offence was importing seditious books into England, and while it would appear

---

78. See Levy, *Origins of the Fifth Amendment* (1968, Oxford). But compare Langbein, "The Historical Origins of the Privilege" (1994), 92 Mich. L. Rev. 1047. And note the comment of Frankfurter, J.: "The privilege against self-incrimination is a specific provision of which it is peculiarly true that 'a page of history is worth a volume of logic'," in *Ullman v. U.S.*, 350 U.S. 422, 438 (1956). See also Morgan, "The Privilege Against Self-Incrimination" (1949), 34 Minn. L. Rev. 1; and 8 Wigmore, *Evidence* (McNaughton Rev.), s. 2250.

that he knew the nature of the charge against him, no bill of complaint was preferred before he was requested to take the oath. Lilburne denied the charges against him but refused to take the oath. Rather than taking this as a confession of guilt, the court found him guilty of contempt and sentenced him to a fine, corporal punishment and imprisonment until he conformed by taking the oath. Lilburne's martyrdom, and his numerous pamphlets against the excesses of the High Commission and Star Chamber smuggled out of his prison caused others to follow his example, public discontent to swell, and the way to be paved for radical reforms. In 1641 the High Commission and Star Chamber were abolished and the *ex officio* oath outlawed. The opposition had been to the far ranging inquiry on oath without benefit of accusation or bill of complaint; but such was the depth of emotion over the excesses of those courts that anything akin to their procedures was regarded as odious. Gradually, in the common law courts, accused persons, even though properly charged, began to resist their questioning on the basis that no man is bound to incriminate himself. By 1700 it was firmly recognized that no person, in any court, whether he be accused or merely witness, could be compelled to answer if the answer would tend to incriminate. The common law privilege was born.

It should be noted, however, that accused persons continued being questioned by examining justices of the peace prior to trial, although that examination was not on oath. The normal criminal trial would begin with a reading of the accused's earlier compulsory examination.[79] The privilege against self-incrimination, at least in its formative years, was confined to foreclose only compulsory examination at trial. It was not until *Jervis's Act* of 1848[80] that we see the accused being advised that he need not make a statement to the examining justices prior to committal.

Until the end of the 19th century the accused was not able to give testimony on oath for two reasons. First, he was regarded as incompetent because of his obvious interest in the outcome of the proceedings. Second, it was regarded as a violation of his privilege against self-incrimination to place him on the horns of a dilemma: should he choose to testify falsely gaining temporal relief but everlasting damnation or testify truthfully and forfeit his liberty? Perhaps a trilemma in that should he choose not to testify, and it being known that he was able, he risked an inference of guilt being drawn from his silence.

(ii) *Canada Evidence Act*

By the end of the 19th century statutory reforms made the accused competent for the defence. The common law position of non-compellability at the instance of the prosecution remained. Section 4 of the Canada Evidence Act provides:

> (1) Every person charged with an offence, and, except as otherwise provided in this section, the wife or husband, as the case may be, of the person so charged, is a competent witness for the defence, whether the person so charged is charged solely or jointly with any other person.

---

79. The compulsory examination was provided for by statute: (1554), 1 & 2 Phil. & Mar., c. 13, s. 4.

80. 11 & 12 Vict., c. 42, s. 18, the predecessor to the present Canadian provision used in the preliminary hearing: see Criminal Code, R.S.C. 1985, c. C-46, ss. 540, 541.

It is important to recognize that this privilege, in its origins and as later interpreted in Canada, operated to protect a person from being compelled to give evidence before a court or like tribunal. It was also restricted to testimonial evidence. Taking bodily samples, fingerprints or photographs were not seen as captured by the privilege.[81] In short, the privilege in Canada was seen to be reflected simply, and solely, in the accused's non-compellability at trial. The accused, pursuant to the legislation, was a competent witness for the defence. It was up to the accused to decide whether he would go into the box.

In Canada, the legislation also provided that no witness, including the accused who chose to become a witness, could refuse to answer a question on the grounds that the answer might tend to criminate. Rather, the legislation provided that he was obliged to answer but the answer could not be used against him in later proceedings. For example, the Canada Evidence Act provides:

> 5.(1) No witness shall be excused from answering any question on the ground that the answer to the question may tend to criminate him, or may tend to establish his liability to a civil proceeding at the instance of the Crown or of any person.

> (2) Where with respect to any question a witness objects to answer on the ground that his answer may tend to criminate him, or may tend to establish his liability to a civil proceeding at the instance of the Crown or of any person, and if but for this Act, or the Act of any provincial legislature, the witness would therefore have been excused from answering the question, then although the witness is by reason of this Act or the provincial Act compelled to answer, the answer so given shall not be used or admissible in evidence against him in any criminal trial or other criminal proceeding against him thereafter taking place, other than a prosecution for perjury in the giving of that evidence or for the giving of contradictory evidence.

Similar provisions exist in provincial legislation.[82]

In *R. v. Mottola*[83] Morden, J.A. explained the proper procedure to be followed:

> An accused person who is a witness and any other witness is not excused from answering incriminating questions. However, if the witness objects to answering a question upon the ground that his answer may tend to incriminate him and he then answers it as he is bound by the Act to do, the answer shall not be used in evidence against him in any criminal proceedings against him thereafter taking place with the necessary exception for a perjury charge in the giving of such evidence. The objection must be taken by the witness to the question. In practice when a witness is being examined upon an incident or series of incidents and he thinks that all or any of his answers might tend to incriminate him, the Judge might of course permit a general objection to the series of such questions and not require a specific objection to each and every question. But the objection cannot be taken before the witness is sworn and before he is asked any questions. Any protection the witness has if he objects to the question, as provided by s. 5(2), is against the use of his answer in independent, contemporaneous or subsequent prosecutions. This protection is conferred by the

---

81. *Marcoux v. R.* (1975), 24 C.C.C. (2d) 1 (S.C.C.).

82. For similar provincial and territorial provisions. see: R.S.A. 1980, c. A-21, s. 6; R.S.B.C. 1979, c. 116, s. 4; R.S.M. 1987, c. E-150, s. 6; R.S.N.B. 1973, c. E-II, s. 6; R.S.N. 1970, c. 115, s. 3A; R.S.N.W.T. 1974, c. E-4, s. 8; R.S.N.S. 1989, c. 154, s. 59; R.S.O. 1990, c. E.23, s. 9; R.S.P.E.I. 1988, c. E-11, s. 6; R.S.S. 1978, c. S-16, s. 37; and R.S.Y.T. 1986, c. 57, s. 7.

83. (1959), 124 C.C.C. 288, 295 (Ont. C.A.).

Act and not by any ruling of the Judge when objection is taken to a question. The procedure followed in the case under appeal was unwarranted. The Magistrate had no authority to confer or withhold "the protection of the Court" upon the witness Boule or upon the appellant Vallee. Both these witnesses could at any time during their examination object to answer questions — they had no right to refuse to answer — but if they would have been excused at common law from answering such questions, their answers could not be used against them in other criminal proceedings. The accused has the same rights in this regard as any other witness at his trial.

Notice that while the federal legislation can only give protection against subsequent use in criminal proceedings, protection in other proceedings is also granted by counterpart legislation of the provinces.[84]

(iii) *Sections 11(c) and 13 of Charter*

Compare the provision in the Charter of Rights, section 13, which provides for blanket exclusion without the necessity of objection.[85] This is an obvious and welcome advance.

The Charter of Rights provides:

11. (*c*) [Any person charged with an offence has the right] not to be compelled to be a witness in proceedings against that person in respect of the offence.

13.   A witness who testifies in any proceedings has the right not to have any incriminating evidence so given used to incriminate that witness in any other proceedings, except in a prosecution for perjury or for the giving of contradictory evidence.

DUBOIS v. R.
[1985] 2 S.C.R. 350, 48 C.R. (3d) 193, 22 C.C.C. (3d) 513

[The accused was convicted by a jury of second degree murder, but the Alberta Court of Appeal granted a new trial on the grounds of misdirection to the jury. At the second trial, held after the proclamation of the Canadian Charter of Rights and Freedoms, the Crown introduced as evidence the accused's testimony, given voluntarily at his first trial, in which he admitted that he had killed the deceased but alleged circumstances of justification. The defence counsel objected, arguing that it was contrary to the right in section 13 of the Charter of a witness who testifies in any proceedings not to have any incriminating evidence used to incriminate that witness in any other proceedings. The trial judge ruled that section 13 did not apply, as the Charter came into force after the accused had testified in his first trial. The accused was again convicted. His appeal, on the ground that his testimony at the first trial should have been excluded, was dismissed. The Alberta Court of Appeal held that the second trial was not "any other proceedings" within the meaning of section 13. The accused appealed further. McIntyre, J., dissenting, would have dismissed the appeal on the basis that a second trial on the same charge would not be "other proceedings" within the meaning of section 13. The majority judgment was given by:]

LAMER J. (DICKSON C.J.C., ESTEY, CHOUINARD, WILSON and LE DAIN JJ. concurring):—

---

84.   See, *e.g.*, the Ontario Evidence Act, R.S.O. 1990, c. E.23, s. 9.
85.   R.S.C. 1985, App. II (Sched. B). See *R. v. Wilson* (1982), 67 C.C.C. (2d) 481 (Ont. Co. Ct.), that by the Charter of Rights no objection is needed.

. . . .

NATURE AND PURPOSE OF S. 13

A plain reading of s. 13 indicates that the guarantee it provides is directed against self-incrimination through the use of one's previous testimony. It is a very specific form of protection against self-incrimination and must therefore be viewed in the light of two closely related rights, the right of non-compellability and the presumption of innocence, set forth in s. 11(*c*) and (*d*) of the Charter:

. . . .

Section 11(*d*) imposes upon the Crown the burden of proving the accused's guilt beyond a reasonable doubt as well as that of making out the case against the accused before he or she need respond, either by testifying or by calling other evidence. As Laskin J. (as he then was) wrote in *R. v. Appleby*, [1972] S.C.R. 303 at 317 [B.C.]:

> The 'right to be presumed innocent' . . . is, in popular terms, a way of expressing the fact that the Crown has the ultimate burden of establishing guilt; if there is any reasonable doubt at the conclusion of the case on any element of the offence charged, an accused person must be acquitted. In a more refined sense, the presumption of innocence gives an accused the initial benefit of a right of silence and the ultimate benefit (after the Crown's evidence is in and as well as any evidence tendered on behalf of the accused) of any reasonable doubt: See *Coffin v. U.S.* (1895), 156 U.S. 432 at 452.

The Crown's "burden of establishing guilt" and the "right of silence", i.e., the concept of a "case to meet", which are essential elements of the presumption of innocence, also underlie the non-compellability right. For, as Professor Ratushny has written, in "The Role of the Accused in the Criminal Process (Ss. 10(*a*) and (*b*), 11(*a*), (*c*) and (*d*), and 13)", in Tarnopolsky and Beaudoin (eds.), The Canadian Charter of Rights and Freedoms: Commentary (1982), at pp. 358-59:

> In many ways, it is the principle of a 'case to meet' which is the real underlying protection which the 'non-compellability' rule seeks to promote. The important protection is not that the accused need not testify, but that the Crown must prove its case before there can be any expectation that he will respond, whether by testifying himself, or by calling other evidence. However, even where a 'case to meet' has been presented, the burden of proof remains upon the Crown to the end.

And in Self-Incrimination in the Canadian Criminal Process (1979), at p. 180:

> The accused need only respond once. The Crown must present its evidence at an open trial. The accused is entitled to test and to attack it. If it does not reach a certain standard, the accused is entitled to an acquittal. If it does reach that standard, then and only then is the accused required to respond or to stand convicted.

As such, the concept of the "case to meet" is common to ss. 11(*c*), 11(*d*) and 13. In the context of ss. 11(*c*) and 13, it means specifically that the accused enjoys "the initial benefit of a right of silence" (*R. v. Appleby*, supra [p. 317]), and its corollary, protection against self-incrimination. Section 13, like s. 11(*c*), is a recognition of the principle (Wigmore on Evidence, McNaughton revision, vol. 8 (1961), p. 318, para. 2251) that:

> . . . the individual is sovereign and that proper rules of battle between government and individual require that the individual not be bothered for less than good reason and not be conscripted by his opponent to defeat himself . . .

Hence the purpose of s. 13, when the section is viewed in the context of s. 11(*c*) and (*d*), is to protect individuals from being indirectly compelled to incriminate themselves, to ensure that the Crown will not be able to do indirectly that which s. 11(*c*) prohibits. It guarantees the right not to have a person's previous testimony used to incriminate him or her in other proceedings.

. . . .

ANY OTHER PROCEEDINGS

Having established that s. 13 is a form of protection against self-incrimination, it is still necessary to consider whether this implies that an accused who has chosen to testify should be protected in a retrial of the same offence or one included therein.

I do not see how the evidence given by the accused to meet the case as it was in the first trial could become part of the Crown's case against the accused in the second trial, without being in violation of s. 11(*d*), and to a lesser extent of s. 11(*c*). For the accused is being *conscripted* to help the Crown in discharging its burden of "*a case to meet*", and is thereby denied his or her right to stand mute until a case has been made out.

To allow the prosecution to use, as part of its case, the accused's previous testimony would, in effect, allow the Crown to do indirectly what it is estopped from doing directly by s. 11(*c*), i.e., to compel the accused to testify. It would also permit an indirect violation of the right of the accused to be presumed innocent and remain silent until proven guilty by the prosecution, as guaranteed by s. 11(*d*) of the Charter.

In *R. v. Mannion* [86] the accused had been convicted of rape. An appeal was allowed and a new trial directed. During the second trial one of the central issues raised concerned the appropriate inferences to be drawn from the accused's hasty departure from Edmonton after the alleged commission of the crime; the inferences depended upon whether he knew of the rape charge before his departure. At the second trial the accused was again convicted. At both trials evidence was led that prior to his arrest and after the accused had left Edmonton no police officer had told him they wanted to investigate his involvement in a rape. At the second trial the Crown confronted the accused with his testimony given at the first trial, in which he had testified that he knew before he left Edmonton that the police wanted to see him concerning a rape. The Supreme Court made a logical extension of *Dubois.* They found that the accused's testimony at the earlier trial, while not introduced by the Crown in chief, was still used to incriminate him. The Crown argued at the second trial that the accused knew that a rape was involved before the police told him, and his precipitate flight from Edmonton displayed a consciousness of guilt. The earlier inconsistent statement, which showed knowledge of the rape, was relied on by the Crown to establish guilt.

R. v. KULDIP
[1990] 3 S.C.R. 618, 1 C.R. (4th) 285, 61 C.C.C. (3d) 385

[The accused was convicted of failing to stop at the scene of an accident contrary to section 233(2) of the Criminal Code. An appeal was allowed and a new trial ordered. On the new trial, Crown counsel sought to cross-examine the accused on testimony he had given at the first trial. At the first trial the accused had testified that following the accident he had attended at a police

---

86.   (1986), 53 C.R. (3d) 193 (S.C.C.).

station and reported what had occurred. The accused also testified that about a month later he went back to the same police station in an attempt to find out to whom he had made the original accident report. The accused testified at the first trial that when he attended on the second occasion he spoke to a particular officer who told the accused that he remembered him being at the police station following the accident. At the second trial, however, the accused discovered, just an hour before he was to testify, that the officer whom he had seen on his second attendance at the station had not been on duty when he claimed to have reported the accident. At the second trial, the accused testified that he had thought this officer was there but he must have been mistaken. Crown counsel cross-examined the accused on the testimony which he had given at the first trial. The accused was again convicted and his appeal to the summary conviction appeal court was dismissed. In the Ontario Court of Appeal, his appeal was allowed on the basis that cross-examination of the accused on the evidence which he had given at the first trial infringed section 13 of the Charter. The Supreme Court allowed the Crown's appeal.]

LAMER C.J.C. (DICKSON, C.J.C., GONTHIER and McLACHLIN, JJ. concurring):—

. . . .

[T]he respondent's prior testimony was used by the Crown to suggest, in effect, that he changed the evidence he gave at his first trial that P.C. Brown was present when he reported the occurrence on February 6, 1983, because he had learned at the subsequent trial that P.C. Brown was not on duty that day. In doing so, the Crown obviously sought to undermine the respondent's credibility in respect of the fact that he had allegedly reported the incident immediately.

. . . .

Using a prior inconsistent statement from a former proceeding during cross-examination in order to impugn the credibility of an accused does not, in my view, incriminate that accused person. The previous statement is not tendered as evidence to establish the proof of its contents, but rather is tendered for the purpose of unveiling a contradiction between what the accused is saying now and what he or she has said on a previous occasion. For example, a situation could arise where A. is charged with murder and B. gives testimony at A.'s trial that B. was with A. in Montreal on the day of the alleged murder committing a bank robbery. B. may subsequently become the accused in a trial for robbery and choose to take the stand in his defence. If B. then testifies that he was in Ottawa on the day of the alleged robbery, the Crown is entitled to cross-examine B. with respect to the discrepancy between his current testimony and his previous testimony. The previous statement is used only to impeach the accused's credibility with respect to his current testimony that he was in Ottawa on the day of the alleged robbery. The previous statement may not be used, however, to establish the truth of its contents; it may not be used to establish that the accused was, in fact, in Montreal on the day of the alleged bank robbery nor can it be used to establish that the accused did, in fact, commit the alleged bank robbery. In the situation just described, it would be incumbent upon the trial judge to give a warning to the jury that it would not be open to it to conclude, on the basis of his previous statement, that the accused was in Montreal on the day of the alleged bank robbery nor to conclude that the accused did, in fact, commit the bank robbery. The jury would have to be warned that the only possible conclusion open to it from such cross-examination would be that the accused was not telling the truth when he said that he was in Ottawa on the day of the robbery and that he was not, in fact, in Ottawa on that day. Of course, this in turn might well enable it to conclude, beyond a reasonable doubt, that B. *was* in Montreal committing the robbery; but this conclusion could only be reached as a result of *other* evidence which will have become uncontradicted evidence as a result of the cross-examination which has impeached the credibility of the accused and thereby caused the jury to disbelieve the accused's current testimony.

. . . .

An accused has the right to remain silent during his or her trial. However, if an accused chooses to take the stand, that accused is implicitly vouching for his or her credibility. Such an accused, like any other witness, has therefore opened the door to having the trustworthiness of his/her evidence challenged. An interpretation of s. 13 which insulates such an accused from having previous inconsistent statements put to him/her on cross-examination where the only purpose of doing so is to challenge that accused's credibility, would, in my view, "stack the deck" too highly in favour of the accused.

. . . .

The [Ontario Court of Appeal's] understanding of the purpose underlying s. 13 and its concern for the inequity which could result if s. 13 were interpreted so as to provide less protection than s. 5 thus caused it to reject the Crown's contention that s. 13 prevents the use of prior inconsistent statements made by an accused in cross-examining him at a later proceeding where the sole purpose of using the statement is to assist the Crown in incriminating the accused.

With all due respect, I am unable to accept the Court of Appeal's method of interpreting s. 13. First, I believe that s. 5(2) of the Act should not be used as an obligatory instrument in the assessment of the ambit of s. 13, even if the necessary result, which I do not admit in this instance, would be that the protection granted by the federal statute is wider than that afforded under the Charter. It is possible that, in certain circumstances, the rights protected by statute will be greater in scope than comparable rights affirmed by our Constitution. The Charter aims to guarantee that individuals benefit from a minimum standard of fundamental rights. If Parliament chooses to grant protection over and above that which is enshrined in our Charter, it is always at liberty to do so.

. . . .

Secondly, and I say this with the utmost respect, I cannot accept the Ontario Court of Appeal's interpretation of s. 5(2) of the *Canada Evidence Act*. In my opinion, the protection offered by s. 5(2), namely, the guarantee that "the answer so given [by the witness] shall not be used or receivable in evidence against him in any criminal trial, or other criminal proceeding against him thereafter taking place . . .", must be interpreted in consideration of the express purpose of allowing the witness to make an objection under s. 5(2). This purpose is expressed clearly in the opening words of s. 5(2) that impose the substantive condition to be fulfilled before the section is made operative: a witness is entitled to object to a question on the grounds that "his answer may tend to criminate him, or may tend to establish his liability to a civil proceeding at the instance of the Crown or of any person. . .". Since the witness is only entitled to object to a question on the grounds that the answer to the question will tend to criminate him, it is only logical that he be guaranteed, in exchange for compelling him to answer the question, that his answer will not be used to criminate him in a subsequent proceeding. A further guarantee that such answer will not be used in cross-examination to challenge the witness's credibility at a later proceeding would extend beyond the purpose of s. 5(2). With respect for contrary views, testimony given by a witness at a proceeding may, notwithstanding an objection under s. 5(2), be used at a subsequent proceeding in cross-examining the witness if the purpose of such use is to impeach his credibility and not to incriminate the witness.

. . . .

In the case at bar, the cross-examination of the respondent at the second trial was clearly for the purpose of undermining his credibility. Therefore, in view of the foregoing analysis, his s. 13 rights were not violated.

. . . .

Consequently, I would allow the appeal and restore the conviction entered by the Provincial Court of Ontario.

[Wilson, La Forest and L'Heureux-Dubé, JJ. agreed with the Court of Appeal.]

The Supreme Court's ruling in *Kuldip* seems to be consistent with principle. Provisions such as section 5(2) of the Canada Evidence Act, and provincial counterparts such as section 9 of the Ontario Evidence Act, modelled after similar legislation in England, had as their purpose the discovery of truth. A blanket ability to refuse to answer any questions on the ground that the answers might tend to incriminate in the future would frustrate present inquiry. From an early time it was not unusual for statutes to grant immunity, or indemnity from prosecution, for any offences arising out of a witness's testimony — if that person would provide truthful evidence against another. Professor Wigmore noted that "[t]he tradition of it as a lawful method of annulling the privilege against self-incrimination is unquestioned in English history."[87] The state would forego prosecution of one offender in the future for the sake of discovering the truth with respect to the instant matter involving another offender. From that position, it was a natural step to replacing statutes which gave complete immunity from prosecution for any offence disclosed by the witness's evidence with legislative provisions which give protection against subsequent use of the witness's testimony, as is done by section 5(2) and by section 13 of the Charter. The protection is clearly much narrower but the thought is the same: get the evidence concerning the matter at issue, advance the inquiry and, in exchange, grant some form of immunity for the witness. Since the purpose of the legislation is pursuit of truth, it would be very odd to allow such legislative provisions to inhibit that search by permitting a witness to tell one story at trial, and a different story at another trial, and yet be shielded from confrontation with the earlier statement. It is one thing to protect the witness against directly incriminating herself by her own words, using her own words as indicative of guilt, and quite another to protect against the use of an earlier statement to expose defects in her credibility.

The decision in *Kuldip* raises an interesting and perhaps even more important question. Suppose an accused person gives a statement to the police during their investigation in such circumstances that a court later declares that a Charter right has been infringed and that the statement ought to be excluded pursuant to section 24(2). Should the prosecution nevertheless be able to confront the accused with his earlier statement in cross-examination should he tell a story at trial which is inconsistent with his earlier statement?

In some jurisdictions in the United States, the prosecution is entitled to use the earlier statement to challenge credibility. In *Miranda v. State of Arizona*,[88] the United States Supreme Court saw the Fifth Amendment's right to be protected against compulsory self-incrimination as the solution to the confession problem. In *Miranda*, the court briefly summarized its holding:

The prosecution may not use statements, whether exculpatory or inculpatory, stemming from custodial interrogation of the defendant unless it demonstrates the

---

87.   8 Wigmore, *Evidence* (McNaughton Rev.), s. 2281.
88.   384 U.S. 436, 86 S.Ct. 1602 (1966).

use of procedural safeguards effective to secure the privilege against self incrimination. . . . Prior to any questioning, the person must be warned that he has a right to remain silent, that any statement he does make may be used against him, and that he has the right to the presence of an attorney, either retained or appointed.[89]

In *Harris v. New York*,[90] statements made by the accused to the police at police headquarters were preceded by defective *Miranda* warnings; the accused was not advised that he had a right to appointed counsel if he could not afford one. The accused testified at his trial. Over his objection, the prosecution introduced the accused's earlier statements which partially contradicted his testimony. The trial judge instructed the jury that it could consider the earlier statements only for the purpose of evaluating the accused's credibility. Harris was convicted. On review, the Supreme Court held that the evidence was properly admitted. In *Miranda*, the court had ruled that both inculpatory and exculpatory statements would be inadmissible if the warnings were not given and noted:

> If a statement made were in fact truly exculpatory it would, of course, never be used by the prosecution. In fact, statements merely intended to be exculpatory by the defendant are often used to impeach his testimony at trial or to demonstrate untruths in the statement given under interrogation and thus to prove guilt by implication. These statements are incriminating in any meaningful sense of the word and may not be used without the full warnings and effective waiver required for any other statement.[91]

Nevertheless, Chief Justice Burger, for the majority in *Harris*, recognizing that "some comments" in *Miranda* could be read as a bar to use of an uncounselled statement for *any* purpose, found the same:

> [N]ot at all necessary to the Court's holding and cannot be regarded as controlling. . . . It does not follow from *Miranda* that evidence inadmissible against an accused in the prosecution's case in chief is barred for all purposes, provided of course that the trustworthiness of the evidence satisfies legal standards.[92]

The court reasoned that the earlier statements would be a valuable aid to the jury in assessing credibility, and that it was not necessary to exclude, since there was sufficient deterrence of improper police activity in the fact that improperly obtained evidence would not be receivable in chief.[93]

---

89.   *Ibid.*, at pp. 444-45.
90.   401 U.S. 222, 91 S.Ct. 643 (1971).
91.   *Supra*, note 88, at p. 477.
92.   *Supra*, note 90, at p. 224.
93.   In *Oregon v. Hass*, the court took *Harris* a step further. In *Hass*, the accused was advised of his rights in accordance with *Miranda* and invoked them. His request for a lawyer was refused, however, and the police continued to interrogate. The court ruled that statements so obtained were receivable to impeach, finding that "the balance was struck in *Harris*" and, that, at p. 722: "Here too the shield provided by *Miranda* is not to be perverted to a license to testify inconsistently or even perjuriously, free from the risk of confrontation with prior inconsistent utterances." For state courts rejecting *Harris* when interpreting their own state constitutions, see *People v. Kimble*, 195 Cal. App. (3d) 1484 (1986); *Com. v. Triplett*, 462 Pa. 244 (1975); and *State v. Santiago*, 53 Haw. 254, 492 P. (2d) 657 (1971). For criticism of my thoughts in this area see Rauf, "Section 13 of the Charter and the Use of an Accused's Prior Testimony: A Reply to Doherty and Delisle" (1991), 4 C.R. (4th) 42.

A Crown counsel tried the argument in Calder.[94] A police officer was charged with procuring the sexual services of a person under 18 and breach of trust. There was evidence in the form of an independent witness and the officer's own notebook that he had met a prostitute late one evening. When senior officers questioned the accused, he denied the meeting. On a pre-trial motion, this statement, tendered as evidence of consciousness of guilt, was excluded as it had been obtained in violation of section 10(b). At trial, the officer testified that he had met with the prostitute but he provided an innocent explanation. The Crown's motion to be permitted to cross-examine on the statement for impeachment purposes was rejected.

The Crown received a measure of success in the Ontario Court of Appeal.[95] The majority decided that there could be circumstances in which Kuldip could be relied upon to cross-examine the accused based on a statement previously ruled inadmissible under section 24(2). Mr. Justice Doherty (McKinlay, J.A. concurring) set out a number of restricted conditions, including that the statement would have to be voluntary. Labrosse, J.A. strongly disagreed. The purpose to which the statement was put was immaterial. Whether used directly to incriminate the accused or to impeach credibility the evidence was only in existence because of a Charter breach and admission would render the trial unfair. McKinlay, J.A. agreed with Doherty, J.A. that there could be cases where cross-examination could be allowed but held that here the facts were not extreme enough.

The further Crown appeal to the Supreme Court closed the Crown's window of opportunity even further. For the 6-1 majority[96] Sopinka, J. rejected the analogy to Kuldip. The test under 24(2) as to the effect of admission on the repute of the administration of justice was different. The "reasonable well-informed citizen who represents community values" would likely find admission of the statement not less fair because it was only used to destroy credibility.

The sole dissenting opinion in Calder was by McLachlin, J.:

> The same concern for getting at the truth may weigh in favour of using the same statement in cross-examination to test the accused's credibility and uncover any inaccuracies or fabrications in his evidence in chief. From the perspective of the individual case, it is important to permit the jury to fairly judge the truthfulness of the witness. From the perspective of the trial process as a whole, it is equally important not to permit witnesses to take the stand and fabricate lies free from the fear that they may be cross-examined on earlier contradictory statements.[97]

The majority's distinction of Kuldip is indeed not compelling. The Calder decision has been criticized on this and other bases.[98] In Calder, Sopinka, J. for

---

94. (1996), 46 C.R. (4th) 133 (S.C.C.).

95. (1994), 32 C.R. (4th) 197 (Ont. C.A.). See David Tanovich, "Calder. Using Unconstitutionally Obtained Evidence to Impeach" (1995), 35 C.R. (4th) 82.

96. Gonthier, Cory, Iacobucci, and Major JJ. concurred as did La Forest J. in a separate opinion.

97. At 149-150.

98. See Ian D. Scott, "Calder. The Charter Trumps the Truth Seeking Tool of Impeaching the Accused with a Prior Inconsistent Statement", (1996) 46 C.R. (4th) 161 and David Rose, "Calder Successes Will Be Rare and the Procedure is Uncertain" (1996), 46 C.R. (4th) 151.

the majority did leave open the possibility of "very limited circumstances" in which a material change of circumstances would warrant reopening the issue of exclusion of evidence under section 24(2). Given the ruling on the facts in *Calder*, it is very difficult to imagine any special circumstances that would warrant a departure from the majority approach.[99] This scepticism was voiced in *Calder* in a concurring opinion of La Forest, J.

(iv) Pre-trial Right to Silence: Charter section 7

The issue in *Hebert* (1990), 77 C.R. (4th) 147 (S.C.C.) was the admissibility of a statement by an accused who had been arrested on a charge of robbery. He gave the statement to an undercover police officer placed in his cell after he had indicated that he did not wish to speak to the police. The Supreme Court of Canada unanimously decided that the statement had been obtained in violation of a breach of the right to silence under section 7 and had been properly excluded under section 24(2).

McLachlin, J. delivered the majority judgment, with six justices concurring.[100] She found in the common law voluntary confession rule and in the privilege against self-incrimination, which granted the accused immunity from incriminating himself at trial, the essence of the right to silence:

> [T]he person whose freedom is placed in question by the judicial process must be given the choice of whether to speak to the authorities or not.

Consideration of other Charter rights suggested that the right to silence of detained persons under section 7 had to be broad enough to accord that person a free choice on the matter of whether to speak to the authorities. The most important function of the right to counsel was to ensure that the accused understood his rights, chief among which was his right to silence. The privilege against self-incrimination enshrined in sections 11(*c*) and 13 of the Charter would be diminished if a person were to be compelled to make statements at the pre-trial stage. The right of a detained person to silence under section 7 had to be viewed as broader in scope than the confession rule existing in Canada at the time of the adoption of the Charter. The right had to reflect the Charter's concern for individual freedom and the integrity of the judicial process, and permit the exclusion of evidence offensive to those values. On a "purposive approach" to the right to silence, the scope of the right had to be extended to exclude police tricks which would effectively deprive the suspect of the choice of remaining silent:

> To permit the authorities to trick the suspect into making a confession to them after he or she has exercised the right of conferring with counsel and declined to make a statement, is to permit the authorities to do indirectly what the Charter does not permit them to do directly. This cannot be in accordance with the purpose of the Charter.

---

99. See however the view of Peter Sankoff, "Carter Should Not Preclude the Re-admission of Real Evidence" (1998), 14 C.R. (5th) 283 suggesting that, where an accused misleads a Court about previously excluded real evidence, judges should be more favourable to a *Calder* application. No such distinction was recognized in *Bisko* (1998), 14 C.R. (5th) 283 (Ont. C.A.).

100. Dickson C.J., Lamer, La Forest, L'Heureux-Dubé, Gonthier and Cory JJ. Wilson and Sopinka JJ. gave separate concurring reasons.

McLachlin, J. had earlier pointed out that *Rothman* had been decided after the majority ruling in *Wray*[101] that a court had no power to exclude admissible and relevant evidence on the basis that the administration of justice would be brought into disrepute. Distinguished scholars and judges had criticized this approach and it could no longer be maintained under the Charter.

Justice McLachlin further determined that her approach was not one of an "absolute right to silence in the accused, capable of being discharged only by waiver." On the subjective approach to waiver defined in *Clarkson*[102] all statements made by detainees not knowingly made to a police officer would be excluded because the Crown could not establish waiver. The majority decided that the scope of the right to silence should not be extended this far.[103]

Madam Justice McLachlin further identified four limits to this newly recognized constitutional right to silence:

1. The police may question the accused in the absence of counsel after the accused has retained counsel:

    Presumably, counsel will inform the accused of the right to remain silent. If the police are not posing as undercover officers and the accused chooses to volunteer information, there will be no violation of the Charter. Police persuasion, short of denying the suspect the right to choose or depriving him of an operating mind, does not breach the right to silence.

2. The right to silence applies only after detention:

    In an undercover operation prior to detention, the individual from whom information is sought is not in the control of the state. There is no need to protect him from the greater power of the state. After detention, the situation is quite different; the state takes control and assumes the responsibility of ensuring that the detainee's rights are respected.

3. The right to silence does not affect voluntary statements to a cell-mate provided that person is not acting as a police informant or an undercover police officer.

4. The right to silence is not violated where undercover agents observe the suspect and do not "actively elicit information in violation of the suspect's choice to remain silent."

Provincial courts have proved reluctant to extend the *Hebert* pre-trial right to silence to situations where the officer is identified. It has been held that non-coercive questioning prior to detention is no violation.[104] In *Smith*,[105] Mr. Justice Doherty for the Ontario Court of Appeal confirmed that a detained person has no absolute right to remain silent. The police are not absolutely prohibited from questioning a detained person and do not have to advise as to the right to remain silent. Where there is no section 10(*b*) right to counsel, as in the case of a motorist

---

101. [1971] S.C.R. 272.
102. [1986] 1 S.C.R. 383.
103. Both Sopinka and Wilson JJ. would have applied the accepted waiver standard.
104. *Hicks* (1988), 64 C.R. (3d) 68 (Ont. C.A.), affirmed (1990), 54 C.C.C. (3d) 575 (S.C.C.). See too *Imeson* (1992), 13 C.R. (4th) 322 (Ont. Gen. Div.).
105. (1996), 46 C.R. (4th) 229 (Ont. C.A.).

asked to perform sobriety tests under the Highway Traffic Act, the section 7 right to make an informed choice as to whether to speak to police required only that the police did not engage in conduct that effectively and unfairly deprives the detainee of the right to choose whether to speak. The Court held that section 7 had not been violated by two simple questions as to whether the motorist had been drinking and as to the quantity.

Recent interpretations of the right to silence in the context of police questioning after the accused has been afforded an opportunity to consult counsel have turned on the following passage of McLachlin, J. in *Hebert*:

> [The] Charter requires that the suspect be informed of his or her right to counsel and be permitted to consult counsel without delay. If the suspect chooses to make a statement, the suspect may do so. But if the suspect chooses not to, the state is not entitled to use its superior power to override the suspect's will and negate his or her choice.[106]

The B.C. Court of Appeal determined in *K. (H.W.)*[107] that the section 7 right to silence was not breached by overriding the accused's choice not to speak where police asked the accused in a murder case whether he wished to take a breathalyser, after assuring the lawyer they would not be interviewing him. Because of the agreement with the lawyer, McEachern, C.J.B.C., for the court, found this case close to the line between "fair and unfair treatment" but noted that the accused had chosen freely and voluntarily to say far more than was necessary to answer the question.[108] So too the B.C. court held there was no right to silence violation in *Ekman*.[109] The accused had indicated that he was only willing to answer questions with his lawyer present, but did so without his lawyer when the police advised him he had no right to the presence of a lawyer and the choice was his. There had been no confusion in the accused's mind as to his rights.

However, in *Otis*,[110] the Quebec Court of Appeal decided that the right to silence should be more meaningful. Although the court decided that the accused had sufficient, though limited, cognitive capacity to make choices Justice Proulx for the court decided that the continued police questioning, after he had asked them to stop four times, violated section 7. The police were not entitled to use their superior power to totally disregard the accused's desires and undermine his choice to remain silent. Once an accused has clearly stated he wishes to remain silent, the police cannot act as if there has been a waiver.

(v) *Principle Against Self-incrimination: Charter section 7*

Since *Hebert*, in a series of complex and split Supreme Court decisions, a majority position has emerged through the judgments of Chief Justice Lamer that within principles of fundamental justice guaranteed by section 7 there is a

---

106. At para. 80.
107. (2000), 32 C.R. (5th) 359 (B.C.C.A.).
108. At para. 18.
109. (2000), 146 C.C.C. (3d) 346 (B.C.C.A.).
110. 433 (2000), 37 C.R. (5th) 320 (Que. C.A.). See Guy Cournoyer, "*Otis*: The Quebec Court of Appeal Asserts a Meaningful Right to Silence Where a Suspect Says No to Interrogation" (2000), 37 C.R. (5th) 342.

"principle against self-incrimination" wider than the pre-trial right to silence, the protections against compellability in section 11(*c*) and the privilege against self-incrimination in section 13. The Chief Justice put it best for the majority of the court in *P. (M.B.)*.[111]

> Perhaps the single most important organizing principle in criminal law is the right of an accused not to be forced into assisting in his or her own prosecution. . . . This means, in effect, that an accused is under no obligation to respond until the state has succeeded in making out a *prima facie* case against him or her. In other words, until the Crown establishes that there is a "case to meet", an accused is not compellable in a general sense (as opposed to the narrow, testimonial sense) and need not answer the allegations against him or her.[112]

The Chief Justice saw the presumption of innocence and the power imbalance between the state and the individual as being at the root of the principle. In a later judgment, he describes the principle against self-incrimination in even broader terms:

> Any state action that coerces an individual to furnish evidence against him or herself in a proceeding in which the individual and the state are adversaries violates the principle against self-incrimination. Coercion means the denial of free and informed consent.[113]

This principle against self-incrimination or a "case to meet" is not merely an organizing principle of existing rules and principles but one that has the capacity to introduce new rules.[114] It is now seen to be the explanation of the recognition of a pre-trial right to silence in *Hebert*.

It also led the court in *B.C. Securities Commission v. Branch*[115] to create a doctrine of derivative use immunity and also a discretion to prevent the compellability of a co-accused. Two officers of a company were served with summonses from the Securities Commission under the provincial Securities Act compelling their attendance for examination and requiring them to produce all records in their possession. When the officers failed to appear, the Commission sought an order from the court committing the officers for contempt. The officers applied for a declaration that the Act violated section 7 of the Charter. The Supreme Court decided that the principle against self-incrimination required that persons compelled to testify be provided with subsequent derivative-use immunity in addition to the use immunity guaranteed by section 13 of the Charter. The accused would have the evidentiary burden of showing a plausible connection between the compelled testimony and the evidence later sought to be adduced.

---

111. (1994), 29 C.R. (4th) 209 (S.C.C.). In *S. (R.J.)* (1995), 36 C.R. (4th) 1 (S.C.C.) Iacobucci, J., speaking for four justices not including Lamer, C.J., expressly adopted the principle of self-incrimination outlined by the Chief Justice in *P. (M.B.)*.
112. At 226.
113. *P. (M.B.)* at 41. This statement was adopted by La Forest, J. for a unanimous Court in *Fitzpatrick* (1995), 43 C.R (4th) 343 (S.C.C.), although distinguished on the facts.
114. Iacobucci, J. in *S. (R J.)* at 49.
115. (1995), 38 C.R. (4th) 133 (S.C.C.), where Sopinka, J. and Iacobucci, J. reached a consensus majority position not evident in the earlier 229-page inconclusively split decision in *S. (R.J.)* (1995), 36 C.R. (4th) 1 (S.C.C.). See further *Jobin* (1995), 38 C.R. (4th) 176 (S.C.C.) and *Primeau* (1995), 38 C.R. (4th) 189 (S.C.C.).

Once this was done, in order to have the evidence admitted, the Crown would have to satisfy the court on a balance of probabilities that the authorities would have discovered the impugned derivative evidence absent the compelled testimony. The court also decided that, in addition, courts can, in certain circumstances, grant exemptions from compulsion to testify. The crucial question was whether the predominant purpose for seeking the evidence is to obtain incriminating evidence against the person compelled to testify or rather for some other legitimate public purpose. That test was seen to strike the appropriate balance between the interests of the state in obtaining the evidence for a valid public purpose on the one hand, and the right to silence of the person compelled to testify on the other.[116]

Branch was distinguished by La Forest, J. for the Court in *Fitzpatrick*,[117] in holding that section 7 did not prevent the Crown from relying on statutorily required fishing logs on a charge of overfishing. The Court held that the principle against self-incrimination should not be applied as rigidly as it might in the context of a purely criminal offence. Fishing logs were required from all commercial fishers as conditions of their license to assist in the routine administration of a regulated industry.

In *G. (S.G.)* (1997),[118] the Supreme Court held 5-2[119] that the discretion to allow the Crown to reopen its case after the defence had begun to answer was extremely narrow and far less likely to be exercised, otherwise the section 7 right of an accused not to be conscripted would be compromised. The minority pointed to the fact the late evidence had been unforeseen, had not arisen through fault of the Crown and should be left to a determination of whether there was prejudice to the defence case.[120]

In *White* (1999),[121] Iacobucci, J. held for a 6-1 majority[122] of the Supreme Court that the section 7 principle against self-incrimination barred the admission of motor vehicle accident reports made under the compulsion of a provincial Motor Vehicle Act at a trial for failing to stop at the scene of an accident under section 252(1)(*a*) of the Criminal Code. To obtain this use immunity, the person who made the statement would have to prove compulsion on a balance of probabilities. The test was whether the declarant held an honest and reasonable belief that he or she was required by law to report the accident to the person to whom the report was given.[123]

---

116. This is further addressed by Cory, J. (Iacobucci and Major, JJ. concurring) in concurring reasons in *Phillips v. Nova Scotia (Commissioner, Public Inquiries Act)* (1995), 39 C.R. (4th) 141 (S.C.C.).
117. *Supra*, note 113.
118. (1997), 8 C.R. (5th) 198 (S.C.C.).
119. Per Cory, J. (Lamer, C.J., Sopinka, J., Iacobucci, J. and Major, J. concurring). McLachlin, J. (L'Heureux-Dubé, J. concurring) dissented on this point.
120. See comment by Delisle, "Annotation", (1997) 8 C.R. (5th) 204 in favour of the majority position.
121. (1999), 24 C.R. (5th) 201 (S.C.C.). See criticism of Steven Penney, "The Continuing Evolution of the s. 7 Self-Incrimination Principle: *R. v. White*" (1999), 24 C.R. (5th) 247 and the reply by Michael Plaxton, "An Analysis and Defence of Free Choice Theory: A Response to Professor Penney" (1999), 27 C.R. (5th) 218.
122. L 'Heureux-Dubé, J. dissented.
123. At 230-232, applied in *Gibb* (1999), 30 C.R. (5th) 189 (Sask. Q.B.) (admitting statement made to parole officer after arrest).

Iacobucci, J. restated the residual principle against self-incrimination in the following broad terms:

> It is now well-established that there exists, in Canadian law, a principle against self-incrimination that is a principle of fundamental justice under s. 7 of the Charter. [The] principle has at least two key purposes, namely to protect against unreliable confessions, and to protect against abuses of power by the state. There is both an individual and a societal interest in achieving both of these protections. Both protections are linked to the value placed by Canadian society upon individual privacy, personal autonomy and dignity. . . . A state which arbitrarily intrudes upon its citizens' personal sphere will inevitably cause more injustice than it cures.
>
> The jurisprudence of this Court is clear that [it] . . . is an overarching principle within our criminal justice system, from which a number of specific common law and Charter rules emanate, such as the confessions rule, and the right to silence, among many others.[124]

However he also added an important general caveat.[125] The fact that the principle against self-incrimination had the status of an overarching principle did not imply that it provided absolute protection for an accused against all uses of information compelled by statute or otherwise. The residual protections were specific, contextually-sensitive and required a balancing process. In some contexts, the factors that favoured the importance of the search for truth would outweigh the factors that favour protecting the individual against undue compulsion by the state.

The principle against self-incrimination has not caught fire in lower courts, but there are some signs of life. The Ontario Court of Appeal seized on Iacobucci, J.'s above caveat in *White* to summarily dismiss an argument that the new DNA warrant powers in the Criminal Code violated the principle against self-incrimination.[126] Justice Finlayson went as far as to say that the principle against self-incrimination was not a right protected under section 7 but was found in section 7 only to the extent that it was a principle of fundamental justice.[127] The Ontario Court had no difficulty in holding that the principle did not bar the admission of a guilty plea at a subsequent criminal proceeding.[128]

So too the B.C. Court of Appeal determined that the principle against self-incrimination did not bar the admissibility of information provided to Revenue Canada in a fraud prosecution.[129] The principle has not availed in the context of compelled testimony under the Mutual Legal Assistance in Criminal Matters Act given the evidentiary immunity provided.[130] On the other hand, the Quebec Court

---

124. At 219-220.
125. At 220-221.
126. *F. (S.) v. Canada (Attorney-General)* (2000), 32 C.R. (5th) 79 (Ont. C.A.).
127. At 93. He also distinguished *Stillman* as grounded in the context of a bodily search without statutory authorization (at 94).
128. *Ford* (2000), 33 C.R. (5th) 178 (Ont. C.A.). See too *Thompson* (2001),151 C.C.C. (3d) 339 (Ont. C.A.) (upholding offence of failing to provide roadside test).
129. *Wilder* (2000), 142 C.C.C. (3d) 418 (B.C.C.A.). See also *Graham* (1997), 121 C.C.C. (3d) 76 (B.C.S.C.).
130. (1995), 41 C.R. (4th) 358 (Que. C.A.), *U.K. v. Hrynyk* (1996), 107 C.C.C. (3d) 104 (Ont. Gen. Div.).

of Appeal excluded the evidence of an accused and his wife compelled at a fire commissioner's inquiry from the subsequent arson trial.[131]

(vi) *No Adverse Inference from Pre-trial Silence*

Can guilt be inferred from pre-trial silence? Should it be? Can pre-trial silence impair credibility about a defence first raised at trial?

R. v. CHAMBERS
[1990] 2 S.C.R. 1293, 80 C.R. (3d) 235, 59 C.C.C. (3d) 321

[The accused was charged with conspiring to import cocaine. At his trial his defence was that he had no intention of carrying out the agreement notwithstanding the appearance of his being an active conspirator. Rather, it was argued that his purpose was to recapture affections of his former mistress who was one of the conspirators. The accused gave evidence of an arrangement with one Kuko to rob one of the conspirators of the cocaine before he flew to Vancouver. Crown counsel cross-examined the accused concerning his failure to advise anyone prior to trial of his real intent. Both counsel eventually requested the trial judge to direct the jury to completely ignore the questions and answers given pertaining to the accused's silence on the issues of guilt or innocence and credibility. The trial judge agreed to do that. The trial lasted 50 days. The trial judge neglected to include these instructions in his charge to the jury and neither counsel reminded him of him of his undertaking.]

CORY, J. (DICKSON, C.J.C., LAMER, C.J.C. and LA FOREST, SOPINKA and MCLACHLIN, JJ. concurring): —

. . . .

Martin J.A. restated his position in *R. v. Symonds*. In that case the Crown led evidence that the accused had refused to say anything to the police after he had been cautioned. Later, during the cross-examination of the accused, the Crown repeatedly asked him why he had not offered his innocent explanation of the events to the police prior to the trial. The trial judge did not instruct the jury that they should not draw any adverse inference from this evidence. At issue was whether the admission of the evidence and the failure of the trial judge to properly instruct the jury constituted a reversible error. At p. 227 Martin J.A. wrote:

> It is fundamental that a person charged with a criminal offence has the right to remain silent and a jury is not entitled to draw any inference against an accused because he chooses to exercise that right. We think that in the absence of some issue arising in the case which makes the statement of an accused, following the giving of a caution, that he has nothing to say relevant to that issue, such evidence is inadmissible. In the present case there was no issue with respect to which the appellant's failure to reply was relevant and the evidence should not have been tendered: *see R. v. Robertson* (1975), 21 C.C.C. (2d) 385.

The court directed a new trial.

In my view, unless the Court can establish a real relevance and a proper basis for their admission, neither the questions by the investigating officers nor evidence as to the ensuing silence of the accused should be admitted. In the case at bar, the Crown agreed

---

131. *Kabbabe* (1997), 6 C.R. (5th) 82 (Que. C.A.).

that the trial judge should have instructed the jury that they were to ignore both the questions and the answers. It can therefore be taken that there was no relevant basis for asking these questions. The questions were improper and the evidence inadmissible. The failure of the trial judge to so instruct the jury, pursuant to his undertaking, compounded the error and caused, I fear, irreparable damage to the defence.

Further, I am in agreement with the conclusion of Lambert J.A. that s. 6l3(1)(b)(iii) cannot be applied to rectify the situation. Without a direction from the trial judge, I would expect that the most reasonable and fair-minded juror might still draw an inference that the appellant should have said something regarding Kuko to persons in authority at the time of his arrest or at least well before trial. A juror could not be expected to understand that in the ordinary course of events neither the questions nor the answers pertaining to situations where the right to silence applied should be admitted. In those circumstances it would be impossible for the Crown to establish, as it must, that despite the error the result must necessarily be the same: see *Colpitts v. R.,* [1965] S.C.R. 739.

The circumstances of this trial aggravated the effect of the omission. Based upon the judge's undertaking to charge with regard to the subject, counsel for the defence did not re-examine. That re-examination in itself might have had a significant effect. It would have demonstrated that the appellant had disclosed his proposed defence some years before the trial. The absence of the re-examination, coupled with the failure to give the requisite instructions on the subject, could only have resulted in a significant injustice. The jury were deprived of the evidence that would establish that the so-called double intent defence to which the "Kuko" evidence related was not of recent concoction. As a result of the Crown's cross-examination, the jury could well have been left with the erroneous impression that Chambers was under a duty to disclose the Kuko story to a person in authority. The failure to disclose a defence of alibi in a timely manner may be considered in assessing the credibility of that defence but that is a unique situation. As a general rule there is no obligation resting upon an accused person to disclose either the defence which will be presented or the details of that defence before the Crown has completed its case. There was clearly no obligation resting upon the appellant to disclose either his defence of double intent or the Kuko story to the Crown or anyone in authority. The failure to correct such an impression by direction from the trial judge rendered the right to silence a snare of silence for the appellant. Without any direction to ignore these questions and answers, it is impossible to say that the verdict would necessarily have been the same.

. . . .

The failure to charge on this issue in the circumstances of the case constituted a serious miscarriage of justice that requires the direction of a new trial.

[L'Heureux-Dubé, J. dissented on the basis that the accused was not unfairly prejudiced by the objectionable questioning and the absence of direction.]

Should adverse inferences be drawn from an accused's failure to testify?

It is very important to distinguish between inferences that might flow from silence during the investigative process and inferences from silence at trial. The appropriateness of drawing such inferences, the fairness, must be judged separately. Many protections available to an accused at trial are not present during police questioning. At trial the accused will normally be represented by counsel. He will then know the charge against him and will have listened to and been able to challenge the evidence against him. The trial is in public and an impartial judge is present to ensure the accused's rights are safe-guarded and the hearing is conducted according to the rules of natural justice. There are certain procedural safeguards in place as to how he may be questioned if he decides to take the stand. Before the accused is called on to answer the judge will have decided that there is a case to meet; the trial judge will have decided that there is evidence upon which a reasonable jury properly instructed could return a verdict of guilty. Finally, it is almost certain that judges and juries will draw adverse inferences from the accused's silence at trial as they personally witness the accused's silence in the face of accusation; there is no need for evidence to be led as to the accused's silence.

(vii) *No Adverse Inference from Trial Silence*

We have seen in *Chambers* that the Supreme Court has determined that normally no adverse inference should be drawn from the accused remaining silent before trial. However, the Supreme Court has suggested that different considerations apply to silence at trial given that the accused is represented, knows the case to meet due to disclosure and there are rules regarding the admissibility of evidence. It appears to be clear from various Supreme Court dicta that adverse inferences can be drawn against an accused for not testifying in some circumstances. What those circumstances are is far less clear. In *Francois*,[132] McLachlin, J. wrote for the majority that:

> subject to the caveat that failure to testify cannot be used to shore up a Crown case which otherwise does not establish guilt beyond a reasonable doubt, a jury is permitted to draw an adverse inference from the failure of an accused person to testify.[133]

In *Lepage*,[134] the Supreme Court divided 3-2 as to whether the trial judge had drawn an adverse inference from the accused's failure to offer an explanation for the presence of his fingerprints but was in agreement that such an inference could be drawn "once the Crown had proved a *prima facie* case".[135] Chief Justice Lamer in *P. (M.B.)* (1994),[136] in describing the "principle against self-incrimination" for the Court, stated the following:

> Once the Crown discharges its obligation to present a *prima facie* case, such that it cannot be non-suited by a motion for a directed verdict of acquittal, the accused can be expected to respond . . . and failure to do so may serve as the basis for drawing adverse inferences. [Once] there is a "case to meet" which, if believed, would result in conviction, the accused can no longer remain a passive participant in the prosecutorial process and becomes — in a broad sense — compellable. That is, the accused must answer the case against him or her, or face the possibility of conviction.[137]

It would appear at this point that the Supreme Court had no objections to adverse inferences based on the accused's failure to testify provided that there is otherwise enough evidence to go to the jury.

However in *Noble* a 5-4 majority abruptly changed course and decided that normally an adverse inference should not be drawn from trial silence.

---

135. (1994), 31 C.R. (4th) 201 (S.C.C.).
136. At 210. La Forest, J., Gonthier, J. and Iacobucci, J. concurred. Major, J. (Sopinka, J. and Cory, J. concurring) dissented.
134. (1995), 36 C.R. (4th) 145 (S.C.C.).
135. Sopinka, J. for the majority at 159, Major, J. for the minority.
136. (1994), 29 C.R. (4th) 209 (S.C.C.).
137. At 227-228.

R. v. NOBLE
[1997] 1 S.C.R. 874, 6 C.R. (5th) 1, 114 C.C.C. (3d) 385

[The manager of an apartment building found two young men in the parking area of his building, one of whom appeared to be attempting to break into a car with a screwdriver. When the manager asked the man for identification, he handed over an expired driver's licence. The manager testified that he thought the photograph on the licence accurately depicted the man in front of him in the garage and told the man that he could retrieve the licence from the police. The accused was eventually charged with breaking and entering and having in his possession an instrument suitable for the purpose of breaking into a motor vehicle. At trial, neither the manager nor anyone else could identify the accused, but the trial judge concluded that he as the trier of fact could compare the picture in the driver's licence with the accused in the courtroom and conclude that the driver's licence accurately depicted the accused. He also was satisfied that the building manager would have carefully examined the licence at the time of the incident. The trial judge noted that the accused faced an overwhelming case to meet as a result of the licence, yet remained silent. In the trial judge's view, he could draw "almost an adverse inference" that "certainly may add to the weight of the Crown's case on the issue of identification". The accused was convicted on both counts. The Court of Appeal set aside the conviction and ordered a new trial. A 5:4 majority of the Supreme Court dismissed the Crown' appeal.]

SOPINKA, J. (L'HEUREUX-DUBÉ, CORY, IACOBUCCI and MAJOR, JJ. concurring): —

. . . .

The right to silence is based on society's distaste for compelling a person to incriminate him- or herself with his or her own words. Following this reasoning, in my view the use of silence to help establish guilt beyond a reasonable doubt is contrary to the rationale behind the right to silence. Just as a person's words should not be conscripted and used against him or her by the state, it is equally inimical to the dignity of the accused to use his or her silence to assist in grounding a belief in guilt beyond a reasonable doubt. To use silence in this manner is to treat it as communicative evidence of guilt. To illustrate this point, suppose an accused did commit the offence for which he was charged. If he testifies and is truthful, he will be found guilty as the result of what he said. If he does not testify and is found guilty in part because of his silence, he is found guilty because of what he did not say. No matter what the non-perjuring accused decides, communicative evidence emanating from the accused is used against him. The failure to testify tends to place the accused in the same position as if he had testified and admitted his guilt. In my view, this is tantamount to conscription of self-incriminating communicative evidence and is contrary to the underlying purpose of the right to silence. In order to respect the dignity of the accused, the silence of the accused should not be used as a piece of evidence against him or her.

The Presumption of Innocence

The presumption of innocence, enshrined at trial in s. 11(d) of the Charter, provides further support for the conclusion that silence of the accused at trial cannot be placed on the evidentiary scales against the accused. . . . If silence may be used against the accused in establishing guilt, part of the burden of proof has shifted to the accused. In a situation where the accused exercises his or her right to silence at trial, the Crown need only prove the case to some point short of beyond a reasonable doubt, and the failure to testify takes it over the threshold. The presumption of innocence, however, indicates that it is not incumbent on the accused to present any evidence at all, rather it is for the Crown to prove him or her guilty. Thus, in order for the burden of proof to remain with the Crown, as required by the Charter, the silence of the accused should not be used against him or her in building the case for guilt. Belief in guilt beyond a reasonable doubt must be grounded on the testimony and any other tangible or demonstrative evidence admitted during the trial.

Some reference to the silence of the accused by the trier of fact may not offend the Charter principles discussed above: where in a trial by judge alone the trial judge is convinced of the guilt of the accused beyond a reasonable doubt, the silence of the accused may be referred to as evidence of the absence of an explanation which could raise a reasonable doubt. If the Crown has proved the case beyond a reasonable doubt, the accused need not testify, but if he doesn't, the Crown's case prevails and the accused will be convicted. It is only in this sense that the accused "need respond" once the Crown has proved its case beyond a reasonable doubt. Another permissible reference to the silence of the accused was alluded to by the Court of Appeal in this case. In its view, such a reference is permitted by a judge trying a case alone to indicate that he need not speculate about possible defences that might have been offered by the accused had he or she testified. . . . Such treatment of the silence of the accused does not offend either the right to silence or the presumption of innocence. If silence is simply taken as assuring the trier of fact that it need not speculate about unspoken explanations, then belief in guilt beyond a reasonable doubt is not in part grounded on the silence of the accused, but rather is grounded on the evidence against him or her. The right to silence and its underlying rationale are respected, in that the communication or absence of communication is not used to build the case against the accused. The silence of the accused is not used as inculpatory evidence, which would be contrary to the right to silence, but simply is not used as exculpatory evidence. Moreover, the presumption of innocence is respected, in that it is not incumbent on the accused to defend him- or herself or face the possibility of conviction on the basis of his or her silence. Thus, a trier of fact may refer to the silence of the accused simply as evidence of the absence of an explanation which it must consider in reaching a verdict. On the other hand, if there exists in evidence a rational explanation or inference that is capable of raising a reasonable doubt about guilt, silence cannot be used to reject this explanation.

. . . .

The principles to which I have referred which derive from ss. 7 and 11(d) of the Charter find ample support in recent case law of this Court. While earlier cases on the appropriate use of silence by the trier of fact are admittedly ambiguous, recent decisions are clear: silence may not be used by the trier of fact as a piece of inculpatory evidence. . . . In my view, these comments clearly indicate that it is not permissible to use the failure to testify as a piece of evidence contributing to a finding of guilt beyond a reasonable doubt where such a finding would not exist without considering the failure to testify. McLachlin J. stated that the failure to testify could not be used to "shore up a Crown case which otherwise does not establish guilt beyond a reasonable doubt". Major J. stated that "this lack of testimony cannot otherwise be used to strengthen the Crown's case where the Crown has fallen short of proving guilt". In my view, these statements indicate that silence cannot be used to take an unproven case to a proven case.

. . . .

There may, however, be confusion over the use of the words "adverse inference" in the above cases. Professor R. J. Delisle, in an annotation to *R. v. François* (1994), 31 C.R. (4th) 203, asked that if an adverse inference is permitted, what inference is relevant if it can only be drawn after guilt beyond a reasonable doubt has been proved? He stated at p. 204:

The essence of a criminal trial is whether the Crown has established its case beyond a reasonable doubt. If a jury cannot use the failure to testify to assist in its determination of whether they are satisfied beyond a reasonable doubt, then pray tell what the permissible adverse inference does? For what else can the jury use it?

As set out above, silence is not inculpatory evidence, but nor is it exculpatory evidence. Thus, as in *Lepage*, if the trier of fact reaches a belief in guilt beyond a reasonable doubt, silence may be treated by the trier of fact as confirmatory of guilt. Silence may indicate, for example, that there is no evidence to support speculative explanations of the Crown's evidence offered by defence counsel, or it may indicate that the accused has not put forward any evidence that would require that the Crown negative an affirmative defence. In this limited sense, silence may be used by the trier of fact. If, however, there is a rational explanation which is consistent with innocence and which may raise a reasonable doubt, the silence of the accused cannot be used to remove that doubt. Thus, there are permissible uses of silence by the trier of fact. However, Delisle is correct in stating that, since these permissible uses only arise after the trier of fact has reached a belief in guilt beyond a reasonable doubt, the uses may be superfluous. I would therefore conclude that courts should generally avoid using the potentially confusing term "inference" in discussing the silence of the accused. "Inference" could be taken to indicate that the trier of fact used silence to help establish the case for guilt beyond a reasonable doubt, which is not a permissible use of silence. Indeed, because of the potential for confusion, discussion of the silence of the accused should generally be avoided. However, where silence is mentioned by the trial judge as confirmatory of guilt given the totality of the evidence, but not as a "make-weight", there is no reversible error. *Lepage* provides an example of such a situation.

. . . .

Thus far in the analysis I have not distinguished cases where the trier of fact is a jury from cases where the trier of fact is a judge. In my view, there is no difference in the principles governing either situation; the trier of fact, whether judge or jury, cannot treat the silence of the accused as a "make-weight". . . . While the principles governing the judge and the jury as trier of fact are identical, it is clear that there are differences between the two in practice. The first difference is found in s. 4(6) of the Canada Evidence Act. Section 4(6), whose validity is not at issue in the present case, prevents a trial judge from commenting on the silence of the accused. The trial judge is therefore prevented from instructing the jury on the impermissibility of using silence to take the case against the accused to one that proves guilt beyond a reasonable doubt. The second practical difference is that while judges give reasons which permit appellate review of the specific basis for a finding of guilt, juries do not give reasons and courts are prohibited from speculating about the reasoning process of a jury in reaching a verdict. These two factors have a significant effect on the potential inferences from the failure to testify in a jury trial: in a jury trial, it is impossible to prevent a jury from drawing whatever inference they please from the failure to testify. They cannot be cautioned against such an inference *ex ante* because of s. 4(6), and they cannot be reversed *ex post* for drawing such an inference because speculation as to the jury's reasoning is forbidden. While there are practical considerations which prevent appellate review of the use of the silence of the accused by a jury, it remains an error of law for the jury to become convinced of guilt beyond a reasonable doubt as the result of the silence of the accused at trial. . . . Because of s. 4(6) and the absence of reasons, there is no practical way of preventing the jury from drawing an improper inference from silence. The fact that the jury is permitted to do so does not elevate the use of silence to a principle of law which should be extended to all triers of fact.

On a related point, I would add that nothing in s. 4(6) or in the analysis thus far prevents the trial judge from telling the jury that the evidence on a particular issue is uncontradicted. In such a circumstance, the judge is not instructing the jury to consider the failure of the accused to testify per se, but rather is simply instructing the jury to take note of the fact that no evidence had been led to contradict a particular point. Rather than inviting the jury to place the failure of the accused on the evidentiary scales, the judge is instructing the jury that it need not speculate about possible contradictory evidence which has not been led in evidence.

. . . .

In support of its contention that silence may be used to build the case against the accused, the appellant pointed to various appellate review cases involving s. 686 of the Criminal Code. Section 686(1)(b)(iii) is a curative provision; notwithstanding errors of law at the trial, if the court of appeal is satisfied that no miscarriage of justice occurred when the conviction was entered, the conviction will be upheld. In applying this curative provision, this Court has established that it is permissible for an appellate court to account for the silence of the accused. . . . Similarly, it has also been established that it is appropriate for an appellate court to account for the accused's failure to testify in assessing the reasonableness of the verdict under s. 686(1)(a)(i). . . . The appellant submitted that since it is permissible for appellate courts to consider silence in assessing the verdict, it must be permissible for the trier of fact to consider silence in reaching a verdict. In my view, the appellate review cases do not contradict the conclusion that silence may not be placed on the evidentiary scales, either by the trier of fact or by appellate courts. Rather, the cases hold that appellate courts, like triers of fact, may refer to the silence of the accused as indicative of the absence of an exculpatory explanation; silence is not inculpatory, but nor is it exculpatory. Nowhere do the appellate review cases outlined above explicitly state that silence may be used as a "make-weight" by the trier of fact, but there is wording that suggests that silence may be used simply in the limited sense of not providing an innocent explanation. . . . The appellate court, and the trier of fact, may consider the silence of the accused as failing to provide an innocent explanation for the existence of otherwise convincing inculpatory evidence.

. . . .

In any event, the principles generally governing appellate review are not necessarily identical to those governing the trial. At trial, the accused is presumed innocent under s. 11(d) of the Charter, but this section does not establish a presumption of innocence in other proceedings such as appeals. . . . In my view, the presumption of innocence does not operate with the same vigour in the context of an appeal of a conviction as it does at trial. After the guilty verdict has been entered, it is no longer incumbent on the Crown to establish guilt — that guilt having already been proved beyond a reasonable doubt — rather it is incumbent on the appellant to demonstrate an error at trial. In such a context, the presumption of innocence is not applied in the same manner as it is at trial. . . . Regardless of the use of silence by the appellate court in exercising its discretion to confirm the conviction or order a new trial, the conviction will not be reached on the basis of the silence of the accused, rather the presumption of guilt established by the guilty verdict will not be dislodged. Thus, even if the appellate review cases go farther than suggesting that silence may be accounted for by the court of appeal only in the limited sense of confirming the absence of innocent explanations, the principles applying to appellate review are not necessarily those that apply to a trial. At trial, which is the context with which the present appeal is concerned, not appellate review, the presumption of innocence and the right to silence are of paramount importance. . . . I leave for another day any final conclusion as to whether the appellate review cases were correct insofar as they implied that silence may be treated as a make-weight by an appellate court.

Alibi Cases

The appellant submitted that *Vézeau v. The Queen*, [1977] 2 S.C.R. 277, held that silence could be treated as a "make-weight". In *Vézeau*, this Court considered the significance of the failure to testify in the context of a defence of alibi. In that case, the defence was alibi, but the accused did not testify. In giving his instructions to the jury, the judge said that they could not draw any conclusion unfavourable to the accused from the fact that he had not testified. The majority of this Court held that, aside from the prohibition of comment on the failure of the accused to testify set out in the Canada Evidence Act, it was an error of law for the trial judge to instruct the jury that they could not consider the absence of testimony by the accused in assessing the alibi. Martland J. stated on behalf of the majority at p. 292 that:

> It was part of the appellant's defence to the charge that he could not have committed the offence because he was in Montreal when the murder occurred. Proof of this alibi was tendered by a witness who claimed to have been with the appellant in Montreal. The direction of the trial judge precluded the jury, when considering this defence, from taking into consideration the fact that the appellant had failed to support his alibi by his own testimony. The failure of an accused person, who relies upon an alibi, to testify and thus to submit himself to cross-examination is a matter of importance in considering the validity of that defence. The jury, in this case, was instructed that they could not take that fact into account in reaching their verdict.

In my view, *Vézeau* set out a narrow exception to the impermissibility of using silence to build the case against the accused at trial. It has clearly been recognized in other contexts that alibi defences create exceptions to the right to silence. . . . In my view, there are two reasons supporting the alibi exception to the right to silence pre-trial which apply also to the right to silence at trial: the ease with which alibi evidence may be fabricated; and the diversion of the alibi inquiry from the central inquiry at trial. I am therefore sympathetic to the view expressed in *Vézeau* that in the limited case of alibi, the failure of the accused at trial to testify and expose him- or herself to cross-examination on the alibi defence may be used to draw an adverse inference about the credibility of the defence. A second reason to permit such a limited exception to the right to silence at trial is that the alibi defence is not directly related to the guilt of the accused; as Gooderson put it, "[a]libi evidence, by its very nature, takes the focus right away from the area of the main facts". Rejecting the alibi defence does not build the case for the Crown in the sense of proving the existence of the required elements of the offence in question, but rather negatives an affirmative defence actively put forward by the accused. Using silence to inform the trier of fact's assessment of the credibility of the accused's affirmative defence of alibi simply goes to the alibi defence itself.

. . . .

On balance, it appears to me that the trial judge used the failure to testify as evidence going to identification which permitted him to reach a belief in guilt beyond a reasonable doubt. Indeed, he stated explicitly that the failure to testify "certainly may add to the weight of the Crown's case" and concluded by finding guilt on the basis of "those reasons", which appeared to include the discussion of the failure to testify. In light of these statements, when the trial judge stated that he "can be" satisfied on the identity issue prior to discussing the failure to testify, in my view he indicated that the evidence before him was consistent with proof of identity, and the failure to testify took belief in identity beyond a reasonable doubt.

. . . Given my conclusion that such reasoning constituted an error of law, I would dismiss the appeal and confirm the judgment of the Court of Appeal ordering a new trial.

LAMER, C.J. (dissenting): — According to Sopinka J. the silence of an accused can only be used by the trier of fact in two very limited senses. The accused's silence may: (1) confirm prior findings of guilt beyond a reasonable doubt; and (2) remind triers of fact that they need not speculate about unstated defences. With greatest respect, this misinterprets the case law. This Court and others have repeatedly held that when the Crown presents a case to meet that implicates the accused in a "strong and cogent network of inculpatory facts", the trier of fact is entitled to consider the accused's failure to testify in deciding whether it is in fact satisfied of his or her guilt beyond a reasonable doubt. . . . None of these early cases suggests that the accused should be compelled to testify or that the accused is anything other than presumed innocent until proven guilty. They merely recognize that when an accused is implicated or "enveloped" in a case of unexplained inculpatory circumstances, there are consequences to silence that trial judges, juries, and appellate courts alike may consider in reaching a verdict. This does not happen in every case. A trier of fact is entitled to draw adverse inferences only where there is a "damning chain of evidence" or more aptly a "strong and cogent network of inculpatory facts". This approach to adverse inferences has been expressly adopted and refined by this Court in a number of judgments in recent years, both before and after the advent of the Charter.

. . . .

Why, one might ask, has this Court commented so frequently on the effect of the accused's silence? Why has it arisen so often as an issue before this Court? The reason is simple: silence can be very probative. Consider, for example, a case of sexual assault where the victim describes her attacker as a man with a very unusual tattoo on the upper portion of his arm. Nothing allows the Crown to call the accused as its first witness, as it could do under an inquisitorial system of criminal justice. However, assuming the Crown, by adducing other evidence, establishes a case to meet (i.e. enough evidence to make a guilty verdict reasonable), would not every man wrongly accused who lacks the described tattoo roll up his sleeve in court to exonerate himself? . . . Recognizing that silence can be probative, this Court has said in the above-mentioned cases that it is a factor that both juries and appellate courts may properly consider.

. . . .

My brother Sopinka disagrees. He asserts that these cases mean only that the silence of the accused can confirm verdicts or at most serve as the basis to refuse to speculate about unstated defences. Nothing, he says, provides that silence can be used as evidence itself. With respect, I find Sopinka J.'s interpretation difficult to support. For one, an inference which merely confirms prior conclusions of guilt is superfluous. As Professor R. J. Delisle has commented:

> The essence of a criminal trial is whether the Crown has established its case beyond a reasonable doubt. If a jury cannot use the failure to testify to assist in its determination of whether they are satisfied beyond a reasonable doubt, then pray tell what the permissible adverse inference does? For what else can the jury use it? (Annotation to *R. v. François* (1994), 31 C.R. (4th) 203, at p. 204.)

Second, I find it illogical for the Court to say that silence may be used by judges and juries but only to the extent that it highlights the fact that the Crown's evidence remains uncontradicted. Uncontradicted by whom? To allow a trial judge to instruct the jury that the evidence remains uncontradicted is just a coded message to remind the jury that the accused has not led any evidence in his or her own defence. The jurisprudence clearly establishes that, once the Crown has proffered a case to meet, the silence of an accused itself can be used in determining whether an accused is guilty beyond a reasonable doubt. I believe that we should be straightforward and say so.

. . . .

With respect, I find it profoundly illogical to say that trial judges and juries must not weigh the silence of the accused on the evidentiary scales, but in reviewing whether their verdicts are reasonable appellate courts can assume that they did. . . . I simply cannot conceive how a trial verdict that is a miscarriage of justice can be cured by an appellate court pursuant to s. 686(1)(b)(iii) because we say that certain Charter rights no longer apply on appeal. I similarly cannot understand how a verdict that would ordinarily be considered unreasonable can magically become reasonable pursuant to s. 686(1)(a)(i) simply because the case has progressed from one level of court to another. If the role of a trier of fact is to have any meaning, appellate courts must undertake their statutory responsibility to review the fitness of verdicts and to cure trial errors on the same understanding of the silence of an accused. I cannot endorse a criminal justice system in which an accused's silence may be used to a greater extent by appellate judges than by triers of fact at the trial level. Otherwise the Court is effectively sanctioning what it says is prohibited — inviting both judges and juries to use silence as evidence, but asking them to keep it quiet.

. . . .

The act of drawing adverse inferences from the silence of an accused is not contrary to the accused's right of non-compellability or the presumption of innocence. This point becomes clear upon a proper understanding of the case to meet. If the Crown establishes a case to meet, such that its case cannot be non-suited by a motion for a directed verdict of acquittal, it has put forth, by definition, sufficient evidence upon which a jury, properly instructed, could reasonably convict. Put differently, when the Crown provides a case to meet, all of the evidence to sustain a conviction has been put forth by the Crown in keeping with its burden of proof. As Professor R. J. Delisle has argued:

> Some object that permitting an inference of guilt modifies the burden of proof. But query whether this is so. The prosecution has the burden of proving the accused's guilt beyond a reasonable doubt and the Crown will not have discharged that burden, if at all, until the end of the case after all the evidence has been heard. The defendant's silence may be treated as a piece of evidence in assisting the discharge of the Crown's burden, it may constitute part of the totality of the evidence, but that does not mean the burden of proof has been shifted.("Silence at Trial: Inferences and Comments" (1997), 1 C.R. (5th) 313, at pp. 318-19.)

. . . .

This approach to adverse inferences is more consistent with the letter and spirit of s. 4(6) of the Canada Evidence Act, R.S.C., 1985, c. C-5, than the approach endorsed by Sopinka J. Section 4(6) currently provides:

> 4.(6) The failure of the person charged, or of the wife or husband of that person, to testify shall not be made the subject of comment by the judge or by counsel for the prosecution.

This rule against commenting on the accused's failure to testify was originally created to ensure that neither the court nor the prosecution would draw unfair attention to the silence of the accused. It was not, however, intended to preclude triers of fact from drawing natural and reasonable inferences from his silence. Under s. 4(6), this Court has said on a number of occasions that a jury is "free to draw" and "frequently does draw" adverse inferences from the failure of the accused to explain. If adverse inferences themselves were impermissible, s. 4(6) would not merely prohibit "comment", it would prohibit the drawing of adverse inferences altogether.

. . . .

I question how Sopinka J.'s position can be reconciled with s. 4(6). Even though s. 4(6) does not prohibit adverse inferences, the intractable rule that emerges from the reasons of Sopinka J. is that no trier of fact can use the accused's silence as inculpatory evidence adding to the weight of the Crown's case. The reason for this rule, he suggests, lies in an accused's fundamental right of non-compellability and the presumption of innocence. However, if this Court is prepared to conclude that the fundamental Charter rights to silence and the presumption of innocence prohibit triers of fact from using the accused's silence as evidence, one would have thought that trial judges would be empowered, if not required, to say so. Similarly, if there are subtle, permissible uses to be made of an accused's silence, trial judges must be able to explain them. ... I cannot reconcile Sopinka J.'s position with s. 4(6) of the Canada Evidence Act. Indeed his reasons indirectly challenge the constitutionality of s. 4(6), which has not been contested at this Court, but which was upheld by Cory J.A. (as he then was) at the Ontario Court of Appeal in *R. v. Boss* (1988),

46 C.C.C. (3d) 523. Other Commonwealth jurisdictions have not only endorsed the act of drawing adverse inferences from the silence of the accused, they affirm that such inferences do not alter the traditional notions of the burden of proof and the right to silence.

. . . .

In my view, the trial judge's use of the accused's silence was proper. Although he could have been more precise, Lemiski Prov. Ct. J. clearly found, without reference to the accused's silence, that the Crown had established an "overwhelming" case to meet. Then, given the network of inculpatory facts, or the "virtual outcry situation" as he referred to it, Lemiski Prov. Ct. J. properly inferred guilt from the silence of the accused. As I have gone to great lengths to discuss, having no doubt concluded that silence was probative in this case, the trial judge's inference was natural and reasonable. Moreover, given the existence of a case to meet, it was perfectly consistent with the respondent's right to silence and the presumption of innocence. For all of these reasons, I would allow the appeal.

LA FOREST, J., GONTHIER, J. concurring: — I agree with the Chief Justice, except that I prefer not to comment on the constitutional validity of s. 4(6) of the Canada Evidence Act, R.S.C., 1985, c. C-5, an issue that is not before us.

McLACHLIN, J. dissenting: — I agree with the Chief Justice that this appeal should be allowed. I add only this. The difference between the positions adopted by Lamer C.J. and Sopinka J. turns on a different conception of the case to meet. . . . In summary, the matter must be viewed in two stages. The first question is whether the Crown has adduced evidence which, if believed, would support a conviction, i.e. prove guilt beyond a reasonable doubt. This is the case to meet. The second question is whether the trier of fact should believe the Crown's evidence. At this second stage, and only at this second stage, the judge or jury may consider the absence of evidence contradicting the Crown's case to meet, including the accused's failure to testify. Any conviction will be based on the Crown's unchallenged evidence. To say that an inference has been drawn from the accused's failure to testify is only to say that the Crown's evidence stands unchallenged. This does not violate the accused's right to silence or presumption of innocence.

For annotations on *Noble* see Delisle and Stuart (1997), 6 C.R. (5th) 5 and 8.

(viii) *Comments on Accused's Failure to Testify*

If triers of fact are entitled to draw inferences tending to guilt should we talk about it openly? The judge in his reasons or the judge in his direction to the jury?

In *Griffin v. California*[138] the accused was convicted of murder. Both the judge and the prosecutor had commented to the jury on the accused's failure to testify. This was in accordance with the State's constitution. The United States Supreme Court, however, decided that this was violative of the Fifth Amendment to the U.S. Constitution as applicable to the states through the Fourteenth Amendment. The dissent argued:

It is not at all apparent to me, on any realistic view of the trial process, that a defendant will be at more of a disadvantage under the California practice than he would be in a court which permitted no comment at all on his failure to take the witness stand. How can it be said that the inferences drawn by a jury will be more detrimental to a defendant under the limiting and carefully controlling language of the instruction here

---

138. 380 U.S. 609 (1964).

involved than would result if the jury were left to roam at large with only its untutored instincts to guide it, to draw from the defendant's silence broad inferences of guilt.[139]

The majority saw quite a difference:

[Comment] is a penalty imposed by courts for exercising a constitutional privilege. It is said however that the inference of guilt from failure to testify as to facts peculiarly within the accused's knowledge is in any event natural and irresistible, and that comment on the failure does not magnify that inference into a penalty. What the jury may infer, given no help from the court, is one thing. What it may infer when the court solemnizes the silence of the accused into evidence is quite another.

The Canada Evidence Act[140] provides: "The failure of the person charged, or of the wife or husband of that person, to testify shall not be made the subject of comment by the judge or by counsel for the prosecution."

The first thing to notice about the Canadian provision is that our courts have decided that the comment is only prohibited in cases of trial by jury and when the comment is made in the presence of the jury. In *R. v. Binder*[141] Roach, J. wrote:

I had always understood that the comment there prohibited was one made by either the Judge or Crown counsel to or in the presence of the jury. I still think so. Counsel for the appellant was unable to refer to any case in which it was held otherwise.

. . . .

It is impossible to think of any other reason for prohibiting such a comment than its improper effect upon a jury.[142]

Perhaps such reasoning was born of a belief that in trials by judge alone the accused's failure to testify could not be magnified out of its proper proportion, since a trial judge is able to place it in its proper perspective.

The next thing to notice is that comment by an accused on his co-accused's failure to take the stand is not foreclosed by the section.[143] In *R. v. Crawford*[144] the accused and another were charged with second degree murder. The accused Crawford made no statement to the police. He testified at trial and blamed the other. He was cross-examined by the other's counsel on his failure to make any statements to the police. The other accused Creighton did not testify at trial. His version of the events was set out in a videotaped statement to the police on his arrest. The Crawford's lawyer said to the jury "an innocent man sitting in Creighton's seat would have gotten into that witness box and sworn that he was not guilty". Only Crawford appealed to the Supreme Court. The Supreme Court was then principally concerned with the extent to which one accused could use

---

139. *Ibid.*, at p. 621.
140. R.S.C. 1985, c. C-5, s. 4(6).
141. (1948), 92 C.C.C. 20 (Ont. C.A.); followed in *Pratte v. Maher*, [1965] 1 C.C.C. 77 (Que. C.A.), *R. v. Bouchard*, [1970] 5 C.C.C. 95 (N.B.C.A.), *Tilco Plastics Ltd. v. Skurjat*, [1967] 1 C.C.C. 131 (Ont. H.C.); affirmed [1967] 2 C.C.C. 196n (Ont. C.A.).
142. *Ibid.*, at pp. 24-25.
143. This appears also to be the approach in England. See *R. v. Wickham* (1971), 55 Crim. App. R. 199 (C.A.); but contrary to the approach in the United States: see *DeLuna v. U.S.*, 308 F.2d 140 (1962).
144. [1995] 1 S.C.R. 858.

his co-accused's silence during the investigation to challenge the credibility of the co-accused's testimony in court. The language of the court, however, appears to accept that comment by one accused on the other's failure to testify was permissible. The court noted in passing that in *R. v. Naglik*[145] the Ontario Court of Appeal had held that neither section 11(*c*) of the Charter nor section 4(6) of the Canada Evidence Act prevented a co-accused's counsel from commenting on an accused's failure to testify. The Court of Appeal in *R. v. Crawford* concluded that: "[I]t was open to counsel for Crawford to comment upon the failure of Creighton to testify on his own behalf."[146]

The next thing to notice about section 4(6) is that there are comments and then there are comments. In *Avon v. R.*[147] the trial judge had said to the jury:

> The accused did not testify. Evidently, he could have done so. He is not obliged to do so. I must tell you immediately, . . . it is not because the accused did not testify that you should believe that he could be guilty. . . . Actually, you have merely the Crown's evidence. The defence did not call witnesses, and the accused did not testify: he did not have to. It is up to the Crown to prove its case.[148]

For the majority Fauteux, C.J.C. wrote:

> I would say that the language used by [the trial judge] is a "statement" of an accused's right not to testify, rather than a "comment" on his failure to do so. In my opinion, the instructions complained of cannot be construed as prejudicial to the accused or such to suggest to the jurors that his silence was used to cloak his guilt.[149]

In *R. v. McConnell* the accused were charged with possession of house-breaking instruments. They had offered an explanation to the police at the time but they did not testify. The trial judge told the jury:

> You are not to be influenced in your decision by either of the accused not going into the witness box and testifying, but the Court does point out that these explanations when made were not made under oath and it is not only for that reason alone, but for any other number of reasons that may occur to you, to decide if you will accept these explanations.[150]

The accused's appeals were dismissed and Justice Ritchie noted:

> [T]he language used by the trial Judge was taken not so much a "comment" on the failure of the persons charged to testify as a statement of their right to refrain from doing so, and it . . . should not be taken to have been the intention of Parliament in enacting s. 4(5) of the *Canada Evidence Act* to preclude Judges from explaining to juries the law with respect to the rights of accused persons in this regard.[151]

In *Vezeau v. R.*[152] the accused was charged with murder. The accused presented an alibi defence but did not testify. The trial judge told the jury that

---

145. (1991), 65 C.C.C. (3d) 272.
146. (1993), 20 C.R. (4th) 331, 348.
147. (1971), 21 D.L.R. (3d) 442 (S.C.C.).
148. *Ibid.*, at p. 445.
149. *Ibid.*, at p. 446.
150. [1968] 4 C.C.C. 257, 260 (S.C.C.).
151. *Ibid.*, at p. 263. For a list of cases setting out what comments are within the section and what are without, see McWilliams, *Canadian Criminal Evidence*, 3d ed., 30:10500.
152. [1977] 2 S.C.R. 277. In *R. v. Boss* (1989), 68 C.R. (3d) 123 (Ont. C.A.) the accused argued

they could not draw any conclusion unfavourable to the accused from the fact he had not testified. He was acquitted. The Court of Appeal reversed and ordered a new trial on the basis that the instruction was an error of law. The Supreme Court unanimously agreed. The dissent thought that the instruction was an error but not such as would warrant a new trial. Justice Martland, for the majority, wrote:

> [I]t is open to a jury to draw an inference from the failure of the accused to testify, and particularly in a case in which it is sought to establish an alibi.
>
> . . . .
>
> [T]he decision of the jury was made in the light of an express direction that they must not, in reaching a decision, draw any unfavourable conclusion from the fact that the appellant had not given evidence. . . . [T]his direction was wrong in law.[153]

On the authority of *Noble*, Canada has a constitutional standard that no adverse inference can be drawn from the accused's silence but a statutory rule in section 4(6) that bars a trial judge from advising the jury not to do so. This appears to be so even if they were to ask "Is it true that the Supreme Court decided that a jury cannot draw an inference of guilt from the accused's silence"? For consistency section 4(6) should be declared unconstitutional.

Reform proposals in this area in Canada and elsewhere have been highly controversial.

In 1972 The Criminal Law Revision Committee in England recommended major changes. The Committee noted:

> The present law and practice are much too favourable to the defence. We are convinced that, when a prima facie case has been made out against the accused, it should be regarded as incumbent on him to give evidence in all ordinary cases. We have no doubt that the prosecution should be entitled, like the judge, to comment on his failure to do so. The present prohibition of comment seems to us wrong in principle and entirely illogical. It may be of little significance if there is no case against him or only a weak one. But the stronger the case is, the more significant will be his failure to give evidence. . . . As to what may be properly included in a comment, we have no doubt that . . . adverse inferences, such as common sense dictates, should be allowed to be drawn from the from the accused's failure to give evidence.[154]

The Committee felt so strongly that it recommended a procedure whereby the accused would be formally called on to give evidence so that his refusal would demonstrate to the jury that the accused had the right to give evidence but declined to do so.[155]

---

unsuccessfully that, as a result of s. 11(*c*) of the Charter of Rights, he had a constitutional right to have the judge charge the jury that no adverse inference should be drawn from the failure of the accused to testify.

153. *Ibid.*, at pp. 288-89.
154. Criminal Law Revision Committee, *Eleventh Report on Evidence (General)*, Cmnd. 4991, s. 110.
155. In 1976 the Republic of Singapore adopted the recommendations of the Committee. See generally Yeo, "Diminishing the Right to Silence: The Singapore Experience" [1983] Crim. L. Rev. 89. Courts in Singapore inform the accused, after the prosecution has rested its case, that if they should "without good cause, refuse to answer any question, the court in determining whether you are guilty of the offence charged may draw such inferences as

Professor Cross, who was a member of the Committee, afterwards defended the Committee's restrictions on the right to silence allowing for such inferences to be drawn as were seen to be proper. He agreed with the critics that the Committee had no empirical data to support the thought that the common law permitted too many wrongful acquittals and that he could not say that the proposed change would lessen the total. But he argued it would at least rid the law of gibberish. The proposed changes would

> spare the judge from talking gibberish to the jury, the conscientious magistrate from directing himself in imbecilic terms and the writer of the law of evidence from drawing distinctions absurd enough to bring a blush to the most hardened academic.[156]

In 1975 the Law Reform Commission of Canada recommended an abolition of section 4(6). In their proposed Code of Evidence, which was never adopted, they provided:

> The accused in a criminal proceeding cannot be compelled to be a witness, but the judge, prosecutor and defence counsel may comment on his failure to testify and the trier of fact may draw all reasonable inferences therefrom.[157]

Nevertheless the Committee's and the Commission's proposals were resisted in England and in Canada. In 1981 the Royal Commission on Criminal Procedure rejected the suggestion for change. Although the Commission noted that objections to adverse inferences regarding silence at trial were not as objectionable as adverse inferences from silence at the investigative stage, still, in their view:

> Any modification to the present law of evidence which aimed at requiring the accused to answer a prima facie case established by the prosecution would be likely to weaken the initial burden of proof that the accusatorial system of trial places upon the prosecution.

In 1982 the Task Force Report on Evidence[158] in Canada recommended that the section prohibiting comment be retained and the jury be advised in neutral terms that the accused has the right to testify but that there is no obligation to do so.

In 1988 the English Parliament imposed restrictions on the right to silence in Northern Ireland.[159] The government maintained it was necessary in order to convict terrorists but the change affected persons charged with any offence. The Order adopted the recommendations of the Revision Committee and judges were

---

appear proper"; see *Haw Tua Tau v. Public Prosecutor*, [1981] 3 All E.R. 14, 18-19 (P.C.). It needs to be noted that jury trials were abolished in Singapore in 1969.

156. Cross, "The Evidence Report: Sense or Nonsense" [1973] Crim. L. Rev. 329 at 332-36.

157. It is noteworthy that the Code also proposed, s. 64(2), that no evidence of the accused's previous convictions could be introduced in attacking the accused's credibility unless the accused had first introduced evidence solely to support his credibility. The Task Force on Evidence, the "successor" to the Commission in recommending changes to the law of evidence, were unanimous in recommending the retention of the existing s. 4(6) forbidding comment by the judge or prosecutor.

158. Report of the Federal/Provincial Task Force on Uniform Rules of Evidence prepared for the Uniform Law Conference, 1982.

159. The Criminal Evidence (N.I.) Order cited in Jackson, "Curtailing the Right to Silence" [1991] Crim. L. Rev. 404.

required to warn accused that adverse inferences might be drawn if they chose not to testify; this warning is to be done in the presence of the jury.[160]

In 1993 the Royal Commission on Criminal Justice concluded that eliminating the right to silence would reduce the prosecution's burden of proof being convicted:

> Given the principle that the burden of proof should rest on the prosecution, it must be wrong for defendants who leave the prosecution to prove its case to be exposed to comment by either the prosecution or the judge to the effect that their failure to enter the witness box corroborates the prosecution case.[161]

The Commission believed that the directions then being given by judges were sufficient:

> The defendant does not have to give evidence. He is entitled to sit in the dock and require the prosecution to prove its case. You must not assume that he is guilty because he has not given evidence. The fact that he has not given evidence proves nothing, one way or the other. It does nothing to establish his guilt. On the other hand, it means that there is no evidence to undermine, contradict, or explain the evidence put before you by the prosecution. [However, you still have to decide whether, on the prosecution's evidence, you are sure of the defendant's guilt.][162]

Some months later, despite the Royal Commission's recommendation to the contrary, the Home Secretary announced his government's plan to seriously limit the right to silence.

The Criminal Justice and Public Order Act, 1994[163] would allow judges and juries to consider a defendant's failure to testify as evidence of his guilt. The Act would extend to England and Wales the reforms accomplished in Northern Ireland in 1988. By section 35, if the accused chooses not to give evidence or, having been sworn, refuses to answer questions, the judge or jury is entitled to draw such inferences as appear to them to be proper. The Act does not require that the judge formally call on the accused to give evidence.

As to what inferences are *proper*, Lord Mustill commented, with respect to the similar Northern Ireland legislation:

> Everything depends on the nature of the issue, the weight of the evidence adduced by the prosecution upon it . . . and the extent to which the defendant should in the nature of things be able to give his own account of the particular matter in question. It is impossible to generalise, for dependent upon circumstances the failure of the defendant to give evidence may found no inference at all, or one which is for all practical purposes fatal.[164]

---

160. Recognizing the certain change in the common law as a result of the Order, see *Murray v. D.P.P.* (1992), 97 Cr. App. R. 151 (H.L.). Professor Dennis notes the possibility of a challenge to the legislation as violative of the European Convention's guarantee to a fair trial which involves the privilege against self-incrimination; see Dennis, "The Criminal Justice and Public Order Act 1994" [1995] Crim. L. Rev. 4.

161. Cmnd. 2263, s. 28.

162. *Ibid.*

163. The Criminal Justice and Public Order Act (Commencement No. 6) Order 1995 provided for the coming into force of the sections relating to inferences from the accused's silence on April 10, 1995.

164. *Murray v. D.P.P., supra,* note 160, at p. 155.

This dictum emphasizes that it will be for the trial judge in each case to decide whether an inference is permissible.

We cannot reliably predict that there will be fewer acquittals of the guilty as a result of commenting on the accused's failure to testify. But we can avoid the various formulae of words which frequently amount to, in the words of Professor Cross, gibberish. It seems to make sense to speak intelligently to the trier about what inferences are proper in the circumstances. Guidance from the judge seems preferable to allowing the jury to roam at large. This comment of course will depend on the trial judge's determination that the particular case is such that a trier would be entitled to draw an adverse inference. If the legislature is not prepared to act then judicial reform is called for.

(f) Compellability of Corporate Officers

R. v. AMWAY CORP.
[1989] 1 S.C.R. 21

[In forfeiture proceedings brought by the government pursuant to the Customs Act, the government applied for an order under Rule 465(1) of the Federal Court Rules that Amway produce one of its officers for examination for discovery. The Federal Court of Appeal reversed the Trial Division's decision to grant the application. Amway argued that Rule 465 infringed section 11(*c*) of the Charter by requiring a corporate defendant to be examined for discovery.]

SOPINKA J. (DICKSON C.J.C., MCINTYRE, LAMER, WILSON, LA FOREST, and L'HEUREUX-DUBÉ JJ. concurring): —

. . . .

Section 11(c) provides:

11. Any person charged with an offence has the right

. . .

(c)   not to be compelled to be a witness in proceedings against that person in respect of the offence;

In order to obtain the benefit of this section of the *Charter* the respondent must establish that it is:

(a)   a person;
(b)   charged with an offence; and
(c)   a witness in proceedings against that person.

With respect to (a) it is neither necessary nor desirable in this case to decide that under no circumstances may a corporation avail itself of the provisions of s. 11. I am also prepared to assume without deciding that the proceedings in question are such that the requirement in (b) is satisfied. In my opinion, however, a corporation cannot be a witness and therefore cannot come within s. 11(*c*).

Pre-*Charter* cases . . . held that an officer of a corporation who testifies in criminal proceedings against the corporation, is the witness. This principle applied equally to an officer who is the directing mind of the corporation. . . .

. . . .

. . . It would be startling to suggest that the officer, if asked a question the answer to which tended to incriminate him, could not avail himself of s. 13 of the *Charter* and s. 5(2) of the *Canada Evidence Act*. If such protection is available, it must be because the officer is a witness. It is hard to rationalize that the officer is a witness and the corporation is a witness. There is only one witness under examination and that is the entity that swore the oath and that would be subject to a penalty for perjury. That is not to say that a witness must be one capable of taking an oath, but where the evidence is sworn evidence, it is my view that the *Charter* intended to protect the person who swore the oath.

. . . .

In my view, it would strain the interpretation of s. 11(*c*) if an artificial entity were held to be a witness. Such a metamorphosis could not be justified on the basis that the rules of evidence on an examination for discovery do not restrict the person testifying to personal knowledge. That person may answer questions based on belief as well as on information obtained from the corporation. There are many proceedings where witnesses are permitted similar latitude. I need only mention public inquiries and proceedings before administrative tribunals to illustrate the point. Traditionally, witnesses in these proceedings have been accorded the protection of s. 5 of the *Canada Evidence Act* (see, for example, *Di Iorio v. Warden of the Montreal Jail*, [1978] 1 S.C.R. 152). The mere fact that rules of evidence permit greater latitude in the source of the information which the witness imparts to the tribunal does not have the effect of transforming the source into a witness.

Applying a purposive interpretation to s. 11(*c*), I am of the opinion that it was intended to protect the individual against the affront to dignity and privacy inherent in a practice which enables the prosecution to force the person charged to supply the evidence out of his or her own mouth. Although disagreement exists as to the basis of the principle against self-incrimination, in my view, this factor plays a dominant role.

. . . .

Accordingly, I am in respectful disagreement with the Federal Court of Appeal that the respondent can obtain the benefit of s. 11(*c*). . . .

R. v. NOVA SCOTIA PHARMACEUTICAL SOCIETY
(1990), 58 C.C.C. (3d) 161 (N.S.T.D.)

[A member of the society sought to quash a subpoena compelling him to testify. The society was charged with conspiracy to unduly lessen competition contrary to section 32(1)(*c*) of the Combines Investigation Act. The member argued that because as a member he could be personally liable for payment of any fine levied against the society he should not be compelled as a witness.]

ROSCOE J.: —

. . . .

Mr. Winsor, the applicant herein, is a pharmacist and from 1979 to 1986 was employed by Maritime Medical Care Inc. and has been subpoenaed by the Crown to testify concerning certain records maintained by the claims department of Maritime Medical Care Inc. during the time that he was employed there. Mr. Winsor has also, since 1979, been a member of the Nova Scotia Pharmaceutical Society and the Pharmacy Association of Nova Scotia, two of the named co-conspirators.

The argument on behalf of the applicant is based upon the common law right not to be compelled to testify against oneself and s. 11(*c*) of the *Canadian Charter of Rights and Freedoms*. . . .

The Nova Scotia Pharmaceutical Society was created by statute of the Legislature of the Province of Nova Scotia on April 4, 1876. That statute creates a body corporate but does not contain any provisions with respect to limited liability of its members for debts and penalties imposed upon the society. . . .

. . . .

The applicant argues that since the Nova Scotia *Pharmacy Act* . . . fails to provide any limitation on the liability of its members, that if the society is found guilty of the offences charged, that Mr. Winsor would be personally liable along with other members of the society for payment of any penalty and, therefore, he should not be compelled to testify against the society.

. . . .

With respect to a common law right not to incriminate oneself, in *Thomson Newspapers Ltd. v. Canada (Director of Investigation & Research [et al.])* (1986), 30 C.C.C. (3d) 145 (Ont. C.A.), where the issue concerned the validity of a section of the *Combines Investigation Act* which allowed the director to summons any person to be examined upon oath, Grange J.A. said at p. 150 C.C.C.:

> While we must now accept that the provisions of ss. 8 to 14 of the Charter are but specific illustrations of the greater rights set forth in s. 7 (see *Reference re s. 94(2) of Motor Vehicle Act* (1985), 24 D.L.R. (4th) 536, particularly *per* Lamer J. at p. 549 D.L.R., nevertheless I am of the view that the only rights against self-incrimination now known to our law are those found in ss. 11(*c*) and 13 of the Charter, namely, the right of a person charged with an offence not to be compelled to be a witness in those proceedings and the right of a witness not to have incriminating evidence given by him used against him in subsequent proceedings.
>
> We in Canada have no modern tradition against a witness incriminating himself by his own testimony. At least since 1893, when the *Canada Evidence Act*, 1893 (Can.), c. 31, was amended to include what is now s. 5 [see R.S.C. 1970, c. E-10] our tradition has been that every witness must answer questions legitimately put to him subject to the protections now found in s. 13 of the Charter and subject to the protection against compelling an accused person to testify in proceedings directed against him (s. 11(*c*) of the Charter). Once he testifies, however, he is no more protected than any other witness. I adopt the conclusion of Professor E. Ratushny found in his work *Self-Incrimination in the Canadian Criminal Process* (1979), p. 92 (with, of course, the necessary changes resulting from the enactment of the Charter) as follows:
>
>> It is clear that the privilege against self-incrimination as it exists in Canada today is an extremely narrow concept. It simply describes two specific procedural and evidentiary rules: the non-compellability of the accused as a witness at his own trial and the section 5(2) protection of a witness not to have testimony used in future proceedings. There is no general principle which can be invoked to achieve a specific result in a particular case.

The issue with respect to whether an officer or employee of a corporate accused is compellable as a Crown witness prior to the enactment of the Charter was determined in *R. v. N.M. Paterson & Sons Ltd.* (1980), 55 C.C.C. (2d) 289. In stating the issue Chouinard J. said at p. 292 C.C.C.:

> Therefore, the true question, in my view, is whether there exists under the criminal law of Canada a rule whereby an officer or employee of a corporation, determined to be the 'directing mind and will' of the corporation, is not compellable as a witness on behalf of the prosecution in a case where the corporation is the accused, on the basis that to rule otherwise would amount to a denial of the privilege of an accused against self-crimination.

The court found that the employee was compellable whether or not the accused employer was a corporate or natural person and the witness being compelled to testify was not an accused for purposes of the privilege of self-incrimination.

. . . .

The applicant herein argues that *Paterson* and *Amway* should be distinguished because in those cases the individual witness is protected from having to pay a penalty if the corporation is found guilty because of the existence of the corporate veil and the limited liability of the witness. In my view, however, the rationale for the decisions is that the witness is a distinct entity separate and apart from the corporation. I see no mention in those cases of the limited liability for the payment of any fine and agree with the Crown submission in this case that the financial effect on Mr. Winsor, if the pharmaceutical society is found guilty, should not be a consideration. But even if it were, his position is not unlike that of a major shareholder or directing mind of a corporate defendant. By virtue of s. 1 of the Act incorporating the pharmaceutical society, the society is a distinct separate entity from its members, and I find that since Mr. Winsor is not personally an accused person, he is a compellable witness for the prosecution.

. . . .

In conclusion, I find that Mr. Winsor is a compellable witness at the trial of this matter and the application to quash the subpoena is dismissed.

[The appeal was dismissed: *R. v. Nova Scotia Pharmaceutical Society* (*sub nom. R. v. Winsor*) (1991), 69 C.C.C. (3d) 136 (N.S.C.A.).]

For the impact of the Charter on the compellability of corporate officers, see *British Columbia Securities Commission v. Branch*,[165] discussed above under Principle Against Self-Incrimination: Charter section 7.

PROBLEMS

Problem 1

John Smith is charged with impaired driving. Constable Jones was the arresting officer. Jones is prepared to testify that when Smith was apprehended he appeared to be unsteady on his feet and that his eyes were glassy. He had followed Smith for three blocks from the parking lot of the Aces Bar and in that time Smith's car was driven in an erratic fashion. When Smith emerged from the driver's seat of the vehicle Jones addressed him: "You've been drinking, haven't you?" but Smith made no reply. Jones told Smith to walk along the white centre-line of the roadway but Smith declined. Jones asked Smith to return with him to the Aces Bar to see the bartender but Smith refused saying that if he was under arrest he must be taken directly to the station. When they arrived at the station Smith refused to take a breath test. Is any of the above evidence receivable at Smith's trial? For what purpose? If Smith does not testify in the face of the admissible evidence would you convict? Compare *Curr v. R.* (1972), 7 C.C.C. (2d) 181 (S.C.C.); *Marcoux v. R.* (1975), 60 D.L.R. (3d) 119 (S.C.C.); *R. v. Shaw* (1964), 48 W.W.R. 190 (B.C.C.A.); *R. v. Eden*, [1970] 2 O.R. 161 (C.A.); *R. v. Itwaru* (1970), 10 C.R.N.S. 184 (N.S.C.A.); *R. v. Robertson* (1975), 21 C.C.C. (2d) 385 (Ont. C.A.); *R. v. Hawke* (1975), 22 C.C.C. (2d) 19 (Ont. C.A.).

---

165. (1995), 38 C.R. (4th) 133 (S.C.C.).

Problem 2

The Smith Glass Company has been charged with resale price maintenance contrary to the Competition Act. At the trial Crown counsel calls as his first witness John Smith, founder, president and sole proprietor of the company. John Smith objects to taking the stand relying on his privilege against self-incrimination. Rule on the objection. Compare *R. v. J.G.S.P.; Ex parte Corning Glass Works Ltd.* (1970), 16 D.L.R. (3d) 609 (Ont. C.A.); leave to appeal refused (1971), 16 D.L.R. (3d) 617n; and *R. v. N.M. Paterson & Sons*, [1979] 1 W.W.R. 5 (Man. C.A.); reversed (1981), 55 C.C.C. (2d) 289 (S.C.C.). See also *Can. v. Amway of Can. Ltd.* (1989), 68 C.R. (3d) 97 (S.C.C.).

Problem 3

You act for John Tracy who is charged with rape. He decided not to testify. The trial judge's charge included the following:

Now, he is charged with rape and I tried to define what rape is to you. You heard the story of this woman, who came on the witness stand here, and her evidence is not denied.

And later the trial judge said:

Now, gentlemen, I am not going into the sordid things that took place there, but I can see nothing in the conduct of this woman that day, according to her evidence — and that is the only evidence we have as to her conduct excepting the other witnesses that came in here to tell the story of what she told them — I see nothing in her conduct that day that should make the jury detract from the truth of anything that she said.

And then again:

It was his doing, according to the evidence and the only evidence we have. . . .

Is there any cause for complaint? Compare *Wright v. R.*, [1945] 2 D.L.R. 523 (S.C.C.); *R. v. Gallagher* (1922), 63 D.L.R. 629 (Alta. C.A.); approved in *Bigaouette v. R.*, [1927] 1 D.L.R. 1147 (S.C.C.).

2. MANNER OF QUESTIONING

The chief source of information for the trier of fact is oral testimony elicited from witnesses called by the parties. The fact that the witnesses are chosen by the parties and may be prepared in advance by them has led to different rules regarding their manner of questioning dependent on who is putting the questions. The witness's description of the incident is first elicited by the party calling him in a process labelled examination-in-chief or direct examination. On the conclusion of direct examination, the adversary engages in cross-examination; the adversary is able to elicit further data concerning the incident from the witness and is also able to question the witness concerning his powers of perception and memory, to demand explicitness in his communication and to explore his sincerity, all in an attempt to challenge the accuracy of his first description. Following cross-examination the witness may be re-examined by the party who called him and permitted to explain or amplify answers given on cross-examination. Further opportunities to cross-examine and re-examine, all at the discretion of the trial judge, are possible.

(a) Leading Questions

A party calling a witness should not ask leading questions. One of the first instances of this rule's articulation provides a good illustrative characterization of the phrase "leading question," and at the same time demonstrates both the rule's justification as well as the frequent irretrievability of the harm done. In the *Trial of Thomas Rosewell*[166] the accused was indicted for High Treason. Witnesses against him had testified that in his preaching he had spoken against Charles I and Charles II as "two wicked Kings." The accused maintained that mention in his sermon of "two wicked Kings" was not concerning Charles I or his present majesty but rather was in reference to Kings referred to in the Book of Chronicles in the Old Testament, i.e., Ahab and his son Ahaziah, whose example he was using to expound on the 20th chapter of Genesis. To make his point the accused called a witness, Hudson, and the transcript reads:

L.C.J. Jeffries:	Come, here is your witness, what say you to him? . . .
Rosewell:	Pray Sir, as to the truth of the business; Did you hear me speak of two wicked Kings? That, my lord, came in, I say upon the second verse of the 20th of Genesis, which I then was expounding.
L.C.J.:	Nay ask him in general what he heard you say; and whether he heard you say anything of two wicked kings, and what it was.
Rosewell:	Ay, about Ahab, and Ahaziah his son —
L.C.J.:	Nay, nay, I must have none of those things, we must have fair questions put; for, as you see we will not admit the king's counsel to put any questions to the witnesses, nor produce any witnesses against you, that are leading, or not proper, so nor must you. But if you have a mind to ask him any questions, what he heard concerning two wicked kings generally, do so.
Hudson:	Upon the second verse he was then.
L.C.J.:	Of what chapter?
Hudson:	Of the 20th of Genesis.[167]

To describe the common law position it would be difficult to improve on the test of Mr. Justice Beck in *Maves v. Grand Trunk Pacific Railway Co.*[168]

> I find the general subject of leading questions dealt with in a most satisfactory way in Best on Evidence, 11th ed., 624 *et seq.* I quote, italicising what I wish to emphasize: —
>
> > The chief rule of practice relative to the interrogation of witnesses is that which prohibits "*leading questions*," *i.e.*, questions which directly or indirectly suggest to the witness the answer he is to give. The rule is, that *on material points* a party must not lead his own witnesses, but may lead those of his adversary; in other words, that leading questions are allowed in cross-examination, but not in examination-in-chief. This seems based on two reasons: first, and principally, on the supposition that the witness has a bias in favour of the party bringing him forward, and hostile to his

---

166. (1684), 10 Howell's State Trials 147 (K.B.).
167. *Ibid.*, at p. 190.
168. (1913), 14 D.L.R. 70, 73-77 (Alta. C.A.). And see Denroche, "Leading Questions" (1963-64), 6 Crim. L.Q. 21.

opponent; secondly, that the party calling a witness has an advantage over his adversary, in knowing beforehand what the witness will prove, or, at least, is expected to prove; and that, consequently, if he were allowed to lead, he might interrogate in such a manner as to extract only so much of the knowledge of the witness as would be favourable to his side, or even put a false gloss upon the whole.

I think a third reason may be added, namely, that a witness, though intending to be entirely fair and honest may, owing, for example, to lack of education, of exactness of knowledge of the precise meaning of words or of appreciation at the moment of their precise meaning, or of alertness to see that what is implied in the question requires modification, honestly assent to a leading question which fails to express his real meaning, which he would probably have completely expressed if allowed to do so in his own words.

. . . .

So that the *general* rule is that in examining one's own witness, not that no leading questions must be asked, but that *on material points* one must *not* lead his own witness but that on points that are *merely introductory and form no part of the substance* of the inquiry one *should* lead.

. . . .

A case which not infrequently arises in practice is that of a witness who recounts a conversation and in doing so omits one or more statements which counsel examining him is instructed formed part of it. The common and proper practice is to ask the witness to repeat the conversation from the beginning. It is often found that in his repetition he gives the lacking statement — possibly omitting one given the first time. This method may be tried more than once, and as a matter of expediency — so as to have the advantage of getting the whole story on the witness' own unaided recollection — counsel might pass on to some other subject and later revert to the conversation, asking him to again state it. But when this method fails, the trial Judge undoubtedly ought to permit a question containing a reference to the subject-matter of the statement which it is supposed has been omitted by the witness. If this method fails, then and not till then — that is when his memory appears to be entirely exhausted, the trial Judge should allow a question to be put to him containing the supposedly omitted matter. It will be, of course, for the jury, or the Judge if there be no jury, to draw a conclusion as to the truthfulness of the witness; although the permitting of a question in a certain form is largely — though I think not wholly — in the discretion of the trial Judge. I should think that, with regard to the class of leading question I have been considering, they should, in every case, be permitted after all the steps which appear to shew the witness' memory to have been exhausted have been taken. If not permitted, great injustice may result. If permitted, the jury or Judge acting as a jury, may, of course, as I have said, disbelieve the answer elicited.

The third reason suggested by Justice Beck for prohibiting leading questions in chief highlights a different kind of leading question from that which directly suggests an answer: a question may be so phrased as to assume within it the truth of some fact which remains controverted between the parties and a witness, not attuned to that fact, may inadvertently agree to its existence. The classic example, of course, is "when did you stop beating your wife?" Another example, "what was the deceased doing when the accused shot her?", in a prosecution where the issue is the identity of the assailant, is equally objectionable as leading, or "misleading," as the witness may unwittingly testify to a fact concerning which he has no knowledge or which he has no wish to concede.

The common law, then, prohibits leading questions but provides exceptions to the general rule. A list of exceptions would include:

a) for introductory, formal or undisputed matters;
b) for the purpose of identifying persons or things;
c) to allow one witness to contradict another regarding statements made by that other;
d) where the witness is either hostile to the questioner or unwilling to give evidence;
e) where it is seen, in the trial judge's discretion, to be necessary to refresh the witness's memory;
f) where the witness is defective in some respect arising from age, education, language or mental capacity;
g) where the matter is of a complicated nature and, in the opinion of the trial judge, the witness deserves some assistance to determine what subject the questioner is asking about.

In exercising his discretion to allow leading questions the trial judge should, however, keep in mind the reasons for the rule canvassed above, and rule not according to a grocery list of exceptions but in accord with the underlying philosophy. The evidence we seek is that of the witness and not that of the questioner. Stating the rule in this open way is preferable, as one could never close the list of exceptions and the matter must be left to the trial judge's discretion. In determining whether a question suggests an answer, much will depend on the character, mood and bias of the witness, and the manner and inflection of the questioner, all matters to be determined in the particular case.[169]

Justice Beck, though admitting that the authorities were not quite clear on the point, suggested that, given the underlying rationale of the rule, the trial judge has a discretion to restrain the cross-examining party from using leading questions when the witness appears to favour him. If the judge does not restrain such leading questions the form of the question may nevertheless detract from the weight of the answer; comment thereon to the jury might be made, and perhaps counsel might be warned of this effect.[170] In *R. v. McLaughlin*,[171] the trial judge, while allowing that the accused could examine his co-accused, held that since the co-accused had not given evidence implicating the accused he had no right to cross-examine. The Court of Appeal held this to be an error in law:

> Undoubtedly occasions will arise during the course of cross-examination of a co-operative co-accused when evidence will be elicited favourable to the accused which, in the absence of a right to cross-examine, would require the testimony of the accused for its proof. In other words, the accused may be able to get his defence before the Court without entering the witness box. I do not regard this as a matter of great concern, because the triers of fact, as in the case of all evidence, will be required to decide what weight is to be attached to it. The impact of evidence on the trier of fact is determined by many factors, including the interest of the witness, his

---

169. See *Reference re R. v. Coffin*, [1956] S.C.R. 191, 211 per Kellock, J.: ". . . while, as a general rule, a party may not either in direct or re-examination put leading questions, the court has a discretion, not open to review, to relax it whenever it is considered necessary in the interests of justice."

170. As an example of such a warning see *R. v. Smuk* (1971), 3 C.C.C. (2d) 457 (B.C.C.A.): failing to call accused as first witness could adversely effect the weight of his evidence.

171. (1974), 2 O.R. (2d) 514 (C.A.).

demeanour, as well as the form in which the questions are put to the witness by counsel.[172]

R. v. ROSE
(2001), 42 C.R. (5th) 183, 153 C.C.C. (3d) 225 (Ont. C.A.)

[The accused was charged with trafficking in cocaine and possession for the purpose of trafficking. The charges arose as a result of police surveillance observations of an alleged drug transaction between the accused and B. B was observed entering a motor vehicle driven by the accused. The motor vehicle was on the fringes of an area known to the police for its high level of crack cocaine selling activity. Shortly after B entered the motor vehicle, the police stopped it. The accused was arrested. After the arrest, money and crack cocaine were found inside the vehicle. B was initially charged jointly with the accused. However, on the first date set for trial, B agreed to give a statement to the police and testify against the accused. It was the Crown's theory that the accused, at the time of his arrest, had just finished selling drugs to B. B testified in accordance with this theory. The accused testified that B was the trafficker and that he was merely an accommodation buyer picking up some drugs for a friend. The trial judge rejected the accused's evidence, found that the accused was the owner of the drugs located in the motor vehicle and that he was the one selling drugs to B on the occasion in question. The accused was convicted. Most of the grounds of appeal related to Crown counsel's conduct of the trial.]

CHARRON, J.A. (FELDMAN and MACPHERSON, JJ.A. concurring): —

Proof of the Crown's Case Through the Use of Leading Questions

A leading question is one that suggests the answer. It is trite law that the party who calls a witness is generally not permitted to ask the witness leading questions. The reason for the rule arises from a concern that the witness, who in many instances favours the party who calls him or her, will readily agree to the suggestions put in the form of a question rather than give his or her own answers to the questions. Of course, the degree of concern that may arise from the use of leading questions will depend on the particular circumstances, and the rule is applied with some flexibility. For example, leading questions are routinely asked to elicit a witness' evidence on preliminary and non-contentious matters. This practice is adopted for the sake of expediency and generally gives rise to no concern. Leading questions are also permitted to the extent that they are necessary to direct the witness to a particular matter or field of inquiry. Apart from these specific examples, the trial judge has a general discretion to allow leading questions whenever it is considered necessary in the interests of justice.

The transcript in this case presents numerous transgressions of this rule by Crown counsel. The appellant relies mainly on the examination-in-chief of the Crown's main witness, Noel Beaudry. Several excerpts are reproduced below. The questions that are most offensive are highlighted.

Q.   All right, and do you recall when — when and how you first met Mr. Rose?
A.   No.

Q.   And what's your connection with Mr. Rose?
A.   What do you mean, connection?

Q.   Well, what do you do with Mr. Rose?

---

172. *Ibid.*, at p. 524.

A.   I talk to him.

Q.   What else do you do with him?

A.   That's about it.

Q.   Does he supply you with crack cocaine?

A.   Sometimes.

Q.   Now, my information is that the police had set up surveillance on yourself and on the 19th of August you got into a motor vehicle with Mr. Rose. The 21st of August you got into a motor vehicle with Mr. Rose.

At this point, defence counsel objected to the leading questions. Crown counsel maintained that his questions were not leading. His submission to the trial judge, in answer to defence counsel's objection, somewhat exemplifies the general approach Crown counsel adopted in questioning not only Beaudry, but all of the Crown witnesses:

[Crown]: Well, this is information I have and I'm asking this witness to either confirm or deny it. If he confirms it, it will become a fact. If he denies it, it won't become a fact. I don't think it's leading at all. It's information I have and I'm asking him to confirm it or deny it. It's not suggesting the answer.

The judge ruled that the question was still incomplete and not objectionable at that point in time. He invited defence counsel to renew his objection if he so wished after hearing the whole question. Crown counsel continued to question the witness much in the same fashion and defence counsel did not renew his objection. Counsel for the appellant relies more particularly on the following excerpts from the examination-in-chief in support of his contention that Crown counsel proved his case through the use of leading questions:

Q.   Mr. Beaudry, I started advising you that my information is that the police were conducting surveillance and on the following dates they saw you get into a motor vehicle which Mr. Rose was driving and those dates were August 19, August 21, September 4, and September 5. Did you, in fact, meet Mr. Rose on those dates?

A.   If it's right there, I guess so. I don't mark it in a book, you know, it's just —

Q.   You didn't mark it. How many times have you purchased crack cocaine from Mr. Rose? You don't have to give me an exact number, give your best estimate or you can give me a range.

A.   Three, four times.

Q.   Three or four times, and do you recall when those three or four times would have been?

A.   No.

Q.   Now, on the 6th of September — or the 5th of September, you were in an automobile with Mr. Rose and the police stopped that automobile?

A.   Yeah.

Q.   You remember that?

A.   Yeah. I don't remember the date, but I remember when they stopped us.

Q.   And there were police cars in front and back of Mr. Rose's car?

A.   Something like that.

Q.   And do you recall what kind of automobile Mr. Rose was driving or drives?

A.   A black car.

Q.   You don't know the make?

A.   No.

Q.   The license number? Has it been — all the times that you've purchased crack cocaine from Mr. Rose, has he been in the same motor vehicle?

A.   Yeah.

Q.   And that's the black car you just indicated?

A.   Black car, yeah.

Q.   Now, when the — on the 5th of September when the police officers stopped the motor vehicle, you were in Mr. Rose's automobile, were you not?

A.   Yeah.

Q.   Mr. Rose was in the automobile?

A.   Yeah.

Q.   Correct, and who was driving the automobile?

A.   Mr. Rose.

Q.   Mr. Rose, and you were in which seat, the front passenger seat?

A.   Yeah. The front seat.

Q.   Was there anyone else in the car?

A.   No.

Q.   All right, and what was your purpose for being in that automobile on that date and time, why were you there?

A.   To tell you the truth, I don't even know because it happened so fast. I didn't have time to say nothing or nothing, you know.

Q.   Well, were you going to purchase crack cocaine from Mr. Rose on that date?

A.   I guess I would have tried.

Q.   Did you have money with you?

A.   Yeah. Of course, it was my rent money, but . . .

Q.   Well, I — is it fair to say that every time you had gotten into Mr. Rose's automobile in the past you purchased crack cocaine from him?

A.   Maybe two out of three.

Q.   Two out of three. Did you have any crack cocaine with you at that time when you got into Mr. Rose's car on the 5th of September?

A.   No.

Q.   You had money with you though?

A.   Yeah.

Q.   Would you agree with me that it's — it seems that you were there to buy crack cocaine from him?

A.   I could have.

Q.   Other than meeting Mr. Rose to buy crack cocaine from him, have you and Mr. Rose ever done anything else together? Do you go to movies together, go to see friends together?

A.   No, we just went for coffee.

Q.   Coffee and when you go for coffee does that end up — is that when you have a conversation about whether —

A.   Sometimes.

Q.   — he has crack cocaine?

A.   Sometimes no. All depends.

Q.   How often would you have gone for coffee with Mr. Rose?

A.   I don't know. Four times, three times.

Q.   Okay, as many times as you've bought crack cocaine from him?

A.   Maybe a little bit less.

Q.   Now, when the police stopped the automobile they found some crack cocaine in the automobile?

A.   That's what they claim.

In my view, Crown counsel's questions to Beaudry were clearly suggestive of the answers. Indeed the entire examination-in-chief reads more like the cross-examination of a witness. This was highly improper particularly in these circumstances where Beaudry, as the trial judge himself stated in his reasons, was "the primary Crown witness" and the questions concerned crucial and contentious matters. The impropriety of Crown counsel's approach is further heightened by the fact that Beaudry's testimony, obtained as it was in return for a stay of the charges against him, was already highly suspect. The manner in which his testimony was elicited could only further undermine its probative value. Consequently, I am of the view that the trial judge erred in ruling against the defence's initial objection and further erred in failing to intervene when Crown counsel continued in this fashion. I do not view defence counsel's failure to renew his objection as an impediment to raising this ground of appeal. In view of the trial judge's failure to appreciate that Crown counsel's questions were indeed leading at the time the objection was made, defence counsel may well have thought that any further objection would be futile.

Virtually all of the incriminating evidence given by Beaudry was elicited through leading questions. Given the circumstances in which he agreed to testify against the appellant, this irregularity raises a real concern that the testimony was proffered, not for its truth, but for the purpose of meeting the expectations of the Crown and the police. The trial judge ultimately accepted some of Beaudry's evidence "as being cogent and vital". Consequently, the finding of guilt may be based, at least in part, on highly questionable evidence.

(b) Refreshing Memory[173]

We have seen above that leading questions may be used sometimes to assist a defective memory. Another important and frequent device, which may or may not stimulate a present recollection, is the use by the witness in the stand of notes made at an earlier time. We should notice that the rules to be discussed

---

173. See generally, Maguire and Quick, "Testimony: Memory and Memoranda" (1957), 3 How. L.J. 1, and Newark and Samuels, "Refreshing Memory," [1978] Crim. L. Rev. 408. See also, *U.S. v. Riccardi*, 174 F. 2d 883 (3d Cir., 1949) per Kalodner, J.

now only apply to "refreshment" in the witness stand.[174] While there are, of course, ethical considerations which forbid placing a story in the mouth of a prospective witness, there are no limitations on the memory aids open for use in preparation for trial.[175]

We have all had the experience in our daily affairs, when seeking to recall a memory, of first recalling a matter associated with it which then triggers or releases the sought item.[176] The triggering device may be a note, a song, a picture:

> . . . memory of things long past can be accurately restored in all sorts of ways. The creaking of a hinge, the whistling of a tune, the smell of seaweed, the sight of an old photograph, the taste of nutmeg, the touch of a piece of canvas, may bring vividly to the foreground of consciousness the recollection of events that happened years ago and which would otherwise have been forgotten. . . . The memory-prodder may itself lack meaning to other persons as a symbol of the past event, as anyone knows who has ever used a knot in his handkerchief as a reminder.[177]

In such a case the witness's memory is truly refreshed. As long as the trier is sure that the witness has a true present memory the device which triggered it is immaterial. Evidently this was the early law. In *Henry v. Lee*,[178] Ellenborough, L.C.J. noted:

> If upon looking at *any* document he can so far refresh his memory as to recollect a circumstance, it is sufficient; and it makes no difference that the memorandum is not written by himself, for it is not the memorandum that is the evidence but the recollection of the witness.

On the other hand, there are instances when the witness has no present memory of the facts in dispute but is able to testify that on an earlier occasion he did have a perfect recollection of the matter and that while he had that recollection he truly recorded the same. In such a case, to use the phrasing of Professor Wigmore, the witness will be allowed to testify as to his "past recollection recorded" since he has no "present memory revived." While the common law was prepared to receive this evidence it noted that the adversary was somewhat prejudiced in his ability to cross-examine the witness, as he could

---

174. The authorities are in conflict as to whether material used to refresh prior to trial should be produced: see and compare *R. v. Musterer* (1967), 61 W.W.R. 63 (B.C. Mag. Ct.); *R. v. Lewis*, [1969] 3 C.C.C. 235 (B.C.S.C.); *R. v. Monfils*, [1972] 1 O.R. 11 (C.A.); *R. v. Bonnycastle* (1969), 3 D.L.R. (3d) 288 (Sask. Q.B.); *R. v. Kerenko* (1965), 49 D.L.R. (2d) 760 (Man. C.A.). See also *Owen v. Edwards* (1983), 77 Cr. App. R. 191 and *R. v. Catling* (1984), 29 C.C.C. (3d) 168 (Alta. Q.B.).

175. See *R. v. Allen (No. 2)* (1979), 46 C.C.C. (2d) 477 (Ont. H.C.) re use of sodium amytol to remove the repression of witness's memory and allow the witness to recall the events. And see *Kowall v. McRae*, [1980] 2 W.W.R. 492 (Man. C.A.) re use of hypnosis for similar purpose. See also *R. v. Pitt*, [1968] 3 C.C.C. 342 (B.C.S.C.). See Haward and Ashworth, "Some Problems of Evidence Obtained by Hypnosis," [1980] Crim. L. Rev. 469. See also *R. v. Clark* (1984), 40 C.R. (3d) 183 (Alta. Q.B.).

176. See Hutchins and Slesinger, "Some Observations on the Law of Evidence — Memory" (1928), 41 Harv. L. Rev. 860 and Gardner, "The Perception and Memory of Witnesses" (1933), 18 Corn. L.Q. 391.

177. Frank, J. in *Fanelli v. U.S. Gypsum*, 141 F. 2d 216, 217 (2d Cir., 1944).

178. (1814), 2 Chitty 124, 125, cited in 3 Wigmore, *Evidence* (Chad. Rev.), s. 759. And see other early English cases to similar effect there cited.

only examine his usual abilities and habits for accuracy.[179] To ensure greater trustworthiness, the common law added further conditions: the earlier recollection must have been recorded while the witness's memory was fresh, i.e., at or near the time of the observation of the matter, and the witness must be prepared to presently vouch for the accuracy of the recording of his recollection and that his then recollection was correct. As described by Meredith, J.A. in *Fleming v. Toronto Railway Co.*:[180]

> On the other branch of the case as well, the defendants are entitled, I think, to a new trial, because of the improper rejection of evidence. The plaintiff made a *primâ facie* case of neglect, on the part of the defendants, to take reasonable care that the car was road-worthy and free from the defect which caused the accident. The defendants then proceeded to meet that case by testimony as to examinations to ensure road-worthiness and freedom from such defect; but, upon objection made on the plaintiff's behalf, the evidence in question was rejected, and rejected upon an erroneous ground, as is now generally admitted. The witness could not, from memory alone, testify to an inspection made shortly before the accident; it would hardly be possible that he could; it was then proposed to put into his hand a report, signed by him in the usual course of his work, shewing that the car had been examined at that time; but, upon such objection, that was prevented. If, looking at the report, the witness could have said, "That is my report, it refers to the car in question, and shews that it was examined at that time, and, though I cannot from memory say that it was then examined, I can now swear that it was, because I signed no report that was untrue, and at the time I signed this report I knew that it was true," that would, of course, be very good evidence, but the defendants were not allowed to get that far; and so the defendants are entitled to a new trial upon this ground also.

While the witness in the latter type of case is not "refreshing his memory," that phrase was used by the courts during the 19th century to describe this process as well as the other. This "unfortunate parsimony of phrase"[181] has been responsible for much of the confusion and apparent conflict in the cases.[182] The further conditions required for past recollection recorded came to be seen by many courts as conditions precedent to the receipt of testimony of present memory revived. This, despite the fact that:

---

179. In a case of "past recollection recorded" the earlier statement is clearly hearsay but it is received because the declarant is there to vouch for the past accuracy.

180. (1911), 25 O.L.R. 317, 325 (C.A.).

181. 3 Wigmore, *Evidence* (Chad. Rev.), s. 735, p. 81.

182. Compare *Reference re R. v. Coffin, supra*, note 169: Crown witness testified at trial somewhat differently than she had at the preliminary a year before and she was asked if she'd like to refresh her memory. She refreshed her memory from the transcript though the same was obviously not recorded at or near the time of the event nor verified by her at the time. See 3 Wigmore, *Evidence* (Chad. Rev.), s. 761, p. 134, that the use of a deposition or report of prior testimony was from earliest times used to refresh memory. To similar effect see cases discussed in *R. v. Muise* (1974), 22 C.C.C. (2d) 487, 496 (N.S.C.A.). And *R. v. Gwozdowski* (1973), 10 C.C.C. (2d) 434 (Ont. C.A.): ". . . there is another reason why the statement . . . should not have been introduced by the Crown, even for the purpose of refreshing the witness' memory. The statement consisted of words written by a police officer, allegedly at the dictation of the witness, some six months after the events being described. Accordingly, it lacked the necessary quality of contemporaneity which is required before such a statement may be shown to a party's own witness, even to refresh his memory."

It is one thing to awaken a slumbering recollection of an event, but quite another to use a memorandum of a recollection, fresh when it was correctly recorded, but presently beyond the power of the witness so to restore that it will exist apart from the record. In the former case it is quite immaterial by what means the memory is quickened; it may be a song, or a face, or a newspaper item, or a writing of some character. It is sufficient that by some mental operation, however mysterious, the memory is stimulated to recall the event, for when so set in motion it functions quite independently of the actuating cause.[183]

A further condition, to promote greater trustworthiness, is that the adversary is entitled to examine the document used to refresh, and to cross-examine the witness on it.[184] Eyre, L.C.J. wrote:

It is always usual and reasonable where a witness speaks from memorandum that counsel should have an opportunity of looking at those memorandum [sic] when he is cross-examining that witness.[185]

And while the evidence in cases of present memory revived was obviously the oral testimony, some courts, because of the confusion, insisted that such was also the case in instances of past recollection recorded;[186] the earlier written statement was ruled inadmissible as the court preferred the present mouthings of the witness. Logically, when the witness has no present independent memory of the event, the writing is the evidence and it deserves to be received as an exhibit. Professor Wigmore wrote:

If by verifying and adopting the record of past recollection the witness makes it usable testimonially, and if by this verification alone can it become so usable, it follows that the record thus adopted becomes to that extent the embodiment of the witness' testimony. Thus, (a) the record verified and adopted, becomes a present evidentiary statement of the witness; (b) and as such it may be handed or shown to the jury by the party offering it.[187]

In *R. v. Green*[188] the Crown called a witness, J., who testified that he had a very limited recollection of the events giving rise to the charge before the court. J. said he had twice read a typed, signed statement he had given to the police but that this did not assist his recollection. It contained considerable detail about the event. J. said that to the best of his knowledge the statement was true when given and was still true although he could not recall most of the events described in the statement. Justice Ferguson decided that the witness was not being candid and he appeared to be unwilling to testify as to the events as opposed to being forgetful. There was then an inconsistency and the Crown therefore was entitled to cross-examine the witness on the statement. After ruling that the Crown could cross-examine the witness on the written statement, the jury was recalled and

---

183. Per Dietrich, J. in *Jewett v. U.S.*, 15 F. 2d 955, 956 (9th Cir., 1926).
184. Even if the refreshing occurred not in the witness stand but before the witness came into the court; see *R. v. Lewis*, [1969] 3 C.C.C. 235 (B.C.S.C.) and *R. v. Catling* (1984), 29 C.C.C. (3d) 168 (Alta. Q.B.).
185. *R. v. Hardy* (1794), 24 Howell's State Trials 199.
186. See *Young v. Denton*, [1927] 1 D.L.R. 426 (Sask. C.A.) and *R. v. Hanaway* (1980), 63 C.C.C. (2d) 44 (Ont. Dist. Ct.). Compare *R. v. Naidanovici*, [1962] N.Z.L.R. 334 (C.A.). But see *Salutin v. R.* (1979), 11 C.R. (3d) 284 (Ont. C.A.).
187. 3 Wigmore, *Evidence* (Chad. Rev.), s. 754. Compare the MacNaughten revision.
188. (1995), 32 C.R. (4th) 248 (Ont. Gen. Div.).

the Crown read to the witness only the portion of the statement which incriminated the accused. The witness acknowledged that he had said that to the police, that he had believed at the time that it was true and that he had signed the statement. However, he said he now had no recollection of the event described in the excerpt read to him. Justice Ferguson saw the statement of the witness to the police as a classic case of past recollection recorded depending on the finding of the jury as to whether the witness adopted the statement as true. In such a case the details of the statement would then be admissible as proof of the facts stated. The jury would have to decide if the witness adopted the statement as true and would also decide what weight to give the evidence contained in the statement. He decided that the jury may not be in a position to make a reasonable decision on either issue unless it had before it the entire statement. Therefore the Crown was ordered to re-open her examination in chief and to adduce the whole statement by having the witness read the entire statement to the jury and if the witness refused or could not do so, the Crown was directed to read the whole statement to the jury. The statement was not given as an exhibit to the jury.

The statement of the witness to the police in *Green* was seen to be a case of past recollection recorded. But the court decided that the statement should not be given as an exhibit to the jury. Rather the statement would go in by having the witness read the entire statement to the jury. If the witness refused the Crown would read the statement to the jury. The procedure adopted seems, *at first blush*, to be fanciful. In a case of past recollection recorded the evidence is the statement and not the present mouthings of the witness. The court in *Green* recognized what the Ontario Court of Appeal had decided in *R. v. Salutin*, that where there was a true case of past recollection recorded: "In such cases the record is the exhibit." One would then expect that in such a case the statement should go in as an exhibit. But there are other considerations that need to be addressed.

In the case of *R. v. McShannock*,[189] cited in *Green*, the complainant described the sexual assault. She had made a lengthy and detailed statement to the police and that statement was entered as an exhibit and went to the jury. Mr. Justice Martin ruled that was improper and quoted the second edition of Professor McCormick's treatise that: "Writings which are merely testimony in a different form should not, by being allowed to the jury be unduly emphasized over other purely oral testimony in the case." That thought is preserved in the fourth edition (1992) in Chapters 2 and 28. In the Federal Rules of Evidence in the United States it is provided that as an exception to the hearsay rule the earlier statement is receivable:

> Rule 803(5) A memorandum or record concerning a matter about which a witness once had knowledge but now has insufficient recollection to enable the witness to testify fully and accurately, shown to have been made or adopted by the witness when the matter was fresh in the witness' memory and to reflect that knowledge correctly. If admitted, the memorandum or record may be read into evidence but may not itself be received as an exhibit unless offered by an adverse party.

In *Weinstein's Evidence*, the commentary to the rule is:

> The refusal to treat a memorandum of past recollection recorded as though

---

189. (1980), 55 C.C.C. (2d) 53 (Ont. C.A.).

it were ordinary documentary evidence that could be marked as an exhibit has been attacked in Wigmore's treartise. The basis for Rule 803(5)'s approach is apparently fear that if the memorandum itself were offered into evidence the jury might give it undue emphasis in relation to other oral testimony. Although the memorandum qualifies as an exception to the hearsay rule, it is viewed as a substitute for the oral testimony. Some members of the Advisory Committee were concerned lest the document be given greater credence than oral testimony of the witness. To prevent overreaching and since oral testimony is normally not taken into the jury room, the draftsmen added this limitation.

By adopting Professor Wigmore's terminology some of the confusion is now being worked out of the system.

R. v. SHERGILL
(1997), 13 C.R. (5th) 160 (Ont. Gen. Div.)

[During the examination-in-chief of a Crown witness the Crown applied for permission to refresh the witness' memory by referring to the transcript of the witness' preliminary inquiry testimony. The preliminary inquiry took place about six and a half years after the alleged offence.]

FERGUSON J.:—

. . . .

A number of lower courts have ruled that a witness may refresh his or her memory by reference to a document even when the contemporaneity requirement cannot be satisfied. In particular, the courts have approved of the practice of permitting the witness to refer to a transcript of the witness' prior testimony. . . The most comprehensive ruling appears to be *R. v. Bengert* (1980), 53 C.C.C. (2d) 481 (B.C. C.A.), leave to appeal to S.C.C. refused, (1980), 53 C.C.C. (2d) 481n (S.C.C.). There the trial judge ruled:

> *Wigmore on Evidence* . . . says that there is no hard and fast rule, that anything in writing may be used to stimulate and revive a recollection. On the other hand, it may be improper in a given instance to allow a witness to refer to something written down. It all depends on the circumstances. Wigmore, as always, provides ample justification in law as well as in common sense for these propositions.

The Court of Appeal approved this ruling in this passage:

> Many lawyers appear to be of the view that a witness may be permitted to refer to notes only if he made the notes reasonably contemporaneously with the event, or if someone else made the notes, he verified the accuracy of the notes when the events were reasonably contemporaneous in his mind. This is a misconception. We agree completely with the trial judge's reasoning.

It is important to bear in mind that on Wigmore's approach the document does not need to be one created by the witness. "It is not so significant when the statement was made or by whom if it serves the purpose to refresh the mind and unfold the truth." *United States v. Riccardi* 174 F.2d 883 (U.S. 3rd Cir. N.J. 1949). One can think of common examples of documents which are not created by the witness: a court transcript, a video statement, a police officer's note of the witness' statement.

. . . .

I believe Wigmore is correct that the conflicts in the authorities arise from a failure to recognize the difference between a situation where the witness is just refreshing memory and the much different situation where the witness has no present memory and the document is being used as a device to introduce past recollection recorded. I agree with

Professor Delisle: . . . . see Delisle, *Canadian Evidence Law in a Nutshell*, Carswell, 1996, at pp. 61-61, and *Evidence: Principles and Problems*, 3rd., Carswell, p.323 ff.

. . . .

I am persuaded that there should be no contemporaneity requirement for documents used to refresh the memory of a witness in the witness stand. That requirement should apply only to cases where the document is being used to introduce past recollection recorded.

. . . .

Will reading the preliminary hearing transcript refresh the witness' memory? This is a factual issue and involves some speculation. It is clear from reading the transcript that the witness did have an independent recollection of events at the time of the preliminary. It took place two years before this trial and some six and a half years after the original events. I find no basis for the contention that the witness now has no memory of the events which could be refreshed. It is clear from her testimony at this trial that she does have a recollection. She just has not recounted all the details or not recounted them in the same way as before. I am satisfied that it is appropriate to refresh the memory of the witness in this case. The events here occurred over 8 years ago and there have been numerous examples during her testimony of her having difficulty recounting all the details she apparently remembers. There is no basis here for believing she lacks any memory of the omitted matters. Defence counsel suggested that before she be allowed to refresh her memory by reference to documents. Crown counsel should first exhaust other attempts to jog her memory so that the jury does not unnecessarily learn that she has previously said the same thing. The defence cited *D. (D.)* where the court stated that the previous statements should not be used to show consistency with the trial testimony and thereby enhance the credibility of the witness. I accepted this suggestion and Crown counsel has tried to lead the witness somewhat. This elicited the omitted matters on some but not all subjects.

[Justice Ferguson then summarized the procedure that should be followed.]

R. v. B. (K.G.)
(1998), 125 C.C.C. (3d) 61 (Ont. C.A.)

[The accused was charged with second degree murder. At his first trial he was acquitted. The Crown's appeal to the Court of Appeal was dismissed. On the Crown's further appeal to the Supreme Court of Canada, the appeal was allowed and a new trial directed. At that trial he was convicted of the included offence of manslaughter. On appeal the accused argued that the trial judge erred in his consideration of the evidence of the mothers of two accomplices of the accused because, before testifying, they had refreshed their memories from statements each had given to the police some considerable time after the events about which they were testifying. The accused argued that the two mothers had little or no independent recollection of the subject events and that their evidence should have been given little or no weight. The mothers each acknowledged that they had refreshed their memories from statements that they had given to the police, two and one-half and three and one-half years after the meeting at which they said that the accused admitted killing the deceased. This is not a case where either witness drew a blank in the witness box and sought to refresh her memory from a previous statement. They refreshed their memories well before the trial.]

OSBORNE J.A. (AUSTIN and GOUDGE JJ.A. concurring):—

. . . .

The trial judge meticulously reviewed the testimony of both Mrs. D. and Mrs. McD. before he accepted it and relied on it. He concluded that the fact that both witnesses had refreshed their memories from statements that they had given to the police could affect the weight of their evidence. Nevertheless, he found as a fact that both witnesses had an independent recollection of the relevant events and that their evidence was reliable. The evidence of both witnesses supports this conclusion. In the end, the trial judge confronted the defence position concerning the weight to be given to Mrs. D.'s and Mrs. McD.'s evidence by stating in his reasons for conviction:

> It is the position of the defence that Mrs. D. and Mrs. McD. were honest but unreliable witnesses. The defence submits that Mrs. D. and Mrs. McD. should not have refreshed their memories from statements which were given to the police a substantial time, two and a half and three and a half years respectively, after the events. While I believe that it is permissible for a witness to refresh his or her memory out of court from notes which were not made contemporaneously with the events about which he or she is testifying it is equally clear that doing so can, and does, affect the weight to be given to the witness's evidence.

I see nothing wrong with either witness reviewing her police statement before testifying. There is also nothing wrong with a defence counsel attempting to determine in cross-examination whether Mrs. D. or Mrs. McD. had a present memory of events about which she testified. What triggers recollection is not significant. This was long ago made clear in 1814 in *Henry v. Lee* (1814), 2 Chitty 124, where Ellenborough L.C.J. said:

> If upon looking at any document he can so far refresh his memory as to recollect a circumstance, it is sufficient; and it makes no difference that the memorandum is not written by himself, for it is not the memorandum that is the evidence but the recollection of the witness.

There is a danger in allowing the phrase "refreshing memory" to apply to those cases where the witness has no present memory, but is able to state that she accurately recorded a past event. In such cases, the witness has no present memory. The evidence, to the extent there is any, is the past record. When a witness refreshes her memory from some external source or event, she has a present memory, albeit one that has been refreshed; how reliable and truthful her recollection is, will be determined by the trier of fact, as happened here.

. . . .

I see nothing wrong with the trial judge's approach to the evidence of Mrs. D. and Mrs. McD. He was alert to all factors that might bear upon the reliability of their evidence, including the fact that both had refreshed their memories from earlier statements that were not made contemporaneously with the events referred to in them. Clearly, the evidence given by Mrs. D. and Mrs. McD. was not their previous statements but their current recollection of the appellant's admission, as refreshed by their earlier review of their statements. Refreshing memory may take place before trial, as happened here, or in some cases, at trial. I would not give effect to this ground of appeal.

While imposing the requirement of contemporaneity to instances of true refreshing of memory may have been "an historical or analytical blunder,"[190] there

---

190. McCormick, *Evidence*, 2d ed., p. 15, amplifies the concern shown by Berger, J. that a witness may not be genuine in his recollection. And see *R. v. Dimmer* (1983), 37 C.R. (3d) 227 (Alta. Q.B.) where the trial judge failed to sufficiently direct his mind to this problem and the conviction was quashed.

was some merit in its imposition to counter any concern that the witness was not genuine in his recollection. Nevertheless there are protections. First, the trial judge may decide from her observation of the witness that the witness's memory is not truly being refreshed by the memorandum and accordingly deny its use; as we noted above, the trial judge has a discretion with respect to all matters of leading the witness and she may decide that the memorandum is too suggestive to be safely used. Second, at common law the adversary has the right to inspect the document and to cross-examine the witness upon it and may then seek to persuade the judge that the document should not be used.[191]

In exercising her discretion the trial judge could benefit by bearing in mind:

Of course, the categories, present recollection revived and past recollection recorded, are clearest in their extremes, but they are, in practice, converging rather than parallel lines; the difference is frequently one of degree. Moreover, it is in complication thereof that a cooperative witness, yielding to suggestion, deceives himself, that a hostile witness seizes an opportunity, or that a writing is used to convey an improper suggestion. Circumstances, or the nature of the testimony, may belie an assertion of present memory; more often the credibility of the witness generally and the cross-examiner's attack upon the reliability of his memory, will decide the claim to an independent recollection.

Properly, the burden to ascertain the state of affairs, as near as may be, devolves upon the trial judge, who should in the first instance satisfy himself as to whether the witness testifies upon a record or from his own recollection. It is upon this satisfaction that the reception of the evidence depends, for if it appear to the court that the witness is wholly dependent for the fact upon the memorandum he holds in his hand, the memorandum acquires a significance which, as stated, brings into operation certain guiding rules. Similarly, the trial judge must determine whether the device of refreshing recollection is merely a subterfuge to improperly suggest to the witness the testimony expected of him. It is axiomatic, particularly with respect to the reception of evidence, that much depends upon the discretion of the trial judge. This is not a new occasion for the exercise of that discretion.[192]

R. v. MATTIS
(1998), 20 C.R. (5th) 93 (Ont. Prov. Div.)

[The accused was charged with trafficking in cocaine. The trial judge considered the evidence of the Crown and of the defence as to what had been observed prior to the accused's arrest.]

BIGELOW J.:—

. . . .

Officers Peters and Berrill whose evidence was clearly crucial to the Crown's case both stated that they had made up their notes of the events separately. In cross-examination they both admitted that their notes with respect to that incident were identical save and except for some short forms of words used by Officer Peters in her notebook. Neither were able to provide any explanation for how this could have occurred.

. . . .

Obviously credibility is a major factor in this case. Mr. Rusonik argues that there are

---

191. See Cross, *Evidence*, 5th ed., p. 234.
192. *U.S. v. Riccardi*, 174 F. 2d 883, 889 (3d Cir., 1949).

significant concerns with respect to the credibility of the police witnesses. As well Ms. Mattis has given evidence on her own behalf contradicting that of the police witnesses.

The only reasonable inference which can be drawn from the fact that the notebooks were identical is that one of the officers copied the notes of the other. In the recent decision of *R. v. Green*, [1998] O.J. No. 3598 (Ont. Ct. Gen. Div.). Malloy, J. commented on the importance of police officers preparing their notes independently:

> There are important reasons for requiring that officers prepare their notes independently. The purpose of notes made by a police officer is to record the observations made by that officer. The notes themselves are not admissible as evidence for the truth of their contents. An officer with relevant evidence to offer may testify at trial as to the act or observations made by him or her. However, that officer is not permitted to testify as to the information received from other officers for the purpose of proving their truth. Such evidence [is] hearsay and inadmissible.

> An officer's notes perform a valuable function at trial. It is usually many months, sometimes years, from the time of an occurrence to the time that the officer is called upon to testify at trial. Without the assistance of notes to refresh his or her memory, the evidence of the officer at trial would inevitably be sketchy at best. If the officer's notes are prepared without any indication of which is the officer's independent recollection and which is somebody else's recollection, there is every likelihood that that officer at trial will be "refreshing" his or her own memory with observations made by someone else. In effect, the officer will be giving hearsay evidence as if it was his or her own recollection rather than the observations of somebody else written into the notes without attribution.

The concerns raised by Malloy, J. are particularly relevant in the present case where it was clear that neither Officer Peters nor Officer Birrell had a clear recollection of the events and both were relying heavily on notes in giving their evidence.

Malloy, J. went on to comment on the effect of collaboration in the making of notes would have on the credibility of the testimony of police officers:

> The fact that officers have collaborated on their notes will always cause a trier of fact to give careful consideration to the reliability of that officer's evidence. There will, however, be situations in which such collaboration, although not good police practice, will not undermine the testimony of the officers. The extent to which the collaboration renders the evidence of the officers' unreliable will depend on the circumstances of each case and the explanation given by the officers.

In the present case no explanation was offered as to how the notebooks could be identical. The obvious fact that the notebooks were copied combined with the lack of any explanation as to how this occurred and the lack of specific recollection by both officers has a significant impact on the reliability of the evidence. Absent confirmation of that evidence in material particulars, it would be unsafe to base a conviction on it.

. . . .

As indicated above absent confirming evidence, it would be dangerous to base of finding of guilt in this case on the evidence of Officers Peters and Birrell. . . . Accordingly, all three charges are dismissed.

R. v. L. (D.O.)
[1993] 4 S.C.R. 419, 25 C.R. (4th) 285, 85 C.C.C. (3d) 289

[The accused was charged with sexual assault alleged to have taken place between September 1985 and March 1988. Following a medical examination of the complainant, a 9-year-old girl, the police began their investigation in May 1988 and a videotaped interview of the complainant took place in August 1988. At the preliminary inquiry, the complainant testified before the court. At trial, the Crown sought to introduce the videotaped interview of the complainant pursuant to s. 715.1 of the Criminal Code. The accused sought a declaration that s. 715.1 was unconstitutional but the trial judge upheld the section. Following a voir dire, the videotaped interview was admitted into evidence and the accused was convicted. The Court of Appeal allowed the accused's appeal and declared s. 715.1 unconstitutional.]

LAMER C.J. (LA FOREST, SOPINKA, CORY, MCLACHLIN and IACOBUCCI JJ. concurring):— I have read the reasons of Justice L'Heureux-Dubé and concur in her result. It is my view that s. 715.1 of the *Criminal Code* . . . is a response to the dominance and power which adults, by virtue of their age, have over children. Accordingly, s. 715.1 is designed to accommodate the needs and to safeguard the interests of young victims of various forms of sexual abuse, irrespective of their sex. By allowing for the videotaping of evidence under certain express conditions, s. 715.1 not only makes participation in the criminal justice system less stressful and traumatic for child and adolescent complainants, but also aids in the preservation of evidence and the discovery of truth.

. . . As s. 715.1 neither offends the principles of fundamental justice nor violates the right a fair trial, it cannot be said to limit the rights guaranteed under s. 7 or 11(*d*) of the *Canadian Charter of Rights and Freedoms*. The respondent has failed to establish that s. 715.1 offends the rules of evidence against the admission of hearsay evidence and prior consistent statements. In addition, as there is no constitutionally protected requirement that cross-examination be contemporaneous with the giving of evidence, the respondent has failed to show that his fundamental right to cross-examine has been violated. The admission of the videotaped evidence does not make the trial unfair or not public, nor does it in any way affect an accused's right to be presumed innocent.

[L'Heureux-Dubé, J., in a lengthy judgment, Gonthier, J. concurring, also found section 715.1 to be not violative of the accused's Charter rights.]

R. v. F. (C.)
[1997] 3 S.C.R. 1183, 11 C.R. (5th) 209, 120 C.C.C. (3d) 225

[The accused was charged with touching his six-year-old daughter for a sexual purpose. The police investigated the complaint the evening it was made and videotaped the complainant's statement describing the incident. At trial, the complainant was shown the videotape following her examination-in-chief. She confirmed that she made the statements on the videotape and that they were true. The trial judge ruled that the complainant had adopted the videotaped statement and admitted it as evidence pursuant to s. 715.1 of the Criminal Code. On cross-examination the complainant made statements which contradicted in part the videotaped statements. The Ontario Court of Appeal overturned the conviction and directed a new trial. The Court of Appeal held that the videotaped evidence that was later disavowed could not be considered as having been adopted under s. 715.1.]

The judgment of the Court was delivered by CORY J.:—

. . . .

The appellate courts of Alberta and Ontario have given different meaning to the word "adopted". What constitutes the adoption of a videotape statement is the first and paramount issue that must be resolved in this appeal. The second is a consideration of what effect, if any, subsequent contradictory evidence of the complainant will have upon the admissibility of the videotape statement.

. . . .

It will be self-evident to every observant parent and to all who have worked closely with young people that children, even more than adults, will have a better recollection of events shortly after they occurred than they will some weeks, months or years later. The younger the child, the more pronounced will this be. Indeed to state this simply expresses the observations of most Canadians. It is a common experience that anyone, and particularly children, will have a better recollection of events closer to their occurrence than he or she will later on. It follows that the videotape which is made within a reasonable time after the alleged offence and which describes the act will almost inevitably reflect a more accurate recollection of events than will testimony given later at trial. Thus the section enhances the ability of a court to find the truth by preserving a very recent recollection of the event in question. . . . The important subsidiary aim of the section is to prevent or reduce materially the likelihood of inflicting further injury upon a child as a result of participating in court proceedings. This will be accomplished by reducing the number of interviews that the child must undergo and thereby diminish the stress occasioned a child by repeated questioning on a painful incident. Further, the videotaping will take place in surroundings that are less overwhelming for a child than the courtroom.

. . . .

Section 715.1 provides that a videotaped statement is admissible in evidence if the complainant "adopts the contents of the videotape" while testifying. What meaning should be attributed to that phrase? . . . . Black's Law Dictionary defines "adopt" as follows:

To accept, appropriate, choose, or select. To make that one's own, property or act, which was not so originally.

Obviously the term "adoption" is capable of several meanings. However, in the context of s. 715.1 the proper interpretation should be one which accords with its aim and purpose. The Alberta and Ontario Courts of Appeal have taken different approaches to the adoption of videotaped evidence. In *R. v. Meddoui* (1990), 61 C.C.C. (3d) 345, the Alberta Court of Appeal found that a witness "adopted" her statement within the meaning of s. 715.1 when she recalled giving the statement and testified that she was then attempting to be honest and truthful. It was held that the complainant need not have a present recollection of the events discussed. The decision approved the use of the videotape as evidence of the events described, even if the complainant is unable to recall the events discussed in the tape which formed the basis for the charge. . . . In *R. v. Toten* (1993), 83 C.C.C. (3d) 5, the Ontario Court of Appeal rejected the *Meddoui* interpretation of "adopts" in favour of a narrower one. It was held that in order to adopt the contents of a videotaped statement, the child complainant must be able, based on a present memory of the events referred to in the videotape, to verify the accuracy and contents of the statement. The child must not only acknowledge making the statement but also the truth of its contents. In light of the clear aim and purpose of s. 715.1, I cannot accept the Ontario Court of Appeal position. . . . S. 715.1 has built-in guarantees of trustworthiness and reliability which eliminate the need for such a stringent requirement for adoption. Further, a lack of present memory or an inability to provide testimony at trial regarding the events referred to in the videotape as a result of the youthfulness and the emotional state of the complainant increases the need to consider the videotaped statement.

The test set out in *Toten* would prevent a child who has little, or no memory of the events from "adopting" the video and it would therefore be inadmissible under s. 715.1. However, it is precisely in this situation that the video is most needed. Children, particularly younger ones, are prone to forget details of an event with the passage of time. A videotape made shortly after the event is more likely to be accurate than the child's viva voce testimony, given months later, at trial. It is quite possible that a young child will have a recollection of going to the police station and making the statement and of her attempt to be truthful at the time yet have no memory of the unpleasant events. This is particularly true where the elapsed time between the initial complaint and the date of trial is lengthy. If effect is to be given to the aims of s. 715.1 of enhancing the truth-seeking role of the courts by preserving an early account of the incident and of preventing further injury to vulnerable children as a result of their involvement in the criminal process, then the videotape should generally be admitted.

. . . .

I recognize that the *Meddoui* approach to "adoption" gives rise to another problem. Specifically, a witness who cannot remember the events cannot be effectively cross-examined on the contents of his or her statement, and therefore the reliability of his or her testimony cannot be tested in that way. However, it was recognized in *R. v. Khan*, [1990] 2 S.C.R. 531; *R. v. Smith*, [1992] 2 S.C.R. 915, and *R. v. B. (K.G.)*, [1993] 1 S.C.R. 740, that cross-examination is not the only guarantee of reliability. There are several factors present in s. 715.1 which provide the requisite reliability of the videotaped statement. They include: (a) the requirement that the statement be made within a reasonable time; (b) the trier of fact can watch the entire interview, which provides an opportunity to observe the demeanor, and assess the personality and intelligence of the child; (c) the requirement that the child attest that she was attempting to be truthful at the time that the statement was made. As well, the child can be cross-examined at trial as to whether he or she was actually being truthful when the statement was made. These indicia provide enough guarantees of reliability to compensate for the inability to cross-examine as to the forgotten events. Moreover, where the complainant has no independent memory of the events there is an obvious necessity for the videotaped evidence. In *Meddoui*, it was recommended that in such circumstances, the trier of fact should be given a special warning (similar to the one given in *Vetrovec v. The Queen*, [1982] 1 S.C.R. 811) of the dangers of convicting based on the videotape alone. In my view, this was sage advice that should be followed.

. . . .

After the videotaped evidence has been admitted, any questions which arise concerning the circumstances in which the video was made, the veracity of the witness' statements, or the overall reliability of the evidence, will be matters for the trier of fact to consider in determining how much weight the videotaped statement should be given. If, in the course of cross-examination, defence counsel elicits evidence which contradicts any part of the video, this does not render those parts inadmissible. Obviously a contradicted videotape may well be given less weight in the final determination of the issues. However, the fact that the video is contradicted in cross-examination does not necessarily mean that the video is wrong or unreliable. The trial judge may still conclude, as in this case, that the inconsistencies are insignificant and find the video more reliable than the evidence elicited at trial. . . . Although each witness' credibility must be assessed, the standard which would be applied to an adult's evidence is not always appropriate in assessing the credibility of young children. This approach to the evidence of children was reiterated in *R. v. W. (R.)*, [1992] 2 S.C.R. 122, at pp. 132-34. There McLachlin J. acknowledged that the peculiar perspectives of children can affect their recollection of events and that the presence of inconsistencies, especially those related to peripheral matters, should be assessed in context. A skilful cross-examination is almost certain to confuse a child, even if she is telling the truth. That confusion can lead to inconsistencies in her testimony. Although the trier of fact must be wary of any evidence which has been contradicted, this is a matter which goes to the weight which should be attached to the videotape and not to its admissibility.

For critical commentary see Moore and Green, "Truth and the Reliability of Children's Evidence: Problems With S. 715 of the Criminal Code" (2000), 30 C.R. (5th) 148.

The Ontario Evidence Act was recently amended to provide:

18.3(1) A videotape of the testimony of a witness under the age of 18 that satisfies the conditions set out in subsection (2) may be admitted in evidence, if the court is of the opinion that this is likely to help the witness give complete and accurate testimony or that it is in the best interests of the witness.

(2) The judge or other person who is to preside at the trial and the lawyers of the parties to the proceeding shall be present when the testimony is given, and the lawyers shall be given an opportunity to examine the witness in the same way as if he or she were testifying in the courtroom.

(3) Subsection 18.4(1) and section 18.5 apply with necessary modifications when testimony is being videotaped.

(4) If a videotape is admitted under subsection (1), the witness need not attend or testify and shall not be summoned to testify.

(5) However, in exceptional circumstances, the court may require the witness to attend and testify even though a videotape of his or her testimony has been admitted in evidence.

(6) With the leave of the court, a videotape of an interview with a person under the age of 18 may be admitted in evidence if the person, while testifying, adopts the contents of the videotape.

(7) Subsection (6) is in addition to any rule of law under which a videotape may be admitted in evidence.

(c) Cross-examination

The purposes of cross-examination, its place in our adversarial system, its scope, and its control may perhaps best be appreciated by examining a few classic quotations:

Professor Wigmore:

For two centuries past, the policy of the Anglo-American system of Evidence has been to regard the necessity of testing by cross-examination as a vital feature of the law. The belief that no safeguard for testing the value of human statements is comparable to that furnished by cross-examination, and the conviction that no statement (unless by special exception) should be used as testimony until it has been probed and sublimated by that test, has found increasing strength in lengthening experience.

Not even the abuses, the mishandlings, and the puerilities which are so often found associated with cross-examination have availed to nullify its value. It may be that in more than one sense it takes the place in our system which torture occupied in the mediaeval system of the civilians. Nevertheless, it is beyond any doubt the greatest legal engine ever invented for the discovery of truth. . . . If we omit political considerations of broader range, then cross-examination, not trial by jury, is the great and permanent contribution of the Anglo-American system of law to improved methods of trial-procedure.[193]

Professor McCormick:

---

193. 5 Wigmore, *Evidence* (Chad. Rev.), s. 1367.

For two centuries, common law judges and lawyers have regarded the opportunity of cross-examination as an essential safeguard of the accuracy and completeness of testimony, and they have insisted that the opportunity is a right and not a mere privilege.[194]

Mr. Justice Dennistoun:

Cross-examination is a powerful weapon of defence, and often its sole weapon. The denial of full opportunity to sift and probe the witnesses of the opposing side has always been regarded with extreme disfavour by British Courts of justice.

Cross-examination may be insisted on for a number of purposes: First, to bring out facts as to which a witness has not been asked to testify, or is anxious to conceal; Second, to show that the witness is unworthy of belief; Third, to adduce facts in mitigation of sentence; Fourth, to adduce facts which in the case of a guilty person may minimize his offence and assist in the rehabilitation of his character.

. . . .

That full cross-examination of an opposite witness should be permitted by the trial Judge is well settled. The Judge may check cross-examination if it become irrelevant, or prolix, or insulting, but so long as it may fairly be applied to the issue, or touches the credibility of the witness it should not be excluded.[195]

Notice particularly that the cross-examiner is not confined to asking questions about matters in issue which arose in examination-in-chief.[196] Notice as well that the trial judge has some discretion to control the questioning if it is unduly lengthy or insulting.[197] Aside from the trial judge's discretion there is an obligation on counsel as well to have concern for the limited time and resources available to the court and also to have some respect for the witness as a fellow human being. As Lord Sankey noted:

It is right to make due allowance for the irritation caused by the strain and stress of a long and complicated case, but a protracted and irrelevant cross-examination not only adds to the cost of litigation, but is a waste of public time. Such a cross-examination becomes indefensible when it is conducted, as it was in this case, without restraint and without the courtesy and consideration which a witness is entitled to expect in a court of law. It is not sufficient for the due administration of justice to have a learned, patient and impartial judge. Equally with him, the solicitors who prepare the case and the counsel who present it to the court are taking part in the great task of doing justice between man and man.[198]

Well prepared and competent counsel should always have a purpose in mind in cross-examining. Not all cross-examination is destructive where the major aim is to impeach, i.e., to seek to destroy credibility. In many cases the aim is

---

194. McCormick, *Evidence*, 2d ed., p. 43.
195. In *R. v. Anderson*, [1938] 3 D.L.R. 317, 319-20 (Man. C.A.). And see *R. v. Roulette* (1972), 7 C.C.C. (2d) 244 (Man. Q.B.) and *R. v. Makow* (1973), 13 C.C.C. (2d) 167 (B.C.C.A.).
196. Compare the U.S. practice: Federal Rules of Evidence, Rule 611(*b*), 28 U.S.C.A. and note Van Pelt, "The Background of Federal Rules 611(*b*) and 607" (1978), 57 Neb. L. Rev. 898.
197. See *Dickinson v. Harvey* (1913), 12 D.L.R. 129, 132 (B.C.C.A.) and *Murray v. Haylow*, [1927] 3 D.L.R. 1036 at 1043 (Ont. C.A.). See also *Fanjoy v. R.* (1985), 21 C.C.C. (3d) 312 (S.C.C.).
198. *Mechanical & Gen. Inventions Co. v. Austin* (1935), 153 L.T. 153, 157 (H.L.) cited with approval in *R. v. Rowbotham (No. 5)* (1977), 2 C.R. (3d) 293 (Ont. Co. Ct.).

merely to use cross-examination for another purpose such as to clarify, pin the witness down, or elicit other evidence. Counsel who called the witness elicited three things in chief. Opposing counsel seeks to elicit three other things the witness observed, which material supports opposing counsel's case.

See generally Younger, *The Art of Cross-examination* (Chicago: A.B.A., Litigation Section, 1976).

Is counsel entitled to put a question on cross-examination although he is not then in a position to prove the same by other evidence? One can imagine the possible impact on a jury of repeated questions suggesting misconduct of some kind on the part of the witness even though such misconduct is denied. And yet there appears to be nothing illegal about such a practice. Lord Radcliffe in *Fox v. General Medical Council*[199] explained:

> An advocate is entitled to use his discretion as to whether to put questions in the course of cross-examination which are based on material which he is not in a position to prove directly. The penalty is that, if he gets a denial or some answer that does not suit him, the answer stands against him for what it is worth.

This position has been adopted in Canada.[200] In England, however, the Bar Council laid down ethical guidelines. Rule Four provides:

> Questions which affect the credibility of a witness by attacking his character, but are not otherwise relevant to the actual inquiry, ought not to be asked unless the cross-examiner has reasonable grounds for thinking that the imputation conveyed by the question is well founded or true.

R. v. HOWARD
[1989] 1 S.C.R. 1337, 69 C.R. (3d) 193, 48 C.C.C. (3d) 38

[The accused and a co-accused, T., had been tried jointly and found guilty of first degree murder. The Court of Appeal found that the trial judge had erred in some respects and ordered a new trial. The co-accused, T., pleaded guilty to second degree murder prior to the second trial. He agreed to a state of facts that put him at the scene of the crime. At the first trial, both the Crown and defence had called experts on footprints to seek to establish or disprove respectively that the footprints found by the body of the victim were made by the co-accused. There was evidence that the accused and T were together on the evening of the killing.

At the second trial, the Crown experts again testified in similar terms. Before the defence expert was to testify, the Crown sought and was granted permission to ask him whether or not the fact that the co-accused had subsequently pleaded guilty to the murder and had accepted a statement of facts that put him at the scene of the crime would change his opinion as given at the first trial. The defence accordingly chose not to call its footprint expert.

The Court of Appeal dismissed accused's appeal from conviction and his appeal to the Supreme Court was by leave. One of the issues before that Court

---

199. [1960] 1 W.L.R. 1017, 1023 (P.C.).
200. See *R. v. Bencardino* (1973), 15 C.C.C. (2d) 342 (Ont. C.A.) and *R. v. Racco (No. 3)* (1975), 23 C.C.C. (2d) 209 (Ont. Co. Ct.). But compare Haines, J. in *R. v. Hawke* (1974), 3 O.R. (2d) 210, 229 (Ont. H.C.).

was whether or not Crown counsel was entitled to refer to the guilty plea entered
by the co-accused in the cross-examination of the expert witness for the defence.]

LAMER J. (MCINTYRE and LA FOREST JJ. concurring):—

. . . .

The issue in this court is: Did the Ontario Court of Appeal err in upholding the trial judge's
ruling that Crown counsel was entitled to adduce through the defence expert, evidence
relating to the plea of the co-accused?

. . . .

The fact that Trudel had pleaded guilty and had acknowledged that the footprint was
his was not, at the time the question was intended to be put to the expert, and was not
going to become, a fact adduced in evidence; nor was it a fact that could fairly be inferred
from the facts in evidence. It is not open to the examiner or cross-examiner to put as a
fact, or even a hypothetical fact, that which is not and will not become part of the case as
admissible evidence. On this ground alone, the question should have been denied.

The only ground upon which I can see the question's being properly put would be to
determine whether the expert took into account facts irrelevant to his expertise.

. . . .

[A] cross-examination may be conducted to determine whether what the expert considered
was relevant, whether there are matters relevant that were not considered and, of course,
whether the expert might have arrived at his conclusion as a *result* of considerations
irrelevant to his particular expertise. An expert may obviously be cross-examined to that
effect, that is whether relevant facts were ignored or disregarded, and whether irrelevant
facts were taken into account, but only irrelevant facts supportive of the conclusion arrived
at. As put by the appellant in his factum:

> Evidence establishing that an expert had failed to form his opinion on a proper
> scientific basis and had considered irrelevant matters is relevant to the validity of
> that opinion. However, it is not relevant to the validity of that opinion that the expert
> had not considered an irrelevant matter. The proposed cross-examination of Dr. Watt
> would establish no more than that he had not considered an irrelevant matter and
> therefore would not impugn the validity of his opinion.

I agree and find the question and answer thereto inadmissible. This is sufficient to dispose
of the matter. However, as this case is to be retried, I should add a comment. At the next
trial Trudel may be called, if the Crown so chooses, to testify to these facts that would
tend to prove that Dr. Watt was wrong in his conclusion. They are facts for the jury's
consideration, not for Dr. Watt, except maybe for the very limited purpose of testing with
the expert the degree of certainty to be given to his science of which he will have testified.

. . . .

I would therefore allow the appeal and order a new trial on the charge of first degree
murder.

L'HEUREUX-DUBÉ J. (dissenting):—

. . . .

The appellant for his part entered a plea of not guilty. His sole defence was in the
nature of an alibi, namely, that at all relevant times he was with Trudel and that neither
Trudel nor he were at the scene of the murder. Giving testimony at his second trial, the
appellant acknowledged being at the Brunswick Hotel with Trudel until closing time,
though he denied getting a cab there. The appellant testified that he and Trudel walked
and eventually hitched a ride to Lambeth in the middle of the night. There, they wandered

around for some two hours before calling a cab which picked them up at approximately 5:00 a.m. Together with Trudel, the appellant said he then proceeded to a bootlegger's home in London where both of them drank beer with another person until 7:00 a.m. During cross-examination, the appellant stated that he did not know what had happened to McCart.

. . . .

PROPOSED CROSS-EXAMINATION OF APPELLANT'S EXPERT

. . . .

In controlling cross-examination, the trial judge enjoys some measure of discretion. In my view there are no inflexible rules prescribing the exact scope of allowable cross-examination in each particular case. An undue restriction on cross-examination may prevent the jury from gauging all the elements relative to the weight of the allowable evidence. Conversely, an overly lenient allowance of cross-examination may distract the jury's focus from the questions of fact it must address. A delicate balance must be struck between the different interests at stake given that arriving at the truth remains a central premise of the administration of criminal justice. Such interests include, among others, the extent to which the credibility of witnesses may be impeached as against the possible risks of encroachment upon the fairness of the trial, including the accused person's right to present a full defence, and the degree of prejudice suffered by the accused.

The balance hinges in great part on the trial judge's assessment of the context of the case, the seriousness of the offence, the nature of the defence and the "atmosphere of the courtroom", that is, the demeanour of witnesses, conduct of counsel and ability of the jury to make a fair assessment of the weight of the evidence discussed or introduced at trial. . . .

In the case of expert testimony, the proper control of cross-examination involves certain special considerations. Specifically, in giving evidence, expert witnesses benefit from a degree of freedom not enjoyed by ordinary witnesses. Experts are mainly called to give their opinion, which is a type of evidence inadmissible when offered by ordinary witnesses.

. . . .

Wigmore has noted that cross-examination is "beyond any doubt the greatest legal engine ever inented for the discovery of truth" (5 Wigmore, Chadbourn rev. (1974), para. 1367, p. 32. One cannot overemphasize the commitment of courts of justice to the ascertainment of the truth. The just determination of guilt or innocence is a fundamental underpinning of the administration of criminal justice. The ends of the criminal process would be defeated if trials were allowed to proceed on assumptions divorced from reality. If a careless disregard for the truth prevailed in the courtrooms, the public trust in the judicial function, the law and the administration of justice would disappear. Though the law of criminal evidence often excludes relevant evidence to preserve the integrity of the judicial process, it is difficult to accept that courts should ever willingly proceed on the basis of untrue facts.

In allowing the proposed cross-examination in the case at bar, the trial judge did not ignore the conflict between, on the one hand, the prejudice caused to the accused by the mention of Trudel's guilty plea, and, on the other, the rule allowing the credibility of an expert witness to be tested on the basis of the expert's opinion. In exercising his discretion to determine the propriety of the question sought to be put to Dr. Watt, the trial judge gave in my view due heed to the interests of the accused and to those of the judicial process as well. He was not blind to the fact that Dr. Watt's evidence would not be put forward as a result of his ruling. He was aware that his ruling left the appellant with a single expert witness instead of the two he had expected to rely upon in support of his defence. But in his discretion the trial judge found that there would be no unduly prejudicial effect on the accused in the circumstances of this case. In the judge's assessment, if the evidence of Dr. Watt were put forward by the defence, it would be necessary to allow the jury to be in a position to attach the appropriate weight to his testimony. On the whole, I agree with this assessment and I am of the view that the trial judge committed no reversible error of law, having exercised his discretion judicially and judiciously.

. . . .

In the result, I would dismiss the appeal.

[For criticism of the majority opinion see Annotation by Brian Gover (1989), 69 C.R. (3d) 194. For adoption of the majority opinion see *R. v. Evans* (1994), 93 Man. R. 77 (Q.B.).]

R. v. WILSON
(1983), 5 C.C.C. (3d) 61 (B.C.C.A.)

[On the accused's trial for rape the complainant testified that she had attended at the accused's home in response to an advertisement for a housekeeper. According to the victim, once she was there she was tied up by the accused, assaulted and forced to have intercourse. The accused denied committing the offence. The accused also called several character witnesses who testified as to his good and non-violent character. At the preliminary inquiry a woman who had been the accused's housekeeper for several days prior to the offence, and who was his housekeeper at the time of his arrest the day following the alleged offence, was called. However, at trial Crown counsel indicated that he did not intend to call the housekeeper because he was of the view that her evidence was unreliable and that she would not assist the Crown's case. He also indicated that the housekeeper had a psychiatric condition and had been charged with obstructing police. However, in cross-examining the accused Crown counsel suggested to him that the accused had, on several occasions, used violence to obtain sexual favours from his housekeeper. The accused denied these suggestions. In his charge to the jury the trial judge repeated that the accused had denied the various suggestions made by Crown counsel. The accused was acquitted of the charge but convicted of indecent assault. The accused appealed.]

. . . .

LAMBERT J.A.: —

. . . .

The accused put his character in issue. His counsel called three witnesses to give evidence that the accused was not a violent or aggressive person, drunk or sober. It is a well-established rule . . . that in those circumstances the Crown is entitled to cross-examine the accused with respect to other incidents of violence or aggression on his part.

But, in my opinion, there is an overriding rule that applies to all such cross-examination. That is, that the cross-examiner who makes a suggestion of prior wrongdoing on the part of the accused must have a proper basis for doing so. If he does not have a proper basis then, as Mr. Justice Anderson has said, there is a risk of unfair prejudice to the accused through a powerfully persuasive innuendo being wafted into the jury-box.

I agree with Mr. Justice Anderson that the questions that were put to the accused by Crown counsel in relation to acts of sexual violence towards Aline Courchesne were gravely prejudicial to the accused. That prejudice was unfair and improper because the Crown did not intend to call Aline Courchesne as a witness and Crown counsel had reached a conclusion that Aline Courchesne would have been an untruthful and unreliable witness. In those circumstances, Crown counsel did not have "reasonable grounds for thinking that the imputation conveyed by the question was well founded or true".

. . . .

I agree with Mr. Justice Anderson that there are situations where the proper course for Crown counsel, who intends to put questions of the kind that were put in this case, is to request a *voir dire*. Of course, a *voir dire* is not necessary in every case, but only in cases where the Crown does not intend to prove the imputation in its question, and there may be unfair prejudice to the accused. And, of course, there will be cases where such a question is asked without any proper basis but where the trial judge will be able to direct the jury in such a way that the prejudice to the accused will be cured. But in other cases, of which this is one, the prejudice will be so grave that it will not be curable by a direction of the trial judge.

. . . .

ANDERSON J.A.: —

. . . .

If there was any evidence available to counsel for the Crown that the appellant had used violence to obtain sexual favours from Courchesne it is obvious that the source of such information was Courchesne herself. Counsel for the Crown cannot on the one hand declare an available witness unreliable when it suits the Crown so to do and declare that witness reliable for purposes favourable to the Crown. That is exactly what counsel for the Crown attempted to do in this case. He knew that if Courchesne testified her evidence would not be favourable to the Crown. In fact he said so. This did not prevent him, however, from suggesting to the jury, on the basis of something said to him or the police or at the preliminary hearing by a completely unreliable witness, that on the very day of the rape the appellant had indecently assaulted or raped that witness, namely, Courchesne.

. . . .

I come now to deal with the effect on the jury of putting such suggestions to the jury. Jurors are not familiar with the rules of evidence and even if the jury are informed by the trial judge that suggestions are not evidence, it is difficult for those with untrained minds to disregard such suggestions. In a case where the suggestions made, as here, go to the heart of the defence, the members of the jury, or some of them, may well think that there is some truth to the suggestions even if they are denied by the accused. Any suggestion made to a jury by an officer of the court, be he prosecutor or counsel for the defence, weighs heavily with the jury. It is for this reason that, in my opinion, suggestions should not be put in cross-examination on vital issues unless counsel conducting the cross-examination has reasonable grounds for believing that the suggestions are true. Information based on rumour or upon a statement made by an unreliable witness (declared so to be by Crown counsel) does not provide a reasonable basis for cross-examination in respect of such information.

There is a dearth of authority on this subject. The method of dealing with such cross-examination in the United States is dealt with by Jackson J. in *Michelson v. United States* (1948), 335 U.S. 469 at pp. 480-1, as follows:

> Wide discretion [to cross-examine on the alleged prior misconduct of the accused] is accompanied by a heavy responsibility on trial courts to protect the practice from any misuse. The trial judge was scrupulous to so guard it in the case before us. He took pains to ascertain, out of presence of the jury, that the target of the question was an actual event, which would probably result in some comment among acquaintances if not injury to the defendant's reputation. He satisfied himself that counsel was not merely taking a random shot at a reputation imprudently exposed *or asking a groundless question to waft an unwarranted innuendo into the jury box.*

(Emphasis mine.)

I pause here to interject that the suggestions made in the case on appeal were designed not only "to waft an innuendo into the jury box" but to have the jury believe that the accused was an aggressive person who used violence to obtain sexual gratification.

In England the Bar Council Rules (1950) deal with this matter. Rule (4) reads as follows:

> (4) Questions which affect the credibility of a witness by attacking his character, but are not otherwise relevant to the actual inquiry, ought not to be asked unless the cross-examiner has reasonable grounds for thinking that the imputation conveyed by the question is well founded or true.

This matter is also dealt with by the Court of Criminal Appeal in *R. v. O'Neill and Ackers* (1950), 34 Cr. App. R. 108 at p. 111, where the judgment of the Lord Chief Justice reads as follows:

> In this case, a violent attack was made on the police. It was suggested that they had done improper things, and indeed, Ackers repeats that suggestion in his notice of appeal. The applicants had the opportunity of going into the box at the trial and explaining and supporting what they had instructed their counsel to say. They did not dare to go into the box, and, therefore, counsel, who knew that they were not going into the box, ought not to have made these suggestions against the police. It is one thing to cross-examine properly and temperately with regard to credit, though it is very dangerous to do so unless you have material on which to cross-examine, and with which you can confront the witness. It is, however, entirely wrong to make such suggestions as were made in this case, namely that the police beat the prisoners until they made confessions, and then, when there is the chance for the prisoners to substantiate what has been said by going into the box, for counsel not to call them. The Court hopes that notice will be taken of this, and that counsel will refrain, if they do not intend to call their clients, from making charges which, if true, form a defence but which, if there is nothing to support them, ought not to be pursued.

In *Fox v. General Medical Council*, [1960] 1 W.L.R. 1017 at p. 1023, the judgment of Lord Radcliffe reads in part as follows:

> An advocate is entitled to use his discretion as to whether to put questions in the course of cross-examination which are based on material which he is not in a position to prove directly. The penalty is that, if he gets a denial or some answer that does not suit him, the answer stands against him for what it is worth.

I note the words "prove directly" used by Lord Radcliffe. I do not suggest that when a prosecutor makes a suggestion in cross-examination that he must be able to "prove the suggestions directly". I do say, however, that the imputation conveyed by the suggestion should be well founded or true and not based on information obtained from an unreliable witness (a witness so unreliable that Crown counsel would not call her as his witness on a matter essential to the unfolding of the narrative).

In Canada, this matter has been dealt with in *R. v. Racco (No. 3)* (1975), 23 C.C.C. (2d) 209, and in *R. v. Bencardino and de Carlo* (1973), 15 C.C.C. (2d) 342. . . .

With respect to the effect of suggestions of improper conduct made by counsel, I adopt the language of Falconbridge C.J. in *Loughead v. Collingwood Shipbuilding Co.* (1908), 16 O.L.R. 64 at p. 65, where he said:

> The mere putting of the question does all the mischief. The jury will draw their own inferences from the objection taken by defendants' counsel and the ruling of the Court. The real defendant is placed in a position of manifest and incurable disadvantage.

In my opinion, while Rule (4) of the Bar Council does not in explicit terms represent the law in British Columbia, there is a general standard governing the course of conduct to be followed by Crown counsel in all criminal trials. This standard has been set by the Supreme Court of Canada in *Boucher v. The Queen* (1954), 110 C.C.C. 263. The judgment of Rand J. in the *Boucher* case reads in part at p. 270 C.C.C. as follows:

> It cannot be over-emphasized that the purpose of a criminal prosecution is not to obtain a conviction; it is to lay before a jury what the Crown considers to be credible evidence relevant to what is alleged to be a crime. Counsel have a duty to see that all available legal proof of the facts is presented: it should be done firmly and pressed to its legitimate strength, but it must also be done fairly. The role of prosecutor excludes any notion of winning or losing; his function is a matter of public duty than which in civil life there can be none charged with greater personal responsibility. It is to be efficiently performed with an ingrained sense of the dignity, the seriousness and the justness of judicial proceedings.

In my opinion, a prosecutor does not act fairly when he makes a suggestion relating to a vital issue in the case, which he knows is based on an unreliable source.

Assuming, however, that the prosecutor was justified in making the suggestions which he did, it was incumbent on the trial judge in the circumstances, to tell the jury in clear and convincing terms that the prosecutor was bound by the answers made in response to the suggestions made by the prosecutor. In other words, he should have directed the jury to completely disabuse their minds of the suggestions alluded to in cross-examination.

In this case not only did the learned trial judge fail to direct the jury on this vital point but on the contrary he repeated the denial made by the accused as follows:

> He denied that she ever, that is the girl, Aline, ever resisted his advances and he denied ever having slapped her or pushed her and he repeated that he was a non-violent person.

Such a repetition could only reinforce in the minds of the jury the suggestion of violence to obtain sexual favours made by the prosecutor. It was at this stage that the jury should have been firmly directed to entirely disregard the suggestions made. To repeat the denial of the suggestions without any direction as to its import could only prejudice the case for the defence.

. . . .

In conclusion, I would suggest that in cases such as the present, in order to avoid the possibility that a mistrial may result, counsel for the Crown should advise the trial judge in the absence of the jury of the relevant circumstances and of the questions he intends to put in cross-examination. The trial judge could then determine whether such questions should be asked. I think that the occasion for such a *voir dire* will be rare because in most cases counsel will have a solid basis for his cross-examination, even though he may not intend or be able to prove the facts implied by the questions he intends to put to a witness or the accused. Even so, counsel should be on his guard to avoid situations which may result in a mistrial.

I would allow the appeal.

R. v. R. (A.J.).
(1994), 94 C.C.C. (3d) 168 (Ont. C.A.)

[The accused was convicted of incest with his daughter and granddaughter, sexual assault and threatening. One of his grounds of appeal concerned the prejudicial effect of the cross-examination of the accused conducted by Crown counsel. He alleged Crown counsel had argued with and demeaned the accused in cross-examining him, inserted editorial comment and gave evidence while cross-examining him, called upon the accused to comment on the veracity of Crown witnesses and conducted an improper attack on the accused's character.]

DOHERTY J.A. (OSBORNE and LASKIN JJ.A. concurring):—

. . . .

The Cross-examination of the Appellant

Counsel for the appellant submits that Crown counsel's cross-examination of the appellant resulted in a miscarriage of justice. He does not base this contention on any isolated feature of the cross-examination or any specific line of questioning, but contends that the overall conduct and tenor of the cross-examination was so improper and prejudicial to the appellant, that it rendered the trial unfair and resulted in a miscarriage of justice. This argument is becoming a familiar one in this court.

Crown counsel conducted an aggressive and exhaustive 141-page cross-examination of the appellant. She was well prepared and well armed for that cross-examination. Crown counsel is entitled, indeed in some cases expected, to conduct a vigorous cross-examination of an accused. Effective cross-examination of an accused serves the truth-finding function as much as does effective cross-examination of a complainant.

There are, however, well-established limits on cross-examination. Some apply to all witnesses, others only to the accused. Isolated transgressons of those limits may be of little consequence on appeal. Repeated improprieties during the cross-examination of an accused are, however, a very different matter. As the improprieties mount, the cross-examination may cross over the line from the aggressive to the abusive. When that line is crossed, the danger of a miscarriage of justice is very real. If improper cross-examination of an accused prejudices that accused in his defence or is so improper as to bring the administration of justice into disrepute, an appellate court must intervene.

After careful consideration of the entire cross-examination of the appellant in the context of the issues raised by his examination-in-chief and the conduct of the entire trial, I am satisfied that the cross-examination must be characterized as abusive and unfair.

From the outset of the cross-examination, Crown counsel adopted a sarcastic tone with the accused and repeatedly inserted editorial commentary into her questions. I count at least eight such comments in the first eight pages of the cross-examination. During that part of the cross-examination, Crown counsel referred to one answer given by the appellant as "incredible". She repeatedly asked the appellant if he "wanted the jury to believe that one too". When questioned as to how he met T., the appellant said he was told by a friend that a relative would be coming to see him, whereupon Crown counsel remarked "so I guess you were expecting some long lost cousin in the old country". After the appellant had described his reaction to being told by T. that she was his daughter, Crown counsel sarcastically said "gee, I guess everybody would react the way you did".

Crown counsel's approach from the very beginning of the cross-examination was calculated to demean and humiliate the appellant. She persisted in that approach throughout. For example, after the appellant said that he had allowed T. to move in with him shortly after they had met, Crown counsel said "you are just a really nice guy". At another point, she said, "tell me sir, do fathers usually have sexual intercourse with their daughters". Still later, after the appellant had testified that his girlfriend had left him but had told him that she wished to come back, Crown counsel said "you just have all these women running after you wanting to come back".

These are but a few of a great many instances where Crown counsel used the pretence of questioning the appellant to demonstrate her contempt for him and the evidence he was giving before the jury. No counsel can abuse any witness. This self-evident interdiction applies with particular force to Crown counsel engaged in the cross-examination of an accused.

The tone adopted by Crown counsel is not the only problem with her cross-examination. Crown counsel repeatedly gave evidence and stated her opinion during cross-examination. She also engaged in extensive argument with the appellant. For example, when the appellant gave contradictory explanations in the course of cross-examination, Crown counsel announced "you were lying", and when the appellant questioned Crown counsel's description of T. as "your victim" Crown counsel replied "certainly she is". Still later, after Crown counsel had very effectively cross-examined the appellant as to when he had learned that T. was his daughter, she proclaimed "you are playing games with me, with this jury". She followed that comment with the admonition "let's try and be honest". In several instances, the cross-examination degenerated into pure argument between the appellant and Crown counsel. After one lengthy exchange, Crown counsel announced: "It is hard to keep up with you sir because you keep changing your story".

Statements of counsel's personal opinion have no place in a cross-examination. Nor is cross-examination of the appellant the time or place for argument.

Crown counsel also repeatedly called upon the appellant to comment on the veracity of Crown witnesses and to explain why these witnesses had fabricated their evidence. Crown counsel pursued this line of questioning in relation to at least four Crown witnesses. With respect to some of the witnesses, the questions were repeated at different points in the cross-examination. For example, Crown counsel asked the appellant whether J. had "totally fabricated that evidence" and then asked him "why that little girl totally fabricated that evidence". After Crown counsel had put the appellant in the position of calling four of the Crown witnesses liars, the trial judge intervened and suggested that the questions were improper. Crown counsel returned to that form of questioning on at least one occasion following the trial judge's admonition.

The impropriety of these questions cannot be doubted and Crown counsel in this court acknowledged that they were improper. Crown counsel submitted that although the questions were improper, they caused no prejudice. She observed, quite accurately, that the defence implicitly involved an assertion that the Crown witnesses and, in particular, T., had concocted the allegations against the appellant.

The nature of the defence advanced will impact on the harm, if any, caused by this type of questioning. Despite the defence advanced, I cannot say that the repeated resort to this technique, whereby the appellant was placed in the position of accusing others, did not prejudice him in the eyes of the jury. By means of these improper questions, Crown counsel was able to paint the appellant as a callous accuser ready to charge virtually everyone, including a terrified, emotionally distraught young child, with deliberately fabricating evidence against him. These improper questions also forced the appellant to offer explanations for the allegedly false testimony offered by the Crown witnesses. In the case of J. and T., the explanations only served to open further fertile grounds for cross-examination.

I am also driven to the conclusion that at many points in the cross-examination, Crown counsel conducted what amounted to an improper and potentially prejudicial attack on the appellant's character and lifestyle. Given the allegations, it was inevitable and essential that the jury learn something of the appellant's sordid lifestyle and character to assess the charges before them properly. The appellant's decision to testify also meant that his lengthy criminal record would be placed before the jury. These conditions created a real danger that the jury could convict based on their assessment of the appellant as a despicable and evil man, rather than on a finding that the Crown had proven any or all of the charges beyond a reasonable doubt. Crown counsel's cross-examination significantly increased this danger.

There are numerous instances in the cross-examination when the questions went beyond the bounds of relevancy and legitimate credibility impeachment and became an attempt to highlight the appellant's bad character and deviant lifestyle. The appellant was cross-examined about whether he had filed income tax returns. He was also questioned about the criminal records of his associates and about his attitudes, as "a former drug dealer", to T.'s use of prescription pills. Still later, Crown counsel asked the appellant about his respect "for the law and court orders". Crown counsel also cross-examined the appellant to show that he was sexually promiscuous and had no sense of responsibility to any of the women with whom he had been involved during his lifetime. At another point in the cross-examination, she referred to the appellant as "a jailhouse lawyer".

The appellant was also cross-examined about the paternity of C., T.'s young son. He denied that he was the father. Crown counsel then gave evidence to the effect that C. could not be adopted because it was believed that he was the product of an incestuous relationship. She then asked the appellant why he did not submit to a blood test so that the question of C.'s paternity could be cleared up and C. could become eligible for adoption. None of this had anything to do with the allegations against the appellant and could only serve to inflame the jury further against the appellant. Defence counsel at trial objected to the question on the basis that it had no evidentiary foundation. The trial judge upheld the objection on the basis of relevancy, however, Crown counsel persisted, asking:

> If you knew you weren't the father of this child, why didn't you ask to take a blood test to show you weren't?

Cross-examination on this issue continued for several more questions. I can see only one purpose to these questions. Crown counsel wanted to demonstrate that the appellant did not have the decency to take the steps necessary to make C. eligible for adoption.

Defence counsel (not Mr. Campbell) did, at a recess, suggest that some of Crown counsel's questions were bringing out "discreditable conduct not covered by the indictment". He referred specifically to the questions about the income tax returns. Crown counsel responded that counsel should object when the questions were asked "not some two hours later". The trial judge made no ruling and when the jury returned Crown counsel continued her cross-examination in the same manner. Crown counsel also asked the appellant on more than one occasion about conversations he had had with his lawyer. These questions were improper in that they invited the appellant to disclose privileged communications or risk appearing non-responsive to the questions. The questions were also totally irrelevant. Defence counsel did eventually object to this type of questioning and Crown counsel did not pursue it. Crown counsel did, however, continue to ask the appellant questions about whether he intended to call certain persons as witnesses. Crown counsel would know full well that such decisions were for counsel and not the appellant. It was unfair to ask the appellant questions which Crown counsel knew he could not answer.

It must be acknowledged that the appellant was a difficult witness and to some extent contributed to the tone of the cross-examination through his own attitude and refusal on several occasions to answer directly the questions put to him. The vast majority of what I have characterized as improper cross-examination was not objected to at trial. Both of these considerations are relevant when deciding the propriety and potential prejudicial effect of a cross-examination. The failure of counsel to object does not, however, give Crown counsel carte blanche at trial or immunize the cross-examination from appellate scrutiny.

Cases like this, where the allegations are particularly sordid, the complainants particularly sympathetic and the accused particularly disreputable, provide a severe test of our criminal justice system. It is very difficult in such cases to hold the scales of justice in balance and to provide the accused with the fair trial to which he or she is entitled. By her cross-examination, Crown counsel skewed that delicate balance. The cross-examination, considered in its totality and in the context of the entire trial, prejudiced the appellant in his defence and significantly undermined the appearance of the fairness of the trial.

. . . .

The cross-examination destroyed the necessary appearance of fairness in the trial and resulted in a miscarriage of justice. The strength of the Crown's case becomes irrelevant in determining the appropriate disposition and s. 686(1)(b)(iii) has no application. The miscarriage of justice lies in the conduct of the proceedings and not in the verdict arrived at by the jury. All of the convictions must be set aside and a new trial ordered on all of those charges.

(d) Duty to Cross-examine — *rule in Brown v. Dunn p-399*

Aside from counsel's right to cross-examine there may at times be a duty to cross-examine.

R. v. McNEILL
(2000), 33 C.R. (5th) 390, 144 C.C.C. (3d) 551 (Ont. C.A.)

[The accused was charged with numerous offences arising out of an alleged abduction of one C. One of people involved in the abduction, B, testified as Crown witness that he was retained by the accused to collect a drug debt from the victim, that he and the accused went to the victim's motel room for that purpose. The appellant testified and denied any involvement in the abduction.]

MOLDAVER, J.A. (MCMURTRY, C.J.O., and GOUDGE, J.A. concurring): —

. . . .

Cross-examination of the Appellant on Defence Counsel's Failure to Pose Specific Questions to the Crown witness Bonello

In his examination-in-chief of the appellant, defence counsel asked whether the appellant had spoken to Bonello after the Cudney incident. The appellant answered in the affirmative and the following series of questions and answers ensued, without objection from Crown counsel:

Q.   And what did Mr. Bonello say about it?

A.   I was — I was probably a little aggressive with him at first, and he became aggressive right back saying that . . . you know . . . I told him that Bob Cudney — you did this for me; and he said: No, no, no, no. This was done for "killer". It had nothing to do with you.

Q.   For who?

A.   "Killer". I know that sounds a little bit cliché, but . . . as you heard other people testify . . . this is actually somebody's name.

Q.   Did you force the issue with Bonello?

A.   I wouldn't force any issue with Bonello. He just told me that it was Cud — or "killer's" beef and it had nothing to do with me.

For reasons unknown, defence counsel did not question Bonello about this conversation. He was obliged to do so under s. 11 of the Canada Evidence Act, R.S.C. 1985, c. C-5, if it was his intention to lead evidence of a prior statement inconsistent with Bonello's testimony. Had Crown counsel raised the appropriate objection, it would have been for the trial judge to decide whether the appellant should be permitted to testify about the purported conversation (see *R. v. P. (G.)* (1996), 112 C.C.C. (3d) 263 at pp. 278-87 (Ont. C.A.)).

Defence counsel's failure to question Bonello about the conversation did not go unnoticed by the Crown. No doubt, she was concerned that Bonello had not been given the opportunity to confirm, deny or explain it. To the extent she felt the matter was worth pursuing, in my view, the proper procedure would have been to raise the issue with the trial judge in the absence of the jury. That way, the trial judge could have determined whether her concern was valid and if so, what steps should be taken to remedy the situation. Regrettably, Crown counsel did not pursue this course. Instead, she chose to confront the appellant with the fact that defence counsel had not questioned Bonello about the purported conversation either at the preliminary hearing or at trial:

Q.   The gentlemen that you named . . . that you said Bonello named as having been the whole cause of the Cudney incident; you said his name was "killer"?

A.   He said it was "killer's gig", that he was involved with Cudney over, not me; "killer's gig".

Q.   You were present at the preliminary hearing as well as at the trial of this matter, isn't that true?

A.   Absolutely.

Q.   You never heard Mr. Bolnello asked if it was "killer's gig" did you?

A.   I never heard him . . . ?

Q.   Anybody ask Bonello anything about "killer's gig", or if he said that to you?

A.   No. I believe "killer" was mentioned somewhere in this. I think by Bob Cudney. I don't believe Bonello ever used his name. He may have but I don't recall off the top of my head.

Q.   That was my point sir. You're telling us about a conversation that you had with Mr. Bonello, but no one ever suggested to Bonello that that conversation occurred, correct?

In my view, this line of questioning was improper because it was capable of leaving the jury with the impression that the appellant should be held responsible for what may have been a tactical decision or mere oversight on the part of defence counsel. As explained, defence counsel's failure to question Bonello about the purported conversation involved a breach of s. 11 of the Canada Evidence Act. That, however, is not the way the issue was presented to us. Rather, it was framed as a breach of the rule in *Browne v. Dunn* (1893), 6 R. 67 (H.L.). Accordingly, I propose to address that rule, primarily with a view to considering the options available when it is breached.

The rule in *Browne v. Dunn* was succinctly stated by Labrosse J.A. in *R. v. Henderson*, *supra*:

> This well-known rule stands for the proposition that if counsel is going to challenge the credibility of a witness by calling contradictory evidence, the witness must be given the chance to address the contradictory evidence in cross-examination while he or she is in the witness-box.

In *R. v. Verney* (1993), 87 C.C.C. (3d) 363 at p. 376 (Ont. C.A.), Finlayson J.A. outlined the purpose and ambit of the rule:

> *Browne v. Dunn* is a rule of fairness that prevents the "ambush" of a witness by not giving him an opportunity to state his position with respect to later evidence which contradicts him on an essential matter. It is not, however, an absolute rule and counsel must not feel obliged to slog through a witness's evidence-in-chief, putting him on notice of every detail that the defence does not accept. Defence counsel must be free to use his own judgment about how to cross-examine a hostile witness. Having the witness repeat in cross-examination, everything he said in chief, is rarely the tactic of choice. For a fuller discussion on this point, see *Palmer and Palmer v. The Queen* (1979), 50 C.C.C. (2d) 193 at pp. 209-10, [1980] 1 S.C.R. 759, 14 C.R. (3d) 22 (S.C.C.).

While these decisions explain the rule and its underlying purpose, they do not address the options available to a party who feels aggrieved by the failure of his or her opponent to adhere to it. To that end, I offer these suggestions. In cases such as this, where the concern lies in a witness's inability to present his or her side of the story, it seems to me that the first option worth exploring is whether the witness is available for recall. If so, then assuming the trial judge is otherwise satisfied, after weighing the pros and cons, that recall is appropriate, the aggrieved party can either take up the opportunity or decline it. If the opportunity is declined, then, in my view, no special instruction to the jury is required beyond the normal instruction that the jury is entitled to believe all, part or none of a witness's evidence, regardless of whether the evidence is uncontradicted.

The mechanics of when the witness should be recalled and by whom should be left to the discretion of the trial judge.

In those cases where it is impossible or highly impracticable to have the witness recalled or where the trial judge otherwise determines that recall is inappropriate, it should be left to the trial judge to decide whether a special instruction should be given to the jury. If one is warranted, the jury should be told that in assessing the weight to be given to the uncontradicted evidence, they may properly take into account the fact that the opposing witness was not questioned about it. The jury should also be told that they may take this into account in assessing the credibility of the opposing witness. Depending on the circumstances, there may be other permissible ways of rectifying the problem. The two options that I have mentioned are not meant to be exhaustive. As a rule, however, I am of the view that they will generally prove to be the fairest and most effective solutions.

Returning to the issue at hand, Ms. Fairburn does not attempt to justify the impugned line of questioning. Instead, she submits that the trial judge's instructions to the jury were sufficient to overcome any prejudice occasioned to the appellant. The trial judge dealt with this issue in general terms as follows:

> The procedure of cross-examination is a procedure I regard as one of fairness; a rule of professional practice. It is applicable where it is intended to suggest the witness is not speaking the truth on a particular point. The question, by the suggestion made, often sets the stage, as I have tried to indicate, for defence evidence to be led in support of the suggestion. If put to a witness in cross-examination, the witness has the opportunity to explain. If not put to the witness in cross-examination, but put later to other witnesses, the suggestion is then perhaps impossible to explain, and triers of fact can be left with the inference that the witness's story is untrue and the witness unworthy of credit . . . believability.

> There is therefore the practice of cross-examining counsel to put to the witness all significant matters upon which they seek to contradict. I emphasize the words "all significant matters", as some matters may be so obvious as not to be of significance, and likewise some matters may be so insignificant or interrelated with other matters so as not to require a singling out, and the use of time that might be involved in that singling out.

> It is for you to decide if there were any significant matters upon which crown witnesses were not cross-examined, which matters were put forward by other witnesses with a view to suggesting the particular crown witness was not worthy of belief. It is for you to decide if there were any such lapses or failure to cross-examine, and if so, what weight to be given to the particular evidence to be called for which there was no opportunity to explain.

In my view, these instructions were deficient in two respects. First, to the extent the jury understood them to relate to defence counsel's failure to question Bonello about the purported conversation, the trial judge left the jury with the impression that Bonello (and inferentially the Crown), was left in the impossible position of being unable to explain the conversation. With respect, that was both inaccurate and misleading. Had Crown counsel wished to have Bonello's explanation before the jury, she could have sought permission to have him recalled. There was nothing to suggest that Bonello was unavailable or that his recall would have posed any difficulty. As it is, she made no effort to do so. Accordingly, it was wrong to leave the jury with the impression that defence counsel's failure to question Bonello rendered it impossible for him to offer an explanation.

Second, although the jury was instructed on the use that could be made of defence counsel's failure to question Bonello, they were not told that the appellant should not be held responsible for what may have been a tactical decision or mere oversight on the part of his counsel.

(e) Collateral Facts Rule

Counsel is entitled in cross-examination to ask questions about matters relevant to the material issues in the case but is also entitled to ask questions about other matters that may be relevant to the witness's credibility. These questions are subject only to the discretion of the trial judge, who will take into account such considerations as time and fairness to the witness. However if the matters concerning which the witness is questioned are not matters that counsel could prove independently, not matters relevant to the material issues, counsel will not be permitted to lead evidence to contradict the answers. These matters concerning which no contradiction is possible are referred to as collateral matters or collateral facts. While counsel may, in cross, put questions concerning collateral facts he must take the answer of the witness.

R. v. CASSIBO
(1982), 70 C.C.C. (2d) 498 (Ont. C.A.)

[After trial by judge alone, the accused was convicted on four counts of incest. One of the grounds of appeal was whether there had been improper curtailment of the cross-examination of the complainants with respect to whether they had read a certain article on incest in a magazine.]

MARTIN J.A:—

Another ground of appeal . . . on which we did not require argument from Crown counsel was that the trial judge had improperly curtailed cross-examination of the complainants with respect to whether they had read a certain article in a magazine on the ground that the cross-examination related to a collateral matter. Rosetta was asked in a cross-examination whether she had read in magazines about fathers having sexual relations with their daughters and she testified that she had not. She was then shown a magazine entitled "True Experience" being the November 1978 . . . issue containing a story captioned "My Daughter's Lies Sent My Husband to Prison!". She said that it probably belonged to her parents but she did not remember seeing it. The trial judge interjected, observing that surely this was cross-examination with respect to a collateral matter. He, nevertheless, permitted defence counsel to introduce the magazine as an exhibit. Darlene, in cross-examination, said that she did not remember seeing the magazine. In cross-examination, the mother of the girls, Elsie Cassibo, testified that she found the magazine in Darlene's bedroom after Darlene had left the family residence.

. . . .

Even if the cross-examination of Rosetta and Darlene with respect to the contents of the magazine related to a collateral matter, counsel is entitled to cross-examine a witness called by the opposite party with respect to collateral matters on the issue of credibility, but, as a general rule, cannot contradict the answers of the witness with respect to collateral matters by the evidence of other witnesses. The cross-examination with respect to whether Rosetta and Darlene had read the article in the magazine did not, however, relate to a collateral matter. The purpose of the cross-examination was to endeavour to show that they had fabricated their testimony with respect to their allegations against the appellant. The cross-examination accordingly did not relate to a collateral matter but related to the truthfulness of their testimony on the very issue before the court. . . . In the result, however, I do not believe that any prejudice was suffered by the appellant since defence counsel was permitted to cross-examine Rosetta and Darlene as to whether they had read the magazine and to elicit from Mrs. Cassibo that she had discovered the magazine in Darlene's room.

Sometimes, but not always, the evidence that counsel wishes to use to contradict amounts to proof of a statement by the witness that is inconsistent with their present testimony. Proof of previous inconsistent statements, we will see, are subject to the collateral facts rule.

(f) Examination by Court and Order of Witnesses

> The Court has, apparently, no power, of its own motion and without the consent of both parties, to direct further evidence to be given: . . . The parties, and not the Court, are *domini litis* in all civil proceedings. If a party comes into Court with an imperfect case, the proper penalty is dismissal.[201]

In a civil case the court has no power to call a witness,[202] but it may do so in a criminal case when it is seen as necessary in the interests of justice.[203] Apparently the interest of the state in securing truth in criminal matters, where the liberty of the subject is at stake, accounts for the difference; in civil trials, while truth is important, justice, in the sense that both litigants feel satisfied that *their* dispute, framed by *them,* was properly settled, is paramount. The power of the court to call witnesses in criminal cases is limited when the defence has closed its case. The prosecution is not entitled to split its case and therefore cannot call further witnesses after the defence has closed its case unless a matter has arisen *ex improviso*, which no human ingenuity could have foreseen.[204] It was seen to be wise to impose the same limitation on the judge's right to call witnesses to avoid injustice to the accused.[205]

Both in civil and criminal cases the court has the right to ask questions to clarify matters and to interrupt if it feels the witness does not understand. In exercising this right the court must be extremely cautious as it does not know

---

201. *Re Fraser* (1912), 26 O.L.R. 508, 521 (C.A.).

202. See also *Fowler v. Fowler*, [1949] O.W.N. 244 (C.A.).

203. See cases collected in Newark and Samuels, "Let the Judge Call the Witness," [1969] Crim. L. Rev. 399. And see *R. v. Bouchard* (1973), 12 C.C.C. (2d) 554 (N.S. Co. Ct.), criticized in Stenning, "One Blind Man to See Fair Play: The Judge's Right to Call Witnesses" (1973), 24 C.R.N.S. 49. See also *R. v. Brouillard*, [1985] 1 S.C.R. 39; *R. v. Roberts* (1984), 80 Cr. App. R. 89 (C.A.); and *R. v. MacPhee* (1985), 19 C.C.C. (3d) 345 (Alta. Q.B.).

204 See *R. v. P. (M.B.)* (1994), 29 C.R. (4th) 209 (S.C.C.), where the court held it to be error to allow the Crown to reopen its case and recall witnesses after the accused had signalled he would be calling an alibi witness.

205. See *R. v. Harris*, [1927] 2 K.B. 587, 594 (C.C.A.). See also *R. v. Cleghorn*, [1967] 2 Q.B. 584 (C.A.) and *R. v. Morin* (1977), 40 C.R.N.S. 378 (Sask. Dist. Ct.). With respect to the Crown improperly splitting its case, see *John v. R.* (1985), 49 C.R. (3d) 57 (S.C.C.); *R. v. Krause* (1986), 54 C.R. (3d) 294 (S.C.C.) and *R. v. Scott* (1984), 79 Cr. App. R. 49 (C.A.). With respect to proper rebuttal see *R. v. Wood* (1986), 28 C.C.C. (3d) 65 (Ont. C.A.) and *R. v. Wagner* (1986), 50 C.R. (3d) 175 (Alta. C.A.). Regarding re-examination and re-cross-examination see *R. v. Tremblay* (1984), 17 C.C.C. (3d) 359 (Que. C.A.) and *R. v. Rochester* (1984), 13 C.C.C. (3d) 215 (Ont. Co. Ct.).

as much about the case as does counsel and interference can have the opposite effect of that intended. In a now-famous dictum, Lord Denning has observed:[206]

> No one can doubt that the judge, in intervening as he did, was actuated by the best motives. He was anxious to understand the details of this complicated case, and asked questions to get them clear in his mind. He was anxious that the witnesses should not be harassed unduly in cross-examination, and intervened to protect them when he thought necessary. He was anxious to investigate all the various criticisms that had been made against the board, and to see whether they were well founded or not. Hence, he took them up himself with the witnesses from time to time. He was anxious that the case should not be dragged on too long, and intimated clearly when he thought that a point had been sufficiently explored. All those are worthy motives on which judges daily intervene in the conduct of cases, and have done for centuries.
>
> Nevertheless, we are quite clear that the interventions, taken together, were far more than they should have been. In the system of trial which we have evolved in this country, the judge sits to hear and determine the issues raised by the parties, not to conduct an investigation or examination on behalf of society at large, as happens, we believe, in some foreign countries. Even in England, however, a judge is not a mere umpire to answer the question "How's that?" His object, above all, is to find out the truth, and to do justice according to law; and in the daily pursuit of it the advocate plays an honorable and necessary role. Was it not Lord Eldon L.C. who said in a notable passage that truth is best discovered by powerful "statements on both sides of the question"?: see *Ex parte Lloyd.* And Lord Greene M.R. who explained that justice is best done by a judge who holds the balance between the contending parties without himself taking part in their disputations? If a judge, said Lord Greene, should himself conduct the examination of witnesses, "he, so to speak, descends into the arena and is liable to have his vision clouded by the dust of conflict": see *Yuill v. Yuill.*[207]

And in Ontario, Evans, J.A. explained:

> There is unquestionably a right to intervene for the purpose of clarification of the evidence, and when the case is highly technical the interventions may be more frequent. No doubt the trial Judge was actuated by the highest motives, but his zealous participation, irrespective of motive, unfortunately caused him to transgress and he lost sight of the issues raised by the parties and launched into an investigation on behalf of Canadian motorists.[208]

While the judge in criminal cases in Canada has no control over the order in which the accused calls his witnesses,[209] many provinces in Canada have enacted in rules of court governing civil cases a power in the court to require that the party be examined before other witnesses on his behalf.[210] Similarly, these rules permit the court to order the exclusion of prospective witnesses until required to give evidence, whether the witness is a party or not.[211] In criminal cases as well the court has an inherent authority to order the exclusion of

---

206. *Jones v. Nat. Coal Bd.,* [1957] 2 Q.B. 55, 63 (C.A.). For an example of descending into the arena see *R. v. Rhodes* (1981), 59 C.C.C. (2d) 426 (B.C.C.A.).
207. [1945] P. 15 (C.A.).
208. *Phillips v. Ford Motor Co.* (1971), 18 D.L.R. (3d) 641, 663 (Ont. C.A.).
209. See *R. v. Smuk* (1971), 3 C.C.C. (2d) 457 (B.C.C.A.) and *R. v. Angelantoni* (1975), 31 C.R.N.S. 342 (Ont. C.A.).
210. See, *e.g.,* Ontario Rule 52.06(2).
211. *Ibid.*

witnesses but since the accused has the right to be present at his trial the exclusion order may not refer to him. If the accused does not testify first and so gains the advantage of listening to his witnesses being examined and cross-examined before going into the witness stand himself he risks a comment being made on his credibility.

R. v. P. (T.L.)

(1996), 193 A.R. 146 (Alta. C.A.)

[The accused was convicted of robbery. She had called witnesses at the trial to established an alibi. The defence called the accused as its last witness and she denied any involvement in the robbery. The trial judge commented before the accused's cross-examination that her evidence would be given very little weight since all the other evidence in the case had been heard by the accused. A new trial was ordered.]

O'LEARY J.A. (CONRAD and KENNY JJ.A. concurring):—

. . . .

There are two aspects of the trial which cause us concern about the manner in which the trial judge assessed the credibility of the witnesses and the evidence. The first arises from comments made by the trial judge after the appellant had been examined-in-chief but before she was cross-examined. After referring to the fact that the appellant had been called as the last defence witness, the trial judge said:

It makes her evidence useless or shall we say I would give very little weight to the accused's evidence.

While it is true that in alibi cases, calling the accused out of order, that is, other than as the first witness, may, and quite frequently does, diminish the weight to be accorded to her evidence, it does not necessarily do so and certainly does not destroy entirely the credibility of that evidence. An accused is entitled to have his or her evidence heard in full and assessed in conjunction with all of the other evidence presented at the trial and in the light of the submissions of counsel. It is quite clear here that the trial judge committed himself to an adverse assessment of the evidence of the appellant in isolation and before hearing the conclusion of her evidence and before hearing the submissions of counsel.

3. IMPEACHMENT

Professor McCormick has provided the outline for this section of the chapter:

> There are five main lines of attack upon the credibility of a witness. The first, and probably the most effective and most frequently employed, is an attack by proof that the witness on a previous occasion has made statements inconsistent with his present testimony. The second is an attack by a showing that the witness is biased on account of emotional influences such as kinship for one party or hostility to another, or motives of pecuniary interest, whether legitimate or corrupt. The third is an attack upon the character of the witness. The fourth is an attack by showing a defect of capacity in the witness to observe, remember or recount the matters testified about. The fifth is proof by other witnesses that material facts are otherwise than as testified to by the witness under attack.[212]

[handwritten in margin: 5 modes of impeachment]

---

212. McCormick, *Evidence* (2d ed.), p. 66.

(a) Prior Inconsistent Statements

Proof that the witness made an earlier inconsistent statement may be gained during cross-examination out of the mouth of the witness himself or, should the witness deny making the statement, by proof from other witnesses. Should the latter mode of contradiction prove necessary, the common law developed some limitations.

The case of *Attorney General v. Hitchcock*[213] illustrates the first limitation. The defendant was tried for a violation of the revenue laws. The Crown witness, who had testified to having observed the violation, was asked in cross-examination whether he had not earlier made a statement that the officers of the Crown had offered him a bribe to give that evidence. The witness denied having said so and defense counsel proposed to call another witness to testify that in fact such a statement was made.

An objection that such evidence was *collateral* and the witness could not thereby be contradicted was allowed and the evidence excluded. It was held that the ruling at trial was correct. Had the evidence been that the witness had made a statement that he had *accepted* a bribe the ruling would have been different as that would have reflected the possibility of bias. The Court saw testimonial factors, bias, interest, corruption, capacity to observe and remember and so forth, as matters "directly in issue before the Court" on which the witness may then be contradicted. Evidence of such matters are proveable independently of the contradiction; they have relevance apart from the simple fact of contradiction. There are then *two* classes of facts which are not collateral: facts which are relevant to a material issue, and facts relevant to a testimonial factor.[214]

Baron Rolfe explained:

> If we lived for a thousand years instead of about sixty or seventy, and every case were of sufficient importance, it might be possible, and perhaps proper, to throw a light on matters in which every possible question might be suggested, for the purpose of seeing by such means whether the whole was unfounded, or what portion of it was not, and to raise every possible inquiry as to the truth of the statements made. But I do not see how that could be; in fact, mankind find it to be impossible. Therefore some line must be drawn.[215]

The common law decided that considerations of economy of time, the danger of confusing the issues before the jury, and fairness to the witness who came prepared to testify to matters framed by the suit, demanded a rule which obliged the cross-examiner to be content with answers given to collateral matters.

The "collateral facts rule" is simple to state but often difficult in its application. The rule forbids the introduction of extrinsic evidence which contradicts a witness's testimonial assertion about collateral facts. A witness is summoned to

---

213. (1847), 154 E.R. 38 (Exch. Ct.).

214. See 3A Wigmore, *Evidence* (Chad. Rev.), ss. 1004-05, and see *R. v. Shewfelt* (1972), 6 C.C.C. (2d) 304 (B.C.C.A.). Compare another approach to the collateral facts rule which renders all facts collateral which are not relevant to a material issue but recognizes exceptions for bias, interest, etc., see Sopinka and Lederman, *The Law of Evidence in Civil Cases* (1974), pp. 511 and 289, following the lead of Phipson, *Evidence*, 11th ed., pp. 660-61.

215. *Supra*, note 213, at pp. 44-45.

court to testify concerning the material facts involved in the suit. In cross-examination the witness may be asked questions concerning the description given in chief, and may also be asked questions that impact solely on the witness's credibility. If the questions regarding credibility are collateral, the cross-examiner must accept the answers given, and cannot lead other witnesses to contradict the first witness on such matters.

The rule is difficult in its application because of the difficulty in determining what is "collateral". The *Hitchcock* case is the classic exposition. Professor McCormick paraphrased it:

> The classical approach is that facts which would have been independently provable regardless of the contradiction are not "collateral".[216]

McCormick goes on to describe three kinds of facts which meet this test. The first kind of facts which are independently provable are facts relevant to the substantive issues in the case. The second kind are not relevant to the substantive issues but are independently provable by extrinsic evidence to impeach the witness; among these facts are facts showing a bias or interest in the witness. The third kind of facts with respect to which the witness might be contradicted are facts about which the witness could not have been mistaken if he really saw what he claims to have seen; contradicting such a fact would "pull out the linchpin of the story."

Another approach is that of Professor Younger:

> We struggled with the problem in law school; we read an English case called Attorney General Hitchcock. You may not recall it because you may not have understood it. If you went back and read it today, you would not understand it. If you read it every day of your life until you die, you would not understand it; there is no meaning to it. The case is important only because it states what seems to be the prevailing rule with respect to the collateral/not collateral distinction: if the witness denies the prior inconsistent statement, the issue may or may not be collateral. Sometimes you may call another witness to prove the prior statement; sometimes you will not be able to call him. The real question is, when will it be collateral, and when will it not be collateral? The answer is simple: when it is important, it is not collateral. When it is unimportant, it is collateral. Ten thousand cases add up to that.[217]

R. v. KRAUSE
[1986] 2 S.C.R. 466, 54 C.R. (3d) 294, 29 C.C.C. (3d) 385

[Accused was questioned by police about a fatal stabbing and charged with murder. At the trial, on a voir dire, the answers of the appellant were held to be voluntary. The Crown made it clear that it did not intend to adduce the questions and answers in evidence-in-chief but that it would use them in cross-examination if the need arose. When appellant testified on his own behalf he gave evidence not only with respect to the circumstances surrounding the murder but also with respect of his involvement with the police during the murder investigation. Crown counsel cross-examined appellant about his statements to police and applied to call rebuttal evidence at the end of the defence case. The rebuttal evidence was to impeach the credit of appellant.]

---

216. McCormick, *Evidence*, 3d ed., p. 110.
217. *The Art of Cross-Examination* (1976).

McIntyre, J. (Dickson, C.J. and Beetz, Chouinard, Lamer, Wilson and Le Dain, JJ. concurring): —

. . . .

The appellant, in addition to giving the evidence summarized earlier, also gave evidence of his involvement with the police during the investigation of the murder. The points of significance for our purposes in this case may be summarized, as follows:

He swore that:

1. It seemed to be a regular thing for the police to come. . . .

2. The police had suggested to him that if he did not tell them where he had sent Hutter to look for marijuana, they were going to "kick in the doors" of known drug dealers and tell them that the appellant sent Hutter there looking for marijuana.

3. The police showed him a photograph of the deceased when they first interviewed him on March 26, 1981.

4. He had not told the police officers that he had never dealt with Hutter in a dope deal, but rather that the statement was taken out of context and that he had told them that he had never dealt with Hutter prior to January, 1981.

In cross-examination the appellant was questioned extensively regarding his statements to the police. It was put to him that he had told the officers that he had never dealt with Hutter in a dope deal when he had told him where to go.. . . .Crown counsel in cross-examining an accused are not limited to subjects which are strictly relevant to the essential issues in a case. Counsel are accorded a wide freedom in cross-examination which enable them to test and question the testimony of the witnesses and their credibility. Where something new emerges in cross-examination, which is new in the sense that the Crown had no chance to deal with it in its case-in-chief (i.e., there was no reason for the Crown to anticipate that the matter would arise), and where the matter is concerned with the merits of the case (i.e., it concerns an issue essential for the determination of the case) then the Crown may be allowed to call evidence in rebuttal. Where, however, the new matter is collateral, that is, not determinative of an issue arising in the pleadings or indictment or not relevant to matters which must be proved for the determination of the case, no rebuttal will be allowed. An early expression of this proposition is to be found in *Attorney-General v. Hitchcock*, [1847] 1 Ex. 91, 154 E.R. 38, and examples of the application of the principle may be found in *R. v. Cargill*, [1913] 2 K.B. 271 (Ct. Crim. App.)*; R. v. Hrechuk* (1951), 58 Man. R. 489 (C.A.); *R. v. Rafael* [1972] 3 O.R. 238 (Ont. C.A.); and *Latour v. The Queen*, [1978] 1 S.C.R. 361. This is known as the rule against rebuttal on collateral issues. Where it applies, Crown counsel may cross-examine the accused on the matters raised, but the Crown is bound by the answers given. This is not to say that the Crown or the trier of fact is bound to accept the answers as true. The answer is binding or final only in the sense that rebuttal evidence may not be called in contradiction. It follows then that the principal issue which arises on this branch of the case is whether the issues arising out of items 1, 2 and 3 are collateral in the sense described or relevant as going to a determinative issue in the case.

. . . .

There was one principal issue raised in this case, that is, did the appellant kill Hutter or did he not. Evidence bearing on that issue would be clearly material and admissible and in no way collateral. The evidence in respect of which rebuttal was allowed dealt in item 1 with the appellant's assertion that the police harassed him before his arrest. He said it seemed to be a regular thing for the police to come and "grab' him and take him down to the station. Item 2 dealt with further harassing and intimidating conduct on the part of the police, an alleged threat to put pressure on other drug dealers, telling them that the appellant had sent Hutter to them to get marijuana. Item 3 dealt with an allegation that during the course of the investigation the police had shown the appellant a gory photograph of Hutter's body. Were the points so raised material and relevant in deciding the issue — did the appellant kill Hutter?

. . . .

The evidence of the appellant reflected on the integrity of the police — though not on that of any police witness who gave evidence as part of the Crown's case-in-chief — but it did not touch upon the question of guilt or innocence. I am unable to say that the rebuttal evidence, which merely answered allegations made by the appellant and did not touch questions relating to his guilt or innocence, was relevant on that issue. The fact that evidence is introduced by the defence-in-chief does not make it a proper subject for rebuttal evidence unless it is otherwise relevant to a matter other than credibility: see *Cargill*, *supra*, and *Hretchuk*, *supra*. In my view, in agreement with Anderson J.A. in his dissent, the issues made the subject of rebuttal were collateral, as being neither material nor relevant on the issue of guilt or innocence. The Crown was entitled to cross-examine and did cross-examine the appellant on this matter. The Crown, however, was bound by the answers and was not entitled to call evidence in rebuttal.

The common law limitation with respect to collateral facts was legislated in England, with respect to statements, in the mid-19th century and that legislation was copied in all common law jurisdictions in Canada. For example, the Canada Evidence Act[218] provides:

> **10.**(1) On any trial a witness may be cross-examined as to previous statements that the witness made in writing, or that have been reduced to writing, or recorded on audio tape or video tape or otherwise, relative to the subject-matter of the case, without the writing being shown to the witness or the witness being given the opportunity to listen to the audio tape or view the video tape or otherwise take cognizance of the statements, but, if it is intended to contradict the witness, the witness' attention must, before the contradictory proof can be given, be called to those parts of the statement that are to be used for the purpose of so contradicting the witness, and the judge, at any time during the trial, may require the production of the writing or tape or other medium for inspection, and thereupon make such use of it for the purposes of the trial as the judge thinks fit.
>
> (2) A deposition of the witness, purporting to have been taken before a justice on the investigation of a criminal charge and to be signed by the witness and the justice, returned to and produced from the custody of the proper officer shall be presumed, in the absence of evidence to the contrary, to have been signed by the witness.
>
> **11.** Where a witness, on cross-examination as to a former statement made by him relative to the subject-matter of the case and inconsistent with his present testimony, does not distinctly admit that he did make the statement, proof may be given that he did in fact make it; but before that proof can be given the circumstances of the supposed statement, sufficient to designate the particular occasion, shall be mentioned to the witness, and he shall be asked whether or not he did make the statement.

---

218. R.S.C. 1985, c. C-5, ss. 10 and 11; 1994, c. 44, s. 86.

— refreshing memory technique

Cross-examination on a prior inconsistent statement can be a highly effective strategy to attack credibility. However it should be attempted with preparation and care. Most advocacy texts (see, for example Lee Stuesser, *An Advocacy Primer* (1990) pp.153-156) identify four separate steps:

1. Anchor the contradiction by first confirming with some precision the witnesses's evidence in chief (e.g. "You testified this morning that the car was black. Is that correct"?).

2. Confront him with the fact that the witness made an earlier statement (e.g. "Do you recall speaking to the officer on the day of the accident and giving a signed statement?" If the witness denies making any statement it would have to be proved by calling the officer.

3. Highlight the contradiction (e.g. "In the statement you said the lighting was bad and you could not see the colour of the vehicle". Or have the witness read that passage out loud.)

4. Decide on a strategy:

   (i) explore the contradiction to show this witness cannot be believed,

   (ii) leave that argument to counsel's final address or

   (iii) get the earlier statement admitted as the truth, either by getting the witness to adopt it as the truth or by making a successful *K.G.B.* application (to be considered later under Hearsay). Only in (iii) can the statement be entered as an exhibit.

Section 10 is concerned with written statements and section 11 with oral; contradictory proof is limited, as it was by the common law, to previous statements which are "relative to the subject-matter of the case."

By the common law,[219] impeachment by proof of a prior contradictory statement could only be done if preceded by a cross-examination of the witness as to the matter thereof. The common law requirement, now seen in the above legislation, saved time and energy, promoted fairness to the witness and eliminated surprise.

Another limitation imposed by the *Queen's Case* was described by Professor Wigmore as

a rule which for unsoundness of principle, impropriety of policy, and practical inconvenience in trials committed the most notable mistake that can be found among the rulings upon the present subject.[220]

The judges had advised in that case that a witness could not be asked any questions in cross-examination about previous written statements without first producing the writing to the witness and allowing him to read it. Acquainting the witness with the writing in advance was seen by the practising bar as severely blunting the effectiveness of cross-examination[221] and the rule was overturned

---

219. *Queen Caroline's Case* (1820), 129 E.R. 976 (H.L.).

220. 4 Wigmore, *Evidence* (Chad. Rev.), s. 1259, p. 610.

221. Wonderful examples of the effectiveness of cross-examination when unhampered by the rule are given in Wigmore, *ibid.*, at pp. 617-26.

by statute in England in 1854. The English Act was later copied in Canadian legislation: Canada Evidence Act, section 10, which is quoted above.

Counsel may cross-examine the witness as to whether the witness has ever described the incident differently without first alerting the witness that he has it in writing. The *Queen's Case* also required that the whole statement be read in if counsel used it in cross-examination. Notice that the legislation leaves it to the trial judge to determine in each case what use will be made of it.

When a witness at trial testifies that the car was black, while on an earlier occasion she had said it was white, there is clearly an inconsistency and the witness is open to impeachment by proof of the earlier statement. Suppose, however, that the witness who earlier stated the car was white now disclaims all knowledge of the car's colour. Professor McCormick states:

> A distinct but somewhat cognate notion is the view that if a party interrogates a witness about a fact which would be favourable to the examiner if true, and receives a reply which is merely negative in its effect on examiner's case, the examiner may not by extrinsic evidence prove that the first witness had earlier stated that the fact was true as desired by the inquirer. An affirmative answer would have been material and subject to be impeached by an inconsistent statement, but a negative answer is not damaging to the examiner, but merely disappointing, and may not be thus impeached. In this situation the policy involved is not the saving of time and confusion, as before, but the protection of the other party against the hearsay use by the jury of the previous statement.[222]

Is the situation different when the trial judge disbelieves the witness's present disclaimer?[223]

(i) *Impeaching One's Own Witness*

By a common law rule obscure in its origin,[224] a party was not permitted to impeach his own witness by attacks on his character. The rule may have been a lingering effect of the older form of trial by wager of law in which issues were decided by parties calling the requisite number of oath-helpers; these were partisan witnesses chosen by the party and it was unseemly for the party to later attack them should they disappoint him. As witnesses changed into their modern form the policy against impeachment was expressed in terms that a party calling a witness vouched for, or guaranteed his credit. Another, and perhaps better, theory advanced was that it was wrong to permit a party to coerce a certain story from his witness by holding, to the sure knowledge of the witness, ammunition in reserve for the destruction of the witness's character should he deviate. Buller, J. wrote in the 18th century:

> A party never shall be permitted to produce general evidence to discredit his own witness; for that would be to enable him to destroy the witness if he spoke against him, and to make him a good witness if he spoke for him, with the means in his hands of destroying his credit if he spoke against him. But if a witness prove

---

222. McCormick, *Evidence* (2d ed.), p. 71.

223. Compare views of Farris, C.J.C. and Martland, J. in *McInroy and Rouse v. R.* (1978), 42 C.C.C. (2d) 481, 494-95 (S.C.C.).

224. See 3A Wigmore, *Evidence* (Chad. Rev.), s. 896; Ladd, "Impeachment of One's Own Witness" (1936-37), 4 U. Chi. L. Rev. 69; and Bryant, "The Common Law Rule Against Impeaching One's Own Witness" (1982), 32 U.T. L.J. 412.

facts in a cause which make against the party who called him, yet the party may call other witnesses to prove that those facts were otherwise; for such facts are evidence in the cause, and the other witnesses are not called directly to discredit the first witness, but the impeachment of his credit is incidental and consequential only.[225]

In the early case of *Wright v. Beckett*[226] in 1833, the plaintiff's witness surprised counsel with evidence opposite to that expected. Over objection he was asked whether he recalled giving a contrary statement to plaintiff's solicitor and on receiving an evasive answer counsel called, again over objection, plaintiff's solicitor to testify to that fact. Denman, L.C.J. charged the jury that they might receive the statement by way of neutralizing the effect of the testimony given in court. On an application for a new trial the same was refused as the court was evenly divided. Denman, L.C.J. explained why the rule against impeaching one's own witness was inapplicable:

> I consider the meaning to be, that no party shall produce a witness whom he knows to be infamous, and whom he has, therefore, the means of discrediting by general evidence. No inference arises, that I may not prove my witness to state an untruth, when he surprises me by doing so, in direct opposition to what he had told me before. In this case, the discredit is consequential, and the evidence is not general but extremely particular, and subject to any explanation which the witness may be able to afford. . . .
>
>   . . . .
>
> . . . it is impossible to conceive a more frightful iniquity, than the triumph of falsehood and treachery in a witness, who pledges himself to depose to the truth when brought into Court, and, in the meantime, is persuaded to swear, when he appears, to a completely inconsistent story.[227]

Demonstrating capacity for error in the witness evidencing two contrary statements does not necessarily reflect on the witness's character — other testimonial factors, for example defects in memory or powers of observation, may account for it. If the rule were otherwise, rather than the witness being at the mercy of the counsel, the counsel would be at the mercy of the witness; he gives counsel one statement prior to trial causing him to be summoned and, with impunity, gives another story at the trial. Baron Bolland, on the other hand, believed that "great weight is due to the argument founded in the danger of collusion" and would foreclose such proof. For him, however, evidence which was directly relevant to the issue might be received though the same contradicted an earlier witness as then the discrediting of the witness was only a collateral effect. It was Bolland's view that prevailed in later cases.

A compromise between these two positions was effected by a statute, giving a discretion to the trial judge to permit contradiction by a previous statement when, in his opinion, the witness proved adverse. The general prohibition against impeachment by evidence of bad character was continued and, despite a legislative "blunder"[228] the statute has been interpreted to continue the common

---

225. Buller's *Nisi Prius*, p. 297, quoted in *Wright v. Beckett* (1833), 174 E.R. 143, 144 (C.C.P.).
226. *Ibid.*
227. *Ibid.*, at p. 144.
228. Per Cockburn, C.J.C. in *Greenough v. Eccles* (1859), 141 E.R. 315 at 321; the "blunder" has been cured in some of the provincial enactments. The "blunder" of course was that a demonstration of adversity should not be, and was not at common law, a pre-condition to contradicting the witness by other evidence.

law allowance of contradicting your own witness by other evidence about the facts. Copied in Canada, a typical provision is section 9(1) of the Canada Evidence Act:[229]

> 9.(1) A party producing a witness shall not be allowed to impeach his credit by general evidence of bad character, but if the witness, in the opinion of the court, proves adverse, such party may contradict him by other evidence, or, by leave of the court, may prove that the witness made at other times a statement inconsistent with his present testimony; but before the last mentioned proof can be given the circumstances of the supposed statement, sufficient to designate the particular occasion, shall be mentioned to the witness, and he shall be asked whether or not he did make the statement.

The only real problem remaining in interpreting this legislation was the meaning to be given to the word "adverse." The orthodox view in Canada equated "adverse" with "hostile" and demanded a demonstration, a showing, of that hostility in the stand; that was the same condition which the common law had earlier erected as a pre-condition to cross-examining one's own witness.[230] In *Hanes v. Wawanesa Mutual Insurance Co.*[231] the majority of the Ontario Court of Appeal interpreted the provincial counterpart of this legislation more liberally; "adverse" was taken to mean "opposed in interest" which would include "hostile" but of course be much broader. Alternatively, if "adverse" were to be confined to "hostile" it was an hostility of mind that need not be solely displayed in the stand. The evidence of adversity might come from the witness's demeanour, or it might be shown to the trial judge by evidence that the witness on an earlier occasion had made a contradictory statement. This is not, despite its critics, a circular position. By the *Hanes* case evidence of a previous contradictory statement would be led on a *voir dire* in the absence of the jury, the witness would be asked concerning it, and if, as a result, the trial judge determined that the witness was adverse he could permit the statement to be proved in evidence to the jury. Notice that the legislation here under review was concerned with the ability to impeach by extrinsic evidence. It was not legislation on counsel's right to cross-examine his own witness; that was the subject of the common law. If, pursuant to section 9(1), he was asked whether he made the statement and admitted the same, he could be questioned in regard to whether it was true and in that sense cross-examination as to the statement, that is asking the witness why he changed his mind, as opposed to cross-examination at large, was permitted.[232]

In 1969, section 9 of the Canada Evidence Act was amended to include subsection 2:

---

229. R.S.C. 1985, c. C-5, s. 9(1); 1994, c. 44, s. 85.
230. See, *e.g., Greenough v. Eccles, supra*, note 231; and see *R. v. McIntyre*, [1963] 2 C.C.C. 380 (N.S.S.C.): refusing to follow *Hanes v. Wawanesa Mutual Insurance Co.*, [1961] O.R. 495 (C.A.), reversed [1963] S.C.R. 154 in a criminal matter. Re courts insisting on a hostile demeanour being displayed, see *R. v. Koester* (1986), 70 A.R. 369 (C.A.).
231. [1961] O.R. 495 (C.A.); and see *Boland v. Globe & Mail Ltd.*, [1961] O.R. 712 (C.A.); *R. v. Gushue (No. 4)* (1975), 30 C.R.N.S. 178, 183 (Ont. Co. Ct.) per Graburn, J.
232. See MacKay, J.A. in *Hanes v. Wawanesa Mutual Insurance Co., supra*, note 230, at pp. 528 and 532-35. For other views on the permitted scope of cross-examination, see Webster, "Cross-Examination on a Finding of Adversity" (1995), 38 C.R. (4th) 35.

(2) Where the party producing a witness alleges that the witness made at other times a statement in writing, reduced to writing, or recorded on audio tape or video tape or otherwise, inconsistent with the witness' present testimony, the court may, without proof that the witness is (adverse,) grant leave to that party to cross-examine the witness as to the statement and the court may consider the cross-examination in determining whether in the opinion of the court the witness is adverse.[233]

The legislation was designed[234] to adopt the wisdom of the *Hanes* case into criminal matters and to thus allow the adversity, demanded by subsection 1, to be demonstrated not only by the witness's demeanour or bearing but also by cross-examination on an alleged prior contradictory statement. Notice that section 9(2) is confined to written statements.[235] The new legislation was interpreted,[236] however, as if it created a new and independent method for impeachment of one's own witness. The cross-examination mentioned in section 9(2) was intended to be in the absence of the jury since its purpose was to enable the court to determine whether the witness was adverse for the purposes of section 9(1). But given the judicial interpretation, it was noted:

> The cross-examination provided for in s. 9(2) must be in the presence of the jury. The purpose of that cross-examination is to attack the credibility of the witness in respect to the evidence already given. As the jury are the judges of credibility, it is obvious the cross-examination would be meaningless if conducted in their absence.[237]

Accordingly, the courts have worked out a code of procedure to be followed when section 9(2) is invoked:

> In my opinion, a procedure that would give effect to the legislation, and at the same time eliminate the possibility of any adverse effect upon the jury, would be as follows:
>
> (1) Counsel should advise the Court that he desires to make an application under s. 9(2) of the *Canada Evidence Act*.
> (2) When the Court is so advised, the Court should direct the jury to retire.
> (3) Upon retirement of the jury, counsel should advise the learned trial Judge of the particulars of the application and produce for him the alleged statement in writing, or the writing to which the statement has been reduced.
> (4) The learned trial Judge should read the statement, or writing, and determine whether, in fact, there is an inconsistency between such statement or writing and the evidence the witness has given in Court. If the learned trial Judge decides there is no inconsistency, then that ends the matter. If he finds there is an inconsistency, he should call upon counsel to prove the statement or writing.
> (5) Counsel should then prove the statement, or writing. This may be done by producing the statement or writing to the witness. If the witness admits the

---

233. Now R.S.C. 1985, c. C-5; 1994, c. 44, s. 85.
234. See legislative history noted in Delisle, "Witnesses — Competence and Credibility" (1978), 16 Osgoode Hall L. J. 337 at 346.
235. See *R. v. Carpenter* (1983), 31 C.R. (3d) 261, 266 (Ont. C.A.). See *R. v. Daniels*, [1984] N.W.T.R. 311 (S.C.), that a taped interview is not a statement reduced to writing.
236. *R. v. Milgaard* (1971), 2 C.C.C. (2d) 206 (Sask. C.A.); leave to appeal to S.C.C. refused (1971), 4 C.C.C. (2d) 566n (S.C.C.). The *Milgaard* view was specifically approved by the Supreme Court of Canada in *McInroy and Rouse v. R.* (1978), 42 C.C.C. (2d) 481.
237. *Ibid.*, at p. 222, per Culliton, C.J.S.

statement, or the statement reduced to writing, such proof would be sufficient. If the witness does not so admit, counsel then could provide the necessary proof by other evidence.

(6)   If the witness admits making the statement, counsel for the opposing party should have the right to cross-examine as to the circumstances under which the statement was made. A similar right to cross-examine should be granted if the statement is provided by other witnesses. It may be that he will be able to establish that there were circumstances which would render it improper for the learned trial Judge to permit the cross-examination, notwithstanding the apparent inconsistencies. The opposing counsel, too, should have the right to call evidence as to factors relevant to obtaining the statement, for the purpose of attempting to show that cross-examination should not be permitted.

(7)   The learned trial Judge should then decide whether or not he will permit the cross-examination. If so, the jury should be recalled.[238]

Crown counsel often have to resort to sections 9(1) and (2) in domestic assault prosecutions where the unfortunate reality is that principal witnesses often recant in whole or in part from previous incriminating statements. The current practice is to first try and coax the witness back by asking the witness to refresh her memory by reading her prior statement. If she persists in contradiction the usual practice is to use the above *Milgaard* procedure for a section 9(2) application. If that is granted, many judges now allow cross-examination at large. However some would require a further section 9(1) application and some even a declaration of hostility at common law before such cross-examination is permitted. The effect of such applications is that the Crown is granted permission to cross-examine their own witness on a prior inconsistent statement. The procedure is similar to any cross-examination under sections 10 and 11 but the strategy here is not to destroy credibility but rather to try to get the witness to adopt the earlier statement as the truth. A new option is to make a *K.G.B.* application: see later under hearsay, which turns on criteria of necessity and reliability.

PROBLEM

You are a Crown counsel prosecuting a serious domestic assault case before judge and jury. The committal to trial after a preliminary inquiry was on consent of the defence counsel. No evidence was heard. A week before the trial you interviewed the principal witness, Jane. She confirmed that on the day in question she was with the accused, Bob, in her apartment where the assault was alleged to have occurred. She admitted to having been in a common law relationship with him. Apart from that she was totally uncooperative and begged you to drop the charges as she is still with him and loves him. After a couple of minutes she walked out of the interview. You see this as a classic domestic assault case and wish to try for a conviction.

The arresting officer will testify that he answered a 911 call and arrived at the apartment to hear the sound of a fight, breaking glass and shouts. He broke the door down to find the complainant sobbing, clutching her side and with blood

---

238. *Ibid.* See *R. v. Williams* (1985), 44 C.R. (3d) 351 (Ont. C.A.); leave to appeal to S.C.C. refused 44 C.R. (3d) 351n where the finding of adversity can only be on the basis of a prior inconsistent statement, the *judge* must be satisfied that the statement was in fact made.

streaming down her face. The accused was sort of crouching over her and took a run at the officer. He was arrested but refused to answer any questions then or later. Another officer arrived on the scene and took Jane to hospital where she was treated for cracked ribs and received 10 stitches for a wound on her cheek. On her release from hospital she gave a signed statement to the second officer.

There were two earlier statements:

(a) an oral statement by Jane to the arresting officer on his entry to the apartment, "Please go easy on Bob. I love him and he did not mean to hit me that hard".

(b) a written statement signed by Jane to the second officer at the hospital in which Jane stated: "He got jealous when I spoke to another guy at a bar. When he is drunk he often gets moody. When we got back to the apartment he immediately picked up a large purple vase and smashed it over my head. He shouted at me "You bitch" and kicked me in the side. I am glad you guys rescued me. I am tired and I want to go to my mother's house".

You expect Jane to fully or partly recant from both statements at trial. Leaving aside the possibility of a *K.G.B.* application, plan your strategy in dealing with her as a witness in as much detail as you can.

(b) Bias

Witnesses are no longer barred from testifying because of some interest they may have in the outcome of the litigation. Feelings for or against a party, though making testimony less than impartial, are not grounds for exclusion. These matters, however, are fruitful areas of exploration for impeachment purposes. The types of facts from which partiality or hostility may be inferred are infinitely varied and little is to be gained by exploring those judicially recognized in the reports. The inference may be made from the witness's circumstances, for example a family or employment relationship with the party, or acts done by the witness, for example offering a bribe to another witness to testify falsely. Since such feelings betray emotional partiality which may impair the witness's testimonial qualifications, evidence of the same is not collateral and may be elicited in cross-examination of the witness *or* by extrinsic proof.[239]

If it is intended to impeach the witness by evidence of his prior conduct illustrating bias, it should be preceded by a cross-examination of the witness concerning the same.[240] If the witness admits his bias that should be the end of it.

---

239. See *A.G. v. Hitchcock* (1847), 154 E.R. 38 (Exch. Ct.). See an application of this in *R. v. Finnessey* (1906), 11 O.L.R. 338 (C.A.) and cases there cited.

240. Compare 3A Wigmore, *Evidence* (Chad. Rev.), s. 953 and McCormick, *Evidence*, 2d ed., p. 80. In the case of *A.G. v. Hitchcock, ibid*, Baron Alderson stated: "In [that case] it was held to be competent for the prisoner to shew that the witness had a spite against him. It was material to shew that the mind of the witness was not in a state of impartiality or equality towards the prisoner. The witness was asked the question in the first instance; but in that case I do not know that it might not have been proved independently of the

In *General Films Ltd. v. McElroy* [241] the Saskatchewan Court of Appeal noted:

> . . . it is . . . only when the witness had denied his bias or partiality that counsel is entitled to adduce evidence to contradict him. In this case the witness deVries had admitted enough upon his cross-examination to show that he was adversely affected towards the plaintiff. Thus he had acknowledged that he was acting for a rival concern, that he was doing all he could to take business away from the plaintiff, and that he was interested in the result of the case . . . Having thus sufficiently established the state of de Vries' mind and feelings towards the litigation, I do not think that plaintiff's counsel should have been allowed to question Widdifield about what de Vries had said at their interview. Such evidence was objectionable . . . because it raised collateral issues which tend to unduly complicate and prolong trials without adequate reason.

A recent recognition of our courts' preference for admitting the possibility of bias affecting credibility in preference to a blanket exclusion occurred in *R. v. Dikah*.[242] In that case the accused were charged with trafficking in cocaine. All charges involved alleged sales of cocaine to a paid police agent identified as Agent 21. The accused sought a stay alleging that the terms of Agent 21's agreement with the R.C.M.P. rendered any proceedings based on his alleged purchases of cocaine from the accused an abuse of process or a breach of the accused's rights under section 7 of the Charter. The agreement provided that the agent could not anticipate full payment of his fees unless the R.C.M.P. were able, through the agent's assistance, to successfully investigate some or all of the subjects identified. The trial judge decided that this paragraph of the agreement invited corruption and prejudiced the informant from the beginning by inviting him to put a spin on his evidence and fabricate it so that charges could be laid and he could pocket more money. The trial judge stayed the proceedings, relying on section 24(1) of the Charter. The Crown appealed successfully. Justice Labrosse wrote:

> To the extent that agents are paid to gather evidence, their testimony must be viewed by the trier of fact with a certain degree of suspicion. While an expectation of financial advantage may reduce the weight of a witness' testimony, it does not render such evidence inadmissible without more.
>
> . . . .
>
> The testimony of some paid agents may be untrustworthy but it cannot be said that, as a category, all paid agents cannot be trusted to tell the truth. To paraphrase Dickson J. [in *Vetrovec*], the construction of a universal rule singling out the testimony of paid police agents as unreliable would reduce the law of evidence to blind and empty formalism.[243]

---

question having been put to him, although, as I have before said, it is only just and reasonable that the question should be put."

241. [1939] 4 D.L.R. 543, 549 (Sask. C.A.).
242. (1994), 31 C.R. (4th) 105 (Ont. C.A.), affirmed (*sub nom. R. v. Naoufal*), [1994] 3 S.C.R. 1020.
243. *Ibid.*, at pp. 113-14.

(i) *Motives of Accused and Complainants*

In *R. v. S. (W.)*,[244] the accused was charged with sexual assault. The trial judge expressed concern as to a lack of motive in the complainant to lie. Finlayson, J.A., concurred in by Brooke and Austin, JJ.A., noted:

> The Crown on appeal conceded that it was improper for the Crown at trial to demand an explanation from the appellant as to why the complainant would make up what counsel referred to as " this horrendous lie". There is no onus on an accused person to explain away the complaints against him or her. . . . [The trial judge] subtly shifted the onus to the appellant, as accused, to give some explanation as to why the complainant would lie. Why would she bring all this grief upon herself and risk jeopardizing the close relationship between the two families if it were not true?[245]

The Court quoted with approval from *R. v. B. (R.W.)*,[246] where that court found that the trial judge had erred in placing too much weight on the complainant's apparent lack of motive to lie. Setting aside the conviction, Rowles, J.A., writing for the court, stated:

> It does not logically follow that because there is no apparent reason for a witness to lie, the witness must be telling the truth. Whether a witness has a motive to lie is one factor which may be considered in assessing the credibility of a witness, but it is not the only factor to be considered. Where, as here, the case for the Crown is wholly dependant upon the testimony of the complainant, it is essential that the credibility and reliability of the complainant's evidence be tested in the light of all of the other evidence presented.[247]

In *R. v. R. (A.)*,[248] the accused was charged with rape alleged to have been committed 20 years previously. The accused in cross-examination was asked if he had any theory or opinion as to why complainant would lie. The court decided that the question was improper. The court decided that the accused could, however, have been asked if he was aware of any facts which supported his assertion that complainant lying. Twaddle, J.A., for the court, wrote:

> The allegedly offending question asked by Crown counsel was this: "I'm compelled to ask because you say that J. was lying, do you have any theory or opinion as to why J. would lie about this?"
> The learned trial judge allowed this question to be asked. He said:
>
>> [T]hat's a perfectly proper question, the foundation has been laid and we have before us this man's evidence of the fact that his daughter lied when she gave her evidence this morning and now (Crown counsel) is asking, as he's entitled to, why would she lie.
>
> This ruling had the advantage of simplicity, but ignored both the form of the question and the irrelevance of the accused's opinion as to the veracity of the complainant.

---

244. (1994), 29 C.R. (4th) 143 (Ont. C.A.).
245. *Ibid.*, at p. 152. Accord *R. v. Vandenberghe* (1996), 96 C.C.C. (3d) 371 (Ont. C.A.) and *R. v. Prescod* [1996] O.J. No. 3714.
246. (1993), 40 W.A.C. 1 (B.C.C.A.).
247. *Ibid.*, at p. 9.
248. (1994), 88 C.C.C. (3d) 184 (Man. C.A.).

As a general rule, the opinion of an accused as to the veracity of a Crown witness is irrelevant. . . . Although the accused had already asserted his belief that the complainant was a liar when asked the question, the cross-examiner was wrong to pursue the issue by inviting the accused to advance a theory or opinion as to the complainant's motives. . . . [T]he question as it was framed was, to use the words of Hewart L.C.J. in *R. v. Baldwin* (1925), 18 Cr. App. R. 175 at p. 178, "really of the nature of an invitation to an argument".

Quite apart from the irrelevancy of the accused's opinion, this type of question is mischievous in that it tends to place an improper burden on the accused to account for another's conduct. The inability of the accused to explain a conflict between his evidence and that of a Crown witness is not, of itself, a ground for disbelieving the accused. Sometimes, the motivation of an untruthful witness is obscure even to the trained mind of a psychologist.[249]

In *R. v. F. (A.)*[250] the court condemned Crown counsel's cross-examination of the accused and his wife where it had been demanded of them why the complainant would make up such allegations. The Court felt that such questions suggested that there was some onus on the accused to provide a motive for the complainant to lie and thus the cross-examination had the effect of undermining the fundamental presumption of innocence:

This kind of examination undermines the fundamental principle of the presumption of innocence. This court has repeatedly held that this type of cross-examination is improper. We think it is unfortunate that Crown counsel persist in this kind of unfair questioning in the face of the many judgments of this court that such questioning is improper. . . . Unless and until Crown counsel stop this kind of improper and prejudicial cross-examination, this court will regrettably have to remit difficult and sensitive cases of this nature back for a new trial at great expense to the emotional well-being of the parties, not to mention the added burden to the administration of justice.[251]

In *R. v. B. (L.)*,[252] on a charge of sexual assault, the trial judge stated that in considering the credibility of the various witnesses he was entitled to take motive into consideration. The judge then stated that the complainant had no motive for testifying to an untruth but the accused "of course, has a motive for not telling the truth, he does not wish to be convicted". This was found to be error as it displaced the presumption of innocence. Arbour, J.A., for the court:

The statement made by the trial judge went beyond the common sense consideration that witnesses may have, to different degrees, an interest in the outcome of the proceedings, and that this is a factor, among others, which the trier of fact may take into account in assessing credibility.

There are many ways in which a witness may have an interest in the case which may be viewed as affecting the weight that the trier of fact may want to place on the witness's evidence. The interest may be pecuniary, as is often the case for both the plaintiff and the defendant in a civil case. In a criminal case, the accused has an obvious direct interest in the outcome of his or her trial, but other witnesses may have a large stake, be it an emotional, a financial or even a penal interest in the trial in which they are mere witnesses. The degree to which the presence of an interest

---

249. *Ibid.*, at pp. 188-89.
250. (1996), 1 C.R. (5th) 382 (Ont. C.A.).
251. *Ibid.*, at pp. 383-84.
252. (1993), 82 C.C.C. (3d) 189 (Ont. C.A.)

in the outcome may affect the assessment of the credibility of a witness varies with the circumstances of each case.

This court held in *R. v. Wood*, February 26, 1992 (unreported), that an accused's interest in the outcome of the trial may be a factor which a jury could legitimately take into account in determining the appropriate weight to place on the accused's testimony. The court referred to this process as common sense, and said that it was not rendered offensive by the trial judge referring to the accused having a "great interest" in the outcome of his trial. In *Wood*, the court observed that the trial judge was careful to warn the jury that, despite the accused's great interest in the outcome of his trial, "that doesn't mean that every accused person's evidence must be necessarily rejected because of an interest in the outcome". . . .

The impugned passage in the trial judge's reasons in this case, in my opinion, goes beyond the permissible consideration of the accused's interest in being acquitted, as one factor to be taken into account when weighing his testimony. It falls into the impermissible assumption that the accused will lie to secure his acquittal, simply because, as an accused, his interest in the outcome dictates that course of action. This flies in the face of the presumption of innocence and creates an almost insurmountable disadvantage for the accused. . . . If the trial judge comes to the conclusion that the accused did not tell the truth in his evidence, the accused's interest in securing his acquittal may be the most plausible explanation for the lie. The explanation for a lie, however, cannot be turned into an assumption that one will occur.[253]

(c) Character of Witness

(i) *Extrinsic Evidence*

In the early common law, a witness's credibility might be impeached by leading extrinsic evidence of his character. Witnesses who had personal knowledge[254] would give their opinion of the witness's character trait for veracity or mendacity. At times the witness would supplement his own knowledge with what he had heard about the witness,[255] but the real question was whether this witness would, based on his knowledge, believe the former witness on his oath.[256] In 1722 in *Layer's Case*[257] the defense called over twenty character witnesses to impeach the credit of the principal Crown witnesses, Lynch and Plunkett. As typical examinations we read:

Defence Counsel:	What character hath Mr. Plunkett?
Witness A:	I have known Mr. Plunkett several years, and that he was an idle, broken man, and a great liar, and not to be believed.
Counsel:	He would lye before and behind, I think you say?
Witness A:	Yes, he did.
Counsel:	Do you think he is to be credited, if he comes to give testimony against a person?
Witness A:	Upon my word I think he is not, but what he told me; because I have found him to lie backwards and forwards.

---

253. *Ibid.*, at pp. 190-91. Accord *R. v. Murray* (1997), 115 C.C.C. (3d) 225 (Ont. C.A.).
254. See *O'Connor's Trial* (1798), 27 Howell's State Trials 1, 32.
255. See variety in examples transcribed in *Layer's Case* (1722), 16 Howell's State Trials 94.
256. See precedents collected in 7 Wigmore, *Evidence* (Chad. Rev.), s. 1982, note 3.
257. *Supra*, note 255, at pp. 254, 247 and 253.

. . .

Defence Counsel:	Is (Lynch) accounted an honest man, or a knave?
Witness B:	I will not trust him for anything.
Counsel:	The wiser you. Is he a man to be credited? Can you believe what he says?
Witness B:	I think I would not believe him.
Counsel:	You are right.

. . .

Defence Counsel:	Is (Mr. Plunkett) a man as may be believed, even upon his oath, or not?
Witness C:	I must tell you, that I found him in so many mistakes about his own wife, that, by God, I would not take his word for a halfpenny. . . .
Counsel:	Go on, but don't swear by God anymore.

The witness's personal opinion was clearly receivable.

In later decisions we see the witness giving his opinion regarding credibility based on his knowledge of the earlier witness's reputation. For example, in *Mawson v. Hartsink* [258] the questions are

Have you the means of knowing what the general character of this witness was?

From such knowledge of his general character would you believe him on his oath?

In *R. v. Watson,*[259] however, the court held it to be satisfactory for the witness to simply state whether he would believe the witness on oath and that form of adducing evidence respecting credibility was later approved in *R. v. Brown & Hedley.*[260] Lord Goddard in *R. v. Gunewardene* [261] recognized the *Brown & Hedley* case as

direct authority that a witness called to impeach the credibility of previous witnesses can express an individual opinion and is not confined to giving evidence of the latter's reputation.

In *Masztalar v. Wiens,*[262] the plaintiff was injured in a motor-vehicle collision. In dismissing the action the trial judge said that the only reliable witness as to how the accident occurred was the defendant. After the close of the defence case, the plaintiff's counsel announced that he intended to call rebuttal evidence. He wished to call three witnesses who would testify that, based on their knowledge of the reputation of the defendant they would not believe him on his oath. The trial judge refused to allow counsel to call these witnesses, refused to allow counsel to make submissions on the issue, and refused to read the authorities which counsel asked him to consider. The Court of Appeal ordered a new trial. Justice Cumming, Locke, J.A. concurring, wrote:

---

258. (1802), 170 E.R. 656.
259. (1817), 2 Stark 116, 152.
260. (1867), L.R. 1 C.C.R. 70.
261. [1951] 2 K.B. 600 (C.C.A.). Compare *R. v. Rowton* (1865), 10 Cox C.C. 25, which surprised the profession (see 7 Wigmore, *Evidence* (Chad. Rev.), p. 210) by confining evidence of character of an *accused* to reputation and foreclosing opinion.
262. (1992), 2 C.P.C. (3d) 294 (B.C.C.A.).

From the very beginning of the modern law of evidence it has been permissible to call a witness to swear that a witness called for the opposing side cannot be believed on his oath. The practice is to ask the witness whether he knows the impugned witness's reputation for veracity and whether, from such knowledge, he would believe the impugned witness on oath.

. . . .

. . . This ancient rule has been much criticized. It was described by Lord Pearce as "not very logical," "not very useful," and by the editor of *Cross on Evidence*, 7th ed. (London: Butterworths) as "cumbersome," "anomalous," "unconvincing" and "very rare in practice" (at p. 319).

It is fair to say, as well, that although of long standing, it has not been adopted in any decision clearly binding on this Court. Nor is it one which need be applied in every case. On the contrary, it is one which should rarely be invoked. It need not be abolished, but it should be retained to be sparingly applied only in the rare case where the interests of justice require it.

. . . .

Undoubtedly, there is a discretion, on proper grounds, to exclude otherwise legally admissible evidence, but in this case I cannot conclude, the record being silent in this regard, that the learned trial judge exercised his discretion to reject the proffered evidence for any acceptable practical or policy reason recognized as appropriate in the passages from *Morris* and *Corbett* to which I have referred. All we can see, from the record before us, is that he rejected it out of hand.[263]

McEachern, C.J.B.C. offered:

[T]rial judges have at least a discretion not to permit this kind of evidence to become legal clutter in a modern courtroom. I do not think it will be wise or necessary to purport to abolish the rule entirely, for there may possibly be circumstances where a judge would allow such evidence to be called. An example might be where a witness has earned a well-known reputation for mendacity through a course of conduct or dealings over a considerable period of time and such witness may be sprung upon a plaintiff who has not been able to obtain adequate instruction for cross-examination.[264]

The rule appears to still exist, though subject to frequent criticism. Justice G.A. Martin, in *R. v. Gonzague*,[265] held that the trial judge had erred in refusing to allow a witness to express their opinion as to the lack of veracity of another witness; the trial judge believed such an opinion could only be expressed when the impeaching witness had knowledge of the other's reputation for veracity. Justice Martin decided that the impeaching witness was not so confined, but expressed the view that such evidence had little weight. Perhaps a sound exercise of discretion, as proposed by Chief Justice McEachern, to foreclose such evidence on the basis of normally trifling value in comparison to the time taken up, is the solution.

In *R. v. Clarke*[266] the Court modified the *Gonzague* position allowing that the first two questions as to whether the witness was aware of the previous witness's

263. *Ibid.*, at pp. 299-303.
264. *Ibid.*, at p. 308.
265. (1983), 34 C.R. (3d) 169 (Ont. C.A.).
266. (1998), 18 C.R. (5th) 219 (Ont. C.A.).

reputation for veracity and that it was bad, could, subject to discretion, be asked. However the third question, as to whether the witness would believe the previous witness on his oath, had little probative value in comparison to its prejudice and therefore should normally be disallowed.

(ii) *Evidence Elicited on Cross-examination*

While extrinsic evidence of specific instances of misconduct was excluded the common law permitted cross-examination of the witness himself regarding the same. The reasons forbidding extrinsic evidence were seen to be not applicable; confusion was minimal as it ended with the question and answer and the witness was not unfairly surprised as he needn't meet other witnesses.[267] In 1746 the Lord Chancellor noted:

> The other party is at liberty to cross-examine him either to the matter of fact concerning which he had been examined, *or any other matter whatsoever* that shall tend to impeach his credit or weaken his testimony.[268]

The only limitation appears to be counsel's imagination, the restraint of ethical considerations and the trial judge's discretion to protect a witness from harassment when the relevance of the questioning is regarded as minimal.[269] Protection for two particular classes of witnesses deserves closer examination: accused persons and complainants in sexual assault cases (see above, Chapter 4, Character Evidence).

(iii) *Accused as Witness*

The accused was rendered a competent witness in Canada in 1893. The statute which accomplished this contained no language which would afford him any protection from cross-examination over and above that available to the ordinary witness.[270] This was early recognized in the cases. In Quebec in 1893 Wurtele, J.A. stated:

> When a person on trial claims the right to give evidence on his own behalf, he comes under the ordinary rule as to cross-examination in criminal cases. He may be asked all questions pertinent to the issue, and cannot refuse to answer those which may implicate him. Under the new law, which protects him from the effect of his evidence in proceedings subsequently brought, but does not do so in the case in which the evidence is given, he may be convicted out of his own mouth. He cannot be compelled

---

267. 3A Wigmore, *Evidence* (Chad. Rev.), s. 981.
268. Hardwicke, L.C. in *Lord Lovat's Trial*, 18 Howell's State Trials 529, 651.
269. See, *e.g.*, the protection for a complainant in a rape prosecution in *Laliberte v. R.* (1877), 1 S.C.R. 117. Compare *R. v. Bradbury* (1973), 23 C.R.N.S. 293 (Ont. C.A.). See generally Stephen, *History of the Criminal Law* (1883), vol. 1, p. 433. Observe the breadth of cross-examination permitted in *R. v. Titus* (1983), 33 C.R. (3d) 17 (S.C.C.); *R. v. Gonzague* (1983), 34 C.R. (3d) 169 (Ont. C.A.) and *A.G. Que. v. Charron* (1984), 43 C.R. (3d) 240 (Que. S.C.).
270. Compare the Criminal Evidence Act, 1898, 61 & 62 Vict., c. 36, s. 1(*f*) in England which forbade cross-examination of the accused regarding his record unless it was admissible as relevant to a fact in issue, the accused led evidence of his own good character or sought to impugn the character of the prosecutor or his witnesses or he has given evidence against a co-accused.

to testify, but when he offers and gives his evidence he has to take the consequences.[271]

In Ontario in 1902, Osler, J.A. noted:

> The right, and if such it can be called, the privilege, of the accused now is to tender himself as a witness. When he does so he puts himself forward as a credible person, and except in so far as he may be shielded by some statutory protection, he is in the same situation as any other witness, as regards liability to and extent of cross-examination.[272]

Nevertheless, after some uncertainty,[273] some courts have recognized that the accused who chooses to become a witness exposes himself to a greater possibility of prejudice than the ordinary witness. In *R. v. Davison,*[274] Martin, J.A. described the accused's position:

> An accused who gives evidence has a dual character. As an accused he is protected by an underlying policy rule against the introduction of evidence by the prosecution tending to show that he is a person of bad character, subject, of course, to the recognized exceptions to that rule. As a witness, however, his credibility is subject to attack. If the position of an accused who gives evidence is assimilated in every respect to that of an ordinary witness he is not protected against cross-examination with respect to discreditable conduct and associations.
>
> If an accused could in every case be cross-examined with a view to showing that he is a professional criminal under the guise of an attack upon his credibility as a witness it would be virtually impossible for him to receive a fair trial on the specific charge upon which he is being tried. It is not realistic to assume that, ordinarily, the jury will be able to limit the effect of such a cross-examination to the issue of credibility in arriving at a verdict.
>
> In my view the policy rule which protects an accused against an attack upon his character lest it divert the jury from the issue which they are called upon to decide, namely, the guilt or innocence of the accused on the specific charge before the Court, is not wholly subordinated to the rule which permits an accused who elects to give evidence to be cross-examined on the issue of his credibility. In this area of the law, as in so many areas, a balance has been struck between competing interests, which endeavours so far as possible to recognize the purpose of both rules and does not give effect to one to the total exclusion of the other.
>
> Consequently, limitations are imposed with respect to the cross-examination of an accused which do not apply in the case of an ordinary witness.[275]

---

271. *R. v. Connors* (1893), 5 C.C.C. 70, 72 (Que. Q.B.).

272. *R. v. D'Aoust* (1902), 5 C.C.C. 407, 411 (C.A.).

273. See, *e.g.,* the judgment of Spence, J. in *Colpitts v. R.,* [1965] S.C.R. 739; and compare *Koufis v. R.,* [1941] S.C.R. 481 and *R. v. McLaughlan* (1974), 20 C.C.C. (2d) 59 (Ont. C.A.).

274. (1974), 20 C.C.C. (2d) 424 (Ont. C.A.). But compare *R. v. Bird* (1973), 13 C.C.C. (2d) 73 (Sask. C.A.).

275. *Ibid.,* at pp. 441-42. This excerpt from *Davison* was quoted and applied in *R. v. Lawrence* (1989), 52 C.C.C. (3d) 452 (Ont. C.A.); the court allowed the accused's appeal from conviction of manslaughter arising out of the death of a child where the Crown had cross-examined accused to show that he was a "biker," drug dealer and welfare cheat. And see *R. v. Geddes* (1979), 52 C.C.C. (2d) 230 (Man. C.A.):

> The accused was convicted on a charge of criminal fraud. At trial the accused testified on his own behalf. In the course of the cross-examination the accused was asked questions regarding previous convictions of fraud and particularly was asked whether

Accordingly it was held that while witnesses generally are open to cross-examination at large as to credit, an accused, aside from questions regarding previous convictions, should not be cross-examined with regard to previous misconduct or discreditable associations unrelated to the charge for the purpose of impeachment. The court, however, went on to add:

> Cross-examination, however, which is directly relevant to prove the falsity of the accused's evidence does not fall within the ban, notwithstanding that it may incidentally reflect upon the accused's character by disclosing discreditable conduct on his part.
>
>   . . . .
>
> Thus, if an accused found in possession of goods recently stolen were to give evidence that he had purchased them from X in good faith without knowing that they were stolen, it would not seem open to doubt that he could be cross-examined for the purpose of showing, if such were the fact, that he had been associated with X in the commission of prior thefts. Such cross-examination would be permissible as being directly relevant to the veracity of the accused's explanation.[276]

R. v. JONES
(1988), 66 C.R. (3d) 54, 44 C.C.C. (3d) 248 (Ont. C.A.)

[The accused was charged that he sexually assaulted an eight-year-old child. The appellant testified on his own behalf and denied assaulting the complainant. He relied upon an alibi.]

GOODMAN J.A.: —

                    . . . .

The appellant testified in his own behalf. At the very outset of his cross-examination the following questions were asked by counsel for the Crown and answers given by the appellant.

Q.   Have you ever been a paedophile in the past?

A.   No.

Q.   Have you ever received treatment as a paedophile?

A.   Yes, I did, once when I was incarcerated I received treatment after the sexual assaults I was convicted of.

---

he had testified on his own behalf in the trial resulting in the seven convictions of fraud. The Court of Appeal held that the latter questions were improper because the jury was being invited to conclude that if the accused was not believed by the judge in the prior case, he ought not to be believed by the jury in this case. Huband J.A. said (at 238):

> The question went beyond what is authorized by s. 12, and into an area which could only reflect on the character, rather than the credit of the accused. Crown counsel was attempting to convey the impression that, since the accused had not been believed at that trial, he should not be believed by the jury in the instant case.

276. *Ibid.*, at p. 444. See *R. v. Conway* (1985), 17 C.C.C. (3d) 480 (Ont. C.A.), denying the right to cross-examine regarding a conditional discharge. Compare *R. v. Cullen* (1989), 52 C.C.C. (3d) 459 (Ont. C.A.): a witness who is not an accused may be cross-examined with respect to the circumstances surrounding a charge which resulted in a conditional discharge. See also *R. v. Tadish* (1985), 18 C.C.C. (3d) 159 (Ont. C.A.), regarding the direction the trial judge must give respecting the jury's use of the previous record.

The appellant had not led any evidence of good character in his own behalf. He had not put his character in issue. It was improper, therefore, for the prosecution to cross-examine him with respect to matters relating to his bad character. No objection was made by defence counsel at the time the evidence was given.

Counsel for the Crown took the position on this appeal that no substantial wrong was occasioned by the impugned cross-examination in that the accused's answer that he was not a paedophile was uncontradicted and it was an insignificant portion of the evidence which was not mentioned by the Crown in argument nor by the trial judge in his reasons. Unfortunately it is not possible to know what weight, if any, the trial judge gave to this evidence standing alone or in conjunction with other evidence as to the issues of commission by the appellant of the acts of assault alleged or credibility of the appellant. In the absence of a statement by the trial judge that he disregarded this evidence in reaching his conclusions, this court is left with the trial judge's assertion quoted above that he found the accused guilty on the basis of all of the evidence.[277]

If the accused is seen as entitled to protection from questions concerning misconduct not resulting in a conviction, should he similarly be entitled to protection against questions regarding convictions for offences which have trifling probative value on the issue of credit? If an accused is charged with assault and testifies in chief that he was acting in self-defence, should the prosecution be entitled to ask him concerning his six previous convictions for assault? Should accused with previous records be obliged to forego the witness-stand? Should the trial judge have a discretion to foreclose such questioning?

By the early 18th century it seems settled that evidence of specific acts of the witness to affect credibility was not receivable.[278] It was regarded as necessary to exclude the same, for otherwise there would be confusion of the issues and unfair surprise to the witness. When counsel in *Rookwood's Trial* in 1696 proposed to lead evidence of a witness's previous actions which though criminal had not been prosecuted, it was said:

> Any man in the world may by this means be wounded in his reputation, and crimes laid to his charge that he never thought of, and he can have no opportunity of giving an answer to it, because he never imagined there would be any such objection. It is killing a man in his good name by a side-wound, against which he has no protection or defence.[279]

Defence counsel objected to what he perceived to be an anomaly:

> My lord, I cannot imagine why a man that has been guilty of any such crimes, and is not taken, should be of greater credit than a man that has been taken and punished. . . .
> I say it is the crime that renders a man infamous, and I do not know why a man that has had the good fortune not to be taken and punished for great crimes by him committed, should be in a better condition as to the credit of his testimony, than one that is taken and undergoes the punishment of law.[280]

---

277. And see *R. v. C. (W.)* (1990), 54 C.C.C. (3d) 37 (Ont. C.A.): on a charge of sexual assault the accused denied the incident. He was persistently cross-examined by the Crown who suggested he was a satanist and that members of that cult practised child abuse as part of their religion. The court decided the cross-examination created unfair prejudice which could not be cured by the proviso.

278. See *Layer's Case, supra*, note 255, at pp. 247 and 256, and *R. v. Rookwood* (1696), 13 Howell's State Trials 139, 209-11.

279. *Ibid.*, at p. 210, per the argument of the Attorney General accepted by the court.

280. *Ibid.*, at p. 211.

The anomaly disappears when we recognize that the evidence is excluded not by reason of a lack of relevance but because of the policy considerations of consumption of time, confusion of issues and fairness to the witness. If the witness has been previously convicted, proof of the same was permitted to impeach[281] as those dangers normally presented by collateral issues were not present; the previous judgment is conclusive, thus not open to dispute and the witness is not surprised. When witnesses who were previously incompetent to testify because of a conviction for an *infamous*[282] crime, were statutorily made competent[283] in 1843 in England, legislation was soon introduced, continuing the common law attitude, to provide for proof of their previous convictions for impeachment purposes.[284] The English Common Law Commissioners recommended in 1853 that cross-examination regarding previous convictions should be restricted to "offences which imply turpitude and want of probity, and more especially absence of veracity — as for instance, perjury, forgery, obtaining money or goods under false pretences and the like." Unfortunately, the legislation that was actually introduced, and which was later copied in Canada to become our section 12, provided no limitation on the nature of the crime to be inquired into. Our section 12 provides:

> 12.(1) A witness may be questioned as to whether the witness has been convicted of any offence, excluding any offence designated as a contravention under the Contraventions Act, but including such an offence where the conviction was entered after a trial on an indictment.
>
> (1.1) If the witness either denies the fact or refuses to answer, the opposite party may prove the conviction.
>
> (2) The conviction may be proved by producing
>
> (a) a certificate containing the substance and effect only, omitting the formal part, of the indictment and conviction, if it is for an indictable offence, or a copy of the summary conviction, if for an offence punishable on summary conviction, purporting to be signed by the clerk of the court or other officer having the custody of the records of the court in which the conviction, if on indictment, was had, or to which the conviction, if summary, was returned; and
>
> (b) proof of identity.[285]

The precursor of section 12 was first enacted at a time when the accused was not a competent witness at his trial. When the accused was made a

---

281. *Lord Castlemaine's Trial* (1680), 7 Howell's State Trials 1067, 1084 per Scroggs, L.C.J.

282. See 2 Wigmore, *Evidence* (Chad. Rev.), s. 520 for discussion of the meaning "infamous crimes."

283. In England in 1843, 6 & 7 Vict., c. 85. In Canada see Canada Evidence Act, R.S.C. 1985, c. C-5, s. 3, for an example of legislation removing such disqualification.

284. In the early 19th century there appears to be recognized in the cases a privilege in the witness to refuse to answer questions which might bring him into disgrace. While Professor Wigmore is unqualified (3A Wigmore, *Evidence* (Chad. Rev.), s. 980) that extrinsic testimony in the form of convictions was receivable to impeach, the issue is not entirely free from doubt. The Common Law Practice Commission in 1853 (quoted in 3A Wigmore, *Evidence* (Chad. Rev.), s. 984) described as the "better authorities" those which allowed the witness to refuse to answer or deny an earlier conviction and prohibited contradiction. Their "compromise" (Common Law Procedures Act, 1854, c. 125) would preserve the privilege but allow contradictory proof.

285. First enacted in 1869: An Act Respecting Procedure in Criminal Cases, 1869, S.C. 32 &

competent witness in England, in 1898, they recognized that the earlier legislation could affect him very differently than other witnesses. They recognized that a jury would find it difficult to confine their use of the previous record to credibility and, despite any limiting instructions from the judge, the jury might use the fact of the previous conviction as indicative of the accused's character and as directly relevant to whether he did the deed alleged at his present trial. That use was prohibited by the rule of evidence which forbade the introduction of the accused's character save in particularly limited instances. The possibility of this prejudicial impact increased dramatically, of course, if the previous conviction resembled the matter at hand. The legislation which made the accused a competent witness in England addressed this concern and provided that an accused who chose to become a witness could not be asked as to his previous record unless the accused had led evidence of his own good character or attacked the character of the prosecution's witnesses; see Criminal Evidence Act, 1898, 61 & 62 Vict., c. 36, section 1. When Canada made the accused a competent witness at his trial, Canada Evidence Act, S.C. 1892, c. 31, section 4, the legislators displayed no similar foresight and no such modification of the existing law occurred.

In Chapter 3 we saw the Supreme Court of Canada recognize in the *Corbett* decision that there was a discretion. The exercise of the discretion has been uneven and many, if not most, trial judges, unfortunately, will not exclude such questioning but there have been exceptions.

In *R. v. P. (G.F.)*,[286] the accused was charged that he had committed sexual assault on his daughter between January 1985 and July 1988. In 1976 the accused had been convicted of two counts of rape and two counts of wounding with intent. Before any evidence was called the accused applied for an order excluding evidence of his two previous rape convictions. The trial judge dismissed the motion without prejudice to it being renewed later. The application was renewed at the close of the Crown's case. The trial judge ruled that keeping relevant evidence from the trier of fact should be avoided except as a last resort and dismissed the application. The Ontario Court of Appeal noted that the decision to be made on a *Corbett* application is a matter of discretion and an appellate court should not interfere in the absence of clear error. In this case the trial judge believed that exclusion of the record should only be granted as a last resort and this was error. The order sought should have been granted. The court also noted that the timing of such an application would depend upon the circumstances of each case but in most cases it should not be dealt with until the Crown's case has concluded.

In *R. v. Bailey*,[287] the defence applied for an order to prohibit cross-examination of the accused on his record. Specifically the defence wanted the word "sexual" deleted from any reference to the accused's previous conviction

---

33 Vict., c. 29, s. 65. For a provincial counterpart see s. 22, Ontario Evidence Act, R.S.O. 1980, c. 145. Concerning the type of offence relevant to credibility compare *Street v. Guelph*, [1965] 2 C.C.C. 215 (Ont. H.C.) and *Clarke v. Holdsworth* (1967), 62 W.W.R. 1 (B.C.S.C.). See also *Morris v. R.* (1979), 6 C.R. (3d) 36 (S.C.C.) re juvenile offences; *R. v. Stratton* (1978), 42 C.C.C. (2d) 449 (Ont. C.A.) re foreign convictions; and *R. v. Boyce* (1974), 28 C.R.N.S. 336 (Ont. C.A.) re ability to ask witness regarding penalty.

286. (1994), 29 C.R. (4th) 315 (Ont. C.A.).
287. (1993), 22 C.R. (4th) 65 (Ont. Gen. Div.).

for sexual assault with a weapon. Justice Zelinski granted the application as a matter of common sense. He wrote:

> If I were about to enter into a transaction . . . the first thing that I would like to know, referable to the person I was dealing with, is whether or not that person had engaged in the very type of activity I was concerned about. This, of course, identifies as propensity. I think even more than wanting to know whether someone has passed a bad cheque or cheated in cards, one would like to know whether or not that person has done something of the very nature as the matter you are concerned with, again, propensity.
>
> . . . .
>
> Of course, in the exercise of discretion as indicated by La Forest J., the more similar the offence is to the subject matter of the charge, the better the reason, on principles of fairness, for excluding it. As he indicated, while it is commonplace to suggest that jurors are capable of understanding a direction that they must only use a prior conviction on issues of credibility, the likelihood is, based on the studies that he referred to, that this will not be the case and this should be realized.
>
> . . . .
>
> I specifically challenged [the Crown] on the fact that her objection to the deletion of the word "sexual" is nothing more than a desire on the part of the Crown to save that word because of its potential identification with the offence before the jury (notwithstanding the charge I must give them, that evidence that a person who has done this or similar, previously, as proven by a conviction, cannot be used as evidence that he is likely to be at it again).[288]

In *R. v. Saroya*[289] the accused appealed from his conviction of assault. He admitted hitting the victim on the head with a bottle of wine but he testified that he did so in order to break up a fight between the victim and another man. One of the issues was with respect to the disclosure of his criminal record which included a conviction for attempted murder. In the Court below, the trial judge in refusing the accused's request for protection against cross-examination on his criminal record, decided:

> In the case at bar the accused has one prior conviction in 1988 for attempt murder. A man wears the chains he forges in life. A conviction is part of the accused's persona that he puts before the jury when he chooses to testify. I have considered all the factors pertaining to the exercise of discretion as set out in *Corbett*. In my view the accused would not be prejudiced by the admission of the prior conviction and in the interests of justice it should he admitted in evidence.[290]

The Court of Appeal decided:

> The balancing exercise is a particularly difficult one in this case. The relevant factors point to both probative value and prejudice. The accused's prior record discloses a conviction for attempted murder in 1988, some four years prior to the trial at issue here. That was his only prior conviction. A conviction for attempted murder cannot be dismissed as having little probative value on the credibility of a witness. Although it is not a so-called offence of dishonesty, which may be probative of deception, attempted murder is such a serious offence that, in itself, it may be taken to indicate

---

288. *Ibid.*, at pp. 67-68.
289. (1992), 18 C.R. (4th) 198 (Ont. Gen. Div.); affirmed (1994), 76 O.A.C. 25 (C.A.).
290. *Ibid.*, at p. 201 (C.R.).

that the prospect of a conviction for perjury is unlikely to keep the witness in line. More significantly, it would be open to a jury to find, on all the relevant evidence, that the witness is unlikely to have more respect for the truth than he has shown for human life.

On the other hand, of course, a conviction for attempted murder shows a capacity for violence against the person, and, on a charge of aggravated assault and assault causing bodily harm invites an inference of guilt through disposition. Not only is the offence for which the appellant was previously convicted very similar to the one that he was facing at trial, but, being of a more serious nature, it would logically support an inference that if the appellant once attempted to kill someone, he would not likely hesitate to commit the types of assaults that he was alleged to have committed.

. . . .

In the end, guidance comes from the *Corbett* decision. In that case, the majority of the Supreme Court ruled in favour of inclusion, in conformity with s. 12 of the *Canada Evidence Act*, of a prior murder conviction when the accused was facing a charge of first degree murder. Although the potential for prejudice was recognized as significant, the Supreme Court held that the potential prejudice could be displaced by a proper instruction to the jury about the impermissible use of the prior record. It is conceded that such proper instruction was given in the present case. As in *Corbett*, we are of the opinion that the deletion of the appellant's record would leave the jury with incomplete and therefore incorrect information about his credibility as a witness. To deprive the jury of that information in the present case, would hinder the jury's ability to correctly appreciate the facts. On balance, we think that the probative value of the appellant's criminal record of the question of his credibility as a witness outweighs the potential risk that the jury might use that prior conviction as evidence that the appellant is the type of person likely to have committed the offences with which he was charged.[291]

In *R. v. Brand*[292] the accused appealed from his conviction by a jury on a charge of trafficking in cocaine. The accused had made a *Corbett* application, submitting that the trial judge should edit the accused's record of criminal convictions. The accused had a very lengthy record which included convictions for crimes of dishonesty but concluded with three convictions for trafficking in narcotics. The trial judge declined to do edit the record holding that such was an exceptional departure from the general rule which should only be invoked when there is some exceptional unfairness. The Court of Appeal decided:

> He was obliged to weigh and balance the risks for and against exclusion, bearing in mind the evidentiary value of previous convictions admitted pursuant to s. 12, and the fair trial of the accused. The three convictions in question had no probative value with respect to the appellant's credibility but were highly prejudicial. On the other hand, the balance of the record included offences that reflected on credibility. Viewed in this way, we think on the facts, this was a proper case to exclude the three convictions for trafficking. To do so would ensure that the jury had sufficiently complete and correct information about the appellant's credibility as a witness and would effectively remove the possibility of any unfairness by the introduction of the evidence in issue.[293]

---

291. *Ibid.*, at p. 28 (O.A.C.).
292. (1995), 40 C.R. (4th) 137 (Ont. C.A.).
293. *Ibid.*, at p. 140.

R. v. UNDERWOOD
[1998] 1 S.C.R. 77, 12 C.R. (5th) 241, 121 C.C.C. (3d) 117

[The accused was charged with first degree murder. After the Crown closed its case, his counsel made a Corbett application to have the accused's lengthy criminal record excluded. The trial judge did not make a ruling at that time, but rather indicated that he would prefer to wait until the accused had given his testimony in chief. The accused elected not to testify. He was later convicted and his conviction was upheld by the Court of Appeal. On further appeal a new trial was ordered.]

The judgment of the Court was delivered by LAMER C.J.C.:—

. . . .

The question which the Court must answer in this case is whether it is an error of law to refuse to make a ruling on a *Corbett* application before the accused has elected to testify and been examined in chief. On the one hand, it would be very undesirable to force the trial judge to make a decision without all the relevant information. On the other hand, the accused must have an opportunity to make an informed decision whether to testify and, accordingly, should know as much as possible about the consequences of that decision in advance of having to make it. A balance must be struck between these two necessities. However, the balance must reflect that the ultimate goal of the procedural and substantive protections in the criminal justice system are to ensure that trials are scrupulously fair. Our criminal process is based upon the principle that before the accused calls evidence in his own defence, he must have knowledge of the case to be met. The extent to which his criminal record will be admissible against him will encompass part of that case. In this context, the case-to-meet principle suggests that the accused should have a right to make a Corbett application, and to know its outcome at the close of the Crown's case. It would be manifestly unfair to force an accused to engage in what the appellant describes as "russian roulette", or what Professor Delisle, in an annotation to *R. v. Hoffman* (1994), 32 C.R. (4th) 396, at p. 398, calls "blind man's bluff".

Although fairness requires that the ruling be made no later than the close of the Crown's case, there is always the possibility that the defence evidence will influence that trial judge's prior evaluation of the probative value and prejudicial effect of the criminal record. There are various ways of dealing with this problem. One is the possibility of making a preliminary ruling, subject to reconsideration if necessary. [But] imagine the possible unfairness that would arise if the accused takes the stand in reliance on a ruling that some or all of his prior convictions will be excluded, and that ruling is subsequently reversed.

In my view, the situation can be resolved by holding a voir dire before the defence opens its case. In this voir dire, the defence will reveal the evidence which it intends to call, either through calling witnesses, or through agreed statements of fact. The trial judge can then consider the factors set out in Corbett (the nature of the previous convictions, the time since the previous convictions, and any attacks made on the credibility of Crown witnesses) in the context of the defence evidence, and make a final ruling on the Corbett application.

I would emphasize that the purpose of this voir dire is not "defence disclosure". It creates no independent rights in the Crown, and, therefore should not be treated as an excuse for the Crown to deeply probe the case for the defence, as the defence is entitled to do to the Crown's case at a preliminary inquiry. The point to to provide the trial judge with the information he or she needs to make an informed decision, but the Crown has no right to require more than that. There may even be cases in which the trial judge believes he or she has sufficient information to make a decision without such disclosure, such as where the nature of the defence is fairly clear or has otherwise been disclosed (e.g. an alibi), or where the outcome of the application is readily apparent without this information. In those cases, disclosure need not be given.

. . . .

In summary, a *Corbett* application should be made after the close of the Crown's case. If the trial judge believes it to be necessary, a voir dire should be held in which the defence discloses what evidence it intends to call, so he or she can make a fully informed ruling on the application. This ruling may be subject to modification if the defence evidence departs significantly from what was disclosed. In this case, the trial judge refused to rule until after the appellant had testified, and in so doing, he erred.

In *Hewson v. R.*,[294] the court decided, 5:4, that an accused could be questioned as to a previous conviction though at the time of the questioning the conviction was subject to a pending appeal. In *Titus v. R.*,[295] the accused had been convicted of murder. The court granted him a new trial because the trial judge had precluded cross-examination by the defence of a Crown witness with respect to an outstanding murder charge preferred against that witness by the same police department that had laid the murder charge against the accused. The court decided that cross-examination of a Crown witness concerning an outstanding indictment against that witness was proper and admissible for the purpose of showing a possible motivation to seek favour with the prosecution. In *R. v. Danson*,[296] the Crown cross-examined the accused as to an incident where he was found guilty of assault and given a conditional discharge. The trial judge treated the discharge as a conviction. The conviction was quashed. The court noted that an accused unlike an ordinary witness, cannot be cross-examined with respect to discreditable acts unrelated to the charge on the issue of credibility unless he puts his character in issue or is examined pursuant to section 12 ; an adjudication of guilt followed by the granting of a discharge is not a conviction. In *Morris v. R.*,[297] the accused was found guilty on a charge of breaking and entering with intent. He appealed on the ground that the trial judge erred by allowing cross-examination of the accused as to his having been having been found guilty, under the Juvenile Delinquents Act, of offences, under the Criminal Code. The Supreme Court, 5:4, dismissed his appeal, saying the word "offence" as used in section 12 includes a delinquency consisting in a violation of the Criminal Code which is enforceable under the Juvenile Delinquents Act, and a finding of delinquency under that Act was equivalent to a conviction within the meaning of section 12. In *R. v. Scott*,[298] counsel for the accused was permitted to cross-examine the 13-year-old complainant on prior convictions as a juvenile delinquent and a young offender and on pending charges. The court decided that section 38 of the Young Offenders Act providing that no person shall "publish" any report of an offence committed or alleged to have been committed by a young person did not prevent such a cross-examination.

(d) Defects in Capacity of Witness

The cross-examiner is always entitled, subject to the trial judge's discretion, to attempt impeachment by questioning the witness's general capacity to observe, recollect and communicate, and his particular ability in the case under review.

---

294. [1979] 2 S.C.R. 82.
295. [1983] 1 S.C.R. 259.
296. (1982), 35 O.R. (2d) 777 (C.A.).
297. [1979] 1 S.C.R. 405.
298. (1984), 16 C.C.C. (3d) 17 (Ont. G.S.P.).

At times the witness may confess the possibility of error. In other instances the very incredibility of a fact deposed to on cross-examination will disclose such obvious error on one point as to cast doubt on the rest of his evidence. The witness's capacities may also be tested in front of the trier of fact by means of an experiment.

May extrinsic evidence by introduced to prove the incapacity alleged?

If the witness testifies that he observed the incident under review clearly because there was then a full moon, then obviously his opponent should be able to introduce contradictory evidence of the moon's illumination on the evening in question to demonstrate that the witness's opportunity for observation was less than full. But if the extrinsic evidence is previous specific instances of error by the witness, should we analogize to specific instances of misconduct and foreclose, or to evidence of bias and receive? If we seek to test the memory of the witness by asking him questions concerning matters which occurred at the same time as the material event, though unconnected with it, can we lead extrinsic evidence to contradict? May we seek to establish by extrinsic evidence that the witness misperceived other matters at other times unconnected with the material issue? Can we enunciate a clear rule or can we do more than simply rest the decision with the discretion of the trial judge who can weigh the probative value towards impeachment against consumption of time, confusion of issues and fairness to the witness?

Is the situation different when the extrinsic evidence on capacity is medical evidence? May a medical witness give his opinion on veracity and state the reasons for his belief? In *R. v. Toohey*[299] the House of Lords analyzing that problem noted:

> This unreliability may have two aspects either separate from one another or acting jointly to create confusion. The witness may, through his mental trouble, derive a fanciful or untrue picture from events while they are actually occurring, or he may have a fanciful or untrue recollection of them which distorts his evidence at the time when he is giving it.
>
> The only general principles which can be derived from the older cases are these. On the one hand, the courts have sought to prevent juries from being beguiled by the evidence of witnesses who could be shown to be, through defect of character, wholly unworthy of belief. On the other hand, however, they have sought to prevent the trial of a case becoming clogged with a number of side issues, such as might arise if there could be an investigation of matters which had no relevance to the issue save in so far as they tended to show the veracity or falsity of the witness who was giving evidence which *was* relevant to the issue. Many controversies which might thus obliquely throw some light on the issues must in practice be discarded because there is not an infinity of time, money and mental comprehension available to make use of them.

and concluded:

---

299. [1965] A.C. 595, 607-08 (H.L.) per Lord Pearce. See Moore, "Note — The Admissibility of Medical Evidence to Impugn the Reliability of a Witness," [1965] Camb. L.J. 176 and "Note, Psychiatric Evaluation of the Mentally Abnormal Witness" (1949-50), 59 Yale L.J. 1324. See also Hoski, "Use of Psychiatric Evidence as to Credibility of Witnesses in Criminal Trials" (1976), 3 Queen's L.J. 40. For Canadian Cases following *Toohey* see *R. v. Dietrich* (1970), 1 C.C.C. (2d) 49 (Ont. C.A.) and *R. v. Hawke* (1975), 22 C.C.C. (2d) 19 (Ont. C.A.). Compare *R. v. Steinberg*, [1931] O.R. 222 (C.A.).

Human evidence shares the frailties of those who give it. It is subject to many cross-currents such as partiality, prejudice, self-interest and, above all, imagination and inaccuracy. Those are matters with which the jury, helped by cross-examination and common sense, must do their best. But when a witness through physical (in which I include mental) disease or abnormality is not capable of giving a true or reliable account to the jury, it must surely be allowable for medical science to reveal this vital hidden fact to them. If a witness purported to give evidence of something which he believed that he had seen at a distance of 50 yards, it must surely be possible to call the evidence of an oculist to the effect that the witness could not possibly see anything at a greater distance than 20 yards, or the evidence of a surgeon who had removed a cataract from which the witness was suffering at the material time and which would have prevented him from seeing what he thought he saw. So, too, must it be allowable to call medical evidence of mental illness which makes a witness incapable of giving reliable evidence, whether through the existence of delusions or otherwise.

4. SUPPORTING CREDIBILITY

(a) General Rule Prohibiting

Speaking generally, evidence in support of credibility is not receivable unless and until credibility has been attacked. When the witness's character for truthfulness has been impeached by evidence of general reputation, opinion or specific instances of misconduct, the witness may be rehabilitated by evidence of good character, but not before.[300] It is not that the evidence of good character is irrelevant but rather that

> there is no reason why time should be spent in proving that which may be assumed to exist. Every witness may be assumed to be of normal moral character for veracity, just as he is assumed to be of normal sanity. Good character, therefore, in his support is excluded *until his character is brought in question* and it thus becomes worthwhile to deny that his character is bad.[301]

So too, if it is offered to show that the witness has previously made statements consistent with his present testimony:

> ... when the witness has merely testified on direct examination, without any impeachment, proof of consistent statements is unnecessary and valueless. The witness is not helped by it; for, even if it is an improbable or untrustworthy story, it is not made more probable or more trustworthy by any number of repetitions of it. Such evidence would ordinarily be cumbersome to the trial and is ordinarily rejected.[302]

Again, it is not irrelevance to credibility that dictates rejection, but superfluity and consumption of time as the matter is simply not in issue. At times it is said that a prior consistent statement is excluded as in its self-serving nature resides the danger of fabrication as the witness is tempted to manufacture evidence for

---

300. See *R. v. Kyselka* (1962), 133 C.C.C. 103 (Ont. C.A.) rejecting psychiatric opinion in support of credibility. See also *R. v. Burkart*, [1965] 3 C.C.C. 210 (Sask. C.A.).

301. 4 Wigmore, *Evidence* (Chad. Rev.), s. 1104 accepted in *R. v. Clarke* (1981), 63 C.C.C. (2d) 224, 233 (Alta. C.A.). See also *R. v. Martin* (1980), 53 C.C.C. (2d) 425 (Ont. C.A.).

302. 4 Wigmore, *Evidence* (Chad. Rev.), s. 1124; note change from the 3d edition.

himself,[303] but the better view is as above, or, as seen in the language of the Privy Council:

> The purpose of such evidence of a witness's previous statements is and can only be to support his credit, when his veracity has been impugned, by showing a consistency in his account which adds some probative value to his evidence in the box. Generally speaking, as is well known, such confirmatory evidence is not admissible, the reason presumably being that all trials, civil and criminal, must be conducted with an effort to concentrate evidence on what is capable of being cogent and . . . it does not help to support the evidence of a witness who is the accused person to know that he has frequently told other persons before the trial what his defence was. *Evidence to that effect is, therefore, in a proper sense immaterial.*[304] [Emphasis added.]

In *Cross on Evidence*,[305] the rule is so justified:

> [Sometimes] the reason given for the ban (sometimes loosely described as "the rule against narrative" or "the rule against self-corroboration") is the ease with which evidence of this nature can be manufactured. . . . A more convincing reason is that in an ordinary case, the evidence would be at least superfluous, for the assertions of a witness are to be regarded in general as true, until there is some particular reason for impeaching them as false. [Emphasis added.]

R. v. KYSELKA
(1962), 133 C.C.C. 103 (Ont. C.A.)

The judgment of the Court was delivered by

PORTER, C.J.O.:—This was an appeal by the three accused from the judgment of the Honourable Mr. Justice Wilson dated September 20, 1961, following a trial with a jury held at the Town of Barrie, whereby the accused were convicted of rape. At the conclusion of the argument before us we allowed the appeal, quashed the convictions, and directed a new trial, for reasons to be delivered later.

---

303. See, *e.g.*, Sopinka and Lederman, *Evidence in Civil Cases* (1974), p. 264 and cases there cited. And see Eyre, C.J. in *Trial of Thomas Hardy* (1794), 24 Howell's State Trials 199: Declarations are evidence against a prisoner and are not evidence for him, because the presumption upon which declarations are evidence is, that no man would declare anything against himself, unless it were true; but that every man, if he was in a difficulty, or in the view to any difficulty, would make declarations for himself. Those declarations, if offered as evidence, would be offered, therefore, upon no ground which entitled to them to credit. That is the general rule.

304. *Fox v. Gen. Medical Council*, [1960] 3 All E.R. 225, 230. See also Cross, *Evidence* (5th ed.), p. 236. In *Notes to Pothier on Obligations*, quoted in *R. v. Giraldi* (1975), 28 C.C.C. (2d) 248 (B.C.C.A.), Evans notes: "In an ordinary case the evidence would be at least superfluous, for the assertions of a witness are to be regarded in general as true until there is some particular reason for impeaching them as false; which reason may be repelled by circumstances . . . either from the inherent nature and complexion of the evidence itself, or it may be indicated by the imputations actually thrown out in cross-examination or otherwise, by the opposite party." But see Martin, J.A., in *R. v. Campbell* (1977), 38 C.C.C. (2d) 6, 18 (Ont. C.A.): "The narration by a witness of earlier statements made to other persons out of Court appears to be excluded . . . because of the general lack of probative value of such evidence, save in certain circumstances, in support of the credibility of the witness."

305. Tapper, ed., 7th ed (London: Butterworths, 1990), p. 281.

The complainant was 16 years of age and mentally retarded. She lived with her parents in the Town of Barrie. The incidents of which she complained occurred on August 22, 1961, at a place in the country outside the town. The three accused, who were complete strangers to her, had driven her to this place in an automobile.

. . . .

Objection was taken by counsel for the accused on this appeal that certain evidence given by Dr. Cardwell was inadmissible. Dr. Cardwell is a qualified psychiatrist, who has worked for the Department of Health in mental hospitals for 31 years, and is now retired. He was called as a witness by the Crown immediately after the complainant gave her evidence. He had examined the complainant as to her mental capacity. The relevant portions of his evidence are as follows:

A. The first time I saw Margaret was on September 7th at my home. A constable brought her, accompanied by her mother. Her mother and she and I sat and talked together. Q. Did you form any opinion, or make any tests at that time? A. Well, this girl reached Grade 6 at fifteen after having repeated a number of grades up to Grade 6, so that she landed at Grade 6, which is about her ability. She was sixteen last June 10th. As far as I know, she has lived at home, and helped her mother with the work and has never gone out to work. Q. Did you determine her I.Q.? A. I would give her an I.Q. of under 60. Q. That is .6? A. With a mental age of between ten and eleven, nearer ten than eleven. Q. I see, What is your experience with these type of people? You say you have spent most of your life working, with your work, with them. What is your experience with respect to them, and the situation you have seen her go through, that is, giving testimony? A. Well, from my experience, and in asking the mother some questions, my experience has been that these children — that is all they are — are honest, easily led, and they can tell us a story in their simple way without elaborating very much. And I listened to Margaret tell her story this morning, and I thought she did remarkably well. Q. What about the ability to fabricate stories with these persons? A. In this type of case, with that degree of intelligence, they are not imaginative enough to concoct stories. Q. They lack imagination? A. They lack imagination. MR. BURBIDGE: Would you think an ordinary individual dealing with Margaret would quickly come to realize her disability? A. I think it was quite apparent in the witness box today.

The purpose of such evidence was clearly to suggest that the witness was because of her mental classification, likely to be a truthful person. The Crown relied upon the case of *Fisher v. The Queen*, [1961] S.C.R. 525. In that case the Supreme Court of Canada held, affirming the judgment of the Court of Appeal, that it was open to the Crown in a prosecution for murder where drunkenness negativing the intent to kill was the main defence to adduce evidence from a psychiatrist to show that the accused had the capacity to form the specific intent to kill. The accused had made a statement to the police which was admitted in evidence. The statement was the accused's version of his course of conduct and actions throughout the evening of the murder. The incidents described in this statement were put to the witness in the form of a hypothetical question. In answer to this question the witness stated that in his opinion, on the assumed state of facts contained in the question, that the accused was capable of forming the intent to kill.

The *Fisher* case is clearly distinguishable from the case at bar. In the former the evidence was introduced by Crown with reference to the accused and was directed to the proof of capacity to form at the material time the intent which was an essential ingredient of the crime charged. In the case at bar the evidence was led by the Crown with reference to the Crown's *own* witness and while based upon capacity, its primary and only function was to bolster up the credibility of the witness by evidence that she was or was likely to be a truthful person. It was not directed to an issue in the crime charged as it was in the *Fisher* case but only to the weight to be attached to the witness's evidence.

While the credit of any witness may be *impeached* by the *opposite party, R. v. Gunewardene,* [1951] 2 All E.R. 290 at p. 294, there is no warrant or authority for such oath-helping as occurred in the circumstances of this case, reminiscent as it is of the method before the Norman Conquest by which a defendant in a civil suit or an accused person proved his case by calling witnesses to swear that the oath of the party was true. If this sort of evidence were admissible in the case of either party no limit could be placed on the number of witnesses who could be called to testify about the credibility of witnesses as to facts. It would tend to produce, regardless of the number of such character witnesses who were called, undue confusion in the minds of the jury by directing their attention away from the real issues and the controversy would become so intricate that truth would be more likely to remain hidden than be discovered. For these reasons this evidence was not admissible.

Appeal allowed; new trial directed.

R. v. TAYLOR
(1986), 55 C.R. (3d) 321, 31 C.C.C. (3d) 1 (Ont. C.A.)

The judgment of the court was delivered by

CORY J.A.:—Following a trial before a judge and jury Stuart Taylor was convicted on two counts of sexual assault. The trial judge directed the jury to return no verdict in relation to two further counts alleging acts of gross indecency with the two complainants. Taylor is appealing his conviction.

During the trial the defence called a great many witnesses who testified they would not believe the testimony of the two complainants. This conclusion was based upon the habit of the complainants to recount somewhat fantastic accounts of sexual assaults. During the reply the Crown called two expert witnesses as to the propensity of young victims of sexual attacks to fantasize in the manner of the complainants. The primary issue to be determined on this appeal is whether the jury received adequate instructions as to the use that could be made of the evidence of the experts called in reply and how they were to assess that evidence.

Factual background

At the time of trial Stuart Taylor was 53 years of age. He had been engaged in child-care work for some 25 years of that time. Since 1971, Taylor and his wife had operated Pony Tail Farms as a group home for emotionally disturbed children. Although both complainants had been residents of the farm, they were there at different times.

For the purposes of this appeal it is sufficient to note that the complainant M.N. was 18 years of age when the incidents involving Taylor are alleged to have occurred. She had left the farm but returned at her own request in January, 1983, and remained until September of that same year. She testified as to six incidents of sexual assault that occurred during this time.

The complainant X.Y. resided at Pony Tail Farms between December 26, 1983 and September, 1984. She was then 13 years of age. She testified as to four incidents of sexual assault by Taylor which occurred during this period.

Primary ground of appeal

The main ground of appeal and primary contention of the appellant is that the charge to the jury lacked a direction as to the proper use that could be made of the reply evidence. It is argued that the trial judge placed undue emphasis upon the testimony of the experts called in reply in that he went so far as to indicate that their evidence could be considered as supporting the testimony of the complainants. The appellant takes the position that the evidence called by the defence and that given in reply brought into question whether the complainants had been sexually assaulted. The charge it is said failed to focus the jury's attention upon the issue as to whether they had been sexually assaulted by Stuart Taylor.

This case is an example of the problems that confront a trial judge and a jury when most of the trial is given over to an attack upon the credibility of vital witnesses followed by the buttressing of the credibility of those same witnesses by evidence given in reply.

The attack upon the credibility of the complainants

Twenty of the defence witnesses testified that they would not believe the testimony of M.N. and X.Y. The foundation for their disbelief was similar for both. They based their opinion upon the tendency of the complainants to recount strange tales of sexual assaults upon them. M.N. was said to have told far-fetched stories of sexual assaults. In one instance she told of pushing her attacker off the roof of a building thus either killing him or rendering him a paraplegic. In another instance she told of being tied to a bed and raped, then killing her attacker with a fireplace utensil. X.Y. was said to have given accounts of being sexually assaulted by her two adoptive brothers, her adoptive father, a neighbour, an 80-year-old man and someone to whom she was delivering the newspaper.

Dr. Perrault, a psychologist, testified for the defence. She had made an assessment of X.Y. in August of 1983. In her report she commented that she had no reason to doubt the validity of X.Y.'s allegations pertaining to her adoptive brothers' sexual activities with her. Dr. Perrault was of the opinion that in August, 1983, X.Y. had a personality bordering between one manifesting a neurotic type of symptomology and schizophrenia. She stated that depending on the situation X.Y. might not know the difference between the truth and untruth. She said that if X.Y. had described some sort of sexual activity there usually would be some air of reality to it but that she might so fantasize about the incident that an innocent act would get blown out of all proportion.

The evidence called in reply

In light of the extensive attack on the complainants' testimony it is not surprising that evidence tending to explain the sexual stories of the complainants and to support their credibility was called in reply. The landlord of M.N. stated that she would believe her testimony given under oath. Not unexpectedly, so too did her fiancé. No objection is taken to the testimony of those witnesses or the charge in their regard.

More importantly two expert witnesses gave evidence. The first was Dr. Mian, a paediatrician and director of the Suspected Child Abuse and Neglect Unit (SCAN) at Sick Childrens' Hospital. She stated that the SCAN unit had assessed X.Y. in late November of 1984. She was of the opinion that X.Y. exhibited symptoms of sexual abuse. She stated that sexually abused children tend to have a rich fantasy life. She said these children often fantasized about situations where they either gain mastery over their abuser or their abuser masters them. In response to a question from the trial judge Dr. Mian said in her experience only one or two per cent of the children who complained of sexual abuse were lying.

Dianne Garrels, a psychometrist and member of the SCAN unit also testified. It was her opinion that borderline personality disorders were consistent with the sexual abuse of a child. During her interview X.Y. had told her that she had been abused by several men including the appellant. Mrs. Garrels testified that it was her impression that X.Y. had in fact been abused by the people she named.

The admissibility of the evidence

The response of Dr. Mian to the question posed by the trial judge was clearly inadmissible. Additionally, the testimony given by Dianne Garrels that it was her impression that X.Y. had in fact been abused by the appellant should not have been admitted. It was conceded by the appellant that the rest of the evidence called in reply was admissible.

It was certainly appropriate for the defence to call witnesses who could testify that the complainants should not be believed under oath. Those same witnesses could testify as to the basis of their opinion, specifically the incredible stories of sexual assaults related to them by the complainants. These witnesses were not recounting the bizarre tales in order to contradict the evidence given by the complainants on collateral issues pertaining to other real or imagined sexual assaults. Rather they were putting forward the fantastic accounts related by the complainants as the basis for their disbelief of their testimony. This they were entitled to do: see *Cross on Evidence,* 6th ed. (1985), pp. 293-4; *Phipson on Evidence,* 13th ed. (1982), pp. 820-1. As well, Dr. Perrault could give her expert opinion that as a result of the borderline schizophrenic personality of X.Y. she might not be able to distinguish the truth from fantasy.

In light of the defence evidence it was appropriate for the Crown to call in reply the two witnesses who stated they would rely on the sworn testimony of M.N. and as well the expert witnesses Dr. Mian and Mrs. Garrels. The testimony offered by the experts tended to explain the stories of earlier sexual assaults related by the complainants. These accounts were in themselves symptomatic of sexual assaults upon M.N. and X.Y. There is a wealth of authority that supports the position that this evidence was admissible in the circumstances: see *Cross on Evidence,* pp. 293-4; *Phipson on Evidence,* pp. 820-1; *Toohey v. Metropolitan Police Com'r,* [1965] A.C. 595, and *R. v. Gonzague* (1983), 4 C.C.C. (3d) 505 at pp. 511-12, 34 C.R. (3d) 169.

At the conclusion of the evidence the trial judge was confronted with an exceedingly difficult situation. The evidence had the effect of confusing the issues. Through no fault of the trial judge much of the evidence had been directed towards other allegations of sexual abuse made by the complainants rather than those involving Stuart Taylor. The reply evidence to a large extent concentrated upon the question whether the complainants had at some time been victims of a sexual assault. The attention of the jury needed to be focused upon the particular charges that faced Stuart Taylor. As well the jury had to be given careful instructions as to the use that might be made of the evidence called in reply.

. . . .

Did the charge adequately instruct the jury as to the use that might properly be made of the evidence given in reply and focus the attention of the jury upon the charges against Stuart Taylor?

What was essential in this case and what is missing from the charge is a clear direction as to the use that could be made of the expert evidence given in reply. The charge should have contained instructions to the effect that the defence had called many witnesses who stated they would not believe the testimony of the complainants because of their fantasizing with regard to other sexual assaults. The charge should have continued that the expert evidence called in reply indicated that such fantasies are in themselves characteristic of sexually abused children. The jury could then have been advised that the medical explanation of the fantastic stories might to some extent reduce the impact this fantasizing would have had on the credibility of the complainants if left unexplained. Further the jury should have been advised that the evidence given in reply could not be used to bolster the credibility of the complainants. The charge omitted these essential directions.

Additionally, the trial judge emphasized the importance of Dr. Mian's evidence. The doctor's reply to the question posed by the trial judge was inadmissible. More will be said of that later. However, let us assume that the trial judge had stressed the importance of the evidence of the doctor which was admissible. Such a reference would make it imperative that a very clear instruction be given as to the limited use the jury could make of her evidence. The failure to give such a direction in the particular circumstances of this case requires that a new trial be ordered.

Before leaving this topic it may be helpful to the judge presiding at the new trial to observe that the nature of this case makes it advisable that a very clear direction be given to the jury that they should consider the testimony of the complainants with great care and caution, in light of their youth and unfortunate background. The appellant does not complain of that aspect of the trial judge's charge but does object to the directions given as to the independent testimony that the jury might look to as providing support for the complainants' evidence. It may be of assistance in the conduct of the new trial to review that submission and some of the other issues raised in this appeal.

The admissibility of the evidence of Dr. Mian given in answer to a question from the trial judge

The statement of Dr. Mian that of the individual children who do complain only one to two per cent were lying about the sexual abuse inflicted upon them was inadmissible. This evidence could ony serve to bolster the credibility of the complainants and really could serve no other purpose. In the circumstances of this case it was inadmissible. It goes without saying that this statement should not have been mentioned in the charge unless it were to be to instruct the jury that it was inadmissible and should be ignored.

Evidence capable of supporting the testimony of the complainants

The trial judge told the jury that the evidence of William Neal was capable of supporting the testimony of X.Y. He also stated that the evidence of Dr. Mian was capable of supporting the testimony of M.N. He was correct with regard to William Neal, but with respect, I believe he was in error with regard to instructions he gave pertaining to the testimony of Dr. Mian.

William Neal gave evidence as to two incidents involving X.Y. and Stuart Taylor. He said on one occasion he was following or chasing after Taylor and X.Y. He saw them go into the barn. Some 15 minutes later he went in and saw them arise from the hay. On another occasion he was in the swimming-pool. He saw Stuart Taylor touch X.Y. in her pubic region.

It was argued that neither of the incidents described by Neal related to specific complaints put forward by X.Y. She had testified that she was in the upper portion of the barn with Stuart Taylor when the sexual assault occurred. The incident described by Neal took place on the lower level. X.Y. had also testified with regard to an incident which had occurred in the swimming-pool when she was swimming underwater, not when she was leaning against the side of the pool as described by Neal. It was said in those circumstances the evidence of Neal could not be taken to support the testimony of X.Y. as to two of the specific incidents about which she complained.

I cannot accept that contention. Neal is clearly describing one incident involving Taylor and X.Y. in the barn and another involving X.Y. and Taylor in the swimming-pool. Both incidents had a strong sexual connotation and occurred in locations where X.Y. complained of being assaulted by Taylor. His evidence was capable of inducing a rational belief that X.Y. was telling the truth and was for that reason corroborative of her evidence. His testimony thus fell within the description of evidence that could be supportive or corroborative as set forth by Dickson J. In *Vetrovec v. The Queen* (1982), 67 C.C.C. (2d) 1 at p. 19.

Dr. Mian's evidence on the other hand was to the effect that sexually abused children often had a rich fantasy life and that for them to fantasize with regard to sexual incidents was common and indeed a characteristic of a sexually abused child. That evidence was too general in nature to be supportive of the testimony of M.N. with regard to the specific incidents of sexual assault by Taylor which she had related. The evidence of Dr. Mian should not have been left to the jury as being capable of supporting the testimony of M.N.

Reply evidence improperly admitted

Evidence was permitted in reply with regard to one matter that was clearly collateral. It involved telephone calls which allegedly had been made by Stuart Taylor to M.N. after she had left Pony Tail Farms and was working as a baby-sitter for the Cirone family. In his cross-examination Stuart Taylor denied making any telephone calls to M.N. requesting her to return to the farm or threatening her if she did not. M.N. was permitted to give evidence regarding his calls as to when she received them and their content. The evidence of Taylor could reasonably have been anticipated by the Crown and thus the testimony of M.N. ought to have been given during her examination-in-chief if it was thought her evidence in this regard was important.

In the result the appeal is allowed, the conviction must be set aside and a new trial directed.

Appeal allowed; new trial ordered.

Early in its judgment, the court notes:

> This case is an example of the problems that confront a trial judge and a jury when most of the trial is given over to an attack upon the credibility of vital witnesses, followed by the buttressing of the credibility of these same witnesses by evidence given in reply.[306]

One can readily agree with this statement, but by its decision the Court of Appeal has inadvertently taken a turn into a new direction which could produce more problems than it tried to solve. The court decided that the 20 defence witnesses were entitled to express their opinions regarding the complainants' credibility *and* to recite the basis for their opinions, together with giving detailed descriptions of stories which the complainants had told about completely unrelated sexual assaults. This holding is not supported by the authorities and, if followed, will cause undue complication of trials and confusion of issues.

The court purported to rely on *Cross on Evidence*, 6th ed. (1985), pp. 293-94, and *Phipson on Evidence*, 13th ed. (1982), pp. 820-21. Those pages state the opposite of the court's holding. In *Phipson*, the editors note that a witness is entitled to express his opinion of another witness's credibility, based upon his personal knowledge, but is not entitled to give the details of that personal knowledge. The editors write:

> The impeaching witness cannot, in direct examination, give particular instances of the other's falsehood or dishonesty, since no man is supposed to come prepared to defend all the acts of his life.[307]

In *Cross* we see a statement of the well-established rule that a witness can express his opinion on the credibility of another if the opinion is based on his own personal knowledge. But there we read about this rule:

> This longstanding rule is to be distinguished from the situation in which the witness's lack of veracity is imputed to some specific *medical* or *mental* condition. It seems clearly right that such evidence should be before the jury, and the possibility in these circumstances of prolonging the trial unduly remote. [Emphasis added.][308]

A lay witness who expresses his opinion on credibility cannot give the details of the basis of his opinion, but a medical witness can. Recall *R. v. Toohey, supra*.

This is one of those unusual instances where the Court of Appeal acted *per incuriam*.

R. v. J. (F.E.)
(1990), 74 C.R. (3d) 269, 53 C.C.C. (3d) 64 (Ont. C.A.)

[The accused was charged with the sexual assault of his daughter. Shortly before the preliminary hearing the child had written a letter to the Children's Aid

---

306. *R. v. Taylor* (1986), 31 C.C.C. (3d) 1, 4 (Ont. C.A.).
307. *Phipson on Evidence*, at p. 820.
308. *Cross on Evidence*, at p. 293.

Society worker to whom she had reported her father's misconduct in which she said "I am sorry but I lied about my dad." When she was cross-examined at trial about the letter the child said the letter was a lie and that she had written it to help her deal with what had occurred. Over the objection of the accused the Crown called a psychologist who had particular experience with the sexual abuse of children. He testified that the letter she had written was fairly typical of recantations commonly seen among children who have been sexually abused, when they realize the problems that the revelations have caused. He also testified that in his experience he had never found a case in which a child was being truthful when she recanted. The accused was convicted and appealed.]

GALLIGAN J.A. (MORDEN, A.C.J.O. and TARNOPOLSKY, J.A. concurring):—

. . . .

Mr. Greenspan argued that the evidence was inadmissible because its purpose was to bolster or enhance the testimonial trustworthiness of M.E. Ms. Ficek contended that the testimony of the psychologist related to "the syndrome of recantation" and was relevant and admissible to explain the significance of the witness's recantation.

There are two lines of authority, which can often co-exist but which in this case seem to come into conflict. The first line of authority is that, generally speaking, expert evidence is not admissible to support the credibility of a witness. The other is that expert evidence is admissible to show that in cases of child abuse certain common psychological and physical conditions occur. I propose to make some brief reference to each of these two lines of authority.

Evidence adduced solely for the purpose of bolstering a witness's credibility is inadmissible. This exclusionary rule has been called the rule against oath-helping. The existence and importance of the rule was emphasized by McIntyre J. speaking for four of the five judges who formed the majority of the Supreme Court of Canada in *R. v. Beland and Phillips* (1987), 36 C.C.C. (3d) 481 at pp. 486-9. Wilson J.'s dissenting judgment on behalf of the minority discloses that she recognized the existence of the rule. Some examples of the rule's application may be seen in the following cases: *R. v. Kyselka* (1962), 133 C.C.C. 103 (C.A.); *R. v. Taylor* (1986), 31 C.C.C. (3d) 1 at pp. 5-6 (C.A.); *R. v. Kostuck* (1986), 29 C.C.C. (3d) 190 (C.A.), and *R. v. Burkart*, [1965] 3 C.C.C. 210 (Sask. C.A.).

The second line of authority is of relatively recent origin and its rationale is explained in the reasons for judgment given by Wakeling J.A., speaking for himself, in *R. v. B. (G.)* (1988), 65 Sask. R. 134 at p. 148 (C.A.):

> I do not need to resort to statistics to establish that there are many more cases now coming to trial involving sexual abuse of children and requiring a very difficult evaluation of youthful testimony. Under these circumstances, it is understandable that the courts should seek as much assistance as possible from those who can be qualified as experts. They can shed some additional light on evidence that would otherwise be of negligible value, so as to assist the judge in reaching a determination of what facts have been adequately corroborated or otherwise established.

In *R. v. Beliveau* (1986), 30 C.C.C. (3d) 193, the British Columbia Court of Appeal ruled that an expert in child abuse could express an opinion that certain behaviour, demeanour and other factors were consistent with the child having been sexually abused. However, it was made clear that opinion evidence could not be given about the truthfulness of the witness. One of the judges who delivered reasons, Craig J.A., held at p. 203 that counsel for the Crown could not ask Crown witnesses whether they considered the child to be a truthful person. The other judge who delivered reasons, Macfarlane J.A., pointed out at p. 207 that the evidence of the expert was not admissible "to establish that the child was a truthful witness".

. . . .

It is not necessary in this case to attempt to list all of the purposes for which that kind of evidence is admissible. It seems from *R. v. Beliveau, supra*, and from the views expressed by Wakeling J.A. in *R. v. B. (G.), supra*, that it can be used to show that certain psychological and physical conditions could be consistent with sexual abuse. If those conditions were proved to exist in a case, they could tend to support the child's evidence that there had been sexual abuse. It is clear, however, from the judgment of this court in *R. v. Taylor, supra*, from the judgment of the British Columbia Court of Appeal in *R. v. Beliveau, supra*, and from the judgment of the Manitoba Court of Appeal in *R. v. Kostuck, supra*, that the opinion of experts, even in a child-abuse case, is not admissible simply to bolster the credibility of the principle Crown witness.

The distinction between those two circumstances may not always be easy to make. At first blush it may appear that there is not much of a difference between admitting expert opinion evidence to bolster credibility and admitting it to show that certain psychological and physical conditions are consistent with sexual abuse and thus capable of supporting the testimony of the child witness. The difference is that in the first case the witness gives his or her expert opinion about truthfulness. In the second, the evidence is only admitted as tending to show a condition consistent with sexual abuse and, therefore, as being capable of supporting the witness's testimony. It remains for the court to decide as a question of fact whether the psychological or physical conditions, as interpreted by the expert, do in fact support the testimony of the child witness. The distinction is crucial and must always be borne in mind.

. . . .

I think it should now be accepted by this court that properly qualified expert opinion evidence about the general behaviourial and psychological characteristics of child victims of sexual abuse is admissible for certain purposes. It would violate the rule against oath-helping if a witness were allowed to express an opinion about the credibility of a particular witness. However, in order to assist a judge or jury in deciding whether, in a particular case, a recantation by a child of his or her allegations of sexual abuse should lead to a doubt about the witness's credibility, expert evidence about the general behaviour patterns of children in similar circumstances could be helpful. The admission of that evidence would fall within the general rule that expert opinions are admissible in order to assist the trier of fact with the significance of proved facts in an area where the expert has special knowledge outside the knowledge of the trier of fact. . . .

I would think that it is probably not generally known that children who have been sexually abused, and have reported it, commonly recant their allegations. Thus, in order for the trial judge in this case to decide whether this child's testimony should have been disbelieved because of the letter, he was entitled to know that recantations are common.

I have not arrived at this conclusion without some reluctance. The admission of evidence of that kind, as well as being probative, could have a very serious prejudicial effect. The crucial issues in the criminal law, the credibility of witnesses and the guilt or innocence of accused persons, must not be decided by expert witnesses, no matter how high their qualifications. An impressively qualified expert must not be allowed to appear to put his or her stamp of approval upon the testimony of a witness. Worrisome as I find those concerns to be, I am unable to say that they could prevent the evidence from being admitted. However, they do call for the greatest care on the part of trial judges in the use of such evidence.

The psychologist in this case, as has been noted, gave evidence not only about the general behaviourial patterns of children involved in sexual-abuse cases, but he also said that he had not seen one case where the recantation was truthful. That latter part of his evidence was clearly inadmissible. Similar comments were held to be inadmissible by this court in *R. v. Taylor, supra*, and by the Manitoba Court of Appeal in *R. v. Kostuck, supra*. In a case such as this, where everything turns upon the credibility of two witnesses, the admission of that evidence might be fatal to the validity of a jury trial. This case, however, was tried by a judge without a jury. In *R. v. Beliveau, supra,* at p. 203, Craig J.A. pointed out that a judge can be expected to ignore inadmissible evidence in coming to his or her decision.

An examination of the reasons for judgment of the trial judge in this case shows that when he decided that M.E.'s letter should not impeach her credibility he did so because the letter was "understandable and consistent with the pattern of behaviour of children in abuse cases". Nowhere does he refer to the psychologist's opinion about the trustworthiness of children in sexual abuse cases. I am satisfied that the admission of that opinion occasioned no prejudice to the appellant.

In this case the trial judge was correct when he admitted the evidence of the psychologist. He disregarded that portion of the expert's evidence which was not admissible. He properly admitted the evidence and he made proper use of it. In my opinion, this ground of appeal must fail.[309]

In *R. v. Marquard*[310] Dr. Mian was called by the defence to testify that the child had made a statement when she arrived at the hospital that she had burned herself while playing with a lighter. The Crown, in cross-examination, asked Dr. Mian if she could account for the inconsistency between that statement and her testimony at trial where she said her grandmother, the accused, had burned her. Dr. Mian gave evidence offering explanations why children sometimes initially lie in these situations. McLachlin, J. for the majority noted:

> The Crown, in cross-examination, elicited from Dr. Mian the opinion that the child was lying when she told her that she had burned herself with a cigarette lighter. She testified that it is quite common that children "will initially ... give the accidental explanation and later on will give us a story that is more consistent with her injury which is then put in a more convincing [manner] which we believe is the first disclosure of what actually happened." She also testified that even if the child's burn had looked like a lighter burn, she would have been suspicious of the child's story "because of the way the child used it. . . ."

> Dr. Mian went on to buttress her view that the child's actual explanation was a lie by reference to the behaviour of abused children:

> > There's another reason [why children initially lie] which is that children who have been abused often feel that they are responsible for the behaviour that was done to them, for the injury that was inflicted on them. . . . Therefore if the care taker then takes them to the hospital and they're feeling that they did something wrong to elicit this punishment, they're certainly not going to want to tell the hospital staff that they did something wrong because they feel if my mom or whoever did this to me because of what I did, I wonder what these people who are strangers are going to do to me because of what I did.

---

309. And see *R. v. H. (E.L.),* [1990] N.S.J. No. 374 (C.A.). The Crown called a social worker trained in counselling families and children. She testified that she interviewed the complainant and others involved in the case and concluded that the child exhibited many of the symptoms often found in children who have been sexually abused, such as depression, attempts to block out recollection of events, low self-esteem, lack of trust in others and an inability to be specific as to details. The court, relying on *R. v. B. (G.)* and *R. v. Lavallee,* held the evidence of the social worker was admissible as it provided assistance to the trial judge in concluding whether an assault had occurred.

310. (1993), 25 C.R. (4th) 1 (S.C.C.).

The purport of this evidence was clear. Dr. Mian was of the view that the child was lying when she told the hospital staff that she had burned herself with a lighter, and that the child's second story — the one she told at trial — was the truth.[311]

For the majority, Dr. Mian had "crossed the line between expert testimony on human behaviour and assessment of credibility of the witness herself." The majority wrote: "Had Dr. Mian confined her comments to expert evidence explaining why children may lie to hospital staff about the cause of their injuries, there could have been no objection to her evidence."[312]

The majority relied on an editorial by Professor Mewett summarizing the law in the area. In dissent, Justice L'Heureux-Dubé, agreed that Professor Mewett's schematic was wise but decided that its dictates were respected in *Marquard*. Justice L'Heureux-Dubé felt that "the relevance of her testimony does not lie in whether or not Dr. Mian thought Debbie-Ann was lying, but rather in her knowledge of the characteristics of abused children." Dr. Mian may be excused for wondering in the future exactly where this difficult line is to be drawn.

(b) Exceptions

To the general rule excluding previous consistent statements, the common law recognized certain exceptions.

(i) To Rebut Allegation of Afterthought

If, in cross-examination, a witness's account of some incident or set of facts is challenged as being a recent invention, thus presenting a clear issue whether, at some previous time, he said or thought what he has been saying at the trial, he may support himself by evidence of earlier statements by him to the same effect. Plainly the rule that sets up the exception cannot be formulated with any great precision, since its application will depend on the nature of the challenge offered by the course of cross-examination and the relative cogency of the evidence tendered to repel it. Its application must be, within limits, a matter of discretion, and its range can only be measured by the reported instances, not in themselves many, in which it has been successfully invoked.[313]

Examples may assist. In *R. v. Neigel*,[314] a Crown witness testified to the accused's confession to murder. He was asked in cross-examination whether he had not on a previous occasion told others that the accused had not confessed to him and, on denying the same, proof of such inconsistent statements was made. It was held that evidence could be received of an even earlier statement consistent with his present testimony. In *R. v. Wannebo*[315] the accused on charges of robbery maintained that he was with his co-accused innocently, unaware that a robbery was being committed. On cross-examination Crown counsel asked him

---

311. *Ibid.*, at pp. 17-18.
312. *Ibid.*, at p. 20.
313. *Fox v. Gen. Medical Council, supra*, note 304, at p. 230.
314. (1918), 39 D.L.R. 154 (Alta. C.A.).
315. (1972), 7 C.C.C. (2d) 266 (B.C.C.A.).

questions which would enable the Court to draw the inference that that defence of what I may call innocent accompaniment of MacLeod was something which had been contrived between the two men after their arrest.[316]

The British Columbia Court of Appeal held it was proper to re-examine the accused:

with a view to showing that, very shortly after the commission of the second robbery and at a time before the appellant would have had an opportunity of consulting, after the robbery, with MacLeod, the appellant had made statements to a Detective Reid to the same effect as he subsequently made in giving evidence at his trial, that is, as to his presence on the two occasions being an innocent one.[317]

R. v. PANGILINAN
(1987), 60 C.R. (3d) 188, 39 C.C.C. (3d) 284

The judgment of the court was delivered by

ESSON J.A.:—Mr. Pangilinan was convicted by a jury of sexual assault and unlawful confinement. The issues on appeal arise from evidence led by the Crown of prior consistent statements by the complainant. The appellant submits that the evidence should not have been admitted and that, even if it was properly admitted, the jury should have been warned that it was not evidence of the truth of the facts stated but only of the consistency of the complainant's testimony.

The complainant was a prostitute. She met Pangilinan in a night spot in Vancouver and travelled with him in his car to a hotel in Richmond, where he said he was staying, for the purpose of providing her services to him. Negotiations took place in the car outside the hotel, resulting in disagreement on price, which led him to say he was not interested and her to demand money for her time and inconvenience. He drove the car a short distance away from the hotel to an industrial area, which was deserted at that time of night, and there stopped the car. She bit his finger, intercourse took place, she got out of the car and walked to the hotel where she spoke to the two employees whose evidence gives rise to the issues on appeal. As to those facts, there is no substantial conflict in the evidence.

The conflict relates to the events which led to the biting and the intercourse. She testified that Pangilinan stopped the car, refused to permit her to leave, said that she was "going to get raped" and struck her a number of times with his fists. The biting took place in the course of the struggle. She said that she submitted to intercourse because she was afraid for her safety. His version was that the complainant was angry at not getting any money, that he did not prevent her from leaving the car and did not assault her, but that she bit him in her anger. He told her that he would sue her and take her to the police. She then calmed down and consented to intercourse.

The two hotel employees met the complainant when she entered the lobby. Their evidence as to her appearance of dishevelment and distress is not objected to. What is objected to is their evidence, led by the Crown, to the effect that she had been raped and that she wanted to call the police and prosecute the man.

There was a faint suggestion on the part of the Crown that this evidence was admissible on the basis of the res gestae exception but that rightly was not pressed. In the circumstances of this case, the only issue is whether the evidence was admissible to rebut an allegation of recent fabrication, contrivance or concoction.

The complainant gave evidence before the hotel employees. In cross-examination, it was put to her that she had concocted her version of the story where it differed from that

---

316. *Ibid.*, at p. 267.
317. *Ibid.*

of the complainant. It is that line of questioning which, the Crown submits, opened the door to calling evidence of the prior consistent statements of the two employees.

It is settled law that, where the credibility of a witness has been challenged by an allegation or suggestion of recent fabrication, a previous consistent statement by that witness is admissible to rebut that suggestion. The allegation need not be express, but may be inferred from the whole circumstances of the case and the conduct of the trial: *R. v. Giraldi*, [1975] W.W.D. 166 (B.C.C.A.).

While the allegation of fabrication was put expressly and in the strongest of terms, that by itself is not enough. It is also necessary that the fabrication be "recent" as that term is employed in the authorities. I see nothing in the cross-examination, or in the conduct of the trial, to suggest that the defence did not accept that the complainant had been consistent in her story from the time of the first opportunity to tell it to anyone, i.e., when she entered the hotel.

In those circumstances, the foundation for calling evidence of prior consistent statements has not been laid. The point was considered by the Ontario Court of Appeal in *R. v. Campbell* (1977), 38 C.C.C. (2d) 6. There, it was the accused rather than the Crown who contended that he should have been permitted to lead prior consistent evidence. That does not affect the principle. Martin J.A., for the court, dealt with this point at p. 20:

> Where the failure of a witness to mention some circumstance on an earlier occasion when he might have done so, is made the basis for a suggestion that he had invented the story since that occasion, then evidence is admissible that on a still earlier occasion, he did mention that circumstance: see *Nominal Defendant v. Clements,* at p. 495. Manifestly, it would also be open to the witness to repel a suggestion of recent fabrication of that kind by introducing evidence that on the very occasion on which it is suggested he omitted to mention the circumstance, he did, in fact, speak of it.
>
> On the other hand, the fact that the whole story of a witness is challenged does not, by itself, constitute an allegation of *recent*fabrication: see *Fox v. General Medical Council, supra*, at p. 1026.
>
> Much of the cross-examination of the appellant was conducted with a view to showing certain improbabilities in his story. If a witness cannot be cross-examined with a view to showing that his story is improbable, without bringing into play the exception arising from a suggestion of recent fabrication, he cannot be cross-examined at all without making the exception operative. Mr. Gold's submissions really amount to this: in every case where the accused denies the truth of the Crown's case, there is an implicit allegation that his story has been recently contrived. I do not think the exception is so broad.

In this case, it is the Crown which seeks to make the exception operative on the basis that the complainant denied the truth of the accused's case, and that there was therefore an implicit allegation that her story had been recently contrived.

It follows that, in my view, the evidence of the two employees as to the prior consistent statements of the complainant was wrongly admitted. That being so, the issue whether a special direction should have been given with respect to it is essentially academic. The Crown does not dispute that such a direction is necessary, but says that no substantial wrong or miscarriage of justice was occasioned by its absence in this case. It does not contend that, if the evidence was wrongly admitted, the provisions of s. 613(1)(*b*)(iii) [of the Criminal Code] should be applied. I do not regard this as an appropriate case for applying those provisions.

I would allow the appeal, set aside the convictions and direct a new trial.

Order accordingly.

(ii) *Prior Identification*

When a witness at trial is asked to identify a person in the courtroom the surrounding circumstances may seriously weaken the weight of the identification. In a criminal trial for assault the identification as the assailant of the person in the prisoner's dock would have little force, as the trier of fact might naturally theorize that the witness is not giving his present recollection of the incident but rather that the witness is concluding from the accused's location that the police have arrested the proper person. As in the previous section, the circumstances of the case may cast doubt on the witness's statement and we therefore receive evidence of any prior identification made when such circumstances were not present; a close examination of the earlier circumstances will enhance or detract from the cogency of the present identification. Viscount Haldane, L.C., in the case of *R. v. Christie*,[318] described the process:

> Had the boy, after he had identified the accused in the dock, been asked if he had identified the accused in the field as the man who assaulted him, and answered affirmatively, then that fact might also have been proved by the policeman and the mother who saw the identification. *Its relevancy is to shew that the boy was able to identify at the time and to exclude the idea that the identification of the prisoner in the dock was an afterthought or a mistake.* [Emphasis added.]

The opportunity for an early identification when the incident is fresh in the witness's mind is not only for the witness's benefit. It is not satisfactory to the prisoner's interests that identification first occur at trial; he should be paraded with others of like characteristics and the witness obliged to "pick him out."[319]

The fact of the previous identification should be made known so that opposite counsel can, through cross-examination, explore the fairness with which that identification was conducted. The witness at trial may in truth be testifying only to his memory of the person he identified at the line-up parade and its surrounding circumstances deserve detailed exploration for the accused's own protection. If the police have used photographs in their investigation:

> There is always the risk that a witness may unconsciously substitute the clear impression gained by looking at a photograph for the perhaps hazy recollection of the face he is trying to recall, and his subsequent identification of the accused may be really the result of a mental comparison with the photograph instead of with the living person. The possibility of error arising from this cause is a thing of which the defence is entitled to take the fullest advantage, and an injustice might be done to the accused if the fact of photographs having been shown to witnesses were not disclosed.[320]

---

318. [1914] A.C. 545, 551 (H.L.).
319. See *R. v. Cartwright* (1914), 10 Cr. App. Rep. 219, 221 per Reading, L.C.J.: ". . . the prisoner was not put with a number of other men so that a witness might be able to identify this man as the guilty man. It would have been infinitely better had this been done." For a recent case regarding defective line-ups see *R. v. Faryna*, [1983] 1 W.W.R. 577 (Man. C.A.). See generally Brooks, *Study Paper of Law Reform Commission of Canada, Pretrial Eyewitness Identification Procedures*, 1984.
320. *R. v. Fannon* (1922), 22 S.R.N.S.W. 427 (C.A.) approved in *R. v. Harrison*, [1928] 3 D.L.R. 224 (B.C.C.A.). There is of course the unavoidable prejudice possibility flowing from the fact that the police had pictures of the accused to use.

(iii) *Recent Complaint*

Until the beginning of the 19th century complaints of rape were received in evidence with little discussion of the underlying principles, their reception apparently justified simply by a tradition that had its roots in the early procedural requirement of the "hue and cry." In the 13th century the hazards of trial were great and it was adjudged that not every complaint would be sufficient to put the antagonist to his proof. Complaint witnesses, suitors, were demanded who would vouch for the plaintiff's cause:[321]

> It is not enough that the plaintiff should tell his tale: he must offer to prove its truth. . . . No one is entitled to an answer if he offers nothing but his bare assertion, his *nude parole*. The procedure in the Appeal of Felony is no real exception to this rule. The appellor alleges, and can be called upon to prove, fresh "suit" with hue and cry, so that the neighbourhood . . . is witness to his prompt action, to the wounds of a wounded man, to the torn garments of a ravished woman. It should not escape us that in this case, as in other cases, what the plaintiff relies on as support for his word is "suit." This suggests that the suitors . . . whom the plaintiff produces in a civil action have been, at least in theory, men who along with him have pursued the defendant.[322]

During the 19th century, we see the courts enunciating principles to explain the reception of this evidence which violated the then crystallized rule against previous consistent statements, and the most common principle announced is akin to the principle underlying the first two exceptions above discussed: the circumstances of a case may cast doubt on the witness's present description of the incident. If a woman has been raped it is assumed that it would be a very natural thing for her to then speak out, and the failure so to do would act to contradict her present accusation. If nothing was said at trial about the fact of an earlier complaint, the trier might then assume there was none and so reject her present testimony. Accordingly, if there was a complaint, evidence of it could be led to counter this assumption;[323] this might be done in chief without the necessity of any allegation of recent invention in cross-examination. During the 19th century the prosecutor was confined to proving the fact of the complaint, but in 1896, in *R. v. Lillyman*,[324] it was decided that the details of the complaint were also receivable:

> In reality, affirmative answers to such stereotyped questions as these, "Did the prosecutrix make a complaint" (a very leading question, by the way) "of something done to herself?" "Did she mention a name?" amount to nothing to which any weight ought to be attached; they tend rather to embarrass than assist a thoughtful jury, for they are consistent either with there having been a complaint or no complaint of the prisoner's conduct. To limit the evidence of the complaint to such questions and answers is to ask the jury to draw important inferences from imperfect materials, perfect materials being at hand and in the cognizance of the witness in the box. In our opinion, nothing ought unnecessarily to be left to speculation or surmise.

Although the details may be received, the complaint was not receivable for the purpose of proving its truth but solely to counter the influence of the assumption

---

321. See Thayer, *Preliminary Treatise on Evidence at the Common Law* (1898), pp. 10-16.
322. Pollock and Maitland, *History of English Law*, 2d ed. (1898), vol. 2, pp. 605-06.
323. See generally 4 Wigmore, *Evidence* (Chad. Rev.), s. 1134-39, discussing this principle and others.
324. [1896] 2 Q.B. 167, 177-78 (C.C.R.). Accord, *R. v. Thomas*, [1952] 4 D.L.R. 306 (S.C.C.).

that might otherwise flow from silence and so confirm, by the victim's conduct, her present testimony.[325]

Belying its origins, the exception during the 19th century was confined to complaints of rape by female complainants. In the 20th century the courts have extended the exception to cover the prosecution of other sexual offences,[326] whether the complainant was male or female.

In *Kribs v. R.*[327] Fauteux, J. explained:

> The principle is one of necessity. It is founded on factual presumptions which, in the normal course of events, naturally attach to the subsequent conduct of the prosecutrix shortly after the occurrence of the alleged acts of violence. One of these presumptions is that she is expected to complain upon the first reasonable opportunity, and the other, consequential thereto, is that if she fails to do so, her silence may naturally be taken as a virtual self-contradiction of her story.
>
> . . . .
>
> . . . by giving evidence of her conduct shortly after the alleged occurrence, the prosecutrix does not, in a sense, enhance or confirm her story any more than she does in reciting all that she did in resistance to the assault, but she rebuts a presumption and, in doing so, adds, for all practical purposes, a virtually essential complement to her story.

The courts held that if there was an absence of complaint at the first reasonable opportunity, the trial judge should charge the jury regarding the adverse inference they may draw against the complainant's credibility.[328]

In 1983 the Criminal Code was amended[329] to provide:

> **246.5** The rules relating to evidence of recent complaint in sexual assault cases are hereby abrogated.

To describe the provision as ambiguous is understatement. Does it mean that evidence of recent complaint cannot be given? Does it mean that no adverse inference is to be taken if complaint was not made?

R. v. O'CONNOR
(1995), 100 C.C.C. (3d) 285 (Ont. C.A.)

[The accused was charged with touching for a sexual purpose a young girl who was a member of a church group of which he was the leader. The accused was tried by a judge sitting without a jury. The defence was that the allegations of sexual activity were fabricated. The Crown asked the complainant during

---

325. See Hawkins, J. in *R. v. Lillyman, ibid.*, at p. 170. See the difficulty experienced by Fauteux, J. in *Kribs, infra*, note 327, seeking to distinguish these two uses. See also in *R. v. Thomas*, [1952] 2 S.C.R. 344, the court allowing the statement to be used to show consistency but denying its use as corroboration. If the complainant doesn't testify the complaint is naturally inadmissible: see *R. v. Cook* (1979), 9 C.R. (3d) 85 (Ont. C.A.) and *R. v. Brasier* (1779), 168 E.R. 202 (Crown Cases).

326. See the history of this development canvassed in *R. v. Lebrun* (1951), 100 C.C.C. 1 (Ont. C.A.). And see *R. v. Christenson*, [1923] 2 D.L.R. 379 (Alta. C.A.) per Beck, J. suggesting the exception should operate in all crimes of violence, sexual or non-sexual.

327. [1960] S.C.R. 400, 405-06. And see *R. v. Boyce* (1975), 23 C.C.C. (2d) 16, 33 (Ont. C.A.).

328. See *Boyce, ibid.*, at p. 33.

329. S.C. 1980-81-82-83, c. 125, s. 19. See now R.S.C. 1985, c. C-46, s. 275.

examination in chief if she had told anyone of her relationship with the accused and received the answer that she had told a camp counsellor and her best friend. Defence counsel objected and stated that no allegation of recent fabrication had been made. The trial judge gave effect to that objection. In cross-examination, defence counsel asked the complainant whether she had told certain persons within a specified time-frame about the sexual acts. The complainant replied that she had not. The trial judge later allowed the camp counsellor to testify as to a complaint to her within three days of the time-frame relied on by the defence to support an adverse inference, and the complainant's stepmother and older sister were permitted to testify that the complainant had told them about the sexual relationship and that they agreed that the stepmother would inform the police.

The accused was convicted and appealed.]

FINLAYSON, J.A.:—

. . . .

The position of the defence that emerges from the record at trial and the argument on appeal is that the testimony of the complainant, to the extent that it recounted sexual abuse, had been made up out of whole cloth. The fabrication was said to be in no sense recent, but defence counsel did not designate its origin as being at any specific time. Put simply, the position is that since the defence had never alleged *recent* fabrication (as opposed to fabrication *ab initio*), the Crown was not entitled to lead any evidence under the rubric of recent fabrication, because no such allegation had been made. Therefore (the submission went) while it was permissible for the defence to demand of the complainant why she had not complained of these assaults to her sister Kelly on a particular day, the Crown was not entitled to bring out in reply, or at all, that she had complained three days later to her camp counsellor and still later to her sister and her stepmother.

In my opinion, this is being too clever by half. "Recent" fabrication is by definition a subset of fabrication generally. One may escape this implication by asserting a challenge to the complainant's credibility based on an allegation of fabrication *simpliciter*, but not when it is coupled with a charge that she had not divulged the fact of the sexual conduct to a person to whom the trier of fact would expect her to complain, *i.e.*, an absence of recent complaint. The law does not require that an allegation of recent fabrication be made explicitly: the court can look at all the circumstances of the case. . .

In this case the whole thrust of the cross-examination relating to Jenny Lamb and the sister Kelly was structured so as to establish the lack of an early complaint to someone whom the trial judge would expect a complaint to be made under the circumstances. The questions as to why no complaints were made were restricted as to person and to time but with the object of leaving the impression that there were no complaints whatsoever. As such, the questioning was designed to give rise to an inference that the complaint was formulated subsequent to the event recounted in her testimony at trial. It clearly implied what is, by any other name, an allegation of recent fabrication.

I am of the view that an allegation of recent fabrication is no more than an allegation that the complainant has made up a false story to meet the exigencies of the case. The word "recent" means that the complainant's evidence has been invented or fabricated after the events in question and thus is a "recent" invention or fabrication. . . .

. . . .

I conclude that the rulings of the trial judge were correct and his use of the statements elicited were in accordance with the principle that he could only rely on the facts of the complaints, not the truth of their contents, in assessing the credibility of the complaint.

Issue (2)

The appellant submits that the trial judge erred in holding that he could draw no adverse inference from the complainant's failure to disclose the occurrence of the offence at a time proximate to its taking place. At trial, defence counsel suggested that the trial judge draw an inference adverse to the complainant with respect to her credibility because she didn't complain to her sister or her best friend in the weeks immediately after the offence occurred. In his reasons for judgment the trial judge said:

> The fact that someone doesn't complain is no longer a valid consideration in this court. . . . The fact that someone doesn't come forward immediately, speak to a mother or a father, another loved one, someone she trusts, a counsellor, a police officer, anybody, no longer is capable of allowing an adverse inference simply because of the fact that no comment was made. There may well be other reasons that an adverse inference be drawn but the fact here, that she didn't speak to Kelly during the summer, and waited until October 24th is really of no significance.

In support of this submission the appellant in this court relies on *R.v. F. (J.E.), supra* . . . :

> On the other hand, there never was a prohibition against the accused attempting to exploit the lack of a recent complaint, and since only the right of the Crown to lead this evidence-in-chief has been negated, the defence can elect whether to open this door or not.

I would note first that there is nothing in this passage or elsewhere in the judgment in *R.v. F. (J.E.)* that requires a judge to draw an adverse inference in the face of a lack of recent complaint. The passage simply notes that the defence may still raise this issue when there is no evidence of a recent complaint. Such an allegation goes directly to the credibility of the complainant and thus the decision to draw such an inference is a matter properly within the discretionary province of the trier of fact. Accordingly, there is no error in the trial judge's refusing to draw the inference in this case.

However, the appellant's contention was advanced on a different footing. The appellant argued that the trial judge erred in instructing himself that as a matter of law it was not open to him to draw an adverse inference on the basis of a lack of recent complaint. I would agree that as a bald assertion of law, it is erroneous to state that a trier of fact is no longer entitled to draw an adverse inference based on an absence of recent complaint. However, when the passage quoted above from the trial judge's lengthy and detailed reasons is read in the light of other conclusions made by him in those reasons and in the course of the proceedings, it is clear that he was not advancing this point as a general proposition of law. As I read the passage, he is simply expressing the opinion based on his experience in this case and one that he heard the day before that the fact that the victims did not complain in either case was not significant.

fairness

    . . . .

GOODMAN, J.A.:— . . . In my opinion, the evidence of the complaints made by the complainant to her sister Kelly, Cynthia Collins and Tanya Kronschnabl, in the circumstances of this case, was not admissible on the basis of the exception to the rule against prior consistent statements resulting from an allegation of recent fabrication but rather on the basis hereinafter set forth.

Prior to the 1983 amendment to the *Criminal Code* . . . , purporting to abrogate the rules relating to evidence of recent complaint . . . , the prosecution was permitted to elicit from the complainant evidence of a complaint of a sexual assault, made at the first reasonable opportunity, to support the credibility of the victim. After the 1983 amendment, the prosecution was no longer permitted to do so.

In my opinion, however, the amendment does not prevent defence counsel from cross-examining a complainant about the lack of recent complaint, but in doing so the door is opened to permit the Crown to adduce evidence of a prior complaint in order to rebut any adverse inference which might be drawn by the fact-finder from the silence alleged by the defence and to rebut the attack on the credibility of the complainant based on the lack of recent complaint.

In Sopinka, Lederman and Bryant, *The Law of Evidence in Canada*, 1992, it is stated at p. 317:

> It appears that the effect of the statutory amendment is that recent complaint evidence may not be led in anticipation of the adverse inference drawn from silence. However, defence counsel are not precluded from cross-examining a complainant about the lack of a prior complaint. If they do, they take the risk that the Crown may adduce a prior complaint to rebut the allegation.

And further at p. 318:

> . . . the ability of the defence to question a complainant on the absence or untimeliness of a complaint has had nothing to do in the past with the doctrine of recent complaint. One of the most common means of suggesting that a witness's testimony is fabricated is to allege failure to speak when it would have been expected, and this has always been recognized.

In the case at bar, defence counsel cross-examined the complainant in a manner which might leave the impression that she had never made a prior complaint or at the very least had not made a timely complaint to a person or persons to whom it was reasonable to expect that she would have complained. In that circumstance it was, in my opinion, permissible for the Crown to re-examine the complainant with respect to the reasons for the lack of complaint to the persons referred to by defence counsel in his cross-examination and to adduce evidence with respect to the prior complaints which had allegedly been made by the complainant prior to the complaint to the police.

. . . .

WEILER, J.A.:— I am in agreement with Finlayson J.A. that the effect of the cross-examination which was conducted by counsel for the defence gave rise to the inference that the complainant had fabricated her evidence after the events in question and, in addition, suggested that there was an absence of any complaint concerning the alleged assault prior to the complaint being made to the police. In these circumstances, I agree with him that it was appropriate for the trial judge to hear evidence of the complainant's meeting with her sister Kelly and the social worker, Cynthia Collins, as well as her complaint to Tanya Kronschnabl. I also agree with Goodman J.A. that the impression resulting from the cross-examination, that there was no complaint made of any sexual assault prior to the complaint to the police, would have made the complainant's evidence of her complaint to Kelly, Cynthia Collins, and Tanya Kronschnabl admissible, quite apart from any suggestion of recent fabrication.

(iv) *Narrative or Principled Approach*

In *R. v. Albert* [330] the accused was charged with sexual assault. The complainant testified that shortly after the alleged rape she made statements to several persons to the effect that she had been raped by the accused. The trial judge permitted several witnesses to testify as to these prior consistent statements. This was held to be error and a new trial was ordered:

> The Crown . . . argues that the prior consistent statements of the complainant were admissible as part of the narrative, or to rebut an allegation of recent fabrication. We disagree.

---

330. (1993), 19 C.R. (4th) 322 (Ont. C.A.).

It was not necessary for the jury to understand the unfolding of events to be apprised of the content of the statements made by the complainant shortly after the alleged offence.

Moreover, there was no suggestion by the defence that the complainant had, at any particular point in time, fabricated the allegation that she had been raped. [Emphasis added.][331]

In *R. v. F. (J.E.)*,[332] the same court, just a year later, dealt with an accused who was charged with sexual assault. The complainant was sixteen years of age at the time that she testified as to a series of sexual assaults by the accused in 1985, 1986 and 1987 commencing when she was nine years old. The trial judge permitted the Crown to lead evidence that the complainant had made prior consistent statements relating to the accused's sexual abuse of her to a number of persons. The accused's appeal was allowed.

The court decided that there were only two exceptions that could possibly have application to the case: (1) where recent fabrication was alleged and (2) where the previous consistent statement could be admitted as part of the res gestae or as part of the narrative. The court noted that if the Crown was relying upon an allegation of recent fabrication as the basis for the admissibility of prior consistent statements, it must wait until the defence has clearly opened this door by making an opening statement, or through cross-examination of the complainant or other Crown witnesses, or by the allegation of fabrication becoming implicit from the defence's conduct of the case. The court decided that in this case the evidence of the previous statements was elicited before any attack was made and recent fabrication could not be relied on to justify receipt. The court also decided that res gestae, a phrase used in the law of evidence to explain the admissibility of words used by a person that shed light upon the quality of the act they accompany, was not a fertile area for enlarging the admissibility of prior consistent statements.

The court then looked to narrative as an exception to the rule against the admission of previous consistent statements for a more hopeful approach to the problem of the evidence of children in sexual assault cases. Justice Finlayson for the court wrote:

It must be a part of the narrative in the sense that it advances the story from offence to prosecution or explains why so little was done to terminate the abuse or bring the perpetrator to justice. *Specifically, it appears to me to be part of the narrative of a complainant's testimony when she recounts the assaults, how they came to be terminated, and how the matter came to the attention of the police.* . . . [N]arrative is justified as providing background to the story — to provide chronological cohesion and eliminate gaps which would divert the mind of the listener from the central issue. It may be supportive of the central allegation in the sense of creating a logical framework for its presentation — but it cannot be used, and the jury must be warned of this, as confirmation of the truthfulness of the sworn allegation. . . . The fact that the statements were made is admissible to assist the jury as to the sequence of events from the alleged offence to the prosecution so that they can understand the conduct of the complainant and assess her truthfulness. However, the jury must be

331. *Ibid.*, at p. 325.
332. (1993), 26 C.R. (4th) 220 (Ont. C.A.).

instructed that they are not to look to the content of the statements as proof that a crime has been committed. [Emphasis added.][333]

The court decided that while the evidence of the complaints was admissible there should be a new trial since there had been no limiting instruction on the use of the statements:

> The jury was never told that the complaints were not admissible for the truth of their contents, and that they were to consider only the fact that the complaints were made to assist them in their understanding of what occurred and why.[334]

In *R. v. Ay* [335] the accused had been convicted of a variety of sexual offences. One of the grounds of appeal was that inadmissible evidence of the complainant's prior out of court consistent statements concerning the allegations of sexual assault, which were made to her mother, the investigating officers and others, was allowed to go before the jury and that the trial judge failed to instruct the jury as to the use which could properly be made of so much of such evidence as was admissible. Justice Wood approved of the Ontario Court of Appeal's decision in *F. (J.E.)* and concluded:

> To summarize, the fact that a prior complaint was made, when it was made, and why it was or was not made in a timely fashion, are all matters relevant and admissible to establish the conduct of the complainant in a criminal case, from which conduct the trier of fact is entitled to draw inferences relative to the credibility of that complainant's evidence. However, the content of any prior statement cannot be used to demonstrate its consistency with, and therefore the probable truthfulness of, the complainant's evidence at trial, and thus such content is inadmissible unless relevant for some other purpose such as providing necessary context for other probative evidence.[336]

Justice Wood decided that it was open to the Crown to lead evidence from the complainant that she eventually disclosed the accused's assaults upon her, first to a family counsellor, then to her mother, then to her therapist, and finally to the police. It was also open to the Crown to lead evidence from those to whom she spoke, confirming the simple fact that such complaints were in fact made. But, he decided, the specific content of such statements, and any other evidence the sole purpose of which was to invite the jury to conclude that these prior statements were both truthful and consistent with her sworn evidence before them, was not admissible.

In *F. (J.E.)* the court says the complaint cannot be used, and the jury must be warned of this, as confirmation of the truthfulness of the sworn allegation. The jury must be instructed that they are not to look to the content of the statements as proof that a crime has been committed. If the jury is not to use the fact of complaint as confirmation of the witness's now story to what is it relevant? If the jury is not to hear the contents, how do they determine whether there is consistency? In *Ay* the court says the fact that a prior complaint was made is relevant and admissible to establish the conduct of the complainant in a criminal case, from which conduct the trier of fact is entitled to draw inferences relative

---

333. *Ibid.*, at pp. 237-41.
334. *Ibid.*, at p. 240.
335. (1994), 93 C.C.C. (3d) 456 (B.C.C.A.).
336. *Ibid.*, at p. 471.

to the credibility of that complainant's evidence. The court, however, says that the content of any prior statement cannot be used to demonstrate consistency. How does the jury infer anything *vis-à-vis* credibility if they aren't told the contents? And if told the contents, that's what demonstrates consistency.

Remember the law relating to recent complaint before it was abrogated by now section 275 of the Criminal Code. If a woman was raped it was assumed that it would be a very natural thing for her to then speak out, and the failure so to do was seen to act to contradict her present accusation. If there was a complaint, evidence of it could be led to support;[337] this might be done in chief without the necessity of any allegation of recent invention in cross-examination. During the 19th century the prosecutor was confined to proving the fact of the complaint, but in 1896, in *R.v. Lillyman*, it was decided that the details of the complaint were also receivable:

> In reality, affirmative answers to such stereotyped questions as these, "Did the prosecutrix make a complaint" (a very leading question, by the way) "of something done to herself?" "Did she mention a name?" amount to nothing to which any weight ought to be attached; they tend rather to embarrass than assist a thoughtful jury, for they are consistent either with there having been a complaint or no complaint of the prisoner's conduct. To limit the evidence of the complaint to such questions and answers is to ask the jury to draw important inferences from imperfect materials, perfect materials being at hand and in the cognizance of the witness in the box. In our opinion, nothing ought unnecessarily to be left to speculation or surmise.[338]

Is the wisdom of *Lillyman* self-evident?

5. DEMEANOUR AS GUIDE TO CREDIBILITY

Lord Devlin, recognized by all as a great trial judge, wrote:

The great virtue of the English trial is said to be the opportunity it gives to the judge to tell from the demeanour of the witness whether or not he is telling the truth. I think that this is overrated. I would adopt in their entirety the words of Mr. Justice MacKenna:

> I question whether the respect given to our findings of fact based on the demeanour of the witness is always deserved. I doubt my own ability and sometimes that of other judges, to discern from a witness's demeanour, or the tone of voice whether he is telling the truth. He speaks hesitantly. Is that the mark of a cautious man, whose statements are for that reason to be respected or is he taking time to fabricate? Is the emphatic witness putting on an act to deceive me, or is he speaking from the fullness of his heart, knowing that he is right? Is he likely to be more truthful if he looks me straight in the face than if he casts his eyes on the ground perhaps from shyness or a natural timidity? For my part I rely on these considerations as little as I can help.[339]

Empirical studies conducted by psychologists confirm Lord Devlin's point.[340] They usually stress that bodily movements and the sound of the voice are better

---

337. See generally, 4 Wigmore, *Evidence* (Chad. Rev.), ss. 1134-39, discussing this principle.
338. *Supra*, note 324, at pp. 177-78.
339. Lord Devlin, *The Judge*, 1979, p. 63.
340. See for example, Ekman and Fresein, "Detecting Deception from the Body or Face" (1974), 29 J. of Personality & Social Psychology 288; Ekman, *Telling Lies: Clues to Deceit in the Marketplace*, Politics and Marriage, Norton, (U.S. 1991), esp. pp. 287-92; Blumenthal, "A Wipe of the Hands, A Lick of the Lips: The Validity of Demeanour Evidence in Assessing

indicators than facial demeanour, but then only if the observer is acquainted with the normal mannerisms of the witness. Professor Ekman's empirical studies indicated that while U.S. Secret Service agents scored very well in accurately picking out liars, judges, trial lawyers, police, forensic psychiatrists and the FBI achieved at a level no better than chance![341]

And yet, the frailty of using demeanour as indicative of credibility, as accepted by Lord Devlin and seemingly established by the psychologists, is certainly at odds with dicta from most trial judges who in their reasons frequently use the same as indicating their acceptance or rejection of the testimony of witnesses. It is also at odds with the deference often paid by appellate courts who frequently say that although they have a transcript of what was said at trial they are disadvantaged in their assessment of the worth of testimonial evidence because they were not present when the testimony was given.

Has the time come for judges to reappraise their attitudes towards demeanour? How might that be done?

R. v. NORMAN
(1993), 26 C.R. (4th) 256, 87 C.C.C. (3d) 153 (Ont. C.A.)

[The accused was charged with raping the complainant, then 13 years old, in 1973. The complainant alleged that she had forgotten the rape, and remembered it in fragments in the course of therapy sessions. The accused testified and denied any sexual contact with the complainant. The trial judge found that the complainant was a credible witness and the accused was convicted.]

The judgment of the court was delivered by FINLAYSON J.A.:—

. . . .

The trial judge in this case seems to have determined credibility solely on the basis of the demeanour of the complainant and Mrs. Goebel. He said that he was impressed with the manner in which the complainant testified: she was straightforward and stood up well in cross-examination, and it appeared to him that she was not being vindictive. As for Mrs. Goebel, he said that she testified in an assured and straightforward manner and impressed him as a credible witness.

In *White v. R.*, [1947] S.C.R. 268 at p. 272, the senior Mr. Justice Estey discussed the issue of credibility. He said it is one of fact and cannot be determined by following a set of rules. He stated in part:

> It is a matter in which so many human characteristics, both the strong and the weak, must be taken into consideration. The general integrity and intelligence of the witness, his powers to observe, his capacity to remember and his accuracy in statement are important. It is also important to determine whether he is honestly endeavouring to tell the truth, whether he is sincere and frank or whether he is biased, reticent and evasive. All these questions and others may be answered from the observation of the witness' general conduct and demeanour in determining the question of credibility.

Witness Credibility" (1993), 72 Nebraska L. Rev. 1157, Stone, "Instant Lie Detection? Demeanour and Credibility in Criminal Trials" (1991), Crim. L. Rev. 821 and Loretta Re, "Oral v. Written Evidence: The Myth of the Impressive Witness" (1983), Aus. L.J. 679.

341. Hunter and Cronin, *Evidence, Advocacy and Ethical Practice* (Butterworths, 1995), p. 329.

I do not think that an assessment of credibility based on demeanour alone is good enough in a case where there are so many significant inconsistencies. The issue is not merely whether the complainant sincerely believes her evidence to be true; it is also whether this evidence is reliable. Accordingly, her demeanour and credibility are not the only issues. The reliability of the evidence is what is paramount. So far as Mrs. Goebel is concerned, her evidence is inherently hard to credit, and should have been subjected to closer analysis. For the purposes of this case, I adopt what was said by O'Halloran J.A., speaking for the British Columbia Court of Appeal in *Faryna v. Chorny* (1951), 4 W.W.R. (N.S.) 171 at p. 174:

> The credibility of interested witnesses, particularly in cases of conflict of evidence, cannot be gauged solely by the test of whether the personal demeanour of the particular witness carried conviction of the truth. The test must reasonably subject his story to an examination of its consistency with the probabilities that surround the currently existing conditions. In short, the real test of the truth of the story of a witness in such a case must be its harmony with the preponderance of the probabilities which a practical and informed person would readily recognize as reasonable in that place and in those conditions.

O'Halloran J.A. pointed out later at p. 175 that "[t]he law does not clothe the trial judge with a divine insight into the hearts and minds of the witnesses."

In *R. v. S. (W.)*[342] Justice Finlayson repeated the thought and explained:

> I am not satisfied that a positive finding of credibility on the part of the complainant is sufficient to support a conviction in a case of this nature where there is significant evidence which contradicts the complainant's allegations. We all know from our personal experiences as trial lawyers and judges that honest witnesses, whether they are adults or children, may convince themselves that inaccurate versions of a given event are correct and they can be very persuasive. The issue, however, is not the sincerity of the witness but the reliability of the witness' testimony. Demeanour alone should not suffice to found a conviction where there are significant inconsistencies and conflicting evidence on the record.[343]

PROBLEMS

Problem 1

Where could (should) objections be made in the following transcript? What contrary arguments might be made and how would you rule?

The plaintiff is suing defendant for damages arising out of a motor-vehicle accident. The plaintiff calls Joseph Smith to the stand:

Clerk: You swear that the evidence to be given by you to the court and jury sworn, touching the matters in question, shall be the truth, the whole truth and nothing but the truth. So help you God.

Witness: I'd rather not swear.

---

342. (1994), 29 C.R. (4th) 143 (Ont. C. A.), leave to appeal refused (1994), 35 C.R. (4th) 402 (note) (S.C.C.).

343. *Ibid.*, at pp. 149-50.

The Court:	Do you affirm?
Witness:	Yes.
The Court:	Fine, proceed.
Q.:	Your name is Joseph Smith?
A.:	Yes.
Q.:	You live at 2236 Princess Street in the city of Kingston?
A.:	Yes.
Q.:	You are employed as a police officer by the municipality of Metropolitan Kingston and have been so employed as a traffic officer for some 22 years and as such have investigated thousands of accidents?
A.:	Yes.
Q.:	You've given evidence in court on numerous occasions?
A.:	Yes.
Q.:	You're wearing a gold pin in your lapel —
A.:	It's my 20 year pin for good service to the force.
Q.:	Fine, thank you officer, now, on the evening in question you were standing on the corner of Princess and North Streets at about 4:12 p.m. when your attention was attracted by a loud noise?
A.:	Yes.
Q.:	Tell the court and the jury what you saw.
A.:	I saw a car driven by the defendant —
Q.:	You mean the person sitting beside my friend Mr. Jones?
A.:	Yes.
Q.:	Continue please.
A.:	I saw his car driving furiously down the street squealing its tires and without any regard for the safety of pedestrians who were already in the cross-walk.
Q.:	Then what happened?
A.:	Well, he mustn't have applied the brakes because he went straight through the cross-walk and ran down the plaintiff. I went over to see if I could help and the defendant got out of his car.
Q.:	How did he get out of his car?
A.:	What do you mean?
Q.:	In what manner did he exit?
A.:	He opened the driver's door and stepped out.
Q.:	Was there anything noticeable about his gait?
A.:	I'm sorry, I don't know what you're driving at.
Q.:	Was the defendant walking with any noticeable characteristic? — a sway, for example.
A.:	Oh yes, I remember now, he staggered as he walked and he brushed against the hood of the car as he came around to see the victim.
Q.:	Anything else?
A.:	Like what?
Q.:	Well, as a result of your observations did you decide to charge the defendant with any offence?

A.:   Yes, I charged him with impaired driving and he was later convicted.

Cross-Examination

Q.:   Why were you at the intersection of Princess and North Streets at 4:42 p.m.?

A.:   I live near there.

Q.:   And you just happened to be there when the accident occurred?

A.:   That's right.

Q.:   Don't you find that to have been just a little convenient?

A.:   I suppose it was for the plaintiff.

Q.:   Don't be smart with me, witness! I suggest to you that you didn't arrive at the scene of the accident until one-half hour after the accident had occurred.

A.:   No, sir.

Q.:   Would you care to think about that for a moment?

A.:   No — there's no need to —

Q.:   Suppose I told you that I'm prepared to call three witnesses to testify that you came running up to them at the scene and shouted "what happened?"

A.:   They'd be lying.

Q.:   Everyone lies but you? All right, let's move on. Isn't it true that you've been on a crusade against teenage drivers ever since your own wife was injured by one and that coloured your thinking about my client who happens to be a teenager?

A.:   No.

Q.:   Aren't you known at the precinct as an officer who keeps score of how many teenagers he tickets a day?

A.:   No.

Q.:   You hate teenagers don't you?

A.:   No.

Q.:   You think they shouldn't be on the road until they're 20 years old?

A.:   No.

Q.:   You think they're dangerous.

A.:   No.

Q.:   I have nothing further at this time but I reserve my right to further cross-examination at a later time.

Problem 2

The defendant is being tried for the theft of a quantity of household goods, the property of Ms. Farid. The defendant had been hired to move these goods from Ms. Farid's former residence to her new address and Ms. Farid maintains that some of her things never arrived. Ms. Farid has testified that as her chattels were being taken out of her house she made longhand notes and later, in anticipation of the trial, she copied these notes on her typewriter. The witness is being examined by the prosecutor:

Q.:   When you look at that typewritten sheet, does that refresh your recollection as to the items therein mentioned?

A.:	It does.
Q.:	In what way?
A.:	Well, every item here — for instance: "2 Chinese vases octagonal shape Satsuma," I remember.
Q.:	You remember these items individually as packed?
A.:	Individually, each one. I lived with these things, your Honour, I know them.
The Court:	You lived with them yourself?
A.:	I did.
The Court:	So when you look at that paper, it does refresh your recollection?
A.:	Absolutely.
Prosecutor:	Your Honour I tender in evidence as proof of the items removed from Ms. Farid's home this typewritten list.

Do you have any objection to make? Do you have any questions to ask? Compare *U.S. v. Riccardi,* 174 F. 2d 883 (3d Cir., 1948). Suppose the typewritten copy had been made by the investigating officer from Ms. Farid's notes: any difference? See *R. v. Kearns,* [1945] 2 W.W.R. 477 (B.C.C.A.). Compare *R. v. Elder,* [1925] 3 D.L.R. 447 (Man. C.A.).

Problem 3

A witness to a hit-run collision recorded the licence number of the fleeing automobile. The witness advised the investigating officer, who made a notation in his note-book; the witness heard the officer correctly broadcast the licence number on the police radio but never looked at his notebook. At trial, the witness, having lost her own note, seeks to refresh her memory from the officer's notebook. How would you rule? Compare *R. v. Davey* (1969), 68 W.W.R. 142 (B.C.S.C.), and *R. v. Mills,* [1962] 3 All E.R. 298 (C.C.A.). See also *R. v. Hanaway* (1980), 63 C.C.C. (2d) 44 (Ont. Dist. Ct.).

Problem 4

On accused's trial for robbery the victim identified the accused as his assailant and further testified to the fact that within days of the incident he picked the accused out of a line-up organized by the police. A defence witness, Casey, testified that the accused had been with him on the evening in question and neither of them had been near the scene of the robbery. On cross-examination he was asked:

Q.:	Have you always described these events as you now testify?
A.:	Yes — I think so.
Q.:	Do you recall giving a statement to the police about the matter?
A.:	Yes.
Q.:	Within two or three days of the incident?
A.:	Yes.
Q.:	Would you agree with me that your memory of the incident was probably better then than it is today?
A.:	Maybe.

Q.:   Would you care to look at your statement to refresh your memory?

A.:   Not particularly.

Q.:   Why not?

A.:   Because I remember very clearly what happened and it's as I now say.

Q.:   I suggest to you that your statement to the police implicates the accused.

A.:   Maybe it does.

Q.:   I'm showing you this statement and am asking you now whether you recognize it.

A.:   I recognize it. I gave that statement.

Q.:   Thank you witness.

The trial judge charged the jury concerning the normal frailties of eye-witness identification evidence but advised them that Casey's statement confirmed the identification. Comment. Compare *R. v. Moore* (1956), 25 C.R. 159 (Ont. C.A.).

Problem 5

A defence witness was cross-examined with respect to a previous statement made by her to the police. Her evidence on cross-examination after she was shown her statement was:

Q.:   And I draw your attention specifically to the narrative on the second page, and I'm just going to read a part to you, if you don't mind.

"I believe I went out while Sue watched the kids but I'm not sure. If I did, I was back around 1:30 p.m. and Sue left."

Have I accurately read to you what was in your statement?

A.:   Yes, you have.

Q.:   And that's what you told Sergeant Oakley, isn't it?

A.:   Yes, it is.

Q.:   And you told him that because you believed it to be the truth?

A.:   Yes.

Is the previous statement receivable for its truth? Compare *R. v. Scott* (1989), 50 C.C.C. (3d) 337 (B.C.C.A.).

Problem 6

In a running-down case the principal witness for the plaintiff, Steve, described the impact by the defendant's car:

A.:   Yes, and this car passed and I lost sight of Steve and all of a sudden I seen his body in the air straight out — the two shoes come off of his feet and the foot come out of his stocking and turned a somersault and he come down on his back.

On cross-examination the witness was asked:

Q.:   And so you say you saw the whole thing quite clearly?

A.:   Yes, I did.

Q.:   Do you recall the police coming on the scene?

A.:   Yes, when they arrived they asked who it was that was hurt and who saw it.

Q.:   What did you do?

A.:   Well I stepped forward and told them I'd seen it. That I saw Steve when his body flew in the air and turned a somersault.

Counsel for the defendant has now called Constable Jones, one of the investigating officers.

Q.:   When you arrived at the scene were you approached by a lady who said she saw the accident?

Plaintiff's
Counsel: Objection, my lord.

Q.:   Did you call for witnesses?

Plaintiff's
Counsel: Same objection.

What is the objection? How would you rule on it? See *Tzagarakis v. Stevens* (1968), 69 D.L.R. (2d) 466 (N.S.C.A.). Compare *Piddington v. Bennett & Wood Pty. Ltd.* (1940), 63 C.L.R. 533 (Aust. H.C.). See also *R. v. Brown* (1861), 21 U.C.Q.B. 330 (C.A.).

Problem 7

In a civil suit for damages the plaintiff's witness has described the motor vehicle accident, which he attributed to the fault of defendant, and is now being cross-examined:

Q.:   Sir, you've testified that you observed this accident which occurred on July 12, 1987. Can you tell us how you happened to be at that location?

A.:   Well, yes, as a matter of fact. The accident occurred near the Exhibition Stadium and I was on my way to see a ball game there.

Q.:   Who was playing?

A.:   The Blue Jays and the Red Sox.

Q.:   And this was on July 12, 1987.

A.:   Yes.

Q.:   You're sure about that.

A.:   I'm sure.

Q.:   You're as sure about it as you are about all the rest of your evidence.

A.:   Yes, I am!

Q.:   Would it surprise you to know that on July 12, 1987, the Jays were in the middle of a road trip to the West Coast and that night they were playing a game in Seattle?

A: It would surprise me very much. I'm certain the Jays were at Exhibition Stadium that night.

Q: You're right about everything.

A: This time I am. I saw the accident, your client was at fault and the Jays were in Toronto.

Counsel: Your honour, I have no more questions of this witness. I do feel obliged to alert the Court and my friend that in presenting my client's case I intend to call evidence that on the evening in question the Toronto Blue Jays were in Seattle.

Counsel
for
Plaintiff: Your honour, our position is that this matter of where the Blue Jays were
playing is collateral to the real issue between the parties, which is who
was at fault in the accident. Being collateral the rules of evidence preclude
the calling of contradictory evidence. My friend must take the answer of
the witness and live with it.

Problem 8

Rattan, an East Indian gentleman, was charged with sexual assault while
threatening to use a weapon. He testified that sexual intercourse had occurred
but that the complainant had consented. Under cross-examination, the
complainant was asked about events which had occurred ten months before the
incident that was the subject-matter of this charge. The cross-examination took
this course:

Q.:   And you complained to the police on that occasion that you had been raped
by two East Indian gentlemen, didn't you?

A.:   No. I didn't say I got raped. They assumed that.

Q.:   You didn't complain to police?

A.:   No.

Q.:   About being sexually assaulted?

A.:   No, that I recall, no.

Q.:   Not that you recall?

A.:   No.

Q.:   You explained to — you complained to Mr. and Mrs. Alvarez who ran the group
home where you lived at the time of that your reason for being late was you'd
been picked up in a car against your will and sexually assaulted by two East
Indian gentlemen, didn't you?

A.:   No. It's been quite a while. I don't remember that.

Q.:   Could you have made that complaint to Mr. and Mrs. Alvarez and also to the
police?

A.:   No.

Q.:   No?

A.:   That I recall, no.

As part of the defence case, counsel for Rattan wished to call evidence
about the events of the evening ten months earlier. Receivable? Compare *R. v.
Rattan* (1988), 68 C.R. (3d) 84 (B.C.C.A.).

Problem 9

The accused was charged with fraud in connection with the operation of a
travel agency. The accused gave evidence and was asked in cross-examination
whether he had filed income tax returns over a period of years. The accused
stated that he had done so except for two or three years when his books were
under seizure by Crown authorities. The Crown proposes to call evidence to
establish that the accused has not filed any income tax returns for a period of
some ten years. The accused objects. Rule on the objection. See *R. v. Rafael*

(1972), 7 C.C.C. (2d) 325 (Ont. C.A.). Would it affect your ruling if the accused's evidence had come out in examination-in-chief? See *R. v. Gross* (1972), 9 C.C.C. (2d) 122 (Ont. C.A.). Compare *R. v. Porter* (1974), 16 C.C.C. (2d) 422 (B.C. Prov. Ct.).

6. CORROBORATION

(a) When Required?

The ecclesiastical and civil law systems of proof provided that a verdict could not be had on the strength of one witness's evidence. For most issues two witnesses were sufficient but in other cases a higher number might be required. In addition, particular witnesses, according to their inherent quality or weakness, would be assigned a particular numerical value, perhaps a quarter or half of a regular witness. The common law generally resisted attempts at any quantitative measurement of the evidence necessary to a finding and the testimony of a single witness was sufficient. Wigmore sees the common law resistance resident in the different nature of the tribunal there present, the jury. As the jury continued being entitled to act as witnesses themselves until the eighteenth century it would have been otiose for the judge to attempt to erect rules of a number.[344] The common law was interested then in the quality of the witnesses tendered and not their number. The judge was entitled to express his opinion regarding that quality, but it was always for the jury, on the basis of their assessment, to accept or reject the testimony. As Greenshields, J. expressed it:

> On questions of fact the presiding Judge is entitled to express an opinion as to the value of testimony offered; he is entitled to give his opinion as to the credibility of any particular witness, always, however, making it reasonably clear to the Jury that it is not bound to accept his opinion with respect to the facts; that it is the province of the Jury, irrespective of the guiding opinion of the Judge, to find upon the facts, particularly to pass upon the guilt or innocence of the accused. The extent to which the trial Judge should dwell upon the facts is largely discretionary, and that discretion rests with the Judge, and will not, if fairly and judicially exercised, be interfered with by an Appellate Court.[345]

The one common law exception to the general rule was the crime of perjury. The crime of perjury had been normally prosecuted in the Court of Star Chamber and that court followed ecclesiastical procedures wherein two witnesses were required. When the Court of Star Chamber was abolished in 1641 the prosecution of perjury in the common law courts incorporated the long established practice of requiring two witnesses as an exception to its normal process. This practice is now reflected in Canada in section 133 of the Criminal Code, which forbids a conviction of perjury "on the evidence of only one witness unless the evidence of that witness is corroborated in a material particular by evidence that implicates the accused."[346] A number of other statutory exceptions to the general rule have

---

344. For the History of Rules of Number, see 7 Wigmore, *Evidence*, 3d ed., s. 2032.
345. *R. v. Gouin* (1926), 41 Que. K.B. 157 (C.A.). See, however, the criticism by O'Halloran, J.A. in *R. v. Pavlukoff* (1953), 10 W.W.R. 26, 40-44 (B.C.C.A.).
346. See *R. v. Doz* (1984), 12 C.C.C. (3d) 200 (Alta. C.A.) and *R. v. Predy* (1983), 17 C.C.C. (3d) 379 (Alta. C.A.).

been created dependent either on the issue being litigated or on the kind of witness tendered. In some instances corroboration is required for a verdict while in others a warning is required that it is unsafe to convict without corroboration but open to the trier to do so.

(i) *Treason*

By the Criminal Code[347] the offence of treason requires corroboration. The roots of this requirement can be traced to a statute of Edward VI in 1547[348] requiring two witnesses in treason trials. The legislators, mindful of the excesses of Henry VIII, apparently saw this as a device to protect themselves against future regal uses of the law of treason. Wigmore wrote:

> The object of the rule requiring two witnesses in treason is plain enough. It is, as Sir William Blackstone said, to "secure the subject from being sacrificed to fictitious conspiracies, which have been the engines of profligate and crafty politicians in all ages.[349]

(ii) *Forgery*

The Criminal Code provided that corroboration was required to convict of forgery.[350] The requirement was an historical accident. This requirement was initially imposed in the Forgery Act of 1869,[351] when it was decided to allow witnesses to testify in such matters though they were interested in the outcome of the litigation.[352] It was, then, an exhibit of the legislators' caution in moving in that direction. Notice that the requirement of corroboration was limited to cases of those witnesses who were interested persons. When the Criminal Code was enacted in 1892 that limitation was abandoned and corroboration was required regardless of the character of the witness. No intelligent reason can presently be advanced for the requirement and the section was repealed in 1994.[353]

(iii) *Accomplices*

It is well recognized that an accomplice who testifies for the prosecution may be purchasing immunity for himself and this particular weakness in his testimony may need to be pointed out to the trier. During the 19th century it became a rule of practice. Lord Abinger wrote in 1837:

> It is a practice which deserves all the reverence of law, that judges have uniformly told juries that they ought not to pay any respect to the testimony of an accomplice, unless the accomplice is corroborated in some material circumstance. . . . The danger is, that when a man is fixed, and knows that his own guilt is detected, he purchases impunity by falsely accusing others.[354]

---

347. R.S.C. 1985, c. C-46, s. 47(2).
348. 1 Edw. VI, c. 12, s. 22, discussed in 7 Wigmore, *Evidence* (3d ed.), s. 2036.
349. 7 Wigmore, *Evidence* (3d ed.), s. 2037.
350. R.S.C. 1985, c. C-46, s. 367(2). See *R. v. Esposito* (1985), 24 C.C.C. (3d) 88 (Ont. C.A.); leave to appeal to S.C.C. refused 24 C.C.C. (3d) 88n.
351. 32 & 33 Vict., c. 19, s. 54.
352. Parties could not testify until 1869: see the Evidence Act, S.O., 33 Vict., c. 13.
353. Criminal Law Amendment Act, S.C. 1994, c. 44, s. 24.
354. *R. v. Farler* (1837), 173 E.R. 418, 419.

This rule of practice became a rule of law in this century;[355] and the judge was required

> to warn the jury of the danger of convicting a prisoner on the uncorroborated testimony of an accomplice or accomplices, and, in the discretion of the judge, to advise them not to convict upon such evidence; but the judge should point out to the jury that it is within their legal province to convict upon such unconfirmed evidence.[356]

Failure to warn would result in the conviction being overturned. The classic definition of corroboration, accepted as gospel by the Canadian courts, was given by Lord Reading in *R. v. Baskerville:*

> We must hold that evidence in corroboration must be independent testimony which affects the accused by connecting or tending to connect him with the crime. In other words it must be evidence which implicates him, that is, which confirms in some material particular not only the evidence that the crime has been committed, but also that the prisoner committed it.[357]

Some courts required the trial judge to also indicate to the jury what evidence in the case was capable of constituting corroboration and to confine the jury to a consideration of those matters when determining if corroboration existed.[358] The law in this area grew into a complexity[359] which belied its humble beginnings as an admirable practice of caution.

VETROVEC v. R.
[1982] 1 S.C.R. 811, 67 C.C.C. (2d) 1, 27 C.R. (3d) 304

[The accused were two of several persons charged with conspiring to traffic in heroin. The principal evidence against the accused was given by an accomplice who testified that he met the accused in Hong Kong and that they supplied him with six pounds of heroin which he then brought into the United States where he again met with the accused, and then into Canada where he again met them. The trial judge directed the jury that it was dangerous to act on the uncorroborated evidence of the accomplice but that certain pieces of evidence indicating that the accused were in Hong Kong at the relevant time and other pieces of evidence referring to subsequent events and indicating that the accused were involved in drug trafficking were all capable of corroborating the accomplice. The accused were convicted. The appeal by the accused was dismissed.]

The judgment of the court was delivered by DICKSON, J.: —

. . . .

I would like to review and reassess general principles relating to the law of

---

355. See *R. v. Baskerville*, [1916] 2 K.B. 658 (C.C.A.); *Davies v. D.P.P.*, [1954] A.C. 378 (H.L.). And see in Canada *R. v. Gouin*, [1926] S.C.R. 539 accepting the *Baskerville* direction as a rule of law.

356. *R. v. Baskerville, ibid.*, at p. 663. See *R. v. Chayko* (1984), 12 C.C.C. (3d) 157 (Alta. C.A.).

357. *Ibid.*, at p. 667.

358. See *R. v. Racine* (1977), 32 C.C.C. (2d) 468 (Ont. C.A.). The Supreme Court of Canada left this point open: see *Kirsch v. R.* (1982), 62 C.C.C. (2d) 86.

359. To see how complex see Branca, *Corroboration in Studies in Canadian Criminal Evidence* (1972), ed. by Salhany & Carter; and Maloney, *Corroboration Revisited, Studies in Criminal Law and Procedure* (1973, C.B.A). See also the book by Wakeling, *Corroboration in Canadian Law* (1977).

corroboration of accomplices. This is one of the most complicated and technical areas of the law of evidence. It is also in need of reform. Both the Law Reform Commission of Canada (Report on Evidence, s. 88(b) of the proposed Code) and the English Criminal Law Revision Committee (11th Report on Evidence 1972, Cmnd 4991, paras. 183-5), have recently recommended a drastic overhaul of the law of corroboration. The Evidence Code proposed by the Law Reform Commission of Canada would contain the following provision:

88. For greater certainty it is hereby provided that:

. . . .

(b) Every rule of law that requires the corroboration of evidence as a basis for a conviction or that requires that the jury be warned of the danger of convicting on the basis of uncorroborated evidence is abrogated.

. . . .

In the case of a jury charge in which a witness who might be regarded as an accomplice testifies, it has become not merely a rule of practice but a rule of law for the trial judge to warn the jury that it is dangerous to found a conviction on the evidence of an accomplice unless that evidence is corroborated in a material particular implicating the accused. The jury may convict in such circumstances but it is dangerous to do so. The judge must determine as a matter of law whether the witness might be an accomplice for the purposes of the rule. The jury must then decide whether he is in fact an accomplice. The judge explains the legal definition of "corroboration" with heavy reliance upon what was said by Lord Reading in *R. v. Baskerville*. The judge lists for the jury the pieces of evidence which are in his view capable of amounting to corroboration. Finally, they are told that it is for the jury to decide whether the evidence to which their attention has been directed does amount to corroboration, As the study paper of the Law Reform Commission of Canada "Evidence: Paper Study 11, Corroboration" dryly observes an "enormous superstructure ... has been erected on the original basic proposition that the evidence of some witnesses should be approached with caution".

The accused is in the unhappy position of hearing the judge draw particular attention to the evidence which tends to confirm the testimony the accomplice has given. Cogent prejudicial testimony is thus repeated and highlighted. For the jury this part of the charge can only be, in the words of Lord Diplock in *Director of Public Prosecutions v. Hester*, [1972] 3 All E.R. 1056 at p. 1075, "a frequent source of bewilderment". The task of a trial judge seeking to identify the evidence capable of amounting to corroboration is unenviable. Lord Reading in the Baskerville case said that it would be in high degree dangerous to attempt to formulate the kind of evidence which could be regarded as corroboration. It is also often a difficult and dangerous exercise identifying what pieces of evidence are capable of being corroborative. To take a simple example.

. . . .

In evaluating the adequacy of the law in this area, the first question which must be answered is a basic one: why have a special rule for accomplices at all? Credibility of witnesses and the weight of the evidence is, in general, a matter for the trier of fact. Identification evidence, for example, is notoriously weak, and yet the trial judge is not automatically required, as a matter of law, to instruct the jury on this point. Similarly, the trial judge is not required in all cases to warn the jury with respect to testimony of other witnesses with disreputable and untrustworthy backgrounds. Why, then, should we automatically require a warning when an accomplice takes the stand.

. . . .

Since the judge's instructions on this issue involve questions of law, numerous technical appeals are taken on the issue of whether a particular item of evidence is "capable" of constituting corroboration. The body of case-law is so complex that it has in turn produced a massive periodical literature. Moreover, the cases are difficult to reconcile. The Law Reform Commission of Canada has described the case-law in the area as full of "subtleties, variations, inconsistencies and great complexities": study paper 11, at p. 7. The result is that what was originally a simple, common-sense proposition — an accomplice's testimony should be viewed with caution — becomes transformed into a difficult and highly technical area of law. Whether this "enormous superstructure" (to use the description of the Law Reform Commission) has any meaningful relationship with the task performed by the jury is unknown.

. . . .

The law of corroboration is unduly and unnecessarily complex and technical. I would hold that there is no special category for "accomplices". An accomplice is to be treated like any other witness testifying at a criminal trial and the judge's conduct, if he chooses to give his opinion, is governed by the general rules. I would only like to add one or two observations concerning the proper practice to be followed in the trial court where as a matter of common sense something in the nature of confirmatory evidence should be found before the finder of fact relies upon the evidence of a witness whose testimony occupies a central position in the purported demonstration of guilt and yet may be suspect by reason of the witness being an accomplice or complainant or of disreputable character. There are great advantages to be gained by simplifying the instruction to juries on the question as to when a prudent juror will seek some confirmation of the story of such a witness, before concluding that the story is true and adopting it in the process of finding guilt in the accused as charged. It does not, however, always follow that the presiding justice may always simply turn the jury loose upon the evidence without any assisting analysis as to whether or not a prudent finder of fact can find confirmation somewhere in the mass of evidence of the evidence of a witness.

Because of the infinite range of circumstance which will arise in the criminal trial process it is not sensible to attempt to compress into a rule, a formula or a direction the concept of the need for prudent scrutiny of the testimony of any witness. What may be appropriate, however, in some circumstances, is a clear and sharp warning to attract the attention of the juror to the risks of adopting, without more, the evidence of the witness. There is no magic in the word corroboration, or indeed in any other comparable expression such as confirmation and support. The idea implied in those words may, however, in an appropriate case, be effectively and efficiently transmitted to the mind of the trier of fact. This may entail some illustration from the evidence of the particular case of the type of evidence, documentary or testimonial, which might be drawn upon by the juror in confirmation of the witness's testimony or some important part thereof. I do not wish to be taken as saying that such illustration must be carried to exhaustion. However, there is, in some circumstances, particularly in lengthy trials, the need for helpful direction on the question of sifting the evidence where guilt or innocence might, and probably will, turn on the acceptance or rejection, belief or disbelief, of the evidence of one or more witnesses. All of this applies equally in the case of an accomplice, or a disreputable witness of demonstrated moral lack, as, for example, a witness with a record of perjury. All this takes one back to the beginning and that is the search for the impossible: a rule which embodies and codifies common sense in the realm of the process of determining guilt or innocence of an accused on the basis of a record which includes evidence from potentially unreliable sources such as an accomplice.

[The Court, in the result, decided that in this case it would have been sufficient for the trial judge simply to have instructed the jury that they should view the testimony of the accomplice with great caution and that it would be wise to look for other supporting evidence before convicting the accused. However, since the trial judge did outline for the jury items of evidence he considered capable of corroborating the accomplice's testimony, the court examined this evidence to ensure that the accused were not prejudiced by the instruction. The Court decided that the evidence referred to by the trial judge was capable of corroborating the accomplice. In the result, the instructions by the trial judge did not prejudice the accused.]

(iv) *Informers*

R. v. BROOKS

[2000] 1 S.C.R. 237, 30 C.R. (5th) 201, 141 C.C.C. (3d) 321

[A 19-month-old child was found murdered in her crib wrapped in a green comforter. Only the accused and the child's mother had access to her on the night of the murder. The Crown led evidence from two jailhouse informants, King and Balogh, who testified that the accused, while incarcerated, had admitted that he had killed the child to stop her crying. Both informants had lengthy criminal records of dishonesty. One unsuccessfully sought a lighter sentence in return for his testimony and had testified as an informant in a prior trial. The other had a history of substance abuse and a psychiatric history highlighted by suicide attempts, paranoia, deep depression and a belief in clairvoyant ability. Both had histories of offering to testify in criminal trials. The trial judge's jury charge did not provide a *Vetrovec* warning to the jury about the danger of relying on the informants' testimonies. Neither counsel requested a warning nor objected to the lack of a warning. The accused was convicted of first degree murder. The Court of Appeal set aside the conviction and ordered a new trial.]

BASTARACHE, J. (GONTHIER, and McLACHLIN, JJ. concurring): —

. . . .

It is my opinion that the decision not to give a *Vetrovec* warning was within the discretion of the trial judge and that the exercise of this discretion should not have been interfered with on appeal. I have reached this conclusion for the reasons I set out below.

In *Vetrovec*, Dickson J. held that a trial judge has the discretion, and not the duty, to give a clear and sharp warning to the jury with respect to the testimony of certain "unsavoury" witnesses. Dickson J. followed what he referred to as the "common sense" approach, moving away from "blind and empty formalism" and "ritualistic incantations". . . . This Court in *Vetrovec* deliberately chose not to formulate a fixed and invariable rule where "clear and sharp" warnings would be required as a matter of course regarding the testimony of certain categories of witnesses. Rather, where a witness occupies a central position in the determination of guilt and, yet, may be suspect because of a disreputable or untrustworthy character, a clear and sharp warning may be appropriate to alert the jury to the risks of adopting the evidence "without more". It is therefore within the trial judge's discretion to give a *Vetrovec* caution. . . . In exercising his or her discretion to warn the jury regarding certain evidence, the trial judge may consider, *inter alia*, the credibility of the witness and the importance of the evidence to the Crown's case. These factors affect whether the *Vetrovec* warning is required. In other words, the greater the concern over the credibility of the witness and the more important the evidence, the more likely the *Vetrovec* caution will be mandatory. Where the evidence of so called "unsavoury witnesses" represents the whole of the evidence against the accused, a "clear and sharp" *Vetrovec* warning may be warranted. Where, however, there is strong evidence to support the conviction in the absence of the potentially "unsavoury" evidence, and less reason to doubt the witness's credibility, the *Vetrovec* warning would not be required, and a lesser instruction would be justified. The trial judge's instruction with respect to the evidence of jailhouse informants must therefore be commensurate with the particular circumstances of the case. For example, the trial judge is not required to give a "clear and sharp" warning on the dangers of convicting on the impugned evidence where, in the circumstances, the trial judge believes that there is no such danger. Similarly, the trial judge may properly decline to give a warning if the warning may prejudice the accused's case rather than assist it. Provided there is a foundation for the trial judge's exercise of discretion, appellate courts should not interfere. Here, that foundation was established having regard to the credibility of the witnesses, the importance of their evidence and the failure to request a warning.

. . . .

To find that the trial judge's failure to provide a "clear and sharp" *Vetrovec* warning in the circumstances of this case amounts to an error of law runs counter to the spirit of *Vetrovec*, which affirmed a judicial discretion to provide warnings only in appropriate circumstances. Provided there is a foundation for the judge's exercise of discretion, appellate courts should not interfere. Here that foundation existed. For these reasons, I am unable to conclude that the failure of the trial judge to give a "clear and sharp" *Vetrovec* warning amounted to an error of law. I would allow the appeal accordingly and restore the conviction entered by the trial judge.

MAJOR, J. (IACOBUCCI and ARBOUR, JJ. concurring): —

. . . .

In my opinion, the trial judge ought to have given a *Vetrovec* warning. In its absence the charge was not the equivalent nor was it adequate. In the result it cannot be said that the verdict would necessarily have been the same and accordingly the appeal should be dismissed.

. . . .

In summary, two main factors are relevant when deciding whether a *Vetrovec* warning is necessary: the witness's credibility, and the importance of the witness's testimony to the Crown's case. No specific threshold need be met on either factor before a warning becomes necessary. Instead, where the witness is absolutely essential to the Crown's case, more moderate credibility problems will warrant a warning. Where the witness has overwhelming credibility problems, a warning may be necessary even if the Crown's case is a strong one without the witness's evidence. In short, the factors should not be looked to independently of one another but in combination.

Recommendations of the Kaufman Report

Since the decisions of this Court in *Vetrovec* and *Bevan*, the extreme dangers of relying on the use of "jailhouse informers" as witnesses in criminal prosecutions has been highlighted in the *Report of The Commission on Proceedings Involving Guy Paul Morin* (the "Kaufman Report") released in 1998 where the Honourable Fred Kaufman, C.M., Q.C., stated at p. 602:

> In-custody informers are almost invariably motivated by self-interest. They often have little or no respect for the truth or their testimonial oath or affirmation. Accordingly, they may lie or tell the truth, depending only upon where their perceived self-interest lies. In-custody confessions are often easy to allege and difficult, if not impossible, to disprove.

and at p. 638:

> The evidence at this Inquiry demonstrates the inherent unreliability of in-custody informer testimony, its contribution to miscarriages of justice and the substantial risk

that the dangers may not be fully appreciated by the jury. In my view, the present law has developed to the point that a cautionary instruction is virtually mandated in cases where the in-custody informer's testimony is contested.

Since the release of the Kaufman Report, the Ministry of the Attorney General of Ontario has revised its internal policies to reflect many of the Report's recommendations. New policies include the establishment of an "In-Custody Informer Committee", the function of which is to review the use of all in-custody informers in criminal trials to determine whether their use as a witness is in the public interest. The Ministry has also adopted into its Policy Manual the Kaufman Report's recommended list of factors to be considered in assessing an informer's reliability or lack thereof. The factors also serve as a useful guide to a trial judge when determining whether a *Vetrovec* warning is necessary.

. . . .

In my opinion the failure of the trial judge to give a *Vetrovec* warning was a misdirection of law. The question is then whether in light of all the evidence the test in *Bevan* is met. Would the result have necessarily been the same?

[Major, J. then examined the other evidence in the case and concluded.]

There was evidence that implicated the accused but with a proper instruction regarding the testimony of the jailhouse informants it is difficult for me to preclude the possibility of a different result. I agree with the Court of Appeal and would dismiss the appeal and confirm the order for a new trial.

BINNIE, J.: —

I agree with the result reached by Justice Bastarache, but I reach that conclusion by a different route. In my view, the evidence of the "jailhouse informants" in this case was tainted by a combination of some of the more notorious badges of testimonial unreliability, including the opportunity to lie for personal benefit, and the jury ought to have been given a clear and sharp warning to that effect. The trial judge erred in law in failing to give such a warning, as found by Justice Major and a majority of the Ontario Court of Appeal. At the same time, I differ, with respect, from the conclusion that this error of law requires a new trial. Given the other evidence against the respondent that was necessarily accepted by the jury in reaching their verdict of first degree murder, I think, with great respect to those of the opposite view, that there is no reasonable possibility that the verdict would have been different had the error of law not been made.

. . . .

[Binnie, J. then reviewed the evidence and concluded.]

For these reasons, I conclude that the failure of the trial judge to give a *Vetrovec* warning was an error of law, but that there is no reasonable possibility the jury would have rendered a different verdict had the proper warning been given. The Crown bears a heavy onus in seeking the application of the curative provision of s. 686(1)(b)(iii) but, for the reasons given, it is my view that justice does not require a new trial on the particular facts of this case. The appeal should therefore be allowed and the respondent's conviction and sentence restored.

(v) *Primary Witnesses in Sex Cases*

In the early common law the testimony of the victim in the trial of a sexual offence was sufficient to support a conviction. In Hale, *Pleas of the Crown,* we read:

> The party ravished may give evidence upon oath and is in law a competent witness; but the credibility of her testimony, and how far forth she is to be believed, must be

left to the jury, and is more or less credible according to the circumstances of fact that concur in that testimony. . . . It is one thing whether a witness be admissible to be heard; another thing, whether they are to be believed when heard. It is true, rape is a most detestable crime, and therefore ought severely and impartially to be punished with death; but it must be remembered that it is an accusation easily to be made and hard to be proved; and harder to be defended by the party accused, tho never so innocent.[360]

By 1925, however, the common law had come to demand a similar warning about the evidence of primary witnesses in sex cases as they had required respecting the evidence of accomplices. Hewart, L.C.J. in *R. v. Jones* wrote:

The proper direction in such a case [where the offence charged is a sexual offence] is that it is not safe to convict upon the uncorroborated testimony of the prosecutrix, but that the jury, if they are satisfied of the truth of her evidence, may, after paying attention to that warning, nevertheless convict.[361]

In Canada the Criminal Code was amended in 1954 to provide that with regard to five sexual offences (rape, attempted rape, sexual intercourse with a female under 14, sexual intercourse with a female between 14 and 16, and indecent assault on a female):

. . . the judge shall, if the only evidence that implicates the accused is the evidence, given under oath, of the female person in respect of whom the offence is alleged to have been committed and that evidence is not corroborated in a material particular by evidence that implicates the accused, instruct the jury that it is not safe to find the accused guilty in the absence of such corroboration, but that they are entitled to find the accused guilty if they are satisfied beyond a reasonable doubt that her evidence is true.[362]

Glanville Williams sought to justify the instruction:

There is sound reason for this, because sexual cases are particularly subject to the danger of deliberately false charges, resulting from sexual neurosis, fantasy, jealousy, spite, or simply a girl's refusal to admit that she consented to an act of which she is now ashamed. Of these various possibilities, the most subtle are those connected with mental complexes.[363]

In 1975 the Criminal Code provision was repealed and, after a period of uncertainty, it now seems settled that the common law requirement of a warning was not thereby revived.[364]

The Criminal Code continued to require corroboration prior to conviction for a number of other sexual offences: per section 139, sexual intercourse with the feeble-minded, incest, seduction of a female between 16 and 18 years of age,

---

360. 1680, Hale, L.C.J., *Pleas of the Crown*, 1, 633, 635 quoted in 7 Wigmore, *Evidence*, 3d ed., s. 2061.

361. (1925), 19 Cr. App. R. 40, 41.

362. See R.S.C. 1970, c. 34, s. 142.

363. "Corroboration — Sexual Cases," [1962] Crim. L. Rev. 662.

364. See *R. v. Camp* (1977), 36 C.C.C. (2d) 511 (Ont. C.A.) and *R. v. Firkins* (1977), 37 C.C.C. (2d) 227 (B.C.C.A.); leave to appeal to S.C.C. refused (1978), 80 D.L.R. (3d) 63n. But compare *R. v. Riley* (1978), 42 C.C.C. (2d) 437 (Ont. C.A.) and *R. v. Curtis*, [1989] N.J. No. 84 (C.A.), regarding the need for caution when relying solely on the evidence of the complainant in a sexual assault case.

seduction under the promise of marriage, sexual intercourse with a step-daughter, seduction of female passengers on vessels, parent or guardian of female person procuring her defilement; per section 195, procuring;[365] per section 253 communicating venereal disease to another person;[366] per section 256 procuring a feigned marriage.[367] Wigmore described statutory requirements of corroboration in sex cases:

> The fact is that, in the light of modern psychology, this technical rule of corroboration seems but a crude and childish measure, if it be relied upon as an adequate means for determining the credibility of the complaining witness in such charges. The problem of estimating the veracity of feminine testimony in complaints against masculine offenders is baffling enough to the experienced psychologist. This statutory rule is unfortunate in that it tends to produce reliance upon a rule of thumb. Better to inculcate the resort to an expert scientific analysis of the particular witness' mentality, as the true measure of enlightenment.[368]

Notice that the requirements here imposed *forbade conviction* even if the trier of fact was satisfied of the accused's guilt beyond a reasonable doubt.

The neanderthal ideas and attitudes above described in this section have now been largely overcome, at least in our legislative provisions. In 1982 section 139 was repealed and section 246.4 enacted. Section 246.4 was later enlarged in 1988 and the counterpart section now provides:

> **274.** Where an accused is charged with an offence under section 151, 152, 153, 155, 159, 160, 170, 171, 172, 173, 212, 271, 272 or 273, no corroboration is required for a conviction and the judge shall not instruct the jury that it is unsafe to find the accused guilty in the absence of corroboration.

R. v. S. (F.)
(1997), 116 C.C.C. (3d) 435 (Ont. C.A.)

[The accused was charged with sexual assault causing bodily harm.]

FINLAYSON J.A. (WEILER and LASKIN JJ.A. concurring):—The complainant's testimony was central to the case for the Crown. However, with the exception of her evidence with respect to the incidents at the motel, her testimony was unsupported by any independent confirmatory evidence. In my opinion this case did call for a "clear and sharp warning" in relation to the testimony of the complainant as called for in *Vetrovec*. Apart from the highly suspect account she gave of the Lake Wilcox incident, the complainant had a lengthy psychiatric history, the details of which were before the jury, and which included "flashback" recollections of certain events. Her past conduct also revealed a pattern of false statements of fact to her doctors.

365. See now R.S.C. 1985, c. C-46, s. 212.
366. *Ibid.*, s. 289.
367. *Ibid.*, s. 292.
368. 7 Wigmore, *Evidence*, 3d ed., s. 2061, p. 354. For a good critical note calling for the repeal of such statutory provisions see "The Rape Corroboration Requirement: Repeal Not Reform" (1972), 81 Yale L.J. 1365. See also Bienen, "A Question of Credibility: John Henry Wigmore's Use of Scientific Authority" (1983), 19 Cal. Western L. Rev. 235.

(vi) *Unsworn Evidence of Children*

If a child is sworn as a witness the judge is directed to warn the jury to treat his evidence with caution much as he would warn them with respect to the testimony of accomplices. In *Kendall v. R.,*[369] Judson, J. explained:

> The basis for the rule of practice which requires the Judge to warn the jury of the danger of convicting on the evidence of a child, even when sworn as a witness, is the mental immaturity of the child. The difficulty is fourfold: 1. His capacity of observation. 2. His capacity of recollection. 3. His capacity to understand questions put and frame intelligent answers. 4. His moral responsibility.

Section 586 of the Criminal Code forbade conviction "upon the unsworn evidence of a child unless the evidence of the child is corroborated in a material particular by evidence that implicated the accused." Provisions in the Canada Evidence Act and in most of the provincial Evidence Acts mirrored this requirement.[370] Notice again that findings were *prohibited* though the trier is satisfied beyond a reasonable doubt.

In 1988 section 586 (659) of the Criminal Code[371] and section 16(2) of the Canada Evidence Act[372] were repealed. While the requirement of corroboration for the unsworn testimony of children was dispensed with, the legislation did not, unlike the new section 246.4, say anything forbidding a cautionary warning. For many, unfortunately, the "wisdom" of *Kendall* will cause many judges and lawyers to continue to be distrustful of the evidence of children. The common sense displayed in *Vetrovec* mandates that we ought not to automatically characterize a witness's capacity for truth-telling depending on whether they belong to a particular class of people. No one should assume that all children are inherently suspect. The child witness should be treated like other witnesses, as an individual with whatever individual shortcomings or individual attributes that are there to be observed. Rather than parroting such phrases as "Out of the mouths of babes can only come truth . . .", or "It is well known that children fantasize (have poor memories, lack perceptual abilities) . . ." we, as lawyers, need to become more aware of the social science literature and the empirical studies that have been done.

R. v. S. (W.)
(1994), 29 C.R. (4th) 143, 90 C.C.C. (3d) 242

[The accused was charged with sexual interference. The complainant, who was 15 years old at the time of the trial, testified that the accused, her uncle by marriage, touched her for a sexual purpose up to 200 times between January 1988 and January 1990 when she stayed overnight as a guest of the accused's family at their farmhouse. The Court of Appeal found that there was a conflict in the evidence about when and in what circumstances the complainant slept downstairs, which was where the interference allegedly took place. The Court expressed a concern that the trial judge, having made a positive finding of credibility in favour of the complainant, did not appear to have given serious

---

369. (1962), 132 C.C.C. 216, 220 (S.C.C.).
370. See Canada Evidence Act, s. 16(2); Ontario Evidence Act, s. 18(2).
371. 1987, c. 24, s. 15; see now R.S.C. 1985, c. C-46, s. 659; 1993, c. 45, s. 9.
372. 1987, c. 24, s. 18.

consideration to the possibility that, on the whole of the evidence, there was a reasonable doubt that the alleged acts did, in fact, occur.]

FINLAYSON J.A.:— . . . .

My concern in this case is that the trial judge, having made a positive finding of credibility in favour of the complainant, does not appear to have given serious consideration to the possibility that, on the whole of the evidence, there is a reasonable doubt that the alleged acts did, in fact, occur. I think that the words of Wood J.A. in *R. v. K. (V.)* (1991), 4 C.R. (4th) 338 (B.C. C.A.), another case involving the alleged sexual touching of a child, are appropriate to bear in mind, where he stated at p. 357:

> I have already alluded to the danger, in a case where the evidence consists primarily of the allegations of a complainant and the denial of the accused, that the trier of fact will see the issue as one of deciding whom to believe. Earlier in the judgment, I noted the gender-related stereotypical thinking that led to assumptions about the credibility of complainants in sexual cases which we have at long last discarded as totally inappropriate. It is important to ensure that they are not replaced by an equally pernicious set of assumptions about the believability of complainants which would have the effect of shifting the burden of proof to those accused of such crimes.

Galligan J.A. alluded to a similar danger in *R. v. J. (F.E.)* (1990), 53 C.C.C. (3d) 64 (Ont. C.A.) at pp. 67-68:

> While there is no scale upon which conflicting evils can be weighed, it should be remembered that revolting as child sexual abuse is, it would be horrible for an innocent person to be convicted of it. For that reason I think the courts must be vigilant to ensure that the zeal to punish child sexual abusers does not erode the rules which the courts have developed over the centuries to prevent the conviction of the innocent.

It is evident from his reasons that the trial judge was impressed with the demeanour of the complainant in the witness box and the fact that she was not shaken in cross-examination. I am not satisfied, however, that a positive finding of credibility on the part of the complainant is sufficient to support a conviction in a case of this nature where there is significant evidence which contradicts the complainant's allegations. We all know from our personal experiences as trial lawyers and judges that honest witnesses, whether they are adults or children, may convince themselves that inaccurate versions of a given event are correct and they can be very persuasive. The issue, however, is not the sincerity of the witness but the reliability of the witness's testimony. Demeanour alone should not suffice to found a conviction where there are significant inconsistencies and conflicting evidence on the record: see *R. v. Norman* (1993), 16 O.R. (3d) 295 at pp. 311-15 for a discussion on this subject.

The Supreme Court of Canada has addressed the issue of the assessment of the evidence of child witnesses in two leading cases dealing with allegations of sexual abuse: *R. v. B. (G.)* (1990), 56 C.C.C. (3d) 200 and *R. v. W. (R.)* (1992), 74 C.C.C. (3d) 134. In *R. v. W. (R.)*, McLachlin J. comments that there have been two major changes in recent years in the approach that courts should take to the evidence of young children. The first is the removal of the notion, found at common law and codified in legislation, that the evidence of children was inherently unreliable and therefore to be treated with special caution. The second is a new appreciation that it may be wrong to apply adult tests for credibility to the evidence of children. With respect to the second change, she cites Wilson J. in *R. v. B. (G.)* at pp. 219-220, where Wilson J. advocates a common sense approach when dealing with the testimony of young children and advises judges not to impose the same exacting standards upon them as upon adults. Wilson J. emphasizes that the courts should continue to carefully assess the credibility of child witnesses and she does not suggest that the standard of proof beyond a reasonable doubt should cease to apply in criminal cases in which young children have been victimized. In *R. v. W. (R.)*, McLachlin J. adds that we should not approach the evidence of children from the perspective of rigid stereotypes and we should adopt a ''common sense'' approach which takes into account the strengths and weaknesses characterizing the evidence offered in the particular case.

As I understand these two judgments, we must assess witnesses of tender years for what they are, children, and not adults. We should not expect them as witnesses to perform in the same manner as adults. This does not mean, however, that we should subject the testimony of children to a lower level of scrutiny for reliability than we would do adults. My concern is that some trial judges may be inadvertently relaxing the proper level of scrutiny to which the evidence of children should be subjected. The changes to the evidentiary rules were intended to make child evidence more readily available to the court by removing the restraints on its use that existed previously but were never intended to encourage an undiscriminating acceptance of the evidence of children while holding adults to higher standards. With respect, I think the case on appeal illustrates the latter approach.[373]

The Court allowed the appeal on the basis that the verdict was unreasonable. The Court recognized the authority of *R. v. W. (R.)*,[374] that an appellate court determining the reasonableness of a verdict is entitled, while giving due deference to the trial judge's advantaged position, to assess findings of credibility made in the court below. To similar effect, with the majority and minority of the appellate court assessing credibility quite differently, see *R. v. François*.[375]

In *R. v. W. (R.)*, McLachlin J. wrote:

The repeal of provisions creating a legal requirement that children's evidence be corroborated does not prevent the judge or jury from treating a child's evidence with caution where such caution is merited in the circumstances of the case.[376]

In *R. v. W. (R.S.)*[377] Justice Twaddle for the Court developed this thought:

Whilst the previously held views as to the unreliability of complaints in cases of sexual assault have now been discarded, it would be foolhardy to assume that the danger once feared in every case now exists in none. The rationale for the old rules of practice requiring corroboration was not grounded in stereotypical thinking alone.[378]

R. v. G. (A.)
(1998), 21 C.R. (5th) 149, 130 C.C.C. (3d) 30 (Ont. C.A.)

[The accused was convicted of sexual assault. The complainant was a niece of the accused. She alleged that on three occasions between December 1986 and March 1988, the accused briefly touched and rubbed her vaginal area while she was fully clothed. The accused denied the assault and led evidence of a motive in the complainant to fabricate. The trial was held in 1996. On appeal the issue was whether the verdict was unreasonable. The majority voted to dismiss the appeal. In the course of his dissenting opinion, Justice Finlayson commented on his understanding of the positions of complainants and accused in sexual assault cases.]

Finlayson J.A.:—

The trial judge failed to approach the complainant's evidence with the scepticism that it deserved in this case. There is not the remotest of supporting evidence that any

373. *Ibid.*, at pp. 148-51.
374. [1992] 2 S.C.R. 122.
375. (1994), 31 C.R. (4th) 201 (S.C.C.).
376. *Supra*, note 374, at p. 266.
377. (1992), 74 C.C.C. (3d) 1, 8 (Man. C.A.).
378. *Ibid.*, at p. 8.

sexual acts took place. The sexual acts are highly ambiguous coming as they do from an uncle and "godfather" to the young girl. Any form of "horseplay" could explain them. Giving the most generous interpretation to the acts as described by the complainant, they are hardly consistent with intent to commit a sexual assault. Even the trial judge noted that at the time of their occurrence, the complainant did not know what the touchings meant. The evidence is very much open to the construction that the appellant could have had some incidental contact with the girl that was entirely innocent.

There is no pattern of abuse here. The appellant must have had more than three opportunities to abuse the girl if he was of a mind to. No explanation is offered for the fact that the assaults simply ceased. On the darker side, the evidence is not inconsistent with the appellant's contention that the complainant had a motive to fabricate, given the appellant's concerns regarding her friendship with N.

Having had the advantage of reading the transcripts of many of what are termed "historical sexual abuse cases" that have come before this court over the last decade, I am concerned that this case does fit a pattern of allegations of sexual abuse that are initiated by ulterior motives. The complaints are usually of this vague and unsubstantiated nature. They are so stale dated and amorphous that it is impossible for the person accused to give a detailed rebuttal to them without arousing suspicion as to why his memory is so precise.

The defence also reveals a pattern. Faced with attempting to recall what must have been a non-event to any normal person, the accused seized upon a material discrepancy in the complainant's evidence and demonstrated objectively that the appellant's story cannot be true in a significant particular. In this case it was the red couch. [The complainant described the assaults as having occurred on a red couch in the basement. Evidence was led that the red couch didn't come onto the premises until well after the complained of incident.] The trial judge at no time stated that he disbelieved the appellant or the other witnesses on this issue (by way of a sidebar, he did not expressly disbelieve the appellant on any, of his evidence). His approach to the red couch evidence was to ignore its importance. He said:

> The complained of detail is this case of course relates to the where of the offence as recounted by a six or seven-year-old as opposed to the who, the who-did-it and what-was-done to her by him.

The criminal courts need a new gatekeeper. Parliament and the judiciary have radically eroded the traditional protection available to the accused in sexual assault cases. My comment does not reflect nostalgia. The changes were long overdue. However, the pendulum must not be allowed to swing too far in the other direction. As I had occasion to observe in *R. v. P. (M.B.)* (1992), 9 O.R. (3d) 424, affirmed [1994] 1 S.C.R. 555 at p. 433:

> In our efforts to protect those most deserving of protection, we must not neglect our traditional role as protectors of the rights of the accused to a fair trial.

The majority of sexual offences are now tried without a jury in the Ontario Court (Provincial Division). There is no preliminary hearing in which both the Crown and the defence can make some assessment of the reliability of the complainant's testimony. In any event, the safeguard of the exercise of prosecutorial discretion in weak cases has fallen victim to the catchword "zero tolerance". The former rules regarding corroboration have been abolished. Despite the obvious need in most cases for some supporting evidence, many judges pay lip service to this admonition. Distortions in the complainant's evidence are too often dismissed as the norm with children. The accused who testifies is granted no such leeway. The burden quickly shifts to him to explain his conduct. Reasonable doubt, the most fundamental concept of British justice, runs the risk of becoming a hollow invocation, rather than the shield against injustice it was meant to be.

There has to be a new gatekeeper and that person is the trial judge. He was not present in this case. The trial judge was prepared to convict the appellant on the flimsiest of evidence. This complaint should not have gone to trial, much less have led to a conviction. Where the trial judge convicts on evidence such as this record displays, the Court of Appeal has more than the right, it has the duty to interfere and, in the interests of justice, quash the verdict as unreasonable.

LABROSSE, BORINS JJ.A. concurring:— . . .

In applying the unreasonable verdict test the appellate court should show great deference to findings of credibility made at trial given the advantage possessed by the trial judge in hearing the evidence and observing the demeanour of the witnesses, I conclude that the trial judge's verdict is supported by the evidence and is not unreasonable, as conceded by counsel for the appellant. I cannot agree with the comments made by Finlayson J.A. with respect to sexual assaults, particularly those found in paragraphs 25 to 26 of his reasons.

With whom do you agree?

(vii) *Miscellaneous Provisions*

A number of statutory provisions exist in provincial legislation which require corroboration for a finding. For example, provisions in a number of Evidence Acts demand corroboration in actions against estates of deceased persons,[379] and in actions by or against the mentally ill.[380]

(b) What is Corroboration?

The classic definition of corroboration given by Lord Reading in *R. v. Baskerville*[381] requires that the corroborative evidence be independent of the principal witness and implicate the accused, that is "confirms in some material particular not only the evidence that the crime has been committed, but also that the prisoner committed it." Many of the statutory provisions requiring corroboration have similar language: "upon the evidence of only one witness, unless the evidence of that witness is corroborated in a material particular by evidence that implicates the accused." It is in the application of this definition to the evidence in the particular case that trial judges have had great difficulty and "probably has given rise to more new trials being ordered by appellate courts than any other branch of the law of evidence."[382] It is difficult, if not impossible, to reconcile all the reported decisions on the application of the definition but the Supreme Court has recently sought to explain.

R. v. B. (G.)
[1990] 2 S.C.R. 3, 77 C.R. (3d) 327, 56 C.C.C. (3d) 161

[The accused was charged with committing an aggravated sexual assault on the complainant, a kindergarten student who was five years old at the time of the alleged offence. The complainant gave unsworn testimony at the trial. There was, then, a need for corroboration, pursuant to the legislation then in existence.]

WILSON J. (L'HEUREUX-DUBÉ, GONTHIER, CORY and MCLACHLIN JJ., concurring):— . . .

---

379. See, *e.g.*, R.S.O. 1980, c. 145, s. 13; R.S.A. 1980, c. A-21, s. 12.
380. See, *e.g.*, R.S.O. 1980, c. 145, s. 14; R.S.N. 1970, c. 115, s. 15.
381. [1916] 2 K.B. 658 (C.C.A.).
382. Task Force Report on Uniform Rules of Evidence (1981), p. 428.

Any review of the case law dealing with corroboration must begin with a discussion of *Baskerville*. . . .

It is the interpretation of [*Baskerville*] which seems to have caused confusion in recent years. . . .

[The Crown] submits that the *Baskerville* rule is open to two interpretations. The first, or narrow rule, sees corroborative evidence as independent evidence that itself implicates the accused. The second, and considerably broader interpretation, is that if the witness identifies the accused and the evidence of the witness is confirmed in some material particular, then there is corroboration in law of that witness's evidence. The Crown advocates the broader interpretation. However, in my view, support for the broader interpretation is not to be found in Lord Reading's judgment. He made it abundantly clear throughout his reasons that there had to be corroborative evidence as to a material circumstance of the crime <u>and</u> as to the identity of the accused in relation to that crime. In *Vetrovec*, Dickson J. shared this view, stating at p. 826:

> Prior to the judgment of Lord Reading, there had been controversy over whether corroborative evidence must implicate the accused, or whether it was sufficient if it simply strengthened the credibility of the accomplice. Lord Reading settled the controversy in favour of the former view.

In the years following *Baskerville* the narrow interpretation of the rule was approved in numerous decisions of this Court. One text writer has commented that this Court acted upon the narrow interpretation of the rule on at least fifteen occasions over a period of sixty years: see Schiff, *Evidence in the Litigation Process* (1988), vol. 1, at p. 613. . . . .

The Court [in *Vetrovec*] expressed a preference for a common sense approach rather than the overly technical approach in *Baskerville*. It found at least three problems with *Baskerville*. The first was that it confuses the reason behind the accomplice warning and prompts the courts to determine whether the corroborative evidence fits the definition rather than deciding whether there is evidence that bolsters the credibility of the accomplice. Secondly, because corroboration became a legal term of art the law in the area became increasingly complex and technical. Thirdly, and most importantly, the Court was of the view that the definition was unsound in principle. Dickson J. stated at p. 826:

> With great respect, on principle Lord Reading's approach seems perhaps over-cautious. The reason for requiring corroboration is that we believe the witness has good reason to lie. We therefore want some other piece of evidence which tends to convince us that he is telling the truth. Evidence which implicates the accused does indeed serve to accomplish that purpose but it cannot be said that this is the only sort of evidence which will accredit the accomplice.

. . . .

It seems to me, therefore, that this Court has clearly rejected an ultra technical approach to corroboration and has returned to a common sense approach which reflects the original rationale for the rule and allows cases to be determined on their merits. . . .

I am, accordingly, in agreement with the Crown's position.

. . . .

Also in favour of the liberal interpretation [of the legislation requiring corroboration] are the presumptions that the law does not require the impossible and the legislator intends only what is just and reasonable. Since the only evidence implicating the accused in many sexual offences against children will be the evidence of the child, imposing too restrictive a standard on their testimony may permit serious offences to go unpunished and perhaps to continue. Moreover, it is reasonable to assume that the legislator did not intend an accused to benefit from the youthful age of his victim by placing unnecessary impediments in the way of prosecuting offences against small children.

8

Hearsay

A picture of the hearsay rule with its exceptions would resemble an old-fashioned crazy quilt made of patches cut from a group of paintings by cubists, futurists and surrealists.[1]

1. THE RULE

(a) History

The hearsay rule was described by Professor Wigmore as "that most characteristic rule of the Anglo-American law of evidence — a rule which may be esteemed, next to jury trial, the greatest contribution of that eminently practical legal system to the world's methods of procedure."[2] It was not always thus, and it may assist our understanding of the rule's present day workings and justifications if we have some regard for its origin.[3]

The exclusionary rule prohibiting hearsay did not come into existence until the latter part of the 17th century as the jury's role in fact resolution completed its evolution into its present form.[4] The jury initially was not to decide issues on the basis of evidence produced in open court; its members were selected because they had knowledge of the facts. Insofar as their knowledge was imperfect it was their function to investigate and gather information from those who were knowledgeable. The members of the jury were witnesses from the community, selected by a public official, who then tried the case.[5]

> We must not think of them as coming into court ignorant, like their modern successors, of the cases about which they will have to speak. . . . Some of the verdicts that are given must be founded on hearsay and floating tradition. Indeed, it is the duty of the jurors, so soon as they have been summoned, to make inquiries about the facts of which they will have to speak when they come before the court. They must collect testimony; they must weigh it and state the net result in a verdict. . . . At the least a fortnight had been given them in which to "certify themselves" of the facts. We know of no rule of law which prevented them from listening during this interval to the tale of the litigants; indeed it was their duty to discover the truth. . . . Separately or collectively, in court or out of court, they have listened to somebody's story and believed it. . . . We may say, if we will, that the old jurors were witnesses; but even

---

1.   Morgan and Maguire, "Looking Backward and Forward at Evidence" (1937), 50 Harv. L.R. 909 at 921.

2.   5 Wigmore, *Evidence* (Chad. Rev.), p. 28.

3.   A full account is provided in 5 Wigmore, *Evidence* (Chad. Rev.), p. 1364. And see Morgan, "History and Theory of the Hearsay Rule", in *Some Problems of Proof under the Anglo-American System of Litigation* (1956), Columbia University Press, pp. 106-40.

4.   Wigmore provides numerous citations to cases where hearsay is being received, despite objections, through the sixteenth and seventeenth centuries and fixes the date of the doctrine as between 1675 and 1690.

5.   See generally, Thayer, "Trial by Jury and Its Development," in *A Preliminary Treatise on Evidence at the Common Law* (1898), Chapter 3.

in the early years of the thirteenth century they were not, and were hardly supposed to be, eye-witnesses.[6]

Witnesses had been called before the jury during the 13th and 14th centuries but these were pre-appointed witnesses; witnesses who had agreed at the time of the transaction to support its credit if later called upon, for example, attesting witnesses to a deed. These witnesses joined with the jurors and conferred privately to make a finding; they did not, until the middle of the 14th century,[7] testify in open court, but rather assisted the jury members with their particular knowledge. Professor Thayer described it:

> In the earlier cases these witnesses sometimes appear to have been conceived of as a constituent part of the jury; it was a combination of business witnesses and community witnesses who tried the case, the former supplying to others their more exact information. . . . But in time the jury and the witnesses came to be sharply discriminated. . . . The charge to the jury is to tell the truth to the best of their knowledge, while that to the witnesses is to tell the truth and loyally inform the inquest, without saying anything about their knowledge; "for the witnesses," says Thorpe, C.J. in 1349, "should say nothing but what they know as certain, i.e., what they see and hear."

It was not until the latter part of the 15th century that ordinary witnesses as we know them today, casual witnesses as Bentham called them, began to testify in open court about disputed facts. It was a natural development that the same requirement of speaking to first-hand knowledge imposed on the pre-appointed witnesses should eventually be placed on the casual witness.

Though witnesses began informing the jury in the latter part of the 15th century, their importance was slight in comparison to the jury's informing itself. This gradually changed during the 16th and 17th centuries, at which time evidence presented in open court became the prime source of information for the jury. The jury ceased to be witness and became solely trier. Coincident with this development came the need for the exclusionary rules of evidence, as the jury was directed to rely only on what it learned publicly in court. There obviously had been little need for exclusionary rules when the jury was informing itself. The earlier prohibition against the pre-appointed witnesses speaking to second-hand information may have caused litigants and judges to be skeptical about the value of hearsay from these new witnesses, and while it was being received there was constant worrying over its worth, and agitation for reform. In 1552[8] the first statutory attempt at reform took place. Although it was confined to treason trials, it demanded the production of the accusers, if then alive, to confront the

---

6.   Pollock and Maitland, *The History of English Law* (2d ed., 1898), Vol. 2, pp. 621-28.
7.   See Thayer, *supra*, note 5 at p. 125.
8.   5 & 6 Edw. VI, c. 11, s. 12. "Which said accusers at the time of the arraignment of the party accused, if they be then living, shall be brought in person before the party so accused, and avow and maintain that which they have to say to prove him guilty." And, in (1554), 1 & 2 Phil. & Mar., c. 10, s. 11: Upon arraignment for treason the persons "or two of them at the least," who shall declare any thing against the accused "shall, if living and within the realm, be brought forth in person before the party arraigned if he require the same, and object and say openly in his hearing what they or any of them can against him."

accused at the trial and maintain their earlier depositions. This requirement was a marked departure from the then normal criminal trial process wherein previously sworn depositions were routinely filed. The celebrated case of Sir Walter Raleigh's prosecution on an indictment for conspiracy to commit various treasons[9] illustrates the practice of the time, the narrow judicial construction given the statutory efforts at reform, and the arguments then being made for change. When Raleigh demanded his statutory right to be confronted with his accuser, Lord Cobham, he was refused:

Raleigh: The Proof of the Common Law is by witness and jury: let Cobham be here, let him speak it. Call my accuser before my face, and I have done. . . . All this is but one Accusation of Cobham's, I hear no other thing; to which accusation he never subscribed nor avouched it. I beseech you, my lords, let Cobham be sent for, charge him on his soul, on his allegiance to the King; if he affirm it, I am guilty. . . . By the rigour and cruelty of the law (the Accusation) may be a forcible evidence.

Popham, L.C.J.: That is not the rigour of the law, but the justice of the law; else when a man hath made a plain Accusation, by practice he might be brought to retract it again.

Raleigh: Oh my lord, you may use equity.

L.C.J.: That is from the King; you are to have justice from us. . . . This thing cannot be granted, for then a number of Treasons should flourish: the Accuser may be drawn by practise, whilst he is in person.

Gawdy, J.: The Statute you speak of concerning two Witnesses in case of Treason, is found to be inconvenient, therefore by another law it was taken away.

Raleigh: The common Trial of England is by Jury and Witnesses.

Warburton, J.:

I marvel, Sir Walter, that you being of such experience and wit, should stand on this point; for so many horse-stealers may escape, if they may not be condemned without witnesses. . . . My Lord Cobham hath, perhaps, been labored withal; and to save you, his old friend, it may be that he will deny all that which he hath said.

Raleigh: I know not how you conceive the Law.

L.C.J.: Nay, we do not conceive the Law, but we know the Law.

Raleigh: Indeed, where the Accuser is not to be had conveniently, I agree with you; but here my Accuser may; he is alive, and in the house. Susanna had been condemned, if Daniel had not cried out, "Will you condemn an innocent Israelite, without examination or knowledge of the truth?" Remember, it is absolutely the Commandment of God: If a false witness rise up, you shall cause him to be brought before the Judges; if he be found false, he shall have the punishment which the accused should have had. It is very sure, for my lord to accuse me is my certain danger, and it may be a means to excuse himself. . . . Good my lords, let my Accuser come face to face, and be deposed.

L.C.J.: You have no law for it.

---

9.   *Sir Walter Raleigh's Trial* (1603), 2 Howell's State Trials 1, 15-19.

Gradually, during the 17th century, the new ideas took hold and concern for the worth of hearsay yielded an exclusionary rule. In the beginning, only oral hearsay was inadmissible. Previously sworn depositions continued to be received, but the practice developed of insisting on the deponent's attendance at trial to confirm the truth of the deposition; over many years, public oral testimony of confirmation became more important than earlier written depositions. In time, earlier writing became receivable only to confirm that what the witness said at trial had always been maintained. With this development toward openness, to publicly presenting the evidence in the presence of the parties, there was increased reliance by the jury on the parties' efforts to inform. As the parties took greater control over what evidence would be presented, and challenged the worth of evidence presented by their opponent, the adversary system and the peculiarly English technique of cross-examination was fashioned. With these developments, the hearsay rule was born as a natural counterpart. Juries were to be informed by witnesses with personal knowledge, speaking on oath, publicly, in their presence and in the presence of the parties, and were to be open to cross-examination when they expressed themselves; if the evidence was otherwise it was to be excluded as hearsay.

Against this background, observe two cases which display the early stated reasons for the hearsay rule. In the trial of Braddon and Speke[10] in 1684, the accused seeks to lead evidence:

Jeffries, L.C.J.:	Does she know anything of her own knowledge?
Braddon:	She can tell what she heard, my lord.
L.C.J.:	'Tis no evidence. . . . Where is the woman that told her? Why is not she brought?
Counsel for Braddon:	They say, she is so big with child she can't come.
L.C.J.:	Why, if that woman were here herself, if she did say it, and would not swear it, we could not hear her; how then can her saying be an evidence before us? I wonder to hear any man that wears a gown, to make a doubt of it.

And later, even though the out-of-court saying was a *sworn* deposition by one with personal knowledge, it was rejected if the party against whom it was tendered was unable to cross-examine the deponent. This other reason for the rule was insisted on in *R. v. Paine*,[11] in 1696. In a prosecution for criminal libel, it was sought to introduce against the accused the deposition of the person to whom the accused had allegedly published the libel. That person had been examined upon oath by the Mayor of Bristol but had since died. The accused objected that he had not been present at the examination and therefore had not been able to cross-examine. The Crown argued that the deposition ought to be received as there was assurance of trustworthiness in that "if such oath should be false, the party might be indicted for perjury." The report noted:

---

10.   *Re Braddon and Speke* (1684), 9 Howell's State Trials 1127, 1188-89.
11.   (1696), 87 E.R. 584, 585 (K.B.).

The court thereupon sent the Puisne Judge to confer with the Justices of the Common Pleas; who returning, the Chief Justice declared, that it was the opinion of both Courts that these depositions should not be given in evidence, the defendant not being present when they were taken before the mayor, and so had lost the benefit of a cross-examination.

The rule is now settled law, and became a source of pride to the English lawyer, as we read in a note from 1730:

The excellency therefore of our laws above others, I take chiefly to consist in that part of them, which regards Criminal Prosecutions: here indeed it may with great truth and justice be said, that we have by far the better of our neighbours, and are deservedly their admiration and envy.

This might be made to appear in many particulars. In other Countries . . . the Witnesses are examined in private, and in the Prisoner's absence; with us they are produced face to face, and deliver their Evidence in open court, the prisoner himself being present, and at liberty to cross-examine them.[12]

(b) Reason for Rule

In Hawkins' *Pleas of the Crown* we read:

It seems agreed, that what a Stranger has been heard to say is in Strictness no manner of Evidence either for or against a Prisoner, not only because it is not upon Oath but also because the other Side hath no opportunity of a cross-examination.[13]

While it is sometimes said[14] that the hearsay rule was fashioned out of a distrust for the lay juror's capacity to properly assess the worth of the evidence, the history noted above confirms Professor Morgan's view that the reasons for the rule given at the time by judges and commentators:

. . . have to do with the credulity not of jurors but of witnesses. . . . Not one of them even suggests a peculiar incapacity of jurors to evaluate such evidence, and so long as jurors could properly rely upon what they learned by inquiry or otherwise outside the presence of the court, any such suggestion would have bordered on absurdity.[15]

Nevertheless, distrust for the jury's capacity to adequately assess hearsay becomes an after-the-fact added justification. The trier of fact will be more assured of accuracy in his decision if descriptions of events are given in open court rather than through an intermediary. Trustworthiness of decision-making is enhanced for a number of reasons which may be grouped under two heads. First, the witness who speaks in open court is subject to a perjury prosecution should he lie; this witness who speaks in open court is encouraged to speak honestly and without exaggeration by the solemnity of the occasion and by the presence of the party against whose interests he speaks; the witness's manner of speaking, his demeanour, will be available for review by the trier of fact, who will thus be better able to evaluate his credibility. The second group of reasons resides in our adversary system and in the faith we repose in "the greatest legal engine

---

12. Emlyn's Preface to the Second Edition of the State Trials, 1 Howell's State Trials, XXV.
13. Hawkins, *Pleas of the Crown* (1716), Book II, c. 46, s. 14 as noted by Morgan, *supra*, note 3 at p. 111.
14. See, *e.g.*, Ewaschuk, "Hearsay Evidence" (1978), Osgoode Hall L.J. 407.
15. Morgan, *supra*, note 3 at p. 112.

ever invented for the discovery of truth"[16] — cross-examination. The description of a past event by a witness has resident within it the possibility of error due to at least four dangers.[17] The description may be defective because first, the witness did not perceive the incident accurately; second, the witness does not now remember the incident accurately; third, the witness's language describing the incident may be ambiguous or otherwise defective and the communication of his thoughts may therefore be misunderstood; fourth, the witness may be presently insincere in his account and wish to deliberately mislead the trier of fact. These four dangers may be guarded against by canvassing their existence through cross-examination which, of course, is only possible when the individual with the personal knowledge is present in the witness stand; the adversary may be greatly prejudiced if the description comes in through the relation of another who has no ability to aid in exposing possible defects in the declarant's perception, memory, communication or sincerity.

If we keep this background of history and reason in mind, we will be better able to deal with the ever recurring problem of identifying whether a particular piece of evidence is hearsay, and we should also be better able to construct arguments for and against the receivability of hearsay evidence in a particular case.

(c) Identifying Hearsay

Professor McCormick defined hearsay:

> (i) Hearsay evidence is testimony in court, or written evidence, of a statement made out of court, the statement being offered as an assertion to show the truth of matters asserted therein, and thus resting for its value upon the credibility of the out-of-court asserter.[18]

Notice particularly the closing lines of that definition, "resting for its value upon the credibility of the out-of-court asserter." Why is that a requirement? Because, as we discussed above, the principal reasons for excluding hearsay evidence are the lack of the protective safeguards of oath and cross-examination, safeguards which are only necessary when the value of the evidence depends on the credibility of the asserter.

A sues B for failure to deliver lumber in accordance with their contract; B defends, denying the existence of any contract. A calls X to testify that he heard B unequivocally and unambiguously agreeing to deliver lumber to A on a certain date for a certain price. Clearly this is <u>not hearsay</u>, as we care not whether B was sincere in expressing his intention to accept the terms. The legal consequences of a valid contract are produced by the fact that B spoke the

---

16.   5 Wigmore, *Evidence* (Chad. Rev.), c. 1367, p. 32.

17.   See the classic exposition by Morgan, "Hearsay Dangers and the Application of the Hearsay Concept" (1948), 62 Harv. L. Rev. 177, of which my note is but an attempted paraphrase.

18.   McCormick, *Evidence*, 2d ed. (1972), p. 584. And see, per Dickson, J. in *R. v. O'Brien* (1977), 38 C.R.N.S. 325, 327 (S.C.C.): "It is settled law that evidence of a statement made to a witness by a person who is not himself called as a witness is hearsay and inadmissible when the object of the evidence is to establish the truth of what is contained in the statement; it is not hearsay and is admissible when it is proposed to establish by the evidence, not the truth of the statement, but the fact that it was made."

words, and the value of the words does not rest on the credibility of the out-of-court asserter.[19] Similarly, proof of statements constituting defamation would not offend the hearsay rule; the proponent of the evidence is obviously not attempting to prove the truth asserted within the statements.[20] Words accompanying actions often characterize the same, and if the substantive law has an objective test of intention, the words are receivable.[21] Statements made by suspects which are established as false during the course of a police investigation may be received as non-hearsay evidencing a consciousness of guilt.[22] The list of situations of relevant non-hearsay statements, and their variety, is limitless, and their identification is only eased when the purpose of the hearsay rule is kept in the forefront.

Identifying whether an out-of-court statement is hearsay or not is seen by many as a difficult exercise and various formulae of words have been used for the purpose. The best way to begin is to ask: Who is the declarant; i.e. who uttered the out-of-court statement? What did he or she say? Why does the proponent want to introduce the statement? What is its relevance?

One popular formula of words is problematic. Ask whether the statement is being tendered for its truth or tendered for the fact that the statement was made. Although this is perhaps a fair description, the formula frequently produces circumlocutions that confound. It is not unusual for counsel to seek an end run around the hearsay rule by insisting that he is not tendering the evidence for the purpose of establishing its truth but rather only for the purpose of establishing that the statement was in fact made. When counsel offers such in justification, the adversary should ask the proponent of the evidence to precisely articulate the relevance in the case resident in the fact that the statement was made. It will often be seen that the only relevance that can be found will reside in accepting the speaker's belief concerning an external event as accurate; the statement will be seen to be of value only if we assume its truth. The statement on close analysis will often be seen to be hearsay.

An example might assist. Dante is charged with the robbery of Harold. When Dante was arrested, he was taken to a detention centre and booked in. Investigating Officer King has testified that the victim Harold gave him a list of the serial numbers of the bills taken from him in the robbery. Harold made the list just before the robbery. King went to the detention centre and, on examining the booking sheet, observed that when Dante was booked in certain personal effects were taken from him. He asked to see those effects. He was given an envelope which had the name "Dante" written thereon. In the envelope were found two bills with serial numbers matching numbers on the list provided by Harold. Harold is prepared to testify, refreshing his memory from the list that he prepared, that these two bills were part of the money taken from him during the robbery. Dante attacks the evidence as hearsay. The Crown argues that the evidence is not hearsay. The Crown argues that the name "Dante" on the envelope is not an out-of-court statement being tendered for the purpose of

19. See *Creaghe v. Iowa Home Mut. Casualty Co.*, 323 F. 2d 981 (10th Cir., 1963).
20. See *Dalrymple v. Sun Life Assur. Co.*, [1966] 2 O.R. 227 (C.A.); affirmed 60 D.L.R. (2d) 192n (S.C.C.).
21. See *Leeson v. Leeson*, [1936] 2 K.B. 156 (C.A.).
22. See *Mawaz Khan v. R.*, [1967] 1 A.C. 454 (P.C.).

proving its truth. It is evidence only that the statement was in fact made. The fact that the statement was made is a piece of original circumstantial evidence from which the trier of fact can infer that the two bills were in Dante's possession when he was arrested. This is quite an attractive argument, at least on the surface, and might be accepted.[23] But closely analyze the situation. How is the fact that the name "Dante" appears on the envelope relevant to the issue? Someone, probably the booking officer, wrote the name "Dante" on the envelope. The fact of the name appearing, the fact that the statement was made, only has relevance if we accept that the writer was accurate when he identified these effects as belonging to Dante. If the booking officer had written on the envelope "I found the contents of this envelope on the person of Dante when he arrived at the booking office" all would quickly see that this was a hearsay statement. The worth of the statement depended on the credibility of the out-of-court asserter, the booking officer, and the adversary, Dante, was prevented from challenging, through cross-examination, the worth of the out-of-court statement.[24]

A better analytical technique for determining whether a statement is hearsay would be framed in terms of the underlying concern of the rule. As with the proper application of all rules of evidence, it is wise to always keep in mind the purpose of the rule. Given the basis for the hearsay rule — the adversary's inability to cross-examine the person with knowledge of the event — we can then construct an analytical tool for identifying hearsay. If there are relevant, meaningful questions that the adversary might wish to ask of the person who made the out-of-court statement, then the out-of-court statement is hearsay; if there are no meaningful questions that can be put, the statement is not hearsay. To properly identify whether or not an out-of-court statement is hearsay keep in mind the reason for the rule.

An example from the cases might assist. In *Subramaniam v. Public Prosecutor*,[25] the accused had been convicted of unlawfully possessing ammunition contrary to Emergency Regulations in Malaya and was sentenced to death. His defence had been duress and he sought to relate conversations he had had with the terrorists who had threatened him; the trial court ruled this evidence was hearsay, and not admissible unless the terrorists were called. The Privy Council held that the trial judge was in error and noted:

> Evidence of a statement made to a witness by a person who is not himself called as a witness may or may not be hearsay. It is hearsay and inadmissible when the object of the evidence is to establish the truth of what is contained in the statement. It is not hearsay and is admissible when it is proposed to establish by the evidence, not the truth of the statement, but the fact that it was made. The fact that the statement was made, quite apart from its truth, is frequently relevant in considering the mental

---

23. For acceptance of such an argument see *R. v. Bastien* (1968), 20 C.C.C. (2d) 562 (B.C. Co. Ct.).

24. For judicial recognition that this is the proper analysis, see *R. v. Lal* (1979), 51 C.C.C. (2d) 336 (B.C.C.A.).

25. [1956] 1 W.L.R. 965, 970 (P.C.). Compare *R. v. Bencardino* (1973), 15 C.C.C. (2d) 342 (Ont. C.A.): a witness had denied being threatened and the court held that another might be called to testify that the same witness had earlier told him he had been threatened "because the evidence will be received not to prove the fact of intimidation but rather to prove [witness's] state of mind of fear." The court relied on *Subramanian*. Do you agree?

state and conduct thereafter of the witness or of some other person in whose presence the statement was made.

The Privy Council then noted that the value of the impugned evidence in this case did not rest on the credibility of the out-of-court asserter; the value of the evidence was in the fact of the statement having been made, since if believed by the accused it would support his defence of duress. The trier of fact would not be misled, nor the adversary prejudiced, by the absence from the witness stand of the terrorist-declarant. If the terrorist were called as a witness, what questions would adversary ask? Could adversary ask the terrorist if he was sincere when he treatened the accused? If he intended to communicate a threat? Surely these questions would be properly objected to as immaterial since the issue before the court was not the terrorist's state of mind but rather the accused's. Since it was the fact of the statement having been made that was relevant, the adversary would be protected and trustworthiness guarded by allowing the accused to testify; the accused is on oath and may be cross-examined regarding his sincerity, perception and memory concerning whether the statement was in fact made.

A more modern example may be seen in the case of *R. v. Dunn*.[26] On a charge of threatening, the Crown needed to establish that the interception of the telecommunication containing the threat was lawfully made. The wiretap provisions of the Criminal Code [27] provide that an intercept is lawfully made if the recipient of the communication has consented to the interception. The prosecution sought to lead evidence of conversations between the police officer and the victim, by then deceased, in which the victim, the recipient of the telecommunication, had given her consent to the interception. The defence objected to this evidence as hearsay, the court agreed, and the evidence was ruled inadmissible. Fortunately, the court found the necessary consent by implication from other evidence, and later confessed its error in identifying the evidence as hearsay. The court had initially failed to recognize that the value of the evidence did not rest on the credibility of the out-of-court asserter. The police officer had been tendered to testify to an objective fact which he had observed, consent given, the relevance of which resided simply in its happening. The adversary was not prejudiced in being unable to cross-examine the complainant regarding what she meant by the words she uttered and the trier of fact could equally well decide, without her presence, whether the words uttered amounted to a valid consent.[28]

Understanding the purpose of the rule is essential to avoid errors in identification of out-of-court statements.[29] Justice MacDonald described it very well:

---

26.   (1975), 28 C.C.C. (2d) 538 (N.S. Co. Ct.).

27.   Section 189.

28.   On the same point the Ontario Court of Appeal properly noted that "consent was an issue of fact in these proceedings and could be proved like any other fact in issue": *R. v. Cremascoli and Goldman* (1977), 38 C.C.C. (2d) 212, 217 per Brooke, J.A. Curiously the Supreme Court of Canada was less than emphatic in its approval: "While I am inclined to agree with that statement, I do not consider it necessary to deal with the point:" (1979), 51 C.C.C. (2d) 1, 25, per McIntyre, J.

29.   For a recent error in identification see the trial judge's ruling in *R. v. Wildman* (1981), 60 C.C.C. (2d) 289, 295 (Ont. C.A.) (reversed [1984] 2 S.C.R. 311).

Essentially it is not the form of the statement that gives it its hearsay or non-hearsay characteristics but the use to which it is put. Whenever a witness testifies that someone said something, immediately one should then ask, "what is the relevance of the fact that someone said something". If, therefore, the relevance of the statement lies in the fact that it was made, it is the making of the statement that is the evidence — the truth or falsity of the statement is of no consequence: if the relevance of the statement lies in the fact that it contains an assertion which is, itself, a relevant fact, then it is the truth or falsity of the statement that is in issue. The former is not hearsay, the latter is.[30]

R. v. EVANS
[1993] 3 S.C.R. 653, 25 C.R. (4th) 46, 85 C.C.C. (3d) 97

[The accused and a co-accused D. were charged with robbery. Witnesses were able to identify D. as one of the robbers. The robbers got into a waiting car, which was driven by a third person. The getaway car had been purchased two days earlier from a married couple. Neither the husband nor the wife was able to make a positive photographic or dock identification. Both testified however that the man who bought the car told them that he worked in chain-link fencing. The wife testified that the man said he had big dogs. The husband testified that the man said his dog was going to have pups. Other evidence showed that the accused had a large dog that was going to have pups and that he had been employed as a chain-link fencer.

The accused was convicted and his appeal was dismissed. He appealed further.]

SOPINKA J. (L'HEUREUX-DUBÉ, GONTHIER, CORY and IACOBUCCI JJ. concurring):—

. . . .

The respondent argued that the statements are not hearsay because the fact that the appellant owned a large pregnant dog and had worked as a chain-link fence installer had been independently proved. This argument was apparently accepted by the Court of Appeal. The appellant argued that the statements are hearsay because they had no probative value unless assumed to be true. Each of these submissions is slightly off the mark.

The ultimate value of these statements was to prove that the appellant and the purchaser of the getaway car were one and the same person. There was independent proof that the appellant worked as a fencer, and that he owned a large pregnant dog. If the purchaser could be proved to have a large pregnant dog and have worked as a fence installer, this would suggest that the appellant was the purchaser. However, there is no proof that the purchaser owned a dog or worked as a fencer unless the statements made to the Boutets are assumed to be true. The statements cannot be used for the truth of their contents unless they are admissible under an exception to the hearsay rule.

That being said, the statements still have some probative value as non-hearsay. Quite apart from the truth of the contents, the statements have some probative value on the issue of identity. On the issue of identity, the fact that certain representations are made is probative as it narrows the identity of the declarant to the group of people who are in a position to make similar representations. The more unique or unusual the representations, the more probative they will be on the issue of identity. I emphasize that the statements are not being used as truth of their contents at this stage.

For example, if a declarant stated: "I have a tattoo on my left buttock which measures 1 centimetre by $1\frac{1}{2}$ centimetres and resembles a four-leaf clover" and it was proved that

---

30. *R. v. Baltzer* (1974), 27 C.C.C. (2d) 118, 143 (N.S.C.A.).

the accused had such a tattoo on his left buttock, the identity of the group to which the declarant belonged would be narrowed to include the accused as the most likely person, and his family or intimate friends, who would be in a position to know this fact. The statement has probative value without assuming the truth of the statement because the mere fact that it was made tells us something relevant about the declarant that connects him to the accused.

. . . .

The admission of this kind of evidence is not hearsay because the only issue is whether the statement was made, and the veracity, perception and memory of the witness relating the statement can be fully tested by cross-examination. Since the truth of the declarant's assertion is not in issue, deprivation of the right to cross-examine the declarant, on which rejection of hearsay is premised, is of no consequence.

. . . .

[The Court then went on to consider whether the statements by the purchaser, if hearsay, were nevertheless admissible as admissions.]

In this case there was evidence that it was the appellant who made the statements to the Boutets. The trial judge should have considered whether this evidence proved on a balance of probabilities that the statements were in fact made by the accused. In this determination he could have relied on the fact that the statements to the Boutets were made. It would be a most unusual coincidence that the purchaser and the accused would each have these two characteristics in combination. If he ruled out coincidence, the trial judge was entitled to consider that this narrowed the group of persons who were in a position to make this statement to the accused or someone who knew this about the accused and had some reason to make the representation as if he were the accused. Considered in light of the other evidence to which I will refer, the most likely person to make the statement was the accused.

. . . .

McLACHLIN J. (MAJOR J. concurring), dissenting:—

. . . .

My colleague concedes that viewed one way, the statements in question are hearsay. However, he says they are admissible as a statement of facts identifying the speaker as X on the ground that the facts could have been known only to X or to a small group of people to which X belongs. . . .

The probative value of such statements depends on the proposition that the person to be identified, here the accused, is one of very few people who would be able to relate the information which was disclosed by the "speaker" (here the perpetrator of the crime). If many people could have made the statement, it loses its force as an indicator that the "speaker" or perpetrator of the offence is the accused. The case my colleague cites of a "speaker" who describes in detail an unusual tattoo on his left buttock — a tattoo which also, it turns out, is possessed by the accused — is an example in point. The statement identifies both the speaker and the accused as members of the very small group of persons who could have known about the tattoo. It would be highly unusual that a "speaker" would describe himself as having such a tattoo, and that a quite different person, the accused, would possess the same characteristic. Because this would be so extraordinary, there is a strong, although not conclusive, inference that they are one and the same person.

The same inference does not follow where the characteristic is one which anyone who cares to inquire may detect. Consider the case of a criminal who wishes to "finger" another for his crime. Knowing that the other person possesses a peculiar tattoo on his left buttock, such a person might indicate in the course of committing the crime that he, the perpetrator, possessed such a tattoo. If the evidence is that only very few people could have known of the tattoo, the inference, as noted above, is strong that the speaker and the person with the tattoo are one and the same. But if the evidence is that many people could have known about the tattoo, the inference is weak. Any one of those people, whether to shift the blame to another or for a variety of other reasons, might have mentioned it. It is for this reason that the cases in which this principle has been applied uniformly insist that the information related be information which only the accused could have known (*McCormick's* formulation) or which, at the very least, only a few people would have known. . . .

This brings me to the information said to identify the accused as the person who bought the getaway vehicle in the case at bar. The person who picked up the getaway vehicle gave the vendor the information that he worked as a chain-link fencer and owned a large pregnant dog. That was not information which only the perpetrator of the offence could have known. Indeed, it was not information which only a small group of people could have known. It was, on the contrary, information which could have been obtained by anyone who had cared to observe or inquire into the accused's affairs. Accordingly, it does not fall within the rule as stated by *McCormick*. . . .

Nor should it. A number of inferences may be drawn from the fact such a statement was made. One is that another chain-link fencer who owned a large pregnant dog (and there may be a number of such persons in a large city like Calgary) bought the car. Yet another inference is that the criminal, seeking to shift blame from himself to the accused Evans, went out of his way to tell the vendors falsely that he worked as a chain-link fencer and owned a large pregnant dog. Yet another is the inference which the trial judge drew — that the person who bought the getaway car and the accused Evans were one and the same person. The fact that the inference of identity is merely one of several plausible inferences which may be drawn from the statement renders it, on the authorities, inadmissible. It does not have the necessary probative value to support a conviction. The danger of an erroneous inference is simply too great.

. . . .

I would allow the appeal and direct a new trial.

———————

Suppose the vendor of the getaway car in *Evans* saw that in the purchaser's truck there was a quantity of chain-link fencing material and that the purchaser also had with him a large pregnant dog. In such a case the vendor would be able to later describe in court what he had seen at the time of the purchase and that evidence, together with evidence that the accused before the court was a chain-link fencer and the owner of a large pregnant dog, would go a long way toward identifying the accused as the purchaser. Suppose the vendor of the getaway car was by himself during the transaction and later told his wife that the purchaser of their car was a chain-link fencer and the owner of a large pregnant dog. No one would suggest that the wife could later come to court and testify that the purchaser of their car was a chain-link fencer and the owner of a large pregnant dog. Her belief would be founded in hearsay. And yet in *Evans* that's exactly what was permitted. *Someone* told the vendor that he, the purchaser, was a chain-link fencer and the owner of a large pregnant dog and the Court decided that the evidence was admissible. The Court decided the vendor could testify to the character of the purchaser though the vendor only knew the same as the result of what was told to him by *someone*. As far as it being classified as an exception, i.e. an admission, where is the evidence that the statements were made by the accused. Without such evidence we have a first-rate bootstrap operation.[31]

UNITED STATES v. BARBATI
(1968), 284 F. Supp. 409 (U.S. Dist. Ct.)

WEINSTEIN, District Judge: —

Having been convicted of passing a Ten Dollar counterfeit bill (18 U.S.C. t472), defendant moves for a new trial on the ground that the verdict rested upon inadmissible hearsay evidence. See Fed. R. Crim. Proc. 33.

A barmaid and a policeman were the chief witnesses for the prosecution. Two counterfeit Ten Dollar bills had been given to the barmaid in payment for drinks by two men sitting together at the bar. She showed the bills to the manager who hailed a passing police car. Within a few minutes of the time the bills were passed, the policeman had arrested the defendant and his companion in the bar.

At the trial the notes were identified by the policeman as those the barmaid had turned over to him. She also identified the notes, relying upon the signature she had affixed at the time of the arrest.

While the barmaid testified that two men had given her the bills and that she had pointed out the men who gave them to her, she could not, at the time of the trial, recognize the defendant or his companion. Testimony by the policeman, however, established that the defendant was the one pointed out to him as soon as he was called into the bar and that, following identification and arrest, the defendant was taken to the stationhouse where he was fingerprinted and booked.

The critical testimony of the barmaid was as follows:

A   . . . they [the police] came and they asked me where I got the money, I showed them.

Q   Did you point out the two men?

A   Yes, I did.

Q   What if anything happened after that?

A   Well, they searched the men.

Q   Did they search the two men that you pointed out?

A   Yes.

Q   Do you see any of them here now?

A   I can't remember them.

Q   You wouldn't remember what the men looked like now?

A   No, it was so long ago.

Q   What if anything did you do with the $10 notes you got from these men, after the police came?

A   I was taken in the back with the money and the police and I signed those notes at that time.

. . . .

Q   Those were the two notes that were given to you in the bar by the two men?

A   Yes.

---

31.   For a detailed criticism of *Evans* see Delisle, "*Evans*: Mixing Authenticity and Hearsay" (1993), 25 C.R. (4th) 62.

Q   What if anything did the police do with the two men that you pointed out in your presence?

A   They put their hands on the walls . . . and they searched them for weapons, I guess and after that I don't know what happened to the two men, I suppose they took them away.

The policeman had no doubt that the defendant was the person identified in the bar by the barmaid. The barmaid had no doubt that the man she pointed out and who was arrested was the person who gave her one of the notes. It is not disputed that the person so identified was physically in police custody until after he was fingerprinted. No one suggests that the person fingerprinted is not the defendant who was tried in this case.

The evidence was highly probative and reliable. No more satisfactory proof was available. The apparatus for testing the credibility of these two key witnesses was available — the oath, cross-examination and presence at the trial where the jury could observe demeanor.

VIOLATION OF CONSTITUTION AND CRIMINAL RULES

[1] Admission of this evidence violated no right protected by written rule or by the Constitution. Since both the policeman and the barmaid testified, there was no violation of Federal Rule of Criminal Procedure 26 — requiring that "the testimony of witnesses shall be taken orally in open court." Nor, for the same reason, was there a violation of the constitutional right of confrontation.

. . . .

VIOLATION OF HEARSAY RULE

There is more force to defendant's contention that the testimony with respect to the identification by the barmaid at the scene of the crime constituted hearsay. Whether made orally, or by pointing him out, the barmaid was then, the argument goes, making an extra-judicial testimonial statement. This out-of-court statement was being relied upon at the trial to prove its truth, namely, that the man she pointed out was the one who passed a counterfeit bill to her. Since its use required reliance upon all elements of her credibility — observation power, memory, truthfulness and ability to communicate — the barmaid's testimony, defendant concludes, involved serious hearsay dangers.

This analysis is not conclusive. Much that might be classified as hearsay is held not to be hearsay. Much that is hearsay is, nonetheless, admissible.

Courts have not hesitated to characterize as non-hearsay evidence whose use involves hearsay dangers when it is highly probative and necessary. Typical are those criminal cases involving conversations received over the telephone at suspected betting parlors. Use of the statements of the assumed betters requires reliance on the callers' credibility to conclude that they intended to place bets and had some reason to believe that they were calling a bookie. Despite the existence of hearsay dangers this evidence is admitted as non-hearsay. See, e.g., State v. Tolisano, 136 Conn. 210, 70 A.2d 118 (1949); Annot., 13 A.L.R.2d 1405 (1950).

The evidence in the case before us can be classified as non-hearsay without doing violence to theory by analogizing it to proof of identification of objects. In a sense the barmaid turned both the bills and the defendant over to the police. She signed the bills but not the defendant. He, however, was taken in hand and the chain of custody continued until he was brought to the police station where he was fingerprinted — the equivalent of being signed. Defendant's subsequent release on his own recognizance does not break the chain of identification-authentication since there is no doubt that he was the one finger-printed. Analytically, the barmaid now testifies from present memory, "I was given a counterfeit bill by a man, X, and I saw the police arrest X." The policeman testifies from present memory, "the man we arrested, X, was the defendant." Neither of these statements is hearsay.

The analogy will become clearer by assuming the case of a blind man who feels a pickpocket taking his wallet. Assume he seizes the thief, holds him, and calls for help and that a policeman comes by immediately and arrests the man being held. No one would apply the hearsay rule to prevent the identification even though the blind man would not be able to recognize the defendant at the trial. His testimony plus that of the arresting officer would suffice.

Despite the fact that a respectable argument can be made that no hearsay is involved in the instant case, the Court prefers to proceed on the more realistic assumption that hearsay was relied upon by the prosecution. Both the policeman and the barmaid were permitted to buttress each other's testimony by testifying, in effect, that the barmaid said, at the time of arrest, "This is the man who gave me these bills."

The current clear tendency is for federal courts to ask whether admissibility will tend to aid in the search for truth. Hearsay is admitted when it is highly reliable, highly probative, and where the opponent has an adequate opportunity to attack it. See, e.g., United States v. Castellana, 349 F.2d 264, 276 (2d Cir. 1965), cert. denied, 383 U.S. 928, 86 S.Ct. 935, 15 L.Ed.2d 847 (1966) "(We are loath to reduce the corpus of hearsay rules to a strait-jacketing, hypertechnical body of semantical slogans to be mechanically invoked regardless of the reliability of the proffered evidence"); Dallas County v. Commercial Union Assurance Co., 286 F.2d 388, 398 (5th Cir. 1961) (hearsay "admissible because it is necessary and trustworthy"); United States v. Schwartz, 252 F.Supp. 866 (E.D.Pa. 1966). Cf. United States v. Nuccio, 373 F.2d 168, 174 (2d Cir.), cert. denied, 387 U.S. 906, 87 S.Ct. 1688, 18 L.Ed.2d 623 (1967) "(the notion that evidentiary use of anything emerging from the mouth is banned unless it comes within an exception to the hearsay rule is as fallacious as it is durable"). Use of necessary and trustworthy hearsay in a criminal case is typified by the *Schwartz* case where the court found that the prior writing of a witness who was "evasive, unresponsive and contradictory" and "apparently a very sick man," was more satisfactory than his testimony on the witness stand; his prior written statement was admitted even though it was hearsay. 252 F.Supp. at 868. The Court pointed out that there was a necessity for his testimony, that the "jurors had the opportunity to observe the witness' demeanor," and that there was a guarantee of trustworthiness in the way that the statement had been prepared. 252 F.Supp. at 868-869.

The matter before us is quite unlike those in the typical common law line of exclusionary cases where identification takes place sometime after the event. See, e.g., Leeper v. United States, 117 U.S.App.D.C. 310, 329 F.2d 878, cert. denied, 377 U.S. 959, 84 S.Ct. 1641, 12 L.Ed.2d 502 (1964) (concurrence) (identification in stationhouse without lineup); Poole v. United States, 97 F.2d 423 (9th Cir. 1938) (same); People v. Caserta, 19 N.Y.2d 18, 277 N.Y.S.2d 647, 224 N.E.2d 82 (1966) (identification of defendant from photograph to buttress credibility); People v. Jung Hing, 212 N.Y. 393, 106 N.E. 105 (1914) (identification at lineup to buttress credibility). The exclusion is warranted in these cases because the reliability of such identifications is uncertain. See generally P. Wall, Eye-Witness Identification in Criminal Cases (1965). Admitting evidence with such questionable probative force, when added to the hearsay dangers, substantially increases the possibility that it will be overvalued by the jury.

[3] Hearsay evidence introduced against a defendant in criminal cases should, of course, be closely scrutinized and controlled by the court. The defendant does not have the same discovery opportunities in federal criminal cases as in civil cases; and we recognize the need to afford the criminal defendant the greatest possible protection against false convictions.

[4, 5] Nonetheless, hearsay should be admitted where, as here, there is no more satisfactory evidence available, probative force is high, and availability of the hearsay declarant for cross-examination makes the possibility of prejudice slight. The statement of the barmaid identifying defendant was spontaneously made within a few moments of the time the bill was passed and while defendant was still in his place at the bar. It is unlikely that her observation of the man who gave her the bill was mistaken — he was

awaiting her return with his change. There was no time for lapse of memory. No reason for her to lie was suggested; in any event, any motive she might have had to falsify, would not have been substantially different at the trial than it was at the time of the event. The process of pointing out the defendant was so simple that an error in communication was improbable. The barmaid was unlikely to have remained silent if the police had collared an innocent bystander rather than the man she intended to point out.

Danger of the jury's overvaluing the hearsay was reduced by giving specific warning. The court pointed out that the patrolman's statement with respect to the barmaid's identification of the defendant was hearsay, that it was dangerous to rely upon it, and that the jury should evaluate it carefully. No inference with respect to the correctness of the identification arose from defendant's constitutionally protected silence. Cf. Di Carlo v. United States, 6 F.2d 364, 366 (2d Cir. 1925).

In view of the admissibility of the identification evidence pursuant to general principle, it is not necessary to decide whether it falls within a specific recognized hearsay exception.

. . . .

We should not blind ourselves to what the law has learned by bitter experience — identification in court is frequently an almost worthless formality. See, e.g., authorities collected in United States v. Wade, 388 U.S. 218, 228-229, nn. 6-7, 87 S.Ct. 1926, 18 L.Ed.2d 1149 (1967), particularly P. Wall, Eye-Witness Identification in Criminal Cases, 26-27 (1965). By the time of trial positions have often become so fixed and memory so attenuated and distorted by subsequent events that witnesses seldom make identifications on the basis of their raw recollection of the original event. Their apparent certitude is often misleading and not infrequently less reliable than earlier reactions. We cannot permit the mechanical and unreasoned application of the hearsay rule to deny evidence vital to our search for the truth.

The motion is denied.
So ordered.

Compare *R. v. Tat* (1997), 14 C.R. (5th) 116 (Ont. C.A.) and see my annotation accompanying that report.

R. v. COOK
(1984), 39 C.R. (3d) 300 (Ont. C.A.)

The judgment of the court was delivered by

MARTIN J.A. (orally):—The respondent was jointly indicted with Raymond Robert Sarginson on a charge that they:

> . . . did conspire together with Maurice Wayne Panchenko and [J.W.] to commit the indictable offence of robbery, contrary to the *Criminal Code* [R.S.C. 1970, c. C-34].

The respondents' co-accused absconded and did not appear for trial. The two named co-conspirators were not before the court at the trial of the respondent. [J.W.] was a juvenile and the charge was withdrawn against Panchenko.

The facts giving rise to the charge are briefly these. Constable John Cornwall of 52 Division, Metropolitan Toronto Police, testified that he was on plainclothes duty with Constable Gordon Laplante at approximately 4:45 p.m. on the afternoon of 19th October 1982, when he visited the Tivoli Restaurant on Yonge Street.

Constable Cornwall testified that he followed the respondent and three other persons as they entered the restaurant and he and his partner occupied a table approximately 2½ feet from the table chosen by the respondent and the three others.

He further testified that the respondent occupied a seat directly behind him and to his left in a seat at the north-east corner of the table, while her co-accused, Sarginson, was seated at the south-west position, [J.W.], a juvenile, was located at the north-west position and Panchenko was located at the south-east position.

Constable Cornwall testified that initially he overheard the co-accused, Sarginson, stating that he had done 15 months' "dead time", but he did not start to make notes until he heard the respondent say: "Look, I know how we can make some fast money. We can roll some fucking tricks."

According to Constable Cornwall, the respondent continued: "Look, you know how we can make some fast money? We can roll some fucking tricks. We can pick up some tricks on Yonge Street and take them to a parking lot and you guys can jump them."

Constable Cornwall testified that he knew it was the respondent talking because she was seated directly behind him and to his left and that he could tell it was her talking. In addition, he looked around and saw that it was her.

Constable Cornwall further testified that after the respondent made that statement Sarginson said, "Or we can take them to my room," and Panchenko added, "Or fags. We can do fags, too. I used to do fags in Florida. I got one and beat the shit out of him for a big score."

At that point, the juvenile, [W.], stated: "I've done that before. I got this Chink in 81 Charles Street and ripped him off for $75. Pepper came and told him to 'fuck off'." The respondent then stated: "I tried to roll a guy in a parking lot and the fucking trick beat me for five fucking minutes." Her co-accused, Sarginson, then replied: "Don't worry, Mo and I will be right there. We'll beat the fuck out of him and take his fucking money and the fucker won't call the cops. Who's going to tell the cops he went to a lot for a blow job and got beaten?" The juvenile then stated: "We'll have to use different lots for each guy." To which Panchenko replied: "We'll use the ones over there."

There then followed a general discussion pertaining to charges outstanding against the co-accused, Sarginson, his need for money and his experiences in jail, as well as the experiences of [J.W.] and the respondent. This discussion was followed by a short period of silence, interrupted by the respondent, who stated: "Okay, we'll go and get the guys and get them in the parking lot."

At that point [J.W.] stated, "We'll stick together," and the co-accused, Sarginson, asked, "You in, Mo?", to which Panchenko replied "Yeah".

Constable Cornwall and Constable Laplante then left their table, and, after discussion of what they heard, Constable Cornwall formed the intention to arrest all four of the co-accused. Having made that decision, he summoned two uniformed patrol officers and approached the four, identifying himself as a police officer, and informing them they were all under arrest for conspiracy to commit a robbery.

The learned trial judge, at the conclusion of the Crown's case, acquitted the respondent.

It is clear from a reading of the trial judge's reasons for judgment in their entirety that he considered the statements of the other alleged co-conspirators related by Constable Cornwall to be mere hearsay and, as such, not admissible against the respondent. He concluded his reasons for judgment by saying:

> Therefore, the evidence of the meeting in the restaurant as witnessed by Constable Cornwall is admissible, as is the evidence that he overheard the four people having a discussion. What he heard the accused say is likewise admissible. However, what he heard [W.], Sarginson and Panchenko say is inadmissible, as it offends the hearsay rule.

The learned trial judge was of the view that, since the statements of Panchenko, Sarginson and [W.] were not declarations made in the furtherance of a conspiracy, they were inadmissible under the exception to the co-conspirator hearsay rule. That issue did not, however, arise in this case. The statements which Constable Cornwall overheard were direct evidence of the formation of a conspiracy and as such no element of hearsay was involved. In McCormick on Evidence, 2nd ed. (1972), at p. 588, the author states:

> When a suit is brought for breach of a written contract, it would not occur to anyone when a writing is offered as evidence of the contract sued on to suggest that it is hearsay. Similarly, proof of oral utterances by the parties in a contract suit constituting the offer and acceptance which brought the contract into being are not evidence of assertions offered testimonially but rather of utterances — verbal conduct — to which the law attaches duties and liabilities.

The gist of the offence of conspiracy is the agreement between two or more persons to commit an unlawful act — in this case to commit robbery. The offence is complete upon the formation of the agreement even though no acts are done in furtherance of that agreement: see *R. v. O'Brien* (1954), 110 C.C.C. 1 at 3.

Consequently, in the present case the offence of conspiracy was complete as soon as the respondent and the other persons present had concluded an agreement to commit the offence of robbery even though no act was done to carry out that agreement. It is, of course, true that in order to constitute a conspiracy the parties must have made a decision to commit robbery. A mere discussion with respect to the possibility of committing a crime would not constitute a conspiracy: see *R. v. O'Brien* (1974), 59 Cr. App. R. 222.

In our view, there was evidence in this case upon which the tribunal of fact was entitled to conclude that an agreement was made to commit the crime of robbery.

Mr. Raczkowski for the respondent, in a very able argument, submitted that, prior to his falling into error in holding that the statements of Panchenko, Sarginson and [W.] were mere hearsay, the trial judge had already found as a fact that no conspiracy existed and that this was a question of fact with respect to which no appeal lies to this court. We are all satisfied, however, that on a fair reading of the judge's reasons he fell into the fundamental error of concluding that the utterances of Panchenko, Sarginson and [W.] overheard by Constable Cornwall were mere hearsay and not admissible against the respondent.

The Crown has discharged its burden of satisfying us that, but for the error, the verdict would not necessarily have been the same.

Accordingly, the appeal is allowed, the acquittal is set aside and a new trial is ordered.

Appeal allowed; new trial ordered.

[A further appeal to the Supreme Court of Canada was dismissed for the reasons given above: (1986), 50 C.R. (3d) 96 (S.C.C.).]

PROBLEMS

Problem 1

Twelve Bishops attended a conference in Toronto. They witnessed a car accident. An hour later each found a Commissioner for Taking Oaths, wrote out, signed and swore to detailed descriptions of the accident. The descriptions in the affidavits are the same. All indicate that Smith caused the accident by running a red light.

(*a*) Can the plaintiff introduce the Bishops' affidavits into evidence in her lawsuit against Smith?

(*b*) Suppose all 12 Bishops were killed in a plane crash on their departure from Toronto?

(*c*) Suppose there are no other witnesses to the event except the plaintiff and Smith and they tell different stories.

Hearsay?

Problem 2

Smith is being prosecuted for operating a common bawdy house. The prosecution has called Sam Jones who is prepared to testify that he lives on the same street as Smith and that Smith's house has a reputation as a house of prostitution.

Hearsay?

Problem 3

For some reason the material issue is whether the plaintiff could speak on March 4, 1993. A witness is prepared to testify that on March 4, 1993, he heard the plaintiff say, "I can speak."

Hearsay?

Problem 4

The plaintiff claims that he entered into a contract with the defendant who agreed to sell his old car to the plaintiff for $500. The plaintiff wants to call a witness to testify that he heard the defendant say to the plaintiff, "I offer to sell you my old car for $500."

Hearsay?

Problem 5

The witness is being examined in chief:

Q.:   Did you see the accident?

A.:   Yes.

Q.:   Who had the green light?

A.:   I can't remember. But I did tell my husband when I got home that day. He reminded me this morning.

Q.:   What did you tell him?

Hearsay?

Problem 6

The accused claims that he was still suffering the effects of provocation when he attacked the victim, Tom Jones. The accused wants to testify that his wife said to him, "Tom Jones assaulted me."

Hearsay?

Problem 7

In a paternity suit, the plaintiff offers evidence that the defendant sent the child a birthday card addressed "To my darling son."

Hearsay?

Problem 8

In a prosecution of Allen for murder, the defence is insanity. Defence counsel, in the absence of the jury, has proposed that he might call Linda and Florence to testify to conversations which they had with Allen some months prior to the killing, which conversations contained comments "of a weird nature." How should the trial judge rule? Compare *R. v. Baltzer* (1974), 27 C.C.C. (2d) 118 (N.S.C.A.) at 141 *et seq.* See also Hinton, "States of Mind and the Hearsay Rule" (1934), 1 U. Chi. L. Rev. 394 at 397-98 and *Sollars v. State*, 316 P. 2d 917 (Nev. Sup. Ct., 1957). Compare *R. v. Kirkby* (1985), 21 C.C.C. (3d) 31 (Ont. C.A.).

Problem 9

Accused is being prosecuted on a charge of possession of a quantity of stolen coats. The prosecution needs to establish that the coats found in accused's possession were, in fact, the property of the alleged victim. The prosecution called two witnesses, employees of the victim, who together identified an inventory sheet which disclosed registration numbers matching the number on the seized coats. They described how the inventory was conducted. Witness M read the number on the ticket attached to the coat and called out the style, registration number and retail price of each coat to witness O, who in turn recorded the number on her inventory sheet. Witness M did not check the inventory sheet to ensure accurate recording of the numbers she had spoken and witness O did not check the coats to ensure accurate observation of the ticket by M. The defence has objected that this evidence is hearsay. What result? Compare *R. v. Penno* (1977), 35 C.C.C. (2d) 266 (B.C.C.A.). Hearsay? Receivable?

Problem 10

A witness to an accident observes the plate number of the offending vehicle, makes a note of it, and communicates the number to another, who in turn records it. At the trial the witness no longer has his note and cannot recall the number, but the other person is prepared to testify to the number related. What result? Compare *R. v. Davey* (1969), 6 C.R.N.S. 288; *Cattermole v. Millar*, [1977] Crim. L. Rev. 553 (Div. Ct.); and *R. v. Schantz* (1983), 34 C.R. (3d) 370 (Ont. Co. Ct.).

Problem 11

Defendant, a power tool manufacturer, was displaying his wares at a hardware exhibition. Plaintiff, a potential customer, while operating defendant's table saw suffered the loss of two fingers for which he now brings suit. Defendant resists plaintiff's claim and maintains he was contributorily negligent. Defendant offers his employee to testify that shortly before plaintiff screamed the employee heard defendant shout "Put the guard down before operating the saw!" Objectionable? Could employee testify that defendant told him "I told that nitwit to put the guard down before operating the saw!" Could defendant testify "I told that nitwit to put the guard down before operating the saw!"

Problem 12

In a murder prosecution the defence is alibi and the time of the alleged killing is therefore very important. A Crown witness who observed the shooting is now testifying:

Crown: And then what happened?

Witness: Well, that's about it — two shots and the victim collapsed right there in the middle of Union Station.

Crown:	And can you tell us what time this occurred?
Witness:	It was exactly 2:15 p.m.
Crown:	And how do you know?
Witness:	I asked a passerby and he told me . . .
Objection:	Clearly hearsay, Your Honour.
Witness:	Well, I heard the conductor call out "All aboard for the 2:15 to Kingston".
Defence:	Same objection, Your Honour.
Witness:	So I looked up at the station clock.
Defence:	Same objection.
Witness:	And then I looked at my own Rolex wristwatch which the jeweller had checked for accuracy the day before.
Defence:	Your Honour, it's clear to me, and I trust it's clear to you, that there is no way this witness can nail down the time.
Crown:	Well perhaps my friend will tell me what would satisfy him.
Defence:	That's not for me to say. It's your case.

Problem 13

The accused is charged with break, enter and theft. The premises entered were those of a coin shop. The Crown has called a second-hand dealer who testifies that on the day of the break-in he purchased a quantity of coins which roughly matched the coins taken. The dealer cannot identify the accused as the seller of the coins but says the seller gave the name Sammy John, a Kingston address, and a social insurance number; this information was recorded in his dealer's log. The Crown notes for the court that the address and social insurance number are those of the accused before the court, John Samuel Benson. The defence argues the dealer's evidence is hearsay. See *R. v. Evans, supra.*

Problem 14

Suppose the issue at trial is whether Smith, a contestant on a T.V. quiz show, was told the answers to questions before they were asked. One of the parties wishes to introduce the following evidence. During one of the shows, Smith whispered to his partner, "I know that the next answer will be 'Jacques Plante'." There will also be evidence that the next question was "Who was the first hockey goaltender to wear a mask?"
Hearsay?

Problem 15

The accused is charged with sexually assaulting a five-year-old girl, Sharon. There is no question that Sharon was assaulted; the only issue is the identity of the perpetrator. The accused was arrested at his place of residence, which is a studio apartment with purple wallpaper, a pink satin couch, a table made out of crushed Budweiser cans, and a picture of Ronald McDonald on the wall. At trial, the prosecution wishes to call Sharon's mother to testify that on the day of the assault, Sharon told her, "I was in a one-room apartment with purple wallpaper, a pink couch, a table made out of crushed Budweiser cans, and a picture of Ronald McDonald on the wall." See *U.S. v. Muscato*, 534 F.Supp. 969 (E.D.N.Y., 1982).

Hearsay?

(d) Implied Assertions

No one would deny that statements can be made otherwise than by words. A nod of the head can communicate assent as readily as the word "yes"; pointing to a suspect can be as devastating as "that is the man." Actions which are intended by the actor to be assertions are obviously then as capable of being characterized as hearsay as verbal utterances.[32]

A much more difficult problem presents itself when there is within the conduct an implied assertion which was never intended:

> ... the supposed conduct of the family or relations of a testator, taking the same precautions in his absence as if he were a lunatic; his election, in his absence, to some high and responsible office; the conduct of a physician who permitted a will to be executed by a sick testator; the conduct of a deceased captain on a question of seaworthiness, who, after examining every part of the vessel, embarked in it with his family; all these, when deliberately considered, are, with reference to the matter in issue in each case, mere instances of hearsay evidence, mere statements, not on oath, but implied in or vouched by the actual conduct of persons by whose acts the litigant parties are not to be bound.[33]

In *Wright v. Doe d. Tatham*[34] the issue was the testamentary capacity of John Marsden. As evidence of his lack of competency, the court received evidence that Marsden was treated as a child by his servant; that in his youth he was called "silly Jack" and "silly Marsden"; that boys shouted after him "there goes crazy Marsden" and threw dirt at him. As evidence of his competency, three letters addressed to Marsden were tendered. The letters contained no express assertions of his competence, but their content and tone suggested beliefs in the writers that Marsden possessed ordinary intelligence and capacity. These letters were held to be inadmissible hearsay. Baron Parke in the Exchequer Chamber noted:

> The conclusion at which I have arrived is, that proof of a particular fact, which is not of itself a matter in issue, but which is relevant only as implying a statement or opinion of a third person on the matter in issue, is inadmissible in all cases where such a statement or opinion not on oath would be of itself inadmissible; and, therefore, in this case the letters which are offered only to prove the competence of the testator, that is the truth of the implied statements therein contained, were properly rejected.[35]

In the House of Lords, Baron Alderson commented:

> If, therefore, the letters are to be used as proofs of the opinion of the writers respecting Mr. Marsden's capacity, the objection to their admissibility is, that this opinion is not

---

32. See *Chandarasekera v. R.*, [1936] 3 All E.R. 865 (P.C.). But see *Johnson v. State*, 36 N.W. 2d 86 (Wisc., 1949) characterizing a pointing as non-hearsay and in turn characterized as displaying "an obtuseness rarely found in a judicial opinion": Morgan, *supra*, note 3 at p. 144; nevertheless followed in *Kinder v. Commonwealth*, 306 S.W. 2d 265 (Ky., 1957).
33. *Wright v. Doe d. Tatham* (1837), 112 E.R. 488, 516 per Baron Parke speaking in the Exchequer Chamber, which judgment was affirmed in the House of Lords, 7 E.R. 559.
34. *Ibid.*
35. *Ibid.*, at pp. 516-17.

upon oath, nor is it possible for the opposite party to test by cross-examination the foundation on which it rests.[36]

Also in the House of Lords, Coleridge, J. writes:

> Suppose, says [counsel], his fellow townsmen had elected Mr. Marsden to be their representative in Parliament, might I not prove that fact as evidence of their opinion of his competency? Assuming, as the argument does, that Mr. Marsden is connected with such election by no act on his part before, at the time or after, I distinctly answer, no. The question seems to me based on the fallacy, that, whatever is morally convincing, and whatever reasonable beings would form their judgments and act upon, may be submitted to a jury.[37]

Is it possible to quarrel with the intellectual validity of the judicial reasoning in this classic case which would classify as hearsay statements implied from conduct though said conduct was not intended to be assertive?

Consider, however, a later House of Lords decision, *Lloyd v. Powell Duffryn Steam Coal Co.*[38] In this case a workman had been killed in the course of his employment and the issue was whether a child, born after his death, was his child and so entitled to compensation. The disputed evidence consisted of statements by the deceased in which he acknowledged an awareness that the mother was pregnant, and promised to marry her. There were no express statements by him that he was the father but his conduct clearly implied the same. On the issue of paternity the Lords held the evidence to be receivable. Lord Atkinson said:

> From these authorities it necessarily follows, in my view, that if a man, with full knowledge of the pregnancy of a woman with whom he has had sexual intercourse, becomes, during her pregnancy, engaged to be married to her, the fact of that contract having been entered into, though not carried out, is a most powerful piece of evidence on both the issues of fact, namely, the dependency and the paternity of the child.
>   ... To treat the statements made by the deceased as ... proof of the facts stated, is wholly to mistake their true character and significance. This significance consists in the improbability that any man would make these statements, true or false, unless he believed himself to be the father of the child of whom Alice Lloyd was pregnant.[39]

Is the workman's belief in paternity relevant in the case except as evidence of the fact that he is the father? If not how does *Lloyd* differ from *Wright*? Are the hearsay dangers minimized in this type of case? How? Are there questions that you, as adversary, would like to put to declarant? For example, "How do you know you're the father?"[40]

---

36.   (1838), 7 E.R. 559, 577.
37.   *Ibid.*, at p. 566.
38.   [1914] A.C. 733 (H.L.).
39.   *Ibid.*, at pp. 739 and 741.
40.   Compare Finman, "Implied Assertions as Hearsay" (1962), 14 Stan. L. Rev. at 682.

R. v. WYSOCHAN
(1930), 54 C.C.C. 172 (Sask. C.A.)

HAULTAIN, C.J.S.:—Appeal against conviction.

The appellant was convicted on March 20, 1930, before Bigelow, J., of the wilful murder of one Antenia Kropa on December 25, 1929, at Humboldt in this Province, and was sentenced to death.

The main ground of appeal raises the question of the admissibility of evidence of words spoken by A. Kropa some time after she was shot. It appears that A. Kropa, her husband S. Kropa, and the appellant were the only persons present at or about the time the shooting took place.

As to what took place at the time, it will be sufficient to say that according to S. Kropa's evidence the shooting must have been done by the appellant, while on the other hand according to the evidence of the appellant the shooting must have been done by S. Kropa.

The evidence shows that S. Kropa ran out of the house at or about the time the shooting took place, and that after reporting the matter to some friends and the police he returned to the house half an hour later.

The evidence objected to relates to words spoken by A. Kropa at the time. The evidence is, that she said to one Tony Sokolowski, "Tony where is my husband" and that when S. Kropa, the husband, was near her she stretched out her hand to him and said:— "Stanley, help me out because there is a bullet in my body." Further, when she was put into a sleigh to be taken to the hospital and was being covered up, she said, "Stanley, help me, I am too hot."

In his charge to the jury the trial Judge, in commenting on this evidence, said as follows:— "Now, if that was so gentlemen, Mr. Wilson has very properly argued that that would be a most unusual and unreasonable, and I think, improbable thing for her to do, if it was her husband who had shot her. There is no doubt that this woman was killed that night, and there are one of two alternatives before you. Either it was Kropa or the accused, and if it was not Kropa, it does not require any argument or logic for you to come to the conclusion it was the accused, and that is why this evidence is put before you to show that when her husband appeared on the scene she stretched out her arms to him and asked for help. Would it not have been a most improbable thing had he been the author of her death that night?"

It may be observed at the outset that the statements in question were not part of a dying declaration, nor were they part of the *res gestae*. They rather come within the class of utterances described in 3 Wigmore on Evidence, Can. ed., p. 2315, para. 1790, as follows:— "Utterances as indicating Circumstantially the Speaker's Own State of Mind. The condition of a speaker's mind, as to knowledge, belief, rationality, emotion, or the like, may be evidenced by his utterances, either used testimonially as assertions to be believed, or used circumstantially as affording indirect inferences. Utterances of the former sort may be received under the Exception for Statements of a Mental Condition (*ante* para. 1714) . . . . The usual resort is to utterances which circumstantially indicate a specific state of mind causing them."

In *Gilbert* v. *The King* (1907), 12 Can. C.C. 127, at pp. 131-2, Harvey, J., is reported as saying in the Court below, as follows:— " 'The charge is one of deliberately shooting the deceased while the defence is that the shooting was purely accidental. If it were shewn that after the shooting the state of mind of the man shot were one of friendliness to the accused, it surely would be deemed to have an important bearing on the question in issue, and in the same way evidence indicating aversion and fear have as important a bearing in the opposite direction. Wigmore, in his work on Evidence, points out very fully the difference between the admission of utterances as proof of the truth of the facts stated and their admission to prove a state of mind which he terms their circumstantial use as opposed to the other or testimonial use, and states, in par. 1790, that to the use circumstantially the hearsay rule makes no opposition "because the utterance is not used for the sake of inducing belief in any assertion it may contain." ' "

The evidence in question seems to come well within the principle above stated. The utterances in question contained no statement of facts necessary to be proved. They are only evidence more or less strong of a certain feeling or attitude of mind, and it was for the jury to decide what inferences might be drawn from them.

A number of objections were taken to the Judge's charge to the jury on the grounds of misdirection and non-direction. The evidence, in the opinion of the Court, was fully stated in the summing-up, and while on certain points the charge was not favourable to the accused, the jury were adequately instructed as to the defences open to him, and were invariably told that they were after all the sole judges of fact, and that they should not convict if they had any reasonable doubt of the prisoner's guilt.

The appeal must therefore be dismissed.

Appeal dismissed.

The court in *Wysochan* reasoned that, on finding that the statements were in fact made, the jury was entitled to infer the state of mind of the victim *and further* to infer from the state of mind what external event had caused the same. To permit this second inference is to say in effect that from the victim's conduct we can imply an assertion about a material fact and logically therefore the evidence, it is suggested, ought to be characterized as hearsay. To approach the problem from another direction, ask yourself whether adversary, defence counsel, was prejudiced by an inability to cross-examine and explore hearsay dangers.

While sincerity and memory may be minimized in the circumstances, what of communication and perception? Can we tell from the evidence whether the victim actually saw who did the killing? Would you feel the need to cross-examine declarant concerning her opportunity to adequately perceive?

Notice that the argument here being made is *not* that the evidence should be automatically rejected but rather that it ought to be correctly analyzed before a decision is taken.

R. v. EDWARDS
(1994), 34 C.R. (4th) 113, 91 C.C.C. (3d) 123 (Ont. C.A.)

[The police conducted a search of the accused's car. They seized a cellular phone and pager. Using them, the police received calls from people ordering small amounts of cocaine. The accused appealed his conviction on various grounds including the receipt into evidence of conversations heard on the the cellular phone.]

McKinlay J.A. (Finlayson and Abella JJ.A. concurring):—

. . . .

The police had been informed that the appellant carried on a business of drug trafficking, using a cellular phone and a pager. Just prior to his arrest, the appellant was observed talking on the cellular phone in Ms. Evers' car. After their seizure, the police monitored both the phone and pager, and on ten occasions people either contacted the police when they answered the telephone or were called by police in response to a pager message. Several of these individuals asked for the appellant and some requested crack cocaine. The appellant takes the position that evidence of these conversations should have been excluded at trial both because they were obtained only as a result of an illegal search and seizure of Ms. Evers' automobile, and because they constitute hearsay. Since the search and seizure of the phone and pager was not illegal, there is no basis for excluding the evidence on that ground.

With respect to the issue of hearsay, the trial judge held that the evidence was not tendered for the truth of its contents, but to show the nature of the business carried on by the appellant. I agree. In this case the requests for drugs would only constitute hearsay evidence if they were tendered to show that the callers did, in fact, desire to purchase crack cocaine. However, the real issue is not whether such requests contained truths or falsehoods, but whether they were in fact made. In this case the fact that the requests were made can only be relevant to determining the nature of the activities of the appellant, who was intended to respond to the requests. See *R. v. Fialkow*, [1963] 2 C.C.C. 42 (Ont. C.A.).

However, even if these requests could be considered hearsay, the Supreme Court of Canada has recently in *R. v. Khan* and in *R. v. Smith* expanded the exceptions to the hearsay rule to include evidence which is both necessary and reliable. In my view, the evidence in issue fulfils these criteria. It was necessary to prove the nature of the appellant's drug activities, and could not have been proven in this case in any other way that was available to the police. They did not know the identity of the callers, and, in any event, it is unlikely the callers would have testified if their identity had been known. The evidence is reliable, because it was made under circumstances which negate the possibility that the requests were spurious ones. The callers were led to believe that the persons to whom they were speaking (the police) were speaking on behalf of the appellant. In my view, the trial judge was correct in admitting this evidence.

R. v. KEARLEY
[1992] 2 All E.R. 345 (H.L.)

[The police raided the accused's flat. They found drugs but not in sufficient quantity to justify an inference that the accused was a dealer. The accused was taken to the station. Over the next few hours the police took telephone calls asking for the accused and asking to buy drugs; there were also seven callers at the door similarly interested. At his trial on charges of possession with intent to supply the Crown called the police officers to testify to the phone calls and visitors received. The defence unsuccessfully objected that this evidence was hearsay. The accused was convicted and his appeal dismissed.]

LORD BRIDGE OF HARWICH: —

. . . .

If the speaker had expressly said to the police officer that the defendant had supplied him with drugs in the past, this would clearly have been inadmissible as hearsay. When the only relevance of the words spoken lies in their implied assertion that the defendant is a supplier of drugs, must this equally be excluded as hearsay? This, I believe, is the central question on which this appeal turns. Is a distinction to be drawn for the purposes of the hearsay rule between express and implied assertions? If the words coupled with any associated action of a person not called as a witness are relevant solely as impliedly asserting a relevant fact, may evidence of those words and associated actions be given notwithstanding that an express assertion by that person of the same fact would only have been admissible if he had been called as a witness? Unless we can answer that question in the affirmative, I think we are bound to answer the certified question in the negative.

The answer to the question given by the English authorities is clear and unequivocal. [See] *Wright v Doe d Tatham* (1837) 7 Ad & El 313. . . .

. . . .

I fully appreciate the cogency of the reasons advanced in favour of a limitation or exception to the operation of the hearsay rule which would allow the admission of implied assertions of the kind in question. But is it open to your Lordships to modify judicially the common law rule as expounded in *Wright v Doe d Tatham* . . .? Such a modification would involve not only overruling *Wright v Doe d Tatham* but also departing, in reliance on the Practice Statement of 1968, . . . from the precedents set by the decisions of this House in both *R v Blastland* and *Myers v DPP*.

. . . .

LORD ACKNER: —

. . . .

[Counsel for the prosecution] frankly concedes that if the inquirer had said in the course of making his request, "I would like my usual supply of amphetamine at the price which I paid you last week" or words to that effect, then, although the inquirer could have been called to give evidence of the fact that he had in the past purchased from the appellant his requirements of amphetamine and had made his call at the appellant's house for a further supply on the occasion when he met and spoke to the police, the hearsay rule prevents the prosecution from calling police officers to recount the conversation which I have described. This is for the simple reason that the request made in the form set out above contains an express assertion that the premises at which the request was being made were being used as a source of supply of drugs and the supplier was the appellant.

If . . . the simple request or requests for drugs to be supplied by the appellant, as recounted by the police, contains in substance, but only by implication, the same assertion, then I can find neither authority nor principle to suggest that the hearsay rule should not be equally applicable and exclude such evidence. What is sought to be done is to use the oral assertion, even though it may be an implied assertion, as evidence of the truth of the proposition asserted. That the proposition is asserted by way of necessary implication rather than expressly cannot, to my mind, make any difference.

. . . .

LORD OLIVER OF AYLMERTON: —

. . . .

My Lords, to any ordinary layman asked to consider the matter, one might think that the resort of a large number of persons to 11 Perth Close, all asking for "Chippie", all carrying sums of cash and all asking to be supplied with drugs, would be as clear an indication as he could reasonably expect to have that 11 Perth Close was a place at which drugs were available; and if he were to be asked whether or not this showed also that "Chippie" was dealing in drugs, I cannot help feeling that his answer would be, "Of course it does." But so simple—perhaps, one might say, so attractively common sense—a layman's approach is not necessarily a reliable guide in a criminal trial. . . .

. . . .

[T]he state of mind of the caller is not the fact in issue and is, in itself, irrelevant, for it is not probative of anything other than its own existence. It becomes relevant only if and so far as the existence of other facts can be inferred from it. So far as concerns anything in issue at the trial, what the caller said and the state of mind which that fact evinces become relevant and probative of the fact in issue (namely the intent of the appellant) only if, or because, (i) what was said amounts to a statement, by necessary implication, that the appellant has in the past supplied drugs to the speaker (as in two cases in which requests were made for "the usual") or (ii) it imports the belief or opinion of the speaker that the appellant has drugs and is willing to supply them. And here, as it seems to me, we are directly up against the hearsay rule which forms one of the major established exceptions to the admissibility of relevant evidence. . . .

The impermissibility of such a course rests upon a well-established principle expounded in the context of civil proceedings some 150 years ago in *Wright v Doe d Tatham*. . . .

. . . .

LORD GRIFFITHS: —

. . . .

Unless compelled to do so by authority I should be most unwilling to hold that such evidence should be withheld from the jury. In my view the criminal law of evidence should be developed along commonsense lines readily comprehensible to the men and women who comprise the jury and bear the responsibility for the major decisions in criminal cases. I believe that most laymen if told that the criminal law of evidence forbade them even to consider such evidence as we are debating in this appeal would reply "Then the law is an ass." If I was driven by authority to hold that the law of evidence had been developed by the judges to the point at which the evidence was inadmissible, then I would think that a powerful case had been made out to re-examine the wisdom of the decision in *Myers v DPP* [1964] 2 All ER 881, in which it was held by a majority of three to two that no further judicial development of the law of hearsay was permissible and that future correction must be left to the legislature. Over a quarter of a century has passed since that decision but no overall legislative review of hearsay evidence in criminal law has been attempted. The hearsay rule was created by our judicial predecessors and if we find that it no longer serves to do justice in certain conditions then the judges of today should accept the responsibility of reviewing and adapting the rules of evidence to serve present society. I find the dissenting speeches of Lord Pearce and Lord Donovan more persuasive than the speeches of the majority and I note that it was this dissenting view that found favour with the Supreme Court of Canada in *Ares v Venner* [1970] S.C.R. 608.

. . . .

[I]t is said that evidence of what was said by those who telephoned or called at the flat asking to be supplied with drugs was evidence of no more than their belief or opinion that they could obtain drugs from the appellant and on the authority of *Wright v Doe d Tatham* to be treated as inadmissible hearsay.

I cannot accept this submission. It is of course true that it is almost certain that the customers did believe that they could obtain drugs from the appellant, otherwise they would not have telephoned or visited his premises. But why did all these people believe they could obtain drugs from the appellant? The obvious inference is that the appellant had established a market as a drug dealer by supplying or offering to supply drugs and was thus attracting customers. There are of course other possible explanations, such as a mistaken belief or even a deliberate attempt to frame the appellant, but there are very few factual situations from which different inferences cannot be drawn and it is for the jury to decide which inference they believe they can safely draw.

The evidence is offered not for the purpose of inviting the jury to draw the inference that the customers believed they could obtain drugs but to prove as a fact that the telephone callers and visitors were acting as customers or potential customers, which was a circumstance from which the jury could if so minded draw the inference that the appellant was trading as a drug dealer, or to put it in the language of the indictment that he was in possession of drugs with intent to supply them to others.

. . . .

LORD BROWNE-WILKINSON: —

. . . .

[T]he fact that there were a number of people seeking to buy drugs was legally relevant and admissible as showing that there was a market to which the accused could sell, even though such evidence was also capable of giving rise to an impermissible secondary inference, viz that the callers believed Chippie supplied drugs. If the callers had themselves given evidence at the trial and said only that on the relevant day they had made a call for the purpose of obtaining drugs from Chippie, I can see no ground on which such evidence could have been excluded as being irrelevant.

. . . .

The letters in *Wright v Doe d Tatham* were being tendered testimonially to prove the belief of the writers: the calls in this case are being tendered to prove a relevant fact and not the belief of the callers. Accordingly, the hearsay rule does not apply.

R. v. McKINNON
(1989), 70 C.R. (3d) 10 (Ont. C.A.)

[The accused appealed against his conviction for first degree murder. The trial judge ruled that although the accused's wife was not a competent witness for the prosecution, evidence that she was with the police when they discovered the victim's body in remote bush was admissible. The accused argued that the evidence was hearsay by conduct.]

FINLAYSON, J.A. (LACOURCIÈRE and McKINLAY, JJ.A. concurring):—

. . . .

The case for the Crown was based largely on circumstantial evidence. One Paul Bisschops testified that in the spring of 1985 the appellant attempted to convince him to participate in the killing and robbing of an old man who had been receiving substantial overpayments from Workers' Compensation. The intended victim was never identified by name to Bisschops, but it is clear that he was Patterson. His body was later found buried in a remote part of the bush.

. . . .

The intended accomplice, Bisschops, testified that he refused to become involved, but there is circumstantial evidence that the appellant went ahead with his plan and that he in fact killed the victim and disposed of his body in the bush. Patterson was last seen alive with the appellant when they were drinking together at Melonies Restaurant. The day after, the latter was in possession of jewellery that had belonged to the victim and traveller's cheques in the name of Patterson, worth $2,000. Human blood matching the victim's blood type was found on a baseball bat near the gravesite and splattered on the walls in the appellant's home. Personal papers of the victim were discovered in a drawer in the appellant's bedroom. Soil from a shovel recovered from the appellant's home was revealed to have characteristics indistinguishable from those of soil taken from the gravesite. There was other evidence.

The accused did not testify, nor did anyone testify on his behalf. The defences were put forward through cross-examination of Crown witnesses, and submissions were made to the jury relying on those portions of all of the evidence which counsel felt supported the defence positions. One suggestion made was that Bisschops might have been the culprit.

This takes us back to the first complaint, which is the evidence that the police officers who discovered the body in a remote portion of the bush some distance from Sudbury were accompanied by the appellant's wife. While there was no evidence as to what conversation took place between them, it is suggested that the jury could only draw the inference that the information which permitted the police officers to find the gravesite must have come from the appellant's wife, who in turn had received it from the appellant. The Crown submits that another inference could have been that she was involved in the killing herself and therefore there would not necessarily have been a communication between husband and wife which might be protected. The Crown wanted the evidence admitted to help negative the inference that the police obtained their information as to the location of the gravesite from Bisschops. It was admissible for that purpose even though an incidental result was that the jury might infer that the appellant was the source of the wife's knowledge.

I regard this as being a false issue. The police officers could not and did not report what the appellant's wife had said to them. This would have violated the hearsay rule. The trial judge had ruled earlier that she was neither a competent nor a compellable witness at the instance of the Crown. She therefore could not testify against her husband and could not relate what, if anything, she had said to the police officers.

This ruling was based on the common law rule that a wife is not a competent witness against her husband. There are common law and statutory exceptions to this rule, notably in s. 4 of the Canada Evidence Act, R.S.C. 1985, c. C-5, but the trial judge held that none of the exceptions applied on the facts of this case. . . .

Notwithstanding s. 4 and the common law rule, if the jury was prepared to draw an inference adverse to the appellant from the fact that his wife was in the company of the police officers when they found the body in a very remote area, then in my opinion it was perfectly entitled to draw such an inference.

Under the provisions of s. 4(3) of the Evidence Act, the wife was not compellable to disclose any communication made to her during their marriage. This does not mean that she was not free to disclose such a communication to the police out of court. In this respect her attendance at the gravesite in no way offends the letter, or indeed the spirit, of s. 4(3).

Under s. 4(6) of the Evidence Act, her failure to testify for the appellant cannot be made the subject of comment by the judge or by counsel for the prosecution. She did not testify, and no comment was made with respect thereto, but appellant's counsel asks us to treat the evidence of her attendance at the gravesite as amounting to "hearsay by conduct". He submits that her physical attendance at the gravesite made it apparent to the jury that she must have disclosed to the police a communication from her husband to herself as to the location of the body. I cannot accept this.

In the first place, her presence was a fact, and was part of the police officers' testimony as to the search and discovery, which search and discovery surely was a relevant fact in the light of the Crown's theory of the "plan" to kill and hide the body. In the second place, her presence in the manner described cannot be characterized as hearsay by conduct. It has always been my understanding that such hearsay usually amounted to a description of actions or behaviour which are themselves means of expression, such as shrugs, headshakes or other gestures that are a substitute for or supplement to oral communication. Evidence of such conduct is tendered as evidence of an assertion by the person who performed the action. As such, it is inadmissible hearsay. On the facts of this appeal I see nothing in the evidence about the wife's accompanying the police officers to the gravesite which amounts to an assertion or a statement that she received information about its location from her husband, from her husband alone, and from no other source. The evidence is not tendered as evidence of an assertion by the wife. It is not hearsay. For a fuller discussion, see McCormick on Evidence, 3rd ed. (1984), at pp. 736-42.

Is *McKinnon* consistent with *Wright v. Doe d. Tatham*? Can one argue that the fact of the wife's attendance in *McKinnon* was not itself a matter

in issue, but was relevant only as implying a statement, or opinion, which statement, if made expressly would have been clearly inadmissible?

The court here recognizes that "the police officers could not report what the appellant's wife had said to them" and yet the court allows that the jury was entitled to infer from her conduct that she was aware of the grave's location because her husband told her.

Is the conduct received into evidence equivalent to a statement which the court recognized as inadmissible?

The court notes that the wife was not a competent or compellable witness for the prosecution; and yet, by introducing evidence of her conduct and permitting the inference that the accused told her of the gravesite, has the Crown in effect called her as a witness against her husband?

Is the result in *McKinnon*, however, to be preferred over the classic reasoning in *Wright v. Doe d. Tatham*?

The hearsay rule was born as the direct result of the evolution of the adversary system. It is seen to be unfair to receive into evidence a statement made out of court which the adversary cannot test on cross-examination. In the *McKinnon* case, however, the declarant, the wife, was available to the accused. The wife, though not compellable at the instance of the Crown, was compellable by the accused. Any unfairness or prejudice to the accused, flowing from the receipt of hearsay, could have been avoided by the accused calling his wife to the stand to explain the meaning of her conduct.

PROBLEMS

Problem 1

The issue is whether the plaintiff's ship was seaworthy when it set sail on a voyage from which it never returned. The plaintiff wants to call a witness who will testify that the captain of the ship inspected the ship the day before it sailed and then took his wife and two small children with him on the ill-fated voyage.
Hearsay?

Problem 2

The issue is whether it was raining at a particular time. Why that's the issue is of no consequence here. Can a witness testify that though she was inside at the time, she saw another person outside put up his umbrella at that time. Suppose the evidence is that several people put up their umbrellas at the same time? Several hundred?
Hearsay?

Problem 3

In a narcotics prosecution a narcotics agent testifies that he and an informer had agreed to a secret code under which the informer would say, "Isn't the moon lovely tonight?" whenever he was standing next to a person from whom he had purchased heroin. The prosecution now wishes to have the agent testify that the informer said to the agent, while standing next to the accused, "Isn't the moon lovely tonight?"

Hearsay?

Problem 4

Which of the following items of evidence are hearsay?

(*a*) Evidence that A punched B, offered to show that A did not like B.

(*b*) Evidence that A said "B is a thief," offered to show that A did not like B.

Problem 5

Plaintiff sues tobacco company for damages resulting from his wife's death which he maintains is due to cancer caused by company's cigarettes. Plaintiff offers evidence of nurse that her employer, a doctor and cancer specialist now deceased, gave wife cobalt treatments. Defendant argues this evidence is hearsay. Suppose the cobalt treatment was painful and plaintiff is seeking damages for his wife's pain and suffering as well as for the actual death by cancer.

Problem 6

The police executed a search warrant upon an apartment solely occupied by the accused. When the accused became aware of their presence, he was seen to scrub an arborite table top which appeared to be covered with figures. The police also found a copy of a racing form in the apartment. While they were in the apartment, the telephone rang ten or 12 times. The police answered the calls, and on three occasions the callers placed bets totalling $29. The others asked about racing information. The defence objects that this evidence is hearsay. What result? See *R. v. Fialkow*, [1963] 2 C.C.C. 42 (Ont. C.A.) and compare *McGregor v. Stokes*, [1952] V.L.R. 347; but contrast *People v. Barnhart*, 153 P. 2d 214 (Cal. Dist. Ct., 1944) per Doran, J. See also Friedland, "Reputation of Disorderly Houses" (1962), 5 Crim. L.Q. 328 and Ladd, "The Hearsay We Admit" (1952), 5 Okla. L. Rev. 271.

Problem 7

Husband and wife were killed in an automobile accident. Plaintiff, seeking to prove that the wife died first, calls a witness to testify that at the scene of the accident he observed the ambulance attendant cover the wife's body with a sheet, draping the same over her face, and later saw the attendant chat briefly with the husband. Hearsay?

Problem 8

The accused is charged with murdering his wife with a shotgun. His defence is that the gun discharged accidentally while he was cleaning it. The deceased had spoken with her father by phone at 1:09 p.m. and her body was discovered by the police at 1:20 p.m. The prosecution seeks to introduce evidence of a phone call received by the operator from the deceased's house at 1:15 p.m. In the absence of the jury he advises the judge that, if permitted, the telephone operator will testify that the caller was a female, seemingly in an hysterical state, and said "Get me the police please." What arguments might you as defence counsel make? See *Ratten v. R.*, [1972] A.C. 378 (P.C.) and *R. v. Wysochan* (1930), 54 C.C.C. 172 (Sask. C.A.).

Problem 9

Defendant leased certain premises from plaintiff for a term of years, and agreed that during that term he would sell only plaintiff's beer on the premises, with the plaintiff agreeing that he would provide a good and marketable product. Plaintiff now brings suit for an injunction to restrain defendant from purchasing another's beer; defendant resists and seeks to show the poor quality of plaintiff's beer. Defence counsel asks defendant's bartender whether the customers regularly complained as to its quality. Objection by plaintiff is sustained. Defence counsel asks bartender what customers did after drinking plaintiff's beer and bartender testifies that they often spat it out and left the premises. Is this evidence objectionable as hearsay? See *Manchester Brewery Co. v. Coombs* (1900), 82 L.T.R. 349 (Ch. D.). In a similar type of suit, may plaintiff elicit evidence that customers never complained? See *Silver v. New York Central Railway Co.*, 105 N.E. 2d 923 (Mass. Sup. Ct., 1952). See also Falknor, "Silence as Hearsay" (1940), 89 U. of Pa. L. Rev. 192.

(e) Approaches to Hearsay

For many years courts in England and Canada were content to limit the admission of hearsay to slowly developed pigeon-hole exceptions which changed little over time. We shall see that Canadian courts have now developed a broad principled approach to admitting hearsay through criteria of reasonable necessity and circumstantial guarantees of reliability.

In *Myers v. D.P.P.*,[41] the majority of the House of Lords refused to create a new exception to the hearsay rule as there had not been a new exception created for some 90 years.[42] The accused had been prosecuted for conspiracy to receive stolen cars and it was necessary to establish that numbers on the cylinder blocks of the seized cars were the same numbers as on the blocks in the stolen cars. The prosecution sought to do this by introducing the business records of the manufacturer. The common law then recognized an exception to the hearsay rule for declarations made in the course of duty provided the declarant was deceased. The prosecution was unable to satisfy this condition as they were unable to identify the declarant who was but a single worker on a mass production assembly line. They tried to justify reception of the evidence on the basis of unavailability of the declarant, the consequent necessity of using the best evidence available, and assurances of trustworthiness arising from the circumstances in which the record was made. The majority insisted that the rule had become so fixed that only the legislature could create new exceptions to meet society's new needs and conditions.[43]

---

41. [1965] A.C. 1001.
42. See *Sugden v. Lord St. Leonard's* (1876), 1 P.D. 154 (C.A.).
43. See the English response in the Civil Evidence Act, 1968, c. 64. Newark and Samuels, "Comment" (1968), 31 Mod. L. Rev. 668.

The law regarding hearsay can produce absurd results if it is slavishly and mechanically applied. As with any rule of evidence, we should always keep in mind the reason for the rule. If the reason for the rule is otherwise satisfied by the circumstances of a particular case the rule need not operate to exclude relevant evidence. The classic Canadian exposition of common sense in this area is seen in one of the first Supreme Court of Canada opinions choosing not to follow the House of Lords' lead.

In *Ares v. Venner*,[44] the Supreme Court of Canada faced the same question of deciding on the proper approach to hearsay. Plaintiff had suffered a broken leg while skiing. At the hospital Dr. Venner attended, reduced the fracture and applied a full-leg plaster cast. The trial judge received in evidence notes which had been made by the attending nurses. These notes described the plaintiff's toes as "blue," "bluish pink," "cool," and "cold," and were relevant to the issue of the doctor's negligence, as the trial court made the crucial finding that:

> The classic signs of circulatory impairment manifested themselves clearly and early.

The trial court described the usual medical practice in response to such signs and observed that the defendant had not followed such practice. The trial judge relied on a passage from Wigmore,[45] which argued for the admissibility of hospital records as an exception to the hearsay rule based on grounds of necessity and circumstantial guarantees of trustworthiness. Professor Wigmore had found the grounds of necessity in the "serious interference with convenience of hospital management," and the circumstances guaranteeing trustworthiness in the fact that they are made and relied on in affairs of life and death. The Alberta Court of Appeal ordered a new trial on the basis that the nurse's notes contained not just numerical data but observations expressed in opinions which would be fruitful areas of cross-examination. It also noted that one of Professor Wigmore's requirements for admissibility, grounds of necessity, was not satisfied here since the nurses had been subpoenaed by the plaintiff and were present throughout the trial. The Supreme Court of Canada restored the trial judgment.

Speaking for a unanimous court, Hall, J. noted that there had been a long felt need for a restatement of the hearsay rule and that there were two schools of thought regarding how the change should come about — by legislative action or judicial action. He noted that in *Myers v. D.P.P.*, the learned Law Lords had split on the question of approach, with the majority agreeing to the need for reform but deciding it must be left to the legislature. Hall, J. decided:

> I am of opinion that this Court should adopt and follow the minority view rather than resort to saying in effect: "This judge-made law needs to be restated to meet modern conditions, but we must leave it to Parliament and the ten legislatures to do the job."[46]

---

44.   (1970), 14 D.L.R. (3d) 4 (S.C.C.).

45.   6 Wigmore, *Evidence* (Chad. Rev.), s. 1707.

46.   *Supra*, note 44, at p. 16. See *Setak Computer Services Corp. v. Burroughs Business Machines Ltd.* (1977), 76 D.L.R. (3d) 641, 646 (Griffiths, J., Ont. H.C.) recognizing that *Ares v. Venner* expressed the common law in Ontario with respect to business records generally. But see *Exhibitors Inc. v. Allen* (1989), 70 O.R. (2d) 103 (Arbour, J., Ont. H.C.) maintaining that *Ares v. Venner* has no place with respect to business records in civil cases in Ontario as the reception of business records is provided for by provincial legislation.

The court in *Ares v. Venner* recognized that the adversary was not prejudiced by the reception of the nurses' notes. If the nurses were in fact called they would have been allowed to "refresh their memory" by having regard to their notes and little would be gained by their attendance as they would ordinarily add little or nothing to the information furnished by the record. The notes were made by trained observers and that should satisfy any concerns regarding the hearsay danger of perception. The notes were made contemporaneously with the observation and so concern for the memory danger should be stilled. Sincerity of the declarant should not be a concern as the nurse was under a duty to record her observations accurately and discipline could flow from any mistakes. The court displayed a common sense, principled approach. The court was aware of the reason for the rule and why that reason was not applicable to the particular factual situation before it.

Another admirable display of common sense, this time from south of the border, comes from the pen of Circuit Judge Wisdom in the case of *Dallas County v. Commercial Union Assurance Co.*[47] The clock tower of the Dallas County Courthouse at Selma, Alabama collapsed on July 7, 1957. Damage to the courthouse exceeded $100,000. An examination of the debris showed the presence of charred timbers. Dallas County concluded that the char was evidence of lightning having struck and decided that a lightning bolt had hit the building causing the collapse. Dallas County carried insurance for loss caused by fire or lightning and claimed from their insurance company. The insurance company's engineers decided that the collapse was due not to lightning, but to structural weaknesses. In their view the char was the result of a fire that had occurred many, many years before. The case went to the jury on one issue: Did lightning cause the collapse of the clock tower? The jury found for the insurers and the County appealed, arguing that the trial judge erred in receiving into evidence a newspaper clipping dated June 9, 1901 describing a fire in the courthouse. Dallas County argued that the clipping was hearsay. Listen to Wisdom, J., dismissing the appeal:

> In the Anglo-American adversary system of law, courts usually will not admit evidence unless its accuracy and trustworthiness may be tested by cross-examination. Here, therefore, the plaintiff argues that the newspaper should not be admitted: "You cannot cross-examine a newspaper." Of course, a newspaper article is hearsay, and in almost all circumstances is inadmissible. However, the law governing hearsay is somewhat less than pellucid. And, as with most rules, the hearsay rule is not absolute; it is replete with exceptions. Witnesses die, documents are lost, deeds are destroyed, memories fade. All too often, primary evidence is not available and courts and lawyers must rely on secondary evidence. . . . There is no procedural canon against the exercise of common sense in deciding the admissibility of hearsay evidence. In 1901 Selma, Alabama, was a small town. Taking a common sense view of this case, it is inconceivable to us that a newspaper reporter in a small town would report there was a fire in the dome of the new courthouse—if there had been no fire. He is without motive to falsify, and a false report would have subjected the newspaper and him to embarrassment in the community. The usual dangers inherent in hearsay evidence, such as lack of memory, faulty narration, intent to influence the court proceedings, and plain lack of truthfulness are not present here. To our minds, the article published in the Selma Morning-Times on the day of the fire is more reliable, more trustworthy,

---

47.   286 F. 2d 388 (5th Circ., 1961).

more competent evidence than the testimony of a witness called to the stand fifty-eight years later.

For 20 years courts balked at applying *Ares v. Venner* in criminal cases. Then came *Khan*.

R. v. KHAN
[1990] 2 S.C.R. 531, 79 C.R. (3d) 1, 59 C.C.C. (3d) 92

[The accused was charged with sexual assault. The alleged victim was three-and-a-half years old at the time of the assault. She attended with her mother at the office of the family doctor for a general examination of the mother and a routine examination of the child. The child was in the doctor's office, alone with the doctor, for five to seven minutes, while the mother undressed and put on a hospital gown. When the mother rejoined her child she noticed the child picking at a wet spot on her sleeve. The spot on the sleeve was determined to have been produced by a deposit of semen and, in some areas, a mixture of semen and saliva that had soaked through the fabric before it dried. The concentration of the mixture suggested to the forensic biologist that the substances were probably mixed before they were applied to the material. Fifteen minutes after they left the doctor's office, the mother and daughter had essentially the following conversation:

MRS. O.: So you were talking to Dr. Khan, were you? What did he say?

T.: He asked me if I wanted a candy. I said "Yes". And do you know what?

MRS. O.: What?

T.: He said, "Open your mouth". And do you know what? He put his birdie in my mouth, shook it and peed in my mouth.

MRS. O.: Are you sure?

T.: Yes.

MRS. O.: You're not lying to me, are you?

T.: No. He put his birdie in my mouth. And he never did give me my candy.

The mother testified that the word "birdie" meant penis to T. At the trial, T. was called as a witness. She was four years and eight months old. The trial judge ruled that she could not give evidence, sworn or unsworn. The trial judge also ruled that the child's statement to her mother was inadmissible hearsay and could not be adduced. The Ontario Court of Appeal held that the trial judge was wrong in not allowing the child to give unsworn evidence. The court also held that the statement to the mother should have been received as falling within the exception for spontaneous declarations. In the Supreme Court it was decided that the Court of Appeal was right in their determination of error regarding the child's right to testify but, while agreeing that the child's statement deserved to be received, the court decided the spontaneous declaration exception was not the appropriate route. Rejecting the Court of Appeal's approach, Madam Justice McLachlin, writing for the court, noted, regarding

statements made by children to others about sexual abuse. Insofar as they are tied to the exception to the hearsay rule of spontaneous declarations . . . they suffer from certain defects. There is no requirement [of necessity].[48]

---

48.   (1991), 79 C.R. (3d) 1, 11.

The court decided it would be more appropriate to adopt the more flexible and principled approach of *Ares v. Venner*. Madam Justice McLachlin, writing for the court, decided that where there were grounds of necessity and circumstances surrounding the making of the statement, the hearsay could come in.]

McLACHLIN J.:—

. . . .

The hearsay rule has traditionally been regarded as an absolute rule, subject to various categories of exceptions, such as admissions, dying declarations, declarations against interest and spontaneous declarations. While this approach has provided a degree of certainty to the law on hearsay, it has frequently proved unduly inflexible in dealing with new situations and new needs in the law. This has resulted in courts in recent years on occasion adopting a more flexible approach, rooted in the principle and the policy underlying the hearsay rule rather than the strictures of traditional exceptions.

This Court took such an approach in *Ares v. Venner*. . . .

. . . .

[There are] two general requirements: necessity and reliability. The child's statement to the mother in this case meets both these general requirements. Necessity was present, other evidence of the event, as the trial judge found, being inadmissible. . . . The evidence also bore strong indicia of reliability. T. was disinterested, in the sense that her declaration was not made in favour of her interest. She made the declaration before any suggestion of litigation. And beyond doubt she possessed peculiar means of knowledge of the event of which she told her mother. Moreover, the evidence of a child of tender years on such matters may bear its own special stamp of reliability.

. . . .

These developments underline the need for increased flexibility in the interpretation of the hearsay rule to permit the admission in evidence of statements made by children to others about sexual abuse. Insofar as they are tied to the exception to the hearsay rule of spontaneous declarations, however, they suffer from certain defects. There is no requirement that resort to the hearsay evidence be necessary. Even where the evidence of the child might easily be obtained without undue trauma, the Crown would be able to use hearsay evidence. Nor is there any requirement that the reliability of the evidence in the particular be established; hence inherently unreliable evidence might be admitted. Finally, the rule being of an absolute "in-or-out" character, there is no means by which a trial judge could attach conditions on the reception of a particular statement which the judge might deem prudent in a particular case, as, for example, the right to cross-examine the deponent referred to in *Ares v. Venner*, supra. In addition to these objections, it can be argued that to extend the spontaneous declaration rule as far as these cases would extend it is to deform it beyond recognition and is conceptually undesirable.

In Canada too, courts have been moving to more flexibility in the reception of the hearsay evidence of children, although not under the aegis of the spontaneous declaration exception to the hearsay rule.

. . . .

These cases point the way in the correct direction. Despite the need for caution, hearsay evidence of a child's statement may be received where the requirements of *Ares v. Venner* are met. The general approach is summed up in the comment of Wilson J. in *R. v. B. (G.)*, [1990] 2 S.C.R. 30 at 55 [Sask.]:

> In recent years we have adopted a much more benign attitude to children's evidence, lessening the strict standards of oath taking and corroboration, and I believe that this is a desirable development.

The first question should be whether reception of the hearsay statement is necessary. Necessity for these purposes must be interpreted as "reasonably necessary". The inadmissibility of the child's evidence might be one basis for a finding of necessity. But sound evidence based on psychological assessments that testimony in court might be traumatic for the child or harm the child might also serve. There may be other examples of circumstances which could establish the requirement of necessity.

The next question should be whether the evidence is reliable. Many considerations, such as timing, demeanour, the personality of the child, the intelligence and understanding of the child, and the absence of any reason to expect fabrication in the statement, may be relevant on the issue of reliability. I would not wish to draw up a strict list of considerations for reliability or to suggest that certain categories of evidence (for example the evidence of young children on sexual encounters) should be always regarded as reliable. The matters relevant to reliability will vary with the child and with the circumstances, and are best left to the trial judge.

In determining the admissibility of the evidence, the judge must have regard to the need to safeguard the interests of the accused. In most cases a right of cross-examination, such as that alluded to in *Ares v. Venner*, would not be available. If the child's direct evidence in chief is not admissible, it follows that his or her cross-examination would not be admissible either. Where trauma to the child is at issue, there would be little point in sparing the child the need to testify in chief only to have him or her grilled in cross-examination. While there may be cases where, as a condition of admission, the trial judge thinks it possible and fair in all the circumstances to permit cross-examination of the child as the condition of the reception of a hearsay statement, in most cases the concerns of the accused as to credibility will remain to be addressed by submissions as to the weight to be accorded to the evidence and submissions as to the quality of any corroborating evidence.

I add that I do not understand *Ares v. Venner* to hold that the hearsay evidence there at issue was admissible where necessity and reliability are established only where cross-examination is available. First, the court adopted the views of the dissenting judges in *Myers v. D.P.P.*, supra, which do not make admissibility dependent on the right to cross-examine. Second, the cross-examination referred to in *Ares v. Venner* was of limited value. The nurses were present in court at the trial, but, in the absence of some way of connecting particular nurses with particular entries, meaningful cross-examination on the accuracy of specific observations would have been difficult indeed.

I conclude that hearsay evidence of a child's statement on crimes committed against the child should be received, provided that the guarantees of necessity and reliability are met, subject to such safeguards as the judge may consider necessary and subject always to considerations affecting the weight that should be accorded to such evidence. This does not make out-of-court statements by children generally admissible; in particular, the requirement of necessity will probably mean that in most cases children will still be called to give viva voce evidence.

I conclude that the mother's statement in the case at bar should have been received. It was necessary, the child's viva voce evidence having been rejected. It was also reliable. The child had no motive to falsify her story, which emerged naturally and without prompting. Moreover, the fact that she could not be expected to have knowledge of such sexual acts imbues her statement with its own peculiar stamp of reliability. Finally, her statement was corroborated by real evidence. Having said this, I note that it may not be necessary to enter the statement on a new trial, if the child's viva voce evidence can be received as suggested in the first part of my reasons.

CONCLUSION

I would dismiss the appeal and direct a new trial.

In *Khan v. College of Physicians & Surgeons (Ontario)*,[49] the Ontario Divisional Court reviewed the decision of the College to revoke Dr. Khan's licence to practice. At the hearing by a panel of the Discipline Committee, T. testified and her mother was permitted to give the statement attributed to T. That hearing was after the Court of Appeal's judgment in the criminal prosecution and before the decision of the Supreme Court of Canada. Writing for the majority, O'Driscoll, J., noted:

> [T]he precondition of "necessity" was absent and, therefore, the out-of-court statement by Tanya to her mother did not qualify as an exception to the rule against hearsay. . . . [C]ounsel for the respondent College submitted that because Tanya, in her evidence before the Discipline Committee, could not recall anything about "ejaculation", it was "necessary" to allow the mother to give the hearsay statement as truth of the facts contained therein. . . .
>
> Whatever may be the outside limit of the meaning of "necessity", in my view, it does not include shoring up and/or filling in aspects of the evidence of Tanya.[50]

The Court of Appeal disagreed. In *Khan v. College of Physicians and Surgeons (Ontario)* (1992), 9 O.R. (3d) 641 (C.A.) Doherty, J.A. decided:

> The fact that the child testifies will clearly impact on the necessity of receiving his or her out-of-court statement. Necessity cannot, however, be equated with unavailability. In *Khan*, McLachlin J. instructs us that necessary means "reasonably necessary" (at p. 546 S.C.R., p. 104 C.C.C.). In the context of cases involving an alleged sexual assault on a child, reasonable necessity refers to the need to have the child's version of events pertaining to the alleged assault before the tribunal charged with the responsibility of determining whether the assault occurred. In my view, if that tribunal is satisfied that despite the *viva voce* evidence of the child, it is still "reasonably necessary" to admit the out-of-court statement in order to obtain an accurate and frank rendition of the child's version of the relevant events, then the necessity criterion set down in *Khan* is satisfied: see Anne McGillivray, "*R. v. Laramee*: Forgetting Children, Forgetting Truth" (1991), 6 C.R. (4th) 325 at pp. 335-41.

In *R. v. Khan*,[51] the retrial following the Supreme Court's dismissal of the accused's appeal, the child T., now aged nine, testified. The Crown was invited to argue necessity but declined. She was cross-examined and discrepancies were pointed out between her evidence at the disciplinary hearing and her evidence at the trial. At the trial, for example, T. testified to the accused putting his penis in her mouth and the accused then wiping her chest with a kleenex. She had not mentioned the ejaculation at the disciplinary hearing. Pointing to this and other discrepancies, defence counsel submitted that it would be dangerous to convict upon T.'s evidence, relying on the rule of practice in *Kendall v. R.*,[52] that it is dangerous to convict on the evidence of a child even when the child had been sworn. The mother, while testifying at the trial about matters that

---

49.   (1990), 43 O.A.C. 130.
50.   *Ibid.*, at p. 137.
51.   [1991] O.J. No. 637.
52.   (1962), 132 C.C.C. 216 (S.C.C.).

she herself had witnessed, did not relate what T. had told her soon after leaving the doctor's office. The accused was convicted and sentenced to four years.

In this situation would it be possible, in reply, to lead evidence of the child's statement?

In *Khan*, in the Supreme Court of Canada, the ruling that the statement could only be received if it was necessary, was a ruling dealing with the admissibility of a statement tendered for the purposes of proving the truth of that statement, i.e., when tendered as a hearsay statement.

R. v. SMITH

[1992] 2 S.C.R. 915, 15 C.R. (4th) 133, 75 C.C.C. (3d) 257

The judgment of the Court was delivered by

LAMER C.J.: — The principal issue raised by this appeal is the admissibility of hearsay evidence as part of the Crown's case in a murder trial, when the declarant is dead.

The Facts

The respondent was convicted of the murder of Aritha Monalisa King and was sentenced to imprisonment for life with no parole eligibility for thirteen years. Both the respondent and Ms. King were American citizens, ordinarily resident in Detroit. At the respondent's trial, the evidence showed that on August 6, 1986, the respondent picked up Ms. King at her mother's house in Detroit. Together, they drove across the border to Canada. The respondent spent the weekend of August 9 and 10 with Ms. King in a hotel in London, Ontario. Ms. King's body was subsequently discovered at approximately 1:30 a.m. on August 11, near a service station at Beechville, Ontario. The body was found lying on a sheet which may have come from the hotel where Ms. King and the respondent had spent the night. Certain fibres found on the sheet matched fibres from the clothing of the respondent and Ms. King. The body's arms had been cut off, and were never found.

The theory of the Crown was that the respondent was a drug smuggler who had travelled to Canada with Ms. King in order to obtain cocaine. The Crown hypothesized that the respondent had asked Ms. King to take the cocaine back to the United States concealed in her body, but that she had refused. According to the Crown, he then abandoned her at the hotel in London. However, he later returned to pick her up, and drove her to a place where he strangled her, cut off her arms to impede identification, and dumped her body.

In support of this theory, the Crown relied upon evidence of four telephone calls made by the deceased to her mother in Detroit at 10:21 p.m., 11:21 p.m., 11:54 p.m. and 12:41 a.m. on the night between August 10 and August 11, 1986. The first two telephone calls were traced to the telephone in Ms. King's room at the hotel in London. Ms. King's mother testified that in the first telephone call, her daughter said that Larry (the respondent) had abandoned her at the hotel in London and that she wanted a ride home. In the second call, Ms. King told her mother that Larry had still not returned. Her mother testified that she then telephoned from Detroit to a taxi company in London to attempt to arrange a ride home for her daughter. A taxi did arrive at the hotel, but refused to take Ms. King because the credit card that she had been using had been confiscated at the hotel.

The third call was traced to a pay telephone in the hotel lobby. Ms. King's mother testified that in this call her daughter told her that Larry had come back for her, and that she would not need a ride home after all. The fourth telephone call was traced to a pay telephone at the service station near which Ms. King's body was found. Ms. King's mother testified that in this call her daughter told her that she was "on her way".

In addition to these calls, there was evidence that a further telephone call had been made shortly after 1:00 a.m. on August 11 from a pay telephone at the service station near which Ms. King's body was later found. This call was traced to the respondent's residence in Detroit. There was no direct evidence as to who made this telephone call, or what was said. However, a witness at the service station testified that he had seen the respondent near the pay telephones at the service station around this time.

The Crown also led evidence from one Hope Denard, a woman who had travelled with the respondent from Detroit to Canada in the month prior to the murder. Ms. Denard testified that the respondent had asked her to smuggle illegal drugs back to the United States for him, and that when she refused, he drove her to Windsor and abandoned her at a restaurant.

The respondent did not testify at his trial, but set up a defence of alibi supported by the evidence of various witnesses who placed him in Windsor or Detroit at or around the time of the murder. Defence counsel did not object to the testimony by Ms. King's mother as to what her daughter told her in the first two telephone calls. Indeed, it was apparently the theory of the defence that the respondent actually did abandon Ms. King at the hotel in London, a hypothesis supported by the evidence of what Ms. King said in the first two telephone calls to her mother. However, the defence contended that after leaving Ms. King, the respondent returned to Detroit and did not return to the hotel, and therefore could not have been with her when she was murdered.

The respondent appealed his conviction to the Ontario Court of Appeal, which allowed the appeal and ordered a new trial. The Court of Appeal found that evidence as to what was said in the telephone calls made by Ms. King to her mother on the night of the murder was hearsay, and therefore was inadmissible unless it fell within some recognized exception to the hearsay rule. The Court of Appeal went on to decide that the evidence as to what was said by Ms. King in the first two telephone conversations was admissible under an exception to the hearsay rule, but only for the purpose of establishing her state of mind at the time when she made the calls, i.e., that she wanted to come home. The evidence as to what was said in the third telephone conversation, however, fell within no exception to the hearsay rule, and was therefore not admissible for any purpose.

The Court of Appeal concluded that the inadmissible hearsay evidence had been so gravely prejudicial to the respondent that it could not say that, had it not been admitted, the verdict would necessarily have been the same. Therefore, notwithstanding the failure of defence counsel to object to the evidence at trial, the Court of Appeal declined to apply the curative provision in s. 686(1)(b)(iii) of the *Criminal Code*, R.S.C. 1985, c. C-46, quashed the respondent's conviction, and ordered a new trial.

. . . .

[The Supreme Court decided that, while the exception to the hearsay rule invoked by the Crown would operate to allow the first two statements into evidence for the purpose of proving that the deceased wanted to return home, the third statement ("Larry has come back") would not have been admissible under that exception for any purpose at all. The court went on, however.]

. . . .

This, however, is not fatal to the appellant's case. This Court has not taken the position that the hearsay rule precludes the reception of hearsay evidence unless it falls within established categories of exceptions, such as "present intentions" or "state of mind." Indeed, in our recent decision in *R. v. Khan*, [1990] 2 S.C.R. 531, we indicated that the categorical approach to exceptions to the hearsay rule has the potential to undermine, rather than further, the policy of avoiding the frailties of certain types of evidence which the hearsay rule was originally fashioned to avoid.

. . . .

The criterion of "reliability"—or, in Wigmore's terminology, the circumstantial guarantee of trustworthiness—is a function of the circumstances under which the statement in question was made. If a statement sought to be adduced by way of hearsay evidence is made under circumstances which substantially negate the possibility that the declarant was untruthful or mistaken, the hearsay evidence may be said to be "reliable", i.e., a circumstantial guarantee of trustworthiness is established. The evidence of the infant complainant in *Khan* was found to be reliable on this basis.

The companion criterion of "necessity" refers to the necessity of the hearsay evidence to prove a fact in issue. Thus, in *Khan*, the infant complainant was found by the trial judge not to be competent to testify herself. In this sense, hearsay evidence of her statements was necessary, in that what she said to her mother could not be adduced through her. It was her inability to testify that governed the situation.

The criterion of necessity, however, does not have the sense of "necessary to the prosecution's case". If this were the case, uncorroborated hearsay evidence which satisfied the criterion of reliability would be admissible if uncorroborated, but might no longer be "necessary" to the prosecution's case if corroborated by other independent evidence. Such an interpretation of the criterion of "necessity" would thus produce the illogical result that uncorroborated hearsay evidence would be admissible, but could become inadmissible if corroborated. This is not what was intended by this Court's decision in *Khan*.

As indicated above, the criterion of necessity must be given a flexible definition, capable of encompassing diverse situations. What these situations will have in common is that the relevant direct evidence is not, for a variety of reasons, available. Necessity of this nature may arise in a number of situations. Wigmore, while not attempting an exhaustive enumeration, suggested at §1421 the following categories:

> (1) The person whose assertion is offered may now be dead, or out of the jurisdiction, or insane, or otherwise unavailable for the purpose of testing [by cross-examination]. This is the commoner and more palpable reason. . . .

> (2) The assertion may be such that we cannot expect, again or at this time, to get evidence of the same value from the same or other sources . . . . The necessity is not so great; perhaps hardly a necessity, only an expediency or convenience, can be predicated. But the principle is the same.

Clearly the categories of necessity are not closed. In *Khan*, for instance, this Court recognized the necessity of receiving hearsay evidence of a child's statements when the child was not herself a competent witness. We also suggested that such hearsay evidence might become necessary when the emotional trauma that would result to the child if forced to give *viva voce* testimony would be great. Whether a necessity of this kind arises, however, is a question of law for determination by the trial judge.

It is now necessary to apply these principles to the evidence in question in this case. In my opinion, the hearsay evidence of what Ms. King said to her mother in the first two telephone conversations on the night of her murder satisfied the criteria of necessity and reliability set out by this Court in *Khan*. In my view, this evidence falls within the same principles. Ms. King is dead, and will never be able to testify as to what happened on the night of August 10 to August 11, 1986. The relevant direct evidence is therefore unavailable. Ms. King's mother's evidence as to what her daughter told her on the telephone that night was clearly necessary, in the sense that there was no possibility that evidence of what was said could be adduced through the declarant.

Moreover, in respect of the first two telephone conversations, there is no reason to doubt Ms. King's veracity. She had no known reason to lie. In my view, the hearsay evidence relating to the first two telephone conversations between Ms. King and her mother could reasonably be relied upon by the jury, as the traditional dangers associated with hearsay evidence—perception, memory and credibility—were not present to any significant degree.

In my view, it would be neither sensible nor just to deprive the jury of this highly relevant evidence on the basis of an arcane rule against hearsay, founded on a lack of faith in the capacity of the trier of fact properly to evaluate evidence of a statement, made under circumstances which do not give rise to apprehensions about its reliability, simply because the declarant is unavailable for cross-examination. Where the criteria of necessity and reliability are satisfied, the lack of testing by cross-examination goes to weight, not admissibility, and a properly cautioned jury should be able to evaluate the evidence on that basis.

However, I arrive at a different conclusion in respect of the contents of the third telephone conversation (''Larry has come back and I no longer need a ride''). While, as in the case of the first two telephone conversations, the unavailability of the declarant to testify satisfies the criterion of necessity, the conditions under which the statement was made do not, in my view, provide that circumstantial guarantee of trustworthiness that would justify its admission without the possibility of cross-examination. On the evidence, I cannot say that I am without apprehensions that Ms. King may have been mistaken, or, indeed, might have intended to deceive her mother on this account.

The evidence at trial disclosed that after making the second telephone call to her mother, Ms. King was observed to leave the hotel and get into a taxi that her mother had arranged to pick her up. She attempted to negotiate a fare to Detroit, but the taxi would not take her because, at this stage, she no longer had a credit card. She was then observed to leave the taxi and proceed immediately to the telephone booth from which she made the third telephone call. It is not, therefore, unreasonable, to ask whether she actually had time to observe the respondent's return. It is at least possible that she was mistaken, and had simply observed a car which resembled the respondent's car. In any case, it does seem somewhat curious that she would make the statement, ''Larry has come back and I no longer need a ride'' before having spoken to the respondent to ascertain whether he proposed to allow her to continue to travel with him.

In my view, it is highly significant that it was suggested in the course of the previous telephone conversations that one Philip come to pick up Ms. King and drive her back to Detroit. She was vehemently opposed to this suggestion, and there was some evidence that Philip had assaulted her on a previous occasion. When faced with the choice between a ride home with a person for whom she apparently had a great dislike, and of whom she was quite possibly frightened, on the one hand, and with telling her mother that Larry would take her home, on the other, Ms. King might well have preferred the latter alternative.

Moreover, with all due respect, it must be recalled that Ms. King was travelling under an assumed name and using a credit card which she knew was either stolen or forged. She was, therefore, at least capable of deceit. It may have been that she decided to lie to her mother to conceal some aspect of her activities or circumstances, or, indeed, simply to allay her mother's fears.

I wish to emphasize that I do not advance these alternative hypotheses as accurate reconstructions of what occurred on the night of Ms. King's murder. I engage in such speculation only for the purpose of showing that the circumstances under which Ms. King made the third telephone call to her mother were not such as to provide that circumstantial guarantee of trustworthiness that would justify the admission of its contents by way of hearsay evidence, without the possibility of cross-examination. Indeed, at the highest, it can only be said that hearsay evidence of the third telephone call is equally consistent with the accuracy of Ms. King's statements, and also with a number of other hypotheses. I cannot say that this evidence could not reasonably have been expected to have changed significantly had Ms. King been available to give evidence in person and subjected to cross-examination. I conclude, therefore, that the hearsay evidence of the contents of the third telephone conversation did not satisfy the criterion of reliability set out in *Khan*, and therefore was not admissible on that basis.

To conclude, as this Court has made clear in its decisions in *Ares v. Venner, supra*, and *R. v. Khan, supra*, the approach that excludes hearsay evidence, even when highly probative, out of the fear that the trier of fact will not understand how to deal with such evidence, is no longer appropriate. In my opinion, hearsay evidence of statements made by persons who are not available to give evidence at trial ought generally to be admissible, where the circumstances under which the statements were made satisfy the criteria of necessity and reliability set out in *Khan*, and subject to the residual discretion of the trial judge to exclude the evidence when its probative value is slight and undue prejudice might result to the accused. Properly cautioned by the trial judge, juries are perfectly capable of determining what weight ought to be attached to such evidence, and of drawing reasonable inferences therefrom.

In the result, therefore, I conclude that the hearsay evidence of what Ms. King told her mother in the first two telephone calls satisfied the criteria of necessity and reliability set out in *Khan*, and was properly admissible on that basis. While the contents of the third telephone call satisfied the criterion of necessity as well, the events surrounding the making of that call were not sufficient to provide that circumstantial guarantee of trustworthiness which would justify their admission without the test of cross-examination. The Crown did not appeal in respect of the fourth telephone conversation, and therefore I make no comment as to the admissibility of hearsay evidence of its contents, other than to say that, in the event of a new trial, it will be governed by the same principles.

[On Smith's new trial the accused was acquitted. During the jury's deliberations they came back with a question: We heard that there were three phone calls that night. Why could we hear the contents of the first two calls but not the contents of the third?]

R. v. KHARSEKIN
(1994), 30 C.R. (4th) 252, 88 C.C.C. (3d) 193 (Nfld. C.A.)

[The accused, a seaman aboard a Russian trawler, was charged with second degree murder. The victim was the chief engineer of the ship. He suffered a stab wound in the right side of his neck. Shortly afterwards he attended the medical centre on the ship. The doctor inquired who had wounded him. The deceased said "I was wounded by the knife from the second electrical mechanic". Just after this statement, he became unconscious. About 15 to 20 minutes later he was revived. Approximately 30 to 35 minutes after he had regained consciousness, the maintenance mechanic, arrived at the medical centre and inquired who had stabbed him. The doctor said it was the second electrical mechanic. The maintenance mechanic asked "was it Kharsekin" and the doctor asked the victim "Kharsekin, is that Kharsekin?" The victim nodded in agreement. The medical evidence was that the victim was fully conscious and understood the questions being asked. The trial judge held that the replies of the deceased were hearsay and were not admissible under any of the exceptions to the hearsay rule. The accused was acquitted and the Crown appealed.]

CAMERON J.A. (O'NEILL and MARSHALL JJ.A. concurring):—

. . . .

The trial judge held in this case that the decision of the Supreme Court of Canada in *Khan* should be confined to the circumstances illustrated by that case. In fairness to the trial judge, he did not, at that time, have the benefit of the decision of the Supreme Court of Canada in *R. v. Smith* . . . , which made it clear that the principle stated in *Khan* was not confined to cases of sexual assault on children. . . .

The respondent concedes that the victim's statements are relevant and meet the criterion of necessity. The person making the statement is dead and unable to give evidence. There is no evidence to suggest that anyone other that the deceased and his assailant were present at the time of the stabbing and there is no evidence of the same value from other sources. In respect of the test of necessity, the facts in this case are similar to those in *Smith* where the test was held to have been met.

The trial judge concluded and the respondent argues that the indicia of reliability should be the same as those for dying declarations. With respect, I cannot agree. The purpose of the development of the *Khan* approach was to adopt a new principled approach as opposed to the narrow rule bound approach of the past. *Khan* and *Smith* make it clear that there is no inviolable list of considerations for reliability. The factors relevant to reliability will vary from case to case. The fact that some courts have continued to analyze cases under the traditional exceptions to the hearsay rule before turning to a *Khan* approach does not limit the application of *Khan* . . . , nor would I conclude that the admissibility of the evidence here would require the criteria of ''hopeless expectation of death'' and ''spontaneity''.

In this case the deceased had a peculiar means of knowledge. Indeed, only he and the person who wounded him had that knowledge. Pedyura's wound and rapid loss of blood when he arrived at the medical centre indicate that the initial statement was made shortly after the wounding and the confirming statements within an hour of the first. There was little time to plan falsification and the medical evidence supports the position that the deceased knew what he was saying. The first statement was in response to a question but it was not a leading question.

There is physical evidence to indicate that there were blood stains on the respondent's pants consistent with that taken from the body of the deceased.

There is nothing in the circumstances to suggest a reason for the deceased to be untruthful. The tests enunciated in *Khan* and *Smith* were met. There was, in the words of Wigmore, circumstantial probability of trustworthiness and the statements were admissible.

Therefore in failing to admit the deceased's statements the trial judge made an error in law.

R. v. CASSIDY
(1993), 26 C.R. (4th) 252 (Ont. Gen. Div.)

[The accused was charged with first degree murder. He admitted killing the victim and the issue was intent. The Crown sought to call hearsay evidence related to two areas. First, statements said to have been made by the victim close to the time of her death to the effect that the accused used the victim's credit card without her consent, and that the victim demanded her money back and threatened to go to the police. Second, statements made by the victim as to threats made by the accused to her. In each case, the statements were tendered for the purpose of establishing the truth of what was said in the statement.]

GRAVELY J.:—

. . . .

The issues are necessity and reliability. In my opinion, the proffered evidence is relevant to the issue of intent which is central to the trial. The victim is dead and the test of necessity is met. As to reliability of the credit card utterances, Crown counsel suggested that the circumstances insure a high degree of reliability. Four different witnesses say the deceased said the same thing on the same day. All four witnesses gave the statement to the police on the same day separately and soon after the victim's death. All witnesses say the utterances of the victim were made within a couple of days of her death. The Crown also points out that the statements are partially corroborated by the admission of the accused that he did use the victim's credit card. Counsel suggests that even though the victim is not available for cross-examination it would be open to the accused to give evidence contradicting the statements and, in any event, a proper warning to the jury would guard against any potential unfairness.

. . . .

It is somewhat difficult to know how to apply the principles of *Smith* but some guidance is given in the treatment by Chief Justice Lamer of the third telephone call, and he said:

> On the evidence, I cannot say that I am without apprehension that Ms. King may have been mistaken or indeed might have intended to deceive her mother on this account. . . . I wish to emphasize that I do not advance these alternative hypotheses as accurate reconstructions of what occurred on the night of Ms. King's murder. I engage in such speculation only for the purpose of showing that the circumstances under which Ms. King made the third telephone call to her mother were not such as to provide that circumstantial guarantee of trustworthiness that would justify the admission of its contents by way of hearsay evidence without the possibility of cross-examination.

I understand that to mean that before letting in hearsay evidence a trial judge is required to conduct a search for hypotheses that could explain the evidence in a fashion inconsistent with reliability. The search must extend to the point of speculation. Only if that search fails can it be said that the evidence meets the test of substantial equivalence to the reliability afforded by cross-examination. . . .

The facts of this case are that the accused had been in a tumultuous emotional relationship with the deceased for some time. It is not unlikely that under the circumstances, the victim's objective judgment could be clouded or her statements made to friends or her family about the accused be exaggerated, immoderate or otherwise unreliable. These then, are not, in my opinion, the kinds of rather straightforward uncomplicated statements given in a situation where reliability is guaranteed as contemplated in *Smith* and in *Kahn* or indeed in their predecessor, *Ares v. Venner*. Without cross-examination here, defence counsel would be virtually powerless to deal effectively with those statements. On the other hand, if the victim had been alive and available for cross-examination, it is not difficult to imagine that defence counsel could have been successful in obtaining admissions which might have changed some of the facts alleged in the statements.

The criterion of reliability then has not been met and I find that all the hearsay statements tendered are not admissible.

R. v. B. (K.G.)
[1993] 1 S.C.R. 740, 19 C.R. (4th) 1, 79 C.C.C. (3d) 257

[The accused and three other young men were involved in a fight with two others. In the course of the fight, one of the four young men pulled a knife and stabbed one of the men in the chest and killed him. The four young men then fled the scene. About two weeks later, the accused's friends were interviewed separately by the police. With the youths' consent the interviews were videotaped. In their statements, they told the police that the accused had made statements to them in which he acknowledged that he had caused the death of the victim. The accused was charged with second degree murder. At trial, the three youths recanted their earlier statements. They said they had lied to the police to exculpate themselves from any possible involvement. The trial judge held that the witnesses' prior inconsistent statements could not be tendered as proof that the accused actually made the admissions. They were, per the orthodox rule, hearsay. They could only be used to impeach the witnesses' credibility by proving that on an earlier occasion the witnesses had in fact made statements inconsistent with their present testimony. In the absence of other sufficient identification evidence, the trial judge acquitted. The Court of Appeal upheld the acquittal.]

LAMER C.J. (SOPINKA, GONTHEIR, McLACKLIN and IACOBUCCI JJ. concurring): —

. . . .

The orthodox rule has been almost universally criticized by academic commentators. Their criticisms can be distilled into the assertion that the hearsay dangers on which the orthodox rule is based are ill-founded or non-existent in the case of prior inconsistent statements. Respecting the oath, commentators discount the significance of the oath in modern society. Stuesser, is representative in arguing that "[t]he unfortunate reality in our modern society is that the power of an oath must be discounted as a means of ensuring reliability for a statement." . . . However, I note that while the witness faces the legal consequences of violating an oath or solemn affirmation at trial, in most cases there is less incentive to be truthful when the statement is made, leading to a natural preference for the testimony at trial if the alternative is unsworn or unaffirmed testimony.

Critics also claim that the lack of opportunity for the trier of fact to observe the demeanour of the witness at the time the statement was made, and thus to assess credibility based on that demeanour, is overstated in its significance. They argue that the opportunity to observe the witness as he or she denies or professes not to remember making the statement can give the trier insight into the truthfulness of the recantation, and therefore also the truthfulness of the prior statement which is denied. This does not obviate the problem of ensuring that the witness's prior statement is fully and accurately reproduced for the trier of fact. Of course, both of these criticisms of the orthodox rule are reinforced when, as in this case, the prior statement is videotaped, allowing the trier of fact to observe the witnesses' demeanour and ensuring that an accurate record of the statement is tendered as evidence.

. . . .

The lack of cross-examination is the most important of the hearsay dangers, but perhaps also the most overstated in the context of prior inconsistent statements. By definition, commentators argue, the maker of the statement is present in court and amenable to vigorous cross-examination respecting his or her recollection, testimonial capacity and bias at the time of the making of the prior statement. As it is argued in McCormick on Evidence, supra, at p. 120:

> The witness who has told one story aforetime and another today has opened the gates to all the vistas of truth which the common law practice of cross-examination and re-examination was invented to explore. The reasons for the change of face, whether forgetfulness, carelessness, pity, terror, or greed, may be explored by the two questioners in the presence of the trier of fact, under oath, casting light on which is the true story and which the false.

. . . .

Furthermore, commentators observe, the witness's recantation has accomplished all that the opponent's cross-examination could hope to: the witness now testifies under oath that the prior statement was a lie, or claims to have no recollection of the matters in the statement, thus undermining its credibility as much as cross-examination could have.

. . . .

Finally, it is clear that the orthodox rule, in so far as it is based on the hearsay rule, has been undermined by the decisions of this Court in *Khan* and *Smith*. In *Smith*, I stated that the decision in *Khan* "should be understood as the triumph of a principled analysis over a set of ossified judicially created categories", and that that decision:

. . . signalled an end to the old categorical approach to the admission of hearsay evidence. Hearsay evidence is now admissible on a principled basis, the governing principles being the reliability of the evidence, and its necessity.

I will return to *Smith* and the principled approach to the hearsay rule as it applies in the particular case of prior inconsistent statements, but it is important to note that any erosion of the categorical approach to the hearsay rule must influence the Court's consideration of the orthodox rule as one instance of that rule.

[The court then examined the role of stare decisis and decided: "The existing rule has been attenuated by developments in the law of hearsay and is somewhat, if not overly, technical, and reforming the rule would not directly expand the scope of criminal liability."]

. . . .

I am of the view that evidence of prior inconsistent statements of a witness other than an accused should be substantively admissible on a principled basis, following this Court's decisions in *Khan* and *Smith*. However, it is clear that the factors identified in those cases — reliability and necessity — must be adapted and refined in this particular context, given the particular problems raised by the nature of such statements. Furthermore, there must be a voir dire before such statements are put before the jury as substantive evidence, in which the trial judge satisfies him or herself that the statement was made in circumstances which do not negate its reliability.

. . . .

(1) Reliability

(i) The oath

It is undeniable that the significance of the oath has drastically changed since its introduction. Originally the oath was grounded upon a belief that divine retribution would visit those who lied under oath. Accordingly, witnesses were required to believe in this retribution if they were to be properly sworn and their evidence admissible. . . .

We no longer require this belief in divine retribution; in *Reference re Truscott*, [1967] S.C.R. 309, at p. 368, this Court stated in the context of child witnesses that the witness need only understand "the moral obligation of telling the truth". In this sense the oath can be said to have a changed significance, and if critics of the oath suggest only that its original supernatural force has disappeared, I agree with that observation.

. . . .

However, there remain compelling reasons to prefer statements made under oath, solemn affirmation or solemn declaration. While the oath will not motivate all witnesses to tell the truth . . . its administration may serve to impress on more honest witnesses the seriousness and significance of their statements, especially where they incriminate another person in a criminal investigation.

In addition to this positive effect on the declarant, the presence of an oath, solemn affirmation or solemn declaration will increase the evidentiary value of the statement when it is admitted at trial. First, it will mean that the trier of fact will not be asked to accept unsworn testimony over sworn testimony; instead, the trier will have the opportunity to choose between two sworn statements, and the trier's ultimate decision will not be made on the basis of unsworn or unaffirmed testimony. Similarly, should the prior statement be decisive, there is no danger of the accused being convicted solely on the basis of unsworn testimony.

Second, the presence of the oath during the making of the prior statement eliminates the explanation offered by many recanting witnesses, including one of the witnesses in this case: when confronted with the prior inconsistent statement, witnesses explain that it was not made under oath, and assert that the oath they took at trial persuaded them to tell the truth. This naturally privileges the trial testimony in the mind of the trier of fact. If both statements were made under oath, such an explanation can no longer be employed. Furthermore, since both statements cannot be true, the trier of fact has an indication of the low regard in which the witness holds the oath. Therefore, while it is true that the oath in itself has no power to ensure truthfulness in some witnesses, the fact that both statements were made under oath removes resort to the absence of an oath as an indicium of the alleged unreliability of the prior inconsistent statement.

The presence of an oath, solemn affirmation or solemn declaration will have yet another positive effect on the declarant's truthfulness and the administration of justice. A sworn prior statement will be highly persuasive evidence in any prosecution against the declarant related to false testimony (whether in the statement or at trial), and the knowledge that this evidence exists for this purpose should weigh heavily on the mind of one who considers lying in a statement, or recanting his or her prior statement to lie at trial.

Of course, the incentives provided by the declarant's exposure to prosecution under ss. 137, 139 and 140 in relation to the first statement, and his or her fear of a perjury prosecution in relation to testimony given at trial, will only be effective if these sanctions are made known to the declarant. For this reason, the witness should be warned by the person taking the statement that the statement may be used as evidence at a subsequent trial if the witness recants (thereby engaging s. 137), and also that severe criminal sanctions will accompany the making of a false statement. This warning should refer specifically to ss. 137, 139 and 140 of the Criminal Code, and repeat the elements of and sanctions for those offences. As does the formal swearing of the witness in the trial process, this warning and the administration of the oath should serve to bring home to the witness the gravity of the situation and his duty to tell the truth.

. . . .

However, I do not wish to create technical categorical requirements duplicating those of the old approach to hearsay evidence. It follows from *Smith* that there may be situations in which the trial judge concludes that an appropriate substitute for the oath is established and that notwithstanding the absence of an oath the statement is reliable. Other circumstances may serve to impress upon the witness the importance of telling the truth, and in so doing provide a high degree of reliability to the statement. While these occasions may not be frequent, I do not foreclose the possibility that they might arise under the principled approach to hearsay evidence.

(ii) Presence

Proponents of the orthodox rule emphasize the many verbal and non-verbal cues which triers of fact rely upon in order to assess credibility. When the witness is on the stand, the trier can observe the witness's reaction to questions, hesitation, degree of commitment to the statement being made, etc. Most importantly, and subsuming all of these factors, the trier can assess the relationship between the interviewer and the witness to observe the extent to which the testimony of the witness is the product of the investigator's questioning. Such subtle observations and cues cannot be gleaned from a transcript, read in court in counsel's monotone, where the atmosphere of the exchange is entirely lost.

All of these indicia of credibility, and therefore reliability, are available to the trier of fact when the witness's prior statement is videotaped. During the course of the hearing, counsel for the appellant screened a brief excerpt from the videotape of one of the interviews. In the main portion of the television screen is a medium-length shot of the witness facing the camera and seated across a table from the interviewing officer, showing the physical relationship between the two people. In one upper corner is a close-up of the witness's face as he or she speaks, capturing nuances of expression lost in the main view. Along the bottom of the screen is a line showing the date and a time counter, with the seconds ticking off, ensuring that the continuity and integrity of the record is maintained.

The audio-visual medium captures other elements of the statement lost in a transcript, such as actions or distinctive motions which the witness demonstrates (as in this case), or answers given by nodding or shaking the head. In other words, the experience of being in the room with the witness and the interviewing officer is recreated as fully as possible for the viewer. Not only does the trier of fact have access to the full range of non-verbal indicia of credibility, but there is also a reproduction of the statement which is fully accurate, eliminating the danger of inaccurate recounting which motivates the rule against hearsay evidence. In a very real sense, the evidence ceases to be hearsay in this important respect, since the hearsay declarant is brought before the trier of fact.

Of course, the police would not resort to this precaution in every case; it may well be reserved for cases such as this, where a major crime such as murder is being investigated, the testimony of the witnesses is important to the Crown's case, and the character of the witnesses suggests that such precautions would be advisable. It is quite possible that such equipment would be available to police of given forces at a central location, and that such crucial though unstable witnesses will be taken to such locations to make their statements, or, where the statements have already been made, to repeat them in a form which may be substantively admissible should the witness recant.

In addition to an oath or solemn affirmation and warning, then, a complete videotape record of the type described above, or one which duplicates the experience of observing a witness in the courtroom to the same extent, is another important indicium of reliability which will satisfy the principled basis for the admission of hearsay evidence.

Again, it may be possible that the testimony of an independent third party who observes the making of the statement in its entirety could, in exceptional circumstances, also provide the requisite reliability with respect to demeanour evidence. I would only note at this point that there are many persons who could serve this function: police stations will have justices of the peace present or available, the witness may have his or her own lawyer present, and ss. 56(2)(c) and 56(2)(d) of the Young Offenders Act, R.S.C., 1985, c. Y-1, provide that a young person making a statement has a right of access to counsel, parents, or adult relatives. It will be a matter for the trial judge to determine whether or not a sufficient substitute for a videotape record has been provided to allow the trier of fact access to sufficient demeanour evidence to make the statement admissible.

(iii) Cross-examination

The final hearsay danger is the lack of contemporaneous cross-examination when the statement is made. The appellant is correct to concede that this is the most important of the hearsay dangers. However, in the case of prior inconsistent statements, it is also the most easily remedied by the opportunity to cross-examine at trial. This is a feature of prior inconsistent statements that conclusively distinguishes them from other forms of hearsay.
. . .

Furthermore, unlike the oath and presence, it is the hearsay danger which is impossible to address outside of judicial or quasi-judicial processes. Whereas the police can easily administer a warning and oath, and videotape a statement in the course of a witness interview, it would restrict the operation of a reformed rule to judicial or quasi-judicial proceedings to require contemporaneous cross-examination, and thereby severely restrict the impact of a reformed rule. Consider the facts of the present case: when the three witnesses were interviewed by the police, no one had yet been charged with an offence. Who could have cross-examined the witnesses at that point? How could cross-examination have been effective before the case to be met was known? These and other practical difficulties in requiring contemporaneous cross-examination tip the balance in favour of allowing cross-examination at trial to serve as a substitute. Again, we must remember that the question is not whether it would have been preferable to have had the benefit of contemporaneous cross-examination, but whether the absence of such cross-examination is a sufficient reason to keep the statement from the jury as substantive evidence. Given the other guarantees of trustworthiness, I do not think that it should be allowed to be a barrier to substantive admissibility. Of course, it will be an important consideration for the trier of fact in deciding what weight to attach to the prior inconsistent statement, and it is likely that opposing counsel will stress the absence of such cross-examination to the trier of fact.

Therefore, the requirement of reliability will be satisfied when the circumstances in which the prior statement was made provide sufficient guarantees of its trustworthiness with respect to the two hearsay dangers a reformed rule can realistically address: if (i) the statement is made under oath or solemn affirmation following a warning as to the existence of sanctions and the significance of the oath or affirmation, (ii) the statement is videotaped in its entirety, and (iii) the opposing party, whether the Crown or the defence, has a full opportunity to cross-examine the witness respecting the statement, there will be sufficient circumstantial guarantees of reliability to allow the jury to make substantive use of the statement. Alternatively, other circumstantial guarantees of reliability may suffice to render such statements substantively admissible, provided that the judge is satisfied that the circumstances provide adequate assurances of reliability in place of those which the hearsay rule traditionally requires. — *normally, must be satisfied it's voluntary*

(2) Necessity

Prior inconsistent statements present vexing problems for the necessity criterion. The necessity criterion has usually been satisfied by the unavailable witness: in *Khan*, the child declarant who could not be sworn, and in *Smith*, the dead declarant. By definition, the declarant in the case of prior inconsistent statements is available at trial; it is his or her prior statement that is unavailable because of the recantation.

However, it is important to remember that the necessity criterion "must be given a flexible definition, capable of encompassing diverse situations" [see *Smith*]. Wigmore, vol. 5 (Chadbourn rev. 1974), § 1421, at p. 253, referred to two classes of necessity:

(1) The person whose assertion is offered may now be *dead*, or out of the jurisdiction, or insane, or *otherwise unavailable* for the purpose of testing. This is the commoner and more palpable reason.

. . . .

(2) The assertion may be such that we cannot expect, again, or at this time, to get *evidence of the same value* from the same or other sources. . . . The necessity is not so great; perhaps hardly a necessity, only an expediency or convenience, can be predicated. But the principle is the same. [Emphasis in original.]

. . . .

The precise limits of the necessity criterion remain to be established in the context of specific cases. It may be that in some circumstances, the availability of the witness will mean that hearsay evidence of that witness's prior *consistent* (the kind of statement at issue in *Khan*) statements will not be admissible. However, I am not prepared, at this point, to adhere to a strict interpretation that makes unavailability an indispensable condition of necessity.

In the case of prior *inconsistent* statements, it is patent that we cannot expect to get evidence of the same value from the recanting witness or other sources: as counsel for the appellant claimed, the recanting witness holds the prior statement, and thus the relevant evidence, "hostage". The different "value" of the evidence is found in the fact that something has radically changed between the time when the statement was made and the trial and, assuming that there is a sufficient degree of reliability established under the first criterion, the trier of fact should be allowed to weigh both statements in light of the witness's explanation of the change.

[The court then described the process that should be followed on the voir dire determining necessity and reliability.]

For an excellent comment see Rosenberg, "*B. (K.G.)* — Necessity and Reliability: the New Pigeonholes" (1993), 19 C.R. (4th) 69.

R. v. U. (F.J.)
[1995] 3 S.C.R. 764, 42 C.R. (4th) 133, 101 C.C.C. (3d) 97

[The accused was arrested for engaging in sexual activities with his 13-year-old daughter. In the interview with the investigating officer, the daughter said that her father had been having sexual intercourse with her on a regular basis. She said that the last time her father had had sex with her was the previous night. The officer then questioned the accused. He admitted that he had had sex with his daughter many times, described the same sexual activities she had described, and stated that the most recent intercourse had been the previous night.

The accused was charged with a number of sexual offences. His statement to the police was admitted as Crown evidence through the testimony of two officers. The daughter said that although she admitted that she had made the allegations against the accused in her statement, the allegations of sexual assault were untrue. The accused testified that while he had made an inculpatory statement to the police, he denied its truth.

The trial judge invited the jury to compare the daughter's unadopted prior inconsistent statement with the accused's unadopted statement to the police in determining if the prosecution had established guilt. The Court of Appeal upheld the conviction on the theory that there was worth solely on the basis that the daughter had made the statement; the statement was not hearsay and therefore was admissible.

The Supreme Court took a different approach: the statement was hearsay but admissible under *B. (K.G.)*].

LAMER, C.J. (SOPINKA, GONTHIER, CORY, IACOBUCCI and MAJOR, JJ. concurring): —

. . . .

The Voir Dire

I set out the proper procedure for the voir dire in my reasons in *B. (K.G.)*. . . . After the calling party invokes s. 9 of the Canada Evidence Act, and fulfils its requirements in the voir dire held under that section, the party must then state its objectives in tendering the statement. If the statement will only be used to impeach the witness, the inquiry ends at this point. If, however, the calling party wishes to make substantive use of the statement, the voir dire must continue so that the trial judge can assess whether a threshold of reliability has been met. The necessity criterion need not be assessed as it is met whenever a witness recants. The first factor contributing to reliability is the cross-examination of the witness. If the witness provides an explanation for changing his or her story, the trier of fact will be able to assess both versions of the story, as well as the explanation. However, where a witness does not recall making an earlier statement, or refuses to answer questions, the trial judge should take into account that this may impede the jury's ability to assess the ultimate reliability of the statement.

If the additional indicia of reliability I specified in *B. (K.G.)* are present, an oath or affirmation following a warning of penal consequences for lying, and a videotape of the statement, the reliability assessment can be relatively easily made. If the reliability criterion is to be met, in rare cases, by the striking similarity between the statement being assessed and another statement which is already clearly substantively admissible, the trial judge must be satisfied on a balance of probabilities that there are striking similarities between the two statements, and that there was neither reason nor opportunity for the declarants to collude and no improper influence by interrogators or other third parties.

At this stage, the trial judge need only be convinced on a balance of probabilities that the statement is likely to be reliable, as this is the normal burden of proof resting upon a party seeking to admit evidence. The trial judge must also ascertain at this stage that the prior statement relates evidence which would be admissible as the witness's sole testimony.

I would also highlight here the proviso I specified in *B. (K.G.)* that the trial judge must be satisfied on the balance of probabilities that the statement was not the product of coercion of any form, whether involving threats, promises, excessively leading questions by the investigator or other person in a position of authority, or other forms of investigatory misconduct.

The trial judge at this stage is not making a final determination about the ultimate reliability and credibility of the statement. The trial judge need not be satisfied that the prior statement is true and should be believed in preference to the witness's current testimony.

If the trial judge determines that the statement meets the threshold reliability criterion and is thus substantively admissible, he or she must direct the trier of fact to follow a two-step process in evaluating the evidence. The trier of fact must first be certain that the statement which is being used as a reliability referent *was made*, without taking into account the prior inconsistent statement under consideration. Once the trier of fact is satisfied that the *other* statement was made, the trier of fact may compare the similarities between the two statements and, if they are sufficiently striking that it is unlikely that two people would have independently fabricated them, the trier of fact may draw conclusions from that comparison about the truth of the statements.

Finally, where the trial judge finds that the statement is not sufficiently reliable to be used substantively, it may still, of course, be used to impeach credibility or for the fact that it was made. In other words, the orthodox rule will still apply if the minimum reliability threshold is not met.

Application to This Appeal

In this case, the recanting witness was cross-examined in detail about her reasons for changing her story at a preliminary inquiry, on a voir dire under s. 9 of the Canada Evidence Act, and before the jury. She provided a comprehensive explanation for changing her story which could be assessed by both the trial judge and the jury and therefore eliminates the most important danger of hearsay evidence. The statements made by the accused and by his daughter contained both a significant number of similarities in detail and the strikingly similar assertion that the most recent sexual contact between the two had been the previous evening. As a voir dire was also held with regard to the accused's statement, there was also sufficient evidence presented to found a conclusion that the accused and his daughter had neither a reason nor an opportunity to collude, and that the accused was not improperly influenced by the police officers who took his statement. On the basis of all these factors, I conclude that her statement was, therefore, substantively admissible at trial.

The jury was not, of course, instructed in accordance with the procedures I have set out here. Nonetheless, the statements in question are so strikingly similar that I am satisfied that had the instruction been given, the jury would inevitably have been satisfied as to their reliability on the basis which I have outlined above. In these circumstances, the absence of a specific instruction in this regard did not occasion any wrong or miscarriage of justice.

L'HÉUREUX-DUBÉ, J.: —

. . . I agree with the Chief Justice that, in the case at hand, the complainant's prior inconsistent statement was admissible for the purpose of comparison with the appellant's confession. However, unlike my colleague, I do not believe that the similarities between the two statements must be "striking" before the jury can be permitted to use the prior inconsistent statement for this purpose. In my view, so long as there are significant similarities between the two statements, as there clearly were in this case, a witness's prior inconsistent statement will be admissible for purposes of comparison with an accused's unadopted confession in order to assess the truth of that confession.

For a description of various *B. (K.G.)* rulings see Delisle, "*Diu*: Inconsistency in *B. (K.G.)* Rulings" (2000), 33 C.R. (5th) 259.

In *R. v. Hawkins*,[53] an earlier statement was received for its truth following a principled analysis. The accused's girlfriend had testified against the accused at his preliminary hearing. By the time of the trial she had married the accused and was therefore not a competent witness against him. The judgment of Lamer C.J.C. and Iacobucci J., dealt with the requirement of reliability:

> The function of the trial judge is limited to determining whether the particular hearsay statement exhibits sufficient indicia of reliability so as to afford the trier of fact a satisfactory basis for evaluating the truth of the statement. . . . The ultimate reliability of the statement, and the weight to be attached to it, remain determinations for the trier of fact.[54]

The most recent Supreme Court decision dealing with *B. (K.G.)* is *R. v. L. (C.)*.[55] The accused was acquitted of sexually assaulting his daughter. The alleged victim had given six statements to various people over a period of time alleging sexual abuse by the accused. At trial, aged 10, she testified that the prior statements were only lies. The trial judge rejected the Crown's offer to put in evidence the six statements. He noted there had been no videotape record and that there was an absence of spontaneity on the part of the declarant. The Quebec Court of Appeal set aside the acquittal and ordered a new trial. The unanimous opinion decided:

> The first statement made to Dr. Gravel who was, in the circumstances, an independent witness, the note from the child to her mother, the statement to the police in the presence of the mother who encouraged, strongly and on several occasions, her child to tell the truth and finally, the unanimous opinion of the three experts as to the state of problematic dependency on the part of the child towards her mother, contained, in the case at bar, sufficient indicia of reliability to satisfy the judge, on a balance of probabilities that it was possible that the prior statements were reliable.[56]

The Supreme Court dismissed the accused's appeal for the reasons given in the Court below.[57]

The Supreme Court has thus been consistent in its view that the application of *B. (K.G.)* demands flexibility and that reliability depends on an assessment on all the circumstances in each individual case and not on any particular formulae of words.

R. v. Tat,[58] was a trial for murder and attempted murder. The principal Crown witness, who had earlier identified the accused, at trial denied that he was the person who had shot him and his friends. The trial judge received the earlier

---

53.   (1997), 2 C.R. (5th) 245 (S.C.C.).
54.   *Ibid.*, at p. 273.
55.   (1996), 112 C.C.C. (3d) 472 (Que. C.A.).
56.   *Ibid.*, at p. 480.
57.   *R. v. L. (C.)*, [1997] 3 S.C.R. 1001.
58.   (1997), 14 C.R. (5th) 116 (Ont. C.A.).

identification as evidence and the accused was convicted. The Ontario Court of Appeal decided this was in error. That Court, reviewing the criteria of *B. (K.G.)* decided that the statement was not sufficiently reliable. In the conclusion, Doherty J.A., for the Court, wisely described the proper approach:

> The reliability assessment is a holistic one which must address the hearsay dangers as they actually arise in the particular case and the indicia of reliability as revealed by the evidence. Each case will be different. There is no single feature which secures the admission for substantive purposes of a prior inconsistent statement or demands the exclusion of such a statement.[59]

In *R. v. Eisenhauer*,[60] the Crown argued that the "threshold reliability" requirement was not satisfied because the earlier statement was not given on oath, no warning was given to the witness regarding the consequences of lying, the interview was not recorded in its entirety and there were no other substitute factors to assure reliability. Justice Cromwell, writing for the Nova Scotia Court of Appeal, emphasized that the admissibility of prior statements must not take on a pigeon-holing approach:

> Although Chisholm was not under oath or told about the penalties for knowingly providing false information to the police, the seriousness and importance of what she was saying could not have been clearer to her. . . . Chisholm had been arrested as a suspect in the killing on the day the interview took place. She was given the usual cautions. She was confronted with the fact that her earlier alibi did not check out. She confirmed that what she said was the truth. Although there is not a complete verbatim record of what was said, the record of the interview was said to be a fair representation of it. The record includes not only the contents of the discussion, but also notes about the witness's demeanour. The officers who questioned her were available to testify about the interview as they did in detail on the *voir dire*.[61]

In the result he decided the trial judge had erred in his approach to admissibility as the trial judge appeared to have considered that the absence of videotaping and the oath was dispositive of the issue.

In *R. v. Conway*,[62] the trial judge decided the earlier statement met the criteria set out in *B. (K.G.)*. The statement was not given on oath nor was it recorded audibly or visually. Neither was the witness warned of the legal peril of providing a false statement. The trial judge decided however there were other indicia of reliability sufficient to allow admission. On appeal the Court expressed concern that the trial judge had discounted the absence of an oath and referred to the positive effects of an oath in promoting reliability. The Court also noted the lack of any adequate warning impressing on the witness the importance of telling the truth. The absence of a video record was also noted and the police descriptions of the witness's demeanour were not regarded as an adequate substitute. The Court said that it was only in exceptional circumstances that such testimony would be a substitute and then the person who observed the making of the statement "must be an independent third party." This latter requirement was seen by the

---

59.   *Ibid.*, at p. 148.
60.   (1998), 14 C.R. (5th) 35 (N.S. C.A.).
61.   *Ibid.*, at p. 66.
62.   (1997), 13 C.R. (5th) 139 (Ont. C.A.).

Court as imposed by a dictum in *B. (K.G.).*[63] Perhaps most importantly for the Court was the fact that cross-examination of the witness at trial was futile as the witness at trial didn't give an inconsistent statement but rather simply professed no memory. In that situation the jury's ability to assess the ultimate reliability of the earlier statement would be seriously impeded. While the inability to cross-examine in such a situation does not automatically lead to inadmissibility for substantive purposes, it does emphasize the need for other indicia of reliability.

B. (K.G.) ushered in a new age with respect to the admissibility of previous inconsistent statements for substantive purposes. It adopted a principled approach to the hearsay statement. As the above cases spell out, this approach, resting on principles, requires a discretionary approach dependent on the particular facts of the case before the court and cannot be nicely tied up into a formulaic expression as was done with the existing categorical exceptions.

B. (K.G.) can be seen as particularly useful in domestic assault cases where the victim recants at trial.

R. v. MOHAMED
[1997] O.J. No. 1287 (Ont. Prov. Div.)

[The accused was charged with break, enter and assault. He broke into his estranged wife's apartment and poured boiling liquid on her causing severe burns. The wife made an audiotaped statement to a police officer while she was in hospital but later recanted the allegations and gave a different story as to how she came about her injuries. The wife was declared an adverse witness. The Crown applied to have the taped statement admitted for the truth of its contents.]

MacDonnell Prov. J.:—

. . . .

In the case at bar, the defence conceded that by reason of the complainant's recantation, necessity was not in issue. The question is whether the reliability of the prior statement has been established. . . . . . Following the release of the reasons in *B. (K.G.)*, there was concern that the Supreme Court might have pitched the requirements for admission of prior inconsistent statements at such a high level that, for practical purposes, few statements could qualify. In particular, some feared that the Court had made the administration of an oath and videotaping preconditions to admissibility. On a fair reading of the Chief Justice's reasons, however, those concerns appear to be unfounded. The Chief Justice made it very clear that while the oath and videotaping would provide the optimum guarantee of reliability, they were not absolute requirements.

. . . .

(a) The Absence of an Oath

Prior to the taking of the statement, no oath or solemn affirmation was administered to the complainant and she was not warned of the potential consequences of lying to the

---

63. In *R. v. B. (K.G.)* (1993), 19 C.R. (4th) 1 at p. 38 (S.C.C.), Lamer C.J. discussed the value of a videotape to communicate the demeanour of the witness, and then said: "It may be possible that the testimony of an independent third party who observes the making of the statement in its entirety could, in exceptional circumstances, also provide the requisite reliability with respect to demeanour evidence." One might wonder whether this dictum should make for an absolute requirement.

police. For the reasons discussed above, however, the absence of an oath and a warning is not fatal to the application to admit the statement for its truth. The question to be addressed is whether there is something in the circumstances surrounding the making of the statement to compensate for those deficiencies. . . . In the present case, the complainant was interviewed from her hospital bed in the Burn Unit of the Wellesley Hospital where she was being treated for very serious injuries. As soon as Detective Gerry entered her room, he identified himself as the officer in charge of the investigation and updated her on the status of the case. He told her that he had just come from the accused's bail hearing, and that the accused had been released on bail. He testified that this news caused the complainant concern. When he went on to advise her that the accused would not be released from custody until a review of the bail order was heard later in the week, she seemed relieved. Gerry also advised the complainant of the security measures in place at the hospital. He had with him a large attaché case containing taperecording equipment. He proceeded to assemble that equipment on the complainant's bed side table. He pinned a microphone to her clothing and to himself. Before commencing the interview, he told her that he wanted her to provide him with a true account of what had happened between her and the accused.

In light of that combination of circumstances, it would have been plain to any person of average intelligence that from the perspective of the police this was a very serious matter.

. . . .

(b) The Lack of Presence

As indicated above, in B. (K.G.) the majority of the Supreme Court of Canada expressed a strong preference for videotaping as the best compensation for the inability of the trier of fact to be present at the time that the statement was made. The interview with the complainant at the hospital was not videotaped, and therefore as the trier of fact I would not be able to observe an image of the complainant making the statement. However, the statement was, apart from certain preliminaries and a brief portion toward the end, audiotaped. I observe, further, that as the trier of fact I would not be left without any indicia of how complainant appeared. She did testify at some length at this trial, and in the course of cross-examination by both Crown counsel and counsel for the accused I had the opportunity to observe her, to hear her voice, to see her reactions, to witness her display good humour on some occasions and anger and defiance on others. It was in that context that the audiotape was played on the *voir dire*. The opportunity to have seen and heard her as she gave her evidence made the voice on the tape recording familiar and recognizable. In my opinion, that went some distance toward overcoming the disadvantages of not having a videotape of the interview.

. . . .

In the circumstances of this case, I am satisfied that the audiotape of the interview, placed into the context I have described, adequately compensates for the inability of the trier of fact to be present at the time the statement was made.

(c) Lack of Contemporaneous Cross-examination

The complainant was and remains available for cross-examination at this trial should her statement to Detective Gerry be admitted into evidence. For the reasons of the Chief Justice in B. (K.G.), the availability of cross-examination at trial is an adequate substitute for the inability of the defence to cross-examine at the time that the statement was made.

(d) Voluntariness

In order to have a prior inconsistent statement admitted for the truth of its contents, the prosecution is obliged to prove that the statement was voluntary in law. There was no suggestion from the defence that the Crown had failed to meet its burden in this respect.

In my opinion, the evidence adduced on the *voir dire* establishes beyond a reasonable doubt that the complainant's statement to Detective Gerry was voluntary.

. . . .

In my opinion, the Crown has established the threshold reliability of the statement to Detective Gerry. The Crown has also established beyond a reasonable doubt that the statement was voluntary. Accordingly, the statement will be admitted in evidence for the truth of its contents.

[The accused, Mohamed, who had been in custody for seven months prior to sentencing, was sentenced to 42 months imprisonment: [1997] O.J. No. 1556 (Ont. Prov. Div.).]

(f) Should Evidence of Reliability Be Restricted?

Is a judge confined to an examination of the circumstances under which the statement was made when she seeks assurances of reliability? Can she look outside for corroboration and take from other evidence in the case that the statement is probably true and therefore the statement deserves receipt? Recall in *Kharsekin*[64] how the Court of Appeal was persuaded as to the reliability of the victim's statement by, among other things, the presence of the victim's blood on the accused's pants. Recall in *Mohamed* how the Court specifically denied that the judge could outside of the circumstances surrounding the making of the statement.

In the seminal decision of *Khan*, the Court decided that the statement of the child was sufficiently reliable to be received under the new principled approach. Note the evidence relied on by Justice McLachlin in making that decision:

> I conclude that the mother's statement should have been received. It was necessary, the child's *viva voce* evidence having been rejected. It was also reliable. The child had no motive to falsify her story, which emerged naturally and without prompting. Moreover, the fact that she could not be expected to have knowledge of such sexual acts imbues her statement with its own peculiar stamp of reliability. *Finally, her statement was corroborated by real evidence.*[65]

Justice McLachlin decided that one could find evidence supporting reliability looking beyond the circumstances under which the statement was made. The child had told her mother: "He put his birdie in my mouth, shook it and peed in my mouth." On the child's jogging suit the police had found a mixture of semen and saliva. Real, tangible evidence, evidence beyond the circumstances surrounding the making of the statement, had corroborated the child's statement.

In *R. v. U. (F.J.)*,[66] the Supreme Court decided to treat the child's statement to the police as hearsay. It then applied a principled approach to decide it was admissible for its truth. The child's earlier statement described regular sexual intercourse with her father and that she had had sex with him the previous night. The father's statement to the police was very similar. The Court found necessity

---

64. (1994), 30 C.R. (4th) 252.
65. (1990), 79 C.R. (3d) 1 (S.C.C.), at p. 15.
66. (1995), 42 C.R. (4th) 133 (S.C.C.).

resident in the fact that she would not repeat the statements at trial. Chief Justice Lamer found reliability resident as:

> The statements made by the accused and by his daughter contained both a significant number of similarities in detail and *the strikingly similar assertion that the most recent sexual contact between the two had been the previous evening.* As a voir dire was also held with regard to the accused's statement, there was also sufficient evidence presented to found a conclusion that the accused and his daughter had neither a reason nor an opportunity to collude, and that the accused was not improperly influenced by the police officers who took his statement. On the basis of all these factors, I conclude that her statement was, therefore, substantively admissible at trial.[67]

Again, the Court in *R. v. U. (F.J.)* went beyond the circumstances under which the statement was made for a determination of reliability and found corroborative evidence in the father's statement.

In *R. v. Conway*[68] the Crown conceded on the appeal that the classical indicia of reliability were weak; there was no oath, no videotape and the opportunity for cross-examination at trial was minimal as the witness at trial did not give a contradictory statement but rather professed no memory of the matter. The Crown argued however that the earlier statement deserved to be received because it was open to the trial judge to look beyond the circumstances under which the statement was made for evidence that would confirm the accuracy of the statement. The Crown referred to evidence gathered by the police, expert evidence and the testimony of one of the accused. The Court of Appeal saw many difficulties with such a position and noted simply that Chief Justice Lamer had said in *R. v. Smith*:

> The criterion of "reliability" is a function of the circumstances under which the statement in question was made.[69]

For the Ontario Court of Appeal this was dispositive of the issue.

Conway is consistent with the United States Supreme Court decision in *Idaho v. Wright*.[70] In that case, a prosecution of sexual assault, the child had made certain statements to a medical doctor. The statements were received under the residual exception to the hearsay rule provided for in the state rules. It was agreed that the classic indicia of reliability were absent; the doctor had blatantly led the child. The statements were not recorded, by audio or video, and the doctor had only dictated notes to summarize the conversation. The trial court decided however that there was confirmation of her accusatory statements resident in the medical evidence which indicated the child had been abused and testimony from another older daughter that the child had been abused by the accused. The conviction was reversed as violative of the Confrontation Clause. The U.S. court decided that to be sufficiently reliable to satisfy the Confrontation Clause a hearsay statement had to either "fall within a firmly rooted hearsay exception or supported by a showing of particularized guarantees of trustworthiness." Justice O'Connor for the majority decided:

---

67.   *Ibid.*, at p. 157. Emphasis added.
68.   (1997), 13 C.R. (5th) 139 (Ont. C.A.).
69.   (1992), 15 C.R. (4th) 133 (S.C.C.) at p. 148.
70.   110 S.Ct. 3139 (1990).

We agree that "particularized guarantees of trustworthiness" must be shown from the totality of the circumstances, but we think the relevant circumstances include only those that surround the making of the statement and that render the declarant particularly worthy of belief. This conclusion derives from the rationale for permitting exceptions to the general rule against hearsay. . . . The circumstantial guarantees of trustworthiness on which the various specific exceptions to the hearsay rule are based are those that existed at the time the statement was made and do not include those that may be added by using hindsight.[71]

The majority decided that admission of what is, after all, a presumptively unreliable statement by "bootstrapping on the trustworthiness of other evidence at the trial" would be a violation of the constitution. They also noted that corroboration of a child's allegations of sexual abuse by medical evidence of abuse, said nothing concerning the reliability of the child's allegations regarding the identity of the abuser but there was a very real danger that a jury might rely on the partial corroboration and infer that the entire statement was trustworthy.

Justice Kennedy, for four judges in dissent, decided the rule adopted, preventing any corroboration by evidence apart from the circumstances surrounding the making of the statement, was too rigid and would prove to be unworkable. He wrote:

In the context of child abuse, if part of the child's hearsay statement is that the assailant tied her wrists or had a scar on his lower abdomen and there is physical evidence or testimony to corroborate the child's statement, evidence which the child could not have fabricated, we are more likely to believe that what a child says is true.[72]

Justice Kennedy noted that most federal courts had previously looked to the existence of corroborating evidence to determine the reliability of hearsay statements which did not fall within one of the traditional exceptions.

The Supreme Court in Canada has decided to embrace "a principled analysis" for dealing with hearsay. There is logic in identifying those principles as resident within the traditional exceptions as was done in *Idaho v. Wright*. But we need to remember that the traditional exceptions, while bringing some assurances of trustworthiness, are not guarantees.[73] What we need to be asking then is whether there are sufficient indicators of trustworthiness that the trier of fact can make an intelligent decision as to the worth of the statement. Chief Justice Lamer said in *B. (K.G.)*:

The ultimate reliability of the statement and the weight to be attached to it remain, as with all evidence, determinations for the trier of fact. What the reliability component of the principled approach to hearsay exceptions addresses is a *threshold* of reliability, rather than ultimate reliability.[74]

In *Hawkins*, he repeated and amplified the thought:

---

71. *Ibid.*, at §§3148-3149.
72. *Ibid.*, at §3153.
73. See Rosenberg, "*B. (K.G.)* — Necessity and Reliability: The New Pigeonholes" (1993), 19 C.R. (4th) 69 at p. 71 for the interesting observation: "It must be open to the courts to revisit any established exception to determine whether that exception can still be justified on the basis of necessity and reliability."
74. (1993), 19 C.R. (4th) 1 (S.C.C.) at p. 34. Emphasis added.

The criterion of reliability is concerned with *threshold* reliability, not ultimate reliability. The function of the trial judge is limited to determining whether the particular hearsay statement exhibits sufficient indicia of reliability so as to afford the trier of fact a satisfactory basis for evaluating the truth of the statement. . . . The ultimate reliability of the statement, and the weight to be attached to it, remain determinations for the trier of fact.[75]

And, finally, in *U. (F.J.)*, Lamer C.J.C. wrote:

The trial judge at this stage is not making a final determination about the ultimate reliability and credibility of the statement. The trial judge need not be satisfied that the prior statement is true and should be believed in preference to the witness's current testimony. If the trial judge determines that the statement meets the *threshold* reliability criterion and [it] is thus substantively admissible.[76]

When a judge determines the admissibility of a statement under one of the traditional exceptions to the hearsay rule she satisfies herself that the conditions of the exception are satisfied. She determines that the conditions surrounding the making of the statement have been satisfied. She determines that the threshold of reliability has been achieved. As to the ultimate reliability of the statement, the trier of fact must decide that. A spontaneous exclamation, a dying declaration, a declaration against interest, is not guaranteed to be reliable. The judge decides that there is sufficient reliability that the adversary is not unduly or unfairly prejudiced by the lack of an opportunity to cross-examine and that the trier of fact will be able to assess the worth of the statement. Perhaps that's all we can expect from a judge when she applies the principled approach.

In *R. v. Starr* (2000), 36 C.R. (5th) 1 (S.C.C.) the matter seems now to have been settled. Justice Iacobucci for the majority, wrote:

At the stage of hearsay admissibility the trial judge should not consider the declarant's general reputation for truthfulness, nor any prior or subsequent statements, consistent or not. These factors do not concern the circumstances of the statement itself. Similarly, I would not consider the presence of corroborating or conflicting evidence. On this point, I agree with the Ontario Court of Appeal's decision in *R. v. C. (B.)* (1993), 12 O.R. (3d) 608; see also *Idaho v. Wright*, 497 U.S. 805 (1990). In summary, under the principled approach a court must not invade the province of the trier of fact and condition admissibility of hearsay on whether the evidence is ultimately reliable. However, it will need to examine whether the circumstances in which the statement was made lend sufficient credibility to allow a finding of threshold reliability.

The citation to *R. v. C. (B.)* is curious as that case did not consider this issue. *Conway* however certainly did.

For good reviews in this area see Lacelle, "The Role of Corroborating Evidence in Assessing the Reliability of Hearsay Statements for Substantive Purposes" (1999), 19 C.R. (5th) 376 and Archibald, "The Canadian Hearsay Revolution: Is Half a Loaf Better Than No Loaf At All?" (1999), 25 Queen's Law Journal 1, especially at 36-39. For a collection of cases that did look outside the circumstances surrounding the making of the statement see *R. v. Nguyen* (2001), 42 C.R. (5th) 35 (Alta. C.A.).

---

75. (1997), 2 C.R. (5th) 245 (S.C.C.) at p. 273. Emphasis added.
76. (1995), 42 C.R. (4th) 133 (S.C.C.) at p. 156. Emphasis added.

(g) Reviewing Exceptions under Principled Approach

R. v. STARR
[2000] 2 S.C.R. 144, 36 C.R. (5th) 1, 147 C.C.C. (3d) 449

[The accused was charged with two counts of first degree murder. It was alleged that he had shot C and W. The accused had been drinking with C and W in a hotel. They left the hotel and then parted company. C and W stopped at an adjacent gas station. G, a girlfriend of C, approached the car and had a conversation with C. She was angry with C because he was out with W rather than with her, and she walked away. C followed her. G asked C why he would not come home with her. G testified that C replied that he had to "go and do an Autopac scam with Robert". She understood "Robert" to be the accused who she saw in another car parked at the station. The Crown's theory was that the killing was a gang-related execution perpetrated by the accused. W was killed simply because she was in the wrong place at the wrong time. The theory was that the accused had suggested an Autopac scam to C as a pretext to get C out into the country. The trial judge decided that G's testimony regarding C?s intended participation in the scam was admissible under the "present intentions" or "state of mind" exception to the hearsay rule.

The accused was convicted and his appeal to the Manitoba Court of Appeal was dismissed.

The Supreme Court reversed and ordered a new trial.]

IACOBUCCI, J. (MAJOR, BINNIE, ARBOUR and LEBEL, JJ. concurring): —

. . . .

. . . I conclude that the Court of Appeal erred in admitting the statement in question under the "present intentions" exception to the hearsay rule. However, *Khan*, supra, and subsequent cases have established that hearsay that does not fit within a traditional exception may nonetheless be admissible if it meets the twin criteria of reliability and necessity. This case therefore requires that we determine the admissibility of evidence under the principled approach, and more particularly, the interaction between the principled approach and the traditional exceptions. In so doing, I conclude that hearsay that *does* fit within a traditional hearsay exception, as currently understood, may still be inadmissible if it is not sufficiently reliable and necessary. The traditional exception must therefore yield to comply with the principled approach.

. . . .

The theory of the Crown at trial was that the killing of Cook was a gang-related execution perpetrated by the appellant. Weselowski was an unfortunate witness who was killed simply because she was in the wrong place at the wrong time. The theory was that the appellant had used an Autopac scam as a pretext to get Cook out into the countryside. Outside the Turskis' home, Cook got into the smaller car and drove it into the ditch, hitting telephone poles in an effort to damage the car. The appellant shot Weselowski twice in the head, then drove Weselowski's station wagon up the road to where Cook had stopped the smaller car in the ditch. When Cook entered the station wagon on the passenger side, the appellant shot him from the driver's seat three times in the head and three times in the chest. He then pushed Cook's body out of the vehicle and drove away, parking near his brother's house, where the appellant abandoned the station wagon.

. . . .

. . . First of all, and with respect for the contrary view, I am of the opinion that the

Court of Appeal erred in finding that Cook's statement to Giesbrecht fit within the present intentions exception to the hearsay rule. I reach this conclusion for two reasons: the statement was made under circumstances of suspicion, and it was used to prove the intentions of someone other than the declarant. Having so concluded, it is necessary to ask whether the statement was admissible under the principled approach, as enunciated in *Khan* and *Smith*, supra. I conclude that it was not, much for the same reasons that it does not fall within the present intentions exception. Answering this question also raises issues respecting the interaction between the principled approach and the existing exceptions. I conclude that in the event of a conflict between the two, it is the principled approach that must prevail. The governing principles for hearsay admissibility must be reliability and necessity.

. . . .

[Iacobucci, J. then analyzed the scope of the present intentions exception to the hearsay rule.]

With great respect to the Court of Appeal, I conclude that the trial judge erred in admitting Cook's statement to Giesbrecht under the present intentions exception and, having admitted it, in not limiting its use by the jury, for three reasons. First, the statement contained no indicia of reliability since it was made under circumstances of suspicion; second, the trial judge failed to instruct the jury that the statement was only admissible as evidence regarding the intentions of Cook, not the appellant; and third, even if it had been properly limited, the evidence was more prejudicial than probative.

Turning first to the circumstances of suspicion, I agree with Twaddle J.A. that the statement lacked circumstantial guarantees of trustworthiness. As Twaddle J.A. noted, Cook and Giesbrecht had been romantically involved for almost two years. Cook had lived with Giesbrecht and her mother for a time, and had spent the night before his murder with Giesbrecht, after getting out of jail. Then, in the early morning hours of August 21, 1994, Giesbrecht observed Cook in the car of another woman, Darlene Weselowski. Giesbrecht testified that she thought Cook might try to "take off on her" if he saw Giesbrecht approaching the car, and she endeavoured not to be seen by Cook until she was close enough to talk to him. After an initial confrontation, Giesbrecht walked away into an alley behind the gas station, where Cook followed her. Their conversation ended in an argument because Cook was with Weselowski. She was angry at Cook for being with another woman, and asked him expressly why Cook would not come home with her rather than remain with Weselowski. It was at this point, and in this heated context, that Cook said he was going to engage in an Autopac scam with the appellant, who was sitting in a car nearby. Giesbrecht testified that it was unusual for Cook to discuss such business matters with her.

Twaddle J.A. found that the circumstances surrounding the making of the statement cast serious doubt upon the reliability of the statement. The possibility that Cook was untruthful could not be said to have been substantially negated. Twaddle J.A. relied, in particular, upon the fact that Cook may have had a motive to lie in order to make it seem that he was not romantically involved with Weselowski, and upon the ease with which Cook could point to the appellant, who was sitting nearby in a car but out of earshot, as being the person with whom he was going to do a scam. In my view, Twaddle J.A. was correct in finding that these circumstances bring the reliability of Cook's statement into doubt. The statement was made under "circumstances of suspicion", and therefore does not fall within the present intentions exception. The statement should have been excluded.

. . . .

Admissibility of Cook's Statement to Giesbrecht Under the Principled Approach

. . . .

. . . [A] fundamental concern with reliability lies at the heart of the hearsay rule. By excluding evidence that might produce unfair verdicts, and by ensuring that litigants will generally have the opportunity to confront adverse witnesses, the hearsay rule serves as a cornerstone of a fair justice system.

. . . .

In addition to improving trial fairness, bringing the hearsay exceptions into line with the principled approach will also improve the intellectual coherence of the law of hearsay. It would seem anomalous to label an approach "principled" that applies only to the admission of evidence, not its exclusion. Rationalizing the hearsay exceptions into the principled approach shows that the former are simply specific manifestations of general principles, rather than the isolated "pigeon-holes" referred to in *U. (F.J.)*, supra, at para. 20.

. . . .

Having recognized the primacy of the principled approach, it is nevertheless important for a court to exercise a certain degree of caution when reconsidering the traditional exceptions. While the exceptions may need to be reexamined in light of the principled approach, their complete abolition is not the answer. Rather, the exceptions continue to play an important role under the principled approach. Our task therefore is to reconcile the traditional exceptions with the principled approach.

One important function that the hearsay exceptions have served has been to add predictability and certainty to the law of hearsay. In light of the exceptions, and regardless of how illogical or arbitrary they may be, litigants can be more or less certain when going into court of the types of issues that will be relevant in debating admissibility in a particular context, and of the likelihood that the evidence will indeed be admitted. This certainty has fostered greater efficiency in the use of court time both at trial and on appeal, and has facilitated the task of the too frequently overburdened trial judge who is called upon to rule on hearsay admissibility with speed and considerable regularity.

. . . .

Second, in addition to serving the utilitarian goals of providing greater certainty and fostering judicial efficiency, the exceptions have served an explanatory or educative function, instructing litigants and judges about the relevant factors to consider in determining whether to admit a *particular type* of hearsay evidence, or whether to admit hearsay in a *particular factual context*. Different hearsay scenarios by their nature raise different reliability concerns, and different issues of necessity. The specific requirements of the individual exceptions have had the useful effect of focussing attention upon the peculiar factors that make it desirable, or undesirable, to admit a particular form of out-of-court statement. This should be no surprise given Lamer C.J.'s statement in *Smith*, supra, that the principled approach is "governed by the principles which underlie the [hearsay] rule and its exceptions alike". Since the principled approach is implicit in most of the exceptions, they are likely to be strong evidence of necessity and reliability.

It is true that there is guidance inherent in the principled approach itself, which directs a court to gauge whether a particular hearsay statement is reliable and whether its admission is necessary in the circumstances. However, the exceptions are more fact-specific and contextually sensitive. Properly modified to conform to the principled approach, the exceptions are practical manifestations of the principled approach in concrete and meaningful form. Indeed, it is precisely to illustrate the form of analysis under the principled approach that must occur in a particular factual context that this Court in its recent cases has outlined carefully the type of inquiry that must occur when dealing with a particular type of hearsay, whether it be the testimony of a child witness (*Khan*, supra), a prior inconsistent statement (*B. (K.G.)*, supra), and (*U. (F.J.)*, supra) or prior testimony (*Hawkins*, supra). . . .

A third important function played by the traditional hearsay exceptions is that they teach us about the historical and contemporary rationale for admitting certain forms of hearsay. It has quite properly been noted that some hearsay exceptions allow for the admission of evidence that is unreliable, unnecessary, or both. In the interest of fairness for the litigant against whom it is used, unreliable hearsay evidence should never be admitted. Apart from that, a review of the traditional exceptions reveals that there are reasons beyond "pure" necessity why a court might wish to admit reliable hearsay evidence. This point was addressed by Lamer C.J. in *B. (K.G.)*, where he explained that the need to permit the admission of certain forms of hearsay can stem not only from the unavailability of the out-of-court declarant, but also from the quality of the evidence itself.

There are other important functions served by the traditional hearsay exceptions, but the issues I have referred to are sufficient to illustrate that it is neither desirable nor necessary to abolish these exceptions outright. The more appropriate approach is to seek to derive the benefits of certainty, efficiency, and guidance that the exceptions offer, while adding the benefits of fairness and logic that the principled approach provides. The task is to rid the exceptions of their arbitrary aspects, in order to avoid admitting hearsay evidence that should be excluded. . . .

For much the same reasons why the statement did not meet the requirements for admissibility under the present intentions exception, I conclude that the statement is not admissible under the principled approach either. This should not be particularly surprising — as I have discussed above, the traditional exceptions are based on the concepts of reliability and necessity. While occasionally, as in *Khan*, a statement not falling within an existing exception will be admissible under the principled approach, this will likely be the exception, not the rule.

The first requirement for admissibility under the principled approach is reliability. Given my conclusion above that Cook's statement was made under "circumstances of suspicion", it follows that the statement was not reliable. Nor are there any other circumstantial guarantees of trustworthiness that could render the statement reliable. Having found that the statement is unreliable, it is unnecessary to go on to ask whether it was necessary or not. I conclude that Cook's statement to Giesbrecht was inadmissible under the principled approach. Since it does not fall under an existing exception either, for all the reasons given above, the courts below erred in admitting this evidence. There being no serious argument that the error was one that could be saved by the curative proviso, s. 686(1)(b)(iii) of the Criminal Code, R.S.C., 1985, c. C-46, the appeal must be allowed.

. . . .

While *Khan* and its progeny have set out the approach for evidence falling outside a traditional exception, I would note that evidence falling within a traditional exception is presumptively admissible. These exceptions traditionally incorporate an inherent reliability component. . . . All this being said, it is also clear that the logic of the principled approach demands that it must prevail in situations where it is in conflict with an existing exception.

. . . .

It is important when examining the reliability of a statement under the principled approach to distinguish between threshold and ultimate reliability. Only the former is relevant to admissibility: see *Hawkins*, supra. Again, it is not appropriate in the circumstances of this appeal to provide an exhaustive catalogue of the factors that may influence threshold reliability. However, our jurisprudence does provide some guidance on this subject. Threshold reliability is concerned not with whether the statement is true or not; that is a question of ultimate reliability. Instead, it is concerned with whether or not the circumstances surrounding the statement itself provide circumstantial guarantees of trustworthiness.

McLACHLIN, C.J., dissenting (BASTARACHE, J. concurring): —

. . . .

In my view, the following principles govern the admissibility of hearsay evidence:

1.   Hearsay evidence is admissible if it falls under an exception to the hearsay rule;

2.   The exceptions can be interpreted and reviewed as required to conform to the values of necessity and reliability that justify exceptions to the hearsay rule;

3.   Where the evidence is admissible under an exception to the hearsay rule, the judge may still refuse to admit the evidence if its prejudicial effect outweighs its probative value;

4.   Where evidence is not admissible under an exception to the hearsay rule, the judge may admit it provided that necessity and reliability are established.

In short, the common law exceptions to the hearsay rule remain the law, as interpreted and updated to conform to the twin requirements of necessity and reliability. Additionally, evidence not falling within an exception may be admitted if the requirements of necessity and reliability are established. This retains the certainty and predictability associated with the common law exceptions to the hearsay rule and avoids the need to hold a voir dire when evidence falls within an established exception. At the same time, it permits the exceptions to evolve and evidence outside the exceptions to be admitted where necessity and circumstantial guarantees of reliability exist. As with all evidence, the trial judge has an overriding discretion to exclude the evidence if its prejudicial effect outweighs its probative value.

Applying these rules to this case, the first question is whether an established exception to the hearsay rule applies to the evidence at issue. The answer in this case is yes. The victim's statement that he intended to do an Autopac scam with the accused later that night is a statement of present intention. Statements of present intention constitute a long-recognized exception to the rule against admitting hearsay evidence. The next question concerns the ambit of the exception of statements of present intention. . . . I conclude that the victim Cook's statement that he intended to do an Autopac scam with the accused was admissible as evidence of the victim's present intention, and that the trial judge's instructions sufficed in the circumstances to obviate the danger of impermissible inferences. In the result, I agree with L'Heureux-Dubé J. that the appeal should be dismissed.

L'HEUREUX-DUBÉ, J. dissenting (GONTHEIR J., concurring): —

. . . .

The end result of Iacobucci J.'s approach is an open invitation to challenge previously admissible hearsay evidence. I do not believe that this approach flows from our previous decisions in *Khan* and *R. v. Smith*. . . . These cases were not about the exceptions to the hearsay rule but about expanding the scope of admissible evidence beyond the boundaries of the traditional categories. They accepted the traditional exceptions as a given but sought other means to admit reliable and necessary evidence through the adoption of a "principled approach" to hearsay. I fear that to adopt the course charted by Iacobucci J. would sacrifice the experience, certainty and predictability of centuries of jurisprudence in the name of a quest for purported intellectual coherence that is untested by the forges of our courtrooms.

. . . .

I would adopt the following framework of analysis for hearsay statements. First, it must be determined whether the statement is hearsay. Second, the trial judge should determine whether the hearsay statement falls within an established exception to the hearsay rule. If it does, the evidence is admissible. Third, if the evidence does not fall within an established exception, the trial judge should determine whether it would still be admissible under the principled approach. Fourth, the trial judge maintains the limited residual discretion to exclude evidence where the risk of undue prejudice substantially exceeds the evidence's probative value. Finally, once the statements are found admissible, it is for the trier of fact to weigh the evidence and make a determination as to the ultimate reliability of the hearsay evidence at issue. . . . In addition, I would allow for the re-evaluation, in a proper case, of a traditional exception under the principled approach. That is to say, I believe that the principled approach may be applied to reconsider the reliability and necessity of the class of statements that are included in a categorical exception to the rule against hearsay. I would not countenance the case-by-case application of the principled approach to statements falling within accepted exceptions to the rule against hearsay. Individual cases may illuminate or illustrate the need to modify a particular traditional exception, but every piece of evidence that falls within a traditional exception should not be subjected to the principled approach and the concomitant voir dire that it may entail. To do so would unnecessarily complicate the trial process and sacrifice experience, certainty and predictability in the name of the vague and uncertain mantra of "principle".

. . . .

I would conclude that the principled necessity-reliability analysis, while appropriate where hearsay evidence does not fall within an established exception to the hearsay rule, has not replaced and should not supplant the traditional exceptions to the hearsay rule. I am not persuaded by Iacobucci J.'s attempt to split the difference and hold that the principled approach applies to the evidence that falls within a traditional exception but that a voir dire may only sometimes be necessary. Either the principled approach applies to the traditional exceptions or it does not. If it does, then a voir dire is required to consider the admissibility of such evidence. . . . The source of the disagreement between my colleague Iacobucci J. and me can be traced to variant understandings of threshold reliability inquiry under the principled approach. The traditional exceptions are built upon a determination that a threshold of reliability is met in particular instances of hearsay statements. Reliability under the principled approach is similarly restricted to a threshold inquiry.

. . . .

Threshold reliability exists where there is a circumstantial guarantee of trustworthiness. It does not mean that the hearsay is true or even likely to be true, but rather it asks whether the circumstances are such that there is sufficient reliability for the hearsay to be properly assessed by the jury. The traditional hearsay exceptions are based on a determination of threshold reliability. These exceptions have historically been founded on truisms common to classes of people or common to circumstances applicable to all people. There is no reason why that should not continue to be the case. I acknowledge that some of the existing exceptions may require fine tuning. It may be that society has changed in such a manner that the rationale for the exception no longer applies. And, there may be circumstances which could arise in an individual case which challenge the inherent reliability that underpins a hearsay exception. However, the court must differentiate between individual circumstances that go to the weight of the evidence (such as motive to lie or other extraneous circumstances unique to the individual) and circumstances that are properly considered at the threshold stage.

. . . .

I would summarize my position in the following terms. . . . First, *Khan* and its progeny permit hearsay evidence to be admitted in new situations where necessary and where indicia of reliability are present, but did not abolish the traditional exceptions. Second, the traditional exceptions are largely consistent with the necessity-reliability criteria and so do not generally require revision. Finally, the traditional exceptions may be modified or supplemented as appropriate to conform to the principled approach (on this last point, see

Rosenberg, "*B. (K.G.)* — Necessity and Reliability: The New Pigeon-holes"). . . . Trial judges should continue to apply the traditional exceptions to the hearsay rule.

[L'Heureux-Dubé, J. then analyzed admissibility under the present intention exception and concluded it deserved to be received under that exception. Her reasons for that will be later examined when we deal with that exception.]

In *R. v. West* (July 31, 2001), (Ont. S.C.J.) the accused had been apprehended in 1999 and charged with the murder of M which murder had been committed in 1970. One aspect of the homicide investigation involved forensic testing related to vaginal swabs from the deceased. The relevant exhibits were tested at the Centre of Forensic Sciences by P, a senior forensic biologist, for the presence of blood and semen. P prepared and signed a report of his findings dated January 25th, 1971. These findings were used by police investigators in attempts to track down a suspect. P died in the 1980's. The essential evidence against the accused was comparative forensic DNA analysis of the accused's blood together with crime scene samples derived from physical exhibits first scientifically analyzed by P long before the advent of DNA profiling. On application by the Crown the forensic report was ruled admissible for the truth of its contents. Justice Hill decided that rather than first measuring the hearsay at hand against any relevant traditional exceptions apparently applicable, for example business records, he would simply proceed directly to the overarching principled analysis with liberal reference to the traditional exceptions advanced by the Crown. He readily found necessity. With respect to reliability he noted that (1) the declarant had peculiar means of knowledge, (2) the declarant was acting under a duty in a routine of assigned duties, (3) the declarant's statement was made contemporaneously with the recorded event, (4) there were no circumstances of suspicion tending to undermine the credibility of the statement and (5) there were circumstances extant relevant to uncovering any mistakes in the statement. Applying these factors to the report in this case the report was determined to be admissible hearsay.

In *R. v. Kimberley and Clancey* (September 13, 2001), (Ont. C.A.) the accused were convicted of murder. Both accused had sought to rely on evidence of a statement by T that he was the person who did the killing. T had committed suicide prior to the commencement of the trial. At trial, counsel argued that the statements were admissible either under the traditional exception for declarations made against penal interest or under the principled approach to the admissibility of hearsay. On appeal, counsel did not rely on the penal interest exception to the rule but focussed exclusively on the necessity/reliability analysis required by the principled approach and the court, per Doherty, J.A., agreed that this was the preferred approach to the admissibility of the statements. The necessity inquiry mandated by the principled approach to hearsay was straightforward. T killed himself prior to trial and was obviously unavailable to testify. The hearsay dangers presented by T's statements were seen to run the full gamut of the dangers associated with hearsay evidence. He was not under oath or any imperative to speak the truth. The statements were not videotaped so there was no basis upon which a jury could assess T's demeanour. There was nothing approaching a detailed summary, much less a verbatim record, of what was said by T. Finally, T was not subject to cross-examination when he made these statements. The rationale that underlies the penal interest exception was seen to only operate where the statement was made in circumstances where the declarant apprehended an immediate vulnerability to penal consequences. T, however, fully intended to plead guilty to another homicide knowing that he would be sentenced to life imprisonment. Any consequences which might flow from his admissions concerning the killing here under review would not really alter his future or impose any additional penal consequences. Consequently, the fact that the statements amounted to confessions to murder made to police officers did not enhance the reliability of those statements.

Both in *Kimberley* and in *West*, two judges, very experienced in criminal law and evidence, take the position that since *Starr* a judge might best proceed directly to the principled approach instead of asking whether the impugned statement fits within one of the traditional exceptions. This appeared to them to be consistent with the admonition of Justice Iacobucci in *Starr* that "Hearsay evidence may only be admitted if it is necessary and reliable, and the traditional exceptions should be interpreted in a manner consistent with this requirement."

Another judge, also accepted as an expert in the law of evidence, offered four reasons why the approach should be to first address the question of whether the hearsay is admissible under statutory or traditional hearsay exceptions; see Justice Cromwell in *Wilcox* (2001), 152 C.C.C. (3d) 157 (N.S.C.A.). He noted (1) that it has become the practice to first examine whether the hearsay fits an existing exception and cited *Starr* as an example of a court doing just that, (2) analysis under traditional exceptions may not only make resort to the principled approach unnecessary but will assist with the principled approach should it become necessary, (3) a further function of the traditional exceptions is to promote predictability and (4) admissibility under traditional exceptions may have a bearing on the necessity criterion under the principled analysis.

Which approach do you favour?

The terms necessity and reliability were first coined by Professor Wigmore in an attempt to bring some seeming order to bear to the many exceptions. But, of course, this was after the fact reasoning. Wigmore's teacher, Professor Thayer, in his historical researches, suggested there was no single theory to explain the various exceptions. The exceptions, like Topsy, "just growed." To like effect, see Morgan and Maguire, in their classic article "Looking Backward and Forward at Evidence" (1937), 50 Harv. L. Rev. 909 at 921. It seems obvious then that as a result, with no single unifying theory underlying their creation, a number of our present exceptions cannot qualify under the principled approach and will need modification. It will be interesting when we come to examine the various exceptions to the hearsay rule, to speculate which exceptions, fashioned without the requirements of necessity and reliability, will go.

R. v. PARROTT
[2001] 1 S.C.R. 178, 39 C.R. (5th) 255, 150 C.C.C. (3d) 449

[A mature woman with a mental disability was seen being put into the accused's car parked outside the psychiatric hospital where the woman resided. After conducting a search which lasted over seven hours, the police located the car, with the woman and the accused, in a remote area. Her shorts and underwear were in disarray. She had bruises and scratches on her body. The woman made out-of-court statements to the police constable who found her and to the doctor who first examined her. Pointing to her injuries, she communicated that the man in the car had done it. The accused was charged with kidnapping and sexual assault. The out-of-court statements were admitted. The accused was convicted of kidnapping, acquitted of sexual assault, but convicted of assault causing bodily harm. The majority of the Court of Appeal held that the trial judge erred in admitting the hearsay evidence when the complainant herself was available to testify and there was no expert suggestion that she would suffer any trauma or adverse effect by appearing in court. The curative proviso of the Criminal Code was applied to maintain the conviction with respect to kidnapping but the conviction with respect to assault causing bodily harm was quashed and a new trial was ordered. The Crown appealed against the setting aside of the assault verdict.]

BINNIE, J. (MAJOR, BASTARACHE, and ARBOUR, JJ. concurring): —

This appeal tests the limits of the principled hearsay exception that allows the Crown in exceptional circumstances to lead the out-of-court evidence of a complainant at a criminal trial without having him or her present in court and available for cross-examination by the defence.

In this case, the complainant in a kidnapping and sexual assault case was a mature woman who had suffered since birth from Down's Syndrome. She was considered mildly to moderately retarded and had been in institutional care for almost 20 years. Expert evidence was called to establish that her mental development was equivalent to that of a three- or four-year-old child and that her memory of events was poor. Her response to even the simplest questions was said to be not very coherent. The complainant herself was never called into the presence of the trial judge so that these attributes could be verified even though she was available and there was no suggestion that she would suffer any trauma or other adverse effect by appearing in court. Instead the court received evidence of out-of-court statements that she had earlier made to the police and to a doctor.

. . . .

About 7:00 p.m. on July 15, 1994, the respondent drove to the Waterford hospital, a psychiatric hospital in St. John's, and was seen talking to a female resident of the hospital who then brought the complainant to his car. James Barry, a psychiatric nursing assistant at the hospital observed these events from a distance of about 200 feet. He shouted at the respondent and the female resident but neither of them acknowledged the shouts. Mr. Barry testified he saw the female resident grip the complainant, seat her in the car and lift her knees and shut the door. He saw the respondent reach over the seat and lock the door. The respondent was observed giving the female resident $20. Mr. Barry reported the incident to his supervisors who called the police. Despite a search effort it took over seven hours to find the complainant. When she was found, both she and the respondent were still in the same car, now located in a remote coastal area at about 2:35 the next morning.

. . . .

The complainant made statements to police at the time of her being found, as well as to the doctor who first examined her. She repeatedly pointed to her injuries and stated "Man did it, bad man, man in car, patient". Police also conducted a videotaped interview the following day. She was questioned for 15 minutes in the presence of two nurses who had known and worked with her. She was asked about the marks on her hands, arm and face to which, in halting broken sentences, she replied that a man "in handcuffs" did it and that he should be "put in jail". She said that it happened "last night" and that he was wearing glasses and a black hat. She also communicated the facts that he scratched her in the car and that he smacked her.

. . . .

Analysis

While in this country an accused does not have an absolute right to confront his or her accuser in the course of a criminal trial, the right to full answer and defence generally produces this result. In this case, unusually, the Crown precipitated an inquiry under s. 16 of the Canada Evidence Act not for the purpose of establishing the testimonial competence of "a proposed witness", namely the complainant, but to lay an evidentiary basis to keep her out of the witness box. Having satisfied the trial judge entirely through expert evidence that the complainant neither understood the nature of an oath nor could communicate her evidence, the Crown used the voir dire as a springboard to establish the admissibility of hearsay evidence of her out-of-court statements under the principles established in *Khan*.

. . . .

This procedure raises two distinct though related issues, firstly the admissibility of the expert evidence at the voir dire, and secondly the admissibility of the complainant's out-of-court statements at the trial. In my view, these issues ought to have been resolved in favour of the respondent, as held by the majority judgment of the Newfoundland Court of Appeal, for the following reasons:

1. The expert evidence was improperly admitted at the voir dire. Trial judges are eminently qualified to assess the testimonial competence of a witness. The trial judge, after all, was to be at the receiving end of the complainant's communication, and could have determined whether or not she was able to communicate her evidence to him. If she had been called and it became evident that the trial judge required expert assistance to draw appropriate inferences from what he had heard her say (or not say), or if either the defence or the Crown had wished to pursue the issue of requiring an oath or solemn affirmation, expert evidence might then have become admissible to assist the judge. At the time the expert testimony was called, it had not been shown that expert evidence as such was necessary, and the testimony of Drs. Gillespie, Morley and Parsons was therefore inadmissible: *R. v. Mohan*, [1994] 2 S.C.R. 9.

2. Consequently, the trial judge erred in ruling at the conclusion of the voir dire that the complainant's out-of-court statements would be admissible at trial. Having dispensed with hearing from the complainant, and the expert medical testimony having been improperly admitted, the trial judge had no admissible evidence on which to exercise a discretion to admit the complainant's out-of-court statements.

3. Even if the expert medical evidence were to be admitted, and accepting the trial judge's conclusion that the out-of-court statements were "reliable" under the first branch of the *Khan* requirements, the trial judge still erred in the circumstances of this case in finding the admission of out-of-court statements to be "necessary" without first hearing from the complainant.

. . . .

Whether a complainant "is able to communicate the evidence" in this broad sense is a matter on which a trial judge can (and invariably does) form his or her own opinion. It is not a matter "outside the experience and knowledge of a judge or jury" (*Mohan*, supra, at p. 23). It is the very meat and potatoes of a trial court's existence.

Necessity

In *Rockey*, supra, Sopinka J. (for the majority) held that because the evidence regarding the child witness' competence to testify was equivocal, the out-of-court statements were not admissible on this basis. However, he further found that there was uncontroverted evidence that the child would be traumatized by giving evidence and decided that the out-of-court statements were necessary for that reason.

The complainant in this case could have been examined before the trial judge in a format that would have attempted to put her at ease. The trial judge could have ensured that nothing, including questions put to her by opposing counsel, would be used to demean or embarrass her. It is possible that, as anticipated by Dr. Gillespie, the complainant might have been incoherent or otherwise unable to communicate whatever she recalled of the events in question. On the other hand, it is also possible that she might, as suggested by Dr. Morley, have been able to give "some account of what happened to her". In the absence of any suggestion of potential trauma or other exceptional circumstances, I think the respondent was entitled to have this issue determined on the basis of the evidence of the complainant rather than on the conflicting opinions, however learned, of her various doctors.

I accept that it was kinder to the complainant to excuse her from appearing at the trial. It is possible, as my colleague LeBel J. suggests at para. 12, that her appearance "would have served no real purpose". But we do not know this. What we do know is that there were very serious accusations made against the respondent. He was confronted with evidence of her out-of-court statements taken in his absence and on which, of course, he could not cross-examine. As a result of the trial, he was sentenced to three years and nine months in jail in addition to the time already served. Compassion for the complainant must be balanced against fairness to the respondent.

While the concept of necessity "must be given a flexible definition capable of encompassing diverse situations" (*R. v. B. (K.G.)*, [1993] 1 S.C.R. 740, at p. 796), it must nevertheless be established on the facts of each particular case. Wells C.J.N., in dissent, observed that the phrase "to communicate the evidence" in s. 16(1)(b) requires exploration of whether the witness is capable of perceiving events, remembering events and communicating events to the court. This is so, but absent special circumstances, the exploration should include hearing from the witness herself.

The *Khan* principles of necessity and reliability were recently applied by a divided Court in *F. (W.J.)*, [1999] 3 S.C.R. 569, where the hearsay evidence of a child complainant was admitted but not until after the child herself had entered the witness box and demonstrated an inability to answer questions about the events surrounding the sexual assault. Even at that, Lamer C.J. dissented on the basis that the trial court had not adequately pursued the reasons why the child appeared unable to provide her recollection of events.

In this case, we are asked to take *F. (W.J.)* one step further. There was no attempt to seek the evidence directly from the witness/complainant even though there was no suggestion that she would suffer adverse effects from appearing in the witness box. No other explanation was given for her non-appearance. The Crown simply decided to relieve the trial judge of the burden of making his own decision, and left him to pick among the competing versions of her testimonial competence offered up by the medical experts.

In my view, if the witness is physically available and there is no suggestion that he or she would suffer trauma by attempting to give evidence, that evidence should generally not be pre-empted by hearsay unless the trial judge has first had an opportunity to hear the potential witness and form his or her own opinion as to testimonial competence. I say generally because there may arise exceptional circumstances where a witness is available and not called and the out-of-court statements may be nevertheless admitted. The Court was careful not to close the door to this possibility in *R. v. Hawkins*, [1996] 3 S.C.R. 1043, at paras. 71-72; *B. (K.G.)*, supra, at pp. 798-99; and *Rockey*, supra, per McLachlin J., concurring in the result, at para. 23. Green J.A. recognized that possibility in the majority judgment in this case (p. 111). The point is that there are no circumstances put in evidence here that would justify such an exceptional procedure.

The Crown in written and oral argument makes several points in justification of the procedure that was followed. It says, first of all, that while there was no evidence that the complainant would suffer trauma, nevertheless the Court can infer the likelihood of something approaching trauma from the video and the nature of the events she was to be asked about. Her otherwise reclusive existence in the Waterford Hospital suggests an inability to cope with the outside world. The Crown submits that "it would have been simply a bit of a circus and a bit of a farce to have gone through the procedure of calling her as a witness simply to be complete in relation to form", and "[i]t would have been, in effect, almost marking her as an exhibit simply for the purpose of bringing her into the Court and showing her to all sides".

Few complainants can welcome a courtroom appearance in a sexual assault charge, but there is no reason to think this complainant was more vulnerable than others on this account. If there was an issue about trauma, it ought not to have been left to inference. Psychiatric evidence was called specifically to address the necessity of having the complainant testify in person, and none of the doctors raised the issue of potential trauma. The onus was on the Crown to meet the *Khan* criteria for the hearsay exception. It was clear that trauma to a potentially vulnerable witness is an important consideration. No such evidence was called.

Further, as Green J.A. pointed out, the Court should not be quick to leap to the assumption that a person with mental disabilities is not competent to give useful testimony. Trauma should not be presumed, not only because such a presumption would deprive the accused of the ability to observe and cross-examine the witness, but also because stereotypical assumptions about persons with disabilities should be avoided. For the same reason, I disagree with my colleague LeBel J. that we should assume that the complainant's appearance in the witness box would be demeaning or an "infringement . . . of her dignity and integrity" (para. 22). Persons with disabilities should not be underestimated.

. . . .

For these reasons the judgment of the Newfoundland Court of Appeal should be affirmed and the Crown's appeal dismissed.

LEBEL, J. (L'HEUREUX-DUBÉ and GONTHIER, JJ. concurring) dissenting:

. . . .

A hallmark of the principled approach to hearsay is flexibility. In moving away from the categorical approach of the past to hearsay exceptions, the Court signalled in the last decade an intention to render the rules governing the reception of hearsay evidence more responsive to individual situations. . . . When dealing with young children or people with mental disabilities, this approach seeks to address the necessity and reliability required for the admission of the evidence while at the same time safeguarding the dignity and integrity of the complainants or witnesses.

. . . .

We are far from the strict approach to hearsay which prevailed in the past. Perhaps the most important aspect of the broad account of necessity quoted above is the fact that "the categories of necessity are not closed". Trial judges now have a much broader discretion to admit evidence which would otherwise be considered as hearsay. This court should not attempt to confine this discretion into limited categories, but should rather content itself with stating broad principles to guide judges in the exercise of their discretion.

. . . .

In this context, the ruling of the trial judge was not a narrow one limited to the application of a test of mental competence as in s. 16 of the Canada Evidence Act, R.S.C. 1985, c. C-5. The trial judge's inquiry was much broader. It sought to examine the whole of the complainant's condition as mandated by our principled approach to hearsay and necessity as discussed above. In that regard, the trial judge did not simply express a preference for the views of one of the experts heard, Dr. Gillespie. Barry J.'s decision examined more broadly the victim's childlike mental condition or mental retardation and its impact on her potential testimony. This careful consideration of the condition of the complainant led the judge to decide that she was incapable (as opposed to the more narrow concept of "incompetence") of testifying. He then decided that the out-of-court statements in the video should be received into evidence, because they met the reliability and necessity tests.

. . . .

This Court has without exception assumed a posture of deference toward a trial judge's assessment of testimonial capacity. As McLachlin J. admonished in *Marquard*, "[m]eticulous second-guessing on appeal is to be eschewed." The majority of the Court of Appeal engaged in just such a re-evaluation of the record and interfered too readily with the trial judge's findings. The trial judge was in a superior position to assess the expert testimony, which obviously confirmed his own observation of the complainant's abilities during her interview with Sergeant Ryan. In my view, the trial judge's decision to admit the hearsay evidence manifests no palpable error.

I would accordingly allow the appeal and restore the respondent's conviction.

R. v. A. (S.) —See last para for test
(1992), 17 C.R. (4th) 233, 76 C.C.C. (3d) 522 (Ont. C.A.)

[The accused was charged with two counts of sexual assault allegedly committed against his three-year-old daughter, J.A., between January 1, 1989 and September 21, 1989. The complainant was aged five at the time of the trial; the trial judge found her incompetent to testify. The trial judge admitted a statement made by the child to her grandmother during bath time and a similar statement made to her mother. These statements, describing the alleged assaults, were made within two weeks of the alleged assaults. The accused was convicted on both counts and appealed. The appeal was allowed and a new trial ordered. The court was invited to provide some guidance as to how juries should be instructed where a child's out-of-court statement is admitted pursuant to the principles enunciated in *Khan*.]   ‖ ISSUE

October 19, 1992 (Per curiam:)—

. . . .

Three concerns arise when a child's out of court statement alleging criminal conduct against an accused is admitted and the child does not testify. The first relates to the reliability of the evidence of the witness who testifies to the making of the statement; the second, to the absence of traditional means of providing for and testing the reliability of the statement itself; and the third, to the features found in the rest of the evidence which may have a bearing on the reliability of the statement. These concerns will exist in varying degrees in most, if not all, cases and each should be brought to the jury's attention.

(a) Was the Statement Made?

It is recommended that the jury be told they must first determine whether the statement was made and, if it was, the content of the statement. This requires a consideration of the credibility of the witness or witnesses who testify to the making of the statement and the reliability of their evidence, particularly as it relates to the making of the statement.

In some cases, the witness testifying as to the out of court statement may have reason to fabricate evidence against the accused. Even where no such motive exists, the witness may be mistaken as to what was said, or may be inadvertently providing his or her interpretation of what was said rather than an actual narrative.

The trial judge should ensure that the jury is aware of the respective positions of the parties on this issue and the evidence relied upon in support of their positions. The jury should also be told that if, upon a consideration of all of the relevant evidence, they are not satisfied that the statement was made, then the contents of the statement cannot be relied on in determining whether the Crown has proved the guilt of the accused.

(b) *The Need for Caution*

Even if the jury is satisfied that the out of court statement was made, that statement cannot be placed on the same footing as a statement made by a witness in the course of his or her testimony. Out of court statements made by persons who do not testify, offered for the truth of their contents, are subject to frailties which warrant a cautious approach by the trier of fact: *R. c. Potvin*, [1989] 1 S.C.R. 525, at p. 555 [S.C.R.]; *R. v. Smith*, a decision of the Supreme Court of Canada, released August 27, 1992 [now reported (1992), 15 C.R. (4th) 133, at p. 152 C.R.]; *Schwartzenhauer v. R.*, [1935] S.C.R. 367, at p. 369; *R. v. Davidson* (1988), 42 C.C.C. (3d) 289 298-300; *R. v. S. (K.O.)* (1991), 4 C.R. (4th) 37, at p. 41 C.R.]. In this case, those frailties were threefold. The statement was not made under oath or affirmation or after making a promise to tell the truth; the jury did not have the opportunity to see and hear the child testify; and she was not subject to cross-examination.

The existence and significance of these shortcomings should be made clear to the jury in language appropriate to the particular case. The jury should be cautioned that the oath, affirmation or promise to tell the truth are regarded as safeguards against false testimony. They should further be cautioned that as they have not had the opportunity to make a first-hand assessment of the credibility of the child or the child's reliability as it relates to the statement, they operate at a disadvantage in attempting to assess the reliability of the statement. That disadvantage, and the absence of any oath, affirmation or promise to tell the truth, dictate that the jury proceed with caution before accepting the statement as evidence of the truth of the allegations in the statement.

Further, the jury should be told that our adversarial system places great reliance on cross-examination as a very effective means of getting at the truth, not only because it gives an accused an opportunity to test the reliability of evidence which inculpates the accused, but also because it provides an avenue by which additional evidence favourable to the accused might be adduced. The absence of cross-examination raises a further need for caution before accepting and acting on the contents of the statement. The trial judge should make it clear to the jury that the absence of any opportunity to cross-examine the child renders the out of court statement less reliable than would be the case had that opportunity existed.

(c) *The Other Evidence Relating to the Reliability of the Statement*

As with any piece of evidence, a child's out of court statement cannot be considered in isolation. The weight to be given to the statement will be affected by the other evidence which may support or undermine the reliability of the statement. The jury should be instructed that they must look to the other evidence when considering the reliability of the child's out of court statement. The more salient features of the evidence which have a potential impact on the reliability of the statement should be brought to the jury's attention.

For example, in this case the medical evidence had the potential impact on the jury's appraisal of the reliability of the child's statement. If accepted, that evidence offered direct confirmation of her allegation that she had been sexually assaulted, but it did not provide similar confirmation as to the identity of her assailant as her father.

Other factors present in this case which may have affected the jury's assessment of the reliability of the statement included the age and immaturity of the child, the language used in the statement, the relative spontaneity of the statement, the passage of time between the statement and the alleged assaults, and the absence of any details in the statement referrable to the time, place or circumstances in which the assault occurred. Depending on the view of the evidence taken by the jury, each of these factors might enhance or detract from the reliability of the child's statement.

We do not suggest that the factors set out above are exhaustive. Each case must be considered on its own facts and the trial judge must be given some latitude in deciding what parts of the evidence should be brought to the jury's attention.

In summary, the jury should understand that they must first determine whether the statement was made. If they are satisfied that it was made, they must determine what weight, if any, to give that statement. In considering the weight to be given to the statement, the jury must proceed with caution for the reasons set out above, and they must look to the rest of the evidence for indicia which tend to support or negate the reliability of the statement. Finally, the jury must be told that having exercised the required caution and considered the statement in the context of the rest of the evidence, it is exclusively for them to decide whether the statement was made and, if so, what weight, if any, to give to the statement in their ultimate determination of whether the Crown has proved the accused's guilt beyond a reasonable doubt.

R. v. FINTA
(1992), 14 C.R. (4th) 1, 73 C.C.C. (3d) 65

[This appeal concerned the first prosecution conducted under the legislative scheme established by Parliament in response to the recommendations of the Report of the Commission of Inquiry on War Criminals, 1986. That legislative scheme now appears as sections 7(3.71) to (3.77) of the Criminal Code. The Crown preferred an indictment containing eight counts, two counts each of forcible confinement, robbery, kidnapping and manslaughter, four of which counts were said to constitute crimes against humanity and the other four to constitute war crimes. The accused was acquitted and the Crown appealed. The evidentiary issue involved the introduction of the statements and minutes of testimony given by a witness, Dallos, at Finta's Hungarian trial in 1947-48. Although incriminating on the robbery count, the Dallos evidence was potentially favourable to the defence in that it pointed to the possibility that someone else was responsible for the unlawful confinement and kidnapping. Dallos had died in 1963. The Crown refused to call this evidence, and the trial judge, at the request of the defence, called it himself.]

ARBOUR, OSBORNE and DOHERTY JJ.A.:

. . . .

Many rules of evidence, in criminal cases, operate differently for the Crown and the defence, for example, compellability of the accused and his or her spouse, character evidence, the discretion of the trial judge to exclude evidence prejudicial to the defence, and the exclusion of evidence obtained in violation of a constitutional right. The hearsay rule, on the other hand, has traditionally been applied with equal vigour in criminal cases, for or against both the Crown and the accused. Indeed, in *R. v. Williams*, . . . Mr. Justice Martin remarked, at p. 337 O.R., p. 367 C.R.:

> I take it to be self-evident that an accused in exercising his right to make full answer and defence must comply with the established rules of procedure and the rules respecting the admissibility of evidence. Generally speaking, an accused is not precluded from making full answer and defence because he is prevented by the laws of evidence from introducing hearsay not falling within an exception to the hearsay rule in support of his defence. In advancing a defence, the accused must comply with the law of evidence, just as the prosecution must prove the accused's guilt by admissible evidence and not by hearsay, unless the evidence comes within a recognized exception to the hearsay rule. Counsel for the appellant did not take issue

with the proposition that the accused in exercising his right to make full answer and defence must, as a general rule, comply with the rules of evidence. He contended, however, that the rules of evidence governing the admissibility of confessions by third persons which exculpate the accused require re-examination in the light of the Charter.

apply same rules to ~~eff~~ Acc & M

This view was adopted by Sopinka J. in *R. v. Dersch*:

— shows inconsistency

> The right to full answer and defence does not imply that an accused can have, under the rubric of the *Charter*, an overhaul of the whole law of evidence such that a statement inadmissible under, for instance, the hearsay exclusion, would be admissible if it tended to prove his or her innocence.

However, in *Williams*, Martin J.A. recognized the need for a flexible application of some rules of evidence in order to prevent a miscarriage of justice. He said, at p. 343 O.R., p. 373 C.R.:

> I would be disposed to hold that, in some circumstances, precluding an accused, by a mechanical application of the adverse witness requirement of s. 9(1), from cross-examining a witness whom he has called with respect to a prior confession made by the witness that he, rather than the accused, had committed the crime might deprive the accused of his constitutional right to a fair trial secured by the Charter. It seems to me that a court has a residual discretion to relax in favour of the accused a strict rule of evidence where it is necessary to prevent a miscarriage of justice and where the danger against which an exclusionary rule aims to safeguard does not exist.

To the same effect, see D. Paciocco, "The Constitutional Right to Present Defence Evidence in Criminal Cases" (1985) 63 Can. Bar Rev. 519.

Apart from a constitutional dimension, there is, at common law, at least one exception to the hearsay rule which presently operates for the sole benefit of the defence and which provides a fruitful analogy. Declarations against both pecuniary and penal interest have been held to be admissible on common law principles: *R. v. O'Brien* (1977), [1978] 1 S.C.R. 591; *R. v. Demeter* (1975), 25 C.C.C. (2d) 417 (C.A.).

However, in *Lucier v. R.*, [1982] 1 S.C.R. 28, statements which were manifestly against the deceased declarant's panel [*sic*] interest, but which also incriminated the accused, were held to be inadmissible when tendered by the Crown. Ritchie J., speaking for the court in *Lucier*, noted that in both *O'Brien* and *Demeter*, the statements made by an unavailable person had been tendered by the accused and had an exculpatory effect. In *Lucier*, the deceased declarant's statements, although against his penal interest, as noted, also had the effect of incriminating Lucier and were tendered by the prosecution for that purpose. Ritchie J. said, at p. 33 [S.C.R.]:

> The difference is a very real one because a statement implicating the accused in the crime with which he is charged emanating from the lips of one who is no longer available to give evidence robs the accused of the invaluable weapon of cross-examination which has always been one of the mainstays of fairness in our courts.

He then concluded that this was not a "proper case" for admitting the statements. . . .

. . . .

. . . The rationale for the court's conclusion in *Lucier* seems to be that it would be unfair to deprive the accused of his right to cross-examine someone on a statement which implicates the accused in the crime with which he is charged.

. . . .

There is no reason in principle why some exceptions to the hearsay rule cannot operate like many other rules of evidence, to give preferential treatment to what Professor

Gold refers to as "the value of liberty," [see, M. Gold, "*Lucier v. The Queen*: Case Comment" (1983), 21 Osgoode Hall L.J. 142 at 146-47] and to address what Ritchie J. perceived as the unfairness, in *Lucier*, of depriving the accused of an opportunity to test such evidence by cross-examination.

In our view, the same unfairness would exist in this case if the Dallos evidence could be called by the prosecution. The evidence of Dallos is sufficiently reliable to justify its admission as an exception to the hearsay rule on behalf of the accused. It dealt relatively contemporaneously with an event which took place 46 years ago and which the declarant, since deceased, had a unique opportunity to observe. The statements were given on a solemn judicial or quasi-judicial occasion by a person who appeared to be opposed to the interest of the party now desirous of having the evidence tendered. Yet it would be unfair and oppressive for the state to prosecute an accused today with the assistance of evidence, however reliable, which has been in existence for some 46 years and which the accused was not given the opportunity to challenge.

(d) *Conclusion*

In our view, the trial judge's ruling that the Dallos statements were admissible at the behest of the defence despite their hearsay nature is supported by the approach to hearsay taken in *Khan*, supra, and *Miller*, supra, and is consistent with the constitutional considerations identified in *Williams*, supra, and reiterated in *R. v. Rowbotham* (1988), 41 C.C.C. (3d) 1, at p. 57.

The trial judge did not err in holding that the evidence was admissible.

[Dubin, C.J.C. and Tarnopolsky, J.A. agreed that the evidence was admissible and also agreed with the majority that the trial judge was wrong to call the evidence himself. They disagreed however that this error did not amount to a miscarriage of justice.]

---

2. EXCEPTIONS

Professor Wigmore[77] sought to provide us with a theory which would explain the various existing exceptions to the hearsay rule and to generate a principled approach to the creation of new exceptions. Having eliminated from the hearsay category admissions and former testimony, he finds first, that with each of the other exceptions there are circumstances surrounding the making of the statement which guarantee its trustworthiness and so dispense with the need for an oath and cross-examination, and second, that some grounds of necessity exist resident in the unavailability of the declarant or the inconvenience in requiring his attendance.[78] But his teacher, Professor Thayer, in his historical researches, suggests no single theory to explain the various exceptions. He notes[79] rather, that along with the development of the hearsay rule in the late 17th century:

---

77.   5 Wigmore, *Evidence* (Chad. Rev.), s. 1420.
78.   See the criticism by Morgan that if this demonstration of the law of hearsay seems rational and consistent, it is only a "seeming", and that Wigmore's theory has sadly encouraged piecemeal rather than fundamental reform: *Some Problems of Proof under the Anglo-American System of Litigation* (1956), Columbia University Press, pp. 167-68.
79.   *Preliminary Treatise on Evidence* (1898), pp. 519-22.

There came a large and miscellaneous number of so-called "exceptions." Some of these, in reality, were quite independent rules, whose operation was rather that of qualifications and abatements to the generality of this other doctrine; rules which were coeval with the doctrine itself or much older. . . . a number of the so-called "exceptions" to the hearsay prohibition came in under the head of written entries or declarations; they came in, or rather, so to speak, stayed in, simply because they had always been received, and no rule against hearsay had ever been formulated or interpreted as applying to them. Such things, continuing at the present day, are, e.g., the admission of old entries and writings in proof of ancient matters, written declarations of deceased persons against interest, and in the course of duty or business; and, to a limited extent, a merchant's own account books to prove his own case. So also of regular entries in public books, a matter probably never even doubted to be admissible in evidence.

As Professors Morgan and Maguire later noted:

There is in truth no one theory which will account for the decisions. Sometimes an historical accident is the explanation; in some instances sheer need for the evidence overrides the court's distrust for the jury; in others only the adversary notion of litigation can account for the reception; and in still others either the absence of a motive to falsify, or a positive urge to tell the truth as the declarant believes it to be, can be found to justify admissibility. Within a single exception are found refinements and qualifications inconsistent with the reason upon which the exception itself is built. In short, a picture of the hearsay rule with its exceptions would resemble an old-fashioned crazy quilt made of patches cut from a group of paintings by cubists, futurists and surrealists.[80]

Nevertheless, Professor Wigmore's justification of the exceptions has become accepted by many as a useful tool for evaluating the creation of new exceptions.[81] The exact number of existing exceptions is unclear and the subject of some debate in the writings. Clearly all are not of equal importance and it is sufficient if the student is simply generally aware of their existence; those exceptions which regularly occur will need some exploration.

(a) Admissions

(i) Generally

The orthodox view is to treat admissions as an exception to the hearsay rule although they do not share the normal attributes, necessity and circumstantial guarantees of trustworthiness, possessed by the others. This fact has led some to suggest that, though admissible, they would be better characterized as non-hearsay.[82] An admission is, very simply, a statement made by a party tendered by the opposing party; the plaintiff or defendant in civil cases and the accused in a criminal case.

---

80. "Looking Backward and Forward at Evidence" (1937), 50 Harv. L. Rev. 909 at 921.
81. See, *e.g., Ares v. Venner*, [1970] S.C.R. 608 and s. 45(3) of the Uniform Evidence Bill.
82. See Federal Rules of Evidence, Rule 801, 28 U.S.C.A. and Advisory Committee Note; see also McCormick, *supra*, note 18 at p. 629; 4 Wigmore, *Evidence* (Chad. Rev.), s. 1048; and Strahorn, "A Reconsideration of the Hearsay Rule and Admissions" (1937), 85 U. Pa. L. Rev. 564.

A number of theories have been suggested to justify the reception of admissions.[83] For this exception only, grounds of necessity obviously do not exist and trustworthiness is not always present, as there is no requirement that the declarant have personal first-hand knowledge.[84] An example of the difference in approach may be seen in the case of *R. v. Peacock*.[85] It is usually accepted that a witness is not permitted to testify to his own age since his knowledge in that regard must clearly be founded on what someone else has told him, i.e., it is hearsay.[86] In *Peacock*, however, it was allowed that a police constable might relate the accused's *extra-judicial statement* of his own age, as such was an admission.

The various theories advanced to justify reception are grounded in ideas of fairness, responsibility and the adversarial nature of our system. Professor Morgan has offered:

> The admissibility of an admission made by the party himself rests not upon any notion that the circumstances in which it was made furnish the trier means of evaluating it fairly, but upon the adversary theory of litigation. A party can hardly object that he had no opportunity to cross-examine himself or that he is unworthy of credence save when speaking under sanction of an oath.[87]

And Professor Maguire:

> Your own words or other actions have turned out helpful to your adversary; because you are their author, evidence of them is admissible against you.[88]

And finally Chafee:

> What is said by a party or a person closely linked with him in respect to the transaction at issue is considered of such especial value that the usual rules are simply disregarded. This attitude is easier to grasp when we remember that a trial is not an abstract search for truth, but an attempt to settle a controversy between two persons without physical conflict.[89]

---

83. See their examination in Pickard, "Statements of Parties" (1978), 41 Mod. L. Rev. 124 together with his own suggested theory.
84. See *Stowe v. Grand Trunk Pacific Railway* (1918), 39 D.L.R. 127 (Alta. C.A.); affirmed 59 S.C.R. 665; *R. v. Schmidt*, [1948] S.C.R. 333; *R. v. Turner* (1910), 3 Cr. App. R. 103, 161; but see *R. v. Marshall*, [1977] Crim. L.R. 106. Compare *Bird v. Adams*, [1972] Crim. L.R. 174 (Div. Ct.) and *R. v. Chatwood*, [1980] Crim. L.R. 46 (C.C.A.). See discussion in Cross, *Evidence*, 5th ed., p. 521. But see *R. v. Rydzanicz* (1979), 13 C.R. (3d) 190 (Ont. C.A.); *R. v. O'Neill* (1976), 31 C.C.C. (2d) 259 (Ont. C.A.). There appears to be a requirement that when the admission is not based on first-hand knowledge the party-opponent must have expressed his belief in the same: see Phipson, *Evidence*, 12th ed., p. 683 and Cross, *Evidence*, 5th ed., p. 522.
85. (1968), 3 C.R.N.S. 103 (Ont. Co. Ct.).
86. See, *e.g.*, *Anthony v. Charter*, [1933] 1 D.L.R. 684 (Alta. C.A.). But compare the enlightened judgment of *R. v. Lachappelle* (1977), 38 C.C.C. (2d) 369 (Que. C.A.). And see the statutory provision in s. 658(2) of the *Criminal Code*.
87. Morgan, *Basic Problems of Evidence* (1962), p. 266.
88. Maguire, *Evidence, Common Sense and Common Law* (1947), p. 143.
89. "Review of Wigmore on Evidence" (1924), 37 Harv. L. Rev. 513 at 519.

General Rule #1

In all fairness, if the adversary chooses to introduce a statement by the party-opponent he must introduce all of the statement and not just the portion which favours him. As noted in *Capital Trust Co. v. Fowler:* [90]

> The law seems quite settled that, if an admission is used by one party, it must be used in its entirety, that is, everything must be read that is necessary to the understanding and appreciation of the meaning and extent of the admission. It is also equally established that, if a party uses an admission, he makes it evidence in the cause both as to himself and as to the opposition party in the litigation as well; but, if he desires to contradict or qualify any statement in it, he may do so. He can therefore give other evidence so to contradict or qualify it, but, if he does not see fit to do so, the whole of the admission remains as evidence in the cause for the benefit of both parties.

While a party may have the right to insist that his adversary introduce the entirety of a single narrative, this governing principle does not, of course, demand that adversary must introduce all statements or none. As Kaufman, J. said:

> A word of warning may be in order. The fact that the prosecution is obliged, where it chooses to offer in evidence a declaration made by the accused, to introduce the whole, and not just parts, does not mean that an accused can create self-serving evidence by writing out a statement and handing it to the police.[91]

R. v. PHILLIPS
[1995] O.J. No. 2985 (Ont. Gen. Div.)

MCISAAC J.:—

The accused, Lenard Roy Phillips, is charged with the murder of Provincial Constable Eric Nystedt as a result of a stabbing incident which took place in the early morning hours of July 3, 1993 in a relatively isolated cottage area near Furnace Falls, in the County of Haliburton. Mr. Phillips fled the scene and was not arrested until noon of the same day. At that time, he was located hiding in a ditch off Highway #503 several kilometres from the scene of the stabbing. The arresting officers, P.C. DeVoss and P.C. McMaster initially advised him at gunpoint that he was being arrested for stabbing a peace officer. That advice was shortly changed to include the killing of an officer. His response at that time was "I guess I really did it this time." He was immediately advised of his rights to counsel and he received the standard primary and secondary cautions. The defence waives the voluntariness of these statements.

When he was placed into the police cruiser, he asked the arresting officers "So who's the guy I murdered?" P.C. McMaster advised him that he should not say anything further when he said "Can I ask another question?" He did not speak further to these officers other than advising them that he wished to call his mother once they arrived at the Coboconk O.P.P. detachment at 12:34 p.m. At that time, he was asked if he wanted to call a lawyer. That led to his speaking to counsel before he was turned over to the investigating officers at 1:16 p.m. During that interview which lasted until 2:55 p.m., Mr. Phillips advanced several theories that either justified his actions by way of mistaken self-defence or partially excused his actions due to the consumption of alcohol or drugs. He claimed amnesia for the stabbing of P.C. Nystedt, but admitted taking a swing at "someone."

---

90.   (1921), 64 D.L.R. 289, 292 (Ont. C.A.).
91.   Kaufman, *The Admissibility of Confessions* (1979), p. 287. See the adoption of this caution in *R. v. Jackson* (1980), 57 C.C.C. (2d) 154 (Ont. C.A.).

— D argues entire "one statement"

Counsel for Mr. Phillips submits that the utterances shortly after noon and the answers given in the interview that took place between 1:16 p.m. and 2:55 p.m. constitute one entire statement and if the former part goes before the jury then they must hear the second part as well. On the other hand, the Crown suggests that the doctrine of severability applies and the second interview should be excluded on the principle that it is self-serving and is in no way explanatory of the statements made to the arresting officers.

In *Wigmore on Evidence* (Chadbourn Rev.), v. VII, at p. 670, the following comments from *Steward v. Sherman* 5 Conn. 244, 245 (1824) are presented as authoritative on the issue:

> The past and future cannot thus be brought together in order to form an artificial identity. The law never intends that a party may make evidence for himself from his own declarations, but merely that the meaning of a conversation shall not be perverted by proof of a part of it only.

My review of the Canadian jurisprudence with these observations of Hosmer, C.J. As one can easily see, the opportunity for reflection militates against the admissibility of such self-serving evidence.

. . . .

one half — not just statement self-serving

In this case, the statement by the accused to the investigating officers took place at least one hour after his initial contact with the arresting officers. In fact, the recorded interview did not begin until 1:33 p.m. It is clear that not only was Mr. Phillips speaking to completely different police personnel, but he had also had ample time for reflection on what he was going to say. Most importantly, he had had the benefit of legal advice in the interim. In my opinion, this is sufficient in itself to destroy any nexus between the two statements. I am not satisfied that anything said to P.C. Harvey and P.C. Bowen was an "amplification, qualification or explanation" of what he had said to P.C. DeVoss and P.C. McMaster at the time of his arrest.

R. v. FERRIS
(1994), 27 C.R. (4th) 141 (Alta. C.A.)

[The accused was charged with murder. The accused had reported the death of P. by telephone to the City Police on the morning of October 22, 1989. When the police responded to P.'s apartment, they found the accused beside P.'s dead body. He was spotted with the deceased's blood. The cause of death was ten stab wounds. He had not been robbed. The suite had not been forcibly entered but there was clear evidence of a violent struggle having taken place within it. The accused and P. had earlier shared the apartment. They fell out and separated under circumstances where P. had occasion to express concern for his own safety. The accused had left the apartment and taken a hotel room while P. had remained. An intense and angry conversation between them in a bar had been witnessed the previous evening. A neighbour testified that she had been awakened on the morning of October 22 by the sound of a thud and P. exclaiming in a loud voice, described as commanding, fearful and surprised, "Michael". Michael was the accused's name.

After being taken into police custody the accused was advised of his right to silence and his right to counsel. The accused asked to make a phone call to his father. The officer heard the accused say the words "I've been arrested" and later the words "I killed David." He testified that he couldn't hear what else was being said. He heard conversation before, after, and in between the two sets of words he heard, but could not hear what was said. No argument was advanced respecting any right to privacy that the accused might have while in the process of contacting someone following receipt of advice of his right to counsel.

A voir dire was held to determine the admissibility of the accused's statements. The trial judge ruled the statements were voluntary and admissible. The accused was convicted and appealed.]

CONRAD J.A. (PICARD J. concurring):—

. . . .

The facts of this case are unique in that there exist no circumstances or context from which the true meaning of the words can be inferred. It is uncontradicted that the words were part of an utterance only, and that other words passed both before and after those words. It is uncontradicted that the words could have come at the beginning of a sentence or at the end of a sentence. In fact, the words may have been a part of a question such as "You don't think I killed David?" or a statement such as "They think I killed David" or "They think I killed David but I didn't". His father could have asked him what the police think he did and he could have replied "I killed David". Those utterances do not prove any fact in issue and are not an admission of guilt. Indeed, on the basis of the uncontradicted evidence, the possibility of statements with the words ". . . I killed David . . ." contained therein are numerous. There is no way of determining the meaning or thought to be attributed to the words. A trial judge could not ascertain, nor could the jury, the meaning of the words. . . . Without meaning being ascertainable the words are not relevant to any fact in issue and they have no probative value.

. . . .

Where one party seeks to tender an admission of the other party into evidence, he must introduce all of the statement and not just the portion which favours the party tendering. [See] *Capital Trust Corp. v. Fowler.*

. . . .

There is a real prejudice of forbidden reasoning here. There would be an enormous temptation for any trier of fact to look at the outside evidence that tends to implicate the accused in the murder, use those facts to conclude that the accused probably committed the murder, and that therefore he admitted that he did. That finding would then be used to raise the probability of guilt to a conclusion of guilt. The danger implicit in that type of circuitous reasoning is obvious.

. . . .

Moreover, and while not strictly speaking necessary, I am of the view that whether one approaches the question of hearsay admissibility using the traditional categories approach or using a principled approach (per *R. v. Khan* and *R. v. Smith* . . .) the statement in question cannot be admitted.

Under the categorical approach, the applicable exception would be the exception for admissions. Thus as it cannot be found to be an admission it could not be admissible under this approach.

Nor in my view would the words in question fall under the principled approach to the admissibility of hearsay as outlined in the recent Supreme Court of Canada decision *R. v. Smith*, ibid., interpreting *R. v. Khan*, supra. The new rule allows for the reception of hearsay evidence where it is both reliable and necessary and subject to the residual discretion of the trial judge to exclude the evidence when its probative value is slight and undue prejudice might result to the accused. . . . It would be impossible to say that the conditions under which the utterance was made in this case affords a greater circumstantial guarantee of trustworthiness than the conditions in *Smith*. The fact that no meaning can reasonably be attributed to the utterance makes it impossible to attach the label of reliability to the words in question here. . . .

Clearly, this evidence was not necessary as it was open to the Crown to call the accused's father for a more accurate account of what was said in that telephone conversation. Instead the Crown has relied on the eavesdropping of Sergeant Schmidt who was not a party to the conversation and by his own admission could hear only a portion of it.

McCLUNG J.A. (dissenting):—

. . . .

In my view, the admission of this statement after voir dire complied with established Canadian criminal trial practice. Putting aside the fact that it was not the traditional admission or confession made to a person in authority, the holding of a voir dire was occasioned to determine if the words, while incomplete, were uttered by the accused, were voluntary and were probative of the facts in issue. The facts in issue, indeed the ultimate issues, were who killed David Parker and under what intention. In the circumstances of David Parker's unexplained death, it is untenable that a voluntary statement which included the words "I killed David" was not relevant and probative.

. . . .

The appellant is not assisted by *Capital Trust Corp. v. Fowler* . . . , a case reaffirming the practice surrounding the use of explanatory evidence in civil cases, where admissions, in that case by interrogatories, were put in. The rule has never been extended to a requirement that the party who tenders the admission is obliged to supplement it by adding evidence that is not, and never was, in his possession, failing which he will lose his proof.

The appellant, had he elected to testify on either the voir dire or on the general issue, could have supplied the remainder of the statement. Had he not wished to testify yet wished to lead evidence of explanatory features of the conversation, he was free to call as a witness the recipient of his telephone call without going into the box himself. In either way the integrity of the statement "I killed David" could have been challenged, modified or confirmed. Indisputably Ferris was free to remain silent during all stages of his trial but that course was not without risk. He chose to remain silent thereby leaving the jury to draw on its own common sense, collective intelligence and the weight of the other Crown evidence in assessing the evidentiary value of the admission. But that — deciding weight — was its role.

. . . .

It is now suggested that the Crown had a legal obligation to call the recipient of Ferris' telephone call before leading evidence of any part of it. In my view this is a new predicate. On purely legal considerations, there is no oblique motive alleged, and none proven, in the Crown's choice of witnesses to prove the fact. On purely practical consideration, it might be remembered that fathers rarely cooperate with the Crown when murder prosecutions are advanced against their sons.

———————

The statement made or adopted by the party is admissible against that party, and in a joint trial an admission is only evidence against the party who made it and the trier of fact must be warned of its limited utility.[92] There remains a large danger that the jury will not follow the limiting instruction when the confession of the co-accused implicates the other. Indeed the limiting instruction has been

———————

92. It is "an advisable practice" that the jury be immediately warned when a confession is received in a joint trial that it is not evidence against a co-accused: see *Schmidt v. R.*, [1945] S.C.R. 438; *Chote v. Rowan*, [1943] O.W.N. 646 (C.A.).

referred to as a "placebo," a "medicinal lie," "a kind of judicial lie,"[93] as it is practically impossible to follow.[94]

The underlying philosophy of admissions which makes admissions only evidence against their makers produces at times "curious, but perfectly logical"[95] results. An admission by the correspondent of adultery with respondent wife is evidence only against him:

> I am obliged to find . . . that there was no evidence that the wife has committed adultery with this co-respondent, but there is evidence that the co-respondent has committed adultery with the wife. It is perfectly logical; that decision means not that what is in effect the same act was committed by the one person but was not committed by the other, it means that it is proved against the one but it is not proved against the other. That is the basis on which the law is administered; cases are decided upon proof and not upon suspicion and hearsay evidence.[96]

Rule #3

In some of the cases we will see this exception characterized as "an admission against interest." This phrasing is confusing as there is no requirement that the statement be "against interest" when made,[97] and with respect to it being "against interest" when tendered, Professor Wigmore has noted:

> . . . in effect and broadly, *anything said by the party-opponent may be used against him as an admission*, provided it exhibits the quality of inconsistency with the facts now asserted by him in pleadings or in testimony. (This proviso never needs to be enforced, because no party offers thus his opponent's statement unless it does appear to be inconsistent.) [Emphasis added.][98]

---

93. Remarks attributed to Learned Hand, J. and Jerome Frank, J. in *Bruton v. U.S.*, 391 U.S. 123 (1968); in that case the U.S. Supreme Court held that a limiting instruction was not sufficient in such a case as the accused was denied his Sixth Amendment right to confront witnesses. It appears, then, that in the U.S. the prosecutor must proceed in separate trials or not tender the confession. It is interesting to note another solution which appears to have been the law in England until 1830: see *R. v. Hearne* (1830), 172 E.R. 676 and *R. v. Clewes* (1830), 172 E.R. 678. In a reporter's note to the latter case we read: "The practice has been, in reading confessions, to omit the names of other accused parties, and where they are used to say 'another person' 'a third person' & etc." In the above two cases Littledale, J. ordered the witnesses to use the names mentioned in the confession of the co-accused as it was seen necessary that the whole be repeated; he later noted that he would "take care to make such observations to the Jury, as will prevent its having any injurious effect against the other prisoners; and I shall tell the jury that they ought not to pay the slightest attention to this letter, except so far as it goes to affect the person who wrote it." *R. v. Fletcher* (1830), 172 E.R. 691.

94. An infrequent but allied problem concerns the use of one accused's pleas of guilty against his co-accused. See *R. v. Lessard* (1979), 50 C.C.C. (2d) 175 (Que. C.A.) and compare *R. v. Vinette* (1974), 19 C.C.C. (2d) 1 (S.C.C.).

95. *Morton v. Morton*, [1937] P. 151, 153.

96. *Ibid.* at 154-55. See also for a similar result *Harris v. Harris*, [1931] 4 D.L.R. 933 (Ont. S.C.).

97. See, *e.g.*, *R. v. Mandzuk* (1945), 85 C.C.C. 158 (B.C.C.A.); but see also *Piche v. R.*, [1970] 4 C.C.C. 27 (S.C.C.). Admissions by accused in criminal prosecutions must also be established as "voluntary", and this aspect will be considered later. Note however that the statement is receivable, as an exception to the hearsay rule, as an admission, though it was exculpatory in nature when made. And see Phipson, *Evidence* (11th ed.), p. 673.

98. 4 Wigmore, *Evidence* (Chad. Rev.), s. 1048(1)(b).

R. v. STREU
[1989] 1 S.C.R. 1521, 70 C.R. (3d) 1, 48 C.C.C. (3d) 321

[The accused was convicted of possession of stolen property having a value in excess of $200. He sold the property to a police officer, who had posed as a purchaser, for $125. The officer testified that the accused, during conversation leading to the sale, had admitted that the tires and rims belonged to a friend who had "ripped them off." In the absence of the accused's statement there would not be evidence, sufficient to meet the criminal standard of proof, that the items were in fact stolen.]

SOPINKA J.: —

. . . .

The evidence at trial indicated that the appellant attempted to sell four tires and rims to a police officer who posed as a purchaser. The police officer testified to the following conversation with the appellant:

I ask him, referring to the wheels: What are these off of? And he replies: A Volkswagen Rabbit. And I ask: Oh, yeah. From the City here? And he replies: I don't know. My friend ripped them off. I ask: Well, where's the other ones? Harv replies: They're in my house. I reply: Oh, I see. Well, I'll give you twenty bucks apiece. And he replies: I can't let them go for that, they are my friend's wheels. I ask: How much did he want. And Harv replies: He priced them out at one hundred and thirty apiece. That's for the rims. I reply: I'm not paying that much. Just yesterday I bought a 1984 Datsun for $180.

. . . .

Harv replies: Well, I know they're hot and all but they're his tires. I reply: Let me talk to your friend then. Harv replies: I know he'll be mad at me if I only get that much.

The appellant and the police officer proceeded to a garage at the end of a lane near the appellant's home to complete the sale. The appellant expressed concern that they not be observed. The police officer further testified that he paid the appellant $125 for the tires and rims.

. . . .

In *R. v. O'Neill* (1976), 13 C.R. (3d) 193 (Ont. C.A.), the only evidence against the accused regarding the theft of a stereo and turntable — the subjects of the charge against her of unlawful possession — was her statement to the police. In response to the question of whether she knew that the items were stolen the accused replied "yes". She then added that she had been given the items by a male friend.

The Court of Appeal followed *R. v. Porter*, [1976] Crim. L.R. 58, in finding that the hearsay statement of the accused was not proof that the items were stolen. The Court, at p.194, cited the editorial commentary following *R. v. Porter* with approval:

It is one thing for the accused to admit facts of which he has personal knowledge, and for an inference to be drawn from those facts that the goods are stolen. It is another thing for the accused to 'admit' facts of which he has no personal knowledge.

In *R. v. Rydzanicz* (1979), 13 C.R. (3d) 190 (Ont. C.A.), the accused was charged with having in his possession a quantity of stolen cigarettes. The accused stated to the police that he saw his friend Mike enter the shopping centre and come out with a whole shopping cart full of cartons of cigarettes. The accused added that he helped Mike put the cigarettes in the back of the truck. The accused also stated that he knew that the cigarettes were stolen when he saw Mike come out of the shopping centre.

The accused was acquitted at trial on the strength of *R. v. O'Neill, supra.* The Court of Appeal overturned the acquittal because the trial judge had overlooked the fact that the accused stated that he saw Mike go into the store and come out with a shopping cart full of cigarettes. The Court of Appeal, at p. 192, held that:

> That admission was based on the personal knowledge of the respondent, and constituted evidence of relevant fact in a chain of circumstances in support of an inference that the cigarettes were stolen.

Aside from the accused's stated belief, sufficient circumstantial evidence existed to support a finding that the goods were stolen. The Court of Appeal added that it is a question of fact whether the inference that the goods were stolen should be drawn by the trier of fact.

In *R. v. Elliott* (1984), 15 C.C.C. (3d) 195 (Alta. C.A.), the accused was charged with possession of certain roof panels, the property of person or persons unknown, knowing them to "have been obtained by the commission in Canada of theft" contrary to s. 312 of the *Criminal Code.* The items involved were worth approximately $1,300 although the accused testified that he paid $150 for them, having purchased them from an unknown person in a bar. He did not receive a sales slip for the goods and the police testified that the accused told them that because of the low price he paid he realized they were "hot". There was no evidence as to where the goods had been obtained or who their owner was. On appeal by the accused from his conviction, the appeal was allowed and an acquittal entered.

The majority held that it was clear that the element of theft can be proved by circumstantial evidence. In this case, the circumstantial evidence was not strong enough to support the inference that the goods were stolen:

> Here the only evidence of theft is proof of purchase for far below value, at a bar, from a stranger, without a bill of sale. Certainly, this gives rise to the suspicion that the goods which are being sold were stolen. Certainly in a civil case a court could prove on a balance of probabilities that a theft had occurred but I am of the opinion that proof of theft beyond all reasonable doubt has not been established by these facts alone. There has to be more. [p. 201]

. . . .

Although they do not always make it clear, some of these authorities deal with the question relating to the use to be made of an admission based on hearsay as a matter of weight, and others, as a matter of admissibility. In deciding which position is correct, account must be taken of the decision of this Court in *R. v. Schmidt,* [1948] S.C.R. 333, a case that apparently was not drawn to the attention of the Court of Appeal and is not referred to in the factum of either party in this Court. . . .

. . . .

The rationale underlying the exclusion of hearsay evidence is primarily the inherent untrustworthiness of an extra-judicial statement which has been tendered without affording an opportunity to the party against whom it is adduced to cross-examine the declarant. This rationale applies equally in both criminal and civil cases. It loses its force when the party has chosen to rely on the hearsay statement in making an admission. Presumably in so doing, the party making the admission has satisfied himself or herself as to the reliability of the statement or at least had the opportunity to do so. The significance of this factor is evident in the decision of this Court in *Ares v. Venner,* [1970] S.C.R. 608, in which evidence was admitted as an exception to the hearsay rule where the party against whom the evidence was tendered had the opportunity to test the accuracy of the evidence.

I agree with the following statement in *Kitchen v. Robbins*, 29 Ga. 713 (1860), cited by 4 *Wigmore, Evidence*, s. 1053 (Chadbourn rev. 1972) for which I am indebted to McWilliams, *Canadian Criminal Evidence* (2nd ed. 1984), at p. 428:

> Are no admissions good against a party, unless founded on his personal knowledge? The admissions would not be made except on evidence which satisfies the party who is making them against his own interest, that they are true, and that is evidence to the jury that they are true.

Accordingly, once it is established that the admission was in fact made, there is no reason in principle for treating it any differently than the same statement would be treated had it been made in the witness box. In the latter case, if a party indicates a belief in or acceptance of a hearsay statement, that is some evidence of the truth of its contents. The weight to be given to that evidence is for the trier of fact. On the other hand, if the party simply reports a hearsay statement without either adopting it or indicating a belief in the truth of its contents, the statement is not admissible as proof of the truth of the contents.

. . . .

Turning to the admission in question in this appeal, it is impossible to read it as merely reporting a hearsay statement without more. Clearly the appellant was relying on the hearsay statement as being true. Either he accepted it as being true or at least believed it to be true.

. . . Any evidentiary weakness in the information on which the admission was based was a matter of weight and not admissibility. This was a matter for the trial judge who considered the statement along with other evidence and concluded that the accused was guilty beyond a reasonable doubt.

Appeal dismissed.

(ii) *Confessions*

In the middle of the 16th century, statutes were enacted[99] requiring justices of the peace to take dispositions from all witnesses to felony, including the accused. The results of the inquisitorial examination of the accused were transmitted to the judge, and his deposition was read to the jury at the outset of the trial. At the trial as well the accused was frequently questioned by the judge. The practice of questioning an accused at trial diminished during the 17th century, and questioning pre-trial diminished during the 18th century. By 1700 questioning at trial had ceased and by the early 19th century the pre-trial examination by the justices was limited to the recording of any statements which the accused volunteered. This new practice of preliminary examination was embodied in statute form in 1848,[100] giving us the form of preliminary inquiry now provided for by the Canadian Criminal Code:

> Having heard the evidence, do you wish to say anything in answer to the charge? You are not bound to say anything, but whatever you do say will be taken down in writing and may be given in evidence against you at your trial. You must clearly understand that you have nothing to hope from any promise of favour and nothing

---

99. (1554), 1 & 2 Phil. & Mar., c. 13, s. 4; (1555), 2 & 3 Phil. & Mar., c. 10, s. 2. See 1 Stephen, *History of The Criminal Law of England* (1883), 237-38; and 4 Holdsworth, *History of the English Law*, 3d. ed. (1945), 529.
100. Jervis's Act, 11 & 12 Vict., c. 42. See now Criminal Code, s. 541.

to fear from any threat that may have been held out to you to induce you to make any admission or confession of guilt, but whatever you now say may be given in evidence against you at your trial notwithstanding the promise or threat.

Two reasons appear to account for the fall-off of judicial questioning. First, the development and growth of professional police lessened the need for an investigative role by the judicial officers,[101] and, second, the growth of the concept known as the privilege against self-incrimination.

Statements of accused obtained by police interrogation were freely admissible at trial as the admissions of a party. Until the late 18th century there does not appear to be any judicial rule foreclosing their receipt.[102] The courts, however, perhaps mindful of the conclusive nature of these admissions and the heavy consequences of a finding of guilt, erected a barrier to their reception, and demanded that admissions of accused persons have an additional assurance of trustworthiness: to be receivable in a criminal prosecution a confession had to be proved voluntary. In 1783 in *R. v. Warickshall*,[103] the accused was charged with possession of stolen goods. She had made a full confession of her guilt, and as a result the goods were found under her bed. The confession had been obtained by promises of favour and the court refused to admit it. Her counsel then argued

> that as the fact of finding the stolen property in her custody had been obtained through the means of an inadmissible confession, the proof of that fact ought also to be rejected; for otherwise the faith which the prosecutor had pledged would be violated, and the prisoner made the deluded instrument of her own conviction.[104]

But the court held:

> It is a mistaken notion, that the evidence of confessions and facts which have been obtained from prisoners by promises or threats, is to be rejected from a regard to public faith: no such rule ever prevailed. The idea is novel in theory, and would be as dangerous in practice as it is repugnant to the general principles of criminal law. Confessions are received in evidence, or rejected as inadmissible, under a consideration whether they are or are not entitled to credit. A free and voluntary confession is deserving of the highest credit, because it is presumed to flow from the strongest sense of guilt, and therefore it is admitted as proof of the crime to which it refers; but a confession forced from the mind by the flattery of hope, or by the torture of fear, comes in so questionable a shape when it is to be considered as the evidence of guilt, that no credit ought to be given to it; and therefore it is rejected. This principle respecting confessions has no application whatever as to the admission or rejection of facts, whether the knowledge of them be obtained in consequence of an extorted confession, or whether it arises from any other source; for a fact, if it exist at all, must exist invariably in the same manner, whether the confession from which it is derived be in other respects true or false. Facts thus obtained, however, must be fully and satisfactorily proved, without calling in the aid of any part of the confession from which they may have been derived; and the impossibility of admitting any part of the confession as a proof of the fact, clearly shews that the fact may be admitted on other evidence; for as no part of an improper confession can be heard,

---

101. See 1 Stephen, *History of Criminal Law, supra*, note 99, at pp. 194-200.
102. See generally regarding the history of confessions, 3 Wigmore, *Evidence* (Chad. Rev.), s. 817.
103. 168 E.R. 234 (Crown Cases).
104. *Ibid.*, at p. 234.

it can never be legally known whether the fact was derived through the means of such confession or not.[105]

During the 19th century, the judicial attitude toward confessions hardened and a great prejudice against them led to the general exclusion of confessions whenever the slightest hope of advantage or fear of prejudice had been held out. For example, in *R. v. Drew*,[106] it was held to be an inducement, rendering the confession inadmissible, to advise the accused:

... not to say anything to prejudice himself, as what he said I should take down, and it would be used for him or against him at his trial,

as, per Coleridge, J.:

I cannot conceive a more direct inducement to a man to make a confession, than telling him that what he says may be used in his favour at the trial.

A few years later in *R. v. Harris*,[107] the accused is advised

that whatever he said would be ... used against him,

but the confession was rejected, as, per Maule, J.:

The prisoner was told that *whatever* he said would be taken down and used against him. I cannot say that that did not induce him to say something which he thought might be favourable to him.

The courts began to develop an attitude that *all* police questioning of accused persons, after they had been taken into custody, was wrong. In *R. v. Mick*,[108] Mellor, J. grudgingly received the accused's statement, given following a proper caution, but admonished the police superintendent:

I think the course you pursued in questioning the prisoner was exceedingly improper. I have considered the matter very much: many Judges would not receive such evidence. The law does not intend you, as a policeman, to investigate cases in that way. I entirely disapprove of the system of police officers examining prisoners. The law has surrounded prisoners with great precautions to prevent confessions being extorted from them, and the magistrates are not allowed to question prisoners, or to ask them what they have to say; and it is not for policemen to do these things. It is assuming the functions of the magistrate without those precautions which the magistrates are required by the law to use, and assuming functions which are entrusted to the magistrates and to them only. The evidence is admissible, but I entirely disapprove of this way of obtaining it.

In *R. v. Gavin*,[109] Smith, J. prevented the receipt of one accused's statement against other accused with the statement:

When a prisoner is in custody the police have no right to ask him questions. ... A prisoner's mouth is closed after he is once given in charge, and he ought not to be asked anything.

---

105. *Ibid.*, at pp. 234-35.
106. (1837), 173 E.R. 433 (N.P.).
107. (1844), 1 Cox C.C. 106, and see *R. v. Furley* (1844), 1 Cox C.C. 76. But, *contra*, see *R. v. Baldry* (1852), 169 E.R. 568 (C.A.).
108. (1863), 176 E.R. 376.
109. (1885), 15 Cox C.C. 656.

The early English decisions were very protective towards the accused, and Lord Hailsham, discussing the confession rule, explained:

> By the judiciary, though it ought not to be extended, it must by no means be whittled down. It bears, it is true, all the marks of its origin at a time when the savage code of the eighteenth century was in full force. At that time almost every serious crime was punishable by death or transportation. The law enforcement officers formed no disciplined police force and were not subject to effective control by the central government, watch committees or an inspectorate. There was no legal aid. There was no system of appeal. To crown it all the accused was unable to give evidence on his own behalf and was therefore largely at the mercy of any evidence, either perjured or oppressively obtained, that might be brought against him. The judiciary were therefore compelled to devise artificial rules designed to protect him against dangers now avoided by other and more rational means. Nevertheless, the rule has survived into the twentieth century, not only unmodified but developed, and only Parliament can modify it now from the form in which it was given classical expression by Lord Sumner.

The early English decisions in the 19th century were by no means unanimous, however,[110] and the courts appear uncertain as to whether the exclusion of confessions is based solely on considerations of reliability, or whether there is an ability to exclude when the questioning is viewed as improper because of a perceived conflict with the accused's privilege against self-incrimination. As late as 1914 in *Ibrahim v. R.*,[111] we see the House of Lords still struggling with the question. The accused in that case, a soldier in the Indian army, was charged with murder. Evidence was admitted at his trial that within 10 or 15 minutes of the murder, the accused being in custody of the guard, was addressed by his commanding officer: "Why have you done such a senseless act?" to which the accused replied "some three or four days he had been abusing me; without a doubt I killed him." Lord Sumner recognized the oft-quoted classic formula:

> It has long been established as a positive rule of English criminal law, that no statement by an accused is admissible in evidence against him unless it is shewn by the prosecution to have been a voluntary statement, in the sense that it has not been obtained from him either by fear of prejudice or hope of advantage exercised or held out by a person in authority. The principle is as old as Lord Hale.[112]

He noted that it was common ground between the parties that in the circumstances receipt of the statement did not breach the rule, but felt it necessary to consider the objection that receipt was foreclosed simply because the prisoner's answer was preceded by and made in answer to a question, and that the question was put by a person in authority and the answer given by a man in his custody. Lord Sumner reviewed the authorities and concluded:

> The English law is still unsettled, strange as it may seem, since the point is one that constantly occurs in criminal trials. Many judges, in their discretion, exclude such

---

110. See, *e.g.*, Parke, B. in *R. v. Baldry* (1852), *supra*, note 107, at p. 574: ". . . I think there has been too much tenderness towards prisoners in this matter. I confess that I cannot look at the decisions without some shame when I consider what objections have prevailed to prevent the reception of confessions in evidence."

111. [1914] A.C. 599 (P.C.).

112. *Ibid.*, at p. 609. This formula, accepted as gospel in Canada today, was first accepted by our courts as "correctly stating the rule" in *Prosko v. R.* (1922), 63 S.C.R. 226.

evidence, for they fear that nothing less than the exclusion of all such statements can prevent improper questioning of prisoners by removing the inducement to resort to it. This consideration does not arise in the present case. Others, less tender to the prisoner or more mindful of the balance of decided authority, would admit such statements, nor would the Court of Criminal Appeal quash the conviction thereafter obtained, if no substantial miscarriage of justice had occurred. If, then, a learned judge, after anxious consideration of the authorities, decides in accordance with what is at any rate a "probable opinion" of the present law, if it is not actually the better opinion, it appears to their Lordships that his conduct is the very reverse of that "violation of the principles of natural justice" which has been said to be the ground for advising His Majesty's interference in a criminal matter. If, as appears even on the line of authorities which the trial judge did not follow, the matter is one for the judge's discretion, depending largely on his view of the impropriety of the questioner's conduct and the general circumstances of the case, their Lordships think, as will hereafter be seen, that in the circumstances of this case his discretion is not shewn to have been exercised improperly.

Having regard to the particular position in which their Lordships stand to criminal proceedings, they do not propose to intimate what they think the rule of English law ought to be, much as it is to be desired that the point should be settled by authority, so far as a general rule can be laid down where circumstances must so greatly vary. That must be left to a Court which exercises, as their Lordships do not, the revising functions of a general Court of Criminal Appeal.[113]

In 1966 in *Commissioners of Customs v. Harz*,[114] Lord Reid reviewed the authorities and concluded:

I do not think that it is possible to reconcile all the very numerous judicial statements on rejection of confessions but two lines of thought appear to underlie them: first, that a statement made in response to a threat or promise may be untrue or at least untrustworthy: and, secondly, that *nemo tenetur seipsum prodere*. It is true that many of the so-called inducements have been so vague that no reasonable man would have been influenced by them, but one must remember that not all accused are reasonable men or women: they may be very ignorant and terrified by the predicament in which they find themselves. So it may have been right to err on the safe side.

The question was squarely put to the Supreme Court of Canada in *R. v. Wray*.[115] The accused was charged with murder. The accused gave a statement to the police which ended as follows:

Q.   What happened to the gun?

A.   I threw it in the swamp.

Q.   Where?

A.   Near Omemee.

Q.   Will you try and show us the spot?

A.   Yes.

Q.   Is there anything else you wish to add to this John?

A.   Not now thank you.

The accused directed the police to the area where the rifle was found and ballistic evidence matched the bullet from the victim's body to the gun. After a lengthy

---

113. *Ibid.*, at p. 614.
114. [1967] 1 A.C. 760, 820 (H.L.).
115. (1970), 11 D.L.R. (3d) 673, 677 (S.C.C.).

voir dire the trial judge ruled the accused's statement was involuntary and hence legally inadmissible.[116] The prosecution then wished to introduce into evidence the accused's involvement in finding the murder weapon and relied on *R. v. St. Lawrence* where McRuer, C.J.H.C. had said:

> Where the discovery of the fact confirms the confession — that is, where the confession must be taken to be true by reason of the discovery of the fact — then that part of the confession that is confirmed by the discovery of the fact is admissible, but further than that no part of the confession is admissible.[117]

St. Lawrence Rule

The trial judge purported to exercise a discretion to disallow this evidence and directed a verdict of acquittal. The Ontario Court of Appeal, while recognizing the validity of the *St. Lawrence* rule, declined to disturb his decision, saying:

> In our view, a trial Judge has a discretion to reject evidence, even of substantial weight, if he considers that its admission would be unjust or unfair to the accused or calculated to bring the administration of justice into disrepute, the exercise of such discretion, of course, to depend upon the particular facts before him. Cases where to admit certain evidence would be calculated to bring the administration of justice into disrepute will be rare, but we think the discretion of a trial Judge extends to such cases.[118]

The Supreme Court of Canada reversed and directed a new trial. Martland, J. reasoned:

> This development of the idea of a general discretion to exclude admissible evidence is not warranted by the authority on which it purports to be based. . . . the exercise of a discretion by the trial Judge arises only if the admission of the evidence would operate unfairly. The allowance of admissible evidence relevant to the issue before the Court and of substantial probative value may operate unfortunately for the accused, but not unfairly. It is only the allowance of evidence gravely prejudicial to the accused, the admissibility of which is tenuous, and whose probative force in relation to the main issue before the Court is trifling, which can be said to operate unfairly.[119]

In a separate concurring opinion, Judson, J. wrote:

> I agree . . . that we ought not to overrule *R. v. St. Lawrence*. This case reviews the law which has stood since *R. v. Warwickshall*, to the effect that even if a confession is inadmissible in evidence, nevertheless facts which become known by means of this confession may be proved on behalf of the prosecution. . . .
>
> The theory for the rejection of confessions is that if they are obtained under certain conditions, they are untrustworthy. This theory has no application whatever to incontrovertible facts, such as the finding of articles. . . .
>
> How are the facts relating to the discovery of the weapon to be put before the jury? The minimum in this case is the account of Wray's trip from Toronto in the

---

116. For a detailed description of how the confession was obtained see Ontario L.R.C. *Report on Evidence* (1976), pp. 74-90.
117. [1949] O.R. 215, 228 (H.C.). Approved in *R. v. Myrby* (1975), 28 C.C.C. (2d) 395 (Alta. C.A.).
118. [1970] 2 O.R. 3, 4 (C.A.).
119. *Supra*, note 115, at pp. 689-90 (S.C.C.).

company of police officers to a swamp 15 miles west of the scene of the crime and the search for and the discovery of the weapon under the direction of the accused.[120]

The Supreme Court here appears then to regard the policy underlying the confession rule as rooted solely in concern for trustworthiness; if the confession is confirmed as true by tangible evidence, there is no need to exclude. In other decisions, however, the court appears to recognize that there must be another basis. On the same day that the court handed down its decision in *Wray* it gave its decision in *Piche v. R.* The accused was there charged with murder. She was interviewed the day following the killing and told the police that when she had left the apartment the deceased was asleep on the chesterfield. At trial the accused testified that she had intended to commit suicide on the evening in question and the gun had accidentally discharged with the bullet striking the deceased whereupon she then left the apartment. The trial judge excluded the accused's statement to the police as involuntary and the accused was acquitted. The Manitoba Court of Appeal reversed saying the statement was exculpatory not inculpatory and therefore not subject to the confession rule. The Supreme Court of Canada reversed. Cartwright, C.J.C. reasoned:

> The main reason assigned for the rule that an involuntary confession is to be excluded is the danger that it may be untrue but, as has been recently reasserted by this Court in *DeClercq v. The Queen*, the answer to the question whether such a confession should be admitted depends on whether or not it was voluntary, not on whether or not it was true.
>
> It appears to me to involve a strange method of reasoning to say that an involuntary statement harmful to the accused's defence shall be excluded because of the danger of its being untrue but that a harmful involuntary statement, of which there is not merely a danger of its being false but which the prosecution asserts to be false, should be admitted merely because, considered in isolation, it is on its facts exculpatory.
>
> If, on the other hand, one regards the rule against the admission of an involuntary statement as being based in part on the maxim *nemo tenetur seipsum accusare*, the right of an accused to remain silent is equally violated whether, when he is coerced into making a statement against his will, what he says is on its face inculpatory or exculpatory. I find it difficult to see how the prosecution can consistently urge that a statement forced from an accused is in reality exculpatory while at the same time asserting that its exclusion has resulted in the acquittal of the accused and that its admission might well have resulted in conviction.[121]

The Crown in *Piche* sought to introduce the accused's earlier statement as a *false* statement to discredit her present testimony, but the confession rule was held to be a bar; guaranteeing truth cannot be the sole reason for the confession rule. In *DeClercq v. R.*,[122] just a year before *Wray*, the court considered whether an accused, testifying on the *voir dire*, could be asked whether his confession was true. Martland, J., for the majority view that such question was admissible, wrote:

---

120. *Ibid.*, at pp. 692 and 695 [citations omitted]. Compare the attitude of the court in *R. v. Warickshall* (1783), 168 E.R. 234 regarding evidence of accused's involvement in the finding of facts. And see the English attitude in *R. v. Barker*, [1941] 3 All E.R. 33 (C.C.A.).
121. (1970), 11 D.L.R. (3d) 700, 701-02 (S.C.C.).
122. (1968), 70 D.L.R. (2d) 530 (S.C.C.).

voluntariness = main issue, not truth [handwritten margin note]

While it is settled law that an inculpatory statement by an accused is not admissible against him unless it is voluntary, and *while the inquiry on a voir dire* is directed to that issue, and not to the truth of the statement, it does not follow that the truth or falsity of the statement must be irrelevant to such an inquiry. [Emphasis added.] [123]

The court in *DeClercq* recognizes the truth of a confession as *relevant* to the inquiry but that voluntariness, and not truth, is the *issue.* By *DeClercq* a confession which the accused subsequently confirms on oath as true may be excluded, though by *Wray* a confession subsequently confirmed by other evidence must be received. By *DeClercq* there must be another basis for the confession rule. More recently, in *Rothman v. R.,*[124] the court again exhibited divided views on the policy underlying the rule. The accused was charged with possession of narcotics for the purpose of trafficking. He declined to make any statement and was placed in the cells. A policeman, acting in an undercover capacity, was placed in the accused's cell with instructions to gain information from him. The accused told the officer that he "looked like a nark" but the officer was able to persuade him that he was not and the accused proceeded to describe his involvement in the trafficking. After a *voir dire* the trial judge ruled the officer was a "person in authority" and ruled the statement inadmissible. The Ontario Court of Appeal reversed; the majority found the confession rule inapplicable as the accused did not consider the undercover officer to be a "person in authority" within the *Ibrahim* rule. Dubin, J.A. dissented on the basis that the *Ibrahim* rule was not exhaustive and

contradiction [handwritten margin note]

> In my respectful opinion, the rules respecting confessions and privilege against self-incrimination are related. I use that term in the sense of the right of a person under arrest to remain silent when questioned by law enforcement officers.
>
> . . . the right to remain silent after arrest in response to police questioning about the subject-matter of the offence alleged is . . . a fundamental principle in the administration of justice. It would, indeed, be a hollow right if one could be deprived of it by the simple device of being falsely persuaded that the questioner was not a police officer.[125]

The Supreme Court of Canada dismissed the accused's appeal. Martland, J. gave the majority judgment which reasoned:

> Lord Sumner's statement [the "rule" in *Ibrahim*] was adopted in this Court in *Boudreau v. The King* and in *R. v. Fitton.*
>
> The first issue to be determined is whether Constable McKnight was a "person in authority" because, except in the case of a statement made to a person in authority, a statement made by an accused against his own interest is admissible against him in criminal proceedings in the same way that it would be in civil proceedings and there are no special conditions requiring the Crown to prove that the statement was voluntary.
>
> Both parties to this appeal agree that the test to be applied in determining this issue is a subjective test, *i.e.,* did the appellant, when he made the statement to McKnight, believe that McKnight was a person in authority. . . .

---

123. *Ibid.*, at p. 537. Compare *Wong Kam-Ming v. R.*, [1980] A.C. 247 (P.C.) specifically disapproving *DeClercq*. See also *R. v. Brophy*, [1981] 2 All E.R. 705 (H.L.). Compare also *Sawchyn v. R.* (1981), 22 C.R. (3d) 34 (Alta. C.A.); and *R. v. Vangent* (1978), 42 C.C.C. (2d) 313 (Ont. Prov. Ct.).

124. (1981), 59 C.C.C. (2d) 30 (S.C.C.).

125. (1978), 42 C.C.C. (2d) 377, 386, 389-90 (Ont. C.A.).

Once it is accepted that the confession of the appellant was not made to a person in authority, it was properly admissible without any requirement for the Crown to establish that it was voluntary . . . .

With great respect to the dissenting opinion of Dubin J.A., it is my view that the privilege against self-incrimination is not relevant in the circumstances of this case. The scope of the privilege against self-incrimination has been clearly defined by my brother Dickson in the case of *Marcoux and Solomon v. The Queen*. . . .

A claim for protection against self-incrimination can only arise where a tribunal or authority is seeking to compel an individual to disclose something which he does not wish to disclose. In the present case, there was no attempt by anyone to compel the appellant to make the disclosure which he did make. The information given by the appellant to McKnight was furnished by the appellant entirely on his own volition.

For these reasons, it is my opinion that this appeal should be dismissed.[126]

In a separate opinion, agreeing in the result, Lamer, J. wrote:

Therefore, the rules regarding the admissibility of statements by an accused to persons in authority may be enunciated in the following manner:

1. A statement made by the accused to a person in authority is inadmissible if tendered by the prosecution in a criminal proceeding unless the Judge is satisfied beyond a reasonable doubt that nothing said or done by any person in authority could have induced the accused to make a statement which was or might be untrue;

2. A statement made by the accused to a person in authority and tendered by the prosecution in a criminal proceeding against him, though elicited under circumstances which would not render it inadmissible, shall nevertheless be excluded if its use in the proceedings would, as a result of what was said or done by any person in authority in eliciting the statement, bring the administration of justice into disrepute.[127]

In a dissenting opinion Estey, J. wrote:

To summarize then:

(a) The exclusionary confession rule applies to statements given before trial by an accused to persons in authority.

(b) The basic reason for the rule is a concern for the integrity of the criminal justice system. Such a system necessarily requires the support and respect of the community it purports to serve. That support and respect can only be maintained if persons in authority conduct themselves in a way that does not bring the administration of justice into disrepute in the community.

(c) The rule and its administration strike a delicate balance between the need to secure the conviction of the guilty, but above all, the avoidance of the conviction of the innocent.

(d) In the realm of confessions, this standard of conduct is reflected in the requirement that an accused's statement be given "voluntarily".

(e) In this appeal, an expressed decision to remain silent was made by the accused to a policeman who was, in the mind of the accused as well as in fact, a person in authority.

(f) The statement ultimately obtained and tendered in Court was the product of

---

126. *Supra*, note 124, at pp. 35-37.
127. *Ibid.*, at pp. 73-74.

a trick and lies by persons in authority, calculated to subvert the appellant's expressed decision to stand mute.

(g)   Such a determined subversion by the police of an expressed right to refuse to make any statement brings the administration of justice into disrepute. Accordingly, such a statement given in these circumstances cannot get over the hurdle of the exclusionary rule.

(h)   This appeal is not concerned with the gathering of evidence by any other means nor with the circumstance where an accused has not announced to persons in authority that he did not wish to make a statement.

For these reasons I would allow the appeal and restore the acquittal at trial.[128]

The "rule" forecloses receipt of confessions unless they are "voluntary." What is the meaning of "voluntary"? The *Shorter Oxford Dictionary* defines voluntary as

(a)   Of feelings, etc.: Arising or developing in the mind without external constraint; purely spontaneous.

(b)   Of actions: Performed or done of one's own free will, impulse, or choice, not constrained, prompted, or suggested by another.

Clearly the courts are not using the word in this sense. In *Boudreau v. R.,*[129] Rand, J. had written:

. . . the rule is directed against the danger of improperly instigated or induced or coerced admissions. It is the doubt cast on the truth of the statement arising from the circumstances in which it is made that gives rise to the rule. What the statement should be is that of a man free in volition from the compulsions or inducements of authority and what is sought is assurance that that is the case. The underlying and controlling question then remains: Is the statement freely and voluntarily made?

In *R. v. Fitton,*[130] Pickup, C.J.O. interpreted this passage:

In my opinion, the Crown does not discharge the onus resting upon it by merely adducing oral testimony showing that an incriminating statement made by an accused person was not induced by a promise or by fear of prejudice or hope of advantage. That statement of the rule of law is too narrow. The admissions must not have been "improperly instigated or induced or coerced": per Rand J. in *Boudreau v. The King, supra*. The admissions must be self-impelled, and the statement must be the statement of a man "free in volition from the compulsions or inducements of authority". The statement must be "freely and voluntarily made".

C/L voluntary confession rule

R. v. OICKLE
[2000] 2 S.C.R. 3, 36 C.R. (5th) 129, 147 C.C.C. (3d) 321

[During a police investigation into a series of fires, the accused agreed to submit to a polygraph. The test was audiotaped. The accused was informed of his rights to silence, to counsel, and his ability to leave at any time. He was also informed that while the interpretation of the polygraph results was not admissible,

128. *Ibid.,* at pp. 58-59.
129. [1949] 3 D.L.R. 81, 88 (S.C.C.).
130. [1956] O.R. 696, 714 (C.A.).

anything he said was admissible. At the end of the test, about 5:00 p.m., the officer conducting the test informed the accused that he had failed. The accused was reminded of his rights and questioned for one hour. At 6:30 p.m., a second officer questioned the accused and, after 30 to 40 minutes, the accused confessed to setting the fire to his fiancée's car and provided the police with a statement. He appeared emotionally distraught at this time. The accused was arrested and warned of his rights. At the police station, he was placed in an interview room equipped with videotaping facilities where he was questioned about the other fires. Around 8:30 p.m. and 9:15 p.m., the accused indicated that he was tired and wanted to go home. He was informed that he was under arrest and he could call a lawyer but that he could not go home. A third officer took over the interrogation at 9:52 p.m. He questioned the accused until about 11:00 p.m., at which time the accused confessed to setting seven of the eight fires. The accused was then seen crying with his head in his hands. The police then took a written statement from the accused. He was placed in a cell to sleep at 2:45 a.m. At 6:00 a.m., a police officer noticed that the accused was awake and asked whether he would agree to a re-enactment. On the tape of the re-enactment, the accused was informed of his rights and was advised that he could stop the re-enactment at any time. The police drove the accused to the various fire scenes, where he described how he had set each fire. The accused was charged with seven counts of arson. The trial judge ruled on a voir dire that the accused's statements, including the video re-enactment, were voluntary and admissible, and subsequently convicted him on all counts. The Court of Appeal excluded the confessions and entered an acquittal.]

IACOBUCCI, J. (L'HEUREUX-DUBÉ, MCLACHLIN, MAJOR, BASTARACHE and BINNIE, JJ. concurring): —

This appeal requires this Court to rule on the common law limits on police interrogation. Specifically, we are asked to decide whether the police improperly induced the respondent's confessions through threats or promises, an atmosphere of oppression, or any other tactics that could raise a reasonable doubt as to the voluntariness of his confessions. I conclude that they did not. The trial judge's determination that the confessions at stake in this appeal were voluntarily given should not have been disturbed on appeal, and accordingly the appeal should be allowed.

In this case, the police conducted a proper interrogation. Their questioning, while persistent and often accusatorial, was never hostile, aggressive, or intimidating. They repeatedly offered the accused food and drink. They allowed him to use the bathroom upon request. Before his first confession and subsequent arrest, they repeatedly told him that he could leave at any time. In this context, the alleged inducements offered by the police do not raise a reasonable doubt as to the confessions' voluntariness. Nor do I find any fault with the role played by the polygraph test in this case. While the police admittedly exaggerated the reliability of such devices, the tactic of inflating the reliability of incriminating evidence is a common, and generally unobjectionable one. Whether standing alone, or in combination with the other mild inducements used in this appeal, it does not render the confessions involuntary.

. . . .

Two Elements of the Rule

As indicated by McLachlin J. . . . in *R. v. Hebert*, [1990] 2 S.C.R. 151, there are two main strands to this Court's jurisprudence under the confessions rule. One approach is narrow, excluding statements only where the police held out explicit threats or promises to the accused. The definitive statement of this approach came in *Ibrahim v. The King*, [1914] A.C. 599 (P.C.), at p. 609:

> It has long been established as a positive rule of English criminal law, that no statement by an accused is admissible in evidence against him unless it is shewn by the prosecution to have been a voluntary statement, in the sense that it has not been obtained from him either by fear of prejudice or hope of advantage exercised or held out by a person in authority.

This Court adopted the "*Ibrahim* rule" in *Prosko v. The King* (1922), 63 S.C.R. 226, and subsequently applied it in cases like *Boudreau v. The King*, [1949] S.C.R. 262, *Fitton*, supra, *R. v. Wray*, [1971] S.C.R. 272, and *Rothman v. The Queen*, [1981] 1 S.C.R. 640.

The *Ibrahim* rule gives the accused only "a negative right — the right not to be tortured or coerced into making a statement by threats or promises held out by a person who is and whom he subjectively believes to be a person in authority": *Hebert*, supra, at p. 165. However, *Hebert* also recognized a second, "much broader" approach, according to which "[t]he absence of violence, threats and promises by the authorities does not necessarily mean that the resulting statement is voluntary, if the necessary mental element of deciding between alternatives is absent". . . .

While not always followed, McLachlin J. noted . . . that this aspect of the confessions rule "persists as part of our fundamental notion of procedural fairness". This approach is most evident in the so-called "operating mind" doctrine, developed by this Court in *Ward*, supra, *Horvath v. The Queen*, [1979] 2 S.C.R. 376, and *R. v. Whittle*, [1994] 2 S.C.R. 914. In those cases the Court made "a further investigation of whether the statements were freely and voluntarily made even if no hope of advantage or fear of prejudice could be found": *Ward*, supra, at p. 40. The "operating mind" doctrine dispelled once and for all the notion that the confessions rule is concerned solely with whether or not the confession was induced by any threats or promises.

These cases focused not just on reliability, but on voluntariness conceived more broadly. None of the reasons in *Ward* or *Horvath* ever expressed any doubts about the reliability of the confessions in issue. Instead, they focused on the lack of voluntariness, whether the cause was shock (*Ward*), hypnosis (*Horvath*), or "complete emotional disintegration" (*Horvath*). Similarly, in *Hobbins v. The Queen*, [1982] 1 S.C.R. 553, at pp. 556-57, Laskin C.J. noted that in determining the voluntariness of a confession, courts should be alert to the coercive effect of an "atmosphere of oppression", even though there was "no inducement held out of hope of advantage or fear of prejudice, and absent any threats of violence or actual violence"; see also *R. v. Liew*, [1999] 3 S.C.R. 227, at para. 37. Clearly, the confessions rule embraces more than the narrow *Ibrahim* formulation; instead, it is concerned with voluntariness, broadly understood.

The Charter Era

The Charter constitutionalized a new set of protections for accused persons, contained principally in ss. 7 to 14 thereof. The entrenchment of these rights answered certain questions that had once been asked under the aegis of the confessions rule. For example, while the confessions rule did not exclude statements elicited by undercover officers in jail cells (*Rothman*, supra), such confessions can violate the Charter: see *Hebert*, supra, and *R. v. Broyles*, [1991] 3 S.C.R. 595.

In *Hebert*, McLachlin J. interpreted the right to silence in light of existing common law protections, such as the confessions rule. However, given the focus of that decision on defining constitutional rights, it did not decide the inverse question: namely, the scope of the common law rules in light of the Charter. One possible view is that the Charter subsumes the common law rules.

But I do not believe that this view is correct, for several reasons. First, the confessions rule has a broader scope than the Charter. For example, the protections of s. 10 only apply "on arrest or detention". By contrast, the confessions rule applies whenever a person in authority questions a suspect. Second, the Charter applies a different burden and standard of proof from that under the confessions rule. Under the former, the burden is on the accused to show, on a balance of probabilities, a violation of constitutional rights. Under the latter, the burden is on the prosecution to show beyond a reasonable doubt that the confession was voluntary. Finally, the remedies are different. The Charter excludes evidence obtained in violation of its provisions under s. 24(2) only if admitting the evidence would bring the administration of justice into disrepute: see *R. v. Stillman*, [1997] 1 S.C.R. 607, *R. v. Collins*, [1987] 1 S.C.R. 265, and the related jurisprudence. By contrast, a violation of the confessions rule always warrants exclusion.

These various differences illustrate that the Charter is not an exhaustive catalogue of rights. Instead, it represents a bare minimum below which the law must not fall. A necessary corollary of this statement is that the law, whether by statute or common law, can offer protections beyond those guaranteed by the Charter. The common law confessions rule is one such doctrine, and it would be a mistake to confuse it with the protections given by the Charter. While obviously it may be appropriate, as in *Hebert*, to interpret one in light of the other, it would be a mistake to assume one subsumes the other entirely.

The Confessions Rule Today

As previously mentioned, this Court has not recently addressed the precise scope of the confessions rule. Instead, we have refined several elements of the rule, without ever integrating them into a coherent whole. I believe it is important to restate the rule for two reasons. First is the continuing diversity of approaches as evidenced by the courts below in this appeal. Second, and perhaps more important, is our growing understanding of the problem of false confessions. As I will discuss below, the confessions rule is concerned with voluntariness, broadly defined. One of the predominant reasons for this concern is that involuntary confessions are more likely to be unreliable. The confessions rule should recognize which interrogation techniques commonly produce false confessions so as to avoid miscarriages of justice.

In defining the confessions rule, it is important to keep in mind its twin goals of protecting the rights of the accused without unduly limiting society's need to investigate and solve crimes. Martin J.A. accurately delineated this tension in *R. v. Precourt* (1976), 18 O.R. (2d) 714 (C.A.), at p. 721:

> Although improper police questioning may in some circumstances infringe the governing [confessions] rule it is essential to bear in mind that the police are unable to investigate crime without putting questions to persons, whether or not such persons are suspected of having committed the crime being investigated. Properly conducted police questioning is a legitimate and effective aid to criminal investigation . . . . On the other hand, statements made as the result of intimidating questions, or questioning which is oppressive and calculated to overcome the freedom of will of the suspect for the purpose of extracting a confession are inadmissible . . . .

All who are involved in the administration of justice, but particularly courts applying the confessions rule, must never lose sight of either of these objectives.

[The Court then reviewed the literature on the problem of false confessions.]

The common law confessions rule is well-suited to protect against false confessions. While its overriding concern is with voluntariness, this concept overlaps with reliability. A confession that is not voluntary will often (though not always) be unreliable. The application of the rule will by necessity be contextual. Hard and fast rules simply cannot account for the variety of circumstances that vitiate the voluntariness of a confession, and would inevitably result in a rule that would be both over- and under-inclusive. A trial judge should therefore consider all the relevant factors when reviewing a confession.

(a) Threats or Promises

This is of course the core of the confessions rule from *Ibrahim*, supra. It is therefore important to define precisely what types of threats or promises will raise a reasonable doubt as to the voluntariness of a confession. While obviously imminent threats of torture will render a confession inadmissible, most cases will not be so clear.

As noted above, in *Ibrahim* the Privy Council ruled that statements would be inadmissible if they were the result of "fear of prejudice or hope of advantage". The classic "hope of advantage" is the prospect of leniency from the courts. It is improper for a person in authority to suggest to a suspect that he or she will take steps to procure a reduced charge or sentence if the suspect confesses. Therefore in *Nugent*, supra, the court excluded the statement of a suspect who was told that if he confessed, the charge could be reduced from murder to manslaughter. . . . Another type of inducement relevant to this appeal is an offer of psychiatric assistance or other counselling for the suspect in exchange for a confession. While this is clearly an inducement, it is not as strong as an offer of leniency and regard must be had to the entirety of the circumstances. . . . Threats or promises need not be aimed directly at the suspect for them to have a coercive effect. In *R. v. Jackson* (1977), 34 C.C.C. (2d) 35 (B.C.C.A.), McIntyre J.A. . . . offered, as examples of improper inducements, telling a mother that her daughter would not be charged with shoplifting if the mother confessed to a similar offence (see *Commissioners of Customs and Excise v. Harz* , [1967] 1 A.C. 760 (H.L.), at p. 821), or a sergeant-major keeping a company on parade until he learned who was responsible for a stabbing (see *R. v. Smith*, [1959] 2 Q.B. 35.

The *Ibrahim* rule speaks not only of "hope of advantage", but also of "fear of prejudice". Obviously, any confession that is the product of outright violence is involuntary and unreliable, and therefore inadmissible. More common, and more challenging judicially, are the more subtle, veiled threats that can be used against suspects. The Honourable Fred Kaufman, in the third edition of *The Admissibility of Confessions* (1979), at p. 230, provides a useful starting point:

> Threats come in all shapes and sizes. Among the most common are words to the effect that "it would be better" to tell, implying thereby that dire consequences might flow from a refusal to talk. Maule J. recognized this fact, and said that "there can be no doubt that such words, if spoken by a competent person, have been held to exclude a confession at least 500 times" (*R. v. Garner* (1848), 3 Cox C.C. 175, at p. 177).

Courts have accordingly excluded confessions made in response to police suggestions that it would be better if they confessed. However, phrases like "it would be better if you told the truth" should not automatically require exclusion. Instead, as in all cases, the trial judge must examine the entire context of the confession, and ask whether there is a reasonable doubt that the resulting confession was involuntary. . . . I agree that "it would be better" comments require exclusion only where the circumstances reveal an implicit threat or promise.

A final threat or promise relevant to this appeal is the use of moral or spiritual inducements. These inducements will generally not produce an involuntary confession, for the very simple reason that the inducement offered is not in the control of the police officers. If a police officer says "If you don't confess, you'll spend the rest of your life in jail. Tell me what happened and I can get you a lighter sentence", then clearly there is a strong, and improper, inducement for the suspect to confess. The officer is offering a quid pro quo, and it raises the possibility that the suspect is confessing not because of any internal desire to confess, but merely in order to gain the benefit offered by the interrogator. By contrast, with most spiritual inducements the interrogator has no control over the suggested benefit. If a police officer convinces a suspect that he will feel better if he confesses, the officer has not offered anything.

. . . .

In summary, courts must remember that the police may often offer some kind of inducement to the suspect to obtain a confession. Few suspects will spontaneously confess to a crime. In the vast majority of cases, the police will have to somehow convince the suspect that it is in his or her best interests to confess. This becomes improper only when the inducements, whether standing alone or in combination with other factors, are strong enough to raise a reasonable doubt about whether the will of the subject has been overborne. On this point I found the following passage from *R. v. Rennie* (1981), 74 Cr. App. R. 207 (C.A.), at p. 212, particularly apt:

> Very few confessions are inspired solely by remorse. Often the motives of an accused are mixed and include a hope that an early admission may lead to an earlier release or a lighter sentence. If it were the law that the mere presence of such a motive, even if promoted by something said or done by a person in authority, led inexorably to the exclusion of a confession, nearly every confession would be rendered inadmissible. This is not the law. In some cases the hope may be self-generated. If so, it is irrelevant, even if it provides the dominant motive for making the confession. In such a case the confession will not have been obtained by anything said or done by a person in authority. More commonly the presence of such a hope will, in part at least, owe its origin to something said or done by such a person. There can be few prisoners who are being firmly but fairly questioned in a police station to whom it does not occur that they might be able to bring both their interrogation and their detention to an earlier end by confession.

The most important consideration in all cases is to look for a quid pro quo offer by interrogators, regardless of whether it comes in the form of a threat or a promise.

(b) Oppression

There was much debate among the parties, interveners, and courts below over the relevance of "oppression" to the confessions rule. Oppression clearly has the potential to produce false confessions. If the police create conditions distasteful enough, it should be no surprise that the suspect would make a stress-compliant confession to escape those conditions. Alternately, oppressive circumstances could overbear the suspect's will to the point that he or she comes to doubt his or her own memory, believes the relentless accusations made by the police, and gives an induced confession.

A compelling example of oppression comes from the Ontario Court of Appeal's recent decision in *R. v. Hoilett* (1999), 136 C.C.C. (3d) 449. The accused, charged with sexual assault, was arrested at 11:25 p.m. while under the influence of crack cocaine and alcohol. After two hours in a cell, two officers removed his clothes for forensic testing. He was left naked in a cold cell containing only a metal bunk to sit on. The bunk was so cold he had to stand up. One and one-half hours later, he was provided with some light clothes, but no underwear and ill-fitting shoes. Shortly thereafter, at about 3:00 a.m., he was awakened for the purpose of interviewing. In the course of the interrogation, the accused nodded off to sleep at least five times. He requested warmer clothes and a tissue to wipe his nose, both of which were refused. While he admitted knowing that he did not have to talk, and that the officers had made no explicit threats or promises, he hoped that if he talked to the police they would give him some warm clothes and cease the interrogation. Under these circumstances, it is no surprise that the Court of Appeal concluded the statement was involuntary. Under inhumane conditions, one can hardly be surprised if a suspect confesses purely out of a desire to escape those conditions. Such a confession is not voluntary. . . . Without trying to indicate all the factors that can create an atmosphere of oppression, such factors include depriving the suspect of food, clothing, water, sleep, or medical attention; denying access to counsel; and excessively aggressive, intimidating questioning for a prolonged period of time.

A final possible source of oppressive conditions is the police use of non-existent evidence. As the discussion of false confessions, supra, revealed, this ploy is very dangerous. The use of false evidence is often crucial in convincing the suspect that protestations of innocence, even if true, are futile. I do not mean to suggest in any way that, standing alone, confronting the suspect with inadmissible or even fabricated evidence is necessarily grounds for excluding a statement. However, when combined with other factors, it is certainly a relevant consideration in determining on a voir dire whether a confession was voluntary.

(c) Operating Mind

This Court recently addressed this aspect of the confessions rule in *Whittle*, supra, and I need not repeat that exercise here. Briefly stated, Sopinka J. explained that the operating mind requirement "does not imply a higher degree of awareness than knowledge of what the accused is saying and that he is saying it to police officers who can use it to his detriment". I agree, and would simply add that, like oppression, the operating mind doctrine should not be understood as a discrete inquiry completely divorced from the rest of the confessions rule. . . . [T]he operating mind doctrine is just one application of the general rule that involuntary confessions are inadmissible.

(d) Other Police Trickery

A final consideration in determining whether a confession is voluntary or not is the police use of trickery to obtain a confession. Unlike the previous three headings, this doctrine is a distinct inquiry. While it is still related to voluntariness, its more specific objective is maintaining the integrity of the criminal justice system. Lamer J.'s concurrence in *Rothman*, supra, introduced this inquiry. In that case, the Court admitted a suspect's statement to an undercover police officer who had been placed in a cell with the accused. In concurring reasons, Lamer J. emphasized that reliability was not the only concern of the confessions rule; otherwise the rule would not be concerned with whether the inducement was given by a person in authority. He summarized the correct approach . . .:

> [A] statement before being left to the trier of fact for consideration of its probative value should be the object of a voir dire in order to determine, not whether the statement is or is not reliable, but whether the authorities have done or said anything that could have induced the accused to make a statement which was or might be untrue. It is of the utmost importance to keep in mind that the inquiry is not concerned with reliability but with the authorities' conduct as regards reliability.

Lamer J. was also quick to point out that courts should be wary not to unduly limit police discretion (at p. 697):

> [T]he investigation of crime and the detection of criminals is not a game to be governed by the Marquess of Queensbury rules. The authorities, in dealing with shrewd and often sophisticated criminals, must sometimes of necessity resort to tricks or other forms of deceit and should not through the rule be hampered in their work. What should be repressed vigorously is conduct on their part that shocks the community. [Emphasis added.]

As examples of what might "shock the community", Lamer J. suggested a police officer pretending to be a chaplain or a legal aid lawyer, or injecting truth serum into a diabetic under the pretense that it was insulin.

In *Hebert*, supra, this Court overruled the result in *Rothman* based on the Charter's right to silence. However, I do not believe that this renders the "shocks the community" rule redundant. There may be situations in which police trickery, though neither violating the right to silence nor undermining voluntariness per se, is so appalling as to shock the community. I therefore believe that the test enunciated by Lamer J. in *Rothman* is still an important part of the confessions rule.

. . . .

Application to the Present Appeal

Applying the foregoing law to the facts of this appeal, and having viewed the relevant video- and audiotapes, I find no fault with the trial judge's conclusion that the respondent's confession was voluntary and reliable. The respondent was fully apprised of his rights at all times; he was never subjected to harsh, aggressive, or overbearing interrogation; he was not deprived of sleep, food, or drink; and he was never offered any improper inducements that undermined the reliability of the confessions. As the Court of Appeal reached a contrary conclusion with respect to a number of these issues, I will address them in turn.

[The Court then analyzed the fact situation under a variety of heads: 1. Minimizing the Seriousness of the Crimes. 2. Offers of Psychiatric Help. 3. "It Would Be Better". 4. Alleged Threats Against the Respondent's Fiancée. 5. Abuse of Trust. 6. Atmosphere of Oppression. And finally, 7. The Use of the Polygraph Test.]

. . . .

Summary on Voluntariness

In summary, there were several aspects of the police's interrogation of the respondent that could potentially be relevant to the voluntariness of his confessions. These include the comments regarding Ms. Kilcup; the suggestions that "it would be better" for the respondent to confess; and the exaggeration of the polygraph's accuracy. These are certainly relevant considerations when determining voluntariness. However, I agree with the trial judge that neither standing alone, nor in combination with each other and the rest of the circumstances surrounding the respondent's confessions, do these factors raise a reasonable doubt about the voluntariness of the respondent's confessions. The respondent was never mistreated, he was questioned in an extremely friendly, benign tone, and he was not offered any inducements strong enough to raise a reasonable doubt as to voluntariness in the absence of any mistreatment or oppression. As I find no error in the trial judge's reasons, the Court of Appeal should not have disturbed her findings.

ARBOUR, J.: — *Dissent*

I have had the benefit of the reasons of my colleague, Justice Iacobucci, on this appeal. With respect, I believe that there were improper inducements held out by the police officers who interrogated the respondent and that these inducements, considered cumulatively and contextually in light of the "failed" polygraph test, require the exclusion of the respondent's statements. Moreover, in my view the proximity and the causal connection between the "failed" polygraph test and the confession also compels this result. Accordingly, I would dismiss the appeal, set aside the convictions and enter acquittals on all counts. . . . Properly understood, this case involves two confessions obtained by the police following the "failure" of a polygraph test and a skillful interrogation which lasted nearly six hours. Repeated threats and promises were made. They were often subtle but in my view, against the backdrop of the polygraph procedure, they overwhelmed the free will of the respondent. These seemingly mild pressures make this case a difficult one in which to apply the confessions rule and demand an attentive appreciation of the full context in which the alleged voluntary, incriminating statements were made. I fully agree with the summary of the applicable law provided by Justice Iacobucci. . . . However, I take a different view of the proper legal characterization of what happened in the course of the many hours during which the respondent was interrogated and of the voluntary quality of his incriminating statements.

[Justice Arbour then analyzed admissibility under the heads of The Administration of the Polygraph Test, The Post-Polygraph Interrogation, Promise of Psychiatric Help, Minimization of the Seriousness of the Crimes, Threat to Interrogate the Accused's Girlfriend, and finally, as another basis for exclusion, Fair Trial Considerations.]

For these reasons I would dismiss the appeal, set aside the convictions and enter acquittals on all counts.

For commentary see Stuart, "*Oickle*: The Supreme Court's Recipe for Coercive Interrogation" (2001), 36 C.R. (5th) 188 and *Charter Justice in Canadian Criminal Law* (3rd ed., 2001) pp. 119-128.

In *Oickle* the Supreme Court confined itself to the common law. What of an argument based on the pre-trial right to silence and/or the principle against self-incrimination under section 7 of the Charter (see above, Chapter 7)?

PROBLEMS

Problem 1

John Howard has asked you to represent him on an anticipated charge of robbery. He assures you that he had nothing to do with the incident but that he understands the police are looking to question him. Contact with the local police has confirmed your client's suspicion and you have resolved to surrender him at the station this afternoon. How should you advise your client regarding the questions which will be forthcoming? Can you demand that the police only question your client in your presence? Are statements receivable if they question him in contravention of your instructions? Compare *R. v. Dinardo* (1981), 61 C.C.C. (2d) 52 (Ont. Co. Ct.); *R. v. Allen*, [1977] Crim. L. Rev. 163. See also *R. v. Letendre* (1975), 25 C.C.C. (2d) 180 (Man. C.A.).

Problem 2

The accused John Bent was arrested and jointly charged with William Tell with robbery. During the course of the first interview at the police station Bent declined to answer any questions. Two hours later the investigating officer returned Bent to the interrogation room and showed Bent a statement, purportedly signed by Tell, in which Bent is described as the prime mover in the robbery with Tell playing only a subsidiary role. In fact Tell had not given a statement to the police and his signature to the document had been forged by the investigating officer. Bent reacted angrily, saying, "I didn't think he'd turn on me — I guess there really is no honour among thieves." Defence counsel has objected to receipt of Bent's statement. Rule on the objection. Compare *R. v. Allen (No. 3)* (1979), 46 C.C.C. (2d) 553 (Ont. H.C.).

Problem 3

The accused was charged with several sexual offences involving young boys. The accused made an inculpatory statement. The accused was convicted and has appealed. Argue the admissibility of the statement, based on the following transcript.

The investigating constable testified:

A. I then approach Cyril and inform him that I would like to speak to him but I made it quite clear that if he didn't wish to speak to me he didn't have to, not without consulting his lawyer, that was made very clear. I told him I was

> investigating this incident, that I in my job wanted to clear it up. I wanted to get his side of the story down on paper.
>
> Q.   Get his side of the story down. Did he express any desire to wait until a lawyer is called or until he saw a lawyer?
>
> A.   None that I can recall.
>
> Q.   Okay. Did you ever tell Cyril he had a problem that you wanted to help him with?
>
> A.   Yes, I did. I stated that I believed what the children were saying was true and based on that I thought he had a problem and I wanted to help him by talking about it. I stated that in perhaps speaking about it he could better understand it. And also I made it quite clear that in speaking about it he would be helping us in our investigation as well.

Compare the differing views of Monnin, C.J.M. and Huband, J.A. in *R. v. Bird* (1989), 50 C.C.C. (3d) 89 (Man. C.A.).

(iii) *Statements Adopted by Party's Conduct*

If an accusation is directed to a party in circumstances in which it would be reasonable to expect a denial should the accusation be untrue, the party's failure to deny will be received against him as an implied admission.[131]

The classic expression of this appears in *R. v. Christie:*

> . . . the rule of law undoubtedly is that a statement made in the presence of an accused person, even upon an occasion which should be expected reasonably to call for some explanation or denial from him, is not evidence against him of the facts stated save so far as he accepts the statement, so as to make it, in effect, his own. If he accepts the statement in part only, then to that extent alone does it become his statement. He may accept the statement by word or conduct, action or demeanour, and it is the function of the jury which tries the case to determine whether his words, action, conduct or demeanour at the time when a statement was made amounts to an acceptance of it in whole or in part. It by no means follows, I think, that a mere denial by the accused of the facts mentioned in the statement necessarily renders the statement inadmissible, because he may deny the statement in such a manner and under such circumstances as may lead a jury to disbelieve him, and constitute evidence from which an acknowledgment may be inferred by them.[132]

It would not be reasonable to take a party's failure to deny as an implied admission if the accusation was made by a police officer. An accused does have, at least on detention, a right to silence,[133] and it would violate that right if adverse inferences were to be drawn from its exercise.[134] There should be evidence that the party heard and understood the statement, and that given his personal characteristics, emotional condition, and situation, a reasonable person would deny. Given the condition of admissibility, the evidence ought not to be received unless the trial judge is first satisfied that there is sufficient evidence from which

---

131. See *R. v. Christie*, [1914] A.C. 545 (H.L.); *R. v. Stein*, [1928] S.C.R. 553.

132. *Ibid.*, at p. 554, per Lord Atkinson.

133. See above Chapter 7.

134. See *R. v. Eden*, [1970] 2 O.R. 161 (C.A.) and *R. v. Chambers* (1990), 80 C.R. (3d) 235 (S.C.C.). Compare *R. v. Conlon* (1990), 1 O.R. (3d) 188 (C.A.), where the accusation was made by the victim; it was there held that failure of the accused to say anything when accused not by the police, but by the complainant, was inconsistent with the conduct of an innocent person.

a jury might reasonably find an acknowledgment.[135] The House of Lords thought this was a salutary rule of practice and, while they were unwilling to constitute it a rule of law, the view is well expressed by the British Columbia Court of Appeal in *R. v. Harrison:*[136]

> But there is a rule of practice that, for fear of prejudice to the accused, in case it is not shown that he has accepted the statement, that such evidence should not be allowed in until a foundation has been laid for its admission by proof of facts from which, in the opinion of the presiding Judge the jury might reasonably draw the inference that the accused had so accepted the statement as to make it in whole or in part his own.

Given the great prejudice that could result from the jury hearing the accusation, it is better to ensure in advance that there is some evidence of acceptance rather than charging them later to disregard in the absence of acquiescence.

Given that oral statements in the presence of the party may be adopted by silence, does the same hold true for written statements? Is it "reasonable to infer" that the recipient by his silence admits the truth of the statement?[137] Consider the following wisdom:

> Men use the tongue much more readily than the pen. Almost all men will reply to and deny or correct a false statement verbally made to them. It is done on the spot and from the first impulse. But when a letter is received making the same statement, the feeling which readily prompted the verbal denial not unfrequently cools before the time and opportunity arrive for writing a letter. Other matters intervene. A want of facility in writing, or an aversion to correspondence, or habits of dilatoriness may be the real causes of the silence. As the omission to reply to letters may be explained by so many causes not applicable to silence when the parties are in personal conversation, we do not think the same weight should be attached to it as evidence.[138]

Nevertheless there are of course certain relationships where there has been mutual correspondence over a period of time which would make it "reasonable to infer" that failing to reply was an admission of the truthful nature of the communication, and each situation must be evaluated according to its own circumstances. For example, it has been noted:

> When a tradesman makes out his statement of account for goods against, and sends it to, a person, and that person takes no objection thereto, such statement and the failure to object are some evidence that the goods were furnished for the credit of that person . . .
>
> . . .
>
> In mercantile matters where an account is rendered it was said as far back as 1741 in *Willis v. Jernegan:* "There is no absolute necessity that it should be signed by the parties who have mutual dealings . . . it is not the signing which will make it

---

135. See McCormick, *Evidence*, 2d ed. (1972), p. 653.
136. [1946] 3 D.L.R. 690, 696. For an example of the importance of ensuring a foundation in advance see *R. v. Hryn* (1981), 63 C.C.C. (2d) 390 (Ont. Co. Ct.).
137. Compare *Bessela v. Stern* (1877), 46 L.J.C.P. 467 (C.A.) with *Wiedeman v. Walpole* (1890), 24 Q.B.D. 537. See also *R. v. Edwards*, [1983] Crim. L.R. 539.
138. *Fenno v. Watson*, 31 Vt. 345, 352 (1858), as quoted in McCormick, *Evidence* (2d. ed.), p. 653.

a stated account but the person to whom it is sent, keeping it by him any length of time . . . which shall bind him."[139]

(iv) *Statements Authorized by Party*

R. v. STRAND ELECTRIC LTD.
(1968), 2 C.C.C. 264 (Ont. C.A.)

MacKay J.A.:—

. . . .

The Crown witness, Mr. McMurray, a duly authorized inspector under the Act, stated that he knew Richards and that he knew Richards was the supervisor on the subcontract for Strand Electric Limited. McMurray's evidence then continued as follows:

Question: Now, Mr. McMurray, did you have some conversation with Mr. Richards?

Answer: I did.

Question: And were the facts that he told you at that time voluntary?

Answer: Yes.

Question: Now, did Mr. Richards indicate to you what use was being made of the scaffold in question, which is shown in exhibits 1 through 4 and about which my learned friend has made certain admissions?

Answer: Mr. Richards admitted that he was engaging men on the scaffold . . .

By the Court: Question: He was what?

Answer: He was using workmen — or — using the scaffold by workmen.

Mr. Glass: Question: Did he make any observations as to who was using the scaffold?

Answer: He did, sir.

Question: And what did he admit to you as to his observations?

Answer: That the Frank Ribes was employed by Richards —

Question: By whom?

Answer: By Strand Electric, I'm sorry. Could I refer to my notes.

Question: Yes. These are notes that were made at the time of your investigation?

Answer: At the inspection, yes, sir. He agreed that Frank Ribes was an employee of Strand Electric and he was fully aware of the condition of the scaffold.

Question: When you say "he", to whom do you refer?

Answer: Mr. Alfred Richards, the super for Strand Electric.

Question: And did he make any observations about Mr. Ribes or about the scaffold or the two of them in combination?

Answer: Just that he was on the stage at the time of the accident. He was within ten feet of the scaffold in question.

Question: And did he make any observations as to who was using the scaffold before the accident, sometime before?

Answer: No, no, sir.

---

139. *Sarbit v. Hanson & Booth Fisheries (Canada) Co.*, [1951] 2 D.L.R. 108, 112 (Man. C.A.) [citation omitted].

Question: Did he tell you or did he make any admissions to you as to what Mr. Ribes was doing?

Answer: Yes. Mr. Richard had mentioned that he was in the process of installing a sling on the top member of the uppermost platform of the scaffold, using the uppermost platform of the scaffold to install this sling.

Question: And did he admit whether or not he was aware that Mr. Ribes was on this scaffold?

Answer: Yes.

Question: I beg your pardon?

Answer: He was fully aware that Mr. Ribes was on the scaffold.

I am of the view that the Court below was right in holding that a supervisor on the location of the work was a person with authority as agent and employee of the appellant to make the admissions he did and that such statements were admissible as evidence as against the appellant company.

I adopt the statement of the author of *Cross on Evidence*, 2nd ed., pp. 441-2, as being a correct statement of the law on this point. The statement in part is:

> Statements made by an agent within the scope of his authority to third persons during the continuance of the agency may be received as admissions against his principal in litigation to which the latter is a party. So far as the reception of admissions is concerned, the scope of authority is a strictly limited conception. It is sometimes said that the agent must be authorised to make the admission, but that is a confusing statement for no one expressly or impliedly authorises others to make informal admissions on his behalf which may be proved against him in subsequent litigation.

> A better way of putting the matter is to say that the admission must have been made by the agent as part of a conversation or other communication which he was authorised to have with a third party.

Cross then refers to the case of *Kirkstall Brewery Co. v. Furness R. Co.* (1874), L.R. 9 Q.B. 468, where the plaintiff claimed damages for loss of a parcel, and it was held that a statement made by the defendants' stationmaster to a policeman suggesting that the goods had been stolen by a servant of the defendants could be proved against the defendants.

MCLENNAN, J.A., agrees with MACKAY, J.A.

LASKIN, J.A. (dissenting):—

. . . .

An accused's admissions are, of course, properly receivable in evidence against him from the mouth of the person to whom they were made. The rationale of the hearsay rule is not involved in the reception of such evidence to prove the truth of what was admitted. Where, as here, the accused is a corporation, it is not the hearsay rule that controls the reception of an admission against it; the question to be determined is by whose admissions and on what matters is the corporation vicariously committed. Principles of agency as well as of evidence must be considered.

. . . .

Two propositions underlie the reception of an agent's admissions against his principal. There must, first, be proof of the agency; and, as the textbooks say, unless the alleged agent testifies himself to his agency, his assertions that he is an agent, offered through the mouth of another, are inadmissible because as hearsay they beg the question: see 4 *Wigmore on Evidence*, 3rd ed., p. 123; *Cross on Evidence*, 3rd ed., p. 442. Second, the admissions of the agent tendered against the principal must have been made to a third party within the scope of his authority during the subsistence of the agency: *Wigmore on*

Evidence, op. cit., p. 119; *Cross on Evidence, op. cit.*, pp. 441-2. The application of the second of these propositions has, in the cases, revealed a different attitude of the Courts to the authority of an agent to ''act'' on behalf of his principal and his authority to ''speak'' on behalf of his principal, as if speech or conversation was not itself an act. There may, indeed, be justification for viewing authority differently in the two situations, but some of the case law exhibits, in relation to the reception of admissions, the same formal requirement of authority that in earlier days limited the develpment of vicarious liability in tort; and see also *Restatement of the Law*, Agency, 2d, ss. 286, 288 (1958).

The concept of authority, taken literally, would exclude as against the principal any admission of an agent tending to show liability in tort or penal liability, unless the agent is shown to have been authorized to make admissions to charge his principal. It would be a rare case to find such authority in any express sense; and, in the result, the admissions would be receivable only to impeach the agent, if, being called as a witness by the principal, he gave evidence with which the admissions were inconsistent. Authority as between agent and principal has in respect of vicarious liability of the principal to third parties, been translated into an issue of the scope of the agent's duties or employment, and I would apply the same test in relation to admissions by an agent which are tendered in evidence against the principal. The fact that penal liability is involved in the present case does not, in my view, make the test inapplicable here.

The approach that I am supporting would still make it necessary to examine carefully the admissible evidence on the scope of an agent's duties or employment lest the principal be charged by an admission not properly receivable against him. Of course, the trier of fact would also have to determine whether the admission offered against a principal was made; and, as in other cases where evidence is formally admissible, weight would have to be assessed. I do not think, therefore, that the test of admissibility that I have indicated would unfairly prejudice a principal who is a party or an accused in a proceeding against him.

In the present case, the fact of agency as between the accused and Richards is not, as I understood the submissions that were made, contested. McMurray, the inspector, testified that Richards was the supervisor for the accused. It does not appear that he was thereby reporting an assertion by Richards himself but rather that this was something that the inspector knew otherwise. I should note, in connection with the inspector's duties generally, that under ss. 12 [am. 1962-63, c. 22, s. 6] and 13 [am. 1965, c. 19, s. 5] of the Act an inspector may enter premises and may require information from any person in relation to any project. Certainly, in the absence of contrary evidence, it is proper to find that Richards was in a relationship of agency with the accused.

I turn, therefore, to the question of the scope of Richards' duties. Here too there is the problem that a finding on this matter cannot be based on the declarations of the agent where it is sought to receive them in evidence as admissions against the principal. So far as the evidence before us goes, it shows only that Richards is a supervisor of the accused, but in what respect and with what responsibilities does not appear. At one stage in the course of proceedings, counsel for the accused referred to Richards as the superintendent of the accused on the site of the project, but there was no indication as to what this title imported, whether it had to do with the disposition of men or material or inspection of the course of the work or anything else.

. . . .

Returning then to the issue of the scope of Richards' duties, the fact is that there was no evidence as to what his function as supervisor involved. I cannot therefore find that the prosecution has established that any workman of the accused was ordered or put on the defective scaffold by an agent acting in the course of his duties for the accused.

Appeal dismissed.

Quaere whether the exception should be limited to statements made to a third party; do not reports made to the party itself carry sufficient guarantees of trustworthiness? As Professor McCormick notes:

> While slightly less reliable as a class than the agent's authorized statements to outsiders, intra-organization reports are generally made as a basis for some action, and when this is so, they share the reliability of business records. They will only be offered against the principal when they admit some fact disadvantageous to the principal, and this kind of statement by an agent is likely to be true. No special danger of surprise, confusion, or prejudice from the use of the evidence is apparent.[140]

To receive vicarious admissions is consistent with the philosophy which underlies the subject as a whole: fairness, responsibility and the adversarial nature of our system. Scope of authority is key. As recited in a U.S. decision:

> The test of admissibility should not rest on whether the principal gave the agent authority to make declarations. No sensible employer would authorize his employee to make damaging statements. The right to speak on a given topic must arise out of the nature of the employee's duties. The errand boy should not be able to bind the corporation with a statement about the issuance of treasury stock, but a truck driver should be able to bind his employer with an admission regarding his careless driving. Similarly, an usher should be able to commit his employer with an observation about a slippery spot on the lobby floor.[141]

Having agreed that scope of authority governs, it is perhaps sufficient to agree with Professor Wigmore that:

> Upon the application of the principle to specific instances, it would be useless here to enter, for only the rules of the substantive law of agency are involved.[142]

One particular form of agency does deserve mention. In a partnership each partner, when acting within the scope of the partnership, is an agent for the other partners and for the partnership. Applying the above principle, then, statements made by a partner while conducting the firm's business are receivable as admissions against the partnership if the existence of the firm is independently established.

(v) *Statements of Person with Common Purpose*

A particular form of partnership, of course, is conspiracy, civil or criminal. Responsibility underlies the receipt of statements of co-conspirators, as

> the basal reason for admitting the evidence of the acts or words of one against the other is that the combination or preconcert to commit the crime is considered as implying an authority to each to act or speak in furtherance of the common purpose on behalf of the others.[143]

Professor Wigmore notes:

---

140. McCormick, *Evidence*, 2d ed., p. 643.
141. *Rudzinski v. Warner Theatres Inc.*, 114 N.W. 2d 466, 471 (Wisc., 1962).
142. 4 Wigmore, *Evidence* (Chad. Rev.), s. 1078, p. 170. As an example of common sense, see *Tesco Supermarkets Ltd. v. Nattrass*, [1972] A.C. 153 (H.L.) restricting company's vicarious liability to acts of senior management.
143. *Tripodi v. R.* (1961), 104 C.L.R. 1, 7 (Aust. H.C.).

A conspiracy makes each conspirator liable under the criminal law for the acts of every other conspirator done in pursuance of the conspiracy. Consequently . . . the admissions of a co-conspirator may be used to affect the proof against the others, on the same conditions as his acts when used to create their legal liability.[144]

The statements to be received must then have been statements made during the term of the conspiracy and in furtherance of it, and not simply a narrative describing it.[145] This preliminary condition of admissibility presents a problem, as it coincides with the very fact sought to be established. When this concurrence exists[146] it seems reasonable that the statements be received if there is *some* other evidence of a conspiracy and indeed the trial judge in his discretion may even have to relax that requirement.[147]

In *R. v. Barrow*[148] the Supreme Court of Canada summarized the proper approach:

1. The trier of fact must first be satisfied beyond reasonable doubt that the alleged conspiracy in fact existed.

2. If the alleged conspiracy is found to exist then the trier of fact must review all the evidence that is directly admissible against the accused and decide on a balance of probabilities whether or not he is a member of the conspiracy.

3. If the trier of fact concludes on a balance of probabilities that the accused is a member of the conspiracy then he or they must go on and decide whether the Crown has established such membership beyond reasonable doubt. In this last step, only the trier of fact can apply the hearsay exception and consider evidence of acts and declarations of co-conspirators done in furtherance of the object of the conspiracy as evidence against the accused on the issue of his guilt.[149]

---

144. 4 Wigmore, *Evidence* (Chad. Rev.), s. 1079, p. 180.
145. See *R. v. Miller* (1975), 63 D.L.R. (3d) 193, 217-21 (B.C.C.A.) and *R. v. Lynch* (1978), 40 C.C.C. (2d) 7, 24 (Ont. C.A.) re the distinction.
146. See generally on this point Cross, *Evidence*, 5th ed., pp. 69-71.
147. See 4 Wigmore, *Evidence* (Chad. Rev.), s. 1079, p. 187. And see *Ford v. Elliott* (1849), 154 E.R. 1132: "It is a mistake to say that a conspiracy must be proved before the acts of the alleged conspirators can be given in evidence. It is competent to prove insulated acts as steps by which the conspiracy itself may be established," as quoted by Hunt, "Evidentiary Rules Peculiar to Conspiracy Cases" (1973-74), 16 Crim. L.Q. 307 at 330. And see *R. v. Parrot* (1979), 51 C.C.C. (2d) 539, 548-49 (Ont. C.A.) where the court was satisfied that there was *prima facie* evidence that the offence charged was the result of a common design in which the appellant and Mr. Walden were participants. Accordingly, writings which constituted acts or declarations by Mr. Walden in furtherance of the common design were admissible against the appellant.
148. [1987] 2 S.C.R. 694, adopted from its earlier decision in *R. v. Carter*, [1982] 1 S.C.R. 938. For another application of *Carter* see *R. v. Jamieson* (1989), 48 C.C.C. (3d) 287 (N.S.C.A.). In *R. v. Henke* (1989), 72 C.R. (3d) 395 (C.A.), the trial judge fell into error in applying *Carter*; though he applied the first two steps correctly, he then used against the probable conspirator, Henke, the statement given to the police by his alleged co-conspirator, Bickford. The statement given to the police was seen by the Court of Appeal to be "not 'declarations performed and made by the co-conspirators in furtherance of the objects of the conspiracy'. The conspiracy was at an end when Bickford talked to the police, and the statements had nothing to do with furthering its objects. The ordinary rules applied, and the statement of one accused, not on oath, was not admissible in evidence against a co-accused." (pp. 399-400)
149. *Barrow, ibid.*, at p. 740.

The court also explained that in taking the first step the jury would not necessarily have to be satisfied beyond a reasonable doubt as to the identity of the persons involved in the conspiracy. It is entirely possible, and not uncommon, to be satisfied beyond a reasonable doubt on all the evidence that a conspiracy for the purposes alleged in the indictment existed while still being uncertain as to the identity of all the conspirators. The hearsay exception would have no application at this stage but could certainly be useful at the third stage, if reached, in satisfying the trier that the accused was a member of the alleged conspiracy. This exception is not confined, of course, to cases where the offence charged is conspiracy, but rather the underlying principle makes it applicable to any offence which has been committed pursuant to some common design.[150]

R. v. VIANDANTE
(1995), 40 C.R. (4th) 353 (Man. C.A.)

[L was convicted of trafficking in cocaine and conspiring to traffic with V. V was convicted on the sole charge against him, which was conspiring to traffic with L. The evidence against both accused had been obtained via A who, in return for $100,000 had offered to obtain information for the police. At trial A gave evidence of a number of drug transactions with L and also testified that L had told him that V was his supplier. The jury was charged with the standard three-step test typically used in conspiracy cases.

Held: Appeal of accused V allowed; appeal of L dismissed.]

HUBAND J.A. (SCOTT C.J.M. and KROFT J.A. concurring):—One of the most daunting tasks that faces a trial judge is instructing a jury in a case involving conspiracy charges. The law itself is not as clear as it might be, and the trial judge has the added problem of instructing the jury as to what evidence can be used for what purpose, and what evidence is in furtherance of the conspiracy and what is not.

. . . .

Much has been written as to the appropriate instructions which a judge should provide to a jury with respect to conspiracy cases.

In *R. v. Carter*, [1982] 1 S.C.R. 938, McIntyre J., writing for a unanimous court, set forth a three-step process.

In the present case the trial judge charged the jury in accordance with *R. v. Carter*. He explained what constituted a conspiracy and then instructed the jury that the first task was to decide, beyond a reasonable doubt, whether a conspiracy existed. If not, each accused must be acquitted.

Potential trouble arose immediately thereafter when the trial judge told the jury that, regardless of the wording of the indictment, the jury should restrict its assessment of the evidence to the question of whether a conspiracy existed between the two co-accused:

. . . just concentrate on whether or not there was a conspiracy between the two accused.

Moments later the trial judge went on to say:

If you are not satisfied that both accused were members of the alleged conspiracy then, of course, the Crown has failed to prove the existence of the conspiracy and both men must be acquitted.

---

150. See cases cited in *R. v. Parrot, supra*, note 147.

Morse J. then instructed the jury that, if satisfied that a conspiracy between the two existed, the jury should go on to decide whether each accused was a probable member of the conspiracy. In accordance with *R. v. Carter*, he went on to tell the jury that in this second stage when considering whether a particular accused was a probable member, the jury must be confined to evidence of his own actions, conduct and declarations:

> You cannot use the out of court acts or statements of the other accused in deciding this issue, but you do not have to look at the statements and actions of a particular accused in isolation. You may use the statements and actions of the other accused to provide a context so that you are able to understand what the statements and actions of the particular accused mean.

The trial judge then reviewed the evidence. Having done so, he then instructed the jury that the next step was to determine whether the Crown had established, beyond reasonable doubt, that the two accused were members of the conspiracy. He told them that in considering this final phase, "You are entitled to consider the acts and statements of each accused in furtherance of the conspiracy in order to decide whether the other accused was a member of the conspiracy."

. . . .

In my opinion, once the conspiracy is brought down to only two persons, namely, the two co-accused, a charge to the jury based on the *Carter* case requires further explanation in order to avoid confusion.

. . . .

In *R. v. Barrow*, [1987] 2 S.C.R. 694, McIntyre J. in his reasons makes it clear that even in a two-person conspiracy it is open to a jury to convict one but not the other. When the three-step directive in *R. v. Carter* is applied, and if the jury finds that a two-man conspiracy existed beyond reasonable doubt, then by necessary implication at least one of the co-conspirators must be found to be a member of the conspiracy, beyond reasonable doubt.
. . .

In determining the existence of the conspiracy, the jury is entitled to consider direct evidence of the conspiracy but not hearsay. In *R. v. Carter*, McIntyre J. speaks of whether "on all the evidence" the jury is satisfied that the conspiracy charged in the indictment existed. In the subsequent decision in *R. v. Barrow*, McIntyre J. explains what is meant by "all the evidence." It means all the admissible evidence, excluding hearsay. . . .

What is direct as opposed to hearsay evidence as to the existence of the conspiracy? If A, one of the alleged conspirators, makes a declaration that he is involved in an illegal conspiracy to traffic in drugs along with B and C, his declaration is surely direct evidence of the existence of the conspiracy (though hearsay as to the participation of B and C in the conspiracy).

What would constitute hearsay evidence as to the existence of the conspiracy? If, in the present case Armstrong had testified that he had heard from other contacts in the drug subculture that Viandante and Lebras were working together in supplying and selling cocaine, that evidence would be hearsay and therefore inadmissible as proof of a conspiracy. But no evidence of that character was tendered.

I do not think any harm flowed from the fact that the trial judge did not instruct the jury to ignore hearsay evidence in determining the existence of a conspiracy. The statements of Lebras to Armstrong implicating Viandante as his supplier are direct evidence of the existence of the conspiracy, and are therefore admissible for the purpose of proving the existence of the conspiracy. Indeed, I can think of no evidence tendered at the trial which should not be considered by the jury in determining whether the conspiracy existed, although the weight to be attributed to certain evidence might be highly questionable.

The problem with the instructions on the first step of the *Carter* process was the failure to instruct the jury that if a conspiracy was found to exist implicating the accused

Lebras, it did not necessarily mean that the participation of Viandante was also established in spite of the fact that only a two-person conspiracy was alleged. The trial judge told them that they must find each accused to be a member of the conspiracy, which is simply incorrect. A charge based upon the *Carter* process, but containing that erroneous instruction, is misleading and confusing. One can picture the members of the jury sitting about a table having decided beyond a reasonable doubt that a two-person conspiracy existed between Lebras and Viandante, and then wondering what to make of the second and third steps in the process when the participation of each accused has already been determined beyond reasonable doubt. To make sense of it all the jury must be told something along the lines of what McIntyre J. wrote in his reasons in *R. v. Barrow* where he explains that even in a two-person conspiracy it is possible to convict one and acquit the other. . . .

Having decided to instruct the jury on the basis of the *Carter* decision, it would have been preferable if the trial judge had dealt with the first stage more summarily, and then proceeded directly, and with detailed reference to the evidence, to the more difficult question raised at the second stage, namely, whether on the direct evidence against him Lebras was a probable member of the conspiracy with Viandante, and whether, oil the direct evidence against him, Viandante was a probable member of a conspiracy with Lebras. And then, of course, on to the third stage if appropriate. The three-step process suggested in *Carter* is a guideline to be used in appropriate cases to ensure that an accused is not implicated in an illegal conspiracy solely on the hearsay testimony of others. In the present case, the danger is that Viandante may have been found to be a co-conspirator at the first stage of the inquiry. That danger was not removed by the charge to the jury.

There was, of course, some evidence indicating that Viandante was a probable participant in the conspiracy. But when the evidence of Armstrong's conversations with Lebras are excluded from consideration, as they must be when considering the evidence against Viandante at the second stage of the *Carter* process, the evidence against Viandante is far from compelling. On the other hand, as against Lebras the evidence to point to his probable membership in a conspiracy with Viandante is overwhelming if the jury believes Armstrong's testimony, and it obviously did. The danger is that Viandante might have been convicted because, at the first stage of the *Carter* process the jury had already concluded that he was a member of a two-person conspiracy with Lebras, based upon hearsay evidence as to Viandante's participation.

The jury may well have been confused by the application of the Carter three-step process without appropriate modifications to fit a two-person conspiracy. On that ground Viandante's conviction must be set aside.

I have no doubt that if the prosecution could overcome the second-stage hurdle and move on to the third stage, there would be ample evidence in the conversations and dealings between Armstrong and Lebras to prove to the satisfaction of any reasonable jury, beyond reasonable doubt, that Viandante was a party to a conspiracy with Lebras to traffic in cocaine. But we never reach the third stage.

While Viandante was improperly convicted, the same cannot be said for Lebras. As noted, it is perfectly proper, depending upon the force of the evidence, that one co-conspirator should be convicted while the other is acquitted. Concerning Lebras, there was overwhelming evidence from his own mouth that be was in a conspiracy with Viandante as his supplier at least during the time surrounding the first two drug transactions with Armstrong. In my opinion, he was not only properly convicted on the trafficking charges but also on the conspiracy charge.

R. v. DUFF
(1994), 32 C.R. (4th) 153, 90 C.C.C. (3d) 460 (Man. C.A.)

[The accused was charged with three counts of trafficking in cocaine. The trial judge, sitting without a jury, found the charges proved after having considered all of the evidence, including the hearsay evidence of the accused's co-conspirators. The accused appealed. The accused argued that the presentation of the hearsay evidence prior to a determination on the first two issues, that is, that a conspiracy did exist, and that the accused was a member of that conspiracy, is prejudicial to an accused. In any other criminal case where a question arises on the admissibility of evidence, the judge determines that issue within the confines of a voir dire in the absence of the jury. The jury does not hear the challenged evidence and the accused is protected from its prejudicial effect until a judge determines the threshold test has been met for its admission. With the rule and co-conspirator exception as developed in our law, the prejudicial hearsay evidence is presented prior to the jury's being told that it can make no use of that evidence until it has determined two preliminary questions. This practice results in immediate prejudice to an accused. The presentation of potentially incriminating hearsay evidence, prior to the jury's directing its mind to the two preliminary issues dealing with the conspiracy, necessarily must colour its determination of those same issues. The jury is forced to address two vital issues with the knowledge that other prejudicial evidence exists on the final issue for its determination. The accused argued that requiring the trial judge, not the jury, to determine the conspiracy issue would provide greater integrity to the institution of trial by jury.]

HELPER J. (LYON and KROFT JJ.A. concurring):—

. . . .

R. v. Carter . . . sets out the test for the admissibility and use of hearsay evidence of co-conspirators.

The Crown presents its entire case, including the hearsay evidence of the alleged co-conspirators. The trier of fact . . . is instructed to ignore the hearsay evidence, to consider only the direct evidence and to determine, beyond a reasonable doubt, whether a conspiracy does exist. If the answer to that inquiry is in the affirmative, the fact finder must then go on to consider, on a balance of probabilities, whether the direct evidence implicates the accused in that conspiracy. Only when the answer to the second inquiry is also in the affirmative does the fact finder then go on to review all of the evidence, including the hearsay evidence of the co-conspirators as it relates to the substantive charge or charges before the court, to determine beyond a reasonable doubt whether the Crown has proved the case.

[The Court reviewed the different approaches in Australia and the United States.]

To accept the appellant's submission that the process approved by the Supreme Court in *Carter* is inherently prejudicial to an accused, I would necessarily have to conclude that juries are unable to perform their functions in accordance with properly formulated instructions from the trial judge.

Despite the caveat issued by the Australia High Court of Appeal, I do not reach that conclusion. . . .

Juries are able to execute their sometimes formidable tasks very well and are able to follow the clear directions trial judges regularly provide to them. They are often instructed to disregard evidence that has improperly been placed before them and they are able to follow that instruction without the need to declare a mistrial. They are instructed to use a piece of evidence for one purpose only, but not to use that same evidence to prove the truth of the events to which the evidence refers.

. . . .

I do not conclude that the process is inherently prejudicial to an accused or that its application in this case resulted in any prejudice to the appellant.

(vi) *Statements by Representative*

At common law:

> What a trustee says or does in the exercise of his duty is evidence against his beneficiaries. But what he says or does in other respects is not.[151]

What a person says may be received in evidence against him, no matter in what capacity he says it. If a person sues or is sued in a representative capacity, for example, trustee, executor or administrator, his statements are only receivable against the party he represents if the statements were made as part of the exercise of his representative capacity. This position is consistent with the general principle that admissions are receivable only against their maker, but is modified to allow for their receipt when the interests of the declarant and the party are identical.

(vii) *Statements by those in Privity with Estate or Interest with Party*

At common law:

> . . . vicarious admissions may become receivable . . . by *privity* (or, identity) of *interest*, i.e., a relation which permits one person's rights, obligations, or remedies to be affected by the acts of another person, and thus also permits resort to such evidence as that other person may have furnished by way of admissions. This privity may be of two sorts, namely, privity of *obligation* and privity of *title*.[152]

An example may assist. *Woolway v. Rowe*[153] was a civil action for trespass wherein the defendant claimed that plaintiff's estate did not extend so far as to cover the property in question. Defendant offered to prove that when plaintiff's father owned the estate he had specifically disavowed any exclusive interest in it. This was objected to on the basis that plaintiff's father was present in court and might be called, and that therefore his earlier declarations were not admissible. The evidence was received and a rule for a new trial refused with the simple statement, "receivable on the ground of identity of interest."[154]

Professor Morgan wrote:

> The dogma of vicarious admissions, as soon as it passes beyond recognized principles of representation, baffles the understanding. Joint ownership, joint obligation, privity of title, each and all furnish no criterion of credibility, no aid in the evaluation of testimony.[155]

---

151. *New's Trustee v. Hunting*, [1897] 1 Q.B. 607, 611, per Vaughan Williams, J.; affirmed [1897] 2 Q.B. 19, 28, 32.
152. 4 Wigmore, *Evidence* (Chad. Rev.), s. 1076, p. 153.
153. (1834), 110 E.R. 1151.
154. *Ibid.*, at p. 1152 per Lord Denman, C.J.
155. "Admissions" (1937), 12 Wash. L. Rev. 181, 202.

PROBLEMS

Problem 1

On a charge of violating the Customs Act, to establish the country of origin, the Crown seeks to introduce the perfume seized from the accused, the bottles of which have attached labels "Made in Paris." Objectionable? The Crown tenders Constable Smith who is prepared to testify that the accused told him the perfume came from France and when asked how he knew, the accused replied, "Look at the label dummy!" Receivable? Would you convict on this evidence? See *Patel v. Comptroller of Customs*, [1966] A.C. 356 (P.C.) and *Comptroller of Customs v. Western Lectric*, [1966] A.C. 367 (P.C.).

Problem 2

Two young boys were playing "Cowboys and Indians" when one was struck in the eye with an arrow. The statement of claim alleges that the adult defendants were negligent in permitting their son to have a bow and arrows. Plaintiff proposes to introduce evidence that defendant paid medical bills incurred as the result of the injury. Admissible? Do you need to know more facts? See *Walmsley v. Humenick*, [1954] 2 D.L.R. 232 (B.C.S.C.).

Problem 3

The accused is charged with murder. The principal Crown witness, Jones, is prepared to testify that the accused's brother advised him some weeks prior to the trial that he should be careful because the accused had "already killed once to save his hide." Jones is also prepared to say that the accused, the night before the trial, phoned him and said, "If you don't want what Smith got, stay out of the stand tomorrow." The Crown is prepared to lead evidence that Smith was murdered by persons unknown some two years ago. Is the above evidence receivable? On what basis? Cf. *Lizotte v. R.*, [1951] 2 D.L.R. 754, 762 (S.C.C.). And see *Greenwood v. Fitts* (1961), 29 D.L.R. (2d) 260 (B.C.C.A.).

Problem 4

The accused was charged with auto theft. The arresting officer testified:

> I apprehended the boys while they were still in the Morris. The other two were in the front and the accused was in the back seat. I ordered them out and told them to sit in the back seat of my cruiser. Well a period of time elapsed, we requested a tow truck and were sitting there and at the time — I can't say who said this, but the three of them were walking down a lane —

Q. You can't recall who said this but someone said what? Is that what you are going to say?

A. Yes, one of them admitted they were walking down the lane to the rear of Annie's Sales when they observed this Morris vehicle parked at the rear with the keys in it and on the spur of the moment they decided to take it and go for a ride.

Q. Were there any denials or objections to that statement made by any of the three persons?

A. No.

Defence counsel objected and the trial judge answered:

> T.J.   I think it is admissible Mr. Smith, not probably as to the truth of it but the fact is the accused heard it?

Was the trial judge correct? See *R. v. Eden*, [1970] 2 O.R. 161 (C.A.).

Problem 5

An 18-year-old girl pleaded guilty on her first appearance on a charge of impaired driving. The magistrate adjourned the matter for three weeks at the request of the Crown so that a check might be made for any prior convictions. On her second appearance, counsel appeared with her and a request was made that she be permitted to withdraw her plea; the magistrate was duly satisfied that it was an appropriate case, permission was granted and the case set over to be tried at a future date by another magistrate. On her trial, the Crown now proposes to call the court reporter to testify to the earlier plea. Objectionable? See *Thibodeau v. R.*, [1955] S.C.R. 646. At a subsequent civil suit for damages arising out of the motor vehicle accident the plaintiff seeks to introduce the plea. Result? See *English v. Richmond*, [1956] S.C.R. 383; *Re Charlton*, [1969] 1 O.R. 706 (C.A.).

Problem 6

Public Vehicle Commercial licences stipulate exactly what products a carrier may transport across the province. Truck driver Smith transporting lumber in contravention of the owner's licence is involved in a minor accident. He offers the other party a sum of money to forget the accident, explaining that otherwise his boss will be in great trouble. Conversation admissible against owner in later prosecution for carrying goods without a licence?

Problem 7

Your client complains that she is not receiving any responses from the manufacturer to her claim for a refund on her return of a defective television set. Draft a letter to the manufacturer.

Problem 8

Jones, a milkman, pleads guilty to a charge of careless driving arising from an accident in which a pedestrian was injured. Jones and his employer, Best Milk Company, are later sued for damages. Is Jones' plea of guilty admissible? Any limiting instruction necessary? If Jones had pleaded not guilty could his conviction be introduced? See *Hollington v. F. Hewthorn & Co.*, [1943] 2 All E.R. 35 (C.A.). Compare *Demeter v. British Pacific Life Insurance Co.* (1984), 2 C.C.L.I. 246 (Ont. H.C.).

Problem 9

A, B, C and D are being tried for conspiracy to sell unwholesome meat. An unindicted co-conspirator X has agreed to testify in exchange for an offer of immunity by the Crown. X testifies that his dealings were always with A and that he never met B, C or D. A was a deadstock dealer who sold deadstock to X who in turn later repackaged the meat and sold it as meat from freshly killed animals. B, C and D were also deadstock dealers who, according to X, supplied A. X testifies that he approached A initially and suggested he was prepared to purchase deadstock meat at 40 cents a pound, though the going rate to pet food dealers was 20 cents; A asked him how he could do that and X let him in on his plan. X testifies that later, A told him not to worry about his running low on supplies because B, C and D had agreed to come in with him and sell as much as he could handle and went on in his testimony: "He said that they also, of course, insisted on a premium. I was going to seek another supplier but with these assurances I continued on with A." X also testifies that, after the preliminary hearing, B approached him and offered him $1,000 if he'd eliminate B and C from his testimony at trial. Comment on the admissibility of the above evidence.

Problem 10

The accused is charged with the armed robbery of the Ajax Paint Company on June 17. At his preliminary inquiry he decides not to testify but calls as a witness Bill Hood. After a few opening questions the following occurs:

Defense Counsel:	Where were you on the evening of the 17th of June?
Hood:	In the city.
Q.C.:	Could you please be more specific?
Hood:	I'd rather not.
The Court:	What's your problem, witness?
Hood:	I'm afraid that if I speak I might you know, incriminate myself.
The Court:	Go ahead and testify, they won't use your testimony against you.
Hood:	O.K. I did the robbery at the paint store on the 17th and I did it alone.

Between the preliminary and the trial Bill Hood has fled the jurisdiction. Comment on the receivability of the above transcript. See *R. v. Coté* (1979), 50 C.C.C. (2d) 564 (Que. C.A.) (leave to appeal to S.C.C. refused 50 C.C.C. (2d) 564n) and *R. v. Chaperon* (1979), 52 C.C.C. (2d) 85 (Ont. C.A.). See now *R. v. Potvin* (1989), 68 C.R. (3d) 193 (S.C.C.).

Problem 11

In a prosecution for assault, a police officer testifies: "I was present during a line-up and I saw the victim point to the accused as the person who bloodied his nose." Defence objects. Rule on the objection.

Problem 12

Plaintiff, a passenger in a street-car owned by defendant corporation, sues for damages for injuries resulting to her when she alighted from the car; the rear door had opened though the car had not actually stopped and the plaintiff had relied on the open door as an invitation that it was safe to leave. Immediately after the plaintiff fell the conductor got off, helped the plaintiff to her feet and in the hearing of many apologized: "It was my fault, I should not have opened the door, but I thought the car had stopped." Defendant corporation objects. Prepare alternate grounds justifying receipt. See *Jarvis v. London Street Railway Co.* (1919), 45 O.L.R. 167 (C.A.).

Problem 13

The accused Butch Cassidy and the Sundance Kid are charged with conspiracy to defraud the Acme Insurance Company. The fraud alleged maintains that Sundance asked Butch to arrange for the "theft" of Sundance's car when Sundance went on a European vacation. It is alleged that Sundance gave Butch a set of keys to facilitate the theft and advised him where at the airport the vehicle would be parked. The Crown has called a single witness, a police officer named Sherlock. Sherlock has testified that while he was acting on an undercover drug assignment Butch enlisted him to steal Sundance's car. Butch persuaded him that the theft would be easy by describing Sundance's involvement in the scheme and Sundance's intention to make a claim against his insurance company, Acme. Sherlock testified that Butch gave him keys for the car, the car was removed from the parking area, and the car is presently in the possession of the police. Defence counsel argues that none of this evidence is receivable against Sundance. How will the court rule? Compare *R. v. Carter*, [1982] 1 S.C.R. 938 and *R. v. Barrow*, [1987] 2 S.C.R. 694.

(b) Exceptions where Declarant or Testimony Unavailable

There are six common law exceptions under this heading which deserve some comment: declarations against interest, dying declarations, declarations in the course of duty, former testimony, declarations as to pedigree and declarations of testators as to their wills. At common law the declarant in each case needed to be deceased.

(i) *Declarations Against Interest*

The common law recognized an exception for a declaration made by a person concerning a matter within his personal knowledge which declaration when made was to the declarant's own prejudice. The "standard" requirements of a hearsay exception are satisfied by this definition. There are clearly grounds of necessity, as the declarant is unavailable, and there are circumstances guaranteeing trustworthiness resident in the thought that a person is unlikely to intentionally misstate a situation against his own position. The hearsay danger of insincerity is guarded against though the dangers in perception, memory and communications are not eliminated. Notice that "collateral matters mentioned" are also receivable though they may not be against interest;[156] it appears to be accepted that the collateral matters draw their assurance of trustworthiness from the proximity to the statements against interest. Commenting on the basis for the exception, Hamilton, L.J. noted:

> The ground is that it is very unlikely that a man would say falsely something as to which he knows the truth, if his statement tends to his own pecuniary disadvantage.

---

156. As an example see *Higham v. Ridgway* (1808), 103 E.R. 717, 721 (K.B.): to establish a child's date of birth the court received the midwife's account book evidencing receipt of payment for services (against interest) for delivery of a baby on a certain day (collateral matter).

As a reason this seems sordid and unconvincing. Men lie for so many reasons and some for no reason at all; and some tell the truth without thinking or even in spite of thinking about their pockets, but it is too late to question this piece of eighteenth century philosophy.[157]

It seemed to be early settled that the interest affected must be a pecuniary or proprietary interest[158] but there have always been arguments for expanding the nature of the interest to include exposure to criminal liability.[159]

R. v. DEMETER
[1978] 1 S.C.R. 538, 38 C.R.N.S. 317, 34 C.C.C. (2d) 137

[Accused was charged with murder. The Crown case was that accused had procured some unknown person to kill his wife. Accused sought to introduce evidence that a person unconnected with him had confessed to the murder of the wife.]

MARTLAND J. (JUDSON, RITCHIE, PIGEON, DICKSON, BEETZ and DE GRANDPRÉ JJ. concurring):—

. . . .

The appellant sought to introduce evidence through the witness Dinardo that one Eper, who was apparently unconnected with the appellant, had confessed to the murder of the appellant's wife. Eper was an escaped convict, who had been serving a sentence for life at the time of his escape, and who had died prior to the trial. Dinardo was his friend and testified that he would not have given evidence implicating Eper in this murder if Eper had still been alive. The trial judge excluded the alleged confession as being hearsay evidence.

. . . .

It has generally been accepted as the law of England since *The Sussex Peerage* case that the exception to the rule excluding hearsay evidence in respect of declarations made against interest is confined to statements made against pecuniary or proprietary interest and does not permit evidence of a statement by a deceased person against his penal interest.

The Court of Appeal . . . . held that, even if a declaration against penal interest was not necessarily inadmissible, the confession of Eper in question here was not a declaration against penal interest. The reason for so holding is stated as follows:

. . . .

At the time of both the alleged declarations in question in this case Eper was an

---

157. See *Lloyd v. Powell Duffryn Steam Coal Co.*, [1913] 2 K.B. 130, 138 (reversed on other grounds [1914] A.C. 733 (H.L.)).

158. *Sussex Peerage Case* (1844), 8 E.R. 1034 (H.L.). See *Watt v. Miller*, [1950] 2 W.W.R. 1144 (B.C.S.C.), holding that a declaration admitting tortious liability is a declaration against pecuniary interest.

159. In a dissenting opinion in *Donnelly v. U.S.*, 228 U.S. 243, 278 (1913), Holmes, J. noted: The confession of Joe Dick, since deceased, that he committed the murder for which the plaintiff in error was tried, coupled with circumstances pointing to its truth, would have a strong tendency to make anyone outside a court of justice believe that Donnelly did not commit the crime . . . No other statement is so much against interest as a confession of murder; it is far more calculated to convince than dying declarations, which would be let in to hang a man.

escaped convict under sentence of life imprisonment. In the result, he could not be sentenced to a consecutive sentence so that there could be no penal consequence for the crime admitted to which he was vulnerable. The completely uncertain effect on his prospects of parole in the event of another conviction is too remote and uncertain to be regarded as a penal consequence. In addition, at the time of the declaration to Dinardo he and Eper had been accomplices in crimes for many years and Dinardo, on his evidence, was acting as an accessory after the fact in assisting concealment of evidence of the crime declared. Dinardo testified he would not have given his evidence if Eper were alive.

The Court of Appeal enunciated a number of principles which would have to be applied in determining whether a declaration is against penal interest which, in its view, would have to be applied in addition to those applicable in determining whether a declaration is against pecuniary or proprietary interest. They are as follows:

1. The declaration would have to be made to such a person and in such circumstances that the declarant should have apprehended a vulnerability to penal consequences as a result.

2. The vulnerability to penal consequences would have to be not remote.

3. The declaration sought to be given in evidence must be considered in its totality. If upon the whole tenor the weight is in favour of the declarant, it is not against his interest.

4. In a doubtful case a Court might properly consider whether or not there are other circumstances connecting the declarant with the crime and whether or not there is any connection between the declarant and the accused.

5. The declarant would have to be unavailable by reason of death, insanity, grave illness which prevents the giving of testimony even from a bed, or absence in a jurisdiction to which none of the processes of the Court extends. A declarant would not be unavailable in the circumstances that existed in *R. v. Agawa*. [Ed. note: *Agawa* was a joint trial and one accused had given a statement exonerating the other.]

These furnish a valuable guide for consideration in the event that this Court should determine that a declaration against penal interest is not to be held inadmissible under the rule against the reception of hearsay evidence.

Finally, in *R. v. O'Brien*,[160] the Supreme Court of Canada agreed:

> The distinction is arbitrary and tenuous. There is little or no reason why declarations against penal interest and those against pecuniary or proprietary interest should not stand on the same footing. A person is as likely to speak the truth in a matter affecting his liberty as in a matter affecting his pocketbook.;[161]

(ii) *Dying Declarations*

At common law a deceased's declaration regarding the cause of his death was receivable in a prosecution for his death provided there was evidence that when he made the declaration he entertained a hopeless expectation of death.[162]

---

160. (1977), 76 D.L.R. (3d) 513 (S.C.C.). See also *Demeter v. R.* (1978), 75 D.L.R. (3d) 251 (S.C.C.).

161. *Ibid.*, at p. 518; the court, however, applying the requirements of the exception outlined by Hamilton, L.J. in *Lloyd v. Powell, supra*, note 157, held that the instant declaration was not knowingly made against the declarant's interest. And see *Lucier v. R.* (1982), 65 C.C.C. (2d) 150 (S.C.C.) prohibiting the use of such statements *against* an accused.

162. Compare Cross, *Evidence*, 5th ed., p. 564.

The ground for this exception was detailed very early in the development of the rules of evidence:

> . . . the general principle on which this species of evidence is admitted is, that they are declarations made in extremity, when the party is at the point of death, and when every hope of this world is gone; when every motive to falsehood is silenced, and the mind is induced by the most powerful considerations to speak the truth; a situation so solemn, and so awful, is considered by the law as creating an obligation equal to that which is imposed by a positive oath administered in a Court of Justice.[163]

The assurance of trustworthiness from the circumstances will only flow if the declarant was aware of his state and the statement would be competent evidence by him in the stand. Chief Justice Duff in the Supreme Court of Canada described the duty of the trial judge:

> First of all, he must determine the question whether or not the declarant at the time of the declaration entertained a settled, hopeless expectation that he was about to die almost immediately. Then, he must consider whether or not the statement would be evidence if the person making it were a witness. . . . a declaration which is a mere accusation against the accused, or a mere expression of opinion, not founded on personal knowledge, as distinguished from a statement of fact, cannot be received.[164]

Because of the curious happenstance in our Criminal Code that criminal negligence causing death may be charged under that head or under the head of manslaughter, the declaration is receivable in a prosecution of the former crime as well as the latter.[165]

Given the assurances or trustworthiness resident in the requirements of the exception, it is difficult to see why the law does not go further and allow reception with respect to *any* charge arising out of the transaction. Indeed it is worth noting that the common law restriction to the use of dying declarations only in homicide cases was the result, as unfortunately is the case with many of our rules of evidence, of an historical accident. Until the nineteenth century, the exception operated both in civil and criminal cases. The source of the restriction appears to be a statement by East in his chapter on Homicide; in that chapter he noted that dying declarations were receivable in homicide prosecutions. By the next generation this statement had been interpreted to mean that dying declarations were *only* receivable in homicide prosecution.[166] Limiting receipt of the dying declaration to those cases where it concerns the *declarant's* death or injuries was described by Wigmore as an "irrational and pitiful absurdity of this feat of legal cerebration."[167]

---

163. *R. v. Woodcock* (1789), 168 E.R. 352, 353, per Eyre, C.B.
164. *Chapdelaine v. R.*, [1935] 2 D.L.R. 132, 136 (S.C.C.). With regard to the immediacy of the death expected see *R. v. Perry*, [1909] 2 K.B. 697 (C.C.A.) and *R. v. McIntosh*, [1937] 4 D.L.R. 478 (B.C.C.A.).
165. See *R. v. Jurtyn*, [1958] O.W.N. 355 (C.A.).
166. See 5 Wigmore, *Evidence* (Chad. Rev.), s. 1431. Against that background it is remarkable to consider the holding in *R. v. Schwartzenhauer*, [1935] 3 D.L.R. 711 (S.C.C.).
167. 5 Wigmore, *Evidence* (Chad. Rev.), s. 1433.

(iii) *Declarations in Course of Duty*

General

Common law declarations of a deceased person were receivable as exceptions to the hearsay rule if they described the deceased's own activities, were made contemporaneously therewith and the deceased was then under a duty to record the same.[168] This common law exception is no longer as important as it once was, as the federal government and most of the provincial governments have enacted statutory provisions regarding business records; the exception, however, operates with respect to oral and written statements while the statutory provisions deal only with the latter. The exception has, however, been considerably broadened by the Supreme Court of Canada in *Ares v. Venner*.[169] The unanimous opinion of the court, delivered by Hall, J., concluded:

> Hospital records, including nurses' notes, made contemporaneously by someone having a personal knowledge of the matters then being recorded and under a duty to make the entry or record should be received in evidence as *prima facie* proof of the facts stated therein.[170]

The exception now does not demand that the declarant be deceased; indeed in this case the declarants, the nurses, were present in the courtroom but neither side wished to call them as their own witnesses. The common law exception required the declarant to be under a duty to do the act and under a duty to record it; in this case the nurses were under a duty to observe and to record their observations, and therefore their observations, clearly opinions, were receivable. The Alberta Court of Appeal in *Ares v. Venner* had seen these opinions as providing "fruitful areas for cross-examination,"[171] but despite that truth the court ordered them received. It is true that Hall, J. continued:

> This should, in no way, preclude a party wishing to challenge the accuracy of the records or entries from doing so. Had the respondent here wanted to challenge the accuracy of the nurses' notes, the nurses were present in court and available to be called as witnesses if the respondent had so wished.[172]

It is difficult to imagine, however, that the bold direction towards reform of the hearsay rule described by the court was only to be applicable when the declarants were present in the court. In the court's recent decision in *R. v. Khan, supra*, that position was specifically disavowed:

> I add that I do not understand *Ares v. Venner* to hold that the hearsay evidence there at issue was admissible where necessity and reliability are established only where

---

168. See Ewart, "Admissibility at Common Law of Records", [1981] Can. Bar Rev. 52.
169. [1970] S.C.R. 608. Accepted as authoritatively stating the common law position in Ontario in *R. v. Laverty (No. 2)* (1979), 47 C.C.C. (2d) 60, 64 (Ont. C.A.) per Zuber, J.A.: ". . . a declaration in the course of a business duty either in its classic form or as enlarged by *Ares v. Venner* . . ." and in *Setak Computer Services Corp. v. Burroughs Business Machines Ltd.* (1977), 15 O.R. (2d) 750, 755 (H.C.) per Griffiths, J.: "that case settles the common law in Ontario." But *contra* see *Exhibitors Inc. v. Allen* (1989), 70 O.R. (2d) 103 (Ont. H.C.) per Arbour, J.
170. *Ibid.*, at p. 626.
171. (1969), 70 W.W.R. 96, 105 (Alta. C.A.).
172. *Supra*, note 169, at p. 626.

cross-examination is available. First, the Court adopted the views of the dissenting judges in *Myers v. D.P.P.* which do not make admissibility dependent on the right to cross-examine. Second, the cross-examination referred to in *Ares v. Venner* was of limited value. The nurses were present in court at the trial, but in the absence of some way of connecting particular nurses with particular entries, meaningful cross-examination would have been difficult indeed.[173]

Business Records

The common law exception for declarations in the course of duty had been fashioned in the 19th century and, if narrowly interpreted, was clearly inappropriate to the business methods which had evolved by the middle of the 20th. The decisions in *Myers v. D.P.P.*[174] caused the legislature to act, both in England[175] and in Canada. In Ontario, for example, the McRuer-Common Committee reported that

> the absurdity of the common law is forcibly exposed in *Myers v. D.P.P.* . . . the law of evidence with respect to the proof of the contents of records kept in the ordinary course of business is quite unrelated to modern scientific developments in the making and the keeping of records.[176]

At the federal level, the then Minister of Justice regretted the fact that Canadian courts were following the *Myers* decision and noted:

> It is therefore apparent that the law in this country has fallen far behind the major changes which the computer age has brought to business methods. Frequently records are kept either entirely or almost entirely by mechanical means, and in such cases it may be difficult and perhaps impossible to produce a witness to testify to the facts of a particular case, as distinct from testifying about the mechanical system under which transactions or events are recorded. Even in the case of records kept manually it is frequently impossible to trace the person, assuming he is still alive, who made the entries originally in the business records. A useful source of evidence is thereby excluded from the courts. It is little wonder that intelligent laymen conclude that, far from being blind, the goddess of justice is looking the wrong way.[177]

Various provinces and the federal government brought in statutory provisions during the late 1960's to ease the introduction of business records as evidence. As an example the Ontario legislation, enacted in 1966, provided:

> **36.**(1) In this section,
>
>> (*a*) "business" includes every kind of business, profession, occupation, calling, operation or activity, whether carried on for profit or otherwise;
>> (*b*) "record" includes any information that is recorded or stored by means of any device.
>
>> (2) Any writing or record made of any act, transaction, occurrence or event is admissible as evidence of such act, transaction, occurrence or event

---

173. (1990), 79 C.R. (3d) 1, 14 (S.C.C.).
174. [1965] A.C. 1001 (H.L.). On the topic of business records see generally, Ewart, "Documentary Evidence: The Admissibility of Documents under Sec. 30 of the Canada Evidence Act," [1979-80] Crim. L.Q. 189.
175. See Criminal Evidence Act, 1965, c. 20 and Civil Evidence Act, 1968, c. 64.
176. Report of the Committee on Medical Evidence in Civil Cases (1965), pp. 64, 77.
177. Hansard, Jan. 20, 1969, p. 4496.

if made in the usual and ordinary course of any business and if it was in the usual and ordinary course of such business to make such writing or record at the time of such act, transaction, occurrence or event or within a reasonable time thereafter.

(3) Subsection 2 does not apply unless the party tendering the writing or record has given at least seven days notice of his intention to all other parties in the action, and any party to the action is entitled to obtain from the person who has possession thereof production for inspection of the writing or record within five days after giving notice to produce the same.

(4) The circumstances of the making of such a writing or record, including lack of personal knowlege by the maker, may be shown to affect its weight, but such circumstances do not affect its admissibility.

(5) Nothing in this section affects the admissibility of any evidence that would be admissible apart from this section or makes admissible any writing or record that is privileged.[178]

The amendment to the Canada Evidence Act[179] provided in part:

29A.(1) Where oral evidence in respect of a matter would be admissible in a legal proceeding, a record made in the usual and ordinary course of business that contains information in respect of that matter is admissible in evidence under this section in the legal proceeding upon production of the record.

. . . .

(12) In this section "business" means any business, profession, trade, calling, manufacture or undertaking of any kind carried on in Canada or elsewhere whether for profit or otherwise, including any activity or operation carried on or performed in Canada or elsewhere by any government, by any department, branch, board, commission or agency of any government, by any court or other tribunal or by any other body or authority performing a function of government;

"record" includes the whole or any part of any book, document, paper, card, tape or other thing on or in which information is written, recorded, stored or reproduced. . .

Ironically of course the Supreme Court of Canada very shortly afterwards decided to follow the dissenting opinion in *Myers* and to reform judicially the hearsay rule to meet modern conditions.[180]

There is apparent conflict between the statutory provisions. The provincial legislation specifically makes lack of personal knowledge by the maker a factor which does not affect admissibility but only weight. The federal legislation has, as a precondition, the requirement that oral evidence of the matter recorded be admissible.

Does this mean that the maker of the record must have had personal knowledge of the event recorded?[181] **Or does it simply mean that the record**

---

178. This Ontario Evidence Act provision (now R.S.O. 1990, c. E.23, s. 35) is based on a provision of the Commonwealth Fund Act, a proposal for reform drafted by Professor Morgan's Committee in 1927; see generally McCormick, *Evidence* (1972), p. 719.

179. S.C. 1968-69, c. 14, s. 4. See now R.S.C. 1985, c. C-5, s. 30.

180. *Ares v. Venner, supra,* note 169, discussed above. Alberta, the birthplace of the *Ares* decision, did not enact business records legislation, seemingly content with the judicial creation.

181. Advancing this interpretation see Lederman, "The Admissibility of Business Records — A Partial Metamorphosis" (1973), 11 Osgoode Hall L.J. 373 at 394-95 and Mewett quoted in McWilliams, *Canadian Criminal Evidence* (1974), pp. 115-16.

must have relevance to the matters in issue and that if *any* witness would be permitted to describe the matter recorded, the record, though double hearsay, is receivable?

R. v. MARTIN
(1997), 8 C.R. (5th) 246 (Sask. C.A.)

[The accused was charged with six counts of defrauding the Wheat Board. The Crown's theory was that the accused dishonestly overstated the amount of wheat and barley he had on hand, causing the Canadian Wheat Board to advance him more money than it would otherwise have done and depriving it of the difference. The Crown sought to introduce evidence of average crop yields for the municipalities where the accused farmed. The Crown called the Director of the Statistics branch at the Saskatchewan Department of Agriculture and Food. Through him, the Crown sought to present to the jury tables of estimated crop yield averages produced by the Statistics Branch from data gathered by Statistics Canada from Saskatchewan farmers. The tables pertained to the rural municipalities where the accused farmed. The trial judge refused to admit the tables because they relied on hearsay information collected by Statistics Canada and no witness could testify as to its accuracy.]

JACKSON J.A. (CAMERON and SHERSTOBITOFF JJ.A. concurring):—

. . . .

Subsection 30(1) of the Canada Evidence Act increased the likelihood of a Court admitting a business record without testimony as to the source of the information contained in the record. It puts forward only two qualifications for admission: (i) the evidence tendered must be "a record made in the usual and ordinary course of business;" and (ii) it must contain the same information "where oral evidence in respect of a matter would be admissible in a legal proceeding." But vestiges of the old law, which resisted the admissibility of documents except under strict circumstances, remained.

The principal issue concerned "double hearsay", i.e., information contained in a record which was given to the record keeper who has no knowledge of its accuracy.

Many of the provincial equivalents of s. 30(1) specifically require a court to overlook double hearsay. For example, s. 31(3) of The Saskatchewan Evidence Act, R.S.S. 1978, c. S-16 provides "[t]he circumstances of the making of a writing or record mentioned in subsection (2), including lack of personal knowledge by the maker, may be shown to affect its weight, but such circumstances do not affect its admissibility." The difference between the provincial and federal legislation appears to lessen the effectiveness of the latter.

Added to this, s. 30(6) of the Canada Evidence Act provides that a court may consider the circumstances in which the information was written to determine whether an provision of s. 30 applies. This lends further weight to the proposition that Parliament intended courts to exclude documents containing double hearsay.

Mr. Ewart (*Documentary Evidence in Canada*, Carswell, 1984) indicated early academic opinion leaned toward the view that s. 30 did preclude the admissibility of records containing double hearsay but the courts did not share that view. In fact, early cases held double hearsay documents to be admissible, as long as they met the twin requirements of s. 30(1), with little comment.

In *R. v. Anthes Business Forms Ltd.* (1975), 19 C.C.C. (2d) 394, aff'd 26 C.C.C. (2d) 349, aff'd 32 C.C.C. (2d) 207 (S.C.C.) the Ontario Court of Appeal considered the admissibility of corporate files which contained third party records showing details of certain transactions. As in the case at bar, the corporate files were developed from information received from someone who in turn had received it from yet another. Houlden J.A., speaking for the Court, said the files were admissible because they were records "made in the usual and ordinary course of business by the persons who prepared them, and oral evidence in respect of the matters contained in them would have been admissible" (see p. 369). Although the Supreme Court of Canada's brief reasons may represent concurrence with the result rather than with the reasons, Houlden J.A.'s statement is significant in that it focused only on the twin requirements of s. 30(1).

Similarly, in *R. v. Penno* (1977), 35 C.C.C. (2d) 266 the British Columbia Court of Appeal also admitted a written record of inventory numbers prepared by one person based on the information of another. The Court relied on *Ares v. Venner* and s. 30(1) of the Canada Evidence Act.

In *R. v. Grimba* (1978), 38 C.C.C. (2d) 469 (Ont. Co. Ct.), the Crown tendered expert fingerprint evidence to demonstrate that the fingerprints taken from the accused were the same as those on a fingerprint record obtained from the United States Federal Bureau of Investigation. The expert had not made the record and had no personal knowledge of its accuracy, but had been with the FBI for eleven years and described the FBI as serving as a repository for fingerprint records. The Court interpreted s. 30(1) to allow the admission of the records even though they contained double hearsay. Callaghan Co. Ct. J. stated (at p. 471):

It would appear that the rationale behind [s. 30(1)] for admitting a form of hearsay evidence is the inherent circumstantial guarantee of accuracy which one would find in a business context from records which are relied upon in the day to day affairs of individual businesses, and which are subject to frequent testing and cross-checking. Records thus systematically stored, produced and regularly relied upon should, it would appear under s. 30, not be barred from this Court's consideration.

This passage characterizes s. 30(1) as providing a clear exception to the hearsay rules.

In *R. v. Biasi* (1982), 62 C.C.C. (2d) 304 (B.C.S.C.) Justice Paris had to decide whether a telephone company's "circuit card security documents" were admissible. Some of the information contained in the cards was provided by the RCMP to the telephone company who then prepared them. With respect to their admissibility Paris J. ruled:

Nor does the fact that when the record was made up the information was received from another party make the record inadmissible as being hearsay. The provisions of the Canada Evidence Act provide for the admissibility of such records as proof of the facts contained in them even if the record maker received his information from another party, as long as the facts recorded on the document would themselves be admissible in evidence.

Since the Ewart text was published, the Alberta Court of Appeal in *R. v. Boles* (1985), 57 A.R. 232 considered the admissibility of hotel records which confirmed the presence of some of the principal conspirators in India. Admissibility was questioned on the basis that the records contained double hearsay, i.e., presumably the information was given to the hotel management by its employees. Relying on each of the above authorities, the Court concluded that s. 30(1) renders admissible a document made in the ordinary course of business notwithstanding that it contains double hearsay. (See also *R. v. Ross* (1992), 92 Nfld. & P.E.I.R. 51 (Nfld. S.C.) where the Court confirmed the admissibility under s. 30 of written records prepared by a manager with information given to him by other employees.)

Turning to apply these authorities to the case at bar, the trial judge ought to have admitted the tables pursuant to s. 30 of the Canada Evidence Act. As Houlden J.A. said in Anthes, s. 30 makes admissible records made in the usual and ordinary course of business where oral evidence in respect of a matter would be admissible in a legal proceeding. The tables in this case were made in the usual and ordinary course of business of Sask. Agriculture and Food. Section 6 of The Department of Agriculture Act mandates the gathering of the statistics which are then used in the department's regular business of administering agricultural programs. Oral evidence would be admissible, but at some considerable cost and inconvenience. To call every farmer who had farmed for the applicable 15 year period in the two rural municipalities would be impossible. In this case, but for the ability to admit these tables, the information they contained would be lost to the court as occurred in this case. The Crown's witness was prepared to testify that the department used these statistics in its work and relied upon them. As Callaghan Co. Ct. J. said in *Grimba*, ''records thus systematically stored, produced and regularly relied upon should not be barred from the courts' consideration.''

The opening words of s. 30(6) appear to permit a consideration of weight to be made when the court considers admissibility. But if this means a court must reject a record because it contains double hearsay, it places documents prepared in the ordinary course of business in a fundamentally different category than documents admitted pursuant to the common law business duty exception. As indicated in *Ares*, weight is an issue to be addressed after the document is accepted as evidence. The circumstances in which the information was gathered or the record produced, or the lack of such evidence, may affect the weight to be given to it by the trier of fact, but it does not affect its admissibility.

As a general rule, documents made in the ordinary course of business are admitted to avoid the cost and inconvenience of calling the record keeper and the maker. As a matter of necessity the document is admitted. Proof that a document is made in the ordinary course of business prima facie fulfils the qualification that in order for hearsay to be admitted it must be trustworthy.

Section 30 would have accomplished little if the author of the data contained in a business record had to be called to testify. The complexity of modern business demands that most records will be composed of information gleaned by the maker from others.

The Ontario-type legislation allows records of "any act, transaction, occurrence or event" and the Canada Act permits records "in respect of a matter." Should records containing opinion be received? McCormick argues:

> In general, the opinion rule should be restricted to governing the manner of presenting courtroom testimony and should have little if any application to the admissibility of out-of-court statements. It would, however, be appropriate to recognize a discretionary power in the trial judge to exclude an entry if the form in which it was made render it so vague or speculative as to cause its probative value to be outweighed by the danger that it would mislead or confuse the jury ... Sustaining an objection to counsel's question to a witness as calling for an "opinion" is usually not a serious matter since counsel can in most cases easily reframe the question to call for the more concrete statement. But to reject the statement of the out-of-court narrative of what he observed on the ground that the statement is too general in form to meet the courtroom rules of interrogation mistakes the function of the opinion rule and may shut-out altogether a valuable item of proof.[182]

In *Adderly v. Bremner*,[183] Brooke, J. wrote:

> As to the question of the admissibility of the hospital record as proof of diagnosis, opinion or impression which are recorded in the hospital record at the time that the diagnosis was made or opinion or impression formed, I should think there is no doubt that the making of medical diagnosis is basic to the business of a hospital and it is made in the usual and ordinary course of that business. However, diagnosis is a

---

182. McCormick, *Evidence* (1972), pp. 41-42 and 721-22.
183. [1968] 1 O.R. 621 (H.C.).

professional opinion, and in my view it is not an act, transaction, occurrence or event within the meaning of the words in this section.[184]

Why? Recall that the judicially created business records exception, *Ares v. Venner*, allowed opinion regarding the colour of the toes!

(iv) *Former Testimony*

At common law:

Where a witness has given his testimony under oath in a judicial proceeding, in which the adverse litigant had the power to cross-examine, the testimony so given will, if the witness himself cannot be called, be admitted in any subsequent suit between the same parties, or those claiming under them, provided it relate to the same subject or substantially involve the same material questions.[185]

Grounds of necessity reside in the declarant's unavailability, and circumstantial guarantees of trustworthiness in the fact that the statement was given under oath and subject to cross-examination. Indeed, Professor Wigmore[186] would say that "if it has been already subjected to proper cross-examination, it has satisfied the rule and needs no exception in its favour." Nevertheless, the orthodox treatment is to characterize it as an exception, as the trier does not have the advantage of observing the evidence being given and tested on cross-examination.

In criminal cases a statutory embodiment of the common law rule presently appears in the Criminal Code:

715.(1) Where, at the trial of an accused, a person whose evidence was given at a previous trial on the same charge, or whose evidence was taken in the investigation of the charge against the accused or on the preliminary inquiry into the charge, refuses to be sworn or to give evidence, or if facts are proved on oath from which it can be inferred reasonably that the person

(*a*) is dead,
(*b*) has since become and is insane,
(*c*) is so ill that he is unable to travel or testify, or
(*d*) is absent from Canada,

and where it is proved that the evidence was taken in the presence of the accused, it may be admitted as evidence in the proceedings without further proof, unless the accused proves that the accused did not have full opportunity to cross-examine the witness.

(2)   Evidence that has been taken on the preliminary inquiry or other investigation of a charge against an accused may be admitted as evidence in the prosecution of the accused for any other offence on the same proof and in the same manner in all respects, as it might, according to law, be admitted as evidence in the prosecution of the offence with which the accused was charged when the evidence was taken.

---

184. *Ibid.*, at pp. 623-24. Followed in *Setak Computer v. Burroughs* (1997), 15 O.R. (2d) 750 at 761 (H.C.).

185. Taylor, *Evidence*, s. 464, as adopted in *Town of Walkerton v. Erdman* (1894), 23 S.C.R. 352.

186. 5 Wigmore, *Evidence* (Chad. Rev.), s. 1370. See *R. v. Speid* (1988), 63 C.R. (3d) 253 (Ont. C.A.).

(3)   For the purposes of this section, where evidence was taken at a previous trial or preliminary hearing or other proceeding in respect of an accused in the absence of the accused, who was absent by reason of having absconded, the accused is deemed to have been present during the taking of the evidence and to have had full opportunity to cross-examine the witness.

R. v. POTVIN
[1989] 1 S.C.R. 525, 68 C.R. (3d) 193, 47 C.C.C. (3d) 289

[The accused was charged with murder. The Crown called a witness who was alleged to have been an accomplice in the commission of the offence. The witness had testified at the preliminary inquiry and was cross-examined by counsel for the accused. He refused to testify at the accused's trial. The trial judge held that since the conditions set out in then section 643 of the Criminal Code had been met the evidence should be admitted. The accused was convicted and his appeal dismissed. He appealed further.]

WILSON J. (LAMER and SOPINKA, JJ. concurring):— The main issue on this appeal is whether the admission at trial of previously taken evidence under s. 643(1) [now section 715(1)] of the *Criminal Code*, R.S.C. 1970, c. C-34, as amended, . . . violates an accused's rights under ss. 7 or 11(*d*) of the *Canadian Charter of Rights and Freedoms*. . . .

. . . .

What rights then does an accused have under s. 7 of the Charter with respect to the admission of previous testimony? It is, in my view, basic to our system of justice that the accused have had a full opportunity to cross-examine the witness when the previous testimony was taken if a transcript of such testimony is to be introduced as evidence in a criminal trial for the purpose of convicting the accused. This is in accord with the traditional view that it is the opportunity to cross-examine and not the fact of cross-examination which is crucial if the accused is to be treated fairly. As Professor Delisle has noted: Annotation (1986), 50 C.R. (3d) 195 at p. 196: "If the opposing party has had an opportunity to fully cross-examine he ought not to be justified in any later complaint if he did not fully exercise that right." . . .

. . . .

With respect to the appellant's submission that he was deprived of a fair trial under s. 11(*d*) of the Charter, I would conclude, for the reasons given above in reviewing his s. 7 claim, that this claim must also fail if his constitutional right to have had a full opportunity to cross-examine the witness on the earlier occasion was respected. . . .

. . . .

It is my view that the word "may" in s. 643(1) is directed not to the parties but to the trial judge. I believe it confers on him or her a discretion not to allow the previous testimony to be admitted in circumstances where its admission would operate unfairly to the accused. . . .

. . . .

What then is the nature and purpose of the discretion conferred in s. 643(1) which enables the trial judge not to allow the evidence in at trial even in cases in which the requirements of the section have been met? In my view, there are two main types of mischief at which the discretion might be aimed. First, the discretion could be aimed at situations in which there has been unfairness in the manner in which the evidence was obtained. Although Parliament has set out in the section specific conditions as to how the previous testimony has to have been obtained if it is to be admitted under s. 643(1) (the most important, of course, being that the accused was afforded full opportunity to cross-examine the witness), Parliament could have intended the judge to have a discretion in those rare cases in which compliance with the requirements of s. 643(1) gave no guarantee that the evidence was obtained in a manner fair to the accused. This would, of course, represent a departure from the traditional common law approach that the manner in which evidence is obtained, with a few well-established exceptions such as the confessions rule, is not relevant to the question of its admissibility but it would be consistent with the contemporary approach to the expanded requirements of adjudicative fairness. An example of unfairness in obtaining the testimony might be a case in which, although the witness was temporarily absent from Canada, the Crown could have obtained the witness's attendance at trial with a minimal degree of effort. Another example might be a case in which the Crown was aware at the time the evidence was initially taken that the witness would not be available to testify at the trial but did not inform the accused of this fact so that he could make best use of the opportunity to cross-examine the witness at the earlier proceeding. These kinds of circumstances related to the obtaining of the evidence on the earlier occasion might have been in the mind of the legislator as triggering the judge's discretion with respect to its admission at the trial.

A different concern at which the discretion might have been aimed is the effect of the admission of the previously taken evidence on the fairness of the trial itself. This concern flows from the principle of the law of evidence that evidence may be excluded if it is highly prejudicial to the accused and of only modest probative value. . . . How the evidence was obtained might be irrelevant under this principle.

. . . .

In my view, once it is accepted that s. 643(1) gives the trial judge a statutory discretion to depart from the purely mechanical application of the section, the discretion should be construed as sufficiently broad to deal with both kinds of situations, namely where the testimony was obtained in a manner which was unfair to the accused or where, even although the manner of obtaining the evidence was fair to the accused, its admission at his or her trial would not be fair to the accused. I would stress that in both situations the discretion should only be exercised after weighing what I have referred to as the "two competing and frequently conflicting concerns" of fair treatment of the accused and society's interest in the admission of probative evidence in order to get at the truth of the matter in issue. . . . Having regard to the reservations that have been expressed over the restrictive formulation of the common law discretion in *Wray*, *supra*, . . . I believe there is no need or justification for importing a similar restriction into the statutorily conferred discretion in s. 643(1). The protection of the accused from unfairness rather than the admission of probative evidence "without too much regard for the fairness of the adjudicative process" . . . should be the focus of the trial judge's concern.

It will follow that I cannot accept the hard and fast rule approach to this issue taken by the Manitoba Court of Appeal in *Sophonow*, *supra*. That court seems to suggest that the very importance of the evidence requires it to be excluded. . . . I believe that this proposition is at odds with the purpose of s. 643(1) in ensuring that evidence, even important and highly probative evidence, is not lost because of the unavailability of a witness at trial. . . .

In the case at bar I am of the view that the trial judge did not instruct himself properly as to the nature and scope of his discretion under s. 643(1). He stressed the high probative value of the evidence of someone who had been in the victim's home at the time the events occurred but failed, in my view, to give adequate consideration to possible unfairness to the accused arising from either the manner in which the evidence was obtained or the effect of its admission on the fairness of the trial. The Court of Appeal proceeded on the basis that the trial judge had no discretion other than the restrictive common law formulation in *Wray.* Neither court applied its mind to the question whether in the circumstances of this case the trial judge should have exercised his statutory discretion in s. 643(1) to exclude the evidence.

There can be no doubt about the fact that the decision whether or not to exercise the statutory discretion in this case would not have been an easy one. In favour of the admission of the evidence is the absence of any allegation that the manner in which Deschênes' testimony was obtained was unfair to the appellant. Moreover, the appellant's counsel exercised his right to cross-examine Deschênes at the preliminary inquiry and there was some cross-examination. There was also a measure of corroboration of Deschênes' testimony (so far as it purported Potvin as the culprit) by the testimony of Thibault at trial. Also favouring admission of Deschênes' testimony was the factor emphasized by the trial judge, namely its high probative value. The testimony purported to be an eyewitness account of the appellant beating and killing the victim. On the other hand, given the appellant's defence that he was a passive observer and that it was Deschênes, the unavailable witness, who did the actual beating and killing, the issue of Deschênes' credibility was obviously critical to the trier of fact's decision whether to accept or reject Deschênes' version of the events. Yet the jury had no opportunity to observe Deschênes' demeanour as an aid in assessing that witness's credibility.

This is not, however, a matter for this court to decide but rather a matter to be referred back to a trial judge properly instructed as to the nature and scope of his or her statutory discretion under s. 643(1).

. . . .

LA FOREST J. (DICKSON, C.J.C. concurring):— I have had the advantage of reading the reasons of my colleague, Wilson J. I agree with her conclusion and, apart from what follows, her reasoning as well. However, I take a different view of s. 643(1) of the *Criminal Code* and, in consequence, of the source of the discretion to exclude the evidence permitted to be adduced under that provision.

As I read s. 643, it is not directly addressed to the prosecution or the judge, although it has, of course, implications for how they perform their duties. The provision is directed at a certain type of evidence. It makes it admissible. The parties to a trial may, therefore, invoke the provision if they wish. But the provision does not provide that the evidence previously taken shall be accepted; it provides, rather, that it may be read as evidence. This leaves room for the operation of the ordinary principles of the law of evidence, including the rule that the trial judge may exclude admissible evidence if its prejudicial effect substantially outweighs its probative value: see *R. v. Corbett.* . . . The case most frequently cited for the discretion to exclude is *R. v. Wray,* . . . where it is referred to in a dictum by Martland J., but it is simply one of the fundamental postulates of the law of evidence.

As my colleague notes, some have interpreted Martland J.'s dictum as limiting the discretion solely to situations where the evidence is highly prejudicial to the accused and is only of modest probative value. I do not accept this restrictive approach to the discretion. As I noted in *Corbett, supra,* at pp. 433-6 C.C.C., pp. 736-40 S.C.R., this narrow view, which can be traced from a statement by Lord du Parcq in *Noor Mohamed v. The King,* [1949] A.C. 182 at p. 192, has now been rejected by the House of Lords: *R. v. Sang,* [1980] A.C. 402 (H.L.). That case, and others there referred to, make it clear that under English law, a judge in a criminal trial always has a discretion to exclude evidence if, in the judge's opinion, its prejudicial effect substantially outweighs its probative value. . . .

. . . As their Lordships make clear, the discretion is grounded in the judge's duty to ensure a fair trial. . . . I am in accord with their view of the nature of the discretion.

. . . [I]t is evident that the trial judge failed to properly instruct himself either about the existence of the discretion or, more likely, about its nature. He repeatedly stresses the relevance of the evidence without any consideration of its prejudicial character. This smacks of the restricted view of the discretion I have rejected. In my view, therefore, the trial judge failed to exercise the discretion which was incumbent upon him to ensure a fair trial.

—————————

The Manitoba Court of Appeal had decided in *R. v. Sophonow*[187] that there was a discretion in the trial judge to exclude previous testimony, as the statutory provision

> was never intended to apply to a crucial witness whose evidence could work an injustice to the accused if the jury were deprived of seeing his demeanour and his reaction to cross-examination.[188]

The Alberta Court of Appeal had decided in *R. v. Kaddoura*[189] that there was no discretion to exclude previous testimony which satisfied the conditions of the statutory provision:

> I would not curtail s. 643(1) by confining its operation to housekeeping witnesses. A comprehensive mechanism for the preservation and admission of previously-taken evidence, especially critical evidence, is essential in any criminal trial regime which may direct a new trial as a remedy for error.[190]

Potvin has asserted a discretion to exclude highly probative evidence when admission at trial would be unfair. The court states that it is not embracing the hard-and-fast rule approach, taken in *Sophonow*, which would always exclude important evidence. The court, however, recognizes that the issue of credibility of the unavailable witness was critical. In *Potvin* the jury had no opportunity to observe that witness's demeanour, and the court decided that the matter therefore must be referred back to the trial judge for an exercise of the broader discretion it now recognizes.

This is a significant break with the past. For hundreds of years previous testimony has been receivable if the party against whom the evidence is led had the opportunity to cross-examine. The section in the Code simply declared the common law. Whether one approaches the previous testimony as not hearsay (Wigmore) or as hearsay but admissible as an exception to the hearsay rule (McCormick), the previous testimony was always receivable. Unlike other hearsay exceptions, the statement was given under oath, the accuracy of the statement has been certified by a written transcript, and the statement was made in the presence of the party against whom it is now sought to introduce it, subject to an opportunity in that party to cross-examine, and given in solemn circumstances which should promote trustworthiness. The only thing lacking is the opportunity for the trier of fact to observe the demeanour of the witness, but the opportunity to observe the demeanour of the witness is *never* available when hearsay evidence is tendered by the Crown and received under any of the other myriad of exceptions to the hearsay rule. The next logical step from *Potvin* might be to recognize a discretion to exclude on the basis of fairness any and all hearsay statements, whether or not they fit within one of our exceptions, which are

—————————

187. (1986), 50 C.R. (3d) 193.
188. *Ibid.*, at p. 209.
189. (1987), 60 C.R. (3d) 393.
190. *Ibid.*, at p. 399.

important to the Crown's case and depend for their worth on the credibility of the out-of-court asserter. And this "logical" extension therefore suggests a concern about the step taken by the court in *Potvin*.

All rules of evidence are grounded in considerations of reliability, efficiency and fairness. One could never quarrel with the court's assertion here that the trial judge should ensure fairness to the accused at the trial. One could argue, however, that fairness to the accused is already assured by the conditions set out in the legislation, and that an additional discretionary power in the trial judge is unnecessary.[191]

PROBLEM

At a sexual assault trial the accused was unrepresented. He was permitted to cross-examine the complainant for two days. The accused was convicted but on appeal the Quebec Court of Appeal ordered a new trial. At the new trial the complainant refused to testify on the basis the experience of the first trial had lead to depression and a suicide attempt. The Crown applies to have the evidence of the complainant at the first trial admitted to prove the truth. Would you as the judge admit the evidence? On what basis? Do different considerations apply to admitting the transcript as distinct from the audio recording? See *R. v. Dégarie, No. 1* (June 28, 2001), (C.Q.), and *R. v. Dégarie, No. 2* (June 29, 2001), (C.Q.).

(c) Exceptions not Dependent on Availability of Declarant

(i) *Declarations as to Physical Sensation*

In *Gilbey v. Great Western Railway* [192] it was alleged that the deceased had suffered his injury on the job and that compensation from his employer was forthcoming. The trial court received in evidence statements made by the deceased to his wife not merely of his sensations but as to the cause of the injury. On appeal it was held, by Cozens-Hardy, M.R.:

> I do not doubt at all that statements made by a workman to his wife of his sensations at the time, about the pain in the side or his head, or what not — whether those statements were made by groans or by actions or were verbal statements — would be admissible to prove the existence of those sensations. But to hold that those statements ought to go further and be admitted as evidence of the facts deposed to is, I think, open to doubt; such a contention is contrary to all authority.

There have never been grounds of necessity, such as death or insanity of the declarant, attached to this exception but it is believed that there is "a fair necessity, in the sense that there is no other equally satisfactory source of evidence either from the same person or elsewhere."[193] Given these grounds of necessity the evidence

> is not to be extended beyond the necessity on which the rule is founded. Anything in the nature of narration or statement is to be carefully excluded, and the testimony

---

191. *Potvin* was applied in *R. v. Syliboy* (1989), 51 C.C.C. (3d) 503 (N.B.C.A.).
192. (1910), 102 L.T. 202 (C.A.); cited with approval by Middleton, J. in *Youlden v. London Guar. Co.* (1912), 4 D.L.R. 721 (Ont. H.C.); affirmed 12 D.L.R. 433 (Ont. C.A.).
193. 6 Wigmore, *Evidence* (Chad. Rev.), s. 1714, p. 90. It is believed that his spontaneous declaration would be superior to his later recounting of the condition in the witness stand.

is to be confined strictly to such complaints, exclamations, and expressions as usually and naturally accompany and furnish evidence of a present existing pain or malady.[194]

Circumstantial guarantees of trustworthiness are resident in the fact that the declarant, if anyone, should be able to perceive his own sensations or feelings; his declaration is of the moment and defects in memory are absent. Arising from the spontaneity of the declaration and lack of opportunity to fabricate there is some assurance of sincerity, though it is recognized that fabrication can occur. Though the statements under review need not be made to a physician, such declarations would carry the further assurance that the declarant is unlikely to mislead the person from whom he seeks assistance.

(ii) Declarations as to Mental or Emotional State

When a person's mental or emotional state is a material issue in the trial, then that person's statements evidencing the same may be received, and for the same reasons as recounted above justifying declarations as to physical sensation. If at trial X's domicile is material, his earlier statement, "I plan to make Canada my home," is receivable to prove his intent, as we see that the hearsay dangers of communication, memory and perception are absent; in a suit for alienation of affections the wife-declarant's earlier statement of "I don't love you anymore" would similarly be receivable under this exception. Notice that these statements will be received though they were made before or after the moment that the state of mind was material; if the trier determines that a certain state of mind existed on Day 1 he will be able to reason that the same state of mind continued to exist to Day 5.

In a prosecution for murder, statements of the accused, "I'll blow his brains out," "I hate him," would also be receivable under this exception as evidence of intent, but since they also constitute admissions, and are receivable under that head, this exception is seldom canvassed. Of course, admissions are only received when tendered *against* the accused. If statements of the accused, "I never meant to do him harm," "I loved him," are tendered under this exception they would be met with the rebuke that they are self-serving and inadmissible on that ground. Self-serving evidence is excluded because of the danger that an accused might manufacture evidence; but to assume the falsity of the evidence is to beg the question. Professor Wigmore comments:

> Because [we say] this accused person *might* be guilty and therefore *might* have contrived these false utterances, therefore we shall exclude them, although without this assumption they indicate feelings wholly inconsistent with guilt, and although, if he is innocent, their exclusion is a cruel deprivation of a most natural and effective sort of evidence. To hold that every expression of hatred, malice and bravado is to be received, while no expression of fear, goodwill, friendship, or the like, can be considered, is to exhibit ourselves the victims of a narrow whimsicality, which might be expected in the tribunal of Jeffreys, going down from London to Taunton with a list of his intended victims already in his pocket, or on a bench "condemning" to order, as Zola said of Dreyfus's military judges.

---

194. Per Bigelow, J. in *Bacon v. Charlton* (1851), 7 Cush. 586, as quoted in 6 Wigmore, *Evidence* (Chad. Rev.), s. 1718.

. . . There is no reason why a declaration of an existing state of mind, if it would be admissible against the accused, should not also be admissible in his favour, except so far as the circumstances indicate plainly a motive to deceive.[195]

Statements evidencing the state of mind of the declarant may be express or implied; for example in the suit for alienation of affections, the wife may have written to her friends about her husband in a contemptuous way. These statements are often not characterized as falling within this hearsay exception, but rather as pieces of original evidence circumstantially indicating the declarant's mental state. Since, in any case, the statements are receivable, does it matter how they are characterized?

In the above instances, the statements are tendered as evidence when state of mind is a material issue. A larger problem develops if the statements are tendered to evidence an existing state of mind which is not itself material but is relevant to a material issue: for example, in a murder prosecution, evidence of the deceased's statement "I want it all to end" indicating her intention to commit suicide as evidence that later she did perform the act; evidence of the deceased's statement that "I'm going to see Joe tonight and have it out with him" as evidence against Joe that the two fought later that evening. The authorities on this point are meagre and in conflict.[196] The classic "text-book" case in this area is *Mutual Life Insurance Co. v. Hillmon.*[197] The plaintiff sought to recover the proceeds from an insurance policy on her deceased husband. The insurance company resisted on the ground that the body found in Crooked Creek, Kansas was not that of Hillmon but that of his travelling companion, Walters. The disputed evidence consisted of letters written by Walters to his fiancee that he intended to go with Hillmon to Crooked Creek. The court held that the letters should have been received:

> The existence of a particular intention in a certain person at a certain time being a material fact to be proved, evidence that he expressed that intention at that time is as direct evidence of that fact as his own testimony that he then had that intention would be. After his death there can hardly be any other way of proving it, and while he is still alive his own memory of his state of mind at a former time is no more likely to be clear and true than a bystander's recollection of what he then said, and is less trustworthy than letters written by him at the very time and under circumstances precluding a suspicion of misrepresentation. The letters in question were competent . . . evidence that . . . he had the intention of going, and of going with Hillmon, which made it more probable both that he did go and that he went with Hillmon than if there had been no proof of such intention.[198]

The hearsay analysis is faultless; the hearsay dangers are minimized. True it is that "it was only a statement of intention which might or might not have been

---

195. 6 Wigmore, *Evidence* (Chad. Rev.), s. 1732, p. 160.
196. Contrast *R. v. Buckley* (1873), 13 Cox C.C. 293 and *R. v. Wainwright* (1875), 13 Cox C.C. 171. See also *R. v. Thomson*, [1912] 3 K.B. 19 (C.C.A.); *Cuff v. Frazee Storage & Cartage Co.* (1907), 14 O.L.R. 263 (C.A.); *R. v. Moghal* (1977), 65 Cr. App. R. 56; *Home v. Corbeil*, [1955] 4 D.L.R. 750 (Ont. H.C.); affirmed 2 D.L.R. (2d) 543 (Ont. C.A.). Recall *Sugden v. Lord St. Leonard's* (1876), 1 P.D. 154 (C.A.) and its view of the pretestamentary declaration. And see *Workman v. R.*, [1963] 1 C.C.C. 297 (Alta. C.A.); affirmed [1963] 2 C.C.C. 1 (S.C.C.).
197. 145 U.S. 285 (1892).
198. *Ibid.*, at p. 295.

carried out"[199] but the problem that the declarant might not follow through with his intention is not a hearsay problem but rather a problem of relevance.

Suppose however that the declaration of mental state is a statement of belief in the declarant as evidence of some past act.[200] In *Shepard v. U.S.*,[201] a murder prosecution, the statement of the deceased was received as a dying declaration: "Dr. Shepard has poisoned me." On appeal, the conditions of that exception were found not to have been met and the prosecution sought to justify the evidence as indicating the deceased's state of mind which was then inconsistent with the defence of suicide. Cardozo, J. wrote:

> There are times when a state of mind, if relevant, may be proved by contemporaneous declarations of feeling or intent. Mutual Life Ins. Co. v. Hillmon. . . . (other examples are then given) . . . The ruling in that case marks the high-water line beyond which courts have been unwilling to go. . . . Declarations of intention, casting light upon the future, have been sharply distinguished from declarations of memory, pointing backwards to the past. There would be an end, or nearly that, to the rule against hearsay if the distinction were ignored.[202]

If an express statement evidencing a belief in the declarant, a mental state, concerning some phenomena external to the declarant is to be rejected as hearsay, should conduct which only has relevance as implying such a statement be treated differently? Recall *R. v. Wysochan*[203] and *Ratten v. R.*,[204] discussed above.

R. v. P. (R.)
(1990), 58 C.C.C. (3d) 334 (Ont. H.C.)

[The accused was charged with murder. The Crown sought to introduce several statements said to have been made by the deceased to various Crown witnesses. These statements were said to be capable of demonstrating her state of mind. They would show her unhappiness and dissatisfaction with the relationship she had with the accused and her determination to end that relationship. The Crown alleged that the accused was motivated to kill the deceased because he was enraged and humiliated by her decision to leave him.]

DOHERTY J.:—

. . . .

Relevant evidence can be defined as evidence having any tendency to make the existence of any fact that is of consequence to the determination of the action more probable

---

199. The reason given by Cockburn, C.J. in *R. v. Wainwright, supra*, note 196, at p. 172, for rejecting such a statement.
200. The problem is canvassed in Seligman, "An Exception to the Hearsay Rule" (1912-13), 26 Harv. L. Rev. 146; and see Maguire, "The Hillmon Case — Thirty-three Years After" (1925), 38 Harv. L. Rev. 709.
201. 290 U.S. 96 (1933).
202. *Ibid.*, at p. 104. But compare *People v. Merkouris*, 344 P. 2d 1 (Cal. S.C., 1959); cert. den. 361 U.S. 943 (1960).
203. (1930), 54 C.C.C. 172 (Sask. C.A.).
204. [1972] A.C. 378 (P.C.).

or less probable than it would be without the evidence: . . . R. Delisle, *"Evidence Principles and Problems"*, 2nd ed. (1989), pp. 9-11.

In the case at bar, relevance has two aspects. Are the statements relevant to the deceased's state of mind in that they permit one to draw a reasonable conclusion as to her state of mind? If so, is her state of mind relevant directly or indirectly to the fact in issue? . . . I have already indicated that the statements clear the first relevance hurdle.

Relevance is a matter of inductive logic requiring that the trial judge examine the proffered evidence in light of his own knowledge and understanding of human conduct: *McCormick, ibid.*, p. 544; *Delisle, ibid.*, p. 10. Relevance is situational and depends not only on the ultimate issue in the case (*e.g.*, identification), but also on the other factual issues which either of the litigants raises as relevant to the ultimate issue. Consequently, the deceased's mental state may bear no direct relevance to the ultimate issue of identification but it will none the less be relevant to that issue if it is relevant to another fact (*e.g.*, motive) which is directly relevant to the ultimate issue of identification.

. . . .

Assuming relevance, evidence of utterances made by a deceased (although the rule is not limited to deceased persons) which evidence her state of mind are admissible. If the statements are explicit statements of a state of mind, they are admitted as exceptions to the hearsay rule. If those statements permit an inference as to the speaker's state of mind, they are regarded as original testimonial evidence and admitted as circumstantial evidence from which a state of mind can be inferred. The result is the same whichever route is taken, although circumstantial evidence of a state of mind poses added problems rising out of the inference drawing process.

. . . .

Evidence of the deceased's state of mind may, in turn, be relevant as circumstantial evidence that the deceased subsequently acted in accordance with that avowed state of mind. Where a deceased says, "I will go to Ottawa tomorrow", the statement affords direct evidence of the state of mind — an intention to go to Ottawa tomorrow — and circumstantial evidence that the deceased in fact went to Ottawa on that day. If either the state of mind, or the fact to be inferred from the existence of the state of mind is relevant, the evidence is receivable subject to objections based on undue prejudice. . . .

An utterance indicating that a deceased had a certain intention or design will afford evidence that the deceased acted in accordance with that stated intention or plan where it is reasonable to infer that the deceased did so. The reasonableness of the inference will depend on a number of variables including the nature of the plan described in the utterance, and the proximity in time between the statement as to the plan and the proposed implementation of the plan.

The rules of evidence as developed to this point do not exclude evidence of utterances by a deceased which reveal her state of mind, but rather appear to provide specifically for their admission where relevant. The evidence is not, however, admissible to show the state of mind of persons other than the deceased (unless they were aware of the statements), or to show that persons other than the deceased acted in accordance with the deceased's stated intentions, save perhaps cases where the act was a joint one involving the deceased and another person. The evidence is also not admissible to establish that past acts or events referred to in the utterances occurred.

. . . .

A trial judge may, in his discretion, exclude evidence which is otherwise admissible where the potential prejudicial effect of that evidence outweighs its potential probative force. [Citations omittted.]

Prejudice can refer to several things. In the context of this case, it means the danger, despite instructions to the contrary, that the jury will use the evidence of the deceased's utterances for purposes other than drawing inferences and conclusions as to her state of mind and as to her subsequent conduct. In particular, the jury may infer from some of the utterances that Mr. P. was a tyrannical person, obsessed with controlling the deceased even to the extent of engaging in illegal and bizarre conduct. From that, they may infer that he is the sort of person who would kill someone who dared challenge his authority over that person. This line of reasoning, while not illogical, is not permitted: *R. v. D. (L.E.)*, *supra*, at p. 157.

The balancing process envisioned by the claim that prejudicial potential outweighs probative potential is no longer designed only to root out the most extreme cases where prejudicial potential is "grave" and probative value is "trifling": *R. v. Wray*, [1970] 4 C.C.C. 1 at p. 17. The onus, however, is on the accused to demonstrate that the balance favours exclusion of otherwise admissible evidence. Where the prejudice asserted rests in the potential misuse of the evidence by the jury, one's assessment of the jury's ability to properly follow directions will play a key role in determining whether the accused has shown that the balance favours exclusion. Views as to the jury's ability to follow the law rather than their instincts or prejudices differ. . . . I incline to the view that lawyers and judges tend to underestimate the intellectual power and discipline of juries.

R. v. JACK
(1992), 70 C.C.C. (3d) 67 (Man. C.A.)

[The accused was charged with the murder of his wife. The body of the deceased was never found. At trial, a great deal of evidence was admitted of statements made by the deceased to her family and friends. This evidence was led in an effort to show that the deceased would not have abandoned her family and friends.]

SCOTT C.J.M.:—

. . . .

Evidence tendered by the Crown disclosed that in and around December, 1988, Christine Jack met and spoke with a number of her friends. She made comments to all of them regarding her feelings and future intentions. Statements to these persons were admitted by the trial judge as original evidence of the state of mind of Christine Jack. . . .

From all of this evidence the picture that emerges is one of a loving, caring mother who would not willingly abandon her children, family and friends whatever the personal provocation. Equally clear is that she had made up her mind the marriage was finished and had determined, once the holiday season was over, to effect a separation.

. . . .

The trial judge admitted some oral statements and excluded others. In doing so he adopted a test of circumstantial trustworthiness depending in essence upon the nature of the relationship between the witness and Christine Jack. The closer and more long-standing the relationship, the stronger the element of trustworthiness. For this reason, certain statements made to casual acquaintances were not allowed in evidence.

. . . .

The accused's position is that the admission of such evidence was an error: first, because it was not relevant to a material issue before the jury, and secondly, because its probative value was outweighed by its potential prejudice to the accused due to his inability to cross-examine the declarant, Christine Jack.

In my opinion, the trial judge was right in admitting evidence of the state of mind/future plans of Christine Jack especially given the fact that there was no *corpus delicti*.

[Scott, C.J.M. then quoted from *R. v. P. (R.)* (1990), 58 C.C.C. (3d) 334, 338 (Ont. H.C.), and *R. v. Smith* (1990), 61 C.C.C. (3d) 232 (Ont. C.A.).]

The approach in *P. (R.)*, *supra*, was expressly approved by the Ontario Court of Appeal in *Smith*, *supra*. Again it was noted that statements could be admitted if they tended to prove the declarant's present intention. They were admissible as original evidence to show state of mind from which an inference might be drawn, but could not be tendered as proof of the truth of past acts.

. . . .

. . . [T]he broad, general rulings made by the trial judge permitting the introduction of state-of-mind/future-intentions evidence based on a witness-by-witness assessment of the circumstantial trustworthiness of the evidence, and the circumstances under which the statement was made, were correct.

PEOPLE v. MERKOURIS
(1959), 344 P. 2d 1 (Ca. S.C.)

[The accused was convicted of murder and appealed. Consider the court's ruling on the following point:]

Third. *Did the trial court err in receiving in evidence, (a) over defendant's objection, statements made by the deceased, Despine and Robert Forbes, through the testimony of Mr. and Mrs. Fairly and Officer Bonk,*

[7] *No.* (a) The testimony of Mr. and Mrs. Fairly and Officer Bonk, of which defendant complains, was to the effect that in August 1948 Despine and Robert Forbes expressed to Mr. and Mrs. Fairly their intent to stay with them awhile because defendant had threatened their lives, and that in 1949 or 1950 Robert Forbes expressed to Officer Bonk his intention to obtain a permit to carry a gun because defendant had been bothering the Forbeses again. This testimony was objected to on the ground that it was immaterial, hearsay, remote, and prejudicial. In overruling the objection, the judge admonished the jury that the evidence was being received for the limited purpose of showing the declaration of intent of the deceased persons and their state of mind and not as to the truth of the statements alleged to have been made.

The trial court's rulings were correct. The victims' assertions of intent to avoid and protect themselves from defendant were admissible under the mental state exception to the hearsay rule as evidence that in fact they had such intent. The existence of that intent evidences the declarants' fear of defendant.

The declarations that defendant had threatened the victims were admissible, not to prove the truth of that fact directly, but to prove the victims' fear.

[8] Where, as here, the identification of defendant as the killer is in issue, the fact that the victims feared defendant is relevant because it is some evidence that they had reason to fear him, that ii, that there is a probability that the fear had been aroused by the victims' knowledge of the conduct of defendant indicating his intent to harm them rather than, e.g., that the victims' fear was paranoid.

R. v. TOY
[1998] A.J. No. 147 (Alta. Q.B.)

[This was a murder case. Within 15 minutes after the stabbing took place, the accused was found by police wielding a blood-stained knife and was arrested. He told police upon his arrest that "I was attacked in apartment 408." The defence sought to have that statement entered into evidence through one of the police officers. The trial judge decided that the statement was admissible.]

ROOKE J.:—It is admissible for the limited purpose of showing the accused's state of mind at the time that it was made. When admitted for this purpose, statements made by an accused cannot be used for the truth of their contents but only to show the declarant's mental or emotional state at the time of the utterance. Such statements are not, strictly speaking, an exception to the hearsay rule at all but are original, circumstantial, evidence. In the instant case, therefore, I find that the impugned statement does not fall under the res gestae exception and cannot be offered for the truth of its contents. However, I also find that the statement does fall under the "state of mind" category or exception. I therefore hold that the statement is admissible, but only for the limited purpose of establishing the accused's mental or emotional state shortly after the stabbings and upon his arrest. Unless the issue is moot, due to the accused's confirmatory testimony, the jury should be cautioned appropriately as to this limited purpose for admission.

How would you charge the jury if the accused doesn't testify?

R. v. STARR
[2000] 2 S.C.R. 144, 36 C.R. (5th) 1, 147 C.C.C. (3d) 449

[The accused was charged with two counts of first degree murder. He was accused of shooting C and W by the side of a highway. C and W had been drinking with the accused in a hotel. C and W drove to a gas station. The accused also drove to that station. There G, a sometime girlfriend of C, angry with C because he was out with W rather than her, confronted C. G asked C why he would not come home with her. According to G, C replied that he had to "go and do an Autopac scam with Robert". She understood "Robert" to be the accused. The Crown's theory was that the killing was a gang-related execution perpetrated by the accused. W was an unfortunate witness who was killed simply because she was in the wrong place at the wrong time. The theory was that the accused had used an Autopac scam as a pretext to get C out into the countryside. The trial judge found that G's anticipated testimony regarding the scam was admissible under the "present intentions" or "state of mind" exception to the hearsay rule. The Court of Appeal, in a majority decision, upheld the accused?s convictions.]

McLACHLIN, C.J., BASTARACHE, J. concurring: —

. . . .

The first question is whether an established exception to the hearsay rule applies to the evidence at issue. The answer in this case is yes. The victim's statement that he intended to do an Autopac scam with the accused later that night is a statement of present intention. Statements of present intention constitute a long-recognized exception to the rule against admitting hearsay evidence. The next question concerns the ambit of the exception of statements of present intention. Here my colleagues differ. L'Heureux-Dubé J. holds that all statements of present intention are admissible. Iacobucci J., following Professor Wigmore's formulation of the exception, holds that statements of present intention are admissible, unless made in circumstances of suspicion. Canadian law has not yet settled this question.

Interpreting the exception in light of the underlying requirements of necessity and reliability, I share Iacobucci J.'s view that statements of present intention presented for the truth of their contents (i.e., to permit inferences as to what the person in fact did) are admissible, provided they were not made in circumstances of suspicion. Contemporaneity is cited as providing a guarantee of trustworthiness for statements of present intention. In the normal course, the words are contemporaneous with a present intention to do that act. If a person as she heads out the door says, "I'm going to the store", there is every reason to believe that is what she intends to do. This flows from the fact that in the great majority of cases, people making such statements actually intend to do the indicated act. The statement of intention is admitted as a statement of mental condition: inferences that may be drawn as to whether the intended act occurred are another matter: *Wigmore on Evidence*, vol. 6 (Chadbourn rev. 1976), at para. 1725, p. 139; R. J. Delisle: "*R. v. Smith*: The Relevance of Hearsay" (1991), 2 C.R. (4th) 260, at p. 264. The reason statements of present intention are generally reliable indicators of the speaker's "present" or contemporaneous state of mind was captured by Gray J. in *Mutual Life Insurance Co. v. Hillmon*. . . .

Sometimes, however, statements of intention may not reflect the actual present intention of the speaker. The circumstances may suggest that the speaker had reason to lie about his or her intentions. In such cases, the circumstantial guarantee of trustworthiness that underlies the exception disappears. This is why Wigmore held that the exception did not apply where the circumstances cast suspicion on whether the statement of intention represented the speaker's actual intention. Where circumstances of suspicion exist, the presumption of reliability that normally underlies the exception is removed, and it would be inconsistent with the principles underlying the exceptions to the hearsay rule to admit the evidence. (Given the presumption of reliability underlying the exception, it falls to the person opposing the evidence to show circumstances of suspicion.) For this reason, I agree with Iacobucci J. that the statements of present intention are admissible, absent circumstances of suspicion.

This brings us to the question of whether there were circumstances of suspicion here that precluded the trial judge from admitting the victim's statement that he was doing an Autopac scam with the accused later that night. The majority of the Court of Appeal held there were not. Iacobucci J., by contrast, finds there were. I find myself in agreement with the Court of Appeal. The victim Cook, who had another woman and two other people in his car, encountered his girlfriend at a service station. They conversed. He told her that he was going to do an Autopac scam with the accused later that night. They parted. The question is whether the circumstances of this encounter cast suspicion on whether the victim's statement represented his actual intention at the time he spoke. It is argued that the circumstances suggest that he may have made up the Autopac scam story to explain or offset the presence of another woman in his car. It is not clear to me how the statement that he intended to do an Autopac scam with the accused explains why another woman would be in the car with him. Nor is it clear how the statement countered the suggestion that the victim was romantically involved with the woman in the car. It begs the question, "If you are doing an Autopac scam with someone else later tonight, why are you with this woman?" If the victim had said he intended to do the scam with the woman, it might have attracted suspicion as to whether it represented his actual intentions. But that is not what occurred. Accordingly, I would admit the statement as evidence of what the deceased intended to do at the time he made the statement.

Iacobucci J. argues that the statement is not admissible for a second reason — because the statement involves the intention to do a joint act with a third person, the accused. In my view, this goes not to admissibility, but to the inferences which may be drawn from the statement.

. . . .

[M]y colleagues suggest that a jury can never infer what a person other than the speaker did from a statement of joint intention. I would not state the matter so categorically. Certainly, such a statement cannot support an inference as to the state of mind of the third party. However, in some circumstances the statement of joint intention can be fairly considered along with other evidence in deciding what the third party did. The declarant's state of mind may be one piece of evidence amongst others for the jury to consider in determining what happened. Viewed thus, Cook's statement may be viewed as one piece of circumstantial evidence supporting the inference that Starr was with the deceased later that night. . . . This said, it may be that where the only source of inference as to the third party's conduct is the statement of joint intention, it would be unsafe to permit the jury to rely on it for that purpose. When this occurs, the jury should be so directed. In my opinion, this was not such a case; the statement was merely one of a matrix of circumstances that the jury could consider in determining whether the accused met Cook later that night as Cook stated was their common intention. Accordingly, I conclude that the trial judge was not required to tell the jury that they could not consider the statement on the question of what the accused in fact did.

. . . .

L'HEUREUX-DUBÉ, J. (GONTHIER, J. concurring): —

. . . .

I would conclude that the principled necessity-reliability analysis, while appropriate where hearsay evidence does not fall within an established exception to the hearsay rule, has not replaced and should not supplant the traditional exceptions to the hearsay rule. . . . The source of the disagreement between my colleague Iacobucci J. and me can be traced to variant understandings of threshold reliability inquiry under the principled approach. The traditional exceptions are built upon a determination that a threshold of reliability is met in particular instances of hearsay statements. Reliability under the principled approach is similarly restricted to a threshold inquiry.

. . . .

Threshold reliability exists where there is a circumstantial guarantee of trustworthiness. It does not mean that the hearsay is true or even likely to be true, but rather it asks whether the circumstances are such that there is sufficient reliability for the hearsay to be properly assessed by the jury. The traditional hearsay exceptions are based on a determination of threshold reliability. . . . These exceptions have historically been founded on truisms common to classes of people or common to circumstances applicable to all people. There is no reason why that should not continue to be the case. I acknowledge that some of the existing exceptions may require fine tuning. It may be that society has changed in such a manner that the rationale for the exception no longer applies. And, there may be circumstances which could arise in an individual case which challenge the inherent reliability that underpins a hearsay exception. However, the court must differentiate between individual circumstances that go to the weight of the evidence (such as motive to lie or other extraneous circumstances unique to the individual) and circumstances that are properly considered at the threshold stage.

. . . .

The only time when a court should entertain a challenge to an existing exception is where there are facts, generally applicable to a class of persons, which weaken the theoretical justification for the exception. If facts arise which demonstrate that within an exception, we no longer think that statements made by a particular class of persons are inherently reliable, then to a certain extent, the rationale for the exception has been displaced and the exception must be modified to exclude people in such circumstances. For example, it may be that a court may wish to reconsider the dying declaration under certain circumstances such as when a dying person is under the influence of powerful drugs. Another exemption that may benefit from re-examination is the business records exception where the records are written by persons who are not disinterested parties. Both of these examples reflect particular circumstances under which reliability may be questioned for all people in such a situation. I believe that this approach will force the courts to reconsider the exceptions only where a problem exists with the theoretical foundation of the exception.

. . . .

Iacobucci J.'s approach neutralizes the utility of the exceptions which provide predictability and a certain degree of swiftness in our trial process. By requiring the negation of the possibility that the declarant was untruthful, Iacobucci J. creates an extremely high threshold for the introduction of previously acceptable hearsay evidence. The possibility of untruthfulness is inherent in every statement. Ascertaining truth is the fundamental task for the trier of fact, not for the trier of law determining threshold reliability. In addition, by adding the requirement that a statement of intention not be made under circumstances of suspicion so as to conform with the principled approach, Iacobucci J. reveals the essential problem with his proposed mode of hearsay analysis. For if each exception is to incorporate a necessity and reliability component in examining each individual statement that comes under the exception, then the end result is the eradication of the exceptions themselves.

. . . .

The "Joint Act" Rule and the "Present Intentions" Exception

It is common cause that the "present intentions" exception may not be used to infer that a third party acted in accordance with the declarant's stated intention. Doherty J. explained the permissible chain of inferences in *P. (R.)*, supra:

> Evidence of the deceased's state of mind may, in turn, be relevant as circumstantial evidence that the deceased subsequently acted in accordance with that avowed state of mind. When a deceased says, "I will go to Ottawa tomorrow", the statement affords direct evidence of the state of mind — an intention to go to Ottawa tomorrow — and circumstantial evidence that the deceased in fact went to Ottawa on that day. If either the state of mind, or the fact to be inferred from the existence of the state of mind is relevant, the evidence is receivable subject to objections based on undue prejudice.

Later Doherty J. wrote:

> The evidence is not, however, admissible . . . to show that persons other than the deceased acted in accordance with the deceased's stated intentions, save perhaps cases where the act was a joint one involving the deceased and another person."

Lamer C.J. adopted this statement of the joint act exception in *Smith*.

This exception simply recognizes basic principles of logic. As Professor R. J. Delisle explains in "*R. v. Smith*: The Relevance of Hearsay" (1991), 2 C.R. (4th) 260, at p. 264:

> The statement of the declarant's then state of mind should be received as evidence of that state of mind . . . . The next step in the chain — whether an inference should be drawn that the deceased acted in accordance with that state of mind, by himself, or jointly with another — presents a problem, not of hearsay, but of relevance and prejudicial value.

Statements of intention may be admissible despite the fact that they refer to a joint act: see the leading cases of *Mutual Life Insurance Co. v. Hillmon*, 145 U.S. 285 (1892), at p. 296; *United States v. Pheaster*, 544 F.2d 353 (9th Cir. 1976), at pp. 374-80; *People v. Alcalde*, 148 P.2d 627 (Cal. 1944), at pp. 631-33. *Alcalde* presented a situation similar to the one before us: the deceased declarant had said that she "was going out with Frank" that evening. The California Supreme Court, over the dissent of Traynor J., held that the statement was admissible to show the decedent's intent that evening. Generally, this sort of evidence is admissible as an indication of the declarant's intention at the time he or she spoke. The inferences to be drawn from the evidence are for the jury, properly cautioned.

I do not believe that the trial judge erred in leaving Cook's statement of intention to the jury. "Properly cautioned by the trial judge, juries are perfectly capable of determining what weight ought to be attached to such evidence, and of drawing reasonable inferences therefrom", *Smith*, supra. The trial judge told the jury that "[t]he Crown says that Ms. Giesbrecht's evidence is the second thread of evidence to link the accused, Robert Starr, with the deaths of Cook and Weselowski. Again, it is for you to decide whether the evidence of Cook's statement about the scam goes as far as the Crown would have you believe". I do not believe that this instruction invited the jury to draw an impermissible inference against the appellant. In examining what the Crown "would have [the jury] believe", the Crown, referring to another statement not at issue here, explained "evidence of intention" as "What was the deceased thinking about just before his death?". The Crown continued:

> The difference between the statement of intention by Mr. Cook to Young and the statement of intention by Mr. Cook to Giesbrecht is that Cook carried the Giesbrecht intention out, didn't he? He ended up in a car, say the prosecution, driving down a ditch, smashing it up outside of the Turski home. He travelled all that way. He had to have; he was found dead there, and the car that was smashed against the pole was the car that Starr had been in, in the Mohawk garage. So that expression of intention appears to have been carried out.

I believe that the Crown was entitled to ask the jury to draw an inference that Cook in fact acted in accordance with his stated intention, even if that stated intention involved a joint act: see *P. (R.)*, supra. In this situation, circumstances of joint intention may be considered along with the other evidence in determining what the third party did. Thus, I do not believe that the Crown asked the jury to draw an impermissible inference nor do I believe that the trial judge erred in instructing the jury on this issue.

IACOBUCCI, J. (MAJOR, BINNIE, ARBOUR and LeBEL, JJ. concurring): —

. . . .

The theory of the Crown at trial was that the killing of Cook was a gang-related execution perpetrated by the appellant. Weselowski was an unfortunate witness who was killed simply because she was in the wrong place at the wrong time. The theory was that the appellant had used an Autopac scam as a pretext to get Cook out into the countryside. Outside the Turskis' home, Cook got into the smaller car and drove it into the ditch, hitting telephone poles in an effort to damage the car. The appellant shot Weselowski twice in the head, then drove Weselowski's station wagon up the road to where Cook had stopped the smaller car in the ditch. When Cook entered the station wagon on the passenger side, the appellant shot him from the driver's seat three times in the head and three times in the chest. He then pushed Cook's body out of the vehicle and drove away, parking near his brother's house, where the appellant abandoned the station wagon.

. . . .

The Crown argued that the "state of mind" or "present intentions" exception to the hearsay rule applied to render Cook's statement to Giesbrecht admissible. This exception was most recently discussed in detail by this Court in *Smith*, supra, where it was recognized that an "exception to the hearsay rule arises when the declarant's statement is adduced in order to demonstrate the intentions, or state of mind, of the declarant at the time when the statement was made". Wigmore has argued that the present intentions exception also includes a requirement that a statement "be of a present existing state of mind, and must appear to have been made in a natural manner and not under circumstances of suspicion": *Wigmore on Evidence*, vol. 6 (Chadbourn rev. 1976), at para. 1725, p. 129. L'Heureux-Dubé J., at para. 63 of her reasons, denies that Wigmore's suggestion has ever been adopted in our jurisprudence. As I will discuss below, regardless of whether the present intentions requirement ever had such a requirement, the principled approach demands that it must have it now. I will therefore examine the admissibility of Cook's statement under the present intentions exception in light of that understanding.

. . . .

It is important to emphasize that even in "cases where the act was a joint one involving the deceased and another person", the hearsay is not generally admissible to show the intentions of a third party. I draw this conclusion for two reasons. First, I can find no support in Canadian jurisprudence for the proposition that statements of intention are admissible against someone other than the declarant, apart from the one comment by Doherty J. noted above. . . . Second, there are very good reasons behind the rule against allowing statements of present intention to be used to prove the state of mind of someone other than the declarant. As noted above, the central concern with hearsay is the inability of the trier of fact to test the reliability of the declarant's assertion. When the statement is tendered to prove the intentions of a third party, this danger is multiplied. If a declarant makes a statement about the intentions of a third party, there are three possible bases for this statement: first, it could be based on a prior conversation with the accused; second, it could be based on a prior conversation with a fourth party, who indicated the third party's intentions to the declarant; or third, it could be based on pure speculation on the part of the declarant. Under the first scenario, the statement is double hearsay. Since each level of double hearsay must fall within an exception, or be admissible under the principled approach, the mere fact that the declarant is making a statement of present intention is insufficient to render it admissible. The second level of hearsay must also be admissible.

The other two scenarios also clearly require exclusion. If the statement about joint acts is based on a conversation with a fourth party, then the statement is triple hearsay, or worse. If, on the other hand, it is based on pure speculation, then it clearly is unreliable and does not fit within the rationale underlying the present intentions exception. In conclusion then, a statement of intention cannot be admitted to prove the intentions of someone other than the declarant, unless a hearsay exception can be established for each level of hearsay. One way to establish this would obviously be the co-conspirator exception: see *R. v. Carter*, [1982] 1 S.C.R. 938; Sopinka, Lederman and Bryant, supra, at pp. 303-7. This is no doubt what Doherty J. was referring to in *P. (R.)*, supra, when he spoke of "cases where the act was a joint one involving the deceased and another person". Barring the applicability of this or some other exception to each level of hearsay involved, statements of joint intention are only admissible to prove the declarant's intentions.

. . . .

With great respect to the Court of Appeal, I conclude that the trial judge erred in admitting Cook's statement to Giesbrecht under the present intentions exception and, having admitted it, in not limiting its use by the jury, for three reasons. First, the statement contained no indicia of reliability since it was made under circumstances of suspicion; second, the trial judge failed to instruct the jury that the statement was only admissible as evidence regarding the intentions of Cook, not the appellant; and third, even if it had been properly limited, the evidence was more prejudicial than probative.

Turning first to the circumstances of suspicion, I agree with Twaddle J.A. that the statement lacked circumstantial guarantees of trustworthiness. As Twaddle J.A. noted, Cook and Giesbrecht had been romantically involved for almost two years. Cook had lived with Giesbrecht and her mother for a time, and had spent the night before his murder with Giesbrecht, after getting out of jail. Then, in the early morning hours of August 21, 1994, Giesbrecht observed Cook in the car of another woman, Darlene Weselowski. Giesbrecht testified that she thought Cook might try to "take off on her" if he saw Giesbrecht approaching the car, and she endeavoured not to be seen by Cook until she was close enough to talk to him. After an initial confrontation, Giesbrecht walked away into an alley behind the gas station, where Cook followed her. Their conversation ended in an argument because Cook was with Weselowski. She was angry at Cook for being with another woman, and asked him expressly why Cook would not come home with her rather than remain with Weselowski. It was at this point, and in this heated context, that Cook said he was going to engage in an Autopac scam with the appellant, who was sitting in a car nearby. Giesbrecht testified that it was unusual for Cook to discuss such business matters with her.

Twaddle J.A. found that the circumstances surrounding the making of the statement cast serious doubt upon the reliability of the statement. The possibility that Cook was untruthful could not be said to have been substantially negated. Twaddle J.A. relied, in particular, upon the fact that Cook may have had a motive to lie in order to make it seem that he was not romantically involved with Weselowski, and upon the ease with which Cook could point to the appellant, who was sitting nearby in a car but out of earshot, as being the person with whom he was going to do a scam. In my view, Twaddle J.A. was correct in finding that these circumstances bring the reliability of Cook's statement into doubt. The statement was made under "circumstances of suspicion", and therefore does not fall within the present intentions exception. The statement should have been excluded.

. . . .

Finally, I would exclude Cook's statement as more prejudicial than probative. The trial judge did not make a finding on the issue of reliability. His focus was upon the impermissible inferences that the jury might draw from otherwise admissible hearsay, and he regarded the primary prejudice to the appellant to be that the jury might infer that he was the type of person likely to commit insurance fraud. However, as noted above, this was not the primary source of prejudice. The trial judge erred by not considering whether "the prejudicial effect of the prohibited use of the evidence [i.e., the appellant's intentions] overbears its probative value on the permitted use [i.e., Cook's intentions]": *Watt's Manual of Criminal Evidence* (1999). The impermissible inferences that the jury might well have drawn from Cook's statement are that the appellant was in the car that followed Cook, that the appellant was alone in the car (since Cook referred only to the appellant), and that the appellant went with Cook as part of a plan to lure Cook to a secluded area and kill him. These were the specific impermissible inferences that the jury might have drawn in this regard — indeed, they are inferences that the Crown specifically invited the jury to draw — quite apart from the inferences that they might have drawn regarding his general criminality. In my view, Twaddle J.A. was correct in finding that the prejudicial effect of the admission of Cook's statement accordingly outweighed the statement's probative value. The statement ought to have been excluded on this basis as well.

(iii) *Spontaneous Statements*

Discretion in this area there must be, but it is best to have guidelines articulated for its exercise; when the guidelines are spelled out in terms of the exception's justification, as in *Ratten*, we are even further advanced. The chief justification lies in the fact that the danger of insincerity is minimized as there has been no opportunity for the declarant to fabricate, and the memory danger is eliminated since the declaration is contemporaneous with the event. A difficulty, of course, remains in the danger of misperception, and deserves stressing when evaluating the worth of the statement: how often have we exclaimed about a situation and found ourselves later saying, "on second thought. . . ." The very fact that the event was startling and caused the viewer to be excited can impair his perceptual abilities.[205]

Establishing the preliminary condition of admissibility, that the declaration was in response to a startling event, can produce a problem. Can we look at the statement itself to determine the relationship? While it appears as a bootstrap operation it appears to be the better view that the statement can be regarded, in the discretion of the trial judge, along with other matters.[206]

---

205. See Hutchins and Slesinger, "Some Observations on the Law of Evidence" (1928), 28 Col. L. Rev. 432 and Stewart, "Perception Memory and Hearsay", [1970] Utah L. Rev. 1 at 28 and Marshall, *Law and Psychology in Conflict* (1969), pp. 19-20.

206. *Ratten, supra*, note 204, at p. 391.

R. v. BEDINGFIELD
(1879), 14 Cox C.C. 341

[The accused was charged with murder. The accused was present with the deceased in the deceased's house. The deceased came suddenly out of the house with her throat cut. She said something, pointing backwards to the house. In a few minutes she was dead. In the course of the opening speech on the part of the prosecution it was proposed to state what she said. It was objected on the part of the prisoner that it was not admissible.]

Cockburn C.J. said he had carefully considered the question and was clear that it could not be admitted and therefore ought not to be stated, as it might have a fatal effect. I regret, he said, that according to the law of England, any statement made by the deceased should not be admissible. Then could it be admissible having been made in the absence of the prisoner, as part of the res gestae but it is not so admissible for it was not part of anything done, or something said while something was being done, but something said after something done. Anything, he said, uttered by the deceased at the time the act was being done would be admissible, as, for instance, if she had been heard to say something, as "Don't, Harry!". But here it was something stated by her after it was all over, whatever it was, and after the act was completed.

It was submitted, on the part of the prosecution, that the statement was admissible as a dying declaration, the case to be proved being that the woman's throat was cut completely and the artery severed, so that she was dying, and was actually dead in a few minutes; but Cockburn C.J. said the statement was not admissible as a dying declaration, because it did not appear that the woman was aware that she was dying.

It was urged that the woman must have known it as she was actually dying at the time, but Cockburn C.J. said that though she might have known it if she had had time for reflection, here that was not so, for at the time she made the statement she had no time to consider and reflect that she was dying; there is no evidence to show that she knew it, and I cannot presume it. There is nothing to show that she was under the sense of impending death, so the statement is not admissible as a dying declaration.

[The statement was later reported to be "See what Harry has done!" In the result the jury nevertheless found him guilty based on the other evidence.]

R. v. CLARK
(1983), 35 C.R. (3d) 357, 7 C.C.C. (3d) 46 (Ont. C.A.)

[On the accused's trial for murder, spontaneous utterances by the deceased made shortly after she had been injured by the accused when the accused in fact was still present including the words "Help, I've been murdered, I've been stabbed", were admitted as evidence of the truth of the facts stated. On appeal it was argued that the statements were improperly admitted.]

DUBIN, J.A. (MACKINNON, A.C.J.O and CORY, J.A. concurring): —

. . . .

The appellant married Mr. Ade in January, 1977. Their marriage was a somewhat stormy and unusual one, and they separated in November, 1977. The appellant testified that she was still very much in love with her husband and during the period of their separation frequently attended upon him with a view apparently of winning him back. The marriage was annulled in April, 1978, and shortly after Mr. Ade began to see the deceased Beverly Ade. The appellant was devastated when he became involved with another woman. She telephoned his office with such frequency that Mr. Ade asked the switchboard operator to stop passing on her calls to him although some calls did get through. She waited outside his place of work, would follow him to the bank, to the parking-lot or to the cafeteria where he was having lunch.

In December, 1978, Mr. Ade married the deceased. The appellant was observed on many occasions loitering in the area of the residence of Mr. Ade and the deceased. She continued to telephone and visited his office and scouted his premises and the area in which he lived.

. . . .

On the morning of July 7th she attended at the residence of the deceased. The appellant testified that she did so to recover two lawn chairs which had been left in Mr. Ade's garage and which, unbeknownst to her, had been given away by him prior to July 7th. . . . It was during that visit that Beverly Ade came to her death as a result of penetrating stab wounds to her heart, admittedly at the hands of the appellant. The deceased had one superficial wound to the back, one to the right side, ten front torso wounds and four wounds to her hands. . . . The appellant's left hand was cut in three places.

The defence was self-defence and/or provocation. The appellant testified that she knocked on the door of the deceased's premises and told the deceased that she wanted the two lawn chairs. They attended at the garage but could not find the chairs. According to the appellant, the deceased said, "Howard's been over you a long time, just don't make anymore excuses." The appellant replied, "Don't be too sure." The appellant testified that as they came out of the garage the deceased gave the appellant a push and said "not to come around anymore". She stated that she then stood with her back to the garage door and with her eyes closed. When she heard footsteps, she opened her eyes and saw the deceased quite close holding a knife. The appellant was startled and afraid. She testified that she grabbed the knife with her left hand and pushed the deceased with the other. The deceased fell. As the appellant tried to run away, she tripped over the deceased and fell down. She was not sure whether she had hit the deceased but saw that her own hand was bleeding. She said that the deceased then grabbed her, and she felt that she was hanging on to the deceased near a chair which was near the garage entrance. She testified that she did not know that she had injured the deceased who was at that time sitting on the chair.

. . . .

Spontaneous exclamations

It was submitted that the learned trial judge erred in admitting certain of the evidence to be found in the testimony of Fawn Pitcher. On July 7, 1980, Miss Pitcher was staying with her aunt who resided across the street from the Ade residence. . . . In order to appreciate the evidentiary issues raised as well as to indicate the over-all importance of her testimony in this case, I set out hereunder in some detail the relevant portions of Miss Pitcher's testimony:

Q.   Okay, just take it slowly and tell the jury please what it was that you heard please.

A.   Okay, I was in the back kitchen making my breakfast. It was around ten o'clock and I heard somebody calling for help. First I thought it was kids fooling around a pool. I was sort of annoyed at it and it kept up and I thought no, so I went outside and I realized it wasn't a child in a pool. I went out the back gate and I realized where the cries were coming from, across the road.

Q.   Fawn, could you tell me then what you saw and heard as you went across the street to find out what was going on?

A.   Okay, as I came out the back gate to my aunt?s place and up her side lawn I saw a woman standing at the top of the driveway in the picture shown and she was yelling: "Help, help I've been murdered. I've been stabbed." And I didn't see anyone else around. I walked across the road, down through their ditch and up into the lawn and I saw the accused sort of agitated going back and forth towards the deceased. . . .

Q.   All right. Now, where was the accused lady when you first saw her?

A.   She was on the grass.

Q.   Yes.

A.   Near a clump of trees or tree and she was moving back and forth towards the deceased and then back on to the lawn again.

Q.   Okay. Did you see the accused lady right away?

A.   Not right away. Not when I first came out I only saw the deceased.

. . . .

Q.   You were then approaching and the jury has seen the angle that you were approaching on, just tell me what happened then as you approached?

A.   Okay, as I approached, I saw only the deceased and she was yelling, "Help I've been murdered, I've been stabbed." I crossed the road, went up onto the lawn of the other house and she seemed to see me then and she said, "Go call the police, go call an ambulance."

Q.   All right, now, what can you tell me about the appearance of the deceased lady at this time when she was saying these things to you?

A.   She seem to be very distressed. I couldn't see at first that there was any injury apparent until I crossed up into her lawn and as I got closer I saw a red circle on the right shoulder and just below her right shoulder.

. . . .

It was the submission by counsel for the appellant that the words spoken by the deceased, "Help I've been murdered, I've been stabbed" were inadmissible hearsay. No objection was taken by counsel at trial to the admissibility of that evidence, but if the evidence was in fact inadmissible and highly prejudicial, the failure to object is not fatal.

[The Court then reviewed *Bedingfield* and English and Canadian cases that had followed it over the years.]

It is to be noted that the admissibility of the statements under consideration in the foregoing cases was dependent upon whether they could be said to be part of the res gestae, a Latin phrase much criticized in *Wigmore on Evidence*, which will be presently commented upon. In order to fit into a res gestae test, the statement had to form part of the transaction or event and if not immediately contemporaneous was held to be outside the otherwise permissible exception to the hearsay rule.

The basis for the admissibility of a spontaneous exclamation, the label assigned by Wigmore to such statements, was considered and expanded upon in *Ratten v. Reginam*, [1971] 3 All E.R. 801. Ratten was charged with the murder of his wife. Her death had been caused by a wound from a shot-gun held by the appellant. His explanation was that the discharge was accidental and had occurred while he was cleaning his gun in the kitchen of his house. He was unable to explain how the gun from which the shot was fired had come to be loaded. He testified that he immediately telephoned for an ambulance and, shortly after, the police had telephoned him, at which time he asked them to come immediately. At about 1:15 p.m. on the day of the alleged offence, a telephone call was made from their premises. The telephone operator who answered had stated in evidence at trial:

I plugged into a number [the appellant's number] . . . and . . . I opened the speak key and I said to the person, "Number please" and the reply I got was "Get me the police please".

The person on the telephone gave her address and hung up. The telephone operator testified that the person on the telephone was in a hysterical state and later added that the person on the telephone sobbed. The telephone operator advised the police of the call. The police telephoned the Ratten house and spoke to the accused. By this time the deceased had been shot.

Objection was taken to the admissibility of the evidence of the telephone operator on the ground that it was hearsay and that it did not come within any of the recognized exceptions to the rule against hearsay, but the objection was overruled. The issue was again raised on appeal on the premise that the trial judge properly instructed the jury that on the evidence they might find the telephone call was made by the deceased woman.

The Privy Council first held that the evidence of the telephone operator was not hearsay evidence but was admissible as evidence of a fact relevant to an issue.

Lord Wilberforce stated at p. 805:

> The mere fact that evidence of a witness includes evidence as to words spoken by another person who is not called is no objection to its admissibility. Words spoken are facts just as much as any other action by a human being. If the speaking of the words is a relevant fact, a witness may give evidence that they were spoken. A question of hearsay only arises when the words spoken are relied on 'testimonially', i.e., as establishing some fact narrated by the words. Authority is hardly needed for this proposition, but their Lordships will restate what was said in the judgment of the Board in *Subramaniam v. Public Prosecutor*, [1956] 1 W.L.R. 965 at 970:
>
> > Evidence of a statement made to a witness by a person who is not himself called as a witness may or may not be hearsay. It is hearsay and inadmissible when the object of the evidence is to establish the truth of what is contained in the statement. It is not hearsay and is admissible when it is proposed to establish by the evidence, not the truth of the statement but the fact that it was made.

He then proceeded, however, to deal with the admissibility of the evidence on the premise that it was put forth as evidence of the truth of the facts asserted by the statement, and on that premise concluded at pp. 806-7 as follows:

> Their Lordships, as already stated, do not consider that there is any hearsay element in the evidence, nor in their opinion was it so presented by the trial judge, but they think it right to deal with the appellant's submission on the assumption that there is, i.e. that the words said to have been used involve an assertion of the truth of some facts stated in them and that they may have been so understood by the jury. The Crown defended the admissibility of the words as part of the "res gestae", a contention which led to the citation of numerous authorities.
>
> The expression "res gestae", like many Latin phrases, is often used to cover situations insufficiently analysed in clear English terms.
>
> . . . .
>
> The possibility of concoction, or fabrication, where it exists, is on the other hand an entirely valid reason for exclusion, and is probably the real test which judges in fact apply. In their Lordships' opinion this should be recognised and applied directly as the relevant test: the test should be not the uncertain one whether the making of the statement was in some sense part of the event or transaction. This may often be difficult to establish: such external matters as the time which elapses between the events and the speaking of the words (or vice versa), and differences in location being relevant factors but not, taken by themselves, decisive criteria. As regards statements made after the event it must be for the judge, by preliminary ruling, to satisfy himself that the statement was so clearly made in circumstances of spontaneity or involvement in the event that the possibility of concoction can be disregarded. Conversely, if he considers that the statement was made by way of narrative of a detached prior event so that the speaker was so disengaged from it as to be able to

construct or adapt his account, he should exclude it. And the same must in principle be true of statements made before the event. The test should be not the uncertain one, whether the making of the statement should be regarded as part of the event or transaction. This may often be difficult to show. But if the drama, leading up to the climax, has commenced and assumed such intensity and pressure that the utterance can safely be regarded as a true reflection of what was unrolling or actually happening, it ought to be received. The expression "res gestae" may conveniently sum up these criteria, but the reality of them must always be kept in mind: it is this that lies behind the best reasoned of the judges' rulings.

And at p. 808:

These authorities show that there is ample support for the principle that hearsay evidence may be admitted if the statement providing it is made in such conditions (always being those of approximate but not exact contemporaneity) of involvement or pressure as to exclude the possibility of concoction or distortion to the advantage of the maker or the disadvantage of the accused.

It is clear in this case that the challenged evidence was tendered as evidence of the truth of that which was stated, and, thus, if admissible, as a true exception to the hearsay rule.

. . . .

[A]lthough what was stated by Chief Justice Robertson in *R. v. Leland*, [1951] O.R. 12, 98 C.C.C. 337, 11 C.R. 152,[one of the Canadian cases that followed the contemporaneity requirement of *Bedingfield*] appears to have been consistent with the then state of the authorities, it cannot, in my respectful opinion, now be viewed as an authoritative statement of the law. This case can, of course, be readily distinguishable from *Leland*, in that, it is apparent from the evidence of Miss Pitcher that the words attributed by her as having been spoken by the deceased were spoken while the event was still transpiring and, thus, contemporaneous with the unfolding events. But I would prefer to rest my judgment on a broader base as it is now apparent from the foregoing that the narrow test of exact contemporaneity should no longer be followed.

The circumstances, as outlined by Miss Pitcher, under which the words were said to have been spoken by the deceased were such as to exclude the possibility of concoction or distortion, and if Miss Pitcher's evidence were accepted by the jury, the words spoken, "Help I've been murdered, I've been stabbed" were evidence of the belief of the deceased as to what had occurred and evidence as to the truth of the facts stated by her as a true exception to the hearsay rule. . . . The words, "Go call the police, go call an ambulance", to which no exception was taken on appeal, were, of course, admissible as a verbal act and not as an exception to the hearsay rule.

For these reasons, I would reject the submission made by counsel for the appellant on this issue.

In *R. v. Andrews*, [1987] A.C. 281 the Law Lords decided, following *Ratten*, that *R. v. Bedingfield* "would not be so decided today".

The common law has received, normally with the appellation *res gestae*, declarations of a present sense of belief concerning a contemporaneous event witnessed by the declarant. For example it was held in *R. v. Graham*[207] in a prosecution for possession of stolen goods:

----

207. (1972), 7 C.C.C. (2d) 93 (S.C.C.).

. . . the respondent's verbal statement made when the attache case was found, that he had never seen it before in his life, *being one which was immediately connected with the initial discovery of the stolen goods,* was properly admitted in evidence. Explanatory statements made by an accused upon his first being found "in possession" constitute a part of the *res gestae* and are necessarily admissible in any description of the circumstances under which the crime was committed. [Emphasis added.][208]

Notice that the presence of a startling event or excitement in the declarant is not necessary; contemporaneity is the key.[209] Professor Morgan offered the justification:

A statement by a person as to external events then and there being perceived by his senses is worthy of credence for two reasons. First, it is in essence a declaration of a presently existing state of mind, for it is nothing more than an assertion of his presently existing sense impressions. As such it has the quality of spontaneity. . . . Second, since the statement is contemporaneous with the event, it is made at the place of the event. Consequently the event is open to perception by the senses of the person to whom the declaration is made and by whom it is usually reported on the witness stand. The witness is subject to cross-examination concerning that event as well as the fact and content of the utterance, so that the extra-judicial statement does not depend solely upon the credit of the declarant. Unless exact contemporaneousness is insisted upon, the first of these guaranties is partially lacking and the second is weakened.[210]

Considering this justification for the exception under review, and remembering the previous exception for declarations as to existing mental states, did the court in *Graham* accurately describe the statement as receivable because it was part of the *res gestae?*

Contemporaneity minimizes the hearsay dangers of perception and memory and sincerity is thought to be enhanced as the declarant does not have time for reflection and deliberation. For example, in *Graham*, while admitting the first statement, contemporaneous with the discovery, the Supreme Court of Canada ruled the accused's later statement inadmissible:

. . . his written statement was not made contemporaneously with the discovery but rather after ample time had elapsed for reflection. In my view if this statement were to be admitted it would mean that any person accused of receiving stolen goods could, after due consideration, devise an explanation which might easily be true for the goods having been found in his possession and could thus avoid the necessity

---

208. *Ibid.,* at p. 99. Applied in a trial for possession of narcotics, *R. v. Risby* (1976), 32 C.C.C. (2d) 242 (B.C.C.A.); affirmed (1978), 39 C.C.C. (2d) 567 (S.C.C.). See also *R. v. Keeler,* [1977] 5 W.W.R. 410 (Alta. C.A.) and *Reference re R. v. Latta* (1976), 30 C.C.C. (2d) 208 (Alta. C.A.).

209. See *Jarvis v. London St. Ry. Co.* (1919), 45 O.L.R. 167, 173 (C.A.) per Middleton, J., holding a statement inadmissible: "The truth is that the statement said to have been made by the conductor formed no part of the *res gestae,* it was a mere narrative or discussion anent a thing then past. . . . [T]o make the statement admissible, it must be an involuntary and contemporaneous exclamation made without time for reflection; it is because the statement is involuntary and contemporaneous that it is received. These characteristics are supposed to impart some indication of its veracity."

210. Morgan, "A Suggested Classification of Utterances Admissible as Res Gestae" (1922), 31 Yale L.J. 229, 236-37.

of presenting himself as a witness and be afforded the full benefit of his explanation without being subjected to cross-examination. Such an explanation is, in my view, inadmissible under the general rule in criminal cases that self-serving statements made by an accused cannot be introduced on the cross-examination of third parties because they cannot themselves be tested by cross-examination of the accused person who made them, and their introduction in such manner deprives the jury of the benefit of appraising his credibility from observing his demeanour.[211]

(d) Exceptions where Declarant Available

The existing common law position in Canada is that a statement does not cease to be hearsay simply by the attendance of the declarant as a witness. As an example of the problem, consider the case of *Deacon v. R.*[212] In a murder prosecution, the chief Crown witness had earlier given a statement to the police identifying the accused as present in the vehicle at the time the deceased was shot, but at trial her story changed. During the course of the cross-examination, the entire statement was read to her and while she admitted having made it, she denied its truth. The trial judge in his charge to the jury treated the incriminating facts contained in the statement as having full testimonial character from which the jury was entitled to extract the truth. A new trial was ordered and the court commented:

> That such statements generally are limited to credibility and cannot be used as evidence of the truth of the facts to which they relate is well established. . . . It is quite true that it may be difficult to dissociate the matters of such statements from the facts brought before the jury by the witness and to nullify the influence they may have on the minds of the jurors in dealing with the evidence as a whole; but anything short of this would expose a person to a fabricated account of events, too dangerous to risk. But the whole field of cross-examination, in the discretion of the Court, is opened and the matters of the statement can thus be brought within the test of the testimonial response of the witness. This might be taken as a reason for leaving all the facts, including the statement, to the consideration of the jury, but the long experience of the Courts is against it.[213]

Although the declarant is presently under oath and subject to cross-examination, the statement when made was not so subject and the orthodox view accordingly rejects its use as substantive evidence.[214] A classic dictum notes:

> The chief merit of cross-examination is not that at some future time it gives the party opponent the right to dissect adverse testimony. Its principal virtue is in its immediate application of the testing process. Its strokes fall while the iron is hot. False testimony is apt to harden and become unyielding to the blows of truth in proportion as the witness has opportunity for reconsideration and influence by the suggestions of others, whose interest may be, and often is, to maintain falsehood rather than truth.[215]

---

211. *Supra*, note 207, at p. 99 per Spence, J.
212. [1947] 3 D.L.R. 772 (S.C.C.). To similar effect see *R. v. Duckworth* (1916), 31 D.L.R. 570 (Ont. C.A.) and *Lizotte v. R.*, [1951] 2 D.L.R. 754 (S.C.C.).
213. *Ibid.*, at pp. 777-78. See also *R. v. Smith* (1985), 66 A.R. 195 (C.A.).
214. The sole exception to this orthodox view appears to be the single opinion of Estey, J. in *McInroy and Rouse v. R.* (1978), 42 C.C.C. (2d) 481, 506 (S.C.C.), but limiting his holding to statements elicited by s. 9(2) of the Canada Evidence Act; see "Note" (1978-79), 21 Crim. L.Q. 162 commenting on the anomaly thereby produced.
215. *State v. Saporen*, 285 N.W. 898 at 901 (Minn., 1939).

The orthodox view has, however, been frequently criticized. Professor Wigmore commented:

> But the theory of the hearsay rule is that an extrajudicial statement is rejected because it was made out of court by an absent person not subject to cross-examination. . . . Here, however, by hypothesis the witness is present and subject to cross-examination. There is ample opportunity to test him as to the basis for his former statement. The whole purpose of the hearsay rule has been already satisfied. Hence there is nothing to prevent the tribunal from giving such testimonial credit to the extrajudicial statement as it may seem to deserve. Psychologically of course, the one statement is as useful to consider as the other; and everyday experience outside of courtrooms is in accord.[216]

Learned Hand, J. noted:

> If, from all that the jury see of the witness, they conclude that what he says now is not the truth, but what he said before, they are none the less deciding from what they see and hear of that person and in court.[217]

Professor McCormick:

> . . . the witness who has told one story aforetime and another today has opened the gates to all the vistas of truth which the common law practice of cross-examination and re-examination was invented to explore. The two questioners will lay bare the sources of the change of face, in forgetfulness, carelessness, pity, terror, or greed, and thus cast light on which is the true story and which the false.[218]

And finally Friendly, J.:

> The rule limiting the use of prior statements by a witness subject to cross-examination to their effect on his credibility has been described by eminent scholars and judges as "pious fraud," "artificial," "basically misguided," "mere verbal ritual," and an anachronism "that still impede(s) our pursuit of the truth." . . . The orthodox rule defies the dictate of common sense that "The fresher the memory, the fuller and more accurate it is. . . . Manifestly, this is not to say that when a witness changes his story, the first version is invariably true and the later is the product of distorted memory, corruption, false suggestion, intimidation, or appeal to sympathy . . . [but] the greater the lapse of time between the event and the trial, the greater the chance of exposure of the witness to each of these influences." . . . As against this, we are bound by the admonition, in Bridges v. Wixon, . . . against allowing "men to be convicted on unsworn testimony of witnesses — a practice which runs counter to the notions of fairness on which our legal system is founded.[219]

It is perhaps the latter admonition which has caused the courts in Canada to resist any change from the orthodox view. Prior to the establishment of the hearsay rule, criminal convictions could be had on the basis of statements made out of court; the development of the hearsay rule demanded that convictions be based on testimony given in open court in the presence of the accused and then

---

216. 3A Wigmore, *Evidence* (Chad. Rev.), s. 1018, p. 996.
217. In *DiCarlo v. U.S.*, 6 F. 2d 364, 368 (2d Cir., 1925).
218. McCormick, *Evidence*, 2d ed. (1972), p. 603.
219. In *U.S. v. DeSisto*, 329 F. 2d 929 (2d Cir., 1964). See also, Morgan, "Hearsay Dangers and the Application of the Hearsay Concept" (1948), 62 Harv. L. Rev. 177, 192-96; McCormick, "The Turncoat Witness" (1947), 25 Texas L. Rev. 573; Davidson, "The Previous Statements of Witnesses" (1958), 32 Aust. L.J. 38.

subject to cross-examination. How effective can cross-examination be in exploring the dangers of perception, memory and communication when the declarant-witness denies having made the statement or professes no present memory?[220] One commentator has asked:

> Consider the irony of allowing a conviction to rest on the unexamined out-of-court testimony of a witness whom the jury has found incredible under oath.[221]

The above of course is now subject to *R. v. B. (K.G.), supra.*

Notice that cross-examination at trial may be severely blunted if the witness denies having made the earlier statement.

R. v. TAT
(1997), 14 C.R. (5th) 116, 117 C.C.C. (3d) 481 (Ont. C.A.)

DOHERTY J.A. (LABROSSE and WEILER JJ.A. concurring):—

The absence of contemporary cross- examination, is said to be the most important of the dangers associated with the admission of hearsay evidence: *R. v. B. (K.G.)*. If the proffered hearsay consists of a previous statement made by a person who testifies, that danger will usually be alleviated by the ability to cross-examine that witness at trial: *R. v. B. (K.G.)*. If, however, the prior statement is one of identification and the witness denies making the identification, special problems arise and cross-examination at trial may not provide a suitable substitute for contemporaneous cross-examination. Cross-examination of the maker of the statement at trial will certainly assist in assessing the credibility of the witness, but may not assist in testing the reliability of the out-of-court statement. Assuming Quach's prior statement was admitted for its truth, defence counsel would have Quach's statement under oath that he did not make the prior identification and his evidence that Long was not one of the shooters. This could lead the jury to conclude that they could not rely on any identification made by Quach at any time. Were the jury to take this view, the defence could have no complaint about their inability to cross-examine Quach when he made the statement.

It could be, however, that the jury would conclude that Quach lied at trial because he was afraid. The jury might decide that Quach was not afraid when he was speaking to Constable Dobro, in apparent confidence, and that his identification of Long was, therefore, a truthful one and that Quach honestly believed that Long was one of the shooters. A finding that Quach's prior identification was an honest identification, would not, however, end the need to evaluate that identification. As with any evidence of identification, its reliability would remain very much in issue. *How could defence counsel cross-examine Quach at trial with a view to undermining the reliability of his January 5 identification when Quach insisted that he had not made the identification and that Long was not one*

---

220. But compare White, J., expressing the views of six members, in *California v. Green*, 399 U.S. 149, 159 (1970): ". . . The inability to cross-examine the witness at the time he made his prior statement cannot easily be shown to be of crucial significance as long as the defendant is assured of full and effective cross-examination at the time of trial. The most successful cross-examination at the time the prior statement was made could hardly hope to accomplish more than has already been accomplished by the fact that the witness is now telling a different, inconsistent story, and — in this case — one that is favourable to the defendant."

221. Lempert and Saltzburg, *A Modern Approach to Evidence* (West, 1977), p. 487. See also for criticism of any change from the orthodox position, Blakey, "Substantive Use of Prior Inconsistent Statements" (1975), 64 Ky. L.J. 3.

of the shooters? Quach's position at trial effectively foreclosed exploration of the reliability of the January 5 identification through cross-examination of Quach. [Emphasis added.]

(i) *Previous Identification* [222]

If a witness has previously identified the accused out-of-court, that fact may be received in evidence at trial to confirm the witness's identification at trial; the dock identification is supported by the fact of the earlier identification. If the witness is unable to identify the accused at trial, there is no present statement to confirm, and an earlier statement of identification has no relevance; to receive it for its truth would violate the hearsay rule since the earlier statement was not made on oath nor subject to cross-examination.[223] Should we create an exception for previous identification and let the present inability to identify affect solely the weight to be attached to the earlier statement? The defence will be able to cross-examine the eye-witness with regard to his *usual* powers of perception and memory and also his sincerity, and to cross-examine the witness who testifies to declarant's earlier identification about the circumstances and fairness of the procedure used to conduct the out-of-court identification.[224]

R. v. LANGILLE
(1990), 59 C.C.C. (3d) 544 (Ont. C.A.)

OSBORNE J.A.:—

. . . .

With respect to the robbery, the witness who identified the appellant was Linda Armas. Ms. Armas gave Constable Smith a description of the robber, the car and the hand-gun displayed. Constable Smith gave evidence of the particulars of those descriptions as he received them during the afternoon of August 11, 1988, starting at 1:21 p.m. when Constable Smith attended at the gas bar and interviewed Ms. Armas.

In summary, Ms. Armas gave descriptions of the robber to Constables Smith and Keenan shortly after the robbery on August 11, 1988. Ms. Armas participated in the preparation of the composite drawing and identified the appellant in a photograph array and at trial. Constables Smith and Kennan [*sic*] gave evidence of the description each of them received from Ms. Armas. Constable Wise gave evidence of Ms. Armas' response to the photograph array.

. . . .

The issue of whether evidence of a prior identification through a police officer was admissible, was considered by the British Columbia Court of Appeal in *R. v. Swanston* (1982), 65 C.C.C. (2d) 453. In *Swanston* the issue was the identity of a male person who had assaulted and robbed the victim. The victim had given a description of the robber to the police shortly after the robbery. At p. 455, Nemetz C.J.B.C. said:

While it is true that there have been two judicial views expressed on the admissibility of extrajudicial statements, it is my opinion that the law now is that evidence of

---

222. See generally, Libling, "Evidence of Past Identification," [1977] Crim. L. Rev. 268.
223. *R. v. McGuire* (1975), 23 C.C.C. (2d) 385 (B.C.C.A.). Contrast *R. v. Osbourne*, [1973] 1 All E.R. 649 (C.A.) and *R. v. Swanston* (1982), 33 B.C.L.R. 391 (C.A.).
224. See *R. v. Swanston, ibid.* and *U.S. v. Barbati*, 284 F. Supp. 409 (Dist. Ct., 1968).

extrajudicial identification is admissible not only to corroborate an identification made at trial but as independent evidence going to identity.

And at pp. 457-8, Nemetz C.J.B.C. went on to refer to the judgment of Traynor J. in *People v. Gould*, 354 P.2d 865 at p. 867 (1960):

Evidence of an extra-judicial identification is admissible, not only to corroborate an identification made at the trial . . . but as independent evidence of identity. Unlike other testimony that cannot be corroborated by proof of prior consistent statements unless it is first impeached . . . evidence of an extra-judicial identification is admitted regardless of whether the testimonial identification is impeached, because the earlier identification has greater probative value than an identification made in the courtroom after the suggestions of others and the circumstances of the trial may have intervened to create a fancied recognition in the witness' mind . . . *The failure of the witness to repeat the extra-judicial* identification in court does not destroy its probative value, for such failure may be explained by loss of memory or other circumstances. The extra-judicial identification tends to connect the defendant with the crime, and the principal danger of admitting hearsay evidence is not present since the witness is available at the trial for cross-examination.

Nemetz C.J.B.C. then concluded by noting at p. 458:

In the case at bar we not only have an extrajudicial identification but an indentification at the preliminary hearing. Almost a year and a half had gone by since the robbery when the doctor testified at trial. To prevent the Crown from adducing the evidence of the police officer who observed the doctor identifying the robber was to deprive the trier of fact of the opportunity to consider all the evidence concerning the identification of the person who assaulted and robbed the victim. This was error in law attributable to the *obiter* quoted above in *McGuire* which in my respectful opinion should no longer be followed. None of the exclusionary rules of evidence is infringed by permitting the identifying witness, who cannot identify the accused in Court, to state that whoever he identified on an earlier occasion was the culprit. The Crown may, then, prove by another witness that the man identified by the identifying witness was the accused in the dock.

. . . .

In *McCormick on Evidence*, 3rd ed., at p. 747, statements of previous identification are viewed in the context of being an exception to the hearsay rule, in this way (footnotes omitted):

Statements of identification. When A testifies that on a prior occasion B pointed to the accused and said, 'That's the man who robbed me,' the testimony is clearly hearsay. If, however, B is present in court, testifies on the subject of identity, and is available for cross-examination, a case within the present section is presented. Similarly if B has himself testified to the prior identification. Admissibility of the prior identification in all these situations has the support of substantial authority in the cases, often without recognition of the presence of a hearsay problem. Justification is found in the unsatisfactory nature of courtroom identification and the safeguards which now surround staged out-of-court identifications.

Because an identification of an accused person for the first time in the dock at trial is notoriously and understandably suspect, . . . the jury ought to hear the identification narrative or process in a case like this where Mr. Armas [*sic*], in particular, gave the police a description of the suspect robber very shortly after the robbery had occurred. This evidence establishes that Ms. Armas was able to offer a description of the robber on the day of the robbery. The jury was entitled to hear what that description was. This evidence, Ms. Armas' identification of the appellant's photograph in a photograph array and her role in the preparation of the composite drawing go to establish that Ms. Armas was able to describe the male person who robbed the gas bar (and as well the gun, the car and part of the rear licence plate number) on the afternoon of August 11, 1988, and that Ms. Armas identified the appellant on an earlier occasion. In my view this evidence is admissible as original evidence. To the extent that evidence of Ms. Armas' description of the suspect and her previous identification of the suspect can be said to be hearsay or a prior consistent statement, this evidence is properly viewed as an exception to the rule against hearsay and the acceptance of prior consistent statements.

[To similar effect as *Langille*, see *R. v. Power* (1987), 67 Nfld. & P.E.I.R. 272 (Nfld. T.D.) and *R. v. Skipper* (1988), 69 Sask. R. 7 (Q.B.).]

R. v. TAT
(1997), 14 C.R. (5th) 116, 117 C.C.C. (3d) 481 (Ont. C.A.)

[The accused T and L were charged with first degree murder and attempted murder. They were alleged to have entered a restaurant and opened fire at a particular table, killing one man and injuring two. The case for the Crown rested on the identification of L by Q and the identification of both accused by JT. At the trial Q testified that much of what he said during his interview with the police was based on things he had been told and not his own observations. He said that he had initially identified a photograph of L but had quickly reconsidered his identification and told the officers that he was wrong and that L was not one of the shooters. The trial judge held that the officer's evidence of Q's identification of L during the interview was admissible to prove that L was one of the shooters. The accused were convicted and appealed.]

DOHERTY J.A. (LABROSSE and WEILER JJ.A. concurring):—

. . . .

In my view, and contrary to what I suggested in *R. v. T. (W.P.)* (1993), 83 C.C.C. (3d) 5 (Ont. C.A.) the circumstances in which out-of-court statements of identification are admitted do not involve a hearsay use of the out-of-court statements. More importantly, the current jurisprudence does not recognize any hearsay exception which admits prior statements of identification where the maker of the statement denies making the previous identification and testifies that the accused are not the persons who committed the offence. For reasons I will develop, the admissibility of such statements as substantive evidence is governed by *R. v. B. (K.G.)*, *supra* and its progeny.

My review of the Canadian case law reveals two situations in which out-of-court statements of identification may be admitted. Firstly, prior statements identifying or describing the accused are admissible where the identifying witness identifies the accused at trial. The identifying witness can testify to prior descriptions given and prior identifications made. Others who heard the description and saw the identification may also be allowed to testify to the descriptions given and the identifications made by the identifying witness. . . . Clearly, the evidence of the prior descriptions given and the prior identifications made by the identifying witness constitute prior consistent statements made by that witness. Generally speaking, evidence that a witness made prior consistent statements is excluded as irrelevant and self-serving. However, where identification evidence is involved, it is the in-court identification of the accused which has little or no probative value standing alone. The probative force of identification evidence is best measured by a consideration of the entire identification process which culminates with an in-court identification. . . . Where a witness identifies the accused at trial, evidence of prior identifications made and prior descriptions given by that witness do not have a hearsay purpose.

. . . .

The second situation in which out-of-court statements of identification have been admitted arises where the identifying witness is unable to identify the accused at trial, but can testify that he or she previously gave an accurate description or made an accurate identification. In these circumstances, the identifying witness may testify to what he or she said or did on those earlier occasions and those who heard the description given by the witness or witnessed the identification made by the witness may give evidence of what the witness said or did.

In *R. v. Swanston* (1982), 25 C.R. (3d) 385 (B.C. C.A.), the victim of a robbery testified that he had previously accurately identified the person who robbed him at a police line-up and at the preliminary inquiry. By the time of trial, the accused had changed his appearance and the witness could not be certain that the accused was the person who robbed him. . . . *Swanston* does not create an unqualified exception to the hearsay rule admitting prior identification evidence. *Swanston* recognizes that where the identifying witness testifies that he or she previously identified the perpetrator of the offence, evidence of out-of-court statements is admissible as original evidence to show who it was that the identifying witness previously identified. *Swanston* vividly demonstrates the difference between an out-of-court statement identifying the person who the identifying witness testifies committed the crime (a non-hearsay use of the evidence), and evidence of an out-of-court statement relied on as evidence that the person identified committed the crime (a hearsay use of the statement). *Swanston* does not support the admissibility of Constable Dobro's evidence as evidence of identification. Constable Dobro's evidence that Q previously identified Long as one of the shooters had no value as original evidence, absent evidence from Q linking the person said to have been previously identified by him to the person who committed the crime. No such link was established given that Q. denied both making the previous identification and testified that Long was not one of the shooters.

Justice Doherty went on to conclude that the evidence of the previous identification was not admissible under the principles enunciated in *R. v. B. (K.G.)*. While conceding that the necessity criterion had been met, the Court was not persuaded as to reliability. The statement was not made under oath or its secular equivalent, the jury did not have an opportunity to observe the demeanour of Q. when he made the statement or the circumstances surrounding the making of the statement, and Q. was not subject to cross-examination by counsel for the appellants at the time he made the statement.

In *R. v. T. (W.P.)* [225] referred to in *Tat*, the accused challenged the constitutionality of s. 715.1 of the Criminal Code. That section provides for the admissibility of videotaped statements made by specified complainants in certain cases. Justice Doherty wrote for a five-person court. In the course of that opinion he wrote:

> The admission of prior consistent statements, referable to the identification of an accused by a witness, provides a good example of a judge-made exception to the rule against prior consistent statements. Judges have long recognized that an in-court identification has little probative value. Consequently, they admitted prior out-of-court statements made by witnesses which were consistent with their in-court identification. These earlier statements are admitted for the truth of their contents, to assist the jury in determining whether the accused was identified by the witness, and to assist in assessing the weight to be given to that identification.

---

225. (1993), 83 C.C.C. (3d) 5 (Ont. C.A.).

It seems that Justice Doherty then saw prior statements of identification as hearsay but receivable when the witness made an in-court identification. He would then have to similarly conclude that statements of prior identification, made by a witness who cannot identify the accused at trial, but who testifies that he identified the accused earlier and was then satisfied that he was being truthful would similarly be classified as hearsay. To be fair, Justice Doherty acknowledges in *Tat* that his position now is not consistent with his earlier position taken in *T. (W.P.)*. I simply say he got it right the first time!

(ii) *Past Recollection Recorded*

In an earlier section we discussed the different meanings of refreshing memory: present memory revised and past recollection recorded. While a witness is allowed to testify having reference to earlier memoranda, though he has no present recollection of the event,[226] this was justified by the witness's present vouching for the accuracy of the earlier statement; by a fiction the earlier record was assimilated to present testimony by the witness and the evidence received was not the record but the mouthings of the witness.[227] This fiction has been the subject of criticism and it does seem preferable and more honest to characterize the writing as the evidence; the adversary is protected as he is able to cross-examine the declarant about his usual habits for accuracy in recording, and the contemporaneous nature of the writing also serves as some assurance.

PROBLEMS

Problem 1

The accused, Butch Cassidy, is charged with the murder of his estranged wife, Jill. The killing occurred in the early morning hours at deceased's front doorway and was the result of several blows to the head with a small hatchet. Jack, 12-year-old son of this union, was aroused from sleep by someone knocking loudly at the front door. He testifies that he heard his mother go downstairs and then heard her screaming: "Butch, what are you doing? No! — No! — No! — Please don't hurt me Butch." Receivable?

Problem 2

Witness observes a hit-run accident and writes down the licence number of the fleeing vehicle. Witness later describes vehicle to investigating officer who makes a note of it. At trial witness has lost her note and cannot remember the licence plate number. May the investigating officer supply the missing number? By what reasoning? Compare *R. v. Davey* (1969), 6 C.R.N.S. 288 (B.C.S.C.) and *Cattermole v. Millar*, [1977] Crim. L.R. 553 (D.C.).

---

226. *Fleming v. Toronto Railway Co.* (1911), 25 O.L.R. 317 (C.A.).
227. See *Young v. Denton*, [1927] 1 D.L.R. 426 (Sask. C.A.), and see generally 3 Wigmore, *Evidence* (Chad. Rev.), s. 754.

9

Opinion Rule and Expert Evidence

1. OPINION RULE

The following hypothetical direct examination of a witness to an automobile accident illustrates the possible bewilderment that may be suffered by a lay witness when in the hands of a trial judge who believes in applying an opinion rule with the utmost rigour:

Q.	What happened then?
A.	The lady in the car that got hit stumbled out of her car and fell in a faint.
Defence Counsel:	Move to strike the opinions of the witness. Let him state the facts.
The Court:	Strike them out. The jury will disregard that answer. [To witness:] You must state the facts and not your conclusions regarding them. You can't give the jury your opinion as to *which* car got hit, *whose* car it was, *how* the lady got out of the car or *why* she fell, if she did fall, — you must state the facts.[1]

Thankfully the English and Canadian courts have not generally applied an exclusionary opinion rule with such strictness and consequently we have had a great deal less trouble with the rule than our American friends.

As suggested by Cowen and Carter:[2]

The opinion rule has appeared to work in England only because it has been laxly applied.

The true scope of an opinion rule in the law of evidence can be properly appreciated only with an awareness of the historical development in this area. The early 18th century announcements of English courts, that witnesses must speak to facts and not to opinion, when read in the context of that age, forbade quite different testimony than is presently thought to be foreclosed by the opinion rule. Samuel Johnson's Dictionary (1st ed., 1755) defined opinion as "Persuasion of the mind without proof of certain knowledge . . . Sentiments, Judgment, Notion," and never referred to "opinion" in the sense of a reasoned conclusion from facts observed.[3] Prior to the close of the eighteenth century there was no opinion rule, as we know it today[4] and statements made at the time, an opinion: "[I]t is mere opinion, which is not evidence"[5] were statements condemning testimony by

---

1. See King & Pillinger, *Opinion Evidence in Illinois* (1942), p. 1.
2. Cowen and Carter, *Essays on the Law of Evidence* (1956), p. 164.
3. See King & Pillinger, *supra*, note 1, at p. 8.
4. See *Phipson on Evidence*, 11th ed. (1970), p. 504, noting that *Gilbert's Evidence* of 1726 and Buller's *Nisi Prius* of 1767 make no mention of such rule with the first appearance of the same apparently in *Peake on Evidence* in 1801.
5. Lord Mansfield in *Carter v. Boehm* (1766), 97 E.R. 1162, 1168.

witnesses who had no personal knowledge of the event and so suffered from the same lack of testimonial qualification as the witness who repeated hearsay. What was being forbidden then were notions, guesses, conjectures; as phrased by Professor Wigmore, they were statements demanding that "the witness must speak as a knower, not merely a guesser."[6]

While judges and writers in Canada still mouth expressions that lay witnesses cannot give their opinions but must state facts, the intrinsic impossibility of the requirement has led in actual practice to the reception of opinion testimony from witnesses who have personal knowledge. The opinion's reception is justified at times as simply a "compendious mode of stating facts," or a "short-hand rendering" or an application of the "congeries of circumstances rule" or "collective fact rule."[7] On other occasions the court simply recognizes that the opinion rule cannot be absolute. For example, in *R. v. German*,[8] in denying any injustice done by the reception of opinion testimony from lay witnesses respecting defendant's intoxicated condition, Chief Justice Robertson noted:

> No doubt, the general rule is that it is only persons who are qualified by some special skill, training or experience who can be asked their opinion upon a matter in issue. *The rule is not, however, an absolute one.* There are a number of matters in respect of which *a person of ordinary intelligence may be permitted to give evidence of his opinion upon a matter of which he has personal knowledge.* Such matters as the identity of individuals, the apparent age of a person, the speed of a vehicle, are among the matters upon which witnesses have been allowed to express an opinion, notwithstanding that they have no special qualifications, other than the fact that they have personal knowledge of the subject matter, to enable them to form an opinion.[9] [Emphasis added.]

The Anglo-Canadian attitude to the opinion rule is justifiable on two bases: first, the impossibility of testifying only to facts and, second, the absence of any justification for totally excluding opinion testimony in the form of reasoned conclusions from witnesses without regard to their testimonial qualifications as observers of the event.

Regarding the impossibility of complying with the admonition to the witness that he must state facts and not opinion, it has been said:

> ... when our judge instructs the witness to "state the facts" it is as though he demanded that the witness fly by flapping his arms. The witness can't state facts and neither can the judge — facts are unspeakable and unstatable. We can't

---

6.   7 Wigmore, *Evidence* (Chad. Rev.), s. 1917.
7.   See Tyree, "The Opinion Rule" (1955), 10 Rutgers L. Rev. 601. See also, *e.g.*, Baron Alderson in *Wright v. Doe d. Tatham* (1838), 7 E.R. 559 at p. 578: ". . . a compendious mode of putting one instead of a multitude of questions to the witness"; relied on in *Robins v. Nat. Trust Co.* (1925), 57 O.L.R. 46 in receiving the opinion of witnesses respecting testator's mental condition when he signed his will.
8.   [1947] O.R. 395 (C.A.); relied on and followed on this point in *R. v. Pollock*, [1947] 2 W.W.R. 973 (Alta. Dist. Ct.) and *R. v. Nagy* (1965), 51 W.W.R. 307 (B.C. Co. Ct.); but *contra* see *R. v. Davies*, [1962] 1 W.L.R. 1111 (C.M.C.A.).
9.   *Ibid.*, at p. 409. And see *Porter v. O'Connell* (1915), 43 N.B.R. 458 (C.A.) where the court held it admissible for the eye-witness to state, in answer to a question respecting the speed of defendant's horse at the time of the accident, "the horse was going that fast I don't think he could be pulled up immediately."

reproduce in language either reality or our perception of reality. All statements in language are statements of opinion, i.e. statements of mental processes or perceptions. So-called "statements of fact" are only more specific statements of opinion.[10]

Professor Thayer remarked:

In a sense all testimony to matter of fact is opinion evidence; i.e., it is a conclusion formed from phenomena and mental impressions. Yet that is not the way we talk in courts or in common life. Where shall the line be drawn? When does matter of fact first become matter of opinion? . . . In the main, any rule excluding opinion evidence is limited to cases where, in the judgment of the court, it will not be helpful to the jury. . . . It is obvious that such a principle must allow a very great range of permissible difference in judgment; and that conclusions of that character ought not, usually, to be regarded as subject to review by higher courts.[11]

The second justification for the Anglo-Canadian attitude rests in Professor Thayer's premise that all that is logically probative is receivable unless excluded by a rule or principle of law.[12] If relevance is equated with logical probity and dictated not by law but by the common sense of experience, is it fair to say that the opinion of one who witnessed an accident that, for example, the plaintiff was driving too fast for the conditions of the road, is not logically probative of fault in the plaintiff? If it is accepted then that opinion is relevant,[13] it is clear that there must be some clear ground of policy to justify exclusion.[14] The theory has sometimes been put forward that to permit the reception of opinion testimony would be to permit the "usurpation of the jury's function."[15] Is this valid? To begin with, the trier of fact has the ability at all times to determine what evidence it will accept or reject and what weight will be given the same and is never bound to agree with the opinion expressed by the witness. The witness could never usurp the function of the trier of fact even if he wanted to.[16] Further, we do countenance the reception of opinion testimony from a class of witnesses whose opinions are the most likely to influence the trier of fact, the expert. Indeed, do we not want the expert to "usurp" the jury's function to a degree as we see the expert as

---

10. King & Pillinger, *supra*, note 1 at p. 4. And see McCormick, *Evidence*, 2d ed., p. 23, discussing the doctrine that a witness must state facts not opinion: "This classic formula, based as it is on the assumption that 'fact' and 'opinion' stand in contrast and hence are readily distinguishable, has proven the clumsiest of all the tools furnished the judge for regulating the examination of witnesses. It is clumsy because its basic assumption is an illusion. . . . There is no conceivable statement, however specific, detailed and 'factual', that is not in some measure the product of inference and reflection as well as observation and memory." See also for like statements, Maguire, *Evidence Common Sense and Common Law* (1947), p. 24 and 7 Wigmore, *Evidence* (Chad. Rev.), s. 1919.

11. *Preliminary Treatise on Evidence* (1898), p. 524.

12. *Ibid.*, at p. 265.

13. See the criticism of Lord Goddard's view by Cecil Wright, *Case and Comment* (1943), 21 C.B.R. 653 at p. 658. And compare *Betterton v. Turner* (1982), 133 D.L.R. (3d) 289 (B.C.S.C.).

14. See Trautman, "Logical or Legal Relevancy — A Conflict in Theory" (1952), 5 Vand. L. Rev. 385.

15. See, *e.g.*, Phipson, *Evidence*, 11th ed., p. 504; *Carter v. Boehm*, *supra*, note 5, at p. 1168.

16. This justification for the opinion rule has been termed "empty rhetoric" by Professor Wigmore in 7 *Evidence* (Chad. Rev.), s. 1920.

more competent to perform that function?[17] It would appear that English and Canadian judicial decisions have received lay opinion evidence from those with personal knowledge when so to do would be helpful to the jury and to otherwise restrict the witness would unduly interfere with the normal manner of communication.

GRAAT v. R.
[1982] 2 S.C.R. 819, 31 C.R. (3d) 289, 2 C.C.C. (3d) 365

21st December 1982. The judgment of the court was delivered by

DICKSON J.:— This appeal [from 17 C.R. (3d) 55] raises the issue whether on a charge of driving while impaired the court may admit opinion evidence on the very question to be decided, namely, Was the accused's ability to drive impaired by alcohol at the time and place stated in the charge?

. . . .

III

THE ONTARIO COURT OF APPEAL

The appellant sought leave to appeal to the Court of Appeal of Ontario and at that time the question was raised as to whether the trial judge had erred in law in relying on the opinion evidence of the two police officers that the appellant's ability to drive a motor vehicle had been impaired by alcohol.

The court dismissed the appeal, saying [p. 442] that the evidence was admissible under the exception to the rule excluding opinion evidence:

> . . . that permits non-expert opinion evidence where the primary facts and the inferences to be drawn from them are so closely associated that the opinion is really a compendious way of giving evidence as to certain facts — in this case the condition of the appellant.

This echoes the words of Parke B. in *Wright v. Tatham* (1838), 4 Bing. N.C. 489 at 543-44 (H.L.):

> . . . and though the opinion of a witness upon oath, as to that fact [testamentary capacity], might be asked, it would only be a compendious mode of ascertaining the result of the actual observation of the witness, from acts done, as to the habits and demeanour of the deceased.

. . . .

CONCLUSION

I have attempted in the foregoing to highlight the opposing points of view as reflected in some of the cases, texts, and reports of the law reform commissions.

We start with the reality that the law of evidence is burdened with a large number of cumbersome rules, with exclusions, and exceptions to the exclusions, and exceptions to the exceptions. The list of subjects upon which the non-expert witness is allowed to give opinion evidence is a lengthy one. The list mentioned in *Sherrard v. Jacob*, supra, is by

---

17.   See Cowen and Carter, *Essays on the Law of Evidence* (1956), p. 170. See also the majority holding in *R. v. Lupien* (1970), 71 W.W.R. 110 (S.C.C.), approving the reception of expert opinion on the "very thing" the jury had to decide because psychiatry had developed to the point that their views would be more competent.

no means exhaustive: (i) the identification of handwriting, persons and things; (ii) apparent age; (iii) the bodily plight or condition of a person, including death and illness; (iv) the emotional state of a person, e.g., whether distressed, angry, aggressive, affectionate or depressed; (v) the condition of things, e.g., worn, shabby, used or new; (vi) certain questions of value; and (vii) estimates of speed and distance. . . .

Except for the sake of convenience there is little, if any, virtue in any distinction resting on the tenuous and frequently false antithesis between fact and opinion. The line between "fact" and "opinion" is not clear.

To resolve the question before the court I would like to return to broad principles. Admissibility is determined, first, by asking whether the evidence sought to be admitted is relevant. This is a matter of applying logic and experience to the circumstances of the particular case. The question which must then be asked is whether, though probative, the evidence must be excluded by a clear ground of policy or of law.

There is a direct and logical relevance between (i) the evidence offered here, namely, the opinion of a police officer (based on perceived facts as to the manner of driving and indicia of intoxication of the driver) that the person's ability to drive was impaired by alcohol, and (ii) the ultimate probandum in the case. The probative value of the evidence is not outweighed by such policy considerations as danger of confusing the issues or misleading the jury. It does not unfairly surprise a party who had not had reasonable ground to anticipate that such evidence will be offered, and the adducing of the evidence does not necessitate undue consumption of time. As for other considerations, such as "usurping the functions of the jury" and, to the extent that it may be regarded as a separate consideration, "opinion on the very issue before the jury", Wigmore has gone a long way toward establishing that rejection of opinion evidence on either of these grounds is unsound historically and in principle. If the court is being told that which it is in itself entirely equipped to determine without the aid of the witness on the point then of course the evidence is supererogatory and unnecessary. It would be a waste of time listening to superfluous testimony.

The judge in the instant case was not in as good a position as the police officers or Mr. Wilson to determine the degree of Mr. Graat's impairment or his ability to drive a motor vehicle. The witnesses had an opportunity for personal observation. They were in a position to give the court real help. They were not settling the dispute. They were not deciding the matter the court had to decide, the ultimate issue. The judge could accept all or part or none of their evidence. In the end he accepted the evidence of two of the police officers and paid little heed to the evidence of the third officer or of Mr. Wilson.

. . . .

A non-expert witness cannot, of course, give opinion evidence on a legal issue as, for example, whether or not a person was negligent. That is because such an opinion would not qualify as an abbreviated version of the witness's factual observations. An opinion that someone was negligent is partly factual, but it also involves the application of legal standards. On the other hand, whether a person's ability to drive is impaired by alcohol is a question of fact, not of law. It does not involve the application of any legal standard. It is akin to an opinion that someone is too drunk to climb a ladder or to go swimming, and the fact that a witness's opinion, as here, may be expressed in the exact words of the Criminal Code does not change a factual matter into a question of law. It only reflects the fact that the draftsmen of the Code employed the ordinary English phrase: "his ability to drive . . . is impaired by alcohol" (s. 234).

In short, I know of no clear ground of policy or of law which would require the exclusion of opinion evidence tendered by the Crown or the defence as to Mr. Graat's impairment.

I conclude with two caveats. First, in every case, in determining whether an opinion is admissible, the trial judge must necessarily exercise a large measure of discretion. Second, there may be a tendency for judges and juries to let the opinion of police witnesses overwhelm the opinion evidence of other witnesses. Since the opinion is admitted under the "compendious statement of facts" exception rather than under the "expert witness" exception, there is no special reason for preferring the police evidence over the "opinion" of other witnesses. As always, the trier of fact must decide in each case what weight to give what evidence. The "opinion" of the police officer is entitled to no special regard. Ordinary people with ordinary experience are able to know as a matter of fact that someone is too drunk to perform certain tasks, such as driving a car. If the witness lacks the relevant experience, or is otherwise limited in his testimonial capacity, or if the witness is not sure whether the person was intoxicated to the point of impairment, that can be brought out in cross-examination. But the fact that a police witness has seen more impaired drivers than a non-police witness is not a reason in itself to prefer the evidence of the police officer. Constables McMullen and Spoelstra were not testifying as experts based on their extensive experience as police officers.

There was some confusion about this matter in this case as appears from the following cross-examination of Mr. Wilson:

Q.   . . . And of course you've not and never have been a police officer. Do you agree or disagree with me? A. No. No.

Q.   You have never been a police officer? A. No.

Q.   And you're not in the habit of checking people as to the amount of alcohol that is consumed in order to make him impaired. Do you agree or disagree with me? A. I have to agree with you?

Q.   Yes. So you're really not in a position to tell us whether or not he was impaired or not impaired by alcohol. Do you agree or disagree with me? A. I was only . . .

Q.   . . . But of course you were in no position to judge as to whether or not he was impaired. Do you agree or disagree with me? A. I don't have any qualifications in that regard, I guess.

Mr. Wilson does not need any special qualifications. Nor were the police officers relying on any special qualifications when they gave their opinions. Both police and non-police witnesses are merely giving a compendious statement of facts that are too subtle and too complicated to be narrated separately and distinctly. Trial judges should bear in mind that this is non-expert opinion evidence, and that the opinion of police officers is not entitled to preference just because they may have extensive experience with impaired drivers. The credit and accuracy of the police must be viewed in the same manner as that of other witnesses and in the light of all the evidence in the case. If the police and traffic officers have been closely associated with the prosecution, such association may affect the weight to be given to such evidence.

The trial judge was correct in admitting the opinions of the three police officers and Mr. Wilson.

For the foregoing reasons, as well as for the reasons given by Howland C.J.O., I would dismiss the appeal.

Appeal dismissed.

2. EXPERT EVIDENCE

Toward the end of the 18th century what appears to be an exception to the general rule forbidding testimony by witnesses who had no personal knowledge of the facts at issue was established. Expert assistance had been furnished to the court from very ancient times but not in the form normally used today.[18] Special juries of experts were commonly used in the 14th century to resolve trade disputes,[19] and as early as 1353 we find the court summoning surgeons to give an opinion on whether a wound amounted to mayhem.[20] The court summoned the expert, and on considering his advice, then directed the jury respecting the major premise that could be used by them in determining the particular fact situation. With the change in the jury system to their being informed by witnesses summoned by the parties rather than investigating themselves,[21] we find, toward the end of the 18th century, experts being called by the parties, testifying as witnesses, and so furnishing their assistance directly to the jury.[22] To justify this apparent exception to the long-standing rule that witnesses have personal knowledge, the courts reasoned that to receive the same was *necessary*.[23] The expert then could give his opinion on matters of science, though he had no personal knowledge of the event being litigated, where to do so would be *helpful* to the jury's decision-making; where the major premise or premises necessary against which the particular instance under review needs to be tested is lacking from the fund of knowledge possessed by the layman.

The expert's testimonial qualifications, just as those of lay witnesses, must be established before the trier of fact. It is for the trial judge in his discretion to rule whether the experiential qualifications of the witness have been made out,[24] and it is for the trial judge to rule whether the evidence will be helpful. As the state of the art varies with time so will the criterion of helpfulness. Professor McGuire wrote:

> The field of expertness is bounded on one side by the great area of the commonplace, supposedly within the ken of every person of moderate intelligence, and on the other by the even greater area of the speculative and uncertain. Of course both these boundaries constantly shift, as the former area enlarges and the latter diminishes. Only a few years ago it would have been necessary to take expert evidence on issues with respect to the operation of motor cars, airplanes, or radios which are now so completely inside the domain of popular understanding that such evidence would be rejected as superfluous. A century ago purportedly expert evidence on these topics

---

18. See generally Hand, "Historical and Practical Considerations Regarding Expert Testimony" (1901), 15 Harv. L. Rev. 40; see also Thayer, *Cases on Evidence*, 2d ed. (1900), at pp. 672-73 and Rosenthal, "The Development of the Use of Expert Testimony" (1935), 2 L. & Contemp. Prob. 403.

19. See Hand, *ibid.*, at pp. 41 and 42. For a more recent example of the empanelling of a special jury see *R. v. Anne Wycherley* (1838), 173 E.R. 486 a jury of married women impanelled to determine if the convicted defendant was with child, the jury "de vente inspiciendo."

20. *Anonymous*, Lib. Ass. 28, pl. 5 (28 Edw. III); see also *Buller v. Crips* (1705), 87 E.R. 793.

21. See generally Holdsworth, *A History of English Law*, 7th ed. (1856), vol. 1, pp. 332 *et seq.*, and *supra*, Chapter 8 — Hearsay.

22. See, *e.g., Folkes v. Chad* (1782), 99 E.R. 589; (1783), 99 E.R. 686.

23. See note to *Carter v. Boehm* in *Smith's Leading Cases*, 13th ed., vol. 1, p. 560.

24. *Preeper v. R.* (1888), 15 S.C.R. 401.

would have been rejected as visionary.[25]

As the "speculative and uncertain" area changes, how should the court rule?[26]

R. v. MELARAGNI
(1992), 76 C.C.C. (3d) 78 (Ont. Gen. Div.)

[Accused police officers were charged as a result of shooting incident. The theory of the defence was that the accused were acting in self-defence when deceased drove his car at them. One issue at trial was whether the accused was entitled to adduce expert evidence to rebut inferences the jury might draw as to abilities of police officers in a stressful situation.]

MOLDAVER J.:—

. . . .

The defence seeks to call expert evidence designed to rebut inferences which the jury might understandably choose to apply based upon their common everyday experience in life. The defence submits that there is a real risk that this jury will assume, absent the proposed evidence, that police officers are trained to react and do react in a cool, calm and deliberate fashion at all times, including situations of great stress, especially since stress is a regular component in the daily makeup of a police officer's existence. The defence submits that the jury would certainly be forgiven for asking questions such as, "How could a trained police officer miss his target by several feet at close range? How could a police officer think he had fired only two bullets when, in fact, he had fired four? How could a police officer possibly miss seeing his partner on the other side of a four and a half foot high motor vehicle if his partner was standing erect?"

The proposed evidence is sought to be tendered to dispell certain misperceptions that might exist in the minds of the jurors regarding these and other matters. While I have not received any evidence which would tend to confirm the existence of such misperceptions in the minds of the public, I cannot help but believe that the concerns expressed are real. As a society, we are generally unfamiliar through our common everyday experience as to just how police officers do react in situations of extreme stress and peril. What knowledge we do have is generally derived from Hollywood where police officers are for the most part portrayed as super human beings possessed of remarkable marksmanship skills with ice-water flowing through their veins. This perception, which I would describe as a myth, is one which the defence ought to be entitled to dispel. I am of the view that the proposed evidence is, therefore, not only relevant, but may well be helpful to the jury in dispelling the myth which I have described and in arriving at their ultimate decision in this case. Therefore, the evidence proposed by the defence is admissible.

R. v. MELARAGNI
(1992), 73 C.C.C. (3d) 348 (Ont. Gen. Div.)

MOLDAVER J.:—The bullet which struck and killed Wade Lawson passed through the rear window of the vehicle which he was driving. The Crown seeks to tender opinion evidence designed to locate that bullet's approximate point of entry in the rear window.

---

25. *Evidence: Common Sense and Common Law* (1947), p. 30.
26. See generally, Paciocco, "Evaluating Expert Opinion Evidence for the Purpose of Determining Admissibility" (1994), 27 C.R. (4th) 302.

The defence has objected to the admissibility of this evidence for the following reasons: (1) that the opinion evidence is completely unreliable since it stems from an unvalidated and speculative hypothesis, and (2) that Mr. Glenn Carroll, the expert proferred by the Crown, is not qualified to give the opinion sought.

I propose to deal with the issue of reliability first. The hypothesis in question may be stated as follows: (1) that linear radial fracture lines fan out in all directions from the point of impact when a high velocity object, such as a bullet, strikes and penetrates tempered glass; (2) that these linear radial fracture lines can and sometimes do spread in a readily observable fashion to the extremities of the piece of tempered glass that has been penetrated, and (3) that even if large portions of the piece of tempered glass have been shattered and dispersed upon impact, so long as the remaining intact portions of the glass contain a sufficient number of observable linear radial fracture lines, these lines may be used to chart the approximate point of impact.

The validity of this proposition has been attested to by both Mr. Carroll and Mr. Haag. Mr. Carroll is a civilian employed by the R.C.M.P. For the past approximate 20 years he has specialized *inter alia* in the field of glass fracture analysis. Mr. Haag is an expert in the field of firearms and ballistics. A significant part of his training and experience has involved the analysis of glass objects which have been penetrated by high velocity objects such as bullets. . . . On behalf of the defence, Professor John Thornton gave evidence. He is undoubtedly a renowned expert in the field of glass fracture analysis. In his examination-in-chief, Professor Thornton took issue with the evidence of both Messrs. Carroll and Haag. In his opinion, the proposition advanced was not only unreliable, given the present body of scientific knowledge, but it was also potentially incapable of validation. The reason for this latter observation stemmed from his opinion that no two pieces of tempered glass were the same. Every piece of such glass was imbued with its own individual characteristics and, therefore, prospective conclusions based upon prior experimentation might prove impossible. Beyond that, Professor Thornton was of the view that even if prospective conclusions could be gleaned from prior experimentation, the experiments performed by Mr. Carroll in this case were woefully inadequate and served to prove little or nothing.

. . . .

It may well be that a jury will side with Professor Thornton, assuming he testifies at trial, and conclude that Mr. Carroll is unable to be so precise in his charting of the point of impact. However, that does not render Mr. Carroll's evidence inadmissible. It simply goes to the weight of his testimony.

I am, therefore, satisfied based upon the evidence of all three experts, that the proposed evidence is sufficiently reliable from a "scientific" point of view that its exclusion for that reason is not warranted. In other words, I am satisfied that the proposition upon which Mr. Carroll bases his evidence amounts to something more than an unvalidated or speculative hypothesis.

That, however, does not end the matter. Merely because the proposed evidence passes some minimum threshold test of reliability does not in and of itself lead to its automatic inclusion. When the Crown seeks to tender evidence which involves a new scientific technique or body of scientific knowledge, it must, of course, establish that the evidence is relevant and that it passes a minimum threshold test of reliability. As well, the evidence must be outside the experience and knowledge of the trier of fact, and it may only be tendered through a properly qualified expert.

Assuming that these pre-conditions have been met, I am of the view that a number of other factors should be canvassed before the evidence is admitted. These include the following considerations:

(1) Is the evidence likely to assist the jury in its fact-finding mission, or is it likely to confuse and confound the jury?

(2) Is the jury likely to be overwhelmed by the "mystic infallibility" of the evidence, or will the jury be able to keep an open mind and objectively assess the worth of the evidence?

(3) Will the evidence, if accepted, conclusively prove an essential element of the crime which the defence is contesting, or is it simply a piece of evidence to be incorporated into a larger puzzle?

(4) What degree of reliability has the proposed scientific technique or body of knowledge achieved?

(5) Are there a sufficient number of experts available so that the defence can retain its own expert if desired?

(6) Is the scientific technique or body of knowledge such that it can be independently tested by the defence?

(7) Has the scientific technique destroyed the evidence upon which the conclusions have been based, or has the evidence been preserved for defence analysis if requested?

(8) Are there clear policy or legal grounds which would render the evidence inadmissible despite its probative value?

(9) Will the evidence cause undue delay or result in the needless presentation of cumulative evidence?

This list is not necessarily exhaustive; furthermore, the importance of any one or more of these factors will vary depending upon the particular circumstances of the case. In arriving at my decision in this case to admit the impugned evidence, I have considered all of these factors, even though not specifically requested to do so by the defence. My analysis has led me to conclude that the proposition which forms the foundation of the proposed evidence is quite reliable when used to determine a zone or area of impact. It may be somewhat less reliable in pinpointing the exact location of impact, but the proposed evidence is not being tendered for that purpose. I am further satisfied that the evidence, if accepted, could assist the jury in its fact-finding mission and it will not confuse or confound the jury. The proposition is readily understandable and its application is for the most part simple and straightforward.

I am equally convinced that the jury will not be overwhelmed by the "mystic infallibility" of the evidence. If anything, just the opposite will occur. I have no doubt that the jury will carefully consider cross-examination designed to weaken or destroy the worth of the proposed evidence. I have every confidence that the jury will pay close attention to an opposing expert, and I am equally confident that the jury will follow legal instruction regarding the worth of expert evidence in general and this evidence in particular.

Moving on from there, the proposed evidence will not, if accepted, conclusively prove an essential element of the crime which the defence contests. It will simply form a basis for additional expert evidence which, if accepted, might lead to an inference that Constable Melaragni intended to shoot at Mr. Lawson. Regarding the availability of experts, the defence has already retained a leading expert. Furthermore, the defence is able to do its own testing to confirm or cast doubt upon the scientific proposition in issue. Beyond that, the evidence upon which the Crown expert formed his opinion remains in existence. The defence may, even at this time, conduct its own tests on the remaining portion of the back window if it wishes.

Finally, there are no legal or policy grounds which would render the evidence inadmissible and the tendering of this evidence will not cause undue delay or result in the needless presentation of cumulative evidence. For all these reasons, I find that the proposed evidence is admissible.

[Justice Moldaver then went on to the second issue, namely, whether the expert proposed by the Crown, was qualified to give the opinion evidence. He was satisfied that his prior training, experience and study in the field of glass fracture analysis had imbued him with the necessary degree of knowledge and skill so as to enable him to give the opinion evidence which the Crown proposes to tender.]

R. v. MOHAN
[1994] 2 S.C.R. 9, 29 C.R. (4th) 243, 89 C.C.C. (3d) 402

[This case was discussed in Chapter 4 with respect to the reception of expert opinion evidence as to character. Here we'll discuss the case as it impacts on the reception of expert evidence generally.

The accused, a practising paediatrician, was charged with four counts of sexual assault on four of his female patients. Counsel for the accused sought to call a psychiatrist who would testify that the perpetrator of the offences alleged to have been committed would be one of a limited and unusual group of individuals, and that the accused did not fall within that narrow class because he did not possess the characteristics belonging to that group.]

SOPINKA J.:—

. . . .

Admission of expert evidence depends on the application of the following criteria:

(a)   relevance;
(b)   necessity in assisting the trier of fact;   ] →probes from hearsay
(c)   the absence of any exclusionary rule;
(d)   a properly qualified expert.

(a) Relevance

Relevance is a threshold requirement for the admission of expert evidence as with all other evidence. Relevance is a matter to be decided by a judge as question of law. Although prima facie admissible if so related to a fact in issue that it tends to establish it, that does not end the inquiry. This merely determines the logical relevance of the evidence. Other considerations enter into the decision as to admissibility. This further inquiry may be described as a cost benefit analysis, that is "whether its value is worth what it costs." See *McCormick on Evidence* (3rd ed. 1984), at p. 544. Cost in this context is not used in its traditional economic sense but rather in terms of its impact on the trial process. Evidence that is otherwise logically relevant may be excluded on this basis, if its probative value is overborne by its prejudicial effect, if it involves an inordinate amount of time which is not commensurate with its value or if it is misleading in the sense that its effect on the trier of fact, particularly a jury, is out of proportion to its reliability. While frequently considered as an aspect of legal relevance, the exclusion of logically relevant evidence on these grounds is more properly regarded as a general exclusionary rule (see *R. v. Morris*, [1983] 2 S.C.R. 190). Whether it is treated as an aspect of relevance or an exclusionary rule, the effect is the same. The reliability versus effect factor has special significance in assessing the admissibility of expert evidence.

There is a danger that expert evidence will be misused and will distort the fact-finding process. Dressed up in scientific language which the jury does not easily understand and submitted through a witness of impressive antecedents, this evidence is apt to be accepted by the jury as being virtually infallible and as having more weight than it deserves. . . . As La Forest J. stated in *R. c. Béland*, [1987] 2 S.C.R. 398, at p. 434, with respect to the evidence of the results of a polygraph tendered by the accused, such evidence should not be admitted by reason of "human fallibility in assessing the proper weight to be given to evidence cloaked under the mystique of science". The application of this principle can be seen in cases such as *R. v. Melaragni* (1992), 73 C.C.C. (3d) 348, in which Moldaver J. applied a threshold test of reliability to what he described as "a new scientific technique or body of scientific knowledge". Moldaver J. also mentioned two other factors, inter alia, which should be considered in such circumstances . . . :

(1)   Is the evidence likely to assist the jury in its fact-finding mission, or is it likely to confuse and confound the jury?

(2)   Is the jury likely to be overwhelmed by the "mystic infallibility" of the evidence, or will the jury be able to keep an open mind and objectively assess the worth of the evidence?

. . . .

(b) *Necessity in Assisting the Trier of Fact*

In *R. v. Abbey, supra*, Dickson J., as he then was, stated:

With respect to matters calling for special knowledge, an expert in the field may draw inferences and state his opinion. An expert's function is precisely this: to provide the judge and jury with a ready-made inference which the judge and jury, due to the technical nature of the facts, are unable to formulate. An expert's opinion is admissible to furnish the Court with scientific information which is likely to be outside the experience and knowledge of a judge or jury. If on the proven facts a judge or jury can form their own conclusions without help, then the opinion of the expert is unnecessary. . . .

This precondition is often expressed in terms as to whether the evidence would be helpful to the trier of fact. The word "helpful" is not quite appropriate and sets too low a standard. However, I would not judge necessity by too strict a standard. What is required is that the opinion be necessary in the sense that it provide information "which is likely to be outside the experience and knowledge of a judge or jury". . . . As stated by Dickson J., the evidence must be necessary to enable the trier of fact to appreciate the matters in issue due to their technical nature. In *Kelliher (Village) v. Smith*, [1931] S.C.R. 672, at p. 684, this court, quoting from *Beven on Negligence* (4th ed. 1928), p. 141, stated that in order for expert evidence to be admissible, "[t]he subject-matter of the inquiry must be such that ordinary people are unlikely to form a correct judgment about it, if unassisted by persons with special knowledge." More recently, in *R. v. Lavallee, supra*, the above passages from *Kelliher* and *Abbey* were applied to admit expert evidence as to the state of mind of a "battered" woman. The judgment stressed that this was an area that is not understood by the average person.

As in the case of relevance, discussed above, the need for the evidence is assessed in light of its potential to distort the fact-finding process. As stated by Lawton L.J. in *R. v. Turner*, [1975] Q.B. 834, at p. 841, and approved by Lord Wilberforce in *Director of Public Prosecutions v. Jordan*, [1977] A.C. 699, at p. 718:

An expert's opinion is admissible to furnish the court with scientific information which is likely to be outside the experience and knowledge of a judge or jury. If on the proven facts a judge or jury can form their own conclusions without help, then the opinion of an expert is unnecessary. In such a case if it is given dressed up in scientific jargon it may make judgment more difficult. The fact that an expert witness has impressive scientific qualifications does not by that fact alone make his opinion on matters of human nature and behaviour within the limits of normality any more helpful than that of the jurors themselves; but there is a danger that they may think it does.

The possibility that evidence will overwhelm the jury and distract them from their task can often be offset by proper instructions.

There is also a concern inherent in the application of this criterion that experts not be permitted to usurp the functions of the trier of fact. Too liberal an approach could result in a trial's becoming nothing more than a contest of experts with the trier of fact acting as referee in deciding which expert to accept.

These concerns were the basis of the rule which excluded expert evidence in respect of the ultimate issue. Although the rule is no longer of general application, the concerns underlying it remain. In light of these concerns, the criteria of relevance and necessity are applied strictly, on occasion, to exclude expert evidence as to an ultimate issue. Expert evidence as to credibility or oath-helping has been excluded on this basis. See *R. v. Marquard*, [1993] 4 S.C.R. 223, per McLachlin J.

(c) *The Absence of any Exclusionary Rule*

Compliance with criteria (a), (b) and (d) will not ensure the admissibility of expert evidence if it falls afoul of an exclusionary rule of evidence separate and apart from the opinion rule itself. For example, in *R. v. Morin*, [1988] 2 S.C.R. 345, evidence elicited by the Crown in cross-examination of the psychiatrist called by the accused was inadmissible because it was not shown to be relevant other than as to the disposition to commit the crime charged. Notwithstanding, therefore, that the evidence otherwise complied with the criteria for the admission of expert evidence it was excluded by reason of the rule that prevents the Crown from adducing evidence of the accused's disposition unless the latter has placed his or her character in issue. The extent of the restriction when such evidence is tendered by the accused lies at the heart of this case and will be discussed hereunder.

(d) *A Properly Qualified Expert*

Finally the evidence must be given by a witness who is shown to have acquired special or peculiar knowledge through study or experience in respect of the matters on which he or she undertakes to testify.

In summary, therefore, it appears from the foregoing that expert evidence which advances a novel scientific theory or technique is subjected to special scrutiny to determine whether it meets a basic threshold of reliability and whether it is essential in the sense that the trier of fact will be unable to come to a satisfactory conclusion without the assistance of the expert. The closer the evidence approaches an opinion on an ultimate issue, the stricter the application of this principle.

[The Court then analyzed the jurisprudence regarding expert evidence as to disposition, discussed in Chapter 4.]

Application to This Case

I take the findings of the trial judge to be that a person who committed sexual assaults on young women could not be said to belong to a group possessing behavioural characteristics that are sufficiently distinctive to be of assistance in identifying the perpetrator of the offences charged. Moreover, the fact that the alleged perpetrator was a physician did not advance the matter because there is no acceptable body of evidence that doctors who commit sexual assaults fall into a distinctive class with identifiable characteristics. Notwithstanding the opinion of Dr. Hill, the trial judge was also not satisfied that the characteristics associated with the fourth complaint identified the perpetrator as a member of a distinctive group. He was not prepared to accept that the characteristics of that complaint were such that only a psychopath could have committed the act. There was nothing to indicate any general acceptance of this theory. Moreover, there was no material in the record to support a finding that the profile of a pedophile or psychopath has been standardized to the extent that it could be said that it matched the supposed profile of the offender depicted in the charges. The expert's group profiles were not seen as sufficiently reliable to be considered helpful. In the absence of these indicia of reliability, it cannot be said that the evidence would be necessary in the sense of usefully clarifying a matter otherwise inaccessible, or that any value it may have had would not be outweighed by its potential for misleading or diverting the jury. Given these findings and applying the principles referred to above, I must conclude that the trial judge was right in deciding as a matter of law that the evidence was inadmissible.

———————

Mohan signals a more cautious approach to the reception of expert testimony. Counsel tendering expert evidence may now be called on to persuade the judge that applying the basic principles of the law of evidence the expert deserves to be heard by the trier of fact. Evidence, to be admissible, must first be relevant to a matter in issue. This basic rule is as applicable to expert evidence as it is to any other form of evidence. Aside from being relevant, it has long been established that expert evidence to be received must be helpful to the trier of fact. Just as it is the judge who determines relevance so too it is the judge who determines the helpfulness of the expert testimony. It is also the judge who determines whether the experiential qualifications of the tendered expert have been made out; that the proposed witness, by virtue of his learning and experience, has knowledge not commonly shared. In making the determination of helpfulness the judge must consider whether the evidence warrants the consumption of time and whether the evidence could actually be less than helpful due to the possibility that it could mislead the trier of fact who might give the evidence even more worth than it actually deserves. In determining helpfulness it is also for the judge to determine the reliability or validity of the science proposed to be elicited. As the judge is the gatekeeper on the other matters it is also sensible that he as well protect the trier from so-called junk science.[27] The question faced by the court in *R. v. Mohan* was whether this determination should be made simply by the application of the rules set out above, relevance and helpfulness, or whether there is an additional, special rule to be formulated and followed.

In the United States a special evidentiary rule was set out in a federal appellate opinion in 1923[28] and despite criticism over the years it lasted until its repudiation by the United States Supreme Court in 1993.[29] That rule, which became known as the *Frye* test, demanded general acceptance in the scientific community before expertise could be admitted. McCormick in the most recent edition recommends:

> The traditional standards of relevancy and the need for expertise — and nothing more — should govern. This method for evaluating the admissibility of scientific evidence is the most appealing. It avoids the difficult problems of defining when "scientific" evidence is subject to the general acceptance requirement and how general this acceptance must be, of discerning exactly what it is that must be accepted, and of determining the "particular field" to which the scientific evidence belongs and in which it must be accepted.[30]

———————

27. See Huber, *Galileo's Revenge: Junk Science in the Courtroom* (Best Books, 1991).
28. *Frye v. United States*, 293 F. 1013.
29. For criticism in the U.S. see, e.g., Gianelli, "The Admissibility of Novel Scientific Evidence" (1980), 80 Col. L. Rev. 1197, and McCormick, "Scientific Evidence" (1982), 67 Iowa L. Rev. 879. The amount of writing on this issue was likened to "an academic cottage industry"; see Vu & Tamor, "Of Daubert, Elvis and Precedential Relevance" (1993), 41 U.C.L.A. L. Rev. 487, 491.
30. *McCormick on Evidence*, 4th ed. (1992) at p. 874.

In 1975 the Federal Rules of Evidence were enacted by Congress. The impetus for these rules had been the United States Supreme Court and indeed the preliminary drafts were written pursuant to that Court's rule-making authority. It was only later that Congress involved itself in legislating the Rules. Rule 702 of the F.R.E. provides:

> If scientific, technical, or other specialized knowledge will assist the trier of fact to understand the evidence or to determine a fact in issue, a witness qualified as an expert by knowledge, skill, experience, training, or education, may testify thereto in the form of an opinion or otherwise.

This enactment caused many courts to disregard the *Frye* test. Finally, after 20 years of the rule's operation, the United States Supreme Court rejected the *Frye* test, saying it had been superseded by the F.R.E. rule.

In *Daubert v. Merrell Dow Pharmaceuticals Inc.*,[31] parents sued on their own behalf and on behalf of their children for birth defects. The plaintiffs maintained that these were due to the ingestion of Bendectin by the mother during her pregnancy. Bendectin was advertised as helpful to deal with morning sickness. The plaintiffs were unsuccessful in the lower courts. The trial court applied the *Frye* doctrine. The trial court granted summary judgment on the basis of an affidavit of a well-credentialed expert who deposed that having reviewed the literature, more than 30 published studies involving 130,000 patients, no study had found Bendectin to be a substance causing malformations in human fetuses. The plaintiffs did not contest this characterization of the published record regarding Bendectin. They responded with eight experts of their own, each with impressive credentials. They had concluded that Bendectin could cause birth defects. Their conclusions were based on animal studies; pharmacological studies of the chemical structure of Bendectin and the reanalysis of previously published, epidemiological, human statistical, studies. The trial court decided that scientific evidence was admissible only if the principle upon which it is based is sufficiently established to have general acceptance in the field to which it belongs. The court decided that the plaintiffs' evidence did not meet that standard. Given the vast body of epidemiological data concerning Bendectin, the court decided that expert opinion which was not based on epidemiological evidence was not admissible to establish causation. The epidemiological analyses were not admissible because they had not been published or subjected to peer review. The Court of Appeals affirmed holding that expert opinion based on a scientific technique is inadmissible unless the technique was generally accepted as reliable in the relevant scientific community.

The Supreme Court granted *certiorari* in light of sharp divisions among the courts regarding the proper standard. When *certiorari* was granted this was front page news in the United States and 22 amicus briefs were filed.[32] The court decided that the *Frye* test was superseded by the Federal Rules and general acceptance in the scientific community was not a prerequisite to admission of scientific evidence. The rejection of the *Frye* test does not mean however that a trial judge is deprived of authority to exclude expert testimony. Justice Blackmun for the court wrote:

---

31.   113 S.Ct. 2786 (1993).
32.   See Imwinkelried, "Frye Is Dead" *Trial* (September 1993) 60.

Nor is the trial judge disabled from screening such evidence. To the contrary, under the rules the trial judge must ensure that any and all scientific testimony or evidence admitted is not only relevant, but reliable.[33]

The court recognized that scientists typically distinguish between "validity": does the principle support what it purports to show?, and reliability: does application of the principle produce consistent results? The court was, however, at pains to point out that when they spoke of the need for reliability they were speaking of evidentiary reliability, i.e., trustworthiness, and that reliability would be based upon scientific validity.

The court recognized that it would be wrong to demand that the subject of scientific testimony be known to a certainty. To qualify as scientific knowledge however an inference or assertion must be derived by the scientific method. The trial judge is expected to assess whether the reasoning or methodology underlying the testimony is scientifically valid and whether that reasoning or methodology can properly be applied to the facts in issue. The court offered some observations as to how a trial judge might go about his task:

> [W]hether a theory or technique is scientific knowledge that will assist the trier of fact will [depend on] whether it can be and has been tested [and] whether the theory or technique has been subjected to peer review and publication. . . . The fact of publication, or lack thereof, in a peer-reviewed journal will be a relevant, though not dispositive, consideration. . . . [T]he court should consider the known or potential rate of error and the existence and maintenance of standards controlling the technique's operation. . . . Finally, "general acceptance" can yet have a bearing.[34]

Counsel for Merrell Dow Pharmaceuticals Inc. argued that abandoning the general acceptance test would result in a "free-for-all" in which juries would be confounded by irrational pseudoscientific assertions. The Court decided that alongwith the screening by the trial judge, the adversary system with vigorous cross-examination and presentation of contrary evidence were appropriate safeguards.

The court in *Mohan* appears to have arrived at the same position as the court in *Daubert*, though with decidedly less fanfare. In *Mohan*, Justice Sopinka, not unnaturally, appears to follow his text[35] in rejecting the wisdom of a special evidentiary rule. There we find:

> The judicial experience in the United States demonstrates that a judicial standard for admissibility is problematic. To date, Canadian courts have not attempted to formulate a single rule for the admissibility of new scientific evidence. Rather, the courts first apply the traditional exclusionary rules, the expert evidence rule, and then invoke policy reasons specific to the particular proffered evidence to determine admissibility. This appears to be the preferable route and it accords with the present trend in the American federal courts.[36]

In Canada, then, expert evidence will be received if it is relevant to a fact in issue, the expert is properly qualified, the expert evidence is helpful to the trier

---

33. *Supra*, note 31 at p. 2795.
34. *Ibid.*, at pp. 2796-97.
35. *The Law of Evidence in Canada*, Sopinka, Lederman & Bryant (Toronto: Butterworths, 1992).
36. *Ibid.*, at p. 569.

of fact and there are no exclusionary rules in operation. The trial judge, the gatekeeper, has the obligation to vet each of these requirements. In determining helpfulness the trial judge must always have regard to the potential of expert evidence to distort the fact-finding process and turn it into a trial of experts, and should exclude when that danger is manifest. Trial judges always have the discretion to exclude even relevant evidence when probative value is overcome by the counterweights of consumption of time, prejudice and confusion. Expert evidence will only be helpful if the trial decides that it passes the threshold of reliability. The court in *Mohan* does not provide much in the way of guidance for the trial judge to determine the reliability of novel scientific evidence. Perhaps some of the general observations in *Daubert* may be useful to counsel in framing their arguments and to trial judges in deciding the matter.

R. v. OLSCAMP
(1994), 35 C.R. (4th) 37, 95 C.C.C. (3d) 466 (Ont. Gen. Div.)

[This was a ruling regarding the admissibility of expert evidence intended to be called by the Crown in support of the complainant's testimony that she had been sexually abused. Dr. W would testify if permitted that the girl displayed symptoms of a child who had been sexually abused.]

CHARRON J.:—

. . . .

[D]efence counsel took serious issue at the hearing of this motion with both Dr. Wieland's personal qualifications and the validity of the theory being advanced. Consequently, Dr. Wieland testified for an additional three and a half days. Ultimately, the determinative question was not so much whether Dr. Wieland could give the proposed opinion evidence but whether anyone could do so having regard to the present state of knowledge in the field.

. . . .

The evidence is uncontroverted that this field of inquiry is a relatively recent one in the behavioural sciences. At the hearing of this motion, Dr. Wieland conceded that there is no existing valid profile of the sexually abused child. One article put to her in cross-examination appears to summarize well the existing state of knowledge in the field. Dr. Herbert N. Weissman in his article entitled "Forensic Psychological Examination of the Child Witness in Cases of Alleged Sexual Abuse" (1991), 61 Amer. J. Orthopsychiat., 48 states as follows at p. 52:

. . . .

Mental health professionals may be called upon to give opinions as to whether abuse has occurred and whether harm exists as an element of abuse. Controversial methods associated with "profile validity" are sometimes applied, where the expert testifies as to the characteristics of abused children or the characteristics of child abusers. . . .

The psycholegal literature illustrates the kinds of misconceptions that are common in this regard. Foremost among these is that there exists some form of valid, generally accepted profile of the child victim and of the child offender. There is none.

. . .

No reliable constellation of historical, demographic, personality, or other factors has been found that accurately characterizes either the child victim or the child offender. Neither is there any reliable psychological or physiological test or method for determining whether a child has been sexually abused or whether someone has committed an act of sexual abuse. . . .

A diverse array of symptoms is found in a relatively small percentage of molested children, ranging from negligible distress to severe disturbance. Symptoms commonly mentioned include fear, anxiety, depression, anger, withdrawal, sexual preoccupation or precocity, and school and sleep difficulties. Symptoms, however, do not imply etiology, and no symptom constellation has been found sufficiently and substantially associated with sexual abuse so as to constitute a syndrome. All of the characteristics enumerated have also been found to be commonly present in child populations with no history of sexual abuse. Therefore, behavior assumed by some to be indicative of sexual abuse may in fact be so related, but may also be attributable to normal developmental variations, emotional or physical abuse, neglect, family conflict and parental discord, and modelling behavior imitative of adults observed in person or on videotapes or television.

. . . .

[The Court then reviewed much of the scientific literature in the field.]

The present state of knowledge in the field is such that the soundness and reliability of any expert opinion purporting to characterize behavioral symptoms as "consistent with sexual abuse" cannot be demonstrated. Indeed, if there is any consensus to be found among the experts, it is that there is no valid profile in existence which can enable one to identify a child who has been sexually abused. While the symptoms that have often been identified as "consistent with abuse" may indeed be related to the fact that a child has been sexually abused, the research shows that no single symptom or constellation of symptoms has been found to have any real discriminant validity, i.e., they do not serve to single out children who have been subjected to sexual abuse from children who have suffered some other kind of abuse or trauma or even from the general population of children.

. . . .

Expert opinion evidence about the general behavioural and psychological characteristics of child victims of sexual abuse has often been admitted in Canadian criminal trials. The admissibility of this kind of evidence for certain purposes has been confirmed by a number of Canadian Courts of Appeal and by the Supreme Court of Canada: see *R. v. Marquard*; *R. v. B. (R.H.)*; *R. v. B. (G.)*; *R. v. F. (J.E.)*; *Khan v. College of Physicians & Surgeons (Ontario)*; *R. v. T. (S.)*; *R. v. C. (R.A.)*; *R. v. H. (E.L.)*; *R. v. Beliveau.* [Citations omitted.] It does not appear however that the validity of the very theory being advanced was contested in any of these reported cases. In this case, it was.

The Supreme Court of Canada recently has reiterated the governing principles for admissibility of expert opinion evidence in its unanimous judgment in *R. v. Mohan.* . . . Although the proposed evidence is certainly logically relevant to an issue in the case, its probative value, for the reasons set out earlier, is extremely limited. On the other hand, its prejudicial value can be overwhelming. This trial will turn on a question of credibility. Although a distinction can be made between evidence going to credibility alone and this kind of evidence admitted in support of the complainant's testimony, the line is a very fine one. The admission of evidence "[d]ressed up in scientific language" . . . in support of the complainant's testimony may well be given far more weight by the jury than it deserves and may even become determinative of the ultimate issue. The prejudicial effect of this evidence so far outweighs its low probative value that the matter cannot simply be left to be remedied by cross-examination and special instructions to the jury. The evidence should not be admitted.

Furthermore, it cannot be said that its admission is necessary for a proper verdict to be arrived at. While the proposed evidence is likely outside the experience and knowledge of the trier of fact, it is not yet within the experience and knowledge of the experts themselves with a sufficient degree of reliability to be useful. The expert's methodology and the validity of the theory advanced would become the central issue on trial and would consume most of the time and effort expended. The resulting cost to the trial process far exceeds any benefit that could be gained.

The proposed expert opinion evidence does not meet the test and is not admissible. Based on the present state of the art, the evidence could not be offered by any expert in the field.

Regarding how evidence rules ought to respond to syndromes, compare Raeder, "The Double-Edged Sword: Admissibility of Battered Woman Syndrome" (1996), 67 U. Col. L. Rev. 789 and Faigman, "The Syndromic Lawyer Syndrome" (1996), U. Col. L. Rev. 817.

R. v. WARREN
35 C.R. (4th) 347 (N.W.T.S.C.)

[The accused was charged with the culpable homicide of nine miners who died in an underground explosion at a mine. He gave a confession to the police. The defence sought to introduce the evidence of a psychologist to testify to the likelihood that the confession was false. The Crown accepted that the witness was an expert who could give opinions in reference to his professional assessment of the accused based on generally well recognized psychological tests and studies. The Crown however objected to opinions based on assessments, tests or studies made for the specific purpose of indicating the probability or possibility that a confession of crime made to the police is unreliable. The Crown submitted that those assessments, tests and studies were, in themselves, lacking in the necessary reliability for expert evidence and would mislead the jury.]

DE WEERDT J.:—Crown counsel objects to the introduction in evidence before the jury of any mention of certain assessments, tests or studies specifically designed to indicate the likelihood that the accused falsely confessed in October 1993 to the culpable homicide of nine miners who died in an underground explosion at Giant Mine near Yellowknife on September 18, 1992.

. . . .

In Crown counsel's submission the disputed evidence would not only take up the time of the Court to no good purpose; it would in all likelihood mislead the jury. It is submitted on behalf of the Crown that this evidence does not satisfy the requirements for admissibility laid down by the Supreme Court of Canada in *R. v. Mohan*.

. . . .

The evidence, as I understand Dr. Ley's outline of it, will show the nature and results of three tests administered to the accused. These consist of (a) "compliance"; (b) "suggestibility"; and (c) "confession" tests, in the form of "true or false" questionnaires. The tests were apparently developed in this form by Dr. Gisli Gudjonsson, a psychologist at the Institute of Psychiatry, De Crespigny Park, Denmark Hill, England, to whom reference is made in *R. v. Raghip*; *R. v. Silcott*; *R. v. Braithwaite*, The Times, December 9, 1991 (C.A.). As yet, I have heard only the outline given by Dr. Ley and have not seen the actual questionnaires.

The tests in question were selected to provide some measure of the degree to which the accused's confession might be classified as unreliable because it was made during a police interview, in a "coerced compliant" manner, according to the typology of alleged "false confessions" developed in S.M. Kassin and L.S. Wrightsman, editors, *The Psychology of Evidence and Trial Procedure* (London: Sage, 1985). This typology has been accepted and used by Dr. Gudjonsson, who is described by Dr. Ley as being by far the outstanding expert in the field. An article in *The Lancet*, vol. 344, No. 8935, pages 1447-50, dated November 26, 1994, states at p. 1448:

A general understanding of the phenomenon of "false confessions" has come about via a series of studies over ten years by Gudjonsson, a forensic psychologist and former police officer. Gudjonsson has provided good empirical evidence to support a theoretical construct of *interrogative suggestibility* — the variable degree to which individuals tend to acquiesce to authority during questioning. . . .

Kassin and Wrightman also suggested, mainly on the basis of anecdotal evidence, that there are two distinct types of false confessions during interrogation, the first based on overt compliance under interrogative pressure, with retention of internal cognitive control (the suspect confesses knowing he or she is innocent), and the second based on suggestibility (the suspect comes to believe inhis or her guilt under questioning). Gudjonsson has been able to observe directly many such cases and to measure separately individuals' "compliance" and "suggestibility". His data suggest that there is no clear distinction between compliant and suggestible individuals who confess falsely, but it is nevertheless useful to distinguish two psychological mechanisms that may be provoked in vulnerable individuals subjected to interrogation: in *coerced-compliant confessions* the suspect yields to the short-term benefits (freedom from further interrogation and conflict, gaining approval from the police) without realising the long-term risks of confessing; and in *coerced-internalised confessions* suspects come to believe in their guilt, either because they have no clear memory of the events concerned, owing to traumatic or toxic amnesia, or because they begin to mistrust their own recollections.

At p. 1449, *The Lancet* sounds a necessary note of caution, however, as follows:

There is no simple way to detect individuals who are vulnerable to the processes leading to false confessions. Gudjonsson has developed two scales designed to measure objectively how likely an individual is to yield to pressure during interrogation and to leading questions. These methods provide a powerful and innovative research tool, but practical application in forensic assessments is limited by the fact that subjects' level of anxiety and general emotional state can strongly influence results. Moreover, it is doubtful whether the test can be used reliably by psychologists without specific training. The potential for misuse and even for preparing subjects to give false-positive results should not be underestimated. All psychological and medical techniques proposed in the past to yield clear answers in criminal cases (e.g. the polygraph, hypnosis, stylometry, and drug-aided interviews) have proved to be potentially unreliable, liable to be manipulated, and subject to both false-positive and false-negative results.

. . . .

It deserves to be noticed in this connection that the accused (on advice of counsel) has refused to be examined (or, I presume, tested) by a Crown psychiatrist (or, presume, a Crown psychologist). No matter how neutrally professional the manner of Dr. Ley undoubtedly was when testing the accused, it is plain that he would have been seen by the accused in a light different from that of a Crown forensic expert.

. . . .

A most disquieting feature of these tests is that there is no indication that they have ever been independently assessed to determine whether they are in fact capable of showing anything more than that those who claim to have made a false confession of some crime at some time in the past tend to score well on the tests. There is apparently nothing to show how far those claims are truthful other than the anecdotal accounts of the subjects themselves. Such cases are not to be confused with those where an individual has been the victim of forged or perjured evidence of a "confession" not in fact made to the police. And they are likewise to be distinguished from cases such as *R. v. Ward* (1992), 96 Cr. App. Rep. 1 (C.A.) and *R. v. Raghip*; *R. v. Silcott*; *R. v. Braithwaite*, where convictions based in part upon confessions were set aside as "unsafe" following inquiry and judicial review going beyond the evidence at trial.

Dr. Ley, who is apparently as knowledgeable as anyone in Canada in reference to the work of Dr. Gudjonsson and its impact on the forensic science community, frankly acknowledged that the present status of the research in this area of psychometry is "still in the toddler stage". No published research in the field is yet available other than that of Dr. Gudjonsson.

. . . .

The ultimate question for the jury, in relation to the identity of the person who set the explosion, is clearly dependent upon the jury's acceptance or rejection of the confession. While Dr. Ley, like Dr. Lohrasbe, may be able to point to features of the accused's mental condition in October 1993 which reflect upon the confession, it is not for Dr. Ley or any other expert to say whether the confession is or is not a true one, or whether it is to be looked on as reliable or unreliable. These are conclusions to be considered by the jury based on all the evidence before them. Dr. Ley will not be heard to express his opinion on any of these issues.

It is not in dispute that the confession evidence now before the jury is the core of the Crown's case against the accused. Without it, or if it is thrown into doubt, the Crown's case against the accused as being the person who set the explosion underground at Giant Mine on September 18, 1992 is no more than purely circumstantial and would probably not support a guilty verdict on either first degree murder, as charged, or any included offence.

While the reliability and truthfulness of the confession is not the ultimate issue for the jury, it is nevertheless the crucial issue in this trial with reference to the identity of the person who caused the fatal explosion.

The leading judicial authority on the reception of expert opinion evidence in Canada is *R. v. Mohan*. Adopting the analysis formulated by Sopinka J. on behalf of the Supreme Court of Canada in that case, I proceed as follows:

1. Relevance

(a)   While there is logical relevance to the proffered evidence of Dr. Ley with respect to the tests and assessment based on the work of Dr. Gudjonsson, that evidence does not meet the criterion of legal relevance.

(b)   The evidence is misleading in the sense that its effect on the jury would be out of all proportion to its reliability. The tests have not been shown to be reliable as yet. Indeed, the contrary appears to be true. Any assessment based upon them must suffer likewise on grounds of unreliability. The probative value of the evidence is accordingly overborne by its prejudicial effect.

2. Necessity in assisting the Jury

It is true that the proffered evidence is likely to be outside the experience and knowledge of the jury. However, as I have mentioned, the evidence is likely to distort the fact-finding process on a crucial point which, to all intents and purposes, may determine the ultimate issue in the case. Instead of assisting the jury, the evidence is likely to distract (and has the potential to confuse) the jury.

Since neither of these criteria is satisfied, I need go no further. The proffered evidence must be ruled inadmissible.

I have, thanks to counsel, had the advantage of reading certain other authorities, such as *R. v. Marquard*, *R. v. Lafferty*, *R. v. Abbey*, and *R. v. Lavallee* in addition to the very useful discussions in *Daubert v. Merrell Dow Pharmaceuticals* [citations omitted]; "Believe It Or Not" by Mark Hansen (1993), 79 A.B.A.J. 64; "The Trial Judge As Gatekeeper For Scientific Evidence" by Michael Lepp and Christopher B. McNeil (1993), 27 Akron L. Rev. 89; "Contemporary Comment: When Plight Makes Right — The Forensic Abuse Syndrome" (1994) 18 Crim. L.J. (Australia) 29; and, not least, "Notes and Comments" by A.D. (1994), Gold 37 Crim. L.Q. 16; and "The Admissibility of Expert Evidence: A New Caution Based on General Principles" by R.J. Delisle (1994), 29 C.R. (4th) 267. These materials have been of considerable assistance to me.

The objection taken by Crown counsel is therefore sustained.

On the accused's unsuccessful appeal this issue was not commented on: *R. v. Warren* (1997), 117 C.C.C. (3d) 418 (N.W.T. C.A.), leave to appeal refused (1998), 228 N.R. 196 (note) (S.C.C.).

R. v. B. (S.C.)
(1997), 10 C.R. (5th) 302, 119 C.C.C. (3d) 530 (Ont. C.A.)

[The accused was charged with sexual assault with a weapon and sexual assault causing bodily harm. The accused called a psychiatrist in an attempt to show that the perpetrator of the offences had to be either a sexual sadist or a person with an anti-social personality disorder and that the accused did not fit the psychiatric profile of the perpetrator. The accused was acquitted.]

DOHERTY and ROSENBERG JJ.A. (MCKINLAY J.A. concurring):—

. . . .

The admissibility of this expert evidence depends on the application of the principles set down in *R. v. Mohan*. Those principles may be summarized as follows:

Psychiatric evidence to the effect that the accused, because of his or her mental makeup, is unlikely to have committed the crime alleged is generally inadmissible.

The defence may, however, lead expert evidence of an accused's disposition where the crime alleged is one that was committed by a person who is part of a group possessing distinct and identifiable behavioural characteristics. In those cases, the defence may lead evidence to show that the accused's mental makeup or behaviourial characteristics excluded him or her from that group.

. . . .

Dr. Motayne described the tests he had performed on the respondent and advanced his opinion that the respondent did not fit within either of the two categories described above. He said that he could not "completely" rule out the possibility that the respondent had committed these acts, but nothing indicated that the respondent endorsed the beliefs of a sexual sadist or suffered from an anti-social personality disorder.

In cross-examination, the following exchange occurred:

Q.   You would agree with me, doctor, that there is another category, a wider category called a rapist. Is that not right?

A.   That is not defined in the SM4. I think when one speaks of a rapist one includes both categories, both the anti-social personality disorder and the sexual sadist.

Q.   Well, is it correct to say that there is no such thing as a typical rapist?

A.   That's a difficult question for me to answer. I can only answer it in terms of what is defined under the SM4 and for me, if somebody would commit extremely violent acts and happen to do a sexual act I would suggest that that person is a psychopath or an anti-social personality disorder. If the act is driven by a sexual drive or the need to satisfy a sexual urge by degrading somebody I would call that individual a sexual sadist.

In holding that the evidence was admissible, the trial judge considered the decision in *Mohan*, supra. He said:

There appears to be, from Dr. Motayne's evidence on the voir dire, a general acceptance in the scientific community through the DSM4 standards that individuals who may have been the perpetrator of this kind of conduct would fall into two broad classifications and one would be the classification referred to as a sexual sadist and the other would be within the classification of an anti-social personality disorder.

With respect, this conclusion overstates Dr. Motayne's evidence. In chief, Dr. Motayne did no more than indicate that some features of the hypothetical presented to him were consistent with the acts of a sexual sadist or a person suffering from an anti-social personality disorder. Dr. Motayne did not suggest that others who did not fall within either of those categories could be excluded as possible perpetrators. Dr. Motayne's evidence-in-chief did not address the question of whether the scientific community has developed "a standard profile for the offender who commits this type of crime". Dr. Motayne's evidence-in-chief went no further than to identify two recognized types of mental disorder and to opine that certain features of the hypothetical were consistent with a person who suffered from one or the other of those disorders. The evidence of Dr. Motayne in cross-examination comes somewhat closer to the Mohan standard, but also falls short of that standard. In cross-examination, Dr. Motayne testified to the effect that he believed that anyone who would commit the kinds of acts described in the hypothetical must fall within one of the two categories he had described. However, Dr. Motayne did not suggest that this view was generally accepted within the psychiatric community. His evidence on cross-examination, set out above, comes down to an assertion of a personal belief and does not meet the standard set down in Mohan. The evidence should have been excluded.

R. v. TERCEIRA
(1998), 15 C.R. (5th) 359, 123 C.C.C. (3d) 1 (Ont. C.A.)

[The accused was convicted of murder. Hair, fibre, blood and DNA evidence which matched the accused was left on the floor at the attack site and on the victim's clothing. One of the main arguments on the appeal related to the admissibility of the DNA evidence and the instruction to the jury respecting it. The Supreme Court in an endorsement agreed with the courts below.]

FINLAYSON J.A. (BROOKE and McKINLAY JJ.A., concurring):—

. . . .

DNA profiling is a comparatively new method of providing identification evidence for use in criminal cases. DNA evidence is used essentially for two purposes. The first use of DNA evidence is as evidence that the suspect's DNA "matches" the DNA found in blood, semen or tissue recovered at a crime scene. In this way, the DNA evidence serves an exclusionary purpose. In the absence of further qualifications, a "match" is no more than a failure to exclude a suspect's DNA from the crime scene. The debate at trial with respect to the determination of a match, as was the case during the trial of this matter, will often focus on the methodology used to determine a match. The second branch of the analysis of DNA evidence involves the application of population genetics. Probability statistics are introduced in an attempt to bolster the significance of a "match". The scientist determines, according to an established database of known DNA samples, the statistical likelihood that another individual person would have the same DNA pattern as that of the suspect. Simply stated, this second branch considers the statistical likelihood of a random DNA match. Cross-examination of the expert tendering DNA evidence serving this second purpose will usually focus on the methodology used to calculate the numbers reflecting the frequency of the DNA pattern. The DNA evidence in the present case was used by the Crown for the above two purposes.

. . . .

Both Crown and defence counsel on the DNA *voir dire* devoted a considerable portion of their submissions to a discussion of the standard to be applied in relation to the admission of novel scientific evidence. Crown counsel discussed the standard of "relevancy and helpfulness" as well as "relevancy and reliability". Defence counsel made submissions in favour of the adoption of the more restrictive "*Frye*" test articulated by the United States Supreme Court in *Frye v. United States*, 293 F.1013. Both counsel explicitly referred the trial judge to the decision in *R. v. Johnston* (1992), 69 C.C.C. (3d) 395, 12 C.R. (4th) 99 (Ont. Gen. Div.), wherein Langdon J. adopted a "reliability" standard. The trial judge characterized the defence position on the voir dire as urging "that the Crown has not produced sufficient evidence on the *voir dire* to support the reliability and admissibility of Pamella Newall's techniques in analysis". The foregoing demonstrates that the trial judge was aware that initial determinations of reliability would be required before the proposed DNA evidence could be proffered at trial. Moreover, the appellant concedes that the trial judge recognized that reliability was a preliminary finding of fact that would need to be made before the proposed DNA evidence was admissible.

. . . .

Relying upon the judgment of the Supreme Court of Canada in *R. v. Mohan*, counsel for the appellant submits that before the jury can be permitted to hear the evidence of DNA testing, the trial judge is required as a matter of law to conduct what he calls a "*Mohan* type hearing" in order to satisfy himself beyond a reasonable doubt as to the reliability of the evidence adduced by the experts for the Crown. By this counsel for the appellant suggests that the trial judge must satisfy himself as to the acceptance of the technology in the scientific community, the expertise of the Crown witnesses in that field, and the accuracy of the tests carried out pursuant to that technology, among other factors. All this to the criminal standard of proof. Then, and only then, can the same evidence be recalled for the consideration of the jury.

I have some considerable difficulty with this submission which, with respect, reflects a misreading of *Mohan*. In my opinion, the rules laid down by Sopinka J. in *R. v. Mohan* do not signify a departure from the common law rules relating to the admission of opinion evidence in a criminal trial, nor do they purport to do so. The four criteria for the admissibility of expert testimony are derived from case-law. . . . Prior to *Mohan*, when relevant expert opinion evidence has been proffered, Canadian courts focused on two factors in determining its admissibility: the special knowledge criterion and the expertise criterion. In *R. v. Abbey*, [1982] 2 S.C.R. 24 at p. 42, Dickson J. provided the following formulation of the "special knowledge" requirement for the admissibility of expert evidence:

> With respect to matters calling for special knowledge, an expert in the field may draw inferences and state his opinion. An expert's function is precisely this: to provide the judge and jury with a ready-made inference which the judge and jury, due to the technical nature of the facts, are unable to formulate. "An expert's opinion is admissible to furnish the Court with scientific information which is likely to be outside the experience and knowledge of a judge or jury. If on the proven facts a judge or jury can form their own conclusions without help, then the opinion of the expert is unnecessary (*R. v. Turner* (1974), 60 Cr. App. R. 80, at p. 83, per Lawton L.J.).

. . . .

It is to be observed that the word "reliable" is not listed among Sopinka J.'s four criteria. It is, however, discussed under "relevance" under his "cost-benefit analysis" as to whether expert evidence that is otherwise logically relevant may be excluded on the basis that its probative value is overborne by its prejudicial effect.

. . . .

In the appeal before this court the tension is between the probative value of the opinion evidence versus its prejudicial effect in the sense that its effect on the jury may be out of proportion to its reliability. *Mohan* stands as authority for the proposition that expert evidence which may be logically probative of an issue at trial may be nonetheless excluded in certain circumstances. Additionally, in light of the judicial reasoning from *Mohan*, since we are confronted with what was at the time of trial perceived to be a novel scientific theory or technique, we are concerned with the threshold issue of reliability, i.e., is the science itself valid. As I understand *Mohan*, with reference to the case in appeal, the requirement of a basic threshold of reliability as a pre-condition to admissibility is met where the trial judge is satisfied as to the reliability of DNA profiling as a novel scientific technique. Where the Crown and defence part company is with respect to the extent of the inquiry necessary to establish this pre-condition.

Our task is considerably narrowed by the concession of appellant's counsel that he is not suggesting that DNA profiling has not been found reliable in other jurisdictions. The appellant does not take issue with the microbiological aspects of DNA profiling. No general concern was raised at trial about the ability of the Centre of Forensic Science ("CFS") to extract DNA from biological substances and to isolate and remove regions on human chromosomes which are suitable for testing nor to determine whether any two samples were a "match" one to the other. Nor is counsel for the appellant suggesting that the process used by the CFS in this case, involving RFLP or "restriction fragment length polymorphism" analysis, is not an accepted methodology for DNA profiling. Rather, the complaint was that the DNA laboratory was only established by the CFS a few months prior to the testing in this case and there was no general acceptance of its specific methodology used to determine the statistical likelihood of a random match. The attack was not upon the technology of DNA profiling per se but upon the ability of the CFS, notably its principal expert Pamella Newall, to reliably utilize it. In addition, the appellant challenged the introduction of the probability figures as their prejudicial effect would exceed the probative value of presenting quantitative statements of random match probability as opposed to qualitative measures.

. . . .

The jury was given frequency numbers that ranged from one in 1,500 to one in 1.8 million. The appellant concedes the admissibility of qualitative expressions of match significance (such as "rare" or "common") without the specifics afforded by statistics where DNA evidence is admitted showing a match between the DNA found on the crime scene and the DNA of a suspect, counsel for the appellant objects simply to the admission of the numbers themselves. In this case, it would be difficult to translate the figures the experts were prepared to use into neutral language, but all that aside, why would the defence want to do so? The fact that there are competing figures which differ so radically should be before the jury for its assessment. The range of numeric frequency determined by the various experts was fertile ground for cross-examination. This is a classic case for the application of the language of Dickson C.J.C. in *R. v. Corbett*, [1988] 1 S.C.R. 670 at p. 692:

> The very strength of the jury is that the ultimate issue of guilt or innocence is determined by a group of ordinary citizens who are not legal specialists and who bring to the legal process a healthy measure of common sense. The jury is, of course, bound to follow the law as it is explained by the trial judge. Jury directions are often

long and difficult, but the experience of trial judges is that juries do perform their duty according to the law. We should regard with grave suspicion arguments which assert that depriving the jury of all relevant information is preferable to giving them everything, with a careful explanation as to any limitations on the use to which they may put that information.

I do not believe that there should be an absolute prohibition against the introduction of specific match figures. The appellant correctly notes that the case-law reflects conflicting conclusions as to the admissibility of DNA probability statistics in this case, and it might be in others. I would leave the matter to the discretion of the trial judge in the particular case.

R. v. McINTOSH
(1997), 117 C.C.C. (3d) 385 (Ont. C.A.)

[The accused were convicted of various offences as a result of a robbery. The case for the Crown consisted primarily of three eyewitnesses. The trial judge refused to admit expert opinion evidence from a defence psychologist tendered on the issue of eyewitness identification. The psychologist had written extensively on the psychology of witness testimony and claimed that it was a specialty which he had pursued over the years. His evidence related to the frailties of eyewitness identification, including factors present at the time of the offence that would impair the witness' ability to make an accurate identification, the problem of cross-racial identification, the quality of memory recall for perceived events over different time spans, and the influence of "post-event information" on memory.]

FINLAYSON J.A. (LABROSSE and AUSTIN JJ.A. concurring):—

. . . .

The general tenor of [the expert's] evidence is summed up in his own words:

Well, the understanding of jurors, and how they perceive is what psychologists spend their lives doing. We hope to be able to assist the judge or the jury on the various levels and factors of what would lead to a good or a poor identification. It is not my job to decide whether or not that is the answer. All I can do is assist the trier in understanding, 'Here are the reasons why it could be a good identification or a poor one'.

I am astonished at the passivity of the Crown at trial and on appeal with respect to this type of evidence. At trial, Crown counsel contented himself with the early observation that the witness had said nothing that would convince him that a psychologist would know what information would be "probative" to the trial. However, he did not cross-examine Dr. Yarmey on his qualifications, or at all, and seemed to accept that the substance of his testimony was properly the subject-matter of expert evidence. On appeal, Crown counsel limited his argument to the submission that we should defer to the trial judge who rejected the evidence in the exercise of her discretion. He was careful, however, to state that there could be cases in which this evidence could be admitted.

This posture is not surprising given the reliance by the Crown on the "soft sciences" in other cases. In *R. v. Norman* (1993), 87 C.C.C. (3d) 153 (C.A.) the Crown introduced psychiatric evidence of child abuse accommodation syndrome which was misused by the trial judge and resulted in this court setting aside the conviction of the accused. In *R. v. Edwards* (1996), 105 C.C.C. (3d) 21 (C.A.) (leave to appeal to S.C.C. refused August 29, 1996) the Crown attempted unsuccessfully to introduce expert testimony in the form of affidavits to support two Crown appeals against sentences imposed upon the respondents following their pleas of guilty to charges of attempted spousal homicide. The affidavits were sworn by three persons with differing professional backgrounds. All three deponents, however, had written extensively on issues relating to spousal abuse. They advocated the need for greater public awareness and participation in dealing with this pressing social problem. This court dismissed the motion for fresh evidence, holding that it was of marginal relevance to the sentencing issue and smacked of special pleading.

In the light of the limited argument before this court on the matter, it is evident that this is not the case to engage in a full-scale analysis as to whether the type of evidence proffered by Dr. Yarmey is admissible in any circumstance. However, I do not intend to leave the subject without raising some warning flags. In my respectful opinion, the courts are overly eager to abdicate their fact-finding responsibilities to "experts" in the field of the behavioural sciences. We are too quick to say that a particular witness possesses special knowledge and experience going beyond that of the trier of fact without engaging in an analysis of the subject-matter of that expertise. I do not want to be taken as denigrating the integrity of Dr. Yarmey's research or of his expertise in the field of psychology, clearly one of the learned sciences, but simply because a person has lectured and written extensively on a subject that is of interest to him or her does not constitute him or her an expert for the purposes of testifying in a court of law on the subject of that specialty. It seems to me that before we even get to the point of examining the witness's expertise, we must ask ourselves if the subject-matter of his testimony admits of expert testimony. Where is the evidence in this case that there is a recognized body of scientific knowledge that defines rules of human behaviour affecting memory patterns such that any expert in that field can evaluate the reliability of the identification made by a particular witness in a given case? Paraphrasing freely from the definition of "science" in *The Shorter Oxford English Dictionary on Historical Principles*, it seems to me that before a witness can be permitted to testify as an expert, the court must be satisfied that the subject-matter of his or her expertise is a branch of study in psychology concerned with a connected body of demonstrated truths or with observed facts systematically classified and more or less connected together by a common hypothesis operating under general laws. The branch should include trustworthy methods for the discovery of new truths within its own domain. I should add that it would be helpful if there was evidence that the existence of such a branch was generally accepted within the science of psychology.

The definitive judgment on the admissibility of expert evidence in criminal cases is *R. v. Mohan* which was relied upon by both parties to this appeal. . . . I would caution courts to scrutinize the nature of the subject-matter of the expert testimony. Any natural or unnatural phenomenon may become the subject of an investigation conducted according to the scientific method. The scientific method requires the formation of a hypothesis, the testing of the hypothesis using reliable methodology, the examination of the results (usually with statistical analysis) and the formation of a conclusion. However, the fact that the testimony recites the application of the scientific method does not necessarily render the original object of study a matter requiring opinion evidence at trial.

As is implicit in what I have written above, I have some serious reservations as to whether the "Psychology of Witness Testimony" is an appropriate area for opinion evidence at all. I acknowledge that the subject is interesting and Dr. Yarmey's presentation is informative. I also applaud his evidence that he lectures on the subject to police officers. We should all be reminded of the frailties of identification evidence. However, I would have to be persuaded that the subject is a recognized branch of psychology. Even if it is, I do not think that it meets the tests for relevance and necessity set out in *Mohan*.

In the case in appeal, I think that I can deal with relevance and necessity together because they appear to overlap. This opinion evidence is noteworthy in that, unlike most expert psychological or psychiatric testimony, it is not directed to making the testimony of a particular witness more understandable to the trier of fact and therefore more believable (e.g., an explanation of repressed memory syndrome or battered spouse syndrome). This opinion evidence is directed to instructing the jury that all witnesses have problems in perception and recall with respect to what occurred during any given circumstance that is brief and stressful. Accordingly, Dr. Yarmey is not testifying to matters that are outside the normal experience of the trier of fact: he is reminding the jury of the normal experience.

Perhaps I can develop this point through illustration. I suggest that it would be a different situation if a Crown witness had demonstrated remarkable memory feats which would strike the normal juror as startling and therefore less capable of belief. In this hypothetical situation, expert evidence might be admissible to show that the witness is an autistic savant and that such exceptional memory feats are often associated with this syndrome. Or to deal with an example closer to the case at hand, Dr. Yarmey was prepared to testify as to the problems of "cross-racial identification": the perception that members of one race tend to think that members of another race "all look alike". Dr. Yarmey's research supports this popular perception and his opinion on the subject is hardly surprising. But before this opinion evidence could be outside the normal experience of the jurors, would he not have had to conclude that the perception was false and that a cross-racial identification problem did not exist?

This is not to say that a reminder as to cross-racial identification is not appropriate in a case where it is an issue. However, the argument that impresses me is that such a reminder from the trial judge is more than adequate, especially when it is incorporated into the well-established warnings in the standard jury charge on the frailties of identification evidence. Writings, such as those of Dr. Yarmey, are helpful in stimulating an ongoing evaluation of the problem of witness identification, but they should be used to update the judge's charge, not instruct the jury. I think that there is a very real danger that such evidence would "distort the fact-finding process".

More than that I am concerned that much of what Dr. Yarmey and those who support him are saying is that our jury system is not adequate to the task of determining the guilt of an accused person beyond a reasonable doubt where identification evidence is pivotal to the case for the Crown. Much of Dr. Yarmey's evidence might well give us pause to consider whether our present jury instruction is adequate to the task, but to admit such evidence in the particular case may foster apprehension in the timorous juror and give him or her an excuse for not discharging that juror's duty to the community that he or she has sworn to serve.

An additional problem is that this evidence introduces yet another potentially contentious issue into the trial. If the defence is entitled to call this opinion evidence, the Crown is entitled to rebut it. This means that the jury has to be instructed as how conflicts in the opinions of experts are to be resolved, and when resolved, as to the limited use of the evidence. The jury must also be told that to the extent that the opinion evidence contradicts anything said by the trial judge in his or her charge, the jury must reject the evidence and accept what is said by the judge. Would it not be simpler to have the trial judge give the instruction in the first place?

In the case in appeal, the trial judge had the benefit of hearing all of Dr. Yarmey's evidence and of listening to full argument as to its merits and admissibility. In the end, she appears to have had the same reservations as I do with respect to its quality. While she premised her ultimate refusal to admit the evidence upon the failure to meet the necessity test in *Mohan*, in the course of delivering her reasons she stated:

> I do not agree, based on the evidence I've heard from Dr. Yarmey, that the science has advanced that far away from the common experience of jurors.

To address the specific ground of appeal in this case, I am of the opinion that the manner in which the issue of identification was handled by the court (and by "court" I mean the trial judge and counsel for the Crown and the defence) was a model of fairness. The trial judge was correct in rejecting the proffered expert evidence. Her charge to the jury, following the very full closing arguments of all counsel, was exemplary. She impressed upon the jury the frailties of witness identification evidence generally and then, in considerable detail, she set out the identification problems as they applied to the particular facts of the case.

. . . .

We were referred to a number of cases from courts in the United States where expert evidence on identification has been accepted. We were also referred to *William Daubert v. Merrell Dow Pharmaceuticals Inc.*, 113 S.Ct. Rep. 2786 (1993), a decision of the United States Supreme Court which considered the admissibility of expert testimony generally under the Federal Rules of Evidence, Rule 702, 28 U.S.C.A. These cases must be approached with caution because the rules of court under consideration are dissimilar to ours. Moreover, juries in this jurisdiction receive significantly more assistance from the trial judge in their instruction than do juries in the United States. For this reason alone, expert testimony on matters which are covered by the jury instruction has less appeal. Our judges are not only encouraged to comment on the evidence, there are some cases in which they are obliged to do so.

This was such a case and the trial judge took full advantage of it. She was in a far better position than any witness or counsel to point out the frailties of the identification evidence, and her opinions, which she expressed, would have a very positive effect on the jury. She was also in a position to place these frailties in the context of the case for the Crown as a whole and she did that as well. This was not a "straight" identification case as counsel for the appellants submitted. After reading the complete charge of the trial judge on all of the evidence, I am left with no concern about the soundness of the verdict in this case. I would reject this ground of appeal.

On the issue of the helpfulness of expert testimony on eye-witness identification, see Loftus and Doyle, *Eyewitness Testimony, Civil and Criminal*, 3d ed. (Lexis Law Publishing, 1997).

R. v. D. (D.)
[2000] 2 S.C.R. 275, 36 C.R. (5th) 261, 148 C.C.C. (3d) 41

[The accused was charged with sexual assault. The complainant alleged that the accused had sexually assaulted her when she was 5 to 6 years old. The complainant told no one about these events for two-and-a-half years. At trial, defence counsel cross-examined the complainant, who was ten years old at the time, on the lengthy delay in reporting the incidents and suggested that she had fabricated the story. The Crown called a child psychologist to testify that a child's delay in alleging sexual abuse does not support an inference of falsehood. During a voir dire, the psychologist gave a general explanation applicable to all children that delayed disclosure could occur for a variety of reasons and did not indicate the lack of truth of an allegation. The trial judge admitted the expert evidence and the jury found the accused guilty of sexual assault and invitation to sexual touching. The Court of Appeal held that the expert evidence should not have been admitted because it was neither relevant nor necessary. The guilty verdict was set aside for this and other reasons, and a new trial was ordered. The Crown appealed from the finding that the expert evidence was inadmissible but agreed that the order for a new trial was warranted based on the Court of Appeal's other reasons for setting aside the verdict.]

McLachlin, C.J. (L'Heureux-Dubé and Gonthier, JJ. concurring), dissenting:—

. . . .

During the voir dire, Dr. Marshall discussed delayed disclosure of child sexual abuse, based on his knowledge of the scientific literature in the area. He testified that there are many factors which can affect the timing of a complaint, including the relationship between the child and the abuser and the nature of the abuse. Some factors might discourage children from reporting abuse, such as embarrassment; fear of getting themselves or others into trouble; bribery or threats by the perpetrator; fear of being punished or sent away; disruption of the family; or fear that they would not be believed. Young children might also not fully comprehend what happened or not see anything wrong with the abuse.

Dr. Marshall also discussed the timing of allegations of abuse and its relevance to determining whether the abuse actually occurred. In his opinion, most sexual abuse is never disclosed, so one cannot assume that disclosure normally happens immediately. He testified that children disclose at various lengths of time after the event, so there is a continuum from immediate disclosure to delayed disclosure to no disclosure. When cross-examined by defence counsel as to whether the profile of a victim of abuse could be developed by reference to the timing of the complaint, Dr. Marshall stated "the fact of the delay . . . doesn't even enter into my thinking as to whether or not it happened. . . . [T]he research says that the length of time before a child reveals something is not diagnostic". The trial judge asked him to clarify what it means when delay is "not diagnostic", to which Dr. Marshall responded "[i]t proves nothing either way".

. . . .

The test for the admissibility of expert evidence was consolidated in *Mohan*. Four criteria must be met by a party which seeks to introduce expert evidence: relevance, necessity, the lack of any other exclusionary rule, and a properly qualified expert. Even where these requirements are met, the evidence may be rejected if its prejudicial effect on the conduct of the trial outweighs its probative value.

The application of the four *Mohan* criteria is case-specific. Determinations of relevance and necessity, as well as the assessment of whether the prejudicial effect of the evidence outweighs its probative value, must be made within the factual context of the trial. . . . The case-specific nature of the inquiry means that an appellate court cannot lay down in advance broad rules that particular categories of expert evidence are always inadmissible. Such a categorical approach would undermine *Mohan*'s requirement of a case-by-case analysis of the four applicable criteria.

It follows that we cannot say as a general rule that expert evidence on a child's delay in reporting sexual assault is always admissible. Nor can we say it is never admissible. We can only say that it may be admissible if the four *Mohan* criteria are satisfied and if the prejudicial impact of the evidence does not outweigh its probative value. The trial judge erred if he took the comments in *Marquard* as indicating as a matter of stare decisis that expert evidence on delayed disclosure always meets the necessity test. By the same token, it would be erroneous to say that such evidence can never be admitted, as the Crown submits the Court of Appeal suggested. Admissibility of expert evidence must be determined on a case-by-case basis in the factual context of the case as it develops.

Against this background, I turn to the issue of whether the *Mohan* criteria for admissibility were met in this case.

A. Relevance

The trial judge found Dr. Marshall's evidence relevant to a fact in issue — the significance of the child's delay in reporting. The Court of Appeal, by contrast, held that the evidence was not relevant to a fact in issue, but only to the complainant's credibility.

In my view, the trial judge was correct in finding that Dr. Marshall's evidence was relevant to a fact in issue at the trial. The trial turned on the credibility of the complainant. If her testimony was believed, the offence was proved as charged. If there was a reasonable doubt about her credibility, the case was not made out. The issue of delay was subsidiary to the complainant's credibility. The "fact in issue" was whether a child's delay in reporting sexual abuse suggests that the alleged abuse did not occur. The defence put that fact in issue by indicating that it would ask the jury to infer from the delay in reporting that the alleged events were not real occurrences but fabrications. According to the defence, the complainant "was not credible because she waited too long". That was the fact in issue.

Dr. Marshall's evidence was relevant to that issue because he discussed reasons other than fabrication, such as fear of not being believed, that might explain why a child would delay reporting sexual abuse.

. . . .

The Court of Appeal reasoned that Dr. Marshall's evidence should be excluded because it represented "a blatant attempt to bolster the credibility of the only witness the Crown had to the alleged assault". Finlayson J.A. noted the principle, with which I agree, that the actual credibility of a particular witness is not generally the proper subject of opinion evidence: see *R. v. Béland*, [1987] 2 S.C.R. 398; *Marquard*, supra; *R. v. B. (F.F.)*, [1993] 1 S.C.R 697; *Mohan*, supra; *R. v. Burns*, [1994] 1 S.C.R. 656. This is known as the rule against oath-helping. In my view, Dr. Marshall's evidence did not violate that principle. In *Marquard*, supra, at p. 249, I noted that

> there is a growing consensus that while expert evidence on the ultimate credibility of a witness is not admissible, expert evidence on human conduct and the psychological and physical factors which may lead to certain behaviour relevant to credibility, is admissible, provided the testimony goes beyond the ordinary experience of the trier of fact.

. . . .

B. Necessity

When it comes to necessity, the question is whether the expert will provide information which is likely to be outside the ordinary experience and knowledge of the trier of fact: *Burns*, supra; *Mohan*, supra; *R. v. Lavallee*, [1990] 1 S.C.R. 852; *R. v. Abbey*, [1982] 2 S.C.R. 24; *Kelliher (Village of) v. Smith*, [1931] S.C.R. 672. "Necessity" means that the evidence must be more than merely "helpful", but necessity need not be judged "by too strict a standard": *Mohan*, supra, at p. 23. Absolute necessity is not required.

. . . .

The issue again may be put in simple terms: was there a sufficient basis for the trial judge to conclude that the issue of the child's delay in disclosure might involve matters beyond the ordinary knowledge and expertise of the jury? Was the evidence necessary to enable the trier of fact to properly dispose of the credibility issue? In answering this question, we must bear in mind that the trial judge is in the best position of determining the level of the jurors' understanding and what may assist them. In my view, there was an ample foundation for the trial judge's conclusion that Dr. Marshall's evidence went beyond the ordinary knowledge and expertise of the jury.

. . . .

Given the additional assistance that Dr. Marshall's testimony may have provided to the jury, I cannot conclude that the trial judge erred by failing to find that it was unnecessary because he could have given a jury warning. This is particularly so in view of the fact that the defence never raised this argument at trial. That said, the trial judge on the new trial should consider whether the expert's testimony is necessary to that trial in light of all the relevant circumstances, including the arguments of counsel and the possibility of a judicial instruction.

C. No Other Exclusionary Rule

The third criterion for admitting expert evidence is that it must not be excluded by the operation of any other rule. The only exclusionary rule raised here is the principle that an expert may not testify on the ultimate issue of credibility. As discussed earlier, this rule was not violated because Dr. Marshall testified on an issue that was subsidiary to the complainant's credibility. He did not express an opinion on whether her allegations were true or false. It was left for the jury to determine whether they accepted all, some or none of the evidence of the complainant.

D. Properly Qualified Expert

The final requirement for admissibility is that the expert be properly qualified. Neither the accused nor the Court of Appeal suggested that Dr. Marshall was not properly qualified to testify on the subject of delayed disclosure.

E. Probative Value Versus Prejudicial Effects

As with the other elements of the *Mohan* test, probative value and prejudicial effects are case-specific. The determinations made by the trial judge deserve appellate deference. In this case, Dr. Marshall's evidence brought relevant facts and opinions to the case that were not within the jury's knowledge and would not otherwise have been available to assist them. Dr. Marshall's qualifications were not questioned. His testimony was understandable and convincing. Taken together, these factors suggest that the expert evidence possessed considerable probative value.

The accused argues that the probative value of the evidence was outweighed by two important prejudicial effects: (1) that Dr. Marshall's evidence would neutralize a legitimate line of argument and interfere with his right of self-defence; and (2) that Dr. Marshall's evidence would distort the trial process through the undue weight the jury may place on expert evidence. The first alleged prejudicial effect does not withstand scrutiny. As the trial judge noted in his decision on the voir dire, admitting Dr. Marshall's evidence would not prohibit defence counsel from making its "common sense" argument that delay casts doubt on whether the alleged assaults occurred. The Crown's expert evidence merely countered that argument by providing evidence that it was contrary to the current consensus in the scientific community. Conflicting evidence and inferences are the natural product of the adversarial nature of the trial process. Each side seeks to bring evidence to support its arguments. Expert witnesses are subject to cross-examination to probe the validity of their evidence and the weight to be assigned to it. At the end of the day, the jury decides what they accept and what they reject. Evidence is neither inadmissible nor unfair simply because it contradicts an argument put by the other side.

The second prejudicial effect merits closer consideration. Low value expert testimony can distort the fact-finding process by taking a relatively simple issue, dressing it up in scientific language and presenting the trier of fact with a ready-made decision. The jury may be tempted to avoid engaging in serious consideration of the actual facts and instead rely on the apparent expertise of the scientist. In effect, the expert may usurp the domain of the jury. Trial judges must take this possibility into account in determining whether the prejudicial effect of expert evidence outweighs its probative value.

Part of this concern is addressed at the necessity stage: a party seeking to call expert evidence must show that the subject matter of the expert's opinion falls outside the likely range of knowledge and experience of the trier of fact. Nonetheless, that may not suffice. Even if expert evidence may assist the judge or jury, that benefit must be balanced against its costs. Can the expert address the issue in understandable terms? Is the judge or jury likely to take the expert's word as unchallengeable truth, or will the trier of fact be able to examine it critically? At the same time, the judge must not underestimate the ability of jurors to assess evidence; they may be quite capable of discerning whether scientific information is legitimate or not, as long as it is presented in accessible language.

The concern that the jury may be misled was not made out in this case. Dr. Marshall testified in a clear and straightforward manner. He avoided scientific terms which might obfuscate the issue and confuse the jury. His evidence was easy to understand and well within the ability of the jury to evaluate. Unlike some expert witnesses, Dr. Marshall did not rely on his credentials or "the mystique of science" to bolster his testimony: see *Béland*, supra, at p. 434. Nor did his testimony verge on advocacy. He neither explicitly nor implicitly commented on the complainant's credibility or the ultimate issue of the guilt or innocence of the accused. Defence counsel engaged Dr. Marshall in cross-examination and did not seem hindered by the scientific nature of the evidence. On the circumstances that prevailed in the trial below, I cannot conclude that the trial judge erred in holding that the probative value of Dr. Marshall's evidence outweighed its prejudicial effects.

MAJOR, J. (IACOBUCCI, BINNIE and ARBOUR, JJ. concurring):—

. . . .

I. General Approach to the Necessity Requirement

A. Standard of Necessity

The second requirement of the *Mohan* analysis exists to ensure that the dangers associated with expert evidence are not lightly tolerated. Mere relevance or "helpfulness" is not enough. The evidence must also be necessary.

I agree with the Chief Justice that some degree of deference is owed to the trial judge's discretionary determination of whether the *Mohan* requirements have been met on the facts of a particular case, but that discretion cannot be used erroneously to dilute the requirement of necessity. *Mohan* expressly states that mere helpfulness is too low a standard to warrant accepting the dangers inherent in the admission of expert evidence. A fortiori, a finding that some aspects of the evidence "might reasonably have assisted the jury" is not enough.

B. Dangers of Expert Evidence

In *Mohan*, Sopinka J. stated that the need for expert evidence must be assessed in light of its potential to distort the fact-finding process. A brief examination of the dangers associated with the admission of expert evidence is helpful to the analysis of this appeal.

A basic tenet of our law is that the usual witness may not give opinion evidence, but testify only to facts within his knowledge, observation and experience. This is a commendable principle since it is the task of the fact finder, whether a jury or judge alone, to decide what secondary inferences are to be drawn from the facts proved.

However, common law courts have since the 14th century recognized that certain exceptional issues require the application of special knowledge lying outside the experience of the usual trier of fact. Expert opinion evidence became admissible as an exception to the rule against opinion evidence in those cases where it was necessary to provide "a ready-made inference which the judge and jury, due to the technical nature of the facts, are unable to formulate" (*R. v. Abbey*, [1982] 2 S.C.R. 24, at p. 42).

Despite the emergence of the exception, it has been repeatedly recognized that the admissibility requirements of expert evidence do not eliminate the dangers traditionally associated with it. Nevertheless, they are tolerated in those exceptional cases where the jury would be unable to reach their own conclusions in the absence of assistance from experts with special knowledge.

Historically, there existed two modes of utilizing such expert knowledge as was available: first, to select jurors who by experience were best suited to deal with the facts before them, and second, to call experts as friends of the court rather than as witnesses for one side or the other. (See Learned Hand, "Historical and Practical Considerations Regarding Expert Testimony" (1901), 15 Harv. L. Rev. 40.) In this manner, the neutrality of the experts was assured. This notion has long disappeared and now the "professional expert witness" has emerged. Although not biased in a dishonest sense, these witnesses frequently move from the impartiality generally associated with professionals to advocates in the case. In some notable instances, it has been recognized that this lack of independence and impartiality can contribute to miscarriages of justice. (See, e.g., *The Commission on Proceedings Involving Guy Paul Morin* (Kaufman Report) (1998), at p. 172.)

The primary danger arising from the admission of any opinion evidence is that the province of the jury might be usurped by that of the witness. This danger is especially prevalent in cases of expert opinion evidence. Faced with an expert's impressive credentials and mastery of scientific jargon, jurors are more likely to abdicate their role as fact-finders and simply attorn to the opinion of the expert in their desire to reach a just result. The danger of attornment to the opinion of the expert is further increased by the fact that expert evidence is highly resistant to effective cross-examination by counsel who are not experts in that field. In cases where there is no competing expert evidence, this will have the effect of depriving the jury of an effective framework within which to evaluate the merit of the evidence.

Additional dangers are created by the fact that expert opinions are usually derived from academic literature and out-of-court interviews, which material is unsworn and not available for cross-examination. Though not properly admissible as evidence for the proof of its contents, this material generally finds its way into the proceedings because "if an expert is permitted to give his opinion, he ought to be permitted to give the circumstances upon which that opinion is based" (*R. v. Dietrich* (1970), 1 C.C.C. (2d) 49 (Ont. C.A.), at p. 65). In many cases, this material carries with it prejudicial effects which require special instructions to the jury (*Abbey*, supra, at p. 45).

Finally, expert evidence is time-consuming and expensive. Modern litigation has introduced a proliferation of expert opinions of questionable value. The significance of the costs to the parties and the resulting strain upon judicial resources cannot be overstated. When the door to the admission of expert evidence is opened too widely, a trial has the tendency to degenerate into "a contest of experts with the trier of fact acting as referee in deciding which expert to accept" (*Mohan*, supra, at p. 24).

. . . .

In my view, the content of the expert evidence admitted in this case was not unique or scientifically puzzling but was rather the proper subject for a simple jury instruction. This being the case, its admission was not necessary.

Distilling the probative elements of Dr. Marshall's testimony from its superfluous and prejudicial elements, one bald statement of principle emerges. In diagnosing cases of child sexual abuse, the timing of the disclosure, standing alone, signifies nothing. Not all victims of child sexual abuse will disclose the abuse immediately. It depends upon the circumstances of the particular victim. I find surprising the suggestion that a Canadian jury or judge alone would be incapable of understanding this simple fact. I cannot identify any technical quality to this evidence that necessitates expert opinion.

. . . .

A trial judge should recognize and so instruct a jury that there is no inviolable rule on how people who are the victims of trauma like a sexual assault will behave. Some will make an immediate complaint, some will delay in disclosing the abuse, while some will never disclose the abuse. Reasons for delay are many and at least include embarrassment, fear, guilt, or a lack of understanding and knowledge. In assessing the credibility of a complainant, the timing of the complaint is simply one circumstance to consider in the factual mosaic of a particular case. A delay in disclosure, standing alone, will never give rise to an adverse inference against the credibility of the complainant.

It was submitted that it is preferable to introduce the concept contained in Dr. Marshall's evidence to the jury by way of expert testimony rather than by judicial instruction. In my view, this argument is flawed. There is nothing to be gained from a cross-examination of the simple and irrefutable proposition advanced in this case by the expert. As well, there is no benefit to be derived from the added flexibility of expert evidence since the undeniable nature of the proposition does not lend itself to future advancements in knowledge and understanding.

A jury instruction, in preference to expert opinion, where practicable, has advantages. It saves time and expense. But of greater importance, it is given by an impartial judicial officer, and any risk of superfluous or prejudicial content is eliminated. In this appeal, the evidence presented by the expert was precisely what the jury would have been instructed by a proper charge. There is no difference of substance between the two.

3. ULTIMATE ISSUE RULE

An issue which we find debated throughout the cases involving expert evidence involves the supposed problem of the expert giving opinion evidence on the ultimate issue. One would have thought that at this stage in our development of the law of evidence, a final disposition of such "problem" could have been made, but still we see this "red herring" being raised. To term this problem a "red herring" is not an original notion but rather conforms to Professor Wigmore's view of the ultimate issue rule as "one of those impracticable and misconceived utterances which lack any justification in principle."[37]

If the "ultimate issue" with respect to which opinion testimony was barred was narrowly construed to prohibit only expressions of opinion on issues which are mixed questions of fact and law, the rule would be justifiable on the general basis that opinion testimony ought to be received when it is necessary and helpful, and only then. An expression of opinion that involves the application of a legal standard ought to be excluded as superfluous since a jury, properly instructed by the trial judge on the law, is as capable of applying the standard as the witness. As described by Bliss, J.:

> No witness should be permitted to give his opinion directly that a person is guilty or innocent, or is criminally responsible or irresponsible, or that a person was negligent or not negligent, or that he had capacity to execute a will, or deed, or like instrument . . . But the reason is that such matters are not subjects of opinion testimony. They are mixed questions of law and fact. When a standard, or a measure, or a capacity has been fixed by law, no witness whether expert or non-expert, nor however qualified, is permitted to express an opinion as to whether or not the person or the conduct, in question, measures up to that standard. On that question the court must instruct the jury as to the law, and the jury must draw its own conclusion from the evidence. However courts have permitted both scientific and practical experts to express their opinion whether a certain method used, or course of conduct was a proper one.[38]

To perpetuate an ultimate issue rule framed any more broadly than this could exclude much that is helpful to a jury without any worthwhile justification; to say its reception would permit the jury's role to be usurped overlooks the fact that opinion evidence, like any other evidence, can always be rejected by the trier of fact.[39] In favour of the narrower view, the judgment of Aylesworth, J.A., in *R. v. Fisher*[40] is noteworthy. Speaking for the majority, he denied defendant's objection that the psychiatrist's opinion was inadmissible as dealing with the very point the jury had to decide by noting:

> . . . the basic reasoning which runs through the authorities here and in England, seems to be that expert opinion evidence will be admitted where it will be helpful to

---

37. 7 Wigmore, *Evidence* (Chad. Rev.), s. 1921.

38. *Grismore v. Consol. Products Co.*, 5 N.W. 2d 646, 663 (Iowa, 1942). To similar effect, see *R. v. Fisher* (1961), 34 C.R. 320, 342 (Ont. C.A.), per Aylesworth, J.A.

39. See *Snow v. Boston & Maine R.R.*, 65 Me. 230, 231 (1875): "The reason for its exclusion given by counsel, that it would instruct the jury as to the amount of the verdict to be rendered, would seem to be a very good reason for its admission. *Instruction is what the jury want.* They would not be bound by it any more than by other testimony, but it would be more or less valuable in enabling them to come to a correct conclusion." [emphasis added]; noted in 7 Wigmore, *Evidence* (Chad. Rev.), s. 1921, p. 26.

40. *Supra*, note 38.

the jury in their deliberations and it will be excluded only where the jury can as easily draw the necessary inferences without it. When the latter is the situation, the intended opinion evidence is superfluous. . . .

In some cases where opinion evidence has been rejected, the ground given is that the giving of the witness's opinion usurped the function of the jury. In other decisions it is said that the evidence tendered constituted an opinion upon the very point or issue which the jury had to decide. *An examination of these authorities, however, discloses, in my view, that the jury or the judge, in cases tried without a jury, would have had no difficulty in arriving at a proper conclusion in the absence of the tendered opinion and that this was the true ground for its rejection* . . .

Where the opinion tendered involves what is a mixed question of law and fact, the opinion is not admissible. [Emphasis added.][41]

A broader formulation of the ultimate issue rule foreclosing other opinion testimony, over and above opinions respecting guilt or innocence, not only lacks justification but, in theory, is unworkable. The doctrines of relevance and materiality dictate that *all* evidence given at a trial must be with respect to matters that are *necessary* to the prosecution or defence of the matter at issue. All testimony is then with respect to an ultimate issue in the sense that failure of proof with respect to anything necessary to a successful prosecution must yield an acquittal. In theory then, no expert, bound by the rules of relevancy and materiality, would be permitted to testify to *anything* under a broad formulation of the ultimate issue rule. In practice, of course, expert opinion testimony is received and the supposed ultimate issue rule which developed in the nineteenth century is seen, to be kind, as amorphous, and is applied or withheld with a great deal of discretion.

Finally, in *Graat v. R.*,[42] Howland, C.J.O., for the court, concluded:

In Canada the ultimate issue doctrine may now be regarded as having been virtually abandoned or rejected. Where evidence has been rejected on the basis of the doctrine, such rejection can be explained on other grounds. In some instances the opinion evidence should be rejected because the trier of fact, whether Judge or jury, is just as well qualified as the witness to draw the necessary inference. Accordingly, the non-expert testimony is superfluous, as it is of no appreciable assistance to the Judge or jury. . . . In the final analysis, even with the benefit of the expert's evidence the jury still has to make the final determination of the issue, so that the expert is not really usurping the jury's function.

---

41. *Ibid.*, at pp. 340-43. And see *Graat v. R.* (1980), 55 C.C.C. (2d) 429, 443 (Ont. C.A.). In the Supreme Court of Canada decision in *R. v. Fisher* (1961), 35 C.R. 107, a decision of a nine-man court, Fauteux, J. delivering the judgment of the court, noted: "With deference to the views of the learned judges who dissented in the court below, we are all in substantial agreement with the reasons expressed by Aylesworth, J.A., who spoke for the majority, and concur in the conclusion which he reached." See also *Preeper v. R.* (1888), 15 S.C.R. 401, per Gwynne, J.: "The question which the jury had to pass upon was the guilt or innocence of the prisoner in respect to the felony with which he was charged. This was not the question upon which the opinion of the surgeon in the present case was called and given."

42. (1980), 55 C.C.C. (2d) 429, 443 (Ont. C.A.); affirmed (1982), 2 C.C.C. (3d) 365 (S.C.C.). See *R. v. Millar* (1989), 71 C.R. (3d) 78 (C.A.), on a trial of manslaughter of a nine-week-old baby, allowing the receipt of expert evidence that, considering the type and frequency of the injuries, the infant was the subject of "child abuse."

4. EXPERT OPINION BASED ON HEARSAY

(a) Introduction

It is commonly said that an expert is confined to expressions of opinion based on facts proved at the trial, proved by the expert when he has had the advantage of personal observation of the facts at issue, or proved through the testimony of other witnesses, with the opinion elicited based on an assumption of their truthfulness using the device of hypothetical questions.[43] To this general proposition there has developed in Canada a seeming exception that, at least with respect to certain experts, an opinion may be expressed though based on facts not otherwise proved; i.e., where the basis for the expert's opinion consists partly of statements made to him prior to trial, and partly of where there are grounds of necessity in so proceeding or circumstances guaranteeing the trustworthiness of such statements.

(b) Learned Treatises

An expert testifying to her opinion, since only permitted so to do when she possesses particular knowledge and experience not shared by the trier of fact, perforce relies on hearsay; in developing her expertise she often has relied on the statements of her instructors at school or those of text writers, without satisfying herself by personal experiment that their instruction is accurate. As Professor Wigmore has noted:

> To deny the competency of a physician who does not know his facts from personal observation alone is to reject medical testimony almost in its entirety. To allow any physician to testify who claims to know solely by personal experience is to appropriate the witness stand to impostors. Medical science is a mass of transmitted and collated data from numerous quarters; the generalizations which are the result of one man's personal observation exclusively are the least acceptable of all.[44]

The reception of expert opinion based on this kind of hearsay was early recognized in England in the case of *Collier v. Simpson*,[45] where the court refused to receive medical books of authority as evidence of proper practice but Tindal, C.J. went on to say:

---

43. See, *e.g.*, Cross, *Evidence*, 5th ed., p. 446 and Phipson, *Evidence*, 11th ed., p. 507.
44. 3 Wigmore, *Evidence* (Chad. Rev.), s. 687. See also 2 Wigmore, *Evidence* (Chad. Rev.), s. 665b, where he comments: "The data of every science are enormous in scope and variety. No one professional man can know from personal observation more than a minute fraction of the data which he must every day treat as working truths. Hence a reliance on the *reported data of fellow scientists*, learned by perusing the reports in books and journals. The law must and does accept this kind of knowledge from scientific men. On the one hand, a mere layman, who comes to court and alleges a fact which he has learned only by reading a medical or mathematical book, cannot be heard. But, on the other hand, to reject a professional physician or mathematician because the fact or some facts to which he testifies are known to him only upon the authority of others would be to ignore the accepted methods of professional work and to insist on cynical and impossible standards."
45. (1831), 172 E.R. 883. Accord, see also *Davie v. Edinburgh Magistrates*, [1953] S.C. 34, and *R. v. Somers*, [1963] 1 W.L.R. 1306 (C.C.A.).

I do not think that the books themselves can be read; but I do not see any objection to your asking Sir Henry Halford his judgment, and the grounds of it, which may be, in some degree, founded on books, as a part of his general knowledge.

Apparently summarizing the Canadian attitude regarding the extent to which an expert can rely on statements of others found in texts, the Alberta Court of Appeal concluded:

> An expert medical witness may, therefore, upon giving his opinion, state in direct examination that he bases his opinion partly upon his own experience and partly upon the opinions of text-writers who are recognized by the medical profession at large as of authority. I think he may name the text-writers. I think he may add that his opinion and that of the text-writers named accords. Further, I see no good reason why such an expert witness should not be permitted, while in the box, to refer to such text-books as he chooses, in order, by the aid which they will give him, in addition to his other means of forming an opinion, to enable him to express an opinion; and again, that the witness having expressly adopted as his own the opinion of a text-writer, may himself read the text as expressing his own opinion.
>
> In cross-examination an expert medical witness having first been asked whether a certain text-book is recognized by the medical profession as a standard author and having said that it is, there may be read to him a passage from the book expressing an opinion, for the purpose of testing the value of the witness' opinion.[46]

(c) Hearsay in General

Should an expert be allowed to testify to her opinion when the same is based not only on her own direct observation and examination but also on the reports of others? May a doctor express her opinion of the plaintiff's condition when she has relied partly on the reports of pathologists or radiologists and those experts are not called to testify to their findings? May the doctor testify to her opinion where she has relied at least in part on statements made to her by the parties to the subsequent suit? Should the courts treat differently expert opinion based on a patient's history where the same was communicated at a time when the patient was seeking treatment as opposed to where the physician-witness examines the patient not for treatment but solely to prepare herself to testify? Where there is no evidence before the jury of the truth of the statements addressed to the expert witness and therefore no way for the jury to evaluate the foundation of the expert testimony, ought the expert opinion to be nevertheless receivable? These are some of the questions raised by this heading on which the case law appears to be somewhat in disarray.

R. v. JORDAN
(1983), 33 C.R. (3d) 394 (B.C. Co. Ct.)

8th March 1983. WETMORE CO. CT. J.:— The accused on arriving on a flight from Tokyo was searched at customs at the Vancouver airport. He was found in possession of narcotics. His statements to the customs officer confirm both the accused's knowledge of

---

46. R. v. Anderson (1914), 16 D.L.R. 203, 219 (Alta. C.A.). Accord, see Brownell v. Black (1890), 31 N.B.R. 594 (S.C.) and C.P.R. v. Jackson (1915), 52 S.C.R. 281. Following Rowley v. London N.W. Ry. (1873), 8 L.R. Ex. 221.

this substance in his luggage and that it was a narcotic. It appears that there was never specific mention of the word "heroin" in the conversation.

The indictment charges importing heroin in count 1 and possession of heroin for the purposes of trafficking in count 2.

The Crown first produced certificates showing the substance to be heroin. The Crown then produced the analyst for cross-examination. It is on the basis of this evidence that the defence says there is no reliable evidence that the substance is heroin.

Mr. Clark, a duly appointed analyst, explained the process of analysis used. In the final analysis the questioned substance in a gaseous state is subjected to a spectrometric comparison with a known standard of heroin. The spectrometric comparisons being identical, heroin is concluded as being the questioned substance. There is a further comparative study made of a standard graph prepared from scientific literature and the spectrophotomatic characteristics of the questioned substance. Again the points of comparison unite.

Mr. Clark testifies that he would not certify the questioned substance as heroin without a positive identity existing in *both* comparative studies.

In operating his apparatus the "known heroin" comes from the crime detection laboratory in Ottawa to the Vancouver laboratory. There, this "known standard" is again analyzed by the same process before use. This is done not by Mr. Clark necessarily but by other analysts in the Vancouver laboratory. He cannot say who did the actual analysis of the known standard prior to its use as the standard in making the comparisons with the exhibits in this case.

Defence counsel therefore argues that the opinion evidence of Mr. Clark is based upon hearsay evidence, which is not admissible, thus destroying the value of his opinion.

The argument is developed from the judgment of Dickson J. in R. v. Abbey, 29 C.R. (3d) 193 (S.C.C.). In that case the accused related several bizarre incidents to the psychiatrist, which the doctor apparently accepted as truthful. The learned judge then dealt with the medical opinion as if those statements had been established as a fact. From pp. 208-14, Dickson J. discusses the problems of hearsay evidence and opinion evidence. He concludes [p. 214], "Before any weight can be given to an expert's opinion, the facts upon which the opinion is based must be found to exist."

It must be remembered that Dickson J. was dealing with a psychiatric opinion based upon facts which are unique to the particular inquiry. He was not commenting upon other types of information. For example, the psychiatrist's opinion in the final analysis is usually derived from three sources, the patient's comments, his own observations and experience, and the medical literature. Both the experience and medical literature elements involve a great deal of hearsay, but surely all knowledge need not be proved by primary research and observation. Indeed, if that were so, no scientific opinion beyond the most elementary could ever be forthcoming. There comes a time, after testing and observation, that some pragmatic conclusions legitimately arise which need no further verification from original sources.

With respect, I think that is the situation in the case at bar. If it had been established that either the spectrometric comparisons with the supplied "known source" or the published scientific journal graph had not all been consistent, a query may well arise which had not been settled by anything more reliable than hearsay evidence. That did not occur.

I can accept hearsay evidence as original evidence insofar as it relates to my evaluation of the expert's opinion. What I cannot do is accept, as proven for itself, the facts in that hearsay statement. What Mr. Clark really says is that in his opinion the fact that he compared the characteristics of this substance with two substances which he, for good reason, believed to be heroin standards satisfied him that the substance he was analyzing was heroin.

What I am then called upon to measure is my own judgment of his decision, that the conclusion was justified.

The standard is prepared in the crime detection laboratory for this specific purpose. It is then further checked for accuracy by analysts in the Vancouver lab. The standard graph from the scientific literature is likewise designed for this specific purpose. Using these techniques, Mr. Clark testifies to having done hundreds of tests of the same nature. Nothing in cross-examination suggests that observations of a suspicious nature relating to accuracy have ever occurred.

I conclude therefore that there is no reason to doubt the opinion of Mr. Clark that the substance involved in this case is heroin.

With respect to defence counsel, I think this sort of evidence is more analogous to such things as marine charts. Nobody suggests that those documents are inadmissible in proving depths of the ocean without calling the actual measurer and cartographer.

In dismissing the accused's appeal in *Jordan*, Anderson, J.A. commented:

... In the case on appeal the analyst testified that the substance received from Ottawa and labelled "heroin" was tested by an analyst in his office. Such a course is perfectly proper. To call the analyst who made the test of the "known" sample is unnecessary. If such an analyst was called, it would, according to the argument of the appellant, be necessary for him to prove that the substance that he used for comparison purposes was heroin, and so on down the line. Such an argument, while logical, cannot be accepted because it would make scientific proof so ponderous and expensive that in reality the evidence of experts could never be used. In my view, the argument that the judgment in *R. v. Abbey*, [1982] 2 S.C.R. 24, applies to scientific tests of the kind under consideration here is unacceptable.[47]

R. v. LAVALLEE
[1990] 1 S.C.R. 852, 76 C.R. (3d) 329, 55 C.C.C. (3d) 97

[On a charge of murder the accused relied on self-defence. The deceased was a man with whom the accused had been living for several years. The accused shot the deceased in the back of the head as he was leaving her room after he had assaulted and threatened her. A statement by the accused to police was introduced into evidence by the prosecution. In the statement the accused admitted the shooting. She told the police that the accused had threatened to kill her when the other visitors to their home left and that she was scared and thinking about all the other times that the accused had beaten her. The defence called a psychiatrist who testified with respect to the "battered-wife syndrome." He testified that the accused felt that unless she defended herself and reacted in a violent way that she would die. He testified that he had spoken to the accused and the accused's mother on several occasions and that he had read the accused's statement to the police and the police reports. Neither the accused nor the accused's mother testified at the trial. The accused was acquitted. An appeal was allowed and a new trial ordered on the basis that the trial judge did not adequately instruct the jury with respect to the evidence of the psychiatrist. The court changed the substantive law regarding self defence and allowed that lay juries needed the advice of experts to understand the woman's perspective; see, *supra*, Chapter 1. The following extract deals only with the expert's ability to rely on hearsay in coming to his opinion and the trial judge's instruction to the jury in that event.]

---

47.   (1984), 39 C.R. (3d) 50, 57 (B.C.C.A.).

WILSON J. (DICKSON, C.J.C. and LAMER, L'HEUREUX-DUBÉ, GONTHIER and MCLACHLIN, JJ. concurring):—

. . . .

The appellant did not testify but her statement made to police on the night of the shooting was put in evidence. Portions of it read as follows:

Me and Wendy argued as usual and I ran in the house after Kevin pushed me. I was scared, I was really scared. I locked the door. Herb was downstairs with Joanne and I called for Herb but I was crying when I called him. I said 'Herb come up here please.' Herb came up to the top of the stairs and I told him that Kevin was going to hit me actually beat on me again. Herb said he knew and that if I was his old lady things would be different, he gave me a hug. OK, we're friends, there's nothing between us. He said 'Yeah, I know' and he went outside to talk to Kevin leaving the door unlocked. I went upstairs and hid in my closet from Kevin. I was so scared . . . My window was open and I could hear Kevin asking questions about what I was doing and what I was saying. Next thing I know he was coming up the stairs for me. He came into my bedroom and said 'Wench, where are you?' And he turned on my light and he said 'Your purse is on the floor' and he kicked it. OK then he turned and he saw me in the closet. He wanted me to come out but I didn't want to come out because I was scared. I was so scared. [The officer who took the statement then testified that the appellant started to cry at this point and stopped after a minute or two.] He grabbed me by the arm right there. There's a bruise on my face also where he slapped me. He didn't slap me right then, first he yelled at me then he pushed me and I pushed him back and he hit me twice on the right hand side of my head. I was scared. All I thought about was all the other times he used to beat me, I was scared, I was shaking as usual. The rest is a blank, all I remember is he gave me the gun and a shot was fired through my screen. This is all so fast. And then the guns were in another room and he loaded it the second shot and gave it to me. And I was going to shoot myself. I pointed it to myself, I was so upset. OK and then he went and I was sitting on the bed and he started going like this with his finger [the appellant made a shaking motion with an index finger] and said something like 'You're my old lady and you do as you're told' or something like that. He said 'wait till everybody leaves, you'll get it then' and he said something to the effect of 'either you kill me or I'll get you' that was what it was. He kind of smiled and then he turned around. I shot him but I aimed out. I thought I aimed above him and a piece of his head went that way.

. . . .

The expert evidence which forms the subject-matter of the appeal came from Dr. Fred Shane, a psychiatrist with extensive professional experience in the treatment of battered wives. At the request of defence counsel Dr. Shane prepared a psychiatric assessment of the appellant. The substance of Dr. Shane's opinion was that the appellant had been terrorized by Rust to the point of feeling trapped, vulnerable, worthless and unable to escape the relationship despite the violence. At the same time, the continuing pattern of abuse put her life in danger. In Dr. Shane's opinion the appellant's shooting of the deceased was a final desperate act by a woman who sincerely believed that she would be killed that night. . . .

Dr. Shane stated that his opinion was based on four hours of formal interviews with the appellant, a police report of the incident (including the appellant's statement), hospital reports documenting eight of her visits to emergency departments between 1983 and 1985, and an interview with the appellant's mother. In the course of his testimony Dr. Shane related many things told to him by the appellant for which there was no admissible evidence. They were not in the appellant's statement to the police and she did not testify at trial. For example, Dr. Shane mentioned several episodes of abuse described by the appellant for which there were no hospital reports. He also related the appellant's disclosure to him that she had lied to doctors about the cause of her injuries. Dr. Shane testified that such fabrication was typical of battered women. The appellant also recounted to Dr. Shane occasions on which Rust would allegedly beat her, then beg her forgiveness and ply her with flowers and temporary displays of kindness. . . . The appellant denied to Dr. Shane that she had homicidal fantasies about Rust and mentioned that she had smoked some marijuana on the night in question. These facts were related by Dr. Shane in the course of his testimony.

. . . .

In *Abbey*, *supra*, this Court addressed the bases upon which expert evidence that relies on hearsay is admissible. The accused in that case was charged with importing cocaine and his defence was insanity. The accused did not testify. A psychiatrist gave his opinion as to the sanity of the accused and, in the course of giving the basis for his conclusions, referred to incidents and hallucinations related to him by the accused for which there was no admissible evidence. The Crown submitted before this court that the trial judge "accepted and treated as factual much of this hearsay evidence" related to the psychiatrist. Dickson J. found that the point was "well taken". This was the preliminary finding on which the case was based and I think it is fair to say that the trial judge in the case at bar clearly did not make the same mistake as did the trial judge in *Abbey*. At pp. 411-2 of his judgment Dickson J. articulated the hazards inherent in admitting expert testimony based on hearsay:

> The danger, of course, in admitting such testimony is the ever present possibility, here exemplified, that the judge or jury, without more, will accept the evidence as going to the truth of the facts stated in it. The danger is real and lies at the heart of this case. Once such testimony is admitted, a careful charge to the jury by the judge or direction to himself is essential. The problem, however, as pointed out by Fauteux J. in *Wilband* resides not in the admissibility of the testimony but rather the weight to be accorded to the opinion. Although admissible in the context of his opinion, to the extent that it is second-hand his testimony is not proof of the facts stated.

. . . .

It was appropriate for the doctors to state the basis for their opinions and in the course of doing so, to refer to what they were told not only by Abbey but by others, but it was error for the judge to accept as having been proved the facts upon which the doctors had relied in forming their opinions. While it is not questioned that medical experts are entitled to take into consideration all possible information in forming their opinions, this in no way removes from the party tendering such evidence the obligation of establishing, through properly admissible evidence, the factual basis on which such opinions are based. Before any weight can be given to an expert's opinion, the facts upon which the opinion is based must be found to exist.

For present purposes I think the ratio of *Abbey* can be distilled into the following propositions:

1. An expert opinion is admissible if relevant, even if it is based on second-hand evidence.

2. This second hand evidence (hearsay) is admissible to show the information on which the expert opinion is based, not as evidence going to the existence of the facts on which the opinion is based.

3. Where the psychiatric evidence is comprised of hearsay evidence, the problem is the <u>weight</u> to be attributed to the opinion.

4. Before any weight can be given to an expert's opinion, the facts upon which the opinion is based must be found to exist.

In the case at bar the trial judge was clearly of the view that Dr. Shane's evidence was relevant. He would not have admitted it otherwise. As I stated above, in light of the evidence of the battering relationship which subsisted between the appellant and the deceased, the trial judge was correct in so doing.

With respect to the second point, the trial judge warned the jury generally that they could not "decide the case on the basis of things the witnesses did not see or hear", which would seem to include those matters which Dr. Shane neither saw nor heard. He then gave the marijuana smoking and the confirmatory evidence of the appellant's mother as two sources of information which were not evidence in the case. In my opinion, it would have been preferable if the trial judge had described the interview with the appellant as a source of inadmissible evidence, the marijuana smoking being an example of inadmissible evidence from that source. Nevertheless, I think the trial judge makes his meaning clear to the jury in the subsequent passage: "In terms of the matters considered by Dr. Shane he is left, therefore, with the deceased's [*sic* — he means accused's] statement, some supplementary information from the police report and his interpretation of the hospital records." The trial judge thus eliminates the interview with the appellant and his conversation with her mother as sources of admissible evidence. Elsewhere he reinforces the rule that the jury can only consider the admissible evidence. He refers to the hospital visits made by the appellant:

> Another evidentiary caution is necessary here. Mr. Brodsky, in his remarks, said, as he did in calling some of the evidence respecting hospital attendances that this is only a representative sample. He ought not to have said that. It is not evidence and must be completely disregarded by you. The only evidence before you are the eight attendances that you heard about and nothing else — eight attendances and nothing else.

The trial judge's instructions regarding the weight attributable to Dr. Shane's opinion also emphasize his distinction between admissible evidence and hearsay:

> *If the premises upon which the information is substantially based has not been proven in evidence, it is up to you to conclude that it is not safe to attach a great deal of weight to the opinion. An opinion of an expert depends, to a large extent, on the validity of the facts assumed by the evidence of the expert.*
>
> If there are some errors and the factual assumptions aren't too important to the eventual opinion, that's one thing. *If there are errors or matters not in evidence and those matters are substantial, in your view, in terms of the impact on the expert's opinion, then you will want to look at the value and weight of that expert's opinion very carefully.* It depends on how important you think the matters were that Dr. Shane relied on that are not in evidence.

(Emphasis added.)

I agree with Huband J.A. that these instructions with respect to weight conform to this court's judgment in *Abbey*. The only complaint can be with the trial judge's attempt to distinguish admissible from inadmissible evidence. The trial judge was certainly not as clear as he might have been but I have no hesitation in finding that a retrial is not warranted on this account.

Given that Dr. Shane relied extensively on his interview with the appellant, the trial judge drew particular attention to the additional element of credibility that could affect the quality of Dr. Shane's opinion: "It is the position of the Crown that Dr. Shane's opinion stands or falls on the veracity of Lyn Lavallee because he relied so heavily and extensively on what she told him and the evidence contained in the statement, Exhibit 16. That's for you to decide." Later in the charge, he elaborates:

> Undoubtably [*sic*] she was a very important source, if not the major source, of his information. Dr. Shane agreed that if what she told him was erroneous, he would have to reassess his position.

On cross-examination he reiterated that in his opinion her action was spontaneous to the moment to try to defend herself. The straw that broke the camel's back was the threat, 'When the others leave you're going to get it', even though similar statements had been made to her on other occasions. According to what she told him, the accused felt compelled to shoot.

Based on the information he had in the interview, it was his opinion that the acts of the accused were impulsive and not premeditated. He disagreed with the Crown's suggestion that Lyn Lavallee took the opportunity when it presented itself.

He conceded that patients had, on occasion, lied and misled him in the past.

The fourth proposition I have extracted from *Abbey* is that there must be admissible evidence to support the facts on which the expert relies before any weight can be attributed to the opinion. The majority of the Manitoba Court of Appeal appears to interpret this as a requirement that each and every fact relied upon by the expert must be independently proven and admitted into evidence before the entire opinion can be given any weight.

Dr. Shane referred in his testimony to various facts for which there was no admissible evidence. The information was elicited from his interviews with the appellant. It included the smoking of marijuana prior to the killing, the deterioration of the intimate relationship between the appellant and Rust, past episodes of physical and psychological abuse followed by intervals of contrition, the apparent denial of homicidal fantasies on the appellant's part, and her remorse after killing Rust.

If the majority of the Court of Appeal is suggesting that each of these specific facts must be proven in evidence before any weight could be given to Dr. Shane's opinion about the accused's mental state, I must respectfully disagree. *Abbey* does not, in my view, provide any authority for that proposition. The court's conclusion in that case was that the trial judge erred in treating as proven the facts upon which the psychiatrist relied in formulating his opinion. The solution was an appropriate charge to the jury, not an effective withdrawal of the evidence. In my view, as long as there is some admissible evidence to establish the foundation for the expert's opinion, the trial judge cannot subsequently instruct the jury to completely ignore the testimony. The judge must, of course, warn the jury that the more the expert relies on facts not proved in evidence the less weight the jury may attribute to the opinion.

On my reading of the record Dr. Shane had before him admissible evidence about the nature of the relationship between the appellant and Rust in the form of the appellant's statement to the police and the hospital records. In addition, there was substantial corroborative evidence provided at trial by Ezako, the emergency-room doctor who testified to doubting the appellant's explanation of her injuries. There was also the evidence of the witnesses on the night of the shooting who testified to the appellant's frightened appearance, tone of voice, and conduct in dealing with Rust. The evidence pointed to the image of a woman who was brutally abused, who lied about the cause of her injuries, and who was incapable of leaving her abuser. As Huband J.A. comments in dissent, if the trial judge erred at all, he was probably remiss in not mentioning the corroborative evidence of Ezako as buttressing the evidentiary foundation on which Dr. Shane premised his opinion.

. . . .

Where the factual basis of an expert's opinion is a mélange of admissible and inadmissible evidence the duty of the trial judge is to caution the jury that the weight attributable to the expert testimony is directly related to the amount and quality of admissible evidence on which it relies. The trial judge openly acknowledged to counsel the inherent difficulty in discharging such a duty in the case at bar. In my view, the trial judge performed his task adequately in this regard. A new trial is not warranted on the basis of the trial judge's charge to the jury.

I would accordingly allow the appeal, set aside the order of the Court of Appeal, and restore the acquittal.

. . . .

SOPINKA J. (concurring in the result):— I have read the reasons of my colleague Justice Wilson, and I agree in the result that this appeal must be allowed. I find it necessary, however, to add a few words concerning the interpretation of this Court's decision in *R. v. Abbey* (1982), 68 C.C.C. (2d) 394.

Abbey has been roundly criticized: see, *e.g.*, Schiff, *Evidence in the Litigation Process*, 3rd ed., vol. I, (1988), pp. 473-6, and Delisle, *Evidence: Principles and Problems*, 2nd ed. (1989), pp. 477-9. The essence of the criticism is that Abbey sets out more restrictive conditions for the use of expert evidence than did previous decisions of this court: *i.e.*, *City of St. John v. Irving Oil Co. Ltd.* (1966), [1966] S.C.R. 581; *Wilband v. The Queen*, [1967] S.C.R. 14, and *R. v. Lupien*, [1970] S.C.R. 263. Upon reflection, it seems to me that the very special facts in *Abbey*, and the decision required on those facts, have contributed to the development of a principle concerning the admissibility and weight of expert opinion evidence that is self-contradictory. The contradiction is apparent in the four principles set out by Wilson J. in the present case, *ante*, pp. 127-8, which I reproduce here for the sake of convenience:

1.   An expert opinion is admissible if relevant, even if it is based on second-hand evidence.

2.   This second-hand evidence (hearsay) is admissible to show the information on which the expert opinion is based, not as evidence going to the existence of the facts on which the opinion is based.

3.   Where the psychiatric evidence is comprised of hearsay evidence, the problem is the weight to be attributed to the opinion.

4.   Before any weight can be given to an expert's opinion, the facts upon which the opinion is based must be found to exist.

The combined effect of Nos. 1, 3 and 4 is that an expert opinion relevant in the abstract to a material issue in a trial but based entirely on unproven hearsay (*e.g.*, from the mouth of the accused, as in *Abbey*) is admissible but entitled to no weight whatsoever. The question that arises is how any evidence can be admissible and yet entitled to no weight. As one commentator has pointed out, an expert opinion based entirely on unproven hearsay must, if anything, be inadmissible by reason of irrelevance, since the facts underlying the expert opinion are the only connection between the opinion and the case: see Wardle, "*R. v. Abbey* and Psychiatric Opinion Evidence: Requiring the Accused to Testify", 17 Ottawa L. Rev. 116 at pp. 122-3 (1984).

The resolution of the contradiction inherent in *Abbey*, and the answer to the criticism *Abbey* has drawn, is to be found in the practical distinction between evidence that an expert obtains and acts upon within the scope of his or her expertise (as in *City of St. John*,) and evidence that an expert obtains from a party to litigation touching a matter directly in issue (as in *Abbey*).

In the former instance, an expert arrives at an opinion on the basis of forms of enquiry and practice that are accepted means of decision within that expertise. A physician, for example, daily determines questions of immense importance on the basis of the observations of colleagues, often in the form of second or third-hand hearsay. For a court to accord no weight to, or to exclude, this sort of professional judgment, arrived at in accordance with sound medical practices, would be to ignore the strong circumstantial guarantees of trustworthiness that surround it, and would be, in my view, contrary to the approach this court has taken to the analysis of hearsay evidence in general, exemplified in *Ares v. Venner*, [1970] S.C.R. 608. In *R. v. Jordan* (1984), 11 C.C.C. (3d) 565 (B.C.C.A.), a case concerning an expert's evaluation of the chemical composition of an alleged heroin specimen, Anderson J.A. held, and I respectfully agree, that *Abbey* does not apply in such circumstances: see also *R. v. Zundel* (1987), 31 C.C.C. (3d) 97 at p. 146 (Ont. C.A.), where the court recognized an expert opinion based upon evidence ". . . of a general nature which is widely used and acknowledged as reliable by experts in that field".

Where, however, the information upon which an expert forms his or her opinion comes from the mouth of a party to the litigation, or from any other source that is inherently suspect, a court ought to require independent proof of that information. The lack of such proof will, consistent with *Abbey*, have a direct effect on the weight to be given to the opinion, perhaps to the vanishing point. But it must be recognized that it will only be very rarely that an expert's opinion is entirely based upon such information, with no independent proof of any of it. Where an expert's opinion is based in part upon suspect information and in part upon either admitted facts or facts sought to be proved, the matter is purely one of weight. In this respect, I agree with the statement of Wilson J., *ante*, p. 130, as applied to circumstances such as those in the present case:

> . . . as long as there is some admissible evidence to establish the foundation for the expert's opinion, the trial judge cannot subsequently instruct the jury to completely ignore the testimony. The judge must, of course, warn the jury that the more the expert relies on facts not proved in evidence the less weight the jury may attribute to the opinion.

As Wilson J. holds, the trial judge's charge to the jury was adequate, and the appeal ought therefore to be allowed.

The dictum in *Abbey*,

[b]efore any weight can be given to an expert's opinion, the facts upon which the opinion is based must be found to exist,

led some to believe that *all* the facts upon which an opinion was based had to be proved in evidence before the opinion could be given "*any weight.*" In *Lavallee*, Madam Justice Wilson says the real ratio of *Abbey* was the fact that the trier there treated as true the facts as related to the psychiatrist. She decides that weight can be given to an opinion, although all the facts that form the basis of the opinion are not independently proved, provided that there is "some admissible evidence to establish the foundation for the expert's opinion" and provided that a careful warning is given to the jury that facts related to the expert which are not independently proved cannot be taken as true. There was admissible evidence in *Lavallee* to support the doctor's opinion and this made *Lavallee* notably different from *Abbey* where the opinion was based entirely on unproven hearsay. A judge should not tell the jury to completely ignore an opinion partially based on inadmissible evidence but rather it is the trial judge's duty to "warn the jury that the more the expert relies on facts not proved in evidence the less weight the jury may attribute to the opinion." The court does recognize, however, "the inherent difficulty in discharging such a duty in the case at bar." The doctor in *Lavallee* did testify that the accused was an important, if not the major, source of his information and that if what she had told him was erroneous he would have to reassess his position. He related to the trier much of what the accused had told him. A careful warning was therefore required by the decision in *Abbey* and, in the view of the Supreme Court, was provided; a view obviously not shared by the majority of the Manitoba Court of Appeal.[48]

The court recognized that the task for the trial judge is one of "inherent difficulty." This was an appellate decision looking back at the whole process and determining whether there ought to be a new trial. Aside from the inherent difficulty

---

48.   See *R. v. Lavallee* (1988), 65 C.R. (3d) 387 (Man. C.A.).

in charging a jury concerning the weight attributable to an expert's opinion when the factual basis for the same is "a melange of admissible and inadmissible evidence," there is also the danger that a jury might not follow the trial judge's limiting instruction and might treat as true the facts related by the expert as the basis for his opinion. In looking ahead, and seeking to avoid difficulties and dangers, might a trial judge, following *Lavallee*, ensure, in the first instance, that the expert's opinion is confined to that which the expert is able to express based solely on admissible evidence which can be tested by the trier for trustworthiness? If there is no admissible evidence to support the opinion, for example if the opinion is based entirely on hearsay, the opinion, one assumes, must be inadmissible. As Justice Sopinka points out in his concurring opinion, there is no point in admitting an opinion which is entitled to no weight. It is irrelevant. For the trial judge to be able to confine the expert to an opinion based on admissible evidence he will need to know what that admissible evidence is. Could the trial judge direct that the expert give his opinion last, after all the other defence witnesses, including the accused if it is determined to call the accused, have testified?

MIZZI v. DEBARTOK
(1992), 9 O.R. (3d) 383 (Ont. Gen. Div.)

THE COURT [DUNNET, J.]:— The plaintiff wishes to call William Franks as his first witness. This is a personal injury action involving closed-head injury, and the plaintiff indicates that he wishes to present the medical evidence of the doctors who assessed the plaintiff at the outset. The defence objects, and says that if the plaintiff is not called first, it would be difficult to cross-examine the doctors on hearsay evidence and without the evidence of the plaintiff to lay the proper foundation for opinion evidence put to the doctors.

The plaintiff contends that the court will be in a better position to understand the nature of the injury to the plaintiff if the expert evidence of the treating doctors is called first, as well as the evidence as to the functioning of the brain, the physical damage that occurred and the psychological consequences.

In my view the plaintiff is a key witness. He is claiming damages and should have the opportunity to tell his story however best he can at the outset of the trial. As well, I find it is necessary for the court for the medical evidence to follow, and the plaintiff, if he is to be called, to be called at the outset of the trial.

Order accordingly.

R. v. SCARDINO
(1991), 6 C.R. (4th) 146 (Ont. C.A.)

[The accused was charged with murder. There was no dispute that the accused killed his wife. There was evidence that his marriage had been rapidly deteriorating and that he was obsessed with his matrimonial problems. There was evidence that there had been had been a marked change in his personality. A psychiatrist called by the defence testified that the accused was suffering from a major mental illness. In reaching his opinion, the doctor relied upon: (1) the accused's account of his conduct and state of mind on the evening of the killing; (2) the evidence he heard at trial; and (3) the medical tests that were performed on the accused. The doctor testified that the central and most important factor in the formation of his opinion was the factual account provided to him by the accused. That narrative was not repeated in the courtroom by the accused. The accused was convicted of second degree murder and appealed. The appeal was dismissed.]

FINLAYSON J.A. (CATZMAN and LABROSSE, JJ.A. concurring):—

. . . .

In her charge to the jury, the trial Judge clearly set out the distinctive features of the three classes of factual underpinning to the opinion of Dr. Oliver. With respect to the medical tests he performed and his observations of the appellant, the jury was told that it could accept his evidence as evidence of the existence of those facts. In regards to statements made to Dr. Oliver by the appellant and others regarding facts about which he had no direct knowledge, the trial Judge stated that while the doctor was entitled to base his opinion on those statements and to describe them to the jury (because they formed the basis of his opinion), the jury were not to regard his evidence as being evidence of the facts contained in those statements. In this respect the trial Judge stated: "[T]hose facts can only be established by the evidence of persons having direct knowledge of them." . . .

It is the following instruction with which counsel for the appellant took particular issue. The trial Judge stated:

All of those matters which Dr. Oliver described the accused as having told him, I tell you as a matter of law are not evidence. None of that has been established in evidence. The degree to which Dr. Oliver's opinion is dependent upon those statements attributed to the accused *is of no weight* because those facts are not before you. [Emphasis added.]

"All those matters" included not only a narrative of the actions of the appellant in shooting his wife, but also his account of how he felt at the time. It was submitted, on the authority of *Kirkby*, supra, that these statements about hearing a voice and having no control over his body were original evidence on the issue of insanity, as distinct from hearsay. They were admissible, not to prove any fact asserted by them, but as circumstantial evidence to support an inference that the appellant suffered from delusions or hallucinations. As to the appellant's narrative as to how the shooting occurred, it was submitted that it was properly used by Dr. Oliver as a basis for his professional opinion and that it was wrong for the trial Judge to have instructed the jury that an opinion based on this evidence was to be given no weight.

Martin J.A., in *Kirkby*, clearly differentiated between contemporaneous utterances indicating delusions and a narrative that purported to describe a hallucinatory or delusional state of mind in the past. The former are original evidence and admissible if they are capable of supporting a finding of mental illness, but the latter remain hearsay and inadmissible. Martin J.A. also made it clear that a psychiatrist's opinion that was based on hearsay alone was to be given no weight. . . .

The specific reference to *Abbey* by Martin J.A. supports his statement of the law.

. . .

In my view there is no error in the trial Judge's charge. Indeed, it is clear that she patterned her instruction on *Kirkby*, which in turn relied on *Abbey*. If any problem arose from *Abbey*, it was a tendency on the part of some judges to rule that before an expert's opinion was admissible in evidence, *all* the facts upon which the opinion was based must be proved in evidence. *Kirkby*, however, makes it clear that the burden is not that onerous. An expert's opinion is admissible in evidence, notwithstanding the absence of proof in some areas relied upon by the expert. However, the weight to be given to the opinion in such cases is diminished, sometimes to the point where the opinion can be given no weight at all. In my opinion, this view is supported by the recent decision of the Supreme Court of Canada in *Lavallee*, supra.

R. v. GIESBRECHT
(1993), 20 C.R. (4th) 73 (Man. C.A.)

[The accused was convicted of murder. His defence of insanity was rejected by the jury. On appeal he challenged the instructions to the jury on the use of psychiatric evidence. It was the accused's submission that the following excerpts from the trial judge's charge constituted a misdirection:

Now, I must tell you this: You have heard the evidence of many doctors. They gave their opinions regarding the condition of the accused and described to you the facts on which they based their opinion. You ask yourselves, were those facts which were observed by the doctors themselves. If they were, then you may accept their evidence as evidence of the existence of such facts. For example, there are the doctors' observations of the accused as they saw him, the emotional effect they may have spoken of to you, but their opinions were also based in large part on statements made to them by the accused himself or other persons regarding facts of which the doctors have no direct knowledge. Although a doctor and here a psychiatrist is entitled to base his opinion on those statements and to describe them to you because they form part of the basis of his opinion, you must not regard his evidence as being evidence of the facts contained in the statement. Those facts can only be established by the evidence of persons having direct knowledge of them.

For example, we might refer here to the delusions of the Accused. Those only come from the accused, what the accused told the doctors, what he told them. You must be very careful before accepting it as true. But I must tell you this: the degree to which the doctor's opinion is dependent upon statements made by the accused is a matter you may consider in deciding the weight to be given to the opinion of the expert. And, again, you should be very careful weighing such evidence before accepting it. It's only hearsay. They are not proved facts, so be careful what you accept as sound in those terms.

And, finally, part of the testimony of the expert witnesses, if you will recall, consisted of conclusions drawn by them from facts which they have assumed to be true and which have been put to them perhaps in the form of hypothetical questions. The weight of such testimony is dependent entirely upon the truth of the facts stated to them in the hypothetical question. I charge you that it is your duty, before accepting the conclusion of the experts on this question, to examine carefully all the facts related to the expert in the hypothetical question to determine whether such facts have been proven to be true.

All right. That's a little difficult, but it's part of your duty to assess and weigh the evidence of the expert witnesses and determine which opinions you, in your mind, in your view, consider as sound.]

HELPER J.A. (SCOTT J.M. and PHILP J.A. concurring):—

. . . .

The appellant argued that the trial judge erred in referring to his statements to Drs. Shane and Hershberg as hearsay. It was his submission that those statements were properly admitted to show state of mind. He went on to argue that the effect of these instructions was a direction to the jury to give no weight to the opinions of the defence experts. The trial judge was obliged to distinguish for the jury the different types of statements made by an accused which are admitted into evidence and to clarify those which are truly hearsay and those which are admissible, as in this case, as going to prove state of mind.

I do not accept that argument. The trial judge made no error in classifying the appellant's statements in this case as hearsay. He directed the jury properly on the use to be made of expert evidence and the weight to be attached to opinions. His directions did not constitute a message to the jury to attach no weight to the opinions of the experts called on behalf of the defence.

. . . .

In the case at bar, however, the only admissible statements of the appellant dealing with his state of mind were those statements elicited from the appellant during interviews with the doctors called by the defence. That situation is to be distinguished from the example of observed conduct by an accused. In the latter case the statements constitute evidence of conduct; in the former case, the case at bar, the statements constitute hearsay evidence on the issue of state of mind.

. . . .

The directions Wilson J. provided in [*R. v. Lavallee*] can be summarized as follows: the expert is called and is allowed to provide an opinion to assist the jury in understanding the mental state of the accused and his or her actions as a result of that mental state. The jury is not compelled to accept the opinions offered by experts. Hearsay evidence is admissible to explain the basis of the expert opinion, but the jury must be cautioned that such evidence is not admitted for the truth of the statements on which the opinion is based and the statements are not proof of the facts contained therein.

In the case at bar, the defence experts relied upon the appellant's statements to them that he believed the town of Altona collectively was going to kill him. The doctors used that information to formulate their opinions that the appellant suffered from a delusion. The appellant's statements were admitted correctly to show some of the information upon which the doctors relied for their opinions. The statements were not admitted to prove the appellant's state of mind which was a question for the jury to determine based upon admissible evidence, relevant to that issue. The experts' opinions were relevant to that issue. The appellant's statements to the experts were relevant only to the experts' opinions.

. . . .

On the issue of the existence of the alleged delusion, the appellant's statements to the doctors constituted hearsay evidence. The ultimate issue for the jury, that is, whether or not the accused suffered from the delusion that rendered him incapable in those circumstances of distinguishing right from wrong, could be proved only by admissible evidence, relevant to that issue. In this case, the experts' opinions and other observed conduct of the appellant was the only evidence available to the jury.

[The Supreme Court agreed. See *R. v. Giesbrecht*, [1994] 2 S.C.R. 482.]

---

5. EXAMINING EXPERT

(a) Hypothetical Questions

The reason for requiring the expert to provide the trier of fact with the basis for his opinion "is not a deduction from the opinion rule, but rests on the principle of testimonial qualifications that a witness's grounds of knowledge must be made to appear."[49] In a civil suit for negligence arising out of a motor vehicle accident, a witness is examined first respecting his past ability to observe the incident and his present ability to recollect and to communicate a description of the event. Without a demonstrated ability to observe and communicate, the witness's testimony is worthless. So, too, an expert's opinion, which rests always on certain

---

49.   7 Wigmore, *Evidence* (Chad. Rev.), s. 1927.

premises of fact, must be directly coupled to those premises and both supplied to the jury.

The premises may be communicated by the same witness who expresses the opinion when the expert has had the opportunity of personal observation and so is able to recount, on request, the details observed forming the foundation of his opinion. It may be, however, that the factual premises are related by one witness and the opinion by another. Since it is the essential nature of an opinion that it is dependent on its premises, and since the premises can always be rejected by the jury whether testified to by the person giving the opinion or by another, it follows that all opinions in a sense are hypothetical. Is it necessary, therefore, that an expert testifying to an opinion based on personal observation must first state not only that he had an opportunity to observe, but also recount all the details of his observation, as premises, before being permitted to express his opinion?

To this Professor Wigmore answers:

> In academic nicety, yes; practically, no; and for the simple reason that either on direct examination or on cross-examination each and every detail of the appearance he observed can be brought out and thus associated with his general conclusion as the grounds for it, and the tribunal will understand that the rejection of these data will destroy the validity of his opinion.[50]

Where the expert is unable to supply from his own knowledge the details constituting his premises, then his opinion must be brought out by hypothetical presentation so that the jury will later be able to decide whether or not his opinion deserves acceptance after considering other testimony to its premises. As Professor Wigmore notes in describing "the orthodox and accepted theory of the hypothetical question":

> The key to the situation, in short is that there may be two distinct subjects of testimony, — premises, and inferences or conclusions; that the latter involves necessarily a consideration of the former; and that the tribunal must be furnished with the means of rejecting the latter if upon consultation they determine to reject the former, i.e. of distinguishing conclusions properly founded from conclusions improperly founded.[51]

Phipson describes the English attitude in a similar way when he notes:

> Where the issue is substantially one of science or skill merely, the expert may, if he has *himself* observed the facts, be asked the very question which the jury have to decide. If, however, his opinion is based merely upon facts proved by *others,* such a question is improper, for it practically asks him to determine the truth of their testimony, as well as to give an opinion upon it; the correct course is to put such facts to him *hypothetically,* but not *en bloc,* asking him to assume one or more of them to be true, and to state his opinion thereon; where, however, the facts are not in dispute, it has been said that the former question may be put as a matter of convenience, though not as of right.[52]

---

50.   2 Wigmore, *Evidence* (Chad. Rev.), s. 675. See also Chadbourn, *Study Relating to the Uniform Rules of Evidence,* commissioned by the California Law Revision Commission, 1964, pp. 937-39. But see *R. v. Turner* (1975), 60 Cr. App. R. 80, 82.

51.   2 Wigmore, *Evidence* (Chad. Rev.), s. 672; text quoted with approval by Ritchie, J., in *Bleta v. R.,* [1965] 48 D.L.R. (2d) 139, 143 (S.C.C.). See also Maule, J., in *M'Naghten's Case* (1843), 10 Cl. & F. 200, 207, 8 E.R. 718, 721.

52.   Phipson, *Evidence,* 11th ed., p. 518.

Where the expert is not speaking with personal knowledge, but basing his opinion on facts proved at the trial by other witnesses, then an expert cannot, where there has been conflict between the witnesses, be simply asked, "Having heard all the evidence led in this case, what is your opinion with respect to X?" As described by Ritchie, J., in *Bleta v. R.*: [53]

> . . . it is obviously unsatisfactory to ask him to express an opinion based upon the evidence which he has heard because the answer to such a question involves the expert in having to resolve the conflict in accordance with his own view of the credibility of the witnesses and the jury has no way of knowing upon what evidence he based his opinion.

On the other hand, the Supreme Court of Canada did recognize in *Bleta* the same relaxation of attitude to hypothetical questions noted by Phipson when the evidence led by the "fact-witness" is all one way; i.e., depending on the particular case the hypothesis on which the expert is proceeding may be so readily apparent to the jury as to permit the trial judge "in the exercise of his discretion in the conduct of the trial"[54] to dispense with the necessity of abiding the formal hypothetical question technique usually demanded.

(b) Use of Text Books

The classic case of *R. v. Anderson*[55] remains instructive regarding the proper use to be made of texts in the examination and cross-examination of experts. Beck, J. summarized the principles:

> When a medical man or other person professing some science is called as an expert witness, it is his opinion and his opinion only that can be properly put before the jury. Just as in the case of a witness called to prove a fact, it is proper in direct examination to ask him not merely to state the fact, but also how he came by the knowledge of the fact, so in the case of an expert witness called to give an opinion, he may in direct examination be asked how he came by his opinion. An expert medical witness may, therefore, upon giving his opinion, state in direct examination that he bases his opinion partly upon his own experience and partly upon the opinions of text-writers who are recognized by the medical profession at large as of authority. I think he may name the text-writers. I think he may add that his opinion and that of the text-writers named accords. Further, I see no good reason why such an expert witness should not be permitted, while in the box, to refer to such text-books as he chooses, in order, by the aid which they will give him, in addition to his other means of forming an opinion, to enable him to express an opinion; and again, that the witness having expressly adopted as his own the opinion of a text-writer, may himself read the text as expressing his own opinion.
> In cross-examination an expert medical witness having first been asked whether a certain text-book is recognized by the medical profession as a standard author and having said that it is, there may be read to him a passage from the book expressing an opinion, for the purpose of testing the value of the witness' opinion.

And Harvey, C.J. agreed:

> I agree with what my brother Beck has said with reference to the use of text-books. As all evidence is given under the sanction of an oath or its equivalent, it is

53.   [1965] 48 D.L.R. (2d) 139, 141; see also *R. v. Holmes*, [1953] 1 W.L.R. 686 (C.C.A.).
54.   *Ibid.*, at p. 143. And see more recently *R. v. Swietlinski* (1978), 5 C.R. (3d) 324 (Ont. C.A.).
55.   (1914), 16 D.L.R. 203, 219-20 (Alta. C.A.).

apparent that text-books or other treatises as such cannot be evidence. The opinion of an eminent author may be, and in many cases is, as a matter of fact, entitled to more weight than that of the sworn witness, but the fact is that, if his opinion is put in the form of a treatise, there is no opportunity of questioning and ascertaining whether any expression might be subject to any qualification respecting a particular case. A witness would not be qualified as an expert if his opinions were gained wholly from the opinions of others and the faith that is to be given to the opinion of an author of a treatise must come through the faith in the witness and the confidence to be placed in the witness's opinion, in theory, is not to be derived from the confidence in the author with whose opinion he agrees. On principle, therefore, nothing may be given from a text-book, other than as the opinion of a witness who gives it. On cross-examination the Judge should be careful to see that an improper use is not made of text-books, practically to give in evidence opinions of absent authors at variance with those of the witness. It is quite apparent that if the witness is asked about a text-book and he expresses ignorance of it, or denies its authority, no further use of it can be made by reading extracts from it, for that would be in effect making it evidence, but if he admits its authority, he then in a sense confirms it by his own testimony, and then may be quite properly asked for explanation of any apparent differences between its opinion and that stated by him.[56]

6. APPOINTMENT OF COURT EXPERTS

Since the 18th century, with the change from the use of court-appointed experts and special juries, to the use of experts called by the parties testifying as witnesses,[57] adverse criticism has been directed at the apparent partisanship displayed by experts. Too often, unfortunately, the criticism has been unfairly aimed at the expert and his profession, which is in no way responsible for the present system. Often, counsel does not seek the best expert to elucidate the matter in issue, but rather the best witness for his cause. Jessel, M.R. condemned this practice, saying:

> . . . I have, as usual, the evidence of experts on the one side and on the other, and, as usual, the experts do not agree in their opinion. There is no reason why they should . . . the mode in which expert evidence is obtained is such as not to give the fair result of scientific opinion to the Court. A man may go, and does sometimes, to half-a-dozen experts. . . . He takes their honest opinions, he finds three in his favour and three against him; he says to the three in his favour, Will you be kind enough to give evidence? and he pays the three against him their fees and leaves them alone; the other side does the same. It may not be three out of six, it may be three out of fifty. . . . I have always the greatest possible distrust of scientific evidence. . . . I am sorry to say the result is that the Court does not get that assistance from the experts which, if they were unbiased and fairly chosen, it would have a right to expect.[58]

---

56. *Ibid.*, at p. 206-07.
57. See Hand, "Historical and Practical Considerations Regarding Expert Testimony" (1901), 15 Harv. L. Rev. 40; and Rosenthal, "The Development of the Use of Expert Testimony" (1935), 2 Law and Contemporary Problems 403.
58. On the hearing of a motion in *Thorn v. Worthing Skating Rink Co.* (1876), 6 Ch. D. 415n, as noted in *Plimpton v. Spiller* (1877), 6 Ch. D. 412, 416 (C.A.). But see *More v. R.*, [1963] S.C.R. 522, 537-38, where the court criticizes the trial judge's instruction to the jury for his "unwarranted disparagement" of the expert evidence: the trial judge had quoted extracts from Phipson, Taylor, and Lord Campbell to the same effect as the statement of Jessel, M.R. See, too, Overholser, *The Psychiatrist and the Law* (1952), pp. 106-14.

It has been said that the role of the trier of fact in weighing such evidence is difficult and that it becomes impossible when two experts express diametrically opposed views. His decision turns out not on facts proved in evidence, but on which expert he believes. Spellman puts it this way:

> This presents a quandary which, except by coincidence, is remote from any concept of justice. The question at bar should be what is the proper conclusion to be drawn from recorded facts. By the nature of the case, no external criteria are available to the fact-finder to enable him to work his way out of the presented dilemma. Thus, strange as it may seem, the fact-finder, as to this phase of the litigation, is basing his finding on a conclusion as to *credibility*.[59]

A partial solution to the problem of inherent bias in an expert called by a party, may be a return to providing the necessary assistance through a court-appointed expert.[60] As the adversary system developed, the power of the trial judge to call witnesses of any kind declined, especially in civil cases. The view was favoured that the judge should determine the dispute on the basis of the issues raised by the parties and in accordance with the evidence they saw fit to introduce.[61] Whether there remains any inherent common law right in the court to appoint experts as assessors to assist the court on its own motion, is a matter of some doubt.[62] The technique followed in civil law jurisdictions is to permit the court to select experts to inform it of their opinion based on their own particular knowledge and experience.[63] Such experts are permitted not only to give their opinions, but also to conduct independent investigations for the purpose of preparing their written reports.[64] Under the federal criminal procedure in the United States, the trial judge is permitted to select an expert[65] in addition to the experts called by the parties. The court's expert may express his opinion and is not confined solely to the role of interpreter.[66] This practice forms the basis for Rule 706 of the Federal Rules of Evidence.[67] The question arises whether it is a

---

59. Spellman, *Direct Examination of Witnesses* (1968), p. 139.
60. See McCormick, "Some Observations Upon the Opinion Rule and Expert Testimony" (1945), 23 Texas L. Rev. 109, 130-36; and 2 Wigmore, *Evidence* (Chad. Rev.), s. 563. For statutory recommendations to such effect see *Uniform Rules of Evidence* (1953), Rules 59, 61; and *Model Code of Evidence* (1942), Rules 403-10. But see Levy, "Impartial Medical Testimony — Revisited" (1961), 34 Temple L.Q. 416.
61. See *Jones v. Nat. Coal Bd.*, [1957] 2 Q.B. 55 (C.A.); *Fowler v. Fowler*, [1949] O.W.N. 244 (C.A.); but seemingly *contra* in criminal cases: see *R. v. Harris*, [1927] 2 K.B. 587 (C.C.A.).
62. See *Phillips v. Ford Motor Co. of Can.*, [1971] 2 O.R. 637, 663 (C.A.).
63. See Hammelmann, "Expert Evidence" (1947), 10 Mod. L. Rev. 32; Ploscowe, "The Expert Witness in Criminal Cases in France, Germany and Italy" (1935), 2 Law and Contemporary Problems 504; and Schroeder, "Problems Faced by the Impartial Expert Witness in Court; The Continental View" (1961), 34 Temple L.Q. 378.
64. See *e.g.*, Quebec *Code of Civil Procedure*, R.S.Q. 1977, c. C-25, ss. 414-425. Compare also the position of assessors in admiralty cases at common law where expert evidence on matters within the sphere of the assessors cannot be led by the parties: see *Halsbury's Laws of England*, 4th ed., vol. 1, para. 443, at p. 283. For Canadian adoption of the English approach, see: *Montreal Harbour Comm. v. The Universe* (1906), 10 Ex. C.R. 305; and *Fraser v. Aztec* (1920), 20 Ex. C.R. 39.
65. See 2 Wigmore, *Evidence* (Chad. Rev.), s. 563.
66. See Beuscher, "The Use of Experts by the Courts" (1941), 54 Harv. L.R. 1105.
67. Fed. Rules Evid., Rule 706, 28 U.S.C.A. But see Wright, *Federal Practice and Procedure: Criminal*, pp. 229-33 to the effect that the rule in federal criminal cases is seldom used.

desirable compromise with the civil law system, since the parties' experts are forced to testify in the face of the testimony of another expert who bears "the accolade flowing from a judicial appointment."[68] As DeParcq, commenting on a similar provision in the Uniform Rules, said:

> Although the rules purport to allow the parties to call other experts of their own, they might just as well save their money. The testimony of the court-appointed expert will be accepted as gospel, while any other expert testimony will be sound and fury, signifying nothing.[69]

This may or may not be true, as the parties may feel that the court's appointed expert is in a preferred evidentiary position to one called by a party. In England, despite similar rules of the Supreme Court permitting the appointment of independent court experts on the application of the parties,[70] the power is seldom used. Lord Denning, M.R. commented in *Re Saxton:*

> . . . neither side has applied for the court to appoint a court expert. It is said to be a rare thing for it to be done. I suppose that litigants realize that the court would attach great weight to the report of a court expert: and are reluctant thus to leave the decision of the case so much in his hands. If his report is against one side, that side will wish to call its own expert to contradict him and then the other side will wish to call one too. So it would only mean that the parties would call their own experts as well. In the circumstances the parties usually prefer to have the judge decide on the evidence of experts on either side, without resort to a court expert.[71]

In 1970 the Law Reform Committee in England considered provisions for the appointment of court experts and concluded that the introduction of a "general 'court expert' system is not desirable."[72] The Committee concluded that its recommendations with respect to the simultaneous disclosure by the parties of experts' reports would obviate the need for court-appointed experts. It found the following objections to such a system compelling:

> [The exchange of experts' reports] we think, will eliminate the need for oral expert testimony except on matters upon which there is room for a genuine difference of expert opinion or where the expert's opinion has to be based upon facts which are in dispute between the parties and of which the true version will only be ascertained in the course of the hearing of the oral evidence of witnesses of fact. The role of a court expert in either type of case presents great practical difficulties. The first problem is the choice of expert. What voice are the parties to have in his selection if they are unable to agree upon who should be appointed? How is the judge to assess the validity of their objections to particular appointees nominated by the court? Next, how is the expert once appointed to inform himself of the facts upon which to base his report? If they are in controversy it would be for the judge to find the facts, not for the expert to hear and determine disputed matters of evidence. His report would have to await the judge's findings. The alternative of inviting him to report in advance on various hypotheses of fact would run the risk that the correct hypothesis, which

---

68. Per Hincks, J., in dissent in *Scott v. Spanjer Bros. Inc.*, 298 F. 2d 928, 933 (2d Cir., 1962).
69. DeParcq, "The Uniform Rules of Evidence: A Plaintiff's View" (1956), 40 Minn. L. Rev. 301, 334.
70. Rules of Supreme Court, 1982, Order 40, Rules 1-6.
71. [1962] 3 All E.R. 92, 95.
72. Seventeenth Report of the Law Reform Committee, *Evidence of Opinion and Expert Evidence*, Cmnd. 4489 (1970), p. 31, fn. 4.

would be known only at the conclusion of the evidence, had not been stated. Finally, there is the problem of the use to be made of his report. Plainly it would be contrary to our system of administering justice if it were final and conclusive on the matters of expertise with which it dealt, without giving to the parties an opportunity in open court to persuade the judge that it was wrong. Is the court expert to be called at the trial to be cross-examined by any party who wishes to do so? And, if so, are the parties to be entitled to call expert evidence in rebuttal?[73]

The Advisory Committee for the Federal Rules in the United States, on the other hand, wrote:

> The practice of shopping for experts, the venality of some experts, and the reluctance of many reputable experts to involve themselves in litigation, have been matters of deep concern. Though the contention is made that court appointed experts acquire an aura of infallibility to which they are not entitled, . . . the trend is increasingly to provide for their use. While experience indicates that actual appointment is a relatively infrequent occurrence, the assumption may be made that the availability of the procedure in itself decreases the need for resorting to it. The ever-present possibility that the judge may appoint an expert in a given case must inevitably exert a sobering effect on the expert witness of a party and upon the person utilizing his services.[74]

7. EXCHANGE OF EXPERTS' REPORTS

In 1953 a Committee in England under the chairmanship of Lord Evershed[75] considered the matter of the exchange of experts' reports and made the following recommendations:

> **289.** In certain classes of cases the evidence of expert witnesses is necessary to explain the working of a machine or describe some process or other technical matter. Without their assistance counsel might not be able even to explain the case to the Court. At present, the reports and proofs and also the plans and drawings of such experts are privileged. They are not disclosed until the expert goes into the witness box except perhaps in the course of cross-examination. Much time is frequently wasted in cross-examination by counsel trying to understand what the expert witness for the other party is really saying and mastering the technical details of his evidence. A party is apt to rely on his expert's evidence as producing an element of surprise. This often leads to a waste of time and does not assist the Court in coming to an accurate decision as to the facts. The element of surprise is no doubt good tactics under the Rules as they exist at present and on the principles generally adopted today in contesting cases. In our view this element of surprise does not conduce to decisions in accordance with the true facts. The more this element is eliminated, the more correct is likely to be the judgment of the Court. It is, therefore, eminently desirable that each party should know what is the expert evidence to be called for the other side.

---

73. *Ibid.*, at p. 8, s. 14. And see Report of the Ontario Attorney General's Committee on *Medical Evidence in Court in Civil Cases* (1965) reviewing the methods of appointing experts in other jurisdictions and rejecting the idea of selection of experts by the court.
74. Advisory Committee's Note, Fed. Rules Evid., Rule 706, 28 U.S.C.A., pp. 517-18.
75. *Final Report of the Committee on Supreme Court Practice and Procedure (Evershed Committee Report)*, Cmnd. 8878 (1953), 97.

290. We recommend that the evidence of an expert should not be receivable in evidence unless a copy of his report has been made available for inspection by the other side at least ten days before the trial, unless for special reasons the Court or a Judge otherwise orders. This Rule should also apply to experts' plans, drawings, and sketches. The majority of the witnesses before us agreed with this suggestion. It would save time at the trial, reduce the element of surprise and in some cases might lead to agreement between the experts, if not in full, at least as to a considerable portion of their reports.

In 1965 the Ontario Attorney General's Committee on Medical Evidence concluded that, in actions involving personal injuries, an exchange of medical reports ought to be a prerequisite to calling medical testimony. They further recommended that to minimize the inconvenience to the medical profession these reports ought to be receivable in evidence without the necessity of calling the doctor as a witness. The Ontario Evidence Act was amended to create:

52.(1) In this section,

"practitioner" means,

    (a) a member of a College as defined in subsection 1(1) of the *Regulated Health Professions Act, 1991*,

    (b) a drugless practitioner registered under the *Drugless Practitioners Act*,

    (c) a person licensed or registered to practise in another part of Canada under an Act that is similar to an Act referred to in clause (a) or (b).

  (2) A report obtained by or prepared for a party to an action and signed by a practitioner and any other report of the practitioner that relates to the action are, with leave of the court and after at least ten days notice has been given to all other parties, admissible in evidence in the action.

  (3) Unless otherwise ordered by the court, a party to an action is entitled, at the time that notice is given under subsection (2), to a copy of the report together with any other report of the practitioner that relates to the action.

  (4) Except by leave of the judge presiding at the trial, a practitioner who signs a report with respect to a party shall not give evidence at the trial unless the report is given to all other parties in accordance with subsection (2).

  (5) If a practitioner is required to give evidence in person in an action and the court is of the opinion that the evidence could have been produced as effectively by way of a report, the court may order the party that required the attendance of the practitioner to pay as costs therefor such sum as the court considers appropriate.[76]

Similar provisions exist in other provinces, though not always restricted to medical experts.

Although the provisions for disclosure of experts' evidence may appear to be novel incursions into the adversary system, they are not without precedent.

---

76. S.O. 1968, c. 36, s. 2; now R.S.O. 1990, c. E.23, s. 52. The Committee's recommendations were first implemented by an amendment to the Evidence Act in 1966 (R.S.O. 1990, c. E.23, s. 52) and the Ontario Rules of Practice were altered accordingly (O. Reg. 207/66, s. 7). The relevant rule was held to be *ultra vires* in *Circosta v. Lilly*, [1967] 1 O.R. 398 (C.A.), since it effected a change in the substantive law. See also s. 657.3 of the Criminal Code.

As early as 1782, in *Folkes v. Chadd*[77] Lord Mansfield permitted the reception of expert opinion evidence from scientists called by the parties. At the first trial, the opinion of Mr. Milne, an engineer, was received as to the cause of the decay of a harbour. The plaintiff obtained a verdict. However, a new trial was granted, on the ground that the defendants were surprised by the doctrine and reasoning of Mr. Milne, and the parties were directed to print and deliver over to the opposite side the opinions and reasonings of the engineers whom they meant to produce on the next trial, so that both sides might be prepared to answer them.

Against compulsory disclosure we have the remarks of Lord Denning:

> . . . the expert should be allowed to give his report fully and frankly to the party who employs him, with all its strength and weakness, and not be made to offer it beforehand as a hostage to the opponent, lest he take unfair advantage of it. In short, it is one of our notions of a fair trial that, except by agreement, one side is not entitled to see the proofs of the other side's witnesses.[78]

PROBLEMS

Problem 1

The defendant was sued for negligence in the operation of his motor vehicle, which negligence allegedly caused death to a pedestrian, the plaintiff's son. There was little dispute concerning the facts. With absolutely no warning the brakes on defendant's vehicle failed due to a break in the mechanism which permitted the fluid in the master cylinder to escape. The defendant, as soon as he realized that the service brake was useless, applied the emergency brake with his left hand keeping his right hand on the steering wheel. The defendant testified that he did not intentionally turn the car but in fact the car did turn, mounted the sidewalk and struck the infant victim. The defendant testified that he couldn't say whether he looked for the emergency brake or automatically reached for it. According to his evidence, "when things came normal again" his car was on the sidewalk. He saw the infant walking in front of him at a distance of about 20 feet. He testified that he did nothing to avoid striking him, that he could have turned his car but that the thought of doing so did not occur to him. The defence pleaded a denial of negligence and a plea of unavoidable accident. The defendant tenders as a witness Mr. Hastings, who is an automotive engineer of high qualifications and great experience who has investigated very many accidents. Hastings is prepared to testify that as a result of a number of tests which he had carried out, he had calculated that there is an interval of time required by a person who is driving a motor car to react to any perceived danger. He would say that the average "reaction time" would be three-quarters of a second and that this standard has been accepted by highway authorities in this country and in other countries. He would say that the reaction time would be lengthened in a case of the brake failing as the first thought is to wonder what happened and what to do about it. He believes the reaction would be lengthened to three seconds. Counsel proposes to ask the witness whether a hypothetical person driving at 20 m.p.h., who would therefore travel some 90 feet during three seconds, could do anything

---

77.   (1782), 3 Dougl. 157, 99 E.R. 589.
78.   *Re Saxton*, [1962] 3 All E.R. 92, 95.

during the reaction period to avoid the danger? Plaintiff's counsel objects. Rule on the objection. Compare the views of the majority and the dissent in *Adam v. Campbell*, [1950] 3 D.L.R. 449 (S.C.C.). And see the views of the English Court of Appeal in *R. v. Oakley* (1979), 70 Cr. App. R. 7. Compare Dixon, J. in *Clark v. Ryan* (1960), 103 C.L.R. 486 (H.C.).

Problem 2

The accused is charged with murder. The Crown proposes to introduce certain letters allegedly written by the accused while he was remanded in custody; these letters are highly incriminating. The Crown has sought your advice as to how he might authenticate these letters. Advise. Are there alternative techniques? See *Pitre v. R.*, [1933] 1 D.L.R. 417 (S.C.C.).

Problem 3

On a charge of murder the defence is insanity. The psychiatrist called by the accused's counsel has described the accused as suffering from a personality disorder at the time of the killing. Defence counsel proposes to ask the psychiatrist whether the personality disorder is a "disease of the mind." The Crown objects. How should the trial judge rule? See *R. v. Simpson* (1977), 35 C.C.C. (2d) 337, 350 (Ont. C.A.) and *Cooper v. R.* (1979), 51 C.C.C. (2d) 129, 143 (S.C.C.). May the Crown psychiatrist testify that in his opinion the personality disorder was not a "disease of the mind"? That the accused was sane at the time of the killing and knew the nature of and intended his act? That the accused is guilty?

Problem 4

The accused was charged with murder. The Crown alleged that he had stabbed the deceased and severed her jugular vein. The defence was accident. The accused maintained that the woman attacked him with a butcher knife and that she was killed accidentally when he was trying to take the knife away from her. The deceased had cuts on the fingers of her right hand and the doctor who testified as to cause of death said that when the right hand was put up to the neck the wounds on the fingers were in the same direction as the wound on the neck. Crown counsel has asked the doctor to give his opinion as to where the victim's hand was when the knife was put on the neck. Defence counsel objects. Rule on the objection. Compare *R. v. Kuzmack* (1954), 110 C.C.C. 338 (Alta. C.A.); affirmed (1955), 111 C.C.C. 1 (S.C.C.) and *Reference re R. v. Truscott* (1967), 62 D.L.R. (2d) 545, 606 (S.C.C.). See also *R. v. Williams* (1985), 44 C.R. (3d) 351 (Ont. C.A.); leave to appeal to S.C.C. refused 44 C.R. (3d) 351n.

Problem 5

The accused was charged with murder. The defence was provocation. The psychiatrist called by the defence testified in chief that the incident as described by the accused would have provoked him as he then suffered a personality problem, namely, a morbid jealousy. In cross-examination the Crown has asked the psychiatrist whether an ordinary man would have reacted in the same fashion. Defence counsel has objected. Rule on the objection. Compare *R. v. Clark* (1974), 22 C.C.C. (2d) 1 (Alta. C.A.) and *R. v. Turner*, [1975] Q.B. 834 (C.A.).

Problem 6

The plaintiff claims damages for an alleged assault by the defendant. The plaintiff maintains his injuries were caused by a baseball bat wielded by defendant. Defendant contends the injuries were caused by a fall for which he was not responsible. The plaintiff has tendered a medical report which states:

> . . . and in conclusion it is my opinion that the nature of the fracture indicates it was sustained by a tremendous blow. It is unlikely that such an injury would result from a fall off a set of stairs.

Admissible? Compare *Kapulica v. Dumancic*, [1968] 2 O.R. 438 (C.A.) and *Forst v. Adelaide Stevedoring Co.* (1940), 64 C.L.R. 538, 573 (H.C.). See also *Smithers v. R.* (1977), 34 C.C.C. (2d) 427 (S.C.C.).

10

Privilege

1. PRIVILEGED COMMUNICATIONS

(a) Introduction

Evidentiary rules respecting privilege differ from the rules we have so far examined in that the earlier rules were, largely, designed to promote an approximation to truth; the rules we are about to examine clearly operate to restrict the search for truth and must, therefore, be justified by some other value. Rand, J. in *R. v. Snider*[1] wrote of privilege:

> It requires as its essential condition that there be a public interest recognized as overriding the general principle that in a Court of justice every person and every fact must be available to the execution of its supreme functions.

R. v. GRUENKE
[1991] 3 S.C.R. 263, 67 C.C.C. (3d) 289, 8 C.R. (4th) 368

[The accused was convicted of first degree murder. The Crown's theory was that the accused had enlisted the aid of her boyfriend in the planning and commission of the murder, which she committed, to stop the victim's sexual harassment of her and to benefit from the provisions of his will. The evidence of the accused's pastor and the lay counsellor, which directly supported the Crown's theory, was ruled admissible at trial. The communications between the accused, the pastor and the lay counsellor took place when the lay counsellor, on hearing of the victim's death two days earlier, visited the accused. When the accused began speaking of her involvement in the murder, the pastor was called and the conversation continued. The accused unsuccessfully appealed her conviction.]

LAMER, C.J. (LA FOREST, SOPINKA, CORY, MCLACHLIN, STEVENSON and IACOBUCCI, JJ. concurring):—

. . . .

This case requires the Court to consider whether a common law prima facie privilege for religious communications should be recognized or whether claims of privilege for such communications should be dealt with on a case-by-case basis.

. . . .

Given that the Wigmorean criteria (for privilege) play a central role in this case, I will set out the 'test' below for ease of reference (Wigmore, *Evidence in Trials at Common Law*, vol. 8, McNaughton Revision, para. 2285):

(1) The communications must originate in a confidence that they will not be disclosed.

(2) This element of confidentiality must be essential to the full and satisfactory maintenance of the relation between the parties.

---

1.   [1954] 4 D.L.R. 483, 486 (S.C.C.)

(3) The relation must be one which in the opinion of the community ought to be sedulously fostered.

✳ (4) The injury that would inure to the relation by the disclosure of the communications must be greater than the benefit thereby gained for the correct disposal of litigation.

Analysis

Before delving into an analysis of the issues raised by this appeal, I think it is important to clarify the terminology being used in this case. The parties have tended to distinguish between two categories: a "blanket", prima facie, common law, or "class" privilege on the one hand, and a "case-by-case" privilege on the other. The first four terms are used to refer to a privilege which was recognized at common law and one for which there is a prima facie presumption of inadmissibility (once it has been established that the relationship fits within the class) unless the party urging admission can show why the communications should not be privileged (i.e., why they should be admitted into evidence as an exception to the general rule). Such communications are excluded not because the evidence is not relevant, but rather, because there are overriding policy reasons to exclude this relevant evidence. Solicitor-client communications appear to fall within this first category. The term "case-by-case" privilege is used to refer to communications for which there is a prima facie assumption that they are not privileged, i.e., are admissible. The case-by-case analysis has generally involved an application of the "Wigmore test", which is a set of criteria for determining whether communications should be privileged (and therefore not admitted) in particular cases. In other words, the case-by-case analysis requires that the policy reasons for excluding otherwise relevant evidence be weighed in each particular case.

Throughout these reasons, I will be using the terms "class privilege" and prima facie privilege to refer to the first category of communications and will generally use the term "case-by-case privilege" to refer to the second category of communications. I should note that some writers tend to use the term "privileged communications" or "privilege" only in relation to communications which are class-based or prima facie inadmissible. I will be using the term "privilege" in relation to both types of communications.

. . . .

Common Law, prima facie Privilege

A prima facie privilege for religious communications would constitute an exception to the general principle that all relevant evidence is admissible. Unless it can be said that the policy reasons to support a class privilege for religious communications are as compelling as the policy reasons which underlay the class privilege for solicitor-client communications, there is no basis for departing from the fundamental "first principle" that all relevant evidence is admissible until proven otherwise.

In my view, the policy reasons which underlay the treatment of solicitor-client communications as a separate class from most other confidential communications, are not equally applicable to religious communications. The prima facie protection for solicitor-client communications is based on the fact that the relationship and the communications between solicitor and client are essential to the effective operation of the legal system. Such communications are inextricably linked with the very system which desires the disclosure of the communication. In my view, religious communications, notwithstanding their social importance, are not inextricably linked with the justice system in the way that solicitor-client communications surely are.

. . . .

Having found no common law, prima facie privilege for religious communications, I will consider whether such communications can be excluded in particular cases by applying the Wigmore criteria on a case-by-case basis.

2. Case-by-Case Privilege

In *Re Church of Scientology and The Queen (No. 6)* the Ontario Court of Appeal recognized the existence of a "priest and penitent" privilege determined on a case-by-case basis, having regard to the Wigmore criteria. This approach is consistent with the approach taken by this Court in *Slavutych v. Baker*, and is, in my view, consistent with a principled approach to the question which properly takes into account the particular circumstances of each case. This is not to say that the Wigmore criteria are now "carved in stone", but rather that these considerations provide a general framework within which policy considerations and the requirements of fact-finding can be weighed and balanced on the basis of their relative importance in the particular case before the court. Nor does this preclude the identification of a new class on a principled basis. Furthermore, a case-by-case analysis will allow courts to determine whether, in the particular circumstances, the individual's freedom of religion will be imperilled by the admission of the evidence.

. . . .

Having found that religious communications can be excluded in particular cases where the Wigmore criteria are satisfied, I turn now to the question of whether the communications involved in this case satisfy the Wigmore criteria.

Application of the Wigmore Criteria

In my opinion, a consideration of the Wigmore criteria and the facts of this case reveals that the communications between the appellant, Pastor Thiessen and Janine Frovich were properly admitted at trial. In my view, these communications do not even satisfy the first requirement; namely, that they originate in a confidence that they will not be disclosed. Leaving aside the other components of the Wigmore test, it is absolutely crucial that the communications originate with an expectation of confidentiality (in order for those communications to be qualify as "privileged" and to thereby be excluded from evidence). Without this expectation of confidentiality, the raison d'être of the privilege is missing.

In the case at bar, there is evidence that Ms. Gruenke's communications to Pastor Thiessen and Ms. Frovich did not originate in a confidence that they would not be disclosed. The testimony of Pastor Thiessen and Janine Frovich indicates that they were unclear as to whether they were expected to keep confidential what Ms. Gruenke had told them about her involvement in the murder. As was stated by Twaddle J.A. in the Court of Appeal judgment at p. 300, "there was no evidence that the accused Gruenke made her admissions to them in the confident belief that they would be disclosed to no one". Ms. Gruenke did not approach Ms. Frovich and the Pastor on the basis that the communications were to be confidential. In fact, Ms. Frovich initiated the meeting and Ms. Gruenke testified that she saw no harm in speaking to Janine Frovich because she had already made up her mind to turn herself in to the police and "take the blame". In my view, the Court of Appeal accurately described these communications as being made more to relieve Ms. Gruenke's emotional stress than for a religious or spiritual purpose. I note that my view is based on the parties' statements and behaviour in relation to the communication and not on the lack of a formal practice of "confession" in the Victorious Faith Centre Church. While the existence of a formal practice of "confession" may well be a strong indication that the parties expected the communication to be confidential, the lack of such a formal practice is not, in and of itself, determinative.

The communications in question do not satisfy the first Wigmore criterion and their admission into evidence does not infringe Ms. Gruenke's freedom of religion. As I have stated above, whether an individual's freedom of religion will be infringed by the admission of religious communications will depend on the particular facts of each case. In the case at bar, there is no such infringement. I would dismiss the appeal.

L'Heureux-Dubé, J., Gonthier, J. concurring, agreed with the majority that the appeal should be dismissed, substantially for the reasons given. However, they would prefer, for utilitarian reasons, to recognize a class privilege for pastor-penitent communications. They concluded:

> In my view, it is more in line with the rationales identified earlier, the spirit of the Charter and the goal of assuring the certainty of the law, to recognize a pastor-penitent category of privilege in this country. If our society truly wishes to encourage the creation and development of spiritual relationships, individuals must have a certain amount of confidence that their religious confessions, given in confidence and for spiritual relief, will not be disclosed. Not knowing in advance whether his or her confession will be afforded any protection, a penitent may not confess, or may not confess as freely as he or she otherwise would. Both the number of confessions and their quality will be affected. The special relationship between clergy and parishioners may not develop, resulting in a chilling effect on the spiritual relationship within our society. In that case, the very rationale for the pastor-penitent privilege may be defeated.

However, L'Heureux-Dubé, J. and Gonthier, J. decided that in the circumstances of this particular case, the communications did not originate in the confidence that they would not be disclosed and therefore the communications were not covered by such a privilege.

We will later further consider Wigmore's case-by-case approach and also the impact of the Charter. We first examine existing class privileges.

(b) Solicitor-Client Privilege

> . . . the first duty of an attorney is to keep the secrets of his client.[2]

In the 16th and 17th centuries the "obligations of honour among gentlemen" were advanced as the basis for a general privilege from disclosure of communications made in confidence. Members of the legal profession qualified as gentlemen and, accordingly, from the earliest times they were permitted the objection.[3] By the end of the 18th century, this basis for a privilege was rejected by the courts as too obstructive to their search for truth, but a new rationale, pertinent only to the attorney, was established. The classic statement of the new rationale is that of Brougham, L.C. in *Greenough v. Gaskell:*

> The foundation of this rule is not difficult to discover. It is not (as has sometimes been said) on account of any particular importance which the law attributes to the business of legal professors, or any particular disposition to afford them protection, though certainly it may not be very easy to discover why a like privilege has been refused to others, and especially to medical advisers.
>
> But it is out of regard to the interests of justice, which cannot be upholden, and to the administration of justice, which cannot go on, without the aid of men skilled in jurisprudence, in the practice of the Courts, and in those matters affecting rights and obligations which form the subject of all judicial proceedings. If the privilege did not exist at all, every one would be thrown upon his own legal resources; deprived of all professional assistance, a man would not venture to consult any skilful person, or would only dare to tell his counsellor half his case.[4]

And Jessel, M.R. later explained it as:

---

2.   Per Gaselee, J., in *Taylor v. Blacklow* (1836), 132 E.R. 401, 406.

3.   See *Berd v. Lovelace* (1576-77), 21 E.R. 33. See generally 8 Wigmore, *Evidence* (McNaughton Rev.), s. 2286.

4.   (1833), 39 E.R. 618, 620-21 (Ch. Div.), approved in *Solosky v. R.* (1979), 50 C.C.C. (2d) 495, 506 (S.C.C.).

The object and meaning of the rule is this: That as, by reason of the complexity and difficulty of our law, litigation can only be properly conducted by professional men, it is absolutely necessary that a man, in order to prosecute his rights or to defend himself from an improper claim, should have recourse to the assistance of professional lawyers, and it being so absolutely necessary, it is equally necessary, to use a vulgar phrase, that he should be able to make a clean breast of it to the gentleman whom he consults with a view to the prosecution of his claim, or the substantiating his defence against the claim of others; that he should be able to place unrestricted and unbounded confidence in the professional agent, and that the communications he so makes to him should be kept secret, unless with his consent (for it is his privilege, and not the privilege of the confidential agent), that he should be enabled properly to conduct his litigation. That is the meaning of the rule.[5]

The privilege now belongs to the client, not the attorney, and protects him from the disclosure of any confidential communications made by him, or his agent, to his solicitor, or communications by the solicitor in response, while the client was engaged in seeking legal advice.

Stephen, J. amplified Lord Brougham's remarks to deal with the situation where the client is actually seeking assistance for a criminal purpose as opposed to seeking legal advice:

The reason on which the rule is said to rest cannot include the case of communications, criminal in themselves, or intended to further any criminal purpose, for the protection of such communications cannot possibly be otherwise than injurious to the interests of justice, and to those of the administration of justice. Nor do such communications fall within the terms of the rule. A communication in furtherance of a criminal purpose does not "come into the ordinary scope of professional employment."[6]

To displace the privilege, a mere allegation of criminal purpose or fraud is not sufficient; there must be evidence from which the judge can infer the illegal purpose.[7]

Consider the following views favouring and opposing the privilege. J.C. McRuer, in his Royal Commission Inquiry into Civil Rights,[8] justified the privilege:

Without the solicitor and client privilege the whole structure of our adversary system of administering justice would collapse, for the object of that system is that the rights of all persons shall be submitted with equal force to the courts. The only way that the imbalance between the learned and the unlearned, the wise and the foolish, can be redressed is that every man's case be brought before the courts with as nearly equal ability as possible. If a lawyer is to give useful service to his client, he must be free to learn the whole of his client's case. The basis of the privilege between solicitor and client is not, therefore, that the relationship is confidential but that confidentiality is necessary to insure that the public, with safety, may substitute legal advisers in their place instead of having to conduct their own cases and advise themselves.

But Jeremy Bentham argued against the privilege:

---

5.   In *Anderson v. Bank of B.C.* (1876), 2 Ch. D. 644, 649 (C.A.).
6.   In *R. v. Cox* (1884), 14 Q.B.D. 153, 167.
7.   See *Re Goodman and Carr and M.N.R.*, [1968] 2 O.R. 814 (H.C.), and *R. v. Giguere* (1978), 44 C.C.C. (2d) 525, 529-30 (Que. S.C.).
8.   Province of Ontario, Vol. 2, Report No. I (1968), at p. 819.

"A counsel, solicitor, or attorney, cannot conduct the cause of his client" (it has been observed) "if he is not fully instructed in the circumstances attending it: but the client" (it is added) "could not give the instructions *with safety*, if the facts confided to his advocate were to be disclosed." Not with safety? So much the better. To what object is the whole system of penal law directed, if it be not that no man shall have it in his power to flatter himself with the hope of safety, in the event of his engaging in the commission of an act which the law, on account of its supposed mischievousness, has thought fit to prohibit? The argument employed as a reason against the compelling such disclosure, is the very argument that pleads in favour of it.[9]

Notice that the client's communication, whether oral or written, is privileged whenever legal advice is sought thereby, whether or not litigation was then contemplated. With respect to communications from third parties to the client's solicitor, however, a limitation was early insisted on by the courts. In *Wheeler v. Le Marchant*, Jessel, M.R. wrote:

The actual communication to the solicitor by the client is of course protected, and it is equally protected whether it is made by the client in person or is made by an agent on behalf of the client, and whether it is made to the solicitor in person or to a clerk or subordinate of the solicitor who acts in his place and under his direction. Again, the evidence obtained by the solicitor, or by his direction, or at his instance, even if obtained by the client, is protected if obtained after litigation has been commenced or threatened, or with a view to the defence or prosecution of such litigation. So, again, a communication with a solicitor for the purpose of obtaining legal advice is protected though it relates to a dealing which is not the subject of litigation, provided it be a communication made to the solicitor in that character and for that purpose. But what we are asked to protect here is this. The solicitor, being consulted in a matter as to which no dispute has arisen, thinks he would like to know some further facts before giving his advice, and applies to a surveyor to tell him what the state of a given property is, and it is said that the information given ought to be protected because it is desired or required by the solicitor in order to enable him the better to give legal advice. It appears to me that to give such protection would not only extend the rule beyond what has been previously laid down, but beyond what necessity warrants.[10]

Communications from third parties, for example private investigators, insurance adjusters, medical advisers, to the client's solicitor in anticipation of litigation is seen in Canada to be embraced within the solicitor-client privilege, though the purpose underlying its protection is obviously quite different.[11]

Clearly not all documents in a solicitor's possession are privileged from disclosure. Only those which were created for the purpose of obtaining legal advice can be characterized as solicitor-client communications.[12] If a client has certain items of evidence which may be subpoenaed or seized by search warrant, he cannot avoid those processes by simply depositing them with his solicitor.[13]

---

9. "Rationale of Judicial Evidence" (1827), 7 The Works of Jeremy Bentham, 475 (Bowring ed., 1842) quoted in 8 Wigmore, *Evidence* (McNaughton Rev.), s. 2291, p. 550.

10. (1881), 17 Ch. D. 675, 682, relied on in *Re Goodman and Carr and M.N.R., supra*, note 7.

11. See the excellent discussion on the difference in the case note by S.N. Lederman in (1976), 54 Can. Bar Rev. 422.

12. See generally, Cross, *Evidence*, 5th ed., pp. 284-86 re multiple purposes of communications.

13. See, *e.g., Re B.X. Dev. and R.* (1976), 31 C.C.C. (2d) 14, 17 (B.C.C.A.).

On the other hand, the fact that a document was not initially produced *solely* for the purpose of legal advice does not deny the possibility of privilege if that was also an important purpose. Robertson, C.J.O., in *Blackstone v. Mutual Life Assurance Co.*, stated:

> . . . it is not essential to the validity of the claim of privilege that the document for which privilege is claimed should have been written, prepared or obtained solely for the purpose of, or in connection with, litigation then pending or anticipated. It is sufficient if that was the substantial, or one of the substantial, purposes then in view.[14]

For the communication to be privileged, the client must be seeking legal advice from one who is, or who the client reasonably believes to be,[15] professionally qualified to practice law.[16] On the other hand, the fact that one party to the communication is professionally qualified does not automatically make the communication privileged; it must be *legal* advice that is being sought. For example, in *Canary v. Vested Estates*[17] the plaintiffs sought to examine for discovery one Brougham, a director of the defendant who was also its solicitor. Brougham resisted the application on the basis that he had acted in the transaction in his legal capacity. MacDonald, C.J.B.C. observed that the character of the particular work performed must be looked at:

> The fact that a person is by profession a solicitor and is intrusted with and performs duties which can be and usually are, performed by an official, servant or agent of a company does not render him immune from examination on discovery if he performs those duties. In this particular transaction I am inclined to believe that the defendant company is advised to take refuge behind one who in reality was an agent or servant engaged for this particular negotiation along with his associate Austin. He was not clothed for this particular transaction with the professional duties of a solicitor by the defendants. Mr. Brougham, as agent or servant or agent *ad hoc* of the defendants being in possession of knowledge which is relevant to the issues herein and which is necessary for the proper and final determination of the matters in dispute, I think must submit to be examined as applied for.[18]

More recently, Lord Denning has observed:

> The law relating to discovery was developed by the Chancery courts in the first half of the 19th century. At that time nearly all legal advisers were in independent practice on their own account. Nowadays it is very different. Many barristers and solicitors are employed as legal advisers, whole time, by a single employer. Sometimes the employer is a great commercial concern. At other times it is a government department or a local authority. It may even be the government itself, like the Treasury Solicitor and his staff. In every case these legal advisers do legal work for their employer and for no one else. They are paid, not by fees for each piece of work, but by a fixed annual salary. They are, no doubt, servants or agents

---

14. [1944] 3 D.L.R. 147, 149 (Ont. C.A.). Compare *Mitchell v.C.N.R.* (1973), 38 D.L.R. (3d) 581, 587 (N.S.S.C.), that the *main* purpose must be obtaining advice. See *Alfred Crompton Amusement Machines Ltd. v. Commissioners of Customs & Excise (No. 2)*, [1973] 2 All E.R. 1169, 1183 (H.L.) leaving the question open.

15. *R. v. Choney* (1908), 17 Man. R. 467 (C.A.): police officer pretended to be agent of accused's solicitor and communications held privileged.

16. See *Naujokat v. Bratushesky*, [1942] 2 W.W.R. 97, 107 (Sask. C.A.) and *U.S. v. Mammoth Oil Co.*, [1925] 2 D.L.R. 966 (Ont. C.A.) and compare *Morrison-Knudsen Co. v. B.C. Hydro* (1971), 19 D.L.R. (3d) 726 (B.C.S.C.).

17. [1930] 3 D.L.R. 989 (B.C.S.C.).

18. *Ibid.*, at p. 990.

of the employer. For that reason the judge thought that they were in a different position from other legal advisers who are in private practice. I do not think this is correct. They are regarded by the law as in every respect in the same position as those who practise on their own account. The only difference is that they act for one client only, and not for several clients. They must uphold the same standards of honour and of etiquette. They are subject to the same duties to their client and to the court. They must respect the same confidences. They and their clients have the same privileges. I have myself in my early days settled scores of affidavits of documents for the employers of such legal advisers. I have always proceeded on the footing that the communications between the legal advisers and their employer (who is their client) are the subject of legal professional privilege; and I have never known it questioned. There are many cases in the books of actions against railway companies where privilege has been claimed in this way. The validity of it has never been doubted. I speak, of course, of their communications in the capacity of legal advisers. It does sometimes happen that such a legal adviser does work for his employer in another capacity, perhaps of an executive nature. Their communications in that capacity would not be the subject of legal professional privilege. So the legal adviser must be scrupulous to make the distinction. Being a servant or agent too, he may be under more pressure from his client. So he must be careful to resist it. He must be as independent in the doing of right as any other legal adviser.[19]

Recently in Canada the courts have extended the application of the privilege so that it may be effective at an earlier time than the introduction of the privileged materials as evidence. In a number of cases[20] it has been recognized that an application to quash a search warrant may be made when the purpose of issuing the warrant was to allow seizure of documents believed "to afford evidence" when such documents are privileged, since the same could not afford evidence at trial. This led some to suggest that the privilege had become a rule of property rather than a rule of evidence,[21] but the Supreme Court of Canada has recently denied that development. In *Solosky v. R.*[22] the appellant, an inmate of a Federal penitentiary, sought a declaration that "properly identified items of correspondence directed to and received from his solicitor shall henceforth be regarded as privileged correspondence and shall be forwarded to their respective destinations unopened." The appellant relied on the "trend" seen in the search warrant cases but the court noted:

> His mail is opened and read, not with a view to its use in a proceeding, but by reason of the exigencies of institutional security. All of this occurs within prison walls and far from a Court or *quasi*-judicial tribunal. It is difficult to see how the privilege can be engaged, unless one wishes totally to transform the privilege into a rule of property, bereft of an evidentiary basis.

---

19. *Alfred Crompton Amusement Machines Ltd. v. Commr. of Customs & Excise (No. 2)*, [1972] 2 All E.R. 353, 376 (C.A.). See also *Re Girouard and R.* (1982), 68 C.C.C. (2d) 261 (B.C.S.C.) leaving open the question of whether communications between the Attorney General and Crown counsel are subject to solicitor-client privilege.
20. For a list of citations see *Solosky v. R.* (1980), 50 C.C.C. (2d) 495, 507.
21. See Chasse, "The Solicitor-Client Privilege and Search Warrants" (1977), 36 C.R.N.S. 349. And see Kasting, "Recent Developments in the Canadian Law of Solicitor-Client Privilege" (1978), 24 McGill L.J. 115.
22. *Supra*, note 20.

... the appellant is seeking in this appeal something well beyond the limits of the privilege, even as amplified in modern cases.[23]

The client is entitled to restrain disclosure of the communication by the solicitor but should his communication be overheard or intercepted or afterwards stolen, the communication may be proved by other evidence. This rather curious result perhaps stems from a remark by Parke, B. for whom the reasonableness of such a result was self-evident:

> Where an attorney intrusted confidentially with a document communicates the contents of it, or suffers another to take a copy, surely the secondary evidence so obtained may be produced. Suppose the instrument were even stolen, and a correct copy taken, would it not be reasonable to admit it?[24]

Professor Wigmore later offered this justification:

> The law provides subjective freedom for the client by assuring him of exemption from its processes of disclosure against himself or the attorney or their agents of communication. This much, but no more, is necessary for the maintenance of the privilege. Since the means of preserving secrecy of communication are largely in the client's hands and since the privilege is a derogation from the general testimonial duty and should be strictly construed, it would be improper to extend its prohibition to third persons who obtain knowledge of the communications. One who overhears the communication, whether with or without the client's knowledge, is not within the protection of the privilege. The same rule ought to apply to one who surreptitiously reads or obtains possession of a document in original or copy.[25]

When privilege has attached to a document it remains attached for the benefit of the client and for his successors; in other words, "as a general rule, one may say once privileged, always privileged."[26] It is recognized, however, that the privilege may cease to exist if it can be demonstrated that the party who asserts it has no longer an interest to protect. For example, in *R. v. Dunbar*[27] the co-accused had been tried for murder along with one Bray; Bray was acquitted and the co-accused convicted. At the trial, communications by Bray to his solicitor to the effect that the co-accused had no knowledge of the killings would be privileged and could not be used to contradict Bray's testimony that the co-accused had done the killings. On a new trial, however, such communications though initially privileged would be admissible as the admission by Bray would assist the co-accused and could not injure Bray.[28]

---

23. *Ibid.*, at p. 509.
24. *Lloyd v. Mostyn* (1842), 152 E.R. 558, 560 (Exch. Ct.).
25. 8 Wigmore, *Evidence* (McNaughton Rev.), s. 2326, quoted with approval in *R. v. Kotapski* (1981), 66 C.C.C. (2d) 78, 81 (Que. S.C.). To the same effect see *R. v. Dunbar* (1982), 68 C.C.C. (2d) 13, 42 (Ont. C.A.); and *Re Girouard and R., supra*, note 19.
26. Lindley, M.R. in *Calcraft v. Guest*, [1898] 1 Q.B. 759, 761 (C.A.).
27. *Supra*, note 25, at p. 44.
28. And see *R. v. Barton*, [1973] 1 W.L.R. 115, seemingly approved in *Dunbar*, that suggests a discretion in a trial judge to deny the privilege when the communication might enable a man to establish his innocence. See also *R. v. Speid* (1983), 43 O.R. (2d) 596 (C.A.).

DESCÔTEAUX v. MIERZWINSKI
[1982] 1 S.C.R. 860, 28 C.R. (3d) 289, 70 C.C.C. (2d) 385

The judgment of the court was delivered by

LAMER J.:— A citizen who lies about his financial means in order to obtain legal aid is committing a crime. This appeal concerns the right of the police to be authorized by a search warrant to search a legal aid bureau and seize the form filled out by the citizen at his interview, for purposes of proving that this crime was committed. This issue raises several others, including, in particular, the scope of and procedures for exercising the authority to search lawyers' offices, in view of the confidential nature of their clients' files. This appeal will also give everyone an opportunity to note the deficiencies in the law in this area and the limited ability of the courts to compensate for them since their role is not primarily legislative.

. . . .

In the Superior Court

After the documents had been seized and sealed, Mr. Descôteaux and the legal aid bureau (Le Centre communautaire juridique de Montréal) presented to a judge of the Superior Court, District of Montreal, a motion for the issuance of a writ of *certiorari* requesting that the seizure be quashed on the grounds of nullity and requesting the Superior Court Judge to order the justice of the peace to return the sealed envelope and its contents to them.

The motion was dismissed, but the judge amended the wording of the warrant, stating that [translation] "the words 'other documents concerning this case' should be struck out and no longer regarded as forming part of the said search warrant".

The Superior Court Judge stated that he was of the view that solicitor-client privilege could be invoked as soon as confidentiality was threatened, "without waiting until the person or persons disregarding the privilege attempted to tender the information thus obtained as evidence". He found, however, that the documents seized were not privileged since they had been prepared before the solicitor-client relationship came into existence.

. . . .

In the Court of Appeal

The Court of Appeal adopted the conclusions of the Superior Court Judge, together with his reasons [16 C.R. (3d) 188]. To these Bélanger J.A. added on behalf of the court that in any event solicitor-client privilege could not have operated to protect the communication, since the latter was precisely what had been resorted to in order to mislead a representative of the legal aid bureau. On that matter, he stated the following (translation) [at p. 192]:

> In the case at bar the communications or documents that are alleged to be confidential are those referred to in the charge as having been used in the commission of the offence in question. Apart from common law principles, they are no more privileged than if the same information and documents had been used to mislead the lawyer himself in order to fraudulently obtain his services on special terms. In either case I do not think that false communications made to the eventual victim who will have to bear the cost of the services are confidential in any way. In short, a communication made to a representative of the Commission des services juridiques [Legal Services Commission] is in no way confidential if it is an element of an offence committed to the latter's prejudice, since in such circumstances there is no confidentiality between solicitor and client.

I think that at this point I should state my findings in the case at bar; I shall give reasons for them later.

In my view, it was correctly decided that it is not necessary to wait for the trial or preliminary inquiry at which the communication is to be adduced or sought in evidence before raising its confidentiality.

. . . .

The right to confidentiality

It is not necessary to demonstrate the existence of a person's right to have communications with his lawyer kept confidential. Its existence has been affirmed numerous times and was recently reconfirmed by this court in *Solosky v. The Queen*, [1980] 1 S.C.R. 821 at p. 839, where Dickson J. stated:

> One may depart from the current concept of privilege and approach the case on the broader basis that (i) *the right to communicate in confidence with one's legal adviser is a fundamental civil and legal right, founded upon the unique relationship of solicitor and client*, and (ii) a person confined to prison retains all of his civil rights, other than those expressly or impliedly taken from him by law.

(Emphasis added.) There is no denying that a person has a right to communicate with a legal adviser in all confidence, a right that is "founded upon the unique relationship of solicitor and client" (*Solosky, supra*). It is a personal and extra-patrimonial right which follows a citizen throughout his dealings with others. Like other personal, extra-patrimonial rights, it gives rise to preventive or curative remedies provided for by law, depending on the nature of the aggression threatening it or of which it was the object. Thus a lawyer who communicates a confidential communication to others without his client's authorization could be sued by his client for damages; or a third party who had accidentally seen the contents of a lawyer's file could be prohibited by injunction from disclosing them. (I am dealing here generally with the effects of the right to confidentiality. In its present state, the rule of evidence, which I shall discuss later, would not prohibit a third party from making such a disclosure: see 8 Wigmore, *Evidence*, §2326, pp. 633-4 (McNaughton Rev. 1961.)

. . . .

There is no doubt that this right belonging to a person in his dealings with others, including the State, is part of our Quebec public law as well as of the common law.

Although we recognize numerous applications of it today, the right to confidentiality did not first appear until the 16th century, and then did so as a rule of evidence: see, *inter alia, Berd v. Lovelace* (1577), Cary 62, 21 E.R. 33; *Dennis v. Codrington* (1580), Cary 100, 21 E.R. 53.

The rule of evidence is well known; it has often been stated. This court referred to it again recently in *Solosky, supra*. That decision sets out the conditions precedent to the existence of the privilege, as well as its limits and exceptions. It should be pointed out that the substantive conditions precedent to the existence of the privilege, which the judges have gradually established and defined, are in fact the substantive conditions precedent to the existence of the right to confidentiality, the former being merely the earliest manifestation of the latter. There is no need to list those conditions exhaustively here or to review all the nuances that have been developed by the courts over the years. It will be sufficient to review them in broad outline and to emphasize certain aspects of particular relevance to this appeal.

The following statement by Wigmore (8 Wigmore, *Evidence*, §2292, p. 554 (McNaughton Rev. 1961)), of the rule of evidence is a good summary, in my view, of the substantive conditions precedent to the existence of the right of the lawyer's client to confidentiality:

> Where legal advice of any kind is sought from a professional legal adviser in his capacity as such, the communications relating to that purpose, made in confidence

by the client, are at his instance permanently protected from disclosure by himself or by the legal adviser, except the protection be waived.

Seeking advice from a legal adviser includes consulting those who assist him professionally (for example, his secretary or articling student) and who have as such had access to the communications made by the client for the purpose of obtaining legal advice.

There are exceptions. It is not sufficient to speak to a lawyer or one of his associates for everything to become confidential from that point on. The communication must be made to the lawyer or his assistants in their professional capacity; the relationship must be a professional one at the exact moment of the communication. Communications made in order to facilitate the commission of a crime or fraud will not be confidential either, regardless of whether or not the lawyer is acting in good faith.

The substantive rule

Although the right to confidentiality first took the form of a rule of evidence, it is now recognized as having a much broader scope, as can be seen from the manner in which this court dealt with the issues raised in *Solosky, supra*.

. . . .

It is quite apparent that the court in that case applied a standard that has nothing to do with the rule of evidence, the privilege, since there was never any question of testimony before a tribunal or court. The court in fact, in my view, applied a substantive rule, without actually formulating it, and, consequently, recognized implicitly that the right to confidentiality, which had long ago given rise to a rule of evidence, had also since given rise to a substantive rule.

It would, I think, be useful for us to formulate this substantive rule, as the judges formerly did with the rule of evidence; it could, in my view, be stated as follows:

1. The confidentiality of communications between solicitor and client may be raised in any circumstances where such communications are likely to be disclosed without the client's consent.

2. Unless the law provides otherwise, when and to the extent that the legitimate exercise of a right would interfere with another person's right to have his communications with his lawyer kept confidential, the resulting conflict should be resolved in favour of protecting the confidentiality.

3. When the law gives someone the authority to do something which, in the circumstances of the case, might interfere with that confidentiality, the decision to do so and the choice of means of exercising that authority should be determined with a view to not interfering with it except to the extent absolutely necessary in order to achieve the ends sought by the enabling legislation.

4. Acts providing otherwise in situations under para. 2 and enabling legislation referred to in para. 3 must be interpreted restrictively.

The rule of evidence

The rule of evidence is formulated by Cross (*Cross on Evidence*, 5th ed. (1979), p. 282), as follows:

In civil and criminal cases, confidential communications passing between a client and his legal adviser need not be given in evidence by the client and, without the client's consent, may not be given in evidence by the legal adviser in a judicial proceeding. . .

The rule of evidence does not in any way prevent a third party witness (I am referring here to someone other than an agent of the client or the lawyer) from introducing in evidence confidential communications made by a client to his lawyer. It is important to note, however, that before allowing such evidence to be introduced and in determining to what extent to allow it, the judge must satisfy himself, through the application of the substantive rule (No. 3), that what is being sought to be proved by the communications is important to the outcome of the case and that there is no reasonable alternative form of evidence that could be used for that purpose.

Confidentiality in the case at bar

In the case at bar the principal issue is to determine when the solicitor-client relationship, which confers the confidentiality protected by the substantive rule and the rule or evidence, arises.

The Superior Court Judge, as we have seen, was of the view that this relationship, and consequently the right to confidentiality, did not arise until the legal aid applicant had been accepted, that is, until the retainer was established.

When dealing with the right to confidentiality it is necessary, in my view, to distinguish between the moment when the retainer is established and the moment when the solicitor-client relationship arises. The latter arises as soon as the potential client has his first dealings with the lawyer's office in order to obtain legal advice.

The items of information that a lawyer requires from a person in order to decide if he will agree to advise or represent him are just as much communications made in order to obtain legal advice as any information communicated to him subsequently. It has long been recognized that even if the lawyer does not agree to advise the person seeking his services, communications made by the person to the lawyer or his staff for that purpose are none the less privileged: *Minter v. Priest*, [1930] A.C. 558; *Phipson on Evidence*, 12th ed. (1976), p. 244, para. 590; 8 Wigmore, *Evidence* §2304, pp. 586-7 (McNaughton Rev. 1961).

. . . .

Conclusion

In summary, a lawyer's client is entitled to have all communications made with a view to obtaining legal advice kept confidential. Whether communications are made to the lawyer himself or to employees, and whether they deal with matters of an administrative nature such as financial means or with the actual nature of the legal problem, all information which a person must provide in order to obtain legal advice and which is given in confidence for that purpose enjoys the privileges attached to confidentiality. This confidentiality attaches to all communications made within the framework of the solicitor-client relationship, which arises as soon as the potential client takes the first steps, and consequently even before the formal retainer is established.

There are certain exceptions to the principle of the confidentiality of solicitor-client communications, however. Thus communications that are in themselves criminal or that are made with a view to obtaining legal advice to facilitate the commission of a crime will not be privileged, *inter alia*.

The fundamental right to communicate with one's legal adviser in confidence has given rise to a rule of evidence and a substantive rule. Whether through the rule of evidence or the substantive rule, the client's right to have his communications to his lawyer kept confidential will have an effect when the search warrant provided for in s. 443 of the *Criminal Code* is being issued and executed.

Thus the justice of the peace has no jurisdiction to order the seizure of documents that would not be admissible in evidence in court on the ground that they are privileged (the rule of evidence).

Before authorizing a search of a lawyer's officer for evidence of a crime, the justice of the peace should refuse to issue the warrant unless he is satisfied that there is no reasonable alternative to the search, or he will be exceeding his jurisdiction (the substantive rule). When issuing the warrant, to search for evidence or other things, he must in any event attach terms of execution to the warrant designed to protect the right to confidentiality of the lawyer's clients as much as possible.

Applying these principles to the case at bar, I have arrived at the following conclusions.

First, all information contained in the form that applicants for legal aid must fill out is provided for the purpose of obtaining legal advice, is given in confidence for that purpose and, consequently, is subject to the applicant's fundamental right to have such communications kept confidential and, as such, is protected by the rule of evidence and the substantive rule.

It is alleged in the information laid that the communications made by Ledoux with respect to his financial means are criminal in themselves since they constitute the material element of the crime charged. This is an exception to the principle of confidentiality and these communications are accordingly not protected (this does not mean that we are expressing an opinion as to the validity of the allegations in the information). However, since the allegation concerns only the information dealing with the applicant's financial means, all other information on the form remains confidential.

Since the part of the form dealing with Ledoux's financial situation was as an exception admissible in evidence, the justice of the peace had jurisdiction to order its seizure.

Acting within his jurisdiction with regard to the rule of evidence, the justice of the peace also exercised his discretion to issue a warrant, judicially having regard to the substantive rule. As a result of the refusal of the legal aid bureau's staff and lawyers to disclose to the investigators the contents of the form, or of the oral statements made to them by Ledoux concerning his financial situation, there was no reasonable alternative to a search. How otherwise could the investigators ascertain that Ledoux's statements were fraudulent? Perhaps, as a result of their investigation, they knew that Ledoux was not eligible for legal aid in view of his financial means, but the crime of which they suspected him and concerning which they were entitled to continue the investigation was that of having concealed his means, ineligibility not being a crime in itself.

I do not know whether the justice of the peace was the originator of the procedure followed for the search and seizure or whether there was an agreement between counsel. In any event, the manner of proceeding in the case at bar was, again having regard to the substantive rule, proper and acceptable and the justice of the peace was or would have been by law empowered to and justified in making it a condition of granting the warrant.

There is one problem, however. The form seized may contain privileged information. I am of the view that the justice of the peace could have, in the presence of everyone — the Crown, the representative of the bar and the legal aid representative — opened the envelope and examined the form to determine whether it contained anything confidential and, if not, dealt with it in accordance with the law like any other thing seized. If he had discovered that the form contained confidential information, he could have (at least this is one of the ways of proceeding) photocopied the part relevant to the applicant's financial means and dealt with that portion of the form like any other thing seized by placing it on the file. He could have placed the original of the document in a sealed envelope also placed on file, ordering that it not be examined without a judge's order.

In the case at bar, if the information on the back of the form in fact consists of professional notes, as indicated by the form, they are confidential. This would still have to be verified, however. As for the front of the form, most of the information requested is relevant to the applicant's financial situation, although some only indirectly. This is not the case, however, with the information required on the parts of the form that I have identified with the letters A and B, where the information essentially concerns the "nature of the case" or the "probable existence of a right". I am therefore of the view that the judge, after verifying the back of the form, and if he ascertains that it contains professional notes, should have the front of the form, except parts A and B, photocopied, and deal with the photocopies and the original of the document as suggested, that is, place the photocopies on the court file and place the original in a sealed envelope, place the envelope on the file and order the court staff not to open it or allow it to be opened without a judge's order. The sealed envelope will eventually be returned to the legal aid bureau, unless Marcellin Ledoux disputes the authenticity of the photocopy should an inquiry or trial be held; were Ledoux to do so, the judge presiding at the trial or the preliminary inquiry would be fully justified in opening the envelope and allowing those concerned to see the form, since Ledoux would then, in my view, have himself by his allegations made it impossible to reconcile his right to confidentiality for the better administration of criminal justice.

Before concluding, I should state that the procedure will vary from one case to another. Here the good faith of counsel was in no way at issue since, as alleged by the police, they were not accomplices of their client but rather his victims. Clearly different execution procedures should be provided for where the information laid alleges that the lawyer participated in the crime. I would also like to add that the justice of the peace from whom a warrant to search a lawyer's office is being sought, if he is not a judge by profession, would be well advised, although in no way obliged to do so, to refer the applicant to a judge of a court of criminal jurisdiction or even a judge of a superior court of criminal jurisdiction.

For these reasons I would dismiss this appeal and refer the matter back to the justice of the peace, ordering him to deal with the envelope and its contents as stated above.

Appeal dismissed.

R. v. LADOUCEUR
[1992] B.C.J. No. 2854 (B.C.S.C.)

[The accused was charged with sexual assault and choking. The accused issued a subpoena to compel the attendance of Dianne Wiedemann, Crown Counsel with the Ministry of Attorney General for British Columbia, to give evidence in his defence. Ms. Wiedemann previously had conduct of this prosecution; in the course of her preparation for an earlier trial date, she interviewed the complainant and wrote a letter to defence counsel disclosing what evidence she expected the complainant to give in addition to her testimony at the preliminary hearing. The accused wanted Ms. Wiedemann's evidence to prove a previous inconsistent statement of the complainant under the procedures set out in s. 11 of the Canada Evidence Act. Counsel on Ms. Wiedemann's behalf, Mr. Gourlay, moved to set aside the subpoena.]

DONALD J.:—

. . . .

The complainant, in her evidence in chief, told the jury that the accused choked her with a rag during the sexual assault. Defence counsel challenged her identification of Exhibit 3, a brown and white checked tea towel, as the rag used in the incident. He confronted her with a previous statement given to Ms. Wiedemann in which she allegedly described the colour of the rag as "yellowish". The complainant denied that she gave that description to Ms. Wiedemann. The disclosure letter dated March 8, 1991 from Ms. Wiedemann to Mr. R.A. Ross, counsel for the accused, contains the following passage:

In addition to the testimony given at the Preliminary Hearing, we anticipate that L. W. will describe the rag used to choke her as squarish, ripped, of woven material, and perhaps yellowish. At this point L.W. has not viewed the items retrieved by Corporal Harrison from the truck.

Operating on the assumption that Ms. Wiedemann obtained this information from the complainant, Mr. Ross issued Ms. Wiedemann a subpoena in order to prove the earlier out of court statement by her testimony.

. . . .

At the outset of his argument, Mr. Gourlay conceded that no question of privilege arose in these circumstances and that the issue is a matter for the court's discretion. He submitted that to uphold the subpoena would offend public policy by setting a dangerous precedent which allowed the calling of Crown counsel to testify as to what witnesses told them in preparation for court. Public policy considerations include:

1. administrative inconvenience in Crown counsel offices and disruption in Court scheduling — lengthening of trials and creating adjournments — if the prosecutor conducting the case must retire from it because he or she has been called as a witness;
2. the inhibiting effect on discussions between prosecutor and Crown witness if they know that the prosecutor may be called to testify as to what the witness said during their interview; and
3. the changes that may have to result in the way witnesses are prepared for court and how disclosure is communicated to the defence. Since some inconsistencies are bound to surface while reviewing a witness's evidence, prosecutors will be reluctant to take notes of the interviews for fear of having to produce them later. Prosecutors may also take a more guarded and restricted approach with disclosure to protect against the possibility of being called as a witness.

Mr. Gourlay referred to *R. v. Stinchcombe* regarding the obligation on the Crown to make full disclosure as a Charter requirement in criminal cases. . . . Given this heightened responsibility, counsel argued against a result which will increase the risk that prosecutors may become involved as witnesses in their cases.

Neither counsel was able to find a case directly on point. That suggests that this problem arises infrequently and that when it does, the lawyers deal with it other than by forcing the defence to subpoena the prosecutor. I cannot see why counsel in this case did not avoid the necessity of calling Ms. Wiedemann by agreeing to the fact that the complainant told her the rag was yellow. Each case must be decided on its own facts and the precedential effect of the decision will be conditioned by those facts. In the case at bar, none of the perils described by Mr. Gourlay actually happened: no change of counsel was necessary and nothing spoken between the prosecutor and Crown witness was revealed which had not already been disclosed to the defence. All that occurred was the verification of a "will say" statement. A careful prosecutor like Ms. Wiedemann can be relied upon to give an accurate "will say" statement after interviewing a witness. I am surprised that the Crown chose not to admit as a fact that the complainant made the statement to Ms. Wiedemann. With respect, this is not the right case to test the reach of subpoenas issued to prosecutors.

SMITH v. JONES
[1999] 1 S.C.R. 455, 22 C.R. (5th) 203, 132 C.C.C. (3d) 225

[The accused was charged with aggravated sexual assault on a prostitute. His counsel referred him to a psychiatrist hoping that it would be of assistance in the preparation of the defence or with submissions on sentencing in the event of a guilty plea. Counsel informed the accused that the consultation was privileged in the same way as a consultation with him would be. During his interview with the psychiatrist, the accused described in considerable detail his plan to kidnap, rape and kill prostitutes. The psychiatrist informed defence counsel that in his opinion the accused was a dangerous individual who would, more likely than not, commit future offences unless he received sufficient treatment. The accused later pled guilty to the included offence of aggravated assault. The psychiatrist phoned defence counsel to inquire about the status of the proceedings and learned that his concerns about the accused would not be addressed in the sentencing hearing. The psychiatrist commenced this action for a declaration that he was entitled to disclose the information he had in his possession in the interests of public safety. He filed an affidavit describing his interview with the accused and his opinion based upon the interview. The trial judge ruled that the public safety exception to the solicitor-client privilege and doctor-patient confidentiality released the psychiatrist from his duties of confidentiality and concluded that he was under a duty to disclose to the police and the Crown both the statements made by the accused and his opinion based upon them. The Court of Appeal allowed the accused's appeal but only to the extent that the mandatory order was changed to one permitting the psychiatrist to disclose the information to the Crown and police.]

CORY, J. (L'HEUREUX-DUBÉ, GONTHIER, MCLACHLIN, IACOBUCCI and BASTARACHE, JJ. concurring):—

. . . .

Dr. Smith reported that Mr. Jones described in considerable detail his plan for the crime to which he subsequently pled guilty. It involved deliberately choosing as a victim a small prostitute who could be readily overwhelmed. He planned to have sex with her and then to kidnap her. He took duct tape and rope with him, as well as a small blue ball that he tried to force into the woman's mouth. Because he planned to kill her after the sexual assault he made no attempt to hide his identity. Mr. Jones planned to strangle the victim and to dispose of her body in the bush area near Hope, British Columbia. He was going to shoot the woman in the face before burying her to impede identification. He had arranged time off from his work and had carefully prepared his basement apartment to facilitate his planned sexual assault and murder. He had told people he would be going away on vacation so that no one would visit him and he had fixed dead bolts on all the doors so that a key alone would not open them. Mr. Jones told Dr. Smith that his first victim would be a "trial run" to see if he could "live with" what he had done. If he could, he planned to seek out similar victims. He stated that, by the time he had kidnapped his first victim, he expected that he would be "in so deep" that he would have no choice but to carry out his plans.

. . . .

Just as no right is absolute so too the privilege, even that between solicitor and client, is subject to clearly defined exceptions. The decision to exclude evidence that would be both relevant and of substantial probative value because it is protected by the solicitor-client privilege represents a policy decision. It is based upon the importance to our legal system in general of the solicitor-client privilege. In certain circumstances, however, other societal values must prevail.

. . . .

Quite simply society recognizes that the safety of the public is of such importance that in appropriate circumstances it will warrant setting aside solicitor-client privilege. What factors should be taken into consideration in determining whether that privilege should be displaced?

There are three factors to be considered: First, is there a clear risk to an identifiable person or group of persons? Second, is there a risk of serious bodily harm or death? Third, is the danger imminent? Clearly if the risk is imminent, the danger is serious.

These factors will often overlap and vary in their importance and significance. The weight to be attached to each will vary with the circumstances presented by each case, but they all must be considered. As well, each factor is composed of various aspects, and, like the factors themselves, these aspects may overlap and the weight to be given to them will vary depending on the circumstances of each case. Yet as a general rule, if the privilege is to be set aside the court must find that there is an imminent risk of serious bodily harm or death to an identifiable person or group.

(a) Clarity

What should be considered in determining if there is a clear risk to an identifiable group or person? It will be appropriate and relevant to consider the answers a particular case may provide to the following questions: Is there evidence of long range planning? Has a method for effecting the specific attack been suggested? Is there a prior history of violence or threats of violence? Are the prior assaults or threats of violence similar to that which was planned? If there is a history of violence, has the violence increased in severity? Is the violence directed to an identifiable person or group of persons? This is not an all-encompassing list. It is important to note, however, that as a general rule a group or person must be ascertainable. The requisite specificity of that identification will vary depending on the other factors discussed here.

The specific questions to be considered under this heading will vary with the particular circumstances of each case. Great significance might, in some situations, be given to the particularly clear identification of a particular individual or group of intended victims. Even if the group of intended victims is large considerable significance can be given to the threat if the identification of the group is clear and forceful. For example, a threat, put forward with chilling detail, to kill or seriously injure children five years of age and under would have to be given very careful consideration. In certain circumstances it might be that a threat of death directed toward single women living in apartment buildings could in combination with other factors be sufficient in the particular circumstances to justify setting aside the privilege. At the same time, a general threat of death or violence directed to everyone in a city or community, or anyone with whom the person may come into contact, may be too vague to warrant setting aside the privilege. However, if the threatened harm to the members of the public was particularly compelling, extremely serious and imminent, it might well be appropriate to lift the privilege. All the surrounding circumstances will have to be taken into consideration in every case.

In sum, the threatened group may be large but if it is clearly identifiable then it is a factor — indeed an essential factor — that must be considered together with others in determining whether the solicitor-client privilege should be set aside. A test that requires that the class of victim be ascertainable allows the trial judge sufficient flexibility to determine whether the public safety exception has been made out.

(b) Seriousness

The "seriousness" factor requires that the threat be such that the intended victim is in danger of being killed or of suffering serious bodily harm. Many persons involved in criminal justice proceedings will have committed prior crimes or may be planning to commit crimes in the future. The disclosure of planned future crimes without an element of violence would be an insufficient reason to set aside solicitor-client privilege because of fears for public safety. For the public safety interest to be of sufficient importance to displace solicitor-client privilege, the threat must be to occasion serious bodily harm or death.

It should be observed that serious psychological harm may constitute serious bodily harm.

(c) Imminence

The risk of serious bodily harm or death must be imminent if solicitor-client communications are to be disclosed. That is, the risk itself must be serious: a serious risk of serious bodily harm. The nature of the threat must be such that it creates a sense of urgency. This sense of urgency may be applicable to some time in the future. Depending on the seriousness and clarity of the threat, it will not always be necessary to impose a particular time limit on the risk. It is sufficient if there is a clear and imminent threat of serious bodily harm to an identifiable group, and if this threat is made in such a manner that a sense of urgency is created. A statement made in a fleeting fit of anger will usually be insufficient to disturb the solicitor-client privilege. On the other hand, imminence as a factor may be satisfied if a person makes a clear threat to kill someone that he vows to carry out three years hence when he is released from prison. If that threat is made with such chilling intensity and graphic detail that a reasonable bystander would be convinced that the killing would be carried out the threat could be considered to be imminent. Imminence, like the other two criteria, must be defined in the context of each situation.

In summary, solicitor-client privilege should only be set aside in situations where the facts raise real concerns that an identifiable individual or group is in imminent danger of death or serious bodily harm. The facts must be carefully considered to determine whether the three factors of seriousness, clarity, and imminence indicate that the privilege cannot be maintained. Different weights will be given to each factor in any particular case. If after considering all appropriate factors it is determined that the threat to public safety outweighs the need to preserve solicitor-client privilege, then the privilege must be set aside. When it is, the disclosure should be limited so that it includes only the information necessary to protect public safety.

The disclosure of the privileged communication should generally be limited as much as possible. The judge setting aside the solicitor-client privilege should strive to strictly limit disclosure to those aspects of the report or document which indicate that there is an imminent risk of serious bodily harm or death to an identifiable person or group. In undertaking this task consideration should be given to those portions of the report which refer to the risk of serious harm to an identifiable group; that the risk is serious in that it involves a danger of death or serious bodily harm; and that the serious risk is imminent in the sense given to that word above. The requirement that the disclosure be limited must be emphasized. For example, if a report contained references to criminal behaviour that did not have an imminent risk of serious bodily harm but disclosed, for example, the commission of crimes of fraud, counterfeiting or the sale of stolen goods, those references would necessarily be deleted.

[In applying the criteria set out the majority found sufficient clarity, seriousness and imminence to satisfy the Public Safety Exception to Solicitor-Client Privilege.]

. . . .

Dr. Smith chose to bring a legal action for a declaration that he was entitled to disclose the information he had in his possession in the interests of public safety. However, this is not the only manner in which experts may proceed. Although it is true that this procedure may protect the expert from legal consequences, there may not always be time for such an action. In whatever action is taken by the expert, care should be exercised that only that information which is necessary to alleviate the threat to public safety is revealed.

It is not appropriate in these reasons to consider the precise steps an expert might take to prevent the harm to the public. It is sufficient to observe that it might be appropriate to notify the potential victim or the police or a Crown prosecutor, depending on the specific circumstances.

. . . .

The order of the British Columbia Court of Appeal is affirmed. . . . Dr. Smith seeks to recover his costs. He should not have them. This case raised the issue of when solicitor-client privilege can be set aside. It has been found that, because of the danger posed by Mr. Jones to the public, solicitor-client privilege, which Mr. Jones had every right to believe attached to Dr. Smith's report, was set aside. This case arises in the context of criminal proceedings and the result may well affect the sentence imposed on Mr. Jones. It would be unfair and unjust in the circumstances to impose the burden of costs on Mr. Jones and I would not do so.

MAJOR, J. (LAMER, C.J. and BINNIE, J. concurring) dissenting):—

. . . .

In my opinion a limited exception which does not include conscriptive evidence against the accused would address the immediate concern for public safety in this appeal while respecting the importance of the privilege. I do not read Cory J.'s reasons as imposing that limitation. This approach will in my view foster a climate in which dangerous individuals are more likely to disclose their disorders, seek treatment and pose less danger to the public.

. . . .

I agree with Cory J. that the standard of a "clear, serious and imminent" danger is the appropriate test for disclosure of privileged communications. There are compelling public policy reasons for limiting disclosure to cases of clear and imminent danger. The record confirms that Mr. Jones only disclosed his secret plans because his lawyer had properly advised him that anything he said to Dr. Smith would be confidential. If Cory J. is correct in holding that, in cases where the necessity test is met, the privilege is overridden to the extent of allowing disclosure of self-incriminating evidence, the result might endanger the public more than the public safety exception would protect them.

If defence counsel cannot freely refer clients, particularly dangerous ones, to medical or other experts without running a serious risk of the privilege being set aside, their response will be not to refer clients until after trial, if at all. This could result in dangerous people remaining free on bail for long periods of time, undiagnosed and untreated, presenting a danger to society.

The chilling effect of completely breaching the privilege would have the undesired effect of discouraging those individuals in need of treatment for serious and dangerous conditions from consulting professional help. In this case the interests of the appellant and more importantly the interests of society would be better served by his obtaining treatment. This Court has recognized that mental health, including those suffering from potentially dangerous illnesses, is an important public good: see *M. (A.) v. Ryan*, [1997] 1 S.C.R. 157, at para. 27.

Although the appellant did not go to Dr. Smith to seek treatment, it is obvious that he is more likely to get treatment when his condition is diagnosed than someone who keeps the secret of their illness to themselves. It seems apparent that society will suffer by imposing a disincentive for patients and criminally accused persons to speak frankly with counsel and medical experts retained on their behalf.

As appealing as it may be to ensure that Mr. Jones does not slip back into the community without treatment for his condition, completely lifting the privilege and allowing his confidential communications to his legal advisor to be used against him in the most detrimental ways will not promote public safety, only silence. For this doubtful gain, the Court will have imposed a veil of secrecy between criminal accused and their counsel which the solicitor-client privilege was developed to prevent. Sanctioning a breach of privilege too hastily erodes the workings of the system of law in exchange for an illusory gain in public safety.

While I agree with Cory J. that the danger in this case is sufficiently clear, serious and imminent to justify some warning to the relevant authorities, I find that the balance between the public interests in safety and the proper administration of justice is best struck by a more limited disclosure than the broader abrogation of privilege he proposes. In particular, Cory J. endorses the trial judge's limitation of Dr. Smith's affidavit to those portions which indicate an imminent risk of serious harm or death. In the result, conscriptive evidence such as the accused's confession can be disclosed. In my opinion, the danger posed by the accused can be adequately addressed by the expression of that opinion by Dr. Smith without disclosing the confession.

. . . .

Courts are obligated to craft the narrowest possible exception to privilege which accomplishes this purpose. Accordingly, Dr. Smith should be permitted to warn the relevant authorities (i.e., the Attorney General and sentencing judge) that Mr. Jones poses a threat to prostitutes in the Vancouver area. However, Dr. Smith should only disclose his opinion and the fact that it is based on a consultation with Mr. Jones. Specifically, he should not disclose any communication from the accused relating to the circumstances of the offence, nor should he be permitted to reveal any of the personal information which the trial judge excluded from his original order for disclosure.

I agree with Cory J. that in rare cases where an individual poses an instant risk such that even an ex parte application to the court is not possible, the person reviewing the otherwise privileged information may issue a timely warning to the police. Otherwise, the scope and timing of disclosures should be dealt with by the courts on a case-by-case basis.

. . . .

I would allow the appeal without costs, confirm the entirety of Mr. Jones's communications to Dr. Smith to be privileged, but permit Dr. Smith to give his opinion and diagnosis of the danger posed by Mr. Jones.

R. v. McCLURE
[2001] 1 S.C.R. 445, 40 C.R. (5th) 1, 151 C.C.C. (3d) 321

[The accused was a librarian and teacher at the school attended by J.C. in the mid-1970s. In 1997, the accused was charged with sexual offences against 11 former students. After reading about the accused's arrest, J.C. gave a statement to the police alleging incidents of sexual touching by the accused. His allegations were later added to the indictment. J.C. also brought a civil action against the accused. The accused sought production of J.C.'s civil litigation file to determine the nature of the allegations and to assess his motive to fabricate or exaggerate incidents of abuse. In his first ruling, the trial judge applied the *O'Connor* test and ordered the production of the appellant's civil litigation file for his review. In a second ruling, he granted the accused access to the file but ordered all references to quantum of settlement and fees deleted from the produced file. The trial judge ruled that certain matters of sequence were significant, and not available to the defence without access to J.C.'s file. The order granting access was stayed pending appeal. J.C., who was not a party in the criminal trial, was granted leave to appeal the order to the Supreme Court pursuant to section 40 of the Supreme Court Act.]

MAJOR, J. (McLACHLIN, C.J. and L'HEUREUX-DUBÉ, GONTHIER, IACOBUCCI, BASTARACHE, BINNIE, ARBOUR and LEBEL, JJ. concurring):—

. . . .

There are two useful tests which help to identify when the right to make full answer and defence will prevail over the need for confidentiality. While useful, neither test sufficiently addresses the unique concerns evoked by solicitor-client privilege and, as explained later, more is needed.

The first test originated in *O'Connor*, relative to procedures to govern production of medical or therapeutic records that are in the hands of third parties. Subsequently,

Parliament codified the procedure in ss. 278.1 to 278.9 of the Criminal Code and its constitutionality was upheld in *R. v. Mills*, [1999] 3 S.C.R. 668. The *O'Connor* test and ss. 278.1 to 278.9 of the Criminal Code were created with the sensitivity and unique character of third party therapeutic records in mind. They focus on an individual's privacy interest and not the broader policy objectives underlying the administration of justice.

The other test is the innocence at stake test for informer privilege, see *Leipert*. This test details the circumstances under which the identity of an informer might have to be revealed. The value of reliable informers to the administration of justice has been recognized for a long time, so much so that it too is a class privilege. This explains why the high standard of showing that the innocence of the accused is at stake before permitting invasion of the privilege is necessary. Should the privilege be invaded, the state then generally provides for the protection of the informer through various safety programs, again illustrating the public importance of that privilege. The threshold created by the innocence at stake test comes the closest to addressing the concerns raised in this appeal as it is appropriately high. Both informer privilege and solicitor-client privilege are ancient and hallowed protections.

The Innocence at Stake Test for Solicitor-Client Privilege

In granting the respondent McClure access to the complainant's civil litigation file, the trial judge applied the *O'Connor* test for disclosure of confidential therapeutic records. With respect, this was an error. The appropriate test by which to determine whether to set aside solicitor-client privilege is the innocence at stake test, set out below. Solicitor-client privilege should be set aside only in the most unusual cases. Unless individuals can be certain that their communications with their solicitors will remain entirely confidential, their ability to speak freely will be undermined.

In recognition of the central place of solicitor-client privilege within the administration of justice, the innocence at stake test should be stringent. The privilege should be infringed only where core issues going to the guilt of the accused are involved and there is a genuine risk of a wrongful conviction.

Before the test is even considered, the accused must establish that the information he is seeking in the solicitor-client file is not available from any other source and he is otherwise unable to raise a reasonable doubt as to his guilt in any other way.

By way of illustration, if the accused could raise a reasonable doubt at his trial on the question of mens rea by access to the solicitor-client file but could also raise a reasonable doubt with the defence of alibi and/or identification, then it would be unnecessary to use the solicitor-client file. The innocence of the accused would not be at stake but instead it is his wish to mount a more complete defence that would be affected. On the surface it may appear harsh to deny access as the particular privileged evidence might raise a reasonable doubt, nonetheless, the policy reasons favouring the protection of the confidentiality of solicitor-client communications must prevail unless there is a genuine danger of wrongful conviction.

The innocence at stake test is applied in two stages in order to reflect the dual nature of the judge's inquiry. At the first stage, the accused seeking production of a solicitor-client communication must provide some evidentiary basis upon which to conclude that there exists a communication that could raise a reasonable doubt as to his guilt. At this stage, the judge has to decide whether she will review the evidence.

If the trial judge is satisfied that such an evidentiary basis exists, then she should proceed to stage two. At that stage, the trial judge must examine the solicitor-client file to determine whether, in fact, there is a communication that is likely to raise a reasonable doubt as to the guilt of the accused. It is evident that the test in the first stage (could raise a reasonable doubt) is different than that of the second stage (likely to raise a reasonable doubt). If the second stage of the test is met, then the trial judge should order the production but only of that portion of the solicitor-client file that is necessary to raise the defence claimed.

(1) Stage #1

The first stage of the innocence at stake test for invading the solicitor-client privilege requires production of the material to the trial judge for review. There has to be some evidentiary basis for the request. This is a threshold requirement designed to prevent "fishing expeditions". Without it, it would be too easy for the accused to demand examination of solicitor-client privileged communications by the trial judge. As this request constitutes a significant invasion of solicitor-client privilege, it should not be entered into lightly. On the other hand, the bar cannot be set so high that it can never be met. The trial judge must ask: "Is there some evidentiary basis for the claim that a solicitor-client communication exists that could raise a reasonable doubt about the guilt of the accused?"

It falls to the accused to demonstrate some evidentiary basis for his claim that there exists a solicitor-client communication relevant to the defence he raises. Mere speculation as to what a file might contain is insufficient.

That is then followed by a requirement that the communication sought by the accused could raise a reasonable doubt as to his guilt. This must be considered in light of what the accused knows. It is likely that the accused who, it must be remembered, has had no access to the file sought, may only provide a description of a possible communication. It would be difficult to produce and unfair to demand anything more precise. It is only at stage two that a court determines conclusively that such a communication actually exists.

The evidence sought should be considered in conjunction with other available evidence in order to determine its importance. It is the totality of the evidence that governs. However, when the accused is either challenging credibility or raising collateral matters, it will be difficult to meet the standards required of stage one.

Where an accused fails to show that the information sought could raise a reasonable doubt as to guilt, the solicitor-client privilege prevails.

(2) Stage #2

Once the first stage of the innocence at stake test for setting aside the solicitor-client privilege has been met, the trial judge must examine that record to determine whether, in fact, there exists a communication that is likely to raise a reasonable doubt as to the accused's guilt. The trial judge must ask herself the following question: "Is there something in the solicitor-client communication that is likely to raise a reasonable doubt about the accused's guilt?"

After a review of the evidence of the solicitor-client communication in question, the judge must decide whether the communication is likely to raise a reasonable doubt as to the guilt of the accused. In most cases, this means that, unless the solicitor-client communication goes directly to one of the elements of the offence, it will not be sufficient to meet this requirement. Simply providing evidence that advances ancillary attacks on the Crown's case (e.g., by impugning the credibility of a Crown witness, or by providing evidence that suggest that some Crown evidence was obtained unconstitutionally) will very seldom be sufficient to meet this requirement.

The trial judge does not have to conclude that the information definitely will raise a reasonable doubt. If this were the case, the trial would effectively be over as soon as the trial judge ordered the solicitor-client file to be produced. There would be nothing left to decide. Instead, the information must likely raise a reasonable doubt as to the accused's guilt. Also, upon reviewing the evidence, if the trial judge finds material that will likely raise a reasonable doubt, stage two of the test is satisfied and the information should be produced to the defence even if this information was not argued as a basis for production by the defence at stage one.

In determining whether or not the solicitor-client communication in question is likely to raise a reasonable doubt as to the guilt of the accused, the trial judge should consider that the communication in the solicitor-client file cannot be marginal but must be sufficient to establish the basis for its admission. It is the totality of the evidence then available that the trial judge considers in determining whether it is likely that the evidence can raise a reasonable doubt.

The difficulties described in successfully overcoming solicitor-client privilege illustrate the importance and solemnity attached to it. As described earlier, it is a cornerstone of our judicial system and any impediment to open candid and confidential discussion between lawyers and their clients will be rare and reluctantly imposed.

Application to the Case at Bar

In this case, the litigation file should not have been produced to the defence. With respect, the trial judge erred in using the earlier *O'Connor* test for the production of third party confidential therapeutic records to govern whether the litigation file should have been produced to the defence.

The first stage of the innocence at stake test for solicitor-client privilege was not met. There was no evidence that the information sought by the respondent McClure could raise a reasonable doubt as to his guilt. Even if the chronology of events in this case — i.e. lawyer, police, therapist, civil suit — was unusual, it does not justify overriding solicitor-client privilege. This "unusual" chronology does not rise to a level that demonstrates that the litigation file could raise a reasonable doubt as to guilt and so fails at the first stage.

In addition, the accused would be able to raise the issue of the complainant's motive to fabricate events for the sake of a civil action at trial from another source, simply by pointing out the sequence of events and the fact that a civil action was initiated.

The third party appellant, J.C., could not appeal the interlocutory order for production of his litigation file because he was not a party in the criminal trial. Instead, he applied directly to this Court pursuant to s. 40(1) of the Supreme Court Act for leave to appeal the final order ordering production of his litigation file. This avenue of appeal is unsatisfactory. The usual avenue for appeal should be to the court of appeal of the province. That court has broad powers of review and is the desirable forum for appeals of first instance. This appeal is not the first demonstration of the anomaly of a direct appeal of an interlocutory order to the Supreme Court of Canada. The only apparent method of resolving this problem is by legislative amendment.

The appeal is allowed and the order for production by Hawkins J. is set aside.

For comments on *McClure* see Manson, "Annotation: *R. v. McClure*" (2001), 40 C.R. (5th) 1 and Layton, "*R. v. McClure*: The Privilege on the Pea" (2001), 40 C.R. (5th) 19.

(c) Marital Privilege

(i) *Marital Communications*

The English Evidence Amendment Act of 1853[29] made spouses of parties competent and compellable witnesses in civil proceedings; as discussed earlier, spouses had been incompetent at common law because of their supposed interest in the outcome of the litigation. The Act then went on to provide:

> Section 3. No husband shall be compellable to disclose any communication made to him by his wife during the marriage, and no wife shall be compellable to disclose any communication made to her by her husband during the marriage.

All Canadian jurisdictions have enacted identical or quite similar provisions. Notice, at the outset, that the privilege provided, unlike the case of solicitor-client

---

29.   Commonly referred to as *Lord Brougham's Act*.

communications, belongs to the recipient of the communication rather than to the communicant; "it is a mystery to me why it was decided to give this privilege to the spouse who is a witness."[30]

There is some dispute as to whether such a privilege ever existed at common law. Professor Wigmore maintains the privilege did exist but was seldom recognized since spouses of parties were incompetent as witnesses and it would be an exceptional case when such a communication would be otherwise admissible in proceedings to which neither was a party.[31] The courts, however, could find no authority for an earlier common law privilege and concluded that any protection from disclosure had to be found within the particular words of the statute.[32]

Notice that the legislation protects "*any* communication." Professor Wigmore suggests that this phrase should be construed in the spirit of the "correct principle" and the protection should be limited to *confidential* communications. He writes:

> The essence of the privilege is to protect *confidences* only. This is required by the very nature of this class of privileges. The purpose is to insure subjectively the unrestrained privacy of communication, free from any fear of compulsory disclosure. It follows that if the communication is not intended to be a private one the privilege has no application to it.
>
> . . . .
>
> No justification for such an extension of the privilege has ever been attempted, and it must be supposed that this broad statutory phrasing originated in inadvertence. It is proper enough to maintain (as already noticed) that all marital communications should be presumed to be confidential until the contrary appears; but if the contrary appears, there is no reason for recognizing the privilege.[33]

The Canadian courts, however, have not seen fit to construe the language narrowly[34] and it is apparently available to *all* communications.

The legislation provides that "no husband" and "no wife" shall be compellable to disclose and if the privilege is solely based in statute, and that statute is literally construed, a widow or divorced spouse cannot claim the privilege. Greene, M.R. in *Shenton v. Tyler*[35] noted:

> If my view is right that the only rule that exists is that contained in s. 3 of the Act of 1853, it remains to consider whether, under that section, upon its true construction, the privilege continues to exist after the marriage has come to an end. In my opinion it does not. The section in terms relates only to husbands and wives; and no principle of construction known to me entitles me to read into the section a reference to widowers or widows or divorced persons.[36]

---

30. Echoing the words of Lord Reid in *Rumping v. D.P.P.* (1962), 46 Cr. App. R. 398, 409 (H.L.).

31. 8 Wigmore, *Evidence* (McNaughton Rev.), s. 2333.

32. See *Rumping v. D.P.P., supra*, note 30; and *Shenton v. Tyler*, [1939] 1 Ch. 620 (C.A.) per Greene, M.R.

33. 8 Wigmore, *Evidence* (McNaughton Rev.), s. 2336.

34. See, *e.g., MacDonald v. Bublitz* (1960), 31 W.W.R. 478 (B.C.S.C.).

35. *Supra*, note 32.

36. *Ibid.*, at p. 641. See also to like effect *R. v. Kanester*, [1966] 4 C.C.C. 231 (B.C.C.A.) per MacLean, J.A.; approved [1967] 1 C.C.C. 97n (S.C.C.); and *Layden v. North American Life Assur. Co.* (1970), 74 W.W.R. 266 (Alta. S.C.). Compare *R. v. Cooper (No. 1)* (1974),

It is noteworthy as well that the legislation does not forbid disclosure by the spouse testifying, that spouse is free to choose, nor does it forbid disclosure by third parties who intercept or overhear the communication. In *Rumping v. Director of Public Prosecutions*[37] the appellant had been convicted of murder. At his trial the prosecution had introduced a letter written by the accused to his wife which letter amounted to a confession. The appellant had given the letter to a fellow employee to post but instead it was turned over to the police. The appellant argued that aside from the statute there was a common law rule which forbade disclosure, but the absence of judicial authorities and the wording of the section convinced the House of Lords that the letter was properly receivable. In *R. v. Kotapski*[38] the accused, charged with armed robbery, had prepared for his lawyer a document giving an account of his movements and activities on the day of the robbery. Kotapski, having decided to retain different counsel, instructed his former lawyer to send a copy of the document to Mrs. Kotapski. During the execution of a search warrant of accused's residence the document was seized and at trial was tendered as evidence. Greenberg, J., relying on *Rumping v. Director of Public Prosecutions*, ruled the document was receivable in that

> even if [it] had been transformed into a matrimonial communication when it was sent by the accused's first attorney to Mrs. Kotapski, I have no choice but to admit it into evidence now that it is in the possession of the police, since the so-called privilege of s. 4(3) of the *Canada Evidence Act* avails only in favour of the recipient spouse, if he or she testifies.[39]

This attitude toward receivability of privileged communications through third parties is, of course, consistent with the treatment of solicitor-client communications, and may be justified by Professor Wigmore's analysis that it is up to the party to take the necessary precautions against being overheard.

With the advance in electronic eavesdropping techniques, is Wigmore's analysis sufficient?

In *Lloyd v. R.*[40] the accused, husband and wife, were convicted of conspiracy to traffic in narcotics. Telephone conversations between the spouses were intercepted by the police pursuant to an authorization granted under the Criminal Code, section 178.12,[41] and were received in evidence. The appellants argued that by the conjoint effect of section 178.16(5)[42] of the Criminal Code and section 4(3) of the Canada Evidence Act,[43] the intercepts were inadmissible. Those provisions read:

> 178.16(5) Any information obtained by an interception that, but for the interception would have been privileged, remains privileged and inadmissible as evidence without the consent of the person enjoying the privilege.

---

19 C.C.C. (2d) 135 (Ont. H.C.) re incompetence surviving divorce, distinguishing *Shenton v. Tyler, supra*, note 32.

37.   [1962] 3 All E.R. 256 (H.L.).
38.   *Supra*, note 25.
39.   *Ibid.*, at p. 90. See also *R. v. Armstrong* (1970), 1 C.C.C. (2d) 106 (N.S.C.A.).
40.   (1982), 64 C.C.C. (2d) 169 (S.C.C.).
41.   See now R.S.C. 1985, c. C-46, s. 185.
42.   *Ibid.*, s. 189(6).
43.   R.S.C. 1970, c. E-10 [now R.S.C. 1985, c. C-5].

> 4.(3) No husband is compellable to disclose any communication made to him by his wife during their marriage, and no wife is compellable to disclose any communication made to her by her husband during their marriage.

The majority in the British Columbia Court of Appeal ruled that while there was a privilege in a spouse to divulge or to refuse to divulge the information conveyed, that did not make the information privileged. Hinkson, J.A. wrote:

> In my view, it is not possible to equate the privilege attaching to a communication between solicitor and client with the privilege attaching to the spouse who is the recipient of a matrimonial communication. In the former case it is the information passing from client to solicitor, or *vice versa*, that is privileged. In the latter case the information conveyed is not privileged; the recipient spouse has a right to divulge or refuse to divulge the information conveyed. This right to choose what course to follow may be called a privilege but that does not make the information privileged in respect of which the right to choose is exercised. In short, it is a privilege attaching to a witness, not to the information. That distinction, it seems to me, is pointed up by the specific wording of s-s. (5).[44]

The majority in the Supreme Court of Canada held that this was too narrow a view and reaffirmed its earlier concurrence with the views of Moir, J.A. in *R. v. Jean:*[45]

> So far as I am aware the only conversations to which s-s. (5) could apply are between solicitor and client and husband and wife. The subsection speaks of information that would have been privileged but for the interception. It seems to me that there was no information that was ever privileged *per se* because if the solicitor and client or husband and wife were overheard there was no privilege. What really occurred was a witness was able to decide whether or not the contents of certain communications were to be revealed. In a solicitor-and-client relationship the client could determine whether or not he would permit the conversation between himself and his lawyer to be revealed. The recipient of the conversation between spouses could decide if they would reveal the communication. In both cases if the party who had the right chose to exercise it the communication could be said to be privileged.
>
> In my opinion, we must make the same sort of deductions to make sense of s-s. (5) of s. 178.16 of the *Code.* Parliament must be taken to have legislated sensibly and thus we must give s-s. (5) a sensible meaning. To do so it must be taken to mean that the so-called "privileged information" is that information that a person has a right not to reveal. Then, if it is intercepted by a wiretap or by other means dealt with in Part IV.1 of the *Criminal Code*, it is inadmissible by reason of s-s. (5) of s. 178.16. This follows from the philosophy of the "Invasion of Privacy" legislation which proceeds on the basis that these two types of information are private and if they are disclosed by a lawful intercept the information cannot be revealed in Court.
>
> Here the wife had a right not to reveal what was said to her by her spouse during marriage. The conversation was overheard on a lawful interception. What was heard cannot be revealed where the wife does not choose to reveal it.[46]

In ruling on admissibility, should the courts distinguish spousal communications which discuss previous illegal acts and those which are plans for future illegal acts? If solicitor-client communications in

---

44. (1980), 53 C.C.C. (2d) 121, 130.
45. (1979), 46 C.C.C. (2d) 176 (Alta. C.A.); affirmed (1980), 51 C.C.C. (2d) 192n (S.C.C.).
46. *Ibid.*, at p. 187.

furtherance of a criminal aim are not protected from disclosure, should marital communications be saved?[47]

In *R. v. St. Jean*[48] the accused was charged with incest and, pursuant to section 4(2) of the Canada Evidence Act, the wife was therefore "a competent and compellable witness for the prosecution without the consent of the person charged." An issue on appeal was whether the spouse could refuse to disclose communications made to her by her husband. For the Quebec Court of Appeal, Kaufman, J.A. ruled:

> It seems to me that it would not make sense to make a spouse competent and compellable, only to put severe restrictions on the scope of his or her testimony. Take, for instance, the case of *R. v. Lonsdale*, where a husband was charged with the attempted murder of his wife. The Alberta Court of Appeal, in a clear and succinct opinion . . . held that in virtue of s. 4(4) of the Act the wife was a competent and compellable witness against the accused. No conversations between husband and wife appear to have taken place at the time of the incident, but supposing the husband, while pointing a gun at his wife, would have made certain remarks indicative of his intent to kill her, could it be seriously said that while the wife could describe her husband's actions she could not repeat his words? I think not.
>
> . . . .
>
> It might be said that to so hold would be to reduce the import of s. 4(3) of the Act. That may be so, but this section will still have its application in cases where a spouse is called by the defence, but even here it must be pointed out that the privilege is that of the witness and not the accused's.[49]

The Crown's appeal from accused's acquittal was accordingly allowed and a new trial was ordered. Prepare an argument on behalf of the accused for the Supreme Court of Canada.[50]

R. v. ZYLSTRA
(1995), 41 C.R. (4th) 130, 99 C.C.C. (3d) 477 (Ont. C.A.)

Per Curiam:—This appeal is from the appellant's conviction of sexual assault. The appellant did not testify. Defence counsel elected not to call the appellant's wife as a defence witness upon receiving a ruling from the trial judge relating to the manner in which she would be obliged to assert spousal privilege. The court received an outline of the testimony that the appellant's wife was prepared to give and it is obvious that it is highly relevant to the issues at trial.

. . . .

At the close of the Crown's case, counsel for the appellant asked the trial judge for an advance ruling as to whether this privilege could be asserted. He received a favourable ruling. The argument of the Crown on appeal notwithstanding, we are all of the view that the ruling was correct. The Crown relied upon the judgment of Kaufman J.A. of the Quebec Court of Appeal in *R. v. St. Jean* (1976), 32 C.C.C. (2d) 438. However, we prefer

---

47. Compare cases cited in 8 Wigmore, *Evidence* (McNaughton Rev.), s. 2338(7), 1982 supplement.
48. (1976), 32 C.C.C. (2d) 438 (Que. C.A.).
49. *Ibid.*, at pp. 441 and 444 [citations omitted].
50. See generally, 8 Wigmore, *Evidence* (McNaughton Rev.), s. 2338.

the reasoning of Moir J.A. of the Alberta Court of Appeal in *R. v. Jean* (1979), 7 C.R. (3d) 338, aff'd 51 C.C.C. (2d) 192 (S.C.C). . . . Section 4(3) is unambiguous and can be given its plain meaning without making it subject to any other subsection. It says simply that where a wife or husband is otherwise compellable or competent to give evidence, there is no compulsion to divulge communications with a spouse.

After receiving this favourable ruling, defence counsel asked for a ruling that the Crown not be permitted to ask questions of Mrs. Zylstra in cross-examination that would force her to assert the privilege in front of the jury. He submitted that the assertion of the privilege was not relevant to any issue in the trial, and that if the wife was obliged to rely upon it in the presence of the jury, the jury would invariably conclude that her husband had confessed to her his responsibility in the sexual assault. The trial judge refused to make such a ruling and stated that if the privilege was asserted, it must be before the jury.

Defence counsel then asked the trial judge to assure him that he would instruct the jury that the wife had a statutory right to invoke the privilege and that they were not to draw an inference adverse to her credibility from the fact that she exercised that right. The trial judge stated that he was not prepared to make any comment on this matter and stated that he was precluded from doing so by s. 4(6) of the Act.

. . . .

We do agree that if the privilege was asserted, it should be done in the presence of the jury. To proceed otherwise might have left the jury in some confusion by the failure of Crown counsel to pursue obvious lines of inquiry in cross-examination because they were not aware that the privilege had been asserted. We agree with the Crown on appeal that openness in the trial process is to be preferred. The Supreme Court of Canada has elected for this option when dealing with the problems of prior criminal convictions (*R. v. Corbett* (1988), 41 C.C.C. (3d) 385) and pre-trial publicity (*Dagenais v. Canadian Broadcasting Corp.* (1995), 94 C.C.C. (3d) 289). However, a special instruction is called for. We do not think that s. 4(6) has any application to a spouse who has testified. The Crown appears to concede this. It suggests the following in its factum:

The jury ought then to be instructed with respect to the following points:

(*a*)   *The privilege in s. 4(3) is a statutory privilege which all legally married witnesses are entitled to assert in a trial; and*

(*b*)   The privilege is one that belongs to the witness, not the accused person, and, as such, the decision whether to assert or waive the privilege lies with the witness, not the accused.

In our opinion, the above represents a minimum requirement for a proper jury instruction. Whether or not the jury should be instructed that they can draw an adverse inference from the assertion of the privilege, we leave to another day. The trial judge should have a discretion as to what instruction is appropriate and we are not prepared to lay down a hard and fast rule in a case where no testimony was given.

The error on the part of the trial judge in stating that he was not prepared to make any comment to the jury in the event Mrs. Zylstra invoked the protection of s. 4(3) of the Act caused defence counsel to withdraw her as a witness. Crown counsel conceded on appeal that if we were of the opinion that some instruction was required, he could not rely upon the proviso in s. 686(1)(*b*)(iii) of the *Criminal Code*, . . . as standing in the way of a new trial. Accordingly, the appeal is allowed, the conviction below is set aside and a new trial is ordered.

(ii) *Sexual Intercourse*

In *Russell v. Russell* [51] the House of Lords ruled that spouses were not competent to give evidence of non-access if such evidence would tend to bastardize children born during the marriage. Most Canadian provinces followed the English lead and sought to abolish the rule in *Russell v. Russell*. For example, the Ontario Evidence Act[52] was amended by adding subsection 2 to section 8 to provide:

> **8.**(1) The parties to an action and the persons on whose behalf it is brought, instituted, opposed or defended are, except as hereinafter otherwise provided, competent and compellable to give evidence on behalf of themselves or of any of the parties, and the husbands and wives of such parties and persons are, except as hereinafter otherwise provided, competent and compellable to give evidence on behalf of any of the parties.
>
> (2) Without limiting the generality of subsection (1), a husband or a wife may in an action give evidence that he or she did or did not have sexual intercourse with the other party to the marriage at any time or within any period of time before or during the marriage.

Unfortunately the language chosen to abrogate the rule in *Russell v. Russell* may be interpreted as creating a privilege in a spouse, whether party to the action or not, to unilaterally decide whether or not to testify to sexual intercourse during marriage. No justification can be advanced for this obstruction to the search for truth.

(d) Privilege for Without Prejudice Communications

MIDDELKAMP v. FRASER VALLEY REAL ESTATE BOARD
(1992), 71 B.C.L.R. (2d) 276 (B.C.C.A.)

[The plaintiffs complained to the Director of the Competition Act about the defendant real estate board's conduct. The Director referred the matter to the Attorney General of Canada who proceeded against the board by way of information. There were lengthy negotiations. In the result there was a consent prohibition order in Federal Court. During the negotiations the board and the federal authorities exchanged numerous documents. In the plaintiffs' civil action against the board, the defendant board claimed privilege with respect these documents on the ground that they were exchanged on a without prejudice basis. An order to produce the documents was made. The defendant successfully appealed.]

McEACHERN C.J.B.C. (PROUDFOOT, GIBBS AND HOLLINRAKE JJ.A. concurring):— Mr. Justice Locke has fully stated the facts of this case which I need not repeat. He bases his judgment upon an immunity equivalent to privilege arising out of the interest the public has in the settlement of disputes. While reaching the same conclusion I prefer, with respect, to base my judgment on slightly different grounds. . . .

I have no doubt that it is in the public interest, that parties to disputes should be free to negotiate *Competition Act* matters and other disputes freely, and without fear of later prejudice arising out of the steps taken during efforts to arrange settlements.

---

51.   [1924] A.C. 687 (H.L.).
52.   R.S.O. 1990, c. E.23.

I am, however, hesitant to establish an immunity other than privilege because parties to negotiations, such as the appellant in this case, have no control over without prejudice communications once they are sent off to the other side, and documents of the kind in question in this case can easily find their way into the hands of strangers to the dispute being settled. There is no effective protection against the prejudice caused by such communications unless they are characterized as privileged.

. . . .

Considering the enormous scope of production which is required by our almost slavish adherence to the *Peruvian Guano* principle, the questionable relevance and value of documents prepared for the settlement of disputes, and the public interest, I find myself in agreement with the House of Lords that the public interest in the settlement of disputes generally requires "without prejudice" documents or communications created for, or communicated in the course of, settlement negotiations to be privileged. I would classify this as a " 'blanket', *prima facie*, common law, or 'class' " privilege because it arises from settlement negotiations and protects the class of communications exchanged in the course of that worthwhile endeavour.

In my judgment this privilege protects documents and communications created for such purposes both from production to other parties to the negotiations and to strangers, and extends as well to admissibility, and whether or not a settlement is reached. This is because, as I have said, a party communicating a proposal related to settlement, or responding to one, usually has no control over what the other side may do with such documents. Without such protection, the public interest in encouraging settlements will not be served.

. . . .

I would allow the appeal accordingly.

LOCKE J.A.:— This appeal deals with a litigant's obligation to produce certain documents for inspection prior to a civil trial when those documents were generated in negotiating the resolution of potential criminal charges against him.

. . . .

The trial judge examined the existing law at some length. He decided he was bound by previous authority in this court. He identified two competing issues: the promotion of negotiations leading to compromise, and the desirability of full discovery. He followed the case of *Derco Industries Ltd. v. A.R. Grimwood Ltd.* (1984), 57 B.C.L.R. 395, and ordered production.

. . . .

[There then follows a very thorough review of the jurisprudence in this area in other provinces and in England.]

This claim for protection from production of documents "without prejudice" is often considered to be one that the documents are "privileged" and the cases and writers on occasion classify it as a branch of this doctrine. This is no doubt satisfactory provided it is understood that the claim rests on a very different theoretical base than those other forms which arise because of the relationship between two parties which prohibits admission of their evidence at trial without the consent of the other: legal professional privilege, marital privilege, and concerning landlord and tenant as against disclosure of title deeds, by way of example. Those arise because society deems the relationships to be of such importance that it will not permit their sanctity to be undermined. The "privilege" with which we are concerned here deals not with a relationship but with competing legal interests, both of which are intrinsically meritorious. But as the doctrine we discuss is not a true "privilege" but really a rule of public policy, in my opinion papers leading up to a settlement, no matter how obtained, could not be produced in evidence at all.

Some of the difficulties of dealing with it as a "privilege" are dealt with in an article entitled " 'Without Prejudice' Communications — Their Admissibility and Effect" (1974), 9 U.B.C. Law Review 85, where the author D. Vaver has this to say at p. 107 of his dissertation:

> The undesirability of calling the "without prejudice" rule a "privilege" may also be pointed out in those cases where inadmissibility depends on irrelevancy and where the assertion of a privilege is an impossibility. Suppose that a motor accident arises involving A, B and C. A alleges that B is at fault and B alleges that C is at fault. C compromises with B, but A sues B alone, claiming the accident was solely B's fault. B calls C to testify as to the fact of the offer of compromise. A is unable to object to the evidence on the grounds of privilege, for B and C alone can claim privilege. However, the evidence ought to be excluded on the grounds of irrelevancy, for a compromise *per se* is not evidence of an admission but merely implies a desire to buy peace. If the offer of compromise did contain an admission of liability by C and was thus admissible, "privilege" being waived by B and C, A could not prevent inclusion of the evidence. He could not claim privilege, since privilege is personal to the parties, and the evidence was clearly relevant. It may therefore be seen that there are good reasons for eschewing the use of the description "privilege" in the context of the "without prejudice" rule and for not considering the basis of the rule as one of "privilege".

. . . .

And so it is seen that the overwhelming current of authority is in favour of endorsing the protection from production with the aim of curtailing or shortening litigation. This has been the underlying object. I have laboriously canvassed all these cases to show that the principle has always been accepted from the earliest times. There has been much litigation, but it has all been to define the scope of the doctrine: Does it apply to arbitrations? Does it apply to opinion evidence? Does it apply to lawyers as well as clients? Does it apply when there has been a concluded settlement? And so on. Never has the principle, which is really one example of applying the principle of economy of means, been doubted.

In later times much intellectual powder has been expended in attempting to state the true theoretical basis for the doctrine. *Hoghton v. Hoghton* in 1852, *Underwood v. Cox* in 1912, one judge in *Schetky v. Cochrane* in 1918, *Scott Paper* in 1927, *Waxman* in 1968 and *Rush v. Tomkins* in 1988 have all placed it in the ground of public interest.

I agree with this. It has to my mind the immense advantage of enabling one to balance competing interests not on forms of words but on intrinsic strengths. One is enabled to apply principle to the kaleidoscope of circumstance.

The present case

. . . .

With all respect I cannot in law see one reason why this province, alone in the Commonwealth, should not recognize the overriding importance of this protection from the eyes of a third party. To refuse it is to inhibit and penalize one who wishes to settle. It is easy to envisage a building owner loath to compromise the minor claim of a small subcontractor, because of concern an admission of fact would be held against him in another major subcontractor's proceeding.

All the cases emphasize that no bars should be placed in the way of one who wishes to compromise, and to allow the production is by definition to inhibit. Such barriers to settlement should only be permitted if the other competing interest absolutely demands it.

. . . .

In my view, the guiding principle and one promising the greatest good for the greatest number of disputants is to shield these documents from production.

R. v. PABANI
(1995), 89 C.C.C. (3d) 437

[The accused was convicted of the second degree murder of his wife. The accused and his wife were married in late 1987. By June of 1988 she had moved out of the home because of marital discord and, it appeared, physical abuse by the accused. While the accused and his wife were separated, a mutual friend tried to assist them in reconciling their differences. Statements, in which the accused acknowledged having assaulted his wife previously, were admitted into evidence at trial. The accused argued that these statements should have been ruled inadmissible, on the basis that they were communications covered by the common law privilege pertaining to settlement talks in civil proceedings. The Court decided that the common law privilege was unavailable to the accused.]

FINLAYSON J.A.:—

. . . .

In June of 1988, the wife moved out of the matrimonial home. Efforts were made, however, to mend the broken marriage. Through the mediation of a mutual friend, Muntaz Merali, the appellant and the deceased agreed to meet in the presence of their priest to discuss the future of their relationship. The priest was Nazim Ali Hirani who occupied the office of Moog, the most senior position of a priest in the Ismaili religion. . . .

Three meetings took place with the Moog and Mrs. Hirani at the Hirani home. Throughout, the wife placed four terms as pre-conditions to her return: first, the appellant would have to agree to cease the violence, on this she was adamant; second, the payment of the money owed by the appellant to his father-in-law would have to take place; third, the deceased's social insurance number would have to be returned to her; and fourth, the appellant's family would have to agree to stop speaking swahili in the wife's presence because this was a language she did not understand. The appellant agreed to all of these conditions. He implicitly conceded that there had been violence in the marriage, and although it was not discussed in great length during the meetings with the Moog, the appellant pledged to discontinue this behaviour. The appellant had previously admitted to Merali that there had been violence in the relationship, but said that his wife had made too much of it.

The content of these meetings was allowed as evidence during the trial of the appellant.

. . . .

The law has always encouraged discussion between parties to civil litigation that is directed to settling their differences. To foster the resolution of these disputes, the parties are encouraged to speak freely and without the concern that statements will be used against them in the event that a settlement is not arrived at. . . . Additionally, in matrimonial disputes, the state is more interested in reconciliation than divorce and the rule as to privilege tends to promote the prospects of reconciliation. . . . There is, however, no such common law position recognized by the criminal law. The compromise of criminal charges has only recently been recognized within the structure of "plea bargaining". At common law, the settling for valuable consideration of felonies and the withdrawing or stifling of prosecutions for misdemeanours could amount to compounding those offences and become criminal offences themselves: see . . . the offence of compounding an indictable offence codified by s. 141. There does not, however, appear to have been any recognition by the criminal law of "without prejudice" statements outside of a plea bargaining structure. The law seems to be accurately summarized by Strong, *McCormick on Evidence*, 4th ed. (St. Paul: West Publishing, 1992), c. 25, para. 266, at p. 198:

> 266. *Compromise evidence in criminal cases.* The policy of protecting offers of compromise in civil cases does not extend to efforts to stifle criminal prosecution by "buying off" the prosecuting witness or victim. Indeed, such efforts are classed as an implied admission and generally admissible. The public policy against compounding crimes is said to prevail. On the other hand, the legitimacy of settling criminal cases by negotiations between prosecuting attorney and accused, whereby the latter pleads guilty in return for some leniency, has been generally recognized. Effective criminal law administration would be difficult if a large proportion of the charges were not disposed of by guilty pleas. Public policy accordingly encourages compromise, and as in civil cases, that policy is furthered by protecting from disclosure at trial not only the offer but also statements made during negotiations.

This policy would seem to have particular application in the case on appeal. It is true that so far as the matrimonial violence was concerned, any admissions by the appellant related to past misconduct which could amount to assault, but the appellant was not tried with respect to past misconduct, but rather was tried for the murder of his wife after an apparent reconciliation. I do not see on what basis he should be protected from utterances and conduct during the reconciliation process that are relevant to a subsequent criminal act of the magnitude of the one under appeal.

Accordingly, this ground of appeal must fail.

R. v. LAKE
[1997] O.J. No. 5447 (Ont. Gen. Div.)

[The accused was charged with murder. R.C., a young person, was charged separately with the murder and was to be tried in Youth Court. R.C. was called by the Crown as a witness at the accused's trial. Although his testimony-in-chief supported some aspects of the Crown's case, in other more important respects, his testimony rebutted the Crown position. Among the applications made by the Crown was an application for a ruling that R.C.'s instructions to his lawyer were admissible at this trial.]

McCombs J.:—

. . . .

In light of R.C.'s testimony the Crown seeks an order admitting for its truth, evidence as to what was said by R.C.'s lawyer to the Crown in the course of resolution discussions initiated by the defence. The Crown's motion is based on the argument that information allegedly conveyed to the Crown by R.C.'s counsel which was attributed to R.C. is not protected by privilege. Further, the Crown position is that the statements that the Crown alleges were attributed to R.C. by his lawyer at the resolution discussions meet the twin test of necessity and reliability, and are therefore admissible in evidence at this trial under the principled exception to the hearsay rule enunciated in *R. v. B. (K.G)*, supra, and related authorities.

Factual Background of the Motion

Crown counsel Mr. Loparco has advised me that Mr. Rotenberg, counsel for R.C., initiated resolution discussions with the Crown, and advised the Crown that if the charge of murder was withdrawn against R.C., he would be prepared to plead guilty to a charge of conspiracy to commit robbery on the following factual basis:

1.   that R.C. had initially agreed to participate with Lake in the robbery of Tom Huston boots, then abandoned the agreement before the robbery.
2.   that he went to the front door of the store while Lake was inside, and saw him "stabbing and stabbing" Louis Ambas.

Mr. Loparco further advises that the alleged offer to plead on that basis was rejected by the Crown.

. . . .

The position of the Crown is that if, in the course of resolution discussions, a lawyer attributes statements to his or her client, both the discussions and the statements are no longer protected by solicitor-client privilege. The Crown further asserts that although the law recognizes a further public interest privilege in protecting the confidentiality of resolution discussions, that privilege is not absolute, and must, in the circumstances of this case, give way to what is submitted to be a more important public interest: ensuring that criminal prosecutions are a search for the truth.

. . . .

There is a type of privilege recognized at common law. That privilege is related to the public interest in preserving plea negotiations as an essential component of the administration of justice. The privilege was recognized recently in *R. v. Bernardo* [May 10, 1994 (Ont. Ct. Gen. Div.), unreported], by LeSage, Assoc. C.J. (as he then was). He stated:

> I agree with the Crown's submissions that there should be a recognized privilege surrounding plea discussions vis-à-vis the accused and the Crown. There are many reasons in the nature of public policy that would suggest that such a privilege does exist or ought to exist in order to encourage Crown and defence to have full, frank, and private negotiations in criminal oases. I believe, as in civil cases, settlement negotiation privilege ought to exist. The rules of this court concerning pre-hearing conferences in criminal matters contemplate that those negotiations will normally occur in private and that they will remain confidential unless a resolution is achieved in which case the discussions would normally be disclosed in court. I am of the view that the public interest is well served by encouraging such frank and full discussions between counsel for the accused and counsel for the Crown. The saving to the public and the resulting benefit to the administration of justice in resolving cases that ought to be resolved is substantial.

. . . .

Recommendation 46 of the *Report of the Attorney General's Advisory Committee on Charge Screening, Disclosure, and Resolution Discussions* (1993) chaired by the Honourable G. Arthur Martin, also recognized the importance of resolution discussions as an essential component of the administration of justice. The recommendation provides:

> The Committee is of the opinion that resolution discussions are in essential part of the criminal justice system in Ontario, and, when properly conducted, benefit not only the accused, but also victims, witnesses, counsel, and the administration of justice.

The Martin Report recognizes that the integrity of the justice system requires that resolution discussions be encouraged. In my view that means that Counsel must be free to approach the Crown with a view to resolving cases, secure in the knowledge that nothing said in that context can be used to the detriment of their clients.

. . . .

In my view, a ruling favourable to the Crown in the circumstances of a case such as this would have a profound chilling effect upon resolution discussions, an essential component of the administration of justice, and would do irreparable damage to the public interest in the proper administration of justice. This public interest is of such importance that it must outweigh all other considerations. In the result, I conclude that the resolution discussions which took place in the circumstances of this case must remain privileged. The Crown's application must therefore be dismissed.

---

2. CROWN PRIVILEGE — PUBLIC INTEREST IMMUNITY[53]

(a) At Common Law

At common law, when the Crown was a party to the suit it could not be required to give discovery of documents; no special reason needed to be pleaded as the Crown simply exercised its prerogative right. When the suit was between private parties and production of an official document was sought, the Crown could object on the ground that production would be injurious to the public interest.[54] Traditionally this ability to resist disclosure is discussed as based on "Crown privilege" but more recently the inaptness of the phrase has been recognized. As Lord Reid observed:

> The ground put forward has been said to be Crown privilege. I think that that expression is wrong and may be misleading. There is no question of any privilege in the ordinary sense of the word. The real question is whether the public interest requires that the letter shall not be produced and whether that public interest is so strong as to override the ordinary right and interest of a litigant that he shall be able to lay before a court of justice all relevant evidence. A Minister of the Crown is always an appropriate and often the most appropriate person to assert this public interest, and the evidence or advice which he gives to the court is always valuable and may sometimes be indispensable. But, in my view, it must always be open to any person interested to raise the question and there may be cases where the trial judge should himself raise the question if no one else has done so.[55]

The difference between private privileges and this immunity have been well summarized by Sopinka and Lederman:

> Unlike the private privileges such as that relating to communications passing between a solicitor and his client, this public privilege belongs not to any private party, nor to any witness. It is usually asserted by the government, but it would appear that even in the absence of governmental objection, the judge should prohibit disclosure if he feels it will be harmful to the fabric of the state. Because production of secondary evidence whether written or oral of original privileged information would serve equally to endanger the public interest, in contradistinction to private privileges, it too is shut out. The government can make claim to the privilege in all proceedings, whether it is a party to them or not. Moreover, any party or witness may draw the court's attention

---

53. See generally, *Freedom of Information: Canadian Perspectives*, J.D. McCamus, ed. (1981), and Mewett, "State Secrets in Canada" (1985), 63 Can. Bar Rev. 358.
54. See generally, *Duncan v. Cammell, Laird & Co.*, [1942] A.C. 624 (H.L.).
55. *Rogers v. Home Secretary*, [1973] A.C. 388, 400 (H.L.). See generally, Tapper, "Privilege and Policy" (1974), 37 Mod. L. Rev. 92.

to the nature of the evidence with a view to its being excluded. It is not a privilege which may be waived.[56]

The English courts have taken to referring to this subject as "public interest immunity,"[57] and recently the Ontario Court of Appeal adopted "the more accurate description of 'public interest privilege'."[58]

The public interest may be adversely affected by disclosure of official documents in two distinct ways. It may be that disclosure of the *contents* of the particular documents would be injurious to the public interest, or the document may belong to a *class* of documents which ought not to be disclosed whether or not there is anything in the particular document disclosure of which would be injurious. In the latter instance, the maintenance of immunity from disclosure is designed to promote candour in the writer, and so to improve efficiency in the public sector. Lord Simon in *Duncan v. Cammell, Laird & Co.* wrote:

> The objection is sometimes based upon the view that the public interest requires a particular class of communications with, or within, a public department to be protected from production on the ground that the candour and completeness of such communications might be prejudiced if they were ever liable to be disclosed in subsequent litigation rather than on the contents of the particular document itself.[59]

The court's approach in reviewing a claim for immunity will vary depending on whether the claim is a "contents" claim or a "class" claim. Lord Reid in *Conway v. Rimmer* [60] observed:

> It does not appear that any serious difficulties have arisen or are likely to arise with regard to [a "contents" claim]. However wide the power of the court may be held to be, cases would be very rare in which it could be proper to question the view of the responsible Minister that it would be contrary to the public interest to make public the contents of a particular document.[61]

He went on to observe, however, that in a "class" claim:

> ... if the Minister's reasons are of a character which judicial experience is not competent to weigh then the Minister's view must prevail; but experience has shown that reasons given for withholding whole classes of documents are often not of that character. For example a court is perfectly well able to assess the likelihood that, if the writer of a certain class of document knew that there was a chance that his report might be produced in legal proceedings, he would make a less full and candid report than he would otherwise have done.[62]

The House of Lords therefore ruled in favour of judicial review of claims for immunity, rejecting the earlier rule in *Duncan v. Cammell, Laird & Co.* that a Minister's certificate was conclusive. Lord Reid reasoned:

---

56.   Sopinka and Lederman, *The Law of Evidence in Civil Cases* (1974), p. 239.
57.   See *Burmah Oil v. Bank of England*, [1979] 3 All E.R. 700, 722 (H.L.): "[T]his appeal is concerned with the legal topic formerly known as Crown privilege and now as public interest immunity," per Lord Keith of Kinkel.
58.   *Smerchanski v. Lewis* (1981), 58 C.C.C. (2d) 328, 331 (Ont. C.A.).
59.   *Supra*, note 54, at p. 635.
60.   [1968] 1 All E.R. 874 (H.L.).
61.   *Ibid.*, at p. 882.
62.   *Ibid.*, at p. 888.

It is universally recognized that here there are two kinds of public interest which may clash. There is the public interest that harm shall not be done to the nation or the public service by disclosure of certain documents, and there is the public interest that the administration of justice shall not be frustrated by the withholding of documents which must be produced if justice is to be done. There are many cases where the nature of the injury which would or might be done to the nation or the public service is of so grave a character that no other interest, public or private, can be allowed to prevail over it. With regard to such cases it would be proper to say . . . that to order production of the document in question would put the interest of the state in jeopardy; but there are many other cases where the possible injury to the public service is much less and there one would think that it would be proper to balance the public interests involved.[63]

. . . it is more than ever necessary that in a doubtful case the alleged public interest in concealment should be balanced against the public interest that the administration of justice should not be frustrated. If the Minister, who has no duty to balance these conflicting public interests, says no more than that in his opinion the public interest requires concealment, and if that is to be accepted as conclusive in this field as well as with regard to documents in his possession, it seems to me not only that very serious injustice may be done to the parties, but also that the due administration of justice may be gravely impaired for quite inadequate reasons.[64]

It is the judge's duty then to balance the competing public interests but, with regard to certain classes of documents it is well recognized that upholding the claim is virtually automatic. As the Ontario Court of Appeal remarked:

Nor is it necessary for the Judge to peruse the documents in every case before reaching a decision. There are certain classes of documents including those relating to Cabinet proceedings, the conduct of foreign affairs, national defence and security which by their very nature are generally acknowledged to be privileged. While certain classes of documents dealing with easily recognizable state secrets are almost automatically recognized as privileged, the obvious tendency of decisions since *Conway v. Rimmer* has been to restrict class privilege.[65]

Normally the claim for immunity will be made by filing a certificate or affidavit of the responsible Minister, but this is not always necessary.[66] In *Smerchanski v. Lewis* the plaintiff in a civil suit learned that in connection with a parallel criminal prosecution the police had taken statements from the defendant. The plaintiff sought production of these statements from the officer of the Ministry of the Attorney General appointed to prosecute the defendant. Cromarty, J. held the statements automatically privileged from production because of the public interest in preventing the prosecution of criminal offences from being compromised by premature disclosure. The Court of Appeal found that he erred in failing to peruse the documents, and sent the question of admissibility back to him for consideration. In discussing the procedure followed the court noted:

The procedure for determining whether documents should be excluded on grounds of public policy usually involves two steps. The first is the filing of an affidavit

---

63. *Ibid.*, at p. 880.
64. *Ibid.*, at p. 887.
65. *Supra*, note 58, at p. 334.
66. See *Rogers v. Home Secretary, supra*, note 55, at p. 406 describing the merits of the proceeding by way of a certificate from the appropriate minister filed with the court by the Attorney General or his representative.

by a responsible Minister or, as is provided in Ontario by s. 31 of the *Evidence Act*, a designated official asserting the grounds on which the claim for non-production is based. The second is the decision of the Judge usually made after inspection of the questioned documents. This is the procedure envisaged in *Conway v. Rimmer*.

. . . .

The privilege can be claimed in any way which the Court considers appropriate. As a general rule it is preferable that it should be based on an affidavit from a Minister because the nature of the documents and the harmful effects of disclosure are matters within his peculiar knowledge. These considerations do not apply in this case. The objection to disclosure was made in Court by counsel for the Attorney-General. The claim for privilege was rooted in concepts basic to the administration of justice and no affidavit evidence was required to inform the Court on the reasons for the objection.[67]

(b) Statutory Provisions

In 1970 the Federal Court Act[68] was enacted and it provided:

41.(1) Subject to the provisions of any other Act and to subsection (2), when a Minister of the Crown certifies to any court by affidavit that a document belongs to a class or contains information which on grounds of a public interest specified in the affidavit should be withheld from production and discovery, the court may examine the document and order its production and discovery to the parties, subject to such restrictions or conditions as it deems appropriate, if it concludes in the circumstances of the case that the public interest in the proper administration of justice outweighs in importance the public interest specified in the affidavit.

(2) When a Minister of the Crown certifies to any court by affidavit that the production or discovery of a document or its contents would be injurious to international relations, national defence or security, or to federal-provincial relations, or that it would disclose a confidence of the Queen's Privy Council for Canada, discovery and production shall be refused without any examination of the document by the court.

In *Attorney General Quebec v. Attorney General Canada*,[69] Pigeon, J. interpreted this legislation:

Although this enactment is in the *Federal Court Act*, the wording makes it clearly applicable to "any court". This makes it applicable not only to the provincial Courts which are, in the main, Courts of general jurisdiction, federal and provincial, but also to any official invested with the powers of a Court for the production of documents.

The court therefore held the section applicable to a provincial commission of inquiry which had sought production of R.C.M.P. files. In *Human Rights Commission v. Attorney General Canada*[70] the constitutionality of section 41(2) was contested; the Commission argued that the provision was *ultra vires* because it trenched on an area exclusively reserved to the Provinces, the administration of justice. The Supreme Court of Canada ruled that the provision was

---

67. *Supra*, note 58, at pp. 333-34.
68. R.S.C. 1970, c. 10 (2nd Supp.).
69. (1978), 43 C.C.C. (2d) 49, 72 (S.C.C.). To the same effect see *Re Royal Amer. Shows Inc. (No. 2)*, [1977] 6 W.W.R. 673 (Alta.).
70. (1982), 134 D.L.R. (3d) 17 (S.C.C.).

constitutional, evidently on the basis that the documents in question originated with or were in the possession of the Government of Canada. The Attorney General of Quebec, intervening on this point submitted that section 41(2) was "ultra vires to the extent that it seeks to forbid review by the competent courts of the constitutional legality of a decision by the executive to refuse to produce documents." He argued that in a federal state, the federal government is constitutionally limited to the objective of safeguarding the "*federal* public interest"; by the privative clause the federal government gives itself the power to decide, with finality, whether the production of documents is or is not within the *federal* public interest; by the clause the federal government is allowed to decide the constitutional legality of its own action without any review possible by the competent courts. The court decided that this argument:

> . . . raise[d] the applicability of the legislative enactment in a given case, not the constitutionality of the provision itself.
>
> It is perhaps conceivable that a case could arise of an abuse . . . in which the Courts would be justified in considering whether s. 41(2) is inapplicable. . . . the case at bar is clearly not such a case. It is apparent from re-reading the affidavit that it relies on the federal public interest.[71]

While section 41(2) appears to make the Ministerial certificate conclusive, there appeared then to be some residual power in the judge to ensure that the documents are of a class amenable to the claim. In *Landreville v. R.*[72] Mahoney, J. wrote:

> Section 41(2) of the *Federal Court Act* renders the Court powerless in the face of a properly composed ministerial objection to production. That is certainly the case where the documents are plainly of a class, as these are, appropriate to the basis upon which the claim of Crown privilege is asserted. . . . I should not wish silence to be taken as acquiescence in the proposition that it is not open to the Court to adjudicate whether or not documents for which such a claim is asserted are, in fact, of a class amenable to the claim.

Section 41 of the Federal Court Act was repealed in 1983 by the Access to Information Act.[73] By that Act the Canada Evidence Act was amended[74] to provide:

37(1) A Minister of the Crown in right of Canada or other person interested may object to the disclosure of information before a court, person or body with jurisdiction to compel the production of information by certifying orally or in writing to the court, person or body that the information should not be disclosed on the grounds of a specified public interest.

(2) Subject to sections 36.2 and 36.3, where an objection to the disclosure of information is made under subsection (1) before a superior court, that court may examine or hear the information and order its disclosure, subject to such restrictions or conditions as it deems appropriate, if it concludes that, in the circumstances of the case, the public interest in disclosure outweighs in importance the specified public interest.

(3) Subject to sections 36.2 and 36.3, where an objection to the disclosure of information is made under subsection (1) before a court, person or body other

---

71. *Ibid.*, at p. 28.
72. (1976), 70 D.L.R. (3d) 122, 125 (Fed. T.D.).
73. S.C. 1980-81-82-83, c. 111, s. 3 [see now R.S.C. 1985, c. A-1].
74. *Ibid.*, s. 4.

than a superior court, the objection may be determined, on application, in accordance with subsection (2) by

    (a) the Federal Court — Trial Division, in the case of a person or body vested with power to compel production by or pursuant to an Act of Parliament if the person or body is not a court established under a law of a province; or

    (b) the trial division or trial court of the superior court of the province within which the court, person or body exercises its jurisdiction, in any other case.

(4) An application pursuant to subsection (3) shall be made within ten days after the objection is made or within such further or lesser time as the court having jurisdiction to hear the application considers appropriate in the circumstances.

(5) An appeal lies from a determination under subsection (2) or (3)

    (a) to the Federal Court of Appeal from a determination of the Federal Court — Trial Division; or

    (b) to the court of appeal of a province from a determination of a trial division or trial court of a superior court of a province.

(6) An appeal under subsection (5) shall be brought within ten days from the date of the determination appealed from or within such further time as the court having jurisdiction to hear the appeal considers appropriate in the circumstances.

(7) Notwithstanding any other Act of Parliament,

    (a) an application for leave to appeal to the Supreme Court of Canada from a judgment made pursuant to subsection (5) shall be made within ten days from the date of the judgment appealed from or within such further time as the court having jurisdiction to grant leave to appeal considers appropriate in the circumstances; and

    (b) where leave to appeal is granted, the appeal shall be brought in the manner set out in subsection 66(1) of the *Supreme Court Act* but within such time as the court that grants leave specifies.

38(1) Where an objection to the disclosure of information is made under subsection 36.1(1) on grounds that the disclosure would be injurious to international relations or national defence or security, the objection may be determined, on application, in accordance with subsection 36.1(2) only by the Chief Justice of the Federal Court, or such other judge of that court as the Chief Justice may designate to hear such applications.

(2) An application under subsection (1) shall be made within ten days after the objection is made or within such further or lesser time as the Chief Justice of the Federal Court, or such other judge of that court as the Chief Justice may designate to hear such applications, considers appropriate.

(3) An appeal lies from a determination under subsection (1) to the Federal Court of Appeal.

(4) Subsection 36.1(6) applies in respect of appeals under subsection (3), and subsection 36.1(7) applies in respect of appeals from judgments made pursuant to subsection (3), with such modifications as the circumstances require.

(5) An application under subsection (1) or an appeal brought in respect of such application shall

(*a*) be heard *in camera;* and

(*b*) on the request of the person objecting to the disclosure of information, be heard and determined in the National Capital Region described in the schedule to the *National Capital Act.*

(6) During the hearing of an application under subsection (1) or an appeal brought in respect of such application, the person who made the objection in respect of which the application was made or the appeal was brought shall, on the request of that person, be given the opportunity to make representations *ex parte.*

39(1) Where a Minister of the Crown or the Clerk of the Privy Council objects to the disclosure of information before a court, person or body with jurisdiction to compel the production of information by certifying in writing that the information constitutes a confidence of the Queen's Privy Council for Canada, disclosure of the information shall be refused without examination or hearing of the information by the court, person or body.

(2) For the purpose of subsection (1), "a confidence of the Queen's Privy Council for Canada" includes, without restricting the generality thereof, information contained in

(*a*) a memorandum the purpose of which is to present proposals or recommendations to Council;

(*b*) a discussion paper the purpose of which is to present background explanations, analyses of problems or policy options to Council for consideration by Council in making decisions;

(*c*) an agendum of Council or a record recording deliberations or decisions of Council;

(*d*) a record used for or reflecting communications or discussions between Ministers of the Crown on matters relating to the making of government decisions or the formulation of government policy;

(*e*) a record the purpose of which is to brief Ministers of the Crown in relation to matters that are brought before, or are proposed to be brought before, Council or that are the subject of communications or discussions referred to in paragraph (*d*); and

(*f*) draft legislation.

(3) For the purposes of subsection (2), "Council" means the Queen's Privy Council for Canada, committees of the Queen's Privy Council for Canada, Cabinet and committees of Cabinet.

(4) Subsection (1) does not apply in respect of

(*a*) a confidence of the Queen's Privy Council for Canada that has been in existence for more than twenty years; or

(*b*) a discussion paper described in paragraph (2)(*b*)

(i) if the decisions to which the discussion paper relates have been made public, or

(ii) where the decisions have not been made public, if four years have passed since the decisions were made.[75]

---

75. *Ibid.*, Schedule III. See now R.S.C. 1985, c. C-5, ss. 37-39. In *Canada (Attorney General) v. Central Cartage Co.* (1990), 71 D.L.R. (4th) 253 (Fed. C.A.) the absolute language of s. 36.3 of the Canada Evidence Act was unsuccessfully challenged as inconsistent with ss. 7 and 15 of the Charter.

GOGUEN v. GIBSON
(1984), 10 C.C.C. (3d) 492 (Fed. C.A.)

MARCEAU J.:— The particular significance of the judgment here under appeal, a judgment rendered by the Chief Justice of the court, can hardly be overstated. Not only does it deal with one of the most delicate situations a court of law may be confronted with, namely, that created by a collision and conflict between a particular public interest and the public interest in the proper administration of justice; it is, most noteworthily, the very first judgment made pursuant to the new s. 36.2, recently incorporated into the *Canada Evidence Act*, R.S.C. 1970, c. E-10 (as amended), in connection with the "disclosure of Government Information".

It will be recalled that Parliament, in November of 1982, in dealing with the general problem of access to government information, brought substantive changes to the rules applicable when a Minister of the Crown, before a court or a tribunal with jurisdiction to compel, objects on grounds of public interest, to the disclosure of some information sought by a litigant. Section 41(1) and (2) of the *Federal Court Act*, R.S.C. 1970, c. 10 (2nd Supp.), in which were set out the rules until then in force in such situations, was repealed and replaced by three new sections inserted into the *Canada Evidence Act*, ss. 36.1, 36.2 and 36.3. According to the new rules, the right to object to disclosure on grounds of public policy is confirmed and even facilitated and extended: it can be exercised orally and not necessarily by the filing of a sworn certificate; it covers any information and is not restricted to documents; it is given to any interested person and not reserved to Ministers of the Crown. But, the objection is definitive and unassailable in the sole case where a confidence of the Queen's Privy Council is involved. In all other cases, including those where international relations or national defence or security are said to be compromised, the objection will be subject to verification. A superior court will have the right to examine the information sought and the power to overrule the objection ". . . if it concludes that, in the circumstances of the case, the public interest in disclosure outweighs in importance the specified public interest". As to the court to which is assigned the duty to appreciate the situation, it will be the superior court before which the objection is taken in all instances except those where international relations or national defence or security could be involved. And here comes into play s. 36.2 which reads as follows:

. . . .

. . . subsection 36.1(7) applies in respect of appeals from judgments made pursuant to subsection (3), with such modifications as the circumstances require.

(5) An application under subsection (1) or an appeal brought in respect of such application shall

    (*a*)   be heard *in camera*; and

    (*b*)   on the request of the person objecting to the disclosure of information, be heard and determined in the National Capital Region described in the schedule to the *National Capital Act*.

(6) During the hearing of an application under subsection (1) or an appeal brought in respect of such application, the person who made the objection in respect of which the application was made or the appeal was brought shall, on the request of that person, be given the opportunity to make representations *ex parte*.

So, the judgment here under appeal is the first ever rendered in application of this new s. 36.2 incorporated into the *Canada Evidence Act* in 1982. The facts that set in motion the procedure have been much in the news. They are set out in the reasons delivered by the Chief Justice; only their main features need to be repeated here.

The appellants are two of 11 active or former members of the Royal Canadian Mounted Police (the R.C.M.P.) similarly charged under the *Criminal Code* with the offences of theft and conspiracy to commit theft. The 11 informations laid in 1981 relate to an incident known as Operation "Ham", which involved the security service of the R.C.M.P. and took place in Montreal, during the night of January 9, 1973, when premises were entered surreptitiously and computer tapes recording membership lists of a political party were removed, taken out, copied and, some hours later, returned to the exact place from which they had been taken. The two appellants after waiving preliminary inquiry have been committed to trial, by a judge and jury, in the Superior Court (Criminal Division) of the District of Montreal, Quebec. The trial of one of the 11 co-accused has already been completed before a judge alone giving rise to a verdict of guilty and a suspended sentence; the trial of another before a judge and jury has aborted after several days of hearing, the prosecution itself being ordered stayed; and finally, a permanent stay of proceedings has just been ordered with respect to seven others. In the case of the two appellants, a joint indictment was prepared by the Attorney-General for the Province of Quebec and after several postponements, their joint trial was set to begin on January 17, 1983.

On January 5, 1983, pursuant to a request by counsel for the appellants, a subpoena *duces tecum* was issued by a judge of the Superior Court, District of Montreal, addressed to the respondent, in his capacity as Deputy Solicitor-General of Canada, and to the Clerk of the Privy Council of Canada, requiring each of them to attend the court and to bring with them a large number of documents enumerated, in the case of the Deputy Solicitor-General, in a list of some 28 items of volumes and files and, in the case of the Clerk of the Privy Council, in a list of some 30 other items, some of which were, apparently, again, volumes.

On January 12, 1983, the respondent filed with the Superior Court, District of Montreal, a certificate objecting to disclosure of the documents listed in the *duces tecum* and the information contained therein on grounds that disclosure would be injurious to national security and international relations. (The certificate is quoted *verbatim* in the judgment under appeal and need not be reproduced again.) An application for determination of the objection in accordance with the new ss. 36.1 and 36.2 of the *Canada Evidence Act* was then presented to the Chief Justice of the Federal Court who established a procedure to be followed by both parties, permitted the filing of the affidavit and other evidence on which the parties intended to refer in support of their respective positions, and set the matter down for hearing commencing on March 1, 1983. Judgment was rendered on April 28, 1983, and in support thereof, lengthy reasons were delivered in which the learned Chief Justice explained how, according to what principles and on what basis, he had come to a conclusion without having to proceed to an examination of the documents. That conclusion was summarized in the final paragraph of his reasons:

> I am accordingly of the opinion that in the circumstances of this case as disclosed by the material before me the importance of the public interest in maintaining the documents and information in them immune from disclosure on the grounds that their disclosure would be injurious to national security and international relations is not outweighed in importance by the public interest in disclosure and I so determine. It follows that the objections taken in the certificate should be upheld and that this application fails and should be dismissed.

This is the judgment here under appeal, an appeal brought pursuant to s. 36.2(3) of the Act, which gave rise to seven full days of argument by counsel and must now be decided.

In my view, this appeal cannot succeed. I see no basis for disagreeing with the approach adopted and the principles applied by the learned Chief Justice in dealing with the matter, and I find no error in his appreciation of the evidence put before him. I do not think there is any need for inspecting the documents sought before confirming his conclusion that the objection to their disclosure ought to be upheld. The reasons he gave to support that conclusion appear to me convincing and, except for a few minor passages (which I will have occasion to discuss later), I readily adopt them. There is not much to add to those reasons in my opinion, but I wish, nevertheless, to emphasize some of the points which appear to me of particular significance in the consideration of the matter.

1. *The meaning of the new rule applicable to claims for immunity based on international relations or national security*

The most substantial change brought by the new legislation respecting disclosure of government information is undoubtedly that objections to disclosure on grounds that international relations or national security might be injured will no longer be treated as absolute like those based on the necessity to keep secret a confidence of the Queen's Privy Council: objections of that type will be subject to verification and examination like any other public interest objections. Is it for a moment thinkable that the reason for such a fundamental change could be that international relations and national security have become, in the minds of the members of Parliament, less critical than before, or less important than any confidence of the Queen's Privy Council? Of course not. That there can be no public interest more fundamental than national security is as true today as it was yesterday.

The essential reason for the change, in my understanding, is that the concepts involved in the formulation of an objection of that nature are so broad and so vague that, in practice, they leave much room for exaggerations and overstatements, not to mention clear abuses, which it was felt desirable to avoid with every respect for the requirements of the due administration of justice. While a confidence of the Queen's Privy Council, with the precisions given in the Act, is readily identifiable, a possible danger to international relations or national security is not so easily capable of being recognized and, as a result, may be feared and evoked somewhat too quickly, albeit in perfect good faith. That is clearly apparent in the field of international relations, but is also true, although to a somewhat lesser degree, in that of national security, and if the possibility of improper use has always been present in the former system, it will, of course, be even more present in the new one where the objection is available not only to ministers but to any person claiming interest.

The new rule, as I view it, is aimed at thwarting those possible exaggerations, overstatements or abuses by giving the court the authority to examine the information and to declare that the public interest involved as the basis for objecting to disclose, although related to international relations or national security, is, in any given instance, outweighed in importance by the public interest in requiring disclosure for the due administration of justice. But I would think that, on it being established as a fact and not as a mere possibility that international relations or national security are to be genuinely affected by disclosure, the harm that may result to the person seeking the information, if that information is denied, will have to be great indeed for the judge to be able to say that the public interest in the due administration of justice in this particular case nevertheless is predominant and requires that the information be disclosed. I cannot express it better than did the Chief Justice when, after having acknowledged the great importance of the public interest in the due administration of justice, specially criminal justice, he goes on to say (p. 12):

> Important as that public interest is, however, I think it is apparent from the nature of the subject-matter of international relations, national defence and national security that occasions when the importance of the public interest in maintaining immune from disclosure information the disclosure of which would be injurious to them is outweighed by the importance of the public interest in the due administration of justice, even in criminal matters, will be rare.

Which brings up the question of the factors that may be taken into account in assessing, weighing and balancing the two public interests involved. It seems to me that these factors cannot be listed or even classified in any useful way since they must be drawn essentially from the circumstances of each case. But looking at one side of the equation, I think with the learned Chief Justice that in assessing the validity and seriousness of the claim for public interest immunity ". . . the circumstance of who it is that asserts the objection and what his interest in and knowledge of the need for maintaining immunity from disclosure may have its bearing" (at p. 8). I will even add that, in my view, in matters of national security, that circumstance may even be the most forceful one, because of the expertise required to properly assess the situation, an expertise a judge normally does not have. And, looking at the other side, I think — here again with the Chief Justice, if I read his reasons correctly — that the weight of the public interest in disclosure can only be assessed *in concreto*, according to the circumstances of the particular case, and more or less regardless of the contention of the applicant since this assessment is here well within the field of expertise of the judge, relating as it does to the immediate purpose for which the litigant requires the information, the importance of the disclosure to achieve that purpose, the relevancy of such purpose in the whole litigation, the interest, financial, social or moral, at stake in that litigation.

2. *The two-stage approach and the test that is implied in it*

The thrust of the appellants' argument in support of the appeal was that the learned Chief Justice was wrong in reaching his conclusion before examining the files and documents sought. It was said that the reasons set out in the certificate establishing the claim and the TOP SECRET affidavit filed to substantiate it should not have been considered sufficiently clear and detailed to dispense with direct verification, the more so since much of the material had already been disclosed to the McDonald Commission. It was said also that the circumstance that the subpoenas were issued on behalf of accused individuals in a criminal case constituted in itself an exceptional circumstance requiring a thorough examination of the information required. But in fact, the main submissions in that regard were much more substantial and complex than those two opening statements and I will endeavour to summarize them briefly as they were presented to us.

The argument goes like this. The appellants, who do not contest their participation in Operation "Ham", intend to offer as a defence to the charges of theft and conspiracy to commit theft laid against them: (a) that the operation was not undertaken fraudulently and without colour of right, and (b) that they themselves did not act fraudulently and without colour of right. This defence, in view of the factors that constitute the crime of theft under the *Criminal Code* and the importance attached to the state of mind of the person doing the act, is a serious one, albeit apparently raised in like circumstances for the first time in a Canadian court. Now, there is absolutely no doubt that the documents sought may help to establish the elements of that defence: the appellants, who are aware, at least generally, of the contents of many of the files, can attest to that fact and, in any event, the affidavit of the respondent confirms it. By requesting the documents, therefore, the appellants are not engaged in a fishing expedition; the information they seek is clearly relevant. That was sufficient to preclude the learned Chief Justice from denying their request without proceeding to an examination of the documents. Indeed, if a two-stage approach appears to be required — the judge having to assess the situation before going into the examination — the second stage should be undertaken as soon as a serious or *prima facie* case for disclosure has been established. Such a test is more in accordance with the spirit of the legislation and the thrust of the common law authorities, as shown in the most recent English case on the subject, *Air Canada et al. v. Secretary of State for Trade (No. 2)*, [1983] 1 All E.R. 910, than the one applied by the learned Chief Justice — namely, that it be immediately shown that the public interest in disclosure is at least equal in importance to that for immunity — a test which placed on the appellants a burden too onerous and too great at that stage.

Some of the propositions advanced by counsel in making this argument on which they mostly rely require special comments, but first I would like to consider generally this two-stage approach referred to and the so-called test implied therein.

That, in the case of a request for disclosure of information in respect of which an objection has been raised under ss. 36.1 and 36.2 of the Act, the court must proceed by way of a potential two-stage determination of the application is to me quite clear. Authority to inspect the documents is vested in the court, but no duty is imposed on it to do so; and it seems to me that an authority of that kind would be abused if it were exercised unreservedly, uselessly and for any other reason than because it is required to arrive at a conclusion. This observation, to me, not only confirms the inevitability of the two-stage approach but, at the same time, indicates the nature of the so-called test that is implied in it. The court will proceed to the second stage and examine the documents if, and only if, it is persuaded that it must do so to arrive at a conclusion or, put another way, if, and only if, on the sole basis of the material before it, it cannot say whether or not it will grant or refuse the application. Now, many reasons may be thought of that may lead the court to reach a conclusion on the sole basis of the material before it: an easy possibility is a lack of seriousness in the contention that, in the circumstances, some public interest requires immunity; another is the frivolity of the request for disclosure, because the information sought would likely have no bearing on the litigation in which the applicant is involved; still another is the unreasonableness of the application, it being clearly of the nature of a fishing expedition. But the reason most likely to come to the fore is certainly the acquired certitude in the mind of the judge that even if the information sought is of the nature or to the effect expected by the applicant, there is no possibility that the importance of the public interest in keeping the information secret will be outweighed by the importance of the public interest in disclosing it. To me, all that is common sense, and I do not read the Chief Justice's comments in support of the approach he was adopting as meaning anything beyond that.

Nor do I read the English cases on the subject as holding a different view. The speeches in the *Air Canada* case, on which the appellants so much rely, contain many passages emphasizing that a likelihood that the documents would support the case of the party seeking discovery has to be established before the court can decide to proceed to inspection, and it is true that this requirement is, at times, presented as a test. I have no difficulty with that, however. It is indeed a test; it is even the most basic one, which was immediately put in question in the minds of their Lordships in the circumstance of that case since discovery and even inspection was there refused simply because it had not been shown that the documents sought, whatever their content, would really help the applicant. But I do not understand the decision as implying that this most basic test had to be seen as the only one or the final and decisive one.

I come now to some specific points made by the appellants in the course of their argument.

(a) The question of where lay the burden of proof was again raised and discussed in an appeal as it had been in first instance. The learned Chief Justice did not consider it necessary to deal at length with it since ". . . in the present case the material put before me by both sides is such that, in my view, nothing any longer turns on a question of onus" (at p. 21). I do not think that I have to dwell on it either but I will permit myself some brief comments. It is trite to say that normally the party whose case depends on the past or actual existence of a fact, which is neither of common knowledge nor presumed by law, has the burden of convincing the judge that such "existence" is at least probable. If the question of where lies the onus here relates to the very conclusion the judge must reach to order disclosure, namely, that the public interest in disclosure outweighs in importance the specified public interest, the answer is necessarily on the applicant; if it relates to intermediate facts, it will obviously vary from one side to the other according to which side will be prejudiced by the particular facts involved remaining doubtful. So, I do not see why the question of onus would have a particular meaning or bearing in an application of the kind here in question and how it could be settled in advance, whether at the first or second stage of the so-called two-staged approach.

(b) As indicated above, the appellants contended that the certificate filed by the respondent and the TOP SECRET affidavit sworn in supplement thereof were lacking in clarity and details and they found support for their contention in the following passage of the judgment (at p. 40):

> . . . I must note, however, without wishing to be critical, that a certificate which identifies as this one does, the information to the disclosure of which objection is taken, by reference to the information in a multitude of documents, some of which

are in themselves voluminous, which has not already been made public by the report of the McDonald Commission, leaves this court as well as the Superior Court with the task of discerning the subject-matter of the objection by reference to a vague formula rather than by an intelligible description by which particular items can be identified. In addition, there is little if anything in the certificate or the secret affidavit or elsewhere in the material to afford a basis for estimating or assessing the gravity of the danger or the injury that might result from disclosure of any particular information.

I confess to having some difficulty with this passage. The appellants claim that, despite the reserve at the outset, the learned judge's comment cannot be understood otherwise than as a general and clear criticism. If it is the case, I will, with respect, disassociate myself from such criticism. I do not see how, in a case where national security is involved and the documents sought are described as files, a certificate, which is to be public, and the affidavit in support thereof, which, although meant to remain secret, is to be analyzed by all lawyers involved, can go into more specifications and details without jeopardizing the very purpose for which immunity is claimed. It is true that the court is thereby left without being able to assess the *gravity* of the risk to national security that might be involved, at least with respect to each document, before proceeding to a full inspection. But then, if such an assessment of the gravity of the risk is required to reach a conclusion, inspection will have to be done, that is all there is to it. It is to be expected, however, that in many cases, such as this one, an assessment of the gravity of the risk will not be considered necessary.

(c) A last point. The appellants have found refuge repeatedly in the fact that they were not on a "fishing operation", it being all but acknowledged that some of the documents sought would be relevant to their case. I agree that this is not a "fishing operation" in the sense usually given to the expression when applied to discovery proceedings: the appellants are not going completely blind. But it seems to me that requiring 7,500 pages of documents in order to locate a few that may be helpful can easily be seen as not so completely different from a fishing expedition.

3. *The learned Chief Justice's appreciation of the evidence before him*

It is well known that on an ordinary appeal from a judgment of first instance, the appellate court's role is not to retry the case on the facts and while it must ascertain that the trial judge had not made some error in his appreciation of the evidence as a whole ". . . it is not . . . a part of its function to substitute its assessment of the balance of probability for the findings of the Judge who presided at the trial". (Ritchie J. delivering the judgment of the court in *Stein v. The Ship "Kathy K"*, [1976] 2 S.C.R. 802 at p. 808.) Is the present appeal governed by the same basic principle?

I think not. Appeals under ss. 36.1(5) or 36.2(3) of the Act, as I understand the new legislation, cannot be treated as ordinary appeals where the preoccupation is strictly to verify whether or not there is error in the judgment appealed from (not whether it was the only or even the best judgment that could have been rendered). They are appeals against the "determination" made, the word being given, as I understand it, a substantial rather than a formal meaning, one that points to the conclusion itself reached by the judge, to his very appreciation of the situation, an appreciation which, to a large extent, remains a moral appreciation based on personal feelings and convictions. In any event, considering that the appeal court is in as good a position as the first judge in so far as the correct perception of the context is concerned, since the whole of the evidence is necessarily written evidence, and considering also that the appreciation to be verified is not susceptible of degrees, it being the result of a straight "balancing", the court must necessarily intervene if its appreciation turns out to be different from that of the trial judge. In other words, because of the particular matters involved and the scheme of the legislation, the appeal requires the court to proceed to an appreciation of its own without having to give special weight to that of the first judge.

I thought I had to take a position on this preliminary question, but, in fact, it could not have much bearing on my attitude in this case since my own appreciation of the situation is, in all respects, parallel to that of the learned Chief Justice, so much so indeed that I wish simply to refer to his analysis of the material put before him and his reactions as to the relative importance of the two conflicting public interests involved.

It would serve no purpose to go through the evidence again but maybe I could very briefly summarize the situation as I see it. The case in favour of immunity is very rapidly, but at once very forcefully, put: national security and international relations will be injured. To what extent? It is not established, but, to a certain extent, undoubtedly, even if disclosure is ordered with respect to single documents only, since these documents, taken from files, will have to be placed into context if they are to be used for their real meaning. The claim is, indeed, a class claim, one based on the character of the document, as well as a content claim. The case in favour of disclosing is much more complex to assess. The appellants are charged with important criminal offences, it is true, although they certainly do not face the prospect of severe punishment nor can they expect great social reprobation; they need the documents for their defence, and they have a fundamental right to resort to any defence that can help them prove their innocence, it is also true, although the particular defence they have in mind, if serious, is nevertheless still problematic as to its legal value. But beyond that and more immediately, what is the real interest that the appellants have in disclosure? It is, as I see it, to buttress their testimonies and to avoid the risk that the jury, at the end of the trial, will come to the unanimous conclusion that the appellants' contentions and those of all the members of the security service of the R.C.M.P. at the time of the events, including the director, contentions confirmed by a series of documents put in evidence and accepted by the McDonald Commission, are unbelievable, unacceptable, made-up excuses and lies; more precisely that Operation "Ham" was not a "Puma" Operation, one of those operations involving surreptitious entries for intelligence-gathering purposes officially established within the R.C.M.P. security service; that this particular operation was not conceived, authorized and undertaken as a means to provide information in the course of an investigation relating to some very specific matters pertaining to the duties of the service. To accept that national security and international relations be injured, even to only the slightest extent, in order that such a remote risk of extreme incredulity on the part of 12 members of a jury be avoided, would appear to me, I say it with respect, totally unreasonable.

I would dismiss the appeal.

Appeal dismissed.

CAREY v. ONTARIO
[1986] 2 S.C.R. 637, 30 C.C.C. (3d) 498

[The government of Ontario increasingly became financially involved with Minaki Lodge, a resort in northwestern Ontario, and eventually became the owner. The previous owner launched a civil suit against the government seeking damages, including exemplary damages, for breach of agreement, deceit and damage to reputation. On examination for discovery, the defendants' witnesses claimed an absolute privilege respecting all documents that went to or emanated from Cabinet and its committees. The claim was not based on the contents of the documents but on the class to which they belonged. Production, it was alleged, would breach confidentiality and inhibit Cabinet discussion of matters of significant public policy.]

The judgment of the Court was delivered by

LA FOREST J.:—

. . . .

It is obviously necessary for the proper administration of justice that litigants have access to all evidence that may be of assistance to the fair disposition of the issues arising in litigation. It is equally clear, however, that certain information regarding governmental activities should not be disclosed in the public interest. The general balance between these two competing interests has shifted markedly over the years. At times the public interest in the need for government secrecy has been given virtually absolute priority, so long as a claim to non-disclosure was made by a Minister of the Crown. At other times a more even balance has been struck.

. . . .

The shift in the balance between the two interests has also been affected by changing social conditions and the role of government in society at various times. When the early cases were decided, the activities of government were restricted to larger political issues. There was no general right to sue the Crown. The issue, therefore, did not frequently arise and when it did, it was often in the context of a suit between private litigants. In that period, it would appear, the tendency of the Crown was to produce evidence requested by litigants in the absence of some compelling reason that could not be disregarded; . . .

With the expansion of state activities into the commercial sphere, different attitudes to suits against the Crown developed and statutes were enacted to make these possible. The general social context also affected attitudes towards government secrecy. One can scarcely expect the views on this issue to be the same in wartime conditions when the total energy of the nation must be concentrated on winning the war, and an era of peace in which government activity impinges on every aspect of our lives and there is in consequence increased demands for more open government. The question, as Lord Upjohn noted in *Conway v. Rimmer*, [1968] A.C. 910 at p. 991, is one that invites periodic judicial reassessment. Not surprisingly, conflicting dicta can scarcely be reconciled.

. . . .

In making a claim of public interest immunity, the Minister (or official) should be as helpful as possible in identifying the interest sought to be protected. . . .

Counsel for Carey argued that Dr. Stewart's affidavit is inadequate in that it does not set forth with sufficient particularity the interests sought to be protected. I suppose the point may be put in this way. Certainly the grounds advanced for protection are, as some cases have put it, somewhat amorphous and as Thorson J.A. pointed out, less helpful than they might be. Nonetheless, it seems to me that Thorson J.A. was correct in his view that in substance what was sought was the protection as a class of what he generally described as "Cabinet documents", i.e. documents prepared by government departments and agencies in formulating government policies, decisions made by Cabinet, and the like. That being so, Dr. Stewart [in this case] did not see it as necessary to particularize the nature of the information sought to be protected as would be necessary if the claim for protection was based on the nature of the contents of the documents. Essentially what the certificate argues is that the process by which government policy is determined by the Executive Council must remain confidential whatever the policy may be and however much time (save when it has become of historical interest only) has elapsed since the policy was developed. . . .

. . . .

The idea that Cabinet documents should be absolutely protected from disclosure has in recent years shown considerable signs of erosion. This development began in the United States in the famous case of *United States v. Nixon*, 418 U.S. 683 (1974), where a subpoena was directed to the former President of that country to produce tape recordings and documents relating to certain conversations and meetings between him and others. The President, claiming executive privilege, filed a motion to have the subpoena quashed, but the Supreme Court of the United States, affirming the courts below, rejected the President's claim.

While there are important differences between the governmental structure of the United States and that of this country, the underlying values concerned are much the same. Consistent with the law in this country, the Court observed that, while it would accord great deference to presidential views, the judiciary, not the President, was the final arbiter of a claim of privilege. In doing this, a court was bound to weigh the conflicting interests.

. . . .

In weighing the competing interests, the Court took account of the fact that the claim to confidentiality was general in nature. It could not be concluded that presidential advisors would be moved to temper their candour by the infrequent occasions of disclosure in judicial proceedings. By contrast, the production of evidence in criminal proceedings was specific and central to the fair adjudication of a particular case.

The Court also took into account that the claim, as in the case here, was made solely on the basis that confidentiality was required to secure the decision-making process generally, not to protect the revelation of any particular action or policy.

[The court then examined developments in England, Australia and New Zealand.]

This Court had occasion to deal with the matter the following year in *Smallwood v. Sparling, supra.* Sparling was appointed under the *Canada Corporations Act* to conduct an investigation for the Restrictive Trade Practices Commission into the management of Canadian Javelin Ltd. A subpoena was issued to Mr. Smallwood, the former Premier of Newfoundland, to give evidence and to bring forth certain particularized documents. Mr. Smallwood then applied for an injunction enjoining Sparling and others from acting upon the subpoena. In support of his application, it was asserted that at the relevant times he had acted solely as Premier, and that any testimony he would be called upon to give or any documents he would be called upon to produce were subject to public interest immunity.

This Court, however, decided against the granting of the injunction. In dealing with these issues, Wilson J., who delivered the judgment, first noted that while a former Minister may, in some circumstances, claim public interest immunity with respect to specific oral or documentary evidence, he cannot claim complete immunity. . . .

. . . .

The foregoing authorities, and particularly, the *Smallwood* case, are in my view, determinative of many of the issues in this case. That case determines that Cabinet documents like other evidence must be disclosed unless such disclosure would interfere with the public interest. The fact that such documents concern the decision-making process at the highest level of government cannot, however, be ignored. Courts must proceed with caution in having them produced. But the level of the decision-making process concerned is only one of many variables to be taken into account. The nature of the policy concerned and the particular contents of the documents are, I would have thought, even more important. So far as the protection of the decision-making process is concerned, too, the time when a document or information is to be revealed is an extremely important factor. Revelations of Cabinet discussion and planning at the developmental stage or other circumstances when there is keen public interest in the subject matter might seriously inhibit the proper functioning of Cabinet government, but this can scarcely be the case when low level policy that has long become of little public interest is involved.

. . . .

In the present case, however, we are dealing with a claim based solely on the fact that the documents concerned are of a class whose revelation might interfere with the proper functioning of the public service. It is difficult to see how a claim could be based on the policy or contents of the documents. We are merely dealing with a transaction concerning a tourist lodge in northern Ontario. The development of a tourist policy undoubtedly is of some importance, but it is hardly world-shaking. Apart from this, are we really dealing with the formulation of policy on a broad basis, or are we simply concerned with a transaction made in the implementation of that policy? . . . Policy and implementation may well be intertwined but a court is empowered to reveal only so much of the relevant documents as it feels it is necessary or expedient to do following an inspection.

. . . .

There is a further matter that militates in favour of disclosure of the documents in the present case. The appellant here alleges unconscionable behaviour on the part of the government. As I see it, it is important that this question be aired not only in the interests of the administration of justice but also for the purpose for which it is sought to withhold the documents, namely, the proper functioning of the executive branch of government. For if there has been harsh or improper conduct in the dealings of the executive with the citizen, it ought to be revealed. The purpose of secrecy in government is to promote its proper functioning, not to facilitate improper conduct by the government. This has been stated in relation to criminal accusations in *Whitlam*, and while the present case is of a civil nature, it is one where the behaviour of the government is alleged to have been tainted.

Divulgence is all the more important in our day when more open government is sought by the public. It serves to reinforce the faith of the citizen in his governmental institutions. This has important implications for the administration of justice, which is of prime concern to the courts. As Lord Keith of Kinkel noted in the *Burmah Oil* case, *supra*, at p. 725, it has a bearing on the perception of the litigant and the public on whether justice has been done.

. . . .

I would, therefore, order disclosure of the documents for the court's inspection. This will permit the court to make certain that no disclosure is made that unnecessarily interferes with confidential government communications. Given the deference owing to the executive branch of government, Cabinet documents ought not to be disclosed without a preliminary judicial inspection to balance the competing interests of government confidentiality and the proper administration of justice.

MacKEIGAN v. HICKMAN
[1989] 2 S.C.R. 796, 72 C.R. (3d) 129, 50 C.C.C. (3d) 449

[The federal Minister of Justice had referred the conviction of Donald Marshall, Jr. to the Appeal Division of the Supreme Court of Nova Scotia pursuant to section 617(*b*) of the Criminal Code for a redetermination. The panel which heard the matter included a justice who had been the Attorney General of Nova Scotia when Marshall was convicted of murder. The court quashed the conviction, but at the end of its judgment it said that Marshall had contributed to his conviction and that any miscarriage of justice was more apparent than real. Marshall received compensation for his lengthy incarceration but the comments of the Court of Appeal had an impact on the quantum of that payment. A Royal Commission was established. The justices who sat on the Reference were asked to attend and Orders to Attend were issued by the Commission when they declined to do so. The justices successfully applied for a declaration that the Commission had no authority to compel their attendance by virtue of judicial immunity. An appeal by the Commissioners to the Appeal Division of the Supreme Court of Nova Scotia was dismissed. A further appeal to the Supreme Court of Canada was dismissed.]

McLachlin J. (L'Heureux-Dubé and Gonthier, JJ. concurring):—

. . . .

. . . [T]he judiciary, if it is to play the proper constitutional role, must be completely separate in authority and function from the other arms of government. It is implicit in that separation that a judge cannot be required by the executive or legislative branches of government to explain and account for his or her judgment. To entertain the demand that a judge testify before a civil body, an emanation of the legislature or executive, on how and why he or she made his or her decision would be to strike at the most sacrosanct core of judicial independence.

I return to ss. 3 and 4 of the *Public Inquiries Act.* Nothing in the language of those sections suggests that the legislators intended to clothe the Commission with power to abrogate the fundamental principle that judges cannot be compelled to testify as to how and why they arrived at their decisions. . . .

. . . .

The next question is whether the general words of ss. 3 and 4 empower the Commission to compel a judge to testify as to why a particular judge sat on a particular case? . . . [T]he Commission presumably wishes to question the Chief Justice as to why he placed Pace J.A. on the panel, given that Pace J.A. had served as Attorney General during critical aspects of the Marshall case.

This question goes to the administrative or institutional aspect of judicial independence. In *Valente v. The Queen* and *Beauregard v. Canada* this Court affirmed in the strongest terms the necessity that the courts control administrative matters related to adjudication without interference from the Legislature or executive. In *Valente v. The Queen* the importance of the courts' having exclusive control over the assignment of judges was considered central to the institutional independence of the judiciary. In *Beauregard v. Canada,* the Chief Justice stated in this respect, at p. 73, that the very role of the courts "as resolver of disputes, interpreter of the law and defender of the Constitution requires that they be completely separate in authority and function from all other participants in the justice system" (his emphasis).

. . . .

It thus appears clear beyond doubt that the assignment of judges is a matter exclusively within the purview of the court. It would be unthinkable for the Minister of Justice or Attorney General to instruct the Chief Justice as to who should or should not sit on a particular case; that prerogative belongs exclusively to the Chief Justice as the head of the Court. To allow the executive a role in selecting what judges hear what cases would constitute an unacceptable interference with the independence of the judiciary. Inquiries after the fact must be similarly barred, in my view. A Chief Justice who knows that he or she may be examined and cross-examined by the executive or its emanation on why he or she assigned a particular judge to a particular case may feel, consciously or unconsciously, pressure to select someone pleasing to the executive. Even if the Chief Justice did not permit himself or herself to be influenced by such a prospect, the public perception that he or she might have been influenced could harm the esteem in which our system of justice is held. In short, the principle of judicial independence which underlies judicial impartiality and the proper functioning of the courts would be threatened by the possibility of public inquiries as to the reason for the assignment of particular judges to particular cases.

In view of these principles, I conclude that ss. 3 and 4 of the *Public Inquiries Act* should not be read as empowering the Commission to tramel on the exclusive right of the judiciary, through its Chief Justices, to control the assignment of judges, free from constraint, whether before or after the event, from other agencies. I should not, however, be taken as suggesting that a judge could never be called to answer in any forum for the process by which the judge reached a decision or the composition of the court on a particular case. I leave to other cases the determination of whether judges might be called on matters such as these before other bodies which have express powers to compel such testimony and which possess sufficient safeguards to protect the integrity of the principle of judicial independence.

. . . .

CORY J. (dissenting in part)— I have read with great interest the reasons of my colleague Justice McLachlin. Although I am in almost complete agreement, I differ in part from the conclusions which she has reached. In the special circumstances of this case I would allow the appeal to the extent necessary to permit interrogation on two of the three questions sought to be posed on behalf of the Commission of Inquiry. Namely, the two questions are those concerning first, the make-up of the appellate panel, particularly the inclusion of Pace J.A. who was Attorney General at the time of Mr. Marshall's conviction, and secondly, the composition of the record before the court at the time of the reference, specifically directed at determining which affidavits formed part of that record.

. . . .

I hasten to agree with my colleague that there is for very good reason an absolute privilege accorded to the judiciary exempting them from testifying as to their mental processes in arriving at a judgment or as to how they reached a decision in any case that came before them.

. . . .

As well a large measure of judicial immunity from testifying in respect of the administration of the work of the courts is an important and necessary factor in the functioning of the judicial system. For example, it would be unthinkable that an outside agency, whether it be a ministry of government, an agency of government or a bar associate, could designate which judge was to hear a particular case or which members of an appellate court were to sit on an appeal of a case. It is important that there be immunity for judges with regard to their conversations with administrative staff, as much as with their colleagues and clerks. Nonetheless there is an important distinction to be drawn between the two types of judicial immunity. There is first the privilege of the judiciary not to be questioned as to the decisions they have made on cases. This adjudicative privilege is of fundamental importance and is absolute in nature. Secondly, there is the privilege as to the administration of the courts. This administrative privilege is not of the same fundamental importance and is qualified in nature.

. . . .

[J]udicial independence may not necessarily be compromised by all executive or legislative action which affects the administration of the courts.

The administrative privilege of judges is not as vital to the integrity of the administration of justice as is the adjudicative privilege.

. . . .

The qualified privilege of judges on administrative matters will clearly apply in most situations. However, there are exceptional cases such as this one where the qualified privilege of immunity from testifying must give way; this will occur when it is necessary to reaffirm public confidence in the administration of justice.

To take an extreme example, if an appeal court panel consisted of three judges, all of whom at one time or another had acted as Crown counsel in the prosecution of the appellant, the judicial immunity from testifying should not prevail. In such circumstances a properly constituted and qualified commission of inquiry (such as the one involved in this case) should be entitled to pose questions and receive answers as to the basis for the make-up of the appellate panel. An administrative decision such as this, unlike a judgment or reasons for judgment, is not subject to review by appeal procedures. A review of administrative decisions by an appropriate body in cases of apparent abuse will have a salutary effect and ensure continued public confidence in the work of the courts. To paraphrase a well known adage, not only must absolute fairness be exercised in making administrative decisions pertaining to the courts, but the public must be able to perceive that there has been absolute fairness exercised in these decisions.

In this case it is appropriate to review some of the administrative decisions. The wrongful conviction of Marshall of the crime of murder in itself called for a public inquiry. Later the composition of the panel which heard his appeal could have been the subject of public criticism. The lack of any certainty as to what material comprised the record on the appeal was disquieting. Like the wrongful conviction, these last two matters are of grave concern. They can probably be readily and completely answered, but answered they should be.

. . . .

LAMER J.— I have read the reasons of my colleagues Justices Wilson, La Forest, Cory and McLachlin. While I agree with the principles set out in my brother Cory's judgment, when applying them to this case, I reach the same conclusion as my colleague McLachlin J. and, accordingly, would dismiss these appeals.

. . . .

WILSON J. (dissenting in part)— I write in support of the judgment of my colleague, Justice Cory, on these appeals. I agree with him and with my other colleagues, that the judiciary enjoys an absolute immunity with respect to its adjudicative function. I also agree with him that the judiciary's immunity with respect to its administrative function is not absolute and that it must give way in circumstances where the administration of justice is itself under review by a body with the constitutional authority to undertake such a review. It would be anomalous indeed if in a case such as the present all aspects of the justice system leading up to the wrongful conviction of Mr. Marshall, his subsequent release and his receipt of compensation could be inquired into by the Commission except the administrative decisions made by the judiciary.

. . . .

LA FOREST J.— I have had the advantage of reading the reasons of my colleagues, Cory and McLachlin JJ. With respect, I agree with McLachlin J. that the Nova Scotia *Public Inquiries Act*, R.S.N.S. 1967, c. 250, is not specific enough to override the fundamental principle of judicial immunity from being compelled to testify about the decision-making process or the reasons for the composition of the court in a particular case.

Though the point was not argued, were the Act sufficiently explicit, I would tend to the view that it was, to that extent, beyond the legislative capacity of the province.

———————————

Most of the provinces in Canada have enacted legislation providing for immunity claims in proceedings where the Crown is a party. For example, the Proceedings Against the Crown Act in Alberta provides:

11.   In proceedings against the Crown the rules of court as to discovery and inspection of documents and examination for discovery apply in the same manner as if the Crown were a corporation, except that the Crown may refuse to produce a document

or to make answer to a question on discovery on the ground that the production of it or the answer would be injurious to the public interest.[76]

In addition, some provinces have enacted legislation regarding the procedure for immunity claims in suits between parties. For example, the Ontario Evidence Act[77] provides:

30.   Where a document is in the official possession, custody or power of a member of the Executive Council, or of the head of a ministry of the public service of Ontario, if the deputy head or other officer of the ministry has the document in his personal possession, and is called as a witness, he is entitled, acting herein by the direction and on behalf of such member of the Executive Council or head of the ministry, to object to producing the document on the ground that it is privileged, and such objection may be taken by him in the same manner, and has the same effect, as if such member of the Executive Council or head of the ministry were personally present and made the objection.

Having observed the detail of the new legislative provisions in the Access to Information Act,[78] consider the following question:

In many ways, as this opinion suggests, the problem of the privilege for official information is not with the law but with the lawyers. Government attorneys, like all attorneys, like to win their cases. If they can win on procedural grounds or enhance their chances for victory by a claim of privilege, they will usually attempt to do so, regardless of whether justice is served. If government lawyers could be trusted to claim a privilege only when official interests are real and compelling, the precise language of the privilege might not be important. Because government lawyers cannot be so trusted, any governmental privilege should contain language that gives the judge substantial discretion and discourages undue judicial deference to governmental claims. Do you agree?[79]

(c) Identity of Informers

An aspect of Crown privilege,[80] or public interest immunity, is the long-established rule that the identity of informers should be protected from disclosure; the information is not protected but only its source, unless disclosure of the former would disclose the latter. In the early case of *R. v. Hardy*, Eyre, L.C.J. wrote:

It is perfectly right that all opportunities should be given to discuss the truth of the evidence given against a prisoner; but there is a rule which has universally obtained on account of its importance to the public for the detection of crime that those persons who are the channel by means of which that detection is made, should not be unnecessarily disclosed: if it can be made appear that really and truly it is necessary to the investigation of the truth of the case that the name of the person should be

---

76.   R.S.A. 1980, c. P-18.
77.   R.S.O. 1990, c. E.23.
78.   S.C. 1980-81-82-83, c. 111, Sched. V, ss. 54-58 proclaimed in force January 14, 1983; ss. 1-53, 59-77 and Schedules I and II proclaimed in force July 1, 1983.
79.   Posed by Lempert and Saltsburg, *A Modern Approach to Evidence* (1977), p. 703.
80.   Speaking for the majority in the Supreme Court of Canada, Martland, J. continues this phrasing: see *Sol. Gen. Can. v. Royal Commn. Re Health Records* (1982), 62 C.C.C. (2d) 193, 226. Compare Lord Reid in *Rogers v. Home Secretary*, [1973] A.C. 388 (H.L.).

disclosed, I should be very unwilling to stop it, but it does not appear to me that it is within the ordinary course to do it.[81]

While the privilege may have initially been recognized as existing only in criminal prosecutions, the Supreme Court of Canada has recently held it to be available in both criminal and civil proceedings.[82]

The public's interest in concealing the identity of informers is well described by Haines, J. in *R. v. Lalonde:*

... without our citizens giving information to the police the investigation of a crime would be seriously impaired or even defeated. Without witnesses our Courts could not function. Those who know of material facts should be able to disclose them to the police with the assurance they will be treated in confidence. In an aggressive community fear of retaliation can be very real.[83]

The privilege is not absolute. Lord Esher in *Marks v. Beyfus* wrote:

I do not say it is a rule which can never be departed from; if upon the trial of a prisoner the judge should be of opinion that the disclosure of the name of the informant is necessary or right in order to shew the prisoner's innocence, then one public policy is in conflict with another public policy, and that which says that an innocent man is not to be condemned when his innocence can be proved is the policy that must prevail. But except in that case, this rule of public policy is not a matter of discretion; it is a rule of law, and as such should be applied by the judge at the trial, who should not treat it as a matter of discretion whether he should tell the witness to answer or not.[84]

R. v. LEIPERT
[1997] 1 S.C.R. 281, 4 C.R. (5th) 259, 112 C.C.C. (3d) 385

[The police received a Crime Stoppers tip that the accused was growing marihuana in his basement. The police walked the street outside the residence with a sniffer dog on four occasions and each time the dog indicated the presence of drugs. On one occasion a police officer smelt marihuana coming from the accused's house. He also observed that the basement windows were covered and one window was barred shut. The officer obtained a search warrant on the basis of the observations. The information to obtain the search warrant also disclosed that the officer had received a Crime Stoppers tip. The search warrant was executed and the accused was charged with cultivation of marihuana and possession of marihuana for the purpose of trafficking. At trial the accused obtained an order for disclosure of the document reporting the Crime Stoppers tip. The Crown had refused disclosure on the ground of informer privilege. The trial judge had attempted to edit out all references to the identity of the informer. The Crown asked to rely on the warrant without reference to the tip. The trial

---

81. (1794), 24 Howell's State Trials 199.
82. *Sol. Gen. Can. v. Royal Commn. Re Health Records, supra*, note 80.
83. (1971), 5 C.C.C. (2d) 168, 179-80 (Ont. H.C.).
84. (1890), 25 Q.B.D. 494, 498 (C.A.). This passage was adopted by the Ontario Court of Appeal in *Humphrey v. Archibald* (1893), 20 O.A.R. 267, 270 and by the Saskatchewan Court of Appeal in *R. v. Blain* (1960), 127 C.C.C. 267. See also *R. v. Davies* (1983), 31 C.R. (3d) 88 (Ont. C.A.). And see Laskin, C.J.C. in *Sol. Gen. Can. v. Royal Commn. Re Health Records, supra*, note 80, at p. 218.

judge refused that request because the accused did not consent. The Crown ceased to tender evidence and the accused was acquitted. The British Columbia Court of Appeal quashed the acquittal and ordered a new trial. The accused appealed. The appeal was dismissed.]

McLACHLIN J. (LAMER C.J.C., LA FOREST, SOPINKA, GONTHIER, CORY, IACOBUCCI and MAJOR JJ. concurring):—

. . . .

The trial judge was faced with two apparently conflicting rules. The first was the rule requiring disclosure to the defence of all information not clearly irrelevant or privileged. The second was the rule of informer privilege. The trial judge attempted to accommodate both rules by editing the tip sheet to remove information that could reveal the tipster's identity and ordering production of the balance of the tip sheet. I share the view of McEachern C.J.B.C. in the Court of Appeal that the trial judge's approach gave insufficient weight to both the importance of maintaining informer privilege and the danger of ordering disclosure of tip sheets containing details which, despite editing, may enable an accused person to identify the informant.

(a) The Importance of Informer Privilege

A court considering this issue must begin from the proposition that informer privilege is an ancient and hallowed protection which plays a vital role in law enforcement. It is premised on the duty of all citizens to aid in enforcing the law. The discharge of this duty carries with it the risk of retribution from those involved in crime. The rule of informer privilege was developed to protect citizens who assist in law enforcement and to encourage others to do the same. As Cory J.A. (as he then was) stated in *R. v. Hunter* (1987), 57 C.R. (3d) 1 (Ont. C.A.), at pp. 5-6:

> The rule against the non-disclosure of information which might identify an informer is one of long standing. It developed from an acceptance of the importance of the role of informers in the solution of crimes and the apprehension of criminals. It was recognized that citizens have a duty to divulge to the police any information that they may have pertaining to the commission of a crime. It was also obvious to the courts from very early times that the identity of an informer would have to be concealed, both for his or her own protection and to encourage others to divulge to the authorities any information pertaining to crimes. It was in order to achieve these goals that the rule was developed.

The rule is of fundamental importance to the workings of a criminal justice system. As described in *Bisaillon v. Keable*, [1983] 2 S.C.R. 60, at p. 105:

> The rule gives a peace officer the power to promise his informers secrecy expressly or by implication, with a guarantee sanctioned by the law that this promise will be kept even in court, and to receive in exchange for this promise information without which it would be extremely difficult for him to carry out his duties and ensure that the criminal law is obeyed.

In *R. v. Scott*, [1990] 3 S.C.R. 979, at p. 994, Cory J. stressed the heightened importance of the rule in the context of drug investigations:

> The value of informers to police investigations has long been recognized. As long as crimes have been committed, certainly as long as they have been prosecuted, informers have played an important role in their investigation. It may well be true that some informers act for compensation or for self-serving purposes. Whatever their motives, the position of informers is always precarious and their role is fraught with danger. The role of informers in drug-related cases is particularly important and dangerous. Informers often provide the only means for the police to gain some

knowledge of the workings of the drug trafficking operations and networks. . . . The investigation often will be based upon a relationship of trust between the police officer and the informer, something that may take a long time to establish. The safety, indeed the lives, not only of informers but also of the undercover police officers will depend on that relationship of trust.

In most cases, the identity of the informer is known to the police. However, in cases like the instant one, the identity of the informer is unknown to everyone including the Crime Stoppers' agent who received the call. The importance of the informer privilege rule in cases where the identity of the informer is anonymous was stressed by the California Court of Appeal in *People v. Callen*, 194 Cal.App.3d 558 (1987). The court, in holding that the police have no duty to determine or disclose the identity of anonymous informers, stated at p. 587:

> Such an investigatory burden would not only be onerous and frequently futile, it would destroy programs such as Crimestoppers by removing the guarantee of anonymity. Anonymity is the key to such a program. It is the promise of anonymity which allays the fear of criminal retaliation which otherwise discourages citizen involvement in reporting crime. In turn, by guaranteeing anonymity, Crimestoppers provides law enforcement with information it might never otherwise obtain. We are satisfied the benefits of a Crimestoppers-type program — citizen involvement in reporting crime and criminals — far outweigh any speculative benefits to the defense arising from imposing a duty on law enforcement to gather and preserve evidence of the identity of informants who wish to remain anonymous.

Informer privilege is of such importance that once found, courts are not entitled to balance the benefit enuring from the privilege against countervailing considerations, as is the case, for example, with Crown privilege or privileges based on Wigmore's four-part test: J. Sopinka, S.N. Lederman and A.W. Bryant, *The Law of Evidence in Canada* (1992), at pp. 805-6. In *Bisaillon v. Keable*, supra, this Court contrasted informer privilege with Crown privilege in this regard. In Crown privilege, the judge may review the information and in the last resort revise the minister's decisions by weighing the two conflicting interests, that of maintaining secrecy and that of doing justice. The Court stated at pp. 97-98:

> This procedure, designed to implement Crown privilege, is pointless in the case of secrecy regarding a police informer. In this case, the law gives the Minister, and the Court after him, no power of weighing or evaluating various aspects of the public interest which are in conflict, since it has already resolved the conflict itself. It has decided once and for all, subject to the law being changed, that information regarding police informers' identity will be, because of its content, a class of information which it is in the public interest to keep secret, and that this interest will prevail over the need to ensure the highest possible standard of justice. Accordingly, the common law has made secrecy regarding police informers subject to a special system with its own rules, which differ from those applicable to Crown privilege.

The Court in *Bisaillon v. Keable* summed the matter up by asserting that the application of informer privilege "does not depend on the judge's discretion, as it is a legal rule of public order by which the judge is bound". In summary, informer privilege is of such importance that it cannot be balanced against other interests. Once established, neither the police nor the court possesses discretion to abridge it.

(b) Who May Claim Informer Privilege?

The privilege belongs to the Crown: *Canada (Solicitor General) v. Royal Commission (Health Records)*, [1981] 2 S.C.R. 494. However, the Crown cannot, without the informer's consent, waive the privilege either expressly or by implication by not raising it: *Bisaillon v. Keable*, supra, at p. 94. In that sense, it also belongs to the informer. This follows from the purpose of the privilege, being the protection of those who provide information to the police and the encouragement of others to do the same. This is the second reason why the police and courts do not have a discretion to relieve against the privilege.

The fact that the privilege also belongs to the informer raises special concerns in the case of anonymous informants, like those who provide telephone tips to Crime Stoppers. Since the informer whom the privilege is designed to protect and his or her circumstances are unknown, it is often difficult to predict with certainty what information might allow the accused to identify the informer. A detail as innocuous as the time of the telephone call may be sufficient to permit identification. In such circumstances, courts must exercise great care not to unwittingly deprive informers of the privilege which the law accords to them.

(c) The Scope of Informer Privilege

Connected as it is to the essential effectiveness of the criminal law, informer privilege is broad in scope. While developed in criminal proceedings, it applies in civil proceedings as well: *Bisaillon v. Keable*, supra. It applies to a witness on the stand. Such a person cannot be compelled to state whether he or she is a police informer: *Bisaillon v. Keable*, supra. And it applies to the undisclosed informant, the person who although never called as a witness, supplies information to the police. Subject only to the "innocence at stake" exception, the Crown and the court are bound not to reveal the undisclosed informant's identity.

Informer privilege prevents not only disclosure of the name of the informant, but of any information which might implicitly reveal his or her identity. Courts have acknowledged that the smallest details may be sufficient to reveal identity.

McEachern C.J.B.C. in the case at bar suggested that an "accused may know that only some very small circle of persons, perhaps only one, may know an apparently innocuous fact that is mentioned in the document". He noted: "The privilege is a hallowed one, and it should be respected scrupulously".

The jurisprudence therefore suggests that the Crown must claim privilege over information that reveals the identity of the informant or that may implicitly reveal identity. In many cases, the Crown will be able to contact the informer to determine the extent of information that can be released without jeopardizing the anonymity of the tipster. The informer is the only person who knows the potential danger of releasing those facts to the accused. The difficulty in this case is that the identity of the informer is unknown. Therefore, the Crown is not in a position to determine whether any part of the information could reveal his or her identity. This led the Crown in the case at bar to claim privilege for all of the information provided by the informer. The extension of privilege to all information that could identify an informant justifies this claim in the case of an anonymous informant.

(d) The "Innocence at Stake" Exception

Informer privilege is subject only to one exception, known as the "innocence at stake" exception. Lord Esher, M.R., described this exception in *Marks v. Beyfus* (1890), 25 Q.B.D. 494 (C.A.), at p. 498:

> If upon the trial of a prisoner the judge should be of opinion that the disclosure of the name of the informant is necessary or right in order to shew the prisoner's innocence, then one public policy is in conflict with another public policy, and that which says that an innocent man is not to be condemned when his innocence can be proved is the policy which must prevail.

In *Bisaillon v. Keable*, supra, this Court held (at p. 93):

> The rule is subject to only one exception, imposed by the need to demonstrate the innocence of an accused person.

As Cory J. stated in *Scott*, supra, at pp. 995-96:

> In our system the right of an individual accused to establish his or her innocence by raising a reasonable doubt as to guilt has always remained paramount.

In order to raise the "innocence at stake" exception to informer privilege, there must be a basis on the evidence for concluding that disclosure of the informer's identity is necessary to demonstrate the innocence of the accused: *R. v. Chiarantano*, [1990] O.J. No. 2603 (C.A.), per Brooke J.A., aff'd [1991] 1 S.C.R. 906. In *Chiarantano*, supra, the possibility that the information provided by the informer regarding the arrival at a residence of drugs later found in the possession of the accused might conflict with the evidence of the accused was held not to raise a basis for disclosure pursuant to the "innocence at stake" exception. The court held that the usefulness of the information was speculative and that mere speculation that the information might assist the defence is insufficient. If speculation sufficed to remove the privilege, little if anything would be left of the protection which the privilege purports to accord.

On the other hand, circumstances may arise where the evidence establishes a basis for the exception, as where the informer is a material witness to the crime or acted as an agent provocateur: see *Scott*, supra. Where such a basis is established, the privilege must yield to the principle that a person is not to be condemned when his or her innocence can be proved.

(e) Informer Privilege and the Charter

It has been suggested (although not by the appellant) that the Canadian Charter of Rights and Freedoms, as interpreted in *Stinchcombe*, supra, has introduced another exception to the informer privilege rule based on the right to full disclosure of documents in the Crown's possession in aid of the Charter guarantee of the right to make full answer and defence: D.M. Tanovich "When Does *Stinchcombe* Demand that the Crown Reveal the Identity of a Police Informer?" (1995), 38 C.R. (4th) 202. According to this argument, "innocence at stake" would no longer be the only exception to the informer privilege rule.

This argument rests on a right to disclosure broader than any which this Court has enunciated. In *Stinchcombe*, supra, the right to disclosure of Crown documents was expressly made subject to two conditions: relevance (to be interpreted generously as including all that is not clearly irrelevant) and privilege. The right to disclosure was not to trump privilege. Any doubt about its application to informer privilege was expressly negated:

> It is suggested that disclosure may put at risk the security and safety of persons who have provided the prosecution with information. No doubt measures must occasionally be taken to protect the identity of witnesses and informers. Protection of the identity of informers is covered by the rules relating to informer privilege and exceptions thereto.

. . . .

I find no inconsistency between the Charter right to disclosure of Crown documents affirmed in *Stinchcombe*, supra, and the common law rule of informer privilege.

(f) Informer Privilege and Challenges to Search Warrants

Where the accused seeks to establish that a search warrant was not supported by reasonable grounds, the accused may be entitled to information which may reveal the identity of an informer notwithstanding informer privilege "in circumstances where it is absolutely essential": *Scott*, supra, at p. 996. "Essential" circumstances exist where the accused establishes the "innocence at stake" exception to informer privilege. Such a case might arise, for example, where there is evidence suggesting that the goods seized in execution of the warrant were planted. To establish that the informer planted the goods or had information as to how they came to be planted, the accused might properly seek disclosure of information that may incidentally reveal the identity of the informer.

Absent a basis for concluding that disclosure of the information that may reveal the identity of the informer is necessary to establish the innocence of the accused, the information remains privileged and cannot be produced, whether on a hearing into the reasonableness of the search or on the trial proper.

(g) Judicial Editing

The ultimate issue on this appeal is whether the trial judge erred in editing the tip sheet to remove references to the informer's identity and in ordering the edited sheet disclosed to the appellant. In addressing this question, I have regard to the following propositions, discussed above. Informer privilege is of great importance. Once established, the privilege cannot be diminished by or "balanced off against" other concerns relating to the administration of justice. The police and the court have no discretion to diminish it and are bound to uphold it. The only exception to the privilege is found where there is a basis to conclude that the information may be necessary to establish the innocence of the accused. The scope of the rule extends not only to the name of the informer, but to any details which might reveal the informer's identity. It is virtually impossible for the court to know what details may reveal the identity of an anonymous informer. The same considerations apply on challenges to search warrants or wiretap authorizations.

These considerations suggest that anonymous tip sheets should not be edited with a view to disclosing them to the defence unless the accused can bring himself within the innocence at stake exception. To do so runs the risk that the court will deprive the informer of the privilege which belongs to him or her absolutely, subject only to the "innocence at stake" exception. It also undermines the efficacy of programs such as Crimestoppers, which depend on guarantees of anonymity to those who volunteer information on crimes.

. . . .

There may be cases where the informer and his circumstances are known, in which the court can be certain that what remains of an informant document after editing will not reveal the informer's identity. When, however, as in the case at bar, it is impossible to determine which details of the information provided by an informer will or will not result in that person's identity being revealed, then none of those details should be disclosed, unless there is a basis to conclude that the innocence at stake exception applies.

(h) Procedure

When an accused seeks disclosure of privileged informer information on the basis of the "innocence at stake" exception, the following procedure will apply. First, the accused must show some basis to conclude that without the disclosure sought his or her innocence is at stake. If such a basis is shown, the court may then review the information to determine whether, in fact, the information is necessary to prove the accused's innocence. If the court concludes that disclosure is necessary, the court should only reveal as much information as is essential to allow proof of innocence. Before disclosing the information to the accused, the Crown should be given the option of staying the proceedings. If the Crown chooses to proceed, disclosure of the information essential to establish innocence may be provided to the accused.

(i) Application to the Case at Bar

The identity of the anonymous informer was protected by informer privilege. The police and the courts were bound to protect the identity of the informant from disclosure. Given the anonymous nature of the tip, it was impossible to conclude whether the disclosure of details remaining after editing might be sufficient to reveal the identity of the informer to the accused and others who might have been involved in this crime and seeking retribution. It follows that the statement should not have been edited and ordered disclosed to the defence. The informer's privilege required nothing short of total confidentiality. As it was not established that the identity was necessary to establish the innocence of the accused, the privilege continued in place.

. . . .

B. Did the Trial Judge Err in Declining to Allow the Crown to Delete the Reference the Informer from the Material in Support of the Warrant?

The trial judge declined to permit the Crown to withdraw the reference to the tip from the "Information to Obtain" and defend the warrant without reference to it. In his view, this could not be done unless the appellant consented. In my view, this was an error.

The issue before the trial judge was whether there were reasonable grounds for the issuance of the warrant. If the Crown wished to limit its defence of the reasonableness of the warrant and subsequent search to particular grounds, it was entitled to do so. At the end of the day, the task of the judge was to make a ruling on reasonableness on the basis of the information relied on by the Crown.

In the case at bar, the appellant has not brought himself within the "innocence at stake" exception. Therefore, the trial judge should have permitted the Crown to defend the warrant on the material in the "Information to Obtain" with the reference to the Crime Stoppers' tip deleted.

3. CASE-BY-CASE PRIVILEGE

Wigmore recognized that to suppress relevant evidence and so inhibit the search for truth required a public interest weightier than the public's general right to everyman's evidence. He suggested then four conditions as necessary to the establishment of a privilege for confidential communications:

(1) The communications must originate in a *confidence* that they will not be disclosed.

(2) This element of *confidentiality must be essential* to the full and satisfactory maintenance of the relation between the parties.

(3) The *relation* must be one which in the opinion of the community ought to be sedulously *fostered.*

(4) The *injury* that would inure to the relation by the disclosure of the communications must be *greater than the benefit* thereby gained for the correct disposal of litigation.

Only if these four conditions are present should a privilege be recognized.[85]

In *Slavutych v. Baker*[86] the appellant appealed against his dismissal as a university professor. Slavutych had been asked for a confidential report on a colleague's suitability for tenure and this report was used against Slavutych to justify his dismissal; the actual charge against Slavutych was that he had in his report, made a "very serious charge on the flimsiest basis." A board of arbitration upheld the dismissal. The Supreme Court of Canada quashed the award of the arbitration board on the substantive law basis that a party who obtains information in confidence shall not be allowed to use it as a springboard for an action against the person who made the confidential communication. It was not necessary then for the court to consider the admissibility of the document as an evidentiary matter

---

85.   8 Wigmore, *Evidence* (McNaughton Rev.), s. 2285.

86.   (1975), 55 D.L.R. (3d) 224 (S.C.C.).

but, speaking for a unanimous court, Spence, J. measured the communication against Wigmore's criteria and concluded:

> . . . considering this matter only an evidentiary one and under the doctrine of privilege as so ably considered in Wigmore the confidential document should have been ruled inadmissible.[87]

The court's lead, adopting Wigmore's criteria as a guide for the recognition of future privileged communications, has since been followed in a number of cases[88] as the courts seemingly agree with the observation of Laskin, C.J.C.:

> What *Slavutych v. Baker* established is that the categories of privilege are not closed.[89]

R. v. S. (R.)
(1985), 45 C.R. (3d) 161, 19 C.C.C. (3d) 115 (Ont. C.A.)

[The accused was charged with sexual offences involving his young step-daughters. The accused had participated in counselling sessions at a family clinic. The prosecution wished to introduce tape recordings of these sessions. During the sessions the accused was mainly silent and did not deny the allegations of sexual misconduct described by the step-daughters. The judgment of the court was delivered by:]

LACOURCIÈRE J.A.:—

. . . .

The issue of medical privilege

As previously mentioned, following the 1973 complaints and Dr. Lamont's examination, the whole family attended counselling sessions at the Chedoke Family Clinic.

---

87. *Ibid.*, at p. 229. In *Re Inquiry into the Confidentiality of Health Records in Ontario* (1979), 98 D.L.R. (3d) 704, 719 (Ont. C.A.), Dubin, J.A. echoed Spence, J.'s opinion and wrote: "The conditions set forth in that text are, in my opinion, the best test to date to determine whether the privilege contended for exists." On appeal to the Supreme Court of Canada, Laskin, C.J.C. wrote: "What *Slavutych v. Baker* . . . established is that the categories of privilege are not closed. . . . This Court, speaking through Spence J. in the *Slavutych* case, was of the opinion that the fourfold test propounded in 8 Wigmore *Evidence*, §2285, p. 527 provided a satisfactory guide for the recognition of a claim of privilege": (1981), 62 C.C.C. (2d) 193, 207 (S.C.C.).

88. See, *e.g.*, *Jones v. Crompton*, [1977] 4 W.W.R. 440 (B.C.S.C.), diary not prepared in a confidence not privileged; *Bergwitz v. Fast* (1979), 97 D.L.R. (3d) 65 (B.C.S.C.); reversed (1980), 108 D.L.R. (3d) 732 (B.C.C.A.), report by investigating committee of College of Dental Surgeons not privileged as "the injury that 'would enure to the relation by the disclosure' of the views of the investigating committee would not be 'greater than the benefit thereby gained for the correct disposal of litigation' "; *Smith v. Royal Columbian Hosp.* (1981), 123 D.L.R. (3d) 723 (B.C.S.C.), report of Credentials Committee privileged as all four criteria satisfied; *R. v. Littlechild* (1979), 108 D.L.R. (3d) 340 (Alta. C.A.), communication with official on legal aid application privileged as all four conditions satisfied; *Re Univ. of Guelph & C.A.U.T.* (1980), 112 D.L.R. (3d) 692 (Ont. H.C.), communications with university promotion and tenure committee privileged as all four conditions satisfied.

89. *Sol. Gen. Can. v. Royal Commn. Re Health Records, supra*, note 80, at p. 207. Compare Lord Hailsham in *D. v. N.S.P.C.C.*, [1978] A.C. 171, 230 (H.L.): "The categories of public interest are not closed, and must alter from time to time whether by restriction or extension as social conditions and social legislation develop."

Again, in 1978, following Dr. Koziak's examination of A.B., the family re-attended at the same clinic on March 9th and 15th. In the course of the trial the presiding judge conducted a *voir dire* to determine the admissibility of the evidence of Dr. Sawa, the clinic's resident in family therapy, and particularly of the tape and transcript of the second session. On the *voir dire*, it came out that the sexual allegations against the appellant were discussed.

At the urging of Dr. Sawa, who wanted to have a more complete understanding of the family situation, the appellant voluntarily attended the second session which he knew had been prompted by the sexual allegation made against him. The 1978 sessions were recorded on tape for the doctor's own personal education and self-improvement.

The Crown sought to adduce evidence of the contents of the March 15th session which was ruled admissible despite the defence objection made on the basis that the appellant's statements were not voluntary, were made to a person in authority and violated principles of natural justice secured by s. 7 of the *Canadian Charter of Rights and Freedoms*. The ruling of the trial judge refusing to give effect to those objections has not been appealed. The only other objection to the evidence overruled by the trial judge and now advanced on appeal is that the communications made at the counselling session constituted privileged communications as between a doctor and his patient.

Dr. Sawa testified that, after giving a general introduction explaining the purpose of the family assessment, he stated his intention to tape the session and that neither the appellant nor the other members of the family objected. The rest of the session was recorded. I have read the entire 54-page transcript of the assessment session. Basically, the appellant remained silent or was non-committal or evasive when issues surrounding his sexual misconduct were discussed in his presence, although he was invited by Dr. Sawa to "talk about it", to state or comment on feelings about what had been said and, after being urged by his wife, to defend himself. In the *voir dire*, the appellant gave several explanations for his silence:

(1)   He was there to help A.B. get at the root of why she was lying and if he spoke, she would "clam up".

(2)   Everyone knew A.B. was lying.

(3)   Dr. Sawa believed A.B. so there was little point in him denying it.

(4)   Dr. Sawa knew that he had already denied it from the information he had received from Mrs. S during the March 9th session so he did not have to repeat it.

(5)   He was not there to respond to lies.

(6)   He was embarrassed to talk about sex.

(7)   He was a man of few words.

All of these explanations were rejected by the trial judge who made adverse findings against the appellant's credibility. There is no doubt that his silence and evasiveness in the face of direct and indirect accusations of sexual misconduct, which reasonably called for some response from him, contributed to these adverse findings and hence to the finding of guilt.

The learned trial judge ruled against the claim for privilege in the following words:

> With respect to the matter of privilege that was raised. While I felt that there was much to be said for the reasoning of the Honourable Mr. Justice Stewart in the case of *Dembie v. Dembie* (1963), 21 R.F.L. 46, on the authorities presented to me, which were numerous, it seemed very clear and I find that there was no doctor-patient privilege existing between Dr. Sawa and Mr. S which would render his statement inadmissible.

Mr. Code, on behalf of the appellant, contended that the classes of privilege traditionally recognized by the common law, such as, national security and communications between solicitor and client and between husband and wife, should be extended to cover communications between a doctor and his or her patient, particularly in the case of confidential psychiatric counselling interviews. Such expansion of the privilege has been traditionally resisted by common law courts: see *D. v. National Society for Prevention of Cruelty to Children*, [1978] A.C. 171, where the immunity from disclosure allowed by law to police informers was extended to persons who give information about neglect or ill-treatment of children to the National Society for the Prevention of Cruelty to Children. The public interest served by such an extension was considered analogous in both cases. See also *Reference re Legislative Privilege* (1978), 39 C.C.C. (2d) 226, and *Solicitor-General of Canada et al. v. Royal Com'n of Inquiry into Confidentiality of Health Records in Ontario et al.* (1981), 62 C.C.C. (2d) 193.

A federal provincial task force as well as the Ontario Law Reform Commission have expressly refused to recommend any statutory extension of the privilege: see Report of the Federal/Provincial Task Force on Uniform Rules of Evidence, Professional Privilege and Ontario Law Reform Commission Report on the Law of Evidence, Private Privilege. The common *rationale* appears to be that the courts, in their search for truth, should not exclude evidence which is relevant and otherwise admissible or close ". . . to the judicial process wide areas in its search for truth": *Ontario Law Reform Commission Report*, at p. 146.

The appellant's best position is that the decision of the Supreme Court of Canada in *Slavutych v. Baker et al.* (1975), 38 C.R.N.S. 306, has left it open to the courts, in the exercise of their judicial discretion, to recognize and give effect to new categories of privilege on a case-by-case basis, provided that the four criteria "so ably considered in Wigmore" (*per* Spence J. at p. 261 S.C.R.) are present: 8 *Wigmore on Evidence*, 3rd ed. (McNaughton rev., 1961), s. 2312. The four criteria are set out in *Slavutych v. Baker*, *supra*, as follows at p. 260 S.C.R.:

> The communications must originate in a *confidence* that they will not be disclosed.
>
> (2) This element of *confidentiality must be essential* to the full and satisfactory maintenance of the relation between the parties.
>
> (3) The *relation* must be one which in the opinion of the community ought to be sedulously *fostered*.
>
> (4) The *injury* that would inure to the relation by the disclosure of the communications must be *greater than the benefit* thereby gained for the correct disposal of litigation.

The respondent conceded that this discretion existed, therefore this Court heard submissions on the applicability of these criteria in the present case.

(1) *Confidence*

In his ruling on the *voir dire*, the trial judge stated that it was "clear that all parties present at the interview felt that what was said would be confidential . . .". Referring to Dr. Sawa's evidence, he stated:

> He did not expressly say, as I recall, that the dealings would be confidential but it was certainly understood by him as it was by all those present and indeed, as in his own words were that he was very shocked to find that he was called upon to attend a trial of this nature by reason of having conducted that interview and assessment.

Ms. Wein, for the Crown, submitted that there was no explicit guarantee of confidentiality and no common understanding to that effect inasmuch as the sexual allegations had already been made to several other persons. Furthermore, she pointed out that at the end of the session Dr. Sawa disclosed his intention to report A.B.'s situation to the Children's Aid Society. There was no objection from anyone, but Ms. Wein concedes that this was perhaps due to the appellant's belief that the doctor's report would be confined to the financial status of A.B. The fact is, however, that Dr. Sawa never did disclose the situation to the Children's Aid Society.

It is relevant, in this context, to refer to the provisions of the *Child Welfare Act*, R.S.O. 1980, c. 66. After defining "abuse" in s. 47(1) as meaning:

(*a*)   physical harm;

(*b*)   malnutrition or mental ill-health of a degree that if not immediately remedied could seriously impair growth and development or result in permanent injury or death; or

(*c*)   sexual molestation.

Section 49 provides as follows:

49(1) Every person who has information of the abandonment, desertion or need for protection of a child or the infliction of abuse upon a child shall forthwith report the information to a society.

(2) Notwithstanding the provisions of any other Act, every person who has reasonable grounds to suspect in the course of the person's professional or official duties that a child has suffered or is suffering from abuse that may have been caused or permitted by a person who has or has had charge of the child shall forthwith report the suspected abuse to a society.

(3) This section applies notwithstanding that the information reported is confidential or privileged and no action for making the report shall be instituted against any person who reports the information to a society in accordance with subsection (1) or (2) unless the giving of the information is done maliciously or without reasonable grounds to suspect that the information is true.

(4) Nothing in this section shall abrogate any privilege that may exist between a solicitor and the solicitor's client.

Mr. Code contended that the information to be reported refers only to the *fact* of suspected abuse, such as, bruises, etc., and not to the communication itself. It would follow from this argument that the appellant was correct in believing that the communications made during the psychiatric session were privileged.

This narrow construction seems to ignore the provisions of s-s. (3). Dr. Sawa was not asked why he did not report the sexual aspect as opposed to the financial situation as he was required to do notwithstanding any notion of confidentiality or privilege.

It was also submitted by the Crown that the present case does not meet Wigmore's first criterion inasmuch as there was no therapeutic relationship between the appellant and the psychiatrist and no communication originating from the appellant. I do not accept this submission because the appellant was a participant in what may be viewed as group therapy and his "eloquent" silence may be viewed as supporting an inference of consciousness of guilt.

Having regard to all the circumstances and to the finding of fact that the appellant, as well as the other "patients" in the group, regarded the group therapy session as confidential, I am satisfied that Wigmore's first criterion has been met.

(2) *Was confidence essential to the maintenance of the relation?*

It seems reasonable to assume that confidentiality is essential to the full and satisfactory maintenance of a relationship between a psychiatrist and the patients in a group therapy session. However, the Crown referred to some academic writing and empirical evidence against the assumption. Reference was made to Shuman and Weiner, "The Privilege Study: An Empirical Examination of the Psychotherapist-Patient Privilege", [1982] N.C.L. Rev. 893 at p. 926 (1982); Manson, "Observations from an Ethical Perspective on Fitness Insanity and Confidentiality" 27 McGill L.J. 196 at pp. 222-32 (1982); Bing Ho, "The Psychiatrist and the Accused", [1980] U. of T. Fac. L.R. 197; Tacon, "A Question of Privilege: Valid Protection or Obstruction of Justice?" 17 O.H.L.J. 332 (1979); Freedman, "Medical Privilege", 32 Can. Bar. Rev. 1 (1954), and

H.A. Hammelmann, "Professional Privilege: A Comparative Study", 28 Can. Bar. Rev. 750 (1950). The article by Professors Shuman and Weiner presents empirical evidence to cast doubt on the theoretical relationship between confidentiality and effective therapy. On the basis of data gathered by means of a questionnaire distributed to a representative cross-section of the population, the authors conclude, *inter alia*, that patients are probably not deterred from seeking psychiatric help, hindered from making free disclosure or caused to prematurely terminate their treatment due to lack of a privilege. Mr. Justice Freedman, in his article, also suggests that confidentiality is not essential to the patient-doctor relationship, basing his statement on the observation that the profession has long functioned without such a privilege. Professor Manson refers to commentators who argue that the benefits of the privilege are questionable and speculative and observes that courts, in the past, have not recognized the importance of confidentiality for effective therapy. But he goes on to argue for an extension of the solicitor-client privilege to cover the psychiatric relationship where it is litigation-related. The remaining three articles would suggest that confidentiality is essential to the relationship.

In view of the lack of unanimity on this point, in the absence of expert evidence on this record and having regard to my conclusion on the fourth criterion, I prefer to express no opinion on the necessary relationship between confidentiality and effective therapy.

(3) Encouragement of family counselling in cases of child abuse

It was conceded by counsel for the Crown that group therapy for the purpose of marital reconciliation involves a relation which in the opinion of the community ought to be sedulously fostered. This view is reflected in s. 21 of the *Divorce Act*, R.S.C. 1970, c. D-8, whereby admissions and communications made in the course of reconciliation proceedings are not admissible in legal proceedings. Similarly, family counselling in cases of child abuse receives community approval and should be encouraged. This encouragement is, however, subject to the proper balancing of benefit against injury set out in the fourth criterion.

(4) Balancing the benefit against the injury

This criterion is at the crux of the appellant's claim for an extension of the privilege. Mr. Code, for the appellant, has suggested that the breach of patient-psychiatrist confidentiality would result in an injury greater than the benefit to the judicial process by drying up the communications necessary to effective therapy. If the communications are not privileged, according to this argument, lawyers will advise their clients against discussing any criminal offence, including child abuse, with the psychiatrist and psychiatrists will not be able to give any valid undertaking to preserve confidentiality. He submitted that the policy of the courts should favour the preservation of confidentiality in those cases. He referred to *Dembie v. Dembie* (1963), 21 R.F.L. 46, a transcript of a hearing before the late Mr. Justice Stewart who refused to compel a psychiatrist to disclose a communication made to him by his patient in breach of the Hippocratic oath. Counsel for the appellant also referred to what may be described as the marital counselling cases: *G. v. G.*, [1964] 1 O.R. 361; *Porter v. Porter* (1983), 40 O.R. (2d) 417, and *Shakotko v. Shakotko and Williamson* (1976), 27 R.F.L. 1. In these cases, communications made in the presence of a marriage counsellor were held to be privileged at common law as well as by the operation of s. 21(2) of the *Divorce Act*. The privilege was extended in these cases not on the basis of a "professional privilege" but because the communications and admissions had been made during the attempt at reconciliation.

In *Re Waterford Hospital and The Queen* (1983), 6 C.C.C. (3d) 481 at pp. 486-7, Mifflin C.J.N., delivering the judgment of the Newfoundland Supreme Court (Court of Appeal) in quashing a search warrant authorizing the search and seizure of medical files arising from a remand for mental examination arising in a murder case, said this:

> In the present case it has to be accepted that the justice of the peace was fully aware of the reason the trial judge committed the accused to the hospital, and, it is

not unreasonable to expect, that he knew generally the method used at the hospital to make the assessment. Therefore, in my view, to sustain the issuance of this warrant this court would have to support the proposition that, when an accused has been commmitted to the hospital for the purpose of determining his or her mental capacity to stand trial, on an information sworn by a peace officer that he had been informed that an accused had made statements relevant to the commission of the offence, that a justice of the peace (who could be the same judge) could issue a warrant to obtain the record of these statements.

That is a proposition to which I cannot subscribe, nor do I think Parliament intended to allow it. It is fundamental to the very purpose of the remand procedure that those who are charged with assessing the patient be at liberty to conduct their examinations and tests without the fear of their methods and results becoming matters of evidence at a trial, and that the confidential atmosphere between doctor and patient be preserved. It seems to me that to permit a search warrant to issue destroys the very efficacy of the remand procedure, and that a justice of the peace is without jurisdiction to issue it.

I do not think that these cases help the appellant's position in the balancing of interests. In my view, the search for truth in the criminal process outweighs the need for family counselling, at least in cases of suspected child abuse. As previously mentioned, the policy of the law has been to limit the categories of privilege, subject to the judicial discretion to refuse to admit evidence obtained in confidence, such as, the penitent's confession to a priest and the spouse's communication to her psychiatrist in *Dembie v. Dembie, supra.*

The provincial Legislature, in the *Child Welfare Act*, has clearly created an obligation to report cases of suspected abuse to a society. While it is clear, for constitutional reasons, that the provincial Legislature cannot affect the admissibility of evidence in criminal cases, the child welfare legislation is nevertheless a strong and useful indication of public policy in these cases. The vital interest of society in protecting children from abuse must, in my view, be superior to the encouragement of patients to seek therapy from psychiatrists with the assurance that their confidential communications will be protected.

For another consideration of the *Slavutych* criteria see *R. v. Delong.*[90] The accused was charged with assaulting police. The question was whether the trial judge should have ordered production of statements given to police complaints investigators for use in the defence of the accused. The statements were those previously given by Crown witnesses to investigators on a complaint made by the accused to the Complaint Investigation Bureau of the Peel Regional Police, arising out of the same circumstances. The court decided that it was doubtful whether there was true confidentiality established by the informal understanding with the police association. Nor was the relationship one which needed to be "sedulously fostered." Finally, the court decided that it was not satisfied that under condition 4, the "injury" that would result to the relationship between the police officers and the Complaint Bureau had a social value that would outweigh the public interest in favour of the accused facing a serious criminal charge, of having the right to disclosure to enable him to make full answer and defence. The court decided that the statements should have been produced and allowed the accused's appeal.

---

90. (1989), 69 C.R. (3d) 147 (Ont. C.A.).

4. BALANCING CHARTER VALUES

The constitutional right to full disclosure has proved particularly controversial where relied upon by defence counsel to gain access to medical records of sexual assault complainants. The matter reached the Supreme Court in *O'Connor* (1996), 44 C.R. (4th) 1 and *A. (L.L.) v. B. (A.)* (1996), 44 C.R. (4th) 91. The court in *O'Connor* announced a special procedure respecting discovery of medical records in the possession of third parties. The decision represents a fundamental broadening of the *Stinchcombe* right to disclosure of material in the Crown's possession or control to a right to discovery .

Through the judgment of Madam Justice L'Heureux-Dubé in *A. (L.L.) v. B. (A.)*, the court unanimously decided that production should not be determined by class or case-by-case privilege. According to L'Heureux-Dubé, J., the creation of a class privilege in favour of private records in criminal law raised concerns relating to

(1) the truth-finding process of our adversarial trial procedure; (2)the possible relevance of some private records;
(3) the accused's right to make full answer and defence;
(4) the categories of actors included in a class privilege; and
(5) the experience of other countries.

Carefully examining case law dealing with privilege and confidential information, including that relating to police informants, solicitor-client privilege and public interest immunity, she points out that the courts have consistently ordered production where necessary to establish innocence. While there was ground to recognize a case-by-case privilege along Wigmore lines for private records in some instances, such exceptions to the general evidentiary rule of admissibility and disclosure "should not be encouraged". The better approach was one of balancing competing Charter rights. L'Heureux-Dubé, J. with La Forest, Gonthier and McLachlin, JJ. concurring, saw the need to balance the accused's right to a fair trial and full answer and defence with the complainant's rights to privacy and to equality without discrimination. The majority through a joint judgment by Lamer, C.J. and Sopinka, J. with Cory, Iacobucci and Major, JJ. concurring, determined that the accused's right to full answer and defence should be balanced against the complainant's rights to privacy under sections 7 and 8. However the majority, in not referring to a section 15 equality right for complainants, although it was fully argued, implicitly reject it.

The court agreed that there should be a two-stage procedure but divided 5-4 as to the precise tests. For the majority Lamer, C.J. and Sopinka, J. decided that when the defence seeks information in the hands of a third party the onus should be on the accused to satisfy a judge that the information is likely to be relevant. In the context of disclosure, the meaning of relevance was whether the information might be useful to the defence. In the context of production, the test of relevance should be higher: the presiding judge must be satisfied that there is a reasonable possibility that the information is logically probative to an issue at trial or the competence of a witness to testify. While likely relevance was the appropriate threshold for the first stage of the two-step procedure, the majority determined that it should not be interpreted as an onerous burden upon the accused. A relevance threshold, at this stage, was simply a requirement to prevent the defence from engaging in speculative, fanciful, disruptive, unmeritorious, obstructive and time-consuming requests for production. The crux of the *O'Connor* regime is the determination by the majority that the first stage of establishing likely relevance had to be a low threshold as the accused might often be in a catch-22 situation where he was disadvantaged by arguing relevance of a document he had not seen. The majority in *O'Connor* disagreed with L'Heureux-Dubé, J.'s position that such records would only be relevant in rare cases. They gave as examples of possible relevance records which may contain information about the unfolding of the complaint, the use of therapy to influence memory and information bearing on credibility. L'Heureux-Dubé, J. thought the Charter mandated less, but she did not carry the day. Upon their production to the court, the judge should examine the records to determine whether, and to what extent, they should be produced to the accused. In making that determination, the judge must examine and weigh the salutary and deleterious effects of a production order and determine whether a non-production order would constitute a reasonable limit on the ability of the accused to make full answer and defence.

. For the minority, L'Heureux-Dubé, J. saw the first stage burden on an accused to demonstrate likely relevance as significant and, if it could not be met, the application for production should be dismissed as amounting to no more than a fishing expedition. The mere fact that the complainant had received treatment or counselling could not be presumed to be relevant to the trial as therapy generally focuses on emotional and psychological responses rather than being oriented to ascertaining historical truth.

There was a further difference of opinion as to the criteria at the production stage. Lamer, C.J. and Sopinka, J., for the majority, agreed with L'Heureux-Dubé, J. that the following factors should be considered:

(1) the extent to which the record is necessary for the accused to make full answer and defence;
(2) the probative value of the record in question;
(3) the nature and extent of the reasonable expectation of privacy vested in that record;
(4) whether production of the record would be premised upon any discriminatory belief or bias; and
(5) the potential prejudice to the complainant's dignity, privacy or security of the person that would be occasioned by production of the record in question.

However, the majority departed from L'Heureux-Dubé, J.'s further view that it was also necessary to balance two other factors:

(1) the extent to which production of records of this nature would frustrate society's interest in encouraging the reporting of sexual offences, and
(2) the acquisition of treatment by victims [and] the effect on the integrity of the trial process of producing, or failing to produce, the record, having in mind the need to maintain consideration in the outcome.

According to the majority the second factor was more appropriately dealt with at the admissibility stage and not in deciding whether the information should be produced. As for society's interest in the reporting of sexual crimes, the majority pointed to other avenues available to the judge to ensure that production does not frustrate the societal interests, such as publication bans and barring spectators.

The majority decided that quite different considerations should apply where records were in the possession of the Crown. In such cases the complainant's privacy interests in medical records would not have to be balanced. The Crown's disclosure obligations established in *Stinchcombe* were not to be affected. Concerns relating to privacy or privilege disappeared when the documents were in the Crown's possession. If the records were in the possession of the Crown their relevance was to be presumed. It was unfair in the adversarial process for the Crown to have knowledge that was not shared with the accused. When the records had been shared with the Crown, an agent of the state, the records had become the property of the public to be used to ensure that justice was done. In deciding whether the complainant had waived any potential claim of privilege the waiver would have to be informed. There was to be an onus on the Crown to inform the complainant of the potential for disclosure. Any form of privilege would in any event have to yield where such a privilege precluded the accused's right to full answer and defence.

The majority opinion that privacy issues disappear where the medical records are in the possession of the Crown is utterly unconvincing and has been strongly criticized. Heather Holmes puts the problem well:

> This reasoning appears to assume a formal investigative dialogue by which relevant information is requested by the police or Crown and either provided or refused by the witness, with full opportunity for discussion of legal consequences. It cannot have been intended to apply to the hurly-burly of ordinary existence. A wide variety of material will make its way into the police or Crown files by accident, inadvertence, or because of an investigator's less than perfect appreciation of relevance.

> Complainants who muster the considerable courage required for the bringing of criminal charges usually do so without counsel. The Crown prosecutor, as the lawyer tasked with presenting the complainant's report to the court, may appear to the complainant to be "her" lawyer. It is not unusual or unreasonable for a complainant to tacitly consider her relationship with the prosecutor to have a special, albeit undefined, legal status, that at the very least provides some basic protection of confidentiality. Waiver is a strained concept in this situation. See Holmes, "An Analysis of Bill C-46, Production of Records . . ." (1997), 2 Can. Crim. L.R. 71.

Even under *Stinchcombe* there is no absolute duty for the Crown to disclose. Disclosure is subject to determinations of relevance and privilege, both issues here predetermined against the Crown. The notion that the complainant no longer has a privacy issue in the records simply because they are in the possession of the Crown is extraordinary. What if they were stolen, given to the Crown by a therapist without the knowledge of the complainant or handed over to the police by the complainant on the basis that there would otherwise be no prosecution. The minority, through L'Heureux-Dubé, J., point out that the majority opinion is obiter as the appeal did not concern the extent of the Crown's obligation to disclose private records in its possession.

Following *O'Connor* the Parliament of Canada passed the comprehensive Bill C-46 to restrict the production of records in sexual offence proceedings.

In essence the legislation now contained in sections 278.1 to 278.9 of the Criminal Code in large measure reflects word for word the minority position of L'Heureux-Dubé, J. in *O'Connor*. In particular:

1. The preamble asserts a section 15 equality right for women and children who are complainants in sexual cases.
2. Although the *O'Connor* likely relevance test is maintained, section 278.3(4) specifies ten assertions which are declared not sufficient on their own to establish

that a record is likely relevant to an issue at trial or to the competence of a witness to testify.

3. Under section 278.5 a trial judge has to balance privacy and the interests of justice before deciding whether to order the production of a record for review by the court.
4. Under section 278.7 the trial judge may only order production to the accused on consideration of all seven factors listed by L'Heureux-Dubé, J. rather than the five adopted by the *O'Connor* majority.
5. Under section 278.2 the two-stage balancing process must be applied to records in the possession of the Crown.

In *Mills* a joint judgment by Justices McLachlin and Iacobucci holds constitutional the more comprehensive Parliamentary scheme for access to complainants' records in sexual assault cases, which had enacted the minority approach in *O'Connor*. Of the *O'Connor* majority, only Lamer, C.J. dissented in *Mills* and only on the issue of applying the balancing of complainants' rights approach to records in the possession of the Crown. Justice Cory chose not to participate before his retirement and Justices Iacobucci and Major no longer supported their earlier positions.

R. v. MILLS
[1999] 3 S.C.R. 668, 28 C.R. (5th) 207, 139 C.C.C. (3d) 321

McLachlin and Iacobucci, JJ. (L'Heureux-Dubé, Gonthier, Major, Bastarache and Binnie, JJ. concurring):—

. . . .

The law develops through dialogue between courts and legislatures: see *Vriend v. Alberta*, [1998] 1 S.C.R. 493. Against the backdrop of *O'Connor*, Parliament was free to craft its own solution to the problem consistent with the Charter. Turning to the legislation at issue in this appeal, we find it constitutional. It is undisputed that there are several important respects in which Bill C-46 differs from the regime set out in *O'Connor*, supra. However, these differences are not fatal because Bill C-46 provides sufficient protection for all relevant Charter rights. There are, admittedly, several provisions in the Bill that are subject to differing interpretations. However, in such situations we will interpret the legislation in a constitutional manner where possible: see *Slaight Communications Inc. v. Davidson*, [1989] 1 S.C.R. 1038, at p. 1078. By so doing, we conclude that Bill C-46 is a constitutional response to the problem of production of records of complainants or witnesses in sexual assault proceedings.

. . . .

Like *O'Connor*, Parliament has set up a two-stage process: (1) disclosure to the judge; and (2) production to the accused. At the first stage, the accused must establish that the record sought is "likely relevant to an issue at trial or to the competence of a witness to testify" and that "the production of the record is necessary in the interests of justice" (s. 278.5(1)). Bill C-46 diverges from *O'Connor* by directing the trial judge to consider the salutary and deleterious effects of production to the court on the accused's right to full answer and defence and the complainant or witness's right to privacy and equality. A series of factors is listed that the trial judge is directed to take into account in deciding whether the document should be produced to the court (s. 278.5(2)). If the requirements of this first stage are met, the record will be ordered produced to the trial judge. At the second stage, the judge looks at the record in the absence of the parties (s. 278.6(1)), holds a hearing if necessary (s. 278.6(2)), and determines whether the record should be produced on the basis that it is "likely relevant to an issue at trial or to the competence of a witness to testify" and that its production is "necessary in the interests of justice" (s. 278.7). Again at this stage, the judge must consider the salutary and deleterious effects on the accused's right to make full answer and defence and on the right to privacy and equality of the complainant or witness, and is directed to "take into account" the factors set out at s. 278.5(2): s. 278.7(2). When ordering production, the judge may impose conditions on production: s. 278.7(3).

The respondent and several supporting interveners argue that Bill C-46 is unconstitutional to the extent that it establishes a regime for production that differs from or is inconsistent with that established by the majority in *O'Connor*. However, it does not follow from the fact that a law passed by Parliament differs from a regime envisaged by the Court in the absence of a statutory scheme, that Parliament's law is unconstitutional. Parliament may build on the Court's decision, and develop a different scheme as long as it remains constitutional. Just as Parliament must respect the Court's rulings, so the Court must respect Parliament's determination that the judicial scheme can be improved. To insist on slavish conformity would belie the mutual respect that underpins the relationship between the courts and legislature that is so essential to our constitutional democracy: *Vriend*, supra . . . .

Relationship Between the Courts and the Legislature Generally

A posture of respect towards Parliament was endorsed by this Court in *Slaight Communications*, supra, at p. 1078, where we held that if legislation is amenable to two interpretations, a court should choose that interpretation that upholds the legislation as constitutional. Thus courts must presume that Parliament intended to enact constitutional legislation and strive, where possible, to give effect to this intention. This Court has also discussed the relationship between the courts and the legislature in terms of a dialogue, and emphasized its importance to the democratic process. In *Vriend*, supra, at para. 139, Iacobucci J. stated:

> To my mind, a great value of judicial review and this dialogue among the branches is that each of the branches is made somewhat accountable to the other. The work of the legislature is reviewed by the courts and the work of the court in its decisions can be reacted to by the legislature in the passing of new legislation (or even overarching laws under s. 33 of the Charter). This dialogue between and accountability of each of the branches have the effect of enhancing the democratic process, not denying it.

See also Peter W. Hogg and Allison A. Bushell, "The Charter Dialogue Between Courts and Legislatures" (1997), 35 Osgoode Hall L.J. 75. If the common law were to be taken as establishing the only possible constitutional regime, then we could not speak of a dialogue with the legislature. Such a situation could only undermine rather than enhance democracy. Legislative change and the development of the common law are different.

. . . .

Courts do not hold a monopoly on the protection and promotion of rights and freedoms; Parliament also plays a role in this regard and is often able to act as a significant ally for vulnerable groups. This is especially important to recognize in the context of sexual violence. The history of the treatment of sexual assault complainants by our society and our legal system is an unfortunate one. Important change has occurred through legislation aimed at both recognizing the rights and interests of complainants in criminal proceedings, and debunking the stereotypes that have been so damaging to women and children, but the treatment of sexual assault complainants remains an ongoing problem.

If constitutional democracy is meant to ensure that due regard is given to the voices of those vulnerable to being overlooked by the majority, then this court has an obligation to consider respectfully Parliament's attempt to respond to such voices.

Parliament has enacted this legislation after a long consultation process that included a consideration of the constitutional standards outlined by this Court in *O'Connor*. While it is the role of the courts to specify such standards, there may be a range of permissible regimes that can meet these standards. It goes without saying that this range is not confined to the specific rule adopted by the Court pursuant to its competence in the common law. In the present case, Parliament decided that legislation was necessary in order to address the issue of third-party records more comprehensively. As is evident from the language of the preamble to Bill C-46, Parliament also sought to recognize the prevalence of sexual violence against women and children and its disadvantageous impact on their rights, to encourage the reporting of incidents of sexual violence, to recognize the impact of the production of personal information on the efficacy of treatment, and to reconcile fairness to complainants with the rights of the accused. Many of these concerns involve policy decisions regarding criminal procedure and its relationship to the community at large. Parliament may also be understood to be recognizing "horizontal" equality concerns, where women's inequality results from the acts of other individuals and groups rather than the state, but which nonetheless may have many consequences for the criminal justice system. It is perfectly reasonable that these many concerns may lead to a procedure that is different from the common law position but that nonetheless meets the required constitutional standards.

We cannot presume that the legislation is unconstitutional simply because it is different from the common law position. The question before us is not whether Parliament can amend the common law; it clearly can. The question before us is whether in doing so Parliament has nonetheless outlined a constitutionally acceptable procedure for the production of private records of complainants in sexual assault trials.

. . . .

Tensions Among Full Answer and Defence, Privacy, and Equality

(a) Balancing Interests and Defining Rights

At play in this appeal are three principles, which find their support in specific provisions of the Charter. These are full answer and defence, privacy, and equality. No single principle is absolute and capable of trumping the others; all must be defined in light of competing claims. As Lamer C.J. stated in *Dagenais*, supra, at p. 877:

When the protected rights of two individuals come into conflict . . . Charter principles require a balance to be achieved that fully respects the importance of both sets of rights.

. . . .

Whether or not all the rights involved are "principles of fundamental justice", Charter rights must always be defined contextually.

. . . .

(b) Nature of the Charter Principles

(i) Full Answer and Defence

It is well established that the ability of the accused to make full answer and defence is a principle of fundamental justice protected by s. 7. . . . Many of these principles of fundamental justice are informed by the legal rights outlined in ss. 8 to 14 of the Charter. . . . Our jurisprudence has recognized on several occasions "the danger of placing the accused in a 'Catch-22' situation as a condition of making full answer and defence". This is an important consideration in the context of records production as often the accused may be in the difficult position of making submissions regarding the importance to full answer and defence of records that he or she has not seen. Where the records are part of the case to meet, this concern is particularly acute as such a situation very directly implicates the accused's ability to raise a doubt concerning his or her innocence. As the Court stated in *R. v. Leipert*, [1997] 1 S.C.R. 281, at para. 24, "[t]his Court has consistently affirmed that it is a fundamental principle of justice, protected by the Charter, that the innocent must not be convicted". Where the records to which the accused seeks access are not part of the case to meet, however, privacy and equality considerations may require that it be more difficult for accused persons to gain access to therapeutic or other records.

That said, the principles of fundamental justice do not entitle the accused to "the most favourable procedures that could possibly be imagined": *R. v. Lyons*, [1987] 2 S.C.R. 309, per La Forest J., at p. 362. This is because fundamental justice embraces more than the rights of the accused. For example, this Court has held that an assessment of the fairness of the trial process must be made "from the point of view of fairness in the eyes of the community and the complainant" and not just the accused: *R. v. E. (A.W.)*, [1993] 3 S.C.R. 155, per Cory J., at p. 198. . . . This spectrum of interests reflected in the principles of fundamental justice highlights the need to avoid viewing any particular principle in isolation from the others.

. . . .

Several principles regarding the right to make full answer and defence emerge from the preceding discussion. First, the right to make full answer and defence is crucial to ensuring that the innocent are not convicted. To that end, courts must consider the danger of placing the accused in a Catch-22 situation as a condition of making full answer and defence, and will even override competing considerations in order to protect the right to make full answer and defence in certain circumstances, such as the "innocence at stake" exception to informer privilege. Second, the accused's right must be defined in a context that includes other principles of fundamental justice and Charter provisions. Third, full answer and defence does not include the right to evidence that would distort the search for truth inherent in the trial process.

(ii) Privacy

Since *Hunter v. Southam Inc.*, [1984] 2 S.C.R. 145, this Court has recognized that s. 8 of the Charter protects a person's reasonable expectation of privacy. This right is relevant to the present appeal, as an order for the production of documents is a seizure within the meaning of s. 8 of the Charter [citations omitted]. Therefore an order for the production of records made pursuant to ss. 278.1 to 278.91 of the Criminal Code, falls within the ambit of s. 8.

. . . .

This Court has most often characterized the values engaged by privacy in terms of liberty, or the right to be left alone by the state. . . . This interest in being left alone by the state includes the ability to control the dissemination of confidential information. These privacy concerns are at their strongest where aspects of one's individual identity are at stake, such as in the context of information "about one's lifestyle, intimate relations or political or religious opinions".

. . . .

In fostering the underlying values of dignity, integrity and autonomy, it is fitting that s. 8 of the Charter should seek to protect a biographical core of personal information which individuals in a free and democratic society would wish to maintain and control from dissemination to the state. This would include information which tends to reveal intimate details of the lifestyle and personal choices of the individual. That privacy is essential to maintaining relationships of trust was stressed to this Court by the eloquent submissions of many interveners in this case regarding counselling records. The therapeutic relationship is one that is characterized by trust, an element of which is confidentiality. Therefore the protection of the complainant's reasonable expectation of privacy in her therapeutic records protects the therapeutic relationship.

. . . .

Given that s. 8 protects a person's privacy by prohibiting unreasonable searches or seizures, and given that s. 8 addresses a particular application of the principles of fundamental justice, we can infer that a reasonable search or seizure is consistent with the principles of fundamental justice. Moreover, as we have already discussed, the principles of fundamental justice include the right to make full answer and defence. Therefore a reasonable search and seizure will be one that accommodates both the accused's ability to make full answer and defence and the complainant's privacy right.

From our preceding discussion of the right to make full answer and defence, it is clear that the accused will have no right to the records in question insofar as they contain information that is either irrelevant or would serve to distort the search for truth, as access to such information is not included within the ambit of the accused's right. . . . The values protected by privacy rights will be most directly at stake where the confidential information contained in a record concerns aspects of one's individual identity or where the maintenance of confidentiality is crucial to a therapeutic, or other trust-like, relationship.

(iii) Equality

Equality concerns must also inform the contextual circumstances in which the rights of full answer and defence and privacy will come into play. In this respect, an appreciation of myths and stereotypes in the context of sexual violence is essential to delineate properly the boundaries of full answer and defence. As we have already discussed, the right to make full answer and defence does not include the right to information that would only distort the truth-seeking goal of the trial process. In *R. v. Osolin*, [1993] 4 S.C.R. 595, Cory J., for the majority on this issue, stated, at pp. 669 and 670:

> The provisions of ss. 15 and 28 of the Charter guaranteeing equality to men and women, although not determinative should be taken into account in determining the reasonable limitations that should be placed upon the cross-examination of a complainant. . . . A complainant should not be unduly harassed and pilloried to the extent of becoming a victim of an insensitive judicial system.

The reasons in *Seaboyer* make it clear that eliciting evidence from a complainant for the purpose of encouraging inferences pertaining to consent or the credibility of rape victims which are based on groundless myths and fantasized stereotypes is improper. The accused is not permitted to "whack the complainant" through the use of stereotypes regarding victims of sexual assault.

. . . .

When the boundary between privacy and full answer and defence is not properly delineated, the equality of individuals whose lives are heavily documented is also affected, as these individuals have more records that will be subject to wrongful scrutiny. Karen Busby cautions that the use of records to challenge credibility at large

> will subject those whose lives already have been subject to extensive documentation to extraordinarily invasive review. This would include women whose lives have been documented under conditions of multiple inequalities and institutionalization such as Aboriginal women, women with disabilities, or women who have been imprisoned or involved with child welfare agencies ("Discriminatory Uses of Personal Records in Sexual Violence Cases" (1997), 9 C.J.W.L.148, at pp. 161-62).

These concerns highlight the need for an acute sensitivity to context when determining the content of the accused's right to make full answer and defence, and its relationship to the complainant's privacy right.

Summary

In summary, the following broad considerations apply to the definition of the rights at stake in this appeal. The right of the accused to make full answer and defence is a core principle of fundamental justice, but it does not automatically entitle the accused to gain access to information contained in the private records of complainants and witnesses. Rather, the scope of the right to make full answer and defence must be determined in light of privacy and equality rights of complainants and witnesses. It is clear that the right to full answer and defence is not engaged where the accused seeks information that will only serve to distort the truth-seeking purpose of a trial, and in such a situation, privacy and equality rights are paramount. On the other hand, where the information contained in a record directly bears on the right to make full answer and defence, privacy rights must yield to the need to avoid convicting the innocent. Most cases, however, will not be so clear, and in assessing applications for production courts must determine the weight to be granted to the interests protected by privacy and full answer and defence in the particular circumstances of each case. Full answer and defence will be more centrally implicated where the information contained in a record is part of the case to meet or where its potential probative value is high. A complainant's privacy interest is very high where the confidential information contained in a record concerns the complainant's personal identity or where the confidentiality of the record is vital to protect a therapeutic relationship.

With this background in mind, we now proceed to discuss the statutory provisions under attack.

· · · ·

The Statutory Provisions

Section 278.3(4) lists a series of "assertions" that cannot "on their own" establish that a record is likely relevant. The respondent submits that on a plain reading, this provision prevents the accused from relying on the listed factors when attempting to establish the likely relevance of the records. This, he argues, interferes with the right to make full answer and defence by restricting what the judge can consider in determining whether the records must be produced to the defence. The legislation raises the bar for production, he asserts, making it difficult if not impossible for the accused to meet the likely relevance test of ss. 278.5 and 278.7. The respondent contends that it is unconstitutional to exclude the assertions listed in s. 278.3(4) as irrelevant.

This submission forgets that when legislation is susceptible to more than one interpretation, we must always choose the constitutional reading. See *Slaight*, supra, at p. 1078. This mistake leads the respondent to overstate the purpose and effect of s. 278.3(4). As has frequently been held, its purpose is to prevent speculative and unmeritorious requests for production [citations omitted]. It does not entirely prevent an accused from relying on the factors listed, but simply prevents reliance on bare "assertions" of the listed matters, where there is no other evidence and they stand "on their own".

The purpose and wording of s. 278.3 does not prevent an accused from relying on the assertions set out in subsection 278.3(4) where there is an evidentiary or informational foundation to suggest that they may be related to likely relevance. . . . The section requires only that the accused be able to point to case specific evidence or information to show that the record in issue is likely relevant to an issue at trial or the competence of a witness to testify, see *Leipert*, supra, at para. 21. Conversely, where an accused does provide evidence or information to support an assertion listed in s. 278.3(4), this does not mean that likely relevance is made out. Section 278.3(4) does not supplant the ultimate discretion of the trial judge. Where any one of the listed assertions is made and supported by the required evidentiary and informational foundation, the trial judge is the ultimate arbiter in deciding whether the likely relevance threshold set out in s. 278.5 and 278.7 is met. We conclude that s. 278.3(4) does not violate ss. 7 or 11(d) of the Charter.

. . . .

Both the majority and minority of this Court in *O'Connor*, supra, held that records must be produced to the judge for inspection if the accused can demonstrate that the information is "likely to be relevant": *O'Connor*, supra, at para. 19, per Lamer C.J. and Sopinka J., and at para. 138, per L'Heureux-Dubé J. The Court defined the standard of likely relevance as "a reasonable possibility that the information is logically probative to an issue at trial or the competence of a witness to testify". Although the majority recognized that complainants have a constitutional right to privacy it held that no balancing of rights should be undertaken at the first stage. This conclusion was premised on the finding that: (1) to require the accused to meet more than the likely relevance stage would be to "put the accused in the difficult situation of having to make submissions to the judge without precisely knowing what is contained in the records"; and (2) there is not enough information before a trial judge at this initial stage of production for an informed balancing procedure to take place. To this end, the majority held that the analysis should be confined to determining "likely relevance" and "whether the right to make full answer and defence is implicated by information contained in the records". In contrast, the minority held that once the accused meets the "likely relevance" threshold, he must then satisfy the judge that the salutary effects of ordering the documents produced to the court for inspection outweigh the deleterious effects of such production, having regard to the accused's right to make full answer and defence, and the effect of such production on the privacy and equality rights of the subject of the records. L'Heureux-Dubé J. found that a sufficient evidentiary basis could be established at this stage through Crown disclosure, defence witnesses, the cross-examination of Crown witnesses at both the preliminary inquiry and the trial and, on some occasions, expert evidence. Parliament, after studying the issue, concluded that the rights of both the complainant and the accused should be considered when deciding whether to order production to the judge. In coming to this conclusion, Parliament must be taken to have determined, as a result of lengthy consultations, and years of Parliamentary study and debate, that trial judges have sufficient evidence to engage in an informed balancing process at this stage. . . . As a result of the consultation process, Parliament decided to supplement the "likely relevant" standard for production to the judge proposed in *O'Connor* with the further requirement that production be "necessary in the interests of justice". The result was s. 278.5. This process is a notable example of the dialogue between the judicial and legislative branches discussed above. This Court acted in *O'Connor*, and the legislature responded with Bill C-46. As already mentioned, the mere fact that Bill C-46 does not mirror *O'Connor* does not render it unconstitutional.

The question comes down to this: once likely relevance is established, is it necessarily unconstitutional that a consideration of the rights and interests of those affected by production to the court might result in production not being ordered? The answer to this question depends on whether a consideration of the range of rights and interests affected, in addition to a finding of likely relevance, will ultimately prevent the accused from seeing documents that are necessary to enable him to defend himself — to raise all the defences that might be open to him at trial. The non-disclosure of third party records with a high privacy interest that may contain relevant evidence will not compromise trial fairness where such non-disclosure would not prejudice the accused's right to full answer and defence.

Section 278.5(1) is a very wide and flexible section. It accords the trial judge great latitude. Parliament must be taken to have intended that judges, within the broad scope of the powers conferred, would apply it in a constitutional manner — a way that would ultimately permit the accused access to all documents that may be constitutionally required. Indeed, a production regime that denied this would not be production "necessary in the interests of justice".

. . . .

While this Court may have considered it preferable not to consider privacy rights at the production stage, that does not preclude Parliament from coming to a different conclusion, so long as its conclusion is consistent with the Charter in its own right. As we have explained, the Bill's directive to consider what is "necessary in the interests of justice", read correctly, does include appropriate respect for the right to full answer and defence.

This leaves the argument that the judge cannot consider the factors listed in s. 278.5(2) without looking at the documents. However, s. 278.5(2) does not require that the judge engage in a conclusive and in-depth evaluation of each of the factors. It rather requires the judge to "take them into account" — to the extent possible at this early stage of proceedings — in deciding whether to order a particular record produced to himself or herself for inspection. Section 278.5(2) serves as a check-list of the various factors that may come into play in making the decision regarding production to the judge. Therefore, while the s. 278.5(2) factors are relevant, in the final analysis the judge is free to make whatever order is "necessary in the interests of justice" — a mandate that includes all of the applicable "principles of fundamental justice" at stake.

Furthermore, contrary to the respondent's submissions, there is a sufficient evidentiary basis to support such an analysis at this early stage. This basis can be established through Crown disclosure, defence witnesses, the cross-examination of Crown witnesses at both the preliminary inquiry and the trial, and expert evidence, see: *O'Connor*, supra, at para. 146, per L'Heureux-Dubé J. As noted by Taylor J. for the British Columbia Supreme Court, "the criminal process provides a reasonable process for the acquisition of the evidentiary basis", *Hurrie*, supra, at para. 39. To this end, as the Attorney of British Columbia submitted: "Laying the groundwork prior to trial, or comprehensive examination of witnesses at trial, will go a long way to establishing a meritorious application under this legislation".

The nature of the records in question will also often provide the trial judge with an important informational foundation. For example, with respect to the privacy interest in records, the expectation of privacy in adoption or counselling records may be very different from that in school attendance records, see for example, *R. v. J.S.P.*, B.C. S.C., Vancouver Registry Nos. CC970130 & CC960237, May 15, 1997. Similarly, a consideration of the probative value of records can often be informed by the nature and purposes of a record, as well as the record-taking practices used to create it. As noted above, many submissions were made regarding the different levels of reliability of certain records. Counselling or therapeutic records, for example, can be highly subjective documents which attempt merely to record an individual's emotions and psychological state. Often such records have not been checked for accuracy by the subject of the records, nor have they been recorded verbatim. All of these factors may help a trial judge when considering the probative value of a record being sought by an accused.

As discussed above in the context of defining the right to full answer and defence, courts must as a general matter ensure that the accused can obtain all pertinent evidence required to make full answer and defence, and must be wary of the danger of putting the accused in a Catch-22 situation in seeking to obtain such evidence. Where there is a danger that the accused's right to make full answer and defence will be violated, the trial judge should err on the side of production to the court. We conclude that s. 278.5 is constitutional.

Once the first hurdle is passed and the records are produced to the judge, the judge must determine whether it is in the interests of justice that they be produced to the defence. Again the judge must be satisfied that the records are "likely relevant" and that production, this time to the accused, is necessary in the interests of justice. In making this decision, the judge must once again consider the factors set out in s. 278.5(2).

The respondent accepts that weighing competing interests is appropriate at this second stage of the analysis. However, the respondent contends that the requirement under s. 278.7(2), that the trial judge take the factors specified in paragraphs s. 278.5(2)(a) to (h) into account, inappropriately alters the constitutional balance established in *O'Connor*. Specifically, the respondent contends that ss. 278.5(2)(f) and (g) elevate the societal interest in encouraging the reporting of sexual offences and encouraging of treatment of complainants of sexual offences, to a status equal to the accused's right to make full answer and defence. This, he suggests, alters the constitutional balance established in *O'Connor*, where the majority specifically determined these factors to be of secondary importance to defence interests in any balancing of competing interests and better taken into account through other avenues. The respondent also contends that s. 278.5(2)(h) unfairly requires trial judges to consider the effect of disclosure on the integrity of the trial process. The respondent submits that this is a question going to admissibility.

These concerns are largely answered by the analysis advanced under s. 278.5(2), discussed at greater length above. Trial judges are not required to rule conclusively on each of the factors nor are they required to determine whether factors relating to the privacy and equality of the complainant or witness "outweigh" factors relating to the accused's right to full answer and defence. To repeat, trial judges are only asked to "take into account" the factors listed in s. 278.5(2) when determining whether production of part or all of the impugned record to the accused is necessary in the interest of justice, s. 278.7(1).

The respondent argues that the inclusion of the societal interest factors in ss. 278.5(2)(f) and (g) alters the constitutional balance established by the *O'Connor* majority. With respect, this argument is unsound. . . . As noted above, when preparing Bill C-46 Parliament had the advantage of being able to assess how the *O'Connor* regime was operating. From the information available to Parliament and the submissions it received during the consultation process, Parliament concluded that the effect of production on the integrity of the trial was a factor that should be included in the list of factors for trial judges to "take into account" at both stages of an application for production. Several interveners have interpreted this factor as requiring courts to consider, along with the other enumerated factors, whether the search for truth would be advanced by the production of the records in question; that is, the question is whether the material in question would introduce discriminatory biases and beliefs into the fact-finding process. We agree with this interpretation of the inquiry required by s. 278.5(2)(h) and believe it to be in keeping with the purposes set out in the preamble of the legislation.

By giving judges wide discretion to consider a variety of factors and requiring them to make whatever order is necessary in the interest of justice at both stages of an application for production, Parliament has created a scheme that permits judges not only to preserve the complainant's privacy and equality rights to the maximum extent possible, but also to ensure that the accused has access to the documents required to make full answer and defence.

LAMER, C.J.:—

. . . .

While I agree with McLachlin and Iacobucci JJ.'s finding that Bill C-46 complies with ss. 7 and 11(d) of the Canadian Charter of Rights and Freedoms as it applies to the production of records in the possession of third parties, I take a different view of the legislative regime's approach to records in the hands of the Crown. In my opinion, Bill C-46's treatment of records that form part of the case to meet tips the balance too heavily in favour of privacy to the detriment of the accused's right to make full answer and defence.

Do you think there should be a presumption of constitutionality in Charter cases? What are the advantages and disadvantages of the new approach of dialogue and deference? What of Chief Justice Dickson's view in *Hunter v. Southam* that the courts should be the guardians of the Constitution?

On the issue of equality why was there no reference to the ten-part test for judging section 15 claims established in *Law v. Minister of Human Resources Development,* [1999] 1 S.C.R. 497 by Justice Iacobucci, J. for a unanimous court, as recently as March, 1999?

The essence of the *Law* test is that there is in fact no Charter guarantee of equality per se. The guarantee is against discrimination within the meaning of section 15. This is set out in part 3 of *Law* as follows:

> (3) Accordingly, a court that is called upon to determine a discrimination claim under s. 15(1) should make the following three broad inquiries:
>
> A. Does the impugned law (a) draw a formal distinction between the claimant and others on the basis of one or more personal characteristics, or (b) fail to take into account the claimant's already disadvantaged position within Canadian society resulting in substantively differential treatment between the claimant and others on the basis of one or more personal characteristics?
>
> B. Is the claimant subject to differential treatment based on one or more enumerated and analogous grounds?
> and
>
> C. Does the differential treatment discriminate, by imposing a burden upon or withholding a benefit from the claimant in a manner which reflects the stereotypical application of presumed group or personal characteristics, or which otherwise has the effect of perpetuating or promoting the view that the individual is less capable or worthy of recognition or value as a human being or as a member of Canadian society, equally deserving of concern, respect, and consideration?

The court in *Law* also requires careful identification of "one or more relevant comparators", discrimination on an enumerated or analogous ground and a consideration of context.

Is the comparator group in *Mills* all other victims of crime or is it male victims of sexual assault? It surely couldn't be the accused given that the context is a criminal trial where the issue is punishment rather than compensation. Is the violation discrimination by gender or age or is it an analogous ground because complainants in sexual assault cases have been discriminated against through myths and stereotypical views?

The implications of an enforceable section 15 claim for complainants in sexual assault cases is left unexplored. The policy issues are far wider than establishing privacy rights for therapeutic and other records of complainants. Can complainants now seek status to be represented throughout a sexual assault trial? How about rights to cross-examine the accused, to challenge the similar fact evidence rule or to reverse the presumption of innocence?

For critical comments on *Mills* see Stuart, "*Mills*: Dialogue with Parliament and Equality by Assertion at What Cost?" (2000), 28 C.R. (5th) 275 and Peter Sankoff, "Crown Disclosure After *Mills*: Have the Ground Rules Suddenly Changed?" (2000), 28 C.R. (5th) 285.

Professor Stephen Coughlan, "Complainants' Records After *Mills*: Same as it Ever Was" (2000), 33 C.R. (5th) 300, has suggested that a close reading of *Mills* is that, although the language is deference to Parliament, the court has read in discretion at every point such that its regime still conforms to its earlier majority judgment in *O'Connor*. Accepting that there is reading down in *Mills*, this appears to place far too little emphasis on the raising of the bar at the first stage of production to the judge. Several courts have already decided that *Mills* has indeed raised that threshold test. See *Batte* (2000), 34 C.R. (5th) 197 (Ont. C.A.) (criticized by Joseph Wilkinson, "*Batte*: Raising the Defence Hurdle for Access to Third Party Records" (2000), 34 C.R. (5th) 257) and *M.(D.)* (2001), 37 C.R. 80 (5th) (Ont. S.C.J.) (denying access to a diary and counselling records because the evidentiary foundation was not laid at the preliminary inquiry). In *Shearing* (2000), 31 C.R. (5th) 177 (B.C.C.A.) (see Delisle, "Annotation" in (2000), 31 C.R. (5th) 179), the B.C Court of Appeal even applied *Mills* to deny the right to cross-examine on the diary of a complainant. The court saw *Mills* as having shifted the balance away from the primary emphasis on the rights of accused to require consideration of equality rights of the complainant. *Shearing* did not involve rape shield laws or the issue of production. The diary in *Shearing* was said to contain an account of the alleged abuse.

Do you agree with the decision that this was not to be disclosed?

The court in *Mills* certainly reads down the "insufficient grounds" section 278.3(4) which declares the long list of assertions which would not meet the likely relevant test. Pointing to words "on their own" the court holds this merely requires an evidentiary foundation. The court sees the purpose of the provision to be the prevention of speculative myths, stereotypes, and generalized assumptions about sexual assault victims and classes of records from forming the entire basis of an otherwise unsubstantiated order for production of private records. The problem, as Kent Roach points out, "Editorial on *Mills*" (2000), 43 Crim. L.Q. 145, is that only some of the prohibited assertions involve sexist rape myths. Those relating to credibility do not. The section requires only, holds the court in reading the section down, that the accused be able to point to case specific evidence or information to show that the record in issue is likely relevant to an issue at trial or the competence of a witness to testify. The court indicates one source of such an evidentiary base to be the preliminary inquiry. The difficulty here is that many sexual assault trials across Canada are now proceeded with, through Crown election, by way of summary proceedings where there is no preliminary (and no jury trial).

In such cases is it a good idea to encourage free-ranging and intrusive inquiries into the existence and type of records presumably necessitating adjournments where production is ordered?

The various other rulings in *Mills* on the records issues are supportable. This includes the acceptance by the majority of Parliament's view that the balancing of rights of complainants must also occur, in the absence of express waiver, where the records are in the possession of the Crown. We have seen that the majority ruling to the contrary in *O'Connor* was obiter and not persuasive in holding that privacy had necessarily been waived by complainants in such cases.

M. (A.) v. RYAN
[1997] 1 S.C.R. 157, 4 C.R. (5th) 220

MCLACHLIN J. (LA FOREST, SOPINKA, CORY, IACOBUCCI and MAJOR JJ. concurring):—After having been sexually assaulted by the respondent Dr. Ryan, the appellant sought counselling from a psychiatrist. The question on this appeal is whether the psychiatrist's notes and records containing statements the appellant made in the course of treatment are protected from disclosure in a civil suit brought by the appellant against Dr. Ryan. Put in terms of principle, should a defendant's right to relevant material to the end of testing the plaintiff's case outweigh the plaintiff's expectation that communications between her and her psychiatrist will be kept in confidence?

. . . .

IV. General Principles

The common law principles underlying the recognition of privilege from disclosure are simply stated. They proceed from the fundamental proposition that everyone owes a general duty to give evidence relevant to the matter before the court, so that the truth may be ascertained. To this fundamental duty, the law permits certain exceptions, known as privileges, where it can be shown that they are required by a "public good transcending the normally predominant principle of utilizing all rational means for ascertaining truth": *Trammel v. United States*, 445 U.S. 40 (1980), at p. 50.

While the circumstances giving rise to a privilege were once thought to be fixed by categories defined in previous centuries — categories that do not include communications between a psychiatrist and her patient — it is now accepted that the common law permits privilege in new situations where reason, experience and application of the principles that underlie the traditional privileges so dictate: *Slavutych v. Baker*, [1976] 1 S.C.R. 254; *R. v. Gruenke*, [1991] 3 S.C.R. 263, at p. 286. The applicable principles are derived from those set forth in *Wigmore on Evidence*, vol. 8 (McNaughton rev. 1961), sec. 2285. First, the communication must originate in a confidence. Second, the confidence must be essential to the relationship in which the communication arises. Third, the relationship must be one which should be "sedulously fostered" in the public good. Finally, if all these requirements are met, the court must consider whether the interests served by protecting the communications from disclosure outweigh the interest in getting at the truth and disposing correctly of the litigation.

It follows that the law of privilege may evolve to reflect the social and legal realities of our time. One such reality is the law's increasing concern with the wrongs perpetrated by sexual abuse and the serious effect such abuse has on the health and productivity of the many members of our society it victimizes. Another modern reality is the extension of medical assistance from treatment of its physical effects to treatment of its mental and emotional aftermath through techniques such as psychiatric counselling. Yet another development of recent vintage which may be considered in connection with new claims for privilege is the Canadian Charter of Rights and Freedoms, adopted in 1982.

. . . .

The first requirement for privilege is that the communications at issue have originated in a confidence that they will not be disclosed. The Master held that this condition was not met because both the appellant and Dr. Parfitt had concerns that notwithstanding their desire for confidentiality, the records might someday be ordered disclosed in the course of litigation. With respect, I do not agree. The communications were made in confidence. The appellant stipulated that they should remain confidential and Dr. Parfitt agreed that she would do everything possible to keep them confidential. The possibility that a court might order them disclosed at some future date over their objections does not change the fact that the communications were made in confidence. With the possible exception of communications falling in the traditional categories, there can never be an absolute guarantee of confidentiality; there is always the possibility that a court may order disclosure. Even for documents within the traditional categories, inadvertent disclosure is always a possibility. If the apprehended possibility of disclosure negated privilege, privilege would seldom if ever be found.

The second requirement — that the element of confidentiality be essential to the full and satisfactory maintenance of the relation between the parties to the communication — is clearly satisfied in the case at bar. It is not disputed that Dr. Parfitt's practice in general and her ability to help the appellant in particular required that she hold her discussions with the appellant in confidence. Dr. Parfitt's evidence establishes that confidentiality is essential to the continued existence and effectiveness of the therapeutic relations between a psychiatrist and a patient seeking treatment for the psychiatric harm resulting from sexual abuse. Once psychiatrist-patient confidentiality is broken and the psychiatrist becomes involved in the patient's external world, the "frame" of the therapy is broken. At that point, it is Dr. Parfitt's practice to discontinue psychotherapy with the patient. The result is both confusing and damaging to the patient. At a time when she would normally find support in the therapeutic relationship, as during the trial, she finds herself without support. In the result, the patient's treatment may cease, her distrustfulness be exacerbated, and her personal and work relations be adversely affected.

The appellant too sees confidentiality as essential to her relationship with Dr. Parfitt. She insisted from the first that her communications to Dr. Parfitt be held in confidence, suggesting that this was a condition of her entering and continuing treatment. The fact that she and Dr. Parfitt feared the possibility of court-ordered disclosure at some future date does not negate the fact that confidentiality was essential "to the full and satisfactory maintenance" of their relationship.

The third requirement — that the relation must be one which in the opinion of the community ought to be sedulously fostered — is equally satisfied. Victims of sexual abuse often suffer serious trauma, which, left untreated, may mar their entire lives. It is widely accepted that it is in the interests of the victim and society that such help be obtained. The mental health of the citizenry, no less than its physical health, is a public good of great importance. Just as it is in the interest of the sexual abuse victim to be restored to full and healthy functioning, so is it in the interest of the public that she take her place as a healthy and productive member of society.

It may thus be concluded that the first three conditions for privilege for communications between a psychiatrist and the victim of a sexual assault are met in the case at bar. The communications were confidential. Their confidence is essential to the psychiatrist-patient relationship. The relationship itself and the treatment it makes possible are of transcendent public importance.

The fourth requirement is that the interests served by protecting the communications from disclosure outweigh the interest of pursuing the truth and disposing correctly of the litigation. This requires first an assessment of the interests served by protecting the communications from disclosure. These include injury to the appellant's ongoing relationship with Dr. Parfitt and her future treatment. They also include the effect that a finding of no privilege would have on the ability of other persons suffering from similar trauma to obtain needed treatment and of psychiatrists to provide it. The interests served by non-disclosure must extend to any effect on society of the failure of individuals to obtain treatment restoring them to healthy and contributing members of society. Finally, the interests served by protection from disclosure must include the privacy interest of the person claiming privilege and inequalities which may be perpetuated by the absence of protection.

As noted, the common law must develop in a way that reflects emerging Charter values. It follows that the factors balanced under the fourth part of the test for privilege should be updated to reflect relevant Charter values. One such value is the interest affirmed by s. 8 of the Charter of each person in privacy. Another is the right of every person embodied in s. 15 of the Charter to equal treatment and benefit of the law. A rule of privilege which fails to protect confidential doctor/patient communications in the context of an action arising out of sexual assault perpetuates the disadvantage felt by victims of sexual assault, often women. The intimate nature of sexual assault heightens the privacy concerns of the victim and may increase, if automatic disclosure is the rule, the difficulty of obtaining redress for the wrong. The victim of a sexual assault is thus placed in a disadvantaged position as compared with the victim of a different wrong. The result may be that the victim of sexual assault does not obtain the equal benefit of the law to which s. 15 of the Charter entitles her. She is doubly victimized, initially by the sexual assault and later by the price she must pay to claim redress — redress which in some cases may be part of her program of therapy. These are factors which may properly be considered in determining the interests served by an order for protection from disclosure of confidential patient-psychiatrist communications in sexual assault cases.

These criteria, applied to the case at bar, demonstrate a compelling interest in protecting the communications at issue from disclosure. More, however, is required to establish privilege. For privilege to exist, it must be shown that the benefit that inures from privilege, however great it may seem, in fact outweighs the interest in the correct disposal of the litigation.

At this stage, the court considering an application for privilege must balance one alternative against the other. The exercise is essentially one of common sense and good judgment. This said, it is important to establish the outer limits of acceptability. I for one cannot accept the proposition that "occasional injustice" should be accepted as the price of the privilege. It is true that the traditional categories of privilege, cast as they are in absolute all-or-nothing terms, necessarily run the risk of occasional injustice. But that does not mean that courts, in invoking new privileges, should lightly condone its extension. In the words of Scalia J. (dissenting) in *Jaffee v. Redmond*, 116 S. Ct. 1923 (1996), at p. 1941:

> It is no small matter to say that, in some cases, our federal courts will be the tools of injustice rather than unearth the truth where it is available to be found. The common law has identified a few instances where that is tolerable. Perhaps Congress may conclude that it is also tolerable. . . . But that conclusion assuredly does not burst upon the mind with such clarity that a judgment in favor of suppressing the truth ought to be pronounced by this honorable Court.

It follows that if the court considering a claim for privilege determines that a particular document or class of documents must be produced to get at the truth and prevent an unjust verdict, it must permit production to the extent required to avoid that result. On the other hand, the need to get at the truth and avoid injustice does not automatically negate the possibility of protection from full disclosure. In some cases, the court may well decide that the truth permits of nothing less than full production. This said, I would venture to say that an order for partial privilege will more often be appropriate in civil cases where, as here, the privacy interest is compelling. Disclosure of a limited number of documents, editing by the court to remove non-essential material, and the imposition of conditions on who may see and copy the documents are techniques which may be used to ensure the highest degree of confidentiality and the least damage to the protected relationship, while guarding against the injustice of cloaking the truth.

It must be conceded that a test for privilege which permits the court to occasionally reject an otherwise well-founded claim for privilege in the interests of getting at the truth may not offer patients a guarantee that communications with their psychiatrists will never be disclosed. On the other hand, the assurance that disclosure will be ordered only where clearly necessary and then only to the extent necessary is likely to permit many to avail themselves of psychiatric counselling when certain disclosure might make them hesitate or decline. The facts in this case demonstrate as much. I am reinforced in this view by the fact, as Scalia J. points out in his dissenting reasons in *Jaffee v. Redmond*, that of the 50 states and the District of Columbia which have enacted some form of psychotherapist privilege, none have adopted it in absolute form. All have found it necessary to specify circumstances in which it will not apply, usually related to the need to get at the truth in vital situations. Partial privilege, in the views of these legislators, can be effective.

The view that privilege may exist where the interest in protecting the privacy of the records is compelling and the threat to proper disposition of the litigation either is not apparent or can be offset by partial or conditional discovery is consistent with this Court's view in *R. v. O'Connor*, [1995] 4 S.C.R. 411. The majority there did not deny that privilege in psychotherapeutic records may exist in appropriate circumstances. Without referring directly to privilege, it developed a test for production of third party therapeutic and other records which balances the competing interests by reference to a number of factors including the right of the accused to full answer and defence and the right of the complainant to privacy. Just as justice requires that the accused in a criminal case be permitted to answer the Crown's case, so justice requires that a defendant in a civil suit be permitted to answer the plaintiff's case. In deciding whether he or she is entitled to production of confidential documents, this requirement must be balanced against the privacy interest of the complainant. This said, the interest in disclosure of a defendant in a civil suit may be less compelling than the parallel interest of an accused charged with a crime. The defendant in a civil suit stands to lose money and repute; the accused in a criminal proceeding stands to lose his or her very liberty. As a consequence, the balance between the interest in disclosure and the complainant's interest in privacy may be struck at a different level in the civil and criminal case; documents produced in a criminal case may not always be producible in a civil case, where the privacy interest of the complainant may more easily outweigh the defendant's interest in production.

My conclusion is that it is open to a judge to conclude that psychiatrist-patient records are privileged in appropriate circumstances. Once the first three requirements are met and a compelling prima facie case for protection is established, the focus will be on the balancing under the fourth head. A document relevant to a defence or claim may be required to be disclosed, notwithstanding the high interest of the plaintiff in keeping it confidential. On the other hand, documents of questionable relevance or which contain information available from other sources may be declared privileged. The result depends on the balance of the competing interests of disclosure and privacy in each case. It must be borne in mind that in most cases, the majority of the communications between a psychiatrist and her patient will have little or no bearing on the case at bar and can safely be excluded from production. Fishing expeditions are not appropriate where there is a compelling privacy interest at stake, even at the discovery stage. Finally, where justice requires that communications be disclosed, the court should consider qualifying the disclosure by imposing limits aimed at permitting the opponent to have the access justice requires while preserving the confidential nature of the documents to the greatest degree possible.

It remains to consider the argument that by commencing the proceedings against the respondent Dr. Ryan, the appellant has forfeited her right to confidentiality. I accept that a litigant must accept such intrusions upon her privacy as are necessary to enable the judge or jury to get to the truth and render a just verdict. But I do not accept that by claiming such damages as the law allows, a litigant grants her opponent a licence to delve into private aspects of her life which need not be probed for the proper disposition of the litigation.

VI. Procedure for Ascertaining Privilege

In order to determine whether privilege should be accorded to a particular document or class of documents and, if so, what conditions should attach, the judge must consider the circumstances of the privilege alleged, the documents, and the case. While it is not essential in a civil case such as this that the judge examine every document, the court may do so if necessary to the inquiry. On the other hand, a judge does not necessarily err by proceeding on affidavit material indicating the nature of the information and its expected relevance without inspecting each document individually. The requirement that the court minutely examine numerous or lengthy documents may prove time-consuming, expensive and delay the resolution of the litigation. Where necessary to the proper determination of the claim for privilege, it must be undertaken. But I would not lay down an absolute rule that as a matter of law, the judge must personally inspect every document at issue in every case. Where the judge is satisfied on reasonable grounds that the interests at stake can properly be balanced without individual examination of each document, failure to do so does not constitute error of law.

VII. Application to This Case

The Court of Appeal declined to order production of Dr. Parfitt's notes to herself on the ground that they were unnecessary given that she would not be called to testify. It ordered the production of notes and records of consultations with the appellant, but under stringent conditions. While the Court of Appeal did not proceed on the basis of privilege, its orders are supported by the principles relating to privilege that I have attempted to set forth.

The interest in preserving the confidentiality of the communications here at issue was, as discussed, compelling. On the other hand, the communications might be expected to bear on the critical issue of the extent to which the respondent Dr. Ryan's conduct caused the difficulties the appellant was experiencing. A court, in a case such as this, might well consider it best to inspect the records individually to the end of weeding out those which were irrelevant to this defence. However, the alternative chosen by the Court of Appeal in this case of refusing to order production of one group of documents and imposing stringent conditions on who could see the others and what use could be made of them cannot be said to be in error. In the end, the only persons to see the documents in question will be the lawyers for the respondent Dr. Ryan and his expert witnesses. Copies will not be made, and disclosure of the contents to other people will not be permitted. In short, the plaintiff's private disclosures to her psychiatrist will be disclosed only to a small group of trustworthy professionals, much in the fashion that confidential medical records may be disclosed in a hospital setting. I am not persuaded that the order of the Court of Appeal should be disturbed.

VIII. Conclusion

I would dismiss the appeal with costs.

[L'Heureux-Dubé J. would have allowed the appeal and set aside the decision of the Court of Appeal. In conclusion she reasoned as follows.]

L'HEUREUX-DUBÉ J.:—

. . . .

The Court of Appeal in the present case allowed the appeal in part. It did so after attempting some balancing of the privacy interests of the plaintiff and the interests in a fair trial. Consequently, it withheld the notes made for diagnostic purposes and restricted the dissemination and reproduction of the records once produced. Nonetheless, it did not review the documents before ordering their production. In my view, such a process does not give due consideration to the appropriate balance of the Charter values engaged by the discovery procedures.

Indeed, in these particular circumstances, and given the nature of the damages claimed and the information sought by the defence, very little meaningful protection has been accorded to these private records. If plaintiffs in such cases know that the entire contents of their discussion with their therapists or any other private records may be revealed to the lawyers and expert witnesses of the defendant, they may very well be deterred from seeking civil remedies. Without anyone reviewing the documents to remove information which is private, irrelevant or of very limited probative value, an order of production constitutes a serious breach of privacy while affording potentially limited benefit to the defence. A hierarchy of Charter values has been created, one where the defence is greatly advantaged while the effect on the plaintiff may be highly detrimental. In striking an appropriate balance of Charter values, such a hierarchy is impermissible. The Court of Appeal's decision must, therefore, be revisited. While the Court of Appeal's general approach was correct and while it did not have the benefit of our judgments in *O'Connor* and *L.L.A.*, at the time its decision was rendered, the process it adopted is infirm.

As regards the first issue, that relating to the privileged nature of the communications between the appellant and Dr. Parfitt, I agree with McLachlin J. that a successful claim of privilege has clearly been established for the records which were exempt from disclosure. I also affirm the Court of Appeal's general conclusion that it had a broader discretion to control the process of discovery for the remaining documents to ensure that it not affect one of the parties unjustly.

The exercise of discretion upon which the order was based did not effect an appropriate balance of the Charter values of privacy, equality, and fair trial. By failing to screen private records in such cases, the court creates a hierarchy of Charter values, where interests in privacy and equality may be seriously affected for records or parts thereof which may provide very little if any benefit to the defence or be unnecessary to ensure the fairness of the proceedings. Procedures adapted to the context of discovery in civil proceedings from the principles developed by this Court in *O'Connor* are in order.

I would allow the appeal with costs. The decision of the Court of Appeal should be set aside, except as regards the notes which were not disclosed, and the matter remitted back to the Master for determination in a manner consistent with the foregoing reasons.

PROBLEMS

Problem 1

John Doe has consulted you with regard to a running-down case. He admits to you that he left the scene of the accident and intends to conceal his identity from the authorities. He wants to know, however, whether the victim will be otherwise compensated. You have advised him that the Accident Compensation Fund will provide a fair settlement for her losses if the hit-and-run driver is not identified. In the subsequent suit to recover from the fund, counsel for the Attorney General has applied for an order compelling you to disclose your client's name and address. Privileged? Compare *Thorson v. Jones* (1973), 38 D.L.R. (3d) 312 (B.C.S.C.).

Problem 2

On August 15, 1983, a coroner's inquest was held for the purpose of investigating the circumstances surrounding the death of John W. Warren. Several days prior to the date of the inquest, Olwell was served with a subpoena *duces tecum*, which said, in part:

> . . . bring you all knives in your possession and under your control relating to Henry LeRoy Gray, Gloria Pugh or John W. Warren.

Thereafter, at the coroner's inquest the following exchange took place between a deputy prosecutor and appellant:

Q.   Now, Mr. Olwell, did you comply with that? [Subpoena]

A.   I do not have any knives in my possession that belong to Gloria Pugh, or to John W. Warren, and I did not comply with it as to the question of whether or not I have a knife belonging to Henry LeRoy Gray.

Q.   Now, I would ask you, do you have a knife in your possession or under your control relating to or belonging to Henry LeRoy Gray?

A.   I decline to answer that because of the confidential relationship of attorney and client; and to answer the question would be a violation of my oath as an attorney.

        . . .

Q.   And for the record, Mr. Olwell, in the event you do have in your possession a knife or knives that would be called for under the subpoena duces tecum, I take it your answer would be that you received these at the time you were acting as the attorney for Mr. Gray, is that correct?

A.   That is correct.

Further, on examination by the coroner, the following occurred:

Mr. Sowers: . . . As the Coroner of King County I order you to do so [answer] under the provisions of the law set forth in the legislature.

Mr. Olwell: I decline to surrender any of my client's possessions, if any, because of the confidential relationship of attorney and client because under the law I cannot give evidence which under the law cannot be compelled from my client himself.

Olwell is now before you cited for contempt. Rule on the citation. Compare *State ex rel. Sowers v. Olwell*, 394 P. 2d 681 (Wash. S.C., 1964). Did Olwell act ethically in receiving the knife? See *Problems in Ethics and Advocacy*, [1969] Special Lectures of L.S.U.C., "Defending a Criminal Case," at pp. 279 and 311. See also *Re Ryder*, 263 F. Supp. 360 (1967); affirmed 381 F. 2d 713 (4th Cir., 1967).

Problem 3

The deceased secured a divorce from appellant on March 25, 1982. That night she was killed, as she lay at home in her bed, as the result of a gunshot wound. From the mattress on her bed, as well as from the bed of her daughter, bullets were recovered which were shown by a firearms expert to have been fired by a .38 special revolver having Colt characteristics. Appellant was shown to have purchased a Colt .38 Detective Special some ten months prior to the homicide.

Marjorie Bartz, a telephone operator in the city of San Angelo, testified that at 2:49 in the morning of March 26, 1982, while on duty, she received a call from the Golden Spur Hotel; that at first she thought the person placing the call was a Mr. Cox and so made out the slip but that she then recognized appellant's voice, scratched out the word Cox and wrote Clark. She stated that appellant told her he wanted to speak to his lawyer, Jimmy Martin in Dallas, and that she placed the call to him at telephone number Victor 1942 in that city and made a record thereof, which record was admitted in evidence. Miss Bartz testified that, contrary to company rules, she listened to the entire conversation that ensued, and that it went as follows:

> The appellant: "Hello, Jimmy, I went to the extremes."
> The voice in Dallas: "What did you do?"
> The appellant: "I just went to the extremes."
> The voice in Dallas: "You got to tell me what you did before I can help."
> The appellant: "Well, I killed her."
> The voice in Dallas: "Who did you kill; the driver?"
> The appellant: "No, I killed her."
> The voice in Dallas: "Did you get rid of the weapon."
> The appellant: "No, I still got the weapon."
> The voice in Dallas: "Get rid of the weapon and sit tight and don't talk to anyone, and I will fly down in the morning."

It was stipulated that the Dallas telephone number of appellant's attorney was Victor 1942.

On appeal it is argued that the court erred in admitting the testimony of the telephone operator because the conversation was privileged. Give judgment. Compare *Clark v. State*, 261 S.W. 2d 339 (Texas C.C.A., 1953); cert. den. 346 U.S. 855, 905.

Problem 4

In a civil action arising out of a motor vehicle accident the defendant was cross-examined regarding his earlier plea of guilty to a charge of dangerous driving arising from the same accident. The defendant explained that he had obtained inadequate legal advice and in fact had been railroaded into his plea by the legal aid lawyer assigned to the case. In reply plaintiff calls the lawyer who acted for defendant in the criminal case. Defendant objects and claims privilege. Rule on the objection. Compare *Harich v. Stamp* (1979), 59 C.C.C. (2d) 87 (Ont. C.A.).

Problem 5

John Doe requests that you act for him on an anticipated charge of murder. He advises you that he intends to kill his wife tomorrow, hopes to get away cleanly but should he be apprehended, instructs you to seek his remand to a psychiatric facility as a first step in the preparation of an insanity defence. What should you do? Cf. *Tarasoff v. Regents of the University of California*, 551 P. 2d 334 (Cal. S.C., 1976).

Problem 6

The local police have asked you for assistance. Last evening they were involved in a high speed chase of a stolen automobile during which a pedestrian was killed. The driver of the vehicle escaped on foot but found in the glove compartment was an appointment card issued out of your office showing an appointment for tomorrow afternoon at 2:00 p.m. The police ask you to examine your diary and give them the name of the person expected. Should you help? They advise that if you are not forthcoming they intend to secure a search warrant for your office. They further advise that they intend to be in your office tomorrow waiting to see who attends. What should you do?

Problem 7

The accused is charged with robbery. The victim has testified that the accused closely resembles his assailant but he cannot be sure of his identification as his assailant had longer hair, did not have a moustache and wore spectacles. The prosecutor seeks to call you, the accused's counsel, to testify concerning the accused's appearance when you were first retained. Objectionable? The prosecutor seeks an order from the court to compel the accused to shave his moustache and to put on a pair of spectacles. Objectionable?

Problem 8

John Doe visited you in your office last night. His clothes were in disarray and he was bleeding heavily from four long scratches across his cheek. He asked you to act for him should he be charged with rape but you declined. Later Doe is arrested for rape alleged to have occurred on the evening he visited. May you testify to his physical condition that evening? Compare *Gosselin v. R.* (1903), 33 S.C.R. 255; *People v. Daghita*, 86 N.E. 2d 172 (N.Y., 1949).

Problem 9

You act for the Municipality of Metropolitan Kingston. John Smith is before the courts on a charge of assaulting a peace officer in your community. When Smith was arrested he filed a complaint with the local Police Bureau. His complaint was duly investigated and reports were taken from the four constables who were present during the incident. The names of those four constables appear on the indictment preferred against Smith. You have been advised by Inspector Clouseau, the person in charge of the complaint bureau, that he has been served with a subpoena requiring his attendance at Smith's trial and the production by him at the trial of the written reports made by the four constables. Advise the Inspector regarding his position. Does it matter that no civil proceedings arising out of Smith's complaint have yet been taken? Compare *R. v. Higgins* (1975), 29 C.C.C. (2d) 314 (Ont. Co. Ct.) and *Neilson v. Laugharne*, [1981] 1 All E.R. 829 (C.A.).

Problem 10

The accused stands charged before you with two criminal offences: the first, that he committed a sexual assault on L.G., and the second, that he unlawfully trafficked in cannabis resin. The principal crown witness with respect to both offences is L.G. At the time these offences are alleged to have occurred, L.G. was in the care of and under the protection of social agencies, from which she had run. Counsel for the accused has subpoenaed a case worker from each of the three agencies that were and had become involved with L.G. They were instructed by each subpoena to bring their files to court. A lawyer has appeared before you on behalf of the Minister of Community Services and claimed privilege over the files in the custody of the case workers. Rule. Compare *R. v. Ryan*, [1991] N.S.J. No. 468 (C.A.)

Problem 11

John Austin was acquitted of murder. During the following week a story appeared in the local newspaper under William French's byline which described the killing in great detail. The story included some details of the manner in which the body was mutilated which had not come out in evidence and had in fact been deliberately suppressed by the police to avoid undue pain and suffering to the victim's family. On appeal from the acquittal the Crown seeks to lead fresh evidence by calling William French and asking him to identify his source. French has publicly stated that he will never reveal his source regardless of any threatened punishment. Is his source privileged? Compare *Attorney General v. Mulholland*, [1963] 1 All E.R. 767 (C.A.). See also Blasi, "The Newsman's Privilege: An Empirical Study" (1971), 70 Mich. L. Rev. 229; Beaver, "The Newsman's Code: The Claim of Privilege and Everyman's Right to Evidence" (1968), 47 Ore. L. Rev. 243; and Kuhn, "Note: The Right of a Newsman to Refrain from Divulging the Sources of his Information" (1950), 36 Va. L. Rev. 61.

Problem 12

John Howard, aged 18, has been charged with indecent assault on a ten-year-old girl. The prosecution has called the accused's father to testify to conversations he had with the accused in his cell while awaiting trial. The father has refused to testify on the basis that what he was told was only following the father's promise of never disclosing the confidence. The prosecution insists on an answer. You are the trial judge. Rule on the request for privilege. Should you rule against the father and if he persists in his refusal, what punishment? See and compare *Re A & M*, 403 N.Y.S. 2d 375 (1978).

Problem 13

John Smith has been charged with the murder of a 14-year-old girl and asks you to defend him. You accept his retainer and during the first interview he admits the killing and discloses the whereabouts of the body. The police have been unable to discover the location of the body; the charge against your client rests largely on the fact that the deceased was last seen arguing with your client. Should you advise the police of the body's location? Should you go to the location described by your client and see whether the body is still hidden there? You read in the newspaper of the mental anguish of the deceased's parents who cannot cope with the problem of not knowing whether their child is dead or alive. Should you advise the parents that the child is dead? See Chamberlain, "Confidentiality in the Case of Robert Garrow's Lawyers" (1976), 25 Buff. L. Rev. 212.

11

Exclusion of Improperly Obtained Evidence

By the common law as developed in Canada, evidenced by the Supreme Court's decision in *R. v. Wray*,[1] the trial judge had no discretion to exclude relevant evidence of real probative worth where he believed the evidence was obtained illegally or improperly. However, the Canadian Charter of Rights and Freedoms, enacted in 1982, provides:

> **24.**(1) Anyone whose rights or freedoms, as guaranteed by this Charter, have been infringed or denied may apply to a court of competent jurisdiction to obtain such remedy as the court considers appropriate and just in the circumstances.
>
> (2) Where, in proceedings under subsection (1), a court concludes that evidence was obtained in a manner that infringed or denied any rights or freedoms guaranteed by this Charter, the evidence shall be excluded if it is established that, having regard to all the circumstances, the admission of it in the proceedings would bring the administration of justice into disrepute.

By the Charter, the focus is on whether admission of the evidence at the trial would bring the administration of justice into disrepute, but the decision will depend on "all the circumstances" surrounding the Charter violation which occurred during the investigation. A trial judge is to be concerned with how the investigation was conducted. The Charter plots a new direction for Canadian courts giving a discretion to exclude based on how the evidence was gathered. Canadian courts have since been endeavouring to fashion the appropriate guidelines for its exercise. As we explain in the preface we are of the view that this topic is better explored in Criminal Procedure courses since one of the main factors is the seriousness of the Charter violation and this requires an assessment of each Charter right. See further Delisle and Stuart, *Learning Canadian Criminal Procedure* (6th ed., 2000) and Stuart, *Charter Justice in Canadian Criminal Law* (3rd ed., 2001), Chapter 11. Here we highlight the major authorities on section 24(2), starting with the leading interpretation in *Stillman*.

R. v. STILLMAN
[1997] 1 S.C.R. 607, 5 C.R. (5th) 1, 113 C.C.C. (3d) 321

[A group of teenagers consumed drugs and alcohol at a camp in the woods. The accused, aged 17, left the group with a 14-year-old girl. When the accused arrived home that night he was obviously cold, shaken and wet from the upper thighs down. He was cut above one eye, and had mud and grass on his pants. The explanation for his condition was that he had been in a fight with five others. His account of where he had last seen the victim varied over time. The girl's body was found near where she had last been seen by the group. The cause of death was a wound or wounds to the head. Semen was found in her vagina and a human bite mark had been left on her abdomen.

---

1. (1970), 11 D.L.R. (3d) 673 (S.C.C.).

A week later the accused was arrested for the murder. At the station, police advised his lawyers that they wished to take hair samples and teeth impressions and to question the accused. The lawyers informed the police in writing that their client had been advised not to consent to providing any bodily samples or to speak to the police without a lawyer being present. Once the lawyers left, the police took bodily samples from the accused under threat of force. A sergeant took scalp hair samples by passing a gloved hand through the accused's hair, as well as by combing, clipping and plucking hairs. The accused was made to pull some of his own pubic hair. Plasticine teeth impressions were then taken. In the absence of the accused's parents or lawyers, a police officer interviewed the accused for an hour in an attempt to obtain a statement. The accused did not say anything but sobbed throughout the interview. When he asked to see a lawyer, the interview stopped and he was permitted to call his lawyer. While waiting for his lawyer, the accused was permitted to use the washroom, escorted by an officer. He blew his nose with a tissue and threw it into a waste bin. The tissue containing mucus was seized by the officer and later used for DNA testing.

The accused was released from custody but was arrested again several months later after the police had received the DNA and ondontology results. Without the accused's consent, impressions of his teeth were taken by a dentist in a procedure which took two hours. More hair was taken, as well as a saliva sample and buccal swabs.

Following a *voir dire* the trial judge found that the hair samples, teeth impressions and buccal swabs had been obtained in violation of the Charter but should nevertheless be admitted. He found that the tissue had not been obtained through a Charter violation. The accused was convicted by a jury of first degree murder. The majority of the New Brunswick Court of Appeal dismissed the appeal.

In the Supreme Court the appeal was allowed; a new trial was ordered at which hair samples, buccal swabs and dental impressions were to be excluded but the tissue was to be admitted. The majority, 7-2, ruled that the evidence of hair samples, buccal swabs and dental impressions could not be authorised as a search incident to arrest and had therefore been obtained in violation of section 8 of the Charter. The majority also found a violation of section 7. Here we consider the majority's ruling on section 24(2).]

CORY J. (LAMER C.J. and LA FOREST, SOPINKA and IACOBUCCI JJ. concurring):—

. . . .

B. Section 24 (2) of the Charter

(1) The Hair Samples, Dental Impressions and Buccal Swabs

The factors outlined by this Court in the trailblazing decision of *Collins* can be divided into three groups based on their effect on the repute of the administration of justice. The first of these categories includes those factors which relate to the fairness of the trial; the second group pertains to the seriousness of the Charter violation; and the third group concerns the possibility that the administration of justice could be brought into disrepute by excluding the evidence even though it was obtained in violation of the Charter. In my view, the trial judge erred in his consideration of the first two factors.

In considering how the admission of the evidence would affect the fairness of the trial, the trial judge erred in concluding that the hair samples and dental impressions existed independently of any Charter breach and were thus admissible. Certainly the appellant's hair samples, dental patterns and saliva existed as "real" evidence. However, the trial judge failed to appreciate the significance of the inescapable conclusion that, in violation of his Charter rights, the appellant was conscripted or forced by the police to provide evidence from his body thus incriminating himself. I have used the term "conscripted" to describe the situation where the police have compelled the accused to participate in providing self-incriminating evidence in the form of a confession or providing bodily samples. It is a term that has been used in other decisions of the Court, including *Collins*, to describe self-incriminating evidence obtained as a result of a Charter breach. In the circumstances, it was unnecessary and inappropriate to consider the seriousness of the breach. However, when he did so, the trial judge focussed exclusively on the conduct of the police. While police conduct is certainly one factor to be considered under this heading, it is not the only consideration. Here it was essential that other factors be considered. It is thus apparent that the trial judge erred in his appreciation and application of the proper legal principles to be considered in applying s. 24(2), and that the admissibility of the impugned evidence must be reconsidered.

There can be no question that the *Collins* decision was the pathfinder that first charted the route that courts should follow when considering the application of s. 24(2). However, subsequent decisions of this Court and their interpretations by the courts below indicate that a further plotting of the course for courts to follow is required, while maintaining the basic principles outlined in *Collins*. For example, confusion has arisen as to what constitutes "real" evidence and in what circumstances its exclusion or admission would render the trial unfair. Perhaps the ensuing review of some decisions and proposed procedure for classifying evidence will be of some assistance.

(a) Fairness of the Trial

A consideration of trial fairness is of fundamental importance. If after careful consideration it is determined that the admission of evidence obtained in violation of a Charter right would render a trial unfair then the evidence must be excluded without consideration of the other *Collins* factors. A fair trial for those accused of a criminal offence is a cornerstone of our Canadian democratic society. A conviction resulting from an unfair trial is contrary to our concept of justice. To uphold such a conviction would be unthinkable. It would indeed be a travesty of justice. The concept of trial fairness must then be carefully considered for the benefit of society as well as for an accused. . . . The primary aim and purpose of considering the trial fairness factor in the s. 24(2) analysis is to prevent an accused person whose Charter rights have been infringed from being forced or conscripted to provide evidence in the form of statements or bodily samples for the benefit of the state. It is because the accused is compelled as a result of a Charter breach to participate in the creation or discovery of self-incriminating evidence in the form of confessions, statements or the provision of bodily samples, that the admission of that evidence would generally tend to render the trial unfair. That general rule, like all rules, may be subject to rare exceptions.

Thus, as a first step in the trial fairness analysis it is necessary to classify the type of evidence in question. Evidence to be considered under "fairness" will generally fall into one of two categories: non-conscriptive or conscriptive. The admission of evidence which falls into the "non-conscriptive" category will, as stated in Collins, rarely operate to render the trial unfair. If the evidence has been classified as non-conscriptive the court should move on to consider the second and third Collins factors, namely, the seriousness of the Charter violation and the effect of exclusion on the repute of the administration of justice. The key, then, is how to distinguish between "non-conscriptive" and "conscriptive" evidence.

. . . .

(i) Classification of the Evidence

. . . .

What has come to be referred to as "real" evidence will not necessarily fall into the "non-conscriptive" category. There is on occasion a misconception that "real" evidence, referring to anything which is tangible and exists as an independent entity, is always admissible. It is for this reason that blood, hair samples or the identity of the accused are often readily, yet incorrectly, classified as "real evidence existing independently of the Charter breach". It is true that all of these examples "exist" quite independently of a Charter breach. Yet, it is key to their classification that they do not necessarily exist *in a useable form*. For example, in the absence of a valid statutory authority or the accused's consent to take bodily samples, the independent existence of the bodily evidence is of no use to the prosecution since there is no lawful means of obtaining it. The crucial element which distinguishes non-conscriptive evidence from conscriptive evidence is not whether the evidence may be characterized as "real" or not. Rather, it is whether the accused was compelled to make a statement or provide a bodily substance in violation of the Charter. Where the accused, as a result of a breach of the Charter, is compelled or conscripted to provide a bodily substance to the state, this evidence will be of a conscriptive nature, despite the fact that it may also be "real" evidence. Therefore, it may be more accurate to describe evidence found without any participation of the accused, such as the murder weapon found at the scene of the crime, or drugs found in a dwelling house, simply as *non-conscriptive* evidence; its status as "real" evidence, *simpliciter*, is irrelevant to the s. 24(2) inquiry.

. . . .

Traditionally, the common law and Canadian society have recognized the fundamental importance of the innate dignity of the individual. There is little likelihood of maintaining any semblance of dignity where, without consent and in the absence of any statutory authorization, intrusive procedures are employed to take bodily substances. to take bodily substances. For example, can there be any respect demonstrated for an individual if against their will women and men accused of a crime can be compelled to provide samples of their pubic hair to the police?

It is repugnant to fair-minded men and women to think that police can without consent or statutory authority take or require an accused to provide parts of their body or bodily substances in order to incriminate themselves. The recognition of the right to bodily integrity and sanctity is embodied in s. 7 of the Charter which confirms the right to life, liberty and the security of the person and guarantees the equally important reciprocal right not to be deprived of security of the person except in accordance with the principles of fundamental justice. This right requires that any interference with or intrusion upon the human body can only be undertaken in accordance with principles of fundamental justice. Generally that will require valid statutory authority or the consent of the individual to the particular bodily intrusion or interference required for the purpose of the particular procedure the police wish to undertake. . . . It follows that the compelled use of the body or the compelled provision of bodily substances in breach of a Charter right for purposes of self-incrimination will generally result in an unfair trial just as surely as the compelled or conscripted self-incriminating statement.

So soon as that is said, it is apparent that a particular procedure may be so unintrusive and so routinely performed that it is accepted without question by society. Such procedures may come under the rare exception for merely technical or minimal violations referred to earlier. For example, assuming that fingerprinting is conscriptive, it is minimally intrusive and has been recognized by statute and practice for such an extended period of time that this Court readily found that it was acceptable in Canadian society. See the carefully crafted reasons of La Forest J. in *Beare*, supra. Similarly, the Criminal Code provisions pertaining to breath samples are both minimally intrusive and essential to control the tragic chaos caused by drinking and driving. . . . In my view, police actions taken without consent or authority which intrude upon an individual's body in more than a minimal fashion violate s. 7 of the Charter in a manner that would as a general rule tend to affect the fairness of the trial. Those opposed to this position may argue that it leads to the requirement that the state will have to justify legislation permitting bodily intrusion. Yet, I do not find that to be an unduly onerous requirement when dealing with bodily intrusions. Although the issue was not raised it would seem that the recent provisions of the Code permitting DNA testing might well meet all constitutional requirements. The procedure is judicially supervised, it must be based upon reasonable and probable grounds and the authorizing judge must be satisfied that it is minimally intrusive. It cannot be forgotten that the testing can establish innocence as readily as guilt as the Guy-Paul Morin case so vividly demonstrates. It seems to me that the requirement of justification is a reasonable safeguard which is necessary to control police powers to intrude upon the body. This is the approach that I would favour.

. . . .

The compulsion which results in self-incrimination by a statement or the taking of bodily substances or the use of the body itself may arise in a number of ways such as the forced participation in a line-up identification (*R. v. Ross*, [1989] 1 S.C.R. 3); providing a breath sample (*R. v. Bartle*, [1994] 3 S.C.R. 173); providing DNA samples — blood (*Borden*, supra); telling the police where to find evidence (*Burlingham*, supra); and making an incriminating statement (*R. v. Manninen*, [1987] 1 S.C.R. 1233). . . . On the other hand, an example of a situation where evidence obtained in violation of a Charter right was admitted because there was no compulsion is *R. v. Wijesinha*, [1995] 3 S.C.R. 422. In that case, the accused, a lawyer, had set up a scheme whereby police officers, for a fee, would refer to him individuals caught driving while impaired. Part of the evidence against the accused were certain statements he made at a meeting he had arranged with a police officer who, unbeknownst to him, was wearing a "body pack" which recorded the conversation. This surreptitious recording was undertaken without a warrant, and hence violated s. 8 of the Charter. Obviously, the accused was not detained at the time he made these statements.

With respect to the first branch of the *Collins* test, it was held at para. 55 that:

> On the first question, it seems readily apparent that the admission of the evidence did not affect the fairness of the trial. The appellant could not by any stretch of the imagination be said to have been conscripted into incriminating himself in these conversations.

. . . .

Derivative Evidence

A subset of conscriptive evidence is "derivative evidence". This is a term frequently used to describe what is essentially conscriptive "real" evidence. It involves a Charter violation whereby the accused is conscripted against himself (usually in the form of an inculpatory statement) which then leads to the discovery of an item of real evidence. In other words, the unlawfully conscripted statement of the accused is the necessary cause of the discovery of the real evidence. An example is provided by *Burlingham* . . . If the evidence under consideration is classified as conscriptive, that is to say self-incriminating, which in the case of statements includes derivative evidence, then it will be necessary to take the second step of the analysis and determine whether the admission of the evidence would render the trial unfair.

(ii) The Discoverability or "But For" Principle

The admission of self-incriminating evidence in the form of statements or bodily substances conscripted from the accused in violation of the Charter and evidence derived from unlawfully conscripted statements will, as a general rule, tend to render the trial unfair. Nevertheless, in recent cases it has been held that the admission of conscriptive evidence will not render the trial unfair where the impugned evidence would have been discovered in the absence of the unlawful conscription of the accused. There are two principal bases upon which it could be demonstrated that the evidence would have been discovered. The first is where an independent source of the evidence exists. The second is where the discovery of the evidence was inevitable. . . . Where it is established that either a non-conscriptive means existed through which the evidence would have been discovered or that its discovery was inevitable, then the evidence was discoverable; it would have been discovered in the absence of the unlawful conscription of the accused. The Crown must bear the onus of establishing discoverability on a balance of probabilities. Where the evidence was "discoverable", even though it may be conscriptive, its admission will not, as a general rule, render the trial unfair. The Court should therefore proceed to consider the seriousness of the violation.

. . . .

(iii) Trial Fairness Summary

. . . .

The summary itself can be reduced to this short form:

1.   Classify the evidence as conscriptive or non-conscriptive based upon the manner in which the evidence was obtained. If the evidence is non-conscriptive, its admission will not render the trial unfair and the court will proceed to consider the seriousness of the breach and the effect of exclusion on the repute of the administration of justice.

2.   If the evidence is conscriptive and the Crown fails to demonstrate on a balance of probabilities that the evidence would have been discovered by alternative non-conscriptive means, then its admission will render the trial unfair. The Court, as a general rule, will exclude the evidence without considering the seriousness of the breach or the effect of exclusion on the repute of the administration of justice. This must be the result since an unfair trial would necessarily bring the administration of justice into disrepute.

3.   If the evidence is found to be conscriptive and the Crown demonstrates on a balance of probabilities that it would have been discovered by alternative non-conscriptive means, then its admission will generally not render the trial unfair. However, the seriousness of the Charter breach and the effect of exclusion on the repute of the administration of justice will have to be considered.

(iv) Application of the Principles Discussed to this Case

The police had no right to obtain the hair samples, teeth impressions or buccal swabs from the appellant without his informed consent. The appellant clearly expressed his refusal to provide bodily samples. Yet, by threat of force the police obtained the sample of scalp hair, buccal swabs and compelled the appellant to pluck his pubic hair to provide as a sample. They proceeded with the lengthy and intrusive process of taking impressions of his teeth. There can be no doubt that the police, by their words and actions, compelled the appellant to participate in providing the evidence. Equally there can be no doubt that the evidence of bodily samples constituted conscriptive evidence.

It is apparent that the impugned evidence would not have been discovered had it not been for the conscription of the accused in violation of s. 7 and s. 8 of the Charter. The appellant was not obliged to provide the hair samples, teeth impressions or buccal swabs. His Charter guarantee of security of the person and the inviolability of his body meant that in the absence of statutory authority the Crown could not undertake the impugned procedure. Quite simply, the police could not, in the absence of valid statutory authority, lawfully obtain the samples without his consent. No independent source existed by which the police could have obtained the impugned evidence. Since the appellant expressly refused to consent to provide samples, the evidence was not discoverable by the state without the conscription of the accused in violation of the Charter. It follows that the admission of the evidence would render the trial unfair. This finding is sufficient to resolve the s. 24(2) issue as the evidence must be excluded: Hebert, supra. However, something should be said of the seriousness of the Charter violation which occurred in this case.

[Cory J. went on to find that the breach was also serious and would shock the conscience of the community.]

. . . .

(2) The Tissue Containing Mucous

In contrast to the hair samples, teeth impressions and buccal swabs, the police did not force, or even request, a mucous sample from the appellant. He blew his nose of his own accord. The police acted surreptitiously in disregard for the appellant's explicit refusal to provide them with bodily samples. However, the violation of the appellant's Charter rights with respect to the tissue was not serious. The seizure did not interfere with the appellant's bodily integrity, nor cause him any loss of dignity. In any event, the police could and would have obtained the discarded tissue. They would have had reasonable and probable grounds to believe that the tissue would provide evidence in their investigation and therefore would have sealed the garbage container and obtained a search warrant in order to recover its contents. Quite simply, it was discoverable. In my view, the administration of justice would not be brought into disrepute if the evidence obtained from the mucous sample were to be admitted.

L'HEUREUX-DUBÉ J. (GONTHIER J. concurring) dissenting:—

. . . .

I find that there was no breach of the appellant's Charter rights in the obtention of the evidence here in question, and that the trial judge and the majority of the Court of Appeal, albeit for different reasons, were correct in finding that such evidence was admissible at trial. Consequently, it is not strictly necessary to deal with a s. 24(2) inquiry. Nevertheless, given the importance of this issue in the reasons of Cory and McLachlin JJ., some comment is in order.

. . . .

The framework set out in *Collins*, in my opinion, represents the proper approach to s. 24(2) and efforts since then to explain, clarify, refine, extend, add to or distinguish *Collins*, have only served to further muddy the waters. . . . I am strongly of the view, in particular, that the classification of evidence proposed by my colleague Cory J., under the trial fairness aspect of the s. 24(2) analysis, in terms of "non-conscriptive 'real' evidence" and "conscriptive evidence" (which includes "derivative evidence"), with their possible extension to all kinds of unforeseen situations, is, in my view, an unfortunate development. . . . I have consistently maintained that the trial fairness concern arises solely where the accused is compelled as a result of a Charter breach to participate in the creation or discovery of self-incriminating evidence, and that this protection against self-incrimination is confined to testimonial evidence. . . . As to whether evidence which affects the fairness of the trial must inevitably be excluded under s. 24(2), I would respond in the negative. Like McLachlin J., I am of the view that a proper consideration of "all the circumstances" demands a balancing of each set of factors set out in *Collins*.

. . . .

McLACHLIN J. (dissenting):—

. . . .

In my respectful opinion, the view expressed in some cases that any evidence which affects the fairness of the trial must be excluded under s. 24(2) should be resisted. First, it runs counter to the spirit and wording of s. 24(2), which requires that judges in all cases balance all factors which may affect the repute of the administration of justice, and elevates the factor of trial unfairness to a dominant and in many cases conclusive status. Second, it rests on an expanded and, with respect, erroneous concept of self-incrimination or conscription which equates any non-consensual participation by or use of the accused's body in evidence gathering with trial unfairness. Third, it erroneously assumes that anything that affects trial fairness automatically renders the trial so fundamentally unfair that other factors can never outweigh the unfairness, with the result that it becomes unnecessary to consider other factors. . . . I would reject the approach to s. 24(2) proposed by the majority on this appeal. In my view, the Court must consider all the circumstances of the case and in light of them, balance the effect of admitting the evidence on the repute of the administration of justice against the effect of rejecting the evidence. The circumstances to be considered include those listed by this Court in *Collins*. It cannot be said as a matter of law that one factor is more important than others, or that one factor will trump the others and render them superfluous. In particular, the dual propositions that all conscripted evidence, including real evidence, is unfair because it requires the accused to incriminate himself or herself and that any evidence that affects trial fairness must automatically be excluded, should be rejected. The principle against self-incrimination does not apply to real evidence, except that which is derivative from compelled testimony, and there are different degrees of trial fairness. Depending on the degree of unfairness and countervailing circumstances, the fairness of the manner in which the evidence was obtained may or may not result in rejection of the evidence under s. 24(2). In an extreme case, where the unfairness casts doubt on the safety of the verdict, it may, as a matter of application of the balancing process, be predicted that the interest in admitting the evidence will never outweigh the harm that would be done by its admission. Similarly, it may be hazarded as a matter of prediction that, to quote Lamer J. in *Collins*, "[r]eal evidence ...obtained in a manner that violated the Charter will rarely operate unfairly for that reason alone" (p. 284). These predictive generalizations, however, do not change the overriding rule that the judge must in each case consider and balance all of the circumstances in determining the admissibility of evidence taken in contravention of Charter guarantees.

[McLachlin J. then reviewed all of the factors set out in *Collins* and decided that the trial judge and the Court of Appeal had not erred.]

Major J.:—I agree with Cory J.'s reasons excluding the conscripted evidence obtained from hair samples, buccal swabs and dental impressions. However, with respect, I do not agree that the tissue containing the mucous sample taken from the wastebasket, after being discarded by the appellant, was obtained in violation of s. 8 of the Canadian Charter of Rights and Freedoms. . . . In the circumstances of this case, the appellant had no reasonable expectation of privacy with respect to the tissue he discarded.

For critical reviews of the s. 24(2) analysis in *Stillman*, see David Paciocco, "Stillman, Disproportion and the Fair Trial Dichotomy under Section 24(2)" (1997), 2 Can. Crim. L.R. 163 and Carol Brewer, "*Stillman* and Section 24(2): Much To-Do About Nothing" (1997), 2 Can. Crim. L.R. 239. Do you find that the majority has drawn a convincing line between conscripted and non-conscripted evidence? Is the doctrine of discoverability outlined in *Stillman* workable and/or wise? See further Stuart, "*Stillman*: Limiting Search Incident To Arrest, Consent Searches and Refining The Section 24(2) Test" (1997), 5 C.R. (5th) 99 at 104-109.

When the Supreme Court decides that the evidence is non-conscripted and therefore does not effect trial fairness the focus is on the second and third *Collins* factors, namely seriousness of the violation and effect on the reputation of the justice system. In such cases the Supreme Court rarely excludes evidence. This is particularly evident in drug cases.

R. v. FEENEY
[1997] 2 S.C.R. 13, 7 C.R. (5th) 101, 115 C.C.C. (3d) 129

[The police, investigating a murder, went to the accused's house. When they received no answer at the door, they entered, roused the accused, touched his leg, ordered him to get up and took him to the front of the trailer for better lighting. The police arrested him after seeing blood on his shirt. Following a caution with respect to the right to counsel but not the right to immediate counsel, the police asked the accused a couple of questions which he answered. The accused's shirt was seized and he was taken to the police detachment. The majority found violations of the accused's Charter rights under sections 8, 9 and 10(b). Here we consider those aspects of the judgment having to do with s. 24(2) of the Charter.]

SOPINKA J. (LA FOREST, CORY, IACOBUCCI and MAJOR JJ. concurring):—

. . . .

Characterizing the evidence in the case at bar, the first step in the trial fairness inquiry, I conclude that the bloody shirt is non-conscriptive, and thus its admission does not go to trial fairness. The bloody shirt existed in a form useable by the state independent of any actions by the state. Moreover, with respect to the bloody shirt, the appellant was not compelled to incriminate himself by means of a statement, the use of the body, or the production of bodily samples. While the appellant was asked to step into the light in order better to see him, equally the police could have simply turned on a light or inspected the shirt closely in order to examine it. The taking of the shirt did not involve the use of the appellant's body or bodily samples in a manner that rendered the evidence conscriptive; his body was not integral to the taking of the bloody shirt and thus the shirt is not conscriptive.

On the other hand, the statements obtained by the police in the trailer in violation of the appellant's s. 10(b) rights are clearly conscriptive evidence. By not informing the appellant of his immediate right to counsel, the police in effect compelled the statements, which statements are paradigmatic self-incriminating evidence. Having found the statements conscriptive, the next question set out in *Stillman* is whether alternative legal means to obtain the conscriptive evidence existed. As the Crown did not attempt to prove that the statements would have been made even in the absence of a violation of s. 10(b) I conclude that the statements were conscriptive and would not have been obtained without breaching the Charter. Thus, following the *Stillman* analysis, the statements were not "discoverable". The admission of the statements therefore would affect the fairness of the trial. Given that no exceptional circumstances exist in this case, the admission of the conscriptive, non-discoverable statements would render the trial unfair; thus the statements are inadmissible under s. 24(2).

The shoes were observed by the police during the initial unconstitutional search of the trailer. The shoes were later seized in a search which I have concluded violated s. 8. The shoes are clearly non-conscriptive evidence, given that they are not compelled statements or bodily samples, and did not involve the use of the appellant's body. The admission of the shoes would thus not affect trial fairness. The cigarettes were also observed by the police in the initial unconstitutional search of the trailer. . . . Their admission would not affect trial fairness. Also in making a conscriptive statement at Williams Lake, the appellant told police that he had stolen cash and had hidden it under his mattress. In the second unconstitutional search of the trailer, the police seized the cash. Like the cigarettes and the shoes, the cash is facially non-conscriptive evidence. Unlike the statement about the cigarettes, however, the conscriptive statement at Williams Lake about the cash was a sufficient cause for obtaining the cash, stating as it did the location of the cash. However, in my view, the statement was not a necessary cause of the taking of the cash. The police clearly intended to search the trailer again and I am satisfied would have done so even in the absence of the statement as to the location of the money. In conducting a second search, in my view they would have located the cash under the mattress. Given that the conscriptive statement was not a necessary cause of the taking of the money, the money was not conscriptive, derivative evidence.

It is important to note the distinction between the test for characterizing evidence as conscriptive, derivative evidence and the test for determining whether conscriptive evidence is discoverable. Discoverability is concerned with whether a Charter breach was necessary to the discovery and obtaining of conscriptive evidence. If the conscriptive evidence would have been obtained even if the Charter had not been breached, the evidence is discoverable and its admission, despite the conscription of the accused, would not affect trial fairness. In determining discoverability, therefore, the alternative means to obtain the evidence must comply with the Charter.

The derivative evidence inquiry, on the other hand, is directed at determining whether a piece of evidence should be viewed as having a conscriptive nature because of its intimate relationship with other conscriptive evidence. Evidence is derivative evidence if it would not have been obtained but for the conscriptive evidence. In analyzing this question, it is not relevant whether the means by which the evidence would have been discovered in the absence of the conscription were constitutional. The inquiry is directed at whether evidence should be treated as a product of the accused's mind or body for the purposes of s. 24(2), which treatment does not depend on the constitutionality of the alternative means of discovery. Thus, in the present case, to conclude that the cash is not derivative evidence, it is sufficient to conclude that the police would have discovered the cash even if the conscripted statement at Williams Lake had not been made. It is irrelevant for the purpose of the derivative evidence inquiry that the police would have found the evidence by unconstitutional means such as the second search. Given the probable, although unconstitutional, discovery of the cash even if the conscripted statement had not been made, the cash was not conceptually a product of the appellant's mind or body. The cash, therefore, should be treated not as derivative evidence, but as non-conscriptive evidence; its admission would not affect trial fairness. I note, of course, that the unconstitutionality of the second search is a factor to be considered under other branches of the *Collins* test.

The fingerprints, as stated above, were taken in violation of the Charter. Moreover, they were conscriptive evidence — the appellant was compelled to provide evidence from his body, his fingerprints, which incriminated him. The police would not have obtained this evidence without violating the appellant's Charter rights as they did not have reasonable and probable grounds to arrest him. The fingerprints were not discoverable. The fingerprints were conscriptive, non-discoverable evidence whose admission, given the absence of exceptional circumstances, would render the trial unfair. Consequently, the fingerprints are inadmissible.

Summarizing the trial fairness analysis, the bloody shirt, the shoes, the cigarettes and the money were not conscriptive evidence and thus their admission would not affect trial fairness; the statements in the trailer, as well as those at the Williams Lake detachment, and the fingerprints were conscriptive and were not discoverable, thus their admission would affect trial fairness. The statements and the fingerprints are inadmissible. The other evidence which does not affect trial fairness must be analyzed in light of the second and third branches. Analyses under these branches of the Collins test may require exclusion of the evidence.

Seriousness of the Violation

The violations were, in my view, very serious in the present case. One of the indicia of seriousness is whether the violations were undertaken in good faith: see *Therens*, supra, at p. 652; *Collins*, supra, at p. 285. One indication of bad faith is that the Charter violation was undertaken without any lawful authority. In *R. v. Genest*, [1989] 1 S.C.R. 59, for example, the Court held that a search in violation of well-known common law principles was performed in bad faith. In the instant case, the police did not even have subjective belief in reasonable and probable grounds for the appellant's arrest prior to their warrantless, forced entry into his dwelling house where he was sleeping. Aside from the impact of the Charter on the requirements for warrantless arrests in dwelling houses, the absence of subjective belief in reasonable grounds indicated that the police could not have lawfully arrested the appellant under s. 495 of the Code even had he been in a public place. That they flagrantly disobeyed the law of warrantless arrests in dwelling houses as set out in *Landry* certainly renders the more serious the violation which directly led to the taking of the bloody shirt, and indirectly led to the taking of the shoes, cigarettes and money.

. . . .

In the present case, the police did not have subjective grounds to arrest, and thus the requirements for a warrantless arrest in a dwelling house set out in *Landry* were not met. Indeed, the statutory requirements to make a warrantless arrest in any location were not met. In these circumstances, as in *Kokesch*, the police either knew they were trespassing, or they ought to have known. The police could not be held to have acted in good faith and the trial judge erred in this respect.

. . . .

The respondent also argued that there were exigent circumstances in this case, which, according to *Silveira*, supra, may be a relevant consideration in a s. 24(2) analysis. As discussed above, in my view exigent circumstances did not exist in this case any more than they would exist in any situation following a serious crime. After any crime is committed, the possibility that evidence might be destroyed is inevitably present. To tend to admit evidence because of the mitigating effect of such allegedly exigent circumstances would invite the admission of all evidence obtained soon after the commission of a crime. In my view, however, there were no exigent circumstances in this case that mitigated the seriousness of the Charter breach. This is not to say that there may not be exigent circumstances arising out of matters other than the recent commission of the offence that serve to mitigate the seriousness of the breach.

. . . .

Effect of Exclusion on the Repute of the Administration of Justice

The admission of the conscriptive evidence, the statements and the fingerprints, would, as discussed above, impact on the fairness of the trial. Consequently, the repute of the administration of justice would be harmed by their admission and they are inadmissible. The other evidence, while not conscriptive, was obtained as the result of a very serious intrusion of the appellant's privacy rights. Moreover, the evidence was associated with serious violations of the appellant's s. 10(b) rights, indicating a pattern of disregard for the Charter by the police in the present case.

While the appellant stood accused of a very serious crime, in my view the following words of Iacobucci J. in *Burlingham*, supra, at p. 242, apply to the present case:

> We should never lose sight of the fact that even a person accused of the most heinous crimes, and no matter the likelihood that he or she actually committed those crimes, is entitled to the full protection of the Charter. Short-cutting or short-circuiting those rights affects not only the accused, but also the entire reputation of the criminal justice system. It must be emphasized that the goals of preserving the integrity of the criminal justice system as well as promoting the decency of investigatory techniques are of fundamental importance in applying s. 24(2).

The serious disregard for the appellant's Charter rights in the case at bar suggests that the admission of the evidence would bring greater harm to the repute of the administration of justice than its exclusion. The shirt, shoes, cigarettes and money were inadmissible under s. 24(2), along with the statements and the fingerprints. If the exclusion of this evidence is likely to result in an acquittal of the accused as suggested by L'Heureux-Dubé, J. in her reasons, then the Crown is deprived of a conviction based on illegally obtained evidence. Any price to society occasioned by the loss of such a conviction is fully justified in a free and democratic society which is governed by the rule of law.

L'HEUREUX-DUBÉ J. (GONTHIER and McLACHLIN JJ. concurring) dissenting:—

. . . .

As I have found that the actions of the police in this case did not breach the Charter, it is unnecessary for me to consider s. 24(2). Had it been necessary, however, I would have concurred with the findings of the trial judge and the Court of Appeal that considering the exigent circumstances and seriousness of the crime, excluding this evidence would clearly bring the administration of justice into disrepute, particularly since this result would likely preclude the appellant, who was convicted by a jury, of being brought to justice.

LAMER C.J. (dissenting):—I have had the benefit of the reasons of both of my colleagues, Justice L'Heureux-Dubé, and Justice Sopinka, and cannot agree with either of them. I do agree with L'Heureux-Dubé, J. in the result, but substantially for the reasons given by Lambert J.A. of the Court of Appeal of British Columbia (1995), 54 B.C.A.C. 228. My reasons and conclusion are not to be taken as disagreeing in any way with the principles of *R. v. Stillman*, [1997] 1 S.C.R. 607, as expressed in the reasons of Sopinka J. I agree with those principles as stated therein. My disagreement is with their application on the facts of this case. I would accordingly dismiss this appeal.

R. v. LEWIS
(1998), 13 C.R. (5th) 34, 122 C.C.C. (3d) 481 (Ont. C.A.)

[The accused was charged with possession of cocaine for the purpose of trafficking. The police received a tip from an anonymous source that a man with the accused's name and matching his description would be taking a certain flight at a certain time accompanied by a two-year-old boy and would be carrying cocaine concealed in a bottle of wine or rum. After identifying the accused based on that description, the police officers escorted him to a baggage room and asked him if he had any drugs in his luggage. The accused opened one of his bags. The officer reached into the bag and removed a bottle of rum which contained almost a pound of 100 per cent pure cocaine. The trial judge found that the accused's rights under ss. 8 and 10(b) of the Canadian Charter of Rights and Freedoms were violated and he excluded the evidence of the cocaine under s. 24(2) of the Charter on the ground that the evidence would not have been found but for the illegal search and that its admission would render the trial unfair. The Crown appealed. The Court of Appeal decided that the investigative detention, which encompassed a search of the accused's luggage, gave rise to an obligation that the police inform the accused of his right to counsel and therefore there was a violation of s. 10(b) of the Charter. Also the accused was subject to an unreasonable search and seizure. The search was a warrantless one, was not the incident of a lawful arrest, and was not preceded by an informed consent. It and the seizure which followed were unreasonable. The Court went on to consider whether the evidence should be excluded under s. 24(2).]

DOHERTY J.A. (McMURTRY C.J.O. and ROSENBERG J.A. concurring):—

. . . .

The trial judge's reliance on a "but for" discoverability test is understandable given the state of the law at the time of the trial. Some cases in this court had adopted that approach: e.g., see *R. v. Zammit*, supra, at p. 124 C.C.C.; *R. v. Acciavatti* (1993), 80 C.C.C. (3d) 109 (Ont. C.A.). More recent decisions of the Supreme Court of Canada, however, have clarified the fair trial component of the s. 24(2) analysis. In *R. v. Stillman*, [1997] 1 S.C.R. 607, Cory J. identified the characterization of the challenged evidence as conscriptive or non-conscriptive as the primary task in the assessment of whether its admission would impair the fairness of the trial.

R. v. Stillman was applied in *R. v. Feeney* and in *R. v. Belnavis* (1997), 118 C.C.C. (3d) 405 at p. 423 (S.C.C.). In both cases, conscriptive evidence was limited to evidence in the form of a statement, a bodily sample or evidence derived from the use of the accused's body. In addition to evidence which is conscriptive by nature, other evidence found as a result of the obtaining of conscriptive evidence may also be regarded as conscriptive for the purposes of s. 24(2): *R. v. Feeney*.

These same cases make it clear that the discoverability of evidence tainted by a Charter violation becomes significant to its admissibility only if that evidence is otherwise properly characterized as conscriptive. The admission of evidence which is conscriptive but discoverable will not affect the fairness of the trial: *R. v. Stillman*.

Mr. Tanovich, for the respondent, submits that when the respondent opened the bag for the police in the course of the search, he was conscripted to assist in obtaining the evidence in the bag. I cannot agree. The respondent was not compelled to open the bag and in opening the bag, he added nothing to the evidentiary value of the cocaine found in the bag. The respondent was not used in any relevant sense in the obtaining of the evidence, nor was he required to incriminate himself. I see no difference for fair trial purposes between a situation in which the police open the bag and a situation in which an accused opens the bag for the police. In either case, it is a police search and the evidentiary value of anything seized in the search has no connection to the accused's physical involvement in the search. Mr. Tanovich's submission would turn an inconsequential feature of the interplay between the respondent and the police into the determining factor in the characterization of the evidence as conscriptive or non-conscriptive. Cory J., in an extrajudicial observation, has also rejected the distinction urged by Mr. Tanovich: see P. Cory, "General Principles of Charter Exclusion", Paper presented at the National Criminal Law Programme 1997, Halifax, Nova Scotia.

The cocaine did not come within any of the three types of conscriptive evidence identified in *Stillman*, *Feeney* and *Belnavis* and it was not discovered as the result of the obtaining of conscriptive evidence. The trial judge erred in law in holding that the admission of the cocaine would impair the fairness of the trial.

. . . .

The breaches of s. 8 and s. 10(b) were not inconsequential. I am satisfied, however, that the trial judge erred in law in failing to appreciate the effect of the respondent's reduced privacy expectations in determining the seriousness of the s. 8 breach. I am also satisfied that he erred in law in his consideration of whether the police reasonably believed that the respondent was willing to let them search his bag.

The third factor to be considered in determining whether evidence should be excluded under s. 24(2) is the effect on the administration of justice of the exclusion of the proffered evidence. In this case, the cocaine was reliable evidence which was essential to the prosecution of a very serious crime. There can be no doubt that the exclusion of this kind of evidence exacts a heavy toll on the repute of the administration of justice. That consequence must be accepted where necessary to preserve trial fairness or where the Charter violations are sufficiently serious to demand the exclusion of the evidence. Trial fairness is not compromised in this case and the seriousness of the breaches is not of a magnitude which warrants the exclusion of this kind of evidence. The cocaine should not have been excluded. I would allow the appeal, set aside the acquittal and direct a new trial.

R. v. DAVIES
(1998), 18 C.R. (5th) 113, 127 C.C.C. (3d) 97 (Y.T. C.A.)

[The central issue was whether evidence seized from the accused by a police officer was conscriptive or non-conscriptive. The evidence was a pair of bolt cutters. Their admission into evidence at trial was crucial to the accused's conviction for possession of a break-in instrument contrary to s. 351(1) of the Criminal Code. The police officer saw the accused and another person late at night and thought they were acting suspiciously. There had been a rash of break and enters of residences and businesses. When speaking to one of the males, the accused started to walk by. He had a backpack with him. The police officer asked the accused what was in the backpack. When the accused said nothing or it was empty, the police officer said, "Then you would not object if I saw what was in it?" The accused opened it and presented it. The police officer saw the bolt cutters in the backpack. On those facts the trial judge held that the officer, having only a suspicion, searched the bag without reasonable and probable grounds. She found that this was not a consensual search because the officer did not inform the accused of his right not to be searched. The Crown did not challenge those findings. The trial judge found that the seizure was unreasonable and violated s. 8 of the Charter but she admitted the bolt cutters under s. 24(2) of the Charter on an application of the *Collins* test and, in particular, the finding that the evidence was real evidence and non-conscriptive.]

DONALD J.A. (HINDS and RICHARD JJ.A. concurring):—

. . . .

Were it not for a recent decision of the Ontario Court of Appeal relying on an extrajudicial statement by Mr. Justice Cory in clarifying the *Stillman* decision, I would have allowed the appeal on the ground that the discovery of the evidence involved the participation of the accused in the course of a Charter breach. I am persuaded, somewhat reluctantly, that the *Stillman* case must be read in a narrower sense than its language would suggest. In that sense, exclusion is limited to discoveries where the accused's participation involves statements, bodily samples or the use of the body as evidence.

. . . .

Since the extrajudicial remarks of Mr. Justice Cory have been judicially applied I think it appropriate to set out the relevant portions of his paper. It will be seen that the hypothetical case given by Mr. Justice Cory illustrating when the *Stillman* formula will not operate is remarkably close to the circumstances in this case. At pp.12-13 of the paper he said:

Third, not all evidence compelled from the accused in violation of the Charter will be classified as "conscriptive" evidence. This label attaches only to three very specific kinds of evidence: statements, the use as evidence of the body and bodily samples. The first of these, statements, is self-explanatory. Where the accused is forced, in violation of the Charter, to make a statement, the statement will be conscriptive and, if it is not "discoverable", can not be admitted at the trial. This situation usually arises in cases where the accused provides a statement as a result of a breach of his right to counsel.

"The use of the body as evidence" will occur in cases such as R. v. Ross and Leclair, where the accused were forced, in violation of their Charter rights, to participate in a police line up. They were thereby forced to allow their bodies to be used as evidence for identification purposes.

Finally, bodily samples consist of parts of an accused's body, such as hair or blood samples, teeth impressions or buccal swabs, taken from him in violation of the Charter.

An alternative approach to "conscriptive" evidence would be to classify any evidence discovered as a result of the forced participation of the accused as "conscriptive". Thus, if the police force the accused to produce the contents of his pocket, the items seized would be classified as "conscriptive" simply because they could not have been seized without the forced participation of the accused. This approach is not the one followed in *Stillman*. On the authority of *Stillman*, the items seized from the accused's pocket would not be classified as "conscriptive" evidence. Although these items may well have been compelled from the accused in violation of the Charter, they do not consist of statements, bodily samples or the use of the body as evidence, and hence are not conscriptive. Of course, whether they would be admitted in evidence would depend upon the other *Collins* factors.

I am unable to find any meaningful difference between Mr. Justice Cory's hypothesis and the facts of this case. Consequently, with the benefit of the clarification of *Stillman*, I cannot uphold the appellant's argument that the evidence was conscriptive. As Mr. Cozens does not contend that the learned trial judge erred in her application of the other branches of the *Collins* test, which were against the appellant, it follows that the appeal must be dismissed. For these reasons I would dismiss the appeal.

INDEX